INTERMEDIATE ACCOUNTING
Comprehensive Volume   Ninth Edition

Jay M. Smith, Jr., PhD, CPA

Brigham Young University

K. Fred Skousen, PhD, CPA

Brigham Young University

Published by

A92 SOUTH-WESTERN PUBLISHING CO.

CINCINNATI   WEST CHICAGO, IL   CARROLLTON, TX   LIVERMORE, CA

PREFACE

The ninth edition of INTERMEDIATE ACCOUNTING represents the most extensive revision in the history of this widely accepted textbook. It provides comprehensive and up-to-date coverage of financial accounting concepts and standards. All relevant FASB pronouncements issued through March 1, 1987, are incorporated in the ninth edition, including the exposure drafts relating to cash flow statements and accounting for deferred income taxes. In addition, relevant provisions of the Tax Reform Act of 1986 are integrated at appropriate points in the text.

While the ninth edition reflects extensive changes, the underlying objective remains the same — to provide the most teachable and student-oriented text on the market. Topics are introduced and developed in a logical sequence and explained in a manner that is clear and understandable to students. Many real-world examples have been added to enhance student understanding and interest. The student-oriented approach of INTERMEDIATE ACCOUNTING is one of the main reasons why it has been a leading intermediate text for so many years. The emphasis on student understanding and teachability has been retained and strengthened in the ninth edition.

IMPORTANT FEATURES OF THE NINTH EDITION

The overall structure of the ninth edition is similar to that of the eighth edition. However, the chapter sequence has been partially revised and several important topics are covered in more depth. Many of the chapters have been significantly revised, and some have been totally rewritten. The revisions reflect extensive feedback from users of the eighth edition and from several accounting educators who reviewed the new and revised material for the ninth edition. Following is a summary of the most significant features of the ninth edition of INTERMEDIATE ACCOUNTING.

Comprehensive Coverage of Topics

The ninth edition has been expanded to provide more comprehensive coverage of important topics and issues in financial accounting and reporting. Many new illustrations, examples, and applications have been added throughout the text to clarify and reinforce discussions and explanations.

Real-World Perspective

Real-world examples and events are used extensively to illustrate important points and to enhance student interest. This new feature enables students to view financial accounting and reporting from a broader, business-oriented perspective.

Current Accounting Standards

The text has been updated to include all current pronouncements of the FASB that are relevant to intermediate accounting. These include the new standards relating to pensions and changing prices and the Board's proposed standards on cash flow statements and deferred income taxes.

End-of-Chapter Materials

Many new and revised cases, exercises, and problems are included at the end of each chapter. The cases provide a vehicle for promoting class discussion of important issues. The exercises and problems have been increased in number to allow instructors more flexibility in making assignments.

Highlights of Specific Changes

The ninth edition of INTERMEDIATE ACCOUNTING consists of twenty-six chapters organized into five logically related parts. Every chapter in the text has been revised, and many have been extensively rewritten. Following is a summary of the most significant content changes.

Accounting Standards and the Underlying Conceptual Framework. Chapters 1 and 2 have been extensively revised to give students a better perspective and understanding of the accounting profession, the standard-setting process, and the underlying conceptual framework of accounting.

Recognition, Measurement, and Reporting of Income. Chapter 4 provides more comprehensive treatment of income and its components — including discontinued operations, extraordinary items, cumulative effects of accounting changes, and intraperiod tax allocation — in one chapter. The chapter also presents an expanded discussion of revenue and expense recognition and measurement, including a discussion of capital maintenance concepts.

Balance Sheet and Statement of Cash Flows. A new section covering disclosure in notes to financial statements has been added to Chapter 5. The chapter introduces the statement of cash flows, which is covered in detail in Chapter 24.

The Time Value of Money. Chapter 6 is a new chapter covering present and future value (formerly covered in an appendix at the end of the text) that can be used as a review of present and future value concepts or as a first exposure to the topic. The chapter focuses on business applications and provides numerous, easy-to-follow examples.

Plant and Intangible Assets. Chapter 11 clarifies and expands the discussion and illustration of capitalization of construction period interest. The chapter has been updated to include accounting for software development expenditures per FASB Statement No. 86. Chapter 12 has been updated to include an explanation of the major changes in ACRS as a result of the Tax Reform Act of 1986.

Earnings Per Share. Chapter 18 provides a clarified discussion of earnings per share that is reinforced with more examples to aid students in understanding this complex topic. An appendix has been added at the end of the chapter which presents a comprehensive illustration of earnings per share computations with multiple potentially dilutive securities.

Income Taxes. Chapter 20 has been reorganized, clarified, and updated to include relevant provisions of the Tax Reform Act of 1986 and the important FASB Exposure Draft, "Accounting for Income Taxes." Both the deferred approach (APB Opinion No. 11) and the liability approach favored by the FASB are presented and illustrated in the chapter. Coverage of computational difficulties related to graduated tax rates has been deleted from the chapter.

Accounting for Leases. Chapter 21 includes more complete discussion and illustration of certain aspects of accounting for leases, such as classification criteria, residual values, initial direct costs, and lease disclosures. The provisions of FASB Statement No. 91 dealing with initial direct costs have been incorporated in the chapter. Discussion of real estate leases is now presented in an appendix to allow instructors more flexibility.

Accounting for Pensions. Chapter 22 has been completely rewritten to reflect the new standards in the pension area (FASB Statements No. 87 and 88). The chapter identifies the issues in accounting for pensions by employers and presents numerous illustrations of how the FASB standards are applied. A glossary of pension terms as defined by the FASB has been included to assist students in studying this complex topic. A new set of questions, cases, exercises, and problems has been included with this chapter.

Accounting Changes and Error Corrections. Chapter 23 is a new chapter that consolidates the discussion of accounting changes and correction of errors.

Statement of Cash Flows. Chapter 24 incorporates the FASB's proposed standard for a new cash flow statement to replace the statement of changes in financial position. The illustrations highlight cash flows from operating, investing, and financing activities. To provide an historical perspective, the chapter also includes a brief explanation and illustration of the working capital concept of funds.

Changing Prices. Chapter 25 incorporates the FASB's most recent conclusions regarding the reporting of price level changes (Statement No. 89). The chapter retains a conceptual discussion of current cost and constant dollar accounting and illustrates the computations involved, but the detailed discussion of the disclosure requirements of FASB Statement No. 33 has been deleted.

SUPPLEMENTARY MATERIALS

An improved and expanded package of supplementary materials is provided with the ninth edition to assist both instructors and students. The package includes new items that have been carefully prepared and reviewed and previously available materials that have been extensively revised.

Materials for Instructors

Solutions Manual. This manual contains the answers to all end-of-chapter questions, cases, exercises, and problems.

Instructor's Resource Manual, prepared by Edward W. Scott, Jr. of Olympic College, Jay M. Smith, Jr., and K. Fred Skousen. This new manual contains teaching outlines, references, descriptions of exercises and problems, estimated time requirements for problems, and other aids which provide a basis for developing class presentations and assigning homework.

Transparencies. Transparencies of solutions for all end-of-chapter exercises and problems are available with the ninth edition of the text.

Examinations. A test bank is available in both printed and microcomputer (MicroSWAT II) versions. The test bank which has been significantly revised and expanded, includes true-false questions, multiple-choice questions, and examination problems for each chapter, accompanied by solutions.

Materials for Students

Study Guide, prepared by Frank J. Imke of Texas Tech University. The study guide provides review and reinforcement materials for each chapter, including learning objectives, a glossary of key terms in the chapter, chapter review outlines, objective questions, and short problems. Answers for all questions and problems are provided in a separate section at the end of the study guide.

Microcomputer Study Guide. A new microcomputer version of the manual study guide can be used with Apple //e and Apple //c, IBM PC and IBM PCjr, and the Tandy 1000 microcomputers.

Practice Case, prepared by Donald C. Dwyer of Berkshire Community College. A new practice case, *SporTime Inc.*, provides a comprehensive review of accounting principles.

Electronic Spreadsheet Applications for Intermediate Accounting, prepared by Gaylord N. Smith of Albion College. This supplemental text-workbook with template diskette includes intermediate accounting applications a Lotus 1-2-3 tutorial. It requires approximately 25-30 hours for completion, and it requires access to Lotus 1-2-3.

Working Papers. Printed forms for solving end-of-chapter problems are contained in a single bound volume and are perforated for easy removal.

Check Figures. Instructors may order check figures for students to use in verifying their solutions to end-of-chapter problems.

Template Diskette. The template diskette is used with Lotus™ 1-2-3™⁴ for solving selected end-of-chapter exercises and problems. The diskette may be ordered free of charge from South-Western Publishing Co.

ACKNOWLEDGEMENTS

Relevant pronouncements of the Financial Accounting Standards Board and other authoritative publications are paraphrased, quoted, discussed, and referenced throughout the textbook. We are indebted to the American Accounting Association, the American Institute of Certified Public Accountants, the Financial Accounting Standards Board, and the Securities and Exchange Commission for material from their publications.

We thank the following faculty who reviewed the eighth edition or manuscript for this edition and provided many helpful comments and suggestions:

James R. Barnhart
Ball State University

Joseph H. Bylinski
University of North Carolina

Don E. Collins
Ithaca College

Linda M. Dykes
College of Charleston

Robert V. Egenolf
The University of Texas at
  San Antonio

Edward B. Grant
Central Michigan University

Larzette Hale
Utah State University

Marshall Hamilton
Texas Wesleyan College

James R. Hemingway
Stephen F. Austin University

Hartwell C. Herring, III
The University of Tennessee

Walter K. Rutledge
University of West Florida

Ted Zielinski
Milwaukee Area Technical College

We also wish to thank the faculty and students who have used INTERMEDIATE ACCOUNTING and volunteered their constructive suggestions for its improvement.

Jay M. Smith, Jr.
K. Fred Skousen

ABOUT THE AUTHORS

Jay M. Smith, Jr., PhD, CPA, is Professor of Accounting at the School of Accountancy, Brigham Young University. He holds a bachelor's and a master's degree from BYU and a PhD from Stanford University. He has thirty years of teaching experience at BYU, Stanford University, the University of Minnesota where he served as department chairman for four years, and at the University of Hawaii. He has received several awards and recognitions in accounting, including fellowships from the Danforth and Sloan Foundations, the Distinguished Faculty Award from the BYU School of Management, and several teaching excellence awards. Professor Smith has written extensively in accounting journals and has been involved in several research projects, including work done on grants from the Ford Foundation, Peat, Marwick, Mitchell & Co., and Arthur Andersen & Co. He served as editor of the Education Research Department of the Accounting Review from 1976 to 1978, as secretary to the Auditing Section of the American Accounting Association, and as a member of the editorial board for the Auditing Section's journal. He is a member of the American Institute of CPAs, the Utah Association of CPAs, and the American Accounting Association and has served on numerous committees of these organizations.

K. Fred Skousen, PhD, CPA, is Peat Marwick Professor and the past Director of the School of Accountancy, Brigham Young University. He holds a bachelor's degree from BYU and the master's and PhD degrees from the University of Illinois. Professor Skousen has taught at the University of Illinois, the University of Minnesota, the University of California at Berkeley, and the University of Missouri. He received Distinguished Faculty Awards at the University of Minnesota and at BYU and was recognized as the National Beta Alpha Psi Academic Accountant of the Year in 1979. Professor Skousen is the author or co-author of over 40 articles, research reports, and books. He served as Director of Research and a member of the Executive Committee of the American Accounting Association and is a member of the American Institute of CPAs, and the Utah Association of CPAs. He is currently serving as president of the UACPA and on Council for the AICPA. Dr. Skousen has also served as a consultant to the Controller General of the United States, the Federal Trade Commission, the California Society of CPAs, and several large companies. He was a Faculty Resident on the staff of the Securities and Exchange Commission and a Faculty Fellow with Price Waterhouse and Co.

CONTENTS IN BRIEF

PART ONE
OVERVIEW OF ACCOUNTING AND ITS THEORETICAL FOUNDATION

1	Accounting in a Complex Business Environment	2
2	A Conceptual Framework of Accounting	28
3	Review of the Accounting Process	62
4	Recognition, Measurement, and Reporting of Income	116
5	The Balance Sheet and Statement of Cash Flows	160
6	The Time Value of Money: Accounting Applications	208

PART TWO
ASSETS

7	Cash and Temporary Investments	241
8	Receivables	285
9	Inventories — Cost Procedures	326
10	Inventories — Estimation and Noncost Valuation Procedures	382
11	Plant and Intangible Assets — Acquisition	428
12	Plant and Intangible Assets — Utilization and Retirement	492
13	Long-Term Investments in Equity Securities and Other Assets	553

PART THREE
LIABILITIES AND EQUITY

14	Liabilities — Current and Contingent	592
15	Accounting for Long-Term Debt Securities	635
16	Owners' Equity — Contributed Capital	691
17	Owners' Equity — Retained Earnings	739
18	Earnings per Share	772

PART FOUR
SPECIAL PROBLEMS IN INCOME DETERMINATION AND REPORTING

19	Revenue Recognition	818
20	Accounting for Income Taxes	862
21	Accounting for Leases	901
22	Accounting for Pensions	956
23	Accounting Changes and Error Corrections	1015

PART FIVE
FINANCIAL REPORTING

24	Statement of Cash Flows	1053
25	Reporting the Impact of Changing Prices	1097
26	Financial Statement Analysis	1154

APPENDIXES

A	Illustrative Financial Statements	1200
B	Index of References to APB and FASB Pronouncements	1218

CONTENTS

PART ONE
OVERVIEW OF ACCOUNTING AND ITS
THEORETICAL FOUNDATION

1 Accounting in a Complex Business Environment   **2**

Accounting and Financial Reporting   3
    Users of Accounting Information 3, Financial Reporting 5
The Accounting Profession   5
    The External Audit Function 6, Other Services Provided by CPAs 7,
The Development of Accounting Standards   9
    Financial Accounting Standards Board 10, The Standard-Setting
    Process 12, American Institute of Certified Public Accountants 14,
    Securities and Exchange Commission 16, American Accounting Asso-
    ciation 17, Other Organizations 18, Impact of Accounting Standards
    19, Standard-Setting in a Complex Environment 22, Conflict Between
    Public and Private Sector 23
Overview of Intermediate Accounting   25

2 A Conceptual Framework of Accounting   **28**

Need for a Conceptual Framework   28
Nature and Components of the FASB's Conceptual Framework   30
    Objectives of Financial Reporting 32, Qualitative Characteristics of
    Accounting Information 38, Elements of Financial Statements 46,
    Recognition, Measurement, and Reporting 46
Traditional Assumptions of Accounting Model   51
Conceptual Framework Summarized   53

3 Review of the Accounting Process   **62**

Overview of the Accounting Process   63
    Recording Phase 66, Summarizing Phase 72
Accrual Versus Cash Basis Accounting   85
Computers and the Accounting Process   85
Appendix A: Special Journals and Subsidiary Ledgers   87
Voucher System   88
Illustration of Special Journals and Subsidiary Ledgers   89
    Sales Journal 89, Cash Receipts Journal 90, Voucher Register 90,
    Cash Disbursements Journal 91, General Journal 91, Subsidiary
    Ledgers 92
Appendix B: Comprehensive Illustration of Accrual Versus
Cash Accounting   93

4   Recognition, Measurement, and Reporting of Income   116

Importance of Recognizing, Measuring, and Reporting Income   116
What Is Income?   117
  Valuation Approach 119, Transaction Approach 120
Reporting of Income   126
  *Form of the Income Statement 127, Content of a Multiple-Step In-
  come Statement 130, Earnings per Share 141*
Reporting Changes in Retained Earnings   142
Reporting Implications of Conceptual Framework   143
Summary   144

5   The Balance Sheet and Statement of Cash Flows   160

Usefulness of the Balance Sheet   161
Elements of the Balance Sheet   162
  *Classified Balance Sheets 163, Current Assets and Current Liabilities
  164, Noncurrent Assets and Noncurrent Liabilities 168, Owners'
  Equity 172, Offsets on the Balance sheet 174, Form of the Balance
  Sheet 175, Additional Disclosure to the Balance Sheet 177*
Limitations of the Balance Sheet   183
Overview of the Statement of Cash Flows   184
  Concept of Funds Flow 186, Format of a Statement of Cash Flows 187

6   The Time Value of Money: Accounting Applications   208

Simple and Compound Interest   210
Future and Present Value Techniques   212
  *Use of Formulas 213, Use of Tables 214, Business Applications 216,
  Determining the Number of Periods, the Interest Rate, or the Rental
  Payment 219*
Additional Complexities   222
  Ordinary Annuity vs. Annuity Due 222, Interpolation 226
Concluding Comment   229

PART TWO
ASSETS

7   Cash and Temporary Investments   242

Cash   242
  *Composition of Cash 243, Compensating Balances 245, Management
  and Control of Cash 247, Petty Cash Fund 248, Bank Reconciliations
  249*
Temporary Investments   256
  *Criteria for Reporting Securities as Temporary Investments 256,
  Recording Purchase and Sale of Marketable Securities 257, Valuation
  of Marketable Securities 259, Evaluation of Methods 264*

8   Receivables   285

Classification of Receivables   285
Accounts Receivable   287
  *Recognition of Accounts Receivable 287, Valuation and Reporting of
  Accounts Receivable 289, Accounts Receivable as a Source of Cash
  296*

Notes Receivable   301
*Valuation of Notes Receivable 301, Notes Receivable as a Source of
Cash 307*
Presentation of Receivables on the Balance Sheet   310

9   Inventories — Cost Procedures   **326**
Nature of Inventory   326
Classes of Inventories   327
Raw Materials 327, Goods in Process 328, Finished Goods 328
Inventory Systems   328
Items to Be Included in Inventory   332
*Goods in Transit 332, Goods on Consignment 333, Conditional and
Installment Sales 333*
Determination of Inventory Cost   333
*Items Included in Cost 334, Discounts as Reductions in Cost 334,
Purchase Returns and Allowances 336*
Traditional Cost Allocation Methods   337
*Specific Identification 338, First-In, First-Out Method 338, Average
Cost Methods 340, Last-In, First-Out Method — Specific Goods 342,
Last-In, First-Out Method — Dollar Value 347*
Comparison of Cost Allocation Methods   353
Income Tax Considerations 355
Evaluation of LIFO as a Cost Allocation Method   357
Major Advantages of LIFO 357, Major Disadvantages of LIFO 357
Other Cost Methods   360
Cost of Latest Purchases 360, Standard Costs 360, Direct Costing 361
Selection of an Inventory Method   362
Appendix: Determination of Price Indexes   363

10   Inventories — Estimation and Noncost Valuation Procedures   **382**
Gross Profit Method   382
Retail Inventory Method   385
*Markups and Markdowns — Conventional Retail 386, Freight, Dis-
counts, Returns, and Allowances 389, Retail Method with Varying
Profit Margin Inventories 390*
Retail-LIFO Method   390
Inventory Valuations at Other than Cost   393
*Inventory Valuation at Lower of Cost or Market 393, Valuation at
Market 399, Losses on Purchase Commitments 401, Valuation of
Trade-Ins and Repossessions 402*
Effects of Errors in Recording Inventory Position   404
Inventories on the Balance Sheet   407

11   Plant and Intangible Assets — Acquisition   **428**
Classification of Plant and Intangible Assets   428
Valuation of Plant and Intangible Assets at Acquisition   429
Real Property 430, Equipment 433, Intangible Assets 434
Recording Acquisition of Plant and Intangible Assets   442
*Purchase on Deferred Payment Contract 443, Acquisition Under
Capital Lease 445, Acquisition by Exchange of Nonmonetary Assets*

446, Acquisition by Issuance of Securities 446, Acquisition by Self-Construction 447, Acquisition by Donation or Discovery 455

Capital and Revenue Expenditures   456
   Research and Development Expenditures 457, Computer Software Development Expenditures 460
Expenditures Subsequent to Acquisition   463
   Maintenance and Repairs 463, Renewals and Replacements 464, Additions and Betterments 465
Summary   465
Appendix: Goodwill Estimation   465
Variables Used in Goodwill Valuation   466
   Estimating the Level of Future Earnings 466, Determining the Appropriate Rate of Return 467
Methods of Valuing Goodwill   467
   Capitalization of Average Net Earnings 468, Capitalization of Average Excess Net Earnings 468, Number of Years' Excess Earnings 469, Present Value Method 470

12   Plant and Intangible Assets — Utilization and Retirement   492

Depreciation of Plant Assets   492
   Factors Affecting the Periodic Depreciation Charge 493, Recording Periodic Depreciation 495, Methods of Depreciation 496
Historical Cost Versus Current Cost Allocation   511
Amortization of Intangible Assets   513
Depletion of Natural Resources   516
   Computing Periodic Depletion 516, Special Problems — Oil and Gas Properties 517
Changes in Estimates of Variables   519
   Change in Estimated Life 519, Change in Estimated Units of Production 520, Impairment of Tangible and Intangible Asset Values 521
Asset Retirements   522
   Asset Retirement by Sale 523, Asset Retirement by Exchange for Other Nonmonetary Assets 523, Asset Retirement by Exchange of Nonmonetary Assets — Special Case 525, Retirement by Involuntary Conversion 528
Balance Sheet Presentation and Disclosure   529
Appendix: Insurance Recovery on Involuntary Conversions   530
   Fire Insurance 530

13   Long-Term Investments in Equity Securities and Other Assets   553

Long-Term Investments in Equity Securities   554
   Acquisition of Stocks 554, Accounting for Long-Term Investments in Stocks 555, The Cost Method 557, The Equity Method 563, Changes Between Cost and Equity Methods 567, Required Disclosures for Long-Term Investments in Stock 570, Accounting for Long-Term Investments in Stocks Summarized 571
Long-Term Investments in Funds   572
   Establishment and Accumulation of Funds 572, Accounting for Funds 573
Cash Surrender Value of Life Insurance   574
Other Long-Term Investments   576
Reporting Long-Term Investments on the Balance Sheet   576

PART THREE
LIABILITIES AND EQUITY

14   Liabilities — Current and Contingent   **592**

Definition of Liabilities   593

Classification and Measurement of Liabilities   594
   Current Versus Noncurrent Classification 594, Measurement of Liabilities 595

Liabilities that Are Definite in Amount   596
   Accounts Payable 596, Short-Term Debt 597, Short-Term Obligations Expected to Be Refinanced 598, Miscellaneous Operating Payables 600, Unearned Revenues 607

Estimated Liabilities   608
   Refundable Deposits 608, Warranties for Service and Replacements 609, Customer Premium Offers 611, Tickets, Tokens, and Gift Certificates Outstanding 613, Compensated Absences 614

Contingent Liabilities   615
   Litigation 617, Self Insurance 619, Loan Guarantees 620

Balance Sheet Presentation   620

15   Accounting for Long-Term Debt Securities   **635**

Financing with Long-Term Debt   635

Accounting for Bonds   636
   Nature of Bonds 637, Market Price of Bonds 640, Issuance of Bonds 642, Accounting for Bond Interest 645, Retirement of Bonds at Maturity 649, Extinguishment of Debt Prior to Maturity 650

Troubled Debt Restructuring   660
   Transfer of Assets in Full Settlement (Asset Swap) 661, Grant of Equity Interest (Equity Swap) 663, Modification of Debt Terms 664

Off-Balance-Sheet Financing   667
   Sale of Receivables with Recourse 667, Captive Finance Companies and Other Unconsolidated Entities 668, Research and Development Arrangements 668, Project Financing Arrangements 669, Reasons for Off-Balance-Sheet Financing 669

Valuation and Reporting of Long-Term Debt Securities on the Balance Sheet   670
   Reporting Bonds and Long-Term Notes as Investments 671, Reporting Bonds and Long-Term Notes as Liabilities 671

Appendix: Accounting for Serial Bonds   673
   Bonds-Outstanding Method 673, Effective-Interest Method 674, Bond Redemption Prior to Maturity — Serial Bonds 675

16   Owners' Equity — Contributed Capital   **691**

Nature and Classifications of Capital Stock   692
   Rights of Ownership 693, Par or Stated Value of Stock 693, Preferred Stock 695, Common Stock 698

Issuance of Capital Stock   699
   Capital Stock Issued for Cash 699, Capital Stock Sold on Subscription 700, Subscription Defaults 701, Capital Stock Issued for Consideration Other Than Cash 703, Issuance of Capital Stock in Exchange for a Business 704

Capital Stock Reacquisition   704
   Stock Reacquired for Immediate Retirement 705, Treasury Stock 706,
   Donated Treasury Stock 710
Stock Rights, Warrants, and Options   710
   Stock Rights 711, Stock Warrants 714, Stock Options Issued to Em-
   ployees 715, Disclosure of Stock Options 721
Stock Conversions   721
Stock Splits and Reverse Stock Splits   722
Balance Sheet Disclosure of Contributed Capital   723

17   Owners' Equity — Retained Earnings   739
Factors Affecting Retained Earnings   739
   Prior Period Adjustments 740, Earnings 741, Dividends 741, Other
   Changes in Retained Earnings 742
Accounting for Dividends   742
   Restrictions on Retained Earnings 743, Recognition and Payment of
   Dividends 744, Cash Dividends 745, Property Dividends 745, Stock
   Dividends 746, Liquidating Dividends 750
Quasi-Reorganizations   751
Reporting Stockholders' Equity   753

18   Earnings per Share   772
Evolution of Requirements for Earnings per Share Disclosure   773
Simple and Complex Capital Structures   775
   The Simple Capital Structure — Computational Guidelines 776, The
   Complex Capital Structure — Computational Guidelines 779
Primary Earnings per Share   779
   Stock Options, Warrants, and Rights 780, Convertible Securities 783,
   Multiple Potentially Dilutive Securities 787
Fully Diluted Earnings per Share   787
   Illustration of Fully Diluted Earnings per Share 788, Effect of Actual
   Exercise or Conversion 789
Effect of Net Losses   790
Summary of Earnings per Share Computations   791
Financial Statement Presentation   792
Appendix: Comprehensive Illustration Using Multiple Potentially
Dilutive Securities   795

PART FOUR
SPECIAL PROBLEMS IN INCOME
DETERMINATION AND REPORTING

19   Revenue Recognition   818
Revenue Recognition Prior to Delivery of Goods or Performance of
Services   819
   General Concepts of Percentage-of-Completion Accounting 820 Nec-
   essary Conditions to Use Percentage-of-Completion Accounting 820,
   Measuring the Percentage of Completion 821, Accounting for Long-
   Term Construction-Type Contracts 823, Income Tax Considerations

829, *Accounting for Long-Term Service Contracts — the Proportional Performance Method* 829, *Evaluation of Proportional Performance Method* 832

Revenue Recognition After Delivery of Goods or Performance of Services   833
Installment Sales Method 834, *Cost Recovery Method* 840, *Cash Method* 841

Methods of Accounting Before Revenue Recognition   842
Deposit Method — General 843, *Deposit Method — Franchising Industry* 843, *Consignment Sales* 845

Concluding Comments   846

20   Accounting for Income Taxes   **862**

Intraperiod Income Tax Allocation   863
Interperiod Income Tax Allocation   864
Permanent Differences 865, *Timing Differences* 866, *Computation of Income Tax Expense and Income Taxes Payable* 867, *Impact of Interperiod Income Tax Allocation* 868, *Comprehensive Illustration of Interperiod Income Tax Allocation* 869, *Interperiod Income Tax Allocation with Changing Income Tax Rates* 872, *Partial vs. Comprehensive Income Tax Allocation* 878

Accounting for Net Operating Losses (NOL's)   879
Net Operating Loss Carryback 879, *Operating Loss Carryforward* 881

Investment Tax Credit   882
Accounting for the Investment Tax Credit 882, *Evaluation of Accounting Treatment of Investment Tax Credit* 883

Disclosure of Income Taxes   884
Concluding Comments   884

21   Accounting for Leases   **901**

Economic Advantages of Leasing   902
Historical Development for Lease Accounting   903
Nature of Leases   904
Lease Classification Criteria   908
Application of Lease Classification Criteria 911

Accounting for Leases — Lessee   913
Accounting for Operating Leases — Lessee 913, *Accounting for Capital Leases — Lessee* 914

Accounting for Leases — Lessor   921
Accounting for Operating Leases — Lessor 923, *Accounting for Direct Financing Leases* 923, *Accounting for Sales-Type Leases* 927, *Sale of Asset During Lease Term* 930

Disclosure Requirements for Leases   930
Lessee 931, *Lessor* 931

Accounting for Sale-Leaseback Transactions   932
Concluding Comment   936
Appendix A: Criteria for Capitalization of Real Estate Leases   936
Leases Involving Land Only or Buildings Only 936, *Leases Involving Land and Buildings* 938, *Leases Involving Real Estate and Equipment* 938, *Profit Recognition on Sales-Type Real Estate Leases* 938

Appendix B: Leveraged Leases   939

22 Accounting For Pensions   **956**

Pension Plans in Our Economy   956
   Regulation of Pension Plans—ERISA 957
Nature and Characteristics of Employer Pension Plans   958
   Funding of Employer Pension Plans 959, Defined Contribution Plans
   959, Defined Benefit Plans 960
History of Pension Accounting Standards   964
Issues in Accounting for Defined Benefit Plans   965
Accounting for Pensions   966
   Determining Net Periodic Pension Cost 966, Determining Pension
   Liability 979, Determining Pension Assets 982, Pension Settlements
   and Curtailments and Termination Benefits 985, Disclosure of Pen-
   sion Plans 988
Multiemployer Pension Plans   991
Postretirement Benefits Other Than Pensions   991
Conclusion   994
Appendix: Glossary of Pension Terms   996

23 Accounting Changes and Error Corrections   **1015**

Treatment of Accounting Changes and Error Corrections   1016
   Change in Accounting Estimate 1018, Change in Accounting Prin-
   ciples 1018, Change in Reporting Entity 1024, Error Corrections 1024
Summary of Accounting Changes and Correction of Errors   1035

PART FIVE
FINANCIAL REPORTING

24 Statement of Cash Flows   **1053**

Historical Perspective   1053
Objectives and Limitations of the Funds Statement   1055
The "All Financial Resources" Concept of Funds   1055
Preparation of Funds Statements   1056
   Funds Defined as Cash 1057, Funds Defined as Working Capital 1062
Comprehensive Illustration of Cash Flow Statement   1064
   Work Sheet Approach to Preparing a Cash Flow Statement 1064
Reporting Cash Flows   1074
Appendix: T-Account Approach to Preparing a Cash Flow Statement   1075

25 Reporting the Impact of Changing Prices   **1097**

Reporting the Effects of Changing Prices   1098
Reporting Alternatives 1099, Historical Perspective 1100
Constant Dollar Accounting   1101
   Price Indexes 1102, Mechanics of Constant Dollar Restatement 1103,
   Purchasing Power Gains and Losses 1105, Arguments for and Against
   Constant Dollar Accounting 1110
Current Cost Accounting   1110
   Concept of Well-Offness 1111, Holding Gains or Losses 1111, Mechan-
   ics of Current Cost Accounting 1113, Arguments for and Against
   Current Cost Accounting 1114

Current Cost/Constant Dollar Accounting 1114
The FASB Experiment 1116
Prospects for the Future 1116
Appendix: Comprehensive Illustration 1117
  Historical Cost/Constant Dollar Basis 1118
    Historical Cost/Constant Dollar Statement of Income and Retained Earnings 1121, Historical Cost/Constant Dollar Balance Sheet 1124
  Current Cost/Nominal Dollar Basis 1125
    Current Cost/Nominal Dollar Statement of Income and Retained Earnings 1125, Current Cost/Nominal Dollar Balance Sheet 1128, Retained Earnings 1129
  Current Cost/Constant Dollar Basis 1130
    Current Cost/Constant Dollar Statement of Income and Retained Earnings 1130, Current Cost/Constant Dollar Balance Sheet 1132

26   Financial Statement Analysis **1154**
Objectives of Financial Statement Analysis 1154
Analytical Procedures 1156
  Comparative Statements 1157, Index-Number Trend Series 1158, Common-Size Financial Statements 1159, Other Analytical Procedures 1161, Liquidity Analysis 1162, Activity Analysis 1164, Profitability Analysis 1169, Capital Structure Analysis 1173, Summary of Analytical Measures 1176
Use of Industry Data for Comparative Analysis 1178
  Segment Reporting 1179, Sources of Industry Data 1180
Interpretation of Analyses 1181

APPENDIXES

A   Illustrative Financial Statements **1200**
B   Index of References to APB and FASB Pronouncements **1218**

Index **1225**

PART ONE
OVERVIEW OF ACCOUNTING AND ITS THEORETICAL FOUNDATION

1   Accounting in a Complex Business Environment

2   A Conceptual Framework of Accounting

3   Review of the Accounting Process

4   Recognition, Measurement, and Reporting of Income

5   The Balance Sheet and Statement of Cash Flows

6   The Time Value of Money: Accounting Applications

1
Accounting In A Complex Business Environment

The time has arrived for United Exploration Inc.'s annual meeting. The purpose of the meeting is to elect members to the Board of Directors, to take care of miscellaneous corporate matters, and to answer stockholders' questions concerning the recently issued financial statements. The attendance at this year's meeting is unusually large because of a significant decline in net income reported for the current year.

Three groups are represented at the meeting: (1) management (2) external auditors, and (3) stockholders. Much of the technical discussion involves the impact of changing the method of depreciation used for the financial statements. Management explains to the stockholders that the new method makes United's statements more comparable to those of competitors. The stockholders are especially concerned because the decline in net income has had a negative effect in the stock market. There is some expressed concern that management is purposefully manipulating income. The stockholders are interested in the impact of the accounting change because they must decide whether to buy additional shares in the company, sell the shares they have, or maintain their present position.

The above scenario describing a stockholders' meeting is repeated hundreds of times each year as various interested parties meet to discuss the financial affairs of their companies. The audited financial statements contained in annual reports are the primary source of financial information available to stockholders about the profitability and financial soundness of a corporation. The accountant's function is considered essential to the smooth operation of our nation's economy. This chapter will explore how the accounting profession has dealt with discharging its important responsibilities.

ACCOUNTING AND FINANCIAL REPORTING

As implied in the above illustration and as indicated in the following quotation, the overall objective of accounting is to provide information that can be used in making economic decisions.

> Accounting is a service activity. Its function is to provide quantitative information, primarily financial in nature, about economic entities that is intended to be useful in making economic decisions — in making reasoned choices among alternative courses of action.[1]

Several key features of this definition should be noted. First, accounting provides a vital **service** in today's business environment. Economists and environmentalists remind us constantly that we live in a world with limited resources. We must use our natural resources, our labor, and our financial wealth wisely so as to maximize their benefit to society. The better the accounting system that measures and reports the cost of using these resources, the better the decisions that are made for allocating them. Second, accounting is concerned primarily with **quantitative financial information** that is used in conjunction with qualitative evaluations in making judgments. Finally, although accountants place much emphasis on reporting what has already occurred, this past information is intended to be useful in making **economic decisions** about the future.

Users of Accounting Information

If accounting is to meet its objective of providing useful information for economic decision making, the following questions must be answered: (1) Who are the users of accounting information, and (2) what information do they require to meet their decision making needs?

User groups are normally divided into two major classifications: (1) **internal users** who make decisions directly affecting the internal operations of the enterprise, and (2) **external users** who make decisions concerning their relationship to the enterprise. Major internal and external user groups are listed in Exhibit 1-1.

Internal users need information to assist in planning and controlling enterprise operations and managing (allocating) enterprise resources. The accounting system must provide timely information needed to control day-to-day operations and to make major planning decisions, such as "Do we

---

[1]*Statement of the Accounting Principles Board No. 4,* "Basic Concepts and Accounting Principles Underlying Financial Statements of Business Enterprises" (New York: American Institute of Certified Public Accountants, 1970), par. 40.

Exhibit 1–1   Internal and External User Groups

Internal users

Company management
Company employees
Board of directors

External users

Creditors
Investors
Potential investors
Governmental agencies
General public

---

make this product or another one? Do we build a new production plant or expand existing facilities? Must we increase prices or can we cut costs?"

The types of decisions made by external users vary widely, thus their information needs are highly diverse. Considerable time and effort have been devoted to studying the information needs of external users.[2] As a result, two groups, creditors and investors, have been identified as the principal external users of financial information. Two reasons cited for the importance of these groups are:[3]

1. Their decisions significantly affect the allocation of resources in the economy.
2. Information provided to meet investors' and creditors' needs is likely to be generally useful to members of other groups who are interested in essentially the same financial aspects of business enterprises as investors and creditors.

Creditors need information about the profitability and stability of the enterprise to answer such questions as: "Do we lend the money, and with what provisions?" Investors (both existing stockholders and potential investors) need information concerning the safety and profitability of their investment. As noted in the introduction to this chapter, stockholders must decide whether to increase, decrease, terminate, or maintain their interest in an enterprise.

---

[2]For example, see Richard S. Savich, "The Use of Accounting Information in Decision Making," *The Accounting Review* (July 1977), p. 642.

[3]*Statement of Financial Accounting Concepts No. 1,* "Objectives of Financial Reporting by Business Enterprises" (Stamford: Financial Accounting Standards Board, 1978), par. 30.

Financial Reporting

The two major classifications of users, internal and external, have led to a distinction between two major areas of accounting. **Management accounting** (sometimes referred to as managerial or cost accounting) is concerned primarily with financial reporting for internal users. Internal users, especially management, have control over the accounting system and can specify precisely what information is needed and how the information is to be reported. **Financial accounting** focuses on the development and communication of financial information for external users in the form of general purpose financial statements. The statements include a balance sheet, income statement, statement of cash flows, and usually a statement of changes in retained earnings or in owners' equity.

Most accounting systems are designed to generate information for both internal and external reporting. Generally, the external information is much more highly summarized than the information reported internally. The internal decisions made by management require information regarding, for example, specific product lines, specific financing alternatives, individual sales territories, detailed expense classifications, and differences between actual and budgeted revenues and costs. The decisions made by external users require broader indications of overall profitability and financial stability.

While internal financial reporting is governed by the needs of management, external financial reporting is governed by an established body of standards or principles[4] that are designed to reflect the external users' needs. The development of these standards is discussed in some detail later in this chapter.

This textbook focuses on financial accounting and external reporting. The remaining chapters present the concepts, standards, and procedures applied in the development of the basic financial statements.

THE ACCOUNTING PROFESSION

Professional accountants perform their work in many different roles and environments. To meet its various reporting needs, a business enterprise may employ **financial accountants,** who are primarily concerned with external financial reporting; **management accountants,** who are primarily concerned with internal financial reporting; and **tax accountants,** who prepare the necessary federal, state, and local tax returns and advise manage-

---

[4]The terms "standards" and "principles" are used interchangeably by the accounting profession and in this text.

ment in matters relating to taxation. In smaller organizations, there is less specialization and more combining of responsibility for the various accounting functions.

Larger business enterprises typically employ **internal auditors** who review the work performed by accountants and others within the enterprise and report their findings to management. In addition to auditing financial reports generated by the accounting system, they review the operational policies of the company and make recommendations for improving efficiency and effectiveness. Although internal auditors are employees of the enterprise, they must be independent with respect to the employees whose work they review. Thus, internal auditors generally report to top management or a special audit committee of the board of directors.

Some accountants, known as Certified Public Accountants (CPAs), do not work for a single business enterprise. Rather, they provide a variety of services for many different individual and business clients. With respect to external financial reporting, the most important service provided by CPAs is the independent audit of financial statements.

The External Audit Function

As independent or external auditors, CPAs play a critical role in the reporting of financial information to external users. Their responsibility is to independently examine the financial statements to be furnished to external users and to express an opinion as to the fairness of the statements in adhering to generally accepted accounting principles. The auditor's opinion is communicated in a report that accompanies the financial statements. The opinion is based on evidence gathered by the auditor from the detailed records and documents maintained by the company and from a review of the controls over the accounting system. An example of the auditor's report for Colgate-Palmolive Company is included on page 8.

The need for independent audits resulted from the emergence of the corporate form of business and the resulting separation of ownership and management. A significant proportion of the productive activity in the United States is conducted by publicly held corporations; that is, by corporations whose securities are sold to the general public. The stockholders who own the corporations are primarily investors and are generally not involved in enterprise operations. These investor-owners rely on management to operate the business and report periodically on the performance and financial status of the enterprise. Those companies registered nationally with the Securities and Exchange Commission are *required* to have an annual external audit as a protection to the stockholders.

Management has control over the information reported to stockholders and other external users and is responsible for the content of the financial statements. They emphasize this responsibility by including a report from management in the annual report to stockholders. (See Report of Management for Colgate-Palmolive Company reproduced on page 8). Management is also accountable for the profitability and financial condition of the enterprise as reflected in the statements. Obviously, there is a motivation on the part of management to present the financial information in the most favorable manner possible. It is the responsibility of the auditors to review management's reports and to independently decide if the reports are indeed representative of the actual conditions existing within the enterprise. The auditor's opinion adds credibility to the financial statements of enterprises, whether large or small, or privately or publicly held.

Other Services Provided by CPAs

In addition to performing independent audits, CPAs assist clients in **tax planning** and reporting to various government entities. CPAs also function as management consultants, offering advice to clients in such areas as systems design, organization, personnel, finance, internal control, and employee benefits. These services are frequently referred to as **management advisory services.** Various accounting services are also provided for smaller, privately owned businesses.

The Practice of Public Accounting. CPAs practice either individually or in firms. Because of the importance of personal liability for professional conduct, public accounting firms are generally organized as either proprietorships or partnerships. Most state laws now permit CPAs to be organized as professional corporations. These corporations provide many of the benefits of the corporate structure, but still retain personal liability for the professionals involved.

Almost all big, publicly held corporations are audited by a few large CPA firms. Listed in alphabetical order, the nine largest firms are Arthur Andersen & Co.; Arthur Young & Company; Coopers & Lybrand; Deloitte Haskins & Sells; Ernst & Whinney; KMG Main Hurdman; Peat, Marwick, Mitchell & Co.; Price Waterhouse & Co.; and Touche Ross & Co. Each of these firms is an international organization with many offices in the United States and abroad.

Many small businesses and nonprofit entities are serviced by regional and local CPA firms, including a large number of sole practitioners. In these firms, the role of auditing is often less important than the areas of tax reporting and planning and systems consulting. A CPA in a smaller firm is expected to be something of an accounting generalist, as opposed to the

REPORT OF MANAGEMENT

The management of Colgate-Palmolive Company has prepared the accompanying financial statements and is responsible for their content and other information contained in this annual report. The Company's financial statements were prepared in accordance with generally accepted accounting principles and include amounts that are based on management's best estimates and judgments. Arthur Andersen & Co., independent accountants, has examined the financial statements and presented an independent opinion thereon.

Colgate-Palmolive maintains a system of internal accounting control designed to provide reasonable assurance that transactions are executed in accordance with proper authorization and are recorded properly, and that assets are safeguarded. Effectiveness of internal controls is enhanced by the communication of formal policies regarding corporate conduct to all levels of employees and by staffing managerial positions with professionally trained and qualified personnel. The control system is monitored by internal auditors who examine financial reports, test the accuracy of transactions and otherwise obtain assurance that the system is operating in accordance with the Company's stated objectives.

The Audit Committee of the Board of Directors is composed entirely of non-employee directors. The Committee meets periodically and independently with management, internal auditors and the independent accountants to discuss the Company's internal accounting controls, auditing and financial reporting matters. The internal auditors and independent accountants have unrestricted access to the Audit Committee.

Reuben Mark
President and Chief
Executive Officer

Paul A. Jones
Executive Vice President and
Chief Financial Officer

REPORT OF INDEPENDENT ACCOUNTANTS

To the Board of Directors and Shareholders of
Colgate-Palmolive Company:

We have examined the consolidated balance sheet of Colgate-Palmolive Company (a Delaware corporation) and subsidiaries as of December 31, 1984 and 1983, and the related statements of income, changes in financial position, retained earnings and changes in capital accounts for each of the three years in the period ended December 31, 1984. Our examinations were made in accordance with generally accepted auditing standards and, accordingly, included such tests of the accounting records and such other auditing procedures as we considered necessary in the circumstances.

In our opinion, the financial statements referred to above present fairly the financial position of Colgate-Palmolive Company and subsidiaries as of December 31, 1984 and 1983, and the results of their operations and the changes in their financial position for each of the three years in the period ended December 31, 1984, in conformity with generally accepted accounting principles applied on a consistent basis.

New York, New York
February 14, 1985   Arthur Andersen & Co.

more specialized positions of CPAs in large regional and national firms. A vital role is played by the smaller public accounting firms in serving the thousands of small entities in the United States that are crucial to the nation's economy.[5]

---

[5]According to a newsnote in *Forbes*, 98% of all the businesses in the United States are private proprietorships or partnerships. They account for one-third of the U.S. output, and 65 of them have revenues over $1 billion. "Who Needs Stockholders?" *Forbes* (November 18, 1985), p. 6.

THE DEVELOPMENT OF ACCOUNTING STANDARDS

Accounting principles and procedures have evolved over hundreds of years. The formal standard-setting process that exists today, however, has developed in the past fifty years. Because accounting grew so rapidly with the advent of the Industrial Revolution, accounting procedures were often developed without extended debate or discussion. Accountants developed methods that seemed to meet the needs of their respective companies, resulting in diverse procedures among companies in accounting for similar activities. The comparability of the resulting financial reports, therefore, was often questionable.

During the 1920's, these differences led to financial statements that were often inflated in value. Market values of stocks rose higher than the underlying real values warranted until the entire structure collapsed in the stock market crash of 1929. The government of the United States, under the leadership of President Franklin D. Roosevelt, vigorously attacked the ensuing depression, and among other things, created the Securities and Exchange Commission (SEC). This new agency was given the responsibility to protect the interests of investors by ensuring full and fair disclosure in the regulation of the capital markets. The broad power granted to the SEC by Congress will be more fully discussed in a separate section. The emergence of the SEC forced the accounting profession to unite and to become more diligent in developing accounting principles and ethics to govern the profession. This led over time to the formation of several different private sector organizations, each having the responsibility of issuing accounting standards. These organizations, their publications, and the time they were in existence are identified in Exhibit 1-2 and discussed in subsequent sections of the chapter.

Exhibit 1–2   Accounting Standard-Setting Bodies

Standard-Setting Body	Date	Authoritative Publications
AICPA Committee on Accounting Procedures	1939–1959	Accounting Research Bulletins
Accounting Principles Board	1959–1973	APB Opinions
Financial Accounting Standards Board	1973–present	Statements of Financial Accounting Standards Interpretations

In the previous pages, three important groups that are involved with general purpose financial statements were identified; users, managers of business enterprises, and external auditors. As has been demonstrated, each of these groups has its own specific function to perform in the complex business environment that constitutes our economy. In many instances, these functions may be in conflict with each other. This condition provides another reason for the establishment of accounting standards—to resolve those different points of view that lead to different accounting methods being applied in similar circumstances.

Standards are designed to help accountants apply consistent principles for different businesses. They are recognized by the profession as representing the generally accepted position of the profession, and must be followed in the preparation of financial statements unless circumstances warrant an exception to a standard. These standards are commonly referred to as **generally accepted accounting principles (GAAP)**. If the management of an enterprise feels the circumstances do not warrant compliance with the standard, an exception can be taken. Under these circumstances, the auditor's report must clearly disclose the nature of and the reason for the exception in the financial statements.[6]

Financial Accounting Standards Board

The **Financial Accounting Standards Board (FASB)** is an independent organization consisting of seven full-time members drawn from professional accounting, business, government, and academia.[7] The members are required to sever all connections with their firms or institutions prior to assuming membership on the Board. Members are appointed for five-year terms and are eligible for reappointment to one additional term. Headquartered in Stamford, Connecticut, the Board has its own research staff and an annual budget in excess of 10 million dollars.

Funding for the FASB is obtained through the **Financial Accounting Foundation (FAF)**, an organization that is also responsible for selecting members of the FASB and its Advisory Council. (See Exhibit 1-3 for Fi-

---

[6]American Institute of Certified Public Accountants, *Code of Professional Ethics,* Rule 203.

[7]Maintaining this independence is sometimes difficult when complex issues affect so many groups in material ways. For example, in 1985, executives of business enterprises openly expressed their desire for more business representation on the FASB to assure that their interests were being considered. In a newspaper article, "The F. A. S. B. Comes Under Fire," Eric Berg, writing for *The New York Times,* stated that "It (business) has deluged foundation members with telephone calls and letters and has formed a committee with some of the most powerful financial executives in America to make sure more business executives get on the board." *The New York Times,* August 18, 1985, Section 3, page 4.

nancial Accounting Foundation organization chart.) The **Advisory Council** consults with the Board on major policy questions, selects major project task forces to work on specific projects, and conducts such other activities as may be requested by the FASB. The Foundation is administered by a Board of Trustees whose 15 members are made up of representatives from eight sponsoring institutions as follows:

American Accounting Association (AAA)

American Institute of Certified Public Accountants (AICPA)

Financial Analysts Federation (FAF)

Financial Executives Institute (FEI)

National Association of Accountants (NAA)

Securities Industry Association (SIA)

National Association of State Auditors, Comptrollers, and Treasurers (NASACT)

Government Finance Officers Association (GFOA)

The latter two organizations were added in 1984 when the Foundation assumed responsibility for selecting members for a newly established organization, the **Governmental Accounting Standards Board (GASB)**. This Board was organized to establish standards in the governmental area.

Exhibit 1–3   Financial Accounting Foundation Organizational Chart

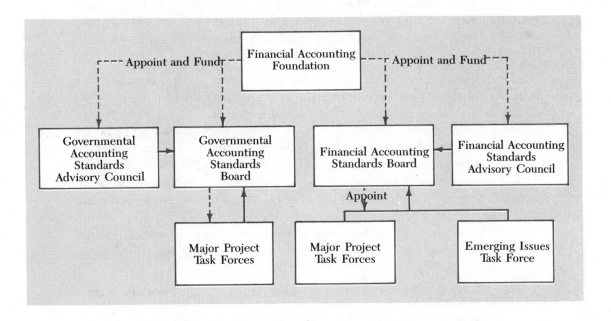

The Standard-Setting Process[8]

The major function of the FASB is to study accounting issues and establish accounting standards. These standards are published as **Statements of Financial Accounting Standards.** The FASB also issues **Statements of Financial Accounting Concepts.** The concepts identified in the statements are intended as guides for establishing standards. That is, they provide a framework within which specific accounting standards can be developed.[9]

Because the actions of the FASB have an impact on many individuals and groups within the economy, the Board follows a standard-setting process that is open to public observation and participation. The Board separates the topics it deals with into two areas: (1) Major Projects and (2) Implementation and Practice Problems. The process for the first area is very extensive and often requires from two to four years or more to complete. For example, significant events in the development of FASB Statement No. 87, issued in late 1985, are listed in Exhibit 1-4. While the eleven years required to complete this project exceed the normal period, this example illustrates how difficult it is to resolve some of the more complex accounting issues. The process for the second area, Implementation and Practice Problems, though still subject to public input, is designed for completion within a six-to twelve-month period.

The long-term nature of the standard-setting process has been one of the principal points of criticism of the Board. There seems to be no alternative to the lengthy process, however, given the philosophy that arriving at a consensus among the members of the accounting profession and other interested parties is important to the Board's credibility.

Major Projects. For each major project undertaken by the Board, a task force of outside experts is appointed to study the existing literature. When available literature is deemed insufficient, additional research is conducted. Subsequently, the Board issues a **Discussion Memorandum** that identifies the principal issues involved with the topic. This document includes a discussion of the various points of view as to the resolution of the issues, but does not include a specific conclusion. An extensive bibliography is usually included. Readers of the discussion memorandum are invited to comment either in writing or orally at a public hearing. Sometimes a topic is not identified well enough to issue a discussion memorandum, and the FASB issues a preliminary document identified as an

---

[8]For a more detailed description of the FASB and its operations see "Facts about FASB," published annually by the Financial Accounting Standards Board.

[9]The conceptual framework of the FASB is discussed fully in Chapter 2.

Exhibit 1–4

Significant Events in the Development of FASB Statement No. 87,
"Employers' Accounting for Pensions"

1974	Pensions added to FASB agenda
1975	Task force appointed
1975	Discussion Memorandum #1 issued
1976	Public hearing #1 held
1977	Exposure Draft #1 issued
1979	Exposure Draft #1 revised
1980	FASB background paper issued
1981	Discussion Memorandum #2 issued
1981	Public hearing #2 held
1982	Preliminary Views document issued
1983	Supplement to Discussion Memorandum #2 issued
1984	Public hearing #3 held
1985	Exposure Draft #2 issued
1985	Public hearing #4 held
1985	Statement No. 87 issued in December

"Invitation to Comment." The topic is briefly discussed in the document, and readers are encouraged to send their comments to the FASB for more definite formulation of specific issues.

After a Discussion Memorandum has been issued and comments from interested parties have been evaluated, the Board meets as many times as necessary to resolve the issues. These meetings are open to the public, and the agenda is published in advance. From these meetings, the Board develops an **Exposure Draft** of a Statement that includes specific recommendations for financial accounting and reporting. A majority of the seven-member Board is required to approve the Exposure Draft for issuance. Again, reaction to this document is requested from the accounting and business community. At the end of the exposure period, usually 60 days or more, all comment papers are reviewed by the Staff and the Board. Further deliberation by the Board leads to either the issuance of a **Statement of Financial Accounting Standards,** to a revised Exposure Draft, or in some cases to abandonment of the project.

The final statement not only sets forth the actual standards, but also establishes the effective date and method of transition, and gives pertinent background information and the basis for the Board's conclusions, including reasons for rejecting significant alternative solutions. If any members dissent from the majority view, they may include the reasons for their dissent as part of the document.

Implementation and Practice Problems. The second category of issues dealt with by the Board involves implementation and practice problems that relate to previously issued standards. Depending on the nature of a problem, the Board may issue a Statement of Financial Accounting Standards or an **Interpretation.** The interpretation may be issued without appointing a task force, issuing a Discussion Memorandum, or holding public hearings. Exposure of these publications, however, to either the public or the Advisory Council is required as part of the due process followed by the Board.

Problems that arise in practice are also addressed in **Technical Bulletins** prepared and issued by the staff of the FASB. The Bulletins, which are reviewed by the Board prior to being issued, provide guidance for particular situations that arise in practice. In contrast with Standards and Interpretations, the staff Technical Bulletins do not have the authority of GAAP.

The procedures of the Board are intended to help accomplish its mission, which is to establish and improve standards of financial accounting and reporting. The credibility of the Board has fluctuated through the years as different issues have been resolved. The FASB has no legislative power, but must depend on the general acceptance of its pronouncements by the accounting profession and other interested groups. This acceptability is directly influenced by two other organizations: the AICPA and the SEC.[10]

American Institute of Certified Public Accountants

The **American Institute of Certified Public Accountants** is the professional organization of practicing CPAs in the United States. The organization was founded in 1887, and publishes a monthly journal, the *Journal of Accountancy*. Membership in the AICPA is voluntary, and over 250,000 CPAs are members.

Prior to the formation of the FASB, accounting principles were established under the direction of the AICPA. From 1939–1959, principles were formed by the **Committee on Accounting Procedures (CAP).** Their pronouncements were known as **Accounting Research Bulletins (ARBs).** From 1959 to 1973, accounting principles were formed by the **Accounting Principles Board (APB)** and issued as **Opinions.** Dissatisfaction with the part-time nature of these boards, their failure to react quickly to some issues, and the lack of broad representation on the boards because of their direct relationship to the AICPA led to the formation in 1973 of the FASB.

---

[10]An evaluation of the FASB's success was undertaken in 1984 by the Harris Research Group. Over 600 individuals were queried on a variety of topics. In response to the query as to the overall view of the FASB, 87% ranked its success as good or excellent. Louis Harris, "A Study of Attitudes Towards an Assessment of the FASB," Executive Summary, *FASB Viewpoints*, p. 4.

Although the FASB replaced the APB as the official standard-setting body for the profession, the AICPA continued to influence the establishment of accounting standards through its issuance of **Accounting and Audit Guides** and **Statements of Position (SOPs).** The Guides were issued by specially appointed committees of the AICPA and dealt with specific industries, such as construction, insurance, banking, and real estate. These Guides not only contained information concerning the auditing of these entities, but also discussed alternative accounting methods that could be employed by the industry. The Guides often recommended a preferred accounting method. The SOPs were issued by the Accounting Standards Executive Committee (AcSEC), an AICPA committee established when the FASB assumed the standard-setting role. SOPs often dealt with emerging issues that had not yet been placed on the FASB agenda, but which needed to be addressed by the profession for improved comparability in financial reporting. While the Guides and SOPs were not part of GAAP, they were considered **Preferable Accounting Principles** and began to be looked upon as another important source of standards guidance.

The FASB became concerned about this growing volume of "other" standards, and in 1979 adopted the Guides and SOPs as officially preferred accounting principles subject to their review and possible subsequent issuance as FASB Statements.[11] Beginning in the early 1980s, many specialized industry guides were adopted as FASB Standards. (See list of FASB standards in Appendix B of the text). Although no longer issuing SOPs, AcSEC still helps the FASB identify emerging issues and communicates the concerns of CPAs on accounting issues to the FASB. Thus, the AICPA continues to influence greatly the establishment of accounting standards.

The AICPA also assumes the major responsibility for establishing standards for auditing, accounting and review services, taxation, and management advisory services. It also is concerned with maintaining the integrity of the profession through its Code of Professional Ethics and through a quality control program that includes a process of peer review of CPA firms conducted by other CPAs. Although membership in the AICPA traditionally has been individual, the influence of the firm has become increasingly important. In the late 1970s the AICPA instituted a firm membership in one of two sections: (1) the **SEC Practice Section (SECPS)** for firms that have clients subject to government regulation through the Securities and Exchange Commission (SEC), and (2) the **Private Companies Practice Section (PCPS)** for firms that do not have clients regulated by the

---

[11]*Statement of Financial Accounting Standards No. 32,* "Specialized Accounting and Reporting Principles and Practices in AICPA Statements of Position and Guides on Accounting and Auditing Matters" (Stamford: Financial Accounting Standards Board, 1979).

SEC. The SEC practice firms are subject to more stringent regulation than the private companies practice firms, although a high quality of performance is expected of all firms. At the present time, membership in these sections is voluntary. A firm may belong to both sections, and most of the larger firms do.

Another important function of the AICPA is preparation and grading of the Uniform CPA examination. This examination, covering two and one half days, is given twice each year simultaneously in all fifty states. In addition to passing all four parts of the examination, an individual must meet the state education and experience requirements in order to obtain state certification as a CPA. Most states now require CPAs to meet continuing education requirements in order to retain their certificate to practice. The AICPA assists its members in meeting these requirements through an extensive Continuing Professional Education (CPE) program that includes course offerings throughout the United States.

Securities and Exchange Commission

The **Securities and Exchange Commission** was created by an act of Congress in 1934. Its primary role is to regulate the issuance and trading of securities by corporations to the general public. Prior to offering securities for sale to the public, a company must file a registration statement with the Commission that contains financial and organizational disclosures. In addition, all publicly held companies are required to furnish annual and other periodical information to the Commission and to have their external financial statements examined by independent accountants.

The Commission's intent is not to prevent the trading of speculative securities, but to insist that investors have adequate information. As a result, the SEC is vitally interested in financial reporting and the development of accounting standards. The Commission carefully monitors the standard-setting process and responds to Discussion Memorandums and Exposure Drafts issued by the FASB. The Commission also brings to the Board's attention emerging problems that need to be addressed.

When the Commission was formed, Congress gave it power to establish accounting principles as follows:

> The Commission may prescribe, in regard to reports made pursuant to this title, the form or forms in which the required information shall be set forth, the items or details to be shown in the balance sheet and the earning statement, and the methods to be followed in the preparation of reports, in the appraisal or valuation of assets and liabilities . . . [12]

---

[12]Securities Exchange Act of 1934, Section 13(b).

The Commission has generally refrained from fully using these powers, preferring to work through the private sector in the development of standards. Throughout its existence, however, the Commission has issued statements pertaining to accounting and auditing issues. Most of them are quite specific in nature and deal with a particular company or a specific situation. At present, SEC statements are referred to as either *Financial Reporting Releases* (FRRs) or *Accounting and Auditing Enforcement Releases (AAERs)*. Previously they were referred to as *Accounting Series Releases* (ASRs). Although the SEC is generally supportive of the FASB, from time to time the Commission intervenes in the standard-setting process. The SEC has been credited, for example, with requiring experimentation with current value disclosure when it appeared that the FASB was going to recommend an alternative approach to reporting inflation information.

American Accounting Association

The **American Accounting Association** is primarily an organization for accounting academicians, although practicing professional accountants also belong in large numbers. A quarterly journal, *The Accounting Review* is published by the AAA. Several specialized sections have been organized within the AAA, and many of these also publish journals. Accounting academicians are very interested in the development of accounting standards. They have the unique position of being professionals not directly involved with the preparation or audit of financial statements. Thus they are able to consider objectively the needs of users as well as business enterprises and auditors. The AAA was instrumental in encouraging development by the FASB of a conceptual framework for accounting that would assist in the development of standards to govern financial reporting. AAA committee members review FASB Discussion Memorandums and Exposure Drafts and respond to the proposals of the FASB. Individual members of the association participate actively in research projects that are used by the FASB as the basis for many of its recommendations.[13]

The American Accounting Association does not claim to serve as a majority voice for accounting academicians. There are many different opinions and points of view represented in its membership. Its major role is to

---

[13]Indicative of this type of research are the following reports commissioned and issued by the FASB as background for its issued Concepts Statement No. 5. Yuji Ijiri, *Recognition of Contractual Rights and Obligations* (Stamford: Financial Accounting Standards Board, 1980); Henry Jaenicke, *Survey of Present Practices in Recognizing Revenues, Expenses, Gains, and Losses* (Stamford: Financial Accounting Standards Board, 1981); L. Todd Johnson and Reed K. Storey, *Recognition in Financial Statements: Underlying Concepts and Practical Conventions* (Stamford: Financial Accounting Standards Board, 1982).

serve as a forum within which individual educators can express their views, either individually or in specially appointed committees. The impact of the academic arm of accounting on the establishment of accounting standards has increased through the years, as evidenced by inclusion of an educator as a member of the FASB and the large number of educators included on FASB task forces and the FASB staff.

Other Organizations

Although the preceding groups have traditionally exercised the most direct influence upon the regulation of accountants and the development of accounting principles, the influence of other groups has also been felt. Professional accountants from business enterprises are represented on the Board of Trustees of the Financial Accounting Foundation by two organizations, the **Financial Executives Institute** and the **National Association of Accountants.**

The FEI is a national organization composed of financial executives employed by large corporations. The FEI membership includes treasurers, controllers, and financial vice-presidents. The FEI has sponsored several research projects through the years related to financial reporting problems.[14]

The NAA is more concerned with the information needs of internal users than with external reporting. Its monthly publication, *Management Accounting,* has traditionally dealt mainly with problems involving information systems and the development and use of accounting data within the business organization. It awards the **Certificate of Management Accounting (CMA)** to those management accountants who pass a 2½-day qualifying examination and meet specified experience requirements. Because a firm's information system usually provides data for both internal and external reporting, the NAA is often concerned about the activities of the FASB and responds to its invitations to comment on issues that are related to internal reporting.

The users of external financial reports are also represented on the Board of Trustees by two organizations. The **Financial Analysts Federation** represents the large number of analysts who advise the investing public on the meaning of the financial reports issued by America's businesses. Members of this group have often been critical of corporate financial reporting practices and have continually requested increased disclosure of pertinent

---

[14]Representative of these reports on vital financial issues are the following: John K. Shank, *Price Level Adjusted Statements and Management Decisions* (New York: Financial Executive Research Foundation, 1975); Allen A. Geed, *Inflation: Its Impact on Financial Reporting and Decision Making* (New York: Financial Executive Research Foundation, 1978).

financial data. The **Securities Industry Associates** is the organization that represents the investment bankers who manage the portfolios of the large institutional investors that have affected the stock market so dramatically in the past decade. The large amount of investment capital controlled by insurance companies and banks has significantly diminished the influence of the small investor in the market. The strong "bull market" of the mid 1980's was characterized by large daily swings in the stock market prices caused by heavy trading by institutional investors. This group of external users of financial information has become increasingly vocal with regard to financial reporting and the establishment of accounting standards.

Although the preceding discussion of accounting standards has focused on reporting by private enterprise businesses, the accounting profession is also concerned with the reporting by the numerous government institutions in our economy. This includes not only the Federal Government and its agencies, but also the large number of states, counties, and municipal governments. It is estimated that the total expenditures by these government organizations exceed 1.5 trillion dollars per year. Two government organizations were added to the list of sponsors of the FAF in 1984 — the **National Association of State Auditors, Treasurers, and Controllers** and the **Government Finance Officers Association.** These organizations are especially interested in the standards issued by the **Government Accounting Standards Board,** a companion board to the FASB organized in 1984 to focus on reporting by the public sector of our economy. Although the statements issued by governmental organizations do not have a direct impact on investors, the magnitude of their impact on such vital economic factors as the interest rate, tax policies, and employment rates cannot be ignored in any financial planning. Creditors are especially affected by the financial activities of governmental units that require funding through various forms of bonds and long-term notes.

Impact of Accounting Standards

As discussed earlier in this chapter, accounting information plays a critical role in the economic decision-making process. Thus, the standards applied in the development of financial information have a significant impact on the allocation of resources in our economy.

Professional Judgment. Many accounting standards provide general guidelines rather than precise rules. The accountant, therefore, must exercise professional judgment in interpreting and applying standards. For example, FASB Statement No. 5, "Accounting for Contingencies," states that a contingent loss and the related liability should be recognized in the financial statements only if it is "probable" that an actual future loss will be sustained. It is up to the accountant and the auditor to decide whether it is "probable" that an event, such as a lawsuit, will result in a definite liability. The accountant's decision has a direct impact on the information reported on the financial statements.

The Manville Corporation provides an interesting example of the difficulty in applying the contingent liability standards. As a principal manufacturer of asbestos used in the construction business, Manville became subject to a large number of lawsuits arising from individuals who claimed they were injured by working with or coming into contact with the dangerous substance. To alert users of the financial statements to this contingent liability, Manville included an extensive note with its 1980 financial statements, part of which is reproduced below. These lawsuits

Manville Corporation

Notes to Financial Statements for 1980

Note 5 — Contingencies

The Company is a defendant or co-defendant in a substantial number of lawsuits brought by present or former insulation workers, shipyard workers, factory workers and other persons alleging damage to their health from exposure to dust from asbestos fiber or asbestos-containing products manufactured or sold by the Company and, in most cases, by certain other defendants. The majority of these claims allege that the Company and other defendants failed in their duty to warn of the hazards of inhalation of asbestos fiber and dust originating from asbestos-containing products. In the opinion of Management, the Company has substantial defenses to these legal actions, resulting in part from prompt warnings of the possible hazards of exposure to asbestos fiber emitted from asbestos-containing insulation products following the 1964 publication of scientific studies linking pulmonary disease in insulation workers to asbestos exposure.

Because of the uncertainties associated with the asbestos/health litigation, and in spite of the substantial defenses the Company believes it has with respect to these claims, the eventual outcome of the asbestos/health litigation cannot be predicted at this time and the ultimate liability of the Company after application of available insurance cannot be estimated with any degree of reliability. No reasonable estimate of loss can be made and no liability has been recorded in the financial statements. Liabilities, if any, relating to asbestos/health litigation will be recorded in accordance with generally accepted accounting principles when such amounts can be reasonably estimated. Depending on how and when these uncertainties are resolved, the cost to the Company could be substantial.

eventually forced Manville Corporation into receivership as indicated in the October 30, 1985 article, reproduced below.

THE WALL STREET JOURNAL WEDNESDAY, OCTOBER 30, 1985   **7**

Manville Had Loss Of $98.6 Million For Third Quarter

By a WALL STREET JOURNAL *Staff Reporter*

DENVER—Manville Corp. reported a third-quarter net loss of $98.6 million, which includes a previously announced $120.1 million write-down from the sale or closing of some operations.

The loss, the company's largest ever, compares with a profit of $28.2 million, or 92 cents a share, in the year-earlier period. The building and forest-products company's revenue in the quarter rose slightly to $515.7 million from $511.9 million in the 1984 third quarter.

Manville said the $120.1 million charge includes the closing of plants in Manville, N.J., and Marrero, La., the shutdown of some residential roofing operations and the sale of most of its Canadian operations and some international businesses. The charge also includes $27.1 million that was set aside to provide for future asbestos-related health claims.

For the nine months, the company reported a net loss of $66 million compared with net income of $59 million, or $1.68 a share, a year earlier. Revenue in the nine months rose 3.5% to $1.45 billion from $1.4 billion a year earlier.

Manville has said it hopes to emerge from bankruptcy-law proceedings next year by creating a $2.5 billion trust fund for asbestos victims. The company filed for protection from its creditors under Chapter 11 of the federal Bankruptcy Code three years ago after thousands of people filed lawsuits claiming they contracted diseases from exposure to Manville-made asbestos products.

Alternative Accounting Principles. In many areas, there is more than one generally accepted principle or standard for reporting events or transactions. Examples include depreciation of plant assets, inventory valuation, and costs of long-term construction contracts. The choice of one standard rather than another can have a material effect on financial statements.

For example, in 1983 Revere Copper and Brass Inc. changed its method of valuing some of its inventory from FIFO to LIFO. The income statement for that year reported net income of $15,042,000 and income tax expense of $1,801,000. Had Revere continued to value its inventories under the FIFO method, net income would have been approximately $20,986,000 and the company would have incurred a much larger tax liability. The balance sheet reported inventories of $90,491,000, whereas using FIFO, inventories would have been reported at approximately $98,000,000.

Reported financial information, particularly net income, can have far-reaching effects. Thus, a decrease in net income could cause a decline in stock prices or a reduction of dividends paid to stockholders. Also, some companies have employee compensation and benefit plans that are directly related to net income. Thus, when employee bonuses or contributions to employee profit-sharing plans are calculated as a percentage of net income, the employees would suffer a direct economic loss as a result of lower reported earnings.

These are just a few examples of the impact of accounting standards and their application. They are intended to underscore the importance of accounting information and the standards applied in developing that information.

Standard-Setting in a Complex Environment

The environment within which business and accounting function has become increasingly complex. One of its characteristic features is the many social, political, legal, and economic influences that create continual change in that environment. Technology has developed new products that have led to a dramatic shift from a capital-intensive industrial economy in the United States to a labor-intensive information technology economy.[15] Government continues to influence the economy through its tremendous federal deficits, tax regulations, international trade policy, and actions to control inflation. World markets have become closer as businesses have increased their international involvement and funds have become increasingly fluid in movement around the world. If accounting is to continue to be the "language of business," it must adapt to these complex, changing relationships.

This dynamic environment means that the standard setters must be continually alert to the effects of the environmental factors upon accounting. For example, the technological revolution of the past few years has included a significant increase in the use of computers, both in business and in the home. The programs that make the computer so adaptable to varied uses are known as "computer software." Thousands of companies, many quite small, have been formed to produce wide varieties of software for public consumption. The accounting issue involved concerns the treatment of costs to develop the software. There is always uncertainty as to whether the cost to develop the software will be recovered in the market place. Should these costs be reported as assets before the judgment of the market

---

[15]John Naisbett, *Megatrends* (New York: Warner Books, 1982).

place is known, or should they be charged to expense and written off against revenue?[16]

Another example of how our complex environment affects accounting is the financial market place. It is continuing to develop new instruments that also adapt to the rapid changes in the economy. Variable interest debt, zero-interest-rate discounted bonds, and leveraged leases describe financial instruments that have emerged in the past few years. Accounting for these instruments on the books of both the lender and the investor must be considered and standards issued where current pronouncements are not deemed sufficient to assure comparable treatment by business enterprises.

The changing environment also creates the need to continually review existing standards to see if they require revision. The FASB has adopted a policy of reviewing its pronouncements to see if modification is needed. As a result of such review, the standards dealing with recording fluctuations in foreign exchange rates were modified after a seven year period of time.[17]

The magnitude of the growth in the standards is demonstrated by the fact that in the first 12 years of the FASB's existence, it issued 88 standards and 38 interpretations of standards. This compares with 31 opinions issued in a similar period by the Accounting Principles Board, predecessor to the FASB. While it is true that some of the FASB standards are quite narrow in their coverage, there is still significantly more output from the FASB than was true of earlier standard-setting bodies.

Conflict between Public and Private Sector

As indicated previously, the SEC has historically left the standard-setting process to the private sector. The Commission's influence, however, has often been felt on specific issues. From time to time, Congress has urged the SEC to exercise a more critical role in setting financial accounting standards and in evaluating the independence and quality control of CPA firms. Over the past two decades, there have been many legal actions brought against CPA firms for failure to fairly disclose the financial condition of a company. These legal actions have become more common, and as they arise, Congress, through its committee structure, again raises difficult questions about whether the system in the private sector is working for the benefit of the public.

---

[16] The FASB responded to this question by issuing *Statement of Financial Accounting Standards No. 86*, "Accounting for Computer Software Costs" (Stamford: Financial Accounting Standards Board, 1985). See Chapter 11 for detailed discussion of this topic.

[17] *Statement of Financial Accounting Standards No. 52*, issued in 1981, replaced *Statement of Financial Accounting Standards No. 8*, issued in 1975.

In 1978 there were two significant Congressional committees that conducted hearings concerning the accounting profession: the Metcalf Committee, chaired by Senator Lee Metcalf (Montana), and the Moss Committee, chaired by Representative John E. Moss (California). A Senate staff report entitled "The Accounting Establishment" was used extensively by the committees as they probed such issues as the possible monopoly position of the eight largest U.S. accounting firms (the "Big 8"); the independence of auditors whose firms employ tax consultants and management advisory counselors who work directly with audit clients; and the poor quality of audit work being performed in some instances. Although no definite legislative action was taken, these committees attracted a great deal of attention from the profession, and several changes were made by the AICPA as a result of these hearings, including its establishment of the firm membership divisions. Also, as a result of these hearings, annual reports from the SEC on the auditing profession are now required by Congress. These reports have generally been positive; however, another increase in business failures in the mid 1980s, including many bank failures, led to another round of hearings under the direction of Representative John Dingell of Michigan. The long-range impact of these Congressional hearings on the regulation of the accounting profession is still to be determined.

Although much attention is paid to the audit function by these congressional committees, there also has been attention paid to the establishment of accounting standards. Critics of standard setting in the private sector ask if it is realistic to assume that the profession can establish and administer standards and still retain an independent posture. Congress continues to prod the SEC to exercise a more active role in assuring that financial reporting is adequately measuring and disclosing the true status of companies and their activities. The FASB has responded to this pressure by its open discussion policy and its attempt to arrive at standards that balance theory and varying user needs.

Regardless of who sets accounting standards, the task is difficult. As will be discussed in the next chapter, there are very few absolutes in accounting principles. As evidenced by the voluminous tax legislation and the extreme difficulty in achieving tax simplification, passing the responsibility for accounting standard setting to the SEC or a similar governmental agency would probably lead to an even greater complexity in financial reporting. If accountants are to retain their role as professionals, they must be able to exercise judgment in applying general guidelines to specific problems. Users, managers of business enterprises, and professional auditors must balance their needs and views and continue to work toward more meaningful accounting and financial reporting. If these users cannot obtain meaningful reports through the private sector organizations such as the FASB, there will be increased demand from the public through Congress to do it by legislation.

OVERVIEW OF INTERMEDIATE ACCOUNTING

This first chapter is designed to emphasize the importance of accounting and financial reporting in today's complex business environment and the challenges that face those who are members of the accounting profession. The remaining chapters of the text cover in depth the elements contained in the basic financial statements presented to external users. To help students realize that the issues discussed are not just textbook issues, extensive examples of actual businesses are included throughout the book.

Although there has been a growing body of standards that constitute GAAP, there are many unresolved areas. In some cases, the existing standards have been questioned, and recommendations for revision of the standards have been made. It is important that those who plan to enter the profession of accounting have a foundation as to not only what GAAP currently is, but also have a theoretical understanding of why it developed to its present state.

QUESTIONS

1. Accounting has been defined as a service activity. Who is served by accounting and how are they benefitted?
2. Accounting is sometimes characterized as dealing only with the past. Give three examples of how accounting information can be of value in dealing with the future.
3. How does the fact that there are limited resources in the world relate to accounting information?
4. Distinguish between management accounting and financial accounting.
5. Contrast the roles of an accountant and an auditor.
6. Why are independent audits necessary?
7. What conditions led to the establishment of accounting standard-setting bodies?
8. What are the differences in purpose and scope of the FASB's Statements of Financial Accounting Standards, Statements of Financial Accounting

Concepts, Interpretations of Financial Accounting Standards, and Technical Bulletins?

9. What characteristics of the standard-setting process are designed to increase the acceptability of standards established by the FASB?
10. What is the relationship of the AICPA and the AAA to the FASB?
11. How does the SEC influence the accounting profession?
12. Why is standard setting such a difficult and complex task?
13. Why is Congress conducting hearings on the accounting profession? What type of legislation has been proposed to increase control over accounting?

DISCUSSION CASES

CASE 1–1   (How should I invest?)

Changing economic conditions have made equity securities (stock) a desirable investment alternative. Assume you have funds to invest in common stock, but you are not sure which companies you should invest in. You send for and receive the annual reports of several companies in three growth industries, but your background in accounting is limited to an introductory course. With your limited experience, what information would you expect to find to assist you in making an investment decision in (a) the balance sheet, (b) the income statement, and (c) the statement of cash flows?

CASE 1–2   (How large is too large?)

The existence of a relatively few large CPA firms that service virtually all of the major industrial and financial firms and thus dominate the accounting profession, has led to criticism through the years. In a staff study for Senator Metcalf and his Subcommittee on Reporting, Accounting, and Management, the following assertion was made:

> The AICPA has developed prestige because of its size, resources, management, and the professional reputation of CPAs for objectivity, which has been accepted by the public and governmental authorities until recent years. Analysis of AICPA activities reveals that the organization primarily promotes the perceived interest of the large national accounting firms. Those interests are generally sympathetic to the management interests of large corporate clients which are primary sources of revenue for large accounting firms. (p. 129, 1976 report)

What dangers do you see from this concentration of power? What advantages are present because of the emergence of a relatively few large firms?

CASE 1–3   (Here comes Congress again!)

Congressional hearings are again being held on the question of control of the accounting profession. There are many critics of accounting who would like to see more government control of accounting standards and of the auditors who examine financial statements of business enterprises.

(a) What points would you expect to hear from the president of the AICPA defending retention of private-sector control?

(b) What points would you expect to hear from a senator advocating installation of government controls over the accounting profession?

CASE 1–4   (What do users need?)

The definition of accounting quoted in this chapter stresses that information generated by an accounting system should be useful for making decisions. There are two basic types of users: those external to the company and those who are within the company, or internal users. Distinguish between the types of information these two user groups would need in order to make their decisions.

CASE 1–5   (SEC: A necessary evil?)

Annette Wilson and Henry Wall were selected to present a case in competition with students from other universities dealing with the need for a government agency oversight responsibility to monitor the quality of accounting in the private sector. Draft an outline showing the points you think Annette and Henry should make.

2
A Conceptual Framework of Accounting

Accounting often is viewed by the general public as a scientific discipline based on a fixed set of rules and procedures. This is a natural perception since the public's exposure to accounting generally relates to financial statements, tax returns, and other reports showing dollar amounts that give an impression of exactness. Those within the profession, however, recognize that accounting is more an art than a science, and that the operating results and other accounting measurements are based on estimates and judgments relative to the measurement and communication of business activity.

Although not an exact science, accounting and financial reporting are governed by a well-established body of "generally accepted accounting principles," referred to as GAAP. As explained in Chapter 1, GAAP includes standards and interpretations issued by the FASB and those pronouncements issued by previous standard-setting bodies that have not been suspended or superseded. Underlying these principles or standards are several fundamental concepts and assumptions that, collectively, provide a theoretical or conceptual framework of accounting. This chapter focuses on the need for such a framework and examines the major components of the FASB's conceptual framework.

NEED FOR A CONCEPTUAL FRAMEWORK

Much has been written about the theoretical foundation or **conceptual framework** that underlies accounting practice. There are several reasons why such a framework is important. One major purpose is to provide broad definitions of the objectives, terms, and concepts involved in the practice of accounting. This definitional aspect of the framework prescribes the boundaries of accounting and financial reporting.[1]

A strong theoretical foundation is essential if accounting practice is to keep pace with a changing business environment. Accountants are continually faced with new situations, technological advances, and business innovations that present new accounting and reporting problems. These problems must be dealt with in an organized and consistent manner. If their impact is sufficiently broad, specific issues may be resolved through the FASB's standard-setting process. The conceptual framework plays a vital role in the development of new standards and in the revision of previously issued standards. Recognizing the importance of this role, the FASB stated that fundamental concepts "guide the Board in developing accounting and reporting standards by providing . . . a common foundation and basic reasoning on which to consider merits of alternatives."[2] In a very real sense, then, the FASB itself is a primary beneficiary of a conceptual framework.

A conceptual framework also brings together the objectives and fundamentals of existing accounting practice and financial reporting. This helps users to better understand the purposes, content, and characteristics of information provided by accounting.

A conceptual framework not only helps in understanding existing practice, but it also provides a guide for future practice. When accountants are confronted with new developments that are not covered by GAAP, a conceptual framework provides a frame of reference for analyzing and resolving emerging issues.

A conceptual framework is also useful in selecting the most appropriate methods for reporting enterprise activity. Often, there is more than one justifiable or generally accepted reporting alternative for a particular transaction or event, and accountants must use their judgment in selecting among available alternatives. Fundamental concepts provide guidance in choosing the alternative that most accurately reflects the financial position and results of operations for the entity given the specific circumstances involved. If businesses and their activities were identical, reporting alternatives could be eliminated. However, that is not the case. Even within a particular industry, companies are not organized in exactly the same way. They do not produce identical products or provide identical services, and their accounting systems and the reports generated therefrom are not uniform. Thus, accountants must exercise professional judgment in ful-

---

[1]See, for example, Paul B. W. Miller, "The Conceptual Framework: Myths and Realities," *Journal of Accountancy* (March, 1985), pp. 62-71.

[2]*Statement of Financial Accounting Concepts No. 6,* "Elements of Financial Statements" (Stamford: Financial Accounting Standards Board, December, 1985), p. i.

filling their roles as suppliers of useful information for decision makers. A conceptual framework helps make the results of the reporting process more comparable than they would be otherwise.

In summary, a conceptual framework of accounting should:

1. define the boundaries of accounting by providing definitions of basic objectives, key terms, and fundamental concepts,
2. assist the FASB in the standard-setting process by providing a basis for developing new and revised accounting and reporting standards,
3. provide a description of current practice and a frame of reference for resolving new issues not covered by GAAP, and
4. assist accountants and others in selecting from among reporting alternatives the method that best represents the economic reality of the situation.

If these purposes are accomplished, the overall result should be a reporting of the most useful information for decision-making purposes, which is the ultimate goal of accounting.

NATURE AND COMPONENTS OF THE FASB'S CONCEPTUAL FRAMEWORK

Serious attempts to develop a theoretical foundation of accounting can be traced to the 1930s. Among the leaders in such attempts were accounting educators, as individuals and collectively as a part of the American Accounting Association (AAA). In 1936, the Executive Committee of the AAA began issuing a series of publications devoted to accounting theory, the last of which was published in 1965 and entitled "A Statement of Basic Accounting Theory." During the period from 1936 to 1973, there were several additional publications issued by the AAA and also by the American Institute of Certified Public Accountants (AICPA), each attempting to develop a conceptual foundation for the practice of accounting.[3]

---

[3]Among the most prominent of these publications were: Maurice Moonitz, *Accounting Research Study No. 1*, "The Basic Postulates of Accounting" (New York: American Institute of Certified Public Accountants, 1961); William A. Paton and A. C. Littleton, *An Introduction to Corporate Accounting Standards*, Monograph 3 (Evanston, Ill.: American Accounting Association, 1940); Thomas H. Sanders, Henry R. Hatfield, and W. Moore, *A Statement of Accounting Principles* (New York: American Institute of Accountants, Inc., 1938); Robert T. Sprouse, and Maurice Moonitz, *Accounting Research Study No. 3*, "A Tentative Set of Broad Accounting Principles for Business Enterprises" (New York: American Institute of Certified Public Accountants, 1962); *Statement of the Accounting Principles Board No. 4*, "Basic Concepts and Accounting Principles Underlying Financial Statements of Business Enterprises" (New York: American Institute of Certified Public Accountants, October 1970); *Report of the Study Group on the Objectives of Financial Statements*, "Objectives of Financial Statements" (New York: American Institute of Certified Public Accountants, October 1973).

While these publications made significant contributions to the development of accounting thought, no unified structure of accounting theory emerged from these efforts. When the Financial Accounting Standards Board was established in 1973, it responded to the need for a general theoretical framework by undertaking a comprehensive project to develop a "conceptual framework for financial accounting and reporting." This project has been described as an attempt to establish a constitution for accounting. The goal of the FASB was to provide "a coherent system of interrelated objectives and fundamentals that is expected to lead to consistent standards and that prescribes the nature, function, and limits of financial accounting and reporting."[4]

The conceptual framework project was one of the original FASB agenda items. It was viewed as a long-term, continuing project to be developed in stages. Because of its significant potential impact on many aspects of financial reporting, and therefore its controversial nature, progress was deliberate. The project had high priority and received a large share of FASB resources. In December, 1985, the FASB issued the last of six Concepts Statements, which provide the basis for the conceptual framework.[5]

The FASB's framework incorporates many widely accepted concepts and principles developed in earlier works. In addition, several traditional assumptions underlying accounting practice are explicitly or implicitly recognized in the framework. The assumptions are discussed later in the chapter and include economic entity, going concern, arm's-length transactions, stable monetary unit, accounting periods, and accrual accounting. The main components of the FASB's conceptual framework, including the underlying assumptions, are presented in Exhibit 2-1.

The first area addressed by the FASB was the basic purposes or **objectives** of financial reporting. The Board sought answers to the questions: Who are the users of accounting information? What kinds of information do they require for decision making? Based on the objectives, the FASB proceeded to develop fundamental concepts that define the important **qualitative characteristics** of useful information and the specific **elements** to be included in financial statements.

---

[4]*Statement of Financial Accounting Concepts No. 6*, p. i.
[5]The six Concepts Statements issued by the FASB are:
   1. Objectives of Financial Reporting by Business Enterprises
   2. Qualitative Characteristics of Accounting Information
   3. Elements of Financial Statements of Business Enterprises
   4. Objectives of Financial Reporting by Nonbusiness Organizations
   5. Recognition and Measurement in Financial Statements of Business Enterprises
   6. Elements of Financial Statements (a replacement of No. 3).

Exhibit 2–1   A Conceptual Framework for Accounting

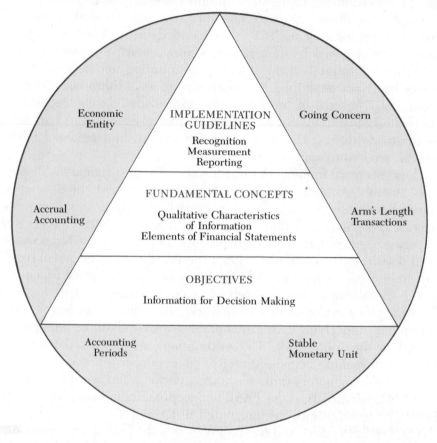

Building on the objectives and fundamental concepts, the FASB addressed the issues of **recognition**, **measurement**, and **reporting**. In this final phase of the framework project, the Board established broad implementation guidelines relating to the questions: When should revenues and expenses be recognized? How should revenues and expenses and other financial statement elements be measured (valued)? How should financial information be reported or displayed?

Each of the framework components is discussed in the following sections. In considering the individual components, the interrelationships become apparent. Decisions concerning one part of the framework influence other parts.

Objectives of Financial Reporting

The starting point for the FASB's conceptual framework was to establish the objectives of financial reporting, since they determine the purposes and overall direction of accounting. Without identifying the goals for financial reporting, e.g., who needs what kind of information and for what reasons, accountants cannot determine the recognition criteria needed, which measurements are useful, or how best to report accounting information.

The financial reporting objectives discussed in this chapter and listed in Exhibit 2–2 are summarized and adapted from FASB Concepts Statement No. 1. Some general observations regarding these objectives should be made. First, because the FASB is currently the primary standard-setting body for accounting in the private sector, the Board's objectives should be considered carefully. However, it should also be recognized that another group might identify somewhat different objectives for financial reporting. The objectives, as well as the other components of the conceptual framework, should therefore not be interpreted as "universal truths."

Exhibit 2–2   Objectives of Financial Reporting

General Objective: Provide useful information for decision making

Specific Objectives: Provide information:
a. For assessing cash flow prospects
b. About financial condition
c. About performance and earnings
d. About how funds are obtained and used

Source: *Statement of Financial Accounting Concepts No. 1*

A second and related point is that the objectives of financial reporting are directly connected with the needs of those for whom the information is intended and must be considered in their environmental context. Financial reporting is not an end in itself, but is directed toward satisfying the need for useful information in making business and economic decisions. Thus, the objectives of financial reporting may change due to changes in the information needs of decision makers and because of changes in the economic, legal, political, and social aspects of the total business environment.

Third, the objectives of financial reporting are intended to be broad in nature. The objectives must be broadly based to satisfy a variety of user needs. Thus, they are objectives for general purpose financial reporting, attempting to satisfy the common interests of various potential users rather than to meet the specific needs of any selected group. The list of potential users includes:[6]

---

[6]*Statement of Financial Accounting Concepts No. 1*, "Objectives of Financial Reporting by Business Enterprises" (Stamford: Financial Accounting Standards Board, November, 1978), par. 24.

1. owners	14. stock exchanges
2. lenders	15. lawyers
3. suppliers	16. economists
4. potential investors	17. taxing authorities
5. creditors	18. regulatory authorities
6. employees	19. legislators
7. management	20. financial press and reporting agencies
8. directors	
9. customers	21. labor unions
10. financial analysts	22. trade associations
11. advisors	23. business researchers
12. brokers	24. teachers and students
13. underwriters	25. the public

While there are many potential users of financial reports, the objectives are directed primarily toward the needs of those external users of accounting data who lack the authority to prescribe the information they desire. For example, the Internal Revenue Service or the Securities and Exchange Commission can require selected information from individuals and companies. Investors and creditors, however, must rely to a significant extent on the information contained in the periodic financial reports supplied by management and, therefore, are the major users toward which financial reporting is directed.

A fourth point is that the objectives pertain to financial reporting in general, which encompasses not only disclosures in financial statements, but also other information concerning an enterprise's financial condition and earnings ability. While financial statements are a primary means of communicating information to external parties, other forms and sources are also used for decision making. The total information spectrum relative to investment, credit, and similar decisions is presented in Exhibit 2–3. This illustrates the overall focus of financial reporting and, more specifically, the areas of primary concern for financial accounting—the financial statements, the notes to financial statements, and supplementary disclosures directly affected by generally accepted accounting principles.

Information for Decision Making. As discussed in Chapter 1, the overall objective of financial reporting is to provide information that is useful for decision making. The FASB states:

> Financial reporting should provide information that is useful to present and potential investors and creditors and other users in making rational investment, credit, and similar decisions. The information should be comprehensible to those who have a reasonable understanding of business and economic activities and are willing to study the information with reasonable diligence.[7]

---

[7]*Statement of Financial Accounting Concepts No. 1,* par. 34.

Exhibit 2–3   Information Spectrum

All Information Useful for Investment, Credit, and Similar Decisions

Financial Reporting

Area Directly Affected by Existing FASB Standards

Basic Financial Statements

Financial Statements

- Statement of Financial Position
- Statements of Earnings and Comprehensive Income
- Statement of Cash Flows
- Statement of Investments by and Distributions to Owners

Notes to Financial Statements (& parenthetical disclosures)

Examples:
- Accounting Policies
- Contingencies
- Inventory Methods
- Number of Shares of Stock Outstanding
- Alternative Measures (market values of items carried at historical cost)

Supplementary Information

Examples:
- Changing Prices Disclosures (FASB Statement 33 as amended)
- Oil and Gas Reserves Information (FASB Statement 69)

Other Means of Financial Reporting

Examples:
- Management Discussion and Analysis
- Letters to Stock-holders

Other Information

Examples:
- Analysts' Reports
- Economic Statistics
- News Articles about Company

Source: Adapted from *Statement of Financial Accounting Concepts No. 5*, p. 5.

The emphasis in this overall objective is on investors and creditors as the primary external users because in satisfying their needs, most other general-purpose needs of external users will be met. The objective also recognizes a fairly sophisticated user of financial reports, one who has a reasonable understanding of accounting and business and who is willing to study and analyze the information presented.

Cash Flow Prospects. Investors and creditors are interested primarily in future cash flows. Thus, financial reporting should **provide information that is useful in assessing cash flow prospects.** Investment and lending decisions are made with the expectation of eventually increasing cash resources. An investor hopes to receive a return on the investment in the form of cash dividends, and ultimately sell the investment for more than it cost. Creditors seek to recover their cash outlays by repayments of the loans and to increase cash resources from interest payments. In making decisions, investors and creditors must consider the amounts, timing, and uncertainty (risk) of these prospective cash flows.

A company is similar to an investor in desiring to recover its investment plus receive a return on that investment. A company invests cash in non-cash resources in order to produce a product or service that it expects to sell for an amount greater than the amount invested, thereby increasing cash resources. To the extent that a company is successful in generating favorable cash flows, it can pay dividends and interest, and the market price of its securities will increase. Thus, as illustrated in Exhibit 2–4, the cash flows to investors and creditors are directly related to the cash flows of business enterprises, and financial reporting should provide information that is useful in assessing the enterprise's prospective cash flows.

Enterprise Financial Condition. Financial reporting should **provide information about an enterprise's assets, liabilities, and owners' equity** to help investors, creditors, and others evaluate the financial strengths and weaknesses of the enterprise and its liquidity and solvency. Such information will help users determine the financial condition of a company, which, in turn, should provide insight into the prospects of future cash flows. It may also help users who wish to estimate the overall value of a business.

Enterprise Performance and Earnings. Another important objective of financial reporting is to **provide information about an enterprise's financial performance during a period.** Performance is evaluated mainly on the basis of enterprise earnings. In fact, the FASB states that "the primary focus of financial reporting is information about an enterprise's performance provided by measures of earnings and its components."[8] There are several

---

[8]*Statement of Financial Accounting Concepts No. 1,* par. 43.

Exhibit 2–4   Enterprise Cash Flows to and from Investors and Creditors

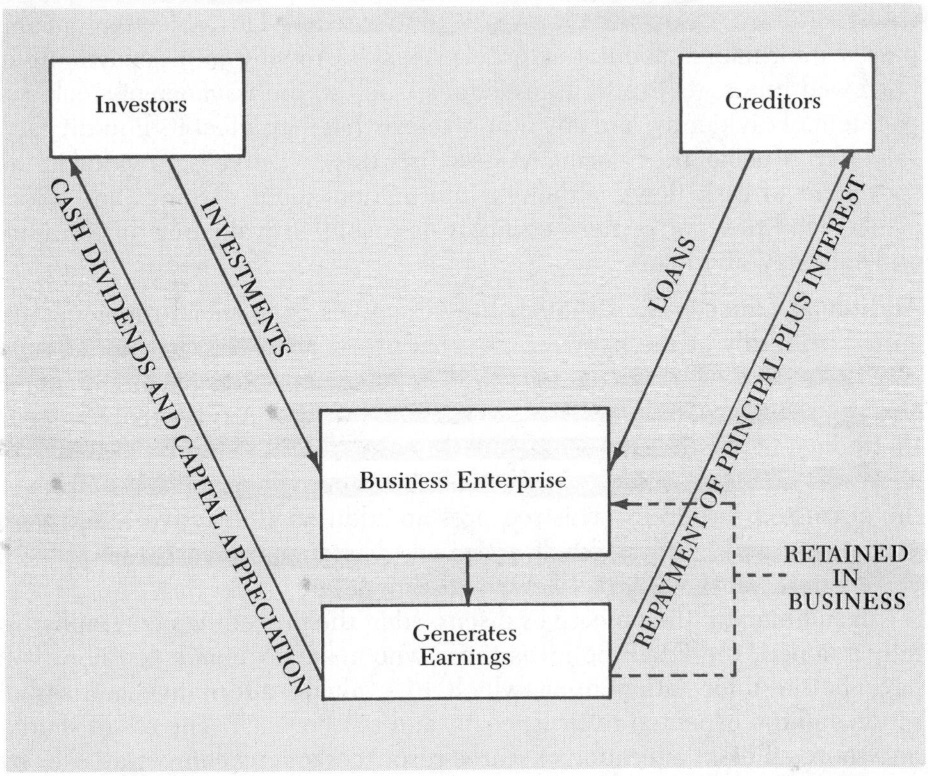

aspects of this important objective. Clearly, investors and creditors are concerned mostly with expectations of future enterprise performance. However, to a large degree, they rely on evaluations of past performance as measures of future performance. The FASB recognizes that investors and creditors want information about earnings primarily as an indicator of future cash-flow potential. The Board concluded, however, that information about enterprise earnings, measured by accrual accounting, generally provides a better indicator of performance than does information about current cash receipts and disbursements.

Investors and creditors use reported earnings and information concerning the components of earnings in a variety of ways. For example, earnings may be interpreted by users of financial statements as an overall measure of managerial effectiveness, as a predictor of future earnings and long-term "earning power," and as an indicator of the risk of investing or lending. The information may be used to establish new predictions, confirm previous expectations, or change past evaluations.

How Funds Are Obtained and Used. Notwithstanding the emphasis on earnings, another objective of financial reporting is to **provide information about an enterprise's cash flows during a period.** This objective encompasses information about the enterprise's borrowing and repayment of borrowed funds; its capital transactions, such as the issuance of stock and payment of dividends; and any other factors that may affect its liquidity and solvency. Much of the information to satisfy this objective is provided in the statement of cash flows, although information about earnings and about assets, liabilities, and owners' equity is also useful in evaluating the liquidity and solvency of a firm.

Additional Objectives. Although the objectives of financial reporting are aimed primarily at the needs of external users, financial reporting should also **provide information that allows managers and directors to make decisions that are in the best interest of the owners.** A related objective is that sufficient **information should be provided to allow the owners to assess how well management has discharged its stewardship responsibility** over the entrusted resources. This requires an additional objective—**financial reporting should include explanations and interpretations to help users understand the financial information provided.**

In summary, if the objectives discussed in the preceding paragraphs are fully attained, the FASB believes those who make economic decisions will have better information upon which to evaluate alternative courses of action and the expected returns, costs, and risks of each. The result should be a more efficient allocation of scarce resources among competing uses by individuals, enterprises, markets, and the government.

Qualitative Characteristics of Accounting Information

Individuals who are responsible for financial reporting should continually seek to provide the best, i.e., most useful, information possible within reasonable cost constraints. The problem is very complex because of the many choices among acceptable reporting alternatives. For example, what items should be capitalized as assets or reported as liabilities? Which revenues and costs should be assigned to a particular reporting period and on what basis? What are the attributes to be measured: historical costs, current values, or net realizable values? At what level of aggregation or disaggregation should information be presented? Where should specific information be disclosed—in the financial statements, in the notes to the financial statements, or perhaps not at all? These and similar choices must be made by policymakers, such as members of the FASB or SEC; by managements as they fulfill their stewardship roles; and by accountants as they assist management in reporting on a company's activities.

To assist in choosing among financial accounting and reporting alternatives, several criteria have been established by the FASB. These criteria relate to the qualitative characteristics of accounting information. A hierarchy of these qualities is presented in Exhibit 2–5 and will be used as a frame of reference in discussing them.

Exhibit 2–5   A Hierarchy of Accounting Information Qualities

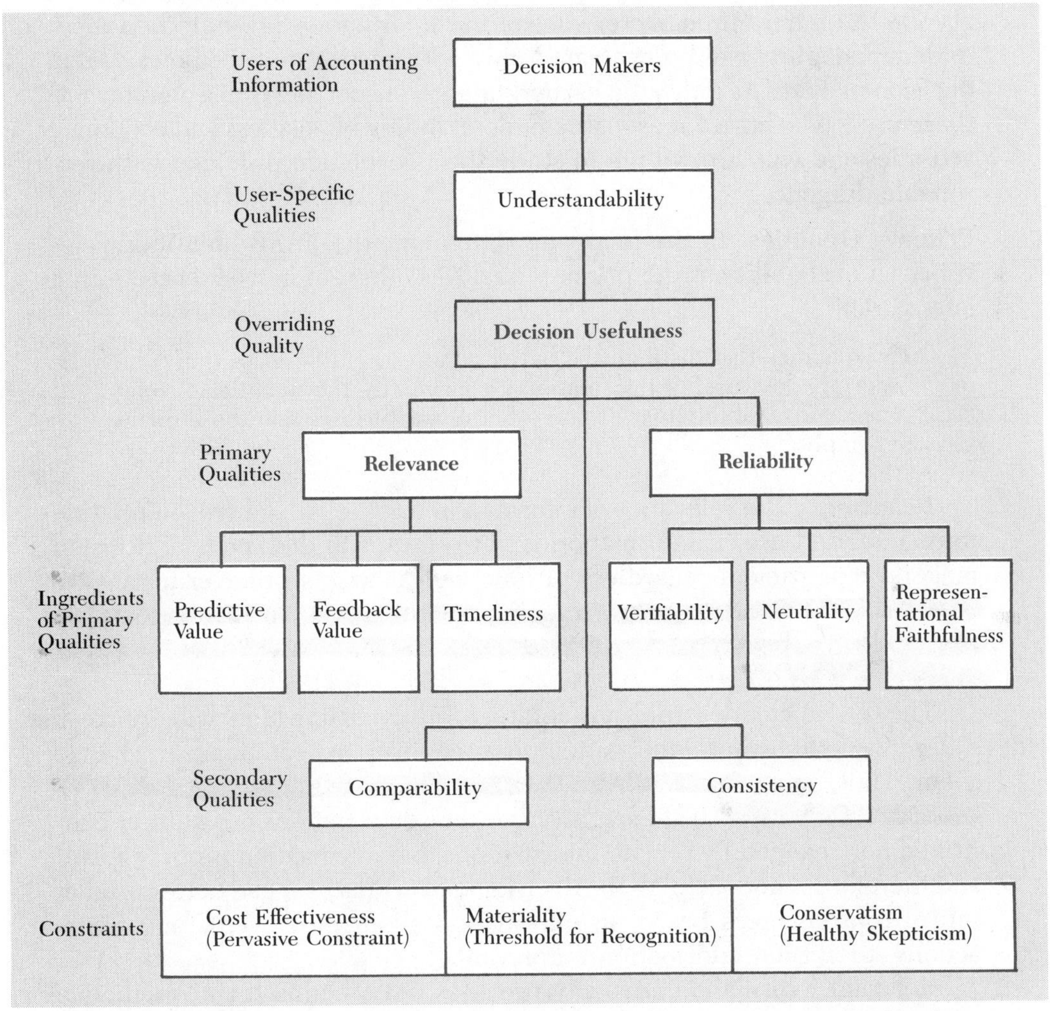

Source: Adapted from FASB Statement of Financial Accounting Concepts No. 2, p. 15.

Decision Usefulness. The overriding quality or characteristic of accounting information is **decision usefulness,** which is central to the hierarchy presented in Exhibit 2–5. All other qualities are viewed in terms of their contribution to decision usefulness. The illustrated hierarchy distinguishes user-specific qualities, such as **understandability**, from qualities inherent in accounting information, such as relevance and reliability. The quality of understandability is essential to decision usefulness. Information cannot be useful to decision makers if it is not understood even though the information may be relevant and reliable. The understandability of information depends on the characteristics of users, e.g., their prior knowledge, and also on the inherent characteristics of the information presented. Hence, understandability can be evaluated only with respect to specific classes of decision makers. As indicated earlier, financial reporting is directed toward those users who have a reasonable understanding of business and economic activities and who are willing to study the information provided with reasonable diligence.

Primary Qualities. In the following statement, the FASB identified **relevance** and **reliability** as the primary qualities inherent in useful accounting information:

> The qualities that distinguish "better" (more useful) information from "inferior" (less useful) information are primarily the qualities of relevance and reliability, with some other characteristics that those qualities imply.[9]

Relevance. The relevance of information may be judged only in relation to its intended use. If information is not relevant to the needs of decision makers, it is useless regardless of how well it meets other criteria. The objective of relevance, then, is to select methods of measuring and reporting that will aid those individuals who rely on financial statements to make decisions.

The FASB defines relevant information as that which will "make a difference." Relevant information may confirm expectations or change them. Thus, relevance is related to the **feedback value** and the **predictive value** of information. If the decision maker's expectations are neither confirmed nor changed by certain information, that information is not relevant and therefore is not useful to the decision maker. If a user can better predict future consequences based on information about past events and transactions, then such information is relevant.[10]

Relevant information normally provides both feedback and predictive value at the same time. Feedback on past events helps confirm or correct

---

[9]*Statement of Financial Accounting Concepts No. 2*, "Qualitative Characteristics of Accounting Information" (Stamford: Financial Accounting Standards Board, May, 1980), par. 15.
   [10]*Ibid.*, pars. 46–50.

earlier expectations. Such information can then be used to help predict future outcomes. For example, when General Motors presents comparative income statements, an investor has information to compare last year's operating results with this year's. This provides a general basis for evaluating prior expectations and for estimating what next year's results might be. The information therefore provides both feedback and predictive value concerning General Motors. As stated by the FASB, "Without a knowledge of the past, the basis for prediction will usually be lacking. Without an interest in the future, knowledge of the past is sterile."[11]

Timeliness is another key ingredient of relevance, relating directly to decision usefulness. Information furnished after a decision has been made is of no value. Again using General Motors as an example, when the company issues interim financial reports, it is attempting to provide information on a timely basis so that the information will be more relevant. Thus, to be relevant, information must offer predictive or feedback value, and it must be presented to users in a timely manner.

Reliability. The second primary quality of accounting information is reliability. Accounting information is reliable if users can depend on it to be reasonably free from error or bias and to be a faithful representation of the economic conditions or events that it purports to represent.[12] Reliability does not mean absolute accuracy. Information that is based on judgments and that includes estimates and approximations cannot be totally accurate, but it should be reliable. The objective, then, is to present the type of information in which users can have confidence. Such information must contain the key ingredients of reliability: verifiability, neutrality, and representational faithfulness.

Verifiability implies objectivity and consensus. Accountants seek to base their findings on facts that are determined objectively and that can be verified by other trained accountants using the same measurement methods. For example, assume that the amount of depreciation expense reported in the current year's income statement for the SAVE ON Company is $125,000. That amount can be verified if it is known that the straight-line method of depreciation was applied to depreciable assets totalling $1,250,000 and that the assets had an estimated useful life of 10 years with no salvage value.

Neutrality relates to information being communicated in an unbiased manner. If financial statements are to satisfy a wide variety of users, the information presented should not be colored in favor of one group of users

---

[11]*Ibid.*, par. 51.
[12]*Ibid.*, par. 63.

to the detriment of others. In this sense, the concept of neutrality is similar to the all-encompassing concept of "fairness."

The ingredient of **representational faithfulness** means that there is agreement between the information being reported and the actual results of economic activity being measured. Thus, the amounts and descriptions reported in the financial statements should reflect the economic reality of what is being represented. For a company to report sales of $3.4 million when they actually had sales of $2.5 million would not be a faithful representation and would cause that information to be unreliable.

Secondary Qualities. In addition to the primary qualities of relevance and reliability, there are two secondary qualities that affect the usefulness of accounting information: comparability and consistency.

Comparability. The essence of **comparability** is that information becomes much more useful when it can be related to a benchmark or standard. The comparison may be with data for other firms or it may be with similar information for the same firm, but for other equivalent periods of time. To illustrate how comparable data can increase the usefulness of information, consider the situation where a company reports current assets of $350,000 and current liabilities of $275,000. The current ratio is 1.27, but does this information reflect a favorable or unfavorable liquidity position? Without knowing comparable data for other companies in the industry or the current ratio of this company for other years, the information is of somewhat limited value. If data were available to show that the average current ratio of all companies in this particular industry is 1.22 and further that this company's current ratio was 1.05 and 1.10, respectively, for the past two years, then it would appear that the company's liquidity position has improved and that it is in relatively good shape.

Given that comparability increases the usefulness of information, financial reports should provide data permitting comparisons among companies and comparison of results of the same company over different time periods. This requires that like things be accounted for in the same manner on the financial statements of different companies and for a particular company for different periods. It should be recognized, however, that uniformity is not always the answer to comparability. Different circumstances may require different treatment.

Still, one of the greatest unsolved problems in accounting is the present acceptance of alternative accounting methods under situations that do not appear to be sufficiently different to warrant different accounting practices. The goal is for basic similarities and differences in the activities of companies to be apparent from the financial statements.

Research in accounting is currently being directed toward identifying circumstances justifying the use of a given method of accounting. If this research is successful, alternative methods can be eliminated where circumstances are found to be the same. In the meantime, current practice requires disclosure of the accounting methods used, as well as the impact of changes in methods when a change can be justified. Although the disclosures currently made do not generally provide enough information for a user to convert the published financial information from one accounting method to another, they do provide information that can assist the user in determining the degree of comparability among enterprises.

Consistency. **Consistency** is another important ingredient of useful accounting information. In view of the number of reporting alternatives, the methods adopted by an enterprise should be consistently employed if there is to be continuity and comparability in the financial statements. In analyzing statements, users seek to identify and evaluate the changes and trends within the enterprise. Conclusions concerning financial position and operations may be materially in error if, for example, accelerated depreciation is applied against the revenue of one year and straight-line depreciation against the revenue of the next year, or if securities are reported under long-term investments in one year and under current assets in the following year.

This is not to suggest that methods once adopted should not be changed. A continuing analysis of the business activities, as well as changing conditions, may suggest changes in accounting methods and presentations leading to more informative statements. These changes should be incorporated in the accounting system and the financial statements. The statements should be accompanied by a clear explanation of the nature of the changes and their effects, where they are material, so that current reporting can be properly interpreted and related to past reporting.

Constraints. Underlying the informational qualities identified in Exhibit 2–5 are three important constraints: (1) cost effectiveness, (2) materiality, and (3) conservatism.

Cost Effectiveness. Information is like other commodities in that it must be worth more than it costs to be desirable. Too often government regulators and others assume that information is a "free" good. Obviously, it is not, and the **cost-benefit relationship** must always be kept in mind when selecting or requiring reporting alternatives. To illustrate, in the early 1970s the Federal Trade Commission proposed that large companies be required to disclose information about lines of business. A group of companies brought court action to prohibit the proposed requirement. A major argument of the companies was that the information would be very costly to prepare, because it was not normally generated by the accounting system. The companies also argued that the line-of-business disclosures in the form proposed by the FTC would not be beneficial to users, because the reported segments would be artificial and not those the companies normally used to report on a less than company-wide basis. Although the FTC prevailed, primarily because of perceived benefits in regulating anti-trust situations, this case underscores an important point — the cost of producing information (including, for example, modification to the existing accounting system, or even additional printing and mailing costs) must be compared to the extra benefits (generally meaning an improvement in specific decisions of users) to determine if the information should be reported.

The difficulty in assessing cost effectiveness is that the costs and benefits, but especially the benefits, are not always evident or easily measured. Notwithstanding this difficulty, cost effectiveness is an important constraint and should be considered when selecting reporting alternatives.

Materiality. Contrary to the belief of many readers of financial statements, the amounts reported in the statements are not always complete and are often not exact. While for many decisions completeness and exactness are not required, there is a point at which information that is incomplete or inexact does influence a decision. This point defines the boundary between information that is material and information that is immaterial.

Materiality is an overriding concept related to, but distinguishable from, the primary qualities of relevance and reliability. Materiality determines the threshold for recognition of accounting items and is primarily a quantitative consideration. While relevance is directed toward the nature of the information, materiality focuses on the size of a judgment item in a given set of circumstances. Materiality deals with the specific question — is the item large enough or the degree of accuracy precise enough to influence the decision of a user of the information? Of course, the degree of influence caused by the size of an item also depends on the nature of the item and the circumstances in which a judgment must be made. For example, a $1 million loss from a product-related lawsuit might be financially devastating for some enterprises, but may not even warrant separate disclosure on Ford Motor Company's financial statements.

At the present time, there are few guidelines to assist preparers of financial reports in applying the concept of materiality. Where materiality guidelines do exist, they are often not uniform. For example, the materiality guideline for reporting by segments of a company suggests that certain information be disclosed for any major segment that accounts for 10% or more of total company sales. On the other hand, for determining the significance of dilution in earnings per share computations, the materiality guideline is 3%. Thus, for these two different reporting areas, the materiality guideline varies from 10% to 3%. Since quantitative guidance concerning materiality is often lacking, managers and accountants must exercise judgment in determining whether a failure to disclose certain data will influence the decisions of the users of financial statements.

Past court cases can help determine what is material by providing examples of where the lack of disclosure of certain information in the financial statements has been considered a material misstatement. The failure to disclose proper inventory values or pending sales of large amounts of assets, the failure to disclose the imminence of a highly profitable transaction or to disclose a significant downward readjustment of reported earnings are a few examples.[13]

In summary, the following point should be kept in mind in making judgments concerning materiality:

> The omission or misstatement of an item in a financial report is material if, in the light of surrounding circumstances, the magnitude of the item is such that it is probable that the judgment of a reasonable person relying upon the report would have been changed or influenced by the inclusion or correction of the item.[14]

Conservatism. Another constraint associated with the characteristics of useful information is **conservatism**. This means that when accountants have genuine doubt concerning which of two or more reporting alternatives should be selected, users are best served by adopting a conservative approach, that is, by choosing the alternative with the least favorable impact on owners' equity. However, conservatism does not mean deliberate and arbitrary understatement of assets and earnings. On the contrary, use of conservative procedures is motivated by not wanting to overstate assets and earnings when dealing in "gray areas."

Conservatism should be used when a degree of skepticism is warranted. For example, generally accepted accounting principles require the expensing of research and development costs on the basis that the future benefits cannot be accurately determined. Since there is often reasonable doubt as to the existence or amount of future benefits, the costs are expensed, and the amount of income reported currently is reduced. Another

---

[13]For additional examples of quantitative materiality considerations, see *Statement of Financial Accounting Concepts No. 2*, Appendix C, par. 165.

[14]*Ibid.*, par. 132.

example of conservatism in accounting practice is reporting short-term marketable equity securities at a lower of cost or market value. If General Mills held short-term marketable equity securities and the market value dropped below cost, the company should report those securities at the lower market value. To continue to report the securities at cost would overstate current assets and might imply to statement users that current assets exceed current liabilities by more than is actually the case.

The constraint of conservatism is a useful one, but one that should be applied carefully and used only as a moderating and refining influence on the information reported. Essentially, conservatism means prudence in financial accounting and reporting.

Elements of Financial Statements

Having identified the qualitative characteristics of accounting information, the FASB in Concepts Statement No. 3 established definitions for the ten basic elements of financial statements of business enterprises. In Concepts Statement No. 6, the FASB expanded the scope of Statement No. 3 to encompass not-for-profit organizations as well. These elements comprise the building blocks upon which financial statements are constructed. The elements are interrelated and collectively report the performance and status of an enterprise. For reference purposes, the FASB definitions of the ten basic elements are listed on page 47. These definitions and the issues surrounding them are discussed in detail as the elements are introduced in later chapters.

Recognition, Measurement, and Reporting

FASB Concepts Statement No. 5 builds on the foundation laid by the previously issued concepts statements and provides broad guidelines for implementing or applying the objectives and fundamental concepts discussed thus far. It provides guidance in determining *what* information should be formally incorporated into financial statements and *when*. Specifically, Statement No. 5 sets forth recognition criteria and discusses certain measurement issues that are closely related to recognition. In addition, this statement addresses financial reporting and identifies the financial statements that should be presented in light of the objectives of financial reporting.

Recognition Criteria. Recognition is the process of formally recording an item and eventually reporting it as one of the elements in the financial statements. Recognition involves both the initial recording of an item and any subsequent changes related to that item. To qualify for recognition, an

Elements of Financial Statements

Assets are probable future economic benefits obtained or controlled by a particular entity as a result of past transactions or events.

Liabilities are probable future sacrifices of economic benefits arising from present obligations of a particular entity to transfer assets or provide services to other entities in the future as a result of past transactions or events.

Equity or **net assets** is the residual interest in the assets of an entity that remains after deducting its liabilities.

Investments by owners are increases in equity of a particular business enterprise resulting from transfers to it from other entities of something valuable to obtain or increase ownership interests (or equity) in it. Assets are most commonly received as investments by owners, but that which is received may also include services or satisfaction or conversion of liabilities of the enterprise.

Distributions to owners are decreases in equity of a particular business enterprise resulting from transferring assets, rendering services, or incurring liabilities by the enterprise to owners. Distributions to owners decrease ownership interests (or equity) in an enterprise.

Comprehensive income is the change in equity of a business enterprise during a period from transactions and other events and circumstances from nonowner sources. It includes all changes in equity during a period except those resulting from investments by owners and distributions to owners.

Change in market fluxuation

Revenues are inflows or other enhancements of assets of an entity or settlements of its liabilities (or a combination of both) from delivering or producing goods, rendering services, or other activities that constitute the entity's ongoing major or central operations.

Expenses are outflows or other using up of assets or incurrences of liabilities (or a combination of both) from delivering or producing goods, rendering services, or carrying out other activities that constitute the entity's ongoing major or central operations.

Gains are increases in equity (net assets) from peripheral or incidental transactions of an entity and from all other transactions and other events and circumstances affecting the entity except those that result from revenues or investments by owners.

Losses are decreases in equity (net assets) from peripheral or incidental transactions of an entity and from all other transactions and other events and circumstances affecting the entity except those that result from expenses or distributions to owners.

Source: *Statement of Financial Accounting Concepts No. 6*, pp. ix–x.

item should meet four fundamental criteria: (1) definition, (2) measurability, (3) relevance, and (4) reliability.[15] For an item to be formally recognized, it must meet one of the definitions of the elements of financial statements, as defined in Concepts Statement No. 6. For example, a receivable must meet the definition of an asset to be recorded and reported as such on a balance sheet. The same is true of liabilities, owners' equity, revenues, expenses, and other elements. As an example of a continuing controversy in this area, some accountants question whether deferred income taxes meet the strict definition of a liability and therefore whether they should be recognized as such. For some companies, the amount is significant. For example, IBM reported a deferred tax credit in 1985 of almost $3.7 billion. If, in fact, this amount does not represent a future outlay or sacrifice, it is misleading even though it is reported in accordance with GAAP.

In addition to qualifying as an element, an item must be objectively measurable in monetary terms to be recognized. Sometimes an item clearly meets the definition criterion but cannot be measured objectively. For example, the president's letter in the annual report of IBM Corporation mentions the significant value of IBM's 405,000 employees. These employees have future benefit to IBM and may be considered assets of high value to that company. Yet, that value is not recognized as an asset on IBM's balance sheet, since it cannot be measured in a reliable manner.

Information about an item must be both relevant and reliable in order for the item to be recognized. Since there are often trade-offs between relevance and reliability, consideration of these primary qualities may affect the timing of recognition. For example, information about a pending lawsuit may be relevant, but its recognition usually is delayed until the amounts and circumstances can be determined with sufficient reliability.

The four fundamental recognition criteria apply to all elements of financial statements. However, since one of the major tasks of accounting is to measure and report net income (loss), proper application of the recognition criteria is particularly important when recognizing revenues and expenses. Generally, under the **revenue recognition principle,** revenues for a period are recorded when two conditions are met: (1) the earnings process is substantially complete, and (2) there is receipt of cash or a near-cash asset, i.e., when revenues are realized or realizable. These two criteria have led to the conventional recognition of revenue at the point of sale, i.e., at the specific point in the earning process when assets are sold

---

[15]*Statement of Financial Accounting Concepts No. 5,* "Recognition and Measurement in Financial Statements of Business Enterprises" (Stamford: Financial Accounting Standards Board, December, 1984), par. 63.

or services are rendered. According to the **matching principle,** expenses for a period are determined by association with specific revenues or a particular time period. The revenue recognition and expense matching principles are discussed and illustrated in Chapter 4.

Measurement Attributes. Closely related to recognition is measurement. There are five different measurement attributes currently used in practice.[16]

Historical cost is the cash equivalent price exchanged for goods or services at the date of acquisition. Land, buildings, equipment, and most inventories are common examples of items recognized using the historical cost attribute.

Current replacement cost is the cash equivalent price that would be exchanged currently to purchase or replace equivalent goods or services. Some inventories are recognized at their current replacement costs.

Current market value is the cash equivalent price that could be obtained by selling an asset in an orderly liquidation. Some investments in marketable securities are reported using current market values.

Net realizable value is the amount of cash expected to be received or paid from the conversion of assets or liabilities in the normal course of business. Generally, this attribute is equal to the sales price less normal costs to sell. Net realizable value is used for recognizing short-term receivables, some inventories, and certain liabilities such as trade payables and warranty obligations.

Present (or discounted) value is the amount of net future cash inflows discounted to their present value. Long-term receivables and long-term payables use this measurement attribute.

It should be noted that different measurement attributes often have the same monetary value, especially at the point of initial recognition. For example, the historical cost and the current replacement cost of a piece of land are the same at the date of acquisition. The amount would also be the current market value of the land at that point in time assuming an arm's-length transaction.

The trade-off between relevance and reliability mentioned earlier is also evident in considering which measurement attribute to use. Current accounting practice is said to be based on historical costs since that is the attribute generally used in the initial recording of transactions. Historical cost is used because it is objective (reliable), being based on an exchange that has taken place between presumably independent parties. In effect, the historical cost is the fair market price of the item involved in the

---

[16]*Ibid.*, par. 67.

transaction at that date. Many accountants feel that current replacement costs or market values are more relevant than historical costs for future-oriented decisions; yet, those attributes often lack reliability. Because it is both reliable and relevant, historical cost has been the valuation basis most commonly used in accounting practice. However, as indicated above, other measurement attributes are used at times and are expected to continue to be used in the future. The "proper" measurement attribute is the one that under the circumstances provides the most useful (relevant and reliable) information at a reasonable cost.

In using historical cost as one (and perhaps the dominant) measurement attribute, the FASB indicated in Concepts Statement No. 5 that it expects nominal units of money to continue to be used in recognizing items in financial reporting. Nominal units of money are unadjusted for general price changes and therefore fluctuate over time in terms of purchasing power. If there is little or no inflation, measurement using nominal dollars is satisfactory. However, if general price levels change significantly, the FASB will probably have to reconsider this decision. The subject of changing prices is discussed fully in Chapter 25.

Financial Reporting. For financial reporting to be most effective, all relevant information should be presented in an unbiased, understandable, and timely manner. This is sometimes referred to as the **full disclosure principle.** Because of the cost-benefit constraint discussed earlier, however, it would be impossible to report *all* relevant information. Further, too much information would adversely affect understandability and, therefore, decision usefulness. Those who provide financial information must use judgment in determining what information best satisfies the full disclosure principle within reasonable cost limitations.

Although guidelines in this area are not well defined, Concepts Statement No. 5 indicates that a "full set of financial statements" is necessary to meet the objectives of financial reporting. Included in the recommended set of general-purpose financial statements are reports that would show:[17]

> Financial position at the end of the period
> Earnings (net income) for the period
> Comprehensive income (total nonowner changes in equity) for
>   the period
> Cash flows during the period
> Investments by and distributions to owners during the period

Current practice generally includes a set of financial statements consisting of (1) an **income statement** presenting the results of operations of

---

[17]*Statement of Financial Accounting Concepts No. 5*, par. 13.

an entity for a reporting period; (2) a **balance sheet** reporting the financial position of a business at a certain date; and (3) a **statement of cash flows** (funds statement) describing the changes in enterprise resources over the reporting period. The three primary statements are referred to as general-purpose finance statements because they are intended for use by a wide variety of external users. Although there has been some discussion as to the need for special purpose statements directed to specific external users, there has been no significant movement toward this in practice.

Sometimes a **retained earnings statement** is provided, or combined with the income statement, showing the changes in retained earnings for the period. When there are changes in owners' equity other than those affecting retained earnings, a supplemental **statement of changes in owners' equity** may be presented to provide a complete reconciliation of the beginning and ending equity balances.

The current general-purpose statements would seem to satisfy the recommendations of Concepts Statement No. 5, with one exception. **Comprehensive income** is a new concept specifically defined in Statement No. 5 as including all changes in owners' equity except investments by and distributions to owners. This concept, which is explained and illustrated in Chapter 4, may require a new statement. While the funds statement was traditionally prepared on a working capital basis by a majority of companies, the emphasis on cash flows in Concepts Statement No. 1 led many companies to switch to a cash concept of funds. In late 1986, the FASB issued a proposed standard that will require all companies to present a statement of cash flows as recommended in Concepts Statement No. 5. This topic is introduced in Chapter 5 and covered in detail in Chapter 24.

In general, the FASB and other standard-setting bodies have been reluctant to specify exact formats for reporting. Instead, they have allowed and encouraged companies to experiment with various reporting (display) techniques. The results are sometimes quite encouraging as companies voluntarily seek new and better ways to present information. For example, the pictorial information on page 52 was presented by IBM, along with its formal funds statement, to assist readers in understanding the sources and uses of funds by IBM during 1985.

TRADITIONAL ASSUMPTIONS OF ACCOUNTING MODEL

The FASB's Conceptual Framework described in the preceding sections is influenced by several underlying assumptions. While not addressed

Summary of Sources of Funds
(Dollars in millions)

Summary of Uses of Funds
(Dollars in millions)

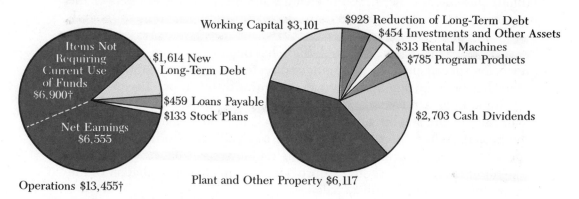

Working Capital $3,101

$928 Reduction of Long-Term Debt
$454 Investments and Other Assets
$313 Rental Machines
$785 Program Products

Items Not Requiring Current Use of Funds $6,900†

$1,614 New Long-Term Debt

$459 Loans Payable
$133 Stock Plans

Net Earnings $6,555

$2,703 Cash Dividends

Operations $13,455†

Plant and Other Property $6,117

†Includes Translation Effects of $677

Source: *IBM 1985 Annual Report.*

explicitly, these traditional assumptions are implicit in the conceptual framework. They, too, help establish generally accepted accounting practice. The following paragraphs briefly describe the six basic assumptions that were identified in Exhibit 2–1 on page 32.

First, the business enterprise is viewed as a specific **economic entity** separate and distinct from its owners and any other business unit. It is the entity and its activities that receive the focus of attention for accounting and reporting purposes.

Second, in the absence of evidence to the contrary, the entity is viewed as a **going concern.** This continuity assumption provides support for the preparation of a balance sheet that reports costs assignable to future activities rather than market values of properties that would be realized in the event of voluntary liquidation or forced sale. This same assumption calls for the preparation of an income statement reporting only such portions of revenues and costs as are allocable to current activities.

Third, the transactions and events of an entity provide the basis for accounting entries, and any changes in resources and equity values are generally not recorded until a transaction has taken place. Furthermore, transactions are assumed to be **"arm's-length" transactions.** That is, they occur between independent parties, each of whom is capable of protecting its own interests. If Entity A is selling goods to Entity B, it will try to sell at a sufficiently high price to make a profit. Entity B, on the other hand, will try to purchase those goods at a reasonably low price. The bargained price arrived at in this arm's-length transaction is assumed to be an objective market valuation at that date, and is considered an objective value for measurement purposes.

Fourth, transactions are assumed to be measured in **stable monetary units.** Because of this assumption, changes in the dollar's purchasing power have traditionally been ignored. Thus, financial statements reflect items that are measured in terms of nominal dollars. To many accountants, this is a serious limitation of the accounting model. As noted earlier, the impact of price changes is discussed in Chapter 25.

Fifth, because accounting information is needed on a timely basis, the life of a business entity is divided into specific **accounting periods.** By convention, the year has been established as the normal period for reporting. Annual statements, as well as statements covering shorter intervals, such as quarters, are provided by entities to satisfy the needs of those requiring timely financial information.

Finally, for each time period, an income measure is determined using **accrual accounting.** This means that revenues are recognized as earned, not necessarily when cash is received; and expenses are recognized when incurred, not necessarily when cash is paid. For most financial reporting purposes, accrual accounting is considered preferable to the cash-basis system of accounting.

In total, these assumptions as well as the concepts discussed earlier in the chapter comprise the current accounting model. They help determine what will be accounted for and in what manner. In effect, they set the boundaries of accounting practice.

CONCEPTUAL FRAMEWORK SUMMARIZED

Exhibit 2–6 summarizes the major components of a conceptual framework of accounting. Such a framework provides a basis for consistent judgments by standard-setters, preparers, users, auditors, and others involved in financial reporting. A conceptual framework will not solve all accounting problems, but if used on a consistent basis over time, it should help improve financial reporting.

The framework discussed in this chapter will be a reference source throughout the text. In studying the remaining chapters, you will see many applications and a few exceptions to the theoretical framework established here. An understanding of the overall theoretical framework of accounting should make it easier for you to understand specific issues and problems encountered in practice.

Exhibit 2–6 A Conceptual Framework of Accounting

I. Objectives of Financial Reporting
   A. General—Provide useful information for decision making
   B. Specific—Provide information:
       1. For assessing cash flow prospects
       2. About financial condition
       3. About performance and earnings
       4. About how funds are obtained and used

II. Fundamental Concepts
   A. Qualitative Characteristics of Accounting Information
       1. Overriding quality—decision usefulness
       2. Primary qualities
           a. Relevance
               ● predictive value
               ● feedback value
               ● timeliness
           b. Reliability
               ● verifiability
               ● neutrality
               ● representational faithfulness
       3. Secondary qualities
           a. Comparability
           b. Consistency
       4. Constraints
           a. Cost effectiveness (pervasive constraint)
           b. Materiality (recognition threshold)
           c. Conservatism (healthy skepticism)
   B. Elements of Financial Statements
       1. Assets   6. Comprehensive income
       2. Liabilities   7. Revenues
       3. Equity   8. Expenses
       4. Investments by owners   9. Gains
       5. Distributions to owners   10. Losses

III. Implementation Guidelines
   A. Recognition Criteria
       1. Definition   3. Relevance
       2. Measurability   4. Reliability
   B. Measurement Attributes
       1. Historical cost   4. Net realizable value
       2. Current replacement cost   5. Present (or dis-
       3. Current market value   counted) value

C. Financial Reporting
   1. Full disclosure
   2. Set of general-purpose financial statements
      a. Financial Position
      b. Earnings (net income or loss)
      c. Comprehensive Income
      d. Cash flows
      e. Investments by and distributions to owners

IV. Traditional Assumptions of Accounting Model
   A. Economic entity
   B. Going concern
   C. Arm's-length transactions
   D. Stable monetary unit
   E. Accounting periods
   F. Accrual accounting

QUESTIONS

1. List and explain the main reasons why a conceptual framework of accounting is important.
2. Why is judgment required by accountants in fulfilling their role as suppliers of information?
3. The FASB's Conceptual Framework project has received considerable attention. What is the project expected to accomplish? What is it not likely to do?
4. Identify the major objectives of financial reporting as specified by the FASB.
5. The overriding quality of accounting information is decision usefulness. How does the user-specific quality of "understandability" affect decision usefulness?
6. Distinguish between the primary informational qualities of relevance and reliability.
7. Does reliability imply absolute accuracy? Explain.
8. Define comparability. How does comparability relate to uniformity?
9. Of what value is consistency in financial reporting?
10. Why is it so difficult to measure the cost effectiveness of accounting information?
11. What is the current materiality standard in accounting?
12. Is it possible for information to be immaterial and yet relevant? Explain.
13. What is conservatism in accounting? When does it become a relevant issue? What are some examples of conservatism in accounting practice?
14. List and define the ten basic elements of financial statements.
15. Identify the criteria that an item must meet to qualify for recognition.
16. Identify and describe five different measurement attributes.

17. FASB Concepts Statement No. 5 indicates that a full set of financial statements is needed to meet the objectives of financial reporting. What are the reports that should be included in the set of general-purpose financial statements?
18. Identify the six traditional assumptions that influence the conceptual framework, and briefly explain how they affect it.

DISCUSSION CASES

Case 2–1 (The establishment of a conceptual framework)

As a student of accounting, you have noticed that a substantial portion of the literature deals with establishing a theoretical framework upon which accounting practice can be based. This is currently the case and has been for the past 50 years. Yet, in discussions with colleagues and friends, you have to admit that the accounting profession has found it difficult to establish an authoritative set of accounting concepts and principles that are universally accepted within the business community. As you think about this problem, at least two questions come to mind: (1) Is an overall conceptual framework of accounting even needed? and (2) What has the FASB done differently, if anything, to succeed in establishing a conceptual framework for accounting where others have failed? Discuss possible answers to these questions.

Case 2–2 (How important are the economic consequences of accounting principles?)

During the 1960s, and again in the 1980s, corporate merger activity increased significantly in the United States. Many of the early mergers involved companies in completely unrelated fields. Accounting for these mergers sometimes enabled a company in a weak financial position to merge with a financially strong company and thus postpone the disclosure of poor management to statement users. In an attempt to clarify the accounting rules and to eliminate financial statement manipulation that did not truly present the entity's financial status, the Accounting Principles Board proposed a change in accounting for mergers. One business executive heavily involved in merger activity commented publicly that the Board had no right to issue such pronouncements. If the accounting requirements were changed, the executive argued, merger activity would decline and economic growth in our economy would stagnate.

More recently, the FASB has issued standards that require companies to account for unfunded pension costs as liabilities. Executives of several large companies, e.g., General Motors, have argued that such accounting will seriously limit the ability of many companies to borrow and will have a serious, negative impact on business activity and, therefore, on society.

Recognizing that accounting rules have an impact on business activity and may affect economic growth, should this result influence the decision by accounting standard-setting bodies as to how transactions should be recorded and reported? Should the impact on society be the most important consideration for an accounting principle?

Case 2–3   (Elements of financial statements)

Conserv Corporation, a computer software company, is trying to determine the appropriate accounting procedure to apply to its software development costs. Management is considering capitalizing the development costs and amortizing them over several years. Alternatively, they are considering charging the costs to expense as soon as they are incurred. You, as an accountant, have been asked to help settle this issue. Which definitions of financial statement elements would apply to these costs? Based on this information, what accounting procedure would you recommend and why?

Case 2–4   (Recognition, measurement, and reporting considerations in financial reporting)

A few years ago, the SEC adopted amendments to Regulation S-X, requiring separate disclosure of preferred stock subject to mandatory redemption requirements, often called "redeemable preferred stock." In taking such action, the SEC noted an increase in the use of complex securities—such as redeemable preferred stock—that exhibit both debt and equity characteristics. The question subsequently considered by the FASB was whether or not such securities should be classified as liabilities rather than as equity securities. How might the FASB's guidelines for recognition, measurement, and reporting assist in resolving this or similar issues?

Case 2–5   (Financial reporting: the difficult task of satisfying diverse informational needs)

Teri Green has recently been promoted. She is now the chief financial officer of Teltrex, Inc. and has primary responsibility for the external reporting function. During the past three weeks, Green has met with: Jeff Thalman, the senior vice president of Westmore First National Bank where Teltrex has a $1,000,000 line of credit; Susan Davis, a financial analyst for Stubbs, Jones, and McConkie, a brokerage firm; and Brian Ellis, who is something of a corporate gadfly and who owns 2 percent of the outstanding common stock of Teltrex. Each of these individuals has commented on last year's annual report of Teltrex, pointing out deficiencies and suggesting additional information they would like to see presented in this year's annual report. From Green's point of view, explain the nature of general purpose financial statements and indicate the informational qualities of the accounting data that she must be concerned with in fulfilling the corporation's external reporting responsibility.

Case 2–6   (Responsibility for financial reporting)

It is apparent from reading the *Wall Street Journal* and other financial publications that an increasing number of law suits are being filed each year against independent accountants (CPAs). Most cases involve accountants who audited the financial statements of companies that subsequently went bankrupt. Who is responsible for a company's financial statements? How might a conceptual framework improve the quality of financial reporting?

EXERCISES

EXERCISE 2–1   (Aspects of the FASB Conceptual Framework)

Determine whether the following statements are true or false. If a statement is false, explain why.

1. Comprehensive income includes changes in equity resulting from distributions to owners.
2. Timeliness and predictive value are both characteristics of relevant information.
3. The tendency to recognize favorable events early is an example of conservatism.
4. Objectives of Concepts Statement No. 1 focus primarily on the needs of internal users of financial information.
5. Statements of Financial Accounting Concepts are considered authoritative pronouncements.
6. The overriding objective of financial reporting is to provide information for making economic decisions.
7. Concepts Statement No. 1 seeks to clarify *how* financial statement reporting should be accomplished, and succeeding Concepts Statements clarify *what* should be reported in financial statements.
8. Certain modifying constraints, such as conservatism, can justify departures from GAAP.
9. Under Concepts Statement No. 5, the term "recognized" is synonymous with the term "recorded."
10. Once an accounting method is adopted, it should never be changed.

EXERCISE 2–2   (Conceptual Framework terminology)

Match the statements on the left with the letter of the terms on the right. An answer (letter) may be used more than once and some terms require more than one answer (letter).

1. Key ingredients in quality of relevance.	a. Cost effectiveness
2. Basic assumptions that influence the FASB's Conceptual Framework.	b. Representational faithfulness
	c. Matching principle
3. The idea that information should represent what it purports to represent.	d. Verifiability
	e. Time periods
4. The most pervasive constraint.	f. Unrealized
5. An example of conservatism.	g. Completeness
6. The availability of information when it is needed.	h. Timeliness
	i. Materiality
7. Associating expense with a particular revenue or time period.	j. Predictive value
	k. Economic entity
8. Determines the threshold for recognition.	l. Lower of cost or market rule
	m. Accrual accounting
9. Implies objectivity and consensus.	n. Arms' length
10. Transactions between independent parties.	

EXERCISE 2–3 (Qualitative characteristics of accounting information)

Identify the qualitative characteristics most likely violated by each of the following situations. (Briefly support your answers.)

a. A prospective purchaser of a company receives only the conventional financial statements.

b. An investor examines the published annual reports of all companies in the steel industry for the purpose of investing in the most profitable one.

c. A company uses the prefix "reserve" for a contra asset, a liability, and a retained earnings appropriation.

d. A company reports all of its land, buildings, and equipment on the basis of a recent appraisal.

e. Management elects to change its method of inventory valuation in order to overcome an unprofitable year from operations. This change enables the company to report a gradual growth in earnings.

EXERCISE 2–4 (Applications of accounting characteristics and concepts)

For each situation listed, indicate by letters the appropriate qualitative characteristic(s) or accounting concept(s) applied. A letter may be used more than once, and more than one characteristic or concept may apply to a particular situation.

a. Understandability
b. Verifiability
c. Timeliness
d. Representational faithfulness
e. Neutrality
f. Relevance
g. Going concern

h. Economic entity *owner & business separate*
i. Historical cost
j. Quantifiability
k. Materiality
l. Comparability
m. Conservatism

_____ 1. Goodwill is only recorded in the accounts when it arises from the purchase of another entity at a price higher than the fair market value of the purchased entity's tangible assets.

_____ 2. Marketable securities are valued at the lower of cost or market.

_____ 3. All payments out of petty cash are debited to Miscellaneous Expense.

_____ 4. Plant assets are classified separately as land or buildings, with an accumulated depreciation account for buildings.

_____ 5. Periodic payments of $1,500 per month for services of H. Hay, who is the sole proprietor of the company, are reported as withdrawals.

_____ 6. Small tools used by a large manufacturing firm are recorded as expenses when purchased.

_____ 7. Marketable securities are initially recorded at cost.

_____ 8. A retail store estimates inventory, rather than taking a complete physical count, for purposes of preparing monthly financial statements.

_____ 9. A note describing the company's possible liability in a lawsuit is included with the financial statements even though no formal liability exists at the balance sheet date.

_____10. Depreciation on plant assets is consistently computed each year by the straight-line method.

EXERCISE 2–5   (Theoretical support for corrected balance sheet)

G. Nielsen prepared the following balance sheet for Nielsen Inc. as of December 31, 1987. Review each item listed, and considering the additional data given, prepare a corrected, properly classified balance sheet. Where a change is made in reporting an item, disclose in a separate note the theoretical support for your suggested change. Record any offsetting adjustments in the Retained Earnings account, except for possible contributed capital changes.

Assets		Liabilities	
Cash................	$ 30,000	Accounts payable ...	$ 85,000
Marketable		Taxes payable......	65,000
securities...........	55,000	Notes payable......	120,000
Notes receivable	40,000	Mortgage payable...	273,000
Accounts receivable	130,000	Capital stock	300,000
Inventories	195,000	Retained earnings...	140,000
Land and buildings	520,000		
Accumulated dep.-			
buildings	(27,000)		
Goodwill..............	40,000		
	$983,000		$983,000

Additional data:

(a) Cash included a bank checking account of $20,000, current checks and money orders on hand of $5,000, and a $5,000 check that could not be cashed. The check was from Davis Co., a customer that had gone out of business. Nielsen feels this $5,000 will probably not be recovered.

(b) Marketable securities are listed at year-end market values. They were purchased early in 1987 for $46,800.

(c) Nielsen estimates that all receivables are collectible except for a three year old past due note of $8,000. Past collection experience indicates that two percent of current notes and accounts prove uncollectible.

(d) Land and buildings are recorded at initial cost. At date of acquisition, land was valued at $70,000 and buildings at $450,000. Building depreciation has been correctly recorded.

(e) Goodwill was recorded when Nielsen received an offer of $40,000 more for the business than the recorded asset values.

(f) Of the notes payable, $30,000 will be due in 1988 with the remainder of the notes coming due in 1989 and 1990.

(g) The mortgage is payable in annual payments of $19,500.

(h) The capital stock has a par value of $100 per share; 2,500 shares are issued and outstanding.

EXERCISE 2–6   (Theoretical support for corrected income statement)

A. Hillstead prepared the following income statement for the calendar year 1987.

Revenues.....	$80,000
Expenses.....	50,000
Net income ...	$30,000

An examination of the records reveals the following:

(a) Hillstead is the sole proprietor.
(b) Business operations include:
    1. A catering service
    2. An equipment rental shop
    3. Rental of a part of Hillstead's home for small receptions
(c) Revenues include:

1. Catering service sales	$50,000
2. Equipment rentals	12,500
3. Reception rental space	17,500
	$80,000

(d) Expenses consisted of:

1. Cost of goods sold (catering)	$15,000
2. Other costs (catering)	11,500
3. Depreciation—equipment rental	1,500
4. Repairs and other costs—equipment rental	2,500
5. Depreciation, $2,000; cleaning, $4,500; and miscellaneous costs, $1,000—reception rental space	7,500
6. Living expenses—family	12,000
	$50,000

Based on the FASB's Conceptual Framework, indicate what changes, if any, you would make in the income statement format and amount of Hillstead's income for 1987 and give theoretical support for your conclusions.

3

Review of the Accounting Process

All business enterprises, regardless of size or the nature of their operations, need accurate records of business transactions. Businesses that do not keep accurate records will not operate as efficiently and profitably as they could otherwise. In addition, the Foreign Corrupt Practices Act of 1977 requires publicly held companies, by law, to keep accurate books and records that fairly reflect business activity.

A variety of reports are prepared from accounting records to assist users in making better economic decisions. As explained in Chapters 1 and 2, general-purpose financial statements are prepared for external user groups, primarily current or potential investors and creditors, who are involved financially with an enterprise, but who are not a part of its management team. User groups within organizations, especially those in managerial positions, receive reports to assist them in planning and controlling the day-to-day operations of their organizations. Tax returns and similar reports must be prepared to comply with Internal Revenue Service (IRS) requirements. Special reports are required by various regulatory agencies such as the Securities and Exchange Commission (SEC).

Each of these reports is based on data that are the result of an accounting system and a set of procedures collectively referred to as the **accounting process**, or the **accounting cycle**. While this process follows a fairly standard set of procedures, the exact nature of the **accounting system** used to collect and report the data will depend on the type of business, its size, the volume of transactions processed, the degree of automation employed, and other related factors. The various routines in each system are developed to meet the special needs of the business unit. Every accounting system, however, should be designed to provide accurate information on a timely and efficient basis. At the same time, the system must provide controls that are effective in preventing mistakes and guarding against dishonesty.

Historically, accounting systems were maintained by hand and referred to as **manual systems**. Such systems continue to be used effectively in many situations. In today's modern business environment, however, most companies use at least some type of automated equipment, such as cash registers or other special-purpose business machines, and many companies have **electronic data processing (EDP) systems** that utilize the capabilities of high-speed computers. Furthermore, the advent of microcomputers has put EDP systems within the reach of almost all smaller companies that previously had to rely on manual or partially mechanized systems. As explained later in the chapter, an EDP system has many advantages and some disadvantages. The important point is that all accounting systems are designed to serve the same information gathering and processing functions. There is no difference in the underlying accounting concepts involved, only in some mechanical aspects of the process and in the appearance of the records and reports. Since it is easier to understand and to illustrate, a manual system will be used for the examples in this chapter and throughout the text.

The purpose of this chapter is to review the basic steps of the accounting process, including a brief review of the mechanics of double-entry accounting. To assist in your review, a list of terms commonly used in the data gathering and reporting process is provided on pages 64 and 65.

OVERVIEW OF THE ACCOUNTING PROCESS

The accounting process consists of two interrelated parts: (1) the recording phase and (2) the summarizing phase. The recording phase is concerned with the collection of information about economic transactions and events. For most businesses, the recording function is based on double-entry accounting procedures. In the summarizing phase, the recorded information is organized and summarized, using various formats for a variety of decision-making purposes. There is an overlapping of the two phases, since the recording of transactions is an ongoing activity that does not cease at the end of an accounting period, but continues uninterrupted while events of the preceding period are being summarized. The recording and summarizing phases of the accounting process are reviewed and illustrated in this chapter. The form and content of the basic financial statements are discussed and illustrated in depth in Chapters 4 and 5.[1]

---

[1]Appendix A at the end of the book provides an illustrated set of financial statements from the 1985 annual report of General Mills, Inc.

Commonly Used Terms in the Accounting Process

Account — an accounting record in which the results of similar transactions are accumulated; a separate account is maintained for each asset, liability, owners' equity, revenue, and expense item, showing increases, decreases, and a balance.

Accrual accounting — a system of accounting in which revenues and expenses are recorded as they are earned and incurred, not necessarily when cash is received or paid.

Adjusting entries — entries required at the end of each accounting period to update the accounts as necessary and to fully recognize, on an accrual basis, revenues and expenses for the period.

Business documents — business records used as the basis for analyzing and recording transactions; examples include invoices, check stubs, receipts, and similar business papers.

Closing entries — entries that reduce all nominal, or temporary, accounts to a zero balance at the end of each accounting period, transferring the pre-closing balances to real, or permanent, accounts.

Control account — a general ledger account that summarizes the detailed information accounted for and reported elsewhere, usually in a subsidiary ledger.

Credit — an entry on the right side of an account.

Debit — an entry on the left side of an account.

Double-entry accounting — a system of recording transactions in a way that maintains the equality of the accounting equation: ASSETS = LIABILITIES + OWNERS' EQUITY.

General-purpose financial statements — reports that reflect the summary of business activity; the statements that traditionally include the *balance sheet* (showing the financial position at the end of a period), *income statement* (showing results of operations for the period), and *cash flow statement (funds statement)*, showing the main sources and uses of funds during a period). A fourth statement showing changes in stockholders' equity is also usually included.

Journal — an accounting record in which transactions are first entered, providing a chronological record of business activity; sometimes referred to as a "book of original entry." *Special journals* may be used to record cash receipts, cash disbursements, sales, and purchases, or a company may only use a *general journal* to record all transactions.

Ledger — a book (or computer printout) of accounts. The *general ledger* includes all asset, liability, owners' equity, revenue, and expense accounts. A *subsidiary ledger* is a group of accounts providing the detail for a specific general ledger control account.

Nominal accounts—accounts that are closed to a zero balance at the end of an accounting period; includes income statement accounts (revenues and expenses) and dividends; also referred to as "temporary" accounts.

Post-closing trial balance—a listing of all real account balances after the closing process has been completed.

Posting—the process of classifying and grouping similar transactions in common accounts by transferring amounts from the journal to the ledger.

Real accounts—accounts that are not closed to a zero balance at the end of each accounting period; also referred to as "permanent" accounts or "balance sheet" accounts.

Reversing entries—entries made at the beginning of a period that exactly reverse certain adjusting entries made at the end of the previous period.

Transactions—exchanges of goods or services between entities, and other events having an economic impact on a business.

Trial balance—a listing of all account balances; provides a means of testing whether total debits equal total credits for all accounts.

Work sheet—a columnar schedule used to summarize accounting data; often used to facilitate the preparation of the financial statements.

The accounting process, illustrated in Exhibit 3–1, generally includes the following steps in well-defined sequence:

Recording Phase
1. Business documents are analyzed. Analysis of the documentation of business activities provides the basis for making an initial record of each transaction.
2. Transactions are recorded. Based on the supporting documents from Step 1, transactions are recorded in chronological order in books of original entry, or journals.
3. Transactions are posted. Transactions, as classified and recorded in the journals, are posted to the appropriate accounts in the general and, where applicable, subsidiary ledgers.

Summarizing Phase
4. A trial balance of the accounts in the general ledger is prepared. The trial balance, usually prepared on a work sheet, provides a summary of the information as classified in the ledger, as well as a general check on the accuracy of recording and posting.
5. Adjusting entries are recorded. Before financial statements can be prepared, all accountable information that has not been recorded must be

determined. Often adjustments are first made on a work sheet, and may be formally recorded and posted at any time prior to closing (Step 7). If a work sheet is not used, the adjusting entries must be recorded and posted at this point so the accounts are current prior to the preparation of financial statements.

6. Financial statements are prepared. Statements summarizing operations and showing the financial position and changes in financial position are prepared from the information on the work sheet or directly from the adjusted accounts.

7. Nominal accounts are closed. Balances in the nominal (temporary) accounts are closed into appropriate summary accounts. As determined in summary accounts, the results of operations are transferred to the appropriate owners' equity accounts.

8. A post-closing trial balance may be taken. A trial balance is taken to determine the equality of the debits and credits after posting the adjusting and closing entries.

9. Selected accounts may be reversed. Accrued and prepaid balances that were established by adjusting entries may be returned to the nominal accounts that are to be used in recording and summarizing activities involving these items in the new period. This step is not required, but may be desirable as a means of facilitating recording and adjusting routines in the succeeding period.

Recording Phase

Accurate financial statements can be prepared only if transactions have been properly recorded. A **transaction** is an event that involves the transfer or exchange of goods or services between two or more entities. Examples of business transactions include the purchase of merchandise or other assets from suppliers and the sale of goods or services to customers. In addition to transactions, other events and circumstances may affect the assets, liabilities, and owners' equity of the business. Such events and circumstances also must be recorded. Examples include the recognition of depreciation on plant assets, a decline in the market value of inventories and investments, or a loss suffered from a flood or an earthquake.

As indicated, the recording phase involves analyzing business documents, journalizing transactions, and posting to the ledger accounts. Before discussing these steps, the system of double-entry accounting will be reviewed, since most businesses use this procedure in recording their transactions.

Double-Entry Accounting. As explained in Chapters 1 and 2, financial accounting rests on a foundation of basic assumptions, concepts, and principles that govern the recording, classifying, summarizing, and reporting

Exhibit 3–1   The Accounting Process

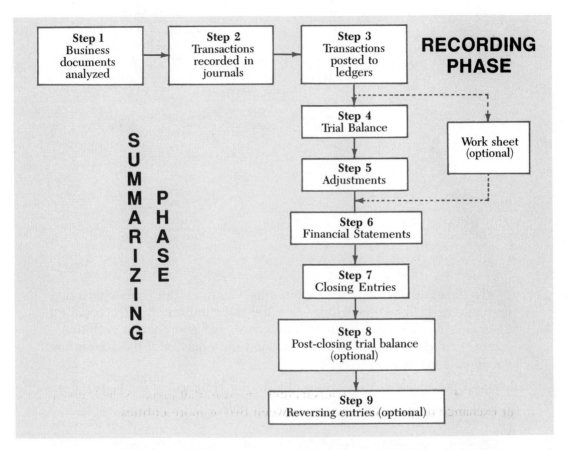

of accounting data. **Double-entry accounting** is an old and universally accepted system for recording accounting data. With double-entry accounting, each transaction is recorded in a way that maintains the equality of the basic accounting equation:

$$Assets = Liabilities + Owners' \ Equity$$

To review how double-entry accounting works, recall that a **debit** is an entry on the left side of an account and a **credit** is an entry on the right side. The debit/credit relationships of accounts were explained in detail in your introductory accounting course. Exhibit 3–2 summarizes these relationships for a corporation. You will note that assets, expenses, and dividends are increased by debits and decreased by credits. Liabilities, owners' equity accounts (capital stock and retained earnings), and revenues are increased by credits and decreased by debits.

Exhibit 3–2   Debit and Credit Relationships of Accounts

Assets			Liabilities			Owners' Equity	
Debit	Credit	=	Debit	Credit	+	Debit	Credit
Increase	Decrease		Decrease	Increase		Decrease	Increase
(+)	(−)		(−)	(+)		(−)	(+)

Retained Earnings			Capital Stock	
Debit	Credit		Debit	Credit
Decrease	Increase		Decrease	Increase
(−)	(+)		(−)	(+)

Dividends			Expenses			Revenues	
Debit	Credit		Debit	Credit		Debit	Credit
Increase	Decrease		Increase	Decrease		Decrease	Increase
(+)	(−)		(+)	(−)		(−)	(+)

To illustrate double-entry accounting, consider the transactions and journal entries shown in Exhibit 3–3 and their impact on the accounting equation. In studying this illustration, you should note that for each transaction, total debits equal total credits and the equality of the accounting equation is maintained.

Exhibit 3–3   Double-Entry Accounting: Illustrative Transactions and Journal Entries

Transaction	Journal Entry			Impact of Transaction on Accounting Equation Assets = Liabilities + Owners' Equity
1. Investment by shareholder in a corporation, $10,000	Cash Capital Stock	10,000	10,000	+10,000 = +10,000
2. Purchase of merchandise on account, $5,000	Inventory Accts Payable	5,000	5,000	+ 5,000 = + 5,000
3. Payment of wages expense, $2,500	Wages Expense Cash	2,500	2,500	− 2,500 = − 2,500 (Increase in an expense reduces Retained Earnings and, therefore, Owners' Equity)
4. Collection of accounts receivable, $1,000	Cash Accts Receivable	1,000	1,000	+ 1,000 = − 1,000
5. Payment of account payable, $500	Accts Payable Cash	500	500	− 500 = − 500
6. Receipt of royalty fees, $20,000	Cash Royalty Revenue	20,000	20,000	+20,000 = +20,000 (Increase in revenue increases Retained Earnings and, therefore, Owners' Equity)

7. Purchase of equipment: $15,000 down payment plus $40,000 long-term note	Equipment
	   Cash
	   Note Payable
		55,000	15,000
			40,000
				+55,000 = +40,000
				−15,000

8. Payment of cash dividends, $4,000	Dividends Cash	4,000	4,000	− 4,000 = − 4,000 (Dividends reduce Retained Earnings and, therefore, Owners' Equity)

To summarize, you should remember the following important features of double-entry accounting:

1. Assets are always increased by debits and decreased by credits.
2. Liability and owners' equity accounts are always increased by credits and decreased by debits.
3. Owners' equity for a corporation includes capital stock accounts and the retained earnings account.
4. Revenues, expenses, and dividends relate to owners' equity through the retained earnings account.
5. Expenses and dividends are increased by debits and decreased by credits.
6. Revenues are increased by credits and decreased by debits.
7. The difference between total revenues and total expenses for a period is net income (loss), which increases (decreases) owners' equity through Retained Earnings.

Analyzing Business Documents. The basic accounting records of a business consist of:

1. The original source material evidencing transactions, called **business** or **source documents**,
2. The records for classifying and recording the transactions, known as **journals** or **books of original entry** and,
3. The records for summarizing the effects of transactions upon individual asset, liability, and owners' equity accounts, known as the **ledgers**.

The recording phase begins with an analysis of the documentation showing what business activities have occurred. Normally, a business document is the first record of each transaction. Such a document offers detailed information concerning the transaction and also fixes responsibility by naming the parties involved. The business documents provide support for the data to be recorded in the journals. Copies of sales invoices or cash register tapes, for example, are the evidence in support of the sales record; purchase invoices support the purchase record; debit and credit memorandums support adjustments in debtor and creditor balances; check stubs and cancelled checks provide data concerning cash disbursements; the corporation minutes book supports entries authorized by action of the board of directors; journal vouchers prepared and approved by appropriate officers are a source of data for adjustments or corrections that are to be reported in the accounts. Documents underlying each recorded transaction provide a means of verifying the accounting records and thus form a vital part of the information and control system.

Journalizing Transactions. Once the information provided on business documents has been analyzed, transactions are recorded in chronological order in the appropriate journals. In some very small businesses, all transactions are recorded in a single journal. Most business enterprises, however, maintain various special journals, designed to meet their specific needs, as well as a general journal. A **special journal** is used to record a particular type of frequently recurring transaction. Special journals are commonly used, for example, to record each of the following types of transactions: sales, purchases, cash disbursements, and cash receipts. A **general journal** is used to record all transactions for which a special journal is not maintained. As illustrated below, a general journal shows the transaction date and the accounts affected, and gives a brief description of each transaction. It also provides debit and credit columns and a posting reference column. When transactions are posted, as explained in the next section, the appropriate ledger account numbers are entered in the posting reference column. Special journals are illustrated and explained in Appendix A at the end of this chapter.

General Journal Page 24

Date		Description	Post Ref.	Debit	Credit
1987 July	1	Dividends	330	25,000	
		Dividends Payable...................	260		25,000
		Declared semiannual cash dividend on common stock.			
	10	Equipment............................	180	7,500	
		Notes Payable	220		7,500
		Issued note for new equipment.			
	31	Payroll Taxes Expense.................	418	2,650	
		Payroll Taxes Payable	240		2,650
		Recorded payroll taxes for month.			

Posting To The Ledger Accounts. An **account** is used to summarize the results of similar transactions. A **ledger** is a collection of all the accounts maintained by a business and may be in the form of a book or a computer printout. The specific accounts required by a business unit vary depending on the nature of the business, its properties and activities, the information to be provided on the financial statements, and the controls to be employed in carrying out the accounting functions. The accounts used by a particular business are usually expressed in the form of a **chart of accounts**. This chart lists all accounts in systematic form with identifying numbers or symbols that provide the framework for summarizing business operations.

Information recorded in the journals is transferred to appropriate accounts in the ledger. This transfer is referred to as **posting**. Ledger accounts for Equipment and Notes Payable are shown on page 71, illustrating the posting of the July 10 transaction from the general journal on page 70. The posting reference (GJ24) indicates that the transaction was transferred from page 24 of the general journal. Note that the account numbers for Equipment (180) and Notes Payable (220) are entered in the posting reference column of the journal.

General Ledger

Account   Equipment   Account   180

Date		Item	Post Ref.	Debit	Credit	Balance
1987 July	1	Balance				10,550
	10	Purchase Equipment	GJ24	7,500		18,050

Account   Notes Payable   Account No. 220

Date		Item	Post Ref.	Debit	Credit	Balance
1987 July	1	Balance				5,750
	10	Purchase Equipment	GJ24		7,500	13,250

It is often desirable to establish separate ledgers for detailed information in support of balance sheet or income statement items. The **general ledger** includes all accounts appearing on the financial statements, while separate **subsidiary ledgers** afford additional detail in support of certain general ledger balances. For example, a single accounts receivable account is usually carried in the general ledger, and individual customers' accounts are recorded in a subsidiary accounts receivable ledger; the capital stock account in the general ledger is normally supported by individual stockholders' accounts in a subsidiary stockholders' ledger. The general ledger account that summarizes the detailed information in a subsidiary ledger is known as a **control account**. Subsidiary ledger accounts are illustrated in Appendix A at the end of this chapter.

Depending primarily on the number of transactions involved, amounts may be posted to ledger accounts on a daily, weekly, or monthly basis. If a computer system is being used, the posting process may be done automatically as transactions are recorded. At the end of an accounting period, when the posting process has been completed, the balances in the ledger accounts are used for preparing the trial balance.

Summarizing Phase

As noted earlier, the objective of the accounting process is to produce financial statements and other reports that will assist various users in making economic decisions. Once the recording phase is completed, the data must be summarized and organized into a useful format. The remaining steps of the accounting process are designed to accomplish this purpose. These steps will be illustrated using data from Rosi, Inc., a hypothetical merchandising company, for the year ended December 31, 1987.

Preparing a Trial Balance. After all transactions for the period have been posted to the ledger acounts, the balance for each account is determined. Every account will have either a debit, credit, or zero balance. **A trial balance** is a list of all accounts and their balances. The trial balance, therefore, indicates whether total debits equal total credits and thus provides a general check on the accuracy of recording and posting. A trial balance for Rosi, Inc., is presented on page 73.

Preparing Adjusting Entries. In order to report information on a timely basis, the life of a business is divided into relatively short time periods, such as a year, a quarter, or a month. While this is essential for the information to be useful, it does create problems for the accountant who must summarize the financial operations for the designated period and report on the financial position at the end of that period. Transactions during the period have been recorded in the appropriate journals and posted to the ledger accounts. At the end of the period, many accounts require adjustments to reflect current conditions. At this time, too, other financial data, not recognized previously, must be entered in the accounts to bring the books up to date. This requires analysis of individual accounts and various source documents. Based on this analysis, **adjusting entries are made, and financial statements are prepared using the adjusted account balances.**

This part of the accounting process is illustrated using the adjusting data for Rosi, Inc. presented on page 74. The data are classified according to the typical areas requiring adjustment at the end of the designated time period, in this case the year 1987. The accounts listed in the trial balance on page 73 do not reflect the adjusting data. The adjusting data must be combined with the information on the trial balance if the resulting financial statements are to appropriately reflect company operating results and financial position.

Asset Depreciation. Charges to operations for the use of buildings, furniture, and equipment must be recorded at the end of the period. In recording asset depreciation, operations are charged with a portion of the

Rosi, Inc.
Trial Balance
December 31, 1987

Cash	83,110	
Accounts Receivable	106,500	
Allowance for Doubtful Accounts		1,610
Inventory	45,000	
Prepaid Insurance	8,000	
Interest Receivable	0	
Notes Receivable	28,000	
Land	114,000	
Buildings	156,000	
Accum. Depr. — Buildings		39,000
Furniture & Equipment	19,000	
Accum. Depr. — Furniture & Equipment		3,800
Accounts Payable		37,910
Unearned Rent Revenue		0
Salaries and Wages Payable		0
Interest Payable		0
Payroll Taxes Payable		5,130
Income Tax Payable		0
Dividends Payable		3,400
Bonds Payable		140,000
Common Stock, $15 par		150,000
Retained Earnings		126,770
Dividends	13,600	
Sales		479,500
Purchases	162,600	
Purchase Discounts		3,290
Cost of Goods Sold	0	
Salaries and Wages Expense	172,450	
Heat, Light, and Power	32,480	
Payroll Taxes Expense	18,300	
Advertising Expense	18,600	
Doubtful Accounts Expense	0	
Depr. Exp. — Buildings	0	
Depr. Exp. — Furniture & Equipment	0	
Insurance Expense	0	
Interest Revenue		1,100
Rent Revenue		2,550
Interest Expense	16,420	
Income Tax Expense	0	
Totals	994,060	994,060

asset's cost, and the carrying value of the asset is reduced by that amount. A reduction in an asset for depreciation is usually recorded by a credit to a contra account, Accumulated Depreciation. **A contra account** (or offset account) is set up to record subtractions from a related account. Certain accounts relate to others, but must be added rather than subtracted on the statements, and are referred to as **adjunct accounts**. Examples include

Adjusting Data for Rosi, Inc.
December 31, 1987

Asset Depreciation:
(a) Buildings, 5% per year.
(b) Furniture and equipment, 10% per year.
Doubtful Accounts:
(c) The allowance for doubtful accounts is to be increased by $1,100.
Accrued Expenses:
(d) Salaries and wages, $2,150.
(e) Interest on bonds payable, $5,000.
Accrued Revenues:
(f) Interest on notes receivable, $250.
Prepaid Expenses:
(g) Prepaid insurance, $3,800.
Deferred Revenues:
(h) Unearned rent revenue, $475.
Income taxes:
(i) Federal and state income taxes, $8,000.
Inventory:
(j) A periodic inventory system is used; the ending inventory balance is $51,000.

Freight In, which is added to Purchases, and Additional Paid-In Capital, which is added to the Capital Stock account balance.

Adjustments at the end of the year for depreciation for Rosi, Inc. are as follows:

(a)	Depreciation Expense-Buildings................................	7,800	
	Accumulated Depreciation-Buildings............................		7,800
	To record depreciation on buildings at 5% per year.		
(b)	Depreciation Expense-Furniture & Equipment	1,900	
	Accumulated Depreciation-Furniture & Equipment................		1,900
	To record depreciation on furniture and equipment at 10% per year		

Doubtful Accounts. Invariably, when a business allows customers to purchase goods and services on credit, some of the accounts receivable will not be collected, resulting in a charge to income for bad debt expense. Under the accrual concept, an adjustment should be made for the estimated expense in the current period, rather than when specific accounts actually become uncollectible. This produces a better matching of revenues and expenses and therefore a better income measurement. Using this procedure, operations are charged with the estimated expense, and receivables are reduced by means of a contra account, Allowance for Doubtful Accounts. To illustrate, the adjustment for Rosi, Inc. at the end of the year, assuming the allowance account is to be increased by $1,100, would be as follows:

(c) Doubtful Accounts Expense 1,100
        Allowance for Doubtful Accounts   1,100
            To adjust for estimated doubtful accounts expense.

Throughout the accounting period, when there is positive evidence that a specific account is uncollectible, the appropriate amount is written off against the contra account. For example, if a $150 receivable were considered uncollectible, that amount would be written off as follows:

Allowance for Doubtful Accounts 150
    Accounts Receivable..   150
        To write off an uncollectible account.

No entry is made to Doubtful Accounts Expense, since the adjusting entry has already provided for an estimated expense based on previous experience for all receivables.

Accrued Expenses. During the period, certain expenses may have been incurred for which payment is not to be made until a subsequent period. At the end of the period, it is necessary to determine and record any expenses not yet recognized. In recording an accrued expense, an expense account is debited and a liability account is credited. The adjusting entries to record accrued expenses for Rosi, Inc. are:

(d) Salaries and Wages Expense................................... 2,150
        Salaries and Wages Payable   2,150
            To record accrued salaries and wages.

(e) Interest Expense... 5,000
        Interest Payable   5,000
            To record accrued interest on bonds.

Accrued Revenues. During the period, certain amounts may have been earned, although collection is not to be made until a subsequent period. At the end of the period, it is necessary to determine and record the earnings not yet recognized. In recording accrued revenues, an asset account is debited and a revenue account is credited. The illustrative entry recognizing the accrued revenue for Rosi, Inc. is as follows:

(f) Interest Receivable... 250
        Interest Revenue..   250
            To record accrued interest on notes receivable.

Prepaid Expenses. During the period, expenditures may have been recorded on the books for commodities or goods that are not to be received or used up currently. At the end of the period, it is necessary to determine the portions of such expenditures that are applicable to subsequent periods and hence require recognition as assets.

The method of adjusting for prepaid expenses depends on how the expenditures were originally entered in the accounts. They may have been recorded originally as debits to (1) an expense account or (2) an asset account.

Original Debit to an Expense Account. If an expense account was originally debited, the adjusting entry requires that an asset account be debited for the amount applicable to future periods and the expense account be credited. The expense account then remains with a debit balance representing the amount applicable to the current period.

Original Debit to an Asset Account. If an asset account was originally debited, the adjusting entry requires that an expense account be debited for the amount applicable to the current period and the asset account be credited. The asset account remains with a debit balance that shows the amount applicable to future periods. An adjusting entry for prepaid insurance for Rosi, Inc. illustrates this situation as follows:

(g)	Insurance Expense	4,200	
	Prepaid Insurance		4,200
	To record expired insurance ($8,000 − $3,800 = $4,200).		

Since the asset account Prepaid Insurance was originally debited, as shown in the trial balance, the amount of the prepayment ($8,000) must be reduced to reflect only the $3,800 that remains unexpired.

Deferred Revenues. Payments may be received from customers prior to the delivery of goods or services. Amounts received in advance are recorded by debiting an asset account, usually Cash, and crediting either a revenue account or a liability account. At the end of the period, it is necessary to determine the amount of revenue earned in the current period and the amount to be deferred to future periods. The method of adjusting for deferred revenues depends on whether the receipts for undelivered goods or services were recorded originally as credits to (1) a revenue account or (2) a liability account.

Original Credit to a Revenue Account. If a revenue account was originally credited, this account is debited and a liability account is credited for the revenue applicable to a future period. The revenue account remains with a credit balance representing the earnings applicable to the current period. As indicated in the trial balance for Rosi, Inc., rent receipts are recorded originally in the Rent Revenue account. Unearned revenue at the end of 1987 is $475 and is recorded as follows:

(h)   Rent Revenue   475
        Unearned Rent Revenue.   475
            To record unearned rent revenue.

Original Credit to a Liability Account. If a liability account was credited originally, this account is debited and a revenue account is credited for the amount applicable to the current period. The liability account remains with a credit balance that shows the amount applicable to future periods.

Income Taxes. When a corporation reports earnings, adjustments must be made for federal and state income taxes. Income Tax Expense is debited and Income Tax Payable is credited. The entry to record income taxes for Rosi, Inc. is as follows:

(i)   Income Tax Expense   8,000
        Income Tax Payable.   8,000
            To record income taxes.

Note that the above entry assumes a single year-end accrual of income taxes. Most companies record income taxes monthly when estimated payments are made to federal and state taxing authorities.

Adjusting the Inventory Account. The type of adjustment required for the inventory account depends on whether a periodic or perpetual inventory system is used. When the periodic inventory method is used, physical inventories must be taken at the end of the period to determine the inventory to be reported on the balance sheet and the cost of goods sold to be reported on the income statement. When perpetual inventory records are maintained, the ending inventory and the cost of goods sold balances appear in the ledger. An adjustment is necessary only to correct the recorded balances for any spoilage or theft that may have occurred, as determined by a physical count of the inventory. The inventory procedures for merchandising companies are reviewed in the following paragraphs. Accounting for inventories of manufacturers is explained in Chapter 9.

Periodic (Physical) Inventories. When using the **periodic inventory system**, all purchases of merchandise during a period are recorded in a Purchases account. At the end of the period, before adjustments are made, the Inventory account still reflects the beginning inventory balance. The ending balance, based on a physical count, may be recorded in the Inventory account by an adjusting entry. At the same time the Inventory account is adjusted, the Purchases account, and any related accounts such as Purchase Discounts or Freight In, may be closed to Cost of Goods Sold. In this way, the amount of Cost of Goods Sold is established through a single adjusting entry.

Using the method just described, an adjustment for Rosi, Inc. would be made to the inventory account by debiting it for $6,000 ($51,000–$45,000), debiting Purchase Discounts for $3,290, crediting Purchases for $162,600, and debiting Cost of Goods Sold for the net amount, $153,310. This would increase Inventory to its ending balance of $51,000, close Purchase Discounts and Purchases, and reflect the amount of Cost of Goods Sold to be reported on the income statement. The adjusting entry would be as follows:

```
(j)  Inventory..............................................    6,000
     Purchase Discounts ......................................    3,290
     Cost of Goods Sold ......................................  153,310
        Purchases.............................................              162,600
           To adjust inventory, cost of goods sold,
           and related accounts.
```

An alternative to the above procedure is to adjust inventory and cost of goods sold through the closing process.

Perpetual Inventories. When a **perpetual inventory system** is maintained, a separate Purchases account is not used. The Inventory account is debited whenever goods are acquired. When a sale takes place, two entries are required: (1) the sale is recorded in the usual manner, and (2) the merchandise sold is recorded by a debit to Cost of Goods Sold and a credit to Inventory. At any time during the period, Inventory reflects the inventory on hand, and Cost of Goods Sold shows the cost of merchandise sold. At the end of the period, no adjustment is needed for inventory, except to adjust for spoilage or theft as noted earlier. Cost of Goods Sold would be debited and Inventory would be credited for the cost of the spoiled or stolen goods.

Preparing Financial Statements. Once all accounts have been brought up to date through the adjustment process, **financial statements** may be prepared. The data may be taken directly from the adjusted account balances in the ledger, or a work sheet may be used.

Using a Work Sheet. An optional step in the accounting process is to use a **work sheet** to facilitate the preparation of adjusting entries and financial statements. A work sheet is an accounting tool that is often used in organizing large quantities of data. However, preparing a work sheet is not a required step. As indicated, financial statements can be prepared directly from data in adjusted ledger account balances.

When a work sheet is constructed, trial balance data are listed in the first pair of columns. The adjusting entries are listed in the second pair of columns. Sometimes a third pair of columns is included to show the trial balance after adjustment. Account balances, as adjusted, are carried forward to the appropriate financial statement columns. A work sheet for a merchandising enterprise will include a pair of columns for the Income Statement accounts and a pair for the Balance Sheet accounts. Two columns for a Statement of Changes in Stockholders' Equity may be placed between the Income Statement and the Balance Sheet columns if desired. There are no columns for the statement of cash flows, because this statement contains a rearrangement of information included in comparative balance sheets and the income statement. The income statement and balance sheet are discussed and illustrated in Chapters 4 and 5, respectively, and the statement of cash flows is discussed in Chapters 5 and 24. A work sheet for Rosi, Inc. is shown on pages 80 and 81. All adjustments illustrated previously are included.

Closing the Nominal Accounts. Once adjusting entries are formally recorded in the general journal and posted to the ledger accounts, the books are ready to be closed in preparation for a new accounting cycle. During this closing process, the **nominal (temporary) account** balances are transferred to a **real (permanent) account**, leaving the nominal accounts with a zero balance. Nominal accounts include all income statement accounts plus the dividends account for a corporation or the drawings account for a proprietorship or partnership. The real account that receives the closing amounts from the nominal accounts is Retained Earnings for a corporation or the respective capital accounts for a proprietorship or partnership. Since they are real accounts, these and all other balance sheet accounts remain open and carry their balances forward to the new period.

The mechanics of closing the nominal accounts are straightforward. All revenue accounts with credit balances are closed by being debited; all expense accounts with debit balances are closed by being credited. This reduces these temporary accounts to a zero balance. The difference between the closing debit amounts for revenues and the credit amounts for expenses is net income (or net loss) and is an increase (or decrease) to Retained Earnings. The closing of Dividends reduces Retained Earnings. Thus, the closing entries for revenues, expenses, and dividends may be made directly to Retained Earnings, as follows:

Revenues...	xx	
Retained Earnings		xx
To close revenues to Retained Earnings.		
Retained Earnings	xx	
Expenses...		xx
To close expenses to Retained Earnings.		
Retained Earnings	xx	
Dividends..		xx
To close the dividends account to Retained Earnings.		

Rosi,
Work
December

	Account Title	Trial Balance		
		Debit	Credit	
1	Cash	83,110		1
2	Accounts Receivable	106,500		2
3	Allowance for Doubtful Accounts		1,610	3
4	Inventory	45,000		4
5	Prepaid Insurance	8,000		5
6	Interest Receivable	0		6
7	Notes Receivable	28,000		7
8	Land	114,000		8
9	Buildings	156,000		9
10	Accum. Depr.—Buildings		39,000	10
11	Furniture & Equipment	19,000		11
12	Accum. Depr.—Furniture & Equipment		3,800	12
13	Accounts Payable		37,910	13
14	Unearned Rent Revenue		0	14
15	Salaries and Wages Payable		0	15
16	Interest Payable		0	16
17	Payroll Taxes Payable		5,130	17
18	Income Tax Payable		0	18
19	Dividends Payable		3,400	19
20	Bonds Payable		140,000	20
21	Common Stock, $15 par		150,000	21
22	Retained Earnings		126,770	22
23	Dividends	13,600		23
24	Sales		479,500	24
25	Purchases	162,600		25
26	Purchase Discounts		3,290	26
27	Cost of Goods Sold	0		27
28	Salaries and Wages Expense	172,450		28
29	Heat, Light, and Power	32,480		29
30	Payroll Taxes Expense	18,300		30
31	Advertising Expense	18,600		31
32	Doubtful Accounts Expense	0		32
33	Depr. Exp.—Buildings	0		33
34	Depr. Exp.—Furniture & Equipment	0		34
35	Insurance Expense	0		35
36	Interest Revenue		1,100	36
37	Rent Revenue		2,550	37
38	Interest Expense	16,420		38
39	Income Tax Expense	0		39
40	Totals	994,060	994,060	40
41	Net Income			41
42				42

Inc.
Sheet
31, 1987

#	Adjustments Debit	Adjustments Credit	Income Statement Debit	Income Statement Credit	Balance Sheet Debit	Balance Sheet Credit	#
1					83,110		1
2					106,500		2
3		(c) 1,100				2,710	3
4	(j) 6,000				51,000		4
5		(g) 4,200			3,800		5
6	(f) 250				250		6
7					28,000		7
8					114,000		8
9					156,000		9
10		(a) 7,800				46,800	10
11					19,000		11
12		(b) 1,900				5,700	12
13						37,910	13
14		(h) 475				475	14
15		(d) 2,150				2,150	15
16		(e) 5,000				5,000	16
17						5,130	17
18		(i) 8,000				8,000	18
19						3,400	19
20						140,000	20
21						150,000	21
22						126,770	22
23					13,600		23
24				479,500			24
25		(j) 162,600					25
26	(j) 3,290						26
27	(j) 153,310		153,310				27
28	(d) 2,150		174,600				28
29			32,480				29
30			18,300				30
31			18,600				31
32	(c) 1,100		1,100				32
33	(a) 7,800		7,800				33
34	(b) 1,900		1,900				34
35	(g) 4,200		4,200				35
36		(f) 250		1,350			36
37	(h) 475			2,075			37
38	(e) 5,000		21,420				38
39	(i) 8,000		8,000				39
40	193,475	193,475	441,710	482,925	575,260	534,045	40
41			41,215			41,215	41
42			482,925	482,925	575,260	575,260	42

An alternative to the closing method described on page 79 is to use an **Income Summary** account. Income Summary is a temporary "clearing" account that is used only to accumulate amounts from the closing entries for revenues and expenses and therefore summarizes the net income or net loss for the period. After revenues and expenses are closed to Income Summary, the balance in that account is then closed to Retained Earnings. Dividends must still be closed directly to Retained Earnings, since dividends do not affect net income and are not closed to Income Summary. If a work sheet is prepared, the balances in the income statement columns provide the data for closing revenues and expenses. The closing entries for Rosi, Inc. are presented below, assuming that an Income Summary account is used.

Closing Entries

1987			
Dec. 31	Sales..	479,500	
	Interest Revenue	1,350	
	Rent Revenue.......................................	2,075	
	Income Summary....................................		482,925
	To close revenue accounts to Income Summary.		
	Income Summary.....................................	441,710	
	Cost of Goods Sold..............................		153,310
	Salaries and Wages Expense		174,600
	Heat, Light, and Power............................		32,480
	Payroll Taxes Expense		18,300
	Advertising Expense		18,600
	Interest Expense		21,420
	Doubtful Accounts Expense...........................		1,100
	Depreciation Expense — Buildings		7,800
	Depreciation Expense — Furniture and Equipment		1,900
	Insurance Expense		4,200
	Income Tax Expense...............................		8,000
	To close expense accounts to Income Summary.		
	Income Summary....................................	41,215	
	Retained Earnings		41,215
	To transfer the balance in Income Summary to Retained Earnings.		
	Retained Earnings	13,600	
	Dividends.......................................		13,600
	To close Dividends to Retained Earnings.		

Note that with the adjusting method illustrated for Inventory, Cost of Goods Sold is already computed. It can then be closed to Income Summary (or directly to Retained Earnings if an Income Summary account is not used) just like any other operating expense.

Preparing a Post-Closing Trial Balance. After the closing entries are posted, a **post-closing trial balance** may be prepared to verify the equality of the debits and credits for all real accounts. The post-closing trial balance for Rosi, Inc. is presented below.

Rosi, Inc.
Post-Closing Trial Balance
December 31, 1987

Cash	83,110	
Accounts Receivable	106,500	
Allowance for Doubtful Accounts		2,710
Inventory	51,000	
Prepaid Insurance	3,800	
Interest Receivable	250	
Notes Receivable	28,000	
Land	114,000	
Buildings	156,000	
Accumulated Depreciation-Buildings		46,800
Furniture and Equipment	19,000	
Accumulated Depreciation—Furniture and Equipment		5,700
Accounts Payable		37,910
Salaries and Wages Payable		2,150
Interest Payable		5,000
Payroll Taxes Payable		5,130
Income Tax Payable		8,000
Dividends Payable		3,400
Bonds Payable		140,000
Unearned Rent Revenue		475
Common Stock, $15 par		150,000
Retained Earnings		154,385
	561,660	561,660

Reversing Entries. At the beginning of a new period, the following types of adjusting entries may be reversed:

1. accrued expenses
2. accrued revenues
3. prepaid expenses when the original debit was to an expense account
4. deferred revenues when the original credit was to a revenue account

Reversing entries are not necessary, but they make it possible to record the expense payments or revenue receipts in the new period in the usual manner. For example, if a reversing entry is not made for accrued expenses, payments in the subsequent period would have to be analyzed as to (1) the amount representing payment of the accrued liability, and (2) the amount representing the expense of the current period. Alternatively, the accrued and deferred accounts could be left unadjusted until the close of the subsequent reporting period when they would be adjusted to their correct balances.

The adjustments establishing accrued and prepaid balances for Rosi, Inc. were illustrated earlier in the chapter. The appropriate reversing entries are shown below.

Reversing Entries

```
1988
Jan. 1  Salaries and Wages Payable ................................  2,150
            Salaries and Wages Expense.............................         2,150
        Interest Payable ...........................................  5,000
            Interest Expense.......................................         5,000
        Interest Revenue...........................................    250
            Interest Receivable....................................          250
        Unearned Rent Revenue....................................    475
            Rent Revenue .........................................          475
```

To illustrate accounting for an accrued expense when (1) reversing entries are made and (2) reversing entries are not made, assume that accrued salaries on December 31, 1987, are $350 and on December 31, 1988, are $500. Payment of salaries for the period ending January 4, 1988, is $1,000. Adjustments are made and the books are closed annually on December 31. The possible entries are shown below:

	(1) Assuming Liability Account Is Reversed	(2) Assuming Liability Account Is Not Reversed	
		(a) Transaction in Next Period Is Analyzed.	(b) Transaction in Next Period is Not Analyzed. Adjustment at Close of Next Reporting Period.
December 31, 1987 Adjusting entry to record accrued salaries.	Salaries ..... 350 Salaries Payable ... 350	Salaries ..... 350 Salaries Payable ... 350	Salaries....... 350 Salaries Payable..... 350
December 31, 1987 Closing entry to transfer expense to the income summary account.	Income Summary .... xxx Salaries ... xxx	Income Summary.... xxx Salaries ... xxx	Income Summary ..... xxx Salaries..... xxx
January 1, 1988 Reversing entry to transfer balance to the account that will be charged when payment is made.	Salaries Payable ..... 350 Salaries ... 350	No entry	No entry
January 4, 1988 Payment of salaries for period ending January 4, 1988.	Salaries ..... 1,000 Cash 1,000	Salaries Payable ..... 350 Salaries ..... 650 Cash...... 1,000	Salaries....... 1,000 Cash 1,000
December 31, 1988 Adjusting entry to record accrued salaries.	Salaries ..... 500 Salaries Payable ... 500	Salaries ..... 500 Salaries Payable ... 500	Salaries....... 150 Salaries Payable..... 150

ACCRUAL VERSUS CASH BASIS ACCOUNTING

The procedures described in the previous sections are those required in a double-entry system based on accrual accounting. **Accrual accounting** recognizes revenues as they are earned, not necessarily when they are received. Expenses are recognized and recorded when they are incurred, not necessarily when they are paid. This provides for a better matching of revenues and expenses during an accounting period and generally results in financial statements that more accurately reflect a company's financial position and results of operations.[2]

Some accounting systems are based on cash receipts and cash disbursements instead of accrual accounting. **Cash basis accounting** procedures frequently are found in organizations not requiring a complete set of double-entry records. Such organizations might include smaller, unincorporated businesses, and some nonprofit organizations. Professionals engaged in service businesses, such as CPAs, dentists, and engineers, also have traditionally used cash accounting systems. Even many of these organizations, however, periodically use professional accountants to prepare financial statements and other required reports on an accrual basis.

A controversy exists currently as to the appropriateness of using cash accounting systems,[3] especially as a basis for determining tax liabilities. The FASB, in Concepts Statement No. 1, indicates that accrual accounting provides a better basis for financial reports than does information showing only cash receipts and disbursements. The AICPA's position, however, is that the cash basis is appropriate for some smaller companies and especially for companies in the service industry. Until this controversy is settled, accountants will continue to be asked to convert cash-based records to generally accepted accrual-based financial statements. The necessary procedures are illustrated and explained in Appendix B at the end of this chapter.

COMPUTERS AND THE ACCOUNTING PROCESS

The usual procedures for recording transactions and the sequence of activities leading to the preparation of financial statements have been

---

[2] In Concepts Statement No. 6, the FASB discusses the concept of accrual accounting and relates it to the objectives of financial reporting. *Statement of Financial Accounting Concepts No. 6*, "Elements of Financial Statements" (Stamford: Financial Accounting Standards Board, December 1985).

[3] For an argument on retaining the cash basis of accounting, see Ronnie G. Flippo, "The President's Tax Proposals: A View from Capitol Hill," *Journal of Accountancy* (September 1985), pp. 86–88.

briefly reviewed in this chapter. These procedures and activities are referred to collectively as the accounting process or accounting cycle. The accounting process begins with the analysis of business documents evidencing the transactions of an entity and concludes with the final summarized financial statements.

As an organization grows in size and complexity, the recording and summarizing processes become more involved, and means are sought for improving efficiency and reducing costs. Some enterprises may find that a system involving primarily manual operations is adequate in meeting their needs. Others find that information processing needs can be handled effectively only through electronic data processing (EDP) equipment.

Companies requiring great speed and accuracy in processing large amounts of accounting data often utilize a **computer system** capable of storing and recalling data, performing many mathematical functions, and making certain routine decisions based on mathematical comparisons. These systems normally include various other machines that can "read" data from disks, magnetic tapes, or punched cards and print information in a variety of forms, all under the control of a computer.

Modern computer systems have vast capabilities. The individual steps involved in recording and summarizing may be combined into one process. The information traditionally recorded in journals and ledgers may be stored in memory banks or on computer disks and recalled as needed. Online, real-time systems have the capability of continuous updating of all relevant files. This makes it possible for reports to be produced on a much more timely basis.

Since the early 1960s, society has been caught in the midst of an ongoing computer revolution. Technological advances in integrated circuitry and microchips led to one of the most significant phenomena of the 1980s — the development of **personal computers** (**PCs**). These compact, relatively inexpensive computers have changed the way in which many companies and individuals keep track of their business activities. It is estimated that in 1985, over 9 million PCs were being used in businesses, and that over 3.4 million PCs were sold in that year alone. These computers are being used for a variety of activities, including financial analysis, accounting functions, word processing, data base management, inventory control, and credit analysis of customers. As uses have expanded, software packages have been developed to meet current and future demand. The impact of PCs is felt not only in business, but in education and in family life. Several colleges now require entering freshmen to purchase their own PCs for use in a variety of business, mathematics, and science courses. Exposure to computers, and especially the PC, is also very common in elementary and secondary school curricula.

This computer revolution is rapidly changing society and along with it, the way business is conducted and, therefore, the way accounting functions are performed. However, despite their tremendous capabilities, computers cannot replace skilled accountants. In fact, their presence places increased demands on the accountant in directing the operations of the computer systems to assure the use of appropriate procedures. Although all arithmetical operations can be assumed to be done accurately by computers, the validity of the output data depends on the adequacy of the instructions given the computer. Unlike a human accountant, a computer cannot think for itself, but must be given explicit instructions for performing each operation. This has certain advantages in that the accountant can be sure every direction will be carried out precisely. On the other hand, this places a great responsibility on the accountant to anticipate any unusual situations requiring special consideration or judgment. Various control techniques also must be developed for checking and verifying data recorded in electronic form.

The significance of the accounting process in our society and its applicability to every business unit, regardless of size, must be appreciated. Although the procedures may be modified to meet special conditions and may be performed through a variety of manual or computer systems, the process reviewed in this chapter is fundamental to the accounting systems of all enterprises.

APPENDIX A

Special Journals and Subsidiary Ledgers

In recording transactions, many companies use **special journals** in addition to the **general journal**. Special journals eliminate much of the repetitive work involved in recording routine transactions. In addition, they permit the recording functions to be divided among accounting personnel, each individual being responsible for a separate record. This specialization often results in greater efficiency as well as a higher degree of control.

Some examples of special journals are the sales journal, the purchases journal, the cash receipts journal, the cash disbursements journal, the payroll register, and the voucher register.

Sales on account are recorded in the **sales journal**. The subsequent collections on account, as well as other transactions involving the receipt of cash, are recorded in the **cash receipts journal**. Merchandise purchases on account are entered in the **purchases journal**. Subsequent payments on account, as well as other transactions involving the payment of cash, are recorded in the **cash disbursements journal** or in the **check register**. A payroll register may be employed to accumulate payroll information, including payroll deductions and withholdings for taxes.

Column headings in the various journals specify the accounts to be debited or credited; account titles and explanations may therefore be omitted in recording routine transactions. A Sundry column is usually provided for transactions that are relatively infrequent, and account titles must be entered in recording such transactions.

The use of special journals facilitates recording and also simplifies the posting process, because the totals of many transactions, rather than separate data for each transaction, can be posted to the ledger accounts. Certain data must be transferred individually—data affecting individual accounts receivable and accounts payable and data reported in the Sundry columns—but the overall volume of posting is substantially reduced.

The format of a particular journal must satisfy the needs of the individual business unit. For example, with an automated or computerized system, the general journal, any specialized journals, and subsidiary ledgers may be modified or eliminated. Recognizing that modifications are necessary for individual systems, the following sections discuss a voucher system and illustrate some special journals that are commonly used with manual accounting systems.

VOUCHER SYSTEM

Relatively large organizations ordinarily provide for the control of purchases and cash disbursements through adoption of some form of a **voucher system**. With the use of a voucher system, checks may be drawn only upon a written authorization in the form of a **voucher** approved by some responsible official.

A voucher is prepared, not only in support of each payment to be made for goods and services purchased on account, but also for all other transactions calling for payment by check, including cash purchases, retirement of debt, replenishment of petty cash funds, payrolls, and dividends. The voucher identifies the person authorizing the expenditure, explains the nature of the transaction, and names the accounts affected by the transaction. For control purposes, vouchers should be prenumbered, checked against purchase invoices, and compared with receiving reports. Upon verification, the voucher and the related business documents are submitted to the appropriate official for final approval. When approved, the pre-numbered voucher is recorded in a voucher register. The voucher register is a book of original entry and takes the place of a purchases journal. Charges on each voucher are classified and recorded in appropriate Debit columns, and the amount to be paid is listed in an Accounts Payable or Vouchers Payable column. After a voucher is entered in the register, it is placed in an unpaid vouchers file together with its supporting documents.

Checks are written in payment of individual vouchers. The checks are recorded in a check register as debits to Accounts Payable or Vouchers Payable and credits to Cash. Since charges to the various asset, liability, or expense accounts, were recognized when the payable was recorded in the voucher register, these accounts need not be listed in the payments record. When a check is issued, payment of the voucher is reported in the voucher register by entering the check number and the payment date. Paid vouchers and supporting documents are removed from the unpaid file, marked "paid," and placed in a separate paid vouchers file. The balance of the payable account, after the credit for total vouchers issued and the debit for total vouchers paid, should be equal to the sum of the unpaid vouchers file. The voucher register, while representing a journal, also provides the detail in support of the accounts payable or vouchers payable total.

ILLUSTRATION OF SPECIAL JOURNALS AND SUBSIDIARY LEDGERS

Assume that SPN Inc. maintains the following books of original entry: sales journal, cash receipts journal, voucher register, cash disbursements journal, and general journal. As noted, the format of a particular journal must satisfy the needs of the individual business unit. Those presented for SPN Inc. are illustrative only.

Sales Journal

The sales journal, as summarized at the end of the month, appears as follows:

SALES JOURNAL

Accts. Rec. Dr.	Date		Description	Sales Cr.
2,100		31	Sales on account for day	2,100
40,150		31	Total	40,150
(116)				(41)

One entry is made to record the sales on account for each day. Accounts Receivable is debited; Sales is credited. Debits are posted to the individual customers' accounts in the Accounts Receivable Subsidiary Ledger directly from the sales invoices. The numbers in parentheses at the bottom of the journal refer to the accounts to which the totals are posted.

Cash Receipts Journal

The cash receipts journal for SPN Inc. appears as follows:

CASH RECEIPTS JOURNAL

Cash Dr.	Sales Disc. Dr.	Date	Description	Post. Ref.	Sundry Cr.	Sales Cr.	Accts. Rec. Cr.
1,960	40	31	Collection on accounts........	√			2,000
2,250		31	Cash sales........	√		2,250	
8,565		31	Notes receivable...	113	8,500		
			Interest revenue ...	72	65		
151,550	395	31	Total		106,245	9,800	35,900
(111)	(42)				(√)	(41)	(116)

One entry is made each day for the total amount collected on Accounts Receivable. In this entry Cash and Sales Discounts are debited, and Accounts Receivable is credited. Credits are posted to the individual customers' accounts in the Accounts Receivable Subsidiary Ledger from a separate list of receipts on account maintained by the cashier. An entry is also made for daily cash sales. A (check mark) under the Sundry column indicates that the amounts in this column are posted individually and not in total. In the illustration, $8,500 was posted to Notes Receivable (account number 113), and $65 was posted to Interest Revenue (account number 72).

Voucher Register

As noted, the voucher register takes the place of a purchases journal, providing a record of all authorized payments to be made by check. The voucher register appears on the following page. For illustrative purposes, separate debit columns are provided for two accounts—Purchases and Payroll. Other items are recorded in the Sundry Dr. column. Additional separate columns could be added for other items, such as advertising, if desired. The total amount of each column is posted to the corresponding account, with the exception of the Sundry Dr. and Cr. columns, which are posted individually.

VOUCHER REGISTER

Date	Vou. No.	Payee	Paid Date	Ck. No.	Accounts Payable Cr.	Purchases Dr.	Payroll Dr.	Account	Post. Ref.	Sundry Amount Dr.	Sundry Amount Cr.
31	7132	Security National Bank.......	7/31	3106	9,120			Notes Payable ...	211	9,120	
31	7133	Payroll	7/31	3107	1,640		2,130	FICA Tax Payable.....	215		90
								Income Tax Payable.....	214		400
31	7134	Far Fabrications			3,290	3,290					
31	7135	Midland Inc. ..			1,500	1,500					
31	7136	Nyland Supply Co. .			5,550	5,550					
31		Total			55,375	24,930	2,130			33,645	5,330
					(213)	(51)	(620)			(√)	(√)

Cash Disbursements Journal

The cash disbursements journal is illustrated below. It accounts for all the checks issued during the period. Checks are issued only in payment of properly approved vouchers. The payee is designated together with the number of the voucher authorizing the payment. The cash disbursements record, when prepared in this form, is frequently called a check register.

CASH DISBURSEMENTS JOURNAL

Date	Check No.	Account Debited	Vou. No.	Accounts Payable Dr.	Purchase Discounts Cr.	Cash Cr.
31	3106	Security National Bank..........	7132	9,120		9,120
31	3107	Payroll	7133	1,640		1,640
31	3108	Pat Bunnell.......	7005	1,500	30	1,470
31		Total.............		61,160	275	60,885
				(213)	(52)	(111)

General Journal

Regardless of the number and nature of special journals, certain transactions cannot appropriately be recorded in the special journals and are recorded in the general journal. A general journal with an illustrative entry during the month of July is illustrated on the following page. This general journal is prepared in two-column form. A pair of debit and credit columns is provided for the entries that are to be made to the general ledger accounts.

General Journal

Date		Description	Post. Ref.	Debit	Credit
1987 July	31	Allowance for Doubtful Accounts	117	1,270	
		Accounts Receivable	116		1,270
		To write off uncollectible account. (Rit-Z Shop)			

Subsidiary Ledgers

As explained in the chapter, subsidiary ledgers provide the detail of individual accounts in support of a control account in the general ledger. Whenever possible, individual postings to subsidiary accounts are made directly from the business documents evidencing the transactions. This practice saves time and avoids errors that might arise in summarizing and transferring this information. If postings to the subsidiary records and to the control accounts are made accurately, the sum of the detail in a subsidiary record will agree with the balance in the control account. A reconciliation of each subsidiary ledger with its related control account should be made periodically, and any discrepancies found should be investigated and corrected.

As an illustration of the relationship of a general ledger control account to its subsidiary ledger accounts, the Accounts Receivable control account is shown below. The three subsidiary accounts are shown on the following page.

General Ledger

Account: **Accounts Receivable**   *Account No.* **116**

Date		Item	Post. Ref.	Debit	Credit	Balance
1987 July	1	Balance				9,200
	31	Sales on account. . .	SJ	40,150		49,350
	31	Collections on account	CRJ		35,900	13,450
	31	Write off of uncollectible account . . (Rit-Z Shop)	GJ		1,270	12,180

Accounts Receivable Subsidiary Ledger

Name: **Stocks and Co.**
Address: **546 South Fox Rd, Chicago, IL   60665**

Date		Item	Post. Ref.	Debit	Credit	Balance
1987						
July	1	Balance				1,000
	10	Purchase..........	SJ	1,525		2,525
	31	Purchase..........	SJ	2,100		4,025

Name: **The Chocolate Factory**
Address: **7890 Redwood Dr, Pittsburgh, PA   15234**

Date		Item	Post. Ref.	Debit	Credit	Balance
1987						
July	2	Purchase	SJ	3,450		3,450
	10	Payment	CRJ		3,450	-0-
	15	Purchase	SJ	2,000		2,000
	31	Payment	CRJ		2,000	-0-

Name: **The Rit-Z Dress Shop**
Address: **789 Cotton Drive, Phoenix, AZ   85090**

Date		Item	Post. Ref.	Debit	Credit	Balance
1987						
July	1	Balance				1,270
	31	Write off of uncol- lectible account (6 months old)	GJ		1,270	-0-

---

APPENDIX B

Comprehensive Illustration of Accrual Versus Cash Accounting

The adjustments required in converting from a cash basis to accrual accounting may be summarized as in Exhibit 3–4. In the exhibit, the

Exhibit 3–4

Cash Basis	± Adjustment Required	= Accrual Basis
Sales Receipts:		
Cash sales + Cash collections of Accounts Receivable	+ Ending Accounts Receivable − Beginning Accounts Receivable	= Net Sales
Other Receipts: (e.g., rent and interest)		
Cash received for rent	+ Beginning Unearned Rent − Ending Unearned Rent	= Rent Revenue
Cash received for interest	+ Ending Interest Receivable − Beginning Interest Receivable	= Interest Revenue
Payments for Goods: Cash purchases + Cash payments for Accounts Payable	+ Ending Accounts Payable − Beginning Accounts Payable + Beginning Inventory − Ending Inventory	= Cost of Goods Sold
Payments for Expenses: Cash paid for rent, utilities, wages, etc.	+ Beginning Prepaid Expenses − Ending Prepaid Expenses + Ending Accrued Expenses − Beginning Accrued Expenses	= Operating Expenses (excludes depreciation and similar noncash expenses)

procedure for computing net sales under the accrual concept is illustrated. The computation of gross sales requires additional adjustment if sales discounts and returns and allowances exist, or if any accounts have been determined to be uncollectible. For example, assume sales data as follows:

Data from cash records:
Cash sales 10,000
Collections on accounts receivable arising from sales 42,000
Data from balance sheets:
Accounts receivable at the beginning of the period 14,300
Accounts receivable at the end of the period 12,500
Supplementary data from special analysis of records:
Accounts determined to be uncollectible during the period 600
Sales discounts allowed customers during the period 850
Sales returns and allowances during the period 300

The supplementary data indicate that uncollectible accounts of $600, sales discounts of $850, and sales returns and allowances of $300 are to be recognized. These amounts must be added to cash collections in arriving at gross sales, for there must have been sales equivalent to the reductions in accounts receivable from these sources. Gross sales for the period are computed as follows:

Cash sales..		$10,000
Sales on account:		
Accounts receivable at the end of the period.....................	$12,500	
Collections on accounts receivable	42,000	
Uncollectible accounts receivable............................	600	
Sales discounts	850	
Sales returns and allowances	300	
	$56,250	
Deduct accounts receivable at the beginning of the period.........	14,300	41,950
Gross sales for the period		$51,950

Similar adjustments would be required for purchase discounts, purchase returns and allowances, and freight in to compute gross purchases on an accrual basis.

To provide a comprehensive illustration of the conversion of cash-based records to accrual-based financial statements, data for BJS Company, a proprietorship, will be used. In making the conversion from cash to accrual, a balance sheet is prepared first. Assets and liabilities at year-end are determined by analysis of the prior year's balance sheet, a review of accounting records and documents, and physical counts of inventories and supplies. Owner's equity is the difference between total assets and total liabilities. Comparative balance sheets for BJS Company appear on page 96.

After the balance sheet is prepared, the next step is to analyze cash records and prepare a summary of cash receipts and cash disbursements for the period, as illustrated below.

Summary of Cash Receipts and Disbursements

Cash Balance, January 1, 1987		$ 3,200
Receipts:		
Cash sales.......................................	$ 9,200	
Collections:		
Accounts receivable arising from sales..............	42,000	
Notes receivable arising from sales.................	6,000	
From rental of store space.........................	1,750	
From interest and dividends........................	400	
From sales of investments (cost $7,500)	6,250	65,600
		$68,800
Disbursements:		
Payments on accounts payable arising from purchases .	$40,000	
For salaries......................................	4,200	
For rent	4,400	
For supplies......................................	1,000	
Acquisition of furniture and fixtures	3,500	
For miscellaneous expense.........................	1,500	
Owner's withdrawals	9,000	63,600
Cash balance, December 31, 1987		$ 5,200

BJS Company
Comparative Balance Sheet Data

	Dec. 31 1987	Dec. 31 1986
Assets		
Current assets:		
Cash..	$ 5,200	$ 3,200
Notes receivable.................................	3,000	2,500
Accounts receivable..............................	4,500	6,000
Interest receivable	50	150
Inventory......................................	24,600	20,000
Supplies	600	400
Prepaid miscellaneous expenses	0	100
Total current assets	$37,950	$32,350
Noncurrent assets:		
Long-term investments	$ 2,200	$ 9,700
Furniture and fixtures (cost less accumulated depreciation)	8,325	5,800
Total noncurrent assets.........................	$10,525	$15,500
Total assets	$48,475	$47,850
Liabilities and Owner's Equity		
Current liabilities:		
Accounts payable................................	$ 9,000	$ 7,500
Salaries payable.................................	250	200
Miscellaneous expenses payable	150	0
Unearned rent revenues	125	150
Total liabilities	$ 9,525	$ 7,850
Owner's Equity:		
Betty Shapiro, capital............................	38,950	40,000
Total liabilities and owner's equity.....................	$48,475	$47,850

Supplementary data developed from an analysis of business documents and the cash records confirm the following:

1. The net amount reported for Furniture and Fixtures in the December 31, 1987 balance sheet was based on the following information: furniture and fixtures were acquired during the year for cash, $3,500; depreciation expense for 1987 is $975.
2. Long-term investments costing $7,500 were sold in 1987 for $6,250.
3. Purchase discounts of $600 were allowed on the payment of creditor invoices during the year. Sales returns and allowances amounted to $1,480.

Based on the information from the balance sheet, the summary of cash receipts and disbursements, and the supplemental data, an income statement can now be prepared for BJS Company. Schedules in support of the income statement balances as well as a summary of the changes in owner's equity are also provided.

BJS Company
Income Statement
For Year Ended December 31, 1987

Revenue from net sales:			
Sales...............................	(A)	$57,680	
Less sales returns and allowances......................		1,480	$56,200
Cost of goods sold:			
Beginning inventory			$20,000
Purchases	(B) $42,100		
Less purchase discounts..........	600	41,500	
Cost of goods available for sale ...		$61,500	
Less ending inventory............		24,600	36,900
Gross profit on sales..............			$19,300
Operating expenses:			
Salaries.........................	(C)	$ 4,250	
Rent expense	(D)	4,400	
Supplies expense................	(E)	800	
Depreciation expense— furniture and fixtures	(F)	975	
Miscellaneous expenses	(G)	1,750	12,175
Operating income			$ 7,125
Other revenues and gains:			
Interest and dividend revenue	(H)	$ 300	
Rent revenue	(I)	1,775	2,075
Other expenses and losses:			
Loss on sale of investments.......	(J)		(1,250)
Income from continuing operations before income taxes			$ 7,950

BJS Company
Summary of Changes in Owner's Equity
For Year Ended December 31, 1987

Betty Shapiro, capital, December 31, 1987........................	$38,950
Betty Shapiro, capital, January 1, 1987	40,000
Net decrease in owner's equity	$ (1,050)
Withdrawals by owner during year	9,000
Net income for year	$ 7,950

(A) Computation of gross sales:

Cash sales...		$ 9,200
Sales on account:		
Notes and accounts receivable, December 31, 1987	$ 7,500	
Collections on notes and accounts receivable	48,000	
Sales returns and allowances	1,480	
	$56,980	
Deduct notes and accounts receivable, January 1, 1987......	8,500	48,480
Gross sales for the year		$57,680

(B) Computation of gross purchases:

Purchases on account:	
Accounts payable, December 31, 1987	$ 9,000
Cash payments on accounts payable.......................	40,000
Discounts allowed on accounts payable	600
	$49,600
Deduct accounts payable, January 1, 1987.................	7,500
Gross purchases for the year..............................	$42,100

Computation of operating expenses:

(C) Salaries:

Salaries payable, December 31, 1987	$ 250
Add payments for salaries	4,200
	$ 4,450
Deduct salaries payable, January 1, 1987..................	200
Salaries expense for the year	$ 4,250

(D) Rent expense:

Payments for rent.......................................	$ 4,400

(E) Supplies expense:

Supplies, January 1, 1987................................	$ 400
Add payments for supplies	1,000
	$ 1,400
Deduct supplies on hand, December 31, 1987..............	600
Supplies used during the year............................	$ 800

(F) Depreciation expense:

Furniture and fixtures (net), January 1, 1987	$ 5,800
Add purchases of furniture and fixtures during year	3,500
	$ 9,300
Deduct furniture and fixtures (net), December 31, 1987.......	8,325
Depreciation expense for the year	$ 975

(G) Miscellaneous expenses:

Prepaid miscellaneous expenses, January 1, 1987...........	$ 100
Add: Miscellaneous expense payments.....................	1,500
Miscellaneous expenses payable, December 31, 1987 ..	150
Miscellaneous expenses for the year	$ 1,750

(H) Computation of interest and dividend revenue:

Interest receivable, December 31, 1987.....................	$ 50
Add Interest and dividend receipts	400
	$ 450
Deduct interest receivable, January 1, 1987................	150
Total interest and dividend revenue for the year	$ 300

(I) Computation of rent revenue:

Unearned rent revenue, January 1, 1987	$ 150
Add rent receipts...	1,750
	$ 1,900
Deduct unearned rent revenue, December 31, 1987..........	125
Total rent revenue for the year............................	$ 1,775

(J) Computation of loss on sale of investments:

Cost of investments sold...................................	$ 7,500
Proceeds from sale	6,250
Loss on sale of investments...............................	$ 1,250

QUESTIONS

1. What type of reports are generated from the accounting system?
2. What are the main similarities and differences between a manual and an automated accounting system?
3. Distinguish between the recording and summarizing phases of the accounting process.
4. List and describe the steps in the accounting process. Why is each step necessary? Which steps are optional?
5. Under double-entry accounting, what are the debit/credit relationships of accounts?
6. Distinguish between: (a) real and nominal accounts, (b) general journal and special journals, and (c) general ledger and subsidiary ledgers.
7. As Beechnut Mining Company's independent certified public accountant, you find that the company accountant posts adjusting and closing entries directly to the ledger without formal entries in the general journal. How would you evaluate this procedure in your report to management?
8. Explain the nature and the purpose of (a) adjusting entries, (b) closing entries, and (c) reversing entries.
9. Give three common examples of contra accounts; explain why contra accounts are used.
10. Payment of insurance in advance may be recorded in either (a) an expense account or (b) an asset account. Which method would you recommend? What periodic entries are required under each method?

11. Distinguish between the procedures followed by a merchandising enterprise using a periodic (physical) inventory system and one using a perpetual inventory system.
12. Describe the nature and purpose of a work sheet.
13. What effect, if any, does the use of a work sheet have on the sequence of the summarizing phase of the accounting process?
14. The accountant for the Miller Hardware Store, after completing all adjustments except for the merchandise inventory, makes the following entry to close the beginning inventory, to set up the ending inventory, to close all nominal accounts, and to report the net result of operations in the capital account.

Inventory (December 31, 1987)	22,500	
Sales	250,000	
Purchase Discounts	2,500	
Inventory (January 1, 1987)		25,000
Purchases		175,000
Selling Expense		25,000
General and Administrative Expense		18,750
Interest Expense		1,875
M. Mills, Capital		29,375

(a) Would you regard this procedure as being acceptable? (b) What alternate procedure could you have followed to close the nominal accounts?

15. From the following list of accounts, determine which ones should be closed and whether each would normally be closed by a debit or credit entry.

Cash	Retained Earnings
Rent Expense	Capital Stock
Accounts Receivable	Interest Revenue
Land	Advertising Expense
Depreciation Expense	Purchase Discounts
Sales Revenue	Notes Payable
Sales Discounts	Dividends
Purchases	Accounts Payable
Freight In	

16. Distinguish between accrual and cash-basis accounting.
17. Is greater accuracy achieved in financial statements prepared from double-entry, accrual data as compared with cash data? Explain.
18. What are the major advantages of electronic data processing as compared with manual processing of accounting data?
19. One of your clients overheard a computer manufacturer sales representative saying the computer will make the accountant obsolete. How would you respond to this comment?
*20. What advantages are provided through the use of: (a) special journals, (b) subsidiary ledgers, and (c) the voucher system?
*21. The Tantor Co. maintains a sales journal, a voucher register, a cash receipts journal, a cash disbursements journal, and a general journal. For each account listed at the top of page 101, indicate the most common journal sources of debits and credits.

(a) Cash
(b) Marketable Securities
(c) Notes Receivable
(d) Accounts Receivable
(e) Allowance for Doubtful Accounts
(f) Merchandise Inventory
(g) Land and Buildings
(h) Accumulated Depreciation
(i) Notes Payable
(j) Vouchers Payable

(k) Capital Stock
(l) Retained Earnings
(m) Sales
(n) Sales Discounts
(o) Purchases
(p) Freight In
(q) Purchase Returns
(r) Purchase Discounts
(s) Salaries
(t) Depreciation

**22. In developing the sales balance, the owner of a business recognizes cash collections from customers and the change in the receivables balance but ignores the write-off of uncollectible accounts. Indicate the effects, if any, that such omissions will have on net income.

*Relates to Appendix A
**Relates to Appendix B

EXERCISES

EXERCISE 3–1   (Journal entries)

Oakley Supply Company, a merchandising firm, engaged in the following transactions during October 1987. The company records inventory using the perpetual system.

1987
Oct. 1 Sold merchandise to the Plough Corporation for $7,500; terms 2/10, n/30, FOB shipping point. Plough paid $100 freight on the goods. The merchandise cost $3,720.
5 Received inventory costing $8,350; terms n/30.
7 Received payment from Plough for goods shipped October 1.
15 The payroll paid for the first half of October was $9,000. (Ignore payroll taxes.)
18 Purchased a machine for $5,200 cash.
22 Declared a dividend of $.60 per share on 45,000 shares of common stock outstanding.
27 Purchased building and land for $150,000 in cash and a $250,000 Mortgage payable, due in 30 years. The land was appraised at $150,000 and the building at $350,000.

Record the above transactions in general journal form (ignore explanations).

EXERCISE 3–2   (Adjusting and reversing entries)

In analyzing the accounts of Loma Corporation, the adjusting data listed at the top of page 102 are determined on December 31, the end of an annual fiscal period.

(a) The prepaid insurance account shows a debit of $2,640, representing the cost of a 2-year fire insurance policy dated July 1.

(b) On September 1, Rent Revenue was credited for $4,000, representing revenue from subrental for a 5-month period beginning on that date.

(c) Purchase of advertising materials for $2,475 during the year was recorded in the advertising expense account. On December 31, advertising materials costing $600 are on hand.

(d) On November 1, $4,500 was paid as rent for a 6-month period beginning on that date. The rent expense account was debited.

(e) Miscellaneous Office Expense was debited for office supplies of $1,350 purchased during the year. On December 31, office supplies of $320 are on hand.

(f) Interest of $235 is accrued on notes payable.

(1) Give the adjusting entry for each item. (2) What reversing entries would be appropriate? (3) What sources would provide the information for each adjustment?

EXERCISE 3–3   (Adjusting entries)

Upon inspecting the books and records for Hamilton Sign Company, for the year ended December 31, 1987, you find the following data.

(a) A receivable of $380 from Clarke Realty is determined to be uncollectible. The company maintains no allowance for such losses.

(b) A creditor, E. J. Stanley Co., has just been awarded damages of $2,200 as a result of breach of contract during the current year by Hamilton Sign Company. Nothing appears on the books in connection with this matter.

(c) A fire destroyed part of a branch office. Furniture and fixtures that cost $10,200 and had a book value of $7,800 at the time of the fire were completely destroyed. The insurance company has agreed to pay $6,500 under the provisions of the fire insurance policy.

(d) Advances of $1,150 to salespersons have been recorded as sales salaries.

(e) Machinery at the end of the year shows a balance of $18,460. It is discovered that additions to this account during the year totaled $4,460, but of this amount $800 should have been recorded as repairs. Depreciation is to be recorded at 10% on machinery owned throughout the year, but at one half this rate on machinery purchased or sold during the year.

What entries are required to bring the accounts up to date? (Ignore income tax consequences.)

EXERCISE 3–4   (Adjusting and closing entries)

Accounts of Pioneer Heating Co. at the end of the first year of operations show the balances at the top of the next page. The end-of-the-year physical inventory is $50,000. Prepaid operating expenses are $4,000 and sales commissions payable are $5,900. Investment revenue receivable is $1,000. Depreciation for the year on buildings is $4,500 and on machinery, $5,000. Federal and state income taxes for the year are estimated at $18,100. Give the entries to adjust and close the books, assuming use of an Income Summary account.

Cash	$ 39,000	
Investments	50,000	
Land.............................	70,000	
Buildings.........................	180,000	
Machinery........................	100,000	
Accounts Payable..................		$ 65,000
Common Stock		320,000
Additional Paid-In Capital		40,000
Sales		590,000
Purchases........................	280,000	
Sales Commissions	200,000	
General Operating Expenses	101,000	
Investment Revenue................		5,000
	$1,020,000	$1,020,000

EXERCISE 3–5   (Adjusting entries)

The following accounts were taken from the trial balance of ABC Company as of December 31, 1987. Given the information below, make the necessary adjusting entries.

Sales Revenue	$45,000
Interest Revenue..................................	2,500
Equipment	23,000
Accumulated Depreciation—Equipment	6,000
Beginning Inventory	10,000
Advertising Expense...............................	1,000
Selling Expense...................................	3,000
Interest Expense..................................	500

(a) The equipment has an estimated useful life of 7 years and a salvage value of $2,000. Depreciation is calculated using the straight-line method.
(b) Ending inventory is $14,000.
(c) $1,000 of selling expense has been paid in advance.
(d) Interest of $100 has been accrued on notes receivable.
(e) $400 of advertising expense was incorrectly debited to selling expense.

EXERCISE 3–6   (Adjusting and reversing entries)

On May 16, 1987, Brenda Sycamore paid insurance for a 3-year period beginning June 1. She recorded the payment as follows:

Prepaid Insurance...................	612	
Cash		612

(1) What adjustment is required on December 31? What reversing entry, if any, would you make?
(2) What nominal account could be debited instead of Prepaid Insurance? What adjusting entry would be needed under these circumstances? What reversing entry, if any, would you make?

EXERCISE 3–7   (Adjusting entries)

The data listed below were obtained from an analysis of the accounts of Noble Distributor Company as of March 31, 1987, in preparation of the annual report.

Noble records current transactions in nominal accounts and *does not* reverse adjusting entries. What are the appropriate adjusting entries?

(a) Prepaid Insurance has a balance of $14,100. Noble has the following policies in force.

Policy	Date	Term	Cost	Coverage
A	1/1/87	2 years	$ 3,600	Shop Equipment
B	12/1/86	6 months	1,800	Delivery Equipment
C	7/1/86	3 years	12,000	Buildings

(b) Subscriptions Received in Advance has a balance of $56,250. The following subscriptions were included in the balance.

Inception	Amount	Term
July 1, 1986	$27,000	1 year
October 1, 1986.............	22,200	1 year
January 1, 1987	28,800	1 year
April 1, 1987	20,700	1 year

(c) Interest Payable has a balance of $825. Noble owes a 10%, 90-day note for $45,000 dated March 1, 1987.

(d) Supplies has a balance of $2,190. An inventory of supplies revealed a total of $1,410.

(e) Salaries Payable has a balance of $9,750. The payroll for the 5-day workweek ended April 3, totaled $11,250.

EXERCISE 3–8   (Closing entries)

An accountant for Jolley, Inc., a merchandising enterprise, has just finished posting all the year-end adjusting entries to the ledger accounts and now wishes to close the appropriate account balances in preparation for the new period.

(1) For each of the accounts listed below, indicate whether the year-end balance should be: (a) carried forward to the new period, (b) closed by debiting the account, or (c) closed by crediting the account. Assume, for this exercise, that the beginning inventory was zero and that the ending inventory amount is adjusted through the closing process by being debited.

(a)	Cash	25,000		(m)	Prepaid Insurance	16,000
(b)	Sales	50,000		(n)	Interest Receivable	2,000
(c)	Dividends	3,000		(o)	Sales Discounts	3,000
(d)	Inventory (Beginning).....	0		(p)	Freight In	4,000
(e)	Selling Expenses.........	3,000		(q)	Interest Revenue	2,000
(f)	Capital Stock	100,000		(r)	Supplies	8,000
(g)	Income Summary	0		(s)	Retained Earnings	6,500
(h)	Wages Expense	10,000		(t)	Accumulated Depreciation	2,000
(i)	Dividends Payable	4,000		(u)	Inventory (Ending)	60,000
(j)	Purchases...............	28,000		(v)	Purchase Returns &	
(k)	Accounts Payable........	12,000			Allowances	4,000
(l)	Accounts Receivable	140,000		(w)	Depreciation Expense........	1,000

(2) Give the necessary closing entries.

EXERCISE 3–9   (Closing entries —
Proprietorship, Partnership, and Corporation)

Lennon's Tannery shows a credit balance in the Income Summary account of $135,200 after the revenue and expense items have been transferred to this account at the end of the fiscal year. Give the remaining entries to close the books assuming:

(a) The business is a sole proprietorship: the owner, D. H. Lennon, has made withdrawals of $28,000 during the year, and this is reported in a drawing account.

(b) The business is a partnership: the owners, D. H. Lennon and B. L. Oster, share profits 5:3; they have made withdrawals of $50,000 and $32,000 respectively, and these amounts are reported in drawing accounts.

(c) The business is a corporation: the ledger reports Additional Paid-In Capital, $500,000, and Retained Earnings, $200,000; dividends during the year of $65,000 were recorded in a Dividends account.

EXERCISE 3–10   (Determining income from equity account analysis)

On November 1, the capital of D. T. Conners was $8,500 and on November 30 the capital was $12,187. During the month, Conners withdrew merchandise costing $500 and on November 25 paid a $4,000 note payable of the business with interest at 10% for three months with a check drawn on a personal checking account. What was Conners' net income or loss for the month of November?

EXERCISE 3–11   (Determining income from equity account analysis)

An analysis of the records of J. L. Kane disclosed changes in account balances for 1987 and the supplementary data listed below. From these data, calculate the net income or loss for 1987.

Cash	3,000 decrease
Accounts receivable.......................	2,000 increase
Merchandise inventory	16,000 increase
Accounts payable.........................	4,000 increase

During the year, Kane borrowed $30,000 in notes from the bank and paid off notes of $20,000 and interest of $1,000. Interest of $375 is accrued as of December 31, 1987. There was no interest payable at the end of 1986.

In 1987, Kane also transferred certain marketable securities to the business and these were sold for $8,000 to finance the purchase of merchandise.

Kane made weekly withdrawals in 1987 of $500.

*EXERCISE 3–12   (Special Journals)

Owen Company uses a general journal, sales journal, cash receipts journal, cash disbursements journal, and a voucher register. For each transaction below, indicate the appropriate journal(s) or register to be used.

(a) Make a credit sale.

(b) Collect cash on an account receivable.

(c) Record bad debt expense.

(d) Write a check for payroll expense.

(e) Purchase raw materials on account.

(continued)

(f) Give a discount on a sale.
(g) Sell equipment on credit.
(h) Make a cash sale.
(i) Borrow $3,000 from the bank.
(j) Record adjusting and closing entries.
(k) Pay a supplier with a check.
(l) Record accrued interest payable.
(m) Sell truck for cash.
(n) Record depreciation expense.
(o) Pay back loan.

Relates to Appendix A

*EXERCISE 3–13   (Cash to Accrual Basis)

The following information is taken from the records of Mario's Tune-up Shop:

	Balance Jan. 1 1987	Balance Dec. 31 1987	Transactions During 1987
Accruals:			
Interest receivable	810	975	
Wages payable............................	1,650	1,725	
Interest payable	1,200	1,425	
Cash receipts and payments:			
Interest on notes receivable.................			1,860
Wages			96,000
Interest on notes payable...................			1,395

Compute the interest revenue, the wages expense, and the interest expense for the year 1987.

Relates to Appendix B

*EXERCISE 3–14   (Account analysis — gross sales)

Total accounts receivable for the Bako Company were as follows: on January 1, $6,000; on January 31, $6,300. In January, $9,500 was collected on accounts, $600 was received for cash sales, accounts receivable of $700 were written off as uncollectible, and sales allowances of $100 were made. What amount should be reported for gross sales on the income statement for January?

Relates to Appendix B

*EXERCISE 3–15   (Comprehensive cash to accrual basis)

The following information for the first quarter of 1987 is obtained from the cash-basis records of Brad Berrett.

	March 31	January 1
Accounts receivable	$26,400	$13,500
Inventory	3,000	11,400
Prepaid operating expense	660	750
Store equipment (net)....................	9,000	9,750
Accounts payable	7,500	10,500
Operating expenses payable	1,500	810

The cashbook shows the following:

Balance, January 1		$ 4,500
Receipts: Accounts receivable	$10,800	
Investment by Berrett	1,800	12,600
		$17,100
Payments: Accounts payable	$15,600	
Operating expenses	2,100	17,700
Balance, March, 31—bank overdraft		$ (600)

Prepare an accrual-basis income statement for the 3-month period accompanied by schedules in support of revenue and expense balances.

Relates to Appendix B

PROBLEMS

PROBLEM 3–1   (Adjusting and reversing entries)

The trial balance of Kohler's Diamonds, shows, among other items, the following balances on December 31, 1987, the end of a fiscal year:

Accounts Receivable	150,000	
9% Century City Bonds	225,000	
Land	275,000	
Buildings	450,000	
Accumulated Depreciation-Buildings		173,250
8% First-Mortgage Bonds Payable		600,000
Rent Revenue		71,500
Office Expense	7,500	

The following facts are ascertained on this date upon inspection of the company's records.

(a) It is estimated that approximately 2% of accounts receivable may prove uncollectible.

(b) Interest is receivable semiannually on the Century City bonds on March 1 and September 1.

(c) Buildings are depreciated at 5% a year; however, there were building additions of $50,000 during the year. The company computes depreciation on asset acquisitions during the year at one half the annual rate.

(d) Interest on the first-mortgage bonds is payable semiannually on February 1 and August 1.

(e) Rent revenue includes $5,100 that was received on November 1, representing rent on part of the buildings for the period November 1, 1987 to October 31, 1988.

(f) Office supplies of $2,000 are on hand at December 31. Purchases of office supplies were debited to the office expense account.

Instructions:

(1) Prepare the journal entries to adjust the books on December 31, 1987.

(2) Give the reversing entries that may be appropriate at the beginning of 1988.

PROBLEM 3–2   (Adjusting entries)

On December 31, the Philips Company noted the following transactions that occurred during 1987, some or all of which might require adjustment to the books.
(a) Payment to suppliers of $1,200 was made for purchases on account during the year and was not recorded.
(b) Building and land were purchased for $175,000. The building's fair market value was $100,000 at the time of purchase. The building is being depreciated over a 20-year life using the straight-line method, and assuming no salvage value.
(c) Of the $34,000 in accounts receivable, 2.5% is estimated to be uncollectible. Currently, the allowance for doubtful accounts shows a debit balance of $290.
(d) On June 10, $25,000 was loaned to a customer on a 6-month note with interest at an annual rate of 15%. Repayment was made on December 10, 1987. The receipt of the interest payment was not recorded.
(e) During 1987, Philips received $2,500 in advance for services to be performed in 1988. The $2,500 was credited to sales revenue.
(f) The interest expense account was debited for all interest charges incurred during the year and shows a balance of $1,100. However, of this amount, $300 represents a discount on a 60-day note payable, due January 30, 1988.

Instructions:
(1) Give the necessary adjusting entries to bring the books up to date.
(2) Indicate the net change in income as a result of the foregoing adjustments.

PROBLEM 3–3   (Transactions based on adjusting entries)

The accountant for Besner Plumbing made the following adjusting entries on December 31, 1987:

(a)	Prepaid Rent	600	
	Rent Expense		600
(b)	Advertising Materials	1,000	
	Advertising Expense		1,000
(c)	Interest Revenue	250	
	Unearned Revenue		250
(d)	Office Supplies	500	
	Office Expense		500
(e)	Prepaid Insurance	525	
	Insurance Expense		525

Further information is provided as follows:
(a) Rent is paid every October 1.
(b) Advertising materials are paid at one time (June 1) and are used evenly throughout the year.
(c) Interest is received every March 1.
(d) Office supplies are purchased every July 1 and used evenly throughout the year.
(e) Yearly insurance premium is payable each August 1.

Instructions: For each adjusting entry, indicate the original transaction entry that was recorded.

PROBLEM 3–4   (Adjusting entries)

The bookkeeper from the Irwin Wholesale Electric Co. prepares no reversing entries and records all revenue and expense items in nominal accounts during the period. The following balances, among others, are listed on the trial balance at the end of the fiscal period, December 31, 1987, before accounts have been adjusted:

	Dr (Cr)
Accounts Receivable	$152,000
Allowance for Doubtful Accounts	(1,000)
Interest Receivable	2,800
Discounts on Notes Payable	300
Prepaid Real Estate and Personal Property Tax	1,800
Salaries and Wages Payable	(4,000)
Discounts on Notes Receivable	(2,800)
Unearned Rent Revenue	(1,500)

Inspection of the company's records reveals the following as of December 31, 1987.
(a) Uncollectible accounts are estimated at 3% of the accounts receivable balance.
(b) The accrued interest on investments totals $2,400.
(c) The company borrows cash by discounting its own notes at the bank. Discounts on notes payable at the end of 1987 are $1,600.
(d) Prepaid real estate and personal property taxes are $1,800, the same as at the end of 1986.
(e) Accrued salaries and wages are $4,300.
(f) The company accepts notes from customers, giving its customers credit for the face of the note less a charge for interest. At the end of each period, any interest applicable to the succeeding period is reported as a discount. Discounts on notes receivable at the end of 1987 are $1,500.
(g) Part of the company's properties had been sublet on September 15, 1986, at a rental of $3,000 per month. The arrangement was terminated at the end of one year.

Instructions: Give the adjusting entries required to bring the books up to date.

PROBLEM 3–5
(Preparation of work sheet and adjusting and closing entries)

Account balances taken from the ledger of the James Corporation on December 31, 1987, are listed at the top of page 110.

Adjustments on December 31, 1987, are required as follows:
(a) The inventory on hand is $87,570.
(b) The allowance for doubtful accounts is to be increased to a balance of $3,000.
(c) Buildings are depreciated at the rate of 5% per year.
(d) Accrued selling expenses are $3,840.
(e) There are supplies of $780 on hand.
(f) Prepaid insurance relating to 1988 and 1989 totals $720.
(g) Accrued interest on long-term investments is $240.
(h) Accrued real estate and payroll taxes are $900.
(i) Accrued interest on the mortgage is $480.
(j) Income tax is estimated to be 40% of the income before income tax.

Accounts Payable	$ 35,000	Land	$ 69,600
Accounts Receivable	72,000	Long-Term Investments	15,400
Accumulated Depreciation-		Mortgage Payable	68,800
Buildings	19,800	Office Expense	21,680
Allowance for Doubtful		Purchases	138,480
Accounts	1,380	Purchase Discounts	2,140
Buildings	72,000	Retained Earnings,	
Capital Stock, $10 par	180,000	December 31, 1986	14,840
Cash	24,000	Sales	246,000
Dividends	13,400	Sales Discounts	5,400
Freight In	3,600	Sales Returns	4,360
Insurance Expense	1,440	Selling Expense	49,440
Interest Expense	2,640	Supplies Expense	5,200
Interest Revenue	660	Taxes-Real Estate and Payroll	7,980
Inventory, Dec. 31, 1986	62,000		

Instructions:
(1) Prepare a trial balance.
(2) Journalize the adjustments.
(3) Journalize the closing entries.
(4) Prepare a post-closing trial balance.

Although not required, the use of a work sheet is recommended for the solution of this problem.

PROBLEM 3–6   (Closing entries and post-closing trial balance)

Real Corporation
Adjusted Trial Balance
December 31, 1987

Cash	$ 22,500	
Accounts Receivable	24,000	
Allowance for Doubtful Accounts		$ 240
Inventory	45,300	
Equipment	210,000	
Accumulated Depreciation—Equipment		84,000
Accounts Payable		28,000
Notes Payable		80,000
Wages Payable		10,000
Income Taxes Payable		8,900
Common Stock		50,000
Retained Earnings		27,310
Sales Revenue		270,000
Interest Revenue		8,000
Cost of Goods Sold	171,250	
Wages Expense	28,000	
Interest Expense	1,500	
Utilities Expense	5,000	
Depreciation Expense	42,000	
Insurance Expense	2,000	
Advertising Expense	6,000	
Income Tax Expense	8,900	
	$566,450	$566,450

Instructions: Given the adjusted trial balance for Real Corporation:
(1) Journalize the closing entries.
(2) Prepare a post-closing trial balance.

PROBLEM 3–7
(Preparation of work sheet and adjusting and closing entries)

The following account balances are taken from the general ledger of the Whitni Corporation on December 31, 1987, the end of its fiscal year. The corporation was organized January 2, 1984.

Cash.	$ 40,250
Notes Receivable	16,500
Accounts Receivable	63,000
Allowance for Doubtful Accounts (credit balance).	650
Inventory, January 1, 1987	88,700
Land.	80,000
Buildings.	247,600
Accumulated Depreciation—Buildings	18,000
Furniture and Fixtures	15,000
Accumulated Depreciation—Furniture and Fixtures	9,000
Notes Payable	18,000
Accounts Payable	72,700
Common Stock, $100 par	240,000
Retained Earnings.	129,125
Sales	760,000
Sales Returns and Allowances.	17,000
Purchases.	479,650
Purchase Discounts	7,850
Heat, Light, and Power.	16,700
Taxes.	10,200
Salaries and Wages Expense.	89,000
Sales Commissions.	73,925
Insurance Expense	18,000
Interest Revenue.	2,600
Interest Expense	2,400

Data for adjustments at December 31, 1987, are as follows:

(a) Merchandise inventory; $94,700.
(b) Depreciation (to nearest month for additions):
        Furniture and fixtures, 10%
        Buildings, 4%. Additions to the buildings costing $150,000 were completed June 30, 1987.
(c) The allowance for doubtful accounts is to be increased to a balance of $2,500.
(d) Accrued expenses:
        Sales commissions, $700
        Interest on notes payable, $45
        Property tax, $6,000
(e) Prepaid expenses: insurance, $3,200.

(f) Accrued revenue: interest on notes receivable, $750.
(g) The following information is also to be recorded:
    (1) On December 30, the board of directors declared a quarterly dividend of $1.50 per share on common stock, payable January 25, 1988, to stockholders of record January 15, 1988.
    (2) Income tax for 1987 is estimated at $15,000.
    (3) The only charges to Retained Earnings during the year resulted from the declaration of the regular quarterly dividends.

Instructions:
(1) Prepare an eight-column work sheet. There should be a pair of columns each for trial balance, adjustments, income statement, and balance sheet.
(2) Prepare all the journal entries necessary to give effect to the foregoing information and to adjust and close the books of the corporation.
(3) Prepare the reversing entries that may appropriately be made.

*PROBLEM 3–8   (Using special journals)

Beesley Distributing, Inc., a fruit wholesaler, records business transactions in the following books of original entry: general journal (GJ); voucher register (VR); cash disbursements journal (CDJ); sales journal (SJ); and cash receipts journal (CRJ). Beesley recorded and filed the following business documents:
(a) Sales invoices for sales on account totaling $4,600.
(b) The day's cash register tape showing receipts for cash sales at $700.
(c) A list of cash received on various customers' accounts totaling $2,930. Sales discounts taken were $30.
(d) The telephone bill for $60 payable in one week.
(e) Vendors' invoices for $5,000 worth of fruit received.
(f) Check stub for payment of last week's purchases from All-Growers Farms, $5,940. Terms were 1/10, n/30 and payment was made within the discount period.
(g) Check stub for repayment of a $10,000, 90-day note to Mercantile Bank, $10,300.
(h) A letter notifying Beesley that Littex Markets, a customer, has declared bankruptcy. All creditors will receive 10 cents on every dollar due. Littex owes Beesley $1,300.

Instructions:
(1) Indicate the books of original entry in which Beesley recorded each of the business transactions. (Use the designated abbreviations.)
(2) Record the debits and credits for each entry as though only a general journal were used. Use account titles implied by the voucher system.

*Relates to Appendix A

*PROBLEM 3–9   (Using special journals)

A fire destroyed Fong Company's journals. However, the general ledger and accounts receivable subsidiary ledger were saved. An inspection of the ledgers reveals the following information:

General Ledger

	Cash					Sales		
May 1	Bal. 8,200						May 31	5,050
31	7,338						31	4,500

	Sales Discounts					Accounts Receivable		
May 3	12			May 1	Bal. 3,100	May 31		2,850
				31	5,050			

Accounts Receivable Ledger

	Customer A					Customer B		
May 1	Bal.	290		May 1	Bal. 1,250	May 13		1,000
5		500			400			

	Customer C					Customer D		
May 2	1,450			May 1	Bal. 1,560	May 11		650

	Customer E			
May 2	1,200	May 3		1,200
12	1,500			

Fong's credit policy is 1/10, n/30.

Instructions: Reconstruct the sales and cash receipts journals from the information given.

Relates to Appendix A

*PROBLEM 3–10   (Cash to Accrual Basis)

Balance sheets for the Fugal Hardware Stores prepared in 1987 report the balances listed at the top of page 114.

An analysis of cash receipts and disbursements discloses the following:

Receipts		Disbursements	
Capital stock..............................	$ 80,000	Trade creditors—notes and accounts......	$210,000
Trade debtors—notes and accounts.......	230,000	Expenses................................	70,000
Cash sales..............................	65,000	Dividends...............................	40,000
Notes receivable discounted:		Equipment..............................	28,000
Face value, $20,000, proceeds..........	19,500	Bonds..................................	50,000
12% note issued to bank, dated March 31,			
1987	30,000		
Sale of investment......................	25,000		

Assets	June 30	January 1
Cash..	$ 84,500	$ 33,000
Notes receivable	21,000	20,000
Accounts receivable	95,000	74,000
Inventory	150,000	160,000
Prepaid expenses	10,000	12,000
Long-term investments (at cost)	10,000	40,000
Buildings and equipment (net)..................	120,000	100,000
	$490,500	$439,000

Liabilities and Stockholders' Equity	June 30	January 1
Notes payable.................................	$ 58,000	$ 75,000
Accounts payable..............................	75,000	60,000
Interest payable	900	—
Expenses payable	3,000	2,000
Bonds payable	—	50,000
Common stock, $100 par.......................	130,000	100,000
Additional paid-in capital.......................	150,000	100,000
Retained earnings	73,600	52,000
	$490,500	$439,000

Instructions:
(1) Prepare an income statement supported by schedules showing computations of revenue and expense balances for the six-month period ended June 30, 1987.
(2) Prove the net income or loss determined in part (1) by preparing a retained earnings statement.

*Relates to Appendix B.

*PROBLEM 3–11   (Cash to Accrual Basis)

The trial balance for Henry Specialty Foods is presented on page 115. This is a calendar-year sole proprietorship, maintaining its books on the cash basis during the year. At year-end, however, Ryan Henry's accountant adjusts the books to the accrual basis for sales, purchases, and cost of sales, and records depreciation to more clearly reflect the business income for income tax purposes.

During 1987 Henry signed a new eight-year lease for the store premises and is in the process of negotiating a loan for remodeling purposes. The bank required Henry to present financial statements for 1987 prepared on the accrual basis. During the course of a compilation engagement, Henry's accountant obtained the following additional information.

(a) Amounts due from customers totaled $7,900 at December 31, 1987.
(b) A review of the receivables at December 31, 1987 disclosed that an allowance for doubtful accounts of $1,100 should be provided. Henry had no bad debt losses from inception of the business through December 31, 1987.
(c) Unpaid vendors' invoices for food purchases totaled $9,650 at December 31, 1987.
(d) On signing the new lease on October 1, 1987, Henry paid $8,400 representing one year's rent in advance for the lease year ending October 1, 1988. The

$7,500 annual rental under the old lease was paid on October 1, 1986, for the lease year ended October 1, 1987.

(e) On April 1, 1987, Henry paid $2,400 to renew the comprehensive insurance coverage for one year. The premium was $2,160 on the old policy which expired on April 1, 1987.

(f) Depreciation on equipment was computed at $5,800 for 1987.

(g) The inventory amounted to $23,000 at December 31, 1987, based on physical count of goods priced at cost. No reduction to market was required.

(h) Accrued expenses at December 31, 1986, and December 31, 1987, were as follows:

	12/31/86	12/31/87
Payroll taxes	$250	$400
Salaries....................	375	510
Utilities	275	450

(i) Accrual purchases are closed to Cost of Goods Sold.

Henry Specialty Foods
Trial Balance
December 31, 1987

Cash	$ 18,500	
Accounts Receivable, 12/31/86	4,500	
Inventory, 12/31/86................................	20,000	
Equipment	35,000	
Accumulated Depreciation, 12/31/86...................		$ 9,000
Accounts Payable, 12/31/86.........................		5,650
Ryan Henry, Drawings..............................	24,000	
Ryan Henry, Capital, 12/31/86		33,650
Sales..		187,000
Purchases	82,700	
Salaries...	29,500	
Payroll Taxes.....................................	2,900	
Rent...	8,400	
Miscellaneous Expense.............................	3,900	
Insurance	2,400	
Utilities	3,500	
	$235,300	$235,300

Instructions:

(1) Prepare a work sheet with the following columns: Cash Basis, Adjustments, and Accrual Basis. Convert the trial balance of Henry Specialty Foods to the accrual basis for the year ended December 31, 1987. Journal entries are not required to support your adjustments.

(2) Prepare the statement of changes in Ryan Henry's capital for the year ended December 31, 1987.

(AICPA Adapted)

Relates to Appendix B.

4
Recognition, Measurement, and Reporting of Income

The title of the newspaper article was eye-catching as all good journalism demands. "Income for X Company Up $1.2 Million Over Prior Year." The article stated that, after three years of losses, X Company was reporting a profit. Further down the newspaper column was some additional information about X Company's profit. "The net income figure includes an extraordinary gain of $.8 million and a credit of $.5 million arising from a gain on disposal of discontinued operations, both after income taxes." With this information, the reader is able to put the headline in perspective. While it is true that income was up $1.2 million, it is also true that $1.3 million of unusual gains were recognized during the year. Income from "normal operations" is actually down by $.1 million. As this case demonstrates, there is more to understanding the income reported by a company than just identifying one number.

IMPORTANCE OF RECOGNIZING, MEASURING, AND REPORTING INCOME

The recognition, measurement, and reporting (display) of business income and its components is regarded as one of the most, if not *the* most, important tasks of accountants. The users of financial statements who must make decisions regarding their relationship with the company are almost always concerned with a measure of its success in using the resources committed to its operation. Has the activity been profitable? What is the trend of profitability? Is it increasingly profitable, or is there a downward trend? What is the most probable result for future years? Will the company be profitable enough to pay interest on its debt and dividends to its stock-

116

holders and still grow at a desired rate? These and other questions all relate to the basic question, what is income?

For many users, only one figure, the "bottom line," is meaningful. They feel uncomfortable trying to analyze additional information. To others, information about the components of income is important and can be used to help predict future income and cash flows. Not only can this information be helpful to a specific user, but it is also of value to the economy. As discussed in Chapter 1, one of the principal tasks facing accountants is to provide information that will assist in allocating scarce resources to the most efficient and effective organizations. If reported income is overstated when compared with the actual underlying situation, a poor allocation will be made. Resources will flow to inefficient entities, while the more efficient entities will suffer due to a lack of resources.

Income figures are also used for purposes other than resource allocation by creditors and investors. Governments, both federal and state, rely heavily on income taxes as a source of their revenues. The income figure used for assessing taxes is based on laws passed by Congress and regulations applied by the IRS and various courts. The income determined for financial reporting, however, is determined by adherence to accounting standards (GAAP) developed by the profession. Thus, the amount of income reported to creditors and investors may not be the same as the income reported for tax purposes. Many items are the same for both types of reporting, but there are some significant differences. Most of these differences relate to the specific purposes Congress has for taxing income. Governments use an income figure as a base to assess taxes, but they must use one that relates closely with the ability of the taxpayer to pay the computed tax. For example, accrual accounting requires companies to defer recognition of revenues that are received before they are earned. Income tax regulations, however, require these unearned revenues to be reported as income as soon as they are received in cash.

This text will focus on the principles of accounting that lead to the preparation of the basic set of financial statements. In Chapter 20, income for tax purposes will be discussed, but only as it is used to determine the tax liability that is reported on the balance sheet.

WHAT IS INCOME?

Although there are varying ways to measure income, all of them share a common basic concept: that income is a return over and above the investment. Economists have defined the concept as the amount that an entity could return to its investors and still leave the entity as well-off at the end of the period as it was at the beginning.[1] But what does it mean to be as "well-off"? This question has given rise to different ways of expressing the basic income concept, and these different ways are often referred to as different "concepts of income."

One popular way of viewing "well-off" is in terms of **financial capital maintenance.** Under this concept, an enterprise earns income "only if the financial (money) amount of an enterprise's net assets at the end of a period exceeds the financial amount of net assets at the beginning of the period after excluding the effects of transactions with owners."[2] For example, if a company has beginning net assets of $262,000, has $25,000 of new owners' investment during the year, and has ending net assets of $310,000, the income for the year is $23,000 ($310,000–$262,000–$25,000). The financial capital maintenance concept does not require any particular method of measurement. It can be applied using historical cost or any of the other measurement attributes described in Chapter 2.

Another way of viewing income is in terms of **physical capital maintenance.** Under this concept, income occurs "only if the physical productive capacity of the enterprise at the end of the period . . . exceeds the physical productive capacity at the beginning of the period, also after excluding the effects of transactions with owners."[3] This concept requires that productive assets (inventories, buildings, and equipment) be valued at current cost. For example, if the company in the previous example has beginning net assets of $262,000 measured using costs at the beginning of year, but $282,000 using costs at the end of the year, has $25,000 of additional owners' investment during the year, and has an ending net asset balance of $310,000, the income for the year is $3,000 ($310,000–$282,000–$25,000). In contrast to the financial capital maintenance concept, adjustments from historical cost to current cost under this concept would *not* be considered part of income, but would be recorded as a direct adjustment to equity. The enterprise would have a return on its investment only after the productive capacity, as measured by net assets of $282,000, had been maintained.

The Financial Accounting Standards Board considered carefully these and other ways of viewing income in their study of the conceptual framework. Ultimately, the FASB adopted the financial capital maintenance approach.

---

[1]Although many economists and accountants have adopted this view, a basic reference is J. R. Hicks' widely accepted book, *Value and Capital,* 2nd edition (Oxford University Press, 1946).

[2]*Statement of Financial Accounting Concepts No. 5,* "Recognition and Measurement in Financial Statements of Business Enterprises" (Stamford: Financial Accounting Standards Board, 1984), par. 47.

[3]*Ibid.*

The financial capital maintenance concept has been applied in various ways. Two widely accepted approaches are:

1. Valuation of an enterprise's net assets (**valuation approach**).
2. Summarizing revenue and expense transactions (**transaction approach**).

Valuation Approach

The valuation approach stresses that income is a residual concept. Operationally, this approach requires measurement of the assets and liabilities of a company at two points of time. If the difference between the assets and liabilities, referred to as "net assets" or equity, has increased after eliminating any new equity investment or distribution, income has resulted. If there has been no change, there is no income. If the equity interest has declined, a negative income, or loss, has been incurred. Because this approach is widely accepted among economists, it is sometimes referred to as the **economic approach**.

The most difficult and controversial issue surrounding this approach concerns the measurement of the assets and liabilities. Since income is a residual concept, the measurement issue focuses on these balance sheet categories. Some would argue that assets should be measured at their unexpired historical cost values. Others feel that replacement values or disposal values should be used. Some would include as assets intangible resources, such as human resources, goodwill, and geographical location, that have been attained over time without specifically identified payments. Others feel that only resources that have been acquired by "arm's-length" exchange activities should be included. Likewise, controversy has developed over the measurement of liabilities. Should future claims against the entity for items such as pensions and warranties be valued at their discounted values, at their future cash values, or eliminated completely until events clearly define the existence of a specific liability? Clearly, income determined under this approach will vary widely depending on how the assets and liabilities are measured.

One of the greatest weaknesses of the valuation approach is that the income figure is computed in one operation. No detail describing how the income is earned is generated through this approach. Income is simply the difference between the net assets at two points in time after eliminating any transactions involving dealings with the owners.

To illustrate, assume that the Bosco Company has an increase in total recorded assets of $1.2 million, an increase in recorded liabilities of $.5 million, additional investment of $.2 million and dividend distribution of $.3 million. How much is the income for the company?

	(millions)
Increase in total assets...	$1.2
Increase in total liabilities..	.5
Increase in net assets...	$ .7
Less additional investment.......................................	(.2)
Plus dividends..	.3
Income...	$ .8

As discussed in Chapters 1 and 2, an important objective of financial reporting is to assist users in predicting future cash flows. The single income amount provided by the valuation approach is not as useful for prediction as is a traditional income statement with several separate sections reporting various components of income. The transaction approach provides the detail necessary to prepare such a statement.

Transaction Approach

While the valuation and transaction approaches yield the same income, assuming the same measurement method is used under each approach, the detail provided by the transaction approach is necessary to meet the objectives of financial reporting. The **transaction approach**, sometimes referred to as the "matching method," focuses on business events that affect certain elements of financial statements, namely, revenues, expenses, gains, and losses. Income is measured as the difference between resource inflows (revenues and gains) and outflows (expenses and losses) over a period of time. Definitions for the four income elements were presented in Chapter 2 and are repeated on page 121 as an aid to the following discussion.

As can be seen from studying these definitions, by defining gains and losses in terms of changes in equity after providing for revenues, expenses, and investments and distributions to the owners, income determined by the transactions approach will be the same income as that determined under the valuation approach. However, by identifying intermediate income components, the transaction approach provides detail to assist in predicting future cash flows.

The key problem in recognizing and measuring income using the transaction approach is deciding when an "inflow or other enhancement of assets" has occurred and how to measure the "outflows or other using up of assets." As discussed in Chapter 2, the first issue is identified as "the revenue recognition" problem, and the second issue is identified as the "expense recognition" or "matching" problem. Rather than concentrating on net asset values as is done under the valuation approach, the transaction approach focuses on the detailed recognition of revenues, expenses, gains, and losses.

> ### Component Elements of Income
>
> **Revenues** are inflows or other enhancements of assets of an entity or settlements of its liabilities (or a combination of both) from delivering or producing goods, rendering services, or other activities that constitute the entity's ongoing major or central operations.
>
> **Expenses** are outflows or other using up of assets or incurrences of liabilities (or a combination of both) from delivering or producing goods, rendering services, or carrying out other activities that constitute the entity's ongoing major or central operations.
>
> **Gains** are increases in equity (net assets) from peripheral or incidental transactions of an entity and from all other transactions and other events and circumstances affecting the entity except those that result from revenues or investments by owners.
>
> **Losses** are decreases in equity (net assets) from peripheral or incidental transactions of an entity and from all other transactions and other events and circumstances affecting the entity except those that result from expenses or distributions to owners.

Source: *Statement of Financial Accounting Concepts No. 6,* "Elements of Financial Statements of Business Enterprises" (Stamford: Financial Accounting Standards Board, 1985), p. x.

Revenue and Gain Recognition. The transaction approach requires a clear definition of when income elements should be recognized, or recorded, in the financial statements. Under the generally accepted accounting principle of accrual, recognition does not necessarily occur when cash is received. The conceptual framework identifies two factors that should be considered in deciding when revenues and gains should be recognized: **realization** and the **earnings process**. Revenues and gains are generally recognized when:[4]

1. they are realized or realizable and
2. they have been earned through substantial completion of the activities involved in the earnings process.

In order for revenues and gains to be **realized**, inventory or other assets must be exchanged for cash or claims to cash. Revenues are **realizable** when assets held or assets received in an exchange are readily convertible to known amounts of cash or claims to cash. The **earnings process** criterion

---

[4]*Statement of Financial Accounting Concepts No. 5,* par. 83.

relates primarily to revenue recognition. Most gains result from transactions and events, such as the sale of land or a patent, that involve no earnings process. Thus, being realized or realizable is of more importance in recognizing gains.

Application of these two criteria to certain industries and companies within these industries has resulted in recognition of revenue at different points in the revenue-producing cycle. This cycle can be a lengthy one. For a manufacturing company, it begins with the development of proposals for a certain product by an individual or by the research and development department and extends through planning, production, sale, collection, and finally expiration of the warranty period. All of these steps are involved in generating sales revenue. If there is a failure at any step, revenue may be seriously curtailed or even completely eliminated. And yet, there is only one aggregate revenue amount for the entire cycle, the selling price of the product.

For a service company, the revenue-producing cycle begins with an agreement to provide a service and extends through the planning and performance of the service to the collection of the cash and final proof through the passage of time that the service has been adequately performed. With increasing legal actions being taken against professionals, such as doctors and accountants, one could argue that the revenue-producing cycle does not end until the possibility of legal claims for services performed is remote.

Although some accountants have argued for recognizing revenue on a partial basis over these extended production or service periods, the prevailing practice has been to select one point in the cycle that best meets the revenue recognition criteria. Both of these criteria are generally met at the **point of sale**, which is generally when goods are delivered or services are rendered to customers. Thus, revenue for automobiles sold to dealers by Ford Motor Company will be recognized when the cars are shipped to the dealers. Similarly, Price Waterhouse and Co. will record its revenue from audit and tax work when the services have been performed and billed. In both examples, the earnings process is deemed to be substantially complete, and the cash or receivable from the customer meets the realization criterion. Although the "point-of-sale" practice is the most common revenue recognition point, there are notable variations to this general rule.

1. If products or other assets are readily realizable because they can be sold at reliably determined prices without significant selling effort, revenues may be recognized at the **point of completed production**. Examples of this situation may occur with certain precious metals and agricultural products that are supported by Government price guarantees. In these situations,

the earnings process is considered to be substantially complete when the mining or production of the goods is complete.

2. If a product or service is contracted for in advance, revenue may be recognized as production takes place or as services are performed, especially if the production or performance period extends over more than one fiscal year. The **percentage of completion** and **proportional performance** methods of accounting have been developed to recognize revenue at several points in the production or service cycle rather than waiting until the final delivery or performance takes place. This exception to the general point-of-sale rule is necessary if the qualitative characteristics of relevance and representational faithfulness are to be met. Construction contracts for buildings, roads, and dams and contracts for scientific research are examples of situations where these methods of revenue recognition occur. In all cases where this revenue recognition variation is employed, a firm, enforceable contract must exist to meet the realizability criterion, and an objective measure of progress toward completion must be attainable.

3. If collectibility of assets received for products or services is considered doubtful, revenues and gains may be recognized as the cash is received. Although the earnings process has been substantially completed, the questionable receivable fails to meet the realization criterion. The **installment sales** and **cost recovery methods** of accounting have been developed to recognize revenue under these conditions. Sales of real estate, especially speculative recreational property, are often recorded using this variation of the general rule.

The general point-of-sale rule will be assumed unless specifically stated otherwise. The variations introduced above are discussed fully in Chapter 19.

Expense and Loss Recognition. In order to determine income, not only must criteria for revenue recognition be established, but the principles for recognizing expenses and losses must be clearly defined. Some expenses are directly associated with revenues and can thus be recognized in the same period as the related revenues. Other expenses are not associated with specific revenues and are recognized in the time period when paid or incurred. Still other expenditures are not recognized currently as expenses because they relate to future revenues and, therefore, are reported as assets. Expense recognition, then, can be divided into three categories: (1) direct matching, (2) immediate recognition, and (3) systematic and rational allocation.

Direct Matching. Relating expenses to specific revenues is often referred to as the "matching" process. For example, the cost of goods sold is clearly a direct expense that can be matched with the revenues produced by the sale of goods and reported in the same time period as the revenues are recognized. Similarly, shipping costs and sales commissions usually relate directly to revenues.[5]

Direct expenses include not only those that have already been incurred, but should also include anticipated expenses related to revenues of the current period. After delivery of goods to customers, there are still costs of collection, bad debt losses from uncollectible receivables, and possible warranty costs for product deficiencies. These expenses are directly related to revenues and should be estimated and matched against recognized revenues for the period.

Immediate Recognition. Many expenses are not related to specific revenues, but are incurred to obtain goods and services which indirectly help to generate revenues. Because these goods and services are used almost immediately, their costs are recognized as expenses in the period of acquisition. Examples include most administrative costs, such as office salaries, utilities, and general advertising and selling expenses.

Immediate recognition is also appropriate when future benefits are highly uncertain. For example, expenditures for research and development may provide significant future benefits, but they are usually so uncertain that the costs are written off in the period in which they are incurred.

Most losses also fit in the immediate recognition category. Because they arise from peripheral or incidental transactions, they do not relate directly to revenues. Examples include losses from disposition of used equipment, losses from natural catastrophes such as earthquakes or tornadoes, and losses from disposition of investments.

Systematic and Rational Allocation. The third general expense recognition category involves assets that benefit more than one accounting period. The cost of assets such as buildings, equipment, patents, and prepaid insurance are spread across the periods of expected benefit in some systematic and rational way. Generally, it is difficult if not impossible to relate these expenses directly to specific revenues or to specific periods, but it is clear that they are necessary if the revenue is to be earned. Examples of expenses that are included in this category are depreciation and amortization.

The methods adopted for recognizing expenses and losses should appear reasonable to an unbiased observer and should be followed consistently unless the underlying conditions surrounding the asset change. Some expenses are related to the goods being produced, and thus may be deferred in inventory values if the goods are unsold at the end of an

---

[5]*Statement of Financial Accounting Concepts No. 6,* par. 144.

accounting period. Examples include depreciation on production machinery and plant insurance. Other expenses are related to periods, and are allocated directly as an expense of the immediate time period. Examples include depreciation of delivery trucks and amortization of bond discount.[6]

Changes in Estimates. In reporting periodic revenues and in attempting to properly match those expenses incurred to generate current period revenues, accountants must continually make judgments. The numbers reported in the financial statements reflect these judgments and are based on estimates of such factors as the number of years of useful life for depreciable assets, the amount of gas or oil to be produced, the amount of uncollectible accounts expected, or the amount of warranty liability to be recorded on the books. These and other estimates are made using the best available information at the statement date. However, conditions may change subsequently, and the estimates may need to be revised. Naturally, if either revenue or expense amounts are changed, the income statement is affected. The question is whether the previously reported income measures should be revised or whether the changes should impact only on current and future periods.

The Accounting Principles Board stated in Opinion No. 20 that changes in estimates should be reflected in the current period (the period in which the estimate is revised) and in future periods, if any, that are affected. No retroactive adjustments are to be made for a change in estimate.[7] These changes are considered a normal part of the accounting process and not errors made in past periods. For example, Murphy Oil Corporation extended the life on its offshore drilling barges from 12 to 16 years. Extending the life increased net income by $13.6 million or $.37 a share in the year of the change.

To illustrate the computations for a change in estimate, assume that Springville Manufacturing Inc. purchased a milling machine at a cost of $100,000. At the time of purchase, it was estimated that the machine would have a useful life of 10 years. Assuming the straight-line method is used, the depreciation expense is $10,000 per year ($100,000 ÷ 10). At the beginning of the fifth year, however, conditions indicated that the machine would only be used for 3 more years. Depreciation expense in the fifth, sixth, and seventh years should reflect the revised estimate, but depreciation expense recorded in the first four years would not be affected. Since the book value at the end of four years is $60,000 ($100,000 − $40,000 accumulated depre-

---

[6] *Ibid.*, par. 147.

[7] *Opinions of the Accounting Principles Board No. 20,* "Accounting Changes" (New York: American Institute of Certified Public Accountants, 1971), par. 31.

ciation), annual depreciation charges for the remaining 3 years of estimated life would be $20,000 ($60,000 ÷ 3). The following schedule summarizes the depreciation charges over the life of the asset.

Year	Depreciation
1	$ 10,000
2	10,000
3	10,000
4	10,000
5	20,000
6	20,000
7	20,000
	$100,000

Effects of Changing Prices. The preceding presentation of revenue and expense recognition has not addressed the question of how, if at all, changing prices are to be recognized under the transaction approach. As indicated in Chapter 2, accountants have traditionally ignored this phenomenon, especially when gains would result from recognition. When an economy experiences high rates of inflation, users of financial statements become concerned that the statements do not reflect the impact of these changing prices. When the inflation rates are lower, this user concern decreases.

The Financial Accounting Standards Board in Statement No. 33 required certain large publicly held companies to disclose selected information about price changes on a supplemental basis. The Board did not require this recognition to be reported in the basic financial statements, but in a supplemental note to the financial statements that did not have to be audited. Subsequently, some of the disclosure requirements were eliminated in Statement No. 82, and all price-level disclosures were made voluntary in Statement No. 89.

The effects of changing prices are discussed and illustrated in Chapter 25. Generally accepted accounting principles are still based primarily on historical exchange prices, and the transaction approach to income determination recognizes price changes only when losses in value are indicated.

REPORTING OF INCOME

After recognition and measurement criteria are established, the manner in which income is to be reported (displayed) must be determined. Although GAAP requires disclosure of many specific items of information, there is no standardized form of the income statement or other general-purpose financial statements. The reporting of income thus raises many questions regarding, for example, the format of the income statement, terminology used to describe the items presented, the level of detail in the statement, and income-related disclosures to be presented in notes to the financial statements. In answering these and other questions regarding the reporting of income, the overriding consideration should be the usefulness of the information for decision making.

In the following sections, current practices in reporting income will be examined and illustrated. Subsequently, the implications of the FASB's conceptual framework for future reporting practices will be considered.

Form of the Income Statement

The income statement traditionally has been prepared in either single-step or multiple-step form. Under the single-step form, all revenues and gains that are identified as operating items are placed first on the income statement followed by all expenses and losses that are identified as operating items. The difference is reported as income from operations. If there are no nonoperating irregular or extraordinary items, this difference may be referred to as net income. The income statement of Mobil Corporation reproduced below illustrates the single-step form.

MOBIL CORPORATION

Consolidated Statement of Income (In millions except for per-share amounts)

Year Ended December 31	1984	1983
Revenues		
Sales and services (including excise and state gasoline taxes: 1984—$3,445; 1983—$3,389; 1982—$3,168)	**$59,492**	$57,996
Interest, dividends, and other revenue	**982**	1,002
Total Revenues	**60,474**	58,998
Costs and Expenses		
Crude oil, products, merchandise, and operating supplies and expenses	**38,705**	38,404
Exploration expenses	**619**	618
Selling and general expenses	**5,329**	4,967
Depreciation, depletion, and amortization	**2,337**	1,892
Interest and debt discount expense	**1,111**	814
Taxes other than income taxes	**8,205**	8,089
Income taxes	**2,900**	2,711
Total Costs and Expenses	**59,206**	57,495
Net Income	**$ 1,268**	$ 1,503
Net Income Per Share	**$3.11**	$3.70

Under the multiple-step form, the income statement is divided into separate sections (referred to as intermediate components in Concepts Statement No. 5), and various subtotals are reported that reflect different levels of profitability. Some of the sections, especially those reported *after* operating income, are specified by FASB pronouncements. Others have become standardized by wide usage. The income statement of the Coca-Cola Company, reproduced below, illustrates one form of a multiple-step income statement. Since the FASB has chosen not to be too specific about display, it is understandable that wide variations of reporting can be found in practice.

Consolidated Statements of Income

The Coca-Cola Company and Consolidated Subsidiaries

(In thousands except per share data)

Year Ended December 31,	1984	1983	1982
Net Operating Revenues	$7,363,993	$6,828,992	$6,021,135
Cost of goods and services	3,992,923	3,772,741	3,310,847
Gross Profit	3,371,070	3,056,251	2,710,288
Selling, administrative and general expenses	2,313,562	2,063,626	1,830,527
Operating Income	1,057,508	992,625	879,761
Interest income	128,837	82,912	106,172
Interest expense	123,750	72,677	74,560
Other income (deductions)—net	5,438	(2,528)	6,679
Income From Continuing Operations			
Before Income Taxes	1,068,033	1,000,332	918,052
Income taxes	439,215	442,072	415,076
Income From Continuing Operations	628,818	558,260	502,976
Income from discontinued operations			
(net of applicable income taxes of			
$414 in 1983 and $4,683 in 1982)	—	527	9,256
Net Income	$ 628,818	$ 558,787	$ 512,232
Per Share:			
Continuing operations	$ 4.76	$ 4.10	$ 3.88
Discontinued operations	—	—	.07
Net income	$ 4.76	$ 4.10	$ 3.95
Average Shares Outstanding	132,210	136,222	129,793

A multiple-step income statement for the Suhaka Corporation, a hypothetical company, is illustrated on page 129. It will be referred to in discussing the content of a multiple-step income statement. To comply with SEC requirements, income statements are usually presented in comparative form for three years. To simplify the illustration, only one year is presented. The illustrated income statement contains more detail than is usually found in actual published financial statements. It has become common practice to issue highly condensed statements, with details and supporting schedules provided in notes to the statements. The potential problem with this practice is that the condensed statements may not provide as much predictive and feedback value as statements that provide more detail about the components of income directly on the statement.

Suhaka Corporation
Income Statement
For Year Ended December 31, 1987

Revenue from net sales:			
Sales...		$800,000	
Less: Sales returns and allowances..............	$ 12,000		
Sales discounts.........................	8,000	20,000	$780,000
Cost of goods sold:			
Beginning inventory.............................		$125,000	
Net purchases................................	$430,000		
Freight in......................................	32,000	462,000	
Cost of goods available for sale.................		$587,000	
Less ending inventory...........................		96,000	491,000
Gross profit on sales.............................			$289,000
Operating expenses:			
Selling expenses:			
Sales salaries.............................	$ 46,000		
Advertising expense........................	27,000		
Miscellaneous selling expenses..............	12,000	$ 85,000	
General and administrative expenses:			
Officers' and office salaries..................	$ 62,000		
Taxes and insurance.......................	26,500		
Depreciation expense.......................	12,000		
Doubtful accounts expense..................	8,600		
Miscellaneous general expense..............	9,200	118,300	203,300
Operating income...............................			$ 85,700
Other revenues and gains:			
Interest revenue...............................		$ 8,750	
Gain on sale of investment.....................		37,000	45,750
Other expenses and losses:			
Interest expense...............................		$ (5,200)	
Loss from fire.................................		(14,300)	(19,500)
Income from continuing operations			
before income taxes..........................			$111,950
Income taxes..................................			44,780
Income from continuing operations................			$ 67,170
Discontinued operations:			
Loss from operations of discontinued business			
segment (net of income tax savings of $14,000)..		$(21,000)	
Loss on disposal of business segment (net of			
income tax savings of $6,400)................		(9,600)	(30,600)
Extraordinary gain from early debt extinguishment			
(net of income taxes of $10,160)................			15,240
Cumulative effect of changing inventory method			
(net of income tax savings of $3,000).............			(4,500)
Net income......................................			$ 47,310
Earnings per common share:			
Income from continuing operations..............			$ 1.34
Discontinued operations........................			−0.61
Extraordinary gain.............................			0.31
Cumulative effect of accounting change..........			−0.09
Net income....................................			$ 0.95

Content of a Multiple-Step Income Statement

The Suhaka Corporation Income Statement has two major categories of income and nine separate sections as follows:

I. Income from continuing operations:
  1. Net sales
  2. Cost of goods sold
  3. Operating expenses
  4. Other revenues and gains
  5. Other expenses and losses
  6. Income tax on continuing operations
II. Irregular or extraordinary items:
  7. Discontinued operations
  8. Extraordinary items
  9. Cumulative effects of changes in accounting principles

There are several important points about this classification. Only one income tax amount is reported for all items included in the income from continuing operations category; it is presented as the last section in the category. In contrast, each item in the irregular or extraordinary items category is reported net of its income tax effect, referred to as "net of tax." This separation of income tax expense into different sections of the income statement is referred to as "intraperiod income tax allocation."

The various types of gains and losses are not reported entirely in one section of the statement. Some are reported as part of income from continuing operations, and others are included in irregular or extraordinary items. If a gain or loss is considered part of the ongoing operations of the company, and if its measurement is not too uncertain, it should be included in the continuing operations category. If a gain or loss relates to operations, but is too irregular to classify with the normal recurring items, it is reported separately in the second category. In addition, some gains and losses have been identified by the FASB as not affecting the income statement at all, but are recorded as direct adjustments to owners' equity. In this category are certain foreign currency translation adjustments and market value declines in long-term securities.

Regardless of where gains and losses are reported, they are usually presented at a net figure, i.e., the difference between gross sales price and cost. This, of course, differs from operating revenues and expenses that are usually reported separately at their gross amounts.

Although the FASB has been very specific about how the irregular and extraordinary items should be displayed, the Board has said little about the display of income from operations. The Suhaka Company illustration, although more detailed than most published statements, demonstrates the use of operating income categories commonly found in practice. As the concepts in the Conceptual Framework project are incorporated into the accounting standards, some increased standardization of an operating income format is likely.

A review of the multiple-step income statement discloses several subtotals, especially in the operating category. These subtotals are identified as follows:

1. Gross profit (Net sales—Cost of goods sold)
2. Operating income (#1—Operating expenses)
3. Income from continuing operations before income tax (#2 + Other revenues and gains − Other expenses and losses)
4. Income from continuing operations (#3 − income tax)
5. Net income (#4 + or − irregular and extraordinary items)

Each of the nine major sections and related subtotals will be discussed separately as a way to better understand current practices in reporting income.

Net Sales. Revenue from net sales reports the total sales to customers for the period. This total should not include additions to billings for sales and excise taxes that the business is required to collect on behalf of the government. These billing increases are properly recognized as current liabilities. Sales returns and allowances and sales discounts should be subtracted from gross sales in arriving at net sales revenue. When the sales price is increased to cover the cost of freight to the customer and the customer is billed accordingly, freight charges paid by the company should also be subtracted from sales in arriving at net sales. Freight charges not passed to the buyer are recognized as selling expenses.

Cost of Goods Sold. In any merchandising or manufacturing enterprise, the cost of goods relating to sales of the period must be determined. As illustrated in the Suhaka Corporation income statement, **cost of goods available for sale** is first determined. This is the sum of the beginning inventory, net purchases, and all other buying, freight, and storage costs relating to the acquisition of goods. The net purchases balance is developed by subtracting purchase returns and allowances and purchase discounts from gross purchases. Cost of goods sold is then calculated by subtracting the ending inventory from the cost of goods available for sale.

When the goods are manufactured by the seller, additional elements enter into the cost of goods sold. Besides material costs, a company incurs labor and overhead costs to convert the material from its raw material state to a finished good. A manufacturing company has three inventories rather than one: raw materials, goods in process, and finished goods. The Suhaka

Corporation is a merchandising company. The cost of goods sold for a manufacturing company is illustrated in Chapter 9.

Operating Expenses. Operating expenses may be reported in two parts: (1) selling expenses and (2) general and administrative expenses. **Selling expenses** include such items as sales salaries and commissions and related payroll taxes, advertising and store displays, store supplies used, depreciation of store furniture and equipment, and delivery expenses. **General and administrative expenses** include officers' and office salaries and related payroll taxes, office supplies used, depreciation of office furniture and fixtures, telephone, postage, business licenses and fees, legal and accounting services, contributions, and similar items. For manufacturing companies, charges related jointly to both production and administrative functions should be allocated in some equitable manner between manufacturing overhead and operating expenses.

Other Revenues and Gains. This section usually includes items identified with the peripheral activities of the company. Examples include revenue from financial activities, such as rents, interest, and dividends, and gains from the sale of assets such as equipment or investments.

Other Expenses and Losses. This section is parallel to the previous one, but results in deductions from, rather than increases to, operating income. Examples include interest expense, bond discount amortization, and losses from the sale of assets.

Income Tax on Continuing Operations. As explained earlier in this chapter, total income tax expense for a period is allocated to various components of income. One amount is computed for income from continuing operations, and separate computations are made for any irregular or extraordinary items. In the Suhaka illustration, an income tax rate of 40% was assumed. Thus, the amount of income tax related to continuing operations is $44,780 ($111,950 × .40).

The same tax rate is applied to all income components in the Suhaka illustration. In practice, however, intraperiod income tax allocation may involve different rates for different components of income. This results from graduated tax rates and special or alternative rates for certain types of gains and losses. In addition, as explained earlier in the chapter, income for tax reporting purposes may differ from income reported in the general-purpose financial statements. This difference gives rise to deferred income taxes, or interperiod income tax allocation, which will be discussed in Chapter 20.

Discontinued Operations. An increasingly common irregular item involves the disposition of a major segment of a business either through sale or abandonment. In 1984, 84 of the 600 surveyed companies in *Accounting Trends and Techniques* reported discontinued operations in their statements. The segment of the company disposed of may be a product line, a division, or a subsidiary company. To qualify as a discontinued operation for reporting purposes, the assets and related activities of the segment must be clearly distinguishable from other assets, operating results, and general activities of the company, both physically and operationally, as well as for financial reporting purposes. For example, closing down one plant of three making the same product, eliminating *part* of a product line, or shifting the production or marketing functions from one location to another would not be classified as discontinued operations.

There are many reasons why management may decide to dispose of a segment. For example:

1. The segment may be unprofitable.
2. The segment may be too isolated geographically.
3. The segment may not fit into the long-range plans for the company.
4. Management may need funds to reduce long-term debt or to expand into other areas.
5. Management may be fearful of a corporate take-over by new investors desiring to gain control of the company.

In the mid 1980's, management of many companies adopted anti-takeover strategies to try to protect their companies. One of the more popular techniques was to sell peripheral operational segments, especially unprofitable ones, that had been acquired during earlier conglomerate years, and to consolidate the company around its principal business operations. One of the companies that did this was General Mills, Inc., whose complete set of statements for 1985 are included in Appendix A. Management's letter to shareholders and employees included in the annual report states:

> In fiscal 1985 General Mills completed a historic corporate restructuring plan. The restructured company will be 90 percent Consumer Foods and Restaurants, which traditionally have been the company's highest return and fastest-growth areas.
>
> The General Mills Board of Directors has approved plans to divest operations representing over 25 percent of both sales and fiscal year-end assets.[8]

As indicated in the company's Consolidated Statement of Earnings, income from discontinued operations net of tax for the fiscal year 1985 was

---

[8]General Mills' annual report for year ending May 26, 1985, p. 1.

$188.3 million, more than 1½ times the earnings from continuing operations. In addition, General Mills streamlined its operations in divisions that were not discontinued. This was referred to as a "redeployment" of assets, and the loss from such redeployment was shown as a separate item in arriving at earnings from continuing operations. Notes 2 and 3 describe the disposition of the toy and fashion segments and redeployment of assets in the retailing and restaurant operations.

Many successful takeovers are financed by financial institutions willing to lend billions of dollars to support the buyout of current stockholders. After the new management assumes control of the company, a common strategy is to sell parts of the company to reduce the debt incurred in the takeover. For example, Allied Corporation purchased Bendix Corporation, a $4.1 billion (revenues) automotive parts, aerospace, and machine tool conglomerate in 1982. Within two years, Allied liquidated a machine tool company, an earthmoving machine business, and a large pipe-bending business. Similarly, in 1985 W. R. Grace & Co. purchased a 26% interest in a West German group and then made plans to sell over $1 billion of assets, including its retail operations that include sporting goods, home centers, and western wear.[9]

Regardless of the reason, the discontinuance of a substantial portion of company operations is a significant event. Therefore, information about discontinued operations should be presented explicitly to readers of financial statements.

Reporting Requirements for Discontinued Operations. When a company discontinues operating a segment of its business, future comparability requires that all elements that relate to the discontinued operation be identified and separated from continuing operations. Thus, in the Suhaka income statement illustrated on page 129, the first category after Income from Continuing Operations is Discontinued Operations. The category is further separated into two subdivisions: (1) the current year income or loss from operating the discontinued segment, or a $21,000 loss, and (2) disclosure of the gain or loss on the actual disposal of the business segment, or a further $9,600 loss.

As previously indicated, the irregular items are all reported net of their respective tax effects. If the item is a gain, it is reduced by the tax on the gain. If the item is a loss, it is deductible against other income and thus its existence *saves* income taxes. The overall company loss can thus be re-

---

[9]"W. R. Grace Plans Asset Sales in 1986 Totaling $1 Billion," *Wall Street Journal,* February 12, 1986, p. 33.

duced by the tax savings arising from being able to deduct the loss from otherwise taxable income.

The income statement for the Suhaka Corporation on page 129 discloses both of these subdivisions. The income tax rate is 40% on all items. Analysis of the income statement shows that Suhaka had an operating loss for the current year of $35,000, but that after a tax savings of $14,000 was deducted, only $21,000 is reported as a loss. The second item discloses that the segment was sold and a loss of $16,000 was experienced on the sale. Application of the income tax rate of 40% reduces this loss to $9,600. If comparative statements are prepared, the same separation between continued and discontinued operations for prior years should be made.

Often a company will decide on a particular date (the **measurement date**) to dispose of a business segment, but will have a phase-out period between that date and the date the segment is actually sold (**disposal date**). The gain or loss on disposal will include any income or loss from operating the segment during the phase-out period. To illustrate using the income statement on page 129, assume Suhaka Corporation decided on July 1, 1987 to phase out a segment of its operation. This date is the measurement date and marks the beginning of the phase-out period.

In computing the gain or loss from disposal of the segment, any operating income or loss during the phase-out period should be included in the gain or loss computation. Thus, the $9,600 loss on disposal reflects both the operating results during phase-out and the gain or loss on final disposal, net of income taxes. The $21,000 loss represents the operating loss (net of income tax savings of $14,000) for the period January 1, 1987, to July 1, 1987.

Further disclosure of discontinued operations can be made in notes to the statements. For example, the note supporting a $45,549,000 loss from discontinued operations for Uniroyal Inc. is reproduced on page 136.

The reporting requirements for discontinued operations are contained in APB Opinion No. 30, "Reporting the Results of Operations."[10] The reporting of discontinued operations can become complex, and only a summary of the guidelines provided by APB Opinion No. 30 is covered here. Application of the guidelines requires judgment. The goal should be to report information that will assist external users in assessing future cash flows by clearly distinguishing normal, recurring earnings patterns from those activities that are irregular yet significant in assessing the total company results of operations.

---

[10] *Opinions of the Accounting Principles Board No. 30*, "Reporting the Results of Operations" (New York: American Institute of Certified Public Accountants, 1973), par. 20.

Uniroyal, Inc.

Discontinued Operations

The company intends to seek purchasers for two segments of its Engineered Products group consisting of its hose and conveyor belting segment, which operates in North America, and its athletic footwear segment. In the intervening period the company intends to continue to improve such businesses to maximize their attractiveness to potential purchasers. In connection with this decision, the company has expensed the unfunded pension costs associated with these businesses. Such pension costs are included in the loss on disposal of discontinued operations.

Sales and losses from operations and disposal of discontinued operations follow:

In thousands	1984	1983	1982
Sales	$ 97,181	104,707	131,220
Loss from operations before income tax benefit	$(19,887)	(19,540)	(8,639)
Income tax benefit	(4,072)	(633)	(2,442)
Loss from operations	(15,815)	(18,907)	(6,197)
Loss on disposal, net of $1,463 income tax benefit	(29,734)	—	—
	$(45,549)	(18,907)	(6,197)

At December 30, 1984 the net assets of discontinued operations were $6.2 million and consisted primarily of receivables, inventories, and property, plant and equipment, net of the related provision for loss on disposal. The decrease from the 1983 balance of $56.1 million reflects the sale of certain hose operations during 1984 and the establishment of the provision for loss on disposals.

Extraordinary Items. According to APB Opinion No. 30, **extraordinary items** are events and transactions that are both **unusual in nature and infrequent in occurrence.** Thus, to qualify as extraordinary, an item must "possess a high degree of abnormality and be of a type clearly unrelated to, or only incidentally related to, the ordinary and typical activities of the entity . . . (and) be of a type that would not reasonably be expected to recur in the foreseeable future . . . ."[11] In addition, the item must be **material** in amount.

The intent of the Accounting Principles Board was to restrict the items that could be classified as extraordinary. The presumption of the Board was that an item should be considered ordinary and part of the company's usual activity unless evidence clearly supported its classification as an extraordinary item. The Board offered certain examples of gains and losses that should *not* be reported as extraordinary items. They include:

1. The write-down or write-off of receivables, inventories, equipment leased to others, or intangible assets.

[11]*Ibid.*, par. 20.

2. The gains or losses from exchanges or translation of foreign currencies, including those relating to major devaluations and revaluations.
3. The gains or losses on disposal of a segment of a business.
4. Other gains or losses from sale or abandonment of property, plant, or equipment used in the business.
5. The effects of a strike.
6. The adjustment of accruals on long-term contracts.

The standard-setting bodies have identified two major items as extraordinary items regardless of whether they meet the dual criteria: (1) material gains and losses from debt extinguishment[12] and (2) net operating loss carryforwards.[13] Since 1980, an increasing number of companies have been reporting extraordinary items. *Accounting Trends and Techniques* reports that of the 600 companies analyzed for its publication, 84 reported extraordinary items in 1984 as compared with 47 in 1980.[14] Most of this increase can be attributed to the two specific items identified by the APB as extraordinary items. In 1984, Uniroyal, Inc. reported extraordinary gains (credits) of $79.2 million from debt extinguishment, income tax carryforwards, and gains from the sale of a foreign subsidiary. The note describing the details of these gains is presented on page 138.

Some items may not meet both criteria for extraordinary items, but may meet one of them. Although these items do not qualify as extraordinary, they should be disclosed separately as part of income from continuing operations, either before or after operating income. Examples of these items include strike-related costs, obsolete inventory write-downs, and gains and losses from sale or abandonment of property, plant, and equipment. Because these items appear before income from operations, they are not adjusted for their income tax effects. United States Steel Corporation listed such items under the heading "Unusual Items" and included provisions for estimated costs related to shutdown of facilities and revaluation of investments and other assets. A partial income statement for United States Steel is reproduced on page 139.

Cumulative Effects of Changes in Accounting Principles. The last item included in the irregular category of the income statement is the effect of changing accounting principles. Although the profession has recognized the desirability of consistency in application of accounting principles, there are occasions where conditions justify a change from one principle to an-

---

[12]*Statement of Financial Accounting Standards No. 4,* "Reporting Gains and Losses from Extinguishment of Debt" (Stamford: Financial Accounting Standards Board, 1975).

[13]*Opinions of the Accounting Principles Board No. 11,* "Accounting for Income Taxes" (New York: American Institute of Certified Public Accountants, 1967), par 47.

[14]*Accounting Trends and Techniques-1985* (New York: American Institute of Certified Public Accountants, 1985), p. 295.

Uniroyal, Inc.

Extraordinary Credits

In 1984 extraordinary credits totaled $79,240,000 and consisted of gains from the sale of a foreign subsidiary, the early retirement of debt and the realization of income tax carryforward benefits.

To comply with Malaysian government policy, the company was required to substantially reduce its ownership in its Malaysian natural rubber plantation. Accordingly, in 1984 the company sold the plantation to Malaysian interests resulting in an extraordinary gain of $52,221,000, after deducting income taxes of $9,476,000. The company received $13,807,000 in cash and recorded a receivable of $67,899,000, of which $56,371,000 was received in February 1985 and $11,528,000 is due through 1988.

In December 1984 the company repurchased $49,820,000 principal amount of its 3¾% and 10⅛% promissory notes before their scheduled maturity, resulting in an extraordinary gain of $7,670,000, after deducting income taxes of $100,000.

In 1984 the company realized income tax carryforward benefits totaling $19,349,000. Such carryforward benefits consisted of $15,881,000 of foreign tax credits, $2,377,000 of foreign subsidiary net operating loss benefits and $1,091,000 of capital loss benefits.

Extraordinary credits of $14,715,000 in 1983 consisted of $9,153,000 applicable to the exchange of 1,233,735 shares of common stock for $27,750,000 principal amount of the company's 3¾% promissory notes and $5,562,000 applicable to the exchange of 1,102,442 shares of common stock for $20,036,000 principal amount of the company's 5½% convertible subordinated debentures. These exchanges were not taxable.

other. Sometimes this condition arises because the standard-setting body issues a new pronouncement requiring a change in principle. If GAAP is to be followed, the company has no choice but to change to conform with the new standard. Sometimes economic conditions change, and a company changes accounting principles so that reporting can be more representative of the actual conditions. For example, when there was double-digit inflation during the late 1970's, many companies changed their inventory methods to LIFO to reduce their income and thus reduce the actual cash payments for income taxes.

When a change in an accounting principle occurs, management must decide whether to reflect the new principle in the current and past financial statements. If the new principle is to be applied only to future operations, no special accounting entries are required in the period of the accounting change. If, however, the entity decides to apply the change to past operations, an entry is needed in the current year to adjust the statements for the cumulative effect of the change adjustment. The Board has recognized two different ways to adjust the current statements: (1) as an adjustment to net income for the period of the change, or (2) as an adjustment to the beginning retained earnings balance. As with discontinued operations and extraordinary items, the adjustment in either case should be net of income taxes.

Consolidated Statement of Income

(Dollars in millions)	1984	1983*	1982*
Sales *(Note 24, page 42)*	**$19,104**	$17,539	$18,919
Operating costs:			
Cost of sales (excludes items below) *(Note 4, page 34)*	**13,538**	12,929	14,194
Selling, general and administrative expenses	**606**	715	750
Pensions, insurance and other employee benefits *(Notes 14 and 15, page 39)*	**479**	770	897
Depreciation, depletion and amortization	**1,241**	1,104	1,031
State, local and miscellaneous taxes *(Note 24, page 24)*	**1,425**	1,332	1,328
Exploration expenses	**249**	232	304
Total operating costs	**17,538**	17,082	18,504
Operating income (excludes items shown below)	**1,566**	457	415
Income (loss) from affiliates — equity method *(Note 5, page 34)*	**35**	(14)	59
Other income *(Note 20, page 40)*	**331**	237	344
Total income from all operations	**1,932**	680	818
Interest and other financial income *(Note 20, page 40)*	**114**	102	291
Interest and other financial costs *(Note 20, page 40)*	**(1,019)**	(856)	(911)
Total income (loss) before unusual items, taxes on income, minority interest and extraordinary gain	**1,027**	(74)	198
Unusual items — *add (deduct):*			
Provision for estimated costs attributable to shutdown of facilities *(Note 16, page 39)*	**—**	(1,149)	(123)
Adjustment to provision for occupational disease claims *(Note 17, page 39)*	**—**	—	31
Revaluation of investments and other assets *(Note 18, page 39)*	**(47)**	—	(30)
Total unusual items	**(47)**	(1,149)	(122)
Total income (loss) before taxes on income, minority interest and extraordinary gain	**980**	(1,223)	76

In the income statement on page 129, the Suhaka Corporation recorded a $4,500 cumulative loss due to changing inventory principles as the last of the irregular or extraordinary items. The pretax loss to Suhaka was $7,500, but income tax savings reduced the reported loss by $3,000.

If Suhaka Corporation had followed the other method of reporting the cumulative effects of the change in accounting principles, there would have been no adjustment to income; instead, the loss would have been recorded as a charge directly to Retained Earnings. The Accounting Principles Board specified different criteria to help accountants determine which approach should be applied under what circumstances. Further discussion of these criteria is included in Chapter 23.

To illustrate the reporting of accounting changes, a partial income statement and pertinent note describing an accounting change by Bethlehem Steel Corporation is included below and on page 141.

BETHLEHEM STEEL CORPORATION

Consolidated Statements of Income

(dollars in millions, except per share data)	Year ended December 31		
	1983	1982	1981
Income (Loss) before Extraordinary Gain and Cumulative Effect of Changes in Accounting Principles ($7.31), $(33.64), $4.83 per share	$ (314.2)	$(1,469.6)	$ 210.9
Extraordinary Gain on Early Extinguishment of Debt ($.53 per share) (Note G)	23.5	—	—
Cumulative Effect of Changes in Accounting Principles ($2.86 per share) (Note B)	127.2	—	—
Net Income (Loss) ($(3.92), $(33.64), $4.83 per share)	$ (163.5)	$(1,469.6)	$ 210.9

NOTES TO CONSOLIDATED FINANCIAL STATEMENTS

B. Accounting Changes

In December 1983, Bethlehem adopted certain changes in accounting for depreciation of property, plant and equipment and for the cost of relining blast furnaces.

The changes in accounting for depreciation were lengthening of the estimated depreciable lives of certain assets, adjusting straight-line depreciation for levels of operation and changing from the composite method of depreciating assets to the unit method. These changes affect mainly steel producing and raw material producing facilities.

The change in the estimated depreciable lives of assets was made to approximate more closely the actual useful lives of facilities. The adjustment of straight-line depreciation for levels of operations gives recognition to the fact that the depreciation of production facilities is related to both usage and the passage of time. This adjustment is limited to not more than a 25% increase or decrease from the depreciation calculated on a straight-line basis. Under the unit method of depreciation, gains and losses on the retirement of assets will be recognized in net income immediately. Under the composite method these gains and losses were credited or charged to accumulated depreciation.

In 1983, Bethlehem also adopted a policy of capitalizing the cost of relining blast furnaces. The capitalized cost is depreciated on the unit-of-production basis. Prior to 1983, Bethlehem charged cost of sales with a provision for future reline cost based upon blast furnace production. Capitalizing the cost of relining blast furnaces will more accurately reflect Bethlehem's investment in property, plant and equipment.

Management believes that these changes will provide a better matching of revenues and expenses. They will also bring Bethlehem's accounting practices in line with those predominant in the steel industry.

A summary of the effect on net income of these accounting changes (which were made in December effective January 1, 1983) for the year 1983 is shown in the table below:

(dollars in millions, except per share data)	Increase (Decrease)	
	Net Income	Per Share
Current Year Adjustments:		
Depreciation Changes		
Lengthening depreciable lives....................	$ 69.5	$ 1.56
Adjustment for levels of operation	37.3	.84
Adopt unit method of depreciation	23.5	.53
Capitalization of expenditures for relining		
blast furnaces.................................	11.8	.27
	$ 142.1	$ 3.20
Cumulative Effect Adjustments:		
Adjustment for levels of operation	$ 106.3	$ 2.39
Adopt unit method of depreciation	(102.8)	(2.31)
Capitalization of expenditures for relining		
blast furnaces.................................	123.7	2.78
	$ 127.2	$ 2.86
Total effect on 1983 net income	$ 269.3	$ 6.06

Earnings per Share

In 1969, the Accounting Principles Board issued Opinion No. 15 that required all companies to include a section in the income statement converting certain income components to earnings per share. Separate earnings-per-share amounts are computed by dividing income from continuing operations and each irregular or extraordinary item by the weighted average number of shares of common stock outstanding for the reporting period.[15]

----

[15]*Opinions of the Accounting Principles Board No. 15*, "Earnings per Share" (New York: American Institute of Certified Public Accountants, 1969), par. 47.

For example, the Suhaka Corporation income statement illustrated on page 129 shows earnings per share of $1.34 for income from continuing operations, $.61 for loss from discontinued operations, $.31 for extraordinary gain, and a loss of $.09 for the cumulative effect of a change in accounting principle, or a total of $.95 for net income. These figures were derived by dividing each identified component of net income by 50,000 shares of common stock outstanding during the period.

APB Opinion No. 15 also requires the presentation of additional earnings-per-share information if there is a potential dilution of earnings due to the existence of convertible securities, stock options, or warrants. This subject is discussed in detail in Chapter 18.

REPORTING CHANGES IN RETAINED EARNINGS

Many corporations include a statement identifying the changes in retained earnings as one of their financial statements. This statement generally begins with the opening balance in the retained earnings account and then shows the additions and deductions to arrive at the ending balance. In many cases, this statement is very simple. Net income is included as an addition, dividend distributions as a deduction, and any special credits or charges are added or subtracted as appropriate. There are two general types of retained earnings adjustments: (1) prior period adjustments, and (2) as indicated earlier, adjustments arising from some changes in accounting principles. Prior period adjustments arise primarily when an error occurs in one period and is not discovered until a subsequent period.

The retained earnings statement for Suhaka Corporation is illustrated below.

Suhaka Corporation Retained Earnings Statement For Year Ended December 31, 1987	
Retained earnings, January 1, 1987............................	$175,000
Add prior period adjustment—correction of inventory under- statement (net of income taxes of $10,000)....................	15,000
Adjusted retained earnings, January 1, 1987....................	$190,000
Add net income from income statement.........................	47,310
	$237,310
Deduct dividends declared.....................................	40,000
Retained earnings, December 31, 1987.........................	$197,310

REPORTING IMPLICATIONS OF
CONCEPTUAL FRAMEWORK

The Financial Accounting Standards Board recommended new terminology to report the changes in owners' equity. One of the ten elements defined in Concepts Statement No. 6 and presented in Chapter 2 was "Comprehensive Income." The Board defined this term as follows:

> Comprehensive Income is the change in equity of a business enterprise during a period from transactions and other events and circumstances from nonowner sources. It includes all changes in equity during a period except those resulting from investments by owners and distributions to owners.[16]

The Board also defined a new term for the bottom line of an income statement. As discussed in the chapter, the last figure on an income statement is usually labeled "Net Income." The Board did not define net income; however, they did recommend adoption of the term earnings. As defined in the Statement, **earnings** is identical with net income as that term is used in practice except that the last irregular item discussed, "Cumulative Effects of Changes in Accounting Principles," is not included in earnings. Thus, the earnings amount for the Suhaka Corporation would be $51,810 ($47,310 + $4,500). In addition to an earnings statement, the Board suggested that a new comprehensive income statement should be prepared. This statement would start with the earnings amount and include all other nonowner changes to owners' equity. This statement would include the cumulative effects of changes in accounting principles. Also included would be any recognized changes in values, such as writedowns of long-term equity investments and foreign translation adjustments.

The Board did not include a display of a suggested statement of comprehensive income in Concepts Statement No. 5, but stated: "This Statement does not consider details of displaying those different kinds of information and does not preclude the possibility that some entities might choose to combine some of that information in a single statement."[17] An example of how a statement of comprehensive income might appear for Suhaka Corporation is included on page 144.

It is important to recognize that the terms "earnings" and "comprehensive income" recommended in the concepts statements are not presently part of GAAP. Not until they are incorporated into a statement of standards will they be required of business management and auditors.

---

[16]*Statement of Financial Accounting Concepts No. 6,* par. 70.
[17]*Statement of Financial Accounting Concepts No. 5,* par 14.

Suhaka Corporation Statement of Comprehensive Income For Year Ended December 31, 1987	
Earnings per earnings statement..............................	$51,810
Cumulative effect of changing inventory method (net of income tax savings of $3,000)...............................	(4,500)
Prior period adjustment—correction of inventory understatement (net of income taxes of $10,000).............................	15,000
Foreign translation adjustment................................	30,000
Comprehensive income..	$92,310

The Board seems willing to let this process evolve in practice. The business world will undoubtedly see experimentation with a variety of terms and formats over the next several years. Only after practice has moved voluntarily toward some of the recommendations will possible standards be considered for publication.

SUMMARY

As indicated in the short case situation that began this chapter, one "bottom line" figure for income can often be misleading and result in an inefficient allocation of resources. Standard-setting bodies have been concerned with the ingredients that enter an income measurement. The FASB has tried to address the related problems of income recognition, measurement, and reporting in their concepts statements. Decision usefulness will be improved if some of these recommendations are incorporated into practice. However, change is always slow, especially when the changes involve entrenched terminology and formats. Many of the income components introduced in this chapter will be explored in greater depth in later chapters of the text. A summary of the treatment of the special items discussed in this chapter is included on page 145.

QUESTIONS

1. Why is it unwise for users of financial statements to focus too much attention on the final "bottom-line" income figure?
2. Income as determined by income tax regulations is not necessarily the same as income reported to external users. Why might there be differences?

Summary of Procedures for Reporting Irregular, Nonrecurring, or Unusual Items*

Where Reported	Category	Description	Examples
Part of income from continuing operations	Changes in estimates	Normal recurring changes in estimating future. Included in normal accounts.	Changes in building and equipment lives, changes in estimated loss from uncollectible accounts receivable, changes in estimate of warranty liability.
	Unusual gains and losses, not considered extraordinary	Unusual or infrequent, but not both. Related to normal business operations. Material in amount. Shown in other revenues and gains or other expenses and losses.	Gains or losses from sale of assets, investments, or other operating assets. Write-off of receivables as uncollectible, inventories as obsolete.
On income statement, but after income from continuing operations	Discontinued operations	Disposal of completely separate line of business. Include gain or loss from operating segment, and gain or loss from sale or abandonment.	Sale by conglomerate company of separate line of business such as milling company selling restaurant segment.
	Extraordinary items	Both unusual and nonrecurring. Not related to normal business operations. Material in amount.	Material gains and losses from early extinguishment of debt, from some casualties or legal claims if meet criteria.
	Changes in accounting principles— general case	Change from one accepted principle to another.	Change from one method of inventory pricing to another, change in depreciation method.
As adjustment to retained earnings on the balance sheet	Prior period adjustments and special case changes in accounting principles.	Material correction of errors, changes in accounting principles that require retroactive adjustment.	Failure to depreciate fixed assets, mathematical error in computing inventory balance, retroactive adjustment for new standard.

*This chart describes usual case. Exceptions to the descriptions occasionally do occur.

3. What are the major differences between the valuation and transaction approaches to income measurement?
4. What different measurement methods may be applied to net assets in arriving at income under the valuation approach?
5. How are revenues and expenses different from gains and losses?
6. What two factors must be considered in deciding the point at which revenues and gains should be recognized? At what point in the revenue cycle are these conditions usually met?

7. What are three specific variations or exceptions to the practice of recognizing revenue at the "point of sale"?

8. What guidelines are used to match costs with revenues in determining income?

9. What are the advantages and disadvantages of a multiple-step income statement over a single-step statement?

10. Identify nine separate sections that may be included in a multiple-step income statement.

11. What is the meaning of "intraperiod" income tax allocation?

12. The Pop-Up Company has decided to sell its lid manufacturing division even though the division is expected to show a small profit this year. The division's assets will be sold at a loss of $10,000 to another company. What information (if any) should Pop-Up disclose in its financial reports with respect to this division?

13. Which of the following would *not* normally qualify as an extraordinary item?
    (a) The write-down or write-off of receivables.
    (b) Major devaluation of foreign currency.
    (c) Loss on sale of plant and equipment.
    (d) Gain from early extinguishment of debt.
    (e) Loss due to extensive flood damage to asphalt company in Las Vegas, Nevada.
    (f) Loss due to extensive earthquake damage to furniture company in Los Angeles, California.
    (g) Farming loss due to heavy spring rains in the Northwest.

14. Explain briefly the difference in accounting treatment of (a) a change in accounting principle, and (b) a change in accounting estimate.

15. What is the general practice in reporting earnings per share?

16. What is comprehensive income? How should it be reported?

DISCUSSION CASES

CASE 4-1   (Are we really better off?)

The Klinko Company Board of Directors finally receives the income statement for the past year from management. Board members are initially pleased to see that after three loss years, the company will be reporting a profit for the current year. Further investigation reveals that depreciation expense is significantly lower than it was last year. Company management, concerned by the losses, decided to change its method of reporting depreciation from an accelerated method to straight-line. If the depreciation method had not been changed, a loss would have resulted for the fourth consecutive year. When questioned by the Board about the accounting change, management replied that the majority of companies in the industry use the straight-line depreciation method, and thus the change makes Klinko's income statement more comparable to the other companies. Since comparability is an important qualitative characteristic of accounting information, should the Board accept the explanation of management? How should the information about the change in the depreciation method be displayed in the financial statements?

CASE 4–2   (What is income?)

Stan Johnson is a renowned sculptor who specializes in American Indian sculptures. Typically, a cast is prepared for each work to permit the multiple reproduction of the pieces. A limited number of copies are made for each sculpture, and the mold is destroyed after the number is reached. Limiting the number of pieces enhances the price, and most of the pieces have initially sold for $2,000 to $4,000. To encourage sales, Stan has a liberal return policy that permits customers to return any unwanted piece for a period of up to one year from the date of sale and receive a full refund. Do you think Stan should recognize revenue: (1) when the piece is produced and cast in bronze, (2) when the goods are delivered to the customer, or (3) when the period of return has passed? Justify your answer in terms of the conceptual framework.

CASE 4–3   (When should revenue be recognized?)

You are engaged as a consultant to Skyways Unlimited, a manufacturer of satellite dishes for television reception. Skyways sells its dishes to dealers who in turn sell them to customers. As an inducement to carry sufficient inventory, the dealers are not required to pay for the dishes until they have been sold. There is no formal provision for return of the dishes by the dealers; however, Skyways has requested returns when a dealer's sales activity is considered to be too low. Overall, returns have amounted to less than 10% of the dishes sent to dealers. No interest is charged to the dealers on their balances unless they do not remit promptly upon the sale to a customer. At what point would you recommend that Skyways recognize the revenue from the sale of dishes to the dealers?

CASE 4–4   (We just changed our minds.)

Management for Dunstead Manufacturing Company decided in 1987 to discontinue one of its unsuccessful product lines. The line was not large enough for it to meet the definition of a business segment. The planned discontinuance involved obsolete inventory, assembly lines, and packaging and advertising supplies. It was estimated that a loss of $250,000 would result from the decision, and this estimate was recorded as a loss in the 1987 income statement. In 1988, new management was appointed and it was decided that maybe the unsuccessful product line could be turned around with a more aggressive marketing policy. The change was made, and indeed, the product began to make money. The new management wants to reverse the adjustment made last year and remove the liability for the estimated loss. How should the 1987 estimated loss be reported in the 1987 income statement? How should the 1988 reversal of the 1987 action be reported in the 1988 financial statements?

CASE 4–5   (The sure-fire computer software)

The Flexisoft Company has had excellent success in developing business software for microcomputers. Management has followed the accounting practice of deferring the development costs for the software until sufficient sales have developed to cover the software cost. Because of past successes, management feels it is improper to charge software costs directly to expense as current GAAP requires. What are the pros and cons of deferring or expensing immediately these developmental costs?

CASE 4–6   (Deferred initial operating losses)

Small loan companies often experience losses in the operation of newly opened branch loan offices. Such results usually can be anticipated by management prior to making a decision on expansion. It has been recommended by some accountants that the operating losses of newly opened branches should be reported as deferred charges during the first twelve months of operation or until the first profitable month occurs. Such deferred charges would then be amortized over a five-year period. Would you support this recommendation? Justify your answer.

CASE 4–7   (What was last year's income?)

The Rolstad Corporation has decided to discontinue an entire segment of its business effective November 1, 1987. It hopes to sell the assets involved and convert the physical plant to other uses within the manufacturing division. The CPA auditing the books indicates that GAAP requires separate identification of the revenues and expenses related to the segment to be sold and their removal from the continuing revenue and expense amounts. The controller objects to this change. "We have already distributed widely last year's numbers. If we change them now, one year later, confidence in our financial statements will be greatly eroded." What are the pros and cons of identifying separately the costs related to the discontinued segment?

CASE 4–8   (How do you like my display?)

David Company's Statements of Income for the years ended December 31, 1987, and December 31, 1986, are presented at the top of page 149.

Additional facts are as follows:
(a) On January 1, 1986, David Company changed its depreciation method for previously recorded plant machinery from the double-declining-balance method to the straight-line method. The effect of applying the straight-line method for the year of and the year after the change is included in David Company's Statements of Income for the year ended December 31, 1987, and December 31, 1986, in "cost of goods sold."
(b) The loss from operations of the discontinued Dex Division from January 1, 1987, to September 30, 1987, (the portion of the year prior to the measurement date) and from January 1, 1986, to December 31, 1986, is included in David Company's Statements of Income for the year ended December 31, 1987, and December 31, 1986, respectively, in "other, net."
(c) David Company has a simple capital structure with only common stock outstanding and the net income per share of common stock was based on the weighted average number of common shares outstanding during each year.
(d) David Company common stock is listed on the New York Stock Exchange and closed at $13 per share on December 31, 1987, and $15 per share on December 31, 1986.

David Company
Statements of Income
For Years Ended December 31,

	1987	1986
	(000 omitted)	
Net sales	$900,000	$750,000
Costs and expenses:		
Cost of goods sold.............................	$720,000	$600,000
Selling, general and administrative expenses........	112,000	90,000
Other, net......................................	11,000	9,000
Total costs and expenses......................	$843,000	$699,000
Income from continuing operations before income taxes...................................	$ 57,000	$ 51,000
Income taxes...................................	23,000	24,000
Income from continuing operations..................	$ 34,000	$ 27,000
Loss on disposal of Dex Division, including provision of $1,500,000 for operating losses during phase-out period, less applicable income taxes of $8,000,000 ...	8,000	—
Cumulative effect on prior years of change in depreciation method, less applicable income taxes of $1,500,000	—	3,000
Net income.....................................	$ 26,000	$ 30,000
Earnings per share of common stock:		
Income before cumulative effect of change in depreciation method....................................	$ 2.60	$ 2.70
Cumulative effect on prior years of change in depreciation method, less applicable income taxes........	—	.30
Net income.....................................	$ 2.60	$ 3.00

Instructions: Determine from the additional facts above whether the presentation of those facts in David Company's Statements of Income is appropriate. If the presentation is appropriate, discuss the theoretical rationale for the presentation. If the presentation is not appropriate, specify the appropriate presentation and discuss its theoretical rationale.

(AICPA adapted)

EXERCISES

EXERCISE 4–1   (Calculation of net income)

Changes in the balance sheet account balances for the Olstead Sales Co. during 1987 were as shown at the top of page 150.

Dividends declared during 1987 were $60,000. Calculate the net income for the year assuming there were no transactions affecting retained earnings other than the dividends.

	Increase (Decrease)
Cash	$ 75,500
Accounts Receivable	92,000
Inventory.........................	(30,000)
Buildings and Equipment (net).....	190,000
Patents	(15,000)
Accounts Payable..................	(65,000)
Bonds Payable	150,000
Capital Stock.....................	100,000
Additional Paid-In Capital	50,000

EXERCISE 4–2   (Recognition of revenue or gain)

Indicate which of the following items involves the recognition of revenue or gain. Give the reasons for your answer.

(a) Land acquired in 1962 at $35,000 is now conservatively appraised at $145,000.

(b) Timberlands show a growth in timber valued at $40,000 for the year.

(c) An addition to a building was self-constructed at a cost of $36,000 after two offers from private contractors for the work at $46,500 and $50,000.

(d) Certain valuable franchise rights were received from a city for payment of annual licensing fees.

(e) A customer owing $4,600, which was delinquent for one year, gave securities valued at $5,000 in settlement of the obligation.

(f) Goods costing $1,000 are sold for $1,600 with a 50% down payment on a conditional sales contract, title to the goods being retained by the seller until the full contract price is collected.

(g) Cash is received on the sale of gift certificates redeemable in merchandise in the following period.

EXERCISE 4–3   (Revenue and expense recognition)

State the amount of revenue and/or expense for 1987 in each of the following transactions of the Monroe Tractor Co. The accounting period ends December 31, 1987. Treat each item individually.

(a) On December 15, 1987, Monroe received $18,000 as rental revenue for a 6-month period ending June 15, 1988.

(b) Monroe, on July 1, 1987, sold one of its tractors and received $10,000 in cash and a note for $50,000 at 12% interest, payable in one year. The fair market value of the tractor is $60,000.

(c) One of Monroe's steady customers is presently in a weak cash flow position. To maintain its goodwill with this customer, Monroe sells them 2 tractors with a normal combined selling price of $112,000, but allows them a special discount of $8,000.

(d) During 1987, tractors sold for $400,000 are accompanied by a Monroe guarantee for one year. Past experience indicates that repairs equal to 2% of sales revenue will be required in year of sale, and an additional 4% of sales revenue will be needed for repairs in the subsequent year.

(e) On December 28, 1987, Monroe sold 7 tractors for a total of $435,000. As of December 31, 1987, 3 of the tractors were still in Monroe's warehouse.

EXERCISE 4–4   (Classification of income statement items)

Where in a multiple-step income statement would each item be reported?
(a) Purchase discounts
(b) Gain on early retirement of debt
(c) Interest revenue
(d) Loss on sale of equipment
(e) Casualty loss from hurricane
(f) Sales commissions
(g) Loss on disposal of segment
(h) Income tax expense
(i) Gain on sale of land
(j) Sales discounts
(k) Loss from long-term investments written off as worthless
(l) Depletion expense
(m) Cumulative effect of change in depreciation method
(n) Vacation pay of office employee
(o) Ending inventory

EXERCISE 4–5   (Analysis and preparation of income statement)

The selling expenses of Robinson Inc. for 1987 are 13% of sales. General expenses, excluding doubtful accounts, are 25% of cost of goods sold, but only 15% of sales. Doubtful accounts are 2% of sales. The beginning inventory was $136,000, and it decreased 30% during the year. Income from operations for the year before income tax of 40% is $160,000. Extraordinary gain, net of tax of 40%, is $20,000. Prepare an income statement, including earnings per share data, giving supporting computations. Robinson Inc. has 110,000 shares of common stock outstanding.

EXERCISE 4–6   (Change in estimate)

The Swalberg Corporation purchased a patent on January 2, 1982, for $375,000. The original life of the patent was estimated to be 15 years. However, in December of 1987, the controller of Swalberg received information proving conclusively that the product protected by the Swalberg patent would be obsolete within three years. Accordingly, the company decided to write off the unamortized portion of the patent cost over four years beginning in 1987. How would the change in estimate be reflected in the accounts for 1987 and subsequent years?

EXERCISE 4–7   (Intraperiod income tax allocation)

The Wright Corporation reported the following income items before tax for the year 1987.

Income from continuing operations before income tax	$210,000
Loss from operations of a discontinued business segment	50,000
Gain from disposal of a business segment	20,000
Extraordinary gain on retirement of debt	100,000

[handwritten: can offset each other]

The income tax rate is 40% on all items. Prepare the portion of the income statement beginning with "Income from continuing operations before income tax" for the year ended December 31, 1987, after applying proper intraperiod income tax allocation procedures.

EXERCISE 4–8   (Reporting items on financial statements)

How would you report each of the following items on the financial statements?
(a) Revenue from sale of obsolete inventory.
(b) Loss on sale of the fertilizer production division of a lawn supplies manufacturer.
(c) Material penalties arising from early payment of a mortgage.
(d) Gain resulting from changing asset balances to adjust for the effect of excessive depreciation charged in error in prior years.
(e) Loss resulting from excessive accrual in prior years of estimated revenues from long-term contracts.
(f) Costs incurred to purchase a valuable patent.
(g) Net income from the discontinued dune buggy operations of a custom car designer.
(h) Costs of rearranging plant machinery into a more efficient order.
(i) Error made in capitalizing advertising expense during the prior year.
(j) Gain on sale of land to the government.
(k) Loss from destruction of crops by a hail storm.
(l) Cumulative effect of changing depreciation method.
(m) Additional depreciation resulting from a change in the estimated useful life of an asset.
(n) Gain on sale of long-term investments.
(o) Loss from spring flooding.
(p) Sale of obsolete inventory at less than book value.
(q) Additional federal income tax assessment for prior years.
(r) Loss resulting from the sale of a portion of a line of business.
(s) Costs associated with moving an American business to Japan.
(t) Loss resulting from a patent that was recently determined to be worthless.

EXERCISE 4–9   (Multiple-step income statement)

From the following list of accounts, prepare a multiple-step income statement in good form showing all appropriate items properly classified, including disclosure of earnings per share data. (No monetary amounts are to be recognized.)

Accounts Payable
Accumulated Depreciation — Office Building
Accumulated Depreciation — Delivery Equipment
Accumulated Depreciation — Office Furniture and Fixtures
Advertising Expense
Allowance for Doubtful Accounts
Cash
Common Stock, $20 par (10,000 shares outstanding)
Delivery Salaries
Depreciation Expense — Office Building
Depreciation Expense — Delivery Equipment
Depreciation Expense — Office Furniture and Fixtures
Dividend Revenue
Dividends Payable
Dividends Receivable
Doubtful Accounts Expense
Extraordinary Gain (net of income tax)

Freight In
Federal Unemployment Tax Payable
Goodwill
Income Tax
Income Tax Payable
Insurance Expense
Interest Expense — Bonds
Interest Expense — Other
Interest Payable
Interest Receivable
Interest Revenue
Inventory
Loss from Discontinued Operations (net of income tax)
Miscellaneous Delivery Expense
Miscellaneous General Expense
Miscellaneous Selling Expense
Office Salaries
Office Supplies
Office Supplies Used

Officers' Salaries
Property Tax
Purchases
Purchase Discounts
Purchase Returns and Allowances
Retained Earnings
Royalties Received in Advance

Royalty Revenue
Salaries and Wages Payable
Sales
Sales Discounts
Sales Returns and Allowances
Sales Salaries and Commissions
Sales Tax Payable

EXERCISE 4–10
(Single-step income statement and statement of retained earnings)

The Ahwatukee Awning Co. reports the following for 1987:

Retained Earnings, January 1	$444,500
Selling expenses	288,200
Sales revenue	1,128,025
Interest expense	13,390
General and administrative expenses	236,400
Cost of goods sold	556,220
Dividends declared this year	23,000
Tax rate for all items	40%
Average shares of common stock outstanding during the year	25,000

Prepare a single-step income statement (including earnings per share data) and a statement of retained earnings for Ahwatukee.

EXERCISE 4–11   (Correction of retained earnings statement)

B. Orton has been employed as a bookkeeper for the Losser Corporation for a number of years. With the assistance of a clerk, Orton handles all accounting duties, including the preparation of financial statements. The following is a "Statement of Earned Surplus" prepared by Orton for 1987.

Losser Corporation
Statement of Earned Surplus
for 1987

Balance at beginning of year		$ 85,949
Additions:		
Amortization overstatement for 1987	$ 2,800	
Gain on sale of land	18,350	
Interest revenue	4,500	
Profit and loss for 1987	13,680	
Total additions		39,330
Total		$125,279
Deductions:		
Increased depreciation due to change in estimated life	$ 5,000	
Dividends declared and paid	10,000	
Loss on sale of equipment	3,860	
Loss from major casualty (extraordinary)	27,730	
Total deductions		46,590
Balance at end of year		$ 78,689

(1) Prepare a schedule showing the correct net income for 1987. (Ignore income taxes.) (2) Prepare a retained earnings statement for 1987. (3) Explain why you have changed the retained earnings statement.

PROBLEMS

PROBLEM 4–1   (Single-step income statement)

The Longview Co. on July 1, 1987, reported a retained earnings balance of $1,525,000. The books of the company showed the following account balances on June 30, 1988:

Sales	$2,500,000
Inventory: July 1, 1987	160,000
June 30, 1988	165,000
Sales Returns and Allowances	30,000
Purchases	1,536,000
Purchase Discounts	24,000
Dividends Paid	260,000
Selling and General Expenses	250,000
Income Taxes	285,200

Instructions: Prepare a single-step income statement and a retained earnings statement. The Longview Co. has 400,000 shares of common stock outstanding.

PROBLEM 4–2
(Revenue recognition and preparation of income statement)

The Richmond Company manufactures and sells robot-type toys for children. Under one type of agreement with the dealers, Richmond is to receive payment upon shipment to the dealers. Under another type of agreement, Richmond receives payments only after the dealer makes the sale. Under this latter agreement, toys may be returned by the dealer. The president of Richmond desires to know how the income statement would differ under these two methods over a two-year period.

The following information is made available for making the computations.

Sales price per unit:	
If paid after shipment	$5
If paid after sale, with right of return	$6
Cost to produce per unit (Assume fixed quantity of toys	
is produced)	$3
Expected bad debt percentage of sales if revenue recognized at time	
of shipment	5%
Expected bad debt percentage of sales if revenue recognized at time	
of sale	1/2%
Selling expense—1987	$25,000
Selling expense—1988	$15,000
General and administrative expense 1987 and 1988	$20,000

Quantity shipped and sold	1987	1988
Units shipped to dealers	25,000	30,000
Units sold by dealers	14,000	22,000

Instructions: (1) Prepare a comparative income statement for 1987 and 1988 for each of the two types of dealer agreements assuming the company began operations in 1987. (2) Discuss the implications of the revenue recognition method used for each of the dealer agreements.

PROBLEM 4–3   (Intraperiod income tax allocation)

The following information relates to Millrace Manufacturing Company for the fiscal year ended July 31, 1987.

	Amount
Taxable income July 31, 1987..................................	$900,000
Unusual items included in taxable income:	
Extraordinary gain...	101,000
Loss from disposal of a business segment.....................	(140,000)
Income tax rates:	
Ordinary rates, including loss on business segment.............	40%
Extraordinary gain rates	28%
Prior year error resulting in income overstatement for fiscal year 1986. Tax refund to be requested............................	$ 75,000

(handwritten:)
900,000
−101,000
+140,000
939,000

Instructions: Prepare the income statement for Millrace Manufacturing beginning with "Income from continuing operations before income taxes" for the fiscal year ended July 31, 1987. Apply proper intraperiod income tax allocation procedures.

PROBLEM 4–4   (Reporting special income items)

Radiant Cosmetics Inc. shows a retained earnings balance on January 1, 1987, of $620,000. For 1987, the income from continuing operations was $210,000 before income tax. Following is a list of special items:

Income from operations of a discontinued cosmetic division.........	$18,000
Loss on the sale of the cosmetics division	50,000
Gain on extinguishment of long-term debt.........................	25,000
Correction of sales understatement in 1985 (net of income taxes of $21,000)	39,000
Omission of depreciation charges of prior years (a claim has been filed for an income tax refund of $8,000)...................	20,000

Income tax paid during 1987 was $82,000, which consisted of the tax on continuing operations, plus $8,000 resulting from operations of the discontinued cosmetics division and $10,000 from the gain from extinguishment of debt, less a $20,000 tax reduction for loss on the sale of the cosmetics division. Dividends of $30,000 were declared by the company during the year (50,000 shares of common stock are outstanding).

Instructions: Prepare the income statement for Radiant Cosmetics Inc. beginning with "Income from continuing operations before income tax." Include an accompanying retained earnings statement.

PROBLEM 4–5 (Income and retained earnings statements)

Selected account balances of Connell Company for 1987 along with additional information as of December 31 are as follows:

Contribution to Employee Pension Fund	$290,000		Loss on Write-Down of Obsolete Inventory	$ 75,000
Delivery Expense	425,000		Inventory, January 1, 1987	850,000
Depreciation Expense— Delivery Trucks	29,000		Miscellaneous General Expense	45,000
Depreciation Expense— Office Building	25,000		Miscellaneous Selling Expense	50,000
Depreciation Expense— Office Equipment	10,000		Officers' and Office Salaries	850,000
Depreciation Expense— Store Equipment	25,000		Purchase Discounts	47,700
Dividends	150,000		Purchases	4,133,200
Dividend Revenue	5,000		Retained Earnings, January 1, 1987	550,000
Doubtful Accounts Expense	32,000		Sales	8,125,000
Federal Income Taxes, 1987	459,600		Sales Discounts	55,000
Freight In	145,000		Sales Returns and Allowances	95,000
Gain on Sale of Office Equipment	10,000		Sales Salaries	521,000
Interest Revenue	1,500		State and Local Taxes	100,000
Loss on Sale of Marketable Securities	50,000		Stores Supplies Expense	60,000

(a) Inventory was valued at year-end as follows:

Cost	$825,000
Write-down of obsolete inventory	75,000
	$750,000

(b) Number of Connell shares of stock outstanding 50,000

Instructions: Prepare statements of income and retained earnings in multiple-step format for the year ended December 31, 1987.

PROBLEM 4–6 (Corrected income statement)

The following is the pre-audit statement for 10 months ended December 31, 1987, of All-Seasons Recreation Inc., a firm which started operations March 4, 1987.

Year-end pre-audit observations:
(a) Factory depreciation was included in general and administrative expenses $11,200
(b) Sales returns and allowances not recorded 2,750
(c) Accrued sales commissions were not recorded as of December 31 5,230
(d) Advertising expense paid on March 1 was for newspaper ads appearing each month for the next 12 months 13,200
(e) Income tax rate 40%
(f) Gain due to change in accounting principles was wrongfully included in miscellaneous general and administrative

ALL-SEASONS RECREATION INC.
Income Statement
For the Period Ended December 31, 1987

Sales...............................		$497,000	
Less sales returns and allowances.....		0	$497,000
Cost of goods sold:			
Completed units — 5,000.............		$401,000	
Less ending inventory — 1,000 units....		80,200	320,800
Gross profit on sales			$176,200
Selling Expenses:			
Advertising expense.................	$13,200		
Selling expense.....................	60,000	$73,200	
General and administrative expenses:			
Salary expense.....................	$32,100		
Depreciation expense	16,900		
Misc. general and administrative			
expenses	3,300	52,300	125,500
Income from continuing operations before			
income taxes.....................			$50,700
Income taxes.........................			0
Income from continuing operations.......			$50,700
Extraordinary loss on strike (net of income			
tax savings of $8,000)...............			(12,000)
Cumulative effect of change in accounting			
method (net of income taxes			
of $4,000).........................			6,000
Net Income			$44,700

expenses. (This item is in addition to $6,000 reported as a cumulative change)	2,000
(g) Losses from strike were erroneously reported as an extraordinary item	12,000

Instructions: Prepare a corrected income statement for the period ended December 31, 1987. (Round to nearest dollar. Ignore earnings per share computations.)

PROBLEM 4–7   (Analysis of income items — multiple-step
income statement preparation)

On December 31, 1987, analysis of the Dille Sporting Goods' operations for 1987 revealed the following:
(a) Total cash collections from customers, $107,770.
(b) December 31, 1986, inventory balance, $10,020.
(c) Total cash payments, $96,350.
(d) Accounts receivable, December 31, 1986, $20,350.
(e) Accounts payable, December 31, 1986, $9,870.
(f) Accounts receivable, December 31, 1987, $10,780.
(g) Accounts payable, December 31, 1987, $5,175.
(h) General and administrative expenses total 20% of sales. This amount includes the depreciation on store and equipment.
(i) Selling expenses of $11,661 total 30% of gross profit on sales.

(j) No general and administrative or selling expense liabilities existed at December 31, 1987.

(k) Wages and salaries payable at December 31, 1986, $3,750.

(l) Depreciation expense on store and equipment total 13.5% of general and administrative expenses.

(m) Shares of stock issued and outstanding, 6,000.

(n) The income tax rate is 40%.

Instructions: Prepare a multiple-step income statement for the year ended December 31, 1987.

PROBLEM 4–8   (Corrected income and retained earnings statements)

Selected account balances and adjusting information of Yvonne's Cosmetics Inc. for the year ended December 31, 1987, follow:

Retained Earnings, January 1, 1987	$440,670
Sales Salaries and Commissions	25,000
Advertising Expense	16,090
Legal Services	2,225
Insurance and Licenses	7,680
Travel Expense — Sales Representatives	4,560
Depreciation Expense — Sales/Delivery Equipment	6,100
Depreciation Expense — Office Equipment	4,200
Interest Revenue	550
Utilities	6,400
Telephone and Postage	1,475
Supplies Inventory	2,180
Miscellaneous Selling Expenses	2,740
Dividends Paid	33,000
Dividend Revenue	5,150
Interest Expense	4,520
Allowance for Doubtful Accounts (Cr Bal)	160
Officers' Salaries	36,600
Sales	451,000
Sales Returns and Allowances	3,900
Sales Discounts	880
Gain on Sale of Assets	7,820
Inventory, January 1, 1987	89,700
Inventory, December 31, 1987	20,550
Purchases	141,600
Freight In	5,525
Accounts Receivable, December 31, 1987	261,000
Gain from Discontinued Operations (before income tax)	40,000
Extraordinary Loss (before income tax)	72,600
Shares of Common Stock Outstanding	39,000

Adjusting information:

(a) Cost of Inventory in the possession of consignees as of December 31, 1987, was not included in the ending inventory balance $18,600

(b) After preparing an analysis of aged accounts receivable, a decision was made to increase the allowance for doubtful accounts to a percent of the ending accounts receivable balance 2%

(c) Purchase returns and allowances were unrecorded. They are computed as a percent of purchases (not including freight in)..   6%

(d) Sales commissions for the last day of the year had not been accrued. Total sales for the day .... $ 3,050
Average sales commissions as a percent of sales 3%

(e) No accrual had been made for a freight bill received on January 3, 1988, for goods received on December 29, 1987 .... $ 570

(f) An advertising campaign was initiated November 1, 1987. This amount was recorded as "prepaid advertising" and should be amortized over a six-month period. No amortization was recorded............................ $ 1,818

(g) Freight charges paid on sold merchandise were netted against sales. Freight charge on sales during 1987 .... $ 3,500

(h) Interest earned but not accrued........................ $ 560

(i) Depreciation expense on new forklift purchased March 1, 1987 had not been recognized. (Assume all equipment will have no salvage value and the straight-line method is used. Depreciation is calculated to the nearest month.)
Purchase price....................................... $ 7,800
Estimated life in years...............................   10

(j) A "real" account is debited upon the receipt of supplies. Supplies on hand at year end.......................... $ 1,225

(k) Income tax rate (on all items)..........................   40%

Instructions: Prepare a corrected multiple-step income statement and a retained earnings statement for the year ended December 31, 1987. Assume all amounts are material.

PROBLEM 4–9   (Comprehensive income statement)

The Blacksburg Company decides to follow the FASB recommendations and prepare both an earnings statement and a statement of comprehensive income. The following information for the year ending December 31, 1987, has been provided for the preparation of the statements.

Sales	$450,000
Cost of goods sold	263,000
Foreign translation adjustment (net of income tax)...........	33,000 (cr.)
Selling expenses...	63,900
Extraordinary gain (net of income tax)	39,400
Correction of inventory error (net of income tax)	28,680 (cr.)
General and administrative expenses......................	58,720
Cumulative effect of change in depreciation method (net of income tax savings)	18,380 (dr.)
Income tax expense	21,500
Gain on sale of investment...............................	6,700
Proceeds from sale of land at cost	75,000
Dividends	8,900

Instructions: Prepare the two statements for the company. Use a single-step approach for the earnings statement.

5

The Balance Sheet and
Statement of Cash Flows

The questions posed by the investor were intriguing ones. How can a company go bankrupt when it has continued to report net income every year? If it is profitable, why isn't it successful? The answer, of course, depends on the circumstances in a particular case. One thing is certain, however; net income is not the only measure of success.

For many years, the income statement has been the dominant financial statement for external decision making. Earnings per share, placement of extraordinary items, and revenue recognition have all been topics of great interest to standard-setting bodies. The financial press has regularly reported quarterly earnings of large corporations as newsworthy events. The income statement, however, tells only part of the financial story. It does not answer questions such as: What is the company doing with the income? How is the company being financed? How far in debt is the company? How liquid are its assets? What are the prospects for cash flows over the next six months? To answer these questions, an external user has to focus on at least two other financial statements: the balance sheet and the statement of changes in financial position. Even though these statements have limitations, they report information that is very important for a user in evaluating the ability of a company to continue in operation.

Over the past several years the financial community has expressed increased interest in the financial conditions of reporting entities, especially their liquidity. The Financial Accounting Standards Board also has devoted considerable attention to evaluating how its standards affect the balance sheet.[1] Recently, the Board turned its attention to the statement of changes in financial position, sometimes called a funds statement. Historically, the funds statement was prepared on a working capital basis. However, in recent years and especially since the FASB stressed the importance of predicting future cash flows in its conceptual framework, the use of some form of cash as the focal point for funds became increas-

---

[1]See for example David E. Hawkins, "Toward the New Balance Sheet," *Harvard Business Review* (November-December 1984), pp. 156–163.

ingly popular. To meet the objectives established in the framework, the FASB has recommended a statement of cash flows to replace the more general statement of changes in financial position as one of the primary financial statements.

The increased interest in the balance sheet and funds statement is partially related to the increased number of companies that have found themselves in financial difficulty. By concentrating too much on profitability at the expense of financial strength, some companies found they had insufficient cash to pay their debts. This chapter focuses on the strengths and weaknesses of the balance sheet and describes how companies report their assets, liabilities, and owners' equity. It also provides an overview of the statement of cash flows.

USEFULNESS OF THE BALANCE SHEET

The **balance sheet**, also known as the **statement of financial position**, reports as of a given point in time the resources of a business (**assets**), its obligations (**liabilities**), and the residual ownership claims against its resources (**owners' equity**). By analyzing the relationships among these items, investors, creditors, and others can assess a firm's **liquidity**, i.e., its ability to meet short-term obligations, and **solvency**, i.e., its ability to pay all current and long-term debts as they come due. The balance sheet also shows the composition of assets and liabilities, the relative proportions of debt and equity financing, and how much of a firm's earnings have been retained in the business. Collectively, this information can be used by external parties to help assess the financial status of a firm at a particular date.

Following the traditional accounting model, the balance sheet is a historical report presenting the cumulative results of all past transactions of a business measured in terms of historical costs. It is an expression of the basic accounting equation: **Assets = Liabilities + Owners' Equity**. The balance sheet shows both the character and the amount of the assets, liabilities, and owners' equity.

Balance sheets, especially when compared over time and with additional data, provide a great deal of useful information to those interested in analyzing the financial well-being of a company. Specific relationships, such as a company's current ratio, its debt to equity ratio, and its rate of return on investment can be highlighted.[2] Future commitments, favorable and unfavorable trends, problem areas in terms of collection patterns, and the relative equity positions of creditors and owners can also be analyzed, all of which assist in evaluating the financial position of a company.

---

[2] These ratios and relationships are discussed in detail in Chapter 26.

Of special interest to both creditors and investors in analyzing the balance sheet is the company's **financial flexibility**. For example, how well could the company weather unexpected losses in assets, damage claims arising from its operations, or significant reductions in sales? Often the negative impact on net assets from such events is so material that the existence of the company is threatened unless it can enter the capital markets for additional funds from either creditors or investors. The problem is that obtaining funds becomes difficult once a company is in trouble. Terms for borrowing, including high interest rates, may be so unfavorable that they create further difficulty for a company. Additional stock issues may only sell at decreased prices, and thus dilute the equity of existing shareholders.

Even large companies are not immune to financial crisis. The names of prominent companies that have had significant shocks to their balance sheets in recent years include Chrysler Corporation, Manville Corporation, and Union Carbide. In the case of Chrysler Corporation, the U.S. Government had to guarantee a sizeable loan in order for the company to be able to continue operations. The loan saved the company and enabled it to once again become solvent. Manville and Union Carbide were both subjected to heavy litigation claims that drained their capital, and in the case of Manville, resulted in a bankruptcy and reorganization.

ELEMENTS OF THE BALANCE SHEET

The three elements found on the balance sheet were defined in Chapter 2. These definitions, which were part of FASB Concepts Statement No. 6, are repeated below.[3]

Elements Related to Balance Sheet

Assets are probable future economic benefits obtained or controlled by a particular entity as a result of past transactions or events.

Liabilities are probable future sacrifices of economic benefits arising from present obligations of a particular entity to transfer assets or provide services to other entities in the future as a result of past transactions or events.

Equity or **net assets** is the residual interest in the assets of an entity that remains after deducting its liabilities. In a business enterprise, the equity is the ownership interest.

---

[3]*Statement of Financial Accounting Concepts No. 6,* "Elements of Financial Statements" (Stamford: Financial Accounting Standards Board, 1985), p. ix.

Assets include those costs that have not been matched with revenues in the past and are expected to provide economic benefits in the production of revenues in the future. Assets include both **monetary assets**, such as cash, certain marketable securities, and receivables, and **nonmonetary assets**—those costs, such as inventories, prepaid insurance, equipment, and patents, that are recognized as recoverable and hence properly assignable to revenues of future periods.

Liabilities measure the claims of creditors against entity resources. As indicated by the definition, the method for settlement of liabilities varies. A liability may call for settlement by cash payment or settlement through goods to be delivered or services to be performed.

Owners' equity measures the interest of the ownership group in the total resources of the enterprise. This interest arises from investment by owners, and is increased by net income and decreased by net losses and distributions to owners. An ownership interest does not call for settlement on a certain date; in the event of business dissolution, it represents a claim on assets only after creditors have been paid in full.

Classified Balance Sheets

Balance sheet items are generally classified in a manner that facilitates analysis and interpretation of financial data. Information of primary concern to all parties is the business unit's liquidity and solvency—its ability to meet current and long-term obligations. Accordingly, assets and liabilities are classified as (1) **current** or **short-term** items and (2) **noncurrent or long-term** items. When assets and liabilities are so classified, the difference between current assets and current liabilities may be determined. This is referred to as the company's **working capital**—the liquid buffer available in meeting financial demands and contingencies of the future.

The importance of an adequate working capital position cannot be minimized. A business may not be able to survive in the absence of a satisfactory relationship between current assets and current liabilities. Furthermore, its ability to prosper is largely determined by the composition of the current asset pool. There must be a proper balance between liquid assets in the form of cash and temporary investments, and receivables and inventories. Activities of the business center around these assets. Cash and temporary investments, representing immediate purchasing power, are used to meet current claims and purchasing, payroll, and expense requirements; receivables are the outgrowth of sales effort and provide cash in the course of operations; inventory is also a source of cash as well as the means of achieving a profit. Management, in setting policies with respect to selling, purchasing, financing, expanding, and the paying of dividends, must work within the limitations set by the company's working capital position.

Some writers have questioned the usefulness of the current/noncurrent distinction for all companies. For example, Loyd Heath argues that since any classification scheme is arbitrary, the classification between current and noncurrent should be abolished. Assets and liabilities could then be listed in the order of their liquidity without arbitrary subtotals.[4] Although there is some arbitrariness in the detailed classifications, the popularity of the current ratio (current assets divided by current liabilities) as a measure of liquidity among users suggests that the classification does meet the test of decision usefulness and should be retained.

Although there are no standard categories that must be used, the following general framework for a balance sheet is representative, and will be used in this text.

Assets

Current assets

Investments

Land, buildings, and equipment

Intangible assets

Other noncurrent assets

Liabilities

Current liabilities

Long-term debt

Long-term lease obligations

Deferred income taxes

Other noncurrent liabilities

Owners' Equity

Contributed capital

Retained earnings

Current Assets and Current Liabilities

Current assets include cash and resources that are reasonably expected to be converted into cash during the normal operating cycle of a business or within one year, whichever period is longer. As depicted on page 165, the **normal operating cycle** is the time required for cash to be converted to inventories, inventories into receivables, and receivables ultimately into

---

[4]Loyd Heath, "Is Working Capital Really Working?" *Journal of Accountancy* (August 1980), pp. 55-62.

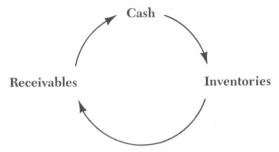

cash. When the operating cycle exceeds twelve months, for example, in the tobacco, distillery, and lumber industries, the longer period is used.

Some exceptions to the general definition of current assets should be noted. Cash that is restricted as to use, e.g., designated for the acquisition of noncurrent assets or segregated for the liquidation of noncurrent debts, should not be included in current assets. Also, in classifying assets not related to the operating cycle, a one-year period is always used as the basis for current classification. For example, a note receivable due in 15 months that arose from the sale of land previously held for investment would be classified as noncurrent even if the normal operating cycle exceeds 15 months.

In addition to cash, receivables, and inventories, current assets typically include such resources as prepaid expenses and marketable securities. Prepayments of such items as insurance and rent are not current assets in the sense that they will be converted into cash but on the basis that, if they had not been prepaid, the use of cash or other current assets during the operating cycle period would have been required. Long-term prepayments should be reported as noncurrent assets and charged to the operations of several years. If securities of companies, whether marketable or not, are acquired for purposes of control rather than conversion back to cash during the normal operating cycle, they should not be designated as current assets. Other items that might be converted into cash, but are not expected to be converted and therefore should not be classified as current assets, include the cash surrender value of life insurance policies, land, and depreciable assets.

Current assets are normally listed on the balance sheet in the order of their liquidity. These assets, with the exception of marketable securities and inventories, are usually reported at their estimated realizable values. Thus, current receivable balances are reduced by allowances for estimated uncollectible accounts. Marketable equity securities should be reported at the lower of aggregate cost or market.[5] Inventories may be reported at cost or on the basis of "cost or market, whichever is lower."

The current asset section of the balance sheet for Metropolitan, Inc., a hypothetical company, is illustrated below.

Current assets:	
Cash..	$ 52,650
Marketable securities (reported at cost;	
market value, $72,600)....................................	67,350
Receivables (net of allowance for doubtful accounts)............	363,700
Inventories (reported at fifo cost or market,	
whichever is lower)......................................	436,100
Prepaid expenses and other...............................	32,900
Total current assets	$952,700

Current liabilities are those obligations that are reasonably expected to be paid using current assets or by creating other current liabilities. Generally, if a liability is reasonably expected to be paid within 12 months, it is probably classified as current. As with receivables, payables arising from the normal operating activities may be classified as current even if they are not to be paid within 12 months, but within the operating cycle if it exceeds 12 months. Items commonly included as current liabilities include:

1. Short-term borrowings
2. Accounts payable
3. Accrued salaries and wages
4. Accrued rental expense
5. Accrued interest expense
6. Accrued taxes
7. Current portion of long-term obligations

The current liability classification, however, generally does not include the following items, since these do not require the use of resources classified as current.

1. Short-term obligations expected to be refinanced.[6]
2. Debts to be liquidated from funds that have been accumulated and are reported as noncurrent assets.
3. Loans on life insurance policies made with the intent that these will not be paid but will be liquidated by deduction from the proceeds of the policies upon their maturity or cancellation.

---

[5]*Statement of Financial Accounting Standards No. 12*, "Accounting for Certain Marketable Securities" (Stamford: Financial Accounting Standards Board, 1975), par. 8.

[6]*Statement of Financial Accounting Standards No. 6*, "Classification of Short-Term Obligations Expected to be Refinanced" (Stamford: Financial Accounting Standards Board, 1975).

4. Obligations for advance collections that involve long-term deferment of the delivery of goods or services.[7]

With respect to short-term obligations that normally would come due within the operating cycle but are expected to be refinanced, i.e., discharged by means of the issuance of new obligations in their place, the FASB has concluded that such obligations should be excluded from current liabilities if the following conditions are met: (1) the intent of the company is to refinance the obligations on a long-term basis, and (2) the company's intent is supported by an ability to consummate the refinancing as evidenced by a post-balance-sheet-date issuance of long-term obligations or equity securities or an explicit financing agreement.[8] In effect, the FASB is recognizing that certain short-term obligations will not require the use of working capital during a period even though they are scheduled to mature during that period. Thus, they should not be classified as current liabilities.

Classification problems can arise when an obligation is **callable** by a creditor because it is difficult to determine exactly when the obligation will be paid. A callable instrument is one that is either (1) payable on demand (has no specified due date), or (2) has a specified due date, but is callable if the debtor violates the provisions of the debt agreement. Any obligation that is due on demand or will become due on demand within one year from the balance sheet date (or operating cycle if longer) should be classified as current.[9]

In addition, a long-term obligation should be classified as current if it is callable at the balance sheet date because the debtor is in violation of a contract provision. For example, some instruments have a specific clause identifying conditions which can cause the debt to be immediately callable, e.g. failure to earn a certain return on assets or failure to make an interest payment. These clauses are referred to as **objective acceleration clauses**. The FASB has stated that if the conditions that trigger the demand have occurred, the debt should be classified as a current debt unless (1) the creditor has waived the right to demand payment for more than one year (or normal operating cycle if longer) from the balance sheet date, or (2) the debtor has cured the deficiency after the balance sheet date but before the

---

[7]*Accounting Research and Terminology Bulletins—Final Edition, No. 43*, "Restatement and Revision of Accounting Research Bulletins" (New York: American Institute of Certified Public Accountants, 1961), Chapter 3, par. 8 and footnotes 2 and 3.

[8]*Statement of Financial Accounting Standards No. 6*, par. 9–11.

[9]*Statement of Financial Accounting Standards No. 78*, "Classification of Obligations That Are Callable by the Creditor" (Stamford: Financial Accounting Standards Board, 1983), par. 5.

statements are issued, and the debt is not callable for a period that extends beyond the debtor's normal operating cycle.[10]

In some cases, the contract does not specifically identify the circumstances under which a payment will be accelerated, but it does indicate some general conditions that permit the lender to unilaterally accelerate the due date. This type of provision is known as a **subjective acceleration clause** because, although the clause may specify certain conditions under which the obligation may be called, the violation of the conditions cannot be objectively determined. The FASB has recommended that if the invoking of the clause is deemed probable, the liability should be classified as a current liability. If the assessment of probability is reasonably possible, only a footnote disclosure is necessary.[11]

The current liability section of the balance sheet for Metropolitan, Inc. is illustrated below:

Current liabilities:

Notes payable	$ 75,000
Accounts payable	312,700
Accrued expenses	86,300
Current portion of long-term debt	62,000
Other current liabilities	28,600
Total current liabilities	$564,600

Noncurrent Assets and Noncurrent Liabilities

Assets and liabilities not qualifying for presentation under the current headings are classified under a number of noncurrent headings. Noncurrent assets may be listed under separate headings, such as "Investments," "Land, buildings, and equipment," "Intangible assets," and "Other long-term assets." Noncurrent liabilities are generally listed under separate headings, such as "Long-term debt," "Deferred income taxes," and "Other noncurrent liabilities."

Investments. Investments held for such long-term purposes as regular income, appreciation, or ownership control are reported under the heading "Investments." Examples of items properly reported under this heading are stocks, bonds, and mortgage holdings; securities of affiliated companies and advances to such companies; sinking fund assets consisting of cash and securities held for the redemption of bonds or stocks, the replacement of buildings, or the payment of pensions; land held for investment purposes;

---

[10]*Ibid.*

[11]*FASB Technical Bulletin 79–3*, "Subjective Acceleration Clauses in Long-Term Debt Agreements" (New York: American Institute of Certified Public Accountants, December, 1979), par. .003.

the cash surrender value of life insurance; and other miscellaneous investments not used directly in the operations of the business. Although many long-term investments are reported at cost, there are modifications to the valuation of some investments that will be discussed in later chapters.

Land, Buildings, and Equipment. Properties of a tangible and relatively permanent character that are used in the normal business operations are reported under "Land, buildings, and equipment" or other appropriate headings, such as property and equipment. Land, buildings, machinery, tools, furniture, fixtures, and vehicles are included under this heading. Most tangible properties except land are normally reported at cost less accumulated depreciation.

Intangible Assets. The long-term rights and privileges of a nonphysical nature acquired for use in business operations are often reported under the heading "Intangible assets." Included in this class are such items as goodwill, patents, trademarks, franchises, copyrights, formulas, leaseholds, and organization costs. Intangible assets are normally reported at cost less amounts previously amortized.

Other Noncurrent Assets. Those noncurrent assets not suitably reported under any of the previous classifications may be listed under the general heading "Other noncurrent assets" or may be listed separately under special descriptive headings. Such assets include, for example, long-term advances to officers and deposits made with taxing authorities and utility companies.

Prepayments for services or benefits to be received over a number of periods are properly regarded as noncurrent. Among these are such items as plant rearrangement costs and developmental and improvement costs. These long-term prepayments are frequently reported under a "Deferred costs" or "Deferred charges" heading. However, objection can be raised to a deferred costs category since this designation could be applied to all costs assignable to future periods including inventories, buildings and equipment, and intangible assets. The deferred costs heading may be avoided by reporting long-term prepayments within the other noncurrent assets section or under separate descriptive headings.

A debit balance in the deferred income tax account may be shown under "Other noncurrent assets" or may be reported separately. Income tax is considered to be prepaid when paid on a computed taxable income that is more than the income reported on the financial statements. The difference between taxable income and income reported from operations may be a temporary timing difference that will be offset in the future. It may be caused by recognizing a taxable item of revenue or expense in one accounting period for tax purposes and in a different accounting period for purposes of reporting operating income. Under these circumstances, matching of income tax expense with revenue requires that the tax paid on taxable income in excess of the book income be deferred and recognized as an addition to tax expense in the period when the income is ultimately recognized on the books. Most of the time, the account Deferred Income Taxes has a credit balance and, as indicated on page 172, is properly shown as a noncurrent liability. Accounting for income tax is considered in detail in Chapter 20.

The noncurrent assets section of the balance sheet for Metropolitan, Inc. is illustrated below:

Noncurrent assets:	
Investments	$ 128,000
Land	76,300
Buildings and equipment (net of accumulated	
depreciation of $228,600)	732,900
Intangible assets...	165,000
Other noncurrent assets	37,800
Total noncurrent assets..................................	$1,140,000

Long-Term Debt. Long-term notes, bonds, mortgages, and similar obligations not requiring the use of current funds for their retirement are generally reported on the balance sheet under the heading "Long-term debt."

When an amount borrowed is not the same as the amount ultimately required in settlement of the debt, and the debt is stated in the accounts at its maturity amount, a debt discount or premium is reported. The discount or premium should be related to the debt item; a discount, then, should be subtracted from the amount reported for the debt, and a premium should be added to the amount reported for the debt. The debt is thus reported at its present value as measured by the proceeds from its issuance.

To illustrate, bond premiums and discounts could be reported as follows:

	Premium	Discount
Bonds Payable......................................	$10,000,000	$10,000,000
Plus Premium	550,000	
Less Discount......................................		600,000
Net obligation	$10,550,000	$ 9,400,000

In many cases, only the net obligation is reported.

Amortization of the discount or premium brings the obligation to the maturity amount by the end of its normal term. When a note, a bond issue, or a mortgage formerly classified as a long-term obligation becomes payable within a year, it should be reclassified and presented as a current liability, except when the obligation is to be refinanced, as discussed earlier, or is to be paid out of a sinking fund.

Long-Term Lease Obligations. Some leases of land, buildings, and equipment are financially structured so that they are in substance a debt-financed purchase. The FASB has established criteria to determine which leases are in effect purchases, or capital leases, rather than ordinary operating leases. The present value of the future minimum lease payments is recorded as a long-term liability. That portion of the present value due within the next year, or normal operating cycle, whichever is longer, is classified as a current liability. As capital leases have become more common, this category appears more often on company balance sheets. The 1985 *Accounting Trends and Techniques* reports that 504 of the 600 companies surveyed reported capital lease obligations on the balance sheet.

Deferred Income Taxes. The credit balance in this account indicates that book income has exceeded taxable income due to timing differences in recognizing revenues and expenses. The most common timing difference occurs in computing depreciation expense for book and tax purposes. Generally, the tax regulations permit a faster write-off than is allowable for financial reporting purposes.

Almost all major companies include this category in their statements. Over the past twenty years, the amounts included in this category have greatly expanded. As companies grow in size, the timing differences also grow. This liability differs from most of the other liabilities in that there is no specific due date for the balance. Only if a company contracts in size, or is liquidated will this deferral require a cash outlay. Because of this, some analysts disregard the balance in this account when analyzing the company's debt position.

Other Noncurrent Liabilities. Those noncurrent liabilities not suitably reported under the separate headings may be listed under this general heading or may be listed separately under special descriptive headings. Such liabilities could include long-term obligations to company officers or affiliated companies, matured but unclaimed bond principal and interest obligations, long-term liabilities under pension plans, and unearned revenues.

Contingent Liabilities. Past activities or circumstances may give rise to possible future liabilities, although legal obligations do not exist on the date of the balance sheet. These possible claims are known as **contingent liabilities**. They are potential obligations involving uncertainty as to possible losses. As future events occur or fail to occur, this uncertainty will be resolved. Thus, a contingent liability is distinguishable from an **estimated liability**. The latter is a definite obligation with only the amount of the obligation in question and subject to estimation at the balance sheet date. There may not be any doubt as to the amount of a contingent liability, for example, a pending lawsuit, but there is considerable uncertainty as to whether the obligation will actually materialize.

In the past, contingent liabilities were not recorded in the accounts nor presented on the balance sheet. When they were disclosed, it was in the notes to the financial statements. As indicated in Chapter 1, since the issuance of FASB Statement No. 5, if a future payment is considered probable, the liability should be recorded by a debit to a loss account and a credit to a liability account.[12] Otherwise, the contingent nature of the loss may be disclosed in a note to the financial statements as discussed on page 181. The noncurrent liabilities section of a balance sheet is illustrated below.

Noncurrent liabilities:
 Long-term debt:
  Notes payable . . . . $ 75,000
  Bonds payable   365,000
 Long-term lease obligations   135,000
 Deferred income taxes   126,700
 Other noncurrent liabilities   72,500
  Total noncurrent liabilities $774,200

Owners' Equity

The method of reporting the owners' equity varies with the form of the business unit. Business units are typically divided into three categories: (1) **proprietorships**, (2) **partnerships**, and (3) **corporations**. In the case of a proprietorship, the owner's equity in assets is reported by means of a single capital account. The balance in this account is the cumulative result of the owner's investments and withdrawals as well as past earnings and losses. In a partnership, capital accounts are established for each partner. Capital account balances summarize the investments and withdrawals and shares of past earnings and losses of each partner, and thus measure the partners' individual equities in the partnership assets.

In a corporation, the difference between assets and liabilities is referred to as **owners' equity**, **shareholders' equity**, or simply, **capital**. In presenting the owners' equity on the balance sheet, a distinction is made between the equity originating from the stockholders' investments, referred to as

---

[12]*Statement of Financial Accounting Standards No. 5,* "Accounting for Contingencies" (Stamford: Financial Accounting Standards Board, 1975), par. 8–13.

contributed capital or **paid-in capital**, and the equity originating from earnings, referred to as **retained earnings**.

The relationship and distinction between the amount of capital contributed or paid in by the owners of the corporation relative to the amount the company has earned and retained in the business is a significant one. Such disclosure helps creditors and investors assess the long-term ability of a company to internally finance its own operations. If the contributed capital of a corporation is large relative to the total owners' equity, it means the corporation has been financed primarily from external sources, usually from the sale of stock to investors. If the earned capital of a corporation is large relative to the total owners' equity, it means the company has been profitable in the past and has retained those earnings in the business to help finance its activities. This distinction between earned and contributed capital is not as important for a proprietorship or partnership because the owners of those types of businesses generally are also involved in their management and therefore are aware of how the company activities are being financed.

Contributed Capital. Contributed or paid-in capital is generally reported in two parts: (1) **capital stock** representing that portion of the contribution by stockholders assignable to the shares of stock issued; (2) **additional paid-in capital** representing investments by stockholders in excess of the amounts assignable to capital stock as well as invested capital from other sources.

Capital stock outstanding having a par value is shown on the balance sheet at par. Capital stock having no par value is stated at the amount received on its original sale or at some other value as stipulated by law or as assigned by action of the board of directors of the corporation. When more than a single class of stock has been issued and is outstanding, the stock of each class is reported separately. **Treasury stock**, which is stock issued but subsequently reacquired by the corporation and not retired or canceled, is subtracted from the total stock issued or from the sum of contributed capital and retained earnings balances. The capital stock balance is viewed as the **legal capital** or **permanent capital** of the corporation.

The amount received in excess of par value on the sale of par-value stock or the amount received in excess of the value assigned to no-par stock is recognized as additional paid-in capital. Additional paid-in capital may also arise from transactions other than the sale of stock, such as from the acquisition of property as a result of a donation or from the sale of treasury stock at more than cost. The additional paid-in capital balances are normally added to capital stock so the full amount of the contributed capital may be reported. Contributed capital is discussed in detail in Chapter 16.

Retained Earnings. The amount of undistributed earnings of past periods is reported as **retained earnings**. The total amount thus shown will probably not represent cash available for payment as dividends since past years' earnings will usually already have been reinvested in other assets. An excess of dividends and losses over earnings results in a negative retained earnings balance called a **deficit**. The balance of retained earnings is added to the contributed capital total in summarizing the stockholders' equity; a deficit is subtracted.

Portions of retained earnings are sometimes reported as restricted and unavailable as a basis for dividends. Restricted earnings may be designated as *appropriations*. Appropriations are sometimes made for such purposes as sinking funds, plant expansion, loss contingencies, and the reacquisition of capital stock. Often such appropriations are disclosed in a note rather than in the accounts. When appropriations have been made in the accounts, retained earnings on the balance sheet consists of an amount designated as appropriated and a balance designated as *unappropriated* or *free*. The term "reserve" should not generally be used to designate appropriations. Retained earnings is fully discussed in Chapter 17.

The Owners' Equity section of the balance sheet of Metropolitan, Inc. is illustrated as follows:

Contributed capital:
Preferred stock, $50 par, 20,000 shares authorized, 2,500 shares issued and outstanding	$125,000
Common stock, $5 par, 100,000 shares authorized, 60,000 shares issued and outstanding	300,000
Additional paid-in capital	120,000
Retained earnings	308,900
Total owners' equity	$853,900

Offsets on the Balance Sheet

As illustrated in the preceding discussion, a number of balance sheet items are frequently reported at gross amounts calling for the recognition of offset balances in arriving at proper valuations. Such offset balances are found in asset, liability, and owners' equity categories. In the case of assets, for example, an allowance for doubtful accounts is subtracted from the sum of the customers' accounts in reporting the net amount estimated as collectible; accumulated depreciation is subtracted from the related buildings and equipment balances in reporting the costs of the assets still assignable to future revenues. In the case of liabilities, reacquired bonds or *treasury* bonds, are subtracted from bonds issued in reporting the amount of bonds outstanding; a bond discount is subtracted from the face value of bonds outstanding in reporting the net amount of the debt. In the stockholders' equity section of the balance sheet, treasury stock is deducted in reporting total stockholders' equity.

The types of offsets described above, utilizing contra accounts, are required for proper reporting of particular balance sheet items. Offsets are improper, however, if applied to different asset and liability balances or to asset and owners' equity balances even when there is some relationship between the items. For example, a company may accumulate cash in a special fund to discharge certain tax liabilities; but as long as control of the cash is retained and the liabilities are still outstanding, the company should continue to report both the asset and the liabilities separately. Or a company may accumulate cash in a special fund for the redemption of preferred stock outstanding; but until the cash is applied to the reacquisition of the stock, the company must continue to report the asset as well as the owners' equity item. A company may have made advances to certain salespersons while at the same time reporting accrued amounts payable to others; but a net figure cannot be justified here, just as a net figure cannot be justified for the offset of trade receivables against trade payables.

Form of the Balance Sheet

The form of the balance sheet presentation varies in practice. Its form may be influenced by the nature and size of the business, by the character of the business properties, by requirements set by regulatory bodies, or by display preferences in presenting key relationships. The balance sheet is prepared in one of two basic forms: (1) the **account form**, with assets being reported on the left-hand side and liabilities and owners' equity on the right-hand side, or (2) the **report form**, with assets, liabilities, and owners' equity sections appearing in vertical arrangement.[13]

The order of asset and liability classifications may vary, but most businesses emphasize working capital position and liquidity, with assets and liabilities presented in the order of their liquidity. An exception to this order is generally found in the Land, Buildings, and Equipment section where the more permanent assets with longer useful lives are listed first. The Balance Sheet for RCA Company reproduced on pages 176 and 177 illustrates the account form reported in the order of liquidity. The balance sheet of General Mills, Inc., reproduced in Appendix A, is an example of the report form. Compare these actual company financial statements and their categories with the Metropolitan, Inc. illustrations included in this

---

[13]These two forms have been equally popular, however, the report form has been increasing in popularity. The *Accounting Trends & Techniques* reported that in 1984, 291 of 600 companies used the account form and 306 the report form. p. 105.

RCA
Consolidated Financial Position

	(In millions)	
December 31	**1984**	1983*

Assets

Current assets

Cash and equivalents	$ 175.3	$ 97.5
Receivables, less allowance for doubtful accounts of $52.7 million (1983—$47.8)	1,650.9	1,287.9
Inventories (Note 4)	758.8	645.9
Rental automobiles of Hertz, at cost less accumulated depreciation of $175.0 million (1983—$133.7)	1,044.4	990.6
Television program costs	399.7	393.4
Prepaid expenses and other	178.4	141.5
Total current assets	4,207.5	3,556.8

Other revenue-earning equipment of Hertz, at cost less accumulated depreciation of $152.0 million (1983—$174.9)	328.9	376.5

Plant and equipment, at cost

Land and buildings	785.5	727.3
Machinery and equipment	2,797.1	2,550.7
	3,582.6	3,278.0
Less accumulated depreciation	1,553.8	1,415.6
	2,028.8	1,862.4

Long-term receivables	84.5	81.4
Investments (Note 3)	1,199.4	1,405.0
Other assets	371.6	366.4
Total assets	$8,220.7	$7,648.5

*Restated, see Note 2.
The accompanying notes are an integral part of this statement.

chapter. The categories used by individual companies vary widely; however, the basic format and structure remain the same.

In some industries the investment in plant assets is so significant that they are placed first on the balance sheet. Also, the equity capital and long-term debt obtained to finance plant assets are listed before current liabilities. The utility industry is a good example of this situation. A balance sheet for the Utah Power and Light Company is illustrated on page 178.

Balance sheets are generally presented in comparative form. With comparative reports for two or more dates, information is made available concerning the nature and trend of financial changes taking place within the periods between balance sheet dates. Currently, a minimum of two years

	(In millions)	
	1984	1983*

Liabilities and Shareholders' Equity

Current liabilities

Notes payable, except Hertz (Note 7)	$ 394.9	$ 343.5
Notes payable of Hertz (Note 8)	299.1	260.2
Accounts payable	747.2	728.5
Accrued compensation	298.6	274.3
Accrued royalties and program costs	274.4	305.9
Other accrued liabilities	880.3	862.7
Income taxes (Note 6)	210.6	143.8
Total current liabilities	3,105.1	2,918.9
Long-term debt, except Hertz (Note 7)	869.2	982.5
Long-term debt of Hertz (Note 8)	727.6	748.5
Other liabilities (Note 12)	394.5	236.8
Deferred income taxes (Note 6)	472.0	297.7
Preference stock subject to mandatory redemption, no par, at stated value net of applicable unamortized discount—authorized: 25,000,000 shares (Note 9)		
$3.65 cumulative preference stock	342.3	339.6
$2.125 cumulative convertible preference stock	220.0	219.0
	562.3	558.6
Shareholders' equity (Note 10)		
Preferred stock, no par, at stated value		
$3.50 cumulative first preferred stock	2.1	2.1
Cumulative series first preferred stock—authorized: 2,000,000 shares:		
$4 convertible first preferred stock	7.6	7.7
Common stock, no par, at stated value—authorized: 125,000,000 shares;		
issued—82,084,018 shares (1983—81,800,067)	54.7	54.5
Additional paid-in capital	598.3	591.5
Retained earnings (Note 7)	1,495.1	1,306.2
Translation adjustment (Note 14)	(67.8)	(56.5)
Total shareholder's equity	2,090.0	1,905.5
Total liabilities and shareholders' equity	$8,220.7	$7,648.5

of balance sheets and three years of income statements and funds statements are required by the SEC to be included in the annual report to shareholders.

Additional Disclosure to the Balance Sheet

Regardless of which form of balance sheet is used, the basic statement does not provide all the information desired by users. Among other things, creditors and investors need to know what methods of accounting were used by the company to arrive at the balances in the accounts. The users often feel they need more information than just account titles and amounts. Sometimes the additional information desired is descriptive and is reported in narrative form. In other cases additional numerical data are reported.

Utah Power & Light Company and Subsidiary
Consolidated Balance Sheets (in thousands of dollars)

December 31,	1984
ASSETS	
Utility Plant (Notes 2, 3, 4 and 11):	
Electric	$3,106,690
Steam heating	1,116
Under construction	61,616
Total	3,169,422
Less accumulated depreciation	608,164
Utility plant—net	2,561,258
Nonutility Property and Investments—at cost:	
Pollution control financing proceeds on deposit with trustee (Note 11)	7,060
Nonutility property and other investments	21,855
Total nonutility property and investments	28,915
Current Assets:	
Cash—including temporary investments (Note 15)	31,276
Receivables—principally customers	107,590
Unbilled revenues (Note 7)	41,686
Fuel—at average cost	28,836
Materials and supplies—utility and coal mine, at average cost	64,092
Prepayments	9,488
Total current assets	282,968
Deferred Debits	26,319
Total	$2,899,460

CAPITALIZATION AND LIABILITIES	
Capital Paid-in and Retained Earnings:	
Cumulative preferred stock—outstanding: 9,000,000 shares (Schedule 1)	$ 225,000
Common stock—outstanding: 1984—53,799,747 shares;	
1983—52,268,200 shares (Note 9)	344,319
Capital paid in excess of par value (Note 9)	483,871
Retained earnings (Notes 10 and 12)	162,667
Total capital paid-in and retained earnings	1,215,857
Long-Term Debt—Excluding currently maturing long-term debt (Note 11) (Schedule 2)	1,083,070
Current Liabilities:	
Currently maturing long-term debt (Schedule 2)	15,000
Notes payable (Note 15)	—
Accounts payable	88,955
Dividends declared	36,438
Taxes accrued	32,309
Interest accrued	27,111
Other—principally tax collections payable	14,199
Total current liabilities	214,012
Deferred Credits:	
Accumulated investment tax credits (Note 5)	161,163
Accumulated deferred income taxes (Note 5)	208,651
Other—principally customer advances	15,153
Total deferred credits	384,967
Reserves	1,554
Commitments and Contingent Liabilities (Note 13)	
Total	$2,899,460

See Notes to Financial Statements

There are at least three principal ways this additional disclosure is provided in the basic financial statements:

1. as parenthetical notations in the body of the statement,
2. as notes to the basic financial statements, and
3. in separate schedules furnished by management that supplement the basic financial statements.

It is generally felt that readers of financial statements are more likely to see the additional information if it is included on the face of the financial statement in a parenthetical notation. However, if the data are lengthy or complex, it is generally better to provide the detail in notes recognized as being an integral part of the statements themselves. Unless specifically excluded, notes are covered by the auditor's opinion. In some instances, the notes include detailed schedules that provide additional information to the serious user. In the examples shown throughout this chapter, several parenthetical notations are included in the illustrations, e.g., in current assets on page 166 there are parenthetical comments concerning valuation. In each case, the same data could have been disclosed in notes.

The following types of notes are typically included by management as support to the basic financial statements.

1. Summary of significant accounting policies.
2. Additional information (both numerical and descriptive) to support summary totals found on the financial statements, usually the balance sheet. This is the most common type of note used.
3. Information about items that are not reported on the basic statements because the items fail to meet the recognition criteria, but are still considered to be significant to users in their decision making.
4. Supplementary information required by the FASB or the SEC to fulfill the full-disclosure principle.

Each of these classifications is briefly discussed in the following paragraphs.

Summary of Significant Accounting Policies. GAAP requires that information about the accounting principles and policies followed in arriving at the amounts in the financial statements be disclosed to the users. The Accounting Principles Board concluded in APB Opinion No. 22:

> . . . When financial statements are issued purporting to present fairly financial position, changes in financial position, and results of operations in accordance with generally accepted accounting principles, a description of all significant accounting policies of the reporting entity should be included as an integral part of the financial statements.[14]

---

[14]*Opinions of the Accounting Principles Board, No. 22,* "Disclosure of Accounting Policies" (New York: American Institute of Certified Public Accountants, 1972), par. 8.

The Board further stated:

> . . . In general, the disclosure should encompass important judgments as to appropriateness of principles relating to recognition of revenue and allocation of asset costs to current and future periods; in particular, it should encompass those accounting principles and methods that involve any of the following: (a) A selection from existing acceptable alternatives; (b) Principles and methods peculiar to the industry in which the reporting entity operates, even if such principles and methods are predominantly followed in that industry; (c) Unusual or innovative applications of generally accepted accounting principles (and, as applicable, of principles and methods peculiar to the industry in which the reporting entity operates).[15]

 *usually footnote #1 required*

Examples of disclosures of accounting policies required by this opinion would include, among others, those relating to depreciation methods, amortization of intangible assets, inventory pricing methods, the recognition of profit on long-term construction-type contracts, and the recognition of revenue from leasing operations.[16]

The exact format for reporting the summary of accounting policies was not specified by the APB. However, the Board recommended such disclosure be included as the initial note or as a separate summary preceding the notes to the financial statements. The summary of significant accounting policies for General Mills, Inc. is presented in Appendix A.

Additional Information to Support Summary Totals. In order to prepare a balance sheet that is brief enough to be understandable but complete enough to meet the needs of users, notes are sometimes added that provide either quantitative or narrative information to support the statement amounts. The General Mills, Inc. notes in Appendix A include a number of examples of this type of note, e.g., Note Seven, Short Term Borrowing; Note Eight, Long-Term Debt; and Note Thirteen, Income Taxes, all provide additional numerical information to support the statement totals. Much of this detail is provided in response to specific disclosure requirements of either the SEC or the FASB. The specific format for the schedules is generally left to management's discretion. Some of the notes that support amounts in the financial statements are primarily descriptive in nature. Examples of this type in the General Mills statements include Note Three, Redeployment Program; Note Eleven, Employees' Retirement Plans; and Note Twelve, Profit-Sharing Plans.

Information about Items Not Included in Financial Statements. As discussed in Chapter 2, items included in the financial statements must meet

---

[15]*Ibid.*, par. 12.
[16]*Ibid.*, par. 13.

certain recognition criteria. Even though an item might not meet the criteria for recognition in the statements, information concerning the item might be relevant to the users. Gain and loss contingencies are good examples of this type of item. **Gain contingencies** relate to possible claims the company has to receive assets, but whose existence is too uncertain to recognize, e.g., a possible favorable court settlement in a lawsuit. **Loss contingencies** relate to possible claims against the company that might require an outflow of assets. In Statement No. 5, the FASB indicated that if the incurrence of a loss is "reasonably possible," the contingency should be disclosed in the notes to the financial statements. The information provided should include as much data as possible to assist the user in evaluating the risk of the loss contingency.[17]

Supplementary Information. The FASB and SEC both require supplementary information that must be reported in separate schedules. For example, the FASB requires the disclosure of quarterly information for certain companies. While the information in these notes is important to the users, it may not be covered by the auditors' opinion. A note that is not covered by the opinion should be clearly marked "unaudited." Examples of such notes in General Mills' statements include Note 16, a schedule of quarterly data, and Note 17, an extensive schedule reporting inflation accounting information.

Subsequent Events. Although a balance sheet is prepared as of a given date, it is usually several weeks and sometimes even months after that date before the financial statements are issued and made available to external users. During this time, the accounts are analyzed, adjusting entries are prepared, and for many companies, an independent audit is completed. Events may take place during this "subsequent period" that have an impact upon the balance sheet and the other basic financial statements for the preceding year. Some of these events may even affect the amounts reported in the statements. These events are referred to in the accounting literature as **subsequent events** or **post-balance-sheet events**.

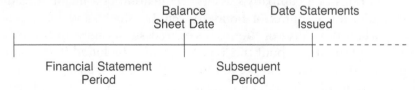

---

[17]*Statement of Financial Accounting Standards No. 5.* Further discussion of loss contingencies and disclosure examples are presented in Chapter 14.

There are two different types of subsequent events that require consideration by management and evaluation by the independent auditor:[18]

1. Those that affect the amounts to be reported in one or more of the financial statements for the preceding accounting period.
2. Those that do not affect the amounts in the financial statements for the preceding accounting period, but that should be reported in the notes to these financial statements.

The first type of subsequent event usually provides additional information that affects the amounts included in the financial statements. The reported amounts in several accounts, such as Allowance for Doubtful Accounts, Warranty Liability, and Income Taxes Payable, reflect estimates of the expected value. These estimates are based on information available as of a given date. If a subsequent event provides information that shows that the conditions existing as of the balance sheet date were different than those assumed when making the estimate, a change in the amount to be reported in the financial statements is required.

To illustrate this type of event, assume that a month after the balance sheet date it is learned that a major customer has filed for bankruptcy. This information was not known as of the balance sheet date, and only ordinary provisions were made in determining the Allowance for Doubtful Accounts. In all likelihood, the customer was already in financial difficulty at the balance sheet date, but it was not general knowledge. The filing of bankruptcy reveals that the conditions at the balance sheet date were different than those assumed in preparing the statements, and a further adjustment to both the balance sheet and income statement is indicated.

The second type of subsequent event does not reveal a difference in the conditions as of the balance sheet date, but involves an event that is considered so significant that its disclosure is highly relevant to readers of the financial statements. These events will usually affect the subsequent year's financial statements and thus may affect decisions currently being made by users. Examples of such events include a casualty that destroys material portions of a company's assets, acquisition of a major subsidiary, sale of significant amounts of bonds or capital stock, and losses on receivables when the cause of the loss occurred subsequent to the balance sheet date. Information about this type of event is included in the notes to the financial statements and serves to put the reader on notice that the predictive value of the statements may be affected by the subsequent event.

---

[18]*AICPA Professional Standards*, AU Section 560, "Subsequent Events" (Chicago: Commerce Clearing House, 1985, par. .02–.05.

There are, of course, many business events that occur during this subsequent period that are related only to the subsequent year and therefore have no impact on the preceding year's financial statements.

The overall objective of note disclosure is clarification of the information presented in the financial statements. Disclosure requirements are so extensive that they cannot be completely discussed in any single chapter. Specific requirements will be noted as appropriate throughout the text.

LIMITATIONS OF THE BALANCE SHEET

Notwithstanding its usefulness, the balance sheet has some serious limitations. External users often need to know a company's worth. The balance sheet, however, does not generally reflect the current values of a business. Instead, the entity's resources and obligations are usually shown at historical costs based on past transactions and events. The historical cost measurements represent market values existing at the dates the transactions or events occurred. However, when the prices of specific assets increase significantly after the acquisition date, as has certainly been the case recently in the United States, then the balance sheet numbers are not relevant for evaluating a company's current worth.

A related problem with the balance sheet is the instability of the dollar, the standard accounting measuring unit in the United States. Because of general price changes in the economy, the dollar does not maintain a constant purchasing power. Yet the historical costs of resources and equities shown on the balance sheet are not adjusted for changes in the purchasing power of the measuring unit. The result is a balance sheet that reflects assets, liabilities, and equities in terms of unequal purchasing power units. Some elements, for example, may be stated in terms of 1960 dollars and some in terms of 1987 dollars. The variations in purchasing power of the amounts reported in the balance sheet make comparisons among companies and even within a single company less meaningful.

An additional limitation of the balance sheet, also related to the need for comparability, is that all companies do not classify and report all like items similarly. For example, titles and account classifications vary; some companies provide considerably more detail than others; and some companies with apparently similar transactions report them differently. Such differences make comparisons difficult and diminish the potential value of balance sheet analysis.

The balance sheet may be considered deficient in another respect. Due primarily to measurement problems, some entity resources and obligations are not reported on the balance sheet. For example, the employees of a company may be one of its most valuable resources; yet, they are not shown on the balance sheet because their future service potentials are not measurable in monetary terms. Similarly, a company's potential liability for polluting the air would not normally be shown on its balance sheet. The assumptions of the traditional accounting model identified in Chapter 2, specifically the requirements of arm's-length transactions or events measurable in monetary terms, add to the objectivity of balance sheet disclosures but at the same time cause some information to be omitted that is likely to be relevant to certain users' decisions.

One author, reflecting on these limitations, wrote the following:

> The current balance sheet published by most corporations is a pathetic financial representation of a company's real resources and obligations. It is a dumping ground for dangling debit and credit entries and a listing of dollar values determined by different, often outmoded, accounting concepts. Users find that the face of such statements often excludes more relevant data than it includes.[19]

This dim view of the balance sheet is not shared by many accountants and users of financial statements. The balance sheet is an important statement for investors and creditors. While its limitations must be understood, it can still provide a user with valuable information for decisions.

The conceptual framework established by the FASB stresses the objective of usefulness of accounting information. During the past few years, the Board has considered several issues that directly affect the balance sheet, using the conceptual framework as a guide in the development of new standards. In some instances, the new standards have a direct impact on the amounts reported on the balance sheet. Notable examples include pensions, receivables with right of return, and interest capitalization. In other instances, the impact has been on required disclosure in notes, such as the requirement for some large companies to disclose segment data. These and other examples will be discussed throughout the text.

OVERVIEW OF THE STATEMENT OF CASH FLOWS

The general purpose financial statements include a statement that reflects the flow of funds of an enterprise over an accounting period. Although this statement is based on the same data as the balance sheet and the income statement, it helps decision makers answer questions that are not addressed directly by the other basic statements. For example, the funds statement helps the reader answer questions such as: How was the income

---

[19]David E. Hawkins, "Towards the New Balance Sheet," *Harvard Business Review,* November–December 1984, p. 156.

used by the company? Why were dividends not larger in view of increased earnings? How can the company distribute dividends in excess of current earnings? How was the plant expansion financed? Why is cash decreasing when earnings are positive and growing? How was bond indebtedness repaid even though the company suffered a substantial operating loss? Will the future funds flow be sufficient to meet the debt repayment provisions?

In 1971, the Accounting Principles Board issued Opinion No. 19 that required inclusion of a funds flow statement with the more traditional balance sheet and income statement. Historically, such a statement had been referred to as a **funds statement**. The APB, however, wanted the statement to be a more complete analysis of all changes in financial position of the entity, and thus recommended a broader title, **statement of changes in financial position**. As indicated earlier, the FASB has recommended replacing the general funds statement, with funds being defined in various ways, with a **statement of cash flows**.[20]

The cash flow statement is intended to provide a summary of cash inflows and outflows for a period of time. Major sources (inflows) and uses (outflows) of cash are shown in Exhibit 5–1. Sources of cash include

Exhibit 5–1   Major Inflows and Outflows of Cash

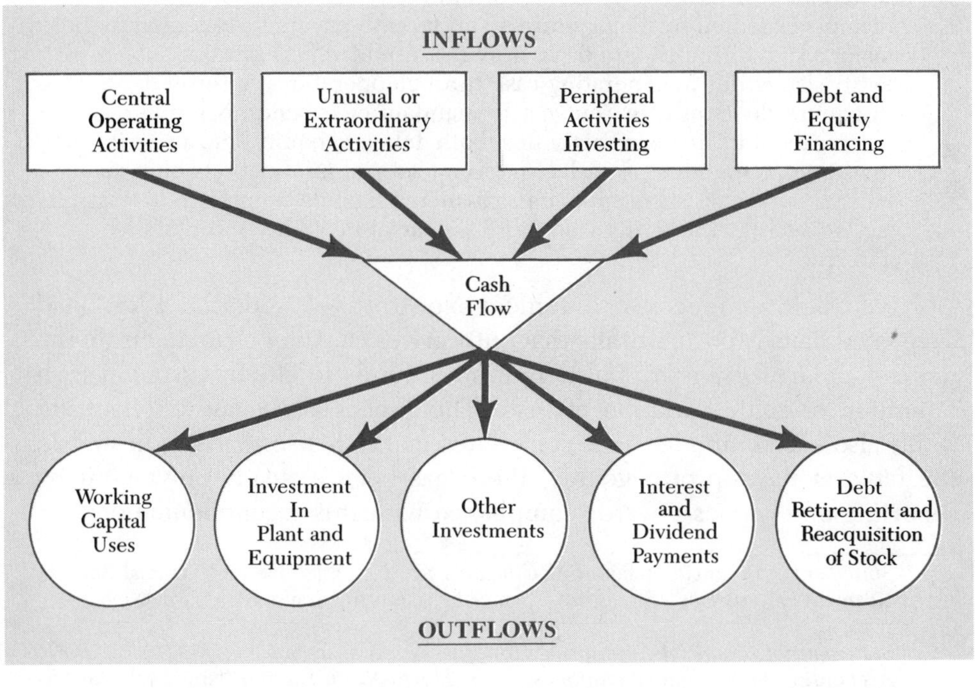

[20] *FASB Exposure Draft*, "Statement of Cash Flows" (Stamford: Financial Accounting Standards Board, 1986).

inflows from the central operating activities of a company, from peripheral activities, such as securities investments, from unusual or extraordinary activities, and from debt and equity financing. Uses of cash include outflows to sustain the central operations, to acquire investments, including plant and equipment, and to service debt and equity financing, including retirement of debt, payment of dividends, and reacquisition of stock.

Concept of Funds Flow

Historically the term "funds" has had many meanings in connection with the statement of changes in financial position. It has been defined as cash, cash plus temporary investments, cash plus receivables, or working capital, with the latter definition of funds being the most popular. However, in Concepts Statement No. 1, the FASB identified as an objective of financial reporting the providing of information that would help a user "assess the amounts, timing, and uncertainty of prospective net cash inflows to the related enterprise."[21] This emphasis upon information about cash flows led to the recommendation by the FASB in Concepts Statement No. 5 that the full set of financial statements (general purpose statements) should include a statement of "cash flows during the period."

> A statement of cash flows directly or indirectly reflects an entity's cash receipts classified by major sources and its cash payments classified by major uses during a period. It provides useful information about an entity's activities in generating cash through operations to repay debt, distribute dividends, or reinvest to maintain or expand operating capacity; about its financing activities, both debt and equity; and about its investing or spending of cash. Important uses of information about an entity's current cash receipts and payments include helping to assess factors such as the entity's liquidity, financial flexibility, profitability, and risk.[22]

Even before Concepts Statement No. 5 was issued, the FASB had suggested in its exposure drafts that enterprises consider changing from the more popular working capital definition of funds to either a straight cash definition or some variation of cash. The Financial Executives Institute (FEI) also recommended that companies make this shift. As indicated in the table at the top of page 187, there has been a steady movement by reporting enterprises towards compliance with this recommendation.[23]

---

[21] *Statement of Financial Accounting Concepts No. 1*, "Objectives of Financial Reporting by Business Enterprises" (Stamford: Financial Accounting Standards Board, November 1978), par 37.

[22] *Statement of Financial Accounting Concepts No. 5*, par. 52.

[23] *Accounting Trends and Techniques, 1985, Thirty-Ninth Edition* (New York: American Institute of Certified Public Accountants, 1985), p. 358.

Funds	1984	1983	1982	1981	1980
Working Capital	244	286	346	466	541
Cash..........................	356	314	264	134	59

To illustrate the special contribution made by the funds statement, consider the needs of a prospective creditor and the means for meeting these needs. An individual or institution asked to make a long-term loan to a company is concerned with the company's proposed use of the borrowed funds, the ability of the company to meet the periodic interest payments on the loan, and the ability of the company ultimately to repay the loan. Balance sheet analysis will provide answers to questions relative to the cash and near-cash items on hand, the working capital of the business—its amount and composition—present long-term indebtedness, and the implications on financial position if the loan is granted. Income statement analysis will provide answers to questions relative to the earnings of the company, the adequacy of earnings to cover interest charges, and the implications as to earnings and interest charges if the loan is granted. Funds statement analysis will indicate the resources available to the company in the past and the uses made of those resources as well as the financing and investing implications if the loan is granted. Finally, funds data can be used in estimating the resources that will be generated in the future and the ability of the company to meet the added indebtedness.

It is obvious that in meeting the requirements of the users of financial statements, funds information will be most useful if offered in comparative form for two or more years. An additional statement reporting forecasted or budgeted funds-flow data may prove of equal or even greater value. Although suggestions have been made that the latter information be made available to the external users of financial information, this practice has not yet been adopted.

Format of a Statement of Cash Flows

In recommending a statement of cash flows, the FASB has not specified an exact format to be used. The Board has suggested, however, that the cash inflows and outflows be classified and reported under three main categories: (1) **operating activities**, (2) **investing activities**, and (3) **financing activities**. The net result of these activities for the period is an increase or decrease in the cash balance. A format that is consistent with the recommendations of the FASB is illustrated on page 188. The General Mills, Inc. statement of funds reproduced in Appendix A, illustrates the application of a similar format.

The statement of cash flows is prepared by analyzing the changes that occurred in all accounts other than cash contained in the enterprise's balance sheet. The operating income of an enterprise is a principal source of cash. Because income as computed under a cash concept differs from that computed using the accrual system, adjustments must be made to the reported income figures to convert them to a cash basis. Usually additional information must be obtained from the accounting records to prepare this statement at the level of detail considered useful. The techniques of preparing and analyzing the statement of cash flows are discussed in detail in Chapter 24.

Staples Corporation
Statement of Cash Flows
For the Year Ended December 31, 1988

Cash flows from operating activities:		
Net income...	$25,000	
Adjustments:		
Depreciation......................................	10,000	
Amortization of patents and goodwill	10,600	
Increase in notes and accounts receivable........	(5,400)	
Decrease in inventory	4,600	
Decrease in notes and accounts payable	(2,500)	
Net cash flow provided (used) by operations		$42,300
Cash flows from investing activities:		
Proceeds from sale of land........................	$30,000	
Purchase of building and equipment................	(42,000)	
Investment in stock of subsidiary..................	(25,000)	
Acquisition of land with common stock..............	(20,000)	
Net cash flow provided (used) by investing activities ..		(57,000)
Cash flows from financing activities:		
Increase in long-term notes payable................	$30,000	
Issuance of common stock to acquire land...........	20,000	
Payment of dividends..............................	(15,000)	
Net cash flow provided (used) by financing activities ..		35,000
Net increase (decrease) in cash		$20,300

QUESTIONS

1. In what way is the balance sheet useful to decision makers?
2. What three elements are contained in the balance sheet?

3. What are the major classifications of (a) assets, (b) liabilities, and (c) owners' equity. Indicate the nature of the items reported within each major classification.

4. (a) Why is the distinction between current and noncurrent assets and liabilities considered to be important? (b) What arguments are there for not making a distinction?

5. What criteria are generally used (a) in classifying assets as current or noncurrent? (b) in classifying liabilities as current or noncurrent?

6. (a) What is a subjective acceleration clause? (b) An objective acceleration clause? (c) How do these clauses in debt instruments affect the classification of a liability?

7. Barker's Inc. reports the cash surrender value of life insurance on company officials as a current asset in view of its immediate convertibility into cash. Do you support this treatment? Explain.

8. Indicate under what circumstances each of the following can be considered noncurrent: (a) cash, (b) receivables.

9. Distinguish between the following: (a) contingent liabilities and estimated liabilities. (b) appropriated retained earnings and unappropriated retained earnings.

10. Under what circumstances may offset balances be properly recognized on the balance sheet?

11. What are the major types of notes attached to the financial statements?

12. Under what circumstances might a parenthetical notation on the balance sheet be preferred to a note?

13. What are some examples of supplementary information that is included in the notes?

14. Under what circumstances does a subsequent event lead to a journal entry for the previous reporting period?

15. What is the basic purpose of the statement of cash flows and what kind of information does this statement provide that is not readily available from the other general purpose statements?

16. Why has the FASB concluded that a cash definition of funds is preferable to a working capital definition?

17. (a) List the three types of activities or functions that provide and use funds. (b) Why is it more informative to separate flows into these three activities than to combine all sources and uses together?

DISCUSSION CASES

CASE 5–1   (How much are we really worth?)

Daylight, Inc. has been fighting several takeover bids, including one from Western Industries. The balance sheet of Daylight shows a net asset position of $35 million. This amounts to a $50 per share book value based on 700,000 shares of common stock issued and outstanding. Western Industries has presented an offer to purchase Daylight's stock from the stockholders for a cash price of $65 per share. Western will finance the purchase by using Daylight's assets as collateral for a bank loan. Why might Western be willing to pay more per share of stock than its book value? If Western Industries is able to purchase Daylight, how would Western's balance sheet probably be affected?

CASE 5-2   (We've got you now!)

The Piedmont Computer Company has brought legal action against ATC Corporation for alleged monopolistic practices in the development of software. The claim has been pending for two years, with both sides accumulating evidence to support their positions. The case is now ready for trial. ATC Corporation has offered to settle out of court for $500,000, but Piedmont is asking for $5,000,000. Piedmont's attorneys feel an award of $2,500,000 from the court is very likely. If financial statements must be issued prior to the court action, how should Piedmont reflect this contingent claim? Support your decision where possible from the conceptual framework.

CASE 5-3   (But what is our liability?)

The Ditka Engineering Co. has signed a third-party loan guarantee for Liberty Company. The loan is from the National Bank of Illinois for $500,000. Liberty has recently filed for bankruptcy, and it is estimated by the company's auditors that creditors can expect to receive no more than 40% of their claims from Liberty. The treasurer of Ditka feels that because of the high uncertainty of final settlement, a liability should be recorded for the entire $500,000. The chief accountant, on the other hand, feels the 40% collection figure is reasonable and proposes that a $300,000 liability be recorded. The president of Ditka does not think a reasonable estimate can be made at this time, and proposes that nothing be accrued for the contingent liability, but that a note be added to the financial statements explaining the situation. As an independent outside auditor, what position would you take? Why?

CASE 5-4   (How much is the cash flow?)

A creditor for Apex Assembly Co. wants to assess the probability of the company being able to meet its debt obligations over the next three years. The debt includes annual interest payments on a 15%, 3-year loan for $500,000 and the principal amount of the loan at the end of the 3-year period. The creditor has examined the balance sheet and income statement, but still doesn't believe it has enough information to evaluate the future cash flow probabilities. Upon further inquiry by the creditor, Apex provides the following statement of changes in financial position.

Apex Assembly Company
Statement of Changes in Financial Position
For the Year Ended December 31, 1987

Funds were provided by:	
Net loss...	$ (5,000)
Add item not using working capital:	
Depreciation expense....................................	10,000
Funds provided by operations...............................	$ 5,000
Proceeds from bank loan....................................	25,000
Proceeds from sale of building.............................	50,000
Total funds provided	$ 80,000
Funds were applied to:	
Purchase of equipment.....................................	$ 60,000
Retirement of stock.......................................	30,000
Total funds applied	$ 90,000
Change in working capital....................................	$(10,000)

What additional data would you desire to better determine both past and future cash flows?

CASE 5–5   (Aren't the financial statements enough?)

Excello Corporation's basic financial statements for the year just ended have been prepared in accordance with GAAP. During the current year, management changed the accounting method for computing depreciation; a major competitor constructed a new plant in the area; three separate lawsuits were brought against the corporation that are not expected to be settled for two years or more; and the corporation continued to use an acceptable revenue recognition principle that differs from that used by most other companies in the industry. Also, after the end of the year, but before the statements were issued, Excello issued additional shares of common stock.

Excello has recently applied for a large bank loan, and the bank has requested a copy of the financial statements. The auditors for Excello have prepared several notes, some quite lengthy, to accompany the financial statements, but Excello's management does not think the loan officer at the bank would understand them and therefore submits the statements without the notes. The bank accepts the statements as submitted.

Which of the events described above should be included in notes to the financial statements? Do you think it is acceptable to delete notes when submitting financial statements to third parties? Substantiate your position.

EXERCISES

EXERCISE 5–1 (Balance sheet classification)

A balance sheet contains the following classifications:

(a) Current assets
(b) Investments
(c) Land, buildings, and equipment
(d) Intangible assets
(e) Other noncurrent assets
(f) Current liabilities

(g) Long-term debt
(h) Unearned revenues
(i) Other noncurrent liabilities
(j) Capital stock
(k) Additional paid-in capital
(l) Retained earnings

Indicate by letter how each of the following accounts would be classified. Place a minus sign (−) after all accounts representing offset or contra balances.

_____ (1) Discount on Bonds Payable
_____ (2) Stock of Subsidiary Corporation
_____ (3) 12% Bonds Payable (due in six months)
_____ (4) U.S. Treasury Notes
_____ (5) Income Tax Payable
_____ (6) Sales Tax Payable
_____ (7) Estimated Claims Under Warranties for Service and Replacements
_____ (8) Accounts Payable (debit balance)
_____ (9) Unearned Rental Revenue (three years in advance)

_____ (10) Long-Term Advances to Officers
_____ (11) Interest Receivable
_____ (12) Preferred Stock Retirement Fund
_____ (13) Trademarks
_____ (14) Allowance for Doubtful Accounts
_____ (15) Dividends Payable
_____ (16) Accumulated Depreciation
_____ (17) Petty Cash Fund
_____ (18) Prepaid Rent
_____ (19) Prepaid Insurance
_____ (20) Organization Costs

EXERCISE 5–2 (Balance sheet classification)

State how each of the following accounts should be classified on the balance sheet.

(a) Accumulated Patent Amortization
(b) Retained Earnings
(c) Vacation Pay Payable
(d) Retained Earnings Appropriated for Loss Contingencies
(e) Allowance for Doubtful Accounts
(f) Liability for Pension Payments
(g) Marketable Securities
(h) Paid-In Capital from Sale of Stock at More Than Stated Value

(i) Unamortized Bond Issue Costs
(j) Goodwill
(k) Receivables — U.S. Government Contracts
(l) Advances to Salespersons
(m) Customers Accounts with Credit Balances
(n) Inventory
(o) Patents
(p) Unclaimed Payroll Checks

(q) Employees Income Tax Payable
(r) Subscription Revenue Received
    in Advance
(s) Interest Payable
(t) Deferred Income Taxes (debit
    balance)

(u) Tools
(v) Deferred Income Taxes (credit
    balance)
(w) Loans to Officers
(x) Leasehold Improvements

EXERCISE 5–3 (Balance sheet preparation — account form)

From the following chart of accounts, prepare a balance sheet in account form showing all balance sheet items properly classified. (No monetary amounts are to be recognized.)

Accounts Payable
Accounts Receivable
Accumulated Depreciation —
    Buildings
Accumulated Depreciation —
    Equipment
Advertising Expense
Allowance for Decline in Value of
    Marketable Securities
Allowance for Doubtful Accounts
Bonds Payable
Buildings
Cash
Common Stock
Cost of Goods Sold
Deferred Income Taxes
    (credit balance)
Depreciation Expense — Buildings
Dividends
Doubtful Accounts Expense
Equipment
Estimated Warranty Expense Payable
    (Current)
Gain on Sale of Land
Gain on Sale of Marketable Securities
Goodwill
Income Summary

Income Tax Expense
Income Tax Payable
Interest Receivable
Interest Revenue
Inventory
Investment in Bonds
Land
Loss on Purchase Commitments
Marketable Securities
Miscellaneous General Expense
Notes Payable
Paid-In Capital from Sale of Common
    Stock at More Than Stated Value
Paid-In Capital from Sale of Treasury
    Stock
Patents
Pension Fund
Premium on Bonds Payable
Prepaid Insurance
Property Tax Expense
Purchases
Purchase Discounts
Retained Earnings
Salaries Payable
Sales
Sales Salaries
Travel Expense

EXERCISE 5–4 (Balance sheet relationships)

For each of the items (a) through (o), indicate the amount that should appear on the balance sheet.

Wolfe and Company Inc.
Consolidated Balance Sheet
December 31, 1987

Assets

Current assets:

Cash		$ (a)
Marketable securities		22,153
Accounts and notes receivable	$ (b)	
Allowance for doubtful accounts and notes receivable	9,622	165,693
Inventories		235,813
Other current assets		10,419
Total current assets		$ (c)
Land, buildings, and equipment	$ (d)	
Accumulated depreciation	352,186	419,418
Other noncurrent assets		9,631
Total assets		$876,312

Liabilities and Owners' Equity

Current liabilities:

Accounts payable		$ 98,670
Payable to banks		22,858
Income taxes payable		8,328
Current installments of long-term debt		(e)
Accrued expenses		6,610
Total current liabilities		$139,186
Long-term debt	$ (f)	
Deferred income taxes	40,406	
Minority interest in subsidiaries	3,309	
Total noncurrent liabilities		(g)
Total liabilities		$308,655

Contributed Capital:

Preferred stock, no par value (authorized 1,618 shares; issued 1,115 shares)		$ 16,596
Common stock, $1 par value per share (authorized 60,000 shares, issued 25,939 shares)	$ (h)	
Additional paid-in capital	(i)	(j)
Total contributed capital		$ (k)

Retained earnings:

Appropriated	$100,000	
Unappropriated	(l)	504,744
Total contributed capital and retained earnings		$ (m)
Less treasury stock, at cost (1,236 shares)		26,688
Total owners' equity		(n)
Total liabilities and owners' equity		$ (o)

EXERCISE 5–5   (Corrected balance sheet)

The bookkeeper for Domino, Inc. submitted the following balance sheet as of December 31, 1987.

Domino Inc.
Balance Sheet
December 31, 1987

Assets		Liabilities and Owners' Equity	
Cash..........................	$ 60,000	Accounts payable—trade.......	$120,000
Accounts receivable—trade	100,000	Salaries payable	40,000
Inventories...................	160,000	Owners' equity................	300,000
Machinery	80,000		
Goodwill.....................	60,000		
	$460,000		$460,000

Reference to the records of the company indicated the following:

(a) Cash included:

Petty cash..	$ 2,000
Payroll account	20,000
Savings account for cash to be used for building remodeling	20,000
General account	18,000
	$60,000

(b) State and local taxes of $4,800 were accrued on December 31. However, $4,800 had been deposited in a special cash account to be used to pay these and neither cash nor the accrued taxes were reported on the balance sheet.

(c) Twenty-five percent of Domino Inc.'s inventory is rapidly becoming obsolete. The obsolete portion of the inventory as of the balance sheet date was worth only one half of what Domino Inc. paid for it.

(d) Goods costing $6,000 were shipped to customers on December 30 and 31, at a sales price of $9,000. Goods shipped were not included in the inventory as of December 31. However, receivables were not recognized for the shipment since invoices were not sent out until January 3.

(e) One of Domino Inc.'s machines costing $25,000 is located on the Autonomous Island Republic, Tropicana. The dictator of Tropicana nationalized several foreign businesses during 1987 and is almost sure to expropriate Domino Inc.'s machinery for personal use. All machinery was acquired in July of 1987 and will not be depreciated this year.

(f) The corporation had been organized on January 1, 1987, by exchanging 22,000 shares of stock with a par value of $10 per share for the net assets of the partnership Knight and Cramer.

Prepare a corrected balance sheet as of December 31, 1987.

EXERCISE 5–6   (Balance sheet schedules)

In its annual report to stockholders, Fowler Inc. presents a condensed balance sheet with detailed data provided in supplementary schedules. From the trial balance of Fowler, prepare the following schedules, properly classifying all accounts as to balance sheet categories:

(a) Current assets
(b) Land, buildings, and equipment
(c) Intangible assets
(d) Total assets

(e) Current liabilities
(f) Noncurrent liabilities
(g) Owners' equity
(h) Total liabilities and owners' equity

Fowler Inc.
Trial Balance
December 31, 1987

Cash	18,500	
Marketable Securities—at cost (market, $23,400)	20,000	
Notes Receivable—trade debtors	30,000	
Accrued Interest on Notes Receivable	1,800	
Accounts Receivable—debit balances	73,000	
Accounts Receivable—credit balances		3,600
Allowance for Doubtful Accounts		4,300
Notes Receivable Discounted		12,000
Inventory	56,900	
Prepaid Expenses	3,100	
Accounts Payable—credit balances		26,500
Accounts Payable—debit balances	7,400	
Notes Payable—trade creditors		12,500
Accrued Interest on Notes Payable		800
Land	80,000	
Buildings	170,000	
Accumulated Depreciation—Buildings		34,000
Equipment	48,000	
Accumulated Depreciation—Equipment		7,600
Patents	20,000	
Accumulated Amortization—Patents		5,000
Franchises	10,000	
Bonds Payable, 8%—issue 1 (mature 12/31/90)		50,000
Bonds Payable, 12%—issue 2 (mature 12/31/99)		100,000
Accrued Interest on Bonds Payable		8,000
Premium on Bonds Payable—issue 1		1,500
Discount on Bonds Payable—issue 2	10,500	
Mortgage Payable		66,000
Accrued Interest on Mortgage Payable		2,160
Capital Stock, par value $25, 10,000 shares authorized, 4,000 shares issued		100,000
Additional Paid-In Capital		16,800
Retained Earnings Appropriated for Bond Redemption		35,000
Unappropriated Retained Earnings		73,440
Treasury Stock—at cost (500 shares)	10,000	
	559,200	559,200

EXERCISE 5–7   (Classification of subsequent events)

The following events occurred after the end of the company's fiscal year, but before the annual audit was completed. Classify each event as to its impact on the financial statements, i.e., (1) reported by changing the amounts in the financial statements (2) reported in notes to the financial statements, (3) does not require reporting. Include support for your classification.

(a) Major customer went bankrupt due to a deteriorating financial condition.
(b) Company sustained extensive hurricane damage to one of its plants.
(c) Company settled a major lawsuit that had been pending for two years.
(d) Increasing U.S. trade deficit may have impact on company's overseas sales.
(e) Company sold a large block of preferred stock.
(f) Preparation of current year's income tax return disclosed an additional $25,000 is due on last year's return.
(g) Company's controller resigned and was replaced by an audit manager from the company's audit firm.

EXERCISE 5–8   (Preparation of financial statement notes)

The following information was used to prepare the financial statements for Payson Chemical Company. Prepare the necessary notes to accompany the statements.

Payson uses the LIFO inventory method on its financial statements. If the FIFO method were used, the ending inventory balance would be reduced by $50,000, and net income for the year would be reduced by $35,000 after taxes. Payson depreciates its equipment using the straight-line method. Revenue is generally recognized when inventory is shipped unless it is sold on a consignment basis. The current value of the equipment is $525,000 as contrasted to its depreciated cost of $375,000.

Payson has borrowed $350,000 on 10-year notes at 14% interest. The notes are due on July 1, 1994. Payson's equipment has been pledged as collateral for the loan. The terms of the note prohibit additional long-term borrowing without the express permission of the holder of the notes. Payson is planning to request such permission during the next fiscal year.

The Board of Directors of Payson is currently discussing a merger with another chemical company. No public announcement has yet been made, but it is anticipated that additional shares of stock will be issued as part of the merger. Payson's balance sheet will report receivables of $126,000. Included in this figure is a $25,000 advance to the president of Payson, $30,000 of notes receivable from customers, $10,000 in advances to sales representatives, and $70,000 of accounts receivable from customers. The reported balance reflects a deduction for anticipated collection losses.

EXERCISE 5–9   (Format of cash flow statement)

From the following information for the Commodore Corporation, prepare a statement of cash flows for the year ended December 31, 1988. Prepare the statement so that it clearly shows cash provided or used by operating, investing, and financing activities.

Amortization of patent.	$ 2,200
Depreciation expense.	7,000
Issuance of common stock	25,000
Issuance of new bonds payable.	15,000
Net income.	55,000
Payment of dividends.	22,500
Purchase of equipment	33,200
Retirement of long-term debt	45,000
Sale of land (includes $6,000 gain).	35,000
Decrease in accounts receivable.	2,100
Increase in inventory.	1,200
Increase in accounts payable.	1,500
Increase in cash	34,900

PROBLEMS

PROBLEM 5–1   (Computing balance sheet components)

Hallis Tractors Inc. furnishes you with the following list of accounts.

Accounts Payable	$ 66,000	Investment in Kaine Oil Co. Stock	
Accounts Receivable	40,000	(70% of outstanding Stock	
Accumulated Depreciation	44,000	owned for control purposes)	$85,000
Advances to Salespersons	5,000	Investment in Siebert Co. Stock	
Advertising Expense	72,000	(current marketable securities)	21,000
Allowance for Doubtful Accounts	8,000	Paid-In Capital in Excess of Par	45,000
Bonds Payable	70,000	Premium on Bonds Payable	6,000
Cash	22,000	Prepaid Insurance Expense	3,000
Certificates of Deposit	31,000	Rent Revenue	37,000
Common Stock (par)	110,000	Rent Revenue Received in	
Customer Accounts with Credit		Advance	2,000
Balances	4,000	Retained Earnings	40,000
Deferred Income Tax (credit		Retained Earnings Appropriated	
balance)	53,000	for Loss Contingencies	30,000
Equipment	164,000	Taxes Payable	10,000
Inventory	49,000	Tools	68,000

Instructions: From the above list of accounts, determine working capital, total assets, total liabilities, and owners' equity per share of stock (75,000 shares outstanding).

PROBLEM 5–2   (Classified balance sheet)

Below is a list of account titles and balances for Johnson Investment Corporation as of January 31, 1987.

Accounts Payable	$ 95,800	Interest Payable	$ 1,900
Accounts Receivable	116,000	Interest Receivable	450
Accumulated Depreciation—		Inventory	184,300
Buildings	141,500	Investments in Undeveloped	
Accumulated Depreciation—		Properties	217,000
Machinery and Equipment	139,000	Land	188,000
Additional Paid-in Capital—		Machinery and Equipment	145,000
Common Stock	62,000	Miscellaneous Supplies	
Allowance for Doubtful Notes		Inventory	6,200
and Accounts Receivable	3,800	Notes Payable (Current)	68,260
Buildings	380,000	Notes Payable (due in 1992)	50,000
Cash in Banks	8,880	Notes Receivable	22,470
Cash on Hand	107,300	Preferred Stock $5 par	320,000
Cash Surrender Value of Life		Prepaid Insurance	4,500
Insurance	17,500	Retained Earnings (Debit	
Claim for Income Tax Refund	4,500	Balance)	11,740
Common Stock $20 par	650,000	Salaries and Wages Payable	9,400
Employees Income Tax Payable	4,780	Temporary Investment in	
Income Tax Payable	24,200	Marketable Securities	156,800

Instructions: Prepare a properly classified balance sheet in report form.

PROBLEM 5–3
(Classified balance sheet — account form including notes)

Account balances and supplemental information for Torrance Research Corp. as of December 31, 1987, are as follows:

Accounts Payable	$ 32,160	Furniture, Fixtures, and Store	
Accounts Receivable — Trade	57,731	Equipment	$769,000
Accumulated Depreciation—		Inventory	201,620
Leasehold Improvements and		Investment in Unconsolidated	
Equipment	579,472	Subsidiary	80,000
Additional Paid-In Capital	125,000	Insurance Claims Receivable	120,000
Allowance for Doubtful Accounts	1,731	Land	6,000
Automotive Equipment	132,800	Leasehold Improvements	65,800
Cash	30,600	7½-12% Mortgage Notes	200,000
Cash Surrender Value of Life		Notes Payable — Banks	17,000
Insurance	3,600	Notes Payable — Trade	63,540
Common Stock	175,000	Patent Licenses	57,402
Deferred Income Tax (credit		Prepaid Insurance	5,500
balance)	45,000	Profit Sharing, Payroll, and	
Dividends Payable	37,500	Vacation Payable	40,000
Franchises	12,150	Retained Earnings	225,800
		Tax Receivable — In Litigation	13,000

Supplemental information:

(a) Depreciation is provided by the straight-line method over the estimated useful lives of the assets.

(b) Common stock is $5 par, and 35,000 of the 100,000 authorized shares were issued and are outstanding.

(c) The cost of an exclusive franchise to import a foreign company's ball bearings and a related patent license are being amortized on the straight-line method over their remaining lives: franchise, 10 years; patents, 15 years.

(d) Inventories are stated at the lower of cost or market: cost was determined by the specific identification method.

(e) Insurance claims based upon the opinion of an independent insurance adjustor are for property damages at the central warehouse. These claims are estimated to be 2/3 collectible in the following year and 1/3 collectible thereafter.

(f) The company leases all of its buildings from various lessors. Estimated fixed lease obligations are $50,000 per year for the next ten years. The leases do not meet the criteria for capitalization.

(g) The company is currently in litigation over a claimed overpayment of income tax of $13,000. In the opinion of counsel, the claim is valid. The company is contingently liable on guaranteed notes worth $17,000.

Instructions: Prepare a properly classified balance sheet in account form. Include all notes and parenthetical notations necessary to properly disclose the essential financial data.

PROBLEM 5–4   (Corrected balance sheet)

The following balance sheet was prepared by the accountant for Bradbury Company.

Bradbury Company
Balance Sheet
June 30, 1988

Assets

Cash	$ 25,500
Marketable securities (includes 30% ownership in stock of Spruce Mountain Developers, at cost of $250,000).	312,000
Inventories (net of amount still due suppliers of $85,000)	624,600
Prepaid expenses (includes a deposit of $10,000 made on inventories to be delivered in 18 months)	32,100
Plant assets (excluding $60,000 of equipment still in use, but fully depreciated).	220,000
Goodwill (based upon estimate of President of Bradbury Company).	50,000
Total assets	$1,264,200

Liabilities and Owners' Equity

Notes payable ($75,000 due in 1990).	$ 135,000
Accounts payable (not including amount due to suppliers of inventory—see above)	142,000
Long-term liability under pension plan	60,000
Appropriation for building expansion.	90,000
Accumulated depreciation—fixed assets	73,000
Taxes payable.	44,500
Bonds payable (net of discount of $10,000)	290,000
Deferred income tax credit	63,000
Common stock ($10,000 shares @ $20 par)	200,000
Additional paid-in capital	50,500
Unappropriated retained earnings.	116,200
Total liabilities and owners' equity.	$1,264,200

Instructions: Prepare a corrected statement in report form using appropriate account titles.

PROBLEM 5–5   (Classified balance sheet—report form)

The financial position of St. Charles Ranch is summarized in the following letter to the corporation's accountant.

Dear Dallas:

The following information should be of value to you in preparing the balance sheet for St. Charles Ranch as of December 31, 1987. The balance of cash as of December 31 as reported on the bank statement was $43,825. There were still outstanding checks of $9,320 that had not cleared the bank, and cash on hand of $3,640 was not deposited until January 4, 1988.

Customers owed the company $40,500 at December 31. We estimated 6% of this amount will never be collected. We owe suppliers $32,000 for poultry feed purchased in November and December. About 75% of this feed was used before December 31.

Because we think the price of grain will rise in 1988, we are holding 10,000 bushels of wheat and 5,000 bushels of oats until spring. The market value at December 31 was $3.50 per bushel of wheat and $1.50 per bushel of oats. We estimate that both prices will increase 15% by selling time. We are not able to estimate the cost of raising this product.

St. Charles Ranch owns 1,850 acres of land. Two separate purchases of land were made as follows: 1,250 acres at $200 per acre in 1970, and 600 acres at $400 per acre in 1975. Similar land is currently selling for $800 per acre. The balance of the mortgage on the two parcels of land is $270,000 at December 31; 10% of this mortgage must be paid in 1988.

Our farm buildings and equipment cost us $176,400 and on the average are 40% depreciated. If we were to replace these buildings and equipment at today's prices, we believe we would be conservative in estimating a cost of $300,000.

We have not paid property taxes of $5,500 for 1988 billed us in late November. Our estimated income tax for 1987 is $18,500. A refund claim for $2,800 has been filed relative to the 1985 income tax return. The claim arose because of an error made on the 1985 return.

The operator of the ranch will receive a bonus of $9,000 for 1987 operations. It will be paid when the entire grain crop has been sold.

As you will recall, we issued 14,000 shares of $10 par stock upon incorporation. The ranch received $275,000 as net proceeds from the stock issue. Dividends of $30,000 were declared last month and will be paid on February 1, 1988.

The new year appears to hold great promise. Thanks for your help in preparing this statement.

Sincerely,
Geneva Adamson
President—St. Charles Ranch

Instructions: Based on this information, prepare a properly classified balance sheet in report form as of December 31, 1987.

PROBLEM 5–6 (Corrected balance sheet—report form)

The bookkeeper for Innovative Computers Inc. reports the following balance sheet amounts as of June 30, 1987:

Current Assets	$254,050
Other Assets	638,550
Current Liabilities	146,600
Other Liabilities	90,000
Capital	656,000

A review of account balances reveals the following data:

(a) An analysis of current assets discloses the following:

Cash	$ 52,250
Marketable securities held as temporary investment	60,000
Trade accounts receivable	56,800
Inventories, including advertising supplies of 2,000	85,000
	$254,050

(b) Other assets include:

Land, buildings, and equipment:		
Depreciated book value (cost, $656,000)		$549,000
Deposit with a supplier for merchandise ordered for August delivery		2,150
Goodwill recorded on the books to cancel losses incurred by the company in prior years		87,400
		$638,550

(c) Current liabilities include:

Payroll payable		$ 7,150
Taxes payable		4,150
Rent payable		11,400
Trade accounts payable:		
Balance	$101,400	
Less debit balance in vendor account due to merchandise return	1,500	99,900
Notes payable		24,000
		$146,600

(d) Other liabilities include:

9% mortgage on land, buildings and equipment, payable in semiannual installments of $9,000 through June 30, 1992	$ 90,000

(e) Capital includes:

Preferred stock: 19,600 shares outstanding ($20 par value)	$392,000
Common stock: 160,000 shares at stated value	264,000
	$656,000

(f) Common shares were originally issued for full consideration, but the losses of the company for the past years were charged against the common stock balance.

Total consideration at time of issuance	$391,000

Instructions: Using the account balances and related data, prepare a corrected balance sheet in report form showing individual asset, liability, and capital balances properly classified.

PROBLEM 5–7   (Corrected balance sheet — report form)

The following balance sheet is submitted to you for inspection and review.

Interstate Freight Company
Balance Sheet
December 31, 1987

Assets		Liabilities and Owners' Equity	
Cash................................	$ 45,050	Miscellaneous liabilities...........	$ 3,600
Accounts receivable..............	112,500	Loan payable	76,200
Inventories......................	204,000	Accounts payable................	75,250
Prepaid insurance	8,800	Capital stock....................	215,000
Land, bldgs, & equip	346,800	Paid-in capital..................	347,100
	$717,150		$717,150

In the course of the review you find the data listed below:
(a) The possibility of uncollectible accounts on accounts receivable has not been considered. It is estimated that uncollectible accounts will total $4,800.
(b) $45,000 representing the cost of a large-scale newspaper advertising campaign completed in 1987 has been added to the inventories, since it is believed that this campaign will benefit sales of 1988. It is also found that inventories include merchandise of $16,250 received on December 31 that has not yet been recorded as a purchase.
(c) Prepaid insurance consists of $1,300, the cost of fire insurance for 1988, and $7,500, the cash surrender value on officers' life insurance policies.
(d) The books show that land, buildings, and equipment have a cost of $526,800 with depreciation of $180,000 recognized in prior years. However, these balances include fully depreciated equipment of $85,000 that has been scrapped and is no longer on hand.
(e) Miscellaneous liabilities of $3,600 represent salaries payable of $9,500, less noncurrent advances of $5,900 made to company officials.
(f) Loan payable represents a loan from the bank that is payable in regular quarterly installments of $6,250.
(g) Tax liabilities not shown are estimated at $15,250.
(h) Deferred income tax (credit) arising from timing differences in recognizing income totals $44,550. This tax was not included in the balance sheet.
(i) Capital stock consists of 6,250 shares of preferred 6% stock, par $20, and 9,000 shares of common stock, stated value $10.
(j) Capital stock had been issued for a total consideration of $253,600, the amount received in excess of the par and stated values of the stock being reported as paid-in capital.

Instructions: Prepare a corrected balance sheet in report form with accounts properly classified.

PROBLEM 5–8 (Corrected balance sheet—account form)

The accountant for the Delicious Bakery prepares the following condensed balance sheet.

Delicious Bakery
Condensed Balance Sheet
December 31, 1987

Current assets	$53,415
Less current liabilities	29,000
Working capital	$24,415
Add other assets	75,120
	$99,535
Deduct other liabilities	3,600
Investment in business	$95,935

A review of the account balances disclosed the following data:

(a) An analysis of the current asset grouping revealed the following:

Cash	$10,600
Trade accounts receivable (fully collectible)	12,500
Notes receivable (notes of customer who has been declared bankrupt and is unable to pay anything on the obligations)	1,000
Marketable securities, at cost (market value $2,575)	4,250
Inventory	20,965
Cash surrender value of insurance on officers' lives	4,100
Total current assets	$53,415

The inventory account was found to include the cost of supplies of $425, a delivery truck acquired at the end of 1987 at a cost of $2,100, and fixtures at a depreciated value of $10,400. The fixtures had been acquired in 1984 at a cost of $12,500.

(b) The total for other assets was determined as follows:

Land and buildings at cost of acquisition, July 1, 1985	$92,000
Less balance due on mortgage, $16,000, and accrued interest on mortgage, $880 (mortgage is payable in annual installments of $4,000 on July 1 of each year together with interest for the year at that time at 11%)	16,880
Total other assets	$75,120

It was estimated that the land, at the time of the purchase, was worth $30,000. Buildings as of December 31, 1987, were estimated to have a remaining life of 17½ years.

(c) Current liabilities represented balances that were payable to trade creditors. Other liabilities consisted of withholding, payroll, real estate and other taxes payable to the federal, state, and local governments. However, no recognition was given the accrued salaries, utilities, and other miscellaneous items totaling $350.

(d) The company was originally organized in 1983 when 5,000 shares of no-par stock with a stated value of $5 per share were issued in exchange for business assets that were recognized on the books at their fair market value of $55,000.

Instructions: Prepare a corrected balance sheet in report form with the items properly classified.

PROBLEM 5–9   (Classified balance sheet—report form)

Tony Akea incorporated his concrete manufacturing operations on January 1, 1987, by issuing 10,000 shares of $10 par common stock to himself. The following balance sheet for the new corporation was prepared.

Wilshire Corporation
Balance Sheet
January 1, 1987

Cash.........................	$ 10,000	Accounts payable—suppliers.....	$ 75,000
Accounts receivable..............	75,000	Capital stock, $10 par............	100,000
Inventory	75,000	Additional paid in capital.........	100,000
Equipment.....................	115,000		
	$275,000		$275,000

During 1987, Wilshire Corporation engaged in the following transactions:
(a) Wilshire Corporation produced concrete costing $270,000. Concrete costs consisted of $200,000, raw materials purchased; $25,000, labor; and $45,000, overhead. Wilshire Corporation paid the $45,000 owed to suppliers as of January 1, and $130,000 of the $200,000 of raw materials purchased during the year. All labor, except for $1,500, and recorded overhead were paid in cash during the year. Other operating expenses of $15,000 were incurred and paid in 1987.
(b) Concrete costing $290,000 was sold during 1987 for $400,000. All sales were made on credit, and collections on receivables were $365,000.
(c) Wilshire Corporation purchased machinery (fair market value = $190,000) by trading in old equipment costing $50,000 and paying $140,000 in cash. There is no accumulated depreciation on the old equipment as it was revalued when the new corporation was formed.
(d) Wilshire Corporation issued an additional 4,000 shares of common stock for $25 per share and declared a dividend of $4 per share to all stockholders of record as of December 31, 1987, payable on January 15, 1988.
(e) Depreciation expense for 1987 was $27,000. The allowance for doubtful accounts after year-end adjustments is $2,500.

Instructions: Prepare a properly classified balance sheet in report form for the Wilshire Corporation as of December 31, 1987.

PROBLEM 5–10   (Analysis of financial position)

Crown Realty Inc., a dealer in land, is searching for funds for a long-term expansion program. Crown must maintain a working capital balance of $12,000,000 to be in a favorable position for borrowing. The post-closing trial balance as of December 31, 1987, is as follows:

Accounts Payable—Trade.		3,678,000
Accounts Receivable.	14,700,000	
Accumulated Depreciation—Office Buildings		24,000,000
Additional Paid-In Capital.		22,500,000
Advances to Affiliates	1,650,000	
Allowance for Doubtful Accounts		189,000
Bonds (payable in installments of $1,500,000 on June 1 of each year).		22,500,000
Cash Surrender Value of Life Insurance.	45,000	
Common Stock, $10 par.		20,000,000
First National Bank Fund for Construction of Office Building	2,400,000	
First National Bank—General Account.	1,866,000	
Income Tax Payable		1,455,000
Land.	42,000,000	
Loans on Life Insurance Policies		30,000
Marketable Securities	9,000,000	
Notes Payable to Bank.		6,000,000
Office Building.	36,000,000	
Office Supplies Inventory	225,000	
Prepaid Insurance	75,000	
Retained Earnings.		7,159,000
Salaries and Wages Payable.		450,000

Additional investigation revealed:

(a) Accounts receivable consist of:

Employee advances—long-term.	$ 1,500,000
Due in 1989 from sale of old office building	3,750,000
Installment notes receivable—trade.	7,500,000
Accounts receivable—trade.	1,950,000
	$14,700,000

(b) Land includes several parcels purchased for $15,000,000, which have become subject to severe flooding, thus lowering the value to $750,000. All the land is for sale except the $15,900,000 site for Crown new office building.

(c) Crown purchased 40% of the voting stock of a savings and loan company for $7,500,000 and included the acquisition in marketable securities.

(d) The loans on the life insurance policies come due in 18 months; the bank notes fall due in 8 months.

Instructions: Show whether Crown Realty Inc. is in a favorable position for borrowing money by computing the working capital. Because of the nature of the business, land for sale is considered inventory.

PROBLEM 5–11 (Preparation of cash flow statement)

The following data were taken from the records of Peabody Produce Company for the year ended June 30, 1987.

Borrowed on long-term notes	$20,000
Issued capital stock.	50,000
Purchased equipment.	27,000
Net income.	37,000
Purchased treasury stock	2,000
Paid dividends.	30,000

Depreciation expense	$12,000
Retired bonds payable	70,000
Goodwill amortization	2,000
Sold long-term investment (at cost)	5,000
Increase in cash	4,000
Decrease in inventories	8,000
Increase in accounts receivable	5,000
Increase in accounts payable	4,000

Instructions:
(1) From the information given, prepare in the form illustrated in the chapter a statement of cash flows.
(2) Briefly explain what an interested party would learn from studying the cash flow statement for Peabody Produce Company.

PROBLEM 5–12   (Preparation of cash flow statement)

The following changes occurred in selected accounts of Affleck Co. for the year ended December 31, 1988.

Increase in long-term debt	$ 57,000
Purchase of treasury stock	52,000
Depreciation and amortization	197,000
Gain on sale of equipment (included in net income)	6,000
Proceeds from issuance of common stock	184,000
Purchase of equipment	634,000
Proceeds from sale of equipment	15,000
Payment of dividends	49,000
Net income	486,000
Increase (decrease) in working capital accounts	
Inventories	275,000
Accounts receivable	229,000
Accounts payable	124,000
Taxes payable	(34,000)
Trade notes payable	167,000
Decrease in cash	49,000

Instructions: From the information given, prepare in the form illustrated in the chapter a statement of cash flows.

6

The Time Value of Money: Accounting Applications

A noted leader in the accounting profession recently observed that the traditional accounting model is badly in need of a tune-up, or perhaps a major overhaul.[1] One recommended change is more complete acceptance and broader use of the **time value of money** concept. This concept is becoming increasingly important in the business world as decision makers try to adjust for the impact of interest and changing economic prices. Consider the following illustrative situations.

- The management of Wheeler Manufacturing Company intends to purchase a new machine. The supplier will accept a $10,000 cash down payment plus a 3-year, 12% note that calls for annual payments of $11,000. Alternatively, the supplier will accept $38,000 cash for the machine. Which alternative purchase plan should Wheeler choose?
- Telluride, Inc. is considering a long-term investment in Sunset Corporation bonds. What is the maximum amount that Telluride will pay for the bonds if they are $20,000 face, 10%, 5-year bonds and if Telluride must earn at least 11% on the investment to meet its corporate investment objectives?
- Pro Shop, Inc. is considering a pension fund for its employees. Management needs to know how much it must invest now in order to establish a fund large enough to pay for the retirement of employees, beginning 12 years from now.
- Med-Cal Corporation, organized by a group of doctors, has entered into a 30-year lease contract on a building. Since this transaction met the requirements of a capital lease, the building and corresponding long-term lease obligation were recorded on the books at a value of

---

[1]Comment by Art Wyatt, member of the Financial Accounting Standards Board, at the Ninth Annual Intermountain Accounting Seminar, Utah State University, Logan, Utah, October 16, 1985.

$150,000. The controller for Med-Cal now needs to prepare a depreciation schedule for the building and an amortization schedule for the lease obligation. What are the procedures for determining the interest and principal portions of the lease payments over the 30-year lease period?

In each of the preceding situations, decisions must be made regarding inflows and outflows of money over an extended period of time. Making correct financial decisions requires that the time value of money be taken into account. This means that dollars to be received or paid in the future must be "discounted" or adjusted to their present values; alternatively, current dollars may be "accumulated" or adjusted to their future values so that comparisons of dollar amounts at different time periods can be meaningful.

In the first example, Wheeler must decide whether to pay $38,000 cash now or pay only $10,000 now and pay $11,000 at the end of each year for 3 years. Assuming Wheeler has sufficient cash, wouldn't it be better to pay $38,000 for the machine instead of $43,000 under the time-payment plan ($10,000 down plus 3 payments of $11,000)? The answer to that question is "not necessarily." This decision requires that the alternatives be made comparable in terms of the time value of money, that is, the two alternatives must be stated at their respective present values.

The present value of the first alternative, the cash purchase, is simply the amount of cash paid, or $38,000. The present value of the second alternative is equal to the $10,000 down payment plus the present values of the three $11,000 payments, as illustrated below.

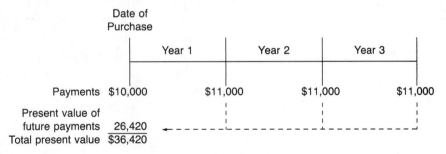

The total present value of three $11,000 payments discounted to the date of purchase at 12% interest is approximately $26,420. This amount plus the down payment of $10,000 equals $36,420, which is less than the $38,000 cash price the supplier is willing to accept. Therefore, assuming other factors equal, for example, that Wheeler can use the $1,580 savings ($38,000 − $36,420) to earn more than the 12% interest it is paying, Wheeler should purchase the machine with the time-payment plan. This conclusion and the other examples in the chapter **ignore any tax implications,** which may modify the decision in actual practice.

As suggested by the previous examples, there are many business situations where present or future value techniques must be used in making financial decisions. Common applications in accounting include the following categories.

1. Valuing long-term notes receivable and payable where there is no stated rate of interest or an inappropriate stated rate of interest.
2. Determining bond prices and using the effective-interest method for amortizing bond premiums or discounts.
3. Determining appropriate values for long-term capital leases and measuring the amount of interest expense and principal amortization applicable to the periodic lease payments.
4. Accounting for pension funds, including interest accruals and amortization entries.
5. Accounting for sinking funds.
6. Analyzing capital budgeting alternatives.
7. Establishing amortization schedules for mortgages and measuring periodic payments on long-term purchase contracts.
8. Determining appropriate asset, liability, and equity values in mergers and business combinations.

Since future and present value techniques are commonly used in business and have become increasingly important for accountants, this chapter explains these techniques and provides several illustrations of their use. The emphasis in the chapter is on present value techniques, since most applications in accounting require future amounts to be discounted to the present. The material presented may be a review for some students; for others, it will add to the theoretical foundation underlying current accounting practice. The techniques explained will be used throughout the text, especially in the chapters dealing with long-term investments and long-term liabilities. Before future and present value techniques can be explained, however, the concept of interest must first be defined.

SIMPLE AND COMPOUND INTEREST

Money, like other commodities, is a scarce resource, and a payment for its use is generally required. This payment (cost) for the use of money is **interest.** For example, if $100 is borrowed, whether from an individual, a business, or a bank, and $110 is paid back, $10 interest has been paid for the use of the $100. Thus, interest represents the excess cash paid or received over the amount of cash borrowed or loaned.

Generally interest is specified in terms of a percentage rate for a period of time, usually a year. For example, interest at 8% means the annual cost of borrowing an amount of money, called the **principal,** is equal to 8% of that amount. If $100 is borrowed at 8% annual interest, the total to be repaid is $108—the amount of the principal, $100, and the interest for a year, $8 ($100 × .08 × 1). Interest on a $1,000 note for 6 months at 8% is $40 ($1,000 × .08 × 6/12). Thus, the formula for computing **simple interest** is

$$i = p \times r \times t,$$
where:

i = Amount of simple interest
p = Principal amount
r = Interest rate (per period)
t = Time (number of periods)

The preceding formula relates to simple interest. Many transactions involve **compound interest**. This means that the amount of interest earned for a certain period is added to the principal for the next period. Interest for the subsequent period is computed on the new amount, which includes both principal and accumulated interest. As an example, assume $100 is deposited in a bank and left for two years at 6% annual interest. At the end of the first year, the $100 has earned $6 interest ($100 × .06 × 1). At the end of the second year, $6 has been earned for the first year, plus another $6.36 interest (6% on the $106 balance at the beginning of the second year). Thus, the total interest earned is $12.36 rather than $12 because of the compounding effect. The table below, based on the foregoing example, illustrates the computation of simple and compound interest for four years.

Year	Simple Interest			Compound Interest		
	Computation	Interest	Total	Computation	Interest	Total
1	($100 × .06)	$6	$106	($100.00 × .06)	$6.00	$106.00
2	(100 × .06)	6	112	(106.00 × .06)	6.36	112.36
3	(100 × .06)	6	118	(112.36 × .06)	6.74	119.10
4	(100 × .06)	6	124	(119.10 × .06)	7.15	126.25

The interest rate used in compound interest problems is the **effective rate of interest** and is generally stated as an annual rate, sometimes called **per annum**. However, if the compounding of interest is for periods other than a year, the stated rate of interest must be adjusted. A comparable adjustment must be made to the number of periods. The adjustments required to the interest rate (i) and to the number of periods (n) for semi-annual, quarterly, and monthly compounding of interest are as follows:

Example	Annual Compounding	Semiannual Compounding	Quarterly Compounding	Monthly Compounding
1.	i = 6%, n = 10	i = 3%, n = 20	i = 1.5%, n = 40	i = .5%, n = 120
2.	i = 12%, n = 5	i = 6%, n = 10	i = 3%, n = 20	i = 1%, n = 60
3.	i = 24%, n = 3	i = 12%, n = 6	i = 6%, n = 12	i = 2%, n = 36

As shown in the table, the semiannual compounding of interest requires the annual interest rate to be reduced by half and the number of periods to be doubled. Quarterly compounding of interest requires use of one-fourth the annual rate and 4 times the number of periods, and so forth. Because of this compounding effect, more interest is earned by an investor with semiannual interest than with annual interest, and more is earned with quarterly compounding than with semiannual compounding.

FUTURE AND PRESENT VALUE TECHNIQUES

Since money earns interest over time, $100 received today is more valuable than $100 received one year from today. Future and present value analysis is a method of comparing the value of money received or expected to be received at different time periods.

Analyses requiring alternative computations in terms of present dollars relative to future dollars may be viewed from one of two perspectives, the future or the present. If a future time frame is chosen, all cash flows must be **accumulated** to that future point. In this instance, the effect of interest is to increase the amounts or values over time so that the future amount is greater than the present amount. For example, $500 invested today will accumulate to a **future value** of $1,079 (rounded) in 10 years if 8% annually compounded interest is paid on the investment.

If, on the other hand, the present is chosen as the point in time at which to evaluate alternatives, all cash flows must be **discounted** from the future to the present. In this instance, the discounting effect reduces the amounts or values. To illustrate, if an investor is earning 10% annual interest on a note receivable that will pay $10,000 in 3 years, what might the investor accept today in full payment, i.e., what is the **present value** of that note? The amount the investor should be willing to accept, assuming a 10% interest rate is satisfactory and that other considerations are held constant, is $7,513 (rounded), which is the discounted present value of the note. The rationale for the investor is that the $7,513 could be invested at 10%, compounded annually, and it would accumulate to $10,000 in 3 years.

As just illustrated, the future and present value situations involving lump-sum amounts are essentially reciprocal relationships, and both future and present values are based on the concept of interest. Thus, if interest can be earned at 8% per year, the future value of $100 one year from now is $108 [$100(1 + .08)]. Conversely, assuming the same rate of interest, the present value of a $108 payment due in one year is $100 [$108 ÷ (1 + .08)]. Similarly, $100 to be received in one year, at a 10% annual interest rate, is worth $90.91 today ($100 ÷ 1.10), because $90.91 invested at 10% will grow to $100 [$90.91(1 + .10)] in one year.

Use of Formulas

There are four common future and present value situations, each with a corresponding formula. Two of the situations deal with one-time, lump-sum payments or receipts[2] (either future or present values), and the other two involve annuities (either future or present values). An **annuity** consists of a **series of equal payments** over a specified number of periods. For example, a contract calling for three annual payments of $3,000 each would be an annuity. However, a similar contract requiring three annual payments of $2,000, $3,000, and $4,000, respectively, would not be an annuity since the payments are not equal.

Without going into the derivation of the formulas, the four common situations are as follows:

1. Future Value of a Lump-Sum Payment: $FV = P(1 + i)^n$
   where:
   FV = Future value
   P = Principal amount to be accumulated
   i = Interest rate per period
   n = Number of periods

   Example: Future value of $1,500 to be accumulated at 10% annual interest for 5 years.
   $FV = \$1,500(1 + .10)^5$
   FV = $2,416 (rounded)

2. Present Value of a Lump-Sum Payment: $PV = A\left[\dfrac{1}{(1 + i)^n}\right]$
   where:
   PV = Present value
   A = Accumulated amount to be discounted
   i = Interest rate per period
   n = Number of periods

---

[2]Hereafter in this chapter, the terms *payments* and *receipts* will be used interchangeably. A payment by one party in a transaction becomes a receipt to the other party and vice versa. The term *rent* is used to designate either a receipt or a payment.

Example: Present value of $2,416 to be discounted at 10% annual interest for 5 years.

$$PV = \$2,416\left[\frac{1}{(1 + .10)^5}\right]$$

PV = $1,500 (rounded)

3. Future Value of an Annuity: $FV_n = R\left[\dfrac{(1 + i)^n - 1}{i}\right]$

where:

FV_n = Future value of an annuity
R   = Annuity payment or periodic rent to be accumulated
i   = Interest rate per period
n   = Number of periods

Example: Future value of annuity of $2,000 for 10 years to be accumulated at 12% annual interest.

$$FV_n = \$2,000\left[\frac{(1 + .12)^{10} - 1}{.12}\right]$$

FV_n = $35,097 (rounded)

4. Present Value of an Annuity: $PV_n = R\left[\dfrac{1 - \dfrac{1}{(1 + i)^n}}{i}\right]$

where:

PV_n = Present value of an annuity
R   = Annuity payment or periodic rent to be discounted
i   = Interest rate per period
n   = Number of periods

Example: Present value of an annuity of $5,000 for 3 years to be discounted at 11% annual interest.

$$PV_n = \$5,000\left[\frac{1 - \frac{1}{(1 + .11)^3}}{.11}\right]$$

PV_n = $12,219 (rounded)

Use of Tables

In the previous examples, formulas were used to make the computations. This is easily accomplished with most modern-day calculators or with microcomputers. Without such tools, however, use of the formulas may be time consuming. Because of this, future and present value tables have been developed for each of the four situations. These tables, such as those provided on pages 230–233, are based on computing the value of $1 for various interest rates and periods of time. Consequently, future and present value computations can be made by multiplying the appropriate table value factor for $1 by the applicable lump-sum or annuity amount involved in the particular situation. Thus, the formulas for the four situations may be rewritten as follows:

1. Future Value of a Lump-Sum Payment:
   $FV = P(1 + i)^n$ or $FV = P(FVF_{\overline{n}|i})$ or simply
   $FV = P$(Table I factor)
   where: $FVF_{\overline{n}|i}$ = Future value factor for a particular interest rate (i) and for a certain number of periods (n) from Table I.

   Example (from page 213):
   $FV = \$1,500$ (1.6105 = Factor from Table I; n = 5; i = 10%)
   $FV = \underline{\$2,416}$ (rounded)

2. Present Value of a Lump-Sum Payment:

   $PV = A\dfrac{1}{(1 + i)^n}$ or $PV = A(PVF_{\overline{n}|i})$ or simply

   $PV = A$(Table II factor)
   where: $PVF_{\overline{n}|i}$ = Present value factor for a particular interest rate (i) and for a certain number of periods (n) from Table II.

   Example (from pages 213–214):
   $PV = \$2,416$ (0.6209 = Factor from Table II; n = 4; i = 10%)
   $PV = \underline{\$1,500}$ (rounded)

3. Future Value of an Annuity:
   $FV_n = R\left[\dfrac{(1 + i)^n - 1}{i}\right]$ or $FV_n = R(FVAF_{\overline{n}|i})$ or simply
   $FV_n = R$(Table III factor)

   Example (from page 214):
   $FV_n = \$2,000$ (17.5487 = Factor from Table III; n = 10; i = 12%)
   $FV_n = \underline{\$35,097}$ (rounded)

4. Present Value of an Annuity:

   $PV_n = R\left[\dfrac{1 - \dfrac{1}{(1 + i)^n}}{i}\right]$ or $PVn = R(PVAF_{\overline{n}|i})$ or simply

   $PV_n = R$(Table IV factor)

   Example (from page 214):
   $PV_n = \$5,000$ (2.4437 = Factor from Table IV; n = 3; i = 11%)
   $PV_n = \underline{\$12,219}$ (rounded)

Note that the answers obtained in the examples by using the tables are the same as those obtained using the formulas with a calculator or microcomputer.

Business Applications

The following examples demonstrate the application of future and present value computations in solving business problems, including each of the four situations just described. Additional applications are provided in later sections as well as in the exercises and problems at the end of the chapter.

Example 1: (Future Value of a Lump Sum)

Marywhether Company loans its president, Celia Phillips, $15,000 to purchase a car. Marywhether accepts a note due in 4 years with interest at 10% compounded semiannually. How much cash does Marywhether expect to receive from Phillips when the note is paid at maturity?

Solution:

This problem involves a lump-sum payment to be accumulated 4 years into the future. In many present and future value problems, a time line is helpful in visualizing the problem:

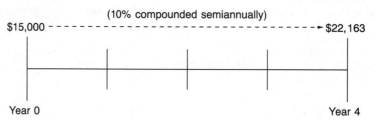

The $15,000 must be accumulated for 4 years at 10% compounded semi-annually. Table I may be used, and the applicable formula is:

$$FV = P(FVF_{\overline{n}|i})$$

where:
FV = The future value of a lump sum
P   = $15,000
n   = 8 periods (4 years × 2)
i   = 5% effective interest rate per period (10% ÷ 2)

FV = $15,000 (Table I $_{\overline{8}|5\%}$)
FV = $15,000 (1.4775)
FV = $22,163 (rounded)

In 4 years, Marywhether will expect to receive $22,163.

Example 2: (Present Value of a Lump Sum)

Edgemont Enterprises holds a note receivable from a steady customer. The note is for $22,000, which includes principal and interest, and is due to be paid in exactly 2 years. The customer wants to pay the note now, and both parties agree that 10% is a reasonable annual interest rate to use in discounting the note. How much will the customer pay Edgemont Enterprises today to settle the obligation?

Solution:

The lump-sum future payment must be discounted to the present at the agreed upon annual rate of interest of 10%. Since this involves a present-value computation of a lump-sum amount, Table II is used, and the applicable formula is:

$$PV = A(PVF_{\overline{n}|i})$$

where:

PV = The present value of a lump sum
A = $22,000
n = 2 periods
i = 10% effective interest rate per period

PV = $22,000 (Table II $_{\overline{2}|10\%}$)
PV = $22,000 (0.8264)
PV = $18,181 (rounded)

The customer will pay approximately $18,181 today to settle the obligation.

Example 3: (Present Value of Series of Unequal Payments)

Casper Sporting Goods Co. is considering a $1 million capital investment that will provide the following expected net receipts at the *end* of each of the next six years.

Year	Expected Net Receipts
1	$195,000
2	457,000
3	593,000
4	421,000
5	95,000
6	5,000

Casper will make the investment only if the rate of return is greater than 12%. Will Casper make the investment?

Solution:

A series of unequal future receipts must be compared with a present lump-sum investment. For such a comparison to be made, all future cash flows must be discounted to the present.

If the rate of return on the investment is greater than 12%, then the total of all yearly net receipts discounted to the present at 12% will be greater than the amount invested. Since the future receipts are not equal, this situation does *not* involve an annuity. Each receipt must be discounted individually. Table II is used, and the applicable formula is:

$PV = A(PVF_{\overline{n}|i})$ where:

(1) Year = n	(2) A (Net Receipts)	(3) Table II $_{\overline{n}|12\%}$	(2) × (3) = (4) PV (Discounted Amount)
1	$195,000	.8929	$ 174,116
2	457,000	.7972	364,320
3	593,000	.7118	422,097
4	421,000	.6355	267,546
5	95,000	.5674	53,903
6	5,000	.5066	2,533
Total			$1,284,515 (Rounded)

The total discounted receipts are greater than the $1 million investment; thus, the rate of return is more than 12%. Therefore, other things being equal, Casper will invest.

Example 4: (Future Value of an Annuity)

Boswell Co. owes an installment debt of $1,000 per quarter for 5 years. The creditor has indicated a willingness to accept an equivalent lump-sum payment at the end of the contract period instead of the series of equal payments made at the end of each quarter. If money is worth 16% compounded quarterly, what is the equivalent lump-sum payment at the end of the contract period?

Solution:

The equivalent lump-sum payment can be found by accumulating the quarterly $1,000 payments to the end of the contract period. Since the payments are equal, this is an annuity. Table III is used, and the applicable formula is:

$$FV_n = R(FVAF_{\overline{n}|i})$$

where:

FV_n = The unknown equivalent lump-sum payment

R = $1,000 quarterly installment to be accumulated

n = 20 periods (5 years × 4 quarters)

i = 4% effective interest rate per period (16% ÷ 4)

FV_n = $1,000 (Table III$_{\overline{20}|4\%}$)

FV_n = $1,000 (29.7781)

FV_n = $29,778 (rounded)

$29,778 paid at the end of 5 years is approximately equivalent to the 20 quarterly payments of $1,000 each plus interest.

Example 5: (Present Value of an Annuity)

Neil Sabin, proprietor of Sabin Appliance, received two offers for his last used, deluxe-model refrigerator. Jerry Sloan will pay $650 in cash.

Elise Jensen will pay $700 consisting of a down payment of $100 and 12 monthly payments of $50. If the installment interest rate is 24% compounded monthly, which offer should Sabin accept?

Solution:

In order to compare the two alternative methods of payment, all cash flows must be accumulated or discounted to one point in time. As illustrated by the time line, the present is selected as the point of comparison.

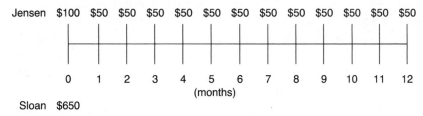

Sloan's offer is $650 today. The present value of $650 today is $650.

Jensen's offer consists of an annuity of 12 payments, plus $100 paid today, which is not part of the annuity. The annuity may be discounted to the present by using Table IV and the applicable formula:

$$PV_n = R(PVAF_{\overline{n}|i})$$

where:

PV_n = Unknown present value of 12 payments

R   = $50 monthly payment to be discounted

n   = 12 periods (1 year × 12 months)

i   = 2% effective interest rate per period (24% ÷ 12)

PV_n = $50 (Table IV$_{\overline{12}|2\%}$)
PV_n = $50 (10.5753)
PV_n = $529

Present value of Jensen's payments	$529
Present value of Jensen's $100 down payment	100
Total present value of Jensen's offer	$629

Therefore Sloan's offer of $650 cash is more desirable than Jensen's offer.

Determining the Number of Periods, the Interest Rate, or the Rental Payment

So far, the examples and illustrations have required solutions for the future or present values, with the other three variables in the formulas being given. Sometimes business problems require solving for the number of periods, the interest rate[3], or the rental payment instead of the future or present value amounts. In each of the formulas, there are four variables. If information is known about any three of the variables, the fourth (unknown) value can be determined. The following examples illustrate how to solve for these other variables.

Example 6: (Determining the Number of Periods)

Rocky Mountain Survey Company wants to purchase new equipment at a cost of $100,000. The company has $88,850 available in cash but does not want to borrow the other $11,150 for the purchase. If the company can invest the $88,850 today at an interest rate of 12% compounded quarterly, how many years will it be before Rocky Mountain will have the $100,000 it needs to buy the equipment?

Solution:

As illustrated below, Rocky Mountain Survey Company can invest $88,850 now at 12% interest compounded quarterly, and needs to know how long it will take for this amount to accumulate to $100,000.

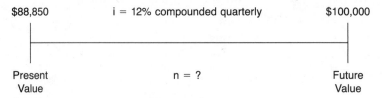

In this situation, involving both present values and future values, either Table I or Table II may be used. If Table I is used, the applicable formula is:

$$FV = PVF_{\overline{n}|i}$$
$$FV = P(\text{Table I factor})$$

The problem would be solved as follows:

$$\frac{FV}{P} = \text{Table I factor}$$

$$\frac{\$100,000}{\$88,850} = 1.1255$$

Reading down the 3% column (12% ÷ 4) in Table I, the factor value of 1.1255 is shown for n = 4. Therefore, it would take 4 periods (quarters)

---

[3]When the interest rate is not known, it is properly called the **implicit rate of interest**, that is, the rate of interest implied by the terms of a contract or situation. (See examples 7 and 10 in this chapter.)

or 1 year for Rocky Mountain to earn enough interest to have $88,850 accumulate to a future value of $100,000.

If Table II were used, the applicable formula is:

$$PV = FVF_{\overline{n}|i}$$
$$PV = A(\text{Table II factor})$$
Solving,
$$\frac{PV}{A} = \text{Table II factor}$$

$$\frac{\$88,850}{\$100,000} = .8885$$

Reading down the 3% column in Table II, the factor of 0.8885 corresponds with n = 4 (quarters) or 1 year. This illustrates again the reciprocal nature of future and present values for lump-sum amounts.

Example 7: (Determining the Interest Rate)

The Hughes family wishes to purchase a baby-grand piano. The cost of the piano one year from now will be $5,800. If the family can invest $5,000 now, how much annual interest must they earn on their investment to have $5,800 at the end of one year?

Solution:

The Hughes family can invest $5,000 now and needs it to accumulate to $5,800 in one year. The rate of annual interest they need to earn can be computed as shown below.

If Table I is used, the applicable formula is:

$$FV = PVF_{\overline{n}|i}$$
$$FV = P(\text{Table I factor})$$
$$\frac{FV}{P} = \text{Table I factor}$$

$$\frac{\$5,800}{\$5,000} = 1.1600$$

Reading across the n = 1 row, the factor value 1.1600 corresponds to an annual effective interest rate of 16%. Therefore, the Hughes family would have to earn 16% annual interest to accomplish their goal. The same result is obtained if Table II is used to solve this problem.

Example 8: (Determining the Rental Payment)

Provo 1st National Bank is willing to lend a customer $75,000 to buy a warehouse. The note will be secured by a 5-year mortgage and carry an annual interest rate of 12%. Equal payments are to be made at the end of each year over the 5-year period. How much will the yearly payment be?

Solution:

This is an example of an unknown annuity payment. Since the present value ($75,000) is known, as well as the interest rate (12%) and the number of periods (5), the annuity payment can be determined using Table IV. The applicable formula is:

$$PV_n = R(PVAF_{\overline{n}|i})$$
$$PV_n = R(\text{Table IV factor})$$
$$\$75,000 = R(3.6048) \text{ (for } n = 5 \text{ and } i = 12\%)$$
$$\frac{\$75,000}{3.6048} = R$$
$$\underline{\$20,806} \text{ (rounded)} = R$$

The payment on this 5-year mortgage would be approximately $20,806 each year.

ADDITIONAL COMPLEXITIES

The illustrations up to this point have been fairly straightforward. In practice, however, complexities can arise that make it somewhat more difficult to use the future and present value tables. Two of these complexities involve: (1) converting ordinary annuity tables to annuity due factor values, and (2) interpolation.

Ordinary Annuity vs. Annuity Due

Annuities are of two types: ordinary annuities (annuities in arrears) and annuities due (annuities in advance). The periodic rents or payments for an **ordinary annuity** are made at the *end of each period,* and the last payment coincides with the end of the annuity term. The periodic rents or payments for an **annuity due** are made at the *beginning of each period,* and one period of the annuity term remains after the last payment. These differences are illustrated below.

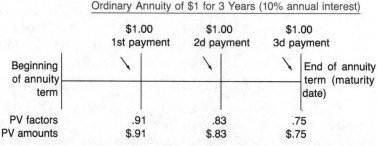

Ordinary Annuity of $1 for 3 Years (10% annual interest)

	$1.00 1st payment	$1.00 2d payment	$1.00 3d payment	
Beginning of annuity term				End of annuity term (maturity date)
PV factors	.91	.83	.75	
PV amounts	$.91	$.83	$.75	

Therefore, assuming a 10% annual interest rate, the present value of an annuity of $1 per year to be received at the *end* of each of the next 3 years is $2.49 ($.91 + $.83 + $.75). Notice that the last $1 is received on the maturity date, or the end of the annuity term.

Again assuming a 10% annual interest rate, the present value of an annuity of $1 per year to be received at the *beginning* of each of the next 3 years is $2.74 ($1.00 + $.91 + $.83). Notice here that the last payment is received 1 year prior to the maturity date.

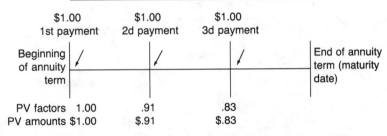

Annuity Due of $1 for 3 Years (10% annual interest)

The difference in the two annuities is in the timing of the payments, and, therefore, how many interest periods are involved. As shown below, both annuities require 3 payments. However, the ordinary annuity payments are at the end of each period so there are only 2 periods of interest accumulation while the annuity due payments are in advance or at the beginning of the period so there are 3 periods of interest accumulation.

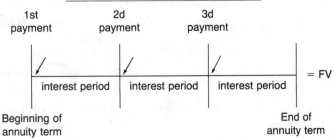

Accumulation of Ordinary Annuity for 3 Years

Accumulation of Annuity Due for 3 Years

The preceding situation is exactly reversed when viewed from a present-value standpoint. The ordinary annuity has 3 interest or discount periods, while the annuity due has only 2 periods, as shown below.

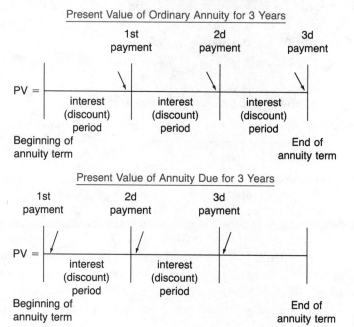

Even though most future and present value annuity tables are computed for ordinary annuities (payments at the end of the periods), these tables can be used for solving annuity due problems where the payments are in advance. However, the following adjustments would be required.

1. To find the **future value of an annuity due** using ordinary annuity table values (Table III), select the appropriate table value for an ordinary annuity for one additional period (n + 1) and subtract the extra payment (which is 1.0000 in terms of the table value for rents of $1.00). The formula is

$$FV_n = R(FVAF_{\overline{n+1}|i} - 1).$$

2. To find the **present value of an annuity due** using ordinary annuity table values (Table IV), select the appropriate table value for an ordinary annuity for one less period (n − 1) and add the extra payment (1.0000). The formula is

$$PV_n = R(PVAF_{\overline{n-1}|i} + 1).$$

By making the above adjustments, when payments are in advance, ordinary annuity tables may be used for all annuity situations. There are special annuity due tables available, but they are not needed if one understands how to convert from ordinary annuity factor values to annuity due factor values.

For example, the table value (Table III) for the future amount of an annuity due for 3 periods at 10% is:

(1) Factor for future value of an ordinary annuity of $1 for 4 periods
    (n + 1) at 10%... 4.6410
(2) Less one payment.. 1.0000
(3) Factor for future value of an annuity due of $1 for 3 periods at 10%......... 3.6410

The table value (Table IV) for the present value of an annuity due for 3 periods at 10% is:

(1) Factor for present value of an ordinary annuity of $1 for two periods
    (n − 1) at 10%... 1.7355
(2) Plus one payment.. 1.0000
(3) Factor for present value of an annuity due of $1 for 3 periods at 10%....... 2.7355

The following examples illustrate the application of converting from ordinary annuity table values to annuity due table values.

Example 9: (Converting from Ordinary Annuity to Annuity Due Table Values for Future Amounts)

The Porter Corporation desires to accumulate funds to retire a $200,000 bond issue at the end of 15 years. Funds set aside for this purpose can be invested to yield 8%. What annual payment starting immediately would provide the needed funds?

Solution:

Annuity payments of an unknown amount are to be accumulated toward a specific dollar amount at a known interest rate. Therefore, Table III is used. Because the first payment is to be made immediately, all payments will fall due at the beginning of each period and an annuity due is used. The appropriate formula is:

$$FV_n = R(FVAF_{\overline{n+1}|i} - 1)$$

where:
FV_n = $200,000
R = Unknown annual payment
n = 15 periods
i   = 8% annual interest

$200,000 = R (Table III $_{\overline{16}|8\%}$ − 1)
$200,000 = R(29.3243)

$$\frac{\$200,000}{29.3243} = R$$

$6,820 = R

Porter Corporation must deposit $6,820 annually, starting immediately, to accumulate $200,000 in 15 years at 8% annual interest.

Example 10: (Converting from Ordinary Annuity to Annuity Due Table Values for Present Values)

Utah Corporation has completed negotiations to lease equipment with a fair market value of $45,897. The lease contract specifies semiannual payments of $3,775 for 10 years beginning immediately. At the end of the lease, Utah Corporation may purchase the equipment for a nominal amount. What is the implicit annual rate of interest on the lease purchase?

Solution:

This is a common application of an annuity due situation in accounting since most lease contracts require payments in advance, i.e., at the beginning of the period rather than at the end of the period. The implicit interest rate must be computed for the present value of an annuity due. The present value is the fair market value of the equipment, and the payment is the lease payment. Table IV is used, and the applicable formula is:

$$PV_n = R(PVAF_{\overline{n-1}|i} + 1)$$

where:

PV_n = $45,897

R = $3,775

n = 20 periods (10 years × 2 payments per year)

i = The unknown semiannual interest rate

$45,897 = $3,775 (Table IV$_{\overline{19}|i}$ + 1)

$$\frac{\$45,897}{\$3,775} = 12.1581 = \text{Table IV}_{\overline{19}|i} + 1$$

11.1581 = Table IV$_{\overline{19}|i}$

Examination of Table IV for 19 periods and a factor of 11.1581 shows Table IV$_{\overline{19}|6\%}$ = 11.1581. Therefore, i = 6%. The implicit annual interest rate is twice the semiannual rate, or 2 × 6% = 12%.

Interpolation

A difficulty in using future and present value tables arises when the exact factor does not appear in the table. One solution is to use the formula. **Interpolation** is another solution. Interpolation assumes the change between two values is linear. Although such an assumption is not totally correct, the margin of error is often insignificant, especially if the table value ranges are not too wide.

For example, determine the table value for the present value of $1 due in 9 periods at 4½%. The appropriate factor does not appear in Table II. However, the two closest values are Table II$_{\overline{9}|4\%}$ = .7026 and Table II$_{\overline{9}|5\%}$ = .6446. Interpolation relates the unknown value to the change in the known values. This relationship may be shown as a proportion:

$$\frac{y}{Y} = \frac{x}{X}$$

4%   4½%   5%

Y

$$\frac{5 - 4½}{5 - 4} = \frac{x}{.7026 - .6446}$$

.7026   ?   .6446

$$\frac{½}{1} = \frac{x}{.0580}$$

X

$$x = .0290$$

The .0290 is the difference between the value for 5% and the value for 4½%. Therefore, the value needed is .0290 + .6446 = .6736. Using the mathematical formula for Table II

$$\left\{ PV = A\left[\frac{1}{(1 + i)^n} \right] \right\},$$

the present value of $1 at 4½% interest for 9 periods is .6729

$$\left\{ PV = 1\left[\frac{1}{(1 + .045)^9} \right] \right\}.$$

The difference (.6736 − .6729 = .0007) is insignificant for most business purposes.

Interpolation is useful in finding a particular unknown table value that lies between two given values. This procedure is also used in approximating the number of periods or unknown interest rates when the table value is known. The following examples illustrate the determination of these two variables.

Example 11: Interpolation: Unknown Number of Periods

The Newbold Foundation contributes $600,000 to a university for a new building on the condition that construction will not begin until the gift, invested at 10% per year, amounts to $1,500,000. How long before construction may begin?

Solution:

This problem involves finding the time (number of periods) required for a lump-sum payment to accumulate to a specified future amount. Table I is used and the applicable formula is:

$$FV = P(FVF_{\overline{n}|i})$$

where:
FV = $1,500,000
P = $600,000
n = Unknown number of periods
i = 10% effective interest rate per year

$$\$1{,}500{,}000 = \$600{,}000 \ (\text{Table I}_{\overline{n}|10\%})$$

$$\frac{\$1{,}500{,}000}{\$\ 600{,}000} = \text{Table I}_{\overline{n}|10\%}$$

$$2.5 = \text{Table I}_{\overline{n}|10\%}$$

Referring to Table I, reading down the $i = 10\%$ column:

n	Table Factor
9 =	2.3579
10 =	2.5937

Interpolating:

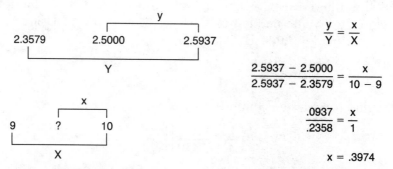

The .3974 is the difference between the number of periods at table factor 2.5937 and the number of periods at table factor 2.5000. Therefore, the number of periods needed is $10.0000 - .3974 = 9.6026$. In other words, about 9.6 periods (in this case, years) are required for $600,000 to amount to $1,500,000 at 10% annual interest.

Example 12: (Interpolation: Implicit Rate of Interest)

Fellmar, Inc. has entered into an automobile lease arrangement. The fair market value of the leased automobile is $15,815 and the contract calls for quarterly payments of $1,525 due at the end of each quarter for 3 years. What is the implicit rate of interest on the lease arrangement?

Solution:

The implicit interest rate must be computed for the present value of an ordinary annuity. The present value is the fair market value of the automobile, and the payment is the lease payment. Table IV is used, and the appropriate formula is given below.

$$PV_n = R(PVAF_{\overline{n}|i})$$
where:
$PV_n = \$15{,}815$
$R\ \ = \$1{,}525$
$n\ \ = 12$ (3 years × 4 payments per year)
$i\ \ \ = $ The unknown quarterly interest rate

$15,815 = \$1,525 \ (\text{Table IV}_{\overline{12}|i})$

$\dfrac{\$15,815}{\$1,525} = \text{Table IV}_{\overline{12}|i}$

$10.3705 = \text{Table IV}_{\overline{12}|i}$

Reading across the $n = 12$ row of Table IV:

i		Table Factor
2% =		10.5753
3% =		9.9540

Interpolating:

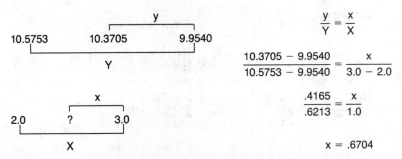

$$\frac{y}{Y} = \frac{x}{X}$$

$$\frac{10.3705 - 9.9540}{10.5753 - 9.9540} = \frac{x}{3.0 - 2.0}$$

$$\frac{.4165}{.6213} = \frac{x}{1.0}$$

$$x = .6704$$

The .6704 is the difference between the interest rate at the table factor 9.9540 and the interest rate at the table factor 10.3705. Therefore, the quarterly implicit interest rate is $3.0000 - .6704 = 2.3296\%$; and the annual implicit interest rate is 9.3184% ($2.3296\% \times 4$).

CONCLUDING COMMENT

As noted in Chapter 2, the FASB's conceptual framework allows for various measurement attributes, one of which is discounted present values. This chapter has illustrated a few of the many business applications of present and future value measurement techniques. As interest rates continue to fluctuate in the world economy, many times reaching double-digit levels, the importance of the time value of money concept will increase. In the remaining chapters of this text, additional illustrations of this important concept will be presented.

TABLE I
Amount of $1 Due in n Periods

n	1%	2%	3%	4%	5%	6%	7%	8%	9%	10%	11%	12%	14%	16%	20%
1	1.0100	1.0200	1.0300	1.0400	1.0500	1.0600	1.0700	1.0800	1.0900	1.1000	1.1100	1.1200	1.1400	1.1600	1.2000
2	1.0201	1.0404	1.0609	1.0816	1.1025	1.1236	1.1449	1.1664	1.1881	1.2100	1.2321	1.2544	1.2996	1.3456	1.4400
3	1.0303	1.0612	1.0927	1.1249	1.1576	1.1910	1.2250	1.2597	1.2950	1.3310	1.3676	1.4049	1.4815	1.5609	1.7280
4	1.0406	1.0824	1.1255	1.1699	1.2155	1.2625	1.3108	1.3605	1.4116	1.4641	1.5181	1.5735	1.6890	1.8106	2.0736
5	1.0510	1.1041	1.1593	1.2167	1.2763	1.3382	1.4026	1.4693	1.5386	1.6105	1.6851	1.7623	1.9254	2.1003	2.4883
6	1.0615	1.1262	1.1941	1.2653	1.3401	1.4185	1.5007	1.5869	1.6771	1.7716	1.8704	1.9738	2.1950	2.4364	2.9860
7	1.0721	1.1487	1.2299	1.3159	1.4071	1.5036	1.6058	1.7138	1.8280	1.9487	2.0762	2.2107	2.5023	2.8262	3.5832
8	1.0829	1.1717	1.2668	1.3686	1.4775	1.5958	1.7182	1.8509	1.9926	2.1436	2.3045	2.4760	2.8526	3.2784	4.2998
9	1.0937	1.1951	1.3048	1.4233	1.5513	1.6895	1.8385	1.9990	2.1719	2.3579	2.5580	2.7731	3.2519	3.8030	5.1598
10	1.1046	1.2190	1.3439	1.4802	1.6289	1.7908	1.9672	2.1589	2.3674	2.5937	2.8394	3.1058	3.7072	4.4114	6.1917
11	1.1157	1.2434	1.3842	1.5395	1.7103	1.8983	2.1049	2.3316	2.5804	2.8531	3.1518	3.4785	4.2262	5.1173	7.4301
12	1.1268	1.2682	1.4258	1.6010	1.7959	2.0122	2.2522	2.5182	2.8127	3.1384	3.4985	3.8960	4.8179	5.9360	8.9161
13	1.1381	1.2936	1.4685	1.6651	1.8856	2.1329	2.4098	2.7196	3.0658	3.4523	3.8833	4.3635	5.4924	6.8858	10.6993
14	1.1495	1.3195	1.5126	1.7317	1.9799	2.2609	2.5785	2.9372	3.3417	3.7975	4.3104	4.8871	6.2613	7.9875	12.8392
15	1.1610	1.3459	1.5580	1.8009	2.0789	2.3966	2.7590	3.1722	3.6425	4.1772	4.7846	5.4736	7.1379	9.2655	15.4070
16	1.1726	1.3728	1.6047	1.8730	2.1829	2.5404	2.9522	3.4259	3.9703	4.5950	5.3109	6.1304	8.1372	10.7480	18.4884
17	1.1843	1.4002	1.6528	1.9479	2.2920	2.6928	3.1588	3.7000	4.3276	5.0545	5.8951	6.8660	9.2765	12.4677	22.1861
18	1.1961	1.4282	1.7024	2.0258	2.4066	2.8543	3.3799	3.9960	4.7171	5.5599	6.5436	7.6900	10.5752	14.4625	26.6233
19	1.2081	1.4568	1.7535	2.1068	2.5270	3.0256	3.6165	4.3157	5.1417	6.1159	7.2633	8.6128	12.0557	16.7765	31.9480
20	1.2202	1.4859	1.8061	2.1911	2.6533	3.2071	3.8697	4.6610	5.6044	6.7275	8.0623	9.6463	13.7435	19.4608	38.3376
21	1.2324	1.5157	1.8603	2.2788	2.7860	3.3996	4.1406	5.0338	6.1088	7.4002	8.9492	10.8038	15.6676	22.5745	46.0051
22	1.2447	1.5460	1.9161	2.3699	2.9253	3.6035	4.4304	5.4365	6.6586	8.1403	9.9336	12.1003	17.8610	26.1864	55.2061
23	1.2572	1.5769	1.9736	2.4647	3.0715	3.8197	4.7405	5.8715	7.2579	8.9543	11.0263	13.5523	20.3616	30.3762	66.2474
24	1.2697	1.6084	2.0328	2.5633	3.2251	4.0489	5.0724	6.3412	7.9111	9.8497	12.2392	15.1786	23.2122	35.2364	79.4968
25	1.2824	1.6406	2.0938	2.6658	3.3864	4.2919	5.4274	6.8485	8.6231	10.8347	13.5855	17.0001	26.4619	40.8742	95.3962
26	1.2953	1.6734	2.1566	2.7725	3.5557	4.5494	5.8074	7.3964	9.3992	11.9182	15.0799	19.0401	30.1666	47.4141	114.4755
27	1.3082	1.7069	2.2213	2.8834	3.7335	4.8223	6.2139	7.9881	10.2451	13.1100	16.7386	21.3249	34.3899	55.0004	137.3706
28	1.3213	1.7410	2.2879	2.9987	3.9201	5.1117	6.6488	8.6271	11.1671	14.4210	18.5799	23.8839	39.2045	63.8004	164.8447
29	1.3345	1.7758	2.3566	3.1187	4.1161	5.4184	7.1143	9.3173	12.1722	15.8631	20.6237	26.7499	44.6931	74.0085	197.8136
30	1.3478	1.8114	2.4273	3.2434	4.3219	5.7435	7.6123	10.0627	13.2677	17.4494	22.8923	29.9599	50.9502	85.8499	237.3763
35	1.4166	1.9999	2.8139	3.9461	5.5160	7.6861	10.6766	14.7853	20.4140	28.1024	38.5749	52.7996	98.1002	180.3141	590.6682
40	1.4889	2.2080	3.2620	4.8010	7.0400	10.2857	14.9745	21.7245	31.4094	45.2593	65.0009	93.0510	188.8835	378.7212	1,469.7716
45	1.5648	2.4379	3.7816	5.8412	8.9850	13.7646	21.0025	31.9204	48.3273	72.8905	109.5302	163.9876	363.6791	795.4438	3,657.2620
50	1.6446	2.6916	4.3839	7.1067	11.4674	18.4202	29.4570	46.9016	74.3575	117.3909	184.5648	289.0022	700.2330	1,670.7038	9,100.4382

TABLE II
Present Value of $1 Due in n Periods

n	1%	2%	3%	4%	5%	6%	7%	8%	9%	10%	11%	12%	14%	16%	20%
1	0.9901	0.9804	0.9709	0.9615	0.9524	0.9434	0.9346	0.9259	0.9174	0.9091	0.9009	0.8929	0.8772	0.8621	0.8333
2	0.9803	0.9612	0.9426	0.9246	0.9070	0.8900	0.8734	0.8573	0.8417	0.8264	0.8116	0.7972	0.7695	0.7432	0.6944
3	0.9706	0.9423	0.9151	0.8890	0.8638	0.8396	0.8163	0.7938	0.7722	0.7513	0.7312	0.7118	0.6750	0.6407	0.5787
4	0.9610	0.9238	0.8885	0.8548	0.8227	0.7921	0.7629	0.7350	0.7084	0.6830	0.6587	0.6355	0.5921	0.5523	0.4823
5	0.9515	0.9057	0.8626	0.8219	0.7835	0.7473	0.7130	0.6806	0.6499	0.6209	0.5935	0.5674	0.5194	0.4761	0.4019
6	0.9420	0.8880	0.8375	0.7903	0.7462	0.7050	0.6663	0.6302	0.5963	0.5645	0.5346	0.5066	0.4556	0.4104	0.3349
7	0.9327	0.8706	0.8131	0.7599	0.7107	0.6651	0.6227	0.5835	0.5470	0.5132	0.4817	0.4523	0.3996	0.3538	0.2791
8	0.9235	0.8535	0.7894	0.7307	0.6768	0.6274	0.5820	0.5403	0.5019	0.4665	0.4339	0.4039	0.3506	0.3050	0.2326
9	0.9143	0.8368	0.7664	0.7026	0.6446	0.5919	0.5439	0.5002	0.4604	0.4241	0.3909	0.3606	0.3075	0.2630	0.1938
10	0.9053	0.8203	0.7441	0.6756	0.6139	0.5584	0.5083	0.4632	0.4224	0.3855	0.3522	0.3220	0.2697	0.2267	0.1615
11	0.8963	0.8043	0.7224	0.6496	0.5847	0.5268	0.4751	0.4289	0.3875	0.3505	0.3173	0.2875	0.2366	0.1954	0.1346
12	0.8874	0.7885	0.7014	0.6246	0.5568	0.4970	0.4440	0.3971	0.3555	0.3186	0.2858	0.2567	0.2076	0.1685	0.1122
13	0.8787	0.7730	0.6810	0.6006	0.5303	0.4688	0.4150	0.3677	0.3262	0.2897	0.2575	0.2292	0.1821	0.1452	0.0935
14	0.8700	0.7579	0.6611	0.5775	0.5051	0.4423	0.3878	0.3405	0.2992	0.2633	0.2320	0.2046	0.1597	0.1252	0.0779
15	0.8613	0.7430	0.6419	0.5553	0.4810	0.4173	0.3624	0.3152	0.2745	0.2394	0.2090	0.1827	0.1401	0.1079	0.0649
16	0.8528	0.7284	0.6232	0.5339	0.4581	0.3936	0.3387	0.2919	0.2519	0.2176	0.1883	0.1631	0.1229	0.0930	0.0541
17	0.8444	0.7142	0.6050	0.5134	0.4363	0.3714	0.3166	0.2703	0.2311	0.1978	0.1696	0.1456	0.1078	0.0802	0.0451
18	0.8360	0.7002	0.5874	0.4936	0.4155	0.3503	0.2959	0.2502	0.2120	0.1799	0.1528	0.1300	0.0946	0.0691	0.0376
19	0.8277	0.6864	0.5703	0.4746	0.3957	0.3305	0.2765	0.2317	0.1945	0.1635	0.1377	0.1161	0.0829	0.0596	0.0313
20	0.8195	0.6730	0.5537	0.4564	0.3769	0.3118	0.2584	0.2145	0.1784	0.1486	0.1240	0.1037	0.0728	0.0514	0.0261
21	0.8114	0.6598	0.5375	0.4388	0.3589	0.2942	0.2415	0.1987	0.1637	0.1351	0.1117	0.0926	0.0638	0.0443	0.0217
22	0.8034	0.6468	0.5219	0.4220	0.3418	0.2775	0.2257	0.1839	0.1502	0.1228	0.1007	0.0826	0.0560	0.0382	0.0181
23	0.7954	0.6342	0.5067	0.4057	0.3256	0.2618	0.2109	0.1703	0.1378	0.1117	0.0907	0.0738	0.0491	0.0329	0.0151
24	0.7876	0.6217	0.4919	0.3901	0.3101	0.2470	0.1971	0.1577	0.1264	0.1015	0.0817	0.0659	0.0431	0.0284	0.0126
25	0.7798	0.6095	0.4776	0.3751	0.2953	0.2330	0.1842	0.1460	0.1160	0.0923	0.0736	0.0588	0.0378	0.0245	0.0105
26	0.7720	0.5976	0.4637	0.3607	0.2812	0.2198	0.1722	0.1352	0.1064	0.0839	0.0663	0.0525	0.0331	0.0211	0.0087
27	0.7644	0.5859	0.4502	0.3468	0.2678	0.2074	0.1609	0.1252	0.0976	0.0763	0.0597	0.0469	0.0291	0.0182	0.0073
28	0.7568	0.5744	0.4371	0.3335	0.2551	0.1956	0.1504	0.1159	0.0895	0.0693	0.0538	0.0419	0.0255	0.0157	0.0061
29	0.7493	0.5631	0.4243	0.3207	0.2429	0.1846	0.1406	0.1073	0.0822	0.0630	0.0485	0.0374	0.0224	0.0135	0.0051
30	0.7419	0.5521	0.4120	0.3083	0.2314	0.1741	0.1314	0.0994	0.0754	0.0573	0.0437	0.0334	0.0196	0.0116	0.0042
35	0.7059	0.5000	0.3554	0.2534	0.1813	0.1301	0.0937	0.0676	0.0490	0.0356	0.0259	0.0189	0.0102	0.0055	0.0017
40	0.6717	0.4529	0.3066	0.2083	0.1420	0.0972	0.0668	0.0460	0.0318	0.0221	0.0154	0.0107	0.0053	0.0026	0.0007
45	0.6391	0.4102	0.2644	0.1712	0.1113	0.0727	0.0476	0.0313	0.0207	0.0137	0.0091	0.0061	0.0027	0.0013	0.0003
50	0.6080	0.3715	0.2281	0.1407	0.0872	0.0543	0.0339	0.0213	0.0134	0.0085	0.0054	0.0035	0.0014	0.0006	0.0001

TABLE III
Amount of an Ordinary Annuity of $1 per Period

	1%	2%	3%	4%	5%	6%	7%	8%	9%	10%	11%	12%	14%	16%	20%
1	1.0000	1.0000	1.0000	1.0000	1.0000	1.0000	1.0000	1.0000	1.0000	1.0000	1.0000	1.0000	1.0000	1.0000	1.0000
2	2.0100	2.0200	2.0300	2.0400	2.0500	2.0600	2.0700	2.0800	2.0900	2.1000	2.1100	2.1200	2.1400	2.1600	2.2000
3	3.0301	3.0604	3.0909	3.1216	3.1525	3.1836	3.2149	3.2464	3.2781	3.3100	3.3421	3.3744	3.4396	3.5056	3.6400
4	4.0604	4.1216	4.1836	4.2465	4.3101	4.3746	4.4399	4.5061	4.5731	4.6410	4.7097	4.7793	4.9211	5.0665	5.3680
5	5.1010	5.2040	5.3091	5.4163	5.5256	5.6371	5.7507	5.8666	5.9847	6.1051	6.2278	6.3528	6.6101	6.8771	7.4416
6	6.1520	6.3081	6.4684	6.6330	6.8019	6.9753	7.1533	7.3359	7.5233	7.7156	7.9129	8.1152	8.5355	8.9775	9.9299
7	7.2135	7.4343	7.6625	7.8983	8.1420	8.3938	8.6540	8.9228	9.2004	9.4872	9.7833	10.0890	10.7305	11.4139	12.9159
8	8.2857	8.5830	8.8923	9.2142	9.5491	9.8975	10.2598	10.6366	11.0285	11.4359	11.8594	12.2997	13.2328	14.2401	16.4991
9	9.3685	9.7546	10.1591	10.5828	11.0266	11.4913	11.9780	12.4876	13.0210	13.5795	14.1640	14.7757	16.0853	17.5185	20.7989
10	10.4622	10.9497	11.4639	12.0061	12.5779	13.1808	13.8164	14.4866	15.1929	15.9374	16.7220	17.5487	19.3373	21.3215	25.9587
11	11.5668	12.1687	12.8078	13.4864	14.2068	14.9716	15.7836	16.6455	17.5603	18.5312	19.5614	20.6546	23.0445	25.7329	32.1504
12	12.6825	13.4121	14.1920	15.0258	15.9171	16.8699	17.8885	18.9771	20.1407	21.3843	22.7132	24.1331	27.2707	30.8502	39.5805
13	13.8093	14.6803	15.6178	16.6268	17.7130	18.8821	20.1406	21.4953	22.9534	24.5227	26.2116	28.0291	32.0887	36.7862	48.4966
14	14.9474	15.9739	17.0863	18.2919	19.5986	21.0151	22.5505	24.2149	26.0192	27.9750	30.0949	32.3926	37.5811	43.6720	59.1959
15	16.0969	17.2934	18.5989	20.0236	21.5786	23.2760	25.1290	27.1521	29.3609	31.7725	34.4054	37.2797	43.8424	51.6595	72.0351
16	17.2579	18.6393	20.1569	21.8245	23.6575	25.6725	27.8881	30.3243	33.0034	35.9497	39.1899	42.7533	50.9804	60.9250	87.4421
17	18.4304	20.0121	21.7616	23.6975	25.8404	28.2129	30.8402	33.7502	36.9737	40.5447	44.5008	48.8837	59.1176	71.6730	105.9306
18	19.6147	21.4123	23.4144	25.6454	28.1324	30.9057	33.9990	37.4502	41.3013	45.5992	50.3959	55.7497	68.3941	84.1407	128.1167
19	20.8109	22.8406	25.1169	27.6712	30.5390	33.7600	37.3790	41.4463	46.0185	51.1591	56.9395	63.4397	78.9692	98.6032	154.7400
20	22.0190	24.2974	26.8704	29.7781	33.0660	36.7856	40.9955	45.7620	51.1601	57.2750	64.2028	72.0524	91.0249	115.3797	186.6880
21	23.2392	25.7833	28.6765	31.9692	35.7193	39.9927	44.8652	50.4229	56.7645	64.0025	72.2651	81.6987	104.7684	134.8405	225.0256
22	24.4716	27.2990	30.5368	34.2480	38.5052	43.3923	49.0057	55.4568	62.8733	71.4027	81.2143	92.5026	120.4360	157.4150	271.0307
23	25.7163	28.8450	32.4529	36.6179	41.4305	46.9958	53.4361	60.8933	69.5319	79.5430	91.1479	104.6029	138.2970	183.6014	326.2369
24	26.9735	30.4219	34.4265	39.0826	44.5020	50.8156	58.1767	66.7648	76.7898	88.4973	102.1742	118.1552	158.6586	213.9776	392.4842
25	28.2432	32.0303	36.4593	41.6459	47.7271	54.8645	63.2490	73.1059	84.7009	98.3471	114.4133	133.3339	181.8708	249.2140	471.9811
26	29.5256	33.6709	38.5530	44.3117	51.1135	59.1564	68.6765	79.9544	93.3240	109.1818	127.9988	150.3339	208.3327	290.0883	567.3773
27	30.8209	35.3443	40.7096	47.0842	54.6691	63.7058	74.4838	87.3508	102.7231	121.0999	143.0786	169.3740	238.4993	337.5024	681.8528
28	32.1291	37.0512	42.9309	49.9676	58.4026	68.5281	80.6977	95.3388	112.9682	134.2099	159.8173	190.6989	272.8892	392.5028	819.2233
29	33.4504	38.7922	45.2189	52.9663	62.3227	73.6398	87.3465	103.9659	124.1354	148.6309	178.3972	214.5828	312.0937	456.3032	984.0680
30	34.7849	40.5681	47.5754	56.0849	66.4388	79.0582	94.4608	113.2832	136.3075	164.4940	199.0209	241.3327	356.7868	530.3117	1181.8816
35	41.6603	49.9945	60.4621	73.6522	90.3203	111.4348	138.2369	172.3168	215.7108	271.0244	341.5896	431.6635	693.5727	1120.7130	2948.3411
40	48.8864	60.4020	75.4013	95.0255	120.7998	154.7620	199.6351	259.0565	337.8824	442.5926	581.8261	767.0914	1342.0251	2360.7572	7343.8578
45	56.4811	71.8927	92.7199	121.0294	159.7002	212.7435	285.7493	386.5056	525.8587	718.9048	986.6386	1358.2300	2590.5648	4965.2739	18281.3099
50	64.4632	84.5794	112.7969	152.6671	209.3480	290.3359	406.5289	573.7702	815.0836	1163.9085	1668.7712	2400.0182	4994.5213	10435.6488	45497.1908

TABLE IV
Present Value of an Ordinary Annuity of $1 per Period

	1%	2%	3%	4%	5%	6%	7%	8%	9%	10%	11%	12%	14%	16%	20%
1	0.9901	0.9804	0.9709	0.9615	0.9524	0.9434	0.9346	0.9259	0.9174	0.9091	0.9009	0.8929	0.8772	0.8621	0.8333
2	1.9704	1.9416	1.9135	1.8861	1.8594	1.8334	1.8080	1.7833	1.7591	1.7355	1.7125	1.6901	1.6467	1.6052	1.5278
3	2.9410	2.8839	2.8286	2.7751	2.7232	2.6730	2.6243	2.5771	2.5313	2.4869	2.4437	2.4018	2.3216	2.2459	2.1065
4	3.9020	3.8077	3.7171	3.6299	3.5460	3.4651	3.3872	3.3121	3.2397	3.1699	3.1024	3.0373	2.9137	2.7982	2.5887
5	4.8534	4.7135	4.5797	4.4518	4.3295	4.2124	4.1002	3.9927	3.8897	3.7908	3.6959	3.6048	3.4331	3.2743	2.9906
6	5.7955	5.6014	5.4172	5.2421	5.0757	4.9173	4.7665	4.6229	4.4859	4.3553	4.2305	4.1114	3.8887	3.6847	3.3255
7	6.7282	6.4720	6.2303	6.0021	5.7864	5.5824	5.3893	5.2064	5.0330	4.8684	4.7122	4.5638	4.2883	4.0386	3.6046
8	7.6517	7.3255	7.0197	6.7327	6.4632	6.2098	5.9713	5.7466	5.5348	5.3349	5.1461	4.9676	4.6389	4.3436	3.8372
9	8.5660	8.1622	7.7861	7.4353	7.1078	6.8017	6.5152	6.2469	5.9952	5.7590	5.5370	5.3282	4.9464	4.6065	4.0310
10	9.4713	8.9826	8.5302	8.1109	7.7217	7.3601	7.0236	6.7101	6.4177	6.1446	5.8892	5.6502	5.2161	4.8332	4.1925
11	10.3676	9.7868	9.2526	8.7605	8.3064	7.8869	7.4987	7.1390	6.8052	6.4951	6.2065	5.9377	5.4527	5.0286	4.3271
12	11.2551	10.5753	9.9540	9.3851	8.8633	8.3838	7.9427	7.5361	7.1607	6.8137	6.4924	6.1944	5.6603	5.1971	4.4392
13	12.1337	11.3484	10.6350	9.9856	9.3936	8.8527	8.3577	7.9038	7.4869	7.1034	6.7499	6.4235	5.8424	5.3423	4.5327
14	13.0037	12.1062	11.2961	10.5631	9.8986	9.2950	8.7455	8.2442	7.7862	7.3667	6.9819	6.6282	6.0021	5.4675	4.6106
15	13.8651	12.8493	11.9379	11.1184	10.3797	9.7122	9.1079	8.5595	8.0607	7.6061	7.1909	6.8109	6.1422	5.5755	4.6755
16	14.7179	13.5777	12.5611	11.6523	10.8378	10.1059	9.4466	8.8514	8.3126	7.8237	7.3792	6.9740	6.2651	5.6685	4.7296
17	15.5623	14.2919	13.1661	12.1657	11.2741	10.4773	9.7632	9.1216	8.5436	8.0216	7.5488	7.1196	6.3729	5.7487	4.7746
18	16.3983	14.9920	13.7535	12.6593	11.6896	10.8276	10.0591	9.3719	8.7556	8.2014	7.7016	7.2497	6.4674	5.8178	4.8122
19	17.2260	15.6785	14.3238	13.1339	12.0853	11.1581	10.3356	9.6036	8.9501	8.3649	7.8393	7.3658	6.5504	5.8775	4.8435
20	18.0456	16.3514	14.8775	13.5903	12.4622	11.4699	10.5940	9.8181	9.1285	8.5136	7.9633	7.4694	6.6231	5.9288	4.8696
21	18.8570	17.0112	15.4150	14.0292	12.8212	11.7641	10.8355	10.0168	9.2922	8.6487	8.0751	7.5620	6.6870	5.9731	4.8913
22	19.6604	17.6580	15.9369	14.4511	13.1630	12.0416	11.0612	10.2007	9.4424	8.7715	8.1757	7.6446	6.7429	6.0113	4.9094
23	20.4558	18.2922	16.4436	14.8568	13.4886	12.3034	11.2722	10.3711	9.5802	8.8832	8.2664	7.7184	6.7921	6.0442	4.9245
24	21.2434	18.9139	16.9355	15.2470	13.7986	12.5504	11.4693	10.5288	9.7066	8.9847	8.3481	7.7843	6.8351	6.0726	4.9371
25	22.0232	19.5235	17.4131	15.6221	14.0939	12.7834	11.6536	10.6748	9.8226	9.0770	8.4217	7.8431	6.8729	6.0971	4.9476
26	22.7952	20.1210	17.8768	15.9828	14.3752	13.0032	11.8258	10.8100	9.9290	9.1609	8.4881	7.8957	6.9061	6.1182	4.9563
27	23.5596	20.7069	18.3270	16.3296	14.6430	13.2105	11.9867	10.9352	10.0266	9.2372	8.5478	7.9426	6.9352	6.1364	4.9636
28	24.3164	21.2813	18.7641	16.6631	14.8981	13.4062	12.1371	11.0511	10.1161	9.3066	8.6016	7.9844	6.9607	6.1520	4.9697
29	25.0658	21.8444	19.1885	16.9837	15.1411	13.5907	12.2777	11.1584	10.1983	9.3696	8.6501	8.0218	6.9830	6.1656	4.9747
30	25.8077	22.3965	19.6004	17.2920	15.3725	13.7648	12.4090	11.2578	10.2737	9.4269	8.6938	8.0552	7.0027	6.1772	4.9789
35	29.4086	24.9986	21.4872	18.6646	16.3742	14.4982	12.9477	11.6546	10.5668	9.6442	8.8552	8.1755	7.0700	6.2153	4.9915
40	32.8347	27.3555	23.1148	19.7928	17.1591	15.0463	13.3317	11.9246	10.7574	9.7791	8.9511	8.2438	7.1050	6.2335	4.9966
45	36.0945	29.4902	24.5187	20.7200	17.7741	15.4558	13.6055	12.1084	10.8812	9.8628	9.0079	8.2825	7.1232	6.2421	4.9986
50	39.1961	31.4236	25.7298	21.4822	18.2559	15.7619	13.8007	12.2335	10.9617	9.9148	9.0417	8.3045	7.1327	6.2463	4.9995

QUESTIONS

1. Explain what is meant by the time value of money concept and describe its impact on business decisions.
2. Identify some common accounting applications of the time value of money concept.
3. Explain the difference between simple interest and compound interest.
4. Determine the amount of interest earned on the following:
   a. $9,000 borrowed from a bank at 10% simple annual interest for 8 months.
   b. $15,000 invested for 2 years at 15% simple annual interest.
   c. $1,500 invested for 26 days at 12% simple annual interest. (Use a 360-day year.)
5. Indicate the rate per period and the number of periods for each of the following:
   a. 10% per year, for 3 years, compounded annually.
   b. 10% per year, for 3 years, compounded semiannually.
   c. 10% per year, for 3 years, compounded quarterly.
   d. 10% per year, for 3 years, compounded monthly.
6. What is meant by *discounting* cash flows?
7. Indicate the table and the table value that would be used in calculating the following:
   a. The value today of $5,000 due in 3 years at 16% interest per year, compounded semiannually.
   b. The value today of 5 future annual payments of $4,000 at 12% interest per year, compounded annually.
   c. The value in ten years of $6,000 deposited today at 10% interest per year, compounded semiannually.
   d. The value in 5 years of quarterly payments of $1,500 for 5 years at 16% interest per year, compounded quarterly.
8. How much interest is earned on the following (round to nearest dollar):
   a. $10,500 borrowed for 5 years at 8% per year, compounded annually.
   b. $7,500 invested for 10 years at 20% per year, compounded semiannually.
   c. $12,000 borrowed for 4 years at 16% per year, compounded quarterly.
   d. $1,750 invested for 1 year at 24% per year, compounded monthly.
9. Determine the table values that would be used for the following:
   a. Present value of a single amount to be received at the end of 2 years at 10% interest compounded annually.
   b. Present value of 14 semiannual payments made at the end of the period at 10% interest compounded semiannually.
   c. Future value of a single amount invested for 5 years at 12% interest compounded annually.
   d. Future value of 6 equal quarterly payments made at the end of the period at 16% interest compounded quarterly.
10. An accounting student bought an inexpensive computer for $260 to assist in homework assignments. The student bought the computer on time, agreeing

to pay $26.12 at the end of each month for 12 months. What approximate monthly interest rate did the student pay?

11. Define an annuity. What is the difference between an "ordinary annuity" and an "annuity due?"

12. Explain how the table values for the future value ordinary annuity table are converted to annuity due values.

13. Explain how the table values for the present value ordinary annuity table are converted to annuity due values.

14. For each of the following, compute the future amount of an ordinary annuity. (Round to nearest dollar.)
    a. 12 annual payments of $100 at 6% per annum, compounded annually.
    b. 8 semiannual payments of $50 at 8% per annum, compounded semi-annually.
    c. 19 quarterly payments of $125 at 12% per annum, compounded quarterly.

15. What are the future amounts in Question 14 if the annuities are annuities due?

16. For each of the following, compute the present value of an ordinary annuity.
    a. $1,000 annually for 10 years at 8% per annum, compounded annually.
    b. $2,050 semiannually for 6 years at 6% per annum, compounded semi-annually.
    c. $5,600 quarterly for 3 years at 8% per annum, compounded quarterly.

17. What are the present values in Question 16 if the annuities are annuities due?

18. What is interpolation, when is it used, and is it 100% accurate (explain)?

19. Determine by interpolation the table value that would be used for the following:
    a. Future value of $1 in 6 years at 13% interest per year, compounded semi-annually.
    b. Future value of $1 paid annually for 10 years at 11% interest per year, compounded annually.
    c. Present value of $1 due in 10 years at 9% interest per year, compounded quarterly.
    d. Present value of semiannual payments of $1 for 10 years at 9% interest per year, compounded semiannually.

20. At what annual rate of interest would an investment of $20,000 accumulate to $38,000 at the end of 5 years? (Hint: Interpolation is needed)

EXERCISES

1. Sells Corporation borrowed $1,500 from its major shareholder, the president of the company, at 12% simple interest. The loan is to be repaid in 18 months. (a) How much will Sells have to pay to settle its obligation? (b) How much of the payment is interest? (c) If Sells Corporation has to borrow the $1,500 from the First State Bank at 16% annual interest compounded quarterly, how much interest would it have to pay?

2. Ryan Henry wants to buy his son a Datsun 300-ZX for his 21st birthday. If Henry's son is 16 now, and interest is 8% per annum, compounded semi-annually, what would Henry's semiannual investment need to be if the car will cost $26,000?

3. Determine the amount that must be deposited now at compound interest to provide the desired sum for each of the following.
   a. Amount to be invested for 10 years at 6% per annum, compounded semiannually, to equal $17,000.
   b. Amount to be invested for 2½ years at 8% per annum, compounded quarterly, to equal $5,000.
   c. Amount to be invested for 15 years at 12% per annum, compounded semiannually, then reinvested at 16% per annum, compounded quarterly, for 5 more years to equal $25,000.
   d. Amount to be invested at 8% per annum, compounded semiannually, for 3 years then $5,000 more added and reinvested at the same rate for another 3 years to equal $12,500.

4. Determine the number of periods the following would have to be invested to accumulate to $10,000. Convert the periods to years.
   a. $5,051 at 10% per annum, compounded semiannually.
   b. $5,002 at 8% per annum, compounded annually.
   c. $5,134 at 16% per annum, compounded quarterly.

5. Determine the annual interest rate that is needed for the following to accumulate to $50,000.
   a. $10,414 for 20 years, interest compounded semiannually.
   b. $7,102 for 10 years, interest compounded quarterly.
   c. $33,778 for 10 years, interest compounded annually.

6. Determine the amount that would accumulate for the following investments.
   a. $10,050 at 10% per annum, compounded annually, for 6 years.
   b. $650 at 12% per annum, compounded quarterly, for 10 years.
   c. $5,000 at 16% per annum compounded annually, for 4 years, and then reinvested at 16% per annum, compounded semiannually, for 4 more years.
   d. $1,000 at 8% per annum, compounded semiannually, for 5 years, an additional $1,000 added and then reinvested at 12% per annum, compounded quarterly for 3 more years.

7. Determine the number of periods $10,000 would have to be invested to accumulate to the following. Convert the periods to years.
   a. $59,360 at 16% per annum, compounded annually.
   b. $43,839 at 12% per annum, compounded quarterly.
   c. $33,864 at 10% per annum, compounded semiannually.

8. Determine the interest rate needed for a $5,000 investment to accumulate to the following. State in annual rates.
   a. $10,718 in 8 years, interest compounded annually.
   b. $12,702 in 4 years, interest compounded quarterly.
   c. $6,341 in 1 year, interest compounded monthly.

9. Baxter Company has $5,000 to invest. One alternative will yield 10% per year for 4 years. A second alternative is to deposit the $5,000 in a bank that will pay 8% per year, compounded quarterly. Which alternative should Baxter select?

10. Compute the amounts to which the following periodic investments would accumulate.
    a. $1,500 semiannual payments for 6 years at 10% per annum, compounded semiannually.

b. $800 monthly payments for 1 year at 24% interest per annum, compounded monthly.

c. $1,705 quarterly payments for 4 years at 16% per annum, compounded quarterly.

11. Compute the amounts in Exercise 10 if the payments are made at the beginning of the period.

12. Determine the amount of the periodic investment for the following. Investments are made at the end of the period.

a. $500,000 at the end of 1 year with monthly payments invested at 24% per annum, compounded monthly.

b. $1,050 at the end of 2 years with quarterly payments invested at 8% per annum, compounded quarterly.

c. $50,500 at the end of 4 years with annual payments invested at 6% per annum, compounded annually.

13. Compute the amount of the periodic investments in Exercise 12 if investments are made at the beginning of the period.

14. Determine the amount of the periodic payments needed to pay off the following purchases. Payments are made at the end of the period.   *ANNUITY IN ARREARS*

a. Purchase of a waterbed for $1,205. Monthly payments are to be made for 1 year with interest at 24% per annum, compounded monthly.

b. Purchase of a motor boat for $26,565. Quarterly payments are to be made for 4 years with interest at 8% per annum, compounded quarterly.

c. Purchase of a condominium for $65,500. Semiannual payments are to be made for 10 years with interest at 10% per annum, compounded semiannually.

15. Compute the amount of the periodic payment for Exercise 14 if the payments are made at the beginning of the period.   *ANNUITY DUE*

16. Determine the purchase price for the different payment plans. Payments are at the end of the period.

a. $25.12 monthly payments for 1 year, with 36% interest per annum, compounded monthly.

b. $1,010.75 semiannual payments for 8 years, with 8% interest per annum, compounded semiannually.

c. $5,801.69 annual payments for 20 years with 12% interest per annum, compounded annually.

17. Determine the purchase price for the payment plans in Exercise 16 if payments are made at the beginning of the period.

18. On July 17, 1986, Brian Carr borrowed $40,000 from his rich Uncle George to open a sporting goods store. Starting July 17, 1987, Brian has to make 5 equal annual payments of $10,500 each to repay the loan. What interest rate is Brian paying? (Interpolation is required.)

19. Regan Company has decided to purchase a new office building. Management signs a bank note to pay the Second State Bank $5,000 every 6 months for 10 years. At the date of purchase, the office building costs $60,000. The first payment is 6 months later. What is the approximate annual rate of interest on the note? (Interpolation is required.)

20. If the payments in Exercise 19 began on the date the papers were signed, what would the annual interest rate be?

PROBLEMS

1. Determine the unknown quantity for each of the following independent situations using the appropriate interest tables.

   a. Marc and JoAnn want to start a trust fund for their newborn son, Jason. They have decided to invest $2,500. If interest is 8% compounded semi-annually, how much will be in the fund when Jason turns 20?

   b. Martin Corporation wants to establish a retirement fund. Management wants to have $500,000 in the fund in 40 years. If fund assets will earn 12% compounded annually, how much will need to be invested now?

   c. How many payments would Stan Company, Inc. need to make if it purchases a new building for $90,000, annual payments are $15,180, and interest is 16% compounded annually?

   d. An investment broker indicates that an investment of $10,000 in a CD for 10 years at the current interest rate will earn $21,589. What is the current annual rate of interest if interest is compounded annually?

2. BD Technical College needs to purchase some computers. Because the college is short of cash, Computer Sales Company has agreed to let BD have the computers now and pay $2,500 per computer 6 months from now. If the current cash price is $2,404, what is the rate of interest BD would be paying?

3. Determine the unknown quantity for each of the following independent situations using the appropriate interest tables.

   a. Sue wants to have $10,000 saved for her college tuition. If Sue enters college in 4 years and interest is 8% compounded annually, how much will Sue need to save each year assuming equal payments?

   b. XYZ Company has obtained a bank loan to finance the purchase of an automobile for one of its executives. The terms of the loan require monthly payments of $585. If the interest rate is 18% compounded monthly, and the car costs $15,850, for how many months will XYZ have to make payments?

   c. Spend Company is offering the following investment plan. If deposits of $250 are made semiannually for the next 9 years, $7,726 will accrue. If interest is compounded semiannually, what is the annual rate of interest on the investment?

   d. Jack wants to buy a beanstalk. He needs to know how long he will have to invest $5,000 in order to accumulate $50,445, the price of the beanstalk, if interest is 12 percent compounded annually?

4. Foot Loose, Inc. needs to purchase a new shoelace making machine. Machines Ready has agreed to sell them the machine for $22,000 down and 4 payments of $5,700 to be paid in semiannual installments for the next 2 years. Do-It-Yourself Machines has offered to sell Foot Loose a comparable machine for $10,000 down and 4 semiannual payments of $9,000. If the current interest rate is 16 percent compounded semiannually, which machine should Foot Loose purchase?

5. Cougar Construction is building a new office building, and management is trying to decide how rent payments for the office space should be structured. The alternatives are:

   a. Annual payments of $12,000 at the end of each year.

   b. Monthly payments of $950 at the end of each month.

   Assuming an interest rate of 12% compounded monthly, which payment schedule should Cougar Construction use?

6. Lori Keller plans to save $500 each year to pay for a two-week trip to Europe. If Lori makes her first deposit on July 1, 1987, and her last deposit on July 1, 1989, how much will she have for her trip on July 1, 1990? Assume that the annual interest rate is 8%.

7. Ed Anderson has $250,000 accumulated in a Keogh investment and plans to receive annual payments of $40,360 at the end of each year. If interest is 12% annually, how many payments will Ed receive? If payments are made at the beginning of the year, how many full payments would he receive, and how much would the last payment be? What would the payments have to be if Ed wants to receive 20 payments at the end of the year? At the beginning of the year?

8. The following payment plans are offered on the purchase of a new freezer.
   a. $375 cash.
   b. 8 monthly payments of $51.
   c. $100 cash down and 6 monthly payments of $49.
   Which payment plan would you choose if interest is 18 percent annually, compounded monthly if you are the purchaser? the seller? (Assume ordinary annuities where applicable.)

9. Jay Company wants to start a sinking fund to cover the retirement of a serial bond issuance. The bonds begin maturing in 15 years at a rate of $30,000 per year for 15 years. Jay Company can earn annual interest of 6 percent for the first 15 years and 10% for the remaining years. How much will Jay Company have to deposit annually under the following assumptions?
   a. Payments into the fund are made at the end of the year and bonds are retired at the end of the year?
   b. Payments into the fund are made at the beginning of the year and bonds are retired at the beginning of the year.
   c. Payments into the fund are made at the beginning of the year and bonds are retired at the end of the year.

10. J & J, Inc. borrowed $4,000 on a note due on August 1, 1987. On that date, J & J was unable to pay the obligation but arranged for Western Loan Company to pay the holder $4,000. J&J agreed to pay Western Loan Company a series of 5 equal annual payments beginning August 1, 1987. Each payment is in part a reduction of principal and in part a payment of interest at 12% annually. What is the amount of each payment?

11. ADC Company purchased a machine on February 1, 1987 and will make 7 semiannual payments of $14,000 beginning 5 years from the date of purchase. The interest rate will be 12% compounded semiannually. Determine the purchase price of the machine.

12. Cline Corporation is considering the acquisition of a company and wants to determine the value of the company based on the following information. (Assume revenues and expenses are received and incurred evenly throughout the year.)

Years	Estimated Interest Rate	Estimated Annual Revenues	Estimated Annual Expenses
1–5	16% compounded annually	$170,000	$140,000 30,000
6–10	12% compounded quarterly	215,000	155,000 60,000
11–15	14% compounded semiannually	245,000	185,000 60,000

13. Dr. Philips is considering the purchase of an insurance policy. The following options are available for payment to the beneficiary upon the death of Dr. Philips.
    a. $100,000 immediately.
    b. $8,000 at the end of each quarter for 4 years.
    c. $30,000 immediately and $5,000 in quarterly payments for 4½ years.
    d. Quarterly payments of $4,350 for the next 10 years.
    Given an annual interest rate of 12%, compounded quarterly, which option would you recommend to Dr. Philips?

14. An office equipment company representative has a machine for sale or lease. If you buy the machine, the cost is $7,596. If you lease the machine, you will have to sign a noncancellable lease and make 5 payments of $2,000 each. The first payment will be paid on the first day of the lease. At the time of the last payment, you will receive title to the machine. Determine the implicit interest rate.   (AICPA adapted)

15. On January 1, 1987, Jorgenson Company lent $120,000 cash to McAllister Company, The promissory note made by McAllister did not bear interest and was due on December 31, 1988. No other rights or privileges were exchanged. The prevailing interest for a loan of this type was 12%. What amount of interest income should Jorgenson recognize for 1987?   (AICPA adapted)

PART TWO
ASSETS

7 Cash and Temporary Investments

8 Receivables

9 Inventories — Cost Procedures

10 Inventories — Estimation and Noncost Valuation Procedures

11 Plant and Intangible Assets — Acquisition

12 Plant and Intangible Assets — Utilization and Retirement

13 Long-Term Investments in Equity Securities and Other Assets

7
Cash and Temporary Investments

The first part of this book has established a perspective of accounting and its theoretical foundation. Part II explores items classified as **assets**, beginning with the most liquid assets: cash and temporary investments.

CASH

Cash is perhaps the single most important item on a balance sheet. Since it serves as the medium of exchange in our economy, cash is involved directly or indirectly in almost all business transactions. Even when cash is not involved directly in a transaction, it provides the basis for measurement and accounting for all other items.

Another reason why cash is so important is that individuals, businesses, and even governments must maintain an adequate liquidity position; that is, they must have a sufficient amount of cash on hand to pay obligations as they come due if they are to remain viable operating entities. The importance of liquidity is illustrated by the following excerpt from a recent article in *The Wall Street Journal*.

> Faced with a congressional deadlock over debt-limit legislation, the Reagan administration this week may begin postponing government payments to businesses, state and local governments, and some individuals. The action will be the latest maneuver in the government's attempts to avoid default without violating the current debt limit of $1.824 trillion. Administration officials say the postponement of spending or "deferrals," will be necessary to keep checks from bouncing on

November 15, when the government expects to run out of cash again
if the debt limit isn't raised.[1]

Unlike the U. S. Government, individuals and businesses cannot periodically request and receive almost automatically a raising of their debt limits.
Instead, they must accurately forecast cash requirements and control expenditures. Thus, the management of cash is a critical business function.

In striking contrast to the importance of cash as a key element in the
liquidity position of an entity is its unproductive nature. Since cash is
the measure of value, it cannot expand or grow unless it is converted into
other properties. Cash kept under a mattress, for example, will not grow
or appreciate, whereas land may increase in value if held. Excessive balances of cash on hand are often referred to as **idle cash.** Efficient cash
management requires available cash to be continuously working in one of
several ways as part of the operating cycle or as a short-term or long-term
investment.

Composition of Cash

Cash is the most liquid of current assets and consists of those items that
serve as a medium of exchange and provide a basis for accounting measurement. To be reported as "cash," an item must be readily available and
not restricted for use in the payment of current obligations. A general
guideline is whether an item is **acceptable for deposit at face value** by a
bank or other financial institution.

Items that are classified as cash include coin and currency on hand, and
unrestricted funds available on deposit in a bank, which are often called
demand deposits since they can be withdrawn upon demand. Petty cash
funds or change funds and negotiable instruments, such as personal checks,
travelers' checks, cashiers' checks, bank drafts, and money orders are also
items commonly reported as cash. The total of these items plus undeposited coin and currency is sometimes called **cash on hand.** Interest-bearing accounts, or **time deposits,** also are usually classified as cash, even
though a bank legally can demand prior notification before a withdrawal can
be made. In practice, banks generally do not exercise this legal right.

Deposits that are not immediately available due to withdrawal or other
restrictions require separate classification as "restricted cash" or "temporary investments." They are not "cash." For example, certificates of
deposit (CDs) generally may be withdrawn without penalty only at specified maturity dates. Thus, CDs, money market funds, money market savings certificates, Treasury Bills, and commercial paper (short-term notes

---

[1]"U.S. May Delay Some Payments to Save Cash," *The Wall Street Journal,* November 4, 1985.

issued by corporations) are more appropriately classified as temporary investments than as cash.

Deposits in foreign banks that are subject to immediate and un-restricted withdrawal generally qualify as cash and are reported at their U.S. dollar equivalents as of the date of the balance sheet. However, cash in foreign banks that is restricted as to use or withdrawal should be designated as receivables of a current or noncurrent character and reported subject to appropriate allowances for estimated uncollectible losses.

Some items do not meet the "acceptance at face value on deposit" test and should not be reported as cash. Examples include postage stamps (which are office supplies) and post-dated checks, IOUs, and not-sufficient-funds (NSF) checks (all of which are in effect receivables).

Cash balances specifically designated by management for special purposes should be reported separately. Those cash balances to be applied to some current purpose or current obligation are properly reported in the current section on the balance sheet. For example, cash funds for employees' travel may be reported separately from cash but still be classified as a current asset. However, restricted cash should be reported as a current item only if it is to be applied to some current purpose or obligation. Classification of the cash balance as current or noncurrent should parallel the classification applied to the liability. Cash balances not available for current purposes require separate designation and classification under a non-current heading on the balance sheet.

A credit balance in the cash account resulting from the issuance of checks in excess of the amount on deposit is known as a **cash overdraft** and should be reported as a current liability. When a company has two or more accounts with a single bank, an overdraft can be offset against an account with a positive balance. If the depositor fails to cover the overdraft, the bank has the legal right to apply funds from one account to cover the overdraft in another. However, when a company has accounts with two different banks and there is a positive balance in one account and an overdraft in the other, both an asset balance and a liability balance should be recognized in view of the claim against one bank and the obligation to the other; if recognition of an overdraft is to be avoided, cash should be transferred to cover the deficiency, because the legal right of offset does not exist between two banks.

In summary, cash is a current asset comprised of coin, currency, and other items that (1) serve as a medium of exchange and (2) provide the basis for measurement in accounting. Most negotiable instruments (e.g., checks, bank drafts, and money orders) qualify as cash because they can be converted to currency on demand or are acceptable for deposit at face value by a bank. Components of cash restricted as to use or withdrawal should be disclosed or reported separately and classified as an investment, a receivable, or other asset. Exhibit 7–1 summarizes the classification of various items that have been discussed. The objective of disclosure is to provide the user of financial statements with information to assist in evaluating the entity's ability to meet obligations (its liquidity and solvency) and in assessing the effectiveness of cash management.

Exhibit 7–1   Classification of Cash and Noncash Items

Item	Classification
Undeposited coin & currency	Cash
Unrestricted funds on deposit at bank (demand deposits)	Cash
Petty cash & change funds	Cash
Negotiable instruments, such as checks, bank drafts, and money orders	Cash
Interest-bearing accounts (time deposits)	Cash
Restricted deposits, such as CDs, money market funds, and money market savings certificates	Temporary Investments
Treasury Bills and commercial paper	Temporary Investments
Deposits in foreign banks:	
Unrestricted	Cash
Restricted	Receivables
Postage stamps	Office Supplies
IOUs, post-dated checks, and not-sufficient-funds (NSF) checks	Receivables
Cash restricted for special purposes	*Restricted Cash
Cash overdraft	Current Liability

*Separately reported as current or noncurrent asset depending on the purpose for which it is restricted.

Since the concept of cash embodies the standard of value, few valuation problems are encountered in reporting those items qualifying as cash. When cash is comprised solely of cash on hand and unrestricted demand deposits, the total generally appears on the balance sheet as a single item "Cash." When other components of cash are significant, they should be disclosed or reported as separate items.

Compensating Balances

In connection with financing arrangements, it is common practice for a company to agree to maintain a minimum or average balance on deposit with a bank or other lending institution. These **compensating balances** are defined by the SEC as " . . . that portion of any demand deposit (or any time deposit or certificate of deposit) maintained by a corporation . . . which constitutes support for existing borrowing arrangements of the corporation...with a lending institution. Such arrangements would include both outstanding borrowings and the assurance of future credit availability."[2]

Compensating balances provide a source of funds to the lender as partial compensation for credit extended. In effect, such arrangements raise the interest rate of the borrower because a portion of the amount on deposit with the lending institution cannot be used. These balances present an accounting problem from the standpoint of disclosure. Readers of financial statements are likely to assume the entire cash balance is available to meet current obligations, when, in fact, part of the balance is restricted.

The solution to this problem is to disclose the amount of compensating balances. The SEC recommends that any "legally restricted" deposits held as compensating balances be segregated and reported separately. If the balances are the result of short-term financing arrangements, they should be shown separately among the "cash items" in the current asset section; if the compensating balances are in connection with long-term agreements, they should be classified as noncurrent, either as investments or "other assets." In many instances, deposits are not legally restricted, but compensating balance agreements still exist. In these situations, the amounts and nature of the arrangements should be disclosed in the notes to the financial statements, as illustrated below for U.S. Steel.

Notes to Consolidated Financial Statements (continued)

3. Cash and Marketable Securities

Cash and marketable securities consist of the following:

(In millions) December 31	1984	1983
Cash	$167	$436
Marketable securities, at cost (approximates market)	188	105
Total	$355	$541

The Corporation is required to maintain average compensating balances on deposit with a number of banks in connection with credit agreements discussed in Note 7, page 35. At December 31, 1984 and 1983, respectively, the amounts were $7 million and $26 million.

At December 31, 1984, marketable securities includes $111 million which is temporarily held in escrow in connection with the sale of certain properties.

---

[2]Securities and Exchange Commission, *Accounting Series Release No. 148*, "Disclosure of Compensating Balances and Short-Term Borrowing Arrangements" (Washington: U.S. Government Printing Office, 1973).

Management and Control of Cash

As noted earlier, a business enterprise must maintain sufficient cash for current operations and for paying obligations as they come due. Any excess cash should be invested temporarily to earn an additional return for the shareholders. Effective cash management also requires controls to protect cash from loss by theft or fraud. Since cash is the most liquid asset, it is particularly susceptible to misappropriation unless properly safeguarded. When computerized accounting systems are used, controls are still necessary and are perhaps even more important than with a strictly manual system, in properly accounting for all inflows, outflows, and balances of cash.

The system for controlling cash must be adapted to a particular business. It is not feasible to describe all the features and techniques employed in businesses of various kinds and sizes. In general, however, systems of cash control deny access to the accounting records to those who handle cash. This reduces the possibility of improper entries to conceal the misuse of cash receipts and cash payments. The probability of misappropriation of cash is greatly reduced if two or more employees must conspire in an embezzlement. Further, systems normally provide for separation of the receiving and paying functions. The basic characteristics of a system of cash control are:

1. Specifically assigned responsibility for handling cash receipts.
2. Separation of handling and recording cash receipts.
3. Daily deposit of all cash received.
4. Voucher system to control cash payments.
5. Internal audits at irregular intervals.
6. Double record of cash — bank and books, with reconciliations performed by someone outside the accounting function.

These controls are more likely to be found in large companies with many employees. Small companies with few employees generally have difficulty in totally segregating accounting and cash-handling duties. Even small companies, however, should incorporate as many control features as possible.

To the extent that a company can incorporate effective internal controls, it can reduce significantly the chances of theft, loss, or inadvertent errors in accounting for and controlling cash. Even the most elaborate control system, however, cannot totally eliminate the possibilities of misappropriations or errors. The use of a petty cash fund and periodic bank reconciliations can help identify any cash shortages or errors that may have been made in accounting for cash.

Petty Cash Fund

Immediate cash payments and payments too small to be made by check may be made from a **petty cash fund**. Under an **imprest system**, the petty cash fund is created by cashing a check for the amount of the fund. In recording the establishment of the fund, Petty Cash is debited and Cash is credited. The cash is then turned over to a cashier or some person who is solely responsible for payments made out of the fund. The cashier should require a signed receipt for all payments made. These receipts may be printed in prenumbered form. Frequently, a bill or other memorandum is submitted when a payment is requested. A record of petty cash payments may be kept in a *petty cash journal*.

Whenever the amount of cash in the fund runs low and also at the end of each fiscal period, the fund is replenished by writing a check equal to the payments made. In recording replenishment, expenses and other appropriate accounts are debited for petty cash disbursements and Cash is credited. When the fund fails to balance, an adjustment is usually made to a miscellaneous expense or revenue account, sometimes called "Cash Short and Over." Unless theft is involved, this will usually involve only a nominal amount arising, for example, from errors in making change.

As noted above, a petty cash fund is usually replenished at the end of each fiscal period. If replenishment does not occur at year-end, however, an adjustment to Petty Cash is required to properly record all expenditures from the fund during the period. The debit entries would be the same as those to record replenishment; the credit entry would be to Petty Cash, reflecting a reduction in that account.

To illustrate the appropriate entries in accounting for petty cash, assume that Keat Company establishes a petty cash fund on January 1 in the amount of $500. The following entry would be made.

Petty Cash	500	
Cash		500
To establish a $500 petty cash fund.		

During the next six months, the person responsible for the fund made payments for office supplies ($245), postage ($110), and office equipment repairs ($25). Receipts for these items are maintained as evidence supporting the petty cash disbursements. On July 1 the fund is replenished. At that time the coin and currency in the fund totaled $115. The entry to record the expenses and replenish the fund would be:

Office Supplies Expense	245	
Postage Expense	110	
Repair Expense	25	
Cash Short and Over (or Misc. Expense)	5	
Cash		385
To record expenses and replenish the petty cash fund.		

After this entry the fund would be restored to its original amount, $500. If Keat Company decided to reduce the fund to $400, an entry would be required as follows:

```
Cash....................................................................  100
    Petty Cash..........................................................        100
        To reduce the petty cash fund from $500 to $400.
```

Assume further that during the next six months, Keat Company used its petty cash fund to purchase additional office supplies ($136), purchase decorations and refreshments for an office party ($89), and pay freight charges ($55). Even though the fund was not replenished on December 31, an entry would be required to properly record the expenditures from the fund for that period, as follows:

```
Office Supplies Expense...............................................  136
Misc. Expenses .......................................................   89
Freight ...............................................................   55
    Petty Cash..........................................................        280
        To record expenses paid from the petty cash fund.
```

The entry to increase a petty cash fund is the same as to establish the fund initially—a debit to Petty Cash and a credit to Cash. However, petty cash funds should only be large enough to cover small expenditures. Large amounts should be disbursed through an authorized voucher system.

Bank Reconciliations

When daily receipts are deposited and payments other than those from petty cash are made by check, the bank's statement of its transactions with the depositor can be compared with the record of cash as reported on the depositor's books. A comparison of the bank balance with the balance reported on the books is usually made monthly by means of a summary known as a **bank reconciliation statement**. The bank reconciliation statement is prepared to disclose any errors or irregularities in either the records of the bank or those of the business unit. It is developed in a form that points out the reasons for discrepancies in the two balances. It should be prepared by an individual who neither handles nor records cash. Any discrepancies should be brought to the immediate attention of appropriate company officials.

When the bank statement and the depositor's records are compared, certain items may appear on one and not the other, resulting in a difference in the two balances. Most of these differences result from temporary timing lags, and are thus normal. Four common types of differences arise in the following situations:

1. A deposit made near the end of the month and recorded on the depositor's books is not received by the bank in time to be reflected on the bank

statement. This amount, referred to as a **deposit in transit**, has to be added to the bank statement balance to make it agree with the balance on the depositor's books.

2. Checks written near the end of the month have reduced the depositor's cash balance, but have not cleared the bank as of the bank statement date. These **outstanding checks** must be subtracted from the bank statement balance to make it agree with the depositor's records.

3. The bank normally charges a monthly fee for servicing an account. The bank automatically reduces the depositor's account balance for this **bank service charge** and notes the amount on the bank statement. The depositor must deduct this amount from the recorded cash balance to make it agree with the bank statement balance. The return of a customer's check for which insufficient funds are available, known as a **not-sufficient-funds (NSF) check**, is handled in a similar manner.

4. An amount owed to the depositor is paid directly to the bank by a third party and added to the depositor's account. Upon receipt of the bank statement (assuming prior notification has not been received from the bank), this amount must be added to the cash balance on the depositor's books. Examples include a direct payroll deposit by an individual's employer and interest added by the bank on a savings account.

If, after considering the items mentioned, the bank statement and the book balances cannot be reconciled, a detailed analysis of both the bank's records and the depositor's books may be necessary to determine whether errors or irregularities exist on the records of either party.

There are two common forms of bank reconciliations: (1) reconciliation of bank and book balances to a corrected balance and (2) reconciliation of the bank balance to the book balance. The first form is prepared in two sections, the bank statement balance being adjusted to the corrected cash balance in the first section, and the book balance being adjusted to the same corrected cash balance in the second section. The first section, then, contains items the bank has not recognized as well as any corrections for errors made by the bank; the second section contains items the depositor has not yet recognized and any corrections for errors made on the depositor's books.

The other form begins with the bank statement balance and reports the adjustments that must be applied to this balance to obtain the cash balance on the depositor's books. The second form, then, simply reports the items accounting for the discrepancy between the bank and book balances. Both forms are illustrated on pages 251 and 252.

The reconciliation of bank and book balances to a corrected balance has two important advantages: it develops a corrected cash figure, and it shows separately all items requiring adjustment on the depositor's books.

Reconciliation of Bank and Book Balances to Corrected Balance

Svendsen, Inc. Bank Reconciliation Statement November 30, 1987		
Balance per bank statement, November 30, 1987........		$2,979.72
Add: Deposits in transit............................	$658.50	
Charge for interest made to depositor's account		
by check in error............................	12.50	671.00
		$3,650.72
Deduct outstanding checks:		
No. 1125...	$ 58.16	
No. 1138...	100.00	
No. 1152...	98.60	
No. 1154...	255.00	
No. 1155...	192.07	703.83
Corrected bank balance		$2,946.89
Balance per books, November 30, 1987		$2,952.49
Add: Interest earned during November	$ 98.50	
Check No. 1116 to Ace Advertising for $46		
recorded by depositor as $64 in error	18.00	116.50
		$3,068.99
Deduct: Bank service charges......................	$ 3.16	
Customer's check deposited November 25 and		
returned marked NSF....................	118.94	122.10
Corrected book balance		$2,946.89

After preparing the reconciliation, the depositor should record any items appearing on the bank statement and requiring recognition on the company's books as well as any corrections for errors discovered on its own books. The bank should be notified immediately of any bank errors. The following entries would be required on the books of Svendsen, Inc. as a result of the November 30 reconciliation:

Cash..	98.50	
Interest Revenue		98.50
To record interest earned during November.		
Cash..	18.00	
Advertising Expense		18.00
To record correction for check in payment of advertising recorded		
as $64 instead of the actual amount, $46.		
Accounts Receivable...	118.94	
Miscellaneous General Expense.................................	3.16	
Cash..		122.10
To record customer's uncollectible check and bank charges for		
November.		

Reconciliation of Bank Balance to Book Balance

Svendsen, Inc.
Bank Reconciliation Statement
November 30, 1987

Balance per bank statement, November 30, 1987........		$2,979.72
Add: Deposits in transit.............................	$658.50	
Charge for interest made to depositor's account by bank in error.............................	12.50	
Bank service charges.........................	3.16	
Customer's check deposited November 25 and returned marked NSF........................	118.94	793.10
		$3,772.82
Deduct: Outstanding checks:		
No. 1125............................	$ 58.16	
No. 1138............................	100.00	
No. 1152............................	98.60	
No. 1154............................	255.00	
No. 1155............................	192.07	$703.83
Check No. 1116 to Ace Advertising for $46 recorded by depositor as $64 in error..........	18.00	
Interest earned during November	98.50	820.33
Balance per books, November 30, 1987		$2,952.49

After these entries are posted, the cash account will show a balance of $2,946.89. If financial statements were prepared at November 30, this is the amount that would be reported on the balance sheet. As noted, these adjustments are clearly distinguishable when using the first form of bank reconciliation. If the second form is used, adjustments can be determined only after careful analysis of all reconciling items. It should be noted that the bank reconciliation statement is not presented to external users. It is used as an accounting tool to determine the adjustments required to bring the cash balance up to date as well as the related account balances.

A bank reconciliation is frequently expanded to incorporate a proof of both receipts and disbursements as separate steps in the reconciliation process. This is often referred to as a **four-column reconciliation** or a **proof of cash**. Two reconciliation forms may be employed here as in the previous examples. The form preferred by the authors develops corrected balances for both receipts and disbursements of the bank and the depositor, as illustrated on page 253.

In a four-column reconciliation, columns are provided for the beginning reconciliation, deposits or receipts, withdrawals or disbursements, and the ending reconciliation. Thus, the four-column approach is really two

Reconciliation of Bank and Book Balances to Corrected Balance

Svendsen, Inc.
Proof of Cash
November 30, 1987

	Beginning Reconciliation October 31	Deposits/ Receipts	Withdrawals/ Disbursements	Ending Reconciliation November 30
Balance per bank statement	$5,895.42	$21,312.40	$24,228.10	$2,979.72
Deposits in transit:				
October 31	425.40	(425.40)		
November 30		658.50		658.50
Outstanding checks:				
October 31	(810.50)		(810.50)	
November 30			703.83	(703.83)
NSF check redeposited during November; no entry made on books for return or redeposit		(100.00)	(100.00)	
Charge for interest made by bank in error			(12.50)	12.50
Corrected bank balance	$5,510.32	$21,445.50	$24,008.93	$2,946.89
Balance per books . . .	$5,406.22	$21,457.00	$23,910.73	$2,952.49
Bank service charges:				
October	(5.90)		(5.90)	
November			3.16	(3.16)
Customer's check deposited November 25 found to be uncollectible (NSF)			118.94	(118.94)
Interest earned:				
October	110.00	(110.00)		
November		98.50		98.50
Check No. 116 for $46 recorded by depositor as $64 in error . .			(18.00)	18.00
Corrected book balance	$5,510.32	$21,445.50	$24,008.93	$2,946.89

Also reconciles Cash receipts and disbursements

reconciliations in one. The first column contains a reconciliation as of the end of the preceding period. The deposits per bank statement or receipts per books for the period are added to the beginning balances, and the withdrawals per bank statement or disbursements per books are subtracted to arrive at the ending balances. Deposits/receipts are reconciled in the second column and withdrawals/disbursements in the third column. The amounts must reconcile both vertically and horizontally for the ending bank and book balances to agree.

In order to complete this type of reconciliation, each adjustment must be carefully analyzed. Note that two columns are always affected for each adjustment. For example, a deposit of $425.40 on October 31, 1987, was recorded by the bank in November and is included in the total bank deposits of $21,312.40 for November. However, the deposit was properly recorded on the books as a receipt in October; thus, the $425.40 is not included in the book receipts of $21,457 for November, but is included in the beginning book balance of $5,406.22. The reconciliation accounts for this by deducting the in-transit deposit from the total bank deposits for November and by adding the deposit to the beginning October 31 bank statement balance. This is the same type of analysis that would have been made on October 31 for a regular bank reconciliation on that date. Similarly, the $658.50 deposit in transit at the end of November is already recorded in the book receipts and ending cash balance as of November 30, but must be added to the bank deposits and ending balance to reconcile to the correct balances as of November 30.

A similar analysis is needed for reconciling the timing differences for outstanding checks. Checks totaling $810.50 were outstanding (had not cleared the bank) on October 31 and therefore should be deducted from the October 31 bank balance. The bank records include those checks as withdrawals for November (that is, the $810.50 is included in the total bank withdrawals of $24,228.10), and so the $810.50 must be subtracted from the November withdrawals to reconcile with the corrected balances. On the other hand, the outstanding checks at the end of November are valid withdrawals for November, and so the $703.83 must be added to the bank withdrawals for November and subtracted from the bank cash balance as of November 30.

The adjustment for a "not-sufficient-funds" (NSF) check depends on how the company and bank records are kept. Typically, a company will periodically deposit its checks, recording them as receipts and additions to the cash balance. The bank will similarly record the deposits as increases in cash for the company. However, when the bank determines that a particular check is not collectible from the maker (an NSF check), it usually will show the check as a withdrawal and thus a reduction in the company's cash balance. If, after checking with the customer, the company determines the check is now good, it may merely redeposit the check without making any entries on the books for the bank's return of the check or the redeposit. The bank, however, will again show the check as a deposit and an increase in the cash balance. After the redeposit, the bank will show the correct cash balance. However, the bank deposits included the check twice, once when originally deposited and a second time upon redeposit, and the bank withdrawals included the check once, when it became an NSF check. Therefore, to reconcile the bank and book deposits/receipts and withdrawals/disbursements, the NSF check ($100 in the example) is subtracted from both the bank deposits and withdrawals. (Alternatively, the $100 NSF check could be added to the book receipts and disbursements to make the books reconcile with the bank records.) The preceding discussion is illustrated in Exhibit 7–2 using (+) and (−) designations to reinforce this point.

Exhibit 7–2
Typical Treatment in Reconciling NSF Check

Bank	Balance (Oct. 31)	Deposits/ Receipts	Withdrawals/ Disbursements	Balance (Nov. 30)
1. Original deposit......		+		+
2. Check becomes NSF.............			+	−
3. Check redeposited ...		+		+
4. Adjustment to reconcile..........		−	−	
Correct balance....		+		+
Books				
1. Original deposit......		+		+
2. Check returned by bank (no book entry).............				
3. Check redeposited (no book entry)........				
Correct balance....		+		+

If a company finds that an NSF check cannot be collected immediately, then instead of redepositing the check, it must record the check amount in accounts receivable on the books. Such is the case for the $118.94 check for Svendsen, Inc. in the illustration. Since the bank will have already shown the check as a withdrawal and a reduction in the cash balance, a similar adjustment must be made to the company records.

Another common type of adjustment may be required for errors made either on the bank or book records. These have to be corrected as illustrated for Svendsen, Inc. Once all adjustments are made, the total corrected balances will be the same for both the bank and book records for all four columns.

The illustrations for Svendsen, Inc. assume adjustments of the book amounts are made in the month subsequent to their discovery. If the adjustments were made in the same month, as might be true at year-end, there would be no adjustments in the first column for the book amounts. For example, the $5.90 October bank service charge in the illustration is recognized on the books in November. If the adjustment had been made at the end of October, the beginning book balance would have already shown $5,400.32 ($5,406.22 − $5.90), and the total book disbursements for November would have been $5.90 less. A similar rationale exists for the $110 interest recorded by the bank for Svendsen in October.

The expanded proof of cash or four-column reconciliation procedure normally reduces the time and effort required to find errors made by either the bank or the depositor. In developing comparisons of both receipts and disbursements, the areas in which errors have been made, as well as the amounts of the discrepancies within each area, are immediately identified. This procedure is frequently used by auditors when there is any question of possible discrepancies in the handling of cash.

TEMPORARY INVESTMENTS

Temporarily available excess cash may be invested in time deposits, various money market funds, and similar instruments, or it may be used to purchase securities. As a result, revenue may be generated that would not be available if cash were left idle. Investments made during seasonal periods of low activity can be converted into cash in periods of expanding operations. Asset items arising from temporary conversions of cash are reported in the "Current assets" section of the balance sheet as "Temporary investments." Accounting and reporting considerations applicable to investments of a long-term nature are discussed in Chapters 13 and 15.

Criteria for Reporting Securities as Temporary Investments

Investments in securities qualify for reporting as **temporary investments** provided (1) there is a ready market for converting such securities into cash, and (2) it is management's intention to sell them if the need for cash arises. Temporary investments generally consist of **marketable**

equity securities (preferred and common stock), **marketable debt securities** (government and corporate bonds), **first-mortgage notes** and **short-term paper** (certificates of deposit, Treasury Bills, and commercial paper).

Securities are considered marketable when a day-to-day market exists and when they can be sold on short notice. The volume of trading in the securities should be sufficient to absorb a company's holdings without materially affecting the market price. Securities having a limited market and fluctuating widely in price are not suitable for temporary investments.

Marketable securities may be converted into cash shortly after being acquired or they may be held for some time. In either case, however, they are properly classified as temporary investments as long as management intends to sell them if the need for cash arises. The deciding factor is management's intent, not the length of time the securities are held. Therefore, the following types of investments do not qualify as temporary investments even though the securities may be marketable: (1) reacquired shares of a corporation's own stock; (2) securities acquired to gain control of a company; (3) securities held for maintenance of business relations; and (4) any other securities that cannot be used or are not intended to be used as a ready source of cash.

Recording Purchase and Sale of Marketable Securities

Stocks and bonds acquired as temporary investments are recorded at cost, which includes brokers' fees, taxes, and other charges incurred in their acquisition. Stocks are normally quoted at a price per single share; bonds are quoted at a price per $100 face value although they are normally issued in $1,000 denominations. The purchase of 100 shares of stock at 5⅛, then, would indicate a purchase price of $512.50; the purchase of a $1,000 bond at 104¼ would indicate a purchase price of $1,042.50.

When interest-bearing securities are acquired between interest payment dates, the amount paid for the security is increased by a charge for accrued interest to the date of purchase. This charge should not be reported as part of the investment cost. Two assets have been acquired — the security and the accrued interest receivable — and should be reported in two separate asset accounts. Upon the receipt of interest, the accrued interest account is closed and Interest Revenue is credited for the amount of interest earned since the purchase date. Instead of recording the interest as a receivable (asset approach), Interest Revenue may be debited for the accrued interest paid. The subsequent collection of interest would then be credited in full to Interest Revenue. The latter procedure (revenue approach) is usually more convenient.

To illustrate the entries for the acquisition of securities, assume that $100,000 in U.S. Treasury notes are purchased at 104¼, including brokerage fees, on April 1. Interest is 9% payable semiannually on January 1 and July 1. Accrued interest of $2,250 would thus be added to the purchase price. The entries to record the purchase of the securities and the subsequent collection of interest under the alternate procedures would be as follows:

Asset Approach:

Apr. 1 Marketable Securities (9% U.S. Treasury Notes)	104,250	
Interest Receivable	2,250	
Cash.		106,500
July 1 Cash.	4,500	
Interest Receivable		2,250
Interest Revenue		2,250

Revenue Approach:

Apr. 1 Marketable Securities (9% U.S. Treasury Notes)	104,250	
Interest Revenue	2,250	
Cash.		106,500
July 1 Cash.	4,500	
Interest Revenue		4,500

The important point is that under either approach, the interest revenue recorded for the period is equal to the interest earned, not the amount received. In this case, the company earned $2,250, representing interest for the period April 1 to June 30.

When such securities are acquired at a higher or lower price than their maturity value and it is expected that they will be held until maturity, periodic amortization of the premium or accumulation of the discount with corresponding adjustments to interest revenue is required. However, when securities are acquired as a temporary investment and it is not likely they will be held until maturity, such procedures are normally not necessary. When a temporary investment is sold, the difference between the sales proceeds and the cost is reported as a gain or loss on the sale. For example, if the U.S. Treasury notes in the preceding illustration were sold on July 1 for $105,000, and the brokerage fees on the sale were $500, the transaction would be recorded as follows:

July 1 Cash.	104,500	
Marketable Securities (9% U.S. Treasury Notes)		104,250
Gain on Sale of Marketable Securities		250

The gain would be reported on the income statement as "Other revenue." Note that the brokerage fees involved in the purchase increase the cost of a temporary investment, while the selling fees reduce the cash proceeds and any recognized gain on the sale.

Valuation of Marketable Securities

Three different methods for the valuation of marketable securities have been advanced: (1) cost, (2) cost or market, whichever is lower, and (3) market.

Cost. Valuation of marketable securities at cost refers to the original acquisition price of a marketable security including all related fees, unless a new cost basis has been assigned to recognize a permanent decline in the value of the security. Cost is to be used unless circumstances require another method as is the case with marketable equity securities, to be explained in the next section. The recognition of gain or loss is deferred until the asset is sold, at which time investment cost is matched against investment proceeds. The cost basis is consistent with income tax procedures, recognizing neither gain nor loss until there is a sale or exchange.

Cost or Market, Whichever is Lower. When using the lower of cost or market method, if market is lower than cost, security values are written down to the lower value; if market is higher than cost, securities are maintained at cost, gains awaiting confirmation through sale.

FASB Statement No. 12, "Accounting for Certain Marketable Securities," requires that **marketable equity securities** be carried at the **lower of aggregate cost or market**.[3] An equity security is defined by the FASB in Statement No. 12 as

> "...any instrument representing ownership shares (e.g., common, preferred, and other capital stock), or the right to acquire (e.g., warrants, rights, and call options) or dispose of (e.g., put options) ownership shares in an enterprise at fixed or determinable prices. The term does not encompass preferred stock that by its terms either must be redeemed by the issuing enterprise or is redeemable at the option of the investor, nor does it include treasury stock or convertible bonds."[4]

FASB Statement No. 12 deals only with marketable *equity* securities. Other marketable securities, primarily marketable debt securities, still may be carried at cost unless there is a substantial decline that is not due to temporary conditions. It seems logical, however, to treat all short-term marketable securities similarly. All temporary investments are acquired for

---

[3]*Statement of Financial Accounting Standards No. 12*, "Accounting for Certain Marketable Securities" (Stamford: Financial Accounting Standards Board, 1975), par. 8.

[4]Ibid, par. 7a.

the same reason—utilization of idle cash to generate a short-term return. Both equity securities and debt securities must meet the same criteria to qualify as temporary investments, and their valuation should reflect a similar concept, i.e., the amount of cash that could be realized upon liquidation at the balance sheet date. Therefore, in the illustrations and end-of-chapter material in this text, the lower of cost or market method is used for *all* short-term marketable securities (i.e., stocks and bonds). It should be recognized, however, that actual practice varies. Some companies interpret FASB No. 12 strictly and account for only marketable equity securities on the lower of cost or market basis.

FASB Statement No. 12 requires that the lower of cost or market method be applied to securities in the **aggregate** and not to individual securities. To illustrate the difference between lower of cost or market on an aggregate basis versus an individual item basis, assume marketable securities with cost and market values on December 31, 1987, as follows:

	Cost	Market	Lower of Cost or Market on Individual Basis
1,000 Shares of Carter Co. common..............	$20,000	$16,000	$16,000
$25,000 10% U.S. Treasury Notes................	25,000	26,500	25,000
$10,000 U.S. Government 8% bonds.............	10,000	7,500	7,500
	$55,000	$50,000	$48,500

The lower of cost or market value on an aggregate basis is $50,000; on an individual basis, $48,500.

An important factor considered by the FASB in choosing the aggregate basis is that many companies view their marketable securities portfolios as collective assets. Further, the Board felt that applying the lower of cost or market procedure on an individual security basis would be unduly conservative.

However, the FASB did recognize that many companies classify separately their current and noncurrent securities portfolios. Therefore, when a classified balance sheet is presented, the lower of aggregate cost or market is to be applied to the separate current and noncurrent portfolios. When an unclassified balance sheet is presented, the entire marketable equity securities portfolio is to be considered a noncurrent asset. The application of FASB Statement No. 12 to long-term marketable equity securities is discussed in detail in Chapter 13.

In adopting the lower of aggregate cost or market method for marketable equity securities, the FASB chose to recognize declines in the realizable value of short-term marketable equity securities portfolios as a charge against income of the current period. The possibility of a future recovery in the market value was not considered sufficient reason to maintain the carrying value at cost.

Recognition of a decline in value on the books calls for a reduction of the asset and a debit to a loss account. Various titles are used for the loss account: Unrealized Loss on Marketable Securities; Loss on Valuation of Marketable Equity Securities; Recognized Decline in Value of Current Marketable Securities. The authors prefer the last title to avoid confusion with the entry required upon the final sale of the securities or with the title used in accounting for long-term marketable equity securities. It should also be noted that the valuation loss is not recognized for income tax purposes, and the basis of the securities for measurement of the ultimate gain or loss on final disposition continues to be cost. Cost can be preserved on the books by the use of a valuation account to reduce the securities to market. The following entry illustrates this procedure.

Recognized Decline in Value of Current Marketable Securities	5,000	
Allowance for Decline in Value of Current Marketable Securities...		5,000

The balance sheet would show:

Current assets:		
Marketable securities (at cost)................................	$55,000	
Less allowance for decline in value of current marketable securities..	5,000	
Marketable securities (at market, December 31, 1987)		$50,000

In practice a shorter form is often used, such as the following:

Current assets:	
Marketable securities (reported at market; cost, $55,000).........	$50,000

The $5,000 loss in the above example would be reported on the current income statement, probably as a charge related to financial management. If in the future there is an increase in the market value of the short-term marketable securities portfolio, the write-down should be reversed to the extent that the resulting carrying value does not exceed original cost. The original write-down is to be viewed as a valuation allowance, representing an estimated decrease in the realizable value of the portfolio. Any subsequent market increase reduces or eliminates this valuation allowance. The reversal of a write-down is considered a change in accounting estimate of an unrealized loss, as was noted in Chapter 4.[5]

In subsequent periods, the portfolio of temporary investments will change through purchases and sales of individual securities. Because cost

---

[5]See *FASB Statement No. 5*, par. 2, and *APB Opinion No. 20*, par. 10.

remains the accepted basis for recognition of gain or loss on final disposition and for income tax purposes, it is preferable to record the sale of marketable securities as though no valuation account existed, i.e., on a cost basis. At the end of each accounting period, an analysis can then be made of cost and aggregated market values for the securities held and the allowance account adjusted to reflect the new difference between cost and market. If market exceeds cost at a subsequent valuation date, the allowance account would be eliminated, and the securities would be valued at cost, the lower of the two values. The offsetting revenue account for the adjustment may be titled Recovery of Recognized Decline in Value of Current Marketable Securities.

To illustrate accounting for subsequent years' transactions, assume in the preceding example that in 1988 the Carter Co. stock is sold for $17,000 and $25,000 of 9% U.S. Treasury notes are purchased for $24,500. The following entries are made:

```
Cash.......................................................    17,000
Loss on Sale of Marketable Securities .............................     3,000
    Marketable Securities (Carter Co. Common) .......................              20,000

Marketable Securities (9% U.S. Treasury Notes) .....................    24,500
    Cash.......................................................              24,500
```

Assuming the market value of the remaining securities in the portfolio is unchanged and the market value of the U.S. Treasury notes remains at cost, the aggregate market value of the temporary investments is $58,500 ($26,500 + $7,500 + $24,500). When comparing the aggregate market value to the aggregate cost value of $59,500 ($25,000 + $10,000 + $24,500), the following adjusting entry would be made at the end of 1988:

```
Allowance for Decline in Value of Current Marketable Securities..........    4,000
    Recovery of Recognized Decline in Value of Current
        Marketable Securities ..........................................              4,000
```

This entry leaves the valuation account with a balance of $1,000 which, when subtracted from cost of $59,500, will report the marketable securities at their aggregate market value of $58,500.

If the aggregate market value of the securities portfolio had fallen during 1988 to $53,000 (compared to cost of $59,500), the adjusting entry would be:

```
Recognized Decline in Value of Current Marketable Securities ...........    1,500
    Allowance for Decline in Value of Current Marketable Securities........              1,500
```

This entry increases the allowance account to $6,500 which, when subtracted from cost of $59,500, will report marketable securities at their aggregate market value of $53,000.

On the other hand, if the aggregate market value of the securities portfolio had risen to $60,000 (compared to cost of $59,500), the adjusting entry at year end would be:

Allowance for Decline in Value of Current Marketable Securities.   5,000
   Recovery of Recognized Decline in Value of Current
    Marketable Securities   5,000

This entry cancels the allowance account since the $59,500 original cost of securities is lower than their current $60,000 aggregate market value.

If the classification of a marketable equity security changes from current to noncurrent or vice versa, the security must be transferred to the applicable portfolio at the lower of cost or market value at date of transfer. If the market value is lower than cost, the market value becomes the new cost basis and a realized loss is to be included in determining net income.[6] In essence, this procedure recognizes the loss upon transfer as though it had been realized. This should reduce the likelihood of income being manipulated through the transfer of securities between current and long-term portfolios.

To summarize the accounting for short-term marketable equity securities under FASB Statement No. 12, securities are originally recorded at cost. Subsequent valuation is at lower of cost or market on an aggregate basis. The adjustment is made at year-end through a valuation allowance account. Any reduction in value is recognized as a current period loss in the income statement; any recovery of the write-down, up to the original cost but no higher, is recognized as a current period recovery in the income statement. These gains or losses would be shown after operating income as "other revenues" or "other expenses." The amount of gain or loss on the ultimate sale of a marketable security is still the difference between the sales price and the original cost of the security without consideration for any previous year-end allowance adjustments. Then, at year-end, the allowance will be adjusted once again to reflect the proper lower of cost or market amount for the remaining securities portfolio.

Any permanent declines in securities values are to be recognized as losses currently, just like any other asset, with the new value being considered cost from thence forward. No subsequent partial recovery would be allowed.

FASB Statement No. 12 requires extensive disclosure of information with respect to marketable equity securities, including aggregate cost and market values, gross unrealized gains and losses, and the amount of net realized gain or loss included in net income.[7] The information included by

---

[6]*Statement of Financial Accounting Standards No. 12, op. cit.,* par. 10.
[7]Ibid., par. 12.

Microdyne Corporation in its annual report, and reproduced on page 265, provides an example of the required disclosures for both current and non-current marketable securities.

Market. Market value refers to the current market price of a marketable security. In applying the market value method, permanent declines in market prices of securities are recognized as losses in the current period. Temporary declines in market values are treated the same as under the lower of cost or market method. That is, security values are written down to market through a valuation adjustment at the end of the accounting period. Where the market method differs is in the valuation of securities whose prices have increased above cost. With the market method, current market prices are recognized as affording an objective basis for the valuation of marketable securities; therefore, such securities would be reported on the balance sheet at their current values, whether higher or lower than cost.

If under the market method marketable securities are to be reported at current values that exceed cost, it is necessary to recognize the increase in the value of the securities. This may be done by debiting the securities and crediting a gain from the appreciation in market values. The gain would be reported in the gains and losses section of the income statement. However, if it is felt that recognition of gains resulting from market value increases should await the sale of securities, a separate capital account, such as Unrealized Appreciation in Value of Marketable Securities, may be credited. When the securities are sold, the unrealized appreciation account is eliminated, and any realized gain or loss is recognized in the income statement. In the interim, the balance in the unrealized appreciation account would be reported in the equity section of the balance sheet.

Market value has been and continues to be an acceptable method for valuing marketable securities within certain industries that follow specialized accounting practices with respect to marketable securities. Enterprises within these industries, such as securities brokers and dealers, that carry marketable equity securities at market value are not required by FASB Statement No. 12 to change to lower of cost or market. For most companies, however, the market value method is not presently considered generally accepted accounting practice, and the lower of cost or market method should be used.

Evaluation of Methods

Valuation at cost finds support on the grounds that it is an extension of the cost principle; the asset is carried at cost until a sale or exchange provides an alternative asset and confirms a gain or loss. The cost method

MICRODYNE CORPORATION

	1984	1983
Current assets:		
Cash..	$ 907,778	$ 218,881
Short-term cash investments....................	35,152	3,914,681
Marketable securities (Note 2).................	160,891	508,275
Accounts receivable, including unbilled receivables of $4,628,001 in 1984 and $2,209,187 in 1983, less allowance for doubtful accounts of $191,500 in 1984 and $316,021 in 1983.................	11,623,830	8,664,760
Inventories....................................	12,853,889	12,829,870
Prepaid expenses	76,362	71,612
Income taxes receivable.......................	1,131,706	605,063
Total current assets..........................	26,789,608	26,813,142

Note 2. Marketable Securities

The current and noncurrent portfolios of marketable equity securities are each carried at their lower of aggregate cost or market at the balance sheet date.

To reduce the carrying amount of the current marketable equity securities portfolio to aggregate market, which was lower than aggregate cost at October 28, 1984 and October 30, 1983, valuation allowances in the amounts of $57,557 and $14,753 were established with a corresponding charge to income at those dates. To reduce the carrying amount of the noncurrent marketable equity securities to aggregate market, which was lower than aggregate cost at October 28, 1984 and October 30, 1983, valuation allowances in the amount of $150,000 and $83,795 respectively, were established by a charge to stockholders' equity representing the net unrealized loss.

The following is a summary of marketable securities:

	1984	Current 1983	1982
Aggregate cost.........................	$218,448	$523,028	$265,000
Aggregate market.......................	160,891	508,275	275,000
Unrealized gain (loss)..................	(57,557)	(14,753)	10,000
Valuation allowance, beginning..........	14,753	—	43,500
Charge (credit) to operations...........	42,804	14,753	(43,500)
Valuation allowance, ending.............	57,557	14,753	—

	1984	Non-current 1983	1982
Aggregrate cost	$500,000	$996,010	—
Aggregate market.......................	350,000	912,215	—
Unrealized (loss)	(150,000)	(83,795)	—
Valuation allowance, beginning..........	83,795	—	—
Charge to stockholders' equity	66,205	83,795	—
Valuation allowance, ending.............	150,000	83,795	—

At October 28, 1984, gross unrealized gains and gross unrealized losses pertaining to marketable equity securities in the portfolios were as follows:

	Gains	Losses
Current................................	—	$ 57,557
Non-current...........................	—	$150,000

Net realized gains of $45,648 and $65,153 and a net realized loss of $7,000 on the sale of marketable equity securities was included in the determination of net income for 1984, 1983 and 1982, respectively. The cost of the securities sold was based on the first-in, first-out method.

offers valuation on a consistent basis from period to period. It is the simplest method to apply and adheres to income tax requirements. However, certain objections to cost can be raised. The use of cost means investments may be carried at amounts differing from values objectively determinable at the balance sheet date, and the integrity of both balance sheet and income statement measurements can be challenged. The use of cost also means identical securities may be reported at different values because of purchases at different prices. A further objection is that management, in controlling the sale of securities, can determine the periods in which gains or losses are to be recognized even though the changes in values may have accrued over a number of periods.

The use of market value is advocated on the basis that there is evidence of the net realizable value of the marketable securities held at the balance sheet date and any changes from previous carrying values should be recognized as gains or losses in the current period. Assuming marketable securities are defined as having a readily available sales price or bid and ask price from one of the national securities exchanges or over-the-counter markets, this method is objective and relatively simple to apply. The major drawback of this method is that gains or losses may be recognized prior to realization, i.e., prior to the actual sale of the securities. In addition, market values fluctuate, often significantly, which would require continual changing of the carrying value of marketable securities on the balance sheet. Market is also challenged as a departure from the cost principle and as lacking in conservatism. Furthermore, market is not acceptable for general accounting or income tax purposes.

The lower of cost or market procedure provides for recognizing market declines and serves to prevent potential mistakes arising in analyzing statements when these declines are not reported. The lower of cost or market is supported as a conservative procedure. This approach may be challenged on the basis that it may be the most complicated method to follow, and it fails to apply a single valuation concept consistently. Securities carried at cost at the end of one period may be reported at market value in the subsequent period. Critics argue that if net realizable value is a desirable measurement concept, its use should not depend on whether portfolio values are greater or less than original cost.

Regardless of the theoretical merits of the three methods, generally accepted accounting principles currently require use of the lower of cost or market method for marketable equity securities and valuation at cost for other temporary investments. With the emphasis in the conceptual framework on decision usefulness, the market valuation method may become more popular in the future.

QUESTIONS

1. Why is cash on hand both necessary and yet potentially unproductive?
2. The following items were included as cash on the balance sheet for the Lawson Co. How should each of the items have been reported?
   (a) Demand deposits with bank
   (b) Restricted cash deposits in foreign banks
   (c) Bank account used for payment of salaries and wages
   (d) Change funds on hand
   (e) Cash in a special cash account to be used currently for the construction of a new building
   (f) Customers' checks returned by the bank marked "Not Sufficient Funds"
   (g) Customers' postdated checks
   (h) IOUs from employees
   (i) Postage stamps received in the mail for merchandise
   (j) Postal money orders received from customers and not yet deposited
   (k) Receipts for advances to customers
   (l) Notes receivable in the hands of the bank for collection
   (m) Special bank account in which sales tax collections are deposited
   (n) Customers' checks not yet deposited
3. On reconciling the cash account with the bank statement, it is found that the general cash fund is overdrawn $436 but the bond redemption account has a balance of $5,400. The treasurer wishes to show cash as a current asset at $4,964. Discuss.
4. The Melvin Company shows in its accounts a cash balance of $66,500 with Bank A and an overdraft of $1,500 with Bank B on December 31. Bank B regards the overdraft as in effect a loan to the Melvin Company and charges interest on the overdraft balance. How would you report the balances with Banks A and B? Would your answer be any different if the overdraft arose as a result of certain checks which had been deposited and proved to be uncollectible and if the overdraft was cleared promptly by the Melvin Company at the beginning of January?
5. Mills Manufacturing is required to maintain a compensating balance of $15,000 with its bank to maintain a line of open credit. The compensating balance is legally restricted as to its use. How should the compensating balance be reported on the balance sheet and why?
6. (a) What are the major advantages in using imprest petty cash funds? (b) What dangers must be guarded against when petty cash funds are used?
7. (a) Give at least four common sources of differences between depositor and bank balances. (b) Which of the differences in (a) require an adjusting entry on the books of the depositor?
8. (a) What two methods may be employed in reconciling the bank and the cash balances? (b) Which would you recommend? Why?
9. (a) What purposes are served by preparing a four-column reconciliation of receipts and disbursements? (b) Why might this form be used by auditors?

10. Tronex Corporation engaged in the following practices at the end of a fiscal year:

    (a) Sales on account from January 1– January 5 were predated as of the month of December.

    (b) Checks in payment of accounts were prepared on December 31 and were entered on the books, but they were placed in the safe awaiting instructions for mailing.

    (c) Customers' checks returned by the bank and marked "Not Sufficient Funds" were ignored for statement purposes.

    (d) Amounts owed to company officers were paid off on December 31 and reborrowed on January 2.

    Explain what is wrong with each of the practices mentioned and give the entries that are required to correct the accounts.

11. Define *temporary investments*. What criteria must be met for a security to be considered a temporary investment?

12. What two methods may be used to record the payment for accrued interest on interest-bearing securities? Which method is preferable?

13. (a) What positions are held with respect to the valuation of marketable securities? (b) What arguments can be advanced in support of each and which position do you feel has the greatest merit?

14. Cintech International reports marketable securities on the balance sheet at the lower of cost or market. What adjustments are required on the books at the end of the year in each situation below:

    (a) Securities are purchased early in 1986 and at the end of 1986 their market value is more than cost.

    (b) At the end of 1987, the market value of the securities is less than cost.

    (c) At the end of 1988, the market value of the securities is greater than at the end of 1987 but is still less than cost.

    (d) At the end of 1989, the market value of the securities is more than the amount originally paid.

15. One of the arguments advanced for using market as the valuation procedure for temporary investments is that it assists in a "proper evaluation of managerial decisions and activities relative to purchases, sales, and holdings of marketable securities." How might you support this statement using the following example? Marketable securities purchased for $500 rose in value to $900 as of the end of the fiscal year, and were sold in the subsequent year for $650.

DISCUSSION CASES

CASE 7–1   (Cash management)

Jack Wilson, manager of Expert Building Company, is a valued and trusted employee. He has been with the company from its start two years ago. Because of the demands of his job, he has not taken a vacation since he began working. He is in charge of recording collections on account, making the daily bank deposits, and reconciling the bank statement.

Late last year, clients began complaining to you, the president, about incorrect statements. As president, you check into this matter. Wilson tells you there is nothing to worry about. The problem is due to the slow mail; customers' payments and statements are crossing in the mail.

Because clients were not complaining last year, you doubt the mail is the primary reason for the problem. What might be some of the reasons for the delay? What are some other problems that might begin to occur? What can be done to remedy the problem? What should be done to make sure the problems are avoided in the future?

CASE 7–2   (Accounting for marketable securities)

PART A:

The Financial Accounting Standards Board issued its Statement No. 12 to clarify accounting methods and procedures with respect to certain marketable securities.

Required:
1. Why does a company maintain an investment portfolio of current securities?
2. What factors should be considered in determining whether investments in marketable equity securities should be classified as current or noncurrent?

PART B:

Presented below are three unrelated situations involving marketable equity securities.

Situation 1

A current portfolio with an aggregate market value in excess of cost includes one particular security whose market value has declined to less than one-half of the original cost. The decline in value is considered to be permanent.

Situation 2

A marketable equity security whose market value is currently less than cost, is classified as noncurrent but is to be reclassified as current.

Situation 3

A company's current portfolio of marketable equity securities consists of the common stock of one company. At the end of the prior year, the market value of the security was fifty percent of original cost. However, at the end of the current year, the market value of the security had appreciated to twice the original cost. The security is still considered current at year end.

Required: What is the effect upon classification, carrying value, and earnings for each of the above situations. Complete your response to each situation before proceeding to the next situation.   (AICPA Adapted)

EXERCISES

EXERCISE 7–1   (Reporting cash on the balance sheet)

1. Indicate how each of the items below should be reported, using the following classifications: (a) cash, (b) restricted cash, (c) temporary investment, (d) receivable, (e) liability, (f) office supplies, or (g) other.

1. Checking account at First Security	$ (20)
2. Checking account at Second Security	350
3. United States savings bonds	650
4. Payroll account	100
5. Sales tax account	150
6. Foreign bank account—unrestricted (in equivalent U.S. Dollars)	750
7. Postage stamps	22
8. Employee's postdated check	30
9. IOU from President's brother	75
10. A wristwatch (reported at market value; surrendered as security by a customer who forgot his wallet)	30
11. Credit memo from a vendor for a purchase return	87
12. Traveler's check	50
13. Not-sufficient-funds check	18
14. Ten cases of empty soft drink bottles (return value)	24
15. Petty cash fund ($16 in currency and expense receipts for $84)	100
16. Money order	36

2. What amount would be reported as Cash on the balance sheet?

EXERCISE 7–2   (Accounting for petty cash)

An examination on the morning of January 2 by the auditor for the Pearson Lumber Company discloses the following items in the petty cash drawer:

Stamps		$ 22.00
Currency and coin		115.66
IOUs from members of the office staff		121.00
An envelope containing collections for a football pool, with office staff names attached		35.00
Petty cash vouchers for:		
Typewriter repairs	$13.00	
Stamps	45.00	
Telegram charges	28.50	
Delivery fees	12.00	98.50
Employee's check postdated January 15		150.00
Employee's check marked "NSF"		189.00
Check drawn by Pearson Lumber Company to Petty Cash		345.00
		$1,076.16

The ledger account discloses a $1,050 balance for Petty Cash. (1) What adjustments should be made on the auditor's working papers so petty cash may be correctly stated on the balance sheet? (2) What is the correct amount of petty cash for the balance sheet? (3) How could the practice of borrowing by employees from the fund be discouraged?

EXERCISE 7–3   (Compensating balances)

Greenfield Company had the following cash balances at December 31, 1987.

Cash in banks	$1,500,000
Petty cash funds (all funds were reimbursed on December 31, 1987)	20,000
Cash legally restricted for additions to plant (expected to be disbursed in 1988)	2,000,000

Cash in banks includes $500,000 of compensating balances against short-term borrowing arrangements at December 31, 1987. The compensating balances are not legally restricted as to withdrawal by Greenfield. In the current asset section of Greenfield's December 31, 1987, balance sheet, what total amount should be reported as cash?   (AICPA adapted)

EXERCISE 7–4   (Bank reconciliation)

In preparing the bank reconciliation for the month of March, Dewey Company has available the following information:

Balance per bank statement 3/31	$25,076
Deposits in transit 3/31.....................................	4,576
Outstanding checks 3/31	3,985
Credit erroneously recorded by bank in Dewey's account 3/12....................................	465
Bank service charge for March...........................	21

What is the correct cash balance at March 31?

(AICPA adapted)

EXERCISE 7–5   (Correct cash balance)

Lee Corporation's checkbook balance on December 31, 1987, was $5,980. In addition, Lee held the following items in its safe on December 31:

Check payable to Lee Corporation, dated January 2, 1988, not included in December 31 checkbook balance	$1,000
Check payable to Lee Corporation, deposited December 20, 1987, and included in December 31 checkbook balance but returned by bank on December 31, marked "NSF". The check was redeposited January 2, 1988, and cleared January 7	400
Postage stamps received from mail order customer	75
Check drawn on Lee Corporation's account, payable to vendor, dated and recorded December 31, but not mailed until January 15, 1988	565

What is the proper amount to be shown as cash on Lee's balance sheet at December 31, 1987?   (AICPA adapted)

EXERCISE 7–6   (Adjusting the cash account)

The accounting department supplied the following data in reconciling the bank statement for Lane Jewelers:

Cash balance per books	$14,692.71
Deposits in transit	2,615.23
Bank service charge	21.00
Outstanding checks	3,079.51
Note collected by bank including $45 interest (Lane not yet notified)	1,045.00
Error by bank—check drawn by Lance Corp. was charged to Lane's account	617.08
Sale and deposit of $1,729.00 was entered in the sales journal and cash receipts journal as $1,792.00	

Give the journal entries required on the books to adjust the cash account.

EXERCISE 7–7   (Bank reconciliation—correct balances)

The Muchmore Manufacturing Co. received its bank statement for the month ending June 30 on July 2. The bank statement indicates a balance of $2,840. The cash account as of the close of business on June 30 has a balance of $435. In reconciling the balances, the auditor discovers the following:

(a) Receipts on June 30 of $9,500 were not deposited until July 1.
(b) Checks outstanding on June 30 were $12,310.
(c) Collection by bank of note for $150 less collection fees of $25, not recorded on the books.
(d) The bank has charged the depositor for overdrafts, $80.
(e) A canceled check to W. E. Lee for $9,618 was entered in cash payments in error as $9,168.

Prepare a bank reconciliation statement. (Use the form reconciling bank and depositor figures to corrected cash balance.)

EXERCISE 7–8   (Bank reconciliation—analysis of outstanding checks)

The following information was included in the bank reconciliation for Rylton, Inc. for June. What was the total of outstanding checks at the beginning of June? Assume all other reconciling items are listed below.

Checks and charges returned by bank in June, including a June service charge of $10	$16,435
Service charge made by bank in May and recorded on the books in June	5
Total of credits to Cash in all journals during June	19,292
Customer's NSF check returned as a bank charge in June (no entry made on books)	100
Customer's NSF check returned in May and redeposited in June (no entry made on books in either May or June)	250
Outstanding checks at June 30	8,060
Deposit in transit at June 30	600

EXERCISE 7–9   (Four-column bank reconciliation — correct balances)

Tyler Corporation began doing business with Security Bank on October 1. On that date the correct balance was $4,000. All cash transactions are cleared through the bank account. Subsequent transactions during October and November relating to the records of Tyler and Security are summarized below.

	Tyler Company Books	Security Bank Books
October deposits.	$7,360	$7,110
October checks.	6,290	6,130
October service charge	- - -	10
October 31 balance	5,070	4,970
November deposits (regular)	8,220	8,280
November checks.	9,410	9,220
November service charge	- - -	15
Note collected by bank (included $15 interest)	- - -	1,015
October service charge	10	- - -
November 30 balance	3,870	5,030

On the basis of the foregoing data: (1) prepare a four-column reconciliation as of November 30, reconciling both bank and book balances to a corrected balance, and (2) assuming November 30 is the end of Tyler's fiscal year, give entries that would be required by the bank reconciliation.

EXERCISE 7–10   (Journalizing marketable securities transactions)

Give the entries necessary to record these transactions of Rexton, Inc.

(a) Purchased $80,000 U.S. Treasury 8% bonds, paying 102½ plus accrued interest of $1,500. Broker's fees were $590. Rexton, Inc. uses the revenue approach to record accrued interest on purchased bonds.
(b) Purchased 1,000 shares of Agler Co. common stock at 175 plus brokerage fees of $1,200.
(c) Received semiannual interest on the U.S. Treasury bonds.
(d) Sold 150 shares of Agler at 185.
(e) Sold $20,000 of U.S. Treasury 8% bonds at 103 plus accrued interest of $275.
(f) Purchased a $15,000, 6-month certificate of deposit.

EXERCISE 7–11   (Realized loss)

During 1987, Anthony Company purchased marketable equity securities as a short-term investment. Pertinent data are as follows:

Security	Cost	Market Value (12/31/87)
A	$20,000	$18,000
B	40,000	30,000
C	90,000	93,000

Anthony appropriately carries these securities at lower of aggregate cost or market value. What is the amount of loss to flow through Anthony's income statement in 1987?   (AICPA adapted)

EXERCISE 7–12   (Accounting for marketable securities)

During 1987, Axton's Hobby Shop purchased the following marketable securities:

	Cost	Year-End Market
Wexler Co. Common..................	$12,000	$14,000
10% U.S. Treasury Notes	18,000	11,000

Marketable securities are to be reported on the balance sheet at the lower of aggregate cost or market. (1) What entry would be made at year-end assuming the above values? (2) What entry would be made during 1988 assuming one half of the Wexler Co. common stock is sold for $7,000? (3) What entry would be made at the end of 1988 assuming (a) the market value of remaining securities is $18,000? (b) The market value of remaining securities is $21,000? (c) The market value of remaining securities is $28,000?

EXERCISE 7–13   (Reporting marketable securities)

Denso Corporation reports on a calendar-year basis. Its December 31, 1987, financial statements were issued on February 3, 1988. The auditor's report was dated January 22, 1988. The following information pertains to Denso's aggregate marketable equity securities portfolio.

Cost...............................	$500,000
Market value (12/31/87)	400,000
Market value (1/22/88)	350,000
Market value (2/3/88).................	300,000

How much should be reported on Denso's balance sheet at December 31, 1987, for marketable equity securities?   (AICPA adapted)

EXERCISE 7–14   (Valuation of marketable securities)

Everston Steel Corp. acquires marketable securities in 1986 at a cost of $200,000. Market values of the securities at the end of each year are as follows: 1986, $195,500; 1987, $219,000; 1988, $211,000. Give the entries at the end of 1986, 1987, and 1988 indicating how the securities would be reported on the balance sheet at the end of each year under each of the following assumptions:

(a) Securities are reported at cost.
(b) Securities are reported at the lower of cost or market on an aggregate basis.
(c) Securities are reported at market, using an unrealized appreciation valuation account.

EXERCISE 7–15   (Multiple-choice review)

For each of the following select the best answer.
1. If a marketable equity security that was classified as noncurrent in a prior period were to be reclassified as current in the current period, what would be the effect upon the valuation allowance attendant to that security assuming no changes in its market value?

(a) The valuation allowance should be reclassified as current also.

(b) The valuation allowance should be recognized as a loss in the current period.

(c) The valuation allowance should be adjusted to zero and the security reclassified at cost.

(d) The valuation allowance should be recognized as a gain in the subsequent period.

2. The Bradley Company's marketable equity securities portfolio, which is appropriately included in current assets, is as follows:

	Cost	Market	Unrealized Gain (Loss)
	December 31, 1986		
Allen, Inc..	$100,000	$100,000	---
Lytle Corp..	200,000	150,000	$(50,000)
Pence Company..	250,000	260,000	10,000
	$550,000	$510,000	$(40,000)

	Cost	Market	Unrealized Gain (Loss)
	December 31, 1987		
Allen, Inc..	$100,000	$120,000	$ 20,000
Lytle Corp..	300,000	260,000	(40,000)
Pence Company..	200,000	240,000	40,000
	$600,000	$620,000	$ 20,000

Ignoring income taxes, what amount should be reported as an adjustment to income in Bradley's 1987 income statement? (a) $0, (b) $10,000, (c) $40,000, (d) $60,000.

3. Accumulated changes in the valuation of a short-term marketable equity security should be a component of:

(a) current assets

(b) current liabilities

(c) noncurrent assets

(d) net income

4. Which of the following conditions generally exists before market value can be used as the basis for valuation of a company's marketable equity securities?

(a) Market value must approximate historical cost

(b) Management's intention must be to dispose of the security within one year.

(c) Market value must be less than cost for each security held in the company's marketable equity security portfolio.

(d) The aggregate valuation of a company's marketable equity security portfolio must be less than the aggregate cost of the portfolio.

5. On January 10, 1987, Wilson Corporation acquired 1,000 shares of Bryant Corporation common stock at $70 per share as a short-term investment. On that date Bryant had 100,000 shares issued and outstanding. On November 1, 1987, Bryant declared and paid cash dividends of $2 per share on its outstanding common stock. On December 31, 1987, the market value of Bryant's

common stock was $62 per share. At what value should Wilson report the investment in common stock of Bryant on its December 31, 1987, balance sheet? (a) $60,000, (b) $62,000, (c) $68,000, (d) $70,000.

6. A marketable equity security must have a ready market in order to be classified as current, and

(a) Be available to management for use in short run operations.
(b) Be traded on a recognized national exchange.
(c) Have a current market value in excess of original cost.
(d) Have been owned less than one year.

(AICPA adapted)

PROBLEMS

PROBLEM 7–1   (Composition of cash and marketable securities)

The balance of $192,200 in the cash account of Thomson Inc. consists of these items:

Petty cash fund	$ 1,000
Receivable from an employee	200
Cash in bond sinking fund	15,000
Cash in a foreign bank unavailable for withdrawal	40,000
Cash in First Bank	120,000
Currency on hand	16,000

The balance in the marketable securities account consists of:

U.S. Treasury bonds	$ 52,600
Voting stock of a subsidiary company (70% interest)	425,000
Advances to a subsidiary company (no maturity date specified)	115,000
A note receivable from a customer	20,500
The company's own shares held as treasury stock	25,000
Stock of Midwest Telephone Co.	64,000

Instructions: Calculate the correct Cash and Marketable Securities balances and state what accounts and in what sections of the balance sheet the other items would be properly reported.

PROBLEM 7–2   (Accounting for petty cash)

On December 1, 1987, LGA Corporation established an imprest petty cash fund. The operations of the fund for the last month of 1987 and the first month of 1988 are summarized below:

Dec. 1 The petty cash fund was established by cashing a company check for $1,500 and delivering the proceeds to the fund cashier.

21 A request for replenishment of the petty cash fund was received by the accounts payable department, supported by appropriate signed vouchers, summarized as follows:

Selling expenses	$ 324
Administrative expenses	513
Special equipment	122
Telephone, telegraph, and postage	48
Miscellaneous expenses	260
Total	$1,267

22 A check for $1,294 was drawn payable to the petty cash cashier.

31 The company's independent certified public accountant counted the fund in connection with the year-end audit work and found the following:

Cash in petty cash fund		$ 655
Employees' checks with January dates (postdated)		85
Expense vouchers properly approved as follows:		
Selling expenses	$146	
Administrative expenses	412	
Office supplies	28	
Telephone, telegraph, and postage	48	
Miscellaneous expenses	120	754
Total		$1,494

The petty cash fund was not replenished at December 31, 1987.

Jan. 15 The employees' checks held in the petty cash fund at December 31 were cashed and the proceeds retained in the fund.

31 A request for replenishment was made and a check was drawn to restore the fund to its original balance of $1,500. The support vouchers for January expenditures are summarized below.

Selling expenses	$ 85
Administrative expenses	312
Telephone, telegraph, and postage	35
Miscellaneous expenses	220
Total	$652

Instructions: Record the transactions in general journal form.

Problem 7–3   (Bank reconciliation—corrected balance)

The cash account of Pate Service, Inc. disclosed a balance of $17,056.48 on October 31. The bank statement as of October 31 showed a balance of $21,209.45. Upon comparing the statement with the cash records, the following facts were developed:

(a) Pate's account had been charged on October 26 for a customer's uncollectible check amounting to $1,143.

(b) A 2-month, 9%, $3,000 customer's note dated August 25, discounted on October 12, had been dishonored October 26, and the bank had charged Pate for $3,050.83, which included a protest fee of $5.83.

(c) A customer's check for $725 had been entered as $625 by both the depositor and the bank but was later corrected by the bank.

(d) Check No. 661 for $1,242.50 had been entered in the cash disbursements journal at $1,224.50 and check No. 652 for $32.90 had been entered as $329. The company uses the voucher system.

✓(e) There were bank service charges for October of $39.43 not yet recorded on the books.

(f) A bank memo stated that M. Sear's note for $2,500 and interest of $62.50 had been collected on October 29, and the bank had made a charge of $12.50 (No entry had been made on the books when the note was sent to the bank for collection.)

✓(g) Receipts of October 29 for $6,850 were deposited November 1.

The following checks were outstanding on October 31:

No. 620	$1,250.00	No. 671	$ 732.50
621	3,448.23	673	187.90
632	2,405.25	675	275.72
670	1,775.38	676	2,233.15

Instructions:

(1) Construct a bank reconciliation statement, using the form where both bank and book balances are brought to a corrected cash balance.

(2) Give the journal entries required as a result of the preceding information.

Problem 7–4   (Bank reconciliation—corrected balance)

The books of Hawkins Company show a cash balance of $17,569 as of July 31. Hawkins' bank statement shows a cash balance for the company of $16,432. Additional information which might be useful in reconciling the disparity between the two balances follows:

(a) A deposit of $1,600 was recorded by the bank on July 3, but it should have been recorded for Hawker Company rather than Hawkins Company.

(b) $425 of Petty Cash was included in the cash balance, but an actual count reveals $516 on hand.

(c) Check No. 315 in payment of electric bill for $125 was correctly recorded by the bank but was recorded in the cash disbursements journal of Hawkins as $215.

(d) The bank statement does not show receipts of $1,250 which were deposited on July 31.

(e) The bank statement indicated a monthly service charge of $21.

(f) A check for $372 was returned marked NSF. The check had been included in the July 24 deposit.

(g) Proceeds from cash sales of $1,530 for July 19 were stolen. The company expects to recover this amount from the insurance company. The cash receipts were recorded in the books, but no entry was made for the loss.

(h) A check for $2,560 cleared the bank on July 29. It was a transfer to the payroll account at the same bank. On July 31, all but $1,255 of payroll checks had been processed at the bank.

(i) Interest of $56 has accrued on funds the bank had invested for Hawkins for the month of July.

(j) Outstanding checks totaled $1,420 as of July 31.

(k) The July 22 deposit included a check for $705 that had been returned on July 15 marked NSF. Hawkins Company made no entry upon return of the check.

Instructions:

(1) Prepare a reconciliation of bank and book balances to a correct balance.

(2) Make the necessary journal entries for Hawkins Company with the information provided on the bank reconciliation.

Problem 7–5 (Four-column bank reconciliation—corrected balance)

The following data are applicable to the Morgan Building Co.

(a) The July 31 bank statement balance of $74,875 included a bank service charge of $235 not previously reported to the company but recorded on the company's books in August.

(b) The cash account balance in the general ledger on July 31 was $66,715.

(c) Outstanding checks at July 31 were $13,475. Deposits in transit on July 31 were $5,080.

(d) The bank statement on August 31 had a balance of $78,265, recognizing deposits of $105,360 and withdrawals of $101,970. The withdrawals included a service charge for August of $270 not yet reported to Morgan Building Co.

(e) The cash account balance in the general ledger on August 31 was $80,435, recognizing receipts of $104,405 for August and checks written during August of $90,450. Deposits in transit on August 31 were $4,125, and checks of $2,225 were outstanding as of that date.

Instructions:

(1) Prepare a four-column bank reconciliation as of August 31. Use the form that reconciles both bank and book balances to correct balances.

(2) Give any entries at August 31 that may be required on the company's books.

Problem 7–6 (Four-column bank reconciliation—corrected balance)

The following information is related to Vincent Office Supplies.

	August	September
Bank statement balance—at month end................	$ 2,412	$ 2,782
Cash account balance—at month end	1,955	2,276
Bank charges for NSF check returned (normally written off in month following return)	38	80
Outstanding checks—at month end....................	600	965
Deposits in transit—at month end	300	470
Bank service charges (normally recorded in month following bank charge).............................	5	9
Drafts collected by bank (not recorded by company until month following collection)	200	150
Total credits to cash account	14,853	17,979
Total deposits on bank statement	?	18,080
Check #411 was erroneously recorded in the company checkbook and journal as $286; the correct amount is $236. (This check was not outstanding on September 30.)		

The outstanding checks on September 30 include a company check for $100 certified by the bank on September 18.

All disbursements were made by check.

Instructions: Prepare a four-column bank reconciliation for the month of September. Use the form where both bank and book balances are brought to corrected cash balances.

Problem 7–7   (Bank reconciliation—bank to book balance)

Bank Reconciliation
December 31

Balance per bank		$25,113.46
Add:		
Collections received on Dec. 31 and debited to Cash on books but not yet deposited	$2,142.25	
Check No. 1209 written for $627 but honored and paid by the bank as $1,627	1,000.00	
Customer's check deposited Dec. 27 and returned marked NSF	360.00	
Bank service charge for December	9.20	3,511.45
		$28,624.91
Deduct:		
Outstanding checks*	$1,967.75	
Check No. 1125 for $164 recorded by depositor as $146	22.00	
Proceeds of a Note Receivable which had been left at the bank for collection but has not yet been recorded as collected	1,500.00	3,489.75
		$25,135.16
Unexplained difference		118.00
Balance per books		$25,017.16

*Outstanding Checks:

No. 1210	$ 65.42		No. 1273	$ 515.64
1223	119.11		1280	269.14
1262	74.30		1291	11.92
1272	1,034.22		Total	$1,967.75

Instructions:

(1) Prepare a corrected reconciliation of bank to book balance.

(2) Prepare the necessary journal entries prior to closing the books.

Problem 7–8   (Accounting for marketable equity securities)

During 1987 Bell Company engaged in the following transactions involving marketable equity securities.

Jan.   1   Purchased 1,200 shares in Corporation X for $6 per share.
May 14   Purchased 2,700 shares in Corporation Y for $12 per share.
Sep. 12   Purchased 1,600 shares in Corporation X for $8.50 per share.
Dec. 31   Sold 1,400 shares in Corporation X for $9 per share.

At the end of 1987, the shares in Corporation Y were selling for $7 per share.
On May 13, 1988, all of Corporation Y shares were sold for $8 each. The shares of Corporation X still on hand at December 31, 1988, were selling for $7 per share.

Assume that all the shares are considered to be current assets, and that Bell Company is *not* part of an industry having specialized accounting for marketable securities.

The company assumes a FIFO flow of marketable securities.

Instructions: Provide the journal entries to be made on December 31, 1987, May 13, 1988, and December 31, 1988.

(AICPA adapted)

Problem 7–9   (Recording and valuing temporary investments)

Myers & Associates reports the following information on the December 31, 1986 balance sheet:

Marketable securities (at cost)....................... $225,850
   Less allowance for decline in value
      of marketable securities........................   2,260 $223,590

Supporting records of Myers' temporary holdings show marketable securities as follows:

	Cost	Market
200 shares of Conway Co. common..................	$ 25,450	$ 24,300
$80,000 U.S. Treasury 7% bonds.....................	79,650	77,400
$120,000 U.S. Treasury 7½% bonds	120,750	121,890
	$225,850	$223,590

Interest dates on the Treasury bonds are January 1 and July 1. Myers & Associates makes reversing entries and uses the revenue approach to recording the purchase of bonds with accrued interest.

During 1987 and 1988 Myers & Associates completed the following transactions related to temporary investments.

1987
Jan.   1   Received semiannual interest on U.S. Treasury bonds. (The entry to reverse the interest accrual at the end of the last year has already been made.)
Apr.   1   Sold $60,000 of the 7½% U.S. Treasury bonds at 102 plus accrued interest. Brokerage fees were $200.
May 21   Received dividends of 25 cents per share on the Conway Co. common stock. The dividend had not been recorded on the declaration date.
July   1   Received semiannual interest on U.S. Treasury bonds, then sold the 7% treasury bonds at 97½. Brokerage fees were $250.

Aug. 15   Purchased 100 shares of Nieman Inc. common stock at 116 plus brokerage fees of $50.

Nov. 1   Purchased $50,000 of 8% U.S. Treasury bonds at 101 plus accrued interest. Brokerage fees were $125. Interest dates are January 1 and July 1.

Dec. 31   Market prices of securities were: Conway Co. common, 110; 7½% U.S. Treasury bonds, 101 3/4; 8% U.S. Treasury bonds, 101; Nieman Inc. common, 116 3/4. Myers & Associates reports all marketable securities at the lower of aggregate cost or market.

1988

Jan. 2   Recorded the receipt of semiannual interest on the U.S. Treasury bonds.

Feb. 1   Sold the remaining 7½% U.S. Treasury bonds at 101 plus accrued interest. Brokerage fees were $300.

Instructions:

(1) Prepare journal entries for the foregoing transactions and accrue required interest on December 31. Give computations in support of your entries.

(2) Show how marketable securities would be presented on the December 31, 1987 balance sheet.

Problem 7–10   (Accounting for marketable equity securities)

Ferguson Corporation invested idle cash resources in acquiring 4,000 units of common stock in another company on May 12, 1986 at a price of $18 per share. By the end of 1986, the shares had dropped to a market price of $10 each. On March 3, 1987, the corporation sold 1,000 of the shares for $12,000; by the end of the year, the shares were selling for $13 each. The price of the shares recovered dramatically during 1988. The corporation sold 1,500 shares for $30,000 on September 5, 1988, and by the end of the year, the shares had a market price of $22 each.

Instructions: Assume that the shares are marketable equity securities and that at all times they are classified as current assets. In accordance with FASB Statement No. 12, give the journal entries to be made for the years 1986, 1987, and 1988.

(AICPA adapted)

Problem 7–11   (Alternative methods of valuing marketable securities)

Dextron Co. made the following investments in marketable securities in 1986:

Martin Inc., 1,400 shares @ 45 3/4	$ 64,050
Smith Corp., 1,750 shares @ 22½	39,375
Walker Bros. first-mortgage 8% bonds,	
105 $1000 bonds at par	105,000
	$208,425

Smith Corp. shares were sold at the end of 1988 for $29,750. The market values of the securities at the end of 1986, 1987, and 1988 were as follows:

	1986	1987	1988
Martin Inc.	$ 68,250	$ 55,650	$ 60,375
Smith Corp.	35,700	30,100	—
Walker Bros.	108,500	110,250	105,350

Instructions: Prepare the necessary entries for 1986, 1987, and 1988 for the valuation and the sale of securities, and show how the securities would be reported on the balance sheets prepared at the end of 1986, 1987, and 1988 under each of the following assumptions.
(a) Securities are valued at cost.
(b) Securities are valued at the lower of cost or market (aggregate basis).
(c) Securities are valued at market, using an unrealized appreciation valuation account.

Problem 7–12   (Correcting entries for temporary investments)

During 1987 and 1988, the Kopson Co. made the following journal entries to account for transactions involving temporary investments.

1987
(a) Nov. 1   Marketable Securities............................ 106,883
                  Cash   106,883
                      To record the purchase of $100,000 of U.S.
                      Treasury bonds at 103¼. Brokerage fees were
                      $300. Interest is payable semiannually on
                      January 1 and July 1.
(b) Dec. 31 Recognized Decline in Value of Current
                  Marketable Securities............................ 4,283
                      Allowance for Decline in Value of
                      Current Marketable Securities   4,283
                          To record the decrease in market value of
                          the current marketable securities based on
                          the following data:

	Cost	Market
Fleming Co. stock	$ 25,250	$ 23,350
Dobson Co. stock.....................	32,450	33,950
10% U.S. Treasury bonds.............	106,883	103,000
	$164,583	$160,300

The beginning allowance account balance was $500. There were no other entries in 1987.

1988
(c) Jan. 1   Cash 5,000
                  Interest Revenue................................   5,000
                      To record interest revenue for six months.
(d) July 1   Cash 5,000
                  Interest Revenue................................   5,000
                      To record interest revenue for six months.
(e) Dec. 6   Marketable Securities............................ 50,000
                  Long-Term Investment in Equity Securities   50,000
                      To record the reclassification of 10,000 shares of
                      Braxton Co. stock, which was selected by manage-
                      ment for sale in 1989. Market price was $4.80
                      per share at the date of reclassification.   *(continued)*

(f)   Dec. 31   Recognized Decline in Value of
                 Current Marketable Securities 5,483
            Allowance for Decline in Value of
                 Current Marketable Securities   5,483
            To record the decrease in the market value
            of the current marketable securities based
            on the following data:

	Cost	Market
Fleming Co. stock	$ 25,250	$ 24,950
Dobson Co. stock.....................	32,450	32,650
10% U.S. Treasury bonds..............	106,883	103,500
Braxton Co. stock....................	50,000	48,000
	$214,583	$209,100

There were no other entries.

Instructions: For each incorrect entry, give the entry that should have been made. Assume the revenue approach and the lower of cost or market method.

8
Receivables

For most businesses **receivables** are a significant item, representing a major portion of the liquid assets of a company. Retail and merchandising companies, such as Sears, Roebuck or J C Penney, typically have 50% to 70% of total current assets tied up in receivables. For some service-type businesses, the percentage is even higher. Receivables also can provide a significant source of revenues from finance charges. In 1984, for example, Sears collected $2.1 billion in finance charges from its customers. On the other hand, a lack of control of receivables can result in substantial losses from uncollectible accounts. Even with good credit policies and collection procedures, bad debt losses often range from one to five percent of total credit sales. Finally, receivables can be used as collateral for a loan or sold to generate funds for operating purposes. During 1985, for example, International Harvester Credit Corporation sold $1.2 billion of receivables, using the proceeds from the sale to reduce the corporation's debt.

As the above examples illustrate, receivables can affect the profitability of company operations in a number of ways. This makes the management, control, and accounting for receivables important tasks. The major considerations in accounting for receivables involve their recognition, classification, valuation, and reporting. Collection of receivables and the use of receivables in financing company operations are also important considerations. All of these issues are addressed in this chapter.

CLASSIFICATION OF RECEIVABLES

In its broadest sense, the term *receivables* is applicable to all claims against others for money, goods, or services. For accounting purposes, however, the term is generally employed in a narrower sense to designate claims expected to be settled by the receipt of cash.

In classifying receivables, an important distinction is made between trade and nontrade receivables. Usually, the chief source of receivables is the normal operating activities of a business, i. e., credit sales of goods and services to customers. These **trade receivables** may be evidenced by a formal written promise to pay and classified as **notes receivable**. In most cases, however, trade receivables are unsecured "open accounts," often referred to simply as **accounts receivable**.

Accounts receivable represent an extension of short-term credit to customers. Payments are generally due within 30 to 90 days. The credit arrangements are typically informal agreements between seller and buyer supported by such business documents as invoices, sales orders, and delivery contracts. Normally trade receivables do not involve interest, although an interest or service charge may be added if payments are not made within a specified period. Trade receivables are the most common type of receivable and are generally the most significant in total dollar amount.

Nontrade receivables include all other types of receivables. They arise from a variety of transactions such as: (1) the sale of securities or property other than inventory; (2) advances to stockholders, directors, officers, employees, and affiliated companies; (3) deposits with creditors, utilities, and other agencies; (4) purchase prepayments; (5) deposits to guarantee contract performance or expense payment; (6) claims for losses or damages; (7) claims for rebates and tax refunds; (8) subscriptions for capital stock; and (9) dividends and interest receivable. Nontrade receivables should be summarized in appropriately titled accounts and reported separately in the financial statements.

Another way of classifying receivables relates to the **current** or short-term versus **noncurrent** or long-term nature of receivables. As indicated in Chapter 5, the "Current assets" classification, as broadly conceived, includes all receivables identified as collectible within one year or the normal operating cycle, whichever is longer. Thus, for classification purposes, all trade receivables are considered current; each nontrade item requires separate analysis to determine whether it is reasonable to assume that it will be collected within one year. Noncurrent receivables are reported under the "Investments" or "Other noncurrent assets" caption, or as a separate item with an appropriate description.

In summary, receivables are classified in various ways, e. g., as accounts or notes receivable, as trade or nontrade receivables, and as current or noncurrent receivables. These categories are not mutually exclusive. For example, accounts receivable are trade receivables and are current; notes receivable may be trade receivables and therefore current in some circumstances, but are nontrade receivables, either current or noncurrent, in other situations. The classifications used most often in practice and throughout this book will be simply *accounts receivable, notes receivable,* and *other receivables*.

ACCOUNTS RECEIVABLE

As indicated earlier, accounts receivable include all trade receivables not supported by a written agreement or "note." The following sections discuss the major accounting problems associated with accounts receivable: (1) when they are to be recognized; (2) how they are to be valued and reported; and (3) how they may be used as a source of cash in financing company operations.

Recognition of Accounts Receivable

The recognition of accounts receivable is related to the recognition of revenue. Since revenues are generally recorded when the earning process is complete and cash is realized or realizable, it follows that a receivable arising from the sale of goods is generally recognized when title to the goods passes to the buyer. Because the point at which title passes may vary with the terms of the sale, it is normal practice to recognize the receivable when goods are shipped to the customer. It is at this point in time that the revenue recognition criteria are normally satisfied. Receivables should not be recognized for goods shipped on approval where the shipper retains title until there is a formal acceptance, or for goods shipped on consignment, where the shipper retains title until the goods are sold by the consignee. Receivables for service to customers are properly recognized when the services are performed. The entry for recognizing a receivable from the sale of goods or services is:

```
Accounts Receivable.............................................  XXX
    Sales.......................................................          XXX
```

When the account is collected, Accounts Receivable is credited and Cash is debited.

For department stores and major oil and gas companies, a significant portion of receivables arise from *credit card sales*.[1] The recognition of such receivables is similar to recognition of other trade receivables.

The treatment of credit card sales for other companies, such as American Express or banks that handle VISA or MasterCard, is somewhat different. These companies are generally responsible for approving

---

[1] It is estimated that annual credit card sales amount to over $170 billion in the United States alone. There are over 200 million credit-card holders of nationally available cards such as VISA, MasterCard, American Express, and Diners Club, not even counting the cards of major retailers, such as Sears and Penneys, or the large oil companies.

customers' credit and collecting the receivables. Consequently, they usually charge a service fee, normally 2% to 5% of net credit card sales. These companies generally follow one of two procedures in reimbursing the retail companies that accept their cards: (1) the retailer must submit the credit card receipts in order to receive payments, or (2) they allow retailers to deposit the receipts directly into a checking account. American Express, Diners Club, Carte Blanche, and other travel and entertainment card companies generally follow the first procedure; bank cards are accounted for with the second method.

As an example of how a retail company would account for credit card sales under these two approaches, assume that Little Italy's Pizza Parlor has American Express drafts that total $1,200 on November 20. The entry to record the sales would be:

```
Accounts Receivable-American Express............................  1,200
    Sales.......................................................          1,200
        To record American Express credit card sales for November 20.
```

Little Italy would then send the receipts to American Express, which would send a check to Little Italy for $1,200 less its service fees. Assuming a 5% service charge, which Little Italy would recognize as a selling expense, the entry to record the payment from Amercian Express would be:

```
Cash........................................................  1,140
Credit Card Service Charge.....................................     60
    Accounts Receivable........................................          1,200
        To record payment from American Express on credit card sales.
```

Continuing the example, assume Little Italy also had VISA charge sales of $2,000. These sales are handled under the second method and are treated like a cash sale. In effect, bank credit card sales, such as VISA and Master-Card, are a form of factoring receivables, which is discussed later in the chapter. The retail company makes out a regular, but separate, bank deposit slip and deposits the credit card receipts as though they were cash. The bank receives the deposit slip and credit card receipts and increases the retailer's checking account balance for the total amount less the bank credit card service charge. Assuming a 4% bank service charge, in our example Little Italy would make the following entry:

```
Cash........................................................  1,920
Credit Card Service Charge.....................................     80
    Sales.......................................................          2,000
        To record VISA credit card sales for November 20.
```

Note that under this method a receivable is never established by the retail companies. The receivables from the customers are the responsibility of the bank that issued the credit card. The customers pay the bank directly and any uncollectibles are losses for the bank.

Valuation and Reporting of Accounts Receivable

Theoretically, all receivables should be valued at an amount representing the present value of the expected future cash receipts. As explained in Chapter 6, the present value of a $1,000 receivable due in 1 year at a 10% interest rate is $909.10 ($1,000 × the present value factor of .9091 from Table IV in Chapter 6). The difference in the present value and the amount to be received in the future ($90.90 in the example) is the implicit interest. Since accounts receivable are short term, usually being collected within 30 to 90 days, the amount of interest is insignificant. Consequently, the accounting profession has chosen to ignore the interest element for these trade receivables.[2]

Instead of valuing accounts receivable at a discounted present value, they are to be reported at their **net realizable or expected cash value**. This means that accounts receivable should be recorded net of estimated uncollectible items, trade discounts, and anticipated sales returns or allowances. The objective is to report the receivables at the amount of claims from customers actually expected to be collected in cash.

Uncollectible Accounts Receivable. Invariably, some receivables will prove uncollectible. The simplest method for recognizing the loss from these uncollectible accounts is to debit an expense account, such as Bad Debt Expense or Uncollectible Accounts Expense, and credit Accounts Receivable at the time it is determined that an account cannot be collected. This approach is called the **direct write-off method** and is often used by small businesses because of its simplicity. While the recognition of uncollectibles in the period of their discovery is simple and convenient, this method does not provide for the matching of current revenues with related expenses and does not report receivables at their net realizable value. Therefore, use of the direct write-off method is considered a departure from generally accepted accounting principles. The following sections describe the procedures used in estimating uncollectibles with the **allowance method**, which is required by GAAP.

Establishing an Allowance for Doubtful Accounts. When using the allowance method, the amount of receivables estimated to be uncollectible is recorded by a debit to Doubtful Accounts Expense and a credit to Allowance for Doubtful Accounts. The terminology for these account titles may vary somewhat. Other possibilities, besides Allowance for Doubtful Accounts, include Allowance for Uncollectible Accounts and Allowance for

---

[2]See *Opinions of the Accounting Principle Board No. 21*, "Interest on Receivables and Payables" (New York: American Institute of Certified Public Accountants, 1971), par. 3(a).

Bad Debts. The expense account title usually is consistent with that of the allowance account. A typical entry, normally made as an end-of-the-period adjustment, would be as follows:

```
Doubtful Accounts Expense.......................................  XXX
   Allowance for Doubtful Accounts ...............................      XXX
      To record estimated uncollectible accounts
      receivable for the period.
```

The expense would be reported as a selling or general and administrative expense, and the allowance account would be shown as a deduction from Accounts Receivable, thereby reporting the net realizable amount of the receivables.

Writing Off an Uncollectible Account under the Allowance Method. When positive evidence is available concerning the partial or complete worthlessness of an account, the account is written off by a debit to the allowance account, which was previously established, and a credit to Accounts Receivable. Positive evidence of a reduction in value is found in the bankruptcy, death, or disappearance of a debtor, failure to enforce collection legally, or barring of collection by the statute of limitations. Write-offs should be supported by evidence of the uncollectibility of the accounts from appropriate parties, such as courts, lawyers, or credit agencies, and should be authorized in writing by appropriate company officers. The entry to write off an uncollectible receivable would be:

```
Allowance for Doubtful Accounts .....................................  XXX
   Accounts Receivable...........................................      XXX
      To record the write-off of an uncollectible account.
```

Note that no entry is made to Doubtful Accounts Expense at this time. That entry was made when the allowance was established. The expense was thus recorded in the period when the sale was made, not necessarily in the period when the account became uncollectible, as with the direct write-off method.

Occasionally, an account that has been written off as uncollectible is unexpectedly collected. Entries are required to reverse the write-off entry and to record the collection. Assuming an account of $1,500 was written off as uncollectible but was subsequently collected, the following entries would be made at the time of collection:

```
Accounts Receivable............................................  1,500
   Allowance for Doubtful Accounts ...............................      1,500
      To reverse the entry made to write off the account.

Cash.......................................................  1,500
   Accounts Receivable...........................................      1,500
      To record collection of the account.
```

Estimating Uncollectibles Based on Sales Percentage. The estimate for uncollectible accounts may be based on sales for the period or the amount of receivables outstanding at the end of the period. When a sales basis is used, the amount of uncollectible accounts in past years relative to total sales provides a percentage of estimated uncollectibles. This percentage may be modified by expectations based on current experience. Since doubtful accounts occur only with credit sales, it would seem logical to develop a percentage of doubtful accounts to credit sales of past periods. This percentage is then applied to credit sales of the current period. However, since extra work may be required in maintaining separate records of cash and credit sales or in analyzing sales data, the percentage is frequently developed in terms of total sales. Unless there is considerable periodic fluctuation in the proportion of cash and credit sales, the total sales method will normally give satisfactory results.

To illustrate, if 2% of sales are considered doubtful in terms of collection and sales for the period are $100,000, the charge for doubtful accounts expense would be 2% of the current period's sales, or $2,000. Note that any existing balance in the allowance account resulting from past period charges to Doubtful Accounts Expense is ignored. The entry for this period would be simply:

```
Doubtful Accounts Expense.......................................    2,000
    Allowance for Doubtful Accounts ...................................        2,000
    ($100,000 × .02 = $2,000)
```

The sales percentage method for estimating doubtful accounts is widely used in practice because it is simple to apply. Companies often use this method to estimate doubtful accounts periodically during the year and then adjust the allowance account at year-end in relationship to the accounts receivable balance, as explained in the next section.

Estimating Uncollectibles Based on Accounts Receivable Balance. Instead of using a percentage of sales to estimate uncollectible accounts, companies may base their estimates on a **percentage of total accounts receivable outstanding**. This method emphasizes the relationship between the Accounts Receivable balance and the Allowance for Doubtful Accounts. For example, if total Accounts Receivable are $50,000 and it is estimated that 3% of those accounts will be uncollectible, then the allowance account should have a balance of $1,500 ($50,000 × .03). If the allowance account already has a $600 credit balance from prior periods, then the current period adjusting entry would be:

```
Doubtful Accounts Expense..........................................    900
    Allowance for Doubtful Accounts ......................................        900
```

After posting the preceding entry, the balance in the allowance account would be $1,500, or 3% of total accounts receivable. Note that this method adjusts the existing balance to the desired balance based on a percentage of total receivables outstanding. If, in the example, the allowance account had a $200 debit balance caused by writing off more bad debts than had been estimated previously, the adjusting entry would be for $1,700 in order to bring the allowance account to the desired credit balance of $1,500, or 3% of total receivables.

The most commonly used method for establishing an allowance based on outstanding receivables involves **aging receivables**. Individual accounts are analyzed to determine those not yet due and those past due. Past-due accounts are classified in terms of the length of the period past due. An analysis sheet used in aging accounts receivable is shown below:

ICO Products, Inc.
Analysis of Receivables—December 31, 1987

Customer	Amount	Not Yet Due	Not More Than 30 Days Past Due	31–60 Days Past Due	61–90 Days Past Due	91–180 Days Past Due	181–365 Days Past Due	More Than One Year Past Due
A. B. Andrews....	$ 450			$ 450				
B. T. Brooks	300				$ 100	$ 200		
B. Bryant..........	200		$ 200					
L. B. Devine	2,100	$ 2,100						
K. Martinez	200							$ 200
M. A. Young	1,400	1,000			100	300		
Total...............	$47,550	$40,000	$3,000	$1,200	$ 650	$ 500	$ 800	$1,400

Overdue balances can be evaluated individually to estimate the collectibility of each item as a basis for developing an overall estimate. An alternative procedure is to develop a series of estimated loss percentages and apply these to the different receivables classifications. The calculation of the allowance on the latter basis is illustrated on page 293.

Just as with the previous method based on a percentage of total receivables outstanding, Doubtful Accounts Expense is debited and Allowance for Doubtful Accounts is credited for an amount bringing the allowance account to the required balance. Assuming uncollectibles estimated at $2,870 as shown at the top of page 293 and a credit balance of $620 in the allowance account before adjustment, the following entry would be made:

Doubtful Accounts Expense..	2,250	
Allowance for Doubtful Accounts		2,250

ICO Products, Inc.
Estimated Amount of Uncollectible Accounts — December 31, 1987

Classification	Balances	Uncollectible Accounts Experience Percentage	Estimated Amount of Uncollectible Accounts
Not yet due	$40,000	2%	$ 800
Not more than 30 days past due	3,000	5%	150
31–60 days past due	1,200	10%	120
61–90 days past due	650	20%	130
91–180 days past due	500	30%	150
181–365 days past due	800	50%	400
More than one year past due	1,400	80%	1,120
	$47,550		$2,870

The aging method provides the most satisfactory approach to the valuation of receivables at their net realizable amounts. Furthermore, data developed through aging receivables may be quite useful to management for purposes of credit analysis and control. On the other hand, application of this method may involve considerable time and cost. This method still involves estimates, and the added refinement achieved by the aging process may not warrant the additional cost.

Corrections to Allowance for Doubtful Accounts. As previously indicated, the allowance for doubtful accounts balance is established and maintained by means of adjusting entries at the close of each accounting period. If the allowance provisions are too large, the allowance account balance will be unnecessarily inflated and earnings will be understated; if the allowance provisions are too small, the allowance account balance will be inadequate and earnings will be overstated.

Care must be taken to see that the allowance balance follows the credit experience of the particular business. The process of aging receivables at different intervals may be employed as a means of checking the allowance balance to be certain that it is being maintained satisfactorily. Such periodic reviews may indicate a need for a correction in the allowance as well as a change in the rate or in the method employed.

When the uncollectible accounts experience approximates the estimated losses, the allowance procedure may be considered satisfactory, and no adjustment is required. When it appears that there has been a failure to estimate uncollectible accounts accurately, resulting in an allowance balance that is clearly inadequate or excessive, an adjustment is in order. Such an adjustment would be considered a change in accounting estimate under APB Opinion No. 20, and the effect would be reported in the current and future periods as an ordinary item on the income statement, usually as an addition to or subtraction from Doubtful Accounts Expense.

The actual write-off of receivables as uncollectible by debits to the allowance account and credits to the receivables account may result temporarily in a debit balance in the allowance account. A debit balance arising in this manner does not mean necessarily that the allowance is inadequate; debits to the allowance account simply predate the end-of-period adjustment for uncollectible accounts. The adjustment, when recorded, should cover uncollectibles already determined as well as those yet to be identified.

Discounts. Many companies bill their customers at a gross sales price less an amount designated as a **trade discount.** The discount may vary by customer depending on the volume of business or size of order from the customer. In effect, the trade discount reduces the "list" sales price to the net price actually charged the customer. This net price is the amount at which the receivable and corresponding revenue should be recorded.

Another type of discount is a **cash discount** or **sales discount** offered to customers by some companies to encourage prompt payment of bills. Cash discounts may be taken by the customer only if payment is made within a specified period of time, generally thirty days or less. Receivables are generally recorded at their gross amounts, without regard to any cash discount offered. If payment is received within the discount period, Sales Discounts (a contra account to Sales) is debited for the difference between the recorded amount of the receivable and the total cash collected. This method, which is simple and widely used, is illustrated below with credit terms of "2/10, n/30" (2% discount if paid within 10 days, net amount due in 30 days):

<u>Cash Discounts — Gross Method</u>

Sales of $1,000; terms 2/10, n/30:

Accounts Receivable	1,000	
Sales		1,000

Payments of $300 received within discount period:

Cash	294	
Sales Discounts	6	
Accounts Receivable		300

Payments of $700 received after discount period:

Cash	700	
Accounts Receivable		700

Sales Returns and Allowances. In the normal course of business, some goods will be returned by customers and some allowances will have to be made for such factors as goods damaged during shipment, spoiled or otherwise defective goods, or shipment of an incorrect quantity or type of goods. When goods are returned or an allowance is necessary, net sales and accounts receivable are reduced. To illustrate, assume merchandise costing $1,000 is sold and later returned. The return would be recorded in the following manner:

```
Sales Returns and Allowances .......................................    1,000
     Accounts Receivable..............................................            1,000
```

While the charge could be made directly to Sales, the use of a separate contra account preserves information that may be useful to management.

Some industries, such as the publishing industry, experience a relatively high rate of sales returns. When expected future returns are likely to have a material impact on the financial statements, an end-of-period adjustment should be made to recognize estimated returns.[3]

To illustrate, assume that Western Publishers began operating in January of 1987, and estimated that 3% of its $2 million accounts receivable outstanding at December 31, 1987, would not be collected due to returns and allowances. For illustrative purposes the amount is considered to have a material effect on the company's income. Therefore, the following year-end adjusting entry is made:

```
Sales Returns and Allowances ......................................    60,000
     Allowance for Sales Returns and Allowances ........................            60,000

Computation:
     3% × $2,000,000 = $60,000
```

During the following year, Western would record various sales returns and allowances as they occur. The valuation account, Allowances for Sales Returns and Allowances, if not adjusted during the year, would still have a $60,000 credit balance at the end of 1988. If the year-end Accounts Receivable balance is $1.5 million and 3% is still deemed an appropriate rate, the allowance account should be adjusted to a credit balance of $45,000 ($1,500,000 × 3% = $45,000) with the following entry:

```
Allowance for Sales Returns and Allowances ..........................    15,000
     Sales Returns and Allowances ....................................            15,000
```

The allowance account is a contra asset valuation account to be deducted from accounts receivable on the balance sheet, thus reporting accounts receivable at their estimated net realizable value. The sales returns and allowances account is subtracted from sales on the income statement. This procedure is consistent with the fundamental matching principle. It is

---

[3]*Statement of Financial Accounting Standards No. 48,* "Revenue Recognition When Right of Return Exists" (Stamford: Financial Accounting Standards Board, 1981).

an attempt to recognize the proper amount of sales revenue for a particular period. The realized revenues can then be properly matched with appropriate expenses to produce a realistic income measurement for the period. Failure to anticipate sales returns and allowances or other charges affecting the realizable value of receivables will have little effect on periodic net income when sales volume and the rate of occurrence of such charges do not vary significantly from period to period. The anticipation of sales returns and allowances is not allowed for income tax purposes.

Accounts Receivable as a Source of Cash

Accounts receivable are a part of the normal operating cycle of a business. Cash is used to purchase inventory, which in turn is often sold on account. The receivables are then collected, providing cash to start the cycle over. Frequently the operating cycle takes several months to complete. Sometimes companies need immediate cash and cannot wait for completion of the normal cycle. At other times companies are not in financial stress but want to accelerate the receivable collection process, shift the risk of credit and the effort of collection to someone else, or merely use receivables from customers as a source of financing.

Receivables financing was once looked upon as a desperate measure. In recent years, however, receivables financing has become quite popular for financing leveraged buyouts and for business expansion. As one executive put it, "receivables financing is no longer viewed as last-resort financing but as a legitimate business tool."[4]

Accounts receivable may be converted to cash in one of three ways: (1) **assignment**, which is a borrowing arrangement with receivables pledged as security on a loan; (2) **factoring**, which is a sale of receivables without recourse for cash to a third party, usually a bank or other financial institution; and (3) the **transfer of receivables with recourse**, which is a hybrid of the other two forms of receivables financing.

Assignment of Accounts Receivable. Loans are frequently obtained from banks or other lending institutions by assigning or pledging accounts receivable as security. The loan is evidenced by a written promissory note that provides for either a general assignment of receivables or an assignment of specific receivables.

With a *general assignment*, all accounts receivable serve as collateral on the note. There are no special accounting problems involved. The books simply report the loan (a debit to Cash and a credit to Notes Payable) and

---

[4]See "Receivables Financing Goes Respectable," *INC*. (July 1983), p. 103.

subsequent settlement of the obligation (a debit to Notes Payable and a credit to Cash). However, disclosure should be made on the balance sheet, by parenthetical comment or note, of the amount and nature of receivables pledged to secure the obligation to the lender.

When there is an *assignment of specific receivables* to a lender, the borrower should transfer the balance of those accounts to a special general ledger control account and clearly identify and account for the individual assigned accounts in the subsidiary ledger. The procedures involved are illustrated in the following example. It is assumed that the assignor (the borrower) collects the receivables, which is often the case.

On July 1, 1987, Provo Mercantile Co. assigns specific receivables totalling $300,000 to Salem Bank as collateral on a $200,000, 12% note. Provo Mercantile does not notify its account debtors and will continue to collect the assigned receivables. Salem assesses a 1% finance charge on assigned receivables in addition to the interest on the note. Provo is to make monthly payments to Salem with cash collected on assigned receivables. The following entries would be made.

Illustrative Entries for Assignment of Specific Receivables

Provo Mercantile Co.			Salem Bank		

Issuance of note and assignment of specific receivables on July 1, 1987:

Cash....................	197,000		Notes Receivable........	200,000	
Finance Charge*........	3,000		Finance Revenue*.....		3,000
Accounts Receivable-			Cash.................		197,000
Assigned..............	300,000				
Notes Payable......		200,000			
Accounts Receivable.		300,000			

*(1% × $300,000)

Collections of assigned accounts during July, $180,000 less cash discounts of $1,000; sales returns in July, $2,000.

Cash....................	179,000			
Sales Discounts.........	1,000		(No Entry)	
Sales Returns...........	2,000			
Accounts Receivable-				
Assigned...........		182,000		

Paid Salem Bank amounts owed for July collections plus accrued interest on note to August 1.

Interest Expense*........	2,000		Cash....................	181,000	
Notes Payable..........	179,000		Interest Revenue......		2,000
Cash.................		181,000	Notes Receivable......		179,000

*($200,000 × .12 × 1/12)

Collections of remaining assigned accounts during August less $800 written off as uncollectible:

Cash...................	117,200		(No Entry)
Allowance for			
Doubtful Accounts	800		
Accounts Receivable-			
Assigned*.........		118,000	

*($300,000 − $182,000)

Paid Salem Bank remaining balance owed plus accrued interest on note to September 1:

Interest Expense*........	210		Cash...................	21,210	
Notes Payable**.........	21,000		Interest Revenue*		210
Cash................		21,210	Notes Receivable**		21,000

* ($21,000 × .12 × 1/12)
**($200,000 − $179,000)

If in the preceding example Salem Bank assumes responsibility for collecting the assigned receivables, the account debtors would have to be notified to make their payments to the bank. Salem would then use a liability account (e. g., Payable to Provo Mercantile) to account for cash collections during the period. Since the receivables are still owned by Provo Mercantile, the bank would not record them as assets. Upon full payment of the note plus interest, the bank would remit to Provo Mercantile any cash collections in excess of the note along with any uncollected accounts.

In disclosing the specifically assigned accounts receivable, Provo Mercantile should report them separately as a current asset if they are material. In addition, the equity in assigned accounts should be disclosed parenthetically or in a note. For example, on July 1, Provo Mercantile had $100,000 equity in its assigned receivables ($300,000−$200,000).

Factoring Accounts Receivable. Certain banks, dealers, and finance companies purchase accounts receivable outright on a nonrecourse basis. **A sale of accounts receivable without recourse**[5] is commonly referred to as accounts receivable **factoring**, and the buyer is referred to as a "factor." Customers are usually notified that their bills are payable to the factor, and this party assumes the burden of billing and collecting accounts. The flow of activities involved in factoring is presented on page 299.

---

[5]Recourse is defined by the FASB as "the right of a transferee of receivables to receive payment from the transferor of those receivables for (a) failure of the debtors to pay when due, (b) the effects of prepayments, or (c) adjustments resulting from defects in the eligibility of the transferred receivables." *Statement of Financial Accounting Standards No. 77*, "Reporting by Transferors for Transfers of Receivables with Recourse" (December, 1983), p. 7.

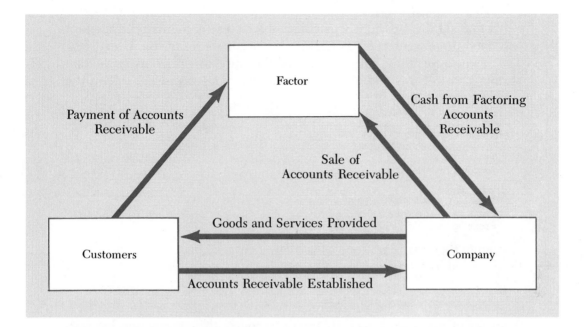

In many cases, factoring involves more than the purchase and collection of accounts receivable. Factoring frequently involves a continuing agreement whereby a financing institution assumes the credit function as well as the collection function. Under such an arrangement, the factor grants or denies credit, handles the accounts receivable records, bills customers, and makes collections. The business unit is relieved of all these activities, and the sale of goods provides immediate cash for business use. Because the factor absorbs the losses from bad accounts and frequently assumes credit and collection responsibilities, the charges associated with factoring generally exceed the interest charges on a loan with an assignment of receivables. Typically the factor will charge a fee of 10% to 30% of the net amount of receivables purchased, except for credit card factoring where the rate is 3% to 5%. The factor may withhold a portion of the purchase price for possible future charges for customer returns and allowances or other special adjustments. Final settlement is made after receivables have been collected.

When receivables are sold outright, without recourse, cash is debited, receivables and related allowance balances are closed, and an expense account is debited for factoring charges. When part of the purchase price is withheld by the factor, a receivable from the factor is established pending final settlement. Upon receipt of the total purchase price from the bank or finance company, the factor receivable account is eliminated. To illustrate, assume that $10,000 of receivables are factored, i. e., sold without recourse, to a finance company for $8,500. An allowance for doubtful accounts equal to $300 was previously established for these accounts. This amount will need to be written off along with the accounts receivable being sold. The finance company withheld 5% of the purchase price as protection against sales returns and allowances. The entry to record the sale of the accounts would be:

```
Cash.............................................................  8,075
Receivable from Factor..........................................    425
Allowance for Doubtful Accounts .................................    300
Loss from Factoring.............................................  1,200
    Accounts Receivable........................................            10,000
```

Computations:
  Cash = $8,500 − $425 = $8,075;
  Factor receivable = $8,500 × 5% = $425;
  Factoring loss = ($10,000 − $300) − $8,500 = $1,200

Assuming there were no returns or allowances, the final settlement would be recorded as follows:

```
Cash.............................................................    425
    Receivable from Factor.......................................            425
```

Transfer of Accounts Receivable with Recourse. The third way that cash can be obtained from accounts receivable financing is by **transferring accounts receivable with recourse**. This is different from factoring, which generally is on a nonrecourse basis. Transferring with recourse means that a transferee (bank or finance company) advances cash in return for accounts receivable, but retains the right to collect from the transferor if debtors (transferor's customers) fail to make payments when due. An important accounting question is whether this type of transaction is a **borrowing transaction** (like an assignment with the receivables as collateral) or a **sale transaction** (like a factoring arrangement). If viewed as a borrowing transaction, a liability should be reported and the difference between the proceeds received and the net receivables transferred is a financing cost (interest). If viewed as a sale, the difference between the amount received from the finance company (the transfer price) and the net amount of the receivables transferred (the gross amount of the receivables adjusted for allowance for doubtful accounts and any finance and service charges) is to be recognized as a gain or loss on the sale, as illustrated previously in the factoring example.

The FASB in Statement No. 77 has concluded that a transfer of receivables with recourse should be accounted for and reported as a sale if all the following conditions are met.

1. The transferor surrenders control of the future economic benefit embodied in the receivables.
2. The transferor's obligation under the recourse provisions can be reasonably estimated.

3. The transferee cannot require the transferor to repurchase the receivables except pursuant to the recourse provisions.[6]

If these conditions are not met, the transfer is reported as a secured loan, i.e., in the same manner as an assignment of receivables discussed previously.

In summary, accounts receivable provide an important source of cash for many companies. The transfer of receivables to third parties in return for cash generally takes the form of an assignment (borrowing with the receivables pledged as collateral) or factoring (a sale without recourse). The financing arrangements are often complex and may involve a transfer of receivables on a recourse basis. Each transaction must be analyzed carefully to see if in form and substance it is a borrowing transaction or a sale transaction, and treated accordingly.

NOTES RECEIVABLE

A **promissory note** is an unconditional written promise to pay a certain sum of money at a specified time. The note is signed by the **maker** and is payable to the order of a specified payee or to bearer. Notes usually involve interest, stated at an annual rate and charged on the face amount of the note. Notes are generally **negotiable**, i.e., legally transferable by endorsement and delivery.

For reporting purposes, **trade notes receivable** should include only negotiable short-term instruments acquired from trade debtors and not yet due. Trade notes generally arise from sales involving relatively high dollar amounts where the buyer wants to extend payment beyond the usual trade credit period of 30 to 90 days. Also, sellers sometimes request notes from customers whose accounts receivable are past due. Most companies, however, have relatively few trade notes receivable.

Nontrade notes receivable should be separately designated on the balance sheet under an appropriate title. For example, notes arising from loans to customers, officers, employees, and affiliated companies should be reported separately from trade notes.

Valuation of Notes Receivable

Notes receivable are initially recorded at their **present value**, which may be defined as the sum of future receipts discounted to the present date

---

[6]*Statement of Financial Accounting Standards No. 77,* "Reporting by Transferors of Transfers of Receivables with Recourse" (December, 1983), par. 5.

at an appropriate rate of interest.[7] In a lending transaction, the present value is the amount of cash received by the borrower. When a note is exchanged for property, goods, or services, the present value equals the current cash selling price of the items exchanged. The difference between the present value and the amount to be collected at the due date or maturity date is a charge for interest.

All notes arising in arm's-length transactions between unrelated parties involve an element of interest. However, a distinction as to form is made between interest-bearing and non-interest-bearing notes. **Interest-bearing notes** are written as a promise to pay a **face amount** plus interest at a specified rate. In the absence of special valuation problems discussed in the next section, the face amount of an interest-bearing note is the present value upon issuance of the note.

Non-interest-bearing notes do not specify an interest rate, but the face amount includes the interest charge. Thus, the present value is the difference between the face amount and the interest included in that amount, sometimes called the *implicit* or *effective* interest.

In recording receipt of a note, Notes Receivable is debited for the face amount of the note. When the face amount differs from the present value, as is the case with non-interest-bearing notes, the difference is recorded as a premium or discount and amortized over the life of the note. In the example to follow, a note receivable is established with credits to Sales and a Discount on Notes Receivable account. The amount of discount is the implicit interest on the note and will be recognized as interest revenue as the note matures.

To illustrate, assume that High Value Corporation sells goods on January 1, 1987, with a price of $1,000. The buyer gives High Value a promissory note due December 31, 1988. The maturity value of the note includes interest at 10 percent. Thus, High Value will receive $1,210 ($1,000 × 1.21)[8] when the note is paid. The following entries show the accounting procedures for an interest-bearing note and one written in a non-interest-bearing form.

Interest-Bearing Note Face Amount = Present Value = $1,000 Stated Interest Rate = 10%		Non-Interest-Bearing Note Face Amount = Maturity = $1,210 No Stated Interest Rate	
1987			
Jan. 1 Notes Receivable.... 1,000		Notes Receivable............. 1,210	
Sales............	1,000	Sales.....................	1,000
		Discount on Notes Receivable	210

To record note received in exchange for goods selling for $1,000.

---

[7]See Chapter 6 for a discussion of present value concepts and applications.

[8]The amount of $1 due in two years at an annual rate of 10% is $1.21. See Table I, Chapter 6.

| Dec. 31 | Interest Receivable .. | 100 | | Discount on Notes Receivable . | 100 | |
| | Interest Revenue .. | | 100 | Interest Revenue .... | | 100 |

To recognize interest earned for one year; $1,000 × .10.

1988

Dec. 31	Cash..............	1,210		Cash.......................	1,210	
	Notes Receivable..		1,000	Discount on Notes Receivable	110	
	Interest Receivable		100	Notes Receivable..........		1,210
	Interest Revenue ..		110	Interest Revenue		110

To record settlement of note at maturity and recognize interest earned
for one year: ($1,000 + $100) × .10.

At December 31, 1987, the unamortized discount of $110 on the non-interest-bearing note would be deducted from notes receivable on the balance sheet. If the non-interest-bearing note were recorded at face value with no recognition of the interest included therein, the sales price and profit to the seller would be overstated. In subsequent periods interest revenue would be understated. Failure to record the discount would also result in an overstatement of assets.

Although the proper valuation of receivables calls for the amortization procedure just described, exceptions may be appropriate in some situations due to special limitations or practical considerations. The Accounting Principles Board in Opinion No. 21 provided guidelines for the recognition of interest on receivables and payables and the accounting subsequently to be employed. However, the Board indicated that this process is not to be regarded as applicable under all circumstances. Among the exceptions are the following:

> . . . receivables and payables arising from transactions with customers or suppliers in the normal course of business which are due in customary trade terms not exceeding approximately one year.[9]

Accordingly, as mentioned earlier, short-term notes and accounts receivable arising from trade sales may be properly recorded at the amounts collectible in the customary sales terms.

Notes, like accounts receivable, are not always collectible. If notes receivable comprise a significant portion of regular trade receivables, a provision should be made for uncollectible amounts and an allowance account established using procedures similar to those for accounts receivable already discussed.

Special Valuation Problems. APB Opinion No. 21 was issued to clarify and refine existing accounting practice with respect to receivables and payables. The opinion is especially applicable to nontrade, long-term notes, such as secured and unsecured notes, debentures (bonds), equipment

---

[9]*Opinions of the Accounting Principles Board, No. 21,* "Interest on Receivables and Payables" (New York: American Institute of Certified Public Accountants, 1971), par. 3(a).

obligations, and mortgage notes. Examples are provided below for notes exchanged for cash and for property, goods, or services.

Notes Exchanged for Cash. When a note is exchanged for cash, and there are no other rights or privileges involved, the present value of the note is presumed to be the amount of the cash proceeds. The note should be recorded at its face amount and any difference between the face amount and the cash proceeds should be recorded as a premium or discount on the note. The premium or discount should be amortized over the life of the note as illustrated previously for High Value Corporation. The total interest is measured by the difference in actual cash received by the borrower and the total amount to be received in the future by the lender. Any unamortized premium or discount on notes is reported on the balance sheet as a direct addition to or deduction from the face amount of the receivables, thus showing their net present value.

Notes Exchanged for Property, Goods, or Services. When a note is exchanged for property, goods, or services in an arm's-length transaction, the present value of the note is usually evidenced by the terms of the note or supporting documents. There is a general presumption that the interest specified by the parties to a transaction represents fair and adequate compensation for the use of borrowed funds.[10] Valuation problems arise, however, when one of the following conditions exists.[11]

1. No interest rate is stated.
2. The stated rate does not seem reasonable, given the nature of the transaction and surrounding circumstances.
3. The stated face amount of the note is significantly different from the current cash equivalent sales price of similar property, goods, or services or from the current market value of similar notes at the date of the transaction.

Under any of the preceding conditions, APB No. 21 requires accounting recognition of the economic substance of the transaction rather than the form of the note. The note should be recorded at (1) the fair market value of the property, goods, or services exchanged or (2) the current market value of the note, whichever is more clearly determinable. The difference between the face amount of the note and the present value is recognized as a discount or premium and amortized over the life of the note.

To illustrate, assume that on July 1 Timberline Corporation sells a tract of land purchased three years ago at a cost of $250,000. The buyer gives Timberline a 1-year note with a face amount of $310,000 bearing interest at a stated rate of 8%. An appraisal of the land prior to the sale indicated

---

[10]*Opinions of the Accounting Principles Board, No. 21,* par. 12.
[11]*Ibid.*

a market value of $300,000, which in this example is considered to be the appropriate basis for recording the sale as follows:

```
1987
July 1   Notes Receivable ...................................   310,000
             Discount on Notes Receivable .......................            10,000
             Land.........................................            250,000
             Gain on Sale of Land .............................             50,000
```

When the note is paid at maturity, Timberline will receive the face value ($310,000) plus stated interest of $24,800. ($310,000 × .08) or a total of $334,800. The interest to be recognized, however, is $34,800 — the difference between the maturity value of the note and the market value of the land at the date of the exchange. Thus, the effective rate of interest on the note is 11.6% ($34,800 ÷ $300,000).

Assuming straight-line amortization of the discount and that Timberline's year-end is December 31, the following entries would be made to recognize interest revenue and to record payment of the note at maturity.

```
1987
Dec. 31   Interest Receivable ...................................   12,400*
              Discount on Notes Receivable .........................    5,000
              Interest Revenue ...................................             17,400
              *($310,000 × .08 × 6/12 = $12,400)

1988
June 30   Cash.........................................   334,800
              Discount on Notes Receivable .........................    5,000
              Notes Receivable....................................            310,000
              Interest Receivable .................................             12,400
              Interest Revenue ...................................             17,400
```

The unamortized discount balance of $5,000 would be subtracted from Notes Receivable on the December 31, 1987, balance sheet.

Imputing an Interest Rate. If there is no current market price for either the property, goods, or services or the note, then the present value of the note must be determined by selecting an appropriate interest rate and using that rate to discount future receipts to the present. The **imputed interest rate** is determined at the date of the exchange and is not altered thereafter.

The selection of an appropriate rate is influenced by many factors, including the credit standing of the issuer of the note and prevailing interest rates for debt instruments of similar quality and length of time to maturity. APB Opinion No. 21 states:

In any event, the rate used for valuation purposes will normally be at least equal to the rate at which the debtor can obtain financing of a similar nature from other sources at the date of the transaction. The objective is to approximate the rate which would have resulted if an independent borrower and an independent lender had negotiated a similar transaction under comparable terms and conditions with the option to pay the cash price upon purchase or to give a note for the amount of the purchase which bears the prevailing rate of interest to maturity.[12]

To illustrate the process of imputing interest rates, assume that Horrocks & Associates surveyed 800,000 acres of mountain property for the Mountain Meadow Ranch. On December 31, 1987, Horrocks accepted a $45,000 note as payment for services. The note is non-interest-bearing and comes due in three yearly installments of $15,000 each beginning December 31, 1988. Assume there is no market for the note and no basis for estimating objectively the fair market value of the services rendered. After considering the current prime interest rate, the credit standing of the ranch, the collateral available, the terms for repayment, and the prevailing rates of interest for the issuer's other debt, a 10% imputed interest rate is considered appropriate. The note should be recorded at its present value and a discount recognized. The computation is based on Present Value Table IV, Chapter 6, as follows:

Face amount of note..	$45,000
Less present value of note:	
$PV_n = R(PVAF)_{\overline{3}\|10\%}$	
$PV_n = \$15,000(2.4869)$...	37,303*
Discount on note	$ 7,697

*Rounded to nearest dollar.

The entry to record the receipt of the note would be:

1987			
Dec. 31	Notes Receivable......................................	45,000	
	Discount on Notes Receivable		7,697
	Service Revenue		37,303
	To record a non-interest-bearing note receivable at its present value based on an imputed interest rate of 10% per year.		

A schedule showing the amortization of the discount on the note is presented below.

	(1) Face Amount Before Current Installment	(2) Unamortized Discount	(3) Net Amount (1) − (2)	(4) Discount Amortization 10% × (3)	(5) Payment Received
December 31, 1988....	$45,000	$7,697	$37,303	$3,730	$15,000
December 31, 1989....	30,000	3,967	26,033	2,603	15,000
December 31, 1990....	15,000	1,364	13,636	1,364	15,000
				$7,697	$45,000

---

[12]*Ibid.*, par. 13.

At the end of each year, an entry similar to the following would be made.

```
1988
Dec. 31  Cash...............................................  15,000
         Discount on Notes Receivable .........................  3,730
              Interest Revenue ...................................        3,730
              Notes Receivable....................................       15,000
                   To record the first year's installment on notes receivable
                   and recognize interest earned during the period.
```

By using these procedures, at the end of the 3 years the discount will be completely amortized to interest revenue, the face amount of the note receivable will have been collected, and the appropriate amount of service revenue will have been recognized in the year it was earned. At the end of each year, the balance sheet will reflect the net present value of the receivable by subtracting the unamortized discount balance from the face amount of the note.

It is necessary to impute an interest rate only when the present value of the receivable cannot be determined through evaluation of existing market values of the elements of the transaction. The valuation and income measurement objectives remain the same regardless of the specific circumstances—to report Notes Receivables at their net present values and to record appropriate amounts of interest revenue during the collection period of the receivables.

Notes Receivable As a Source of Cash

As discussed earlier in the chapter, accounts receivable can be a source of immediate cash. A company can also obtain cash by "discounting" notes receivable. The discounting of notes receivable, sometimes called bank discounting, is not to be confused with the discounting of future cash receipts to arrive at present value or with the discount deducted from Notes Receivable on the balance sheet as discussed previously. **Bank discounting** involves the transfer of negotiable notes to a bank or other financial institution willing to exchange such instruments for cash.

When discounting an interest-bearing note, which is the usual situation, the following steps are taken to determine the amount to be received from the bank (the proceeds).[13]

1. Determine the maturity value of the note.
   Maturity value = Face amount + Interest
   Interest = Face amount × Interest rate × Interest period
   Interest period = Date of note to date of maturity

---

[13] The same procedures apply to the discounting of a non-interest-bearing note, except that the maturity value does not have to be computed (Step 1), since the face amount equals the maturity value.

2. Determine the amount of discount.
   Discount = Maturity value × Discount rate × Discount period
   Discount period = Date of discount to Date of maturity
3. Determine the proceeds.
   Proceeds = Maturity value − Discount

Once the proceeds are determined, the transaction can be recorded, recognizing the applicable liability and net interest revenue or expense (if a borrowing transaction) or the gain or loss (if a sale transaction).

If a note is transferred **without recourse**, i.e., the bank assumes the risk of uncollectibility, the transaction should be recorded as a sale, much like the factoring of accounts receivable discussed earlier. If the note is transferred **with recourse**, which is the usual case, the discounting transaction may be recorded as a sale or a borrowing transaction, depending on the terms and conditions. The criteria for classifying a transfer of accounts receivable with recourse, set forth in FASB Statement No. 77 and presented on pages 300 and 301, also apply to transfers of notes receivable with recourse.

To illustrate the recording of a transfer (discounting) of notes receivable with recourse, assume that Meeker Corporation received a 90-day, $5,000, 10% note from a customer on September 1 to settle a past-due account receivable. The note is discounted at a bank after 10 days at a discount rate of 15%. The transaction would be treated as a sale only if the FASB Statement No. 77 criteria are met. Otherwise, the transfer is recorded as a borrowing transaction. The journal entries for both a sale and borrowing transaction would be as follows:

Discounting Notes Receivable With Recourse

Transaction Recorded as Sale	Transaction Recorded as Borrowing

Received a 90-day, $5,000, 10% note from a customer on September 1:

Notes Receivable.........	5,000		Notes Receivable.........	5,000	
Accounts Receivable.....		5,000	Accounts Receivable.....		5,000

Discounted customer's note at bank on September 11 at a discount rate of 15%:

Cash.....................	4,955		Cash.....................	4,955	
Loss on Sale of Note........	45		Interest Expense	45	
Notes Receivable........		5,000	Obligation on Discounted		
			Notes Receivable......		5,000

Computations (rounded to nearest dollar):
  Maturity value = $5,000 + Interest ($5,000 × .10 × 90/365 = $123) = $5,123
  Discount = $5,123 × .15 × 80/365 = $168
  Proceeds = $5,123 − $168 = $4,955
  Loss/Interest Expense = $168 − $123 = $45

If maturity value of note paid to bank by customer on due date, November 29:

	Obligation on Discounted	
(No entry)	Notes Receivable........ 5,000	
	Notes Receivable......	5,000

If customer defaults and bank collects from Meeker Corporation on November 29 the maturity value ($5,123) plus a $25 protest fee:

Notes Receivable—		Notes Receivable—	
Past Due............... 5,148		Past Due............... 5,148	
Cash................	5,148	Cash................	5,148
		Obligation on Discounted	
		Notes Receivable........ 5,000	
		Notes Receivable......	5,000

Several important points can be observed in the example. First, the loss or net interest expense recognized at the date of discounting ($45) is the difference between the amount charged by the bank to discount the note (in effect, interest expense of $168) and the amount of interest revenue the company would have earned if it had held the note to maturity ($123). Alternatively, the loss or net interest expense is the difference between the face amount of the note ($5,000) and the proceeds received from the bank ($4,955). Depending on how long the note is held prior to discounting and on the difference between the interest rate on the note and the discount rate charged by the bank, it is possible for the proceeds to be greater than the face amount of the note, which would result in a gain or net interest revenue being recorded. For example, if the Meeker Corporation had held the note for 60 days prior to discounting, the entries on September 11 would be:

Transaction Recorded as Sale		Transaction Recorded as Borrowing	
Cash.................... 5,060		Cash.................... 5,060	
Gain on Sale of Note.....	60	Interest Revenue	60
Notes Receivable........	5,000	Obligation on Discounted	
		Notes Receivable......	5,000

Computations (rounded to nearest dollar):
Maturity value (same) = $5,123
Discount = $5,123 × .15 × 30/365 = $63
Proceeds = $5,123 − $63 = $5,060
Gain/Interest Revenue = $123 − $63 = $60

As indicated in the Meeker example, when a note is discounted with recourse, the bank will require payment from the company that discounted the note if the maker of the note defaults on payment at maturity (often referred to as *dishonoring* the note). In addition, the bank generally will charge a protest fee, which in the example is $25. Subsequently, the company will attempt to collect from the customer and, if unsuccessful, will eventually write off the note as uncollectible.

If the note had been discounted without recourse, the transaction would have been recorded in exactly the same manner as shown for a sale in the example. However, no entries would be required after the discounting transaction is recorded on September 30, since the company has no liability with regard to the note after the transfer.

PRESENTATION OF RECEIVABLES ON THE BALANCE SHEET

The receivables qualifying as current items may be grouped for presentation on the balance sheet in the following classes: (1) notes receivable — trade debtors, (2) accounts receivable — trade debtors, and (3) other receivables. Alternatively, trade notes and accounts receivable can be reported as a single amount. The detail reported for other receivables depends on the relative significance of the various items included. Valuation accounts are deducted from the individual receivable balances or combined balances to which they relate.

When notes receivable have been discounted with recourse, a liability (e.g., Obligation on Discounted Notes Receivable) is reported in the balance sheet if the discounting is treated as borrowing. If treated as a sale, no liability is recognized, but a contingent liability should be disclosed in the notes to the financial statements or parenthetically on the balance sheet with notes receivable. If notes are discounted without recourse, there is no contingent liability. If notes or accounts receivable have been pledged to secure a loan, the amount should be disclosed.

Accounts and notes receivable as presented by LSB Industries in its 1984 annual report are shown below. An alternative disclosure method would be to show net trade receivables on the balance sheet and present the detailed information in a note to the financial statements. This latter approach is illustrated on page 311 for Pioneer Hi-Bred International, Inc.

LSB INDUSTRIES, INC.

	1984	1983
Current Assets:		
Cash	$ 2,492,861	$ 1,978,997
Accounts and notes receivable:		
Trade, less allowance for doubtful accounts of $2,979,706 in 1984 and $3,325,050 in 1983	19,704,213	9,692,224
Other, less allowance for doubtful accounts of $20,000 in 1984 and $545,203 in 1983	917,028	397,764
Inventories	43,319,967	34,966,186
Prepaid expenses and supplies	2,512,974	1,089,298
Total current assets	68,947,043	48,124,469

PIONEER HI-BRED INTERNATIONAL, INC.

	1984	1983
Current Assets:		
Cash..	$ 5,754,402	$ 1,724,827
Marketable securities.........................	18,684,951	6,489,833
Receivables:		
Trade	44,701,282	40,525,360
Other......................................	2,000,090	4,390,434
Inventories..................................	213,685,893	271,543,088
Prepaid expenses	8,499,573	9,146,520
Deferred income tax charges, net..............	16,280,133	—
Total current assets......................	$309,606,324	$333,820,052

NOTES TO FINANCIAL STATEMENTS

Note 1 (In Part): Significant Accounting Policies

Receivables:

Receivables are stated net of an allowance for doubtful accounts of $2,138,081 and $1,651,217 at August 31, 1984 and 1983, respectively.

QUESTIONS

1. Explain how each of the following factors affects the classification of a receivable (a) the form of a receivable, (b) the source of a receivable, and (c) the expected length of time to maturity or collection.
2. (a) Describe the methods for establishing and maintaining an allowance for doubtful accounts. (b) How would the percentages used in estimating uncollectible accounts be determined under each of the methods?
3. Identify and explain two items that are deducted in reducing accounts receivable to a net realizable value.
4. An analysis of the accounts receivable balance of $8,702 on the records of Jorgenson, Inc. on December 31 reveals the following:

Accounts from sales of last three months (appear to be fully
   collectible) $7,460
Accounts from sales prior to October 1 (of doubtful value) 1,312
Accounts known to be worthless........................... 320
Dishonored notes charged back to customers' accounts 800
Credit balances in customers' accounts 1,190

(a) What adjustments are required?
(b) How should the various balances be shown on the balance sheet?

5. In what section of the income statement would you report (a) doubtful accounts expense, (b) sales discounts?
6. How are attitudes regarding the financing of accounts receivable changing? Why do you think this is so?
7. Explain the difference between the general assignment of accounts receivable and specific assignment of accounts receivable with regard to (a) collateral and (b) disclosure on financial statements.
8. (a) Distinguish between the practices of (1) assignment of accounts receivable, (2) transfer of accounts receivable with recourse, and (3) factoring accounts receivable. (b) Describe the accounting procedures to be followed in each case.
9. According to FASB Statement No. 77, what three conditions must be met to record the transfer of receivables with recourse as a sale?
10. The Bockweg Co. enters into a continuing agreement with Goessling Financial Services, whereby the latter company buys without recourse all of the trade receivables as they arise and assumes all credit and collection functions. (a) Describe the advantages that may accrue to Bockweg Co. as a result of the factoring agreement. (b) Are there any disadvantages? Explain.
11. Comment on the statement, "There is no such thing as a non-interest-bearing note."
12. (a) When should a note receivable be recorded at an amount different from its face amount? (b) Describe the procedures employed in accounting for the difference between a note's face amount and its recorded value.
13. What is meant by imputing a rate of interest? How is such a rate determined?
14. The Lambert Optical Co. discounts at 20% the following three notes at the Security First Bank on July 1 of the current year. Compute the proceeds on each note using 360 days to a year.
    (a) A 90-day, 13% note receivable for $24,000 dated June 1.
    (b) A 6-month, 11% note receivable for $16,000 dated May 13.
    (c) Its own 4-month note payable dated July 1 with face value of $8,000 and no stated interest rate.
15. Distinguish between accounting procedures for (a) a note receivable discounted with recourse that is subsequently dishonored, and (b) a note receivable discounted without recourse that is subsequently dishonored.
16. Identify alternative methods for presenting information on the balance sheet relating to (a) notes receivable discounted, and (b) assigned accounts receivable.

DISCUSSION CASES

CASE 8–1   (Accounting for uncollectibles)

During the audit of accounts receivable of Williams Company, the new CEO, Bill Davis, asked why the company had debited the current year's expense for doubtful accounts on the assumption that some accounts will become uncollectible next year. Davis also said he believed the financial statements should be based on verifiable, objective evidence. In his opinion it would be more objective to wait until specific accounts become uncollectible before the expense is recorded. What accounting issues are involved? Which method of accounting for uncollectible accounts would you recommend and why?

CASE 8–2   (Accounts receivable as a source of cash)

Assume you are the treasurer for Fullmer Products Inc., and one of your responsibilities is to ensure that the company always takes available cash discounts on purchases. The corporation needs $150,000 within one week in order to take advantage of current cash discounts. The lending officer at the bank insists on adequate collateral for a $150,000 loan. For various reasons, your plant assets are not available as collateral, but your accounts receivable balance is $205,000. What alternatives would you consider for obtaining the necessary cash?

CASE 8–3   (Selling receivables instead of merchandise)

The following excerpts are from an article printed in the *Wall Street Journal*.

Sears, Roebuck & Co. said it arranged to sell $550 million of customer accounts receivable to a group of 16 institutional investors headed by Continental Illinois National Bank & Trust Co.

Under the plan, the investors will assume ownership of the receivables, representing about 8% of Sears' total receivables outstanding as well as additions resulting from new purchases. The receivables will be sold to the institutional investors without recourse. And they will receive subsequent finance charge income on the accounts.

Edward R. Telling, Sears chairman, said the agreement calls for the sale by Sears of additional receivables each month with the total to be sold expected to reach $625 million by February 1, 1979. Subject to further negotiations, the total could reach $1 billion by 1983, he added.

The initial $550 million will be sold at 99.015% of face value with Sears receiving an administrative fee from the institutional buyers for handling the accounts. Initially, the fee will equal 5.62% of the unpaid balance.

What aspects appear to be unique in this actual example of the sale of receivables?

EXERCISES

EXERCISE 8–1   (Multiple choice)

For each of the following, select the **one** best answer.
(1) At the beginning of 1985, Dunkin Company received a 3-year non-interest-bearing $1,000 trade note. The market rate for equivalent notes was 12% at

that time. Dunkin reported this note as a $1,000 trade note receivable on its 1985 year-end statement of financial position and $1,000 as sales revenue for 1985. What effect did this accounting for the note have on Dunkin's net earnings for 1985, 1986, and 1987, and its retained earnings at the end of 1987, respectively?

    (a) Overstate, understate, understate, zero.
    (b) Overstate, understate, understate, understate.
    (c) Overstate, overstate, understate, zero.
    (d) No effect on any of these.

(2) At the close of its first year of operations December 31, 1987, the Harris Company had accounts receivable of $250,000, which were net of the related allowance for doubtful accounts. During 1987, the company had charges to bad debt expense of $40,000 and wrote off, as uncollectible, accounts receivable of $10,000. What should the company report on its balance sheet at December 31, 1987, as accounts receivable before the allowance for doubtful accounts?

    (a) $250,000.
    (b) $260,000.
    (c) $280,000.
    (d) $300,000.

(3) For the month of December 1987, the records of Forest Corporation show the following information:

Cash received on accounts receivable	$35,000
Cash sales	30,000
Accounts receivable, December 1, 1987	80,000
Accounts receivable, December 31, 1987	74,000
Accounts receivable written off as uncollectible	1,000

The corporation uses the direct write-off method in accounting for uncollectible accounts receivable. What are the gross sales for the month of December 1987?

    (a) $59,000.
    (b) $60,000.
    (c) $65,000.
    (d) $72,000.

(4) The Benson Company received a 7-year non-interest-bearing note on February 22, 1986, in exchange for property it sold to the Crispin Company. There was no established exchange price for this property and the note has no ready market. The prevailing rate of interest for a note of this type was 10% on February 22, 1986, 10.2% on December 31, 1986, 10.3% on February 22, 1987, and 10.4% on December 31, 1987. What interest rate should be used to calculate the interest revenue from this transaction for the years ended December 31, 1987 and 1986, respectively?

    (a) 0% and 0%.
    (b) 10% and 10%.
    (c) 10% and 10.3%.
    (d) 10.2% and 10.4%.

(5) The following accounts were abstracted from the trial balance of Harrison Company at December 31, 1987:

	Debit	Credit
Gross sales............		$500,000
Sales Discounts........	$10,000	

On January 1, 1987, Allowance for Doubtful Accounts had a credit balance of $12,000. During 1987, $20,000 of accounts receivable deemed uncollectible were written off.

Historical experience indicates that 3% of gross sales proved uncollectible. What should be the balance in Allowance for Doubtful Accounts after the current provision is made?

(a) $6,700.
(b) $7,000.
(c) $14,700.
(d) $23,000.   (AICPA adapted)

EXERCISE 8–2   (Computing the accounts receivable balance)

The information below, pertaining to the Stalker Company's first year of operations, is to be used in testing the accuracy of Accounts Receivable, which has a balance of $32,000 at December 31, 1987.

(a) Collections from customers, $58,000
(b) Merchandise purchased, $91,000
(c) Ending merchandise inventory, $26,000
(d) Goods sell at 50% above cost
(e) All sales are on account

Compute the balance that Accounts Receivable should show and determine the amount of any shortage or overage.

EXERCISE 8–3   (Recording credit card sales)

Barbara Crane owns a gift shop at the airport. She accepts only cash or Visa and Mastercard credit cards. During the last month the gift shop had a total of $38,000 in sales. Of this amount 75% were credit card sales. The bank charges a 3% fee on net credit card sales. Make the monthly summary entry to reflect the above transactions.

EXERCISE 8–4   (Estimating doubtful accounts)

Accounts Receivable of the Fakler Manufacturing Co. on December 31, 1987, had a balance of $200,000. The Allowance for Doubtful Accounts had a $7,500 debit balance. Sales in 1987 were $1,725,000 less sales discounts of $14,000.
Give the adjusting entry for estimated doubtful accounts expense under each of the following assumptions:

(1) One half of 1% of 1987 net sales will probably never be collected.
(2) Two percent of outstanding accounts receivable are doubtful.
(3) An aging schedule shows that $9,500 of the outstanding accounts receivable are doubtful.

EXERCISE 8–5   (Journal entries for doubtful accounts)

Harry's Gas Station had gross sales of $555,000 during 1987, 30% of which were on credit. Accounts receivable outstanding at December 31, 1987, totaled

$28,000, and the allowance for doubtful accounts had a $400 credit balance. Cash discounts taken by credit customers who paid within the discount period amounted to $10,000. $6,000 of merchandise was returned by dissatisfied customers, 30% of which were by credit customers.

Give the adjusting entry for doubtful accounts expense, assuming:
(1) 1% of net credit sales will be uncollectible.
(2) 2½% of current accounts receivable are doubtful.

EXERCISE 8–6
(Estimating doubtful accounts—percentage of sales method)

Prior to 1987, Jenkins, Inc. followed the percentage-of-sales method of estimating doubtful accounts. The following data are gathered by the accounting department:

	1984	1985	1986	1987
Total sales...	$1,050,000	$2,100,000	$3,600,000	$6,300,000
Credit sales..	600,000	960,000	1,950,000	3,600,000
Accounts receivable (end-of-year balance)................	186,000	234,000	360,000	750,000
Allowance for doubtful accounts (end-of-year credit balance).	3,000	18,000	12,000	66,000
Accounts written off....................................	27,000	6,000	42,000	9,000

(1) What amount was debited to expense for 1985, 1986, and 1987?
(2) Compute the balance in the valuation account at the beginning of 1984 assuming there has been no change in the percentage of sales used over the four-year period.
(3) What explanation can be given for the fluctuating amount of write-off?
(4) Why do the actual write-offs fail to give the correct charge to expense?

EXERCISE 8–7   (Aging accounts receivable)

Ivan Company's accounts receivable subsidiary ledger reveals the following information:

Customer	Account Balance December 31, 1987	Invoice Amounts and Dates	
Allison, Inc.	$ 8,795	$3,500	12/6/87
		5,295	11/29/87
Banks Bros.	5,230	3,000	9/27/87
		2,230	8/20/87
Barker & Co.	7,650	5,000	12/8/87
		2,650	10/25/87
Marrin Co.	11,285	5,785	11/17/87
		5,500	10/9/87
Ring, Inc.	7,900	4,800	12/12/87
		3,100	12/2/87
West Corp.	4,350	4,350	9/12/87

Ivan Company's receivable collection experience indicates that, on the average, losses have occurred as follows:

Age of Accounts	Uncollectible Percentage
0–30 days	.7%
31–60 days	1.4%
61–90 days	3.5%
91–120 days	10.2%
121 days and over	60.0%

The Allowance for Doubtful Accounts credit balance on December 31, 1987, was $2,245 before adjustment.

(1) Prepare an accounts receivable aging schedule.
(2) Using the aging schedule from part (1), compute the Allowance for Doubtful Accounts balance as of December 31, 1987.
(3) Prepare the end-of-year adjusting entry.
(4) (a) Where accounts receivable are few in number, such as in this exercise, what are some possible weaknesses in estimating doubtful accounts by the aging method? (b) Would the other methods of estimating doubtful accounts be subject to these same weaknesses? Explain.

EXERCISE 8–8   (Analysis of allowance for doubtful accounts)

The Transtech Publishing Company follows the procedure of debiting Doubtful Accounts Expense for 2% of all new sales. Sales for four consecutive years and year-end allowance account balances were as follows:

Year	Sales	Allowance for Doubtful Accounts End-of-Year Credit Balance
1984	$2,100,000	$21,500
1985	1,975,000	35,500
1986	2,500,000	50,000
1987	2,350,000	66,000

(1) Compute the amount of accounts written off for the years 1985, 1986, and 1987.
(2) The external auditors are concerned with the growing amount in the allowance account. What action do you recommend the auditors take?
(3) What arguments might Transtech use to justify the balance in the valuation account? Allowance for Doubtful Accounts is the only accounts receivable valuation account used by Transtech Publishing.

EXERCISE 8–9   (Accounts receivable as a source of cash)

The Alpha Corporation decides to use accounts receivable as a basis for financing. Its current position is as follows:

Accounts receivable...	$80,000	Cash overdraft.....	$ 400
Inventories	81,000	Accounts payable ..	57,500

Prepare a statement of its current position, assuming cash is obtained as indicated in each case below:

(1) Cash of $60,000 is borrowed on short-term notes and $35,000 is applied to the payment of creditors; accounts of $70,000 are assigned to secure the loan.

(2) Cash of $60,000 is advanced to the company by Beta Finance Co., the advance representing 80% of accounts transferred on a recourse basis. (Assume the transfer meets the FASB conditions to be accounted for as a sale.)

(3) Cash of $60,000 is received on factoring of $78,000 of accounts receivable.

EXERCISE 8–10   (Accounting for a non-interest-bearing note)

Anderson Corporation sells equipment with a book value of $8,000, receiving a non-interest-bearing note due in three years with a face amount of $10,000. There is no established market value for the equipment. The interest rate on similar obligations is estimated at 12%. Compute the gain or loss on the sale and the discount on notes receivable, and make the necessary entry to record the sale.

EXERCISE 8–11   (Accounting for an interest-bearing note)

Samuel Company purchased a truck from Davis Company for $30,000. Samuel Company, lacking sufficient funds to pay the entire $30,000 in cash, paid $5,000 in cash and the remaining $25,000 was paid by issuing a 6-month, 12% note for that amount. Make the entries to record (1) the purchase of the truck and the settlement of the note on Samuel's books and (2) the settlement of the note on Davis Company's books.

EXERCISE 8–12   (Discounting notes — computations)

On December 21, the following notes are discounted by the bank at 15%. Determine the cash proceeds, rounded to the nearest dollar, from each note using a 365-day year.

(1) 30-day, $4,500, non-interest-bearing note dated December 15.
(2) 60-day, $3,379, 9% note dated December 1.
(3) 60-day, $15,000, 13% note dated November 6.
(4) 90-day, $6,775, 19% note dated November 24.

EXERCISE 8–13   (Accounting for notes receivable discounted)

James Company accepted a $20,000, 90-day, 12% interest-bearing note dated September 1, 1987, from a customer for the sale of a piece of machinery. The machinery cost $25,000 and was 50% depreciated. On October 15, 1987, James discounted the note, with recourse, at First National Bank at a 15% discount rate. The customer paid the note at maturity. Based on a 360-day year, make the entries necessary to record the above transactions on James Company's books. (Assume the transfer of the note does not meet FASB criteria for recording as a sale.)

EXERCISE 8–14   (Accounting for notes receivable discounted)

R. Almond received from H. Jarman, a customer, a 90-day, 12% note for $6,000, dated June 6, 1987. On July 6, Almond had Jarman's note discounted at 10% and recorded the discounting as a sale in accordance with FASB Statement No. 77. The bank protested nonpayment of the note and charged Almond with protest fees of $10 in addition to the maturity value of the note. On September 28, 1987, the note was collected by Almond with interest at 15% from the maturity date to the date of collection. What entries would appear on Almond's books as a result of the foregoing? (Assume a 360-day year.)

EXERCISE 8–15   (Discounting a note receivable)

On June 1, 1987, Flint Company received a $5,200, 90-day, 11% interest-bearing note from a customer on an overdue account receivable. Flint discounted the note, with recourse, immediately at State Bank at a discount rate of 15%. The discounting transaction did not meet FASB criteria for recording as a sale. At the date of maturity the bank notified Flint that the note had not been paid and that the amount of the note plus a $25 protest fee had been charged to its account. Flint is unable to collect from the customer. (1) How much money will Flint receive upon discounting the note? (2) What is the effective rate of interest the bank will earn on the note? (3) Prepare the journal entries to record the events described above. (Assume a 360-day year.)

PROBLEMS

PROBLEM 8–1   (Journal entries and balance sheet presentation)

The balance sheet for the Canton Cosmetic Corporation on December 31, 1986, includes the following receivables balances:

Notes receivable (including notes discounted with recourse, $15,500)		$36,500
Accounts receivable	$85,600	
Less allowance for doubtful accounts	4,150	81,450
Interest receivable		525

Current liabilities reported in the December 31, 1986 balance sheet included:

Obligation on discounted notes receivable	$15,500

Transactions during 1987 included the following:
(a) Sales on account were $767,000.
(b) Cash collected on accounts totaled $576,500, which included accounts of $93,000 on which cash discounts of 2% were allowed.
(c) Notes received in settlement of accounts totaled $82,500.
(d) Notes receivable discounted as of December 31, 1986, were paid at maturity with the exception of one $3,000 note on which the company had to pay the bank $3,090, which included interest and protest fees. It is expected that recovery will be made on this note early in 1988.

(e) Customers' notes of $60,000 were discounted with recourse during the year, proceeds from their transfer being $58,500. (All discounting transactions were recorded as loans.) Of this total, $48,000 matured during the year without notice of protest.

(f) Customers' accounts of $8,720 were written off during the year as worthless.

(g) Recoveries of doubtful accounts written off in prior years were $2,020.

(h) Notes receivable collected during the year totaled $27,000 and interest collected was $2,450.

(i) On December 31, accrued interest on notes receivable was $630.

(j) Uncollectible accounts are estimated to be 5% of the December 31, 1987, Accounts Receivable balance.

(k) Cash of $35,000 was borrowed from the bank, accounts receivable of $40,000 being pledged on the loan. Collections of $19,500 had been made on these receivables (included in the total given in transaction [b]) and this amount was applied on December 31, 1987, to payment of accrued interest on the loan of $600, and the balance to partial payment of the loan.

Instructions:

1. Prepare journal entries summarizing the transactions and information given above.
2. Prepare a summary of current receivables for balance sheet presentation.

PROBLEM 8–2   (Accounting for receivables — journal entries)

The following transactions affecting the accounts receivable of Southern States Manufacturing Corporation took place during the year ended January 31, 1988:

Sales (cash and credit).	$591,050
Cash received from credit customers (customers who paid $298,900 took advantage of the discount feature of the corporation's credit terms 2/10, n/30)	302,755
Cash received from cash customers	205,175
Accounts receivable written off as worthless	4,955
Credit memoranda issued to credit customers for sales returns and allowances	56,275
Cash refunds given to cash customers for sales returns and allowances	16,972
Recoveries on accounts receivable written off as uncollectible in prior periods (not included in cash amount stated above).	10,615

The following two balances were taken from the January 31, 1987 balance sheet:

Accounts receivable.	$95,842
Allowance for doubtful accounts	9,740 (credit)

The corporation provides for its net uncollectible account losses by crediting Allowance for Doubtful Accounts for 1½% of net credit sales for the fiscal period.

Instructions:

1. Prepare the journal entries to record the transactions for the year ended January 31, 1988.
2. Prepare the adjusting journal entry for estimated uncollectible accounts on January 31, 1988.

PROBLEM 8–3
(Estimating uncollectible accounts by aging receivables)

Sun Company, a wholesaler, uses the aging method to estimate bad debt losses. The following schedule of aged accounts receivable was prepared at December 31, 1988.

Age of Accounts	Amount
0–30 days	$561,600
31–60 days	196,100
61–90 days	88,400
91–120 days	18,500
More than 120 days	9,600
	$874,200

The following schedule shows the year-end receivables balances and uncollectible accounts experience for the previous five years.

Loss Experience-Percent of Uncollectible Accounts

Year	Year-End Receivables	0–30 days	31–60 days	61–90 days	91–120 days	Over 120 days
1987	$780,700	.5%	1.0%	10.2%	49.1%	78.2%
1986	750,400	.4	1.1	10.0	51.2	77.3
1985	681,400	.6	1.2	11.0	51.7	79.0
1984	698,200	.5	.9	10.1	52.3	78.5
1983	723,600	.4	1.0	8.9	49.2	77.6

The unadjusted Allowance for Doubtful Accounts balance on December 31, 1988, is $31,796.   AVG: .48%   1.04%   10.04%   50.7%   78.12%

Instructions: Compute the correct balance for the allowance account based on the average loss experience for the last five years and prepare the appropriate end-of-year adjusting entry.

PROBLEM 8–4
(Accounting for assignment of specific accounts receivable)

On July 1, 1987, Turbine, Inc. assigns specific receivables totaling $250,000 to Fort Union Bank as collateral on a $150,000, 16% note. Turbine, Inc. will continue to collect the assigned receivables. Besides the interest collected, Fort Union also receives a 1.5% finance charge on all assigned receivables. Additional information for Turbine, Inc. is as follows:

(a) July collections amounted to $145,000, less cash discounts of $750.
(b) On August 1, paid bank amount owed for July collections and accrued interest on note to August 1.
(c) Collected the remaining assigned accounts during August except for $550 written off as uncollectible.
(d) On September 1, paid bank the remaining amount owed plus accrued interest.

Instructions: Make the entries necessary to record the above information on the books of both Turbine, Inc. and Fort Union Bank.

PROBLEM 8–5 (Assigning and factoring accounts receivable)

During its second year of operations, Shank Corporation found itself in financial difficulties. Shank decided to use its accounts receivable as a means of obtaining cash to continue operations. On July 1, 1987, Shank factored $75,000 of accounts receivable, for cash proceeds of $69,500. On December 27, 1987, Shank assigned the remainder of its accounts receivable, $250,000 as of that date, as collateral on a $125,000, 12% annual interest rate loan from Sandy Finance Company. Shank received $125,000 less a 2% finance charge. Additional information is as follows:

Allowance for Doubtful Accounts, 12/31/87 . . . . . $3,200 (credit)
Estimated uncollectibles, 12/31/87 . . . .   3% of Accounts Receivable
Accounts Receivable (not including factored
and assigned accounts) 12/31/87 . . . . $50,000
None of the assigned accounts had been collected by the end of the year.

Instructions:
1. Prepare the journal entries to record the receipt of cash from (a) factoring and (b) assignment of the accounts receivable.
2. Prepare the journal entry necessary to record the adjustment to Allowance for Doubtful Accounts.
3. Prepare the accounts receivable section of Shank's balance sheet as it would appear after the above transactions.
4. What entry would be made on Shank's books when the factored accounts have been collected?

PROBLEM 8–6 (Discounting notes)

Dival Marketing Corporation completed the following transactions, among others:

May 5 Received a $5,000, 60-day, 10% note dated May 5 from R. D. Spears, a customer.
   24 Received an $1,800, 90-day, non-interest-bearing note dated May 23 from B. Collins as settlement for unpaid balance of $1,752.
   25 Had Spears' note discounted at the bank at 13%.   *selling*
June 7 Had Collins' note discounted at the bank at 15%.
   25 Received from J. L. Smith, a customer, a $7,000, 90-day, 12% note dated June 5, payable to J. L. Smith and signed by the Racine Corp. Upon endorsement, gave the customer credit for the maturity value of the note less discount at 13%.
   29 Received a $3,500, 60-day, 9% note dated June 29 from B. Grady, a customer.
July 5 Received notice from the bank that Spears' note was not paid at maturity. Protest fees of $15 were charged by the bank.
   21 Received payment from Spears on the dishonored note, including interest at 16% on the balance from maturity date to payment date.

Instructions:
1. Give the journal entries to record the above transactions. Assume notes discounted with recourse and do not meet the FASB criteria for recording

as a sale. (Show data used in calculations with each entry and assume a 360-day year.)

2. Give the adjusting entries required on July 31.

PROBLEM 8–7 (Accounting for discounted notes)

The following transactions were completed by M. D. Ellis over a three-month period:

Nov. 10 Received from G. R. Kack, a customer, a $5,000, 60-day, 9% note dated Nov. 9.

   11 Received from M. C. Leckner on account, a $2,100, 60-day, 12% note dated Nov. 10.

   20 Discounted Leckner's note, without recourse, at the bank at 11%.

   24 Discounted Kack's note, with recourse, at the bank at 10%.

Dec. 3 Received a $2,950, 30-day, non-interest-bearing note dated Dec. 1 from M. Ichtemple, crediting Ichtemple's account at face value.

    7 Discounted Ichtemple's note, with recourse, at the bank at 12%.

   29 Received from S. E. Dillhunt, a $500, 90-day, 12% note dated Dec. 14 and made by Bell Realty Inc. Gave the customer credit for the maturity value of the note less discount at 10%.

   29 Received a $4,000, 10-day, 8% note dated Dec. 29 from M. L. Reinhard, a customer.

Jan. 10 Received notice from the bank that Kack's note was not paid at maturity. A protest fee of $15 was charged by the bank.

   22 Received a $25,000, 120-day, 9% note dated Jan. 22 from V. M. Cherry, a customer.

   28 Received payment on Reinhard's note, including interest at 10%, the legal rate, on the face value from the maturity date.

Instructions:

1. Give the entries to record the preceding transactions. Assume that notes discounted with recourse do not meet FASB criteria for recording as a sale. (Show data used in calculations with each entry; round amounts to nearest dollar and assume a 360-day year.)

2. Give the necessary adjusting entries on January 31. Assume all notes discounted are paid when due unless otherwise indicated.

PROBLEM 8–8 (Accounting for non-interest-bearing note)

On January 1, 1987, Austin Manufacturing sold a tract of land to three doctors as an investment. The land, purchased ten years ago, was carried on Austin's books at a value of $55,000. Austin received a non-interest-bearing note for $110,000 from the doctors. The note is due December 31, 1988. There is no readily available market value for the land, but the current market rate of interest for comparable notes is 12%.

Instructions:

1. Give the journal entry to record the sale of land on Austin's books.

2. Prepare a schedule of discount amortization for the note with amounts rounded to the nearest dollar. *(continued)*

3. Give the adjusting entries to be made at the end of 1987 and 1988 to record the effective interest earned.

PROBLEM 8–9   (Non-interest-bearing note)

On January 1, 1987, the Denver Company sold land to the Boise Company which originally cost Denver $400,000. Boise gave Denver a $600,000, non-interest-bearing note payable in six equal annual installments of $100,000, with the first payment due and paid on December 31, 1987. There was no established exchange price for the property and the note has no ready market. The prevailing rate of interest for a note of this type is 12%. The present value of an annuity of $1 in advance for six periods at 12% is 4.1114.

Instructions:
1. Prepare a schedule computing the balance in Denver's net receivable (face amount of note less unamortized discount) from Boise at December 31, 1988, based on the above facts. Show supporting computations in good form.
2. Give the entries required on Denver's books for the life of the note.

(AICPA adapted)

PROBLEM 8–10   (Factoring receivables)

Freemont Factors Inc. was incorporated December 31, 1986. The capital stock of the company consists of 200,000 shares of $10 par value common, all of which were sold at par. The company was organized for the purpose of factoring the accounts receivable of various businesses requiring this service.

Freemont Factors Inc. charges a commission to its clients of 15% of all receivables factored and assumes all credit risks. Besides the commission, an additional 10% of gross receivables is withheld on all purchases and is credited to Client Retainer. This retainer is used for merchandise returns, etc., made by customers of the clients for which a credit memo would be due. Payments are made to the clients by Freemont Factors Inc. at the end of each month to adjust the retainer so that it equals 10% of the unpaid receivables at month end.

Based on the collection experience of other factoring companies in this area, officials of Freemont Factors Inc. have decided to make monthly provisions to Allowance for Doubtful Accounts based on 2% of all receivables purchased. The company also decided to recognize commission revenue on only the factored receivables which have been collected; however, for bookkeeping simplicity, all commissions are originally credited to Commission Revenue and an adjustment is made to Unearned Commissions at the end of each quarter based on 3% of receivables then outstanding.

Operations of the company during the first quarter of 1987 resulted in the following:

Accounts receivable factored:

January	$500,000
February	400,000
March	600,000

Collections on the above receivables totaled $1,200,000.

General and administrative expenses paid during the period:

Salaries.	$18,000
Office rent.	9,000
Advertising	2,500
Equipment rent	6,600
Miscellaneous	4,000

On February 1, 1987, a 3-month 10% bank loan was obtained for $800,000 with interest payable at maturity.

For the first 3 months of the year, the company rented all of its office furniture and equipment; however, on March 31, 1987, it purchased various equipment at a cost of $60,000, the liability for which had not been recorded as of March 31.

Instructions:
1. Give all entries necessary to record the above transactions and to close the books as of March 31, 1987. (Disregard all taxes.)
2. Prepare a balance sheet and an income statement as of March 31, 1987.

(AICPA adapted)

9
Inventories — Cost Procedures

The primary source of revenue for a business entity is the sale of goods or services. For a nonservice enterprise, the cost of the goods or inventory sold and the value of the unsold inventory are significant items in the measurement of income and the determination of financial position. Because of the wide variety of nonservice businesses, many different inventory valuation methods have developed. Some of these are unique to the United States, and have developed in the economic circumstances of changing prices and the income tax laws. Others have developed within industries and have become generally accepted over time.

While the general valuation rule for accounts receivable was identified in Chapter 8 as net realizable value, the general valuation rule for inventories is some measure of cost. Goods are marked up in price to permit a company to recover its direct and indirect costs and to earn a profit. Until a sale of the inventory occurs that meets the revenue recognition criteria discussed in Chapter 4, inventory is valued on some cost basis, modified in some instances by a reduction to a lower market price. This chapter focuses on the various inventory cost procedures and allocation methods that are employed in practice. Chapter 10 presents some additional valuation issues relating to inventory including the lower of cost or market rule for adjusting cost valuation downward.

NATURE OF INVENTORY

The term **inventory** designates goods held for sale in the normal course of business and, in the case of a manufacturer, goods in production or to be placed in production. The nature of goods classified as inventory varies widely with the nature of business activities, and in some cases includes assets not normally thought of as inventory. For example, land and buildings held for resale by a real estate firm, partially completed buildings to be sold in the future by a construction firm, and marketable securities held for resale by a stockbroker are all properly classified as inventory by the respective firms.

Inventory represents one of the most active elements in business operations, being continuously acquired or produced and resold. A large part of a company's resources is frequently invested in goods purchased or manufactured. The cost of these goods must be recorded, grouped, and summarized during the accounting period. At the end of the period, costs must be allocated between current and future activities, i.e., between goods sold during the current period and the inventory, i.e., those goods on hand to be sold in future periods.

If inventory costs remained constant, this allocation would prove to be rather simple. But when inflationary and deflationary pressures cause changes in inventory costs, a more normal condition, the allocation of historical cost to revenues of the current and future periods challenges the most experienced accountant. Failure to allocate costs properly can result in serious distortion of financial position and operating performance.

CLASSES OF INVENTORIES

The term **inventory** or **merchandise inventory** is generally applied to goods held by a merchandising firm, either wholesale or retail, when such goods have been acquired in a condition for resale. The terms **raw materials, goods in process**, and **finished goods** refer to the inventories of a manufacturing enterprise. The latter items require description.

Raw Materials

Raw materials are goods acquired for use in the production process. Some raw materials are obtained directly from natural sources. More often, however, raw materials are acquired from other companies and represent the finished products of the suppliers. For example, newsprint is the finished product of the paper mill but represents raw material to the printer who acquires it.

Although the term raw materials can be used broadly to cover all materials used in manufacturing, this designation is frequently restricted to materials that will be physically incorporated in the products being manufactured. The term **factory supplies**, or **manufacturing supplies**, is then used to refer to auxiliary materials, i.e., materials that are necessary in the production process but are not directly incorporated in the products. Oils and fuels for factory equipment, cleaning supplies, and similar items fall into this grouping since these items are not incorporated in a product but simply facilitate production as a whole. Raw materials directly used in the production of certain goods are frequently referred to as **direct materials**; factory supplies are referred to as **indirect materials**.

Although factory supplies may be summarized separately, they should be reported as a part of a company's inventories since they will ultimately be consumed in the production process. Supplies purchased for use in the delivery, sales, and general administrative functions of the enterprise should not be reported as part of the inventories, but as prepaid expenses.

Goods in Process

Goods in process, alternately referred to as **work in process**, consists of materials partly processed and requiring further work before they can be sold. This inventory includes three cost elements: (1) **direct materials**, (2) **direct labor**, and (3) **factory overhead** or **manufacturing overhead**. The cost of materials directly identified with the goods in production is included under (1). The cost of labor directly identified with goods in production is included under (2). The portion of factory overhead assignable to goods still in production forms the third element of cost.

Factory overhead consists of all manufacturing costs other than direct materials and direct labor. It includes factory supplies used and labor not directly identified with the production of specific products. It also includes general manufacturing costs such as depreciation, maintenance, repairs, property taxes, insurance, and light, heat, and power, as well as a reasonable share of the managerial costs other than those relating solely to the selling and administrative functions of the business.

Finished Goods

Finished goods are the manufactured products awaiting sale. As products are completed, the costs accumulated in the production process are transferred from Goods in Process to the finished goods inventory account. The diagram at the top of page 329 illustrates the basic flow of product costs through the inventory accounts of a manufacturer.

INVENTORY SYSTEMS

Inventory records may be maintained on either a **periodic** or **perpetual** basis. A **periodic inventory system** requires a **physical inventory**, i.e., a

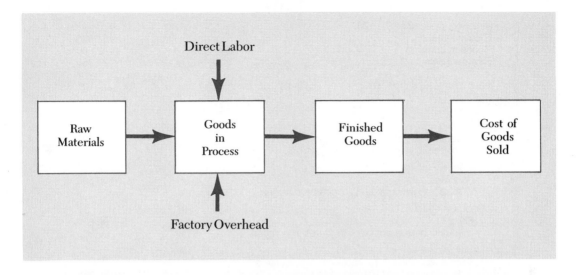

counting, measuring, or weighing of goods, at the end of the accounting period to determine the quantities on hand. Values are then assigned to the quantities to determine the portion of the recorded costs to be carried forward. The entries to adjust the inventories under a periodic inventory system are illustrated in Chapter 3, page 78.

The **perpetual inventory system** requires the maintenance of records that provide a continuous summary of inventory items on hand. Individual accounts are kept for each class of goods. Inventory increases and decreases are recorded in the individual accounts, the resulting balances representing the amounts on hand. Perpetual records may be kept in terms of quantities only or in terms of both quantities and costs. In a manufacturing organization, a perpetual system applied to inventories requires recording the full movement of goods through individual accounts for raw materials, goods in process, and finished goods. To illustrate, assume the following data for the Darnett Corporation, a manufacturing company that uses a perpetual inventory system:

Inventories, January 1, 1987:	
Finished goods..	$ 45,000
Goods in process...	29,400
Raw materials..	21,350
Charges incurred during 1987:	
Raw materials purchased......................................	107,500
Raw materials used...	106,500
Direct labor	96,850
Factory overhead..	134,055
Cost of goods completed in 1987...................................	340,305
Cost of goods sold in 1987	334,305

Inventories, December 31, 1987:

Finished goods.	51,000
Goods in process.	26,500
Raw materials.	22,350

Summary entries to record the preceding data for 1987 would be as follows:

(a) Raw Materials   107,500
     Accounts Payable   107,500
       To record purchases of raw materials.

(b) Goods in Process   106,500
     Raw Materials   106,500
       To record raw materials used in production.

(c) Goods in Process   96,850
     Payroll   96,850
       To distribute direct labor to goods in process.

(d) Factory Overhead   134,055
     Various accounts (e.g., liabilities, accumulated
       depreciation, and prepaid expenses)   134,055
       To record factory overhead charges.

(e) Goods in Process   134,055
     Factory Overhead   134,055
       To apply factory overhead to goods in process.

(f) Finished Goods   340,305
     Goods in Process   340,305
       To transfer completed goods.

(g) Cost of Sales   334,305
     Finished Goods   334,305
       To record the cost of goods sold.

After posting, the inventory and cost of sales accounts would appear in the ledger as follows:

Raw Materials				Goods in Process		
Jan. 1	21,350	(b) 106,500		Jan. 1	29,400	(f) 340,305
(a)	107,500			(b)	106,500	
Dec. 31	22,350			(c)	96,850	
				(e)	134,055	
				Dec. 31	26,500	

Finished Goods				Cost of Goods Sold	
Jan. 1	45,000	(g) 334,305		(g) 334,305	
(f)	340,305				
Dec. 31	51,000				

When preparing the income statement for a manufacturing company, it is useful to prepare a separate manufacturing schedule that shows the detail supporting the cost of goods completed and transferred to Finished Goods. An illustration of this schedule, based on the preceding data and additional factory overhead detail, follows:

Darnett Corporation Schedule of Cost of Goods Manufactured For Year Ended December 31, 1987		
Direct materials:		
Raw materials inventory, January 1, 1987............	$ 21,350	
Purchases	107,500	
Cost of raw materials available for use	$128,850	
Less raw materials inventory, December 31, 1987	22,350	
Raw materials used in production.....................		$106,500
Direct labor..		96,850
Factory overhead:		
Indirect labor	$ 40,000	
Factory supervision	29,000	
Depreciation expense—factory buildings and equipment.....................................	20,000	
Light, heat, and power.............................	18,000	
Factory supplies expense	15,000	
Miscellaneous factory overhead.....................	12,055	134,055
Total manufacturing costs...........................		$337,405
Add goods in process inventory, January 1, 1987.......		29,400
		$366,805
Less goods in process inventory, December 31, 1987 ...		26,500
Cost of goods manufactured		$340,305

Even when a perpetual system is employed, physical counts of the units on hand should be made at least once a year to confirm the balances on the books. The frequency of physical inventories will vary depending on the nature of the goods, their rate of turnover, and the degree of internal control. A plan for continuous counting of inventory items on a rotation basis is frequently employed. Variations may be found between the recorded amounts and the amounts actually on hand as a result of recording errors, shrinkage, breakage, theft, and other causes. The inventory accounts should be adjusted to agree with the physical count when a discrepancy exists. To illustrate, assume that a physical inventory of raw materials resulted in a value that is $2,500 less than the recorded inventory. The entry to adjust the inventory account would be:

Inventory Adjustment...	2,500	
Raw Materials Inventory..		2,500

Normal inventory adjustments for shrinkage and breakage are reported as adjustments to cost of goods sold. Abnormal shortages or thefts may be reported separately as operating expenses.

Practically all large trading and manufacturing enterprises and many relatively small organizations have adopted the perpetual inventory system as an integral part of their record keeping and internal control. This system offers a continuous check and control over inventories. Purchasing and production planning are facilitated, adequate inventories on hand are assured, and losses incurred through damage and theft are fully disclosed. The additional costs of maintaining such a system are usually well repaid by the benefits provided to management.

ITEMS TO BE INCLUDED IN INVENTORY

As a general rule, goods should be included in the inventory of the party holding title. The passing of title is a legal term designating the point at which ownership changes. In some situations, the legal rule may be waived for practical reasons or because of certain limitations in its application. When the rule of passing title is not observed, there should be appropriate disclosure on the statements of the special practice followed and the factors supporting such practice. Application of the legal test under a number of special circumstances is described in the following paragraphs.

Goods in Transit

When terms of sale are **FOB (free on board) shipping point**, title passes to the buyer with the loading of goods at the point of shipment. Under these terms, application of the legal rule to a year-end shipment calls for recognition of a sale and an accompanying decrease in goods on hand on the books of the seller. Since title passes at the shipping point, **goods in transit** at year-end should be included in the inventory of the buyer despite the lack of physical possession. A determination of the goods in transit at year-end is made by a review of the incoming orders during the early part of the new period. The purchase records may be kept open beyond the fiscal period to permit the recognition of goods in transit as of the end of the period, or goods in transit may be recorded by means of an adjusting entry.

When terms of a sale are **FOB destination**, application of the legal test calls for no recognition of the transaction until goods are received by the buyer. In this case, because of the difficulties involved in ascertaining whether goods have reached their destination at year-end, the seller may prefer to ignore the legal rule and employ shipment as a basis for recognizing a sale and the accompanying inventory decrease. In some cases, title to goods may pass before shipment takes place. For example, if goods are produced on special customer order, they may be recorded as a sale as soon as they are completed and segregated from the regular inventory. If the sale is recognized upon segregation by the seller, care must be taken to exclude such goods from the seller's inventory. The buyer, on the other hand, could recognize the in-transit goods as a purchase and thus part of its inventory.

Goods on Consignment

Goods are frequently transferred to a dealer (**consignee**) on a consignment basis. The shipper (**consignor**) retains title and includes the goods in inventory until their sale by the consignee. **Consigned goods** are properly reported at the sum of their cost and the handling and shipping costs incurred in their transfer to the consignee. The goods may be separately designated on the balance sheet as merchandise on consignment. The consignee does not own the consigned goods; hence neither consigned goods nor obligations for such goods are reported on the consignee's financial statements. Accounting for consignments is discussed in Chapter 19. Other merchandise owned by a business but in the possession of others, such as goods in the hands of salespersons and agents, goods held by customers on approval, and goods held by others for storage, processing, or shipment, should also be shown as a part of the owner's ending inventory.

Conditional and Installment Sales

Conditional sales and installment sales contracts may provide for a retention of title by the seller until the sales price is fully recovered. Under these circumstances, the seller, who retains title, may continue to show the goods, reduced by the buyer's equity in such goods as established by collections; the buyer, in turn, can report an equity in the goods accruing through payments made. However, in the usual case when the possibilities of returns and defaults are very low, the test of passing of title should be relinquished and the transaction recorded in terms of the expected outcome: the seller, anticipating completion of the contract and the ultimate passing of title, recognizes the transaction as a regular sale involving deferred collections; the buyer, intending to comply with the contract and acquire title, recognizes the transaction as a regular purchase. Installment sales are discussed in detail in Chapter 19.

DETERMINATION OF INVENTORY COST

After the goods to be included as inventory have been identified, the accountant must assign a dollar value to the physical units. As indicated earlier, the profession has historically favored retention of some measure of cost, generally historical cost for this purpose. Attention is directed in this chapter to identifying the elements that comprise cost, and to a consideration of how to determine the portion of historical costs to be retained as the inventory amount reported on the balance sheet and the amount to be charged against current revenues.

Items Included in Cost

Inventory costs consists of all expenditures, both direct and indirect, relating to inventory acquisition, preparation, and placement for sale. In the case of raw materials or goods acquired for resale, cost includes the purchase price, freight, receiving, storage, and all other costs incurred to the time goods are ready for sale. Certain expenditures can be traced to specific acquisitions or can be allocated to inventory items in some equitable manner. Other expenditures may be relatively small and difficult to allocate. Such items are normally excluded in the calculation of inventory cost and are thus charged in full against current revenue as **period costs.**

The charges to be included in the cost of manufactured products have already been mentioned. Proper accounting for materials, labor, and factory overhead items and their identification with goods in process and finished good inventories is best achieved through adoption of a cost accounting system designed to meet the needs of a particular business unit. Certain costs relating to the acquisition or the manufacture of goods may be considered abnormal and may be excluded in arriving at inventory cost. For example, costs arising from idle capacity, excessive spoilage, and reprocessing are normally considered abnormal items chargeable to current revenue. Only those portions of general and administrative costs that are clearly related to procurement or production should be included in inventory cost.

In practice, companies take different positions in classifying certain costs. For example, costs of the purchasing department, costs of accounting for manufacturing activities, and costs of pensions for production personnel may be treated as inventoriable costs by some companies and period costs by others.

Discounts as Reductions in Cost

Discounts treated as a reduction of cost in recording the acquisition of goods should similarly be treated as a reduction in the cost assigned to the inventory. **Trade discounts** are discounts converting a catalog price list to the prices actually charged to a buyer. The discount available may vary with such factors as the quantity purchased. Thus, trade discounts are frequently stated in a series. For example, given trade discount terms based on the quantity ordered of 30/20/10, a customer would be entitled to a discount of either 30%, 30% and 20%, or 30% and 20% and 10%, depending on the size of the order. Each successive discount is applied to the net invoice cost after deducting any earlier discounts. To illustrate, assume that an inventory item is listed in a catalog for $5,000 and a buyer is given terms of 20/10/5. The net invoice price is calculated as follows:

	Discount	Net Invoice Amount
$5,000 × 20%	$1,000	$5,000 − $1,000 = $4,000
$4,000 × 10%	$ 400	$4,000 − $ 400 = $3,600
$3,600 × 5%	$ 180	$3,600 − $ 180 = $3,420

An alternative approach to the preceding computation is to compute a composite discount rate which can be applied to the initial gross amount. The following computation could be made for the above invoice:

Discount Rate	×	Percentage of Original Invoice Cost	=	Composite Discount Rate
20%		100%		20.00%
10%		80%(100% − 20%)		8.00
5%		72%(80% − 8%)		3.60
		Composite rate		31.60%

Computation of discount: $5,000 × 31.6% = $1,580 discount
Net price = $5,000 − $1,580 = $3,420

The advantage of the composite approach is that once a composite rate is computed, it can be used directly for all purchases that have the same trade discount terms.

Cost is defined as the list price less the trade discount. No record needs to be made of the discount, and the purchases should be recorded at the net price of $3,420.

Cash discounts are discounts granted for payment of invoices within a limited time period. Business use of such discounts has declined in popularity over the past years, although they are still found in some industries. Cash discounts are usually stated as a certain percentage rate to be allowed if the invoice is paid within a certain number of days, with the full amount due within another time period. For example, 2/10, n/30 (two ten, net thirty) means that 2% is allowed as a cash discount if the invoice is paid within 10 days after the invoice date, but that the full or "net" amount is due within 30 days. Terms of 3/10 eom mean a 3% discount is allowed if the invoice is paid within 10 days after the end of the month in which the invoice is written.

Theoretically, inventory should be recorded at the discounted amount, i.e., the gross invoice price less the allowable discount. This **net method** reflects the fact that discounts not taken are in effect credit-related expenditures incurred for failure to pay within the discount period. They are recorded in the discounts lost account and reported as a separate item on the income statement. Discounts lost usually represent a relatively high rate of interest. To illustrate, assume a purchase of $10,000 provides for payment on a 2/10, n/30 basis. This means that if the buyer pays for the purchase by the tenth day, only $9,800 must be paid. Twenty days later the full $10,000 is due. Thus, a discount of $200 is earned for 20 days advance payment. The implicit annual interest rate in this arrangement is 36% (360/20 × 2%), clearly a desirable rate even if a loan is necessary to obtain the cash for the advance payment. Failure on the part of financial management to take a cash discount usually represents carelessness in considering payment alternatives.

The inefficiency of not taking cash discounts is not reflected when inventory records are maintained at the gross unit price for convenience, as is often the case. Under the **gross method** cash discounts taken are reflected through a contra purchases account, Purchase Discounts, when a periodic inventory system is used. With a perpetual inventory system, discounts are credited directly to Inventory.

Because of its control features, the net method of accounting for purchases is strongly preferred; however, many companies still follow the historical practice of recognizing cash discounts only as payments are made. If the payment is made in the same period the inventory is sold, use of either method will result in the same net income. However, if inventory is sold in one period and payment is made in a subsequent period, net income is affected and a proper matching of costs against revenue will not take place. If the net method is used, an adjusting entry should be made at the end of each period to record the discounts lost on unpaid invoices for which the discount period has passed.

The entries required for both the gross and net methods are illustrated at the top of page 337. A perpetual inventory method is assumed.

Purchase Returns and Allowances

Adjustments to invoice cost are also made when merchandise either is damaged or is of a lesser quality than ordered. Sometimes the merchandise is physically returned to the supplier. In other instances, a credit is allowed to the buyer by the supplier to compensate for the damage or the inferior quality of the merchandise. In either case, the liability is reduced and a credit is made either directly to the inventory account under a perpetual inventory system, or to a contra purchases account, Purchase Returns and Allowances, under a periodic inventory system.

Transaction	Purchases Reported Net		Purchases Reported Gross	
Purchase of merchandise priced at $2,500 less trade discount of 30/20 and a cash discount of 2%: $2,500 less 30% = $1,750 $1,750 less 20% = $1,400 $1,400 less 2% = $1,372	Inventory .... 1,372 Accounts Payable. .	1,372	Inventory .... 1,400 Accounts Payable ..	1,400
(a) Assuming payment of the invoice within discount period.	Accounts Payable.... 1,372 Cash	1,372	Accounts Payable .... 1,400 Inventory .... Cash.............	28 1,372
(b) Assuming payment of the invoice after discount period.	Accounts Payable.... 1,372 Discounts Lost ...... 28 Cash	1,400	Accounts Payable .... 1,400 Cash.............	1,400
(c) Required adjustment at the end of the period assuming that the invoice was not paid and the discount period has lapsed.	Discounts Lost ...... 28 Accounts Payable. .	28	No entry required	

TRADITIONAL COST ALLOCATION METHODS

Four commonly applied allocation methods are discussed in this section: (1) **specific identification**, (2) **first-in, first-out (FIFO)**, (3) **average cost**, and (4) **last-in, first-out (LIFO)**. Each has certain characteristics that make it preferable under certain conditions. One of them, the last-in, first-out method, was specifically developed as an attempt to reduce the impact of changing prices on net income. All four methods have in common the fact that inventory cost, as defined in this chapter, is allocated between the income statement and the balance sheet. No adjustment for price changes is made to the total amount to be allocated.

Except for specific identification, all the cost methods are frequently encountered in practice. Many companies use more than one method, applying different methods to different classes of inventory. *Accounting Trends and Techniques* reported the following data regarding the inventory methods used by the 600 companies surveyed.[1]

Method	Number of Companies—1984
Last-in, first-out (LIFO)	400
First-in, first-out (FIFO)	377
Average cost	223
Other	54
Total	1,054

[1]*Accounting Trends and Techniques—1985*, (New York: American Institute of Certified Public Accountants, 1985), p. 116.

There have been few guidelines developed by the profession to assist companies in choosing among these alternative cost allocation methods. Some accountants have suggested that, conceptually, costs attach to the inventory as they are incurred and thus should follow the inventory to its disposition. This argument suggests that methods that allocate the cost of inventory sold according to the physical flow of goods would be preferred. Other writers have emphasized capital maintenance concepts and suggest the use of methods that provide for maintenance of a physical quantity of inventory before recognizing income from its sale. The following discussion of the allocation methods demonstrates how each method relates to these different viewpoints.

Specific Identification

Costs may be allocated between goods sold during the period and goods on hand at the end of the period according to the actual cost of specific units. This **specific identification** method requires a means of identifying the historical cost of each unit of inventory up to the time of sale. With specific identification, the flow of recorded costs matches the physical flow of goods.

The specific identification method is a highly objective approach to matching historical costs with revenues. As stated in Accounting Research Study No. 13, "There appears to be little theoretical argument against the use of specific identification of cost with units of product if that method of determining inventory costs is practicable."[2] Application of this method, however, is often difficult or impossible. When inventory is composed of a great many items or identical items acquired at different times and at different prices, cost identification procedures are likely to be slow, burdensome, and costly. Furthermore, when units are identical and interchangeable, this method opens the doors to possible profit manipulation through the selection of particular units for delivery. Finally, significant changes in costs during a period may warrant charges to revenue on a basis other than past identifiable costs. Interstate Bakeries Corporation uses specific identification for part of its inventories as shown at the top of the next page.

First-In, First-Out Method

The **first-in, first-out (FIFO) method** is based on the assumption that costs should be charged to revenue in the order in which incurred. Inven-

---

[2]Horace G. Barden, *Accounting Research Study No. 13*, "The Accounting Basis of Inventories" (New York: American Institute of Certified Public Accountants, 1973) p. 83.

INTERSTATE BAKERIES CORPORATION

	1984	1983
Current assets:		
Cash and short-term investments..........	$ 4,017,000	$ 6,226,000
Accounts and notes receivable, less		
allowance for doubtful accounts of		
$1,418,000 ($1,317,000 in 1983).........	43,837,000	42,210,000
Inventories..............................	16,658,000	16,523,000
Prepaid expenses	1,251,000	1,455,000
Recoverable pension assets	37,000,000	—
Total current assets....................	102,763,000	66,414,000

NOTES TO CONSOLIDATED FINANCIAL STATEMENTS

Inventories — Inventories are stated at the lower of cost or market. Specific invoiced costs are used with respect to ingredients such as flour and sugar and average costs are used for other inventory items.

---

tories are thus stated in terms of most recent costs. To illustrate the application of this method, assume the following data:

Jan.	1 Inventory	200 units at $10	$ 2,000
	12 Purchase..............	400 units at 12	4,800
	26 Purchase..............	300 units at 11	3,300
	30 Purchase..............	100 units at 12	1,200
	Total	1,000	$11,300

A physical inventory on January 31 shows 300 units on hand. The most recent costs would be assigned to the units as follows:

Most recent purchase, Jan. 30...	100 units at $12	$1,200
Next most recent purchase,		
Jan. 26	200 units at 11	2,200
Total......................	300	$3,400

If the ending inventory is recorded at $3,400, cost of goods sold is $7,900 ($11,300 − $3,400). Thus, revenue is charged with the earliest costs incurred.

When perpetual inventory accounts are maintained, a form similar to that illustrated on page 340 is used to record the cost assigned to units issued and the cost relating to the goods on hand. The columns show the quantities and values of goods acquired, goods issued, and balances on hand. It should be observed that identical values for physical and perpetual inventories are obtained when FIFO is applied.

FIFO can be supported as a logical and realistic approach to the flow of costs when it is impractical or impossible to achieve specific cost identification. FIFO assumes a cost flow closely paralleling the usual physical

COMMODITY: X(FIFO)

DATE	RECEIVED			ISSUED			BALANCE		
	QUANTITY	UNIT COST	TOTAL COST	QUANTITY	UNIT COST	TOTAL COST	QUANTITY	UNIT COST	TOTAL COST
Jan. 1							200	$10	$2,000
12	400	$12	$4,800				200	10	2,000
							400	12	4,800
16				200	$10	$2,000			
				300	12	3,600	100	12	1,200
26	300	11	3,300				100	12	1,200
							300	11	3,300
29				100	12	1,200			
				100	11	1,100	200	11	2,200
30	100	12	1,200				200	11	2,200
							100	12	1,200

flow of goods sold. Revenue is charged with costs considered applicable to the goods actually sold; ending inventories are reported in terms of most recent costs — costs closely approximating the current value of inventories at the balance sheet date. FIFO affords little opportunity for profit manipulation because the assignment of costs is determined by the order in which costs are incurred.

Average Cost Methods

The **weighted average method** is based on the assumption that goods sold should be charged at an average cost, such average being influenced or *weighted* by the number of units acquired at each price. Inventories are stated at the same weighted average cost per unit. Using the cost data in the preceding section, the weighted average cost of a physical inventory of 300 units on January 31 would be as follows:

Jan. 1 Inventory	200 units at $10	$ 2,000
12 Purchase	400 units at 12	4,800
26 Purchase	300 units at 11	3,300
30 Purchase	100 units at 12	1,200
Total	1,000	$11,300

Weighted average cost .... $11,300 ÷ 1,000 = $11.30.
Ending inventory .... 300 units at $11.30 = $3,390.

The ending inventory is recorded at a cost of $3,390; cost of goods sold is $7,910 ($11,300 − $3,390), thus charging revenue with a weighted average cost. The calculations above were made for costs of one month. Similar calculations could be developed for a periodic inventory system in terms of data for a quarter or for a year.

When a perpetual inventory system that records both quantities and amounts is used, a variation of the weighted average method is required. A new weighted average amount is calculated after each new purchase, and this amount is used to cost each subsequent sale until another purchase is made. Because this method results in continuous updating of the average, it is referred to as the **moving average method**. The use of this method is illustrated below.

COMMODITY: X(moving average)

DATE	RECEIVED			ISSUED			BALANCE		
	QUANTITY	UNIT COST	TOTAL COST	QUANTITY	UNIT COST	TOTAL COST	QUANTITY	UNIT COST	TOTAL COST
Jan. 1							200	$10.00	$2,000
12	400	$12	$4,800				600	11.33	6,800
16				500	$11.33	$5,665	100	*11.35	1,135
26	300	11	3,300				400	11.09	4,435
29				200	11.09	2,218	200	11.09	2,217
30	100	12	1,200				300	11.39	3,417

*Increase in unit cost due to rounding.

On January 12 the new unit cost of $11.33 was found by dividing $6,800, the total cost, by 600, the number of units on hand. Then on January 16, the balance of $1,135 represented the previous balance of $6,800, less $5,665, the cost assigned to the 500 units issued on this date. New unit costs were calculated on January 26 and 30 when additional units were acquired.

With successive recalculations of cost and the use of such different costs during the period, the cost identified with the ending inventory will differ from that determined when cost is assigned to the ending inventory in terms of average cost for all goods available during the period. A physical inventory and use of the weighted average method resulted in a value for the ending inventory of $3,390; a perpetual inventory and use of the moving average method resulted in a value for the ending inventory of $3,417.

The average cost approach can be supported as realistic and as paralleling the physical flow of goods, particularly where there is an intermingling of identical inventory units. Unlike the other inventory methods, the average approach provides the same cost for similar items of equal utility. The method does not permit profit manipulation. Limitations of the average method are inventory values that perpetually contain some degree of influence of earliest costs and inventory values that may lag significantly behind current prices in periods of rapidly rising or falling prices.

Last-In, First-Out Method—Specific Goods

The **last-in, first-out (LIFO) method** is based on the assumption that the latest costs of a specific item should be charged to cost of goods sold. Inventories are thus stated at earliest costs. Using the cost data in the preceding section, a physical inventory of 300 units on January 31 would have a cost as follows:

Earliest costs relating to goods, Jan. 1......	200 units at $10	$2,000
Next earliest cost, Jan. 12.................	100 units at 12	1,200
Total................................	300	$3,200

The ending inventory is recorded at a cost of $3,200 and cost of goods sold is $8,100 ($11,300 − $3,200). Thus, revenue is charged with the most recently incurred costs.

When perpetual inventories are maintained, it is necessary to calculate costs on a last-in, first-out basis using the cost data on the date of each issue as illustrated at the top of the next page.

It should be noted that LIFO values obtained under a periodic system will usually differ from those determined on a perpetual basis. In the example, a cost of $3,200 was obtained for the periodic inventory, whereas $3,300 was obtained when costs were calculated as goods were issued. This difference results because it was necessary to "dip into" the beginning inventory layer and charge 100 units of the beginning inventory at $10 to the issue of January 16. The ending inventory thus reflects only 100 units at the beginning unit cost.

These temporary liquidations of inventory frequently occur during the year, especially for companies with seasonal business. These liquidations cause monthly reports prepared on the LIFO basis to be unrealistic and meaningless. Because of this, most companies using LIFO maintain their internal records using other inventory methods, such as FIFO or weighted average, and adjust the statements to LIFO at the end of the year with a **LIFO allowance** account. Companies frequently refer to this account as the *LIFO reserve* account. Because the profession has recommended that the word *reserve* not be used for asset valuation accounts, the term allowance is used in this text. The Parker Pen Company includes a note to its balance sheet that itemizes its inventories at FIFO cost or market, and then includes a separate allowance account to reduce the inventory to LIFO cost.

COMMODITY: X(**LIFO**)

DATE	RECEIVED			ISSUED			BALANCE		
	QUANTITY	UNIT COST	TOTAL COST	QUANTITY	UNIT COST	TOTAL COST	QUANTITY	UNIT COST	TOTAL COST
Jan. 1							200	$10	$2,000
12	400	$12	$4,800				200 400	10 12	2,000 4,800
16				400 100	$12 10	$4,800 1,000	100	10	1,000
26	300	11	3,300				100 300	10 11	1,000 3,300
29				200	11	2,200	100 100	10 11	1,000 1,100
30	100	12	1,200				100 100 100	10 11 12	1,000 1,100 1,200

PARKER PEN COMPANY

NOTES TO CONSOLIDATED FINANCIAL STATEMENTS

Inventories

Inventories consisted of the following:

(In thousands)	1984	1983
At lower of cost (FIFO) or market		
Finished products.	$20,590	$16,134
Work in process	7,930	7,894
Raw materials and supplies.	20,787	17,963
	49,307	41,991
Excess of FIFO over LIFO cost of certain		
domestic inventories	(4,380)	(7,481)
	$44,927	$34,510

Inventories are valued at the lower of cost or market and include the cost of material, labor and manufacturing overhead. Domestic writing instrument and packaging inventories (19 percent of total inventories in 1984 and 37 percent in 1983) are valued on the last-in, first-out (LIFO) basis, and all other inventories are on a first-in, first-out (FIFO) basis. Reductions of certain inventory quantities in 1984 resulted in a liquidation of LIFO inventory quantities carried at costs prevailing in prior years which are lower than current costs. The effect of this reduction was to increase net earnings by approximately $1,200,000 in 1984. This was a planned reduction in inventory and management believes the reduced levels are appropriate for operating purposes.

Assuming the allowance was used by Parker Pen for the first time in 1983, the entry to record the allowance would be as follows:

```
Cost of Goods Sold.................................................   7,481
     Excess of FIFO over LIFO cost...................................        7,481
```

In 1984, the difference was less, therefore, the adjusting entry would reduce the allowance account to its new difference.

```
Excess of FIFO over LIFO cost......................................   3,101
     Cost of Goods Sold..............................................        3,101
```

Each year, the allowance would be adjusted in this manner to properly record the LIFO inventory on the financial statements.

LIFO Conformity Rule. The LIFO inventory method was developed in the United States during the late 1930s as a method of permitting deferral of illusory inventory profits during periods of rising prices. Petition was made to Congress by companies desiring to use this method for tax purposes, and in the Revenue Act of 1938, it became an acceptable tax method. There was, however, a unique provision attached to the use of the LIFO inventory method. It has become known as the **LIFO conformity rule** and specifies that only those taxpayers who use LIFO for financial reporting purposes may use it for tax purposes. LIFO inventory is the only accounting method that must be reported the same way for tax and book purposes. In the early years, the rule was strictly applied. Companies were not permitted to report inventory values using any other method either in the body of the financial statements or in the attached notes. This provision was to avoid the implication that some value other than LIFO was really a better one. Over time, the IRS has gradually relaxed the conformity rule. In 1981, the IRS regulations were further relaxed by (1) permitting companies to provide non-LIFO disclosures as long as they are not presented on the face of the income statement, and (2) allowing companies to apply LIFO differently for book purposes than for tax purposes as long as they use some acceptable form of LIFO.[3]

Prior to the relaxation of the LIFO conformity rule, the income tax regulations became the governing rules for book purposes. The accounting standards bodies elected not to address the method except to recognize that LIFO was an acceptable inventory method.[4] Now that companies may apply LIFO differently for book and tax purposes, both the SEC and the AICPA have addressed the LIFO issue for financial statement reporting purposes. In July 1981 the SEC issued ASR No. 293 that provided guide-

---

[3]Treasury Decision 7756, Title 26 CFR 1.472-2(e), (Washington, D.C.: U.S. Government Printing Office, 1981).

[4]*Accounting Research Bulletin No. 43*, "Restatement and Revision of Accounting Research Bulletins" (New York: American Institute of Certified Public Accountants, 1953), Chapter 4, par. 6.

lines for companies to follow in making supplemental non-LIFO income disclosures. They also included several examples of what they labeled inappropriate use of the LIFO method. Their concern with LIFO as applied was stated as follows:

> For too long, the application of the LIFO method for financial accounting and reporting has been unduly influenced by the tax application. Most explanations or analyses of LIFO in textbooks and articles have been oriented toward tax implications, rather than financial accounting and reporting. With few exceptions, the accounting profession has deferred to the IRS in this area; indeed many accountants appear to view IRS LIFO regulations as if they were generally accepted accounting principles ("GAAP"). The Commission disagrees with this approach and believes that since LIFO may now be applied differently for book accounting and tax accounting, it is appropriate for the current practices used in the application of LIFO to be examined.[5]

The AICPA responded to this request, and under the direction of the Accounting Standards Executive Committee, appointed a nine-person Task Force on LIFO Inventory Problems to study the area. Their study resulted in the publication in November 1984 of an Issues Paper, "Identification and Discussion of Certain Financial Accounting and Reporting Issues Concerning LIFO Inventories." The task force addressed over fifty separate issues, and reported by vote their views on the topic. Although the task force did not have the power to establish definitive accounting standards, the SEC has accepted their report as authoritative pending review of this area by the FASB. Where applicable, the views of the task force will be referenced in the detailed discussion of LIFO that follows.

Specific-Goods LIFO Pools. With large and diversified inventories, application of the LIFO procedures to specific goods is extremely burdensome. Because of the complexity and cost involved, companies frequently selected only a few very important inventory items, usually raw materials, for application of the LIFO method. As a means of simplifying the valuation process and extending its applicability to more items, an adaptation of LIFO applied to specific goods was developed and approved by the IRS. This adaptation permitted the establishment of **inventory pools** of substantially identical goods. At the end of a period, the quantity of items in the pool is determined, and costs are assigned to those items. Units equal to the beginning quantity in the pool are assigned the beginning unit costs. If the number of units in ending inventory exceeds the number of begin-

---

[5]*Accounting Series Release No. 293*, "The Last-In, First-Out Method of Accounting for Inventories" (Washington, D. C.: US Printing Office, 1981), section II.

ning units, the additional units are regarded as an incremental **layer** within the pool.

The unit cost assigned to the items in the new layer may be based on one of three measurements:

1. actual costs of earliest acquisitions within the period (LIFO),
2. the weighted average cost of acquisitions within the period, or
3. actual costs of the latest acquisitions within the period (FIFO).

Increments in subsequent periods form successive inventory layers. A decrease in the number of units in an inventory pool during a period is regarded as a reduction in the most recently added layer, then in successively lower layers, and finally in the original or base quantity. Once a specific layer is reduced or eliminated, it is not restored.

To further illustrate the LIFO valuation process, assume that a company uses three inventory pools. The changes in the pools are as listed below. The inventory calculations that follow the listing are based on the assumption that weighted average costs are used in valuing annual incremental layers.

Inventory pool increments and liquidations:

	Inventory Pool A	Inventory Pool B	Inventory Pool C
Inv., Dec. 31, 1986	3,000 @ $6	3,000 @ $5	2,000 @ $10
Purchases—1987	3,000 @ $7	2,000 @ $6	3,000 @ $11
	1,000 @ $9		
Total available for sale	7,000	5,000	5,000
Sales—1987	3,000	1,000	3,500
Inv., Dec. 31, 1987	4,000	4,000	1,500
Purchases—1988	1,000 @ $8	2,000 @ $6	3,000 @ $11
	3,000 @ $10		
Total available for sale	8,000	6,000	4,500
Sales—1988	3,500	2,500	2,000
Inv., Dec. 31, 1988	4,500	3,500	2,500

Inventory valuations using specific-goods LIFO pools:

	Inventory Pool A		Inventory Pool B		Inventory Pool C	
Inv., Dec. 31, 1986	3,000 @ $6	$18,000	3,000 @ $5	$15,000	2,000 @ $10	$20,000
Inv., Dec. 31, 1987	3,000 @ $6	$18,000	3,000 @ $5	$15,000	1,500 @ $10	$15,000
	1,000 @ $7.50[1]	7,500	1,000 @ $6	6,000		
	4,000	$25,500	4,000	$21,000	1,500	$15,000
Inv., Dec. 31, 1988	3,000 @ $6	$18,000	3,000 @ $5	$15,000	1,500 @ $10	$15,000
	1,000 @ $7.50	7,500	500 @ $6	3,000	1,000 @ $11	11,000
	500 @ $9.50[2]	4,750				
	4,500	$30,250	3,500	$18,000	2,500	$26,000

[1]Cost of units acquired in 1987, $30,000, divided by number of units acquired, 4,000, or $7.50.
[2]Cost of units acquired in 1988, $38,000, divided by number of units acquired, 4,000, or $9.50.

The layer process for LIFO inventories may be further illustrated as shown below.

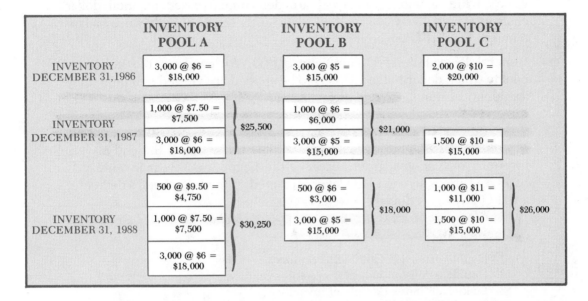

A new layer was added to Inventory Pool A each year. Previously established layers were reduced in 1988 for Inventory Pool B and in 1987 for Inventory Pool C.

Last-In, First-Out Method—Dollar Value

Even the grouping of substantially identical items into quantity pools does not produce all the benefits desired from the use of the LIFO method. Technological changes sometimes introduce new products thus requiring the elimination of inventory in old pools, and requiring the establishment of new pools for the new product that no longer qualifies as being substantially identical. For example, the introduction of synthetic fabrics to replace cotton meant that "cotton" pools were eliminated and new "synthetic fabric" pools established. This change resulted in the loss of lower LIFO bases by companies changing the type of fabrics they used. To overcome this type of problem and to further simplify the clerical work involved, the **dollar-value LIFO inventory method** was developed.[6] Under this method,

---

[6]When new items are introduced, the dollar-value LIFO method does not give the same result as the specific-goods LIFO method. See D. R. Bainbridge, "Is Dollar-Value LIFO Consistent with Authoritative GAAP?" *Journal of Accounting, Auditing, and Finance* (Summer 1984), pp. 334-346, for a discussion as to why dollar-value LIFO may violate the historical cost principle and the concept of financial capital maintenance.

the unit of measurement is the dollar rather than the quantity of goods. All similar items, such as all raw materials for a given line of business, are grouped into a pool, and layers are determined based on total dollar changes. The dollar-value method is currently the most widely used adaptation of the LIFO concept.[7]

General Procedures—Dollar-Value LIFO. All goods in the inventory pool to which dollar-value LIFO is to be applied are viewed as though they are identical items. To determine if the dollar quantity of inventory has increased during the year, it is necessary to value the ending inventory in a pool at the base-year prices and compare the total with that at the beginning of the year, also valued at base-year prices. If the end-of-year inventory at base-year prices exceeds the beginning-of-year inventory at base-year prices, a new LIFO layer is created. If there has been a decrease, a LIFO layer is reduced.

The following four techniques are applied in practice to determine the ending inventory at base-year prices:

1. Double extension (100% of inventory)
2. Double extension index (sample of inventory)
3. Link-chain index (sample of inventory)
4. Externally published index

The income tax regulations specify that the preferred technique is **double extension**. This technique results in a direct computation of the ending inventory at base-year prices because it requires extending *all* items in the ending inventory at both the base-year and the end-of-year prices. Because the double extension technique is time consuming when there are many inventory items, the IRS has permitted the use of an index approach to compute the ending inventory at base-year prices. The IRS has ruled that the preferred index is an internal one developed from a sample of items from the company inventory. Under certain conditions, the IRS has permitted the use of an externally published index.

In practice, most companies have adopted some form of an index method, therefore, the examples and discussion that follow are based on the use of indexes. A further discussion of different types of indexes is included in the Appendix to this chapter.

Assume the index numbers and inventories at end-of-year prices for Ahlander Wholesale Co. are as follows:

---

[7]Maurice E. Stark, "A Survey of LIFO Inventory Application Techniques," *The Accounting Review* (January, 1978), pp. 182–185.

Date	Year-End Price Index[1]	Inventory at End-of-Year Prices
December 31, 1984	1.00	$38,000
December 31, 1985	1.20	54,000
December 31, 1986	1.32	66,000
December 31, 1987	1.40	56,000
December 31, 1988	1.25	55,000

[1]Many published indexes appear as percentages without decimals, e.g., 100, 120, 132, 140, 125.

The effects of adding or deleting inventory layers in this situation can be most easily observed by preparing a work sheet that includes the following steps:

1. Determine the ending inventory in the pool at year-end prices.
2. Convert the ending inventory to base-year prices using the year-end price index.
3. Determine the inventory layers in base-year dollars.
4. Adjust the inventory to dollar value LIFO layers by applying appropriate indexes to each base-year layer.

The work sheet shown below follows these steps and is based on the assumed data for Ahlander.

Date	Inventory at End-of-Year Prices		Year-End Price Index		Inventory at Base-Year Prices	Layers in Base-Year Prices		Incremental Layer Index		Dollar-Value LIFO Cost
December 31, 1984	$38,000	÷	1.00	=	$38,000	$38,000	×	1.00	=	$38,000
December 31, 1985	$54,000	÷	1.20	=	$45,000	$38,000	×	1.00	=	$38,000
						7,000	×	1.20	=	8,400
						$45,000				$46,400
December 31, 1986	$66,000	÷	1.32	=	$50,000	$38,000	×	1.00	=	$38,000
						7,000	×	1.20	=	8,400
						5,000	×	1.32	=	6,600
						$50,000				$53,000
December 31, 1987	$56,000	÷	1.40	=	$40,000	$38,000	×	1.00	=	$38,000
						2,000	×	1.20	=	2,400
						$40,000				$40,400
December 31, 1988	$55,000	÷	1.25	=	$44,000	$38,000	×	1.00	=	$38,000
						2,000	×	1.20	=	2,400
						4,000	×	1.25	=	5,000
						$44,000				$45,400

Reflects inflation & deflation

The following items should be observed in the example:

December 31, 1985 — With an ending inventory of $45,000 in terms of base prices, the inventory has increased in 1985 by $7,000; however, the $7,000 increase is stated in terms of the base year and needs to be restated in terms of 1985 year-end prices which are 120% of the base level.

December 31, 1986 — With an ending inventory of $50,000 in terms of base prices, the inventory has increased in 1986 by another $5,000; however, the $5,000 increase is stated in terms of the pricing when LIFO was adopted and needs to be restated in terms of 1986 year-end costs which are 132% of the base level.

December 31, 1987 — When the ending inventory of $40,000 (expressed in base-year dollars) is compared to the beginning inventory of $50,000 (also expressed in base-year dollars), it is apparent that the inventory has been decreased by $10,000, in base-year terms. Under LIFO procedures, the decrease is assumed to take place in the most recently added layers, reducing or eliminating them. As a result, the 1986 layer, priced at $5,000 in base-year terms, is completely eliminated, and $5,000 of the $7,000 layer from 1985 is eliminated. This leaves only $2,000 of the 1985 layer, plus the base-year amount. The remaining $2,000 of the 1985 layer is multiplied by 1.20 to restate it to 1985 dollars, and is added to the base-year amount to arrive at the ending inventory amount of $40,400.

December 31, 1988 — The ending inventory of $44,000 in terms of the base prices indicates an inventory increase for 1988 of $4,000; this increase requires restatement in terms of 1988 year-end prices which are 125% of the base level.

As discussed earlier, the Internal Revenue Service allows the incremental LIFO layer to be valued using FIFO, average, or LIFO costing. Thus, the incremental index used to compute the new layer may be (1) a beginning-of-year index representing costs in the order of acquisition during the year (LIFO costing); (2) an average index, based on an average purchase price during the year (average costing); or (3) a year-end index, based on the latest acquisition price (FIFO costing).[8]

When FIFO costing is used to value the incremental layer, as in the previous example, the incremental index is the same as the year-end index

---

[8]The Task Force on LIFO Inventory Problems considered this issue from an accounting principles standpoint, and unanimously agreed that "the order of acquisition approach (LIFO costing) generally is most compatible with the LIFO objective but as a practical matter, any of the three pricing approaches consistently applied may be used for financial reporting purposes." *Issues Paper*, "Identification and Discussion of Certain Financial Accounting and Reporting Issues Concerning LIFO Inventories." (New York: American Institute of Certified Public Accountants, 1984), p. 9.

used to determine if a new layer exists. However, if average or LIFO costing is used to compute the new layer, the incremental index will differ from the year-end index. To illustrate, using data from the preceding example, assume that LIFO costing is used to value incremental inventory layers. The beginning-of-year indexes, representing the earliest purchases in each year, are follows:

Date	Price Index Beginning-of-Year Purchases
December 31, 1985	1.02
December 31, 1986	1.21
December 31, 1987	1.35
December 31, 1988	1.38

The computation of year-end inventories would then be made as follows:

Date	Inventory at End-of-Year Prices		Year-End Price Index		Inventory at Base-Year Prices	Layers in Base-Year Prices		Incremental Layer Index		Dollar-Value LIFO Cost
December 31, 1984	$38,000	÷	1.00	=	$38,000	$38,000	×	1.00	=	$38,000
December 31, 1985	$54,000	÷	1.20	=	$45,000	$38,000	×	1.00	=	$38,000
						7,000	×	1.02	=	7,140
						$45,000				$45,140
December 31, 1986	$66,000	÷	1.32	=	$50,000	$38,000	×	1.00	=	$38,000
						7,000	×	1.02	=	7,140
						5,000	×	1.21	=	6,050
						$50,000				$51,190
December 31, 1987	$56,000	÷	1.40	=	$40,000	$38,000	×	1.00	=	$38,000
						2,000	×	1.02	=	2,040
						$40,000				$40,040
December 31, 1988	$55,000	÷	1.25	=	$44,000	$38,000	×	1.00	=	$38,000
						2,000	×	1.02	=	2,040
						4,000	×	1.38	=	5,520
						$44,000				$45,560

In some cases, the index for the first year of the LIFO layers is not 1.00. This is especially true when an externally generated index is used. When this occurs, it is simpler to convert all inventories to a base of 1.00 rather than to use the index for the initial year of the LIFO layers. The computations are done in the same manner as in the previous example except the inventory is stated in terms of the base year of the index, not the first year of the inventory layers. To illustrate, assume the same facts as stated for the example on page 349 except that the base year of the external index is 1980; in 1984, the index is 1.20; and, in 1985, it is 1.44. The schedule showing the LIFO inventory computations would be modified as follows for the first two years. Note that the inventory cost is the same under either situation.

Date	Inventory at End-of-Year Prices		Year-End Price Index		Inventory at Base = 1.00 (1980 Prices)	Layers in Base = 1.00 (1980 Prices)		Incremental Layer Index		Dollar-Value LIFO Cost
December 31, 1984	$38,000	÷	1.20	=	$31,667	$31,667	×	1.20	=	$38,000
December 31, 1985	$54,000	÷	1.44	=	$37,500	$31,667	×	1.20	=	$38,000
						5,833	×	1.44	=	8,400
						$37,500				$46,400

Selection of Pools. The selection of inventory pools is critical in dollar value LIFO. A company should have a minimum number of pools to benefit most by the use of the LIFO method. For manufacturers and processors, **natural business unit pools** are recommended. If it can be shown that a business has only one natural business unit, one pool may be used for all its inventory, including raw materials, goods in process, and finished goods. If, however, a business enterprise is composed of more than one natural business unit, more than one pool will be required. If the company maintains separate divisions for internal management purposes, has distinct production facilities and processes, or maintains separate income records for different units, more than one business unit pool is inferred. The Income Tax Regulations give the following example of a company with more than one natural business unit pool:

> A corporation manufactures, in one division, automatic clothes washers and driers of both commercial and domestic grade as well as electric ranges, mangles, and dishwashers. The corporation manufactures, in another division, radios and television sets. The manufacturing facilities and processes used in manufacturing the radios and television sets are distinct from those used in manufacturing the automatic clothes washers, etc. Under these circumstances, the enterprise would consist of two business units and two pools would be appropriate, one consisting of all of the LIFO inventories entering into the manufacture of clothes washers and driers, electric ranges, mangles, and dishwashers and the other consisting of all of the LIFO inventories entering into the production of radio and television sets.[9]

A manufacturer or processor may choose to use **multiple pools** rather than include all inventory in natural business units. Each pool should consist of inventory items that are substantially similar, including raw materials.

Pools for wholesalers, retailers, etc., are usually defined by major lines, types, or classes of goods. The departments of a retail store are examples of

---

[9]*Ibid.*, Sec. 1.472.8(b) (2) (ii).

separate pools for these entities. The number and propriety of inventory pools is reviewed periodically by the IRS, and continued use of established pools is subject to the results of the evaluation.

The Economic Recovery Tax Act of 1981 simplified the selection of pools for smaller businesses. Any business with average gross receipts not in excess of $2 million for the three most recent taxable years may elect to use a single inventory pool rather than identifying natural product pools.

COMPARISON OF COST ALLOCATION METHODS

In using first-in, first-out, inventories are reported on the balance sheet at or near current costs. With last-in, first-out, inventories not changing significantly in quantity are reported at more or less fixed amounts relating back to the earliest purchases. Use of the average method generally provides inventory values closely paralleling first-in, first-out values, since purchases during a period are normally several times the opening inventory balance and average costs are thus heavily influenced by current costs. Specific identification can produce any variety of results depending on the desires of management. When the prices paid for merchandise do not fluctuate significantly, alternative inventory methods may provide only minor differences on the financial statements. However, in periods of steadily rising or falling prices, the alternative methods may produce material differences.

Differences in inventory valuations on the balance sheet are accompanied by differences in earnings on the income statement for the period. Use of first-in, first-out in a period of rising prices matches oldest low-cost inventory with rising sales prices, thus expanding the gross profit margin. In a period of declining prices, oldest high-cost inventory is matched with declining sales prices, thus narrowing the gross profit margin. Using an average method, the gross profit margin tends to follow a similar pattern in response to changing prices. On the other hand, use of last-in, first-out in a period of rising prices relates current high costs of acquiring goods with rising sales prices. Thus LIFO tends to have a stabilizing effect on gross profit margins.

The application of the different methods, excluding specific identification, in periods of rising and falling prices is illustrated in the following example. Assume that the Wisconsin Sales Co. sells its goods at 50% over prevailing costs from 1985 to 1988. The company sells its inventories and terminates activities at the end of 1988. Sales, costs, and gross profits using each of the three methods are shown in the following tabulation.

	FIFO		Weighted Average[1]			LIFO	
1985:							
Sales, 500 units @ $9		$4,500			$4,500		$4,500
Inventory, 200 units	@ $5 $1,000		200 © $5	$1,000		200 @ $5 $1,000	
Purchases, 500 units	@ $6 3,000		500 @ $6	3,000		500 @ $6 3,000	
Goods available for sale	$4,000			$4,000		$4,000	
Ending Inv., 200 units	@ $6 1,200		200 @ $5.71 ($4,000 ÷ 700)	1,142		200 @ $5 1,000	
Cost of goods sold		2,800			2,858		3,000
Gross profit on sales		$1,700			$1,642		$1,500
1986:							
Sales, 450 units @ $12		$5,400			$5,400		$5,400
Inventory, 200 units	@ $6 $1,200		200 @ $5.71	$1,142		200 @ $5 $1,000	
Purchases, 500 units	@ $8 4,000		500 @ $8	4,000		500 @ $8 4,000	
Goods available for sale	$5,200			$5,142		$5,000	
Ending Inv., 250 units	@ $8 2,000		250 @ $7.35 ($5,142 ÷ 700)	1,838		200 @ $5 ⎱ 50 @ $8 ⎰ 1,400	
Cost of goods sold		3,200			3,304		3,600
Gross Profit on Sales		$2,200			$2,096		$1,800

[1]Totals in the illustration are calculated to the nearest dollar.

	FIFO		Weighted Average			LIFO	
1987:							
Sales, 475 units @ $10.50		$4,988			$4,988		$4,988
Inventory, 250 units	@ $8 $2,000		250 @ $7.35	$1,838		200 @ $5 ⎱ 50 @ $8 ⎰ 1,400	
Purchases, 450 units	@ $7 3,150		450 @ $7	3,150		450 @ $7 3,150	
Goods available for sale	$5,150			$4,988		$4,550	
Ending Inv., 225 units	@ $7 1,575		225 @ $7.13 ($4,988 ÷ 700)	1,604		200 @ $5 ⎱ 25 @ $8 ⎰ 1,200	
Cost of goods sold		3,575			3,384		3,350
Gross profit on sales		$1,413			$1,604		$1,638
1988:							
Sales, 625 units @ $7.50		$4,688			$4,688		$4,688
Inventory, 225 units	@ $7 $1,575		225 @ $7.13	$1,604		200 @ $5 ⎱ 25 @ $8 ⎰ $1,200	
Purchases, 400 units	@ $5 2,000		400 @ $5	2,000		400 @ $5 2,000	
Cost of goods sold		3,575			3,604		3,200
Gross profit on sales		$1,113			$1,084		$1,488

The foregoing transactions are summarized in the table at the top of page 355.

Although the different methods give the same total gross profit on sales for the four-year period, use of first-in, first-out resulted in increased gross profit percentages in periods of rising prices and a contraction of gross profit percentages in periods of falling prices, while last-in, first-out resulted in relatively steady gross profit percentages in spite of fluctuating prices. The weighted average method offered results closely comparable to those

Year	Sales	FIFO			Weighted Average			LIFO		
		Cost of Goods Sold	Gross Profit on Sales	Gross Profit % to Sales	Cost of Goods Sold	Gross Profit on Sales	Gross Profit % to Sales	Cost of Goods Sold	Gross Profit on Sales	Gross Profit % to Sales
1985	$ 4,500	$ 2,800	$1,700	37.8%	$ 2,858	$1,642	36.5%	$ 3,000	$1,500	33.3%
1986	5,400	3,200	2,200	40.7	3,304	2,096	38.8	3,600	1,800	33.3
1987	4,988	3,575	1,413	28.3	3,384	1,604	32.2	3,350	1,638	32.8
1988	4,688	3,575	1,113	23.7	3,604	1,084	23.1	3,200	1,488	31.7
	$19,576	$13,150	$6,426	32.8%	$13,150	$6,426	32.8%	$13,150	$6,426	32.8%

obtained by first-in, first-out. Assuming operating expenses at 30% of sales, use of last-in, first-out would result in a net income for each of the four years; first-in, first-out would result in larger net incomes in 1985 and 1986, but net losses in 1987 and 1988. Inventory valuation on the last-in, first-out basis tends to smooth the peaks and fill the troughs of business fluctuations.

Income Tax Considerations

The preceding comparison of cost methods was made without considering the income tax impact of the method used. As indicated earlier, if a company elects to use LIFO for tax purposes, it must also use some form of LIFO in its financial reports. In a period of inflation, the lower reported profit using LIFO results in lower income taxes. Thus, the tax liability on gross profit, assuming a 45% tax rate, for the three illustrated methods over the four-year period would be as follows:

	FIFO	Weighted Average	LIFO
1985	$ 765	$ 739	$ 675
1986	990	943	810
1987	636	722	737
1988	501	488	670
Total	$2,892	$2,892	$2,892

In this example, a complete cycle of price increases and decreases occurred over the four-year period; thus the total income tax liability for the four years was the same under each method. However, by using LIFO to defer part of the tax during 1985 and 1986, more cash was available to the company for operating purposes. In periods of constantly increasing inflation, the deferral tends to become permanent and is a condition sought by many companies. When inflation started to accelerate in the United

States in the mid 1970's, many companies began to report larger net incomes primarily caused by the illusory influence of holding gains. To protect their cash flows, a significant number of companies changed to LIFO inventory to reduce their present and future tax liabilities. These changes had to be approved by the Internal Revenue Service, and were subject to specific rules governing adoption of the LIFO method. The complexity of some of these rules deterred other companies from making the change even though the tax consequences promised to be favorable.[10]

When a company changes its method of valuing inventory, the change is accounted for as a change in accounting principle. If the change is *to* average cost or FIFO, both the beginning and ending inventories can usually be computed on the new basis. Thus, the effect of changing inventory methods can be determined and reported in the financial statements as explained in Chapter 23. If the change is *to* LIFO from another method, however, a company's records are generally not complete enough to reconstruct the prior years' inventory layers. Therefore, the base-year layer for the new LIFO inventory is the opening inventory for the year in which LIFO is adopted (also the ending inventory for the year *before* LIFO is adopted). There is no adjustment to the financial statements to reflect the change to LIFO. However, the impact of the change on income for the current year must be disclosed in a note to the statements. In addition, the note should explain why there is no effect on the financial statements. Required disclosures for a change to LIFO are illustrated in the following note from the 1985 annual report of The Pillsbury Company.

Inventories

Inventories are valued at the lower of cost or market, except grain inventories which are stated on the basis of market prices at May 31, including adjustment to market of open contracts for grain purchases and sales.

During Fiscal 1985, the Company changed its method of determining cost for substantially all domestic inventories, except grain inventories, from the first-in, first-out (FIFO) method to the last-in, first-out (LIFO) method. The Company believes LIFO results in a better matching of current costs and revenues.

---

[10]A survey in 1980 of 213 companies who were not using LIFO indicated many different reasons for their decision. Principal among them were (1) the company had no tax liability, (2) prices were declining in their industry, and (3) the change to LIFO would have an immaterial impact because of rapid inventory turnover. Michael H. Granof and Daniel G. Short, "Why Do Companies Reject Lifo?" *Journal of Accounting, Auditing, and Finance* (Summer 1984), pp. 323-333.

This accounting change increased inventories at May 31, 1985 and earnings before taxes on income in Fiscal 1985 by $2.3 million ($1.2 million net earnings—3 ¢ per share). The adoption of LIFO did not affect prior years' financial results because it does not change the opening inventory valuation.

EVALUATION OF LIFO AS A COST ALLOCATION METHOD

Because so many companies have resorted to LIFO as a means of reducing income and, consequently, their income tax liability, it is important to identify the advantages and disadvantages of this unique inventory method. Because it allocates only the incurred cost between the balance sheet and the income statement, it can only partially account for the effects of inflation.

Major Advantages of LIFO

The advantages of LIFO may be summarized as follows:

Tax Benefits. Temporary or permanent deferrals of income taxes can be achieved with LIFO, resulting in current cash savings. These deferrals continue as long as the price level is increasing and inventory quantities do not decline. The improved cash flow enables a company to either decrease its borrowing and reduce interest cost, or invest the savings to produce revenue.

Better Measurement of Income. Because LIFO allocates the most recently incurred costs to cost of sales, this method produces an income figure that tends to report only the operating income and defers recognition of the holding gain until prices or quantities decline. The illusory inflation profits discussed earlier tend not to appear as part of net income when LIFO inventory is used.

Major Disadvantages of LIFO

The disadvantages of LIFO are more subtle than the advantages. Companies adopting LIFO sometimes realize too late that LIFO can produce some severe side effects.

Reduced Income. The application of the most recent prices against current revenue produces a decrease in net income in an inflationary period. If management's goal is to maximize reported income, the adoption of LIFO will produce results that are in opposition to that goal.

Investors and other users of financial statements frequently base their evaluations of a company's performance on the "bottom line" or net income. Failure on the part of users to recognize that a lower net income is due to the use of LIFO rather than a decline in operating proficiency may have a depressing effect on the market price of a company's stock. The reduced income may be perceived as a failure on the part of management. Further, the use of LIFO will reduce bonus payments to employees that are based on net income and could reduce the amount of dividends distributed to shareholders.

Unrealistic Inventory Balances on the Balance Sheet. The allocation of older inventory costs to the balance sheet can cause a serious under-statement of inventory values. Depending on the length of time the LIFO layers have been developing and the severity of the price increase, the reported inventory values can be substantially lower than current replace-ment values. For example, Note 5 to the General Mills statements re-produced in Appendix A at the end of the text states that if the FIFO method had been used, inventories would be $47.5 million higher in 1985 than the reported LIFO inventory. This is approximately 28% of the LIFO valued inventory. Because inventory costs enter into the determination of working capital, the current ratio can be seriously distorted under a LIFO inventory system. Although this discussion of LIFO assumes an inflationary economy, if prices were to decrease, LIFO would produce inventory values higher than current replacement costs. It is fair to assume that should this occur, there would be strong pressure for special action to permit the write-down of inventory balances to replacement cost.

Unanticipated Profits Created by Failing to Maintain Inventory Quan-tities. The income advantages summarized previously will be realized only if inventory quantity levels are maintained. If the ending inventory quan-tities decline, the layers of cost eliminated are charged against current revenue. If the inventory costs of these layers are significantly less than the current replacement costs, the reported profit will be artificially increased by the failure to maintain inventory levels.

Two specific examples may clarify this weakness.

1. Many companies who rely upon steel as a basic raw material for their production processes use the LIFO inventory method. Assume that during an extended steel strike many manufacturing companies find their steel stock dwindling as their fiscal year-end approaches. Unless they can restock their inventories, they will be forced to match lower inventory costs against current revenue, thus reporting a substantial holding gain in current profit. Assume, for instance, that company sales for the year are $6,000,000 and that the cost of goods sold using current year prices is $5,000,000 but using

a mixture of current year and earlier years' lower priced LIFO layers, the cost of goods sold is $4,000,000. The resulting increase in profit of $1,000,000 is caused solely by the inability of the company to replace its normal stocks.

2. The failure to protect LIFO layers may be caused by a timing error in requesting shipments of purchases. Assume that a lumber company normally received its lumber by ship, but that at year-end, orders were mishandled and a boat load was not received as planned. The company, in failing to record the boat load of lumber as a current year purchase, would have to apply older LIFO costs against sales. The resulting profit could lead to conclusions that would not be justified by the facts.

To avoid the distortion caused by a temporary reduction of LIFO layers at the end of a year, some accountants advocate establishing a replacement allowance that charges the current period for the extra replacement cost expected to be incurred in the subsequent period when the inventory is replenished. However, the use of an allowance for temporary liquidation of LIFO layers, sometimes referred to as the **base-stock method**, is not currently acceptable for financial reporting or tax purposes. The use of this type of allowance on the books could disqualify a company from filing its tax returns on the LIFO basis, and therefore, it is seldom used in practice.

Unrealistic Flow Assumptions. The cost assignment resulting from the application of LIFO does not normally approximate the physical movement of goods through the business. One would seldom encounter in practice the actual use or transfer of goods on a last-in, first-out basis.

Companies using LIFO cost in their statements sometimes justify the method in the notes to the statements. In a note to the 1984 financial statements (see below), Magic Chef, Inc. not only justified use of LIFO, but also discussed the impact of reductions in LIFO layers.

MAGIC CHEF, INC.

Inventories:

Inventories are generally stated at last-in, first-out cost (LIFO) which is not in excess of market. (See Note 5 to the consolidated financial statements.)

NOTES TO CONSOLIDATED FINANCIAL STATEMENTS

5. Inventories and Cost of Sales

The components of inventories are as follows:

	1984	1983	1982
	(000 Omitted)		
Finished goods.......................	$140,832	$ 78,049	$ 87,014
Work-in-process......................	13,517	7,462	8,220
Raw materials and supplies............	52,964	39,044	38,011
Total................................	$207,313	$124,555	$133,245

Inventories are generally computed using the LIFO inventory method, which the Company believes more realistically matches current costs and current revenues. Had the Company's inventories been valued on the FIFO method, inventories would have been $29,247,000, $27,491,000 and $29,130,000 higher at June 30, 1984, July 2, 1983 and July 3, 1982, respectively. Net income would have been higher by approximately $948,000 ($.10 per share) and $2,558,000 ($.33 per share) in 1984 and 1982, respectively, and lower by $886,000 ($.11 per share) in 1983.

When using the LIFO method, reductions in inventory quantities will generally result in an increase in net income. This occurs because quantities being reduced flow through cost of goods sold at costs from prior years rather than at current costs. The increase in net income as a result of LIFO inventory liquidations was $635,000 ($.07 per share), $699,000 ($.09 per share) and $1,785,000 ($.23 per share) for fiscal years 1984, 1983 and 1982, respectively. During 1984, the Company began using the practical capacity method as the basis for fixed cost application. The effect of the change was to reduce net income by $1,581,000 ($.16 per share). These amounts were considered in determining the effect on net income above.

OTHER COST METHODS

The methods previously described for arriving at inventory cost are the ones most widely used. Several other methods are sometimes encountered and deserve mention.

Cost of Latest Purchases

Sometimes goods are valued at cost of the latest purchase regardless of quantities on hand. When the inventory consists largely of recent purchases, this method may give results closely approximating those obtained through specific cost identification or first-in, first-out procedures with considerably less work. However, when the quantities of goods on hand are significantly in excess of the latest quantities purchased and major price changes have taken place, use of latest costs may result in significant cost misstatement.

Standard Costs

Manufacturing inventories are frequently reported at **standard costs** — predetermined costs based on representative or normal conditions of efficiency and volume of operations. Differences between actual costs and standard costs for materials, labor, and factory overhead result in **standard cost variances** indicating favorable and unfavorable operational or cost experiences. Excessive materials usage, inefficient labor application, excessive spoilage, and idle time, for example, produce unfavorable variances, and these would be separately summarized in variance accounts.

Standard costs are developed from a variety of sources. Past manufacturing experiences may be carefully analyzed; time and motion studies, as well as job and process studies, may be undertaken; data from industry and economy-wide sources may be consulted. Standards should be reviewed at frequent intervals to determine whether they continue to offer reliable cost criteria. Changing conditions require adjustment in the standards, so that at the balance sheet date, standard costs will reasonably approximate costs computed under one of the recognized costing methods.

Direct Costing

A practice widely debated for many years is referred to as **direct costing, marginal costing,** or **variable costing.** Inventories under direct costing are assigned only the variable costs incurred in production — direct materials, direct labor, and the variable components of factory overhead. Fixed costs are treated as period charges and assigned to current revenue. Only costs directly related to output are assigned to goods and charged to the period in which the goods are sold; costs that are a function of time and that are continuing regardless of the volume of output — for example, supervisory salaries, depreciation, and property tax — are charged against revenue of the period in which they are incurred rather than in the period when goods are sold.

Support for direct costing is made on the grounds that it provides more meaningful and useful data to management than full costing. Direct costing enables management to appraise the effects of sales fluctuations on net income. Sales, current and potential, can be evaluated in terms of out-of-pocket costs to achieve such sales. The direct costing approach becomes a valuable tool for planning and control and is used by management to analyze cost, price, and volume relationships.

Although no objection can be raised to the use of direct costing when it is used for internal reporting and as a means for assisting management in decision-making, objection can be raised to the extension of direct costing procedures to the annual financial statements. In measuring financial position and the results of operations, inventories must carry their full costs including a satisfactory allocation of the fixed overhead costs. Fixed costs, no less than variable costs, are incurred in contemplation of future benefits and should be matched against the revenues ultimately produced through such efforts. When inventories are valued by direct costing procedures for internal reporting, they should be restated in terms of full costing whenever financial statements are to be prepared.

SELECTION OF AN INVENTORY METHOD

As indicated in this chapter, companies have many alternative ways to value inventories. Guidelines for the selection of a proper method are very broad, and a company may justify almost any accepted method. After a lengthy study of inventory practices, Horace Barden, retired partner of Ernst and Whinney, concluded his Research Study by stating:

> . . . one must recognize that no neat package of principles or other criteria exists to substitute for the professional judgment of the responsible accountant. The need for the exercise of judgment in accounting for inventories is so great that I recommend to authoritative bodies that they refrain from establishing rules that, in isolation from the conditions and circumstances that may exist in practice, attempt to determine the accounting treatment to be applied under any and all circumstances.[11]

Many companies use more than one method. For example, General Mills values some domestic inventories at the lower of LIFO cost or market and other inventories at the lower of FIFO cost or market.[12] The decision as to which method to use depends on not only the tax consequences but also the nature of the inventories themselves. Except for LIFO, a company may use a different inventory method for tax purposes than it uses for reporting purposes. This creates a timing difference and a need for interperiod income tax allocation. (See Chapter 20.)

Companies sometimes change their inventory methods, especially as economic conditions change. When inventories are a material item, a change in the inventory method by a company may impair comparability of that company's financial statements with prior years' statements and with the financial statements of other entities. Such changes require careful consideration and should be made only when management can clearly demonstrate the preferability of the alternative method. This position was emphasized by the Accounting Principles Board in Opinion No. 20 with the statement, "The burden of justifying other changes rests with the entity proposing the change."[13] If a change is made, complete disclosure of the impact of the change is encouraged by the FASB.

---

[11]Barden, p. 141.

[12]See Appendix A at the end of the text. Note 1D and Note 5.

[13]*Opinions of the Accounting Principles Board, No. 20,* "Accounting Changes" (New York: American Institute of Certified Public Accountants, 1971), par. 16.

APPENDIX
Determination of Price Indexes

The chapter illustrated the use of an index method to compute the ending inventory at base-year prices. There are two common approaches for determining price indexes for a particular inventory: (1) developing a specific internal index from the company's inventory records; or (2) using a published external index relating to the inventory.

Internal Indexes. A widely used technique for developing internal indexes for dollar-value LIFO is double extension. A **double extension index** is computed by extending a representative sample of a specific ending inventory pool at both base-year and end-of-year prices. An index can then be computed applying the following formula:

$$\text{Double extension index} = \frac{\text{Inventory extended at year-end prices}}{\text{Inventory extended at base-year prices}}$$

To illustrate, assume an inventory pool contained ten items. The following sample of four items was drawn to compute a double-extension index.

Item	Ending Quantity	Year-End Price	Base-Year Price	Extended Year-End	Extended Base-Year
A	200	$ 50	$30	$10,000	$ 6,000
B	500	70	40	35,000	20,000
C	150	30	25	4,500	3,750
D	200	100	60	20,000	12,000
Total				$69,500	$41,750

$$\text{Double extension index} = \frac{\$69,500}{\$41,750} = 1.66$$

The Internal Revenue Service has stated that a nonstatistical sample must include at least 50% of the items and represent 70% or more of the dollar value. Fewer items are necessary if a carefully constructed random sample is used.

The double extension index has two principal disadvantages: (1) it is time consuming and costly for companies having a large number of different inventory items; and (2) if new inventory items are being added, it may be difficult to determine base year prices for them. This latter disadvantage is overcome with the **link-chain index**. This modification of the double extension index requires extending a statistically representative portion of the ending inventory at end-of-year prices and beginning-of-year, rather than base-year prices. The index computed from this valuation is then multiplied by a cumulative index carried forward from previous years to determine the current index.

Using the inventory data on page 363, assume that the cumulative link-chain index at the beginning of the current year was 1.51. The following illustrates the computation of the yearly index, i.e., the new "link," and a new cumulative index to use for dollar-value LIFO purposes.

Item	Ending Quantity	Year-End Price	Beginning-of-Year Price	Extended Year-End	Extended Beginning-of-Year
A	200	$ 50	$46	$10,000	$ 9,200
B	500	70	65	35,000	32,500
C	150	30	30	4,500	4,500
D	200	100	85	20,000	17,000
Total				$69,500	$63,200

$$\text{Yearly Index} = \frac{\$69,500}{\$63,200} = 1.10 \text{ (new link)}$$

$$\text{Link-Chain Index} = 1.51 \times 1.10 = 1.66$$

This approach has the advantage of simplicity because historical records of base-year costs are not necessary. It permits adding new inventory items without causing difficulty in computing base-year prices for the new items. A company may change from the double extension index method to the link-chain index if it has had at least a 90% turnover of inventory items in the preceding five-year period.

External Indexes. Although many price-level indexes are published by governmental and private agencies, only the Bureau of Labor Statistics' (BLS) department store indexes were automatically acceptable for income tax purposes until the Economic Recovery Tax Act of 1981 was passed. This Act directed the IRS to prescribe regulations providing for an expansion of external indexes for use by LIFO companies. As a result, regulations were issued in 1982 permitting small businesses with annual sales of $2 million or less to use either monthly consumer price indexes (CPI) or monthly producer price indexes (PPI).[14] Companies that do not qualify as small businesses may use these same indexes, but they may only incorporate in their inventory calculations 80 percent of the reported change in the index being used. A separate index must be used for each inventory item that comprises more than 10 percent of the total inventory value. However, aggregation is permitted of each item comprising less than 10 percent of the total inventory value.

---

[14]*IRS Income Tax Regulations*, Section 1.472-8(e)(3)

The BLS department store indexes that are still acceptable for retail department stores are divided into twenty groups, and each group becomes a separate dollar-value pool.

The increased number of external indexes available was intended to make the LIFO method more feasible for smaller companies by reducing the cost of implementation required if an internal index must be developed. For this reason, the use of the additional external indexes is referred to as "simplified LIFO." The IRS has decided that adoption of these external indexes in place of internal indexes is a change in accounting method. Except for limited situations, companies making the change must obtain prior approval from the Commissioner of Internal Revenue.

The AICPA Task Force on LIFO Inventory considered the use of external indexes and recommended that the IRS regulations concerning their use be accepted for financial reporting except for the limitation on companies that do not qualify as small businesses and thus can incorporate only 80% of the index change in the inventory. By a vote of 5 to 3, the Task Force did not accept the limitation on the use of the external index for reporting purposes.[15]

QUESTIONS

1. What economic conditions make the allocation of inventory costs most difficult?
2. (a) What are the three cost elements entering into goods in process and finished goods? (b) What items enter into factory overhead?
3. Distinguish between raw materials and factory supplies. Why are the terms direct and indirect materials often used to refer to raw materials and factory supplies, respectively?
4. What are the advantages of using the perpetual inventory system as compared with the periodic system?

---

[15]Issues Paper, Task Force on LIFO Inventory, Accounting Standards Division, AICPA, "The Acceptability of "Simplified LIFO" for Financial Reporting Purposes" (New York: American Institute of Certified Public Accountants, 1982), p. 9.

5. Does the adoption of a perpetual inventory system eliminate the need for a physical count or measurement of inventories? Explain.

6. Under what conditions is merchandise in transit legally reported as inventory by the (a) seller? (b) buyer?

7. How should the following items be treated in computing year-end inventory costs: (a) segregated goods? (b) conditional sales?

8. State how you would report each of the following items on the financial statements.
   (a) Manufacturing supplies.
   (b) Goods on hand received on a consignment basis.
   (c) Materials of a customer held for processing.
   (d) Goods received without an accompanying invoice.
   (e) Goods in stock to be delivered to customers in subsequent periods.
   (f) Goods in hands of agents and consignees.
   (g) Deposits with vendors for merchandise to be delivered next period.
   (h) Goods in hands of customers on approval.
   (i) Defective goods requiring reprocessing.

9. (a) What are the two methods of accounting for cash discounts? (b) Which method is generally preferred? Why?

10. Theoretically, there is little wrong with inventory costing by the specific cost identification method. What objections can be raised to the use of this method?

11. What advantages are there to using the average cost method of inventory pricing?

12. The Wallace Co. decides to adopt specific goods LIFO as of the beginning of 1987, and determines the cost of the different kinds of merchandise carried as of this date. (a) What three different methods may be employed at the end of a period in assigning costs to quantity increases in specific lines? (b) What procedure is employed at the end of each period for quantity decreases of specific items?

13. (a) What is the LIFO conformity rule? (b) How has the rule changed since it was first adopted? (c) How might the changes in the conformity rule affect LIFO inventories reported on the financial statements?

14. What are the major advantages of dollar-value LIFO over specific goods LIFO?

15. Indexes are used for two different purposes in computing the layers of a dollar-value LIFO pool. Clearly distinguish between these uses and describe how the indexes are applied.

16. The selection of inventory pools is very important in using the dollar-value LIFO method of inventory costing. What factors should be considered in identifying the pools for a specific company.

17. Discuss the advantages and disadvantages of LIFO as a cost allocation method.

18. (a) What type of company is likely to use standard costs? (b) What precautions are necessary in the use of standard costs?

*19. Identify the three different types of indexes that can be used in applying dollar-value LIFO. What are the advantages and disadvantages of each?

*Relates to Appendix

DISCUSSION CASES

CASE 9–1   (Should we adopt LIFO?)

You are the controller of the Ford Steel Co. Assume the economy enters a period of rapidly increasing inflation. The turnover of inventory in your company occurs about once every nine months. The inflation is causing revenue to rise more rapidly than the historical cost of the goods sold. Although profits are higher this year than last, you realize that the cost to replace the sold inventory is also higher. You are aware that many companies are changing to the LIFO inventory method. But you are concerned that what goes up will eventually come down, and when prices decline, the LIFO method will result in high profits and taxes. Since declining prices are usually equated with economic recession, it is likely that the higher taxes will have to be paid at a time when revenues are declining.

What factors should you consider before making a change to LIFO? Based on the above considerations, what would you recommend?

CASE 9–2   (What is an inventoriable cost?)

You have been hired by Midwestern Products Co. to work in their accounting department. As part of your assignment, you have been asked to review the inventory costing procedures. In the past, the company has attempted to keep its inventory as low as possible to hedge against future declines in demand. One way of doing this has been to charge off as many costs as can be justified as expenses of the current period. Sales have declined, however, and the controller wants to include as high an ending inventory valuation as possible to show the stockholders a better income figure for the current year. Your study shows the following costs have been consistently treated as period costs:

Depreciation of plant
Fringe payroll benefits for factory personnel
Repairs of equipment
Salaries of foremen
Warehouse rental for storage of finished products
Pension costs for factory personnel
Training program—all employees
Cafeteria costs—all employees
Interest expense
Depreciation and maintenance of fleet of delivery trucks

Which of the items do you suggest could be deferred by including them as inventoriable costs? Evaluate the wisdom and propriety of making the suggested changes.

CASE 9–3   (How do we record cash discounts?)

Taylor Company, a household appliances dealer, purchases its inventories from various suppliers. Taylor has consistently stated its inventories at the lower of cost (FIFO) or market. Taylor is considering alternate methods of accounting for the cash discounts it takes when paying its suppliers promptly. From a theoretical standpoint, discuss the acceptability of each of the following methods:

1. Financial income when payments are made.
2. Reduction of cost of goods sold for period when payments are made.
3. Direct reduction of purchase cost.   (AICPA adapted)

CASE 9–4   (Which method shall we use?)

The Watts Corporation began operations in 1987. A summary of the first quarter appears below:

Purchases	Units	Total Cost
January 2	250	$23,250
February 11	100	9,500
February 20	400	38,400
March 21	200	19,600
March 27	225	22,275

Other Data	Sales in Units	Sales Price per Unit	Operating Expenses
January	200	$140	$9,575
February	225	142	7,820
March	350	145	7,905

The Watts Corporation used the LIFO perpetual inventory method and computed an inventory value of $38,300, at the end of the first quarter. Management is considering changing to a FIFO costing method. They have also considered using a periodic system instead of the perpetual system presently being used. You have been hired to assist management in making the decision. What would you advise?

CASE 9–5   (Must we lose LIFO layers?)

The Innovative Production Co. has used the LIFO method of valuing its inventories for several years. Layers for some of the inventory items are valued at amounts ⅓ to ½ of the current market price. The products manufactured and marketed by the company are subject to rapid technological obsolescence, and the company is continually developing new products and phasing out old ones. As items are discontinued, the company finds its income and taxes increasing as old costs are matched against current revenues. However, since new products must be produced at higher costs, it has been difficult to maintain a positive cash flow for the company. The president of Innovative Production, having heard a competitor mention dollar-value LIFO, approaches you, the chief accountant, with the following questions. "Would this help us? What differences are there between our LIFO system and dollar-value LIFO?"

EXERCISES

EXERCISE 9–1   (Passage of title)

The management of Wittusen Company has engaged you to assist in the preparation of year-end (December 31) financial statements. You are told that on November 30, the correct inventory level was 150,000 units. During the month of December sales totaled 50,000 units including 25,000 units shipped on consignment to Tippetts Company. A letter received from Tippetts indicates that as of December 31, they had sold 12,000 units and were still trying to sell the remainder. A review of the December purchase orders, to various suppliers, shows the following:

Date of Purchase Order	Invoice Date	Quantity in Units	Date Shipped	Date Received	Terms
12-2-87	1-3-88	10,000	1-2-88	1-3-88	FOB shipping point
12-11-87	1-3-88	8,000	12-22-87	12-24-87	FOB destination
12-13-87	1-2-88	13,000	12-28-87	1-2-88	FOB shipping point
12-23-87	12-26-87	12,000	1-2-88	1-3-88	FOB shipping point
12-28-87	1-10-88	10,000	12-31-87	1-5-88	FOB destination
12-31-87	1-10-88	15,000	1-3-88	1-6-88	FOB destination

Wittusen Company uses the "passing of legal title" for inventory recognition. Compute the number of units which should be included in the year-end inventory.

EXERCISE 9–2   (Passage of title)

The Oliver Manufacturing Company reviewed its in-transit inventory and found the following items. Indicate which items should be included in the inventory balance at December 31, 1987. Give your reasons for the treatment you suggest.

(a) Merchandise costing $2,350 was received on January 3, 1988, and the related purchase invoice was recorded January 5. The invoice showed the shipment was made on December 29, 1987, FOB destination.

(b) Merchandise costing $625 was received on December 28, 1987, and the invoice was not recorded. The invoice was in the hands of the purchasing agent; it was marked "on consignment."

(c) A packing case containing a product costing $816 was standing in the shipping room when the physical inventory was taken. It was not included in the inventory because it was marked "Hold for shipping instructions." The customer's order was dated December 18, but the case was shipped and the customer billed on January 10, 1988.

(d) Merchandise received on January 6, 1988, costing $720 was entered in the purchase register on January 7. The invoice showed shipment was made FOB shipping point on December 31, 1987. Since it was not on hand during the inventory count, it was not included.

(e) A special machine, fabricated to order for a particular customer, was finished and in the shipping room on December 30. The customer was billed on that date and the machine was excluded from inventory although it was shipped January 4, 1988.   (AICPA adapted)

EXERCISE 9–3   (Trade and cash discounts)

Wakefield Hardware regularly buys merchandise from Valley Suppliers and is allowed a trade discount of 20/10/10 from the list price. Wakefield uses the net method to record purchases and discounts. On August 15, Wakefield Hardware purchased material from Valley Suppliers. The invoice received by Valley showed a list price of $2,500, and terms of 2/10, n/30. Payment was sent to Valley Suppliers on August 28. Prepare the journal entries to record the purchase and subsequent payment. (Round to nearest dollar).

EXERCISE 9–4   (Net and gross methods-entries)

On December 3, Harold Photography purchased inventory listed at $8,600 from Haines Photo Supply. Terms of the purchase were 3/10, n/20. Harold Photography also purchased inventory from Glindmeyer Wholesale on December 10, for a list price of $7,500. Terms of the purchase were 3/10 eom. On December 16, Harold paid both suppliers for these purchases. Harold does not use a perpetual inventory system.

1. Give the entries to record the purchases and invoice payments assuming that (a) the net method is used, (b) the gross method is used.
2. Assume that Harold has not paid either of the invoices at December 31. Give the year-end adjusting entries, if the net method is being used. Also assume that Harold plans to pay Glindmeyer Wholesale within the discount period.

EXERCISE 9–5   (Inventory computation using different cost flows)

The Francum Store shows the following information relating to one of its products.

Inventory, January 1	300 units @ $17.50
Purchases, January 10.	900 units @ $18.00
Purchases, January 20.	1200 units @ $18.25
Sales, January 8	200 units
Sales, January 18	600 units
Sales, January 25	1000 units

What are the values of ending inventory under (1) perpetual and (2) periodic methods assuming the cost flows below? (Carry your unit costs to four places and round to three.)
   (a) FIFO
   (b) LIFO
   (c) Average

EXERCISE 9–6   (Inventory computation using different cost flows)

Diamond Corporation had the following transactions relating to Product A during September.

Date		Units	Unit Cost
September 1	Balance on hand	500 units	$5.00
September 6	Purchase	100 units	4.50
September 12	Sale..................	300 units	
September 13	Sale..................	200 units	
September 18	Purchase	200 units	6.00
September 20	Purchase	200 units	4.00
September 25	Sale..................	200 units	

Determine the ending inventory value under each of the following costing methods:

(1) FIFO (perpetual)
(2) FIFO (periodic)
(3) LIFO (perpetual)
(4) LIFO (periodic)

EXERCISE 9–7   (LIFO inventory computation)

Oldham Farm Supply's records for the first three months of its existence show purchases of Commodity AB as follows:

	Number of Units	Cost
August	5,500	$29,975
September	8,000	41,600
October	5,100	27,030

The inventory at the end of October of Commodity AB using FIFO is valued at $35,350. Assuming that none of Commodity AB was sold during August and September, what value would be shown at the end of October if LIFO cost was assumed?

EXERCISE 9–8   (Dollar-value LIFO inventory method)

The Johnson Manufacturing Company manufactures a single product. The management, Ron and Ken Johnson, decided on December 31, 1985 to adopt the dollar-value LIFO inventory method. The inventory value on that date using the newly adopted dollar-value LIFO method was $500,000. Additional information follows:

Date	Inventory at End-of-Year Prices	Relevant Price Index
Dec. 31, 1986	$583,000	1.10
Dec. 31, 1987	597,360	1.14
Dec. 31, 1988	681,250	1.25

Compute the inventory value at December 31 of each year using the dollar-value method, assuming incremental layers are costed at year-end prices.

EXERCISE 9–9   (Dollar-value LIFO inventory method)

Ella Ann Inc. adopted dollar-value LIFO on December 31, 1985. Data for 1985–1988 follow:

Inventory and index on the adoption date, December 31, 1985:
Dollar-value LIFO inventory. $250,000
Price index at year end (the base year) 1.00

Inventory information in succeeding years:

Date	Inventory at End-of-Year Prices	Year-End Index	Incremental Layer Index
Dec. 31, 1986	$314,720	1.12	1.01
Dec. 31, 1987	347,400	1.20	1.14
Dec. 31, 1988	353,822	1.27	1.20

(1) Compute the inventory value at December 31 of each year under the dollar-value method, assuming incremental layers are costed at beginning-of-year prices.
(2) Compute the inventory value at December 31, 1988 assuming that dollar-value procedures were adopted at December 31, 1986 rather than in 1985.

EXERCISE 9–10   (Inventory computation from incomplete records)

A flood recently destroyed many of the financial records of Gomez Manufacturing Company. Management has hired you to re-create as much financial information as possible for the month of July. You are able to find out that the company uses a weighted average inventory costing system. You also learn that Gomez makes a physical count at the end of each month in order to determine monthly ending inventory values. By examining various documents you are able to gather the following information:

Ending inventory at July 31. . . . .   50,000 units
Total cost of units available for sale in July $118,800
Cost of goods sold during July. . . . . $ 99,000
Cost of beginning inventory, July 1 . . . .   35¢ per unit
Gross margin on sales for July. $101,000

July Purchases

Date	Units	Unit Cost
July 4	60,000	$0.40
July 11	50,000	0.41
July 15	40,000	0.42
July 16	50,000	0.45

You are asked to provide the following information:
(1) Number of units on hand, July 1.
(2) Units sold during July.
(3) Unit cost of inventory at July 31.
(4) Value of inventory at July 31.

EXERCISE 9–11
(Computation of beginning inventory from ending inventory)

The Dayton Company sells Product Z. During a move to a new location, the inventory records for Product Z were misplaced. The bookkeeper has been able to gather some information from the sales records, and gives you the data shown below:

July sales: 53,500 units at $10.00
July purchases:

Date	Quantity	Unit Price
July 5	10,000	$6.50
July 9	12,500	6.25
July 12	15,000	6.00
July 25	14,000	6.20

On July 31, 15,000 units were on hand with a total value of $92,800. Dayton has always used a periodic FIFO inventory costing system. Gross profit on sales for July was $205,875. Reconstruct the beginning inventory (quantity and dollar value) for the month of July.

EXERCISE 9–12   (Impact on profit of failure to replace LIFO layers)

Broadbent Lumber Company uses a periodic LIFO method for inventory costing. The following information relates to the plywood inventory carried by Broadbent Lumber.

Plywood Inventory

	Quantity	LIFO Costing Layers
May 1.............	600 Sheets	300 Sheets at $ 8.00
		225 Sheets at 11.00
		75 Sheets at 13.00

Plywood Purchases

May 8.........................	115 Sheets at $14.00
May 17.........................	95 Sheets at $15.00
May 29.........................	200 Sheets at $14.50

All sales of plywood during May were at $20 per sheet. On May 31, there were 310 sheets of plywood in the storeroom.

(1) Compute the gross profit on sales for May, as a dollar value and as a percent of sales.
(2) Assume that because of a lumber strike, Broadbent Lumber is not able to purchase the May 29 order of lumber until June 10. If sales remained the same, recompute the gross profit on sales for May, as a dollar value and as a percent of sales.
(3) Compare the results of part (1) and part (2) and explain the difference.

EXERCISE 9–13   (Income differences — FIFO vs. LIFO)

First-in, first-out has been used for inventory valuation by the Arbon Co. since it was organized in 1985. Using the data that follow, redetermine the net incomes for each year on the assumption of inventory valuation on the last-in, first-out basis:

	1985	1986	1987	1988
Reported net income (FIFO basis)....	$15,500	$ 40,000	$ 34,250	$ 44,000
Reported ending inventories—				
FIFO basis........................	61,500	102,000	126,000	120,000
Inventories—LIFO basis	56,500	75,100	95,000	105,000

*EXERCISE 9–14 (Double extension and link-chain indexes)

On December 31, 1987, the controller of S & W Enterprises selected six items to use as a representative sample of the company's inventory. Information relative to these products was compiled and summarized in the following schedule.

Base year....................................... 1982
January 1, 1987 cumulative index................... 1.15

	Products in Sample Inventory					
	1	2	3	4	5	6
Historical cost..................	$ 20	$ 45	$10	$ 60	$100	$85
January 1, 1982 price...........	20	50	8	50	92	60
January 1, 1987 price...........	24	51	13	60	102	71
December 31, 1987 price........	26	55	17	66	111	78
December 31, 1987 quantity.....	400	530	60	180	780	30

(1) Compute a price index for use in determining the December 31, 1987 inventory:
   (a) at base-year prices assuming the use of double extension.
   (b) at beginning-of-year prices assuming the use of link-chain.
(2) Compute the link-chain index at January 1, 1988.

*Relates to Appendix

*EXERCISE 9–15 (Link-chain indexes)

On December 31, 1987, Irene's Toy Store took a statistical sample of its inventory. The inventory revealed the following information:

	Quantity		Cost	
	Dec. 31, 1986	Dec. 31, 1987	Dec. 31, 1986	Dec. 31, 1987
Transforming robots	600	750	$10.00	$12.60
Dolls...................	290	250	4.50	5.75
Stuffed elephants	260	140	7.10	7.80
Puzzles	440	376	3.50	3.90

The link-chain cumulative price index at December 31, 1986 was 1.51. Compute the cumulative index at December 31, 1987.

*Relates to Appendix

*EXERCISE 9–16 (Dollar-value LIFO inventory; link-chain indexes)

Stephanie's Fashion Clothing Store has hired you to assist with some year-end financial data preparation. The company's accountant quit three weeks ago and left many items incomplete. Information for computation of yearly price indexes and the inventory summary is in the table below. Stephanie's uses the link-chain index for LIFO inventory valuation.

	1986	1987	1988
Ending inventory at beginning-of-year prices (December 31)	$155,000	?	$191,500
Ending inventory at end-of-year prices......	?	$188,600	?
Beginning cumulative index at January 1 ...	?	?	1.775
Yearly price index........................	1.100	1.060	?
Cumulative index at end of current year	?	1.775	1.955

Determine the inventory data that are missing from the table. Carry each index to three decimal places.

Relates to Appendix

PROBLEMS

PROBLEM 9–1   (Inventory computation using different cost flows)

The Nemelka Corporation uses Part 210 in a manufacturing process. Information as to balances on hand, purchases, and requisitions of Part 210 are given in the following table:

	Quantities			Unit Price
Date	Received	Issued	Balance	of Purchase
January 8	—	—	200	$1.55
January 29	200	—	400	1.70
February 8	—	80	320	—
March 20	—	160	160	—
July 10	150	—	310	1.75
August 18	—	110	200	—
September 6	—	75	125	—
November 14	250	—	375	2.00
December 29	—	200	175	—

Instructions: What is the closing inventory under each of the following pricing methods? (Carry unit costs to four places and round.)
(1) Perpetual FIFO   (4) Periodic LIFO
(2) Periodic FIFO   (5) Moving average
(3) Perpetual LIFO   (6) Weighted average

PROBLEM 9–2   (Inventory computation using different cost flows)

Records of the Swasey Sales Co. show the following data relative to Product A:

March 2 Inventory... 325 units at $25.50	March 3 Sales .. 300 units at $37.50
6 Purchase... 300 units at 26.00	20 Sales .. 200 units at 35.70
13 Purchase... 350 units at 27.00	28 Sales .. 125 units at 36.00
25 Purchase... 50 units at 27.50	

Instructions: Calculate the inventory balance and the gross profit on sales for the month on each of the following bases:

(1) First-in, first-out. Perpetual inventories are maintained and costs are charged out currently.
(2) First-in, first-out. No book inventory is maintained.
(3) Last-in, first-out. Perpetual inventories are maintained and costs are charged out currently.
(4) Last-in, first-out. No book inventory is maintained.
(5) Moving average. Perpetual inventories are maintained and costs are charged out currently. (Carry calculations to four places and round to three.)
(6) Weighted average. No book inventory is maintained.

PROBLEM 9–3   (Inventory calculation — LIFO and FIFO)

The Stokes Manufacturing Co. was organized in 1986 to produce a single product. The company's production and sales records for the period 1986–1988 are summarized below:

	Units Produced		Sales	
	No. of Units	Production Costs	No. of Units	Sales Revenue
1986	320,000	$144,000	200,000	$173,000
1987	310,000	161,200	290,000	230,000
1988	270,000	153,900	260,000	221,000

Instructions: Calculate the gross profit for each of the three years assuming that inventory values are calculated in terms of:
(1) Last-in, first-out. (Average cost used for incremental layers.)
(2) First-in, first-out.

PROBLEM 9–4   (Computation of LIFO inventory with LIFO pools)

The Shurtliff Company sells three different products. Five years ago management adopted the LIFO inventory method and established three specific pools of goods. Shurtliff values all incremental layers of inventory at the average cost of purchases within the period. Information relating to the three products for the first quarter of 1988 is given below.

	Product 400	Product 401	Product 402
Purchases:			
January	1,000 @ $12.00	500 @ $25	5,000 @ $5.30
February.	1,500 @ $12.50	250 @ $26	4,850 @ $5.38
March	1,200 @ $12.25	—	3,500 @ $5.45
First quarter sales (units)	2,850	775	10,750
January 1, 1988 inventory	950 @ $11.50	155 @ $24	3,760 @ $5.00

Instructions: Compute the ending inventory value for the first quarter of 1988. (Round unit inventory values to the nearest cent and final inventory values to the nearest dollar.)

PROBLEM 9-5
(Computation of inventory from balance sheet and transaction data)

A portion of the Howe Company's balance sheet appears below:

	December 31, 1988	December 31, 1987
Assets:		
Cash......................	$353,300	$ 50,000
Notes receivable	-0-	25,000
Inventory	To be determined	199,875
Liabilities:		
Accounts payable...........	To be determined	$ 50,000

Howe Company pays for all operating expenses with cash, and purchases all inventory on credit. During 1988, cash totaling $471,700 was paid on accounts payable. Operating expenses for 1988 totaled $220,000. All sales are cash sales. The inventory was restocked by purchasing 1,500 units per month, and valued by using periodic FIFO. The unit cost of inventory was $32.60 during January 1988 and increased $.10 per month during the year. All sales are made for $50 per unit. The ending inventory for 1987 was valued at $32.50 per unit.

Instructions:
(1) Compute the number of units sold during 1988.
(2) Compute the December 31, 1988 accounts payable balance.
(3) Compute the beginning inventory quantity.
(4) Compute the ending inventory quantity and value.
(5) Prepare an income statement for 1988 (including a detailed cost of goods sold section). Ignore income tax.

PROBLEM 9-6   (Impact of LIFO inventory system)

The Ortiz Corporation sells household appliances and uses LIFO for inventory costing. The inventory contains ten different products, and historical LIFO layers are maintained for each of them. The LIFO layers for one of their products, Magic Chef, were as follows at December 31, 1987:

1986 layer	4,000 @ $90
1981 layer	3,500 @ $85
1977 layer	1,000 @ $75
1975 layer	3,000 @ $48

Instructions:
(1) What was the value of the ending inventory of Magic Chefs at December 31, 1987?
(2) How did the December 31, 1987 quantity of Magic Chefs compare with the December 31, 1986 quantity?
(3) What was the value of the ending inventory of Magic Chefs at December 31, 1988, assuming that there were 10,800 units on hand?

(4) How would income in part (3) be affected if, in addition to the quantity on hand, 1,250 units were in transit to Ortiz Corporation at December 31, 1988? The shipment was made on December 26, 1988, terms FOB shipping point. Total invoice cost was $131,250.

PROBLEM 9–7   (Dollar value LIFO inventory method)

Clifford's Repair Shop began operations on January 1, 1983. After discussing the matter with his accountant, Clifford decided dollar-value LIFO should be used for inventory costing. Information concerning the inventory of Clifford's Repair Shop is shown below:

Date	Inventory at End-of-Year Prices	Year-End Index
Dec. 31, 1983	$16,500	1.00
Dec. 31, 1984	32,000	1.18
Dec. 31, 1985	55,600	1.36
Dec. 31, 1986	32,300	1.14
Dec. 31, 1987	72,250	1.72
Dec. 31, 1988	42,100	2.05

Instructions: Compute the inventory value at December 31 of each year under the dollar-value LIFO inventory method, assuming incremental layers are costed at end-of-year prices.

PROBLEM 9–8   (Dollar value LIFO inventory method)

The Schroeder Company manufactures a single product. The company adopted the dollar-value LIFO inventory method on December 31, 1983. More information "concerning Schroeder Company is shown below:"

Inventory and index on the adoption date, December 31, 1983
Dollar-value LIFO inventory $300,900
Price index at year end (the base year) 1.18

Inventory information in succeeding years:

Date	Inventory at End-of-Year Prices	Year-End Price Index	Incremental Layer Index
Dec. 31, 1984	$363,000	1.320	1.240
Dec. 31, 1985	420,206	1.445	1.368
Dec. 31, 1986	435,095	1.505	1.452
Dec. 31, 1987	417,073	1.543	1.515
Dec. 31, 1988	451,627	1.588	1.552

Instructions: Compute the inventory value at December 31 of each year under the dollar-value LIFO inventory method.

PROBLEM 9–9   (LIFO inventory pools — unit LIFO)

On January 1, 1984, Burgess Company changed its inventory cost flow method from FIFO to LIFO for its raw material inventory. The change was made for both financial statement and income tax reporting purposes. Burgess uses the multiple-pools approach under which substantially identical raw materials are grouped into LIFO inventory pools; weighted average costs are used in valuing annual incremental layers. The composition of the December 31, 1986, inventory for the Class F inventory pool is as follows:

	Units	Weighted Average Unit Cost	Total Cost
Base year inventory — 1984	9,000	$10.00	$ 90,000
Incremental layer — 1985	3,000	11.00	33,000
Incremental layer — 1986	2,000	12.50	25,000
Inventory, December 31, 1986	14,000		$148,000

Inventory transactions for the Class F inventory pool during 1987 and 1988 were as follows:
1987
Mar. 1   4,800 units were purchased at a unit cost of $13.50 for $64,800.
Sept. 1   7,200 units were purchased at a unit cost of $14.00 for $100,800.
A total of 15,000 units were used for production during 1987.
1988
Jan. 10   7,500 units were purchased at a unit cost of $14.50 for $108,750.
May 15   5,500 units were purchased at a unit cost of $15.50 for $85,250.
Dec. 29   7,000 units were purchased at a unit cost of $16.00 for $112,000.
A total of 16,000 units were used for production during 1988.

Instructions:
(1) Prepare a schedule to compute the inventory (unit and dollar amounts) of the Class F inventory pool at December 31, 1987. Show supporting computations in good form.
(2) Prepare a schedule to compute the cost of Class F raw materials used in production for the year ended December 31, 1987.
(3) Prepare a schedule to compute the inventory (unit and dollar amounts) of the Class F inventory pool at December 31, 1988. Show supporting computations in good form.

(AICPA adapted)

PROBLEM 9–10   (Change from FIFO to LIFO inventory)

The Whitewater Manufacturing Company manufactures two products: Raft and Float. At December 31, 1987, Whitewater used the first-in, first-out (FIFO) inventory method. Effective January 1, 1988, Whitewater changed to the last-in, first-out (LIFO) inventory method. The cumulative effect of this change is not determinable and, as a result, the ending inventory of 1987 for which the FIFO method was used, is also the beginning inventory for 1988 for the LIFO method. Any layers added during 1988 should be costed by reference to the first acquisitions of 1988 and any layers liquidated during 1988 should be considered a permanent liquidation.

The following information was available from Whitewater inventory records for the two most recent years:

	Raft		Float	
	Units	Unit Cost	Units	Unit Cost
1987 purchases:				
January 7	5,000	$4.00	22,000	$2.00
April 16	12,000	4.50		
November 8	17,000	5.00	18,500	2.50
December 13	10,000	6.00		
1988 purchases:				
February 11	3,000	7.00	23,000	3.00
May 20	8,000	7.50		
October 15	20,000	8.00		
December 23			15,500	3.50
Units on hand:				
December 31, 1987	15,000		14,500	
December 31, 1988	16,000		13,000	

Instructions: Compute the effect on income before income taxes for the year ended December 31, 1988, resulting from the change from the FIFO to the LIFO inventory method.

(AICPA adapted)

*PROBLEM 9–11   (Link-chain index)

On December 31, 1988 Vellinga Architectural Supply took a statistical inventory items for the sample of its inventory. The inventory revealed the following information:

	Dec. 31, 1986		Dec. 31, 1987		Dec. 31, 1988	
	Quantity	Cost	Quantity	Cost	Quantity	Cost
Pencil leads	2,000	$ 5.00	2,000	$ 5.50	2,200	$ 5.40
Masking tape	1,000	3.00	1,000	3.30	800	3.50
Pink erasers	5,000	4.00	5,000	4.40	5,500	4.75
Vellum paper	3,000	12.00	3,000	13.20	3,200	14.00
Sketch pads	6,000	8.00	6,000	8.80	5,000	9.00
Triangles	1,000	8.00	1,000	8.80	1,000	8.50
Cost of Total Inventory at year-end prices		$750,000		$950,000		$1,020,000

Instructions:

(1) Compute the cumulative index for Vellinga Architectural Supply at December 31, 1987 and 1988 using the link-chain method. Assume the cumulative index at December 31, 1986 was 1.5.

(2) Compute the LIFO inventory at December 31, 1988. Assume the December 1986 LIFO inventory at base-year prices was $500,000, and the balance reported on the balance sheet was $625,000.

*Relates to Appendix

*PROBLEM 9–12   (Double extension index)

Sonja's Cosmetics Supply is interested in generating price indexes for inventory. To aid in accomplishing this task, on December 31, 1987, the controller assembled information on various inventory items.

	Dec. 31, 1984	Dec. 31, 1985		Dec. 31, 1986		Dec. 31, 1987	
	Cost	Quantity	Cost	Quantity	Cost	Quantity	Cost
Base make up.......	$ 8.00	2,000	$8.80				
Body lotion.........	4.50	1,000	4.80	1,500	$ 5.25		
Eye shadow........	6.00	5,000	6.15	5,025	6.35		
Bath oil............	5.50	3,000	5.70	3,200	5.90	3,500	$ 5.85
Blush..............	8.50	6,000	8.55	6,600	8.80	6,200	9.00
Facial cream.......	6.20	1,000	6.60	1,200	6.80	1,600	7.40
Carrying cases	14.00			2,000	14.80	2,200	15.75
Compacts..........	17.50					3,100	19.00
Mascara...........	3.25					5,500	3.95

The controller indicated that 1984 is the base year.

Instructions: Using the double extension method, compute the year-end price index at December 31, 1985, 1986, and 1987.

*Relates to Appendix

10

Inventories — Estimation and Noncost Valuation Procedures

Many difficult accounting issues can arise in measuring and recording inventory values. In Chapter 9, the basic cost flow methods were introduced and explained. This chapter introduces some inventory estimation techniques and addresses some specific valuation issues.

GROSS PROFIT METHOD

Estimates are frequently employed in developing inventory quantities and costs. The **gross profit method** of estimation is based on an assumed relationship between gross profit and sales. A gross profit percentage is applied to sales to determine cost of goods sold; then cost of goods sold is subtracted from the cost of goods available for sale to arrive at an estimated inventory balance.

The gross profit method is useful when:

1. A periodic system is in use and inventories are required for interim statements or for the determination of the week-to-week or month-to-month inventory position, and the cost of taking physical inventories would be excessive for such purposes.
2. Inventories have been destroyed or lost by fire, theft, or other casualty, and the specific data required for inventory valuation are not available.
3. It is desired to test or check the validity of inventory figures determined by other means. Such application is referred to as the **gross profit test**.

The gross profit percentage used must be a reliable measure of current experience. In developing a reliable rate, reference is made to past rates and these are adjusted for variations considered to exist currently. Past gross profit rates, for example, may require adjustment when inventories are valued at last-in, first-out, and significant fluctuations in inventory position and/or prices have occurred. Current changes in cost-price relationships or in the sales mix of specific products also create a need for modifying past rates.

The calculation of cost of goods sold and inventory depends on whether the gross profit percentage is developed and stated in terms of sales or in terms of cost. The procedures to be followed in each case are illustrated below.

Example 1: Gross profit as a percentage of sales.

Assume sales are $100,000 and goods are sold at a gross profit of 40% of sales.

If gross profit is 40% of sales, then cost of goods sold must be 60% of sales.

Sales......................	100%		Sales......................	100%
Cost of goods sold...........	?	=	Cost of goods sold...........	60%
Gross profit.................	40%		Gross profit.................	40%

Cost of goods sold, then, is 60% of $100,000, or $60,000. Goods available for sale less the estimated cost of goods sold gives the estimated cost of the remaining inventory. Assuming the cost of goods available for sale is $85,000, this balance less the estimated cost of goods sold, $60,000, gives an estimated inventory of $25,000.

Example 2: Gross profit as a percentage of cost (or markup on cost).

Assume sales are $100,000 and goods are sold at a gross profit that is 60% of their cost.

If sales are made at a gross profit that is 60% of cost, then sales must be equal to the sum of cost, considered 100%, and the gross profit on cost, 60%. Sales, then, are 160% of cost:

Sales......................	?		Sales......................	160%
Cost of goods sold...........	100%	=	Cost of goods sold...........	100%
Gross profit.................	60%		Gross profit.................	60%

To find cost, or 100%, sales may be divided by 160 and multiplied by 100, or sales may simply be divided by 1.60. Cost of goods sold, then, is $100,000 ÷ 1.60 = $62,500. This amount is subtracted from the cost of goods available for sale to determine the estimated inventory.

When various lines of merchandise are sold at different gross profit rates, it may be possible to develop a reliable inventory value only by making separate calculations for each line. Under such circumstances, it is necessary to develop summaries of sales, goods available for sale, and gross profit data for the different merchandise lines.

A common application of the gross profit method is the estimation of inventory when a physical count is impossible due to the loss or destruction of goods. For example, assume that on October 31, 1987, a fire in the warehouse of a wholesale distributing company totally destroyed the contents, including many accounting records. Remaining records indicated that the last physical inventory was taken on December 31, 1986, and that the inventory at that date was $329,500. Microfilm bank records of canceled checks disclosed that during 1987 payments to suppliers for inventory items were $1,015,000. Unpaid invoices at the beginning of 1987 amounted to $260,000, and communication with suppliers indicated a balance due at the time of the fire of $315,000. Bank deposits for the ten months amounted to $1,605,000. All deposits came from customers for goods purchased except for a loan of $100,000 obtained from the bank during the year. Accounts receivable at the beginning of the year were $328,000, and an analysis of the available records indicated that accounts receivable on October 31 totaled $275,000. Gross profit percentages on sales for the preceding four years were:

1983	28%	1985	23%
1984	25%	1986	24%

From these facts, the inventory in the warehouse at the time of the fire could be estimated as follows:

Estimate of sales January 1 to October 31, 1987

Collection of accounts receivable ($1,605,000 − $100,000)....		$1,505,000
Add accounts receivable balance at October 31, 1987		275,000
		$1,780,000
Deduct accounts receivable balance at January 1, 1987.......		328,000
Estimate of sales January 1 to October 31, 1987		$1,452,000

Average gross profit percentage on sales for past 4 years

$$\left(\frac{.28 + .25 + .23 + .24}{4}\right) \dots\dots\dots\dots\dots\dots\dots\dots\dots \quad 25\%$$

Average cost percentage on sales for past 4 years	75%
Estimate of cost of goods sold to October 31, 1987 ($1,452,000 × 75%)	$1,089,000

Estimate of inventory on October 31, 1987

Inventory January 1, 1987		$ 329,500
Add: Payments to suppliers—1987........................	$1,015,000	
Amounts payable to suppliers, October 31, 1987	315,000	
	$1,330,000	
Deduct accounts payable to suppliers, January 1, 1987	260,000	
Estimate of purchases January 1 to October 31, 1987		1,070,000
Goods available for sale...................................		$1,399,500
Estimate of cost of goods sold for 1987 (from above)		1,089,000
Estimated inventory, October 31, 1987		$ 310,500

RETAIL INVENTORY METHOD

The **retail inventory method** is widely employed by retail concerns, particularly department stores, to arrive at reliable estimates of inventory position whenever desired. This method, like the gross profit method, permits the calculation of an inventory amount without the time and expense of taking a physical inventory or maintaining a detailed perpetual inventory record for each of the thousands of items normally included in a retail inventory. When this method is used, records of goods purchased are maintained at two amounts — cost and retail. The computer has now made it feasible to maintain cost records for the thousands of items normally included in a retail inventory. A **cost percentage** is computed by dividing the goods available for sale at cost by the goods available for sale at retail. This cost percentage can then be applied to the ending inventory at retail, an amount that can be readily calculated by subtracting sales for the period from the total goods available for sale at retail.

The computation of retail inventory at the end of a month is illustrated by the following example:

	Cost	Retail
Inventory, January 1	$30,000	$45,000
Purchases in January	20,000	35,000
Goods available for sale	$50,000	$80,000
Cost percentage ($50,000 ÷ $80,000) = 62.5%		
Deduct sales for January		25,000
Inventory, January 31, at retail		$55,000
Inventory, January 31, at estimated cost ($55,000 × 62.5%)	$34,375	

The effect of the above procedure is to provide an inventory valuation in terms of average cost. No cost sequence, such as LIFO or FIFO, is recognized in the preceding computation; the percentage of cost to retail for the ending inventory is the same as the percentage of cost to retail for goods sold.

Use of the retail inventory method offers the following advantages:

1. Estimated interim inventories can be obtained without a physical count.
2. When a physical inventory is actually taken for periodic statement purposes, it can be taken at retail and then converted to cost without reference to individual costs and invoices, thus saving time and expense.
3. Shoplifting losses can be determined and monitored. Since physical counts of inventory should agree with the calculated retail inventory, any difference not accounted for by clerical errors in the company records must be attributable to actual physical loss by shoplifting or employee theft.

Although this method permits the estimation of a value for inventory, errors can occur in accounting for the dual prices and in applying the retail method. Thus, a physical count of the inventory to be reported on the annual financial statements is required at least once a year. Retail inventory records should be adjusted for variations shown by the physical count so that records reflect the actual status of the inventory for purposes of future estimates and control.

The accounting entries for the retail inventory method are similar to those made using a periodic inventory system. The retail figures are part of the analysis necessary to compute the cost of the inventory; however, they do not actually appear in the accounts. Thus, the following entries would be made to record the inventory data included in the preceding example.

```
Purchases .................................................  20,000
    Accounts Payable .....................................              20,000

Accounts Receivable.......................................  25,000
    Sales.................................................              25,000

Inventory ................................................  34,375
Cost of Goods Sold........................................  15,625
    Inventory ............................................              30,000
    Purchases ............................................              20,000
        To record ending inventory and cost of goods sold for year, and
        close out beginning inventory and purchases.
```

Markups and Markdowns—Conventional Retail

In the earlier inventory calculations, it was assumed that there were no changes in retail prices after the goods were originally recorded. Frequently, however, retail prices do change because of changes in the price level, shifts in consumer demand, or other factors. The following terms are used in discussing the retail method:

1. **Original retail**—the initial sales price, including the original increase over cost referred to as the **markon** or **initial markup**.
2. **Additional markups**—increases that raise sales prices above original retail.
3. **Markup cancellations**—decreases in additional markups that do not reduce sales prices below original retail.
4. **Net markups**—Additional markups less markup cancellations.
5. **Markdowns**—decreases that reduce sales prices below original retail.
6. **Markdown cancellations**—decreases in the markdowns that do not raise the sales prices above original retail.
7. **Net markdowns**—markdowns less markdown cancellations.

The difference between cost and actual selling price as adjusted for the described changes is referred to as the **maintained markup**.

To illustrate the use of these terms, assume that goods originally placed for sale are marked at 50% above cost. Merchandise costing $4 a unit, then, is marked at $6, which is the **original retail**. The **initial markup** of $2 is referred to as a "50% markup on cost" or a "33⅓% markup on sales price." In anticipation of a heavy demand for the article, the retail price is subsequently increased to $7.50. This represents an **additional markup** of $1.50. At a later date the price is reduced to $7. This is a **markup cancellation** of 50 cents and not a markdown since the retail price has not been reduced below the original sales price. But assume that goods originally marked to sell at $6 are subsequently marked down to $5. This represents a **markdown** of $1. At a later date the goods are marked to sell at $5.25. This is a **markdown cancellation** of 25 cents and not a markup, since sales price does not exceed the original retail.

Retail inventory results will vary depending on whether net markdowns are used in computing the cost percentage. When applying the most commonly used retail method, net markups are added to goods available for sale at retail before calculating the cost percentage; net markdowns, however, are not deducted in arriving at the percentage. This method, sometimes referred to as the **conventional retail inventory method**, is illustrated in the following example:

Net markdowns not deducted to calculate cost percentage (Conventional retail):

	Cost	Retail
Beginning inventory	$ 8,600	$ 14,000
Purchases	72,100	110,000
Additional markups		13,000
Markup cancellations		(2,500)
Goods available for sale	$80,700	$134,500
Cost percentage ($80,700 ÷ $134,500) = 60%		
Deduct: Sales		$108,000
Markdowns		4,800
Markdown cancellations		(800)
		$112,000
Ending inventory at retail		$ 22,500
Ending inventory at estimated cost ($22,500 × 60%)	$13,500	

The conventional retail method results in a lower cost percentage and, correspondingly, a lower inventory amount and a higher cost of goods sold than would be obtained if net markdowns were deducted before calculating the cost percentage. This latter method is illustrated at the top of page 388.

The lower inventory obtained with the conventional retail method approximates a **lower of average cost or market** valuation. The lower of cost or market concept, discussed in detail later in this chapter, requires recognition of declines in the value of inventory in the period such declines occur. Under the conventional retail method, markdowns are viewed as

Net markdowns deducted to calculate cost percentage:

	Cost	Retail
Beginning inventory	$ 8,600	$ 14,000
Purchases	72,100	110,000
Net markups		10,500
Net markdowns		(4,000)
Goods available for sale	$80,700	$130,500
Cost percentage ($80,700 ÷ $130,500) = 61.84%		
Deduct sales		108,000
Ending inventory at retail		$ 22,500
Ending inventory at estimated cost ($22,500 × 61.84%)	$13,914	

indicating a decline in the value of inventory and are deducted as a current cost of sales. When markdowns are included in the cost percentage computation, the result is an average cost allocated proportionately between cost of sales and ending inventory. Thus, only a portion of the decline in value is charged in the current period. The remainder is carried forward in ending inventory to be charged against future sales.

Markdowns may be made for special sales or clearance purposes, or they may be made as a result of market fluctuations and a decline in the replacement cost of goods. In either case their omission in calculating the cost percentage is necessary in order to value the inventory at the lower of cost or market. This is illustrated in the two examples that follow:

Example 1: Markdowns for special sales purposes.

Assume that merchandise costing $50,000 is marked to sell for $100,000. To dispose of part of the goods immediately, one fourth of the stock is marked down $5,000 and is sold. The cost of the ending inventory is calculated as follows:

	Cost	Retail
Purchases	$50,000	$100,000
Cost percentage ($50,000 ÷ $100,000) = 50%		
Deduct: Sales		$ 20,000
Markdowns		5,000
		$ 25,000
Ending inventory at retail		$ 75,000
Ending inventory at estimated cost ($75,000 × 50%)	$37,500	

If cost, $50,000, had been related to sales price after markdowns, $95,000, a cost percentage of 52.6% would have been obtained, and the inventory, which is three fourths of the merchandise originally acquired, would have been reported at 52.6% of $75,000, or $39,450. The inventory would thus be stated above the $37,500 cost of the remaining inventory and cost of goods sold would be understated by $1,950. A markdown relating to goods no longer on hand would have been recognized in the development of a cost percentage to be applied to the inventory. Reductions in the goods available at sales prices resulting from shortages or damaged goods should likewise be disregarded in calculating the cost percentage.

Example 2: Markdowns as a result of market declines.

Assume that merchandise costing $50,000 is marked to sell for $100,000. With a drop in replacement cost of merchandise to $40,000, sales prices are marked down to $80,000. Three fourths of the merchandise is sold. The cost of the ending inventory is calculated as follows:

	Cost	Retail
Purchases	$50,000	$100,000
Cost percentage ($50,000 ÷ $100,000) = 50%		
Deduct: Sales		$ 60,000
Markdowns		20,000
		$ 80,000
Ending inventory at retail		$ 20,000
Ending inventory at estimated cost ($20,000 × 50%)	$10,000	

If cost, $50,000, had been related to sales price after markdowns, $80,000, a cost percentage of 62.5% would have been obtained and the inventory would have been reported at 62.5% of $20,000, or $12,500. The use of the 50% cost percentage in the example reduces the inventory to $10,000, a balance providing the usual gross profit in subsequent periods if current prices and relationships between cost and retail prices prevail.

Freight, Discounts, Returns, and Allowances

In calculating the cost percentage, **freight in** should be added to the cost of the purchase; purchase discounts and returns and allowances should be deducted. A purchase return affects both the cost and the retail computations, while a purchase allowance affects only the cost total unless a change in retail price is made as a result of the allowance. Sales returns are proper adjustments to gross sales since the inventory is returned; however, sales discounts and sales allowances are *not* deducted to determine the estimated ending retail inventory. The deduction is not made because the sales price of an item is added into the computation of the retail inventory when it is purchased and deducted when it is sold, all at the gross sales price. Subsequent price adjustments included in the computation would leave a balance in the inventory account with no inventory on hand to represent it. For example, assume the sales price for 100 units of Product A is $5,000. When these units are sold for $5,000, the retail inventory balance would be zero. Subsequently, if an allowance of $100 is granted to the customer, the allowance would not be included in the computation of the month-end retail inventory balance. It would be recorded on the books, however, in the usual manner: debit Sales Allowances and credit Accounts Receivable.

Retail Method with Varying Profit Margin Inventories

The calculation of a cost percentage for all goods carried in inventory is valid only when goods on hand can be regarded as representative of the total goods handled. Varying markon percentages and sales of high- and low-margin items in proportions that differ from purchases will require separate records and the development of separate cost percentages for different classes of goods. For example, assume that a store operates three departments and that for July the following information pertains to these departments:

	Department A		Department B		Department C		Total	
	Cost	Retail	Cost	Retail	Cost	Retail	Cost	Retail
Beginning inventory..........	$20,000	$ 28,000	$10,000	$15,000	$16,000	$ 40,000	$ 46,000	$ 83,000
Net purchases...............	57,000	82,000	20,000	35,000	20,000	60,000	97,000	177,000
Goods available for sale......	$77,000	$110,000	$30,000	$50,000	$36,000	$100,000	$143,000	$260,000
Cost percentage.............	70%		60%		36%		55%	
Sales......................		80,000		30,000		40,000		150,000
Inventory at retail............		$ 30,000		$20,000		$ 60,000		$110,000
Inventory at cost.............		$ 21,000		$12,000		$ 21,600		$ 60,500

$54,600

Because of the range in cost percentages from 36% to 70% and the difference in mix of the purchases and ending inventory, the ending inventory balance, using an overall cost percentage, is $5,900 higher ($60,500 − $54,600) than when the departmental rates are used. When material variations exist in the cost percentages by departments, separate departmental rates should be computed and applied.

The retail method is acceptable for income tax purposes, provided the taxpayer maintains adequate and satisfactory records supporting inventory calculations and applies the method consistently on successive tax returns.

RETAIL-LIFO METHOD

The dollar value LIFO procedures described in Chapter 9 can be applied to the retail inventory method in developing inventory values reflecting a last-in, first-out valuation approach. The **retail-LIFO method** requires that index numbers be applied to inventories stated at retail in arriving at the quantitative changes in inventories. After the retail-LIFO layers have been identified and priced at the incremental layer index, a further adjustment is needed to state the inventory at cost. This is done by multiplying the retail inventory of each layer by the incremental cost percentage.

The incremental cost percentages for the retail-LIFO method are computed in a slightly different manner from that done for the conventional retail method. The two principal differences are:

1. Beginning inventory values are disregarded. The LIFO inventory is composed of a base cost and subsequent cost layers that have not been assigned to revenues. Because costs for prior periods remain unchanged, only the cost of a current incremental layer requires calculation.
2. Markdowns, as well as markups, are recognized in calculating the cost percentage applicable to goods stated at retail. Markdowns were not recognized in arriving at the cost percentage when the objective was to arrive at a lower of cost or market valuation. However, because LIFO measurements require inventory valuation in terms of cost, the recognition of both markups and markdowns is appropriate.

Even though the beginning inventories are not included in the computation of the cost percentage, they are used to determine the amount of retail inventory that should be on hand at the end of the period. Because the retail inventory is adjusted for markups and markdowns, the ending inventory is automatically stated at year-end retail prices.

To illustrate the computation of the retail-LIFO incremental cost percentage, the ending inventory at year-end retail prices, and the inventory at retail-LIFO, assume that the following retail-LIFO layer data apply to Morris Department Stores Inc. as of December 31, 1987.

Layer Year	Year-End and Incremental Price Index	Incremental Cost Percentage	Inventory at End-of-Year Retail Prices
1983	1.00	.60	$60,000
1984 (no layer)			
1985	1.05	.62	69,300
1986	1.10	.64	77,000
1987	1.12	.65	77,280

Assume that the 1988 year-end price index is 1.08. The incremental cost percentage and 1988 ending inventory at end-of-year retail prices are computed as follows:

	Cost	Retail
Beginning inventory—December 31, 1987		$ 77,280
Purchases.	$63,000	$ 98,000
Purchase returns.	(2,000)	(3,000)
Purchase discounts	(1,000)	
Freight in.	2,220	
Markups, net of cancellations.		8,000
Markdowns, net of cancellations		(1,000)
Totals to determine incremental cost percentage—retail-LIFO.	$62,220	$102,000
Incremental cost percentage ($62,220 ÷ $102,000) = 61%		
Goods available for sale		$179,280
Deduct: Sales		100,980
Ending inventory at retail (year-end prices).		$ 78,300

From these data, a worksheet similar to that illustrated in Chapter 9 for dollar-value LIFO can be constructed to determine the retail-LIFO inventory layers. One additional column is necessary to record the incremental cost percentage that will reduce the retail inventory to cost. It is important to note that the incremental cost percentage is used only if an incremental layer is added to the inventory in the current period. In the example, this situation occurred in 1984 when no layer was added. If the inventory level has declined, previous inventory levels will be reduced using the respective years' incremental layer index and incremental cost percentage.

Retail-LIFO Computation

Date	Inventory at End-of-Year Retail Prices		Year-End Price Index		Inventory at Base-Year Retail Prices	Layers		Incremental Layer Index		Incremental Cost Percentage		Retail-LIFO Cost
December 31, 1983	$60,000	÷	1.00	=	$60,000	$60,000	×	1.00	×	.60	=	$36,000
December 31, 1984	no layer											
December 31, 1985	$69,300	÷	1.05	=	$66,000	$60,000	×	1.00	×	.60	=	$36,000
						6,000	×	1.05	×	.62	=	3,906
						$66,000						$39,906
December 31, 1986	$77,000	÷	1.10	=	$70,000	$60,000	×	1.00	×	.60	=	$36,000
						6,000	×	1.05	×	.62	=	3,906
						4,000	×	1.10	×	.64	=	2,816
						$70,000						$42,722
December 31, 1987	$77,280	÷	1.12	=	$69,000	$60,000	×	1.00	×	.60	=	$36,000
						6,000	×	1.05	×	.62	=	3,906
						3,000	×	1.10	×	.64	=	2,112
						$69,000						$42,018
December 31, 1988	$78,300	÷	1.08	=	$72,500	$60,000	×	1.00	×	.60	=	$36,000
						6,000	×	1.05	×	.62	=	3,906
						3,000	×	1.10	×	.64	=	2,112
						3,500	×	1.08	×	.61	=	2,306
						$72,500						$44,324

INVENTORY VALUATIONS AT OTHER THAN COST

The basic cost procedures for determining inventory values have been discussed in this and the previous chapter. In some cases, generally accepted accounting principles permit deviations from cost, especially if a write-down of inventory values is warranted. The following sections of this chapter discuss some of these departures from historical cost and the circumstances under which they are appropriate.

Inventory Valuation at Lower of Cost or Market

The accounting profession has not permitted the recognition of unrealized holding gains on inventories, i.e., goods on hand cannot be "written up" to reflect price-level increases prior to sale. Conversely, however, the recognition of unrealized losses is required under generally accepted accounting principles. This is a reflection of the long-standing and often debated tradition of conservatism in asset valuation and income recognition.

Recognition of a decline in the value of inventory as a loss in the period in which the decline occurs is referred to as **valuation at cost or market, whichever is lower**, or simply **valuation at the lower of cost or market (LCM)**. The American Institute of Certified Public Accountants (AICPA) sanctioned this departure from cost in the following statement:

> A departure from the cost basis of pricing the inventory is required when the utility of the goods is no longer as great as its cost. Where there is evidence that the utility of goods, in their disposal in the ordinary course of business, will be less than cost, whether due to physical deterioration, obsolescence, changes in price levels, or other causes, the difference should be recognized as a loss of the current period. This is generally accomplished by stating such goods at a lower level commonly designated as market.[1]

In applying the lower of cost or market rule, the cost of the ending inventory, as determined under an appropriate cost allocation method, is compared with market value at the end of the period. If market is less than cost, an adjusting entry is made to record the loss and restate ending inventory at the lower value. It should be noted that no adjustment to LIFO cost is permitted for tax purposes; however, for financial reporting purposes, the lower of cost or market rule applies to all inventories. Appli-

---

[1]*Accounting Research and Terminology Bulletins—Final Edition*, No. 43, "Restatement and Revision of Accounting Research Bulletins" (New York: American Institute of Certified Public Accountants, 1961), Ch. 4, statement 5.

cation of LCM to LIFO inventories for financial reporting purposes does not violate the "LIFO conformity" rules if IRS approval is obtained.

Definition of Market. Market in "lower of cost or market" is interpreted as replacement cost with upper and lower limits that reflect estimated realizable values. This concept of market was stated by the AICPA as follows:

> As used in the phrase *lower of cost or market,* the term *market* means current replacement cost (by purchase or by reproduction, as the case may be) except that:
> (1) Market should not exceed the net realizable value (i.e., estimated selling price in the ordinary course of business less reasonably predictable costs of completion and disposal); and
> (2) Market should not be less than net realizable value reduced by an allowance for an approximately normal profit margin.[2]

Replacement cost, sometimes referred to as **entry cost**, includes the purchase price of the product or raw materials plus all other costs incurred in the acquisition or manufacture of goods. Because wholesale and retail prices are generally related, declines in entry costs usually indicate declines in selling prices or **exit values**. However, exit values do not always respond immediately and in proportion to changes in entry costs. If selling price does not decline, there is no loss in utility and a write-down of inventory values would not be warranted. On the other hand, selling prices may decline in response to factors unrelated to replacement costs. Perhaps an inventory item has been used as a demonstrator which reduces its marketability as a new product. Or perhaps an item is damaged in storage or becomes shopworn from excessive handling.

The AICPA definition considers exit values as well as entry costs by establishing a ceiling for the market value at sales price less costs of completion and disposal and a floor for market at sales price less both the costs of completion and disposal and the normal profit margin. The ceiling limitation is applied so the inventory is not valued at more than its net realizable value (NRV). Failure to observe this limitation would result in charges to future revenue that exceed the utility carried forward and an ultimate loss on the sale of the inventory. The floor limitation is applied so the inventory is not valued at less than its net realizable value minus a normal profit. The concept of normal profit is a difficult one to measure objectively. Profits vary by item and over time. Records are seldom accurate enough to determine a normal profit by individual inventory item. Despite these difficulties, however, the use of a floor prevents a definition of market that would result in a write-down of inventory values in one period to create an abnormally high profit in future periods.

---

[2] *Ibid.*, statement 6.

Application of the LCM rule may be summarized in the following four steps:

1. Define pertinent values: cost, replacement cost, upper limit (NRV), lower limit (NRV − normal profit).
2. Determine "market" (Replacement cost as modified by upper or lower limits).
3. Select the lower of cost or market (as defined in 2 above).
4. If write-down is required, prepare the entry.

To illustrate these steps, assume that a certain commodity sells for $1; selling expenses are $.20; the normal profit is 25% of sales or $.25. The lower of cost or market as modified by the upper and lower limits is developed in each case as shown in the illustration below.

			Market			
Case	Cost	Replacement Cost	Floor (Estimated sales price less selling expenses and normal profit)	Ceiling (Estimated sales price less selling expenses)	Market (Limited by floor and ceiling values)	Lower of Cost or Market
A	$.65	$ .70	$.55	$.80	$.70	$.65
B	.65	.60	.55	.80	.60	.60
C	.65	.50	.55	.80	.55	.55
D	.50	.45	.55	.80	.55	.50
E	.75	.85	.55	.80	.80	.75
F	.90	1.00	.55	.80	.80	.80

A: Market is not limited by floor or ceiling; cost is less than market.
B: Market is not limited by floor or ceiling; market is less than cost.
C: Market is limited to floor; market is less than cost.
D: Market is limited to floor; cost is less than market.
E: Market is limited to ceiling; cost is less than market.
F: Market is limited to ceiling; market is less than cost.

The following dollar line graphically illustrates the floor and ceiling range. B and A replacement costs clearly are within bounds and therefore are defined as market. D and C are below the floor and thus the market is the floor; E and F are above the ceiling and market therefore is the ceiling.

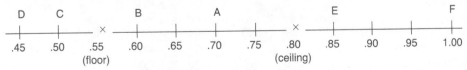

Note that the market value is always the middle value of three amounts: replacement cost, floor, and ceiling.

The last step is to prepare the journal entry to record the adjustment. Assume that the cost of the inventory at year-end was $75,000, and the market was $66,000. A reduction of $9,000 would normally be recorded as follows:

Inventory Loss Due to Write-down of Cost to Market............... 9,000
   Allowance for Write-down of Inventory to Market 9,000

The charge would be recorded in the income statement and the credit would be reported as a contra valuation account on the balance sheet.

Applying Lower of Cost or Market Method. The lower of cost or market method may be applied to each inventory item, to the major classes or categories of inventory items, or to the inventory as a whole. Application of this procedure to the individual inventory items will result in the lowest inventory value. However, application to inventory groups or to the inventory as a whole may provide a more representative valuation with considerably less effort. For example, assume that balanced stocks of raw materials are on hand, some have declined in value and others have gone up. When raw materials are used as components of a single finished product, a loss in the value of certain materials may be considered to be counterbalanced by the gains that are found in other materials, and the lower of cost or market applied to this category as a whole may provide an adequate measure of the utility of the goods.

The following illustration shows the valuation procedure applied to (1) individual inventory items, (2) independent classes of the inventory, and (3) inventory as a whole.

In valuing manufacturing inventories, raw materials declines are applicable to the raw materials inventory and also to raw materials costs in goods

| | | | | | | Cost or Market, Whichever is Lower | | |
| | | | | | | (1) If Applied to Individual Inventory Items | (2) If Applied to Inventory Classes | (3) If Applied to Inventory as a Whole |
	Quantities	Unit Cost	Market	Total Cost	Total Market			
Material A	4,000	$1.20	$1.10	$ 4,800	$ 4,400	$ 4,400		
Material B	5,000	.50	.40	2,500	2,000	2,000		
Material C	2,000	1.00	1.10	2,000	2,200	2,000		
Total raw materials........				$ 9,300	$ 8,600		$ 8,600	
Goods in Process D	10,000	1.60	1.40	$16,000	$14,000	14,000		
Goods in Process E	12,000	1.00	1.20	12,000	14,400	12,000		
Total goods in process				$28,000	$28,400		28,000	
Finished Goods F	3,000	2.00	1.70	$ 6,000	$ 5,100	5,100		
Finished Goods G	2,000	1.50	1.60	3,000	3,200	3,000		
Total finished goods........				$ 9,000	$ 8,300		8,300	
				$46,300	$45,300			$45,300
Inventory valuation.........						$42,500	$44,900	$45,300

in process and finished goods inventories. Declines in direct labor and factory overhead costs also affect the values of goods in process and finished goods, but these are usually ignored when they are relatively minor.

The method that is chosen for reducing an inventory to a lower value should be applied consistently in successive valuations. When valuing inventories by individual items, a lower market value assigned to goods at the end of a period is considered to be its cost for purposes of inventory valuation in subsequent periods; cost reductions once made, then, are not restored in subsequent inventory determinations. This restriction cannot be applied to inventories valued by major classes or as a whole when a record of the individual price changes is not maintained.

Accounting for Declines in Inventory Value. In valuing inventories at the lower of cost or market, a decline in asset value may be reflected directly in the inventory account or in a separate inventory valuation account. The loss on the decline in market value may be shown as a separate item in the income statement after cost of goods sold. Alternatively, the loss may be reflected directly in the cost of goods sold section by valuing the ending inventory at market rather than cost. Separate reporting of these changes has the advantage of providing readers with increased information to forecast operations and cash flows.

Conflict Between Tax Laws and Lower of Cost or Market Rule. A decline in inventory value may be deducted for federal income tax purposes as a loss in the taxable year in which such decline occurs. However, the deductible loss must be computed on an individual item basis. Thus, a company that applies the lower of cost or market rule to classes of inventory or to inventory as a whole for financial reporting purposes must make a separate item-by-item computation to obtain a tax deduction.

Disputes between taxpayers and IRS as to what constitutes a recognizable decline in inventory value have led to a number of court decisions. An important tax case in this area was settled by the U.S. Supreme Court in 1979.[3] The taxpayer, Thor Power Tool Co., had followed the practice of writing down the value of spare parts inventories that were being held to cover future warranty requirements. Although the sales price did not decline, the probability of the parts being sold, and thus the net realizable value, decreased as time passed. The write-down to reflect the current decline in value is consistent with the accounting principle of matching current costs and revenues. The Supreme Court, however, upheld the IRS position that recognition of declines in inventory values

---

[3]Thor Power Tool Company vs. Commissioner of Internal Revenue, *United States Supreme Court Reports*, Vol. 439, p. 532 (1979).

for tax purposes must await actual decline in the sales price for the parts in question.

This case is another illustration of a situation in which tax and financial accounting practices differ. Because the objective of levying taxes is not always compatible with an attempt to measure results of operations, differences will probably always exist. As explained in Chapter 20, this creates a constant need for interperiod tax allocation under the assumption that taxes are accruable as an expense. The U.S. Supreme Court recognized this difference in objectives in their conclusion to the Thor case as follows:

> Given this diversity, even contrariety, of objectives, any presumptive equivalency between tax and financial accounting would be unacceptable.[4]

Evaluation of Lower of Cost or Market Rule. As mentioned earlier, the lower of cost or market rule is evidence of the concept of accounting conservatism. Its strict application has been applied to avoid valuing inventory on the balance sheet at more than replacement cost. Also as discussed earlier, the AICPA replaced this strict entry valuation with a utility measure that relies partially upon exit prices. If selling prices for the inventory have declined and the decline is expected to hold until the inventory is sold, the adjustment of income in the period of the decline seems justified. The value of the inventory has been impaired, which requires current adjustment. However, care must be taken in using this method not to manipulate income by allowing excessive charges against income in one period to be offset by excessive income in the next period.

Some accountants have argued against the use of cost or market because it violates the cost concept. Market valuations are often subjective and based on expectations. To the extent these expectations are not realized, misleading financial statements will be produced. To illustrate, assume that activities summarized in terms of cost provide the following results over a three year period:

	1986		1987		1988	
Sales...........................		$200,000		$225,000		$250,000
Cost of goods sold:						
Beginning inventory............	$ 60,000		$ 80,000		$127,500	
Purchases....................	120,000		160,000		90,000	
Goods available for sale........	$180,000		$240,000		$217,500	
Less ending inventory..........	80,000	100,000	127,500	112,500	92,500	125,000
Gross profit on sales............		$100,000		$112,500		$125,000
Operating expenses.............		80,000		90,000		100,000
Net income		$ 20,000		$ 22,500		$ 25,000
Rate of income to sales		10%		10%		10%

---

[4]*Ibid.*, pp. 542–3.

Assume estimates as to the future utility of ending inventories indicated market values as follows:

1986	1987	1988
$75,000	$110,000	$92,500

If the expected decline in selling prices did not occur, inventory valuation at the lower of cost or market would provide the following results.

	1986		1987		1988	
Sales..........................		$200,000		$225,000		$250,000
Cost of goods sold:						
Beginning inventory............	$ 60,000		$ 75,000		$110,000	
Purchases....................	120,000		160,000		90,000	
Goods available for sale........	$180,000		$235,000		$200,000	
Less ending inventory..........	75,000	105,000	110,000	125,000	92,500	107,500
Gross profit on sales............		$ 95,000		$100,000		$142,500
Operating expenses.............		80,000		90,000		100,000
Net income		$ 15,000		$ 10,000		$ 42,500
Rate of income to sales		7.5%		4.4%		17.0%

Reduction of an inventory below cost reduces the net income of the period in which the reduction is made and increases the net income of a subsequent period over what it would have been. In the example just given, total net income for the three-year period is the same under either set of calculations. But the reduction of inventories to lower market values reduced the net income for 1986 and for 1987 and increased the net income for 1988. The fact that inventory reductions were not followed by decreases in the sales prices resulted in net income determinations that varied considerably from those that might reasonably have been expected from increasing sales and costs that normally vary with sales volume.

Objection to valuation at the lower of cost or market is also raised on the grounds it produces inconsistencies in the measurements of both the financial position and the operations of the enterprise. Market decreases are recognized, but increases are not. Although this system does produce some inconsistent application to the upward and downward movement of market, the authors feel that the lower of cost or market concept is preferable to a strict cost measurement. A loss in the utility of any asset should be reflected in the period the impairment is first recognized and a reasonable estimate of its significance can be determined.

Valuation at Market

When inventory prices are rising, there is pressure on accountants from management to move from the lower of cost or market method of valuing inventories and cost of sales toward a market valuation. Unlike the cost methods discussed in Chapter 9, a market method is not a cost allocation method and is thus not generally accepted for accounting purposes in most instances. However, because discussion of the market method is still prevalent, the application of it will be illustrated in this chapter.

Since both the cost of goods sold and the remaining inventory are valued at market prices (usually replacement costs), their sum will exceed the cost of the inventory purchased. The use of replacement cost to record the cost of goods sold permits the division of the gross profit into two parts: (1) the difference between the purchase cost and the replacement cost at the time of sale, referred to as a **holding gain**; and (2) the difference between the replacement cost and the selling price, which is the **operating profit**. Holding gains must be used to replace the sold inventory, and thus they are not available to pay dividends to stockholders.

This can be diagrammed as follows:

To illustrate this division, assume that a company purchased 100 units of inventory for $10 each or a total of $1,000. At the time of the purchase, it was anticipated that the inventory would be sold for $12.50 per unit, a markup on cost of 25%. Assume further that, prior to resale, the cost to acquire identical goods increased to $12 per unit, and the resale price was increased to $15 per unit to maintain the 25% markup. If the 100 units were sold, historical cost accounting would recognize sales revenue of $1,500 and cost of $1,000, or a gross profit of $500. However, replacement of the 100 units now requires $1,200 of the proceeds. Thus, $200 of the reported profit is really a holding gain and $300 is operating profit.

Using market valuation for inventories recognizes another holding gain during a time of rising prices; the gain on inventories not yet sold. These gains are referred to as **unrealized holding gains** because the inventory has not been sold. Continuing the above example, if only 80 units of inventory are sold, an unrealized holding gain of $2 per unit exists on the remaining 20 units, or $40. The $40 unrealized holding gain would be reported as revenue on the income statement under the financial capital maintenance income concept advocated by the FASB. On the other hand, if the physical capital maintenance concept were adopted, the credit entry would be made directly to the equity section.

There are a few instances where market valuation has become accepted for certain types of inventories. For example, market valuation has become an accepted practice within the mining industry for products such as gold and silver for which market is readily defined and tends to fluctuate dramatically, often in response to speculative trading activity. Similar conditions have led to the widespread use of market in valuing inventories of agricultural commodities. As discussed in Chapter 7, market is an acceptable method for valuing inventories of securities held by financial institutions and brokers and dealers in securities. These have been recognized by the accounting profession as special cases, acceptable within the framework of GAAP.

In the absence of general acceptance of using market prices to value inventories, accountants have frequently adopted some of the LIFO cost variations discussed in Chapter 9. As was observed in discussing LIFO inventory, this method approximates market on the income statement under some conditions. However, since LIFO is a cost allocation method, balance sheet valuations differ significantly from market prices when prices are changing.

The FASB and SEC require supplementary market inventory values for certain larger companies. The authors believe that financial information would be more realistic and relevant if a market-based accounting system were adopted for use on the books and in the general statements. Only when market valuation is uniformly adopted for all purposes can users of financial statements clearly evaluate the impact of inflation on a specific company. Such a step would eliminate the various alternative cost allocation methods currently used. Because market can be defined in different ways, the use of market valuation would not totally eliminate differences among companies, nor would it eliminate completely opportunities for manipulation of net income. However, issuance of specific guidelines by the FASB for applying market valuation could reduce the severity of these problems.

Losses on Purchase Commitments

Another special problem deals with purchase commitments. These contracts are frequently made for the future purchase of goods at fixed prices. No entry is required to record the purchase prior to delivery of the goods. However, when price declines take place subsequent to such commitments, it is considered appropriate to measure and recognize these losses on the books just as losses on goods on hand are recognized. A decline is recorded by a debit to a special loss account and a credit to either a contra asset account or an accrued liability account, such as Estimated Loss on Purchase Commitments. Acquisition of the goods in a subsequent period is recorded by a credit to Accounts Payable, a debit canceling the credit balance in the contra asset or accrued liability account, and a debit to Purchases for the difference.

For example, assume that Rollins Manufacturing Company entered into a purchase contract for $120,000 of materials to be delivered in March of the following year. At the end of the current year, the market price for this order had fallen to $100,000. The entries to record this decline and subsequent delivery of the materials would be as follows:

Dec. 31	Loss on Purchase Commitments		20,000	
	Estimated Loss on Purchase Commitments			20,000
Mar. 1	Estimated Loss on Purchase Commitments		20,000	
	Purchases		100,000	
	Accounts Payable			120,000

The loss is thus assigned to the period in which the decline took place, and a subsequent period is charged for no more than the economic utility of the goods it receives. Current loss recognition would not be appropriate when commitments can be canceled, when commitments provide for price adjustment, when hedging transactions[5] prevent losses, or when declines do not suggest reductions in sale prices. No adjustments are customarily made if a recovery occurs prior to delivery.

Valuation of Trade-Ins and Repossessions

When goods are acquired in secondhand condition as a result of repossessions and trade-ins, they should be recorded at their estimated cash purchase price. In some industries, these prices are defined and made available to dealers. One of the more organized used markets is that for automobiles. A book, published frequently in the various geographical markets of the country, lists low, medium, and high market values for the different models and makes of cars. It also distinguishes between retail and wholesale values. Similar lists are provided for machinery and equipment in some lines. When these publications exist, the prices listed may be used to value repossessed or trade-in inventory.

When published prices are not available, it is more difficult to measure the equivalent cash purchase price of the inventory. Under these conditions, the consistent use of **floor values**—amounts that, after adding reconditioning charges and selling expenses, will permit the recognition of normal profits—would be appropriate.

The accounting for trade-ins is illustrated by the following example: Christensen Department Store sells a new washing machine to a customer

---

[5]Purchases or sales entered into for the purpose of balancing, respectively, sales or purchases already made or under contract, in order to offset the effects of price fluctuations.

for $350 cash and a trade-in of an old washer. It is estimated that a realistic floor value for the trade-in is $50. Reconditioning costs of $30 are incurred after which the trade-in washer is sold for $120, an amount that provides a normal profit. Perpetual inventory records are maintained for trade-ins but not for the regular inventory. The entries shown below reflect these transactions:

Cash..	350	
Trade-In Inventory	50	
Sales..		400
Trade-In Inventory	30	
Cash...		30
Cash..	120	
Sales — Trade-Ins		120
Cost of Trade-Ins Sold	80	
Trade-In Inventory		80

Another approach to valuing trade-in inventories is to establish clearly the sales price of the new inventory being sold, and charge the trade-in inventory for the difference between a cash sales price and the cash required with the trade-in. Assume in the case of the washing machine that the regular cash sales price without a trade-in could be established at $390. The value assigned to the trade-in would thus be $40, the difference between $390 and $350.

Accounting for repossessions requires a slightly different approach. Assume Christensen Department Store sold another washing machine on account for $350 plus interest on the unpaid balance. The customer made principal payments of $200 on the machine and then defaulted on the contract. The machine was repossessed and overhauled at a cost of $40. It was then sold for $150, a price that provided a normal profit of 50% on cost.

The following entries reflect the repossession and subsequent resale.

Loss on Repossession	90	
Repossessed Inventory.....................................	60	
Accounts Receivable.....................................		150

Computation:
Value of repossession established to permit 50% normal profit on cost.
  (33⅓% on selling price.)

Selling price.....................................	$150
Less profit at 33⅓%	50
Cost of repossessed goods sold..................	$100
Less cost of overhaul	40
Value of repossessed inventory	$ 60

Repossessed Inventory.....................................	40	
Cash...		40
Cost to overhaul repossessed washing machine.		

Cash... 150
    Sales — Repossessed Inventory........................... 150
      Sale of repossessed washing machine.

Cost of Repossessed Goods Sold........................ 100
    Repossessed Inventory................................. 100
      Cost of repossessed washing machine.

EFFECTS OF ERRORS IN RECORDING INVENTORY POSITION

Failures to report the inventory position accurately result in misstatements on both the balance sheet and the income statement. The effect on the income statement is sometimes difficult to evaluate because of the different amounts that can be affected by an error. Analysis of the impact is aided by recalling the structure of the cost of goods sold section of the income statement:

Beginning Inventory
+
Purchases
=
Goods Available for Sale
−
Ending Inventory
=
Cost of Goods Sold

An overstatement of the beginning inventory will thus result in an overstatement of goods available for sale and cost of goods sold. Because the cost of goods sold is deducted from sales to determine the gross profit, the overstated cost of goods sold results in an understated gross profit and finally an understated net income. Sometimes an error may affect two of the amounts in such a way that they offset each other. For example, if a purchase in transit under the FIFO method is neither recorded as a purchase nor included in the ending inventory, the understatement of purchases results in an understatement of goods available for sale; however, the understatement of ending inventory subtracted from goods available for sale offsets the error and creates a correct cost of goods sold, gross profit, and net income. Inventory and accounts payable, however, will be understated on the balance sheet.

Because the ending inventory of one period becomes the beginning inventory of the next period, undetected accounting errors affect two accounting periods. If left undetected, the errors will offset each other under a FIFO or average method. Errors in LIFO layers, however, may perpetuate themselves until the layer is eliminated.

This type of analysis is required for all inventory errors. It is unwise to try to memorize the impact an error has on the financial statements. It is preferable to analyze each situation. The following analyses of four typical inventory errors, with their impact on both the current and succeeding years, provide additional opportunity for students to practice the above type of analysis.

1. Overstatement of the ending inventory through errors in the count of goods on hand, pricing, or the inclusion in inventory of goods not owned or goods already sold:

   Current year:

   Income statement—overstatement of the ending inventory will cause the cost of goods sold to be understated and the net income to be overstated.

   Balance sheet—the inventory will be overstated and the owners' equity will be overstated.

   Succeeding year:

   Income statement—overstatement of the beginning inventory will cause the cost of goods sold to be overstated and the net income to be understated.

   Balance sheet—the error of the previous year will have been counterbalanced on the succeeding income statement and the balance sheet will be correctly stated.

2. Understatement of ending inventory through errors in the count of goods on hand, pricing, or the failure to include in inventory goods purchased or goods transferred but not yet sold:

   Misstatements indicated in (1) above are reversed.

3. Overstatement of ending inventory accompanied by failure to recognize sales and corresponding receivables at end of period:

   Current year:

   Income statement—sales are understated by the sales price of the goods and cost of goods sold is understated by the cost of the goods relating to the sales; gross profit and net income are thus understated by the gross profit on the sales.

   Balance sheet—receivables are understated by the sales price of the goods and the inventory is overstated by the cost of the goods that were sold; current assets and owners' equity are thus understated by the gross profit on the sales.

   Succeeding year:

   Income statement—sales of the preceding year are recognized in this year in sales and cost of sales; gross profit and net income, therefore, are overstated by the gross profit on such sales.

Balance sheet—the error of the previous year is counterbalanced on the succeeding income statement and the balance sheet will be correctly stated.

4. Understatement of ending inventory accompanied by failure to recognize purchases and corresponding payables at end of period:

Current year:

Income statement—purchases are understated, but this is counterbalanced by the understatement of the ending inventory; gross profit and net income are correctly stated as a result of the counterbalancing effect of the error.

Balance sheet—although owners' equity is reported correctly, both current assets and current liabilities are understated.

Succeeding year:

Income statement—the beginning inventory is understated, but this is counterbalanced by an overstatement of purchases, as purchases at the end of the prior year are recognized currently; gross profit and net income are correctly stated as a result of the counterbalancing effect of the error.

Balance sheet—the error of the previous year no longer affects balance sheet data.

This analysis can be summarized in tabular form as shown at the top of the next page; (+) indicates overstatement, (−) indicates understatement, and (0) indicates no effect.

The correcting entry for each of these errors depends on when the error is discovered. If it is discovered in the current year, adjustments can be made to current accounts, and the reported net income and balance sheet amounts will be correct. If the error is not discovered until the subsequent period, the correcting entry qualifies as a prior period adjustment if the net income of the prior period was misstated. The error to a prior years' income is corrected through retained earnings. To illustrate these entries, assume that error number three has occurred. The correcting entries required, depending on when the error is discovered, would be as follows. Assume the use of a perpetual inventory system.

Error discovered in current year (cost of inventory $1,000; sales price of inventory, $1,500).

Accounts Receivable	1,500	
Cost of Goods Sold	1,000	
Inventory		1,000
Sales		1,500

Error discovered in subsequent year (sale has been recorded in subsequent year).

	Current year						Subsequent year					
	Assets	Lia-bili-ties	Equity	Sales	Cost of goods sold	Net income	Assets	Lia-bili-ties	Equity	Sales	Cost of goods sold	Net income
(1) Overstatement of ending inventory	+	0	+	0	−	+	0	0	0	0	+	−
(2) Understatement of ending inventory	−	0	−	0	+	−	0	0	0	0	−	+
(3) Overstatement of ending inventory and understatement of sales	−	0	−	−	−	−	0	0	0	+	+	+
(4) Understatement of ending intory and understatement of purchases	−	−	0	0	0	0	0	0	0	0	0	0

Summary of Impact of Inventory Errors on Financial Statements

Sales	1,500	
Cost of Goods Sold		1,000
Retained Earnings		500

If trend statistics are included in the annual reports, prior years' balances should be adjusted to reflect the correction of the error. Present-day audit techniques can substantially reduce the probability of material inventory errors.

INVENTORIES ON THE BALANCE SHEET

It is customary to report both trading and manufacturing inventories as current assets even though in some situations, considerable time will elapse before portions of such inventories are realized in cash. Among the items that are generally reported separately under the inventories heading are merchandise inventory or finished goods, goods in process, raw materials, factory supplies, goods and materials in transit, goods on consignment, and goods in the hands of agents and salespersons. Inventories are normally listed in the order of their liquidity. Any advance payments on purchase commitments should be reported separately and should not be included with inventories. Such advances are preferably listed after inventories in the current asset section since they have not entered the inventory phase of the operating cycle.

The valuation procedures employed must be disclosed in a note to the financial statements outlining all significant accounting policies followed.[6] The basis of valuation (such as cost or lower of cost or market), together with the method of arriving at cost (LIFO, FIFO, average, or other method), should be indicated. The reader of a statement may assume that the valuation procedures indicated have been consistently applied and financial statements are comparable with those of past periods. If this is not the case, a special note should be provided stating the change in the method and the effects of the change upon the financial statements.

If significant inventory price declines take place between the balance sheet date and the date the statement is prepared, such declines should be disclosed by parenthetical remark or note. When relatively large orders for merchandise have been placed by the reporting company in a period of widely fluctuating prices, but the title to such goods has not yet passed, such commitments should be described by special note. Information should also be provided concerning possible losses on purchase commitments. Similar information may be appropriate for possible losses on sales commitments.

Replacement costs of inventories may be disclosed in a note to the financial statements. Until such time as market valuation of inventories becomes generally acceptable for reporting purposes, only supplemental disclosure of current values is permitted.

When inventories or sections of an inventory have been pledged as security on loans from banks, finance companies, or factors, the amounts pledged should be disclosed either parenthetically in the inventory section of the balance sheet or in the notes. The United Foods, Inc. note reproduced below illustrates the disclosure requirements for inventories.

---

[6]*Opinions of the Accounting Principles Board*, No. 22, "Disclosure of Accounting Policies" (New York: American Institute of Certified Public Accountants, 1972), par. 12.

United Foods, Inc.

Inventory Valuation

Finished product and raw material inventories are valued at cost (last-in, first-out), not in excess of market. Maintenance, operating and other sundry supplies are valued at the lower of cost (first-in, first-out) or market.

NOTES TO CONSOLIDATED FINANCIAL STATEMENTS

Note 1—Inventories

Inventories are summarized as follows:

	February 29 or 28,	
	1984	1983
Finished products.	$28,320,801	$48,204,416
Raw materials.	5,117,548	3,541,176
Merchandise and supplies	859,882	1,274,086
Inventories.	$34,298,231	$53,019,678

Finished product and raw material inventories are valued at cost (last-in, first-out), not in excess of market. If current costs had been used, inventories would have been approximately $6,300,000, $6,600,000 and $5,100,000 higher than reported at February 29 or 28, 1984, 1983 and 1982, respectively, and net income would have decreased approximately $162,000 or $.01 per share for fiscal 1984 and $256,000 or $.02 per share for fiscal 1982, and net income would have increased approximately $810,000 or $0.6 per share for fiscal 1983.

During the three years ended February 29, 1984, the Company reduced certain inventory quantities, primarily finished products. This reduction resulted in a liquidation of LIFO inventory layers carried at lower costs prevailing in prior years as compared with the average unit cost of current year procurements and production. The effect of this inventory liquidation was to reduce cost of sales by approximately $1,462,000, $532,000 and $1,210,000 in fiscal 1984, 1983 and 1982, respectively, and to increase net income by approximately $917,000 or $.07 per share in fiscal 1984, $287,000 or $.02 per share in fiscal 1983, and $620,000 or $.04 per share in fiscal 1982.

Substantially all of the inventories are pledged to collateralize long-term debt (see Note 3).

QUESTIONS

1. What is meant by the term "gross profit test"?
2. Distinguish between: (a) gross profit as a percentage of cost and gross profit as a percentage of sales; (b) the gross profit method of calculating estimated inventory cost and the retail inventory method of calculating estimated inventory cost.

3. What effect would the use of the LIFO inventory method have upon the applicability of the gross profit method of valuing inventory?
4. Define (a) initial markup, (b) additional markup, (c) markup cancellation, (d) markdown, (e) markdown cancellation, and (f) maintained markup.
5. (a) How are markdowns treated under the conventional retail method? (b) What costing method is approximated by this approach?
6. How are purchase discounts and sales discounts treated in using the retail inventory method?
7. (a) Describe retail LIFO. (b) How does the retail LIFO cost percentage differ from the conventional retail cost percentage?
8. Under what circumstances would a decline in replacement cost of an item not justify a departure from the cost basis of valuing an inventory?
9. The use of cost or market, whichever is lower, is an archaic continuation of conservative accounting. Comment on this view.
10. Why is a ceiling and floor limitation on replacement cost considered necessary by the AICPA?
11. The Berg Corporation began business on January 1, 1986. Information about inventories, as of December 31 for three consecutive years, under different valuation methods is shown below. Using this information and assuming that the same method is used each year, you are to choose the phrase which best answers each of the following questions:

	LIFO Cost	FIFO Cost	Market	Lower of Cost or Market*
1986	$10,200	$10,000	$ 9,600	$ 8,900
1987	9,100	9,000	8,800	8,500
1988	10,300	11,000	12,000	10,900

*FIFO cost, item by item valuation.

(a) The inventory basis that would result in the highest net income for 1986 is: (1) LIFO cost, (2) FIFO cost, (3) Market, (4) Lower of cost or market.
(b) The inventory basis that would result in the highest net income for 1987 is: (1) LIFO cost, (2) FIFO cost, (3) Market, (4) Lower of cost or market.
(c) The inventory basis that would result in the lowest net income for the three years combined is: (1) LIFO cost, (2) FIFO cost, (3) Market, (4) Lower of cost or market.
(d) For the year 1987, how much higher or lower would net income be on the FIFO cost basis than on the lower of cost or market basis? (1) $400 higher, (2) $400 lower, (3) $600 higher, (4) $600 lower, (5) $1,000 higher, (6) $1,000 lower, (7) $1,400 higher, (8) $1,400 lower.
12. (a) Distinguish between holding gains and operating profit. (b) Are holding gains really "gains"? Explain.
13. There has been increasing support for the use of market values in reporting inventories on the financial statements. What are the major arguments that are raised in supporting such use?
14. How does the accounting treatment for losses on purchase commitments differ between actual losses which have already occurred and losses which may occur in the future?
15. What is the justification for valuing trade-ins or repossessions so that a normal profit can be realized upon their sale?

16. How should repossessed goods be valued for inventory purposes? Give reasons for your answers.
17. How would you recommend that the following items be reported on the balance sheet?
    (a) Unsold goods in the hands of consignees.
    (b) Purchase orders outstanding.
    (c) Advance payments on purchase commitments.
    (d) Raw materials pledged by means of warehouse receipts on notes payable to bank.
    (e) Raw materials in transit from suppliers.
    (f) Goods produced by special order and set aside to be picked up by customer.
    (g) Finished parts to be used in the assembly of final products.
    (h) Office supplies.
18. State the effect of each of the following errors made by Cole Inc. upon the balance sheet and the income statement (1) of the current period and (2) of the succeeding period:
    (a) The company fails to record a sale of merchandise on account; goods sold are excluded in recording the ending inventory.
    (b) The company fails to record a sale of merchandise on account; the goods sold are included, however, in recording the ending inventory.
    (c) The company fails to record a purchase of merchandise on account; goods purchased are included in recording the ending inventory.
    (d) The company fails to record a purchase of merchandise on account; goods purchased are not recognized in recording the ending inventory.
    (e) The ending inventory is understated as the result of a miscount of goods on hand.

DISCUSSION CASES

CASE 10–1   (Where has the inventory gone?)

Harvest Department Store uses the retail inventory method. Periodically, a physical count is made of the inventory and compared with the book figure computed from the company sales and purchase records. This year the extended valuation of the physical count resulted in a total inventory value 10% lower than the book figure. Martha Frost, the controller, is concerned by the variance. A 2 to 3% loss from shoplifting has been tolerated through the years. But 10% is too much. The branch manager, Nick Ward, who is summoned to account for the discrepancy, insists that the book figures must be wrong. He is confident that the shortage could not be that high, but that bookkeeping errors must be at fault. Frost, however, is not satisified with the explanation, and asks Ward to outline specifically what types of errors could have caused such a variance.

CASE 10–2   (Inventory valuation without records)

The Ma & Pa Grocery Store has never kept many records. The proceeds from sales are used to pay suppliers for goods delivered. When the owners, Mark &

Lucy Klein, need some cash, they withdraw it from the till without any record being made of it. The Kleins realize that eventually tax returns must be filed, but for three years "they just don't get around to it." Finally, the Internal Revenue Service catches up with the Kleins, and an audit of the company records is conducted. The auditor requests the general ledger, special journals, inventory counts, and supporting documentation — very little of which is available. Records of expenditures are extremely sketchy because most expenses are paid in cash. If you were the IRS auditor, what might you do to make a reasonable estimate of income for the company.

CASE 10–3   (Have we really had a loss?)

The Flyer Company is experiencing an unusual inventory situation. The replacement cost of its principal product has been declining, but because of a unique market condition, Flyer has not had to reduce the selling price of the item. Jim Hansen, company controller, is aware that GAAP requires the valuation of inventory at the lower of cost or market. He considers market to be replacement cost, and is concerned that to reduce the ending inventory to replacement cost will improperly reduce net income for the current period. Has an inventory loss occurred? Discuss.

CASE 10–4   (What value should we place on the clunker?)

The Dayton Automobile Agency is an exclusive agency for the sales of foreign sports automobiles. As part of its sales strategy, Dayton allows liberal trade-ins on the sale of its new cars. A used car division of the company sells these trade-ins at a separate location, usually at an amount significantly lower than the trade-in allowance. This division is continually showing large losses because the cars are charged to the division at their trade-in values. John Snowden, manager of the used car division, has requested that the costing procedure be changed, and that trade-ins be recorded at a price sufficiently below expected retail to allow a reasonable profit to his division. Barbara Eastwood, controller of the agency, acknowledges that some adjustment needs to be made to the inflated trade-in values, but feels that expected retail value should be used without allowance for a profit. What value should be used on the financial statements for the ending inventory of trade-ins? Discuss the reasonableness of this method for internal management evaluations.

EXERCISES

EXERCISE 10–1   (Inventory loss — gross profit method)

On August 15, 1987, a hurricane damaged a warehouse of Naranjo Merchandise Company. The entire inventory and many accounting records stored in the warehouse were completely destroyed. Although the inventory was not insured, a portion could be sold for scrap. Through the use of microfilmed records, the following data are assembled:

Inventory, January 1	$ 275,000
Purchases, January 1–August 15	1,185,000
Cash sales, January 1–August 15.......................	225,000
Collection of accounts receivable, January 1–August 15	1,732,000
Accounts receivable, January 1	187,500
Accounts receivable, August 15........................	265,000
Salvage value of inventory	3,500
Gross profit percentage on sales.......................	32%

Compute the inventory loss as a result of the hurricane.

EXERCISE 10–2   (Inventory loss—gross profit method)

On June 30, 1987, a flash flood damaged the warehouse and factory of Pendleton Corporation, completely destroying the work-in-process inventory. There was no damage to either the raw materials or finished goods inventories. A physical inventory taken after the flood revealed the following valuations:

Finished goods.............................	$112,000
Work in process	-0-
Raw materials.............................	52,000

The inventory on January 1, 1987, consisted of the following:

Finished goods.............................	$120,000
Work in process	115,000
Raw materials.............................	28,500
	$263,500

A review of the books and records disclosed that the gross profit margin historically approximated 30% of sales. The sales for the first six months of 1987 were $365,000.

Raw material purchases were $96,000. Direct labor costs for this period were $90,000, and factory overhead has historically been applied at 50% of direct labor.

Compute the value of the work-in-process inventory lost at June 30, 1987. Show supporting computations in good form.   (AICPA adapted)

EXERCISE 10–3   (Retail inventory method)

Wilson Department Store uses the retail inventory method. On December 31, 1987, the following information relating to the inventory was gathered:

	Cost	Retail
Inventory, January 1, 1987	$ 26,550	$ 45,000
Sales		350,000
Purchases.............................	262,000	395,000
Purchase Discounts	4,200	
Freight in.............................	2,350	
Net markups...........................		30,000
Net markdowns		10,000
Sales discounts		5,000

Compute the ending inventory value at December 31, 1987, using the conventional retail inventory method.

EXERCISE 10–4   (Retail inventory method)

The High Quality Clothing Store values its inventory under the retail inventory method at the lower of cost or market. The following data are available for the month of November 1987:

	Cost	Selling Price
Inventory, November 1................	$ 53,800	$ 76,000
Markdowns...........................		5,700
Markups.............................		11,200
Markdown cancellations...............		2,200
Markup cancellations		5,600
Purchases...........................	157,304	223,600
Sales		244,000
Purchase returns.....................	3,000	3,600
Sales returns		12,000
Sales allowances.....................		6,000

Based upon the data presented above, prepare a schedule in good form to compute the estimated inventory at November 30, 1987, at the lower of cost or market under the retail inventory method.   (AICPA adapted)

EXERCISE 10–5   (Retail-LIFO inventory method)

The Picayune Department Store began using the retail-LIFO method in 1986 for determining inventory values. In 1986, the cost percentage was computed at 65%. Information relating to the inventory for 1987 is given below:

	Cost	Retail
Inventory, January 1...................	$ 29,510	$ 45,400
Purchases...........................	120,000	172,000
Freight in............................	16,100	
Purchases returns....................	3,500	5,000
Sales		190,000
Net markups.........................		40,000
Net markdowns		10,950
Price index:		
1986 — All year 1.00		
1987 — December 31 1.05		

(1) Compute the cost percentage for 1987. (Round to two decimal places.)
(2) Compute the inventory value to be reported at December 31, 1987, assuming incremental layers are costed at end-of-year prices.

EXERCISE 10–6   (Retail LIFO inventory method)

On July 31, 1988, Kinateder, Smart & Associates compiled the following information concerning inventory for five years. They use the retail-LIFO inventory method.

Date	Year-End Price Index	Incremental Layer Index	Incremental Cost Percentage	Inventory at Retail
Dec. 31, 1983	1.00	1.00	71%	$155,000
Dec. 31, 1984	1.04	1.02	74%	188,600
Dec. 31, 1985	1.12	1.09	64%	192,500
Dec. 31, 1986	1.10	1.11	60%	194,200
Dec. 31, 1987	1.14	1.12	67%	195,800

Compute the inventory cost at the end of each year under the retail-LIFO method. (Round all dollar amounts to the nearest dollar.)

EXERCISE 10–7   (Lower of cost or market valuation)

Determine the proper carrying value of the following inventory items if priced in accordance with the recommendations of the AICPA.

Item	Cost	Replacement Cost	Sales Price	Cost of Completion	Normal Profit
Product 561	$1.85	$1.82	$2.30	$.35	$.20
Product 562	.69	.65	1.00	.30	.04
Product 563	.31	.24	.59	.15	.07
Product 564	.92	.84	1.05	.27	.05
Product 565	.84	.82	1.00	.19	.09
Product 566	1.19	1.15	1.43	.13	.09

EXERCISE 10–8   (Computation of inventory holding gains)

The Winterton Company chief accountant has been concerned that rising inventory prices have resulted in an overstatement of true income during the past year. She has decided to separate the holding gains and operating profit for analysis purposes and assembles the following data (assume there was no opening inventory).

Purchase cost of inventory acquired during year	$673,000
Replacement cost at time of sale of inventory sold during year	$624,000
Purchase cost of ending inventory.	$126,500
Replacement cost of ending inventory	$154,000
Sales for the period.	$786,900

Compute (a) the realized holding gain, (b) the unrealized holding gain, and (c) the operating profit for the period.

EXERCISE 10–9   (Loss on purchase commitments)

On October 1, 1987, Nixon Paper, Inc. entered into a six-month $500,000 purchase commitment for a supply of Product A. On December 31, 1987, the market value of this material has fallen so that current acquisition of the ordered quantity would cost $453,000. It is anticipated that a further decline will occur during the next three months and that market at date of delivery will be approximately $412,000. What entries would you make on December 31, 1987, and on March 31, 1988, assuming the expected decline in prices did occur?

EXERCISE 10–10   (Valuation of trade-in)

Bijoux Inc. sells new equipment with a $28,000 list price. Assume that Bijoux sells one unit of equipment and accepts a trade-in plus $25,200 in cash. The expected sales price of the reconditioned equipment is $2,600, the reconditioning expenses are estimated to be $400, and normal profit is 30% of the sales price.

(1) Prepare the journal entry to record the sale assuming that floor values are used.

(2) Prepare the journal entry to record the sale assuming that the sale of new equipment is recorded at its normal list price.

(3) Evaluate the entries.

EXERCISE 10–11   (Repossessed inventory)

Orton Equipment Inc. sells its inventory on a time basis. In about 5% of the sales, the customer defaults in the payments and the equipment must be repossessed. Assume that equipment was sold for $21,000 which included interest of $2,250 (company uses an allowance for unearned finance charges account). The customer defaulted after making payments of $10,350 which included $1,350 interest. The equipment was repossessed and overhauled at a cost of $2,700. It was then sold on a thirty day account for $16,500, a price that provided a normal profit of 25% on cost. What journal entries would be required to record the repossession and subsequent resale of the equipment?

EXERCISE 10–12   (Correction of inventory errors)

Annual income for the Miner Co. for the period 1983–1987 appears below: However, a review of the records for the company reveals inventory misstatements as listed. Calculate corrected net income for each year.

	1983	1984	1985	1986	1987
Reported net income (loss)	$18,000	$20,000	$2,000	$(7,500)	$16,000
Inventory overstatement, end of year. . .		5,500			3,600
Inventory understatement, end of year .	3,200			10,500	

EXERCISE 10–13   (Effect on net income of inventory errors)

The Oman Company reported income before taxes of $394,000 for 1986, and $459,000 for 1987. A later audit produced the following information:

(a) The ending inventory for 1986 included 2,000 units erroneously priced at $5.90 per unit. The correct cost was $9.50 per unit.

(b) Merchandise costing $17,500 was shipped to the Oman Company, FOB shipping point, on December 26, 1986. The purchase was recorded in 1986, but the merchandise was excluded from the ending inventory since it was not received until January 4, 1987.

(c) On December 28, 1986, merchandise costing $2,900 was sold to Cole Paint Shop. Cole had asked Oman to keep the merchandise for him until January 2, when he would come and pick it up. Because the merchandise was still in the store at year-end, the merchandise was included in the inventory count. The sale was correctly recorded in December 1986.

(d) Holt Company sold merchandise costing $1,500 to Oman Company. The purchase was made on December 29, 1986, and the merchandise was shipped on December 30. Terms were FOB shipping point. Because the Oman Co. bookkeeper was on vacation, neither the purchase nor the receipt of goods was recorded on the books until January 1987.

Assuming all amounts are material and a physical count is taken every December 31,

(1) Compute the corrected income before taxes for each year.

(2) By what amount did the total net income change for the two years combined?

(3) Assume all errors were found in January 1988, before the books were closed for 1987; what journal entry would be made?

EXERCISE 10–14   (Correction of LIFO inventory)

The Romero Products Company's inventory record appears below:

	Purchases		Sales
	Quantity	Unit Cost	Quantity
1985	9,000	$5.60	6,500
1986	9,500	5.75	10,000
1987	7,200	5.82	6,000

The company uses a LIFO cost flow assumption. It reported ending inventories as follows:

1985.................	$14,000
1986.................	11,600
1987.................	18,600

Determine if the Romero Products Company has reported its inventory correctly. Assuming that 1987 accounts are not yet closed, make any necessary correcting entries.

PROBLEMS

PROBLEM 10–1   (Inventory fire loss)

Merkley Manufacturing began operations five years ago. On August 13, 1987, a fire broke out in the warehouse destroying all inventory and many accounting records relating to the inventory. The information available is presented below. All sales and all purchases are on account.

	January 1, 1987	August 13, 1987
Inventory	$128,590	
Accounts receivable	130,590	$107,320
Accounts payable............................	88,140	122,850
Collection on accounts receivable, January 1– August 13.................................		753,800
Payments to suppliers, January 1–August 13 ...		487,500
Goods out on consignment at August 13, at cost		32,500

Summary of previous years sales:

	1984	1985	1986
Sales............................	$626,000	$675,000	$680,000
Gross profit on sales	194,060	182,250	217,600

Instructions: Determine the inventory loss suffered as a result of the fire.

PROBLEM 10–2   (Interim inventory computation — gross profit method)

The following information was taken from the records of the Bloom Company.

	1/1/86–12/31/86	1/1/87–9/30/87
Sales (net of returns).....................	$2,500,000	$1,500,000
Beginning inventory	420,000	730,000
Purchases	2,152,000	1,061,000
Freight in	116,000	72,000
Purchase discounts	30,000	15,000
Purchase returns.........................	40,000	13,000
Purchase allowances.....................	8,000	5,000
Ending inventory.........................	752,500	
Selling and general expenses	450,000	320,000

Instructions: Compute by the gross-profit method the value to be assigned to the inventory as of September 30, 1987, and prepare an interim statement summarizing operations for the nine-month period ending on this date.

PROBLEM 10–3   (Inventory theft loss)

In December, 1987, Target Merchandise Inc. had a significant portion of its inventory stolen. The company determined the cost of inventory not stolen to be $45,700. The following information was taken from the records of the company.

	January 1, 1987 to Date of Theft	1986
Purchases	$154,854	$167,540
Purchase returns and allowances...............	7,225	8,420
Sales..	236,012	261,800
Sales returns and allowances	2,882	2,600
Salaries......................................	9,600	10,800
Rent...	6,480	6,480
Insurance	1,160	1,178
Light, heat, and water	1,361	1,525
Advertising...................................	5,100	3,216
Depreciation expense	1,506	1,536
Beginning inventory	57,456	59,040

Instructions: Estimate the cost of the stolen inventory.

PROBLEM 10–4   (Retail inventory method)

The Rex Clothing Store values its inventory under the retail inventory method. The following data are available for 1987:

	Cost	Selling Price
Inventory, January 1.	$ 54,579	$ 79,100
Additional markdowns		21,000
Additional markups.		40,600
Markdown cancellations		13,000
Markup cancellations.		9,000
Purchases	150,179	221,600
Sales.		246,500
Purchases returns.	4,000	6,000
Sales allowances		12,000
Freight in	14,600	

Instructions:
(1) Prepare a schedule to compute the estimated inventory at December 31, 1987, at the lower of average cost or market under the retail method. *Test Method*
(2) Prepare the summary accounting journal entries to record the above inventory data (include entries to record the purchases, sales, and closing of inventory to income summary).
(3) What gross profit on sales would be reported on the income statement for 1987?

PROBLEM 10–5   (Retail inventory method)

The following information was taken from the records of Monk Inc. for the years 1986 and 1987.

	1987	1986
Sales.	$138,600	$135,600
Sales discounts.	1,840	1,200
Sales returns.	2,100	1,600
Freight in	4,000	3,640
Purchases (at cost)	78,000	68,560
Purchases (at retail).	100,500	92,480
Purchase discounts	4,155	1,000
Beginning inventory (at cost)		65,600
Beginning inventory (at retail).		87,520

Instructions: Compute the value of the inventory at the end of 1986 and 1987 using the conventional retail inventory method.

PROBLEM 10–6   (Retail-LIFO inventory method)

In 1985, Erdmann Inc. adopted the retail-LIFO inventory method. The January 1, 1985 price index was 1.00. The following data are available for a four-year period ending December 31, 1988.

		Cost	Retail
1985	Inventory, January 1	$141,750	$225,000
	Purchases	387,500	625,000
	Sales		575,000
	Year-end price index		1.10
1986	Purchases	363,000	550,000
	Sales		593,125
	Year-end price index		1.06
1987	Purchases	390,000	650,000
	Sales		625,375
	Year-end price index		1.08
1988	Purchases	504,000	800,000
	Sales		762,500
	Year-end price index		1.12

Instructions: Calculate the inventories to be reported at the end of 1985, 1986, 1987, and 1988. Incremental layers are costed at end-of-year prices.

PROBLEM 10–7   (Retail-LIFO inventory method)

The Timp View Sports Shop values its inventory on the retail-LIFO basis. Incremental inventory layers are costed at end-of-year prices. At December 31, 1986, the inventory was valued as follows:

LIFO Layer Year	Cost	Year-End Retail	Year-End Price Index	Retail at Base of 1.00
1980	$14,760	$24,600	1.00	$24,600
1982	9,482	13,545	1.05	12,900
1984	13,442	26,884	1.03	26,100
1985	4,500	6,000	1.10	5,454
	$42,184	$71,029		$69,054

The December 31, 1986, inventory at 1986 retail prices was $77,340. Information relating to 1987 transactions follows:

Purchases—cost	455,850
Purchases—selling price	673,845
Freight in	9,900
Sales returns	11,220
Sales discounts	1,950
Markups	4,740
Markup cancellations	1,080
Markdowns	2,505
Gross sales	702,000
Year-end price index for 1987	1.08

Instructions: Based on the above information, compute:
(1) The 1987 cost ratio.
(2) The inventory amount that would be reported on the balance sheet at December 31, 1987.

PROBLEM 10–8   (Lower of cost or market valuation)

Osborn Inc. carries four items in inventory. The following data are relative to such goods at the end of 1987.

			Per Unit			
	Units	Cost	Replacement Cost	Estimated Sales Price	Selling Cost	Normal Profit
Commodity A	2,000	$5.50	$5.00	$ 8.00	$ .90	$2.00
Commodity B	1,650	6.00	6.00	10.00	.80	1.25
Commodity C	5,000	2.50	2.00	4.75	.95	.50
Commodity D	3,250	7.00	7.50	7.50	1.20	1.75

Instructions: Calculate the value of the inventory under each of the following methods:
(1) Cost.
(2) The lower of cost or market without regard to market floor and ceiling limitations, applied to the individual inventory items.
(3) The lower of cost or market without regard to market floor and ceiling limitations applied to the inventory as a whole.
(4) The lower of cost or net realizable value applied to the individual inventory items.
(5) The lower of cost or market recognizing floor and ceiling limitations applied to the individual inventory items.

PROBLEM 10–9   (Lower of cost or market valuation)

Tropical Supplies Co. uses the first-in, first-out method in calculating cost of goods sold for three of the products that Tropical handles. Inventories and purchase information concerning these three products are given for the month of August.

		Product A	Product B	Product C
Aug. 1	Inventory	5,000 units at $6.00	3,000 units at $10.00	6,500 units at $ .90
Aug. 1–15	Purchases	7,000 units at $6.50	4,500 units at $10.50	3,000 units at $1.25
Aug. 16–31	Purchases	3,000 units at $7.50		
Aug.	Sales	10,000 units	5,000 units	4,500 units
Aug. 31	Sale Price	$8.00 per unit	$11.00 per unit	$2.00 per unit

On August 31, Tropical suppliers reduced their price from the last purchase price by the following percentages: Product A, 20%; Product B, 10%; Product C, 8%. Accordingly Tropical decided to reduce their sales prices on all items by 10% effective September 1. Tropical's selling cost is 10% of sales price. Products A & B have a normal profit (after selling costs) of 30% on sales prices, while the normal profit on Product C (after selling costs) is 15% of sales price.

Instructions:
(1) Calculate the value of the inventory at August 31, using the lower of cost or market method (applied to individual items).
(2) Calculate the FIFO cost of goods sold for August and the amount of inventory write-off due to the market decline.

PROBLEM 10–10   (Trade-ins and repossessed inventory)

The Nusink Appliance Company began business on January 1, 1986. The company decided from the beginning to grant allowances on merchandise traded in as part payment on new sales. During 1987 the company granted trade-in allowances of $64,035. The wholesale value of merchandise traded in was $40,875. Trade-ins recorded at $39,000 were sold for their wholesale value of $27,000 during the year.

The following summary entries were made to record annual sales and trade-in sales for 1987:

Accounts Receivable	439,890	
Trade-In Inventory	64,035	
Sales		503,925
Cash	27,000	
Loss on Trade-In Inventory	12,000	
Trade-In Inventory		39,000

When a customer defaults on the accounts receivable contract, the appliance is repossessed. During 1987 the following repossessions occurred:

	Original Sales Price	Unpaid Contract Balance
On 1986 contracts	$37,500	$20,250
On 1987 contracts	24,000	18,750

The wholesale value of these goods is estimated by the trade as follows:
  (a) Goods repossessed during year of sale are valued at 50% of original sales price.
  (b) Goods repossessed in later years are valued at 25% of original sales price.

Instructions:
(1) At what values should Nusink Appliance report the trade-in and repossessed inventory at December 31, 1987?
(2) Give the entry that should have been made to record the repossessions of 1987.
(3) Give the entry that is required to correct the trade-in summary entries.

PROBLEM 10–11   (Inventory transactions — journal entries)

The Buck Company values its perpetual inventory at the lower of FIFO cost or market. The inventory accounts at December 31, 1986, had the following balances:

Raw materials	$ 81,000
Allowance to Reduce Raw Material Inventory from Cost to Market	5,700
Work in Process	131,520
Finished Goods	205,200

The following are some of the transactions that affected the inventory of the Buck Company during 1987:

Feb. 10 Purchased raw materials at an invoice price of $30,000; terms 3/15, n/30. Buck Company uses the net method of valuing inventories.

Mar. 15 Buck Company repossessed an inventory item from a customer who was overdue in making payment. The unpaid balance on the sale was $190. The repossessed merchandise is to be refinished and placed on sale. It is expected that the item can be sold for $300 after estimated refinishing cost $75. The normal profit for this item is considered to be $40.

Apr. 1 Refinishing costs of $80 are incurred on the repossessed item.

Apr. 10 The repossessed item is resold for $300 on account; 20% down.

May 30 A sale on account is made of finished goods that have a list price of $740 and a cost of $480. A reduction from the list price of $100 is granted as a trade-in allowance. The trade-in item is to be priced to sell at $80 as is. The normal profit on this type of inventory is 25% of the sales price.

Nov. 30 Ordered materials to be delivered January 31, 1988, at a cost of $21,600. No discount terms were included.

Dec. 31 The following information was available to adjust the accounts for the annual statements:
   (a) The market value of the items ordered on November 30 had declined to $18,000.
   (b) The raw material inventory account had a cost balance of $110,400. Current market value was $101,400.
   (c) The finished goods inventory account had a cost balance of $177,600. Current market value was $189,000.

Instructions: Record this information in journal entry form, including any required adjusting entries at December 31, 1987.

PROBLEM 10–12 (Inventory error correction)

The Kirkpatrick Corporation has adjusted and closed its books at the end of 1987. The company arrives at its inventory position by a physical count taken on December 31 of each year. In March of 1988, the following errors were discovered.

(a) Merchandise which cost $2,500 was sold for $3,400 on December 29, 1987. The order was shipped December 31, 1987, with terms of FOB shipping point. The merchandise was not included in the ending inventory. The sale was recorded on January 12, 1988, when the customer made payment on the sale.

(b) On January 3, 1988, Kirkpatrick Corporation received merchandise which had been shipped to them on December 30, 1987. The terms of the purchase were FOB shipping point. Cost of the merchandise was $1,750. The purchase was recorded and the goods included in the inventory when payment was made in January of 1988.

(c) On January 8, 1988, merchandise which had been included in the ending inventory was returned to Kirkpatrick because the consignee had not been able to sell it. The cost of this merchandise was $1,200 with a selling price of $1,800.

(d) Merchandise costing $950, located in a separate warehouse, was overlooked and excluded from the 1987 inventory count.

(e) On December 26, 1987, Kirkpatrick Corporation purchased merchandise from a supplier costing $1,175. The order was shipped December 28 (terms FOB destination) and was still "in-transit" on December 31. Since the invoice was received on December 31, the purchase was recorded in 1987. The merchandise was not included in the inventory count.

(f) The corporation failed to make an entry for a purchase on account of $835 at the end of 1987, although it included this merchandise in the inventory count. The purchase was recorded when payment was made to the supplier in 1988.

(g) The corporation included in its 1987 ending inventory, merchandise with a cost of $1,290. This merchandise had been custom-built and was being held until the customer could come and pick up the merchandise. The sale, for $1,825, was recorded in 1988.

Instructions: Give the entry in 1988 (1987 books are closed) to correct each error. Assume that the errors were made during 1987 and all amounts are material.

PROBLEM 10–13   (Inventory error correction)

The Veeter Corporation adjusted and closed its books on December 31, 1987. Net income of $60,000 was reported for the year. Several months later, the independent auditors discovered the following material errors. Veeter used a periodic inventory method.

(a) 3,000 units of Product A, costing $8.95, were recorded at a unit cost of $8.59 in summarizing the ending inventory.

(b) A sale of merchandise shipped on January 3, 1988, was included in the ending inventory count. The cost of this merchandise was $4,750, and the sale was properly recorded at $5,950 on December 31, 1987.

(c) Merchandise costing $5,550 was included in the inventory although it was shipped to a customer on December 31, 1987, with terms of FOB shipping point. The corporation recorded the sale ($7,400) on January 3, 1988.

(d) Merchandise in the storeroom on December 31 (costing $1,500) was included in the 1987 ending inventory although the purchase invoice was not received or recorded until January 5, 1988.

(e) Merchandise in the hands of a consignee, costing $4,000, was included in the inventory; however, $2,400 of the merchandise had been sold as of December 31. The sale was not recorded until January 31, 1988, when the consignee made a full remittance of $3,200 on the merchandise sold.

(f) On December 31, 1987, a purchase of merchandise costing $2,500 was still in a delivery truck parked in the corporation's receiving dock. Because of the rush at year-end, the truck had not been unloaded. The terms of the purchase were FOB destination. The merchandise was not included in the ending inventory, but the purchase was recorded in the books in 1987.

Instructions:
(1) Compute the corrected net income for 1987.
(2) Give the entries that are required in 1988 to correct the accounts.

PROBLEM 10–14   (Inventory error corrections—cut-off)

The Batavia Company is a wholesale distributor of automotive replacement parts. Initial amounts taken from Batavia's accounting records are as follows:

Inventory at December 31, 1987 (based on physical count of goods in
Batavia's warehouse on December 31, 1987) $1,250,000

Accounts payable at December 31, 1987:

Vendor	Terms	Amount
Holly Company	2% 10 days, net 30	$ 265,000
Marie Inc.	Net 30	210,000
Becca Corporation	Net 30	300,000
Steve Company	Net 30	225,000
Bob Bottle Company	Net 30	—
		$1,000,000

Sales in 1987 . . . . $8,500,000

Additional information is as follows:

(a) Parts held on consignment from Marie to Batavia, the consignee, amounting to $125,000, were included in the physical count of goods in Batavia's warehouse on December 31, 1987, and in accounts payable at December 31, 1987.

(b) $22,000 of parts which were purchased from Bob Bottle and paid for in December 1987 were sold in the last week of 1987 and appropriately recorded as sales of $28,000. The parts were included in the physical count of goods in Batavia's warehouse on December 31, 1987, because the parts were on the loading dock waiting to be picked up by customers.

(c) Parts in transit on December 31, 1987, to customers, shipped FOB shipping point on December 28, 1987, amounted to a cost of $34,000. The customers received the parts on January 6, 1988. Sales of $40,000 to the customers for the parts were recorded by Batavia on January 2, 1988.

(d) Retailers were holding $210,000 at cost ($250,000 at retail) of goods on consignment from Batavia, the consignor, at their stores on December 31, 1987.

(e) Goods were in transit from Marie to Batavia on December 31, 1987. The cost of the goods was $25,000, and they were shipped FOB shipping point on December 29, 1987. The transaction was recorded when the goods were received.

(f) A freight bill in the amount of $2,000 specifically relating to merchandise purchases in December 1987, all of which were still in the inventory at December 31, 1987, was received on January 3, 1988. The freight bill was not included in either the inventory or in accounts payable at December 31, 1987.

(g) All of the purchases from Holly occurred during the last seven days of the year. These items have been recorded in accounts payable and accounted for in the physical inventory at cost before discount. Batavia's policy is to pay invoices in time to take advantage of all cash discounts, adjust inventory accordingly, and record accounts payable, net of cash discounts.

Instructions: Prepare a schedule of adjustments to the initial amounts using the format shown below. Show the effect, if any, of each of the transactions separately and if the transactions would have no effect on the amount shown, state NONE.

	Inventory	Accounts Payable	Sales
Initial amounts	$1,250,000	$1,000,000	$8,500,000
Adjustments			
Total adjustments			
Adjusted amounts	$	$	$

(AICPA adapted)

PROBLEM 10–15   (Gross profit method)

The Hurley Corporation is an importer and wholesaler. Its merchandise is purchased from a number of suppliers and is warehoused by Hurley Corporation until sold to consumers.

In conducting the audit for the year ended June 30, 1988, the company's CPA determined that the system of internal control was good. Accordingly, the physical inventory was observed at an interim date, May 31, 1988, instead of at year end.

The following information was obtained from the general ledger:

Inventory, July 1, 1987	$ 87,500
Physical inventory, May 31, 1988	95,000
Sales for 11 months ended May 31, 1988	840,000
Sales for year ended June 30, 1988	960,000
Purchases for 11 months ended May 31, 1988 (before audit adjustments)	675,000
Purchases for year ended June 30, 1988 (before audit adjustments)	800,000

The CPA's audit disclosed the following information:

Shipments received in May and included in physical inventory but recorded as June purchases	$ 7,500
Shipments received in unsalable condition and excluded from physical inventory.	
Credit memos had not been received nor had chargebacks to vendors been recorded.	
Total at May 31, 1988	1,000
Total at June 30, 1988 (including the May unrecorded chargebacks)	1,500
Deposit made with vendor and charged to purchases in April, 1988.	
Product was shipped in July, 1988	2,000
Deposit made with vendor and charged to purchases in May 1988.	
Product was shipped, FOB destination, on May 29, 1988, and was included in May 31, 1988, physical inventory as goods in transit	5,500
Through the carelessness of the receiving department a June shipment was damaged by rain. This shipment was later sold in June at its cost of $10,000.	

In audit engagements in which interim physical inventories are observed, a frequently used auditing procedure is to test the reasonableness of the year-end inventory by the application of gross profit ratios.

Instructions: Prepare the following schedules:
(1) Computation of the gross profit ratio for 11 months ended May 31, 1988.
(2) Computation by the gross profit method of cost of goods sold during June 1988.
(3) Computation by the gross profit method of the inventory at June 30, 1988.

(AICPA adapted)

PROBLEM 10–16   (Retail and retail-LIFO inventory methods)

Bateman Department Store converted from the conventional retail method to the retail-LIFO method on January 1, 1987. Management requested during your examination of the financial statements for the year ended December 31, 1988 that you furnish a summary showing certain computations of inventory costs for the past three years.

Available information follows:

(a) The inventory at January 1, 1986, had a retail value of $45,000 and a cost of $27,500 based on the conventional retail method. (There were no markdowns in 1985.)

(b) Transactions during 1986 were as follows:

	Cost	Retail
Gross purchases	$282,000	$490,000
Purchase returns	6,500	10,000
Purchase discounts	5,000	
Gross sales (exclusive of employee discounts)		492,000
Sales returns.....................................		5,000
Employee discounts..............................		3,000
Freight in	26,500	
Net markups		25,000
Net markdowns....................................		10,000

(c) The retail value of the December 31, 1987 inventory was $56,100, the cost percentage for 1987 under the retail-LIFO method was 62%, and the regional price index was 102% of the January 1, 1987 price level.

(d) The retail value of the December 31, 1988 inventory was $48,300, the cost percentage for 1988 under the retail-LIFO method was 61%, and the regional price index was 105% of the January 1, 1987 price level.

Instructions:

(1) Prepare a schedule showing the computation of the cost of inventory on hand at December 31, 1986, based on the conventional retail method.

(2) Prepare a schedule showing the computation of the cost of inventory on hand at the store on December 31, 1986, based on the retail-LIFO method. Bateman Department Store does not consider beginning inventories in computing its retail-LIFO cost ratio. Assume that the retail value of the inventory on December 31, 1986, was $50,000.

(3) Without prejudice to your solution to part (2), assume that you computed the inventory on December 31, 1986, (retail value $50,000) under the retail-LIFO method at a cost of $28,000. Prepare a schedule showing the computations of the cost of the 1987 and 1988 year-end inventories under the retail-LIFO method.   (AICPA adapted)

11
Plant and Intangible Assets—Acquisition

Many billions of dollars are invested each year in new property, plant, equipment, and intangible assets. Enterprises must continually make choices as to how they will invest their limited resources to acquire the operating assets needed to reach their goals and objectives. Capital budgets are prepared by management to help evaluate the available alternatives and to identify the priorities for implementation.

Many accounting questions are introduced with the acquisition of assets whose lives and economic benefits extend beyond one year, including:

1. How should the various categories of plant and intangible assets be recorded on the balance sheet?
2. Which costs should be capitalized as assets and which ones should be recognized as expenses in the period of disbursement?
3. At what amounts should the assets be recorded under various methods of purchase?
4. How should expenditures made subsequent to acquisition be recorded?
5. What recognition should be given to changes in either the value of the dollar or the replacement cost of new assets?

These are the central issues concerning the acquisition of plant and intangible assets that will be explored in this chapter.

CLASSIFICATION OF PLANT AND INTANGIBLE ASSETS

Accountants divide **noncurrent operating assets** into two basic categories, plant assets and intangible assets. **Plant assets** are tangible and thus can be observed by one or more of the physical senses. They may be seen and touched and, in some environments, heard and smelled. They have the common characteristic of providing future economic benefits to the enterprise. Common reporting classifications for plant assets include "land, buildings, and equipment" and "property, plant, and equipment." Specific assets that are commonly reported in this category include: land, buildings, and various types of equipment, such as automobiles and trucks, machinery, patterns and dies, furniture and fixtures, and returnable containers.

Intangible assets cannot be directly observed. Evidence of the asset in the form of agreements, contracts, or patents sometimes exists, but the asset itself has no physical existence. It meets the definition of an asset because of the future benefits expected from the item. The following specific assets are commonly reported as intangible assets: patents, copyrights, franchises, trademarks and trade names, organization costs, software development costs, and goodwill.

VALUATION OF PLANT AND INTANGIBLE ASSETS AT ACQUISITION

Plant assets and intangible assets are recorded initially at cost — the initial bargained or cash sales price. The **cost** of property includes not only the original purchase price or equivalent value, but also any other expenditures required in obtaining and preparing it for its intended use. Any taxes and duties, freight, installation, and other expenditures related to the acquisition should be included in the asset cost. In a competitive economy, the cost should be representative of the market value of the asset at the date of acquisition.

An asset acquired in used condition should be recorded at its cost without reference to the balance on the seller's books. Generally, expenditures to repair, recondition, or improve the asset before it is placed in use should be capitalized as part of the cost. It must be assumed that the buyer knew additional expenditures would be required when the purchase was made.

As suggested in Chapter 9, sound accounting theory requires discounts on purchases to be regarded as reductions in cost; earnings arise from sales, not from purchases. In applying this theory, any available discounts on property acquisitions should be treated as reductions to asset cost rather than reported as immediate revenue. Failure to take such discounts should be reported as Discounts Lost or Interest Expense.

In some purchases, a number of assets may be acquired for one lump sum. Some of the assets in the group may be depreciable, others nondepreciable. Depreciable assets may have different useful lives. If there is to be accountability for the assets on an individual basis, the total purchase price must be allocated among the individual assets. When part of a purchase price can be clearly identified with specific assets, such a cost assignment should be made and the balance of the purchase price allocated among the remaining assets. When no part of the purchase price can be related to specific assets, the entire amount must be allocated among the different assets acquired. Appraisal values or similar evidence provided by a competent independent authority should be sought to support such allocation.

To illustrate the allocation of a joint asset cost, assume that land, buildings, and equipment are acquired for $160,000. Assume further that assessed values for the individual assets as reported on the property tax bill are considered to provide an equitable basis for cost allocation. The allocation is made as shown below.

	Assessed Values	Cost Allocation According to Relative Assessed Values	Cost Assigned to Individual Assets
Land	$ 28,000	28,000/100,000 × $160,000	$ 44,800
Buildings	60,000	60,000/100,000 × $160,000	96,000
Equipment	12,000	12,000/100,000 × $160,000	19,200
	$100,000		$160,000

The entry to record this acquisition, assuming a cash purchase, would be as follows:

```
Land ...................................................   44,800
Buildings ..............................................   96,000
Equipment ..............................................   19,200
  Cash ................................................           160,000
```

Some considerations relative to determining the acquisition cost of specific plant and intangible assets are discussed in the following sections.

Real Property

All property is divided into two basic categories—real property and personal property. **Real property**, alternatively referred to as realty or real estate, includes land and most things affixed to it, primarily buildings, building fixtures such as plumbing that cannot be removed without damage to the structure, and most land improvements such as trees, shrubs, and sidewalks. All other property is **personal property**.

Land. When land is purchased, its cost includes not only the negotiated purchase price but also all other costs related to the acquisition, including brokers' commissions, legal fees, title, recording, and escrow fees, and surveying fees. Any existing unpaid tax, interest, or other liens on the property assumed by the buyer are added to cost.

Costs of clearing, grading, subdividing, or otherwise permanently improving the land after its acquisition should also be treated as increases in the cost of land. When a site acquired for a new plant is already occupied by a building that must be torn down, the cost of removing the old structure less any recovery from salvage is added to land cost. If salvage exceeds the cost of razing buildings, the excess may be considered a reduction of land cost. Special assessments by local governments for certain benefits, such as streets and sidewalks, lighting, and sewers and drainage systems that will be maintained by the government, are regarded as permanently improving land and thus chargeable to the asset. When expenditures are incurred for land improvements that will not be maintained by the government and will require ultimate replacement as, for example, paving, fencing, water and sewage systems, and landscaping, such costs should be summarized separately in an account entitled Land Improvements and depreciated over the estimated useful life of the improvements. The useful life of some improvements may be limited to the life of the buildings on the land; other improvements may have an independent service life.

Land qualifies for presentation in the land, buildings, and equipment category only when it is being used in the normal activities of the business. Land held for future use or for speculation should be reported under the investments heading; land held for current sale should be reported as a current asset. A descriptive account title should be used to distinguish land not used in normal operations from the land in use.

Buildings. A purchase involving the acquisition of both land and buildings requires the cost to be allocated between the two assets. Allocable cost consists of the purchase price plus all charges incident to the purchase. The cost allocated to buildings is increased by expenditures for reconditioning and repairs in preparing the asset for use as well as by expenditures for improvements and additions.

When buildings are constructed, their costs consist of materials, labor, and overhead related to construction. Costs of excavation or grading and filling required for purposes of the specific project, rather than for making land usable, are charged to buildings. Charges for architects' fees, building permits and fees, workers' compensation and accident insurance, fire insurance for the period of construction, and temporary buildings used for construction activities, form part of the total building cost. Tax on property improvements and interest costs during a period of construction (discussed later in the chapter) are generally capitalized as a cost of buildings.

It was suggested earlier that when land and buildings are acquired and buildings are immediately demolished, the cost of demolishing buildings is added to land as a cost of preparing land for its intended use. However, the cost of demolishing buildings that have been previously occupied by the company requires different treatment. This is a cost that should be identified with the original buildings. The recovery of salvage upon asset retirement serves to reduce the cost arising from the use of an asset and is frequently anticipated in calculating periodic charges for depreciation; a cost arising from asset retirement serves to increase the cost of asset use but is seldom anticipated in developing periodic charges.

In some cases, careful analysis is required in determining whether an expenditure should be recognized as buildings or whether it should be classified as equipment. For example, expenditures for items such as shelving, cabinets, or partitions are normally reported as buildings, but these would be properly reported as equipment items when they are movable, can be used in different locations, and are considered to have independent lives. Frequently, alternative classifications can be supported and the ultimate choice will be a matter of judgment.

Third-Party Financing of Land and Buildings. Real property is usually purchased through a real estate broker in conjunction with a bank or other financial institution. Frequently the financial institution holds the down payment "in escrow" prior to transfer of the property and prepares the necessary documents to complete the transfer. At the time of settlement, the financial institution acts as a third-party intermediary for the collection of funds from the buyer and disbursement of funds to the seller, the real estate broker, and other payees such as attorneys and taxing authorities.

Generally, both buyer and seller must pay certain costs in connection with the transaction. These costs and the settlement between the buyer and seller are summarized in an **escrow statement** prepared by the financial institution. An example of such a document showing both the seller's and the buyer's interest in the transaction is presented on page 433. Usually, however, each party to the transaction receives a separate statement.

The escrow statement is somewhat confusing at first glance, but it is not difficult to interpret after becoming familiar with the terminology. Two columns are provided for each party—one representing the charges and the other the credits. The mortgage balance owed by the seller and closing costs allocated to the seller are charged against the selling price, unexpired fire insurance as of the settlement date is credited to the seller, and the balance of $420,900 is paid to the seller by the financial institution. The seller's costs include property taxes of $7,000 and mortgage interest of $700 accrued as of the transfer date, both of which will be paid by the buyer when due. The balance to be paid by the buyer to the financial institution is $267,000—the selling price plus the buyer's closing costs less the credits for the mortgage assumed, the deposit, and the accrued taxes and interest.

Mountain West Escrow Company Escrow Statements				
	Statement of Seller		Statement of Buyer	
	Charges	*Credits*	*Charges*	*Credits*
Selling price..............		$739,600	$739,600	
Mortgage assumed by buyer ..	$276,200			$276,200
Property taxes — pro rata (to be paid by buyer)............	7,000			7,000
Commission..............	30,000			
Title insurance (cost split).....	4,000		4,000	
Fire insurance — pro rata (paid by seller)...............		1,200	1,200	
Title search (cost split).......	2,000		2,000	
Escrow fee (buyer pays all) ...			4,000	
Interest — pro rata (to be paid by buyer)	700			700
Recording fee			100	
Deposit placed in escrow				200,000
Cash to balance accounts.....	420,900			267,000
	$740,800	$740,800	$750,900	$750,900

The entry for the buyer to record the acquisition would be as follows, assuming the land portion of the purchase is $100,000 with the remainder assigned to the building.

Land..	100,000	
Unexpired Insurance..	1,200	
Building	649,700	
Escrow Deposit...		200,000
Mortgage Payable		276,200
Taxes Payable		7,000
Interest Payable		700
Cash..		267,000

Equipment

Equipment covers a wide range of items that vary with the particular enterprise and its activities. The discussion in the following paragraphs is limited to machinery, patterns and dies, furniture and fixtures, automobiles and trucks, and returnable containers.

Machinery of a manufacturing concern includes such items as lathes, stamping machines, ovens, and conveyor systems. The machinery account is debited for all expenditures identified with the acquisition and the preparation for use of factory machines. Machinery cost includes the purchase price, tax and duties on purchase, freight charges, insurance charges while in transit, installation charges, expenditures for testing and final preparation for use, and costs for reconditioning used equipment when purchased.

Patterns and dies are acquired for designing, stamping, cutting, or forging out a particular object. The cost of patterns and dies is either a purchase cost or a developmental cost composed of labor, materials, and overhead. When patterns and dies are used in normal productive activities, their cost is reported as an asset and the asset values are written off over the period of their usefulness. When the use of such items is limited to the manufacture of a single job, their cost is recognized as a part of the cost of that job.

Furniture and fixtures include such items as desks, chairs, carpets, showcases, and display fixtures. Acquisitions should be identified with production, selling, or general and administrative functions. Such classification makes it possible to assign depreciation accurately to the different business activities. Furniture and fixtures are recorded at cost, which includes purchase price, tax, freight, and installation charges.

Automobile and truck acquisitions should also be identified with production, selling, or general and administrative functions. Depreciation can then be accurately related to the different activities. Automotive equipment is recorded at its purchase price increased by any sales and excise tax and delivery charges paid. When payment for equipment includes charges for items, such as current license fees, personal property tax, and insurance, these should be recognized separately as expenses relating to both the current and the future use of the equipment.

Goods are frequently delivered in containers to be returned and reused. **Returnable containers** consist of such items as tanks, drums, and barrels. Containers are depreciable assets used in the business and are included in the equipment group. Adjustments must be made periodically to reduce the asset account and its related accumulated depreciation for containers not expected to be returned. The reduction is reported as a current loss.

Intangible Assets

Valuation at cost applies to the acquisition of intangible assets as well as plant assets. Some considerations relative to cost determination for specific types of intangible assets are presented in the following sections.

Patents. A **patent** is an exclusive right granted by the government to an inventor enabling the inventor to control the manufacture, sale, or other use of the invention for a specified period of time. The United States Patent Office issues patents that are valid for seventeen years from the date of issuance. Patents are not renewable although effective control of an invention is frequently maintained beyond the expiration of the original patent through new patents covering improvements or changes. The owner of a patent may grant its use to others under royalty agreements or the patent may be sold.

The issuance of a patent does not necessarily indicate the existence of a valuable right. The value of a patent stems from whatever advantage it might afford its owner in excluding competitors from utilizing a process resulting in lower costs or superior products. Many patents cover inventions that cannot be exploited commercially and may actually be worthless.

Patents are recorded at their **acquisition costs**. When a patent is purchased, it is recorded at the new owner's purchase price. When a patent is developed through company-sponsored research, the costs are expensed as required by FASB Statement No. 2, "Accounting for Research and Development Costs," described later in the chapter. Only patent licensing and related legal fees are included as its costs. All related experimental and developmental expenditures, along with the cost of models and drawings not required by the patent application, are considered research and development costs and are to be debited to expense when incurred.

The validity of a patent may be challenged in the courts. The cost of successfully prosecuting or defending infringement suits is regarded as a cost of establishing the legal rights of the holder and may be added to the other costs of the patent. In the event of unsuccessful litigation, the litigation cost, as well as other patent costs, should be written off as a loss.

Copyrights. A **copyright** is an exclusive right granted by the federal government permitting an author, composer, or artist to publish, sell, license, or otherwise control a literary, musical, or artistic work. In 1978, a new copyright law became effective in the United States. Under the new law, a copyright expires 50 years after the death of the creator of the work. Formerly, copyrights expired after a maximum of 56 years from the time they were granted. The new law permits the United States to be part of the Bern Union, the most widely recognized international copyright agreement.

The cost assigned to a copyright consists of those charges required to establish the right. When a copyright is purchased, it is recorded at its purchase price. The cost of any subsequent litigation to protect the copyright, if successful, should be capitalized as an additional cost of the copyright.

Trademarks and Trade Names. **Trademarks** and **trade names**, together with distinctive symbols, labels, and designs, are important to all companies that depend on public demand for their products. By means of distinctive markings, such as McDonald's golden arches, Levi's pocket patch, and the Chrysler star, particular products are differentiated from competing brands. In building the reputation of a product, relatively large costs may be incurred. The federal government offers legal protection for trademarks through their registry with the United States Patent Office. Prior and continuous use is the important factor in determining the ownership of a particular trademark. The right to a trademark is retained as long as continuous use is made of it. Protection of trade names and brands that cannot be registered must be sought in the common law. Distinctive trademarks, trade names, and brands can be assigned or sold.

The cost of a trademark consists of those expenditures required to establish it, including filing and registry fees, and expenditures for successful litigation in defense of the trademark. When a trademark is purchased, it is recorded at its purchase price.

Organization Costs. In forming a corporation, certain **organization costs** are incurred including legal fees, promotional costs, stock certificate costs, underwriting costs, and state incorporation fees. The benefits to be derived from these expenditures normally extend beyond the first fiscal period. Further, the recognition of these expenditures as expenses at the time of organization would commit the corporation to a deficit before it actually begins operations. These factors support the practice of recognizing the initial costs of organization as an intangible asset.

Expenditures relating to organization may be considered to benefit the corporation during its entire life. Thus, there is theoretical support for carrying organization costs as an intangible asset until the corporation is dissolved or becomes inactive. On the other hand, it may be argued that the organizational and start-up costs of a business are of primary benefit during the first few years of operation. Beyond that point, these costs generally become insignificant in terms of impact on the success or failure of the enterprise.

In addition to organization costs as defined above, some development stage companies in the past deferred many other costs, without regard to recoverability or matching, on the basis that they were not yet fully operating enterprises. Advocates of this approach maintain that all charges for interest, taxes, and general and administrative services during the development stage of a new company should be capitalized. Support for this procedure is based on the theory that future periods are benefited by necessary initial costs, and it is unreasonable to assume losses have been incurred before sales activities begin. The Financial Accounting Standards Board reviewed this practice and concluded that accounting principles for companies in the organizational or developmental stage should be the same as for more mature companies. No special rules or principles should apply.

Therefore, capitalization policies would not be different for these companies, and expenditures for interest, taxes, and administration should be expensed in the period incurred, unless their deferral can be justified by identifiable future benefits.[1]

Franchises. A **franchise** is an exclusive right or privilege received by a business or individual (**franchisee**) to perform certain business functions or use certain products or services, usually in a specified geographical area. The **grantor** of the franchise (**franchisor**) usually specifies a period of time over which the right may be exercised and the conditions under which the franchise can be revoked.

Franchise operations have become so common in our everyday life that often we don't realize we are dealing with them. When we purchase gas from a Phillips 66 station, stay overnight at a Best Western Motel, eat dinner at a Chi-Chi's Mexican restaurant, or shop at a 7-11 convenience store, we are dealing with a franchise operation. Grantors may be business entities or governmental units such as municipalities. In the latter case, governmental units frequently grant business concerns the right to use public property to provide services such as cable TV, power and gas lines, garbage collection, and public transportation.

The cost of a franchise includes any sum paid specifically for a franchise as well as legal fees and other costs incurred in obtaining it. Although the value of a franchise at the time of its acquisition may be substantially in excess of its cost, the amount recorded should be limited to actual outlays. When a franchise is purchased from another company, the amount paid is recorded as the franchise cost.

A franchise agreement may require that periodic payments be made to the grantor. Payments may be fixed amounts or they may be variable amounts depending on revenue, utilization, or other factors. These payments should be recognized by the franchisee as charges to periodic revenue. When certain property improvements are required under terms of the franchise, the costs of the improvements should be capitalized and charged to revenue over the life of the franchise. The revenue recognition problems related to the franchisor are discussed in Chapter 19.

Software Development Costs. In recent years, the tremendous growth in the computer industry, particularly in microcomputers, raised some significant accounting issues relating to expenditures for the development and production of computer software. The FASB has recently addressed this

---

[1]*Statement of Financial Accounting Standards No. 7,* "Accounting and Reporting by Development Stage Enterprises" (Stamford: Financial Accounting Standards Board, 1975), par. 10.

area and established standards which require capitalization of certain software development costs as an intangible asset. The accounting and reporting issues related to software development expenditures are discussed in detail later in the chapter.

Goodwill. Of all the intangible assets, goodwill is perhaps the most controversial. In a general sense, **goodwill** is often referred to as that "intangible something" that makes the sum of the whole company worth more than its individual parts. It includes all the special advantages, not otherwise identifiable, enjoyed by an enterprise, such as a good name, capable staff and personnel, high credit standing, reputation for superior products and services, and favorable location. Unlike most other assets, tangible or intangible, goodwill cannot be transferred without transferring the entire business.

From an accounting point of view, goodwill is recognized as the ability of a business to earn above-normal earnings with the identifiable assets employed in the business. Above-normal earnings mean a rate of return greater than that normally required to attract investors into a particular type of business.

The recording of goodwill has been the subject of many discussions and publications. Under currently accepted accounting principles, goodwill is recorded on the books only when it is **acquired by purchase** or otherwise established through a business transaction. The latter condition includes its recognition in connection with a merger or a reorganization of a corporation or a change of partners in a partnership.

The recognition of goodwill on the company books only when it is acquired in an arm's-length transaction makes it more difficult to compare a company that has recorded goodwill and one that doesn't. Just because a company has not purchased another company does not mean it does not have goodwill as defined above. Thus, current accounting principles may result in misleading users as far as goodwill is concerned. On the other hand, to allow companies to place a value on their own goodwill would undoubtedly lead to abuse. These difficulties have led some accountants to suggest that all purchased goodwill should be written off to expense as soon as it is acquired. Advocates of this position include the authors of Accounting Research Study No. 10, "Accounting for Goodwill," whose justification for immediate write-off was given as follows:

1. Goodwill is not a resource or property right that is consumed or utilized in the production of earnings. It is the result of expectations of future earnings by investors and thus is not subject to normal amortization procedures.
2. Goodwill is subject to sudden and wide fluctuations. That value has no reliable or continuing relation to costs incurred in its creation.

3. Under existing practices of accounting, neither the cost nor the value of nonpurchased goodwill is reported in the balance sheet. Purchased goodwill has no continuing, separately measurable existence after the combination and is merged with the total goodwill value of the continuing business entity. As such, its write-off cannot be measured with any validity.
4. Goodwill as an asset account is not relevant to an investor. Most analysts ignore any reported goodwill when analyzing a company's status and operations.[2]

This position has been consistently rejected by the accounting principles-setting bodies, and the immediate write-off of purchased goodwill is not permitted under GAAP. They maintain that a price has been paid for the excess earnings power, and it should be recognized as an asset. Because of the poor connotative image the term *goodwill* has acquired, some companies use more descriptive titles for reporting purposes, such as "Excess of Cost over Net Assets of Acquired Companies."

In the purchase of a going business, the actual price paid for goodwill usually results from bargaining and compromises between the parties concerned. A basis for negotiation in arriving at a price for goodwill could involve many variables:

1. The level of projected future earnings.
2. An appropriate rate of return.
3. Current valuation of the net business assets other than goodwill.

Several ways in which these variables may be used to aid in the negotiations are presented in the Appendix to this chapter. These are not really accounting methods, but financial models that utilize accounting data.

When a lump-sum amount is paid for an established business and no explicit evaluation is made of goodwill, goodwill may still be recognized. In this case the identifiable net assets require appraisal, and the difference between the full purchase price and the value of identifiable net assets can be attributed to the purchase of goodwill. In appraising properties for this purpose, current market values should be sought rather than the values reported in the accounts. Receivables should be stated at amounts estimated to be realized. Inventories and securities should be restated in terms of current market values. Land, buildings, and equipment may require special appraisals in arriving at their present replacement or reproduction values. Intangible assets, such as patents and franchises, should be included at their current values even though, originally, expenditures were

---

[2]George R. Catlett and Norman O. Olson, "Accounting for Goodwill," *Accounting Research Study No. 10* (New York: American Institute of Certified Public Accountants, 1968).

reported as expenses or were reported as assets and amortized against revenue. Care should be taken to determine that liabilities are fully recognized. Assets at their current fair market values less the liabilities to be assumed provide the net assets total that, together with estimated future earnings, is used in arriving at a purchase price.

To the extent possible, the amount paid for any existing company should be related to identifiable assets. If an excess does exist, the use of a term other than goodwill can avoid the implication that only companies that purchase other companies have goodwill.

To illustrate the purchase and recording of an ongoing business, assume that Airnational Corporation purchases the net assets of Speedy Freight Airlines for $675,000 cash. A schedule of net assets for Speedy Freight at the time of acquisition is presented below:

Speedy Freight Airlines **Schedule of Net Assets** **December 31, 1988**		
Assets		
Cash and temporary investments	$ 21,000	
Receivables	146,000	
Inventory	292,000	
Investments	72,000	
Land, buildings, and equipment (net)	489,200	
Patents, trademarks, and trade names	16,500	$1,036,700
Liabilities		
Current liabilities	$286,000	
Long-term debt	183,500	469,500
Net assets		$ 567,200

Analysis of the $107,800 difference between the purchase price ($675,000) and the net asset book value ($567,200) reveals the following differences between the recorded costs and market values of the assets.

	Cost	Market
Inventory	$292,000	$327,000
Investments	72,000	85,000
Land, buildings, and equipment	489,200	504,500
Patents	7,000	12,000
Trademarks and trade names	9,500	10,000
Franchises		5,000
Totals	$869,700	$943,500

The identifiable portion of the $107,800 difference amounts to $73,800 ($943,500 − $869,700), and is allocated to the respective assets. The remaining difference of $34,000 is recorded as an intangible asset, Goodwill.

The entry to record the purchase is as follows:

Cash and Temporary Investments	21,000	
Receivables	146,000	
Inventory	327,000	
Investments	85,000	
Land, Buildings, and Equipment	504,500	
Patents	12,000	
Trademarks and Trade Names	10,000	
Franchises	5,000	
Goodwill (Excess of market value over cost paid for net assets)	34,000	
Current Liabilities		286,000
Long-Term Debt		183,500
Cash		675,000

Negative Goodwill. Occasionally, the amount paid for another company is less than the fair market value of the net assets of the acquired company. This condition can arise when economic conditions are depressed, and where bargain purchases are possible. The accounting profession has discussed from time to time how such **negative goodwill** should be recorded. Some accountants have suggested that it should be recorded as part of owners' equity.

The APB, however, did not want the total assets to be recorded at an aggregate amount that exceeded cost. The Board decided, therefore, to require the allocation of the excess against all acquired noncurrent assets, except for noncurrent marketable equity securities. If this allocation reduces the noncurrent assets to a zero balance, any remaining excess is credited to a deferred credit account and amortized against revenue over the period benefitted.[3] The method used is similar to the allocation of a lump-sum acquisition price, but with the excess cost being *subtracted* from the market value of the assets on a pro rata basis.

For example, assume Goodtime, Inc. purchases the net assets of Funtime, Inc. for $500,000. The fair market value of Funtime's assets are as follows:

Cash and temporary investments	$ 75,000
Receivables	125,000
Inventories	160,000
Plant and equipment	250,000
Investment in noncurrent marketable equity securities	75,000
Other investments	50,000
	$735,000

---

[3]*Opinions of the Accounting Principles Board No. 16*, "Business Combinations" (New York: American Institute of Certified Public Accountants, 1970), par. 91.

Offsetting the above assets are the following liabilities:

Current liabilities	$ 50,000
Noncurrent liabilities	125,000
	$175,000

The market value of net assets for Funtime is thus $560,000 ($735,000 − $175,000), and the negative goodwill is $60,000 ($560,000 − $500,000). The only noncurrent assets that would meet the Board's criteria for adjustment would be plant and equipment and other investments. The allocation of the $60,000 would be performed as follows:

Plant and equipment	$250,000	5/6
Other investments	50,000	1/6
Total	$300,000	

The $60,000 negative goodwill is thus allocated $50,000 ($60,000 × 5/6) against plant and equipment and $10,000 ($60,000 × 1/6) against other investments. The acquisition is then recorded as follows:

Cash and Temporary Investments	75,000	
Receivables	125,000	
Inventories	160,000	
Plant and Equipment	200,000	
Investment in Noncurrent Marketable Equity Securities	75,000	
Other Investments	40,000	
Cash		500,000
Current Liabilities		50,000
Noncurrent Liabilities		125,000
To record acquisition of Funtime, Inc.		

The following note describing an actual negative goodwill transaction was included in the 1984 annual report for Zondervan Corporation.

> On October 1, 1983, the Company also acquired the remaining 49% interest in the Benson Company, Inc. for 66,666 shares of common stock which were recorded at the approximate market value of the stock at that date. This acquisition was accounted for by the purchase method and resulted in negative goodwill of approximately $1,094,000 which was primarily offset against noncurrent assets acquired.

RECORDING ACQUISITION OF PLANT AND INTANGIBLE ASSETS

When an asset is purchased for cash, the acquisition is simply recorded at the amount of cash paid, including all outlays relating to its purchase and preparation for intended use. Assets can be acquired under a number of other arrangements, however, some of which present special problems relating to the cost to be recorded. The acquisition of assets is discussed under the following headings:

1. Purchase on deferred payment contract
2. Acquisition under capital lease
3. Acquisition by exchange of nonmonetary assets
4. Acquisition by issuance of securities
5. Acquisition by self-construction
6. Acquisition by donation or discovery

Purchase on Deferred Payment Contract

The acquisition of real estate or other property frequently involves deferred payment of all or part of the purchase price. The indebtedness of the buyer is usually evidenced by a note, debenture, mortgage, or other contract that specifies the terms of settlement of the obligation. The debt instrument may call for one payment at a given future date or a series of payments at specified intervals. Interest charged on the unpaid balance of the contract should be recognized as an expense.

To illustrate the accounting for a deferred payment purchase contract, assume that land is acquired for $100,000; $35,000 is paid at the time of purchase and the balance is to be paid in semiannual installments of $5,000, plus interest on the unpaid principal at an annual rate of 10%. Entries for the purchase and for the first payment on the contract are shown below.

Transaction	Entry		
January 2, 1987 Purchased land for $100,000 paying $35,000 down, the balance to be paid in semiannual payments of $5,000 plus interest at 10%.	Land .... Cash .... Note Payable	100,000	35,000 65,000
June 30, 1987 Made first payment. Amount of payment: $5,000 + $3,250 (5% of $65,000) = $8,250	Interest Expense .... Note Payable .... Cash	3,250 5,000	8,250

In the preceding example, the contract specified both a purchase price and interest at a stated rate on the unpaid balance. Sometimes, however, a contract may simply provide for a payment or series of payments without reference to interest, or may provide for a stated interest rate that is unreasonable in relation to the market. As indicated in Chapter 8, APB No. 21, "Interest on Receivables and Payables," requires that in these circumstances, the note, sales price, and cost of the property, goods, or services exchanged for the note should be recorded at the fair market value of the property, goods, or services or at the current market value of the note, whichever value is more clearly determinable.[4] Application of Opinion No. 21 with respect to the seller was illustrated in Chapter 8. The following example illustrates the accounting by the purchaser.

Assume that certain equipment, which has a cash price of $50,000, is acquired under a deferred payment contract. The contract specifies a down payment of $15,000 plus seven annual payments of $7,189.22 each, or a total price, including interest, of $65,324.54. Although not stated, the effective interest rate implicit in this contract is 10%, the rate that discounts the annual payments of $7,189.22 to a present value of $35,000, the cash price less the down payment.[5] As specified in APB Opinion No. 21, if the cash equivalent price, that is, the fair market value of the asset, varies from the contract price because of delayed payments, the difference should be recorded as a discount (contra liability) and amortized over the life of the contract using the implicit or effective interest rate. The entries to record the purchase, the amortization of the discount for the first two years, and the first two payments would be as shown at the top of page 445.

When there is no established cash price for the property, goods, or services, and there is no stated rate of interest on the contract, or the stated rate is unreasonable under the circumstances, an imputed interest rate must be used. A discussion of the determination and application of imputed interest rates is included in Chapter 8.

Property is often acquired under a conditional sales contract whereby legal title to the asset is retained by the seller until payments are completed. The failure to acquire legal title may be disregarded by the buyer and the transaction recognized in terms of its substance—the acquisition of an asset and assumption of a liability. The buyer has the possession and use of the asset and must absorb any decline in its value; title to the asset

---

[4]The term *notes* is used by the Board in Opinion No. 21 as a general term for contractual rights to receive money or contractual obligations to pay money at specified or determinable dates.

[5]As illustrated in Chapter 6, the effective or implicit interest rate is computed as follows:

$$PV_n = R(PVAF_{\overline{n}|i})$$
$$\$50,000 - \$15,000 = \$7,189.22 \ (PVAF_{\overline{7}|i})$$
$$PVAF_{\overline{7}|i} = \frac{\$35,000.00}{\$7,189.22}$$
$$PVAF_{\overline{7}|i} = 4.8684$$

From Table IV, Chapter 6, the interest rate for the present value of 4.8684 when $n = 7$ is 10%. Additional examples of computing an implicit rate of interest are presented in Chapter 6.

Transaction	Entry		
January 2, 1987 Purchased equipment with a cash price of $50,000 for $15,000 down plus seven annual payments of $7,189.22 each, or a total contract price of $65,324.54.	Equipment................ 50,000.00 Discount on Note Payable .... 15,324.54 Note Payable .... Cash................	50,000.00 15,324.54	50,324.54 15,000.00
December 31, 1987 Made first payment of $7,189.22 Amortization of debt discount: 10% × $35,000 = $3,500 ($50,324.54 − $15,324.54 = $35,000)	Note Payable .... 7,189.22 Cash................... Interest Expense .... 3,500.00 Discount on Note Payable	7,189.22 3,500.00	7,189.22 3,500.00
December 31, 1988 Made second payment of $7,189.22. Amortization of debt discount: 10% × $31,310.78* = $3,131.08	Note Payable .... 7,189.22 Cash................... Interest Expense .... 3,131.08 Discount on Note Payable	7,189.22 3,131.08	7,189.22 3,131.08

*$50,324.54 − $7,189.22 = $43,135.32 Note payable
$15,324.54 − $3,500.00 =   11,824.54 Discount on note payable
                          $31,310.78 Present value of note payable end of first year

is retained by the seller simply as a means of assuring payment on the purchase contract.

Acquisition under Capital Lease

A **lease** is a contractual agreement whereby a **lessee** is granted a right to use property owned by the **lessor** for a specified period of time for a specified periodic cost. Many leases, referred to as **capital leases**, are in effect purchases of property. In such cases, the property should be recorded on the lessee's books as an asset at the present value of the future lease payments. Because lease accounting is a complex area, an entire chapter (Chapter 21) is devoted to accounting for leases. Even when a lease is not considered to be the same as a purchase and the periodic payments are written off as rental expense, certain lease prepayments or improvements to the property by the lessee may be treated as capital expenditures. Since leasehold improvements, such as partitions in a building, additions, and attached equipment, revert to the owner at the expiration of the lease, they are properly capitalized on the books of the lessee and amortized over the remaining life of the lease. Some lease costs are really expenses of the period and should not be capitalized. This includes improvements that are made in lieu of rent; e.g., a lessee builds partitions in a leased warehouse for storage of its product. The lessor allows the lessee to offset the cost against rental expense for the period. These costs should be expensed by the lessee.

Acquisition by Exchange of Nonmonetary Assets

In some cases, an enterprise acquires a new asset by exchanging or trading existing nonmonetary assets.[6] Generally, the new asset should be valued at its fair market value or at the fair market value of the asset given up, whichever is more clearly determinable.[7] If the nonmonetary asset is used equipment, the fair market value of the new equipment is generally more clearly determinable, and therefore used to record the exchange. It should be observed that determining the fair market value of a new asset can sometimes be difficult.

The quoted or list price for an asset is not always a good indicator of the market value and is often higher than the actual cash price for the asset. An inflated list price permits the seller to increase the indicated trade-in allowance for a used asset. The price for which the asset could be acquired in a cash transaction is the fair market value that should be used to record the acquisition.

To illustrate, assume the sticker on the window of a new car sitting in a dealer's showroom lists a total selling price of $13,500. The sticker includes a base price plus an itemized listing of all the options that have been added. If you, as a buyer, approached the dealer with your old clunker as a trade-in, you might be surprised to be offered $2,000 for a car you know is worth no more than $1,000. If you offered to pay cash for the new car with no trade-in, however, you could probably buy it for approximately $12,500 or the list price reduced by the inflated amount of allowance offered for the trade-in. The fair market value of the new asset is thus not the list price of $13,500, but the true cash price of $12,500.

If the nonmonetary asset given up to acquire the new asset is also property or equipment, a disposition of a plant asset occurs simultaneously with the acquisition. Because of the need to first discuss depreciation methods and practices before presenting the disposition of assets, the full discussion of acquisition and disposition by exchange is covered in Chapter 12.

Acquisition by Issuance of Securities

A company may acquire certain property by issuing its own bonds or stocks. When a market value for the securities can be determined, that value is assigned to the asset; in the absence of a market value for the

---

[6]Monetary assets are those assets whose amounts are fixed in terms of currency, by contract, or otherwise. Examples include cash and short- or long-term accounts receivables. Nonmonetary assets include all other assets, such as inventories, land, buildings, and equipment.

[7]*Opinions of the Accounting Principles Board, No. 29*, "Accounting for Nonmonetary Transactions" (New York: American Institute of Certified Public Accountants, 1973), par. 18.

securities, the fair market value of the asset acquired would be used. If bonds or stocks are selling at more or less than par value, Bonds Payable or Capital Stock should be credited at par and the difference recorded as a premium or discount. To illustrate, assume that a company issues 1,000 shares of $25 par stock in acquiring land; the stock is currently selling on the market at $45. An entry should be made as follows:

Land	45,000	
Capital Stock		25,000
Paid-In Capital in Excess of Par		20,000

When securities do not have an established market value, appraisal of the acquired assets by an independent authority may be required to arrive at an objective determination of their fair market value. If satisfactory market values cannot be obtained for either securities issued or the assets acquired, values may have to be established by the board of directors for accounting purposes. The source of the valuation should be disclosed on the balance sheet. Assignment of values by the board of directors is normally not subject to challenge unless it can be shown that the board has acted fraudulently. Nevertheless, evidence should be sought to validate the fairness of original valuations, and if, within a short time after an acquisition, the sale of stock or other information indicates that original valuations were erroneous, the affected asset and owners' equity accounts should be adjusted.

Property is frequently acquired in exchange for securities in conjunction with a corporate merger or consolidation. When such combination represents the transfer of properties to a new owner, the combination is designated a *purchase* and the acquired assets are reported at their cost to the new owner. But when such combination represents essentially no more than a continuation of the original ownership in the enlarged entity, the combination is designated a *pooling of interests,* and accounting authorities have approved the practice of recording properties at the original book values as shown on the books of the acquired company. Specific guidelines for distinguishing between a purchase and a pooling of interests are included in APB Opinion No. 16 and are discussed in detail in advanced accounting texts.[8]

Acquisition by Self-Construction

Sometimes buildings or equipment items are constructed by a company for its own use. This may be done to save on construction costs, to utilize idle facilities, or to achieve a higher quality of construction.

---

[8]See, for example, Paul M. Fischer, William James Taylor, and J. Arthur Leer, *Advanced Accounting* (Cincinnati: South-Western Publishing Co., 1986).

A number of special problems arise in determining the cost of self-constructed assets.

Overhead Chargeable to Self-Construction. All costs that can be related to construction should be charged to the assets under construction. There is no question about the inclusion of charges directly attributable to the new construction. However, there is a difference of opinion regarding the amount of overhead properly assignable to the construction activity. Some accountants take the position that assets under construction should be charged with no more than the incremental overhead—the increase in a company's total overhead resulting from the special construction activity. Others maintain that overhead should be assigned to construction just as it is assigned to normal operations. This would call for the inclusion of not only the increase in overhead resulting from construction activities but also a pro rata share of the company's fixed overhead.

The argument for limiting overhead charges to incremental amounts is that the cost of construction is actually no more than the extra costs incurred. Charges should not be shifted from normal operations to construction activities. Management is aware of the cost of normal operations and decides to undertake a project on the basis of the anticipated added costs. The position that construction should carry a fair share of the fixed overhead if the full cost of the asset is to be reported is based on the premise that overhead has served a dual purpose during the construction period and this is properly reflected in reduced operating costs. The latter argument may be particularly persuasive if construction takes place during a period of subnormal operations and utilizes what would otherwise represent idle capacity cost, or if construction restricts production or other regular business activities.

The assignment to construction of normal overhead otherwise chargeable to current operations will increase net income during the construction period. The recognition of a portion of overhead is postponed and related to subsequent periods through charges in the form of depreciation.

The accounting profession has not been successful in coming to an agreement on the issue. Authors of a research study for the AICPA have suggested the following criteria to help resolve the issue.

> ... in the absence of compelling evidence to the contrary, overhead costs considered to have "discernible future benefits" for the purpose of determining the cost of inventory should be presumed to have "discernible future benefits" for the purpose of determining the cost of a self-constructed depreciable asset.[9]

---

[9]Charles Lamden, Dale L. Gerboth, and Thomas McRae, "Accounting for Depreciable Assets," *Accounting Research Monograph No. 1* (New York: American Institute of Certified Public Accountants, 1975), p. 57.

This criterion would charge both normal and incremental overhead costs to self-constructed fixed assets and has the advantage of providing consistency within a company in the treatment of overhead costs.

Saving or Loss on Self-Construction. When the cost of self-construction of an asset is less than the cost to acquire it through purchase or construction by outsiders, the difference for accounting purposes is not a profit but a savings. The construction is properly reported at its actual cost. The savings will emerge as income over the life of the asset as lower depreciation is charged against periodic revenue. Assume, on the other hand, the cost of self-construction is greater than bids originally received for the construction. There is generally no assurance that the asset under alternative arrangements might have been equal in quality to that which was self-constructed. In recording this transaction, just as in recording others, accounts should reflect those courses of action taken, not the alternatives that might have been selected. However, if there is evidence indicating cost has been materially excessive because of certain construction inefficiencies or failures, the excess is properly recognized as a loss; subsequent periods should not be burdened with charges for depreciation arising from costs that could have been avoided.

Interest During Period of Construction. In public utility accounting, interest during a period of construction has long been recognized as a part of asset cost. This practice applies both to interest actually paid and to an implicit interest charge if the public utility uses its own funds. Interest costs, then, are charged to expense through depreciation over the useful life of the asset. Service rates established by regulatory bodies are based on current charges, including depreciation, and thus provide for a recovery of past interest costs.

In some circumstances, generally accepted accounting principles permit the capitalization of construction-period interest by nonutility companies. Only interest costs actually incurred are capitalized, and no implicit interest on internal funds is recognized. The practice of capitalizing interest as part of asset cost is supported on the grounds that interest is a legitimate cost of construction, and the proper matching of revenues and expenses suggests that interest be deferred and charged over the life of the constructed asset. It can also be argued that if buildings or equipment were acquired by purchase rather than by self-construction, a charge for interest during the construction period would be implicit in the purchase price.

Arguments advanced against this practice are:

1. It is difficult to follow cash once it is invested in a firm. Is the interest charge really related to the constructed asset, or is it a payment made to meet general financial needs? Even when a loan is made for specific purposes, it frees cash raised by other means to be used for other projects.
2. To be consistent, implicit interest on all funds used, not just borrowed funds, should be charged to the asset cost. This practice is followed in utility accounting and requires determining a cost of capital for internal funds used, a very difficult task.

Historically, interest capitalization was not a common practice outside the public utility industry. Beginning in the mid 1970's, however, an increasing number of nonutility companies changed their accounting method to a policy of capitalizing interest, an action that tended to increase net income. In reaction to these changes, the Securities and Exchange Commission, in 1974, declared a moratorium on companies changing their methods of accounting for interest costs pending study of the issue by the Financial Accounting Standards Board.[10]

Such a study was conducted, and in October 1979, FASB Statement No. 34 was issued recommending limited capitalization of interest cost. If the development of an asset for use or in limited cases, for sale or lease, requires a significant period of time between the initial expenditure related to its development and its readiness for intended use, interest cost on borrowed funds should be capitalized as part of the asset cost.

The amount of interest to be capitalized is

> . . . that portion of the interest cost incurred during the assets' acquisition periods that theoretically could have been avoided (for example, by avoiding additional borrowings or by using the funds expended for the assets to repay existing borrowings) if expenditures for the assets had not been made.[11]

Capitalization of interest is permitted for assets, such as buildings and equipment, that are being self-constructed for an enterprise's own use and assets that are intended to be leased or sold to others that can be identified as **discrete projects**, that is, projects that can be clearly identified as to the

---

[10]Securities and Exchange Commission, *Accounting Series Release No. 163,* "Capitalization of Interest by Companies Other than Public Utilities" (Washington: U.S. Government Printing Office 1974).

[11]*Statement of Financial Accounting Standards No. 34,* "Capitalization of Interest Cost" (Stamford: Financial Accounting Standards Board, 1979), par. 12.

assets involved. The construction project should have the following characteristics before interest charges are capitalized:[12]

1. Costs are separately accumulated.
2. Construction covers an extended period of time.
3. Construction costs are substantial.

Interest should not be capitalized for inventories manufactured or produced on a repetitive basis, for assets that are currently being used, or for assets that are idle and are not undergoing activities to prepare them for use. Thus, real property that is being held for future development does not qualify for interest capitalization.[13]

Once it is determined that the construction project qualifies for interest capitalization, the amount of interest to be capitalized must be determined. The following basic principles govern the computation of capitalized interest.[14]

1. Only **interest expense actually incurred** can be capitalized. There is no provision for including an interest cost on equity capital.
2. The **maximum interest** that can be capitalized is the **total interest expense paid or accrued** for the year. In consolidated companies, this includes all interest paid by the parent and subsidiaries.
3. Interest charges begin when the first expenditures are made on the project and continue as long as the activities to get the asset ready for its intended use are in progress, and until the asset is completed and actually ready for use.
4. The **average amount of accumulated expenditures** is used as the cost on which to compute the interest charge. This can be computed for each expenditure or can be estimated using the assumption that costs are being incurred evenly over the construction period. Expenditures mean cash disbursements, not accruals.
5. If the construction period covers more than one fiscal period, accumulated expenditures include prior years' capitalized interest.
6. The **interest rates** to be applied to the average accumulated expenditures are applied in a priority order as follows:
   (a) Rate incurred for any debt specifically incurred for funds used on the project.
   (b) Weighted average rate from all other enterprise borrowings regardless of use of funds.
7. If borrowed funds are invested awaiting expenditure on the project, revenue from the investment is not offset against the interest expense in deter-

---

[12]Alex T. Arcady and Charles Baker, "Interest Cost Accounting: Some Practical Guidance," *Journal of Accountancy* (March 1981), p. 64.

[13]*Statement of Financial Accounting Standards No. 34*, par. 10.

[14]All of the items in the list are included in FASB Statement No. 34 except as otherwise noted.

mining the actual interest expense incurred, unless the funds came from tax-exempt borrowings.[15]

8. Disclosure must be made of the total interest expense incurred for the period and the portion that was included as a capitalized cost.

The following illustration demonstrates the application of these guidelines. Cutler Industries, Inc. has decided to construct a new computerized assembly plant. It is estimated that the construction period will be two years, and that the cost of construction will be $6 million. A 12% construction loan for $2 million will be obtained at the beginning of construction.

In addition to the construction loan, Cutler has the following outstanding debt during the construction period:

5-year notes payable, 11% interest .... $ 750,000
Mortgage on other plant, 9% interest................................... $1,200,000

Expenditures on the project are incurred evenly throughout the period, beginning January 1, 1987 and ending on December 31, 1988. The accumulated expenditures at December 31, 1987 amounted to $3,000,000.

Computation of Maximum Interest That Can Be Charged Each Year

Loan	Amount	Interest Rate	Annual Interest
Construction	$2,000,000	12%	$240,000
Notes Payable	750,000	11%	82,500
Mortgage..	1,200,000	9%	108,000
Maximum Interest..............................			$430,500

Computation of Weighted-Average Accumulated Expenditures-1987

Expenditure total, January 1, 1987......................................	0
Expenditure total, December 31, 1987.................................	$3,000,000
	÷ 2
Average accumulated expenditures	$1,500,000

---

[15]*FASB Technical Bulletin 81-5,* "Offsetting Interest to be Capitalized with Interest Income" (Stamford: Financial Accounting Standards Board, 1981) as amended by *Statement of Financial Accounting Standards No. 62,* "Capitalization of Interest Cost in Situations Involving Certain Tax-Exempt Borrowings and Certain Gifts and Grants" (Stamford: Financial Accounting Standards Board, 1982).

Computation of Weighted-Average Interest Rate

Loan	Principal	Rate	Interest Cost
Notes Payable	$ 750,000	11%	$ 82,500
Mortgage	1,200,000	9%	108,000
	$1,950,000	9.8%*	$190,500

*Weighted average rate = $190,500 ÷ $1,950,000 = 9.8% (rounded)

Computation of Interest Eligible for Capitalization-1987

$$\$1,500,000 \quad \times \quad 12\% \quad = \quad \$180,000$$

Since $180,000 is less than the actual interest expense, the $180,000 is capitalized as interest cost.

Computation of Weighted-Average Accumulated Expenditures-1988

Expenditure total, December 31, 1987..................................	$3,000,000
1987 capitalized interest...	180,000
Adjusted expenditure total, December 31, 1987	$3,180,000
Expenditure total, December 31, 1988,	
including 1987 capitalized interest	6,180,000
	$9,360,000
	÷ 2
Average accumulated expenditures.....................................	$4,680,000

Computation of Interest Eligible for Capitalization-1988

$2,000,000	×	12%...............	$240,000
2,680,000	×	9.8%..............	262,640
			$502,640

Since $502,640 is more than the actual interest expense of $430,500, the actual interest expense is capitalized.

There are several important observations about this example. In 1987, the interest expense actually incurred exceeded the amount of interest computed on the average accumulated expenditures. The computed interest amount was therefore capitalized. In 1988, however, more of the company's internal funds were used for the construction, and the computation of interest that could have been capitalized exceeded the interest actually paid. The interest actually paid was therefore capitalized. The example assumed no new loans during 1988. If additional monies were borrowed specifically for the project, the rate on the new borrowings would have been applied to expended funds before applying the weighted average rate on all other borrowings. If additional general borrowings were made, a new computation of the weighted average rate would have been necessary. The example assumed expenditures were made evenly throughout the construction period. If only a few identifiable payments were made, computation of the weighted average accumulated expenditures could have been made by weighting each expenditure separately.

FASB Statement No. 34 requires disclosure of the total interest expense for the year and the amount capitalized. This disclosure can be made either in the body of the income statement or in a note to the statements.

To illustrate these two methods, assume that Cutler Industries reported the 1987 interest information in the income statement and the 1988 information in a note as follows:

Cutler Industries Income Statement-1987

Operating income		xxxxx
Other expenses and losses:		
Interest expense	$430,500	
Less capitalized interest	180,000	250,500
Income before income taxes		xxxxx
Income taxes		xxxxx
Net income		xxxxx

Cutler Industries Notes-1988

Note X-Interest expense

Total interest expense of $430,500 was capitalized as part of the cost of construction for the computerized assembly line building in accordance with the requirements of FASB Statement No. 34.

Another example of note disclosure, reproduced from the 1984 annual report of International Paper Co., appears on page 455.

The capitalization of interest costs as part of the cost of self-constructed assets has been subject to much criticism. The initial acceptance vote of the FASB was by a 4 to 3 margin, the minimum acceptable. The conceptual question that still remains is whether the interest added to asset cost truly

---

INTERNATIONAL PAPER CO.

Interest costs are capitalized on the construction of certain long-term assets. The capitalized interest is recorded as part of the asset to which it is related and is depreciated over the asset's estimated useful life. The Company incurred interest costs of $100 million in 1984, $95 million in 1983, and $86 million in 1982; of these amounts $19 million, $30 million, and $10 million, respectively, have been capitalized.

---

adds to the expected future benefit of the constructed asset. For now the profession has specified the conditions where the answer is yes.

Acquisition by Donation or Discovery

When property is received through donation by a governmental unit or other source, there is no cost that can be used as a basis for its valuation. It is classified as a **nonreciprocal transfer of a nonmonetary asset**.[16] Even though certain expenditures may have to be made incident to the gift, these expenditures are generally considerably less than the value of the property. Here cost obviously fails to provide a satisfactory basis for asset valuation.

Property acquired through donation should be appraised and recorded at its **fair market value**.[17] A donation increases owners' equity, therefore Donated Capital is credited. To illustrate, if the Beverly Hills Chamber of Commerce donates land and buildings appraised at $400,000 and $1,500,000 respectively, the entry on the books of the donee would be:

Land	400,000	
Buildings	1,500,000	
Donated Capital		1,900,000

Depreciation of an asset acquired by gift should be recorded in the usual manner, the value assigned to the asset providing the basis for the depreciation charge.

If a gift is contingent upon some act to be performed by the donee, the contingent nature of the asset and the capital item should be indicated in the account titles. Account balances should be reported "short" or a special note should be made on the balance sheet. When conditions of the gift have been met, both the increase in assets and in owners' equity should be recognized in the accounts and on the financial statements.

Occasionally, valuable resources are discovered on already owned land. The discovery greatly increases the value of the property. However,

---

[16]*Opinions of the Accounting Principles Board, No. 29*, par. 3(d).
[17]*Ibid.*, par. 18.

because the cost of the land is not affected by the discovery, it is common practice to ignore this increase in value. Similarly, the increase in value for assets that change over time, such as growing timber or aging wine, is ignored in common practice. Failure to recognize these discovery or accretion values ignores the economic reality of the situation and tends to materially understate the assets of the entity. More meaningful decisions could probably be made if the user of the statements was aware of these changes in value.

CAPITAL AND REVENUE EXPENDITURES

The decision as to whether a given expenditure is a capital or revenue expenditure is one of the many areas in which an accountant must exercise judgment. If the expenditure is expected to contribute to the production of revenues for more than one fiscal year, it is referred to as a **capital expenditure**, and the cost is recorded as an asset. If the expected future benefits are highly uncertain, then the item is referred to as a **revenue expenditure** and written off immediately as an expense.

Income cannot be fairly measured unless expenditures are properly identified. For example, an incorrect debit to an equipment account instead of an expense account results in the overstatement of current earnings on the income statement and the overstatement of assets and owners' equity on the balance sheet. As the charge is assigned to operations in subsequent periods, earnings of such periods will be understated; assets and equity on the successive balance sheets will continue to be overstated, although by lesser amounts each year, until the asset is written off and the original error is fully counterbalanced. On the other hand, an incorrect debit to an expense instead of an equipment account results in the understatement of current earnings and the understatement of assets and equity. Earnings of subsequent periods will be overstated in the absence of debits for depreciation or amortization; assets and equity will continue to be understated, although by lesser amounts each year, until the original error is completely offset.

In many companies, not all expenditures for assets that have future benefits are recorded in the plant accounts. A lower limit to the definition of a capital expenditure is established to avoid the excessive costs of accounting for relatively small deferred costs. Thus, any expenditure under the established limit is always expensed currently even though future benefits are expected from that expenditure. This practice is justified on the grounds of expediency and materiality. The amount of the limit varies with the size of the company. Limits of $100, $500, and $1,000 are not unusual. This treatment is acceptable as long as it is consistently applied and no material misstatements arise due to unusual expenditure patterns or other causes.

Previous sections of the chapter have described the types of expenditures that are typically capitalized as cost for various types of assets and under various types of acquisition arrangements. The remainder of the chapter focuses on areas where some special problems and considerations arise in determining whether an expenditure is a capital or revenue expenditure. These areas are: research and development expenditures, computer software development expenditures, and expenditures made subsequent to asset acquisition.

Research and Development Expenditures

Historically, expenditures for **research and development (R & D)** purposes were reported sometimes as capital expenditures and sometimes as revenue expenditures. The FASB inherited this problem from the Accounting Principles Board and made this area the subject of their first definitive standard.[18] The Board defined **research activities** as those undertaken to discover new knowledge that will be useful in developing new products, services, or processes or that will result in significant improvements of existing products or processes. **Development activities** involve the application of research findings to develop a plan or design for new or improved products and processes. Development activities include the formulation, design, and testing of products, construction of prototypes, and operation of pilot plants.

In general, the FASB concluded that research and development expenditures should be expensed in the period incurred.[19] This decision was reached after much analysis and after many attempts to establish criteria for selectively capitalizing some research and development expenditures and expensing others. Among the arguments for expensing these costs was the frequent inability to find a definite causal relationship between the expenditures and future revenues. Sometimes very large expenditures do not generate any future revenue, while relatively small expenditures lead to significant discoveries that generate large revenues. The Board found it difficult to establish criteria that would distinguish between those research and development expenditures that would most likely benefit future periods and those that would not.

---

[18]*Statement of Financial Accounting Standards No. 2*, "Accounting for Research and Development Costs" (Stamford: Financial Accounting Standards Board, 1974).

[19]*Ibid.*, par. 12.

As defined by the FASB in Statement No. 2, research and development costs include those costs of materials, equipment, facilities, personnel, purchased intangibles, contract services, and a reasonable allocation of indirect costs that are specifically related to research and development activities and that have no alternative future uses.[20] Such activities include:

1. Laboratory research aimed at discovery of new knowledge.
2. Searching for applications of new research findings or other knowledge.
3. Conceptual formulation and design of possible product or process alternatives.
4. Testing in search for or evaluation of product or process alternatives.
5. Modification of the formulation or design of a product or process.
6. Design, construction, and testing of pre-production prototypes and models.
7. Design of tools, jigs, molds, and dies involving new technology.
8. Design, construction, and operation of a pilot plant that is not of a scale economically feasible to the enterprise for commercial production.
9. Engineering activity required to advance the design of a product to the point that it meets specific functional and economic requirements and is ready for manufacture.[21]

The Board stipulated, however, that expenditures for certain items having alternative future uses, either in additional research projects or for productive purposes, can be capitalized and allocated against future projects or periods as research and development expense. This exception permits the deferral of costs incurred for materials, equipment, facilities, and purchased intangibles, but only if an alternative use can be identified.

The Board was very careful to distinguish between research and development expenses and other expenditures that are related to research activities but classified in other categories. These other expenditures are also usually regarded as expenses in the period incurred, but not as research and development expenses. To illustrate how research related expenditures are recorded under current GAAP, assume the Robotics Corporation made the expenditures listed at the top of page 459 during 1987 related to the development of robots for commercial and productive use.

Evaluation of FASB Position. Research and development costs vary widely among companies. Many expenditures do have future worth, while others are so highly uncertain as to future worth that capitalization is clearly improper. For the FASB to ignore these differences and issue a blanket rule that all research and development expenditures should be handled the

---

[20]*Ibid.*, par. 11.
[21]*Ibid.*, par. 9.

ROBOTICS CORPORATION

Description of Expenditure	**Accounting Treatment per GAAP**
1. Purchase of land to construct research facility.	1. Capitalize as land.
2. Self-construction of building to use in all robotic research.	2. Capitalize as building and depreciate as R & D expense.
3. Purchase of special equipment to be used solely for the development of a robot for the space program. The equipment is not expected to have any use beyond this project.	3. Expense immediately as R & D.
4. Purchase of more generalized equipment that can be used for a wide variety of robotic projects.	4. Capitalize as equipment and depreciate as R & D expense.
5. Research salaries dedicated to improvement of general robotic technology.	5. Expense immediately as R & D.
6. Purchase of patent for innovative construction of arm and hand segments.	6. Capitalize as patent and amortize as cost of production.
7. Labor and material costs incurred in building a prototype model of a robot for space travel.	7. Expense immediately as R & D.
8. Costs to produce ten robots to specified design.	8. Include in cost of goods manufactured. Report as inventory on balance sheet until sold.
9. Salary of marketing executive assigned to find customers for the space robot.	9. Expense immediately as marketing expense.
10. Costs of testing the prototype robot under simulated space travel conditions.	10. Expense immediately as R & D.
11. Legal costs to protect patents purchased.	11. Capitalize as patent and amortize as cost of production.
12. Legal costs of filing for patent on space robot.	12. Capitalize as patent and amortize as cost of production.
13. Research costs for Japanese manufacturer who has contracted with Robotics Corporation for research technology.	13. Record as receivable for contracted amount.

same seems arbitrary and without theoretical support. The International Accounting Group studying this area disagreed with the FASB and identified general situations in which they felt capitalization and deferral of development costs would be justified:

> Development costs of a project may be deferred to future periods if all the following criteria are satisfied:
>
> (a) the product or process is clearly defined and the costs attributable to the product or process can be separately identified;
> (b) the technical feasibility of the product or process has been demonstrated;
> (c) the management of the enterprise has indicated its intention to produce and market, or use, the product or process;
> (d) there is a clear indication of a future market for the product or process or, if it is to be used internally rather than sold, its usefulness to the enterprise can be demonstrated; and

(e) adequate resources exist, or are reasonably expected to be available, to complete the project and market the product or process.[22]

While guidelines to help distinguish between capital and revenue expenditures are desirable, specific rules, such as those issued for research and development expenditures, that mandate by definition the treatment of all expenditures ignore the reality of the great diversity of conditions existing in practice.

Computer Software Development Expenditures

In the best seller, *Megatrends*, John Naisbitt described the significant trend in the United States away from production intensive industries, such as steel, mining, and machine tools, to information processing industries, such as communications, computers, and service.

> The real increase has been in information occupations. In 1950, only about 17 percent of us worked in information jobs. Now more than 65 percent of us work with information as programmers, teachers, clerks, secretaries, accountants, stock brokers, managers, insurance people, bureaucrats, lawyers, bankers, and technicians. And many more workers hold information jobs within manufacturing companies. Most Americans spend their time creating, processing, or distributing information . . . David L. Birch of MIT reports that, as of May 1983, only 12 percent of our labor force is engaged in manufacturing operations today.[23]

As this trend has emerged over the past decade, new accounting issues have arisen that have required special attention. One of these has been accounting for the cost of computer software.

The computer industry has become divided into two major components: hardware and software. Computer hardware consists of the equipment such as consoles, boards, printers, and monitors that are produced and sold by a fairly small number of computer manufacturers. The development of the microcomputer led to the formation of several new hardware manufacturers. However, as the microcomputer explosion spread, the number of computer hardware producing firms decreased through mergers and dissolutions.

Computer software, on the other hand, consists of the programs that have been developed to be used with the hardware to accomplish specific tasks. The development of software requires little in the way of initial

---

[22]*International Accounting Standard, No. 9*, "Accounting for Research and Development Activities" (London, England: International Accounting Standards Committee, 1978), par. 17.

[23]John Naisbitt, *Megatrends: Ten New Directions Transforming Our Lives*, 6th ed. (New York: Warner Books, 1983), pp. 4–5.

capital investment, and thus has led to the formation of hundreds of small software companies, each developing its own special software programs. Scores of computer magazines advertising these programs have emerged in the last decade as businesses and households have purchased their own micros. Software programs such as *Lotus 1-2-3*, *Wordperfect*, *Supercalc*, and *Peachtree* have magnified the power of the computer for everyday use. Specialized accounting, tax, architectural, library, medical, educational, and recreational software packages have been developed by these hundreds of companies and marketed throughout the world.

A major accounting question related to the development of computer software has been how to account for the costs of development and production of the finished product. Many companies considered the development costs as research and development and expensed them in the period incurred as required by FASB Statement No. 2, discussed in the previous section. Other companies argued that these costs should be capitalized and written off against future revenues. Since these costs were a very significant part of the total expenditures of a software company, the alternate methods used to account for them created considerable differences among the financial statements of the various companies. The FASB, with strong support from the SEC, addressed this issue and in 1985 issued FASB Statement No. 86, "Accounting for the Costs of Computer Software to be Sold, Leased, or Otherwise Marketed."

The Board's conclusions concerning computer software costs are summarized in Exhibit 11-1.

Exhibit 11–1   Development of Successful Software

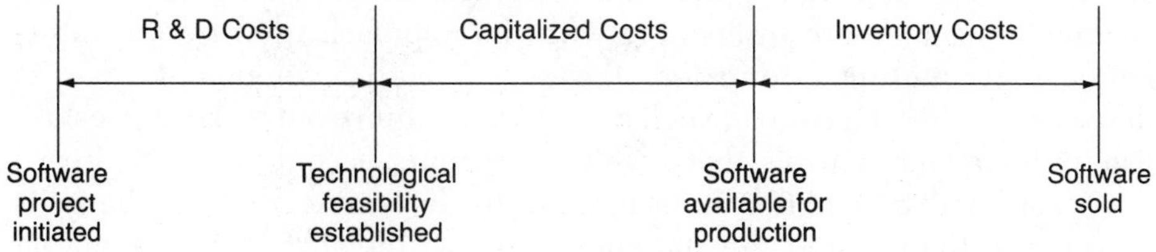

| R & D Costs | Capitalized Costs | Inventory Costs |

| Software project initiated | Technological feasibility established | Software available for production | Software sold |

As demonstrated by Exhibit 11–1, all costs incurred up to the point where technological feasibility is established are to be expensed as research and development. They include costs incurred for planning, designing, and testing activities. Costs incurred after this point up until the product is ready for general release to customers, such as further coding, testing, and production of masters, are to be capitalized as an intangible asset. Additional costs to actually produce software from the masters and package the software for distribution are inventoriable costs and will be charged against revenue as the product is sold.

Considerable judgment is required to determine when technological feasibility has been established. The Board attempted to assist in the judgment with specific definitions and examples as follows:

At a minimum, **technological feasibility** shall be attained when an enterprise has produced either[24]

1. **A detail program design** of the software establishing that the necessary skills, hardware, and software technology are available to the enterprise to produce the product. (Includes coding and testing necessary to resolve uncertainties for high-risk development issues), or
2. **A working model** of the software has been completed and tested.

If an enterprise purchases computer software externally for further development and resale, it should be accounted for in the same manner as described above for internally developed software. While Statement No. 86 does not directly address accounting for costs of computer software that is to be *used* internally by an enterprise as opposed to being *sold* externally, the Board indicated that the rather "high capitalization threshold" of the Statement would "likely be applied to costs incurred in developing software for internal use as well as for sale or lease to others."[25]

The treatment of computer software development costs by the FASB demonstrates how the more general research and development guidelines of FASB Statement No. 2 may be applied in future specific situations. By establishing two transitional points (technological feasibility and availability for general release to customers), the Board has recognized a separation between costs that are identified as being expense and those that are assets to be capitalized and amortized against future revenues.[26] This treatment seems more in keeping with the approach used by the International Accounting Group for all research and development costs as described earlier. Of course, such distinctions require enterprises to establish systems and controls that result in a proper accounting. The Board must continue to monitor its standards to determine that the benefits accruing to the users of the statements exceed the cost of implementing the standards.

---

[24]*Statement of Financial Accounting Standards No. 86,* "Accounting for the Costs of Computer Software to Be Sold, Leased, or Otherwise Marketed" (Stamford: Financial Accounting Standards Board, 1985), par. 4.

[25]*Ibid.*, par. 26.

[26]FASB Statement No. 86 includes a detailed discussion of recommended amortization procedures for capitalized costs. See Chapter 12 for discussion of these provisions.

EXPENDITURES SUBSEQUENT TO ACQUISITION

Over the useful lives of plant assets, regular as well as special expenditures are incurred. Certain expenditures are required to maintain and repair assets; others are incurred to increase their capacity or efficiency or to extend their useful lives. Each expenditure requires careful analysis to determine whether it should be assigned to revenue of the current period, hence charged to an expense account, or whether it should be assigned to revenue of more than one period, which calls for a debit to an asset account or to an accumulated depreciation account. In many cases the answer may not be clear, and the procedure chosen may be a matter of judgment.

The terms maintenance, repairs, betterments, improvements, additions, and rearrangements are used in describing expenditures made in the course of asset use. These are described in the following sections. Exhibit 11–2 summarizes the accounting for these subsequent expenditures.

Exhibit 11–2   Summary of Expenditures Subsequent to Acquisition

Type of Expenditure	Definition	Accounting Treatment
Maintenance and repairs	Normal cost of keeping property in operating condition.	Expense as incurred.
Renewals and replacements		
1. No extension of useful life or increase in future cash flows.	Unplanned replacement. Expenditure needed to fulfill original plans.	Expense as incurred.
2. Extends useful life or increases future cash flows.	Improvement resulting from replacement with better component.	Capitalize by one of two methods: (1) If cost of old component is known: Remove cost of old part and its accumulated depreciation, recognizing gain or loss. Capitalize cost of new component. (2) If cost of old component is not known: Deduct cost of new component from accumulated depreciation.
Additions and betterments	Expenditures that add to asset usefulness by either extending life or increasing future cash flows. No replacement of component involved.	Capitalize by adding to the cost of the asset.

Maintenance and Repairs

Expenditures to maintain plant assets in good operating condition are referred to as **maintenance**. Among these are expenditures for painting, lubricating, and adjusting equipment. Maintenance expenditures are ordinary and recurring and do not improve the asset or add to its life; therefore, they are recorded as expenses when they are incurred.

Expenditures to restore assets to good operating condition upon their breakdown or to restore and replace broken parts are referred to as **repairs**. These are ordinary and recurring expenditures that benefit only current operations, thus they are also debited to expense immediately.

Renewals and Replacements

Expenditures for the overhauling of plant assets are frequently referred to as **renewals**. Substitutions of parts or entire units are referred to as **replacements**. If these expenditures are necessary to achieve the original plans and do not change the original estimates of useful life or cash flows, they should be expensed. If, however, these expenditures extend the life of the asset or increase the cash flows generated by the asset, they should be capitalized by either adding them to the asset value or deducting them from accumulated depreciation.

Theoretically, if a part is removed and replaced with a superior part, the cost and accumulated depreciation related to the replaced part should be removed from the accounts, a loss recognized for the undepreciated book value, and the expenditure for the replacement added to the asset value. Often it is not possible to identify the cost related to a specific part of an asset. In these instances, by debiting accumulated depreciation, the undepreciated book value is increased without creating a build-up of the gross asset values. When this entry is made, no immediate loss related to the removal of the old asset is recognized.

To illustrate replacements, assume the Mendon Fireworks Company replaces the roof of its manufacturing plant for $40,000 and extends the estimated life of the building by five years. Assume that the original cost of the building was $1,600,000 and it is ¾ depreciated. If the original roof cost $20,000, the following entry could be made to remove the undepreciated book value of the old roof and record the expenditure for the new one.

Buildings (new roof)	40,000	
Accumulated Depreciation (old roof)	15,000	
Loss from Replacement of Roof	5,000	
Buildings (old roof)		20,000
Cash		40,000

If Mendon could not identify the cost of the old roof, the following entry would be made:

Accumulated Depreciation	40,000	
Cash		40,000

The book value of the building after the first entry is $435,000 ($1,600,000 − $1,200,000 + $40,000 − $5,000). Assuming the second entry is made, the book value would be $440,000 ($1,600,000 − $1,200,000 + $40,000). The $5,000 additional cost would be reflected in higher depreciation charges over the remaining life of the building.

Additions and Betterments

Enlargements and extensions of existing facilities are referred to as **additions**. Changes in assets designed to provide increased or improved services are referred to as **betterments**. If the addition or betterment does not involve a replacement of component parts of an existing asset, the expenditure should be capitalized by adding it to the cost of the asset. If a replacement is involved, it is accounted for as discussed in the previous section.

SUMMARY

The most challenging issue facing accountants in the area of asset acquisitions is which costs should be deferred and matched against future revenue, and which should be expensed immediately. Costs to acquire new property items with lives in excess of one fiscal period should clearly be capitalized and charged against future periods. Accounting for repairs, additions, and similar costs incurred subsequent to the initial acquisition is less clear, and such expenditures must be individually evaluated in light of existing conditions. The historical acquisition cost of the asset is widely accepted as the basis for the gross investment, whether for tangible or intangible assets. Methods for matching these costs against future revenues will be discussed in the next chapter, as well as accounting for the retirement of assets.

APPENDIX

GOODWILL ESTIMATION

As indicated previously, there are many factors that can be considered in determining the purchase price for a business. In deciding whether more than the current value of identifiable net assets should be paid, management may utilize one or more of the following goodwill valuation methods:

1. Capitalization of average net earnings
2. Capitalization of average excess net earnings
3. Number of years' excess earnings
4. Present value of future excess net earnings

VARIABLES USED IN GOODWILL VALUATION

Before discussing these methods, two variables that are used in all methods are discussed: (1) an estimate of future earnings and (2) the appropriate rate of return.

Estimating the Level of Future Earnings

Past earnings ordinarily offer the best basis on which to develop an estimate of the level of future earnings. In considering past earnings as a basis for projection into the future, reference should be made to earnings most recently experienced. A sufficient number of periods should be included in the analysis so a representative measurement of business performance is available and significant trends are observable. In certain instances, it may be considered necessary to restate revenue and expense balances to give effect to alternative depreciation or amortization methods, inventory methods, or other measurement processes considered desirable in summarizing past operations. Irregular or extraordinary gains and losses that cannot be considered a part of regular activities would be excluded from past operating results. Depending on the circumstances, these items may include gains and losses from the sale of investments and land, buildings, and equipment, gains and losses from the retirement of debt, and losses from casualties.

The regular earnings from operations should be analyzed to determine their trend and stability. If earnings over a period of years show a tendency to decline, careful analysis is necessary to determine whether this decline may be expected to continue. There may be greater confidence in possible future earnings when past earnings have been relatively stable rather than widely fluctuating.

Any changes in the operations of the business that may be anticipated after the transfer of ownership should also be considered. The elimination of a division, the disposal of substantial property items, or the retirement of long-term debt, for example, could materially affect future earnings.

The regular earnings of the past are used as a basis for estimating earnings of the future. Business conditions, the business cycle, sources of supply, demand for the company's products or services, price structure, competition, and other significant factors must be studied in developing data making it possible to convert past earnings into estimated future earnings.

Determining the Appropriate Rate of Return

The existence of above-normal earnings, if any, can be determined only by reference to a normal rate of return. The **normal earnings rate** is that which would ordinarily be required to attract investors in the particular type of business being acquired. In judging this rate, consideration must be given to such factors as money market rates, business conditions at the time of the purchase, competitive factors, risks involved, entrepreneurial abilities required, and alternative investment opportunities.

In general, the greater the risk entailed in an investment, the higher the rate of return required. Because most business enterprises are subject to a considerable amount of risk, investors generally expect a relatively high rate of return to justify their investment. A long history of stable earnings or the existence of certain tangible assets that can be easily sold reduce the degree of risk in acquiring a business and thus reduce the rate of return required by a potential investor.

If goodwill is to be purchased, it should be looked upon as an investment and must offer the prospect of sufficient return to justify the commitment. Special risks are associated with goodwill. The value of goodwill is uncertain and fluctuating. It cannot be separated from the business as a whole and sold, as can most other business properties. Furthermore, it is subject to rapid deterioration and may be totally lost in the event of business sale or liquidation. As a result of the greater risk, a higher rate of return would normally be required on the purchase of goodwill than on the purchase of other business properties.

METHODS OF VALUING GOODWILL

Assume that the following information is available for Company A:

Net earnings after adjustment and elimination of unusual and extraordinary items:

1984	$120,000
1985	80,000
1986	110,000
1987	75,000
1988	115,000
Total	$500,000

Average net earnings 1984–1988: $500,000 ÷ 5 = $100,000. Net assets as appraised on January 2, 1989, before recognizing goodwill, $1,000,000. (Land, buildings, equipment, inventories, and receivables, $1,200,000; liabilities to be assumed by purchaser, $200,000.)

The average net earnings figure of $100,000 for the five-year period 1984–1988 was used in arriving at an estimate of the probable future net earnings.

Different goodwill amounts may be computed using these data depending on which of the four valuation methods listed on page 466 is used. Each of these will be described and illustrated with examples.

Capitalization of Average Net Earnings

The amount to be paid for a business may be determined by capitalizing expected future earnings at a rate representing the required return on the investment. Capitalization of earnings, as used in this sense, means calculation of the principal value that will yield the stated earnings at the specified rate indefinitely or in perpetuity. This is accomplished by dividing the earnings by the specified rate.[27] The difference between the amount to be paid for the business as thus obtained and the appraised values of the individual property items may be considered the price paid for goodwill.

If, in the example, a return of 8% were required on the investment and earnings were estimated at $100,000 per year, the business would be valued at $1,250,000 ($100,000 ÷ .08). Since net assets, with the exception of goodwill, were appraised at $1,000,000, goodwill would be valued at $250,000. If a 10% return were required on the investment, the business would be worth only $1,000,000. In acquiring the business for $1,000,000, there would be no payment for goodwill.

Capitalization of Average Excess Net Earnings

In the above method, a single rate of return was applied to the estimated annual earnings in arriving at the value of the business. No consideration was given to the extent the earnings were attributable to net identifiable assets and the extent the earnings were attributable to goodwill. It would seem reasonable, however, to expect a higher return on a investment in goodwill than on the other assets acquired. To illustrate, assume the following facts:

	Company A	Company B
Net assets as appraised	$1,000,000	$500,000
Estimated future net earnings	100,000	100,000

---

[27]This may be shown as follows: P = principal amount or the capitalized earnings to be computed; r = the specified rate of return; E = expected annual earnings. Then, $E = P \times r$, and $P = E \div r$.

If the estimated earnings are capitalized at a uniform rate of 8%, the value of each company is found to be $1,250,000. The goodwill for Company A is then $250,000, and for Company B, $750,000 as shown:

	Company A	Company B
Total net asset valuation (earnings capitalized at 8%)...................................	$1,250,000	$1,250,000
Deduct net assets as appraised	1,000,000	500,000
Goodwill...	$ 250,000	$ 750,000

These calculations ignore the fact that the appraised value of the net assets identified with Company A exceed those of Company B. Company A, whose earnings of $100,000 are accompanied by net assets valued at $1,000,000, would certainly command a higher price than Company B, whose earnings of $100,000 are accompanied by net assets valued at only $500,000.

Satisfactory recognition of both earnings and asset contributions is generally effected by (1) requiring a fair return on identifiable net assets, and (2) viewing any excess earnings as attributable to goodwill and capitalizing the excess at a higher rate in recognition of the degree of risk that characterizes goodwill. To illustrate, assume in the previous cases that 8% is considered a normal return on identifiable net assets and that excess earnings are capitalized at 20% in determining the amount to be paid for goodwill. Amounts to be paid for Companies A and B would be calculated as follows:

	Company A	Company B
Estimated net earnings....................................	$ 100,000	$ 100,000
Normal return on net assets:		
Company A—8% of $1,000,000	80,000	
Company B—8% of $ 500,000		40,000
Excess net earnings	$ 20,000	$ 60,000
Excess net earnings capitalized at 20%	÷ .20	÷ .20
Value of goodwill	$ 100,000	$ 300,000

	Company A	Company B
Value of net assets offering normal return of 8%	$1,000,000	$ 500,000
Value of goodwill, excess net earnings capitalized at 20%....	100,000	300,000
Total net asset valuation.................................	$1,100,000	$ 800,000

Number of Years' Excess Earnings

Behind each of the capitalization methods just described, there is an implicit assumption that the superior earning power attributed to the existence of goodwill will continue indefinitely. The very nature of goodwill, however, makes it subject to rapid decline. A business with unusually high earnings may expect the competition from other companies to reduce earnings over a period of years. Furthermore, the high levels of earnings may frequently be maintained only by special efforts on the part of the new owners, and they cannot be expected to pay for something they themselves must achieve.

As the goodwill being purchased cannot be expected to last beyond a specific number of years, one frequently finds payment for excess earnings stated in terms of *years* of excess earnings rather than capitalization in perpetuity.[28] For example, if excess annual earnings of $20,000 are expected and payment is to be made for excess earnings for a five-year period, the purchase price for goodwill would be $100,000. If the excess annual earnings are expected to be $60,000 and the payment is to be made for four years' excess earnings, the price for goodwill would be $240,000.

The years of excess earnings method has the advantage of conceptual simplicity. It is related to the common business practice of evaluating investment opportunities in terms of their *payback period* — the number of years expected for recovery of the initial investment.

Present Value Method

The concept of number of years' purchase can be combined with the concept of a rate of return on investment. Excess earnings can be expected to continue for only a limited number of years, but an investment in these earnings should provide an adequate return, considering the risks involved. The amount to be paid for goodwill, then, is the discounted or present value of the excess earnings amounts expected to become available in future periods.

To illustrate the calculation of goodwill by the present value method, assume the earnings of Company A exceed a normal return on the net identifiable assets used in the business by $20,000 per year. These excess earnings are expected to continue for a period of five years, and a return of 12% is considered necessary to attract investors in this industry. The amount to be paid for goodwill, then, may be regarded as the discounted value at 12% of five installments of $20,000 to be received at annual intervals. Present value tables may be used in determining the present value of the series of payments. The present value of 5 annual payments of $1 each, to provide a return of 12%, is found to be 3.6048.[29] Goodwill would be

---

[28]Calculation of goodwill in terms of number of years of excess earnings will yield results identical to the capitalization method when the number of years used is equal to the reciprocal of the capitalization rate. Payment for the five years' earnings, for example, is equivalent to capitalizing earnings at a 20% rate ($1 \div .20 = 5$). Payment of four years' earnings is equivalent to capitalization at a 25% rate ($1 \div .25 = 4$).

[29]See Table IV, Chapter 6.

computed as the present value of five payments of $20,000 each, or $20,000 × 3.6048 = $72,096.

The principal advantage of the present value method is the explicit recognition of the anticipated duration of excess earnings together with the use of a realistic rate of return. Thus, it focuses on the factors most relevant to the goodwill evaluation.

QUESTIONS

1. In the balance sheet of many companies, the largest classification of assets in amount is plant assets. Name the items, in addition to the amount paid to the former owner or contractor, that may be properly included as part of the acquisition cost of the following property items: (a) land, (b) buildings, and (c) equipment.
2. What procedure should be followed to allocate the cost of a lump-sum purchase of assets among specific accounts?
3. What costs are capitalized as (a) copyrights, (b) franchises, (c) trademarks?
4. How would a trademark worth $5,000,000 be reported on the balance sheet if (a) the trademark were purchased for $5,000,000 or (b) the trademark gradually became identified over the years as a company symbol?
5. How should development stage enterprises report (a) their organization costs and (b) net operating losses?
6. (a) Under what conditions may goodwill be reported as an asset? (b) The Roper Company engages in a widespread advertising campaign on behalf of new products, charging above-normal expenditures to goodwill. Do you approve of this practice? Why or why not?
7. How should negative goodwill be reported in the financial statements?
8. What special accounting problems are introduced when a company purchases equipment on a deferred payment contract rather than with cash?
9. (a) Why is the "list price" of an asset often not representative of its fair market value? (b) Under these conditions, how should a fair market value be determined?
10. Bessie Corp. decides to construct a building for itself and plans to use whatever plant facilities it has to further such construction. (a) What costs will enter into the cost of construction? (b) What two positions can the company take with respect to general overhead allocation during the period of construction? Evaluate each position and indicate your preference.

11. What characteristics must a construction project have before interest can be capitalized as part of the project cost?

12. What are the general guidelines for determining the amount of interest that can be capitalized?

13. What are the principal arguments against capitalizing interest as presently mandated by the FASB?

14. The Parkhurst Corporation acquires land and buildings valued at $250,000 as a gift from Industrial City. The president of the company maintains that since there was no cost for the acquisition, neither cost of the facilities nor depreciation needs to be recognized for financial statement purposes. Evaluate the president's position assuming (a) the donation is unconditional, (b) the donation is contingent upon the employment by the company of a certain number of employees for a ten-year period.

15. Why do some companies expense capital expenditures that are under an established monetary amount?

16. Indicate the effects of the following errors on the balance sheet and the income statement in the current year and succeeding years:
    (a) The cost of a depreciable asset is incorrectly recorded as a revenue expenditure.
    (b) A revenue expenditure is incorrectly recorded as an addition to the cost of a depreciable asset.

17. (a) What type of activities are considered to be research and development expenditures? (b) Under what conditions, if any, are research and development costs capitalized?

18. What conceptual modification to the FASB standard on research and development costs is apparent in the later standard on accounting for computer software development costs?

19. Which of the following items would be recorded as an expense and which would be recorded as a capital item?
    (a) Cost of installing machinery
    (b) Cost of unsuccessful litigation to protect patent
    (c) Extensive repairs as a result of a fire
    (d) Cost of grading land
    (e) Insurance on machinery in transit
    (f) Bond discount amortization during construction period
    (g) Cost of major unexpected overhaul on machinery
    (h) New safety guards on machinery
    (i) Commission on purchase of real estate
    (j) Special tax assessment for street improvements
    (k) Cost of repainting offices

20. Why are some capital expenditures made subsequent to acquisition recorded as an increase in an asset account and others are recorded as a decrease in accumulated depreciation?

*21. What factors should be considered in estimating the future earnings of a business in order to develop a fair valuation of goodwill?

*22. (a) Identify and discuss four methods for arriving at a goodwill valuation using estimated future earnings as a basis for these calculations. (b) Which method do you think would give the most relevant valuation of goodwill?

Relates to Appendix

DISCUSSION CASES

CASE 11-1   (Where should we charge it?)

Bachus Energy Corp. has recently purchased the assets of a small local company, Hopkins Inc., for $556,950 cash. The chief accountant of Bachus has been given the assignment of preparing the journal entry to record the purchase. An investigation disclosed the following information about the assets of Hopkins Inc.:

(a) Hopkins owned land and a small manufacturing building. The book value of the property on Hopkins' records was $115,000. An appraisal for fire insurance purposes had been made during the year. The building was appraised by the insurance company at $175,000. Property tax assessment notices showed that the building's worth was five times the worth of the land.

(b) Hopkins' equipment had a book value of $75,000. It is estimated by Hopkins that it would take six times the amount of book value to replace the equipment new. The old equipment is, on the average, 50% depreciated.

(c) Hopkins had a franchise to produce and sell solar energy units from another company in a set geographic area. The franchise was transferred to Bachus as part of the purchase. Hopkins carried the asset on its books at $40,000, the amortized balance of the original cost of $90,000. The franchise is for an unlimited time. Similar franchises are now being sold by the company for $120,000 per geographic area.

(d) Hopkins had two excellent research scientists who were responsible for much of the company's innovation in product development. They are each paid $50,000 per year by Hopkins. They have agreed to work for Bachus Energy at the same salary.

(e) Hopkins held two patents on its products. Both had been fully amortized and were not carried as assets on Hopkins' books. Hopkins feels they could have been sold separately for $75,000 each.

Evaluate each of the above items and prepare the journal entry that should be made to record the purchase on Bachus' books.

CASE 11-2   (How much does it cost?)

The Robbins Co. decides to construct a piece of specialized machinery using personnel from the maintenance department. This is the first time the maintenance personnel have been used for this purpose, and the cost accountant for the factory is concerned as to the accounting for costs of the machine. Some of the issues raised by the maintenance department management are highlighted below:

(a) The supervisor of the maintenance department has instructed the workers to schedule work so all the overtime hours are charged to the machinery. Overtime is paid at 150% of the regular rate, or at a 50% premium.

(b) Material used in the production of the machine is charged out from the materials storeroom at 125% of cost, the same markup used when material is furnished to subsidiary companies.

(c) The maintenance department overhead rate is applied on maintenance hours. No extra overhead is anticipated as a result of constructing the machine.

(d) The maintenance department personnel is not qualified to test the machine on the production line. This will be done by production employees.

(e) Although the machine will take about one year to build, no extra borrowing of funds will be necessary to finance its construction. The company does, however, have outstanding bonds from earlier financing.

(f) It is expected that the self-construction of the machinery will save the company at least $20,000.

What advice can you give the cost accountant to help in the determination of a proper cost for the machine?

CASE 11–3   (But computer software is my inventory)

Educo, Inc. was organized by Sarah Felix and Ivan Corbett, two students working their way through college. Both Sarah and Ivan had played with computers while in high school and had become very proficient users. Sarah had a special ability for designing computer software games that challenged the reasoning power of players. Ivan could see great potential in marketing Sarah's product to other computer buffs, and so the two began Educo. Sales have exceeded expectations, and they have added ten employees to their company to design additional products, debug new programs, and produce and distribute the final software product.

Because of its growing size, increased capital is needed for the company. The partners decide to apply for a $100,000 loan to support the growing cost of research. As part of the documentation to obtain the loan, the bank asked for audited financial statements for the past year. After some negotiations, Al Price, CPA, was hired. Educo produced a preliminary income statement that reported net income of $35,000. After reviewing the statements, Price indicates that the company actually had a $10,000 loss for the year. The major difference related to $45,000 of wage and material costs that Educo had capitalized as an intangible asset but that Price determined should be expensed. "It's all research and development," Price insisted. "But we'll easily recoup it in sales next year," countered Ivan. "I thought you accountants believed in the matching principle. Why do you permit me to capitalize the equipment we're using, but not our software development costs? We'll never look profitable under your requirements."

What major issues are involved in this case? Which position best reflects the FASB Statement relating to software development costs?

CASE 11–4   (Why can't I capitalize the value of that gold?)

The Comstock Company owned several mining claims in Nevada and California. The claims are carried on the books at the cost paid to acquire them ten years ago. At that time, it was estimated that the claims represented ore reserves valued at $250,000, and the price paid for the properties reflected this value. Subsequent mining and exploration activities have indicated values up to four times the original estimate. Additional capital is needed to pursue the claims, and Comstock has decided to issue new shares of common stock. The company wants to report the true value of the claims in the financial statements in order to make the stock more attractive to potential investors. The accountant, Phyllis Green, realizes that the cost basis of accounting does not permit the recording of discovery values. On the other hand, she believes that to ignore the greatly increased value of the claims would be misleading to users. Isn't there some way the asset values can be increased to better reflect future cash flows arising from the claims?

You are hired as an accounting consultant to assist Comstock in its fund raising. What recommendations can you make to them?

CASE 11–5   (Is it an asset or not?)

The Wilton Company has developed a computerized machine to assist in the production of appliances. It is anticipated that the machine will do well in the marketplace; however, the company lacks the necessary capital to produce the machine. Lois Hicks, the Secretary-Treasurer of the Wilton Company, has offered to transfer land to the company to be used as collateral for a bank loan. Consideration for the transfer is an employment contract for five years and a percentage of any profits earned from sales of the new machine. The title to the land is to be transferred unconditionally. In the event Wilton defaults on the employment contract, a lump-sum cash settlement for lost wages will be paid to Hicks.

What are the arguments for and against recording the land as an asset on Wilton's books? Is it a contingent asset? What effect does the provision for a cash settlement in the event of default have on your decision?

EXERCISES

EXERCISE 11–1   (Lump-sum acquisition)

The Hampton Shipping Co. acquired land, buildings, and equipment at a lump-sum price of $410,000. An appraisal of the assets at the time of acquisition disclosed the following values:

Land................................	100,000
Buildings	150,000
Equipment..........................	250,000

What cost should be assigned to each asset?

EXERCISE 11–2   (Lump-sum acquisition)

The Fortin Corporation purchased land, a building, a patent, and a franchise for the lump sum of $975,000. A real estate appraiser estimated the building to have a resale value of $400,000 (⅔ of the total worth of land and building). The franchise had no established resale value. The patent was valued by management at $275,000. Give the journal entry to record the acquisition of the assets.

EXERCISE 11–3   (Cost of specific plant items)

The following expenditures were incurred by the Littlefield Food Co. in 1988: purchase of land, $300,000; land survey, $1,500; fees for search of title for land, $350; building permit, $500; temporary quarters for construction crews, $10,750; payment to tenants of old building for vacating premises, $2,000; razing of old building, $25,000; excavation of basement, $10,000; special assessment tax for street project, $2,000; dividends, $5,000; damages awarded for injuries sustained in construction, $4,200 (no insurance was carried; the cost of insurance would have been $200); costs of construction, $750,000; cost of paving parking lot adjoining building, $40,000; cost of shrubs, trees, and other landscaping, $5,000. What is the cost of the land, land improvements, and building?

EXERCISE 11–4   (Determining cost of patent)

Chen King Enterprises Inc. developed a new machine that reduces the time required to insert the fortunes into their fortune cookies. Because the process is considered very valuable to the fortune cookie industry, Chen King had the machine patented. The following expenses were incurred in developing and patenting the machine.

Research and development laboratory expenses	$15,000
Metal used in the construction of machine	5,000
Blueprints used to design the machine	1,500
Legal expenses to obtain patent	10,000
Wages paid for employees' work on the research, development, and building of the machine (60% of the time was spent in actually building the machine).	30,000
Expense of drawings required by the patent office to be submitted with the patent application	150
Fees paid to government patent office to process application.	500

One year later, Chen King Enterprises Inc. paid $12,000 in legal fees to successfully defend the patent against an infringement suit by the Dragon Cookie Co.

Give the entries on Chen King's books indicated by the above events. Ignore any amortization of the patent or depreciation of the machine.

EXERCISE 11–5   (Correcting organization costs account)

The Baymaster Manufacturing Co. was incorporated on January 1, 1987. In reviewing the accounts in 1988, you find the organization costs account appears as follows:

Account   **Organization Costs**

Item	Debit	Credit	Balance	
			Debit	Credit
Incorporation fees.....................	3,750		3,750	
Legal fees relative to organization	21,150		24,900	
Stock certificate cost	6,000		30,900	
Cost of rehabilitating building acquired at end of 1987.....................	165,600		196,500	
Advertising expenditures to promote company products	18,000		214,500	
Amortization of organization costs for 1987, 20% of balance of organization cost (per board of directors' resolution).........		42,900	171,600	
Net loss for 1987	25,000		196,600	

Give the entry or entries required to correct the account.

EXERCISE 11–6
(Equipment purchase on deferred payment contract)

Wolcott Co. purchases equipment costing $110,000 with a down payment of $20,000 and sufficient semiannual installments of $7,000 (including interest on the unpaid principal at 10% per year) to pay the balance.

(1) Give the entries to record the purchase and the first two semiannual payments.
(2) Assume that there was no known cash price and twenty semiannual installments were to be made in addition to the $20,000 down payment. Give the entries to record the purchase and the first two semiannual payments.

EXERCISE 11–7   (Exchange of nonmonetary assets)

Franklin Analysis Inc. purchased a new computer from a dealer. The following data relate to the purchase:
(a) List price of new computer with trade-in — $45,000
(b) Cash price of new computer with no trade-in — $39,500
(c) Franklin Analysis Inc. received a trade-in allowance (based on list price) of $10,000 on a machine costing $25,000 new and having a present book value of $12,000. The balance was paid in cash.
(d) The Express Delivery Service charged Franklin $1,200 to deliver the computer.

Determine the cost to be recorded for the new computer.

EXERCISE 11–8   (Lump-sum acquisition with stock)

On January 31, 1987, Fontanella Corp. exchanged 10,000 shares of its $25 par common stock for the following assets:

(a) A trademark valued at $120,000.
(b) A building, including land, valued at $650,000 (20% of the value is for the land).
(c) A franchise right. No estimate of value at time of exchange.

Fontanella Corp. stock is selling at $86 per share on the date of the exchange. Give the entries to record the exchange on Fontanella's books.

EXERCISE 11–9   (Purchase of building with bonds and stock)

The Juergatis Co. enters into a contract with the Hyde Construction Co. for construction of an office building at a cost of $720,000. Upon completion of construction the Hyde Construction Co. agrees to accept in full payment of the contract price Juergatis Co. 10% bonds with a face value of $300,000 and common stock with a par value of $300,000 and no established fair market value. Juergatis Co. bonds are selling on the market at this time at 102. How would you recommend the building acquisition be recorded?

EXERCISE 11–10
(Acquisition of land and building for stock and cash)

Summerville's Music Store acquired land and an old building in exchange for 50,000 shares of its common stock, par $8, and cash of $60,000. The auditor ascertains that the company's stock was selling on the market at $15 when the purchase was made. The following additional costs were incurred to complete the transaction.

Escrow cost to complete transaction.................	$10,000
Property tax for previous year......................	30,000
Cost of building demolition	13,000
Salvage value of demolished building...............	6,000

What entry should be made to record the acquisition of the property?

EXERCISE 11–11
(Cost of self-constructed asset including interest capitalization)

The Elgin Manufacturing Company has constructed its own special equipment to produce a newly developed product. A bid to construct the equipment by an outside company was received for $620,000. The actual costs incurred by Elgin to construct the equipment were as follows:

Direct material.......................	$220,000
Direct labor..........................	120,000

It is estimated that variable overhead costs amount to 125% of direct labor costs. In addition, nonvariable costs (exclusive of interest) of $700,000 were incurred during the construction period and allocated to production on the basis of total prime costs (direct labor plus direct material). The prime costs incurred to build the new equipment amounted to 20% of the total prime costs incurred for the period. The company follows the policy of capitalizing all possible costs on self-construction projects.

In order to assist in financing the construction of the equipment, a $300,000, 10% loan was acquired at the beginning of the six-month construction period. The company carries no other debt except for trade accounts payable. Assume expenditures were incurred evenly over the six-month period, and interest charges were to be capitalized in accordance with FASB Statement No. 34. Compute the cost to be assigned to the new equipment.

EXERCISE 11-12   (Capitalization of interest)

Home Department Stores Inc. constructs its own stores. In the past, no cost has been added to the asset value for interest on funds borrowed for construction. Management has decided to change its policy and desires to include interest as part of the cost of a new store just being completed. (a) Based on the following information, how much interest would be added to the cost of the store in 1987? (b) In 1988?

Total construction expenditures:

January 2, 1987	$200,000	*1,300,000*
May 1, 1987	600,000	
November 1, 1987	500,000	
March 1, 1988	700,000	
September 15, 1988	400,000	
December 31, 1988	500,000	
	$2,900,000	

Outstanding company debt:
  Mortgage related directly to new store:
    interest rate 12%; term, five years from beginning of construction .. $1,000,000
  General bond liability:
    Bonds issued just prior to construction of store;
      interest rate 10% for ten years .... $ 500,000
    Bonds issued previously—8%, mature in five years $1,500,000
  Estimated cost of equity capital. 14%

Total debt 2,000,000

EXERCISE 11-13   (Research and development costs)

In 1987 the Armstrong Corporation incurred research and development costs as follows:

Materials and equipment	$130,000
Personnel	100,000
Indirect costs	50,000
	$280,000

These costs relate to a product that will be marketed in 1988. It is estimated that these costs will be recouped by December 31, 1991.

(1) What is the amount of research and development costs which should be charged to income in 1987?

(2) Assume that of the above costs, equipment of $75,000 can be used on other research projects. Estimated useful life of the equipment is five years, and it was acquired at the beginning of 1987. What is the amount of research and development costs that should be charged to income in 1987 under these conditions? Assume depreciation on all equipment is computed on a straight-line basis.   (AICPA adapted)

EXERCISE 11–14   (Capital vs. revenue expenditures)

One of the most difficult problems facing an accountant is the determination of which expenditures should be deferred as assets and which should be immediately charged off as expenses. What position would you take in each of the following instances?

(a) Painting of partitions in a large room recently divided into four sections.
(b) Labor cost of tearing down a wall to permit extension of assembly line.
(c) Replacement of motor on a machine. Life used to depreciate the machine is 8 years. The machine is 4 years old. Replacement of the motor was anticipated when the machine was purchased.
(d) Cost of grading land prior to construction.
(e) Assessment for street paving.
(f) Cost of tearing down a previously occupied old building in preparation for new construction; old building is fully depreciated.

*EXERCISE 11–15   (Calculation of normal pretax earnings)

In analyzing the accounts of Gimble's Inc. in an attempt to measure goodwill, you find pretax earnings of $700,000 for 1987 after debits and credits for the items listed below. Land, buildings, and equipment are appraised at 40% above cost for purposes of the sale.

Depreciation of land, buildings, and equipment (at cost)	$ 75,000
Special year-end bonus to president of company	40,000
Gain on sale of securities	45,000
Gain on revaluation of securities	20,000
Write-off of goodwill	130,000
Amortization of patents and leaseholds	62,500
Income tax refund for 1985	20,000

What is the normal pretax earnings balance for purposes of your calculations?

*EXERCISE 11–16   (Calculation of goodwill—various methods)

The appraised value of net assets of the Fietkau Co. on December 31, 1987, was $800,000. Average net earnings for the past 5 years after elimination of unusual or extraordinary gains and losses were $135,000. Calculate the amount to be paid for goodwill under each of the following assumptions.

(a) Earnings are capitalized at 15% in arriving at the business worth.
(b) A return of 9% is considered normal on net assets at their appraised value; excess earnings are to be capitalized at 15% in arriving at the value of goodwill.
(c) A return of 10% is considered normal on net assets at their appraised value; goodwill is to be valued at 5 years' excess earnings.
(d) A return of 10% is considered normal on net identifiable assets at their appraised value. Excess earnings are expected to continue for six years. Goodwill is to be valued by the present value method using a rate of 12%. (Use present value table in Chapter 6).

*Relates to Appendix

*EXERCISE 11–17   (Computation of goodwill — decision)

Because of superior earning power, Ficklegruber Inc. is considering paying $603,830 for B & J Properties with the following assets and liabilities:

	Cost	Fair Market Value
Accounts receivable	$240,000	$220,000
Inventory	140,000	150,000
Prepaid insurance	10,000	10,000
Buildings and equipment (net)	170,000	300,000
Accounts payable	(160,000)	(160,000)
Net assets	$400,000	$520,000

Estimated future earnings are expected to exceed normal earnings by $27,600 for four years. Ficklegruber Inc. uses the present value method of valuing goodwill. Ficklegruber is willing to purchase B & J if the normal rate of return for B & J exceeds 10%. Should Ficklegruber purchase B & J Properties? (Use present value table in Chapter 6.)

*EXERCISE 11–18   (Computation of goodwill)

The owners of the Levine Clothing Store are contemplating selling the business to new interests. The cumulative earnings for the past 5 years amounted to $600,000 including extraordinary gains of $40,000. The annual earnings based on an average rate of return on investment for this industry would have been $76,000. Excess earnings are to be capitalized at 20%. What is the amount of implied goodwill?   (AICPA adapted)

Relates to Appendix.

PROBLEMS

PROBLEM 11–1   (Lump-sum acquisition of plant)

The Sevier Wholesale Company incurred the following expenses in 1987 for their office building acquired on July 1, 1987, the beginning of its fiscal year:

Cost of land	$ 60,000
Cost of building	540,000
Remodeling and repairs prior to occupancy	67,500
Escrow fee	10,000
Landscaping	25,000
Unpaid property tax for period prior to acquisition	15,000
Real estate commission	30,000

The company signed a non-interest-bearing note for $500,000 on the acquisition. The implicit interest rate is 10%. Payments of $25,000 are to be made semiannually beginning January 1, 1988, for 10 years.

Instructions: Give the required journal entries to record (1) the acquisition of the land and building (assume that cash is paid to equalize the cost of the assets and the present value of the note), and (2) the first two semiannual payments, including amortization of note discount for 1987 and 1988.

PROBLEM 11–2   (Correcting plant capitalization)

On December 31, 1987, the Bushman Co. shows the following account for machinery it had assembled for its own use during 1987:

Account   **Machinery (Job Order #962)**

Item	Debit	Credit	Balance Debit	Balance Credit
Cost of dismantling old machine	12,480		12,480	
Cash proceeds from sale of old machine		10,000	2,480	
Raw materials used in construction of new machine	63,000		65,480	
Labor in construction of new machine ...	49,000		114,480	
Cost of installation	11,200		125,680	
Materials spoiled in machine trial runs...	2,400		128,080	
Profit on construction..................	24,000		152,080	
Purchase of machine tools	16,000		168,080	

An analysis of the detail in the account disclosed the following:

(a) The old machine, which was removed in the installation of the new one, had been fully depreciated.

(b) Cash discounts received on the payments for materials used in construction totaled $2,500 and these were reported in the purchase discounts account.

(c) The factory overhead account shows a balance of $292,000 for the year ended December 31, 1987; this balance exceeds normal overhead on regular plant activities by approximately $14,800 and is attributable to machine construction.

(d) A profit was recognized on construction for the difference between costs incurred and the price at which the machine could have been purchased.

Instructions:

(1) Determine the machinery and machine tools balances as of December 31, 1987.

(2) Give individual journal entries necessary to correct the accounts as of December 31, 1987, assuming that the nominal accounts are still open.

PROBLEM 11–3   (Acquisition of plant)

The Triad Co. planned to open a new store. The company narrowed the possible sites to two lots and decided to take purchase options on both lots while they studied traffic densities in both areas. They paid $7,200 for the option on Lot A and $14,400 for the option on Lot B. After studying traffic densities, they decided to purchase Lot B. The company opened a single real estate account that shows the following:

Debits: Option on Lot A . . . . $ 7,200
        Option on Lot B   14,400
        Payment of balance on Lot B 155,000
        Title insurance   2,100
        Assessment for street improvements.   5,100
        Recording fee for deed.   600
        Cost of razing old building on Lot B.   9,000
        Payment for erection of new building. 300,000
Credit: Sale of salvaged materials from old building   5,000

The salvage value of material obtained from the old building and used in the erection of the new building was $6,000. The depreciated value of the old building, as shown by the books of the company from which the purchase was made, was $54,000. The old building was razed immediately after the purchase.

Instructions:
(1) Determine the cost of the land, listing the items included in the total.
(2) Determine the cost of the new building, listing the items included in the total.

PROBLEM 11–4   (Transactions involving plant)

The following transactions were completed by the Futuristic Toy Co. during 1987:

Mar. 1   Purchased real property for $624,250 which included a charge of $14,250 representing property tax for March 1–June 30 that had been prepaid by the vendor; 20% of the purchase price is deemed applicable to land and the balance to buildings. A mortgage of $375,000 was assumed by the Futuristic Toy Co. on the purchase. Cash was paid for the balance.

2–30 Previous owners had failed to take care of normal maintenance and repair requirements on the building, necessitating current reconditioning at a cost of $24,900.

May 15   Garages in the rear of the building were demolished, $4,500 being recovered on the lumber salvage. The company proceeded to construct a warehouse. The cost of such construction was $37,500 which was almost exactly the same as bids made on the construction by independent contractors. Upon completion of construction, city inspectors ordered extensive modifications in the buildings as a result of failure on the part of the company to comply with the Building Safety Code. Such modifications, which could have been avoided, cost $9,600.

June   1   The company exchanged its own stock with a fair market value of $35,000 (par $30,000) for a patent and a new plastic robot making machine. The machine has a market value of $25,000.

July   1   The new machinery for the new building arrived. In addition to the machinery a new franchise was acquired from the manufacturer of the machinery to produce toy robots. Payment was made by issuing bonds with a face value of $50,000 and by paying cash of $15,000. The value of the franchise is set at $20,000 while the fair market value of the machine is $40,000.

Nov. 20   The company contracted for parking lots and landscaping at a cost of $45,000 and $9,600 respectively. The work was completed and billed on November 20.

Dec. 31   The business was closed to permit taking the year-end inventory. During the taking of the inventory, required redecorating and repairs were completed at a cost of $6,000.

Instructions: Give the journal entries to record each of the preceding transactions. (Disregard depreciation.)

PROBLEM 11–5   (Acquisition of land and construction of plant)

The Feist Corporation was organized in June, 1987. In auditing the books of the company, you find a land, buildings, and equipment account with the following details:

Account   **Land, Buildings, and Equipment**

Date		Item	Debit	Credit	Balance Debit	Balance Credit
1987 June	8	Organization fees paid to the state	20,000		20,000	
	16	Land site and old building ...	315,000		335,000	
	30	Corporate organization costs	10,000		345,000	
July	2	Title clearance fees	8,400		353,400	
Aug.	28	Cost of razing old building ...	20,000		373,400	
Sept.	1	Salaries of Feist Corporation executives	56,000		429,400	
	1	Cost to acquire patent for special equipment	70,000		499,400	
Dec.	12	Stock bonus to corporate promoters, 2,000 shares of common stock, $40 par ...	80,000		579,400	
	15	County real estate tax.......	14,400		593,800	
	15	Cost of new building completed and occupied on this date.................	1,600,000		2,193,800	

An analysis of the foregoing account and of other accounts disclosed the following additional information:

(a) The building acquired on June 16, 1987, was valued at $35,000.
(b) The company paid $20,000 for the demolition of the old building, then sold the scrap for $1,000 and credited the proceeds to Miscellaneous Revenue.
(c) The company executives did not participate in the construction of the new building.
(d) The county real estate tax was for the six-month period ended December 31, 1987, and was assessed by the county on the land.

Instructions: Prepare journal entries to correct the books of the Feist Corporation. Each entry should include an explanation.

PROBLEM 11–6   (Acquisition of intangible assets)

In your audit of the books of Whipple Corporation for the year ending September 30, 1987, you found the following items in connection with the company's patents account:

(a) The company had spent $102,000 during its fiscal year ended September 30, 1986, for research and development costs and debited this amount to its patent account. Your review of the company's cost records indicated the company had spent a total of $123,500 for the research and development of its patents, of which only $21,500 spent in its fiscal year ended September 30, 1985, had been debited to Research and Development Expense.
(b) The patents were issued on April 1, 1986. Legal expenses in connection with the issuance of the patents of $14,280 were debited to Legal and Professional Fees.
(c) The company paid a retainer of $10,000 on October 5, 1986, for legal services in connection with an infringement suit brought against it. This amount was debited to Deferred Costs.
(d) A letter dated October 15, 1987, from the company's attorneys in reply to your inquiry as to liabilities of the company existing at September 30, 1987, indicated that a settlement of the infringement suit had been arranged. The other party had agreed to drop the suit and to release the company from all future liabilities for $20,000. Additional fees due to the attorneys amounted to $1,260.

Instructions: From the information given, prepare correcting journal entries as of September 30, 1987.

PROBLEM 11–7   (Acquisition of intangible assets)

Transactions during 1987 of the newly organized Finn Corporation included the following:

Jan.   2 Paid legal fees of $15,000 and stock certificate costs of $3,200 to complete organization of the corporation.

  15 Hired a clown to stand in front of the corporate office for two weeks and hand out pamphlets and candy to create goodwill for the new enterprise. Clown cost $1,000, candy and pamphlets, $500.

Apr. 1 Patented a newly developed process with the following costs:

Legal fees to obtain patent....................	$22,400
Patent application and licensing fees	3,200
Total.......................................	$25,600

It is estimated that in five years other companies will have developed improved processes making the Finn Corporation process obsolete.

May 1 Acquired both a license to use a special type of container and a distinctive trademark to be printed on the container in exchange for 600 shares of Finn Corporation no par common stock selling for $80 per share. The license is worth twice as much as the trademark, both of which may be used for 6 years.

July 1 Constructed a shed for $75,000 to house prototypes of experimental models to be developed in future research projects.

Dec. 31 Salaries for an engineer and a chemist involved in product development totaled $100,000 in 1987.

Instructions:

(1) Give journal entries to record the foregoing transactions. (Give explanations in support of your entries.)

(2) Present in good form the "Intangible assets" section of the Finn Corporation balance sheet at December 31, 1987.

PROBLEM 11–8
(Income statement for computer software company)

The Microword Company is engaged in developing computer software for the small business and home computer market. Most of the computer programmers are involved in developmental work designed to produce software that will perform fairly specific tasks in a user-friendly manner. Extensive testing of the working model is performed before it is released to production for preparation of masters and further testing. As a result of careful preparation, Microword has produced several products that have been very successful in the marketplace.

The following costs were incurred during 1987.

Salaries and wages of programmers doing research....................	$235,000
Expenses related to projects prior to establishment of technological feasibility	$78,400
Expenses related to projects after technological feasibility has been established but before software is available for production	$49,500
Amortization of capitalized software development costs from current and prior years...	$26,750
Costs to produce and prepare software for sale	$56,300

Additional data for 1987 include:

Sales of products for the year..	$515,000
Beginning inventory...	$142,000
Portion of goods available for sale sold during year....................	60%

Instructions: Prepare an income statement for Microword for the year 1987. Income tax rate is 40%. (Ignore earnings per share computations.)

PROBLEM 11–9   (Valuation of plant assets)

At December 31, 1986, certain accounts included in the property, plant, and equipment section of the Cummings Company's balance sheet had the following balances:

Land	$100,000
Buildings	900,000
Leasehold Improvements	500,000
Machinery and Equipment	600,000

During 1987 the following transactions occurred:

(a) Land site number 653 was acquired for $1,500,000. Additionally, to acquire the land Cummings paid a $90,000 commission to a real estate agent. Costs of $15,000 were incurred to clear the land. During the course of clearing the land, timber and gravel were recovered and sold for $10,000.

(b) A second tract of land (site number 654) with a building was acquired for $400,000. The closing statement indicated that the land value was $260,000 and the building value was $140,000. Shortly after acquisition, the building was demolished at a cost of $30,000. A new building was constructed for $200,000 plus the following costs.

Excavation fees	$11,000
Architectural design fees	8,000
Building permit fee	1,000
Imputed interest on funds used during construction	6,000

The building was completed and occupied on September 30, 1987.

(c) A third tract of land (site number 655) was acquired for $600,000 and was put on the market for resale.

(d) Extensive work was done to a building occupied by Cummings under a lease agreement that expires on December 31, 1996. The total cost of work was $125,000, which consisted of the following:

Painting of ceilings	$ 10,000	(estimated useful life is one year)
Electrical work	35,000	(estimated useful life is ten years)
Construction of extension to current working area	80,000	(estimated useful life is thirty years)
	$125,000	

The lessor paid ½ of the costs incurred in connection with the extension to the current working area.

(e) During December 1987 costs of $65,000 were incurred to improve leased office space. The related lease will terminate on December 31, 1989, and is not expected to be renewed.

(f) A group of new machines was purchased under a royalty agreement which provides for payment of royalties based on units of production for the machines. The invoice price of the machines was $75,000, freight costs were $2,000, unloading charges were $1,500, and royalty payments for 1987 were $13,000.

Instructions:

(1) Prepare a detailed analysis of the changes in each of the following balance sheet accounts for 1987: Land, Buildings, Leasehold Improvements, and Machinery and Equipment. (Disregard the related accumulated depreciation accounts.)

(2) List the items in the fact situation which were not used to determine the answer to (1), and indicate where, or if, these items should be included in Cumming's financial statements.   (AICPA adapted)

PROBLEM 11–10   (Self-construction of equipment)

National Corporation received a $400,000 low bid from a reputable manu-facturer for the construction of special production equipment needed by National in an expansion program. Because the company's own plant was not operating at capacity, National decided to construct the equipment there and recorded the following production costs related to the construction:

Services of consulting engineer	$ 10,000
Work subcontracted...	20,000
Materials	200,000
Plant labor normally assigned to production....................	65,000
Plant labor normally assigned to maintenance..................	100,000
Total	$395,000

Management prefers to record the cost of the equipment under the incremental cost method. Approximately 40% of the corporation's production is devoted to government supply contracts which are all based in some way on cost. The contracts require that any self-constructed equipment be allocated its full share of all costs related to the construction.

The following information is also available:

(a) The above production labor was for partial fabrication of the equipment in the plant. Skilled personnel were required and were assigned from other projects. The maintenance labor would have been idle time of nonproduction plant employees who would have been retained on the payroll whether or not their services were utilized.

(b) Payroll taxes and employee fringe benefits are approximately 30% of labor cost and are included in manufacturing overhead cost. Total manufacturing overhead for the year was $5,630,000 including the $100,000 maintenance labor used to construct the equipment.

(c) Manufacturing overhead is approximately 50% variable and is applied on the basis of production labor cost. Production labor cost for the year for the corporation's normal products totaled $6,810,000.

(d) General and administrative expenses include $22,500 of executive salary cost and $10,500 of postage, telephone, supplies, and miscellaneous expenses identifiable with this equipment construction.

Instructions:

(1) Prepare a schedule computing the amount that should be reported as the full cost of the constructed equipment to meet the requirements of the government contracts. Any supporting computations should be in good form.

(2) Prepare a schedule computing the incremental cost of the constructed equipment.

(3) What is the greatest amount that should be capitalized as the cost of the equipment? Why?   (AICPA adapted)

PROBLEM 11–11   (Capital vs. revenue expenditures)

The Togo Company completed a program of expansion and improvement of its plant during 1987. You are provided with the following information concerning its buildings account:

(a) On October 31, 1987, a 30-foot extension to the present factory building was completed at a contract cost of $108,000.

(b) During the course of construction, the following costs were incurred for the removal of the end wall of the building where the extension was to be constructed:

 (1) Payroll costs during the month of April arising from employees' time spent in removing of the wall, $6,940.

 (2) Payments to a salvage company for removing unusual debris, $780.

(c) The cost of the original structure allocable to the end wall was estimated to be $26,400, with accumulated depreciation thereon of $11,100: $7,080 was received by Togo Company from the construction company for windows and other assorted materials salvaged from the old wall.

(d) The old flooring was covered with a new type long-lasting floor covering at a cost of $5,290. Cost of old flooring not available.

(e) The interior of the plant was repainted in new bright colors for a contract price of $5,375.

(f) New and improved shelving was installed at a cost of $1,212. Cost of old shelving not determinable.

(g) Old electrical wiring was replaced at a cost of $10,218. Cost of the old wiring was determined to be $4,650 with accumulated depreciation to date of $2,055.

(h) New electrical fixtures using fluorescent bulbs were installed. The new fixtures were purchased on the installment plan; the schedule of monthly payments showed total payments of $9,300, which included interest and carrying charges of $720. The old fixtures were carried at a cost of $2,790 with accumulated depreciation to date of $1,200. The old fixtures had no scrap value.

Instructions: Prepare journal entries including explanations for the above information. Briefly justify the capitalization vs. revenue decision for each item.

*PROBLEM 11–12   (Computation of goodwill)

The Elgin Corp. in considering acquisition of the Weiser Company assembles the following information relative to the company.

Weiser Company
Balance Sheet
December 31, 1988

Assets	Per Company's Books	As Adjusted by Appraisal and Audit
Current assets..............................	$ 96,000	$ 92,000
Investments..................................	32,000	28,000
Land, buildings, and equipment (net)..............	279,200	260,000
Goodwill......................................	64,000	64,000
	$471,200	$444,000
Liabilities and Stockholders' Equity		
Current liabilities..............................	$ 15,000	$ 15,000
Long-term liabilities...........................	160,000	160,000
Capital stock.................................	160,000	160,000
Retained earnings...........................	136,200	109,000
	$471,200	$444,000

An analysis of retained earnings discloses the following information:

	Per Company's Books	As Adjusted by Appraisal and Audit
Retained earnings, January 1, 1986.................	$115,560	$ 85,600
Add net income, 1986–1988*......................	49,440	52,200
Deduct dividends 1986–1988......................	(28,800)	(28,800)
Retained earnings, December 31, 1988..............	$136,200	$109,000
*Loss on sale of plant assets in 1988, included in net income...	$ 48,960	$ 52,800

Instructions:
(1) Calculate the amount to be paid for goodwill, assuming that earnings of the future are expected to be the same as average normal earnings of the past three years, 10% is accepted as a reasonable return on net assets other than goodwill as of December 31, 1988, and average earnings in excess of 10% are capitalized at 16% in determining goodwill.
(2) Give the entry on the books of the Elgin Corp., assuming purchase of the assets of the Weiser Company and assumption of its liabilities on the basis as indicated in (1). Cash is paid for net assets acquired.

*Relates to Appendix

*PROBLEM 11–13   (Computation of goodwill)

East Coast Industries Inc. assembles the following data relative to the Arlington Corp. in determining the amount to be paid for the net assets and goodwill of the latter company:

Assets at appraised value (before goodwill)	$1,800,000
Liabilities...	760,000
Stockholders' equity	$1,040,000

Net earnings (after elimination of extraordinary items):

1984	$180,000
1985	139,000
1986	194,000
1987	175,000
1988	202,000

Instructions: Calculate the amount to be paid for goodwill under each of the following assumptions:

(1) Average earnings are capitalized at 16% in arriving at the business worth.
(2) A return of 12% is considered normal on net assets at appraised values, goodwill is valued at 5 years' excess earnings.
(3) A return of 14% is considered normal on net assets at appraised values; excess earnings are to be capitalized at 20%.
(4) Goodwill is valued at the sum of the earnings of the last 3 years in excess of a 10% annual yield on net assets at appraised values. (Assume that net assets are the same for the 3-year period.)
(5) A return of 10% is considered normal on net identifiable assets at their appraised values. Excess earnings are expected to continue for 10 years. Goodwill is to be valued by the present value method using a 20% rate. (Use Chapter 6 present value table.)

Relates to Appendix

12
Plant and Intangible Assets—
Utilization and Retirement

A fundamental characteristic of plant and intangible assets is that they are used to produce revenues over more than one accounting period. Another characteristic common to these assets is that they have limited economic or useful lives. A notable exception to this generalization is land—even farm land can be kept productive indefinitely with proper fertilization and care. All other plant assets, however, have limited lives. The economic benefits provided by intangible assets are, in some cases, limited to a period of time specified by law or contract. Some intangible assets, on the other hand, tend to decline in usefulness with the passage of time.

In order to match costs with related revenues, the cost of an operating asset (other than land) must be allocated in some manner over the estimated useful life of the asset. In practice, three different terms have evolved to describe this **cost allocation process** depending on the type of asset involved. The allocation of **plant asset costs** is referred to as **depreciation**. For mineral and other **natural resources**, the cost allocation process is appropriately called **depletion**. For **intangible assets**, such as patents, copyrights, and goodwill, the process is referred to as **amortization**. Sometimes the latter term is used generically to encompass all the other terms. Because the principles underlying each of these terms are similar, they are discussed together in this chapter.

DEPRECIATION OF PLANT ASSETS

Depreciation is the systematic and rational allocation of asset cost over the periods benefited by the use of the asset. There has been a tendency, however, on the part of many readers of financial statements to interpret depreciation accounting as somehow related to the accumulation of a fund for asset replacement. Terminology used in the past, such as "provision for depreciation" and "reserve for depreciation" has contributed toward this misinterpretation. These have been replaced by more descriptive terms, i.e., "depreciation expense" and "accumulated depreciation."

The charge for depreciation is the recognition of the declining service potential of an asset. The nature of this charge is no different from those made to recognize the expiration of insurance premiums or patent rights. It is true that revenues equal to or in excess of expenses for a period result in a recovery of these expenses; salary expense is thus recovered by revenues, as is insurance expense, patent amortization, and charges for depreciation. But this does not mean that cash equal to the recorded depreciation will be segregated for property replacement. Revenues may be applied to many uses: to the increase in receivables, inventories, or other working capital items; to the acquisition of new property or other noncurrent items; to the retirement of debt or the redemption of stock; or to the payment of dividends. If a special fund is to be established for the replacement of property, specific authorization by management would be required. Such a fund is seldom found, however, because fund earnings would usually be less than the return from alternative uses of the resources.

Factors Affecting the Periodic Depreciation Charge

Four factors must be recognized in determining the periodic charge for depreciation: (1) **asset cost**, (2) **residual or salvage value**, (3) **useful life**, and (4) **pattern of use**.

Asset Cost. The **cost** of an asset includes all the expenditures relating to its acquisition and preparation for use as described in Chapter 11. The cost of an asset less the expected residual value, if any, is the **depreciable cost** or **depreciation base**, i.e., the portion of asset cost to be charged against future revenues.

Residual or Salvage Value. The **residual (salvage) value** of a plant asset is an estimate of the amount that can be realized upon retirement of the asset. This depends on the retirement policy of the company as well as market conditions and other factors. If, for example, the company normally uses equipment until it is physically exhausted and no longer serviceable, the residual value, represented by the scrap or junk that can be salvaged, may be nominal. But if the company normally replaces its equipment after a relatively short period of use, the residual value, represented by the selling price or trade-in value, may be relatively high. From a theoretical point of view, any estimated residual value should be subtracted from cost in arriving at the portion of asset cost to be allocated.

In practice, however, residual values are frequently ignored in determining periodic depreciation charges. This practice is not objectionable when residual values are relatively small or not subject to reasonable estimation, and when it is doubtful whether more useful information will be provided through such refinement.

Useful Life. Plant assets other than land have a limited **useful life** as a result of certain physical and functional factors. The **physical factors** that limit the service life of an asset are (1) *wear and tear,* (2) *deterioration and decay,* and (3) *damage or destruction.* Everyone is familiar with the processes of wear and tear that render an automobile, a typewriter, or furniture no longer usable. A tangible asset, whether used or not, is also subject to deterioration and decay through aging. Finally, fire, flood, earthquake, or accident may reduce or terminate the useful life of an asset.

The **functional factors** limiting the lives of these assets are (1) *inadequacy* and (2) *obsolescence.* An asset may lose its usefulness when, as a result of altered business requirements or technical progress, it no longer can produce sufficient revenue to justify its continued use. Although the asset is still usable, its inability to produce sufficient revenue has cut short its service life. An example of rapid obsolescence can be observed in the computer industry. The rapid technological changes in this field have rendered perfectly good electronic equipment obsolete for efficient continued use long before the physical asset itself wore out.

Both physical and functional factors must be considered in estimating the useful life of a depreciable plant asset. This recognition requires estimating what events will take place in the future and requires careful judgment on the part of the accountant.[1] Physical factors are more readily apparent than functional factors in predicting asset life. But when functional factors are expected to hasten the retirement of an asset, these must also be recognized.

In practice, many companies as a matter of policy dispose of certain classes of assets after a predetermined period, without regard to the serviceability of individual assets within a class. Company automobiles, for example, may be replaced routinely every two or three years.

---

[1]Although the concept of useful life is generally recognized to be difficult to apply, there has been relatively little written on it in accounting literature. For a thorough discussion of the topic, see Charles Lamden, Dale L. Gerboth, and Thomas McRae, "Accounting for Depreciable Assets," *Accounting Research Monograph No. 1* (New York: American Institute of Certified Public Accountants, 1975), Ch. 5.

The useful life of a depreciable plant asset may be expressed in terms of either an estimated time factor or an estimated use factor. The **time factor** may be a period of months or years; the **use factor** may be a number of hours of service or a number of units of output. The cost of the asset is allocated in accordance with the lapse of time or extent of use. The rate of cost allocation may be modified by other factors, but basically depreciation must be recognized on a time or use basis.

Pattern of Use. In order to match asset cost against revenues, periodic depreciation charges should reflect as closely as possible the **pattern of use**. If the asset produces a varying revenue pattern, then the depreciation charges should vary in a corresponding manner. When depreciation is measured in terms of a time factor, the pattern of use must be estimated. Because of the difficulty in identifying a pattern of use, several somewhat arbitrary methods have come into common use. Each method represents a different pattern and is designed to make the time basis approximate the use basis. The time factor is employed in two general classes of methods, **straight-line depreciation** and **decreasing-charge depreciation**. When depreciation is measured in terms of a use factor, the units of use must be estimated. The depreciation charge varies periodically in accordance with the services provided by the asset. The use factor is employed in **service-hours depreciation** and in **productive-output depreciation**.

Recording Periodic Depreciation

The periodic allocation of plant asset costs is made by debiting either a production overhead cost account or a selling or administrative expense account, and crediting an allowance or contra asset account. If the charge is made to a production overhead account, it becomes part of the cost of the finished and unfinished goods inventories and is deferred to the extent inventory has not been sold or completed. If the charge is made to selling or administrative expenses, it is considered to be a period cost and is written off against revenue as an operating expense of the current period.

The valuation or allowance account that is credited in recording periodic depreciation is commonly titled Accumulated Depreciation. The accumulation of expired cost in a separate account rather than crediting the asset account directly permits identification of the original cost of the asset and the accumulated depreciation. The FASB requires disclosure of both cost and accumulated depreciation for plant assets on the balance sheet or notes to the financial statements. This enables the user to estimate the relative age of all assets and provides some basis for evaluating the effects of price-level changes on the company's plant assets.

Methods of Depreciation

There are a number of different methods for allocating the costs of depreciable assets. The depreciation method used in any specific instance is a matter of judgment and should be selected to most closely approximate the actual pattern of use expected from the asset. The following methods are described in this chapter:

Time-Factor Methods
1. Straight-line depreciation
2. Decreasing-charge (accelerated) depreciation
    (a) Sum-of-the-years-digits method
    (b) Declining-balance methods
3. Accelerated cost recovery system (ACRS)

Use-Factor Methods
1. Service-hours method
2. Productive-output method

Group-Rate and Composite-Rate Methods
1. Group depreciation
2. Composite depreciation

The examples that follow assume the acquisition of a polyurethane plastic molding machine at the beginning of 1987 by Schuss Boom Ski Manufacturing, Inc., at a cost of $100,000 with an estimated residual value of $5,000. The following symbols are used in the formulas for the development of depreciation rates and charges:

C = Asset cost
R = Estimated residual value
n = Estimated life in years, hours of service, or units of output
r = Depreciation rate per period, per hour of service, or per unit of output
D = Periodic depreciation charge

Time-Factor Methods. The most common methods of cost allocation are related to the passage of time. In general, a productive asset is used up over time. Possible obsolescence due to technological changes is also a function of time. Of the time-factor methods, straight-line depreciation has been by far the most popular. Accounting Trends and Techniques reported that 567 of the 600 survey companies used the straight-line method in their 1984 financial statements.[2]

The use of decreasing-charge or "accelerated depreciation" methods is based largely on the assumption that there will be rapid reductions in asset efficiency, output, or other benefits in the early years of an asset's life. Such

---

[2]*Accounting Trends and Techniques* (New York: American Institute of Certified Public Accountants, 1985), p. 268.

reductions may be accompanied by increased charges for maintenance and repairs. Charges for depreciation decline, then, as the economic advantages afforded through ownership of the asset decline. The most commonly used decreasing-charge methods are sum-of-the-years-digits and some variation of a declining-balance method.

Straight-line Depreciation. **Straight-line depreciation** relates cost allocation to the passage of time and recognizes equal periodic charges over the life of the asset. The allocation assumes equal usefulness per time period, and in applying this assumption, the charge is not affected by asset productivity or efficiency variations. In developing the periodic charge, an estimate is made of the useful life of the asset in terms of months or years. The difference between the asset cost and residual value is divided by the useful life of the asset in arriving at the cost assigned to each time unit.

Using data for the machine acquired by Schuss Boom Ski Manufacturing (see page 496) and assuming a 5-year life, annual depreciation is determined as follows:

$$D = \frac{C - R}{n}, \quad \text{or} \quad \frac{\$100,000 - \$5,000}{5} = \$19,000$$

Annual depreciation can also be computed by applying a percentage, or **depreciation rate**, to depreciable cost. The rate is the reciprocal value of the useful life expressed in periods, or r (per period) $= 1 \div n$. In the example, the depreciation rate would be $1 \div 5 = 20\%$, and annual depreciation can be computed as follows:

$$\$95,000 \times 20\% = \$19,000$$

A table summarizing the cost allocation process for the asset in the example, using the straight-line method, follows:

Asset Cost Allocation—Straight-Line Method

End of Year	Depreciation Computation		Amount	Accumulated Depreciation	Asset Book Value
					$100,000
1987	$95,000 ÷ 5	=	$19,000	$19,000	81,000
1988	95,000 ÷ 5	=	19,000	38,000	62,000
1989	95,000 ÷ 5	=	19,000	57,000	43,000
1990	95,000 ÷ 5	=	19,000	76,000	24,000
1991	95,000 ÷ 5	=	19,000	95,000	5,000
			$95,000		

It was indicated earlier that residual value is frequently ignored when it is a relatively minor amount. If this were done in the example, depreciation would be recognized at $20,000 per year instead of $19,000.

Sum-of-the-Years-Digits Method. The **sum-of-the-years-digits method** provides decreasing charges by applying a series of fractions, each of a smaller value, to depreciable asset cost. Fractions are developed in terms of the sum of the asset life periods. The numerators are the years-digits listed in reverse order. The denominator for the fraction is obtained by adding these digits.

For example, given an asset with a 3-year life, the denominator, which is the same each year, would be 6, the "sum-of-the-years-digits" (1 + 2 + 3). Since the numerators, which decrease each year, are the years-digits in reverse order (3, 2, 1), the fractions would be: 3/6 for the first year; 2/6 for the second year; and 1/6 for the third year. The total of these fractions is 1.00; thus 100% of the depreciable cost is charged to expense at the end of 3 years. The following formula can be used to facilitate computation of the denominator:

$$[(n + 1) \div 2] \times n$$

If useful life is 15 years, the denominator, determined by the formula, is: $[(15 + 1) \div 2] \times 15 = 120$. The fraction applied to depreciable cost in the first year would be 15/120, in the second year, 14/120, and so on.

In the Schuss Boom example, useful life is 5 years, and the denominator of the fraction is: $[(5 + 1) \div 2] \times 5 = 15$. Alternatively, the denominator can be found by adding the years digits (1 + 2 + 3 + 4 + 5 = 15). Depreciation using the sum-of-the-years-digits method is summarized in the table below:

Asset Cost Allocation — Sum-of-the-Years-Digits Method

End of Year	Depreciation Computation		Amount	Accumulated Depreciation	Asset Book Value
					$100,000
1987	$95,000 × 5/15	=	$31,667	$31,667	68,333
1988	95,000 × 4/15	=	25,333	57,000	43,000
1989	95,000 × 3/15	=	19,000	76,000	24,000
1990	95,000 × 2/15	=	12,667	88,667	11,333
1991	95,000 × 1/15	=	6,333	95,000	5,000
			$95,000		

Note that under this method, the annual charge to depreciation expense declines by 1/15 of the depreciation asset base each year, or by $6,333.

Declining-Balance Methods. The **declining-balance methods** provide decreasing charges by applying a constant percentage rate to a declining asset book value. The most popular rates are 1.5 times the straight-line rate, often referred to as "150% declining balance," and 2 times the straight-line rate, often referred to as **double-declining-balance**.[3] Residual value is not used in the computations under this method; however, it is generally recognized that depreciation should not continue once the book value is equal to the residual value. The percentage to be used is a multiple of the straight-line rate, calculated for various useful lives as follows:

Estimated Useful Life in Years	Straight-Line Rate	1.5 times Straight-Line Rate	2.0 times Straight-Line Rate
3	33 1/3%	50%	66 2/3%
5	20	30	40
6	16 2/3	25	33 1/3
8	12 1/2	18 3/4	25
10	10	15	20
20	5	7 1/2	10

Depreciation using the double-declining-balance method for the asset described earlier is summarized in the table that follows.

End of Year	Depreciation Computation		Amount	Accumulated Depreciation	Asset Book Value
					$100,000
1987	$100,000 × 40%	=	$40,000	$40,000	60,000
1988	60,000 × 40	=	24,000	64,000	36,000
1989	36,000 × 40	=	14,400	78,400	21,600
1990	21,600 × 40	=	8,640	87,040	12,960
1991	12,960 × 40	=	5,184	92,224	7,776
			$92,224		

It should be noted that the rate of 40% is applied to the decreasing book value of the asset each year. This results in a declining amount of depreciation expense. In applying this rate, the book value after 5 years exceeds the residual value by $2,776 ($7,776 − $5,000). This condition arises whenever residual values are relatively low in amount. Since it is impossible to bring a value to zero by using a constant multiplier, most adopters of this method switch to either the straight-line or the sum-of-the-years-digits method when the remaining annual depreciation computed using these methods exceeds the depreciation computed by continuing to apply the declining-balance rate. In the above example, the depreciation expense for 1991 would be $7,960 if a switch were made from double-declining

---

[3]The pure declining-balance method computes a constant rate that, when applied to a declining book value, will cause the book value to equal the estimated residual value at the end of estimated useful life. The formula to arrive at this rate is $1 - \sqrt[n]{R \div C}$, where R is the residual value, C is cost of the asset, and n is the life of the asset. This method is seldom used in practice because it often exceeds the double-declining-balance rate, a limit imposed in the past through the tax code.

balance to straight-line. This would reduce the book value of the asset to its $5,000 residual value.

Accelerated Cost Recovery System (ACRS). The Economic Recovery Tax Act (ERTA) of 1981 introduced a new time-factor method of computing depreciation for tax purposes called the **accelerated cost recovery system (ACRS).** The term "cost recovery" was used in the tax regulations to emphasize that ACRS was not a standard depreciation method since the system was not based on asset life or pattern of use. ACRS has largely replaced traditional depreciation accounting for tax purposes. The new method was intended to both simplify the computation of depreciation and provide for a more rapid writeoff of asset cost to stimulate investment.

In general, the system as it was originally created required that most property acquired after December 31, 1980, be depreciated for tax purposes over one of three **recovery periods**: three, five, or fifteen years, depending on the nature of the property. Examples of 3-year recovery property included automobiles, light-duty trucks, and machinery and equipment used in connection with research and experimentation. The 5-year property class included most machinery, equipment, and furniture. The 15-year class included all real property, i.e., buildings and building improvements.

Cost recovery tables were prepared by the IRS for each class of property, specifying the percentage of cost recovery for each year. The tables developed for this purpose provided for a 150% declining balance pattern of depreciation in the early years of asset use, with built-in switches to straight-line depreciation to assure 100% recovery in the time specified. The tables generally provided for one-half year's depreciation in the year of acquisition for 3- and 5-year property. For 15-year property, the tables were prepared on a monthly basis and the percentage to apply depended on the month of acquisition. It is important to note that residual values are ignored under ACRS, and the recovery percentages are applied to the asset's original cost.

The following cost percentages apply to 3- and 5-year property acquired before 1987:

Year	3-Year Property	5-Year Property
1	25%	15%
2	38	22
3	37	21
4		21
5		21
	100%	100%

To illustrate application of ACRS, assume that the machine used in previous examples was purchased in 1986 and classified as 5-year recovery property under the ACRS guidelines. Depreciation charges on the machine for tax purposes would be as follows:

Year	Cost	Recovery Percentage	ACRS Depreciation
1986	$100,000	15%	$ 15,000
1987	100,000	22	22,000
1988	100,000	21	21,000
1989	100,000	21	21,000
1990	100,000	21	21,000
		100%	$100,000

The depreciation charge for the first year is 15% regardless of when the machine was purchased during 1986. At the end of the fifth year, the entire cost of the machine has been written off, for tax purposes, without regard to residual value.

Amendments to the income tax laws in 1984 and 1985 extended the recovery period for real property to 18 years and 19 years, respectively. A much more significant revision of ACRS, however, resulted from the Tax Reform Act of 1986. The provisions of the 1986 Act apply to assets acquired after December 31, 1986. Thus, ACRS depreciation on assets placed in service prior to 1987 will continue to be computed under the guidelines in effect at the time of acquisition.

Under the provisions of the Act, most 3-year property was reclassified to 5-year property, and most machinery and equipment moved from the 5-year class to a new 7-year class. The method of computing depreciation for these assets was changed to 200% declining balance, switching to straight-line in subsequent years. As noted earlier, a 150% declining-balance method was applicable to these assets under the original ACRS provisions. Thus, even though the cost of most machinery and equipment acquired after 1986 must be written off for tax purposes over a longer period, the effects are offset somewhat in the early years by applying the 200% declining-balance method.

The Tax Reform Act of 1986 had the greatest impact on real property. Under the provisions of the Act, the recovery period for nonresidential real property was increased to 31.5 years, with depreciation computed on a straight-line basis. This is a drastic change from the original ACRS provisions which permitted recovery over 15 years using 150% declining balance in the early years.

When ACRS was first adopted, the goal was to provide incentives for businesses to invest in new productive assets by allowing rapid writeoffs of asset cost. Subsequently, Congress became more concerned with increasing tax revenues to offset the rapidly growing federal deficit. Lengthening the cost recovery periods for depreciable assets was one means of increasing revenues without increasing tax rates. It is expected that such tinkering with ACRS will continue from year to year as the economy ebbs and flows. It is clear that, in this area, Congress is concerned with increasing tax revenues and not with accounting principles. Asset life and pattern of use are not considered important in establishing the recovery periods or the percentages.

Both the AICPA and the FASB have expressed concern over ACRS, and have stated that it should be used for financial reporting only if the lives and patterns of use inherent in the ACRS provisions coincide closely with the actual asset lives and patterns of use. This seldom occurred when the method was first introduced. If Congress continues to lengthen recovery periods, ACRS may approximate useful lives and patterns of use for some classes of assets. The inconsistency and unpredictability of ACRS rules changes, however, demonstrates the wisdom of the decision made by the AICPA not to accept ACRS as an acceptable depreciation method for financial reporting purposes.

Comparison of Time-Factor Methods. Exhibit 12-1 illustrates the pattern of depreciation expense for the time-factor methods discussed in the

Exhibit 12–1   Time-Factor Methods: Depreciation Patterns Compared

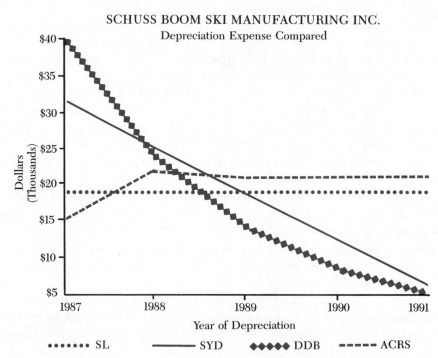

preceding sections. Note that when the straight-line method is used, depreciation is a constant or fixed charge each period. When the life of an asset is affected primarily by the lapse of time rather than by the degree of use, recognition of depreciation as a constant charge is generally appropriate. However, net income measurements become particularly sensitive to changes in the volume of business activity. With above-normal activity, there is no increase in the depreciation charge; with below-normal activity, revenue is still charged with the costs of assets standing ready to serve.

Straight-line depreciation is a widely used procedure for financial reporting purposes. It is readily understood and frequently parallels asset use. It has the advantage of simplicity and under normal conditions offers a satisfactory means of cost allocation. Normal asset conditions exist when (1) assets have been accumulated over a period of years so that the total of depreciation plus maintenance is comparatively even from period to period, and (2) service potentials of assets are being steadily reduced by functional as well as physical factors. The absence of either of these conditions may suggest the use of some depreciation method other than straight line.

Decreasing-charge methods can be supported as reasonable approaches to cost allocation when the annual benefits provided by an asset decline as it grows older. These methods, too, are suggested when an asset requires increasing maintenance and repairs over its useful life.[4] When straight-line depreciation is employed, the combined charges for depreciation, maintenance, and repairs will increase over the life of the asset; when the decreasing-charge methods are used, the combined charges will tend to be equalized. Exhibit 12–2 illustrates this relationship.

Other factors suggesting the use of a decreasing-charge method include: (1) the anticipation of a significant contribution in early periods with the extent of the contribution to be realized in later periods less definite; (2) the possibility that inadequacy or obsolescence may result in premature retirement of the asset.

Depreciation for Partial Periods. The discussion thus far has assumed that assets were purchased on the first day of a company's fiscal period. In

---

[4]The AICPA Committee on Accounting Procedure has stated, "The declining-balance method is one of those which meets the requirements of being 'systematic and rational.' In those cases where the expected productivity or revenue-earning power of the asset is relatively greater during the earlier years of its life, or where maintenance charges tend to increase during the later years, the declining-balance method may well provide the most satisfactory allocation of cost." The Committee would apply these conclusions to other decreasing-charge methods, including the sum-of-the-years-digits method, that produce substantially similar results. See *Accounting Research and Terminology Bulletins–Final Edition*, "No. 44 (Revised), Declining-Balance Depreciation" (New York: American Institute of Certified Public Accountants, 1961), par. 2.

Exhibit 12–2 Decreasing-Charge Depreciation and Repairs and Maintenance Expense

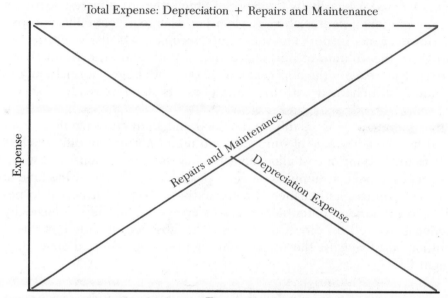

Total Expense: Depreciation + Repairs and Maintenance

reality, of course, asset transactions occur throughout the year. When a time-factor method is used, depreciation on assets acquired or disposed of during the year may be based on the number of days the asset was held during the period. When the level of acquisitions and retirements is significant, however, companies often adopt a less burdensome policy for recognizing depreciation for partial periods. Some alternatives found in practice include the following:

1. Depreciation is recognized to the nearest whole month. Assets acquired on or before the 15th of the month are considered owned for the entire month; assets acquired after the 15th are not considered owned for any part of the month. Conversely, assets sold on or before the 15th of the month are not considered owned for any part of the month; assets sold after the 15th are considered owned for the entire month.

2. Depreciation is recognized to the nearest whole year. Assets acquired during the first six months are considered held for the entire year; assets acquired during the last six months are not considered in the depreciation computation. Conversely, no depreciation is recorded on assets sold during the first six months and a full year's depreciation is recorded on assets sold during the last six months.

3. One-half year's depreciation is recognized on all assets purchased or sold during the year. A full year's depreciation is taken on all other assets.

4. No depreciation is recognized on acquisitions during the year but depreciation for a full year is recognized on retirements.

5. Depreciation is recognized for a full year on acquisitions during the year but no depreciation is recognized on retirements.

Methods 2 through 5 are attractive because of their simplicity. However, Method 1 provides greater accuracy and its use is assumed in the examples and problems in the text unless otherwise specified.

If a company uses the sum-of-the-years-digits method of depreciation and recognizes partial year's depreciation on assets in the year purchased, the depreciation expense for the second year must be determined by the following allocation procedure. Assume that the asset acquired by Schuss Boom Ski Manufacturing (see page 496) was purchased ¾ of the way through the fiscal year. The computation of depreciation expense for the first two years would be as follows:

First Year:
Depreciation for full year (See page 498) $31,667
One-fourth year's depreciation ($31,667 ÷ 4) .... $ 7,917

Second Year:
Depreciation for balance of first year ($31,667 − $7,917) $23,750
Depreciation for second full year (See page 498) $25,333
One-fourth year's depreciation ($25,333 ÷ 4) 6,333
    Total depreciation—second year $30,083

From this point, each year's depreciation will be $\frac{1}{15}$ of the original depreciable asset base ($6,333) less than the previous year. A summary of the depreciation charges for the five-year period is as follows:

Year 1 .... $ 7,917
Year 2 30,083
Year 3 23,750
Year 4 17,417
Year 5 11,083
Year 6 4,750
   Total $95,000

If a company uses a declining-balance method of depreciation, the computation of depreciation when partial years are involved is more straightforward. After the first year's depreciation is computed, the remaining years are calculated in the same manner as illustrated above; a constant percentage is multiplied by a declining book value. Again assuming a purchase ¾ of the way through the fiscal year, the double-declining balance depreciation expense for the asset described on page 496 would be as follows:

Year 1   ($100,000 × .40 × 1/4) $10,000
Year 2   ($90,000 × .40) 36,000
Year 3   ($54,000 × .40) 21,600
Year 4   ($32,400 × .40) 12,960
Year 5   ($19,440 × .40) 7,776
Year 6   ($11,664 × .40 × 3/4) 3,499
   Total depreciation $91,835

Note that the book value at the end of the 5-year life is $8,165 ($100,000 − $91,835) and would require a switch to a straight-line rate to bring the book value to the residual value as was true in the previous double-declining-balance example on page 499.

Use-Factor Methods. Use factor methods view asset exhaustion as related primarily to asset use or output and provide periodic charges varying with the degree of such service. Service life for certain assets can best be expressed in terms of hours of service; for others in terms of units of production.

Service-Hours Method. **Service-hours depreciation** is based on the theory that purchase of an asset represents the purchase of a number of hours of direct service. This method requires an estimate of the life of the asset in terms of service hours. Depreciable cost is divided by total service hours in arriving at the depreciation rate to be assigned for each hour of asset use. The use of the asset during the period is measured, and the number of service hours is multiplied by the depreciation rate in arriving at the periodic depreciation charge. Depreciation charges against revenue fluctuate periodically according to the contribution the asset makes in service hours.

Using asset data previously given and an estimated service life of 20,000 hours, the rate to be applied for each service hour is determined as follows:

$$\text{r (per hour)} = \frac{C - R}{n}, \quad \text{or} \quad \frac{\$100,000 - \$5,000}{20,000} = \$4.75$$

Allocation of asset cost in terms of service hours is summarized in the table below.

Asset Cost Allocation — Service-Hours Method

End of Year	Service Hours	Depreciation Computation		Amount	Accumulated Depreciation	Asset Book Value
						$100,000
1987	3,000	3,000 × $4.75	=	$14,250	$14,250	85,750
1988	5,000	5,000 × $4.75	=	23,750	38,000	62,000
1989	5,000	5,000 × $4.75	=	23,750	61,750	38,250
1990	4,000	4,000 × $4.75	=	19,000	80,750	19,250
1991	3,000	3,000 × $4.75	=	14,250	95,000	5,000
	20,000			$95,000		

It is assumed that the original estimate of service hours is confirmed and the asset is retired after 20,000 hours are reached in the fifth year. Such precise confirmation would seldom be found in practice.

It should be observed that straight-line depreciation resulted in an annual charge of $19,000 regardless of fluctuations in productive activity. When asset life is affected directly by the degree of use, and when there are significant fluctuations in such use in successive periods, the service-hours method, which recognizes hours used instead of hours available for use, normally provides the more equitable charges to operations.

Productive-Output Method. **Productive-output depreciation** is based on the theory that an asset is acquired for the service it can provide in the form of production output. This method requires an estimate of the total unit output of the asset. Depreciable cost divided by the total estimated output gives the equal charge to be assigned for each unit of output. The measured production for a period multiplied by the charge per unit gives the charge to be made against revenue. Depreciation charges fluctuate periodically according to the contribution the asset makes in unit output.

Using the previous asset data and an estimated productive life of 2,500,000 units, the rate to be applied for each thousand units produced is determined as follows:

$$r \text{ (per thousand units)} = \frac{C - R}{n}, \quad \text{or} \quad \frac{\$100,000 - \$5,000}{2,500} = \$38.00$$

A table for the productive-output method would be similar to that prepared for the service-hours method.

Evaluation of Use-Factor Methods. When quantitative measures of plant asset use can be reasonably estimated, the use-factor methods provide highly satisfactory approaches to asset cost allocation. Depreciation as a fluctuating charge tends to follow the revenue curve: high depreciation charges are assigned to periods of high activity; low charges are assigned to periods of low activity. When the useful life of an asset is affected primarily by the degree of its use, recognition of depreciation as a variable charge is particularly appropriate.

However, certain limitations in applying the use-factor methods need to be pointed out. Asset performance in terms of service hours or productive output is often difficult to estimate. Measurement solely in terms of these factors could fail to recognize special conditions, such as increasing maintenance and repair costs, as well as possible inadequacy and obsolescence. Furthermore, when service life expires even in the absence of use, a use-factor method may conceal actual fluctuations in earnings; by relating periodic depreciation charges to the volume of operations, periodic operating results may be smoothed out, thus creating a false appearance of stability.

Group and Composite Methods. It was assumed in preceding discussions that depreciation expense is associated with individual assets and is applied to each separate unit. This practice is commonly referred to as **unit depreciation.** However, there may be certain advantages in associating depreciation with a group of assets and applying a single rate to the collective cost of the group at any given time. Group cost allocation procedures are referred to as **group depreciation** and **composite depreciation.**[5]

Group Depreciation. When useful life is affected primarily by physical factors, a group of similar items purchased at one time should have the same expected life, but in fact some will probably remain useful longer than others. In recording depreciation on a unit basis, the sale or retirement of an asset before or after its anticipated lifetime requires recognition of a gain or loss. Such gains and losses, however, can usually be attributed to normal variations in useful life rather than to unforeseen disasters and windfalls.

The **group-depreciation** procedure treats a collection of similar assets as a single group. Depreciation is accumulated in a single valuation account, and the depreciation rate is based on the average life of assets in the group. Because the accumulated depreciation account under the group procedure applies to the entire group of assets, it is not related to any specific asset. Thus, no book value can be calculated for any specific asset and there are no fully depreciated assets. To arrive at the periodic depreciation charge, the depreciation rate is applied to the recorded cost of all assets remaining in service, regardless of age.

When an item in the group is retired, no gain or loss is recognized; the asset account is credited with the cost of the item and the valuation account is debited for the difference between cost and any salvage. With normal variations in asset lives, the losses not recognized on early retirements are offset by the continued depreciation charges on those assets still in service after the average life has elapsed. Group depreciation is generally computed as an adaptation of the straight-line method, and the illustrations in this chapter assume this approach.[6]

To illustrate, assume that 100 similar machines having an average expected useful life of 5 years are purchased at the beginning of 1987 at a total cost of $2,000,000. Of this group, 30 machines are retired at the end of 1990, 40 at the end of 1991, and the remaining 30 at the end of 1992. Based on the average expected useful life of 5 years, a depreciation charge

---

[5] These methods are sometimes referred to as multiple-asset methods of depreciation. See Stephen T. Limberg and Bill N. Schwartz, "Should You Use Multiple Asset Accounts?" *The CPA Journal* (October 1981), pp. 25–31.

[6] The multiple-asset approach may be modified for unusual retirements. In order to preserve the average life computations, retirements arising from involuntary conversion or other such unusual causes may be recorded at a loss. In order to do this, however, there must be enough detail in the records to approximate the book value of the item at the date of the loss.

of 20% is reported on those assets in service each year. The charges for depreciation and the changes in the group asset and accumulated depreciation accounts are summarized below.

Asset Cost Allocation—Group Depreciation

End of Year	Depreciation Expense (20% of Cost)	Asset			Accumulated Depreciation			Asset Book Value
		Debit	Credit	Balance	Debit	Credit	Balance	
		$2,000,000		$2,000,000				$2,000,000
1987	$ 400,000			2,000,000		$ 400,000	$ 400,000	1,600,000
1988	400,000			2,000,000		400,000	800,000	1,200,000
1989	400,000			2,000,000		400,000	1,200,000	800,000
1990	400,000		$ 600,000	1,400,000	$ 600,000	400,000	1,000,000	400,000
1991	280,000		800,000	600,000	800,000	280,000	480,000	120,000
1992	120,000		600,000	—	600,000	120,000	—	—
	$2,000,000	$2,000,000	$2,000,000		$2,000,000	$2,000,000		

It should be noted that the depreciation charge is exactly $4,000 per machine-year. In each of the first four years, 100 machine-years of service[7] are utilized, and the annual depreciation charge is $400,000. In the fifth year, when only 70 machines are in operation, the charge is $280,000 (20% of $1,400,000). In the sixth year, when 30 units are still in service, a proportionate charge for such use of $120,000 (20% of $600,000) is made.

If the 30 machines retired in 1990 had been sold for $50,000, the entry to record the sale using the group depreciation method would have been as follows:

```
Cash.....................................................   50,000
Accumulated Depreciation—Equipment..........................  550,000
    Equipment...............................................            600,000
```

Because no gain or loss is recognized, the debit to accumulated depreciation is the difference between the cost of the equipment and the cash received.

The preceding example assumed that no new assets were added to the group. This is referred to as a "closed" group. Companies may create such a group, for example, for all furniture acquired in a given year. The group method may also be applied to an "open-ended" group. In this case, additions are made to the group and, thus, the accounts are never "closed." Assume the previous example is changed to include additions

---

[7]It should be observed that in the example the original estimates of an average useful life of 5 years is confirmed in the use of the assets. Such precise confirmation would seldom be the case. In instances where assets in a group are continued in use after their cost has been assigned to operations, no further depreciation charges would be recognized. On the other hand, where all of the assets in a group are retired before their cost has been assigned to operations, a special charge related to such retirement would have to be recognized.

of 20 machines at the end of 1988 at a cost of $425,000, 30 machines at the end of 1991 at a cost of $650,000, and 50 machines at the end of 1992 at a cost of $1,100,000. Assume that all retired machines are from the initial purchase. The charges for the first 6 years under these assumptions are summarized below.

Asset Cost Allocation — Open-Ended Group Depreciation

End of Year	Depreciation Expense (20% of cost)	Asset Debit	Asset Credit	Asset Balance	Accumulated Depreciation Debit	Accumulated Depreciation Credit	Accumulated Depreciation Balance	Asset Book Value
		$2,000,000		$2,000,000				$2,000,000
1987	$400,000			2,000,000		$400,000	$ 400,000	1,600,000
1988	400,000	425,000		2,425,000		400,000	800,000	1,625,000
1989	485,000			2,425,000		485,000	1,285,000	1,140,000
1990	485,000		$600,000	1,825,000	$600,000	485,000	1,170,000	655,000
1991	365,000	650,000	800,000	1,675,000	800,000	365,000	735,000	940,000
1992	335,000	1,100,000	600,000	2,175,000	600,000	335,000	470,000	1,705,000

Application of the group depreciation procedure under circumstances such as the foregoing provides an annual charge that is more closely related to the quantity of productive facilities being used. Gains and losses due solely to normal variations in asset lives are not recognized, and operating results are more meaningfully stated. The convenience of applying a uniform depreciation rate to a number of similar items may also represent a substantial advantage.

Composite Depreciation. The basic procedures employed under the group method for allocating the cost of substantially identical assets may be extended to include dissimilar assets. This special application of the group procedure is known as **composite depreciation**. The composite method retains the convenience of the group method, but because assets with varying service lives are aggregated to determine an average life, it is unlikely to provide all the reporting advantages of the group method.

A composite rate is established by analyzing the various assets or classes of assets in use and computing the depreciation as an average of the straight-line annual depreciation as follows:

Asset	Cost	Residual Value	Depreciable Cost	Estimated Life in Years	Annual Depreciation Expense (Straight-line)
A	$ 2,000	$ 120	$ 1,880	4	$ 470
B	6,000	300	5,700	6	950
C	12,000	1,200	10,800	10	1,080
	$20,000	$1,620	$18,380		$2,500

Composite depreciation rate to be applied to cost: $2,500 ÷ $20,000 = 12.5%
Composite or average life of assets: $18,380 ÷ $2,500 = 7.35 years.

It will be observed that a rate of 12.5% applied to the cost of the assets, $20,000, results in annual depreciation of $2,500. Annual depreciation of $2,500 will accumulate to a total of $18,380 in 7.35 years; hence 7.35 years may be considered the composite or average life of the assets. Composite depreciation would be reported in a single accumulated depreciation account. Upon the retirement of an individual asset, the asset account is credited and Accumulated Depreciation is debited with the difference between cost and residual value. As with the group procedure, no gains or losses are recognized at the time individual assets are retired.

After a composite rate has been set, it is ordinarily continued in the absence of significant changes in the lives of assets or asset additions and retirements having a material effect upon the rate. It is assumed in the preceding example that the assets are replaced with similar assets when retired. If they are not replaced, continuation of the 12.5% rate will misstate depreciation charges.

HISTORICAL COST VERSUS CURRENT COST ALLOCATION

A difficult problem in accounting for plant asset utilization arises in determining the periodic charges to revenues in periods of changing prices. In accounting practice, depreciation, depletion, and amortization have traditionally been viewed as an allocation of the acquisition cost over the life of the asset. This meaning can be observed in the definition of depreciation accounting adopted by the Committee on Terminology in the 1940's and still accepted today:

> *Depreciation accounting* is a system of accounting which aims to distribute the cost or other basic value of tangible capital assets, less salvage (if any), over the estimated useful life of the unit (which may be a group of assets) in a systematic and rational manner. It is a process of allocation, not of valuation. *Depreciation for the year* is the portion of the total charge under such a system that is allocated to the year. Although the allocation may properly take into account occurrences during the year, it is not intended to be a measurement of the effect of all such occurrences.[8]

Under this allocation view, the total amount charged against revenue is fixed by the acquisition cost less any estimated residual value. While the pattern of charges may vary with the allocation method used, the total

---

[8]*Accounting Research and Terminology Bulletins* — Final Edition, "Accounting Terminology Bulletins, No. 1, Review and Résumé" (New York: American Institute of Certified Public Accountants, 1961), par. 56.

amount charged against revenue cannot exceed the historical cost of the asset. For any group of assets at any given time, the cumulative amount charged against past revenues plus the remaining asset carrying or book value will equal the original acquisition cost adjusted by any additions or betterments.

As has been discussed previously, there are many accountants who advocate a charge against revenue based on a current asset value, i.e., the **replacement cost** or **current cost**. This allocation approach matches current rather than past costs against current revenues, resulting in a net income figure that better reflects income available for dividends and that is more useful for estimating future cash flows of a business entity. Plant assets, like inventories, must be replaced, and that portion of current and future earnings needed for replacement will not be available for distribution to owners or for payments to creditors.

This problem has been recognized as a particularly serious one for utilities, since they must obtain approval from regulatory commissions for any changes in the rates they charge to customers. One of the significant cost factors used in determining the rate base is depreciation. The telecommunications area has been especially hard hit in the 1980's as the divestitures arising from the court-ordered breakup of American Telephone and Telegraph Company have placed new strains on the pricing structure. The following quotation summarizes the problem as it relates to depreciation:

Traditional Depreciation Can't Keep Up

Depreciation is a big-ticket issue. The problem is that rapid technological advances and competition among telephone companies are making large portions of their plant and equipment obsolete long before the expiration of useful lives that are calculated under traditional depreciation accounting methods.

For more than a decade, the depreciation charges regulators have allowed telephone companies to pass on to their customers have fallen below what the companies need to recover their investment. The growing depreciation expense now represents by far the largest component of rising phone bills—far outstripping the cost added by divestiture. This has created a gap that some estimate as high as $25 billion between the reserves telephone companies have set aside for depreciation and the amounts they calculate they should have available to replace outmoded equipment.[9]

Historical cost is still the basis for financial statement reporting. However, various attempts have been made to modify the application of historical cost allocation to partially account for the impact of changing prices.

---

[9] Touche Ross & Co., *Washington Briefing* (January 1986), p. 4.

Emphasis in this chapter is on the methods used to allocate the historical acquisition cost against revenue and the modifications made to consider price changes. Supplemental disclosures for price changes are discussed and illustrated in Chapter 25.

AMORTIZATION OF INTANGIBLE ASSETS

The life of an intangible asset is usually limited by the effects of obsolescence, shifts in demand, competition, and other economic factors. Because of the difficulty in estimating such highly uncertain future events, companies sometimes did not amortize the cost of intangible assets, but assumed their value was never used up. This practice was frequently followed for trademarks, goodwill, and some franchises. The Accounting Principles Board, however, felt that eventually all intangible assets became of insignificant worth to the company. The Board, therefore, issued Opinion No. 17, requiring that the recorded costs of all intangible assets acquired after October 31, 1970–the effective date of the Opinion–be amortized over the estimated useful life.[10] Many companies do not amortize certain intangibles, notably goodwill, acquired prior to November 1, 1970, although amortization of these assets was encouraged by the Board. (See note for American Broadcasting Companies, Inc. on page 515.)

The useful life of an intangible asset may be affected by a variety of factors, all of which should be considered in determining the amortization period. Useful life may be limited by legal, regulatory, or contractual provisions. These factors, including options for renewal or extension, should be evaluated in conjunction with the economic factors noted above and other pertinent information. A patent, for example, has a legal life of 17 years; but if the competitive advantages afforded by the patent are expected to terminate after 5 years, then the patent cost should be amortized over the shorter period.

Although the life of an intangible asset is to be estimated by careful analysis of the surrounding circumstances, a maximum life of 40 years was established for amortization purposes. APB Opinion No. 17 included this limitation as follows:

> The cost of each type of intangible asset should be amortized on the basis of the estimated life of that specific asset and should not be written off in the period of acquisition. . . .

---

[10]Opinions of the Accounting Principles Board, No. 17, "Intangible Assets" (New York: American Institute of Certified Public Accountants, 1970).

The period of amortization should not, however, exceed forty years. Analysis at the time of acquisition may indicate that the indeterminate lives of some intangible assets are likely to exceed forty years and the cost of those assets should be amortized over the maximum period of forty years, not an arbitrary shorter period.[11]

The requirement that the recorded cost of all intangible assets be amortized and the arbitrary selection of a 40-year life are of questionable theoretical merit. An analysis of the expected future benefits to be derived from a particular asset should be the basis for capitalizing and amortizing the cost of any asset, whether tangible or intangible.

The establishment by the APB of a 40-year maximum period for the amortization of intangible assets was not intended to determine the normal write-off period as 40 years. However, for some assets, such as goodwill and franchise costs, 40 years has become the most popular period to use. While it is difficult to determine exactly how long goodwill benefits a company, the amortization period should be established based on sound reasoning, not some arbitrary period of time. Some accountants feel that a five- to ten-year period should be used because after that period, a company has probably built its own goodwill based on expenditures and actions during that period. Others feel that goodwill should be written off immediately against Retained Earnings because of the lack of comparability among companies, some of whom report purchased goodwill and others who do not.

The degree of diversity in the amortization of intangible assets, especially goodwill, suggests that further guidelines are needed in this area.[12]

Amortization, like depreciation, may be charged as an operating expense of the period or allocated to production overhead if the asset is directly related to the manufacture of goods. In practice the credit entry is often made directly to the asset account rather than to a separate allowance account. This practice is arbitrary, and there is no reason why charges for amortization cannot be accumulated in a separate account in the same manner as depreciation. The FASB requires disclosure of both cost and accumulated depreciation for plant assets, but does not require similar

---

[11]*Ibid.*, pars. 28–29.

[12] The standard-setting organization for Great Britain considered the goodwill issue in the early 1980's, and issued an official pronouncement in 1984 that recognized two methods of amortizing goodwill: either an immediate write-off against Retained Earnings, which they preferred, or an amortization period of no more than 40 years. The second position agrees with the United States standard. The first position was carefully considered by the APB, and although it was recommended by the authors of Accounting Research Study No. 10, it was rejected as an acceptable alternative.

disclosure for intangible assets. When amortization is recorded in a separate account, such account is typically called Accumulated Amortization.

Amortization of intangible assets is made evenly in most instances, or on a straight-line allocation basis. APB Opinion No. 17 states:

> The Board concludes that the straight-line method of amortization—equal annual amounts—should be applied unless a company demonstrates that another systematic method is more appropriate.[13]

Although practice favors straight-line amortization, analysis of many intangibles such as patents, franchises, and even goodwill suggests that greater benefit is often realized in the early years of the asset's life than in the later years. In those instances, a decreasing-charge amortization seems justified. American Broadcasting Companies, Inc. summarized its procedures for amortizing intangibles in the following note:

AMERICAN BROADCASTING COMPANIES, INC.

	1984	1983	1982
	(Dollars in thousands)		
Other assets:			
Intangibles, at cost, less amortization (Note A)	$247,680	$66,316	$69,828
Program rights, non-current	309,210	300,359	379,865
Deferred charges	19,535	7,646	11,116

Note A (In Part): Summary of Significant Accounting Policies

Intangibles, Less Amortization

Intangibles represent the unamortized excess of cost over underlying net tangible assets of companies acquired. Intangibles amounting to $14,674,000 ($15,034,000 in 1983 and 1982), acquired prior to 1970, which are considered to have continuing value, are not being amortized. The remaining intangibles amounting to $233,006,000 at December 29, 1984 ($51,282,000 at December 31, 1983 and $54,794,000 at January 1, 1983) are being amortized on the straight-line method based on their estimated useful lives not exceeding forty years. Amortization of intangibles amounted to $5,795,000, $3,697,000 and $4,287,000 for 1984, 1983 and 1982, respectively. Intangibles amounting to $360,000 in 1984 and $50,000 in 1982, considered to have no continuing value, were written off.

---

[13]*Opinions of the Accounting Principles Board, No. 17,* par. 30.

DEPLETION OF NATURAL RESOURCES

Natural resources, also called **wasting assets**, move toward exhaustion as the physical units representing these resources are removed and sold. The withdrawal of oil or gas, the cutting of timber, and the mining of coal, sulphur, iron, copper, or silver ore are examples of processes leading to the exhaustion of natural resources. Depletion expense is a charge for the using up of the resources.

Computing Periodic Depletion

The computation of depletion expense is an adaptation of the productive-output method of depreciation. Perhaps the most difficult problem in computing depletion expense is estimating the amount of resources available for economical removal from the land. Generally, a geologist, mining engineer, or other expert is called upon to make the estimate, and it is subject to continual revision as the resource is extracted or removed.

Developmental costs, such as costs of drilling, sinking mine shafts, and constructing roads should be capitalized and added to the original cost of the property in arriving at the total cost subject to depletion. These costs are often incurred before normal activities begin.

To illustrate the computation of depletion expense, assume the following facts: Land containing mineral deposits is purchased at a cost of $5,500,000. The land has an estimated value after removal of the resources of $250,000; the natural resource supply is estimated at 1,000,000 tons. The unit depletion charge and the total depletion charge for the first year, assuming the withdrawal of 80,000 tons are calculated as follows:

Depletion charge per ton: ($5,500,000 − $250,000) ÷ 1,000,000 = $5.25
Depletion charge for the first year: 80,000 tons × $5.25 = $420,000

The following entries should be made to record these events.

Land..	250,000	
Mineral Deposits...	5,250,000	
Cash..		5,500,000
Purchase of mineral rights.		
Depletion Expense...	420,000	
Accumulated Depletion (or Mineral Deposits)		420,000
Depletion expense.		

If the 80,000 tons are sold in the current year, the entire $420,000 would be included as part of the cost of goods sold. If only 60,000 tons are sold, $105,000 is reported as part of ending inventory on the balance sheet.

When buildings and improvements are constructed in connection with the removal of natural resources and their usefulness is limited to the duration of the project, it is reasonable to recognize depreciation on such properties on an output basis consistent with the charges to be recognized for the natural resources themselves. For example, assume buildings are constructed at a cost of $250,000; the useful lives of the buildings are expected to terminate upon exhaustion of the natural resource consisting of 1,000,000 units. Under these circumstances, a depreciation charge of $.25 ($250,000 ÷ 1,000,000) should accompany the depletion charge recognized for each unit. When improvements provide benefits expected to terminate prior to the exhaustion of the natural resource, the cost of such improvements should be allocated on the basis of the units to be removed during the life of the improvements or on a time basis, whichever is considered more appropriate.

Special Problems — Oil and Gas Properties

The preceding discussion relates to depletion of all natural resources. Special problems exist in the oil and gas industry in the determination of the asset cost to be used in computing depletion. Even though apparently valuable property rights are acquired, no one can truly measure their value until exploratory activities have been completed. The nature of oil exploration generally results in several dry wells for each "gusher" that is discovered. The accounting question is, "How should these exploratory costs be recorded? Are they part of the asset cost regardless of their success, or are they a period expense?"

Two methods of accounting have developed to account for exploratory costs. The first method is the full cost approach, and the second method is the successful efforts approach. Under the **full cost approach**, all exploratory costs are capitalized and written off against revenues as depletion expense. Under the **successful efforts approach**, exploratory costs for unsuccessful projects are expensed, and only exploratory costs for successful projects are capitalized. Most large, successful oil companies follow the second approach. For example, E.I. Du Pont De Nemours and Company included the following explanation of its depletion method in the notes to the 1984 financial statements:

E.I. DU PONT DE NEMOURS AND COMPANY

Oil and Gas Properties

The company's exploration and production activities are accounted for under the successful efforts method. Costs of acquiring unproved properties are capitalized, and impairment of those properties, which are individually insignificant, is provided for by amortizing the cost thereof based on past experience or the estimated holding period. Geological, geophysical and delay rental costs are expensed as incurred. Costs of exploratory dry holes are expensed as the wells are determined to be dry. Costs of productive properties, production and support equipment, and development costs are capitalized and amortized on a unit-of-production basis.

For smaller companies, the full cost approach has been popular. This method encourages such companies to continue exploration without the severe penalty of recognizing all costs of unsuccessful projects as immediate expenses. Proponents of the full cost approach argue that often valuable exploratory information is discovered even when a "dry hole" is drilled. The cost of a producing well, therefore, should include these unsuccessful costs. The Galaxy Oil Company explains its use of full cost as follows:

GALAXY OIL COMPANY

The Company follows the "full cost method" of accounting whereby all the costs of exploration for and development of oil and gas reserves, including both evaluated and unevaluated costs, are capitalized as incurred. The evaluated capitalized costs applicable to oil and gas properties and related future development costs are amortized on a company-wide unit-of-production method (physical units are determined on the basis of relative energy content, which is estimated by the Company to be 6 MCF of gas to each barrel of oil) based on independent petroleum engineers' estimates of proved oil and gas reserves attributable to the properties.

The issue of how to account for exploratory costs of the oil and gas industry has attracted the attention of the FASB, the SEC, and even the U.S. Congress. When an apparent oil shortage developed in the 1970's, there was strong pressure placed on oil companies to expand their exploration to discover new sources of oil and gas. The Financial Accounting Standards Board was encouraged to identify one of the two alternatives for recording exploratory costs as preferred. In 1977, they selected a form of the successful efforts approach, and issued FASB Statement No. 19, "Financial Accounting and Reporting by Oil and Gas Producing Companies." The smaller companies objected to this standard, and in 1979, the SEC issued its own standard that rejected both alternatives, and suggested adoption of a new method they called **Reserve Recognition Accounting (RRA)**. This method was in reality a form of **discovery accounting** that would recognize as an asset the value of the reserves rather than their cost. Under public and congressional pressure, the FASB issued its Statement

No. 25 that suspended its earlier standard, and effectively permitted again the use of either the full cost or successful efforts approach.[14]

As oil and gas prices declined in recent years, the SEC withdrew its support of RRA. However, the Commission still recommends that current values of reserves be disclosed.

CHANGES IN ESTIMATES OF VARIABLES

The allocation of asset costs benefiting more than one period cannot be precisely determined at acquisition because so many of the variables cannot be known with certainty until a future time. Only one factor in determining the periodic charge for depreciation, amortization or depletion is based on historical information — asset cost. Other factors — residual value, useful life or output, and the pattern of use or benefit — must be estimated. The question frequently facing accountants is how adjustments to these estimates, which arise as time passes, should be reflected in the accounts. As indicated in Chapter 4, a change in estimate is normally reported in the current and future periods rather than as an adjustment of prior periods. This type of adjustment would be made for residual value and useful life changes. However, a change in the cost allocation method based on a revised expected pattern of use, is a change in accounting principle and is accounted for in a different manner. Changes in accounting principles are discussed in Chapter 23.

Change in Estimated Life

To illustrate the procedure for a change in estimate affecting allocation of asset cost, assume that a company purchased $50,000 of equipment and estimated a ten-year life for depreciation purposes. Using the straight-line method with no residual value, the annual depreciation would be $5,000. After four years, accumulated depreciation would amount to $20,000, and the remaining undepreciated book value would be $30,000. Early in the fifth year, a re-evaluation of the life indicates only four more years of service can be expected from the asset. An adjustment must therefore be made for the fifth and subsequent years to reflect the change. A new annual depreciation charge is calculated by dividing the remaining book value by the remaining life of four years. In the illustration above, this would result in an annual charge of $7,500 for the fifth through eighth years ($30,000 ÷ 4 = $7,500).

---

[14]*Statement of Financial Accounting Standards No. 25*, "Suspension of Certain Accounting Requirements for Oil and Gas Producing Companies," (Stamford: Financial Accounting Standards Board, 1979).

Asset Cost Allocation
Change in Estimated Life — Straight-Line Method

End of Year	Depreciation		Accumulated Depreciation
	Computation	Amount	
1987	$50,000 ÷ 10	$ 5,000	$ 5,000
1988	$50,000 ÷ 10	5,000	10,000
1989	$50,000 ÷ 10	5,000	15,000
1990	$50,000 ÷ 10	5,000	20,000
1991	($50,000 − $20,000) ÷ 4	7,500	27,500
1992	($50,000 − $20,000) ÷ 4	7,500	35,000
1993	($50,000 − $20,000) ÷ 4	7,500	42,500
1994	($50,000 − $20,000) ÷ 4	7,500	50,000
		$50,000	

A change in the estimated life of an intangible asset is accounted for in the same manner, i.e., the unamortized cost is allocated over the remaining life based on the revised estimate. Because of the uncertainties surrounding the estimation of the life of an intangible asset, frequent evaluation of the amortization period should be made to determine if a change in estimated life is warranted. For example, assume a patent costing $51,000 is being amortized over 17 years. Amortization per year would be $3,000($51,000 ÷ 17). If, at the end of 5 years, the patent is estimated to have a remaining life of 4 years, the book value of $36,000 [$51,000 − ($3,000 × 5)] will be amortized over 4 years at $9,000 per year.

Change in Estimated Units of Production

Another change in estimate occurs in accounting for wasting assets when the estimate of the recoverable units changes as a result of further discoveries, improved extraction processes, or changes in sales prices that indicate changes in the number of units that can be extracted profitably. A revised depletion rate is established by dividing the remaining resource cost balance by the estimated remaining recoverable units.

To illustrate, assume the facts used in the example on page 516. Land is purchased at a cost of $5,500,000 with estimated residual value of $250,000. The original estimated supply of natural resources in the land is 1,000,000 tons. As indicated previously, the depletion rate under these conditions would be $5.25 per ton, and the depletion charge for the first year when 80,000 tons were mined would be $420,000. Assume that in the second year of operation, 100,000 tons of ore are withdrawn, but before the books are closed at the end of the second year, appraisal of the expected recoverable tons indicates a remaining tonnage of 950,000. The new depletion rate and the depletion charge for the second year would be computed as follows:

Cost assignable to recoverable tons at the beginning of the second year:
Original costs applicable to depletable resources $5,250,000
Deduct depletion charge for the first year   420,000

Balance of cost subject to depletion $4,830,000

Estimated recoverable tons as of the beginning of the second year:
Number of tons withdrawn in the second year   100,000
Estimated recoverable tons as of the end of the second year   950,000

Total recoverable tons at the beginning of the second year   1,050,000

Depletion charge per ton for the second year: $4,830,000 ÷ 1,050,000 = $4.60
Depletion charge for the second year: 100,000 × $4.60 = $460,000.

Sometimes an increase in estimated recoverable units arises from additional expenditures for capital developments. When this occurs, the additional costs should be added to the remaining recoverable cost and divided by the number of tons remaining to be extracted. To illustrate this situation, assume in the preceding example that $525,000 additional costs had been incurred at the beginning of the second year. The preceding computation of depletion rate and depletion expense would be changed as follows:

Cost assignable to recoverable tons as of the beginning of the second year:
Original costs applicable to depletable resources $5,250,000
Add additional costs incurred in the second year   525,000

$5,775,000
Deduct depletion charge for the first year   420,000

Balance of cost subject to depletion $5,355,000

Estimated recoverable tons as of the beginning of the second year; as
above: 1,050,000

Depletion charge per ton for the second year: $5,355,000 ÷ 1,050,000 = $5.10
Depletion charge for the second year: 100,000 × $5.10 = $510,000

Impairment of Tangible and Intangible Asset Values

Events sometimes occur after the purchase of an asset and before the end of its expected life that impair its value and require an immediate writedown of the asset rather than making a normal allocation over a period of time. This type of impairment can occur with any asset, but it occurs with more frequency in relation to goodwill. Excerpts from financial statements for two companies illustrate the varying conditions that can create the need for recording an immediate loss.

GALAXY OIL COMPANY—1984 Financial Statements

...During 1983 the Company charged $6,500,000 against operations relating to the cost of undeveloped exploratory acreage located in Alabama, California, and Nevada which it determined, considering the industry environment at the time, to be significantly impaired. The Company has no future plans to develop this acreage due to the limitation contained in its bank loan agreements.

INTER-CITY GAS CORPORATION—1983 Financial Statements

Pursuant to this reorganization and as a result of the losses incurred by KeepRite in the past two years, the Company has re-assessed its investment in KeepRite Inc. As a result of this re-assessment, it has been determined that the value of the underlying assets in KeepRite have been impaired by an amount of $4,697,000. Accordingly, the Company has written off goodwill of $4,697,000 as an extraordinary charge against income.

The timing for recognizing the impairment of an asset value is a matter of judgment. Continued consideration of reported asset values is necessary to assure that there still are future benefits to justify the asset amount. The writedown of an asset may be classified as an extraordinary item or as a special charge to operations depending upon the materiality of the item and the circumstances surrounding the impairment. The write-down of Galaxy Oil assets was a charge against operations, while the write-down of the goodwill for Inter-City Gas Corporation was an extraordinary charge.

Accounting is made up of many estimates. The procedures outlined in this section are designed to prevent the continual restating of reported income from prior years. Adjustments to prior period income figures are made only if actual errors have occurred, not when reasonable estimates have been made that later prove inaccurate.

ASSET RETIREMENTS

Assets may be retired by sale, exchange, or abandonment. Generally, when an asset is disposed of, any unrecorded depreciation or amortization for the period is recorded to the date of disposition. A book value as of the date of disposition can then be computed as the difference between the cost of the asset and its accumulated depreciation. If the disposition price exceeds the book value, a **gain** is recognized. If the disposition price is less than the book value, a **loss** is recorded. The gain or loss is reported on the income statement as "other revenues and gains" or "other expenses and losses" in the year of asset disposition. As part of the disposition entry, the balances in the asset and accumulated depreciation accounts for the asset are canceled. The following sections illustrate the asset retirement process under varying conditions.

Asset Retirement by Sale

If the proceeds from the sale of an asset are in the form of cash or a receivable (**monetary asset**), the recording of the transaction follows the order outlined in the previous paragraph. For example, assume that on April 1, 1987, Firestone Supply Co. sells for $43,600 manufacturing equipment that is recorded on the books at cost of $83,600 and accumulated depreciation as of January 1, 1987, of $50,600. The company depreciates its manufacturing equipment on the books using a straight-line, 10% rate. It follows the policy of depreciating its assets to the nearest month.

The following entries would be made to record this transaction.

Depreciation Expense—Machinery	2,090	
Accumulated Depreciation—Machinery		2,090
To record depreciation for three months in 1987.		
Cash	43,600	
Accumulated Depreciation—Machinery	52,690	
Machinery		83,600
Gain on Sale of Machinery		12,690
To record sale of machinery at a gain.		

Computation of gain:	
Sales price	$43,600
Book value ($83,600 − $52,690)	30,910
Gain on sale	$12,690

The preceding entries could be combined in the form of a single compound entry as follows:

Cash	43,600	
Depreciation Expense	2,090	
Accumulated Depreciation—Machinery	50,600	
Machinery		83,600
Gain on Sale of Machinery		12,690

Asset Retirement by Exchange for Other Nonmonetary Assets

As indicated in Chapter 11, when plant assets are acquired in exchange for other nonmonetary assets, the new asset acquired is generally recorded at its fair market value or the fair market value of the nonmonetary asset given in exchange, whichever is more clearly determinable. This treatment is referred to as the "general case" and is the more common exchange transaction.

When accounting for exchanges of plant assets, two questions must be asked: (1) Are the assets being exchanged similar in nature? and (2) Are the parties involved in the exchange similar in position, i.e., are they both either dealers of the assets or nondealers? If the answers to both of these questions is affirmative, and if the transaction results in a gain, a "special case" approach is used to record the exchange. The general case will be illustrated first.

The entries required to record the general case for an exchange involving nonmonetary assets are identical to those illustrated in the previous section except that a nonmonetary asset is increased rather than a monetary one. Gains and losses arising from the exchange are recognized when the exchange takes place.

To illustrate, assume in the previous example that the retirement of the described asset was effected by exchanging it for delivery equipment that had a market value of $43,600. The entries would be the same as illustrated except that instead of a debit to Cash, Delivery Equipment would be debited for $43,600. The gain would still be computed by comparing the book value of the machine and the market value of the asset acquired in the exchange.

Delivery Equipment	43,600	
Depreciation Expense	2,090	
Accumulated Depreciation—Machinery	50,600	
Machinery		83,600
Gain on Exchange of Machinery		12,690

If the machinery's fair market value were more clearly determinable than the value of the delivery equipment, the value of the machinery would be used to compute the gain or loss and to determine the value for the delivery equipment. Assume the delivery equipment is used and has no readily available market price, but the machinery had a market value of $25,000. Under these circumstances, a loss of $5,910 ($30,910 − $25,000) would be indicated, and the combined entry to record the exchange would be as follows:

Delivery Equipment	25,000	
Depreciation Expense	2,090	
Accumulated Depreciation—Machinery	50,600	
Loss on Exchange of Machinery	5,910	
Machinery		83,600

Often the exchange of nonmonetary assets includes a transfer of cash, since the nonmonetary assets in most exchange transactions do not have equivalent market values. The cash part of the transaction adjusts the market values of the assets received to those of the assets given up. Thus, if in the previous example the exchange of delivery equipment were accompanied by cash of $3,000, the loss would be reduced to $2,910 and the combined entry would be as follows:

Cash	3,000	
Delivery Equipment	25,000	
Depreciation Expense	2,090	
Accumulated Depreciation—Machinery	50,600	
Loss on Exchange of Machinery	2,910	
Machinery		83,600

In this example, the exchange involved assets that were dissimilar in nature; delivery equipment and machinery. If the exchange involved similar assets, i.e., a used truck for a new one, the same accounting entries would be required unless the exchange is between two parties in similar positions. This special case is discussed in the following section.

Asset Retirement by Exchange of Nonmonetary Assets—Special Case

Not all exchanges of nonmonetary assets have the features to justify the recognition of a gain. Sometimes an exchange of **similar assets** is made to facilitate one of the parties to the exchange in making a sale to an ultimate consumer. For example, the Tri-City Cadillac dealership has a buyer for a blue Eldorado but has only a red one in stock. Another dealership in a nearby town has a blue Eldorado and is willing to exchange its car for Tri-City's red one. This exchange of similar assets is not intended to be an earnings transaction for either party and, therefore, should not reflect any gain, even if the market values of the cars have increased since they were originally acquired from the manufacturer. Another example of such an exchange would occur if two manufacturing companies exchanged similar equipment which both companies used in the production process.

In both of these illustrations, similar assets were transferred between parties in similar business situations. In the first instance, both parties were dealers of automobiles. In the second example, both parties were nondealers of machines being used in the production process. In neither case was the earning process culminated.

When the Accounting Principles Board studied the exchange of nonmonetary assets issue, they determined that an exception to the general rule was needed when the exchange did not culminate the earning process for either party and a gain was otherwise indicated.[15] The exception provided that **no gain** is to be recognized for these special exchanges unless

---

[15]*Opinions of the Accounting Principles Board, No. 29,* "Accounting for Nonmonetary Transactions," (New York: American Institute of Certified Public Accountants, 1973), par. 20–23.

cash is received as part of the exchange. If cash is received, a proportionate share of the gain should be recognized. If the transaction indicates that a loss has occurred, the exception does not apply and the exchange is recorded as illustrated in the previous section. Thus, three conditions must exist for the special case to apply:

1. The assets must be similar in nature; i.e., be expected to fulfill similar functions in the entity.
2. The parties to the transaction must be similar in position; i.e. both be dealers or both be nondealers.
3. A gain must be indicated in the transaction; i.e., the market value of the assets received must exceed the book value of the assets surrendered.

To illustrate the special case, two examples are included below. In the first example, no cash is involved in the exchange. In the second example, the exchange includes a transfer of cash.

Example 1

The Republic Manufacturing Company owns a special molding machine that it no longer uses because of a change in products being manufactured. The machine still has several years of service remaining. Discussion with other companies in the industry has located a buyer, Logan Square Company. However, Logan Square is low on funds and suggests an exchange for one of its machines that could be used in Republic's packaging department. It is decided that both machines meet the definition of being similar in use and have the same market values. The following cost and market data relate to the two machines:

	Republic	Logan
Costs of machines to be exchanged	$46,000	$54,000
Book values of machines to be exchanged	$14,000	$18,000
Market values of machines to be exchanged	$16,000	$16,000

The entry on Republic's books to record the exchange is as follows:

Machinery (new)	14,000	
Accumulated Depreciation on Machinery ($46,000 − $14,000)	32,000	
Machinery (old)		46,000

The entry on Logan's books to record the exchange is as follows:

Machinery (new)	16,000	
Accumulated Depreciation on Machinery ($54,000 − $18,000)	36,000	
Loss on Exchange of Machines	2,000	
Machinery (old)		54,000

Note that in Republic's entry, the special case is used. All three conditions are present: the machines are similar, both parties are nondealers, and the market value of the asset received exceeds the book value of Republic's molding machine, so a gain is indicated. Thus, the value assigned to Republic's newly acquired packaging machine is the book value of its old molding machine.

In Logan's entry, however, the general case is used. The market value of the asset exchanged is less than the book value, so a loss is indicated. The molding machine, therefore, is recorded on Logan's books at its market value, the general case solution.

Example 2

Assume the same facts as in Example 1, except that it is decided the molding machine has a market value of $16,000 and the packaging machine is worth $20,000. To make the exchange equal, Republic agrees to pay Logan Square $4,000 cash in addition to the molding machine.

The entry on Republic's books for Example 2 is as follows:

Machinery (new)...	18,000	
Accumulated Depreciation on Machinery ($46,000 − $14,000).........	32,000	
Machinery (old)...		46,000
Cash..		4,000

As was true for Example 1, the facts of this case require Republic to use the special case. The market value of the machine received ($20,000) exceeds the book value of the molding machine being exchanged plus the cash paid, ($14,000 + $4,000). A $2,000 gain is thus indicated. The machines are similar in use and the parties are both nondealers. The gain, therefore, is deferred and not recognized. The new machine is recorded at $18,000, the market value of the asset received in the exchange ($20,000) less the deferred gain ($2,000).

In Example 2, the book value of the packaging machine on Logan Square's books is less than the market value, indicating a gain ($20,000 − $18,000, or $2,000). The similar assets and similar parties indicate the special case; however, because Logan Square received cash as part of the transaction, generally accepted accounting principles specify that a portion of the $2,000 **indicated gain** should be recognized as having been earned. The amount to be recognized is computed using the following formula:

$$\frac{\text{Recognized}}{\text{Gain}} = \frac{\text{Cash Received}}{\text{Cash + Market Value of Acquired Asset}} \times \frac{\text{Total}}{\text{Indicated}}_{\text{Gain}}$$

Using the figures from Example 2, Logan Square, therefore, would recognize $400 of the gain computed as follows:

$$\frac{\$4,000}{\$4,000 + \$16,000} \times \$2,000 = \$400$$

The recorded value of the molding machine on Logan's books is $14,400, the book value of the packaging machine exchanged less the cash received plus the gain recognized, ($18,000 − $4,000 + $400). Another way of computing the recorded value is by deducting the **deferred gain** from the book value of the exchanged asset ($18,000 − $3,600 or $14,400).

The entry on Logan Square's books to record the exchange is as follows:

Cash..	4,000	
Machinery (new).......................................	14,400	
Accumulated Depreciation on Machinery ($54,000 − $18,000).........	36,000	
Machinery (old).......................................		54,000
Gain on Exchange of Machinery..................................		400

While the exceptions to the general case seem complex, they occur in relatively rare instances. The general effect of the special case is to defer any indicated gain until the new asset is disposed of through sale, trade, or abandonment.[16]

Retirement by Involuntary Conversion

Sometimes retirement of plant assets occurs because of extensive damage caused by such events as a fire, earthquake, flood, or condemnation. Retirements caused by these types of uncontrollable events have been classified as **involuntary conversions**. Some of these events are insurable risks, and the occurrence of the event triggers reimbursement from an insurance company. If the proceeds exceed the book value of the destroyed assets, a gain is recognized on the books. If the proceeds are less than the book value, a loss is recorded.

If the loss was either not insurable, or a company failed to carry insurance on the property, the remaining book value of the asset should be recorded as a loss. Because these types of events are unusual and infrequent, the gains and losses realized are often recorded as an extraordinary item. Of course, if the event has a high probability of recurrence, i.e., a factory built in a low area that frequently experiences flooding, the gain or loss may be classified as an ordinary item.

To illustrate the recording of an involuntary conversion, assume that a flood destroyed a factory building with a $1,200,000 cost and a book value of $350,000. If $400,000 was recovered from the flood insurance policy, the entry to record the loss would be as follows:

Receivable from Insurance Company	400,000	
Accumulated Depreciation—Building	850,000	
Building		1,200,000
Gain on Involuntary Conversion		50,000

---

[16]For a further discussion of the special case, see James B. Hobbs and D. R. Bainbridge, "Nonmonetary Exchange Transactions: Clarification of APB Opinion No. 29," *Accounting Review* (January 1982), pp. 171–175.

Some special problems can arise when provisions of the insurance policy include a coinsurance provision. These complications are addressed in the Appendix to this chapter.

In some cases, the involuntary conversion is caused by government condemnation of private property. Usually such proceedings require the condemning party to pay a fair market value for the assets seized. This generally results in a recognized gain. Some accountants have argued that since these proceeds are often reinvested in similar assets, the gain on such conversion should be deferred by reducing the cost of the new asset. The FASB, however, has indicated that the condemnation and the acquisition of new assets should be viewed as two separate transactions.[17] Thus, the gain is recognized on the condemnation, and the new assets are recorded at their acquisition cost.

For example, assume that the Valley Mining Company had land condemned by the state for a state park. The cost of the land to Valley was $50,000. The agreed upon market value was $260,000. The entry to record the cash receipt would be as follows:

Cash	260,000	
Land		50,000
Gain on Condemnation		210,000

BALANCE SHEET PRESENTATION AND DISCLOSURE

Plant assets, natural resources, and intangible assets are usually shown separately on the balance sheet. As indicated earlier in this chapter, both the gross cost and accumulated depreciation must be disclosed for plant assets. Such disclosure is not required for intangible assets and natural resources, and many companies report only net values for these assets. Because of the alternative cost allocation methods available to compute the charges for depreciation, amortization, and depletion, the methods used must be disclosed in the financial statements. Without this information, a user of the statements might be misled in trying to compare the financial results of one company with another. Cost allocation methods are normally reported in the first note to the financial statements, "Summary of Significant Accounting Policies."

Selected portions of such a note for International Paper Company are reproduced on page 530. Notice the detailed discussion of the methods used for depreciation.

---

[17]*FASB Interpretation No. 30*, "Accounting for Involuntary Conversions of Nonmonetary Assets to Monetary Assets," (Stamford: Financial Accounting Standards Board, 1979).

INTERNATIONAL PAPER COMPANY

STATEMENT OF SIGNIFICANT ACCOUNTING POLICIES

Plants, Properties, and Equipment

Plants, Properties, and Equipment are stated at cost, less accumulated depreciation.

For financial reporting purposes, IP uses the unit-of-production method for depreciating its pulp and paper mills and certain wood products facilities, and the straight-line method for other plants and equipment. When appropriate, additional depreciation is provided on particular assets to recognize reductions in the estimated economic lives of such assets.

Straight-line depreciation rates for financial reporting purposes are as follows: buildings 2½ percent; machinery and equipment 5 percent to 33 percent; woods equipment 10 percent to 16 percent. For tax purposes, depreciation is computed utilizing accelerated methods.

Start-up costs on major projects are capitalized and charged to earnings over a five-year period. These costs are an integral part of the process of bringing a facility into commercial production and therefore benefit future periods. At December 31, 1984 and 1983, unamortized start-up costs were $57 million and $55 million, respectively.

APPENDIX

INSURANCE RECOVERY ON INVOLUNTARY CONVERSIONS

Most companies carry insurance to cover losses from many types of involuntary conversions, especially those that are defined as casualty losses.

The most common casualty loss incurred by a business is that from fire. Of all of the various types of protection offered by insurance, fire is the risk most widely covered. Because of the importance of fire insurance in business and because of special accounting problems that arise in the event of fire, a discussion of this matter is included in this appendix.

Fire Insurance

Fire insurance policies are usually written in $100 or $1,000 units for a period of three years. Insurance premiums are normally paid annually in advance. The amount of the premium is determined by the conditions prevailing in each case.

The insurance contract may be canceled by either the insurer or the insured. When the insurance company cancels the policy, a refund is made on a pro rata basis. When the policyholder cancels the policy, a refund may be made on what is known as a short-rate basis that provides for a higher insurance rate for the shorter period of coverage.

A **coinsurance clause** is frequently written into a policy by the insurance companies to offset the tendency by the buyer to purchase only a minimum insurance coverage. A business with assets worth $100,000 at fair market value, for example, may estimate that any single loss could not destroy more than one half of these assets and might consider itself adequately protected by insurance of $50,000. With an 80% coinsurance clause, however, the business would have to carry insurance equal to 80% of the fair market value of the property, or $80,000, to recover the full amount on claims up to the face of the policy. When less than this percentage is carried, the insured shares in the risk with the insurer.

To illustrate the calculation of the amount recoverable on a policy failing to meet coinsurance requirements, assume the following: assets are insured for $70,000 under a policy containing an 80% coinsurance clause; on the date of a fire, assets have a fair market value of $100,000. Because insurance of only $70,000 is carried when coinsurance requirements are $80,000, any loss will be borne ⅞ by the insurance company and ⅛ by the policyholder; furthermore, whatever the loss, the maximum to be borne by the insurance company is $70,000, the face of the policy. The amount recoverable from the insurance company if a fire loss is $50,000, for example, is calculated as follows:

$$\frac{\$70,000 \text{ (policy)}}{\$80,000 \text{ (coinsurance requirement)}} \times \$50,000 \text{ (loss)} = \$43,750$$

The same calculations are made when the loss is greater than the face of the policy. Assume the same facts given above, but assume a fire loss of $75,000. The amount recoverable from insurance is calculated as follows:

$$\frac{\$70,000 \text{ (policy)}}{\$80,000 \text{ (coinsurance requirement)}} \times \$75,000 \text{ (loss)} = \$65,625$$

In the preceding example, application of the formula gives an amount still less than the face of the policy and hence fully recoverable. But if application of the formula results in an amount exceeding the face value of the policy, the claim is limited to the latter amount. If, for example, the loss is $90,000, the following calculation is made:

$$\frac{\$70,000 \text{ (policy)}}{\$80,000 \text{ (coinsurance requirement)}} \times \$90,000 \text{ (loss)} = \$78,750$$

Recovery from the insurance company, however, is limited to $70,000, the ceiling set by the policy.

When the insurance coverage is equal to or greater than the percentage required by the coinsurance clause, the formula need not be applied since any loss is paid in full up to the face value of the policy. It is important to note that coinsurance requirements are based not on the cost or book value of the insured property but upon the actual market value of the property on the date of a fire. If coinsurance requirements are to be met, a rise in the value of insured assets requires that insurance coverage be increased.

The following general rules may be formulated:

1. In the absence of a coinsurance clause the amount recoverable is the lower of the loss or the face of the policy.
2. When a policy includes a coinsurance clause, the amount recoverable is the lower of the loss as adjusted by the coinsurance formula or the face of the policy.

Insurance policies normally include a **contribution clause** that provides that if other policies are carried on the same property, recovery of a loss on a policy shall be limited to the ratio which the face of the policy bears to the total insurance carried. Such a limitation on the amount to be paid eliminates the possibility of recovery by the insured of amounts in excess of the actual loss. When coinsurance clauses are found on the different policies, the recoverable amount on each is limited to the ratio of the face of the policy to the higher of (a) the total insurance carried, or (b) the total insurance required to be carried by the policy. To illustrate the limitations set by contribution clauses, assume a fire loss of $30,000 on property with a value of $100,000 on which policies are carried as follows: Co. A, $50,000; Co. B, $15,000; Co. C, $10,000.

1. Assuming policies have no coinsurance clauses, amounts that may be recovered from each company are as follows:

Co. A: $\dfrac{\$50,000 \text{ (policy)}}{\$75,000 \text{ (total policies)}} \times \$30,000 \text{ (loss)}$ $20,000

Co. B: $\dfrac{\$15,000 \text{ (policy)}}{\$75,000 \text{ (total policies)}} \times \$30,000 \text{ (loss)}$ 6,000

Co. C: $\dfrac{\$10,000 \text{ (policy)}}{\$75,000 \text{ (total policies)}} \times \$30,000 \text{ (loss)}$ 4,000

Total amount recoverable $30,000

2. Assuming each policy includes an 80% coinsurance clause, coinsurance requirements on each policy would exceed the total insurance carried and amounts recoverable from each company are as follows:

Co. A: $\dfrac{\$50,000 \text{ (policy)}}{\$80,000 \text{ (coinsurance requirement)}} \times \$30,000 \text{ (loss)}$ $18,750

Co. B: $\dfrac{\$15,000 \text{ (policy)}}{\$80,000 \text{ (coinsurance requirement)}} \times \$30,000 \text{ (loss)}$ 5,625

Co. C: $\dfrac{\$10,000 \text{ (policy)}}{\$80,000 \text{ (coinsurance requirement)}} \times \$30,000 \text{ (loss)}$ 3,750

Total amount recoverable $28,125

3. Assuming each policy includes a 70% coinsurance clause, total insurance carried exceeds coinsurance requirements on each policy and amounts recoverable from each company are the same as in (1).

4. Assuming that coinsurance requirements are Co. A—none, Co. B—70%, and Co. C—80%, recovery on each policy is based on its relationship to the total insurance carried or the coinsurance requirement where this is higher, as follows:

Co. A: $\dfrac{\$50,000 \text{ (policy)}}{\$75,000 \text{ (total policies)}} \times \$30,000 \text{ (loss)}$ $20,000

Co. B: $\dfrac{\$15,000 \text{ (policy)}}{\$75,000 \text{ (total policies)}} \times \$30,000 \text{ (loss)}$ 6,000

Co. C: $\dfrac{\$10,000 \text{ (policy)}}{\$80,000 \text{ (coinsurance requirement)}} \times \$30,000 \text{ (loss)}$ 3,750

Total amount recoverable $29,750

QUESTIONS

1. Distinguish among depreciation, depletion, and amortization expense.
2. What factors must be considered to determine the periodic depreciation charges that should be made for a company's depreciable plant assets?
3. Distinguish between the functional and physical factors affecting the useful life of a plant asset.
4. What role does residual or salvage value play in the various methods of time-factor depreciation?
5. Distinguish between time-factor and use-factor methods of depreciation.
6. The accelerated cost recovery system of depreciation is used for income tax purposes but is usually not acceptable for financial reporting. Why is this true?

7. The certified public accountant is frequently called on by management for advice regarding methods of computing depreciation. Although the question arises less frequently, of comparable importance is whether the depreciation method should be based on the consideration of the property items as units, as groups, or as having a composite life.
   (a) Briefly describe the depreciation methods based on recognizing property items as (1) units, (2) groups, or (3) as having a composite life.
   (b) Present the arguments for and against the use of each of these methods.
   (c) Describe how retirements are recorded under each of these methods.
8. What arguments can be made for charging more than an asset's cost against revenue?
9. What factors determine the period and method for amortizing intangible assets?
10. What procedures must be followed when the estimate of recoverable natural resources is changed due to subsequent development work?
11. Under what circumstances should an asset's remaining book value be immediately written off as a loss?
12. Why is 40 years used as the maximum number of years for amortizing an intangible asset?
13. (a) Distinguish between the "full cost" and "successful efforts" approaches to recording exploratory costs for oil and gas properties. (b) The SEC recommended a third approach be followed. What were its distinguishing characteristics?
14. Under what circumstances is a gain or loss recognized when a productive asset is exchanged for a similar productive asset?
15. (a) What are some types of involuntary conversions that can take place with property? (b) What are the arguments for and against recognizing gains and losses on such conversions.
16. Machinery in the finishing department of Jamison Co., although less than 50% depreciated, has been replaced by new machinery. The company expects to find a buyer for the old machinery, and on December 31 the machinery is in the yards and available for inspection. How should it be reported on the balance sheet?
17. How should plant assets, wasting assets, and intangibles be reported on the balance sheet? What footnote disclosure should be made for these assets?
*18. (a) What is a coinsurance clause and why is it found in fire insurance policies?
   (b) What is a contribution clause and how does it affect recovery of a loss?

*Relates to Appendix

DISCUSSION CASES

CASE 12–1   (We don't need depreciation!)

The managements of two different companies argue that because of specific conditions in their companies, recording depreciation expense should be suspended for 1987. Evaluate carefully their arguments.

1. The president of Midas Co. recommends that no depreciation be recorded for 1987 since the depreciation rate is 5% per year, and price indexes show that prices during the year have risen by more than this figure.
2. The policy of Liebnitz Co. is to recondition its building and equipment each year so that they are maintained in perfect repair. In view of the extensive periodic costs incurred in 1987, officials of the company feel that the need for recognizing depreciation is eliminated.

CASE 12–2 (Why write off goodwill?)

The Reno Corporation purchased the Stardust Club for $500,000, which included $100,000 for goodwill. Reno Corporation incurs large promotional and advertising expenses to maintain Stardust Club's popularity. As the annual financial statements are being prepared, the CPA of the Reno Corporation, Alice Boggs, insists that some of the goodwill be amortized against revenue. Boggs cites APB Opinion No. 17 that requires all intangible assets to be written off over a maximum life of 40 years. Phil Brooks, the Reno Corporation controller, feels that amortization of the purchased goodwill in the same periods as heavy expenses are incurred to maintain the goodwill in effect creates a double charge against income of the period. Brooks argues that no write-off of goodwill is necessary. Indeed, goodwill has increased in value and should even be increased on the books to reflect this improvement. Evaluate the logic of these two positions.

CASE 12–3 (Do shorter lives overcome the impact of inflation?)

After several years of proposed legislation to accelerate depreciation for productive assets, the Economic Recovery Tax Act of 1981 adopted an accelerated cost recovery system. One of the arguments given in support of its adoption was that it would help overcome the impact of inflation in depreciation. Evaluate the reasonableness of this argument.

CASE 12–4 (Should alternative methods of depreciation be eliminated?)

The FASB receives recommendations from its Advisory Board as to areas it should consider for study. Depreciation accounting has not been addressed as a separate topic by the FASB, and several alternative methods are used for recording this expense on the books. Recognizing this situation, a recommendation is made to the Board that a study be made of depreciation accounting with the objective of selecting one method as the only acceptable one. Those making the recommendation reasoned that only then could comparability in financial statements be achieved. Present the arguments for and against the FASB following the recommendation. If you were a member of the FASB, what would be your position?

CASE 12–5 (Which depreciation method should we use?)

The Egnew Manufacturing Company purchased a new machine especially built to perform one particular function on the assembly line. A difference of opinion has arisen as to the method of depreciation to be used in connection with this machine. Three methods are now being considered.

(a) The straight-line method

(continued)

(b) The productive-output method
(c) The sum-of-the-years-digits method

List separately the arguments for and against each of the proposed methods from both the theoretical and practical viewpoints.

EXERCISES

EXERCISE 12–1
(Computation of asset cost and depreciation expense)

A machine is purchased at the beginning of 1987 for $31,000. Its estimated life is 6 years. Freight in on the machine is $1,400. Installation costs are $800. The machine is estimated to have a residual value of $2,000 and a useful life of 40,000 hours. It was used 6,000 hours in 1987.

(1) What is the cost of the machine for accounting purposes?
(2) Compare the depreciation charge for 1987 using (a) the straight-line method, and (b) the service-hours method.

EXERCISE 12–2 (Computation of depreciation expense)

The Ragsdale Company purchased a machine for $120,000 on June 15, 1987. It is estimated that the machine will have a 10-year life and will have a salvage value of $12,000. Its working hours and production in units are estimated at 36,000 and 600,000 respectively. It is the company's policy to take a half-year's depreciation on all assets for which they use the straight-line or double-declining-balance depreciation method in the year of purchase. During 1987, the machine was operated 4,000 hours and produced 67,000 units. Which of the following methods will give the greatest depreciation expense for 1987? (1) double-declining balance; (2) productive-output; or (3) service-hours. (Show computations for all three methods.)

EXERCISE 12–3 (Computation of depreciation expense)

Johnson Construction purchased a concrete mixer on July 15, 1987. Company officials revealed the following information regarding this asset and its acquisition:

Purchase price............................	$125,000
Residual value.............................	$18,000
Estimated useful life........................	10 years
Estimated service hours.....................	38,000
Estimated production in units................	500,200 yards

The concrete mixer was operated by construction crews in 1987 for a total of 5,225 hours and it produced 77,000 yards of concrete.

It is company policy to take a half-year's depreciation on all assets for which they use the straight-line or double-declining-balance depreciation method in the year of purchase.

Calculate the resulting depreciation expense for 1987 under each of the following methods and specify which method allows the greatest depreciation expense.

(1) double-declining balance
(2) productive-output
(3) service-hours
(4) straight-line

EXERCISE 12–4 (Computation for book and tax depreciation)

Mountain States Manufacturing purchased factory equipment on March 15, 1986. The equipment will be depreciated for financial purposes over its estimated useful life, counting the year of acquisition as one-half year. The company accountant revealed the following information regarding this machine:

Purchase price............................	$55,000
Residual value............................	$9,000
Estimated useful life......................	10 years

(1) What amount should Mountain States Manufacturing record for depreciation expense for 1987 using the (a) double-declining-balance method? (b) sum-of-the-years-digits method?
(2) Assuming the equipment is classified as 5-year property under the accelerated cost recovery system (ACRS), what amount should Mountain States Manufacturing deduct for depreciation on its tax return in 1987?

EXERCISE 12–5
(Productive-output depreciation and asset retirement)

Equipment was purchased at the beginning of 1985 for $50,000 with an estimated product life of 300,000 units. The estimated salvage value was $5,000. During 1985, 1986, and 1987, the equipment produced 80,000 units, 120,000 units, and 40,000 units respectively. The machine was damaged at the beginning of 1988, and the equipment was scrapped with no salvage value.

(1) Determine depreciation using the productive-output method for 1985, 1986, and 1987.
(2) Give the entry to write off the equipment at the beginning of 1988.

EXERCISE 12–6 (Composite depreciation)

The Medallion Co. records show the following assets:

	Acquired	Cost	Salvage	Estimated Useful Life
Machinery......................	7/1/86	$105,000	$9,000	8 years
Equipment	1/1/87	33,000	1,500	5 years
Fixtures........................	1/1/87	45,000	4,500	4 years

For 1987, what is (a) the composite depreciation rate to be applied to cost using the straight-line method and (b) the composite life of the assets?

EXERCISE 12–7   (Composite depreciation)

A schedule of machinery owned by Webster Manufacturing Company is presented below:

	Total Cost	Estimated Salvage Value	Estimated Life in Years
Machine A........................	$550,000	$70,000	12
Machine B........................	200,000	20,000	8
Machine C........................	40,000	—	5

Webster computes depreciation on the straight-line method. Based on the information presented, calculate the composite depreciation rate and the composite life of these assets.

EXERCISE 12–8   (Group depreciation—closed group)

The CFS Continental Co. maintains its tools and dies on a closed group basis. A new group is created for each year's purchase of tools and dies. The assets are depreciated at a 25% rate beginning in the year following the acquisition. Any gain or loss is deferred until final disposition of the entire group of assets. Assume that for 1986, $150,000 was spent for tools and dies. Disposition of these tools and dies was made as follows (assume that disposals occurred at the beginning of each year):

Year	Cost	Disposition Cash Price
1987................	$ 3,000	$ 2,000
1988................	22,000	9,000
1989................	53,000	22,000
1990................	42,000	17,500
1991................	10,000	3,000
1992................	20,000	1,000

Prepare all journal entries required to account for tools and dies for the years 1987–1992. All tools and dies are disposed of by the end of 1992.

EXERCISE 12–9   (Group depreciation entries—open group)

Carson, Inc. uses the group depreciation method for its furniture account. The depreciation rate used for furniture is 21%. The balance in the Furniture account on December 31, 1986, was $125,000, and the balance in Accumulated Depreciation—Furniture was $61,000. The following purchases and dispositions of furniture occurred in the years 1987–1989 (assume that disposals occurred at the beginning of each year):

Year	Purchase Cost (Cash)	Sales (Cost)	Selling Price (Cash)
1987..............	$35,000	$27,000	$7,000
1988..............	27,600	15,000	6,000
1989..............	20,900	32,000	8,000

(1) Prepare the summary journal entries Carson should make each year (1987–1989) for the purchase, disposition, and depreciation of furniture.

(2) Prepare a summary of the furniture and accumulated depreciation accounts for the years 1987–1989.

EXERCISE 12–10   (Depreciation of special components)

Quasar Manufacturing acquired a new milling machine on May 1, 1982. The machine has a special component that requires replacement before the end of the useful life. The asset was originally recorded in two accounts, one representing the main unit and the other for the special component. Depreciation is recorded by the straight-line method to the nearest month, residual values being disregarded. On May 1, 1988, the special component is scrapped and is replaced with a similar component. This component is expected to have a residual value of approximately 25% of cost at the end of the useful life of the main unit and because of its materiality, the residual value will be considered in calculating depreciation. Specific asset information is as follows:

Main milling machine:	
Purchase price in 1982	$32,400
Residual value	$4,400
Estimated useful life	10 years
First special component:	
Purchase price	$9,790
Residual value	$250
Estimated useful life	6 years
Second special component:	
Purchase price	$15,250
Residual value	?

What are the depreciation charges to be recognized for the years (1) 1982, (2) 1988, and (3) 1989.

EXERCISE 12–11   (Accounting for patents)

The Far West Co. applied for and received numerous patents at a total cost of $30,345 at the beginning of 1982. It is assumed the patents will be useful evenly during their full legal life. At the beginning of 1984, the company paid $7,875 in successfully prosecuting an attempted infringement of these patent rights. At the beginning of 1987, $25,200 was paid to acquire patents that could make its own patents worthless: the patents acquired have a remaining life of 15 years but will not be used.

(1) Give the entries to record the expenditures relative to patents.
(2) Give the entries to record patent amortization for the years, 1982, 1984, and 1987.

EXERCISE 12–12   (Depletion and depreciation expense)

On July 1, 1987, Eureka Mining, a calender-year corporation, purchased the rights to a copper mine. Of the total purchase price, $3,000,000 was appropriately allocable to the copper. Estimated reserves were 600,000 tons of copper. Eureka expects to extract and sell 5,000 tons of copper per month. Production began immediately. The selling price is $20 per ton.

To aid production, Eureka also purchased some new equipment on July 1, 1987. The equipment cost $152,000 and had an estimated useful life of 8 years. However, after all the copper is removed from this mine, the equipment will be of no use to Eureka and will be sold for an estimated $8,000.

If sales and production conform to expectations, what is Eureka's depletion expense on this mine and depreciation expense on the new equipment for financial accounting purposes for the calender year 1987?

EXERCISE 12–13
(Computation and recording of depletion expense)

Goldfinger Mining sought to increase reserves of a special mineral resource. During 1985, the company purchased a piece of property that was expected to retain some value after removal of the mineral resources was complete. Company records reveal the following:

In the year 1985:

Purchase price for property	$4,450,000
Estimated supply of mineral resource	3,500,000 tons
Estimated property value after removal of mineral resource	$650,000
Total resource removal this year	0 tons

In the year 1986:

Developmental costs	$750,000
Total resource removal this year	0 tons

In the year 1987:

Total resource removal this year	550,000 tons

In the year 1988:

Estimated total resources to be recovered in future years (based on new discoveries)	3,660,000 tons
Additional developmental costs	$961,000
Total resource removal this year	700,000 tons

Show computations and entries made to recognize depletion for (1) 1987, (2) 1988.

EXERCISE 12–14   (Change in estimated useful life)

Dietler Corporation purchased a machine on January 1, 1982, for $225,000. At the date of acquisition, the machine had an estimated useful life of 15 years with no salvage value. The machine is being depreciated on a straight-line basis. On January 1, 1987, as a result of Dietler's experience with the machine, it was decided that the machine had an estimated useful life of 10 years from the date of acquisition. What is the amount of depreciation expense on this machine in 1987 using a new annual depreciation charge for the remaining 5 years?

EXERCISE 12–15 (Change in estimated useful life)

Decker Corporation purchased a machine on July 1, 1984, for $90,000. The machine was estimated to have a useful life of 10 years with an estimated salvage value of $10,000. During 1987 it became apparent that the machine would become uneconomical after December 31, 1991, and that the machine would have no scrap value. Decker uses the straight-line method of depreciation for all machinery. What should be the charge for depreciation in 1987 under a new annual depreciation charge for the remaining life? (AICPA adapted)

EXERCISE 12–16 (Recording the sale of equipment with note)

On December 31, 1987, Bellweather Corporation sold for $12,000 an old machine having an original cost of $50,000 and a book value of $6,000. The terms of the sale were as follows: $4,000 down payment, $4,000 payable on December 31 of the next two years. The agreement of sale made no mention of interest; however, 10% would be a fair rate for this type of transaction. Give the journal entries on Bellweather's books to record the sale of the machine and receipt of the two subsequent payments. (Round to the nearest dollar.)

EXERCISE 12–17 (Recording the sale of equipment)

Carter, Inc. purchased equipment costing $100,000 on June 30, 1986, having an estimated life of 5 years and a residual value of $10,000. The company uses the sum-of-the-years-digits method of depreciation, and takes one-half year's depreciation on assets in the year of purchase. The asset was sold on December 31, 1988, for $31,000. Give the entry to record the sale of the equipment.

EXERCISE 12–18 (Exchange of machinery)

Assume that Cooper Corporation has a machine that cost $52,000, has a book value of $35,000, and has a market value of $40,000. The machine is used in Cooper's manufacturing process. For each of the following situations, indicate the value at which Cooper should record the new asset and why it should be recorded at that value.

(a) Cooper exchanged the machine for a truck with a list price of $43,000.
(b) Cooper exchanged the machine with another manufacturing company for a similar machine with a list price of $41,000.
(c) Cooper exchanged the machine for a newer model machine from a dealer. The new machine had a list price of $60,000, and Cooper paid cash of $15,000.
(d) Cooper exchanged the machine plus $3,000 cash for a similar machine from Nutter Inc., a manufacturing company. The newly acquired machine is carried on Nutter's books at its cost of $55,000 with accumulated depreciation of $42,000; its fair market value is $43,000. In addition to determining the value, give the journal entries for both companies to record the exchange.

EXERCISE 12–19 (Exchange of truck)

On January 2, 1987, Winkler Delivery Company traded with a dealer an old delivery truck for a newer model. Data relative to the old and new trucks follow:

Old truck:

Original cost	$8,000
Accumulated depreciation as of January 2, 1987	6,000
Average published market price	1,700

New truck:

List price	$10,000
Cash price without trade-in	9,000
Cash paid with trade-in...	7,800

(1) Give the journal entries on Winkler's books to record the purchase of the new truck.

(2) Give the journal entries on Winkler's books if the cash paid was $6,800.
(AICPA adapted)

EXERCISE 12–20 (Exchange of assets)

The Mapleton Equipment Company exchanged the following assets during 1987. Prepare the journal entries on Mapleton's books for each exchange.

(a) Exchanged with Springville Equipment Company (dealer to dealer) a similar machine. Cost of machine exchanged, $25,000; book value of machine exchanged, $13,000; market value of machine exchanged, $16,000. No cash received.

(b) Same as in (a), except received $4,000 cash and machine with market value of $12,000.

(c) Purchased from Provo Manufacturing Company (dealer to nondealer) a new machine with a $50,000 list price. Paid $35,000 cash and a similar used machine; cost of machine exchanged, $40,000; book value of machine exchanged, $12,000; market value of machine exchanged, $10,000.

*EXERCISE 12–21
(Computation of fire loss and insurance proceeds)

Christensen Inc. purchased a building for $500,000 on August 1, 1977. Depreciation was recorded at 3% a year. On October 31, 1987, 50% of the building was destroyed. On this date the building had a fair market value of $1,200,000. A policy for $500,000 was carried on the building, the policy containing an 80% coinsurance clause. What entries would be made to record (a) the loss from destruction of the building and (b) the amount due from the insurance company? (Assume the company's fiscal period is the calendar year.)

*Relates to Appendix

*EXERCISE 12–22 (Coinsurance computations)

Higginson Corporation had a fire which destroyed their warehouse No. 12 to the extent that it will have to be torn down. The fair market value of the building was $150,000. The contents were valued at $50,000; however, $20,000 was salvaged in a fire-goods sale. The corporation had two insurance policies on the building: one with Saginaw Mutual for $100,000, and one with All State, Inc. for $90,000. What amount will each company pay to Higginson assuming: (a) Both companies require 80% coinsurance? (b) Saginaw Mutual requires 90% coinsurance and All State, Inc. requires 100% coinsurance?

Relates to Appendix

PROBLEMS

PROBLEM 12–1   (Time-factor methods of depreciation)

A delivery truck was acquired by Lancaster Inc. for $14,000 on January 1, 1986. The truck was estimated to have a 3-year life and a trade-in value at the end of that time of $2,000. The following depreciation methods are being considered.

(a) Depreciation is to be calculated by the straight-line method.
(b) Depreciation is to be calculated by the sum-of-the-years-digits method.
(c) Depreciation is to be calculated by the 150% declining-balance method.
(d) Depreciation is to be calculated using the accelerated cost recovery system for 3-year recovery property.

Instructions: Prepare tables reporting periodic depreciation and asset book value over the 3-year period for each assumption listed.

PROBLEM 12–2
(Maintenance charges and depreciation of components)

A company buys a machine for $25,400 on January 1, 1985. The maintenance costs for the years 1985–1988 are as follows: 1985, $1,500; 1986, $1,200; 1987, $7,300 (includes $6,100 for cost of a new motor installed in December 1987); 1988, $2,100.

Instructions:
(1) Assume the machine is recorded in a single account at a cost of $25,400. No record is kept of the cost of the component parts. Straight-line depreciation is used and the asset is estimated to have a useful life of 8 years. It is assumed there will be no residual value at the end of the useful life. What are the total expenses related to the machine for each of the first 4 years?
(2) Assume the cost of the frame of the machine was recorded in one account at a cost of $19,600 and the motor was recorded in a second account at a cost of $5,800. Straight-line depreciation is used with a useful life of 10 years for the frame and 4 years for the motor. Neither item is assumed to have any residual value at the end of its useful life. What are the total expenses and losses related to the machine?
(3) Evaluate the two methods.

PROBLEM 12–3   (Group depreciation and asset retirement)

The Bogart Manufacturing Co. acquired 20 similar machines at the beginning of 1983 for $50,000. Machines have an average life of 5 years and no residual value. The group-depreciation method is employed in writing off the cost of the machines. Machines were retired as follows:

2 machines at the end of 1985   9 machines at the end of 1987
4 machines at the end of 1986   5 machines at the end of 1988

Assume the machines were not replaced.

Instructions: Give the entries to record the retirement of machines and the periodic depreciation for the years 1983–1988 inclusive.

PROBLEM 12–4   (Composite depreciation)

Machines are acquired by Swillinger Inc. on March 1, 1987, as follows:

	Cost	Estimated Residual Value	Estimated Life in Years
Machine 301	$46,000	$6,000	5
302	20,000	2,000	6
303	12,000	800	8
304	18,000	1,500	6
305	6,000	None	10

Instructions:
(1) Calculate the composite depreciation rate for this group.
(2) Calculate the composite or average life in years for the group.
(3) Give the entry to record the depreciation for the year ending December 31, 1987.

PROBLEM 12–5   (Computation of asset cost and depreciation)

Granville Corporation, a manufacturer of steel products, began operations on October 1, 1986. The accounting department of Granville has started the plant asset and depreciation schedule presented on page 545. You have been asked to assist in completing this schedule. In addition to ascertaining that the data already on the schedule are correct, you have obtained from the company's records and personnel the information shown below and on page 545.

(a) Depreciation is computed from the first of the month of acquisition to the first of the month of disposition.
(b) Land A and Building A were acquired from a predecessor corporation. Granville paid $812,500 for the land and building together. At the time of acquisition, the land had an appraised value of $72,000 and the building had an appraised value of $828,000.
(c) Land B was acquired on October 2, 1986, in exchange for 3,000 newly issued shares of Granville's common stock. At the date of acquisition, the stock had a par value of $5 per share and a fair value of $25 per share. During October, 1986, Granville paid $15,200 to demolish an existing building on this land so it could construct a new building.

Granville Corporation
Plant Asset and Depreciation Schedule
For Years Ended September 30, 1987, and September 30, 1988

Assets	Acquisition Date	Cost	Salvage	Depreciation Method	Estimated Life in Years	Depreciation Expense Year Ended September 30, 1987	1988
Land A.............	October 1, 1986	$ (1)	N/A*	N/A	N/A	N/A	N/A
Building A	October 1, 1986	(2)	$47,500	Straight line	(3)	$20,000	(4)
Land B............	October 2, 1986	(5)	N/A	N/A	N/A	N/A	N/A
Building B	Under Construction	210,000 to date	—	Straight line	30	—	(6)
Donated Equipment ..	October 2, 1986	(7)	2,000	Double-declining balance	10	(8)	(9)
Machinery A	October 2, 1986	(10)	5,500	Sum-of-the years-digits	10	(11)	(12)
Machinery B	October 1, 1987	(13)	—	Straight line	12	—	(14)

*N/A—Not Applicable

(d) Construction of Building B on the newly acquired land began on October 1, 1987. By September 30, 1988, Granville had paid $210,000 of the estimated total construction costs of $300,000. Estimated completion and occupancy are July, 1989.

(e) Certain equipment was donated to the corporation by a local university. An independent appraisal of the equipment when donated placed the fair value at $23,000 and the residual value at $2,000.

(f) Machinery A's total cost of $110,000 includes installation expense of $550 and normal repairs and maintenance of $11,000. Salvage value is estimated at $5,500. Machinery A was sold on April 1, 1988.

(g) On October 1, 1987, Machinery B was acquired with a down payment of $4,000 and the remaining payments to be made in ten annual installments of $4,000 each beginning October 1, 1988. The prevailing interest rate was 8%.

Instructions: For each numbered item on the plant asset and depreciation schedule, determine the correct amount. (Round each answer to the nearest dollar.)

(AICPA adapted)

PROBLEM 12–6 (Accounting for patents)

On January 10, 1980, the Richards Company spent $36,000 to apply for and obtain a patent on a newly developed product. The patent had an estimated useful life of 10 years. At the beginning of 1984, the company spent $18,000 in successfully prosecuting an attempted infringement of the patent. At the beginning of 1985, the company purchased for $30,000 a patent that was expected to prolong the life of its original patent by 5 years. On July 1, 1988, a competitor obtained rights to a patent which made the company's patent obsolete.

Instructions: Give all the entries that would be made relative to the patent for the period 1980–1988, including entries to record the purchase of the patent, annual patent amortization, and ultimate patent obsolescence. (Assume the company's accounting period is the calendar year.)

PROBLEM 12–7   (Financial statements for mining company)

The Frazier Corp. was organized on January 2, 1987. It was authorized to issue 92,000 shares of common stock, par $50. On the date of organization it sold 20,000 shares at par and gave the remaining shares in exchange for certain land bearing recoverable ore deposits estimated by geologists at 900,000 tons. The property is deemed to have a value of $3,600,000 with no residual value.

During 1987 mine improvements totaled $226,000. During the year 75,000 tons were mined; 8,000 tons of this amount were on hand unsold on December 31, the balance of the tonnage being sold for cash at $17 per ton. Expenses incurred and paid for during the year, exclusive of depletion and depreciation, were as follows:

Mining	$173,500
Delivery	20,000
General and administrative	19,500

Cash dividends of $2 per share were declared on December 31, payable January 15, 1988.

It is believed that buildings and sheds will be useful only over the life of the mine; hence depreciation is to be recognized in terms of mine output.

Instructions: Prepare an income statement and a balance sheet for 1987. Submit working papers showing the development of statement data.

PROBLEM 12–8   (Computation of depletion and depreciation)

The Flying Dutchman Mining Company paid $2,700,000 in 1986 for property with a supply of natural resources estimated at 2,000,000 tons. The estimated cost of restoring the land for use after the resources are exhausted is $225,000. After the land is restored, it will have an estimated value of $325,000. Equipment was purchased at a cost of $825,000. Buildings, such as bunk houses and mess hall, were constructed on the site for $175,000. The useful lives of the buildings and equipment are expected to terminate upon exhaustion of the natural resources. Operations were not begun until January 1, 1987. In 1987, resources removed totaled 600,000 tons. During 1988, an additional discovery was made indicating that available resources subsequent to 1988 will total 1,505,000 tons. 770,000 tons of resources were removed during 1988.

Instructions: Compute the amount of depletion expense and depreciation expense for 1986, 1987, and 1988.

PROBLEM 12–9   (Computation of depreciation and depletion)

The following independent situations describe facts concerning the ownership of various assets.

(a) The Millett Company purchased a tooling machine in 1977 for $60,000. The machine was being depreciated on the straight-line method over an estimated useful life of 20 years, with no salvage value. At the beginning of 1987, when the machine had been in use for 10 years, Millett paid $10,000 to overhaul the machine. As a result of this improvement, Millett estimated that the useful life of the machine would be extended an additional 5 years.

(b) McCroby Manufacturing Co., a calendar-year company, purchased a machine for $65,000 on January 1, 1985. At the date of purchase, McCroby incurred the following additional costs:

Loss on sale of old machinery..................	$1,500
Freight in	500
Installation cost..............................	2,000
Testing costs prior to regular operation..........	400

The estimated salvage value of the machine was $5,000 and McCroby estimated that the machine would have a useful life of 20 years, with depreciation being computed on the straight-line method. In January 1987, accessories costing $5,400 were added to the machine in order to reduce its operating costs. These accessories neither prolonged the machine's life nor did they provide any additional salvage value.

(c) On July 1, 1987, Lund Corporation purchased equipment at a cost of $34,000. The equipment has an estimated salvage value of $3,000 and is being depreciated over an estimated life of eight years under the double-declining-balance method of depreciation. For the six months ended December 31, 1987, Lund recorded one-half year's depreciation.

(d) The Abbott Company acquired a tract of land containing an extractable natural resource. Abbott is required by its purchase contract to restore the land to a condition suitable for recreational use after it has extracted the natural resource. Geological surveys estimate that the recoverable reserves will be 4,000,000 tons, and that the land will have a value of $500,000 after restoration. Relevant cost information follows:

Land	$9,000,000
Estimated restoration costs	$1,500,000
Tons mined and sold in 1987...............	800,000

(e) In January 1987, Zufeldt Corporation entered into a contract to acquire a new machine for its factory. The machine, which had a cash price of $200,000, was paid for as follows:

Down payment	$ 30,000
Notes payable in 10 equal monthly installments, interest 10%	150,000
500 shares of Zufeldt common stock with an agreed value of $50 per share	25,000
Total	$205,000

Prior to the machine's use, installation costs of $7,000 were incurred. The machine has an estimated useful life of 10 years and an estimated salvage value of $10,000. The straight-time method of depreciation is used.

Instructions: In each case, compute the amount of depreciation or depletion for 1987.   (AICPA adapted)

PROBLEM 12–10   (Exchange of assets)

A review of the books of Longview Electric Co. disclosed that there were five transactions involving gains and losses on the exchange of fixed assets. The transactions were recorded as indicated in the following ledger accounts.

Cash		Plant Assets		Accum. Depr. — Plant Assets	
(2) 5,000	(5) 1,000	(1) 10,000	(3) 118,000	(3) 110,000	
(3) 6,000		(2) 25,000	(4) 300,000	(4) 390,000	

Intangible Assets		Gain on Exchange — Plant Assets		Loss on Exchange — Plant Assets	
(5) 1,000			(1) 10,000	(3) 2,000	
			(2) 30,000		
			(4) 90,000		

Investigation disclosed the following facts concerning these dealer-dealer transactions:

(1) Exchanged a piece of equipment with a $50,000 original cost, $20,000 book value, and $30,000 current market value for a piece of similar equipment owned by Fox Electric that had a $60,000 original cost, $10,000 book value, and a $30,000 current market value.

(2) Exchanged a machine, cost $70,000, book value $10,000, current market value $40,000, for a similar machine, market value $35,000, and $5,000 in cash.

(3) Exchanged a building, cost $150,000, book value $40,000, current market value $30,000, for a building with market value of $24,000 plus cash of $6,000.

(4) Exchanged a factory building, cost $850,000, book value $460,000, current market value $550,000, for equipment owned by Romeo Inc. that had an original cost of $900,000, accumulated depreciation of $325,000, and current market value of $550,000.

(5) Exchanged a patent, cost $12,000, book value $6,000, current market value $3,000 and cash of $1,000 for another patent with market value of $4,000.

Instructions: Analyze each recorded transaction as to its compliance with generally accepted accounting principles. Prepare adjusting journal entries where required.

PROBLEM 12–11   (Exchange of assets)

The Galenka Development Co. acquired the following assets in exchange for various nonmonetary assets.

1987

Mar. 15   Acquired from another company a computerized lathe in exchange for 3 old lathes. The old lathes had a total cost of $35,000 and had a remaining book value of $13,000. The new lathe had a market value of $20,000, approximately the same value as the three old lathes.

June 1 Acquired 200 acres of land by issuing 2,000 shares of common stock with par value of $10 and market value of $90. Market analysis reveals that the market value of the stock was a reasonable value for the land.

July 15 Acquired a used piece of heavy earth-moving equipment, market value $100,000, by exchanging a used molding machine with a market value of $20,000 (book value $8,000; cost $40,000) and land with a market value of $100,000 (cost $40,000). Cash of $20,000 was received by Galenka Development Co. as part of the transaction.

Aug. 15 Acquired a patent, franchise, and copyright for 2 used milling machines. The book value of each milling machine was $1,500 and each had originally cost $10,000. The market value of each machine is $12,500. It is estimated that the patent and franchise have about the same market values, and the market value of the copyright is 50% of the market value of the patent.

Nov. 1 Acquired from a dealer a new packaging machine for 4 old packaging machines. The old machines had a total cost of $50,000 and a total remaining book value of $20,000. The new packaging machine has an indicated market value of $25,000, approximately the same value of the four old machines.

Instructions: Prepare the journal entries required on Galenka Development Co. books to record the exchanges.

PROBLEM 12–12
(Balance sheet presentation of plant and intangible assets)

The following account balances pertain to the Lomax Company.

Account Title	Dr.	Cr.
Equipment	675,000	
Goodwill	435,000	
Inventory	90,000	
Land	300,000	
Franchises	360,000	
Cash	65,000	
Accounts Receivable	137,000	
Buildings	1,400,000	
Patents	15,000	
Notes Receivable	456,000	
Accumulated Depreciation — Equipment		365,000
Accounts Payable		147,000
Notes Payable		1,500,000
Accumulated Depreciation — Buildings		385,000

Additional information:

(a) $600,000 of the notes payable are secured by a direct lien on the building.

(b) The company uses the sum-of-the-years-digits method of cost allocation for buildings and equipment and uses straight-line for patents, franchises, and goodwill.

(c) Inventory valuation was made using the retail method.

Instructions: Prepare the land, buildings, and equipment section and the intangible asset section of the balance sheet.

*PROBLEM 12–13 (Computation of fire loss)

The Golden Corporation is a small manufacturing company producing a highly flammable cleaning fluid. On May 31, 1987, the company had a fire which completely destroyed the processing building and the in-process inventory; some of the equipment was saved.

The cost of the fixed assets destroyed and their related accumulated depreciation accounts at May 31, 1987, were as follows:

	Cost	Accumulated Depreciation
Buildings	$120,000	$74,000
Equipment	45,000	13,125

At present prices, the cost to replace the destroyed property would be: building, $240,000; equipment, $112,500. At the time of the fire, it was determined that the destroyed building was 62½% depreciated, and the destroyed equipment was 33⅓% depreciated.

After the fire a physical inventory was taken. The raw materials were valued at $60,000, the finished goods at $100,000 and supplies at $10,000.

The inventories on January 1, 1987 consisted of:

Finished goods	$140,000
Goods in process	100,000
Raw materials	30,000
Supplies	4,000
Total	$274,000

A review of the accounts showed that the sales and gross profit for the last five years were:

	Sales	Gross Profit
1982	$300,000	$ 86,200
1983	320,000	102,400
1984	330,000	108,900
1985	250,000	62,500
1986	280,000	84,000

The sales for the first five months of 1987 were $150,000. Raw materials purchases were $50,000. Freight on purchases was $5,000. Direct labor for five months was $40,000; for the past five years manufacturing overhead was 50% of direct labor.

Insurance on the property and inventory was carried with three companies. Each policy included an 80% coinsurance clause. The amount of insurance carried with the various companies was:

	Buildings and Equipment	Inventories
Sun Mutual Co.	$90,000	$76,000
Casualty Inc.	60,000	70,000
Fireman's Fund	45,000	70,000

The cost of cleaning up the debris was $21,000. The value of the scrap salvaged from the fire was $1,800.

Instructions:
(1) Compute the value of inventory lost.
(2) Compute the expected recovery from each insurance company.

(AICPA adapted)

Relates to Appendix.

PROBLEM 12–14   (Computation of depreciation and amortization)

Information pertaining to Blake Corporation's property, plant and equipment for 1987 is presented below.

Account balances at January 1, 1987

	Debit	Credit
Land.	$ 150,000	
Building	1,200,000	
Accumulated depreciation		$263,100
Machinery and equipment	900,000	
Accumulated depreciation		250,000
Automotive equipment	115,000	
Accumulated depreciation		84,600

	Depreciation Method	Useful Life
Building	150% declining balance	25 years
Machinery and equipment	Straight-line	10 years
Automotive equipment	Sum-of-the-years' digits	4 years
Leasehold improvements	Straight-line	

The salvage value of the depreciable assets is immaterial. Depreciation is computed to the nearest month.

Transactions during 1987 and other information:
(a) On January 2, 1987, Blake purchased a new car for $10,000 cash and trade-in of a two-year-old car with a cost of $9,000 and a book value of $2,700. The new car has a cash price of $12,000; the market value of the trade-in is not known.
(b) On April 1, 1987, a machine purchased for $23,000 on April 1, 1982, was destroyed by fire. Blake recovered $15,500 from its insurance company.
(c) On May 1, 1987, costs of $168,000 were incurred to improve leased office premises. The leasehold improvements have a useful life of eight years. The related lease, which terminates on December 31, 1993, is renewable

for an additional six-year term. The decision to renew will be made in 1993 based on office space needs at that time.

(d) On July 1, 1987, machinery and equipment were purchased at a total invoice cost of $280,000; additional costs of $5,000 for freight and $25,000 for installation were incurred.

(e) Blake determined that the automotive equipment comprising the $115,000 balance at January 1, 1987, would have been depreciated at a total amount of $18,000 for the year ended December 31, 1987.

Instructions:

(1) For each asset classification prepare schedules showing depreciation and amortization expense, and accumulated depreciation and amortization that would appear on Blake's income statement for the year ended December 31, 1987, and balance sheet at December 31, 1987, respectively.

(2) Prepare a schedule showing gain or loss from disposal of assets that would appear in Blake's income statement for the year ended December 31, 1987.

(3) Prepare the property, plant and equipment section of Blake's December 31, 1987, balance sheet.   (AICPA adapted)

13

Long-Term Investments in Equity Securities and Other Assets

When individuals speak of investments, they generally are referring to such items as stocks and bonds, real estate, certificates of deposit, or other similar items that they have purchased. The investment is made with the intent of receiving the purchase price back (return *of* investment) plus an increase (return *on* investment) in the form of dividends, interest, or gains from appreciation upon sale or maturity of the investment.

Companies also make investments for similar reasons, i.e., to receive a return of the investment as well as to earn a return on the investment. In addition, a company may invest in the stock of another company as a means of diversifying its products or services or to exercise significant influence over that company. For example, if Company A buys most of its raw materials from Company B, Company A may seek to purchase a substantial amount of Company B's stock to insure a source for its raw materials at favorable prices. Another similar reason is to insure a distribution outlet for a company's finished product.

The investment in stock of another company represents an ownership interest in the net operating assets of that company. Sometimes an investment involves the acquisition of all the stock of a company, and therefore represents a 100% ownership interest in the assets and liabilities of the acquired company. This is referred to as a **merger**, as, for example, when General Electric Company purchased RCA Corporation in 1985 for over $6 billion in the largest nonoil and gas related merger in U.S. history.

From the standpoint of the owner, investments are either temporary or long-term. As discussed in Chapter 7, investments are classified as temporary or current only where they are (1) readily marketable and (2) it is

553

management's intent to use them in meeting current cash requirements. The general guideline is whether the investment is expected to be converted to cash within a year or the operating cycle, whichever is longer. Investments not meeting these tests are considered **long-term** or **non-current investments** and are usually reported on the balance sheet under a separate noncurrent heading, as illustrated in this chapter and in the balance sheet for General Mills, Inc., reproduced in Appendix A.

Long-term investments include a variety of assets. Among the most common are:

1. Equity securities, including both preferred and common stock.
2. Bonds, mortgages, and similar debt instruments.
3. Funds, e.g., for debt retirement, stock redemption, or other special purposes.
4. Miscellaneous items, such as real estate held for appreciation, advances to affiliates, equity in joint ventures and partnerships, and interests in life insurance contracts or in trusts and estates.

The primary emphasis in this chapter will be on accounting for long-term investments in equity securities. Accounting for funds and for the cash surrender value of life insurance will also be discussed briefly. The accounting problems relating to bonds and long-term notes are considered in Chapter 15.

LONG-TERM INVESTMENTS IN EQUITY SECURITIES

One of the characteristics of a free enterprise economy is the considerable level of intercorporate investment. As indicated previously, a corporation may acquire securities of another established corporation for a variety of reasons. Whatever the specific objective, an investment in the securities of another corporate entity is expected to enhance the economic well-being of the acquiring company. The accounting and reporting issues for long-term investments in equity securities (stocks) are discussed in the following sections:

1. Acquisition of stocks
2. Accounting for long-term investments in stocks—consolidation, cost method, and equity method
3. Disclosures for long-term investments in equity securities

Acquisition of Stocks

The acquisition of long-term investments in stocks follows the same general principles as those for temporary investments in stocks, as explained in Chapter 7.

Shares of stock are usually purchased for cash through stock exchanges (e.g., New York, American, or regional exchanges) and from individuals and institutional investors rather than from the corporations themselves. The investment is recorded at the amount paid, including brokers' commissions, taxes, and other fees incidental to the purchase price. Even when part of the purchase price is deferred, the full cost should be recorded as the investment in stock, with a liability account established for the amount yet to be paid. If stock is acquired in exchange for properties or services instead of cash, the fair market value of the consideration given or the value at which the stock is currently selling, whichever is more clearly determinable, should be used as the basis for recording the investment. If two or more securities are acquired for a lump-sum price, the cost should be allocated to each security in an equitable manner, as illustrated in earlier chapters.

Accounting for Long-Term Investments in Stocks

In accounting for long-term investments in stocks, one of three basic methods must be used: consolidation, cost, or equity. Which method is appropriate depends on the **control or degree of influence exercised by the acquiring company (investor) over the acquired company (investee)**.

Choosing Among Consolidation, Cost, and Equity Methods. When one company acquires a majority voting interest in another company through the acquisition of **more than 50 percent** of its voting common stock, the acquiring company has **control** over the acquired company. The investor and investee are referred to respectively as the **parent company** and the **subsidiary company**. Where control exists, the proper accounting method is **consolidation**, which means that the financial statement balances of the parent and subsidiary companies are added together or consolidated. In the consolidation process, any intercompany transactions are eliminated, e.g., any sales and purchases between the parent and subsidiary companies. By eliminating all intercompany transactions, the combined balances or consolidated totals appropriately reflect the financial position and results of operation of the total economic unit. This treatment reflects the fact that majority ownership of common stock assures control by the parent over the decision-making processes of the subsidiary. In certain limited situations, the financial statements of a subsidiary are not consolidated with those of the parent. Generally, however, the reporting entity is the total economic unit consisting of the parent and all its subsidiaries. Accounting for consolidated entities is covered in advanced accounting texts.[1]

---

[1] See, for example, Paul M. Fisher, William James Taylor, and J. Arthur Leer, *Advanced Accounting* (Cincinnati: South-Western Publishing Co., 1986).

Consolidated financial statements are appropriate only when the investor holds a majority voting interest (more than 50%) in the investee. A considerable degree of control may be exercised, however, by an investor owning **50 percent or less** of the common stock of the investee. If conditions indicate that the acquiring company exercises **significant influence** over the financial and operating decisions of the other company, the basic accounting principle of substance over form suggests that accounting methods should be used that parallel as closely as possible those followed when actual voting control exists and consolidated statements are prepared. The **equity method** of accounting is used to produce these results.

When the acquiring company **does not exercise significant influence** over the acquired company, accounting for the investment should recognize the separate identities of the companies. This is accomplished by the **cost method** of accounting. Since preferred stock is generally nonvoting stock and does not provide for significant influence, the cost method is always used for investments in preferred stock.

The ability of the investor to exercise significant influence over such decisions as dividend distribution and operational and financial administration may be indicated in several ways: e.g., representation on the investee's board of directors, participation in policy-making processes, material intercompany transactions, interchange of managerial personnel, or technological dependency of investee on investor. Another important consideration is the **extent of ownership** by an investor in relation to the concentration of other stockholdings. While it is clear that ownership of over 50% of common stock assures control by the acquiring company, ownership of a lesser percentage may give effective control if the remaining shares of the stock are widely held, and no significant blocks of stockholders are consistently united in their ownership.

The Accounting Principles Board, in Opinion No. 18, recognized that the degree of influence and control will not always be clear and that judgment will be required in assessing the status of each investment. To achieve a reasonable degree of uniformity in the application of its position, the Board set 20% as an ownership standard; the ownership of **20% or more** of the voting stock of the company carries the presumption, in the absence of evidence to the contrary, that an investor has the ability to exercise significant influence over that company. Conversely, ownership of **less than 20%** leads to the presumption that the investor does not have the ability to exercise significant influence unless such ability can be demonstrated.[2]

---

[2]*Opinions of the Accounting Principles Board, No. 18,* "The Equity Method of Accounting for Investments in Common Stock" (New York: American Institute of Certified Public Accountants, 1971).

In May 1981, the FASB issued Interpretation No. 35 to emphasize that the 20% criterion is only a guideline and that judgment is required in determining the appropriate accounting method in cases where ownership is 50% or less. Interpretation No. 35 lists five illustrative examples of circumstances that might indicate that the investor does not have significant influence, regardless of the percentage of ownership[3]:

1. Opposition by the investee, such as litigation or complaints to governmental regulatory authorities.
2. An agreement between the investor and investee under which the investor surrenders significant rights as a shareholder.
3. Majority ownership of the investee is concentrated among a small group of shareholders who operate the investee without regard to the views of the investor.
4. The investor needs or wants more financial information to apply the equity method than is available to the investee's other shareholders (for example, the investor wants quarterly financial information from an investee who publicly reports only annually), tries to obtain the information, and fails.
5. The investor tries and fails to obtain representation on the investee's board of directors.

While the FASB examples may be helpful in some cases, evaluating the degree of investor influence is often a very subjective process. As a result, the percentage-of-ownership criterion set forth in APB Opinion No. 18 has been widely accepted as the basis for determining the appropriate method of accounting for long-term investments in equity securities when the investor does not possess absolute voting control. Thus, in the absence of persuasive evidence to the contrary, the **cost method** is used when ownership is **less than 20%**; **the equity method**, when ownership is **20% to 50%**. These relationships dealing with the effect of ownership interest and control or influence and the proper accounting method to be used are summarized in Exhibit 13–1 on page 558.

This chapter discusses and illustrates the accounting and reporting issues encountered with the cost and equity methods. The cost method is presented first, followed by the more complex equity method.

The Cost Method

When a long-term investment in another company's stock does not involve either a controlling interest or significant influence, the investment should be accounted for using the cost method. The procedures are essen-

---

[3]*FASB Interpretation No. 35*, "Criteria for Applying the Equity Method of Accounting for Investments in Common Stock" (Stamford: Financial Accounting Standards Board, 1981), par. 4.

Exhibit 13–1
Effect of Ownership Interest and Control or Influence
on Accounting for Long-Term Investments in Common Stocks

Ownership Interest	Control or Degree of Influence	Accounting Method
More than 50%	Control	Consolidated statements
20 to 50%	Significant influence	Equity method
Less than 20%	No significant influence	Cost method

---

tially the same as those described in Chapter 7 for temporary investments in stocks. The investment is initially recorded at cost including commissions and other related expenditures. Revenue is recognized when dividends are received from the investee. Declines in market value are recognized according to the lower-of-cost-or-market (LCM) valuation rule for all marketable equity securities on a portfolio or aggregate basis. Upon sale, the difference between the proceeds received and the cost of the investment is realized as a gain or loss and recorded under "other revenues" or "other expenses" in the income statement.

Temporary Changes in Market Value of Noncurrent Marketable Equity Securities. While the above procedures are generally the same as those followed in accounting for temporary investments in equity securities, there is one major difference in the valuation of current versus noncurrent marketable equity securities. To review the valuation discussion in Chapter 7, current marketable equity securities are valued at LCM, and an allowance account is used to reduce the cost to market. If the market value recovers, the securities may be written back up, but not above original cost. Any change in the allowance account is recognized in the income statement in the period of change.

When marketable equity securities are classified as long-term investments because it is not management's intent to use the securities as a current source of cash, a somewhat different treatment is required by FASB Statement No. 12.[4] Temporary declines in the value of noncurrent marketable equity securities are still reflected in an allowance account,

---

[4]*Statement of Financial Accounting Standards No. 12,* "Accounting for Certain Marketable Securities" (Stamford: Financial Accounting Standards Board, 1975), par. 9.

which is deducted from the long-term investment account on the balance sheet. This is the same as for current marketable equity securities. However, the loss on writedown to LCM is treated differently. Stock prices can fluctuate greatly while the stock is being held, and if the investment is to be retained for a long period, the impact of gains or losses on net income from valuation adjustments could be misleading. Therefore, adjustments for temporary changes in value of noncurrent marketable equity securities are not reflected in current income as are adjustments for current marketable equity securities. Instead a **contra stockholders' equity account** is created for changes in noncurrent securities. This account, which in FASB Statement No. 12 is entitled "Net Unrealized Loss on Noncurrent Marketable Equity Securities," is to be deducted from the total stockholders' equity reported in the balance sheet. Both the allowance account that reduces the investment to market and the contra stockholders' equity account should have the same balance at all times. As the market price of the noncurrent equity securities portfolio fluctuates, these accounts will be adjusted to bring the valuation to the lower of aggregate cost or market. When equity securities are sold, the transaction is recorded on the historical cost basis and a gain or loss recognized. Then at year end, an adjustment is made to the allowance and contra stockholders' equity accounts based on the remaining portfolio of investments. These procedures are illustrated in the following example.

A company carries a noncurrent marketable equity securities portfolio that has a cost of $125,000. At December 31, 1987, the market value of the securities held has fallen to $110,000. The decline is judged to be temporary. The following entries would be required to reduce the securities valuation from cost to market.

Net Unrealized Loss on Noncurrent Marketable Equity Securities.......	15,000
Allowance for Decline in Value of Noncurrent Marketable Equity	
Securities...	15,000

The applicable disclosures on the balance sheet might be shown as follows:

Investments:		
Noncurrent investments in marketable equity securities (cost)	$125,000	
Less allowance for decline in value of noncurrent marketable equity securities....................	(15,000)	110,000
Total assets		$xxx,xxx
Stockholders' Equity:		
Total capital stock and retained earnings............	$xxx,xxx	
Less net unrealized loss on noncurrent marketable equity securities	(15,000)	
Total stockholders' equity and liabilities		$xxx,xxx

If during 1988 one of the securities costing $25,000 was sold for $30,000, the transaction would be recorded based on the original cost as follows:

```
Cash.......................................................    30,000
    Investment in XYZ Stock (original cost)..........................        25,000
    Gain on Sale of Investment.....................................         5,000
```

Assume further that during 1988, two other marketable equity securities were purchased as long-term investments at a total cost of $35,000. Assume the aggregate market value of the portfolio at the end of 1988 is $132,000. Therefore, the amount in the allowance account and in the contra equity account would need to be adjusted to $3,000 ($125,000 beginning cost − $25,000 cost of security sold + $35,000 purchases = $135,000 ending cost − $132,000 end-of-year aggregate market value). The entry would be:

```
Allowance for Decline in Value of Noncurrent Marketable Equity
    Securities.....................................................   12,000
        Net Unrealized Loss on Noncurrent Marketable Equity Securities...        12,000
```

The long-term investments would be shown on the balance sheet at the lower of cost or market value, $132,000 (cost of $135,000 less allowance of $3,000), and the stockholders' equity contra account would reduce total stockholders' equity by the $3,000. Note that the $5,000 gain on the actual sale would be reported as additional income for 1988. Also note that the Allowance for Decline and Net Unrealized Loss accounts can be adjusted upward, but only to a zero balance. If market is equal to or exceeds cost, no adjustment is made due to the practice of conservatism in accounting.

Permanent Declines in Market Value. Sometimes the market price of stock declines due to economic circumstances that are unlikely to improve. For example, low oil prices have caused the stocks of some oil companies to decrease significantly without much expectation that they will ever recover. If a decline in the market value of an individual security in a portfolio is judged to be permanent, the cost basis of that security should be reduced by crediting the investment account rather than an allowance account. In addition, the write-down should be recognized as a loss and charged against current income.[5] The new cost basis for the security may not be adjusted upward to its original cost for any subsequent increases in market value.

To illustrate the accounting for a permanent decline, assume that the portfolio of a company at the end of its first year of operations contains the following noncurrent marketable equity securities:

---

[5]*Ibid.*, par. 21.

	Cost	Market
Company A	$ 50,000	$ 40,000
Company B	30,000	35,000
Company C	100,000	60,000
Total	$180,000	$135,000

On an aggregate basis, the allowance adjustment would be for the difference between cost and market, or $45,000. However, if evaluation of market conditions for the securities of Company C indicates that the decline in value is permanent, the security should be written down to market, which becomes the new cost basis, and a reevaluation made of the balance of the portfolio to determine the need for an allowance. The write-down entry would be as follows:

Recognized Loss from Permanent Decline in Market Value of Noncurrent Marketable Equity Securities................................. 40,000
    Long-Term Investments in Marketable Equity Securities...........   40,000

The recognized loss account would be closed to Income Summary at the end of the year, reducing net income by $40,000. The portfolio of long-term securities would now appear as follows:

	Cost	Market
Company A	$ 50,000	$ 40,000
Company B	30,000	35,000
Company C	60,000	60,000
Total	$140,000	$135,000

At this point, an adjustment would be required to the Allowance for Decline and Net Unrealized Loss accounts to bring them to a $5,000 balance, which is the remaining difference in cost and market values.

Change in Classification Between Current and Noncurrent. As noted in Chapter 7, if there is a change in the classification of a marketable equity security between current and noncurrent assets, the transfer should be made at the lower of cost or market value of the security at the date of the reclassification. This amount becomes the new cost basis with any loss being recorded in the current period as was done for permanent declines in value.

Summary of Marketable Equity Securities Valuation. The valuation of marketable equity securities as discussed on the preceding pages is summarized in the flowchart in Exhibit 13–2. By studying the flowchart carefully in conjunction with the discussion and examples, the decision points and accounting treatment can be more clearly understood.

The Financial Accounting Standards Board, in Statement No. 12, places a high premium on the classification of marketable equity securities.

Exhibit 13–2
Flowchart of Valuation for Marketable Equity
Securities as Prescribed by FASB Statement No. 12

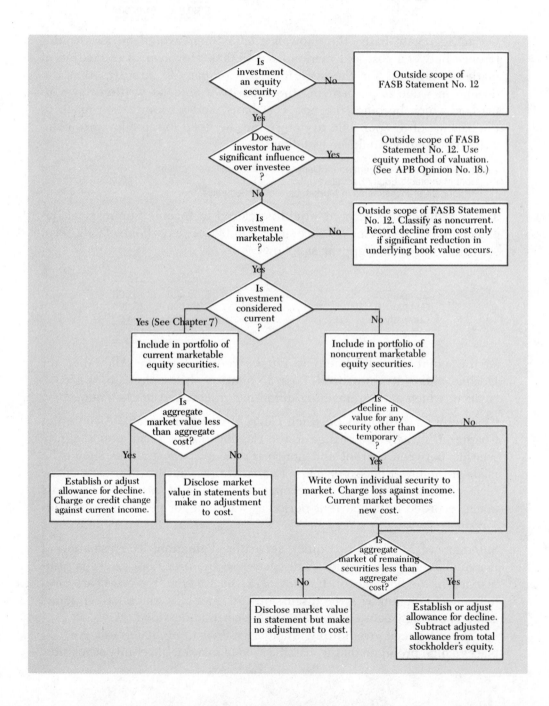

Because the classification is determined on the basis of subjective criteria, e.g., the intent of management to hold or sell, there is concern that the classification can be used to manipulate reported net income. In the authors' opinion, the adoption of a consistent valuation approach for all investments, regardless of their classification, seems preferable to the differentiated treatment for current and noncurrent securities outlined in Statement No. 12.

The Equity Method

The **equity method** of accounting for long-term investments in common stock reflects the economic substance of the relationship between the investor and investee rather than the legal distinction of the separate entities. The objective of this method is to reflect the underlying claim by the investor on the net assets of the investee company.

Under the equity method, just as under the cost method, the investment is initially recorded at cost. However, with the equity method, the investment account is periodically adjusted to reflect changes in the underlying net assets of the investee. The investment balance is increased to reflect a proportionate share of the earnings of the investee company, or decreased to reflect a share of any losses reported. If preferred stock dividends have been declared by the investee, they must be deducted from income reported by the investee before computing the investor's share of investee earnings or losses. When dividends are received by the investor, the investment account is reduced. Thus, the equity method recognizes that investee earnings increase the investee net assets that underlie the investment; similarly, investee losses and dividends paid out reduce the investee net assets and hence the equity in the investment.

Cost and Equity Methods Compared. To contrast and illustrate the accounting entries under the cost and equity methods, assume that Powell Corporation purchases 5,000 shares of San Juan Company common stock on January 2 at $20 per share, including commissions and other costs. San Juan has a total of 25,000 shares outstanding, thus the 5,000 shares represent a 20% ownership interest. As discussed earlier in the chapter, the equity method is used when ownership is 20% to 50% unless there is persuasive evidence that the investor does not have significant influence over the investee. The appropriate entries under both the cost and equity methods are shown in Exhibit 13–3. The actual method used would depend on the degree of influence exercised by the investor as indicated by a consideration of all relevant factors, as well as the percentage owned. Exhibit 13–3 highlights the basic differences in accounting for long-term

Exhibit 13–3   Comparison of Cost and Equity Methods

Cost Method   **Equity Method**

Jan. 2 Purchased 5,000 shares of San Juan Company common stock at $20 per share.

Investment in San Juan				Investment in San Juan		
Company Stock	100,000			Company Stock	100,000	
Cash		100,000		Cash		100,000

Oct. 31 Received dividend of $.80 per share from San Juan Company ($.80 × 5,000 shares).

Cash	4,000			Cash	4,000	
Dividend Revenue		4,000		Investment in San Juan		
				Company Stock		4,000

Dec. 31 San Juan Company announces earnings for the year of $60,000.

No Entry	Investment in San Juan	
	Company Stock	12,000
	Income from Investment in	
	San Juan Company Stock	12,000
	(.20 × $60,000)	

Dec. 31 Market value of San Juan Company common stock is $18.50 per share.

Net Unrealized Loss on			No Entry
Noncurrent Marketable			
Equity Securities	7,500		
Allowance for Decline in Value			
of Noncurrent Marketable			
Equity Securities		7,500	
[($20 − $18.50) × 5,000 shares]			

Carrying value (book value) of investment at year-end:

Cost	$100,000	Cost	$100,000
Less allowance for decline in		Dividend revenue	(4,000)
value	7,500	Share of investee earnings	12,000
	$ 92,500		$108,000

investments under the cost and equity methods. Under both methods, the investment is originally recorded at cost. Dividends received are recognized as dividend revenue under the cost method and as a reduction in the investment account under the equity method. The earnings of the investee company are recorded as an increase to the investment account under the equity method, while no entry is required for this event under the cost method. Under the cost method, an adjustment to lower of cost or market may be required, while no entry is needed under the equity method, since the investment value has already been adjusted to reflect the underlying value of the net assets of the investee. The carrying value under the cost method is cost less any applicable allowance for decline in value; under the equity method, the carrying value is original cost plus any increases from the proportionate share of investee earnings less any dividends received.

Complexities Under the Equity Method. When a company is purchased by another company, the purchase price usually differs from the recorded book value of the underlying net assets of the acquired company. For example, assume Snowbird Company purchased 100% of the common stock of Ski Resorts International for $8 million, although the book value of Ski Resorts' net assets is only $6.5 million. In effect, Snowbird is purchasing some undervalued assets, above-normal earnings potential, or both.

As explained in Chapter 11, during the consolidation process, if the purchase price exceeds the recorded value, the acquiring company must allocate this purchase price among the assets acquired using their current market values as opposed to the amounts carried on the books of the acquired company. If part of the purchase price cannot be allocated to specific assets, that amount is recorded as goodwill. If the purchase price is less than recorded net asset value, the assets acquired must be recorded at an amount less than their carrying value on the books of the acquired company. Whether assets are increased or decreased as a result of the purchase, future income determination will use the new (adjusted) values to determine the depreciation and amortization charges (see the goodwill discussion and illustrations in Chapter 11).

When only a portion of a company's stock is purchased and the equity method is used to reflect the income of the partially owned company, an adjustment to the investee's reported income, similar to that just described, may be required. In order to determine whether such an adjustment is necessary, the acquiring company must compare the purchase price of the common stock with the recorded net asset value of the acquired company at the date of purchase. If the purchase price exceeds the investor's share of book value, the computed excess must be analyzed in the same way as described above for a 100% purchase. Although no entries to adjust asset values are made on the books of either company, an adjustment to the investee's reported income is required under the equity method for the investor to reflect the economic reality of paying more for the investment than the underlying net book values. If depreciable assets had been adjusted to higher market values on the books of the investee to reflect the price paid by the investor, additional depreciation would have been taken by the investee company. Similarly, if the purchase price reflected goodwill, additional amortization would have been required. These adjustments would have reduced the reported income of the investee. To reflect this condition, an adjustment is made by the investor to the income reported by the investee in applying the equity method. This adjustment serves to meet the objective of computing the income reported using the equity method in the same manner as would be done if the company were 100% purchased and consolidated financial statements were prepared.

To illustrate, assume that the book value of common stockholders' equity (net assets) of Stewart Inc. was $500,000 at the time Phillips Manufacturing Co. purchased 40% of its common shares for $250,000. Based on a 40% ownership interest, the market value of the net assets of Stewart Inc. would be $625,000 ($250,000 ÷ .40), or $125,000 more than the book value. Assume that a review of the asset values discloses that the market value of depreciable properties exceeds the carrying value of these assets by $50,000. The remaining $75,000 difference ($125,000 − $50,000) is attributed to goodwill. Assume further that the average remaining life of the depreciable assets is 10 years and that goodwill is amortized over 40 years. Phillips Manufacturing Co. would adjust its share of the annual income reported by Stewart Inc. to reflect the additional depreciation and the amortization of goodwill as follows:

$$
\begin{array}{l}
\text{Additional depreciation } (\$50,000 \times 40\%) \div 10 \text{ years} = \$2,000 \\
\text{Goodwill amortization } \ (\$75,000 \times 40\%) \div 40 \text{ years} = \underline{750} \\
 \$2,750
\end{array}
$$

Each year for the first 10 years, Phillips would make the following entry:

Income from Investment in Stewart Inc. Stock.	2,750	
Investment in Stewart Inc. Stock.		2,750
To adjust share of income on Stewart Inc. common stock for		
proportionate depreciation on excess market value of depreciable		
property, $2,000, and for amortization of goodwill from acquisition of		
the stock, $750.		

After the tenth year, the adjustment would be for $750 until the goodwill amount is fully amortized.

To illustrate, assume that the purchase was made January 2, 1988; Stewart Inc. declared and paid dividends of $70,000 to common stockholders during 1988; and Stewart Inc. reported net income of $150,000 for the year ended December 31, 1988. At the end of 1988, the investment in Stewart Inc. common stock would be reported on the balance sheet of Phillips Manufacturing Co. at $279,250, computed as shown at the top of page 567.

This illustration assumes that the fiscal years of the two companies coincide and that the purchase of the stock is made at the first of the year. If a purchase is made at a time other than the beginning of the year, the income earned up to the date of the purchase is assumed to be included in

Investment in Stewart Inc. Common Stock
<u>Investment in Stewart Inc. Common Stock</u>

Acquisition cost.		$250,000	
Add: Share of 1988 earnings of investee company ($150,000 × .40)		60,000	$310,000
Less: Dividends received from investee ($70,000 × .40)	$ 28,000		
Additional depreciation of undervalued assets	2,000		
Amortization of unrecorded Goodwill	750	30,750	
Year-end carrying value of investment (equity in investee company)			$279,250

the cost of purchase. Only income earned by the investee subsequent to acquisition should be recognized by the investor.

The adjustment for additional depreciation and goodwill amortization is needed only when the purchase price is greater than the underlying book value at the date of acquisition. If the purchase price is less than the underlying book value at the time of acquisition, it is assumed that specific assets of the investee are overvalued or that there is negative goodwill as discussed in Chapter 11, and an adjustment is necessary to reduce the depreciation or amortization included in the reported income of the investee. The journal entry to reflect this adjustment is the reverse of the one illustrated previously. The computations would also be similar except that the adjustments for overvalued assets would be added to (instead of subtracted from) the carrying value of the investment.

As noted earlier in the chapter, during the consolidation process, adjustments must be made to eliminate any intercompany sales, costs, and profits. Under the equity method, if the investor and investee are engaged in intercompany revenue-producing activities, similar adjustments must be made to the investment account by the investor to eliminate the effects of intercompany transactions. A more complete description of these intercompany problems is found in advanced accounting texts.

Changes Between Cost and Equity Methods

Variations in percentage of ownership caused by additional purchases or sales of stock by the investor or by the additional sale or retirement of stock by the investee may require a change in accounting method. For example, if the equity method has been used but subsequent events reduce the investment ownership below 20%, a change should be made to the cost method effective for the year when the reduced ownership occurs. Similarly, if the cost method has been used but subsequent acquisitions increase the investment ownership to 20% or more, a change should be made to the equity method. The required accounting is different depending on whether the change is from the equity method to the cost method or vice versa.

Change from Equity to Cost Method. If an investment in equity securities has been accounted for under the equity method, but circumstances dictate a change to the cost method, no adjustment to the investment account is needed. At the time of change, the carrying amount of the investment, as determined by the equity method for prior years, becomes the new basis for applying the cost method. From that time forward, the investment account would not be adjusted for a proportionate share of investee earnings, nor would any adjustments be made for additional depreciation or amortization of undervalued or unrecorded assets, and dividends received would be credited to a revenue account, not the investment account. Thus, once the equity method is no longer appropriate, the cost method is applied just as in any other situation where the cost method is used.

Change from Cost to Equity Method. Accounting for a change from the cost method to the equity method is more complex. **A retroactive adjustment** is required for prior years to reflect the income that would have been reported using the equity method. This adjustment modifies the carrying value of the investment, in effect restating it on an equity basis, as if the equity method had been used during the previous periods that the investment was held. The offsetting entry for the adjustment is to Retained Earnings. From the date of change forward, the equity method is applied normally.

To illustrate, assume that MTI Corporation acquired stock of Excellcior Inc. over the three-year period 1986–1988. Purchase, dividend, and income information for these years are as follows (the purchases were made on the first day of each year):

Year	Percentage Ownership Acquired	Purchase Price*	Excellcior Inc. Dividends Paid Dec. 31	Income Earned
1986	10%	$ 50,000	$100,000	$200,000
1987	5	30,000	120,000	300,000
1988	15	117,000	180,000	400,000

*Purchase price equal to underlying book value at date of purchase.

The following entries would be made on the books of MTI Corporation to reflect the cost method for the years 1986 and 1987.

```
1986
Jan. 1   Investment in Excellcior Inc. Stock........................   50,000
              Cash.................................................              50,000
                  To record purchase of 10% interest.

Dec. 31  Cash....................................................   10,000
              Dividend Revenue....................................              10,000
                  To record receipt of dividends from Excellcior Inc. (10% ×
                  $100,000).
```

```
1987
Jan. 1   Investment in Excellcior Inc. Stock.......................   30,000
            Cash...............................................              30,000
               To record purchase of 5% interest. (Total ownership in-
               terest is now 15%.)

Dec. 31  Cash.................................................   18,000
            Dividend Revenue ....................................              18,000
               To record receipt of dividends from Excellcior Inc. (15% ×
               $120,000).
```

The additional acquisition of stock at the beginning of 1988 increases ownership to 30%, and a retroactive adjustment to change to the equity method must be made at the time of acquisition. The adjustment is for the difference between the revenue reported using the cost method and that which would have been reported if the equity method had been used. The adjustment would be computed as follows:

Year	Percentage Ownership	Revenue Recognized-Cost Method	Revenue Recognized-Equity Method	Required Retroactive Adjustment
1986	10%	$10,000	$20,000[1]	$10,000
1987	15%	18,000	45,000[2]	27,000
		Total Adjustment		$37,000

[1]$200,000 × 10%
[2]$300,000 × 15%

The following entries would be made on the books of MTI Corporation to reflect the equity method for 1988:

```
1988
Jan. 1   Investment in Excellcior Inc. Stock.......................  117,000
            Cash...............................................             117,000
               To record purchase of 15% interest. (Total ownership in-
               terest is now 30%.)

Jan. 1   Investment in Excellcior Inc. Stock.......................   37,000
            Retained Earnings ...................................              37,000
               To retroactively reflect revenue for 1986 and 1987 for in-
               vestment in Excellcior Inc. as if the equity method had
               been used.

Dec. 31  Investment in Excellcior Inc. Stock.......................  120,000
            Income from Investment in Excellcior Inc. Stock..........             120,000
               To record 30% of income earned by Excellcior Inc.
               using equity method.

Dec. 31  Cash.................................................   54,000
            Investment in Excellcior Inc. Stock......................              54,000
               To record receipt of dividend from Excellcior Inc. using
               equity method (30% × $180,000).
```

Note that in the above example the retroactive adjustment restates the investment account to an equity basis. From that point on, the equity method is applied in a normal manner. For simplicity, the illustration assumed a purchase price equal to the underlying book value at date of purchase. If this were not the case, an adjustment to income for depreciation and amortization would be needed as discussed in an earlier section.

Required Disclosures for Long-Term Investments in Stock

Since the financial position and operating results of the investor can be significantly affected by the method used in accounting for and reporting long-term investments in stocks, it is important that proper disclosures be made. These disclosures may be included parenthetically in the financial statements or more commonly in a note to the financial statements.

FASB Statement No. 12 sets forth disclosure requirements for equity securities accounted for under the cost method and valued at lower of cost or market. These disclosure requirements were discussed and illustrated in Chapter 7. Another example of disclosure for noncurrent equity securities is reproduced from the 1984 annual report of Anchor Hocking Corporation and presented below.

ANCHOR HOCKING CORPORATION

NOTES TO FINANCIAL STATEMENTS

Note 4—Long-term Investment

During 1982, the Company acquired 800,700 shares of Towle Manufacturing Company common stock. Towle, located in Boston, Massachusetts, is engaged in the manufacture and sale of giftware products, primarily sterling silver flatware and holloware, silverplated holloware, pewter holloware, cutlery and other related consumer products. The investment represents 16.6% of the outstanding common shares and 14.1% of the outstanding voting shares of Towle. At December 31, 1983, this investment was recorded at its cost of $18,166,000 which approximated market. At December 31, 1984, the cost of this investment exceeded its market value and a $7,630,000 valuation allowance was established to reduce the carrying amount. The establishment of the valuation allowance resulted in a charge to common stockholders' equity representing the net unrealized loss. Dividends received from Towle are included in other income and amounted to $264,000 in 1984 and $352,000 in 1983. Towle did not declare a dividend in the fourth quarter of 1984.

Because the equity method is generally more complex than the cost method, the disclosures associated with the equity method are usually more detailed. APB Opinion No. 18 provides some recommendations for disclosures applicable to the equity method, including:[6] names of investees and the related percentages of ownership interest, and the difference, if

---

[6]*Opinions of the Accounting Principles Board, No. 18,* "The Equity Method of Accounting for Investments in Common Stock" (New York: American Institute of Certified Public Accountants, 1971), par. 20.

any, between the carrying value of the investment and the underlying equity in net assets of the investee. In addition, if an investor has more than 20% ownership but chooses not to use the equity method, the reasons for the decision should be disclosed. Similarly, if the equity method is used in cases where there is less than 20% ownership, those reasons should also be disclosed. An example of this latter type of disclosure, involving a 15% ownership interest, is included in the partial note from the 1984 financial statements of The Greyhound Corporation, presented below.

THE GREYHOUND CORPORATION

SIGNIFICANT ACCOUNTING POLICIES

Principles of Consolidation:

The consolidated financial statements include the accounts of Greyhound and its subsidiaries, except for its Financial Group subsidiaries. All material intercompany transactions and accounts are eliminated in consolidation.

Investments in Financial Group subsidiaries and in affiliates 20 to 50 percent owned are reflected in the accounts on the equity method. In addition, the investment in ConAgra, Inc. ("ConAgra") (15% owned) is included in the accounts on the equity method. Greyhound's membership both on the Board of Directors and on the Executive Committee of the Board of Directors of ConAgra and its substantial voting rights provide the ability to significantly influence the operating and financial affairs of ConAgra. Equity in net income of ConAgra is recognized after provisions for amortization of intangibles and for income taxes.

Accounting for Long-Term Investments in Stocks Summarized

In summary, the main guidelines for accounting for long-term stock investments are as follows:

1. Investments in stock are always initially recorded at cost, which includes commissions and similar expenditures.

2. Revenue is recognized through (a) consolidation when the investor controls the investee or (b) by the cost or equity method, depending on the degree of ownership influence.

3. If the cost method is used in accounting for long-term marketable equity securities, such securities are valued at the lower of cost or aggregate market, with any write-down reported as a reduction to stockholders' equity rather than charged to income as is the case for short-term marketable equity securities.

4. If the equity method is used, no valuation adjustment to lower of cost or market is needed, since the investment account is increased to reflect a proportionate share of investee income and decreased to reflect investee losses and dividends received from the investee.

5. As with any asset, significant permanent declines in the value of long-term investments are recognized as a loss in the year they occur.

6. When long-term investments are eventually sold, the difference between the carrying value of the investment and the proceeds from the sale is recognized as a realized gain or loss.

LONG-TERM INVESTMENTS IN FUNDS

Cash and other assets set apart for certain common purposes are called **funds**, **sinking funds**, or **redemption funds**. Some funds are to be used for specific current obligations, and are appropriately reported as current assets. Examples of these are petty cash funds, payroll funds, interest funds, dividend funds, and withholding, social security, and other tax funds. Other funds are accumulated over a long term for such purposes as the acquisition or replacement of properties, retirement of long-term debt, the redemption of capital stock, operation of a pension plan, or possible future contingencies. These funds are properly considered noncurrent and are reported under the long-term investment heading.

Establishment and Accumulation of Funds

A fund may be established through the voluntary action of management, or it may be established as a result of contractual requirements. The fund may be used for a single purpose, such as the redemption of preferred stock, or it may be used for several related purposes, such as the periodic payment of interest on bonds, the retirement of bonds at various intervals, and the ultimate retirement of the remaining bond indebtedness.

When a fund is voluntarily created by management, control of the fund and its disposition are arbitrary matters depending on the wishes of management. When a fund is created through some legal requirement, it must be administered and applied in accordance therewith. Such a fund may be administered by one or more independent trustees under an agreement known as a **trust indenture**. If the trustee assumes responsibility for fulfillment of the requirement, as may be true for a bond retirement or pension program, neither the fund nor the related liability is carried on the company's books. However, if the indenture does not free the company from further obligation, the fund must be accounted for as if there were no trustee.

When a corporation is required by agreement to establish a fund for a certain purpose, such as the retirement of bonds or the redemption of stock, the agreement generally provides that fund deposits (1) shall be fixed amounts, (2) shall vary according to gross revenue, net income, or units of product sold, or (3) shall be equal periodic sums that, together with earnings, will produce a certain amount at some future date. The latter arrangement is based on compound-interest factors, and, as noted in Chapter 6, compound interest or annuity tables may be used to determine the equal periodic deposits. For example, in order to accumulate a fund of $100,000 by a series of 5 equal annual deposits at 8% compounded annually, a periodic deposit of $17,045.65 is required.[7]

A schedule can be developed to show the planned fund accumulation through deposits and earnings. Such a schedule is illustrated below:

Fund Accumulation Schedule

Year	Earnings on Fund Balance for Year	Amount Deposited in Fund	Total Increase in Fund for Year	Accumulated Fund Total
1		$17,045.65	$17,045.65	$ 17,045.65
2	$1,363.65	17,045.65	18,409.30	35,454.95
3	2,836.40	17,045.65	19,882.05	55,337.00
4	4,426.96	17,045.65	21,472.61	76,809.61
5	6,144.74	17,045.65	23,190.39	100,000.00

Assuming deposits at the end of each year, the table shows a fund balance at the end of the first year of $17,045.65 resulting from the first deposit. At the end of the second year, the fund is increased by (1) earnings at 8% on the investment in the fund during the year, $1,363.65, and (2) the second deposit to the fund, $17,045.65. The total in the fund at this time is $35,454.95. Fund earnings in the following year are based on a total investment of $35,454.95 as of the beginning of the year.

The schedule is developed on the assumption of annual earnings of 8%. However, various factors, such as fluctuations in the earnings rate and gains and losses on investments, may provide earnings that differ from the assumed amounts. If the fund is to be maintained in accordance with the accumulation schedule, deposits must be adjusted for earnings that differ from estimated amounts. Smaller deposits, then, can be made in periods when earnings exceed the assumed rate; larger deposits are necessary when earnings fail to meet the assumed rate.

Accounting for Funds

A fund is usually composed of cash and securities, but could include other assets. The accounting for stock held in a fund is the same as that described earlier in this chapter except the securities are reported as part

---

[7]This amount can be determined from Table III in Chapter 6. The rent or annual payment for an annuity of $100,000 at 8% for 5 periods is computed as follows:

$$R = \frac{FV_n}{FVAF_n} = \frac{FV_n}{\text{Table III}_{\overline{5}|8\%}} = \frac{\$100,000}{5.8666} = \$17,045.65$$

of the fund balance. The accounting for investments in bonds will be discussed in Chapter 15.

To illustrate the accounting for a fund held by a company, assume that a preferred stock redemption fund is established with annual payments to the fund of $20,000. The fund administrator invests 90% of its assets in stock and places the remainder in bank certificates of deposit paying 10% interest. Journal entries for the first year's transactions are as follows:

Stock Redemption Fund Cash..	20,000	
Cash...		20,000
Annual fund contribution.		
Stock Redemption Fund Securities	18,000	
Stock Redemption Fund Cash..................................		18,000
Investment of fund cash in securities.		
Stock Redemption Fund Certificates of Deposit	2,000	
Stock Redemption Fund Cash..................................		2,000
Investment of fund cash in certificates of deposit.		
Stock Redemption Fund Cash....................................	1,400	
Stock Redemption Fund Revenue		1,400
Dividends on fund securities.		
Stock Redemption Fund Cash....................................	200	
Stock Redemption Fund Revenue		200
Interest on certificates of deposit.		
Stock Redemption Fund Expenses	200	
Stock Redemption Fund Cash..................................		200
Expenses to operate fund.		

At the end of the year, the stock redemption fund assets are as follows:

Stock redemption fund cash	$ 1,400
Stock redemption fund certificates of deposit.........................	2,000
Stock redemption fund securities	18,000
Total	$21,400

This total amount would be reported under the "investments" heading on the balance sheet.

Stock redemption fund revenue for the year is $1,600 and stock redemption fund expense is $200, resulting in a net income from the fund operation of $1,400. This amount is reported on the income statement as other revenue. When stock is redeemed, the payment is made from Stock Redemption Fund Cash after the securities are converted to cash.

CASH SURRENDER VALUE OF LIFE INSURANCE

Many business enterprises carry life insurance policies on the lives of their executives because the business has a definite stake in the continuing services of its officers. In some cases the insurance plan affords a financial cushion in the event of the loss of such personnel. In other instances the insurance offers a means of purchasing the deceased owner's interest in the business, thus avoiding a transfer of such interest to some outside party or the need to liquidate the business in effecting a settlement with the estate of the deceased. In these cases, the company is the beneficiary.

Insurance premiums normally consist of an amount for insurance protection and the balance for a form of investment. The investment portion is the **cash surrender value** available to the policyholder in the event of policy cancellation. If this cash surrender value belongs to the business, it should be reported as a long-term investment. Insurance expense for a fiscal period is the difference between the insurance premium paid and the increase in the cash surrender value of the policy.

An insurance policy with a cash surrender value also has a **loan value**. The amount an insurance company will lend on a policy is normally limited to the cash surrender value at the end of the policy year less discount from the loan date to the cash surrender value date. For example, assume a cash surrender value of $3,000 at the end of the fifth policy year. The maximum loan value on the policy at the beginning of the fifth year, assuming the insurance premium for the fifth year is paid, is $3,000 discounted for one year. If the discount rate applied by the insurance company is 5%, the policy loan value is calculated as follows: $3,000 ÷ 1.05 = $2,857.14.

When the policyholder uses the policy as a basis for a loan, such a loan may be liquidated by payments of principal and interest, or the loan may be continuing, to be applied against the insurance proceeds upon policy cancellation or ultimate settlement. Although it is possible for the policyholder to recognize policy loan values instead of cash surrender values, the latter values are generally used.

The policyholder may authorize the insurance company to apply any dividends declared on insurance policies to the reduction of the annual premium payment or to the increase in cash surrender value, or the dividends may be collected in cash. Dividends should be viewed as a reduction in the cost of carrying insurance rather than as a source of supplementary revenue. Hence, if dividends are applied to the reduction of the annual premium, Insurance Expense is simply debited for the net amount paid. If the dividend is applied to the increase in the policy cash surrender value or if it is collected in cash, it should still be treated as an offset to the periodic expense of carrying the policy; the cash surrender value or Cash is debited and Insurance Expense is credited. After a number of years, the periodic dividends plus increases in cash surrender value may exceed the premium payments, thus resulting in revenue rather than expense on policy holdings.

Collection of a policy upon death of the insured requires cancellation of any cash surrender balance. The difference between the insurance proceeds and the balances relating to the insurance policy is recognized as a gain in the period of death. The nature of the insurance policies carried and their coverage should be disclosed by appropriate comment on the balance sheet.

The entries to be made for an insurance contract are illustrated in the following example. The Pro Style Company insured the life of its president, Tom Jolly, on January 1, 1986. The amount of the policy was $50,000; the annual premiums were $2,100 to be paid in advance.

Policy Year	Gross Premium	Dividend	Net Premium	Increase in Cash Value	Insurance Expense
1	$2,100	—	$2,100	—	$2,100
2	2,100	—	2,100	$1,150	950
3	2,100	$272	1,828	1,300	528

The fiscal period for the company is the calendar year. Jolly died on July 1, 1988. The premium rebate for the period July 1 to December 31, 1988 is $1,050, and the dividend accrued as of July 1, 1988 is $210. The entries made in recording transactions relating to the insurance contract are shown on page 577. The procedures illustrated involve certain concessions in theoretical accuracy but are normally preferred because of their practicality.

OTHER LONG-TERM INVESTMENTS

In addition to securities, funds, and insurance, a company may have other long-term investments. Real estate held as an investment, advances to subsidiaries that are of a long-term nature, deposits made to guarantee contract performance, and equity interests in partnerships, trusts, and estates are all examples. Most of these assets either produce current revenues or have a favorable effect on the investor's business in some other way. Cost is generally the underlying basis for these miscellaneous investments, and a gain or loss is recognized upon sale for the difference between the sales proceeds and the carrying amount of the investment. When available, market or appraised values may be reported parenthetically.

REPORTING LONG-TERM
INVESTMENTS ON THE BALANCE SHEET

Long-term investments are generally reported on the balance sheet immediately following the current assets classification. The investment

Transaction	Entry		
January 1, 1986 Paid first annual premium, $2,100.	Prepaid Insurance .... Cash...........................	2,100	2,100
December 31, 1986 To record insurance expense for 1986.	Life Insurance Expense .... Prepaid Insurance	2,100	2,100
January 1, 1987 Paid second annual premium, $2,100 Premium............................ $2,100 Less cash surrender value.............. 1,150 Net insurance charge .... $ 950	Cash Surrender Value of Life Insurance (as of 12/31/87)....... Prepaid Insurance .... Cash...........................	1,150 950	2,100
December 31, 1987 To record insurance expense for 1987.	Life Insurance Expense .... Prepaid Insurance	950	950
January 1, 1988 Paid third annual premium, $2,100. Premium........................... $2,100 Less: Cash Surrender value .... $1,300 Dividend............... 272 1,572 Net insurance charge .... $ 528	Cash Surrender Value of Life Insurance (as of 12/31/88)....... Prepaid Insurance .... Cash...........................	1,300 528	1,828
July 1, 1988 To record insurance expense for Jan. 1–July 1: ½ × $528 = $264.	Life Insurance Expense .... Prepaid Insurance	264	264
July 1, 1988 To record cancellation of policy upon death of insured: Amount recoverable on policy: Face of policy........................ $50,000 Premium rebate for period July 1– Dec. 31 and current year dividend......................... 1,260 $51,260 Cancellation of asset values: Cash surrender value .... $ 2,450 Prepaid insurance .... 264 $ 2,714 Gain on policy settlement.............. $48,546	Receivable from Insurance Co ..... Cash Surrender Value of Life Insurance.................... Prepaid Insurance .... Gain on Settlement of Life Insurance....................	51,260	2,450 264 48,546

section should not include temporary investments held as a ready source of cash. Headings should be provided for the different long-term investment categories and individual long-term investment costs should be supplemented by market quotations in parenthetical or note form if market exceeds cost. Information concerning the pledge of long-term investments as collateral on loans should be provided. When long-term investments are carried at amounts other than cost, the valuation that is employed should be described.

In reporting funds to be applied to specific purposes or paid to specific parties, disclosure should be made by special note of the conditions relative to their establishment and ultimate application. A fund arrearage or other failure to meet contractual requirements should be pointed out; deposit requirements in the succeeding fiscal period should also be disclosed when material. Offset of a fund balance against a liability item is proper only when an asset transfer to a trustee is irrevocable and actually serves to discharge the obligation.

The "Investments" section of a balance sheet might appear as follows:

Investments:		
Affiliated companies:		
Investment in Salt River Co. common stock, reported by the equity method (investment consists of 90,000 shares representing a 40% interest acquired on July 1, 1986, for $1,500,000)................................	$1,548,000	
Advances to Salt River Co	115,000	$1,663,000
Miscellaneous stock investments at cost (stock has an aggregate quoted market value of $112,000).................................		100,000
Stock redemption fund, composed of:		
Cash	$ 15,000	
Stocks and bonds, at cost (aggregate quoted market value, $420,000)	410,500	
Dividends and interest receivable	4,500	430,000
Investment in land and unused facilities		125,000
Cash surrender value of life insurance carried on officers' lives		12,500
Total investments		$2,330,500

QUESTIONS

1. (a) Distinguish between long-term (or noncurrent) and short-term (or current) investments.
   (b) List several types of long-term investments.
2. Why would a company invest in the stock of another company?
3. David Giles purchases 1,000 shares of Bart Motors at $90 a share in November, paying his broker $65,000. The market value of the stock on December 31 is $125 a share; Giles has made no further payment to his broker. On this date he shows on his balance sheet Bart Motors stock, $100,000, the difference between market value and the unpaid balance to the broker. Do you approve of this treatment? Explain.
4. Define: (a) parent company and (b) subsidiary company.

5. What is the general rule used for determining the appropriate method of accounting for investments in equity securities when the investor does not possess absolute voting control?

6. (a) What factors may indicate the ability of an investor owning less than a majority voting interest to exercise significant influence on the investee's operating and financial policies?
(b) What factors may indicate the investor's inability to exercise significant influence?

7. Distinguish between the method used to account for a temporary decline in the market value of stock under the equity method and under the cost method.

8. How is a permanent decline in the value of long-term stock investments recorded?

9. What adjustment is needed to record the change in classification of an investment in marketable equity securities between current and noncurrent assets?

10. What adjustment needs to be made when a company switches from (a) the equity method to the cost method and (b) the cost method to the equity method of valuing securities?

11. What disclosures are recommended in APB Opinion No. 18 when using the equity method?

12. Identify and describe examples of funds that would be listed as current assets and those that would be listed as investments.

13. (a) Distinguish between life insurance cash surrender value and loan value.
(b) How is the loan value on a life insurance policy calculated?

14. Describe several items properly reported under the "Investments" heading on the balance sheet.

DISCUSSION CASES

CASE 13–1   (Classification of investments)

Hawkes Systems, Inc., a chemical processing company, has been operating profitably for many years. On March 1, 1988, Hawkes purchased 50,000 shares of Diversified Insurance Company stock for $2,000,000. The 50,000 shares represented 25% of Diversified's outstanding stock. Both Hawkes and Diversified operate on a fiscal year ending August 31.

For the fiscal year ended August 31, 1988, Diversified reported net income of $800,000 earned ratably throughout the year. During November, 1987, and February, May, and August, 1988, Diversified paid its regular quarterly cash dividend of $100,000.

What criteria should Hawkes consider in determining whether its investment in Diversified should be classified as (1) a current asset, or (2) a noncurrent asset? Confine your discussion to the decision criteria for determining the balance sheet classification of the investment.   (AICPA adapted)

CASE 13–2   (What is significant influence?)

The Crest Corporation's Board of Directors has been wrestling with a basic decision concerning its involvement with other business entities. Jim Wallace, President, wants to acquire controlling interest (more than 50%) in several companies that serve as suppliers of basic materials used by Crest and other companies that are distributors of its various products. Gail Brewer, Chairman of the Board, feels part of the capital required to obtain more than 50% ownership should be used to expand Crest's working capital. Brewer argues that significant influence over vital operating decisions can be obtained with far less than 50% of the stock. By reducing the investment cost, more funds can be freed for other vital needs. Both Wallace and Brewer are concerned about the impact of stock acquisitions on company profits, especially the effects of different accounting methods, as more substantial investments in other companies are made. They have come to you as the controller of Crest to shed some light on this issue and to obtain your recommendation as to the direction they should go. What factors would you stress in your answer to them?

CASE 13–3   (How does increased ownership in another company affect our books?)

For the past five years Apton Corp. has maintained an investment (properly accounted for and reported upon) in Clarke Co. reflecting a 10% interest in the voting common stock of Clarke. The purchase price was $700,000 and the underlying net equity in Clarke at the date of purchase was $620,000. On January 2 of the current year, Apton purchased an additional 15% (total ownership interest is now 25%) of the voting common stock of Clarke for $1,200,000; the underlying net equity of the additional investment at January 2 was $1,000,000. Clarke has been profitable and has paid dividends annually since Apton's initial acquisition.

Discuss how this increase in ownership affects the accounting for and reporting on the investment in Clarke. Include in your discussion adjustments, if any, to the amount shown prior to the increase in investment to bring the amount into conformity with generally accepted accounting principles. Also include how current and subsequent periods would be reported on.   (AICPA adapted)

CASE 13–4   (Cash surrender value)

During your examination of the financial statements of Jones Paint, which has never before been audited, you discover that the cash surrender value of $500,000 life insurance policy on the president, for which Jones was the beneficiary, had not been recorded in the accounting records. The president stated that the total premium on the policy was charged to the insurance expense account each year because the company had no intention of "cashing in" the policy or of using the cash surrender value as collateral for a loan from the insurance company or a bank. Therefore, asserted the president, it would be misleading for the company to record as an asset an amount never expected to be realized or used by the company.

Evaluate the position of the president of Jones Paint.

EXERCISES

EXERCISE 13–1 (Long-term investments in stocks—cost method)

Prepare journal entries to record the following long-term investment transactions. (Assume that the cost method is used.)

(a) Purchased 2,000 shares of Lynx Company common stock at $65.25 per share, including brokerage fees of $500.
(b) Received a cash dividend of $2 per share from Lynx Company.
(c) Sold 500 shares of Lynx Company Stock at $70 per share, less $300 in brokerage fees.
(d) The end-of-year market value of Lynx Company stock is $60.25. The decline in market value is considered temporary.

EXERCISE 13–2 (Long-term investments in stocks—equity method)

On January 1, 1987, Biro Corporation purchased 10,000 shares of JWS Corporation common stock for $30 per share. JWS had a total of 40,000 shares of stock outstanding at the acquisition date. Additional transactions and data for the year are as follows:

Oct. 31 JWS paid a $1 per share dividend
Dec. 31 JWS reported net income for 1987 of $160,000
Dec. 31 The market value of JWS Corporation stock is $25 per share

Record the above transactions on Biro's books and show how Biro would report its investment in JWS stock on its December 31, 1987, balance sheet. (You may ignore explanations to journal entries, but should show computations.)

EXERCISE 13–3
(Investment in common stock—cost and equity methods)

On January 10, 1987, Farley Corporation acquired 16,000 shares of the outstanding common stock of Davis Company for $800,000. At the time of purchase, Davis Company had outstanding 80,000 shares with a book value of $4 million. On December 31, 1987, the following events took place:

(a) Davis reported net income of $180,000 for the calendar year 1987.
(b) Farley received from Davis a dividend of $.75 per share of common stock.
(c) The market value of Davis Company stock had temporarily declined to $45 per share.

Give the entries that would be required to reflect the purchase and subsequent events on the books of Farley Corporation, assuming (1) the cost method is appropriate; (2) the equity method is appropriate.

EXERCISE 13–4
(Investment in common stock—unrecorded goodwill)

Alpha Co. acquired 20,000 shares of Beta Co. on January 1, 1987, at $12 per share. Beta Co. had 80,000 shares outstanding with a book value of $800,000. There were no identifiable undervalued assets at the time of purchase. Beta Co. recorded earnings of $260,000 and $290,000 for 1987 and 1988, respectively, and paid per share dividends of $1.60 in 1987 and $2.00 in 1988. Assuming a 40-year straight-line amortization policy for goodwill, give the entries to record the purchase in 1987 and to reflect Alpha's share of Beta's earnings and the receipt of the dividends for 1987 and 1988.

EXERCISE 13–5
(Valuation of long-term marketable equity securities)

The long-term marketable equity securities portfolio for Mountain Industries Inc. contained the following securities at December 31, 1986 and 1987:

Marketable Equity Securities (Common Stock)	Initial Cost	Market Value 12/31/86	Market Value 12/31/87
Slaydon Co........................	$10,000	$12,000	$15,000
Smith Co..........................	7,000	3,000	2,000
Taylor Co.........................	21,000	18,000	22,000

(1) Assuming all declines in market value are considered temporary, what is the effect of the changes in market values on the 1986 and 1987 financial statements? Give the valuation entries for these years.

(2) Assume that at December 31, 1987, management believed that the market value of the Smith Co. common stock reflected a permanent decline in the value of that stock. Give the entries to be made on December 31, 1987, under this assumption. How would the marketable securities affect the 1987 financial statements?

EXERCISE 13–6
(Valuation of long-term marketable equity securities)

Bridgeman Paper Co. reported the following selected balances on its financial statements for each of the four years 1985–1988.

	1985	1986	1987	1988
Allowance for Decline in Value of Noncurrent Marketable Equity Securities.................................	0	$25,000	$18,000	$30,000
Recognized Loss from Permanent Decline in Market Value of Noncurrent Marketable Equity Securities.................................	0	0	$ 4,000	0
Allowance for Decline in Value of Current Marketable Equity Securities.................................	0	$ 5,000	$ 8,000	$ 3,000

Based on these balances, reconstruct the valuation journal entries that must have been made each year.

EXERCISE 13–7
(Investment in common stock—equity to cost method)

Siler Co. purchased 100,000 shares of Toppler Manufacturing Co. common stock on July 1, 1987, at $16.50 per share, which reflected book value as of that date. Toppler Manufacturing Co. had 400,000 common shares outstanding at the time of the purchase. Prior to this purchase, Siler Co. had no ownership interest in Toppler. In its second quarterly statement, Toppler Manufacturing Co. reported net income of $168,000 for the six months ended June 30, 1987. Siler Co. received a dividend of $21,000 from Toppler on August 1, 1987. Toppler reported net income of $360,000 for the year ended December 31, 1987, and again paid Siler Co. dividends of $21,000. On January 1, 1988, Siler Co. sold 40,000 shares of Toppler Manufacturing Co. common stock for $17 per share. Toppler reported net income of $372,000 for the year ended December 31, 1988, and paid Siler Co. dividends of $24,000. Give all entries Siler Co. would make in 1987 and 1988 in regard to the Toppler Manufacturing Co. stock.

EXERCISE 13–8
(Investment in common stock—cost to equity method)

Devers Corporation purchased 5% of the 100,000 outstanding common shares of Milo Inc. on January 1, 1986, for a total purchase price of $7,500. Net assets of Milo Inc. at the time had a book value of $150,000. Net income for Milo Inc. for the year ended December 31, 1986, was $50,000. Devers received dividends from Milo during the year of $1,500. There was no change of Devers ownership of Milo Inc. during 1987, and Milo reported net income of $70,000 for the year ended December 31, 1987. Devers received dividends of $2,000 from Milo for that year. On January 1, 1988, Devers purchased an additional 20% of Milo Inc.'s common stock or 20,000 shares for a total price of $40,000. Milo Inc.'s net asset book value at the time of the purchase was $200,000. For the year ended December 31, 1988, Milo Inc. reported net income of $100,000; Devers received dividends from Milo Inc. totaling $10,000 for the year ended December 31, 1988.

Prepare journal entries for Devers Corporation to reflect the preceding transactions, including adjusting entries necessary to reflect the change from the cost method to the equity method of accounting for Devers Corporation's investment in Milo Inc.

EXERCISE 13–9   (Fund investments)

On December 31, 1987, Turpin Corporation set up a stock redemption fund, with an initial deposit of $150,000. On February 1, 1988, Turpin Corporation invested $127,500 stock redemption fund cash in 10% preferred stock of Jerome Inc., par value of $75,000. Jerome normally declares and pays dividends on the preferred stock semiannually: March 1 and September 1. On April 1, 1988, Turpin exchanged the stock with another investor for 4,000 shares of Rolfe Corporation common stock. The market value of the common stock at the date of exchange was $35 per share. Give all the entries necessary to record the preceding transactions assuming semiannual dividends were paid.

EXERCISE 13–10   (Sinking fund accumulation schedule)

Sinking fund tables show that 5 annual deposits of $16,379.75 accruing interest at 10% compounded annually will result in a total accumulation of $100,000 immediately after the fifth payment. (a) Prepare a fund accumulation schedule showing the theoretical growth of a property acquisition fund over the 5-year period. (b) Give all of the entries that would appear on the books for the increases in the property acquisition fund balance for the first 3 years.

EXERCISE 13–11 (Cash surrender value)

The JLK Company follows the practice of taking out whole-life insurance policies on its key employees. The annual premium of $4,200 is paid on May 1. The cash surrender value at December 31, 1987 was $19,700. At the end of 1988, the cash surrender value had increased to $20,600. Give the journal entries for 1988.

EXERCISE 13–12 (Multiple choice)

(1) When an investor uses the cost method to account for investments in common stock, cash dividends received by the investor from the investee should normally be recorded as
  A. Dividend revenue
  B. An addition to the investor's share of the investee's profit
  C. A deduction from the investor's share of the investee's profit
  D. A deduction from the investment account.

(2) Ownership of 51% of the outstanding voting stock of a company would result in
  A. The use of the cost method
  B. The use of the lower of cost or market method
  C. The equity method
  D. A consolidation.

(3) The equity method of accounting for an investment in the common stock of another company should be used when the investment
  A. Is composed of common stock and it is the investor's intent to vote the common stock
  B. Ensures a source of supply such as raw material
  C. Enables the investor to exercise significant influence over the investee
  D. Is obtained by exchange of stock for stock.

(4) A net unrealized loss on a company's long-term portfolio of marketable equity securities should be reflected in the current financial statements as
  A. An extraordinary item shown as a direct reduction from retained earnings
  B. A current loss resulting from holding marketable equity securities
  C. A footnote or parenthetical disclosure only
  D. A valuation allowance and included in the equity section of the statement of financial position.

(5) Which of the following might indicate the ability to exercise significant influence according to APB Opinion No. 18?
  A. Ownership of a 20% interest
  B. Representation of the board of directors
  C. Material intercompany transactions
  D. Participation in policy-making processes
  E. Any one of the above.   (AICPA adapted)

PROBLEMS

PROBLEM 13–1   (Investments in common stock)

Wesley Inc. and the Brill Corp. each have 100,000 shares of no-par common stock outstanding. Zimmerman Inc. acquired 10,000 shares of Wesley stock and 25,000 shares of Brill stock in 1984. Changes in retained earnings for Wesley and Brill for 1986 and 1987 are as follows:

	Wesley Inc.	Brill Corp.
Retained earnings (deficit), January 1, 1986	$200,000	$(35,000)
Cash dividends, 1986	(25,000)	—
	$175,000	$(35,000)
Net income, 1986.	40,000	65,000
Retained earnings, December 31, 1986	$215,000	$30,000
Cash dividends, 1987	(30,000)	(10,000)
Net income, 1987.	60,000	25,000
Retained earnings, December 31, 1987	$245,000	$45,000

Instructions: Give the entries required on the books of Zimmerman Inc. for 1986 and 1987 to account for its investments.

PROBLEM 13–2
(Long-term investments in stock — equity method)

On January 1, 1987, Computer Co. bought 30% of the outstanding common stock of Finance Corp. for $258,000 cash. Computer Co. accounts for this investment by the equity method. At the date of acquisition of the stock, Finance Corp.'s net assets had a carrying value of $620,000. Assets with an average remaining life of five years have a current market value that is $130,000 in excess of their carrying values. The remaining difference between the purchase price and the value of the underlying stockholders' equity cannot be attributed to any tangible asset; however, Finance Corp. is carrying goodwill of $40,000 on its books, which is being amortized at the rate of $1,250 per year for 32 more years. Computer Company has a policy of amortizing goodwill over 40 years. At the end of 1987, Finance Corp. reports net income of $180,000. During 1987, Finance Corp. declared and paid cash dividends of $20,000.

Instructions: Give the entries necessary to reflect Computer Co.'s investment in Finance Corp. for 1987.

PROBLEM 13–3   (Investment in common stock)

On July 1 of the current year, Byron Co. acquired 30% of the outstanding shares of common stock of Douglas International at a total cost of $750,000. The underlying equity (net assets) of the stock acquired by Byron was only $600,000.

Byron was willing to pay more than book value for the Douglas stock for the following reasons:

(a) Douglas owned depreciable plant assets (10-year remaining economic life) with a current fair value of $60,000 more than their carrying amount.

(b) Douglas owned land with a current fair value of $300,000 more than its carrying amount.

(c) Byron believed Douglas possessed enough goodwill to justify the remainder of the cost. Byron's accounting policy with respect to goodwill is to amortize it over 40 years.

Douglas International earned net income of $540,000 evenly over the current year ended December 31. On December 31, Douglas declared and paid a cash dividend of $120,000 to common stockholders. Both companies close their accounting records on December 31.

Instructions:
1. Compute the total amount of goodwill of Douglas International based on the price paid by Byron Co.
2. Prepare all journal entries in Byron's accounting records relating to the investment for the year ended December 31, under the cost method of accounting.
3. Prepare all journal entries in Byron's accounting records relating to the investment for the year ended December 31, under the equity method of accounting.

PROBLEM 13–4   (Accounting for marketable equity securities)

The Blanket Trust Co. owns both temporary and long-term investments in marketable equity securities. The following securities were owned on December 31, 1986:

Temporary Investments

Security	Shares	Total Cost	Market Value Dec. 31, 1986
Albert Groceries, Inc..................	600	$ 9,000	$11,500
West Data, Inc.......................	1,000	27,000	18,000
Steel Co	450	9,900	10,215

Long-Term Investments

Security	Shares	Total Cost	Market Value Dec. 31, 1986
Dairy Products.......................	2,000	$ 86,000	$ 90,000
Vern Movies, Inc.	15,000	390,000	345,000
Disks, Inc	5,000	60,000	80,000

The following transactions occurred during 1987:

(a) Sold 500 shares of West Data for $9,500.
(b) Sold 200 shares of Disks, Inc. for $3,000.
(c) Transferred all of Albert Groceries to long-term portfolio when the total market value was $12,900.
(d) Transferred the remaining shares of Disks, Inc. to the temporary investment portfolio when the market price was $20 per share. These shares were subsequently sold for $18 per share.

At December 31, 1987, market prices for the remaining securities were as follows:

Security	Market Price Per Share
Albert Groceries..................	$22
West Data, Inc	15
Steel Co........................	21
Dairy Products	42
Vern Movies, Inc	28

Instructions: Prepare all journal entries necessary to record Blanket Trust's marketable equity securities transactions and year-end adjustments for 1987. Assume all declines in market value are temporary.

PROBLEM 13–5
(Valuation of long-term marketable equity securities)

The long-term investment portfolio of Camden Inc. at December 31, 1987, contains the following securities:

Opus Company common, 3% ownership, 5,000 shares;
  cost, $100,000; market value, $95,000.
Garrod Inc. preferred, 2,000 shares; cost, $40,000;
  market value, $43,000.
Sherrill Inc. common, 30% ownership, 20,000 shares;
  cost, $1,140,000; market value, $1,130,000.
Jennings Co. common, 15% ownership, 25,000 shares; cost,
  $67,500; market value, $50,000.

Instructions:
1. Give the valuation adjustment required at December 31, 1987, assuming market values in the past for the long-term investment portfolio have always exceeded cost and none of the indicated declines in market value are considered permanent.
2. Assume the Jennings Co. common stock market decline is considered permanent. Give the valuation entries required at December 31, 1987, under this change in assumption.
3. Assume the market values for the long-term investment portfolio at December 31, 1988, were as follows:

Opus Co. Common..................................	$ 102,000
Garrod Inc. Preferred...............................	43,000
Sherrill Inc. Common...............................	1,115,000
Jennings Co. Common	45,000

Give the valuation entries at Dec. 31, 1988, assuming all declines in 1987 and 1988 are temporary except for the 1987 decline in Jennings Co. stock.

PROBLEM 13–6 (Change from cost to equity method)

On January 1, 1987, Loren Inc. paid $700,000 for 10,000 shares of Keller Company's voting common stock, which was a 10% interest in Keller. At this date, the net assets of Keller totaled $6 million. The fair values of all of Keller's identifiable assets and liabilities were equal to their book values. Loren does not have

the ability to exercise significant influence over the operating and financial poli-
cies of Keller. Loren received dividends of $.90 per share from Keller on
October 1, 1987. Keller reported net income of $400,000 for the year ended
December 31, 1987.

On July 1, 1988, Loren paid $2,300,000 for 30,000 additional shares of Keller
Company's voting common stock, which represents a 30% interest in Keller. The
fair value of all Keller's identifiable assets, net of liabilities, was equal to their book
values of $6,500,000. As a result of this transaction, Loren has the ability to
exercise significant influence over the operating and financial policies of Keller.
Loren received a dividend of $.10 per share from Keller on April 1, 1988, and
$1.35 per share from Keller on October 1, 1988. Keller reported net income of
$500,000 for the year ended December 31, 1988, and $200,000 for the six months
ended December 31, 1988. Loren amortizes goodwill over a 40-year period.

Instructions: Loren issues comparative financial statements for 1987 and 1988.
Prepare schedules showing the income or loss before income taxes for the years
ended December 31, 1987 and 1988, that Loren should report from its investment
in Keller. Show supporting computations in good form.   (AICPA adapted)

PROBLEM 13–7
(Investment in common stock — cost to equity to cost method)

Cook Inc. wants to gain a controlling interest in Fox Chemical Co. in order to
assure a steady source of a raw material manufactured by Fox. The following
transactions occurred with respect to Cook and Fox. Both companies keep their
books on a calendar-year basis.

1984

Jan.   2   Cook purchased 5,000 shares (5%) of Fox common stock for $10 per
           share. The assets of Fox had a net carrying value of $800,000. At that
           date, certain depreciable equipment owned by Fox had a fair market
           value $30,000 in excess of its carrying value, with an estimated remain-
           ing useful life of 10 years. Fox also carried land on its books that had a
           fair market value $70,000 in excess of its book value. The balance of the
           excess of the cost of the stock over the underlying equity in net assets
           was attributable to goodwill, which is amortized over 40 years. (Unless
           circumstances indicate otherwise, Cook's policy is to amortize any rec-
           ognized goodwill evenly over a 40-year period from date of acquisition.)

Feb. 15   Cook received a dividend of $3,000 representing a distribution from
           income earned in 1983.

July   1   Cook purchased 10,000 additional shares of Fox stock for $11 per share.
           Fox's net income for the first six months of 1984 was $150,000. The net
           carrying value of Fox stockholders' equity at July 1, 1984, was $890,000.
           The difference between the fair market value of Fox's depreciable assets
           and their carrying value at this date was $30,000, and the equipment had
           an estimated remaining useful life of 9.5 years from the date of pur-
           chase. The market value of the land remained $70,000 over book value.
           Fox had not issued any new stock during the past six months.

Dec. 31   Fox reported net income for the year of $260,000.

1985
Feb. 15   Cook received a cash dividend from Fox of $18,000.
Dec. 31   Fox reported net income for the year of $320,000.

1986
Jan.   2   Cook purchased 20,000 additional shares of Fox stock for $13 per share, which permitted Cook to exercise significant influence over Fox. At this time Fox was experiencing a boycott of its products that was expected to last indefinitely. Although the difference between the fair market value of its assets and their carrying values remained the same, Fox's boycott problems detracted from the long-term attractiveness of its shares, and no implied goodwill was included in the purchase price. (There has been no change in the estimated useful lives of depreciable assets from the date of the original purchase on January 2, 1984).
Feb. 15   Cook received a cash dividend of $49,000 from Fox Co.
Dec. 31   Fox reported net income of $280,000. In view of Fox's boycott situation, Cook decided to write off remaining goodwill over a period of 10 years, beginning this year.

1987
Feb. 15   Cook received a cash dividend of $39,200 from Fox.
Apr.   1   Cook, after experiencing a series of reversals in the marketplace, ceased manufacturing the product containing the raw material from Fox. On this date, Cook sold 20,000 shares of Fox stock for $12 per share. Cook used the average cost of its investment in Fox in calculating its cost basis per share in the investment. Assume Fox had no income for the first quarter of 1987.
Dec. 31   Fox reported net income of $295,000 for the year ended December 31, 1987.

1988
Feb. 15   Cook received a dividend of $17,700 from Fox.
Mar. 20   Cook sold its remaining 15,000 shares of Fox stock for $11.50 per share.

Instructions: Give all the entries necessary to record these transactions on the books of Cook Inc. (Round computations to the nearest dollar.)

PROBLEM 13–8   (Fund accumulation)

On December 31, 1984, a four-payment fund is set up to redeem $50,000 of preferred stock. The fund is guaranteed to earn 8% compounded annually and must generate enough income to enable the company to retire the stock after the fourth payment. The annual installments paid to the fund trustee are $11,096.07. The first deposit is made immediately.

Instructions:
1. Give the journal entries in connection with the fund for the years 1984 and 1985. (Assume the company keeps its books on the calendar year basis.)
2. Suppose that on December 31, 1987, the fund balance of $50,000 consisted of $12,000 cash and $38,000 in securities. The securities are sold for $44,000. Give all the journal entries that would be made to record the sale of the securities, retire the $50,000 of preferred stock, and liquidate any balance in the fund account.

PROBLEM 13–9   (Cash surrender value)

During the course of the audit of Huff Inc., which closes its accounts on December 31, you examine the life insurance policies, premium receipts, and confirmations returned by the insurance companies in response to your request for information. You find that in 1987 the company had paid premiums on the life of the president, Bill Huff, as shown below:

Sole Owner and Beneficiary	Face of Policy	Billed Premium 1987	Dividend Used to Reduce Premium	Annual Premium Date	Cash Surrender Value December 31	
					1986	1987
(1) Huff Inc.	$500,000	$5,000	$2,000	Aug. 30	$126,000	$130,000
(2) Sue Huff, wife of Bill Huff	200,000	4,500	750	Sept. 30	50,000	53,000
(3) Huff Inc.	50,000	2,500	250	Mar. 1	15,000	16,500

Instructions:
1. Prepare all journal entries required for the year 1987.
2. What balances relating to these insurance policies would appear on the balance sheet prepared on December 31, 1987?

PART THREE
LIABILITIES AND EQUITY

14 Liabilities — Current and Contingent

15 Accounting for Long-Term Debt Securities

16 Owners' Equity — Contributed Capital

17 Owners' Equity — Retained Earnings

18 Earnings Per Share

14
Liabilities — Current and Contingent

Part Two focused on the assets of a company, or the debit side of the balance sheet. Liabilities and owners' equity, the credit side of the balance sheet, are considered in Part Three. In this chapter, the general nature of liabilities is discussed as well as how to account for current and contingent liabilities. Subsequent chapters focus on noncurrent liabilities, including bonds, leases, and pensions, that are relatively complex in nature and, in some cases, directly related to asset accounts.

To illustrate the importance of accurately reporting the liabilities of a company, consider the following hypothetical, but realistic, situation.

Judge E. J. Wright is currently deliberating over a type of case that is becoming increasingly common in our society. A suit has been filed by three stockholders against Transcontinental Corporation alleging that Transcontinental's year-end balance sheet was misleading because it did not accurately reflect the financial position of the company at that date. The stockholders relied on the published financial statements and subsequently lost money on their investments in Transcontinental. Two specific points are at issue. First, Transcontinental chose not to estimate its liability under certain warranty provisions, accounting for warranty expenses on a cash basis. The plaintiffs contend that the warranties were in fact liabilities and should have been reported as such under accrual accounting procedures. Second, Transcontinental did not report a contingent liability relating to a significant, pending lawsuit with a supplier, which Transcontinental subsequently lost. Plaintiffs contend again that this information was material and relevant, and should have been disclosed.

Although hypothetical, the above situation is typical of many lawsuits being filed against companies, accountants, underwriters, and financial analysts and advisers. With respect to liabilities, the basic questions are:

- What is a liability?
- When and how should liabilities be disclosed?

These questions relate to definition, recognition, measurement, and reporting addressed by the FASB's Conceptual Framework, as discussed in Chapter 2.

DEFINITION OF LIABILITIES

Liabilities have been defined by the FASB as "probable future sacrifices of economic benefits arising from present obligations of a particular entity to transfer assets or provide services to other entities in the future as a result of past transactions or events."[1] This definition contains significant elements that need to be explored before individual liability accounts are discussed.

A liability is a result of **past transactions or events**. Thus, a liability is not recognized until incurred. This part of the definition excludes contractual obligations from an exchange of promises if performance by both parties is still in the future. Such contracts are referred to as **executory contracts**. This aspect of the liability definition has been subject to much discussion in accounting. The signing of a labor contract that obligates both the employer and the employee does not give rise to a liability in current accounting practice, nor does the placing of an order for the purchase of merchandise. However, under some conditions, the signing of a lease is recognized as an event that requires the current recognition of a liability even though a lease is essentially an executory contract. Clarification of this area is needed.

A liability must involve a **probable future transfer of assets or services**. Although liabilities result from past transactions or events, an obligation may be contingent upon the occurrence of another event sometime in the future. When occurrence of the future event seems probable, the obligation is defined as a liability. Although the majority of liabilities are satisfied by payment of cash, some obligations are satisfied by transferring other types of assets or by providing services. For example, revenue received in advance requires recognition of an obligation to provide goods or services in the future. Usually, the time of payment is specified by a debt instrument, e.g., a note requiring payment of interest and principal on a given date or series of dates. Some obligations, however, require the

---

[1] *Statement of Financial Accounting Concepts No. 6*, "Elements of Financial Statements" (Stamford: Financial Accounting Standards Board, December 1985), par. 35.

transfer of assets or services over a period of time, but the exact dates cannot be determined when the liability is incurred, e.g., obligations to provide parts or service under a warranty agreement.

A liability is the **obligation of a particular entity**, i.e., the entity that has the responsibility to transfer assets or provide services. As long as the payment or transfer is probable, it is not necessary that the entity to whom the obligation is owed be identified. Thus, a warranty to make any repairs necessary to an item sold by an entity is an obligation of that entity even though it is not certain which customers will receive benefits. Generally, the obligation rests on a foundation of legal rights and duties. However, obligations created, inferred, or construed from the facts of a particular situation may also be recognized as liabilities. For example, if a company regularly pays vacation pay or year-end bonuses, accrual of these items as a liability is warranted even though no legal agreement exists to make these payments.

Although the FASB's definition is helpful, the question of when an item is a liability is still not always easy to answer. Examples of areas where there is continuing controversy include the problems associated with off-balance sheet financing (discussed in Chapter 15), deferred income taxes (see Chapter 20), leases (see Chapter 21), pensions (see Chapter 22), and even some equity securities such as redeemable preferred stock (discussed in Chapter 16). Once an item is accepted as having met the definition of a liability, there is still the need to appropriately classify, measure, and report the liability.

CLASSIFICATION AND MEASUREMENT OF LIABILITIES

For reporting purposes, liabilities are usually classified as **current** or **noncurrent**. The distinction between current and noncurrent liabilities was introduced and discussed in Chapter 5, where it was pointed out that the computation of working capital is considered by many to be a useful measure of the liquidity of an enterprise.

Current Versus Noncurrent Classification

As noted in Chapter 5, the same rules generally apply for the classification of liabilities as for assets. If a liability arises in the course of an entity's normal operating cycle, it is considered current if current assets will be used to satisfy the obligation within one year or one operating cycle, whichever period is longer. On the other hand, bank borrowings, notes, mortgages, and similar obligations are related to the general financial condition of the entity rather than directly to the operating cycle, and are classified as current only if they are to be paid with current assets within one year.

When debt that has been classified as noncurrent will mature within the next year, the liability should be reported as a current liability in order to reflect the expected drain on current assets. However, if the liability is to be paid by transfer of noncurrent assets that have been accumulated for the purpose of liquidating the liability, the obligation continues to be classified as noncurrent.

Measurement of Liabilities

The distinction between current and noncurrent liabilities is also an important consideration in the measurement of liabilities. Obviously, before liabilities can be reported on the financial statements, they must be stated in monetary terms. The measurement used for liabilities is the **present value of the future cash outflows** to settle the obligation. Generally, this is the amount of cash required to liquidate the obligation if it were paid today.

If a claim isn't to be paid until sometime in the future, as is the case with noncurrent liabilities, the claim should either provide for interest to be paid on the debt, or the obligation should be reported at the discounted value of its maturity amount. Current obligations that arise in the course of normal business operations are generally due within a short period, e.g., 30 days, and normally are not discounted.[2] Thus, trade accounts payable are not discounted even though they carry no interest provision. However, this is an exception to the general rule; most nonoperating business transactions such as the borrowing of money, purchase of assets over time, and long-term leases, do involve the discounting process. The obligation in these instances is the present value of the future resource outflows.

For measurement purposes, liabilities can be divided into three categories:

1. Liabilities that are definite in amount.
2. Estimated liabilities.
3. Contingent liabilities.

The measurement of liabilities always involves some uncertainty since a liability, by definition, involves a *future* outflow of resources. However, for the first category above, both the existence of the liability and the

---

[2]*Opinions of the Accounting Principles Board No. 21*, "Interest on Receivables and Payables" (New York: American Institute of Certified Public Accountants, 1971), par. 3.

amount to be paid are determinable because of a contract, trade agreement, or general business practice. An example of a **liability that is definite in amount** is the principal payment on a note.

The second category includes items that are definitely liabilities, i.e., they involve a definite future resource outflow, but the actual amount of the obligation cannot be established currently. In this situation, the amount of the liability is estimated so that the obligation is reflected in the current period, even though at an approximated value. A warranty obligation that is recorded on an accrual basis is an example of an **estimated liability**.

Generally, liabilities from both of the first two categories are reported on a balance sheet as claims against recorded assets, as either current or noncurrent liabilities as appropriate. However, items that resemble liabilities, but are contingent upon the occurrence of some future event, are not recorded until it is probable that the event will occur. Even though the amount of the potential obligation may be known, the actual existence of a liability is questionable since it is contingent upon a future event for which there is considerable uncertainty. An example of a **contingent liability** is a pending lawsuit. Only if the lawsuit is lost, or is settled out of court, will a liability be recorded. While not recorded in the accounts, some contingent liabilities should be disclosed in a note to the financial statements, as discussed and illustrated later in the chapter.

LIABILITIES THAT ARE DEFINITE IN AMOUNT

Representative of liabilities that are definite in amount and that are reported on the balance sheet are accounts payable, notes payable, and miscellaneous operating payables including salaries, payroll taxes, property and sales taxes, and income taxes. Some liabilities accrue as time passes. Most notable in this category are interest and rent, although the latter is frequently paid in advance. Some of the problems arising in determining the balances to be reported for liabilities that are definite in amount are described in the following sections.

Accounts Payable

Most goods and services in today's economic environment are purchased on credit. The term **accounts payable** usually refers to the amount due for the purchase of materials by a manufacturing company or merchandise by a wholesaler or retailer. Other obligations, such as salaries and wages, rent, interest, and utilities are reported as separate liabilities in accounts descriptive of the nature of the obligation. Accounts payable are not recorded when purchase orders are placed, but only when legal title to the goods passes to the buyer. The rules for the customary recognition of legal passage of title were presented in Chapter 9. If goods are in transit at year-end, the purchase should be recorded if the shipment terms indicate that title has passed. This means that care must be exercised to review the purchase of goods and services near the end of an accounting period to assure a proper cut-off and reporting of liabilities and inventory.

It is customary to report accounts payable at the expected amount of the payment. Because the payment period is normally short, no recognition of interest by reporting the present value of the liability is required. As indicated in Chapter 9, if cash discounts are available, the liability should be reported net of the expected cash discount. Failure to use the net method in recording purchases usually reports liabilities in excess of the payment finally made.

Short-Term Debt

Companies often borrow money on a short-term basis for operating purposes other than the purchase of materials or merchandise involving accounts payable. Collectively, these obligations may be referred to as **short-term debt**. In most cases, such debt is evidenced by a **promissory note**, a formal written promise to pay a sum of money in the future, and is usually reflected on the debtor's books as **Notes Payable**.

Notes issued to trade creditors for the purchase of goods or services are called **trade notes payable**. Notes issued to banks or to officers and stockholders for loans to the company, and those issued to others for the purchase of plant assets, are called **nontrade notes payable**. It is normally desirable to classify current notes payable on the balance sheet as trade or nontrade, since such information would reveal to statement users the sources of indebtedness and the extent to which the company has relied on each source in financing its activities.

The problems encountered in the valuation of notes payable are the same as those discussed in Chapter 8 with respect to notes receivable. Thus, a short-term note payable is recorded and reported at its present value, which is normally the face value of the note. This presumes that the note bears a reasonable stated rate of interest. However, if a note has no stated rate of interest, or if the stated rate is unreasonable, then the face value of the note would need to be discounted to its present value to reflect the effective rate of interest implicit in the note. This is accomplished by debiting Discount on Notes Payable when the note is issued, and by writing off the discount to Interest Expense over the life of the note, in the same manner as was illustrated for the discount on notes receivable in Chapter 8.

Discount on Notes Payable is a contra account to Notes Payable and would be reported on the balance sheet as follows:

Current liabilities:
Notes payable.................................... $100,000
Less discount on notes payable 10,000 $90,000

Short-Term Obligations Expected to be Refinanced

As noted at the beginning of the chapter, omissions or misrepresentation in the reporting of liabilities can create serious problems for users of financial statements. A similar problem can result from the misclassification of liabilities. Since the "current" classification is reserved for those obligations that will be satisfied with current assets within a year, a short-term obligation that is expected to be refinanced on a long-term basis should not be reported as a current liability. This applies to the currently maturing portion of a long-term debt and to all other short-term obligations except those arising in the normal course of operations that are due in customary terms. Similarly, it should not be assumed that a short-term obligation will be refinanced, and therefore classified as a noncurrent liability, unless the refinancing arrangements are secure. Thus, to avoid potential manipulation, the refinancing expectation must be realistic and not just a mere possibility.

An example will illustrate this last point and show the importance of proper classification. Assume that a company borrows a substantial amount of money that it expects to pay back at the end of 5 years. The president of the company signs a 6-month note, which the loan officer at the bank verbally agrees will be renewed "automatically" until the actual maturity date in 5 years. The only current obligation expected is payment of the accrued interest each renewal period. Under these circumstances the company reports the obligation as noncurrent, except for the accrued interest obligation. Assume further that the loan officer leaves the bank and that the new bank official will not allow the short-term note to be refinanced. The financial picture of the company is now dramatically changed. What was considered a long-term obligation because of refinancing expectations is suddenly a current liability requiring settlement with liquid assets in the near future. This hypothetical situation is similar to what actually happened to Penn Central Railroad before it went bankrupt.

To assist with this problem, the FASB in 1975 issued Statement No. 6, which contains the authoritative guideline for classifying short-term obligations expected to be refinanced. According to the FASB, *both* of the following conditions must be met before a short-term obligation may be properly excluded from the current liability classification.[3]

1. Management must *intend to refinance* the obligation on a long-term basis.
2. Management must *demonstrate an ability to refinance* the obligation.

Concerning the second point, an ability to refinance may be demonstrated by:

a. Actually refinancing the obligation during the period between the balance sheet date and the date the statements are issued.
b. Reaching a firm agreement that clearly provides for refinancing on a long-term basis.

The terms of the refinancing agreement should be noncancelable as to all parties and extend beyond the current year. In addition, the company should not be in violation of the agreement at the balance sheet date or the date of issuance, and the lender or investor should be financially capable of meeting the refinancing requirements.

If an actual refinancing does occur before the balance sheet is issued, the portion of the short-term obligation that is to be excluded from current liabilities cannot exceed the proceeds from the new debt or equity securities issued to retire the old debt. For example, if a $400,000 long-term note is issued to partially refinance $750,000 of short-term obligations, only $400,000 of the short-term debt can be excluded from current liabilities.

An additional question relates to the timing of the refinancing. If the obligation is paid prior to the actual refinancing, the obligation should be included in current liabilities on the balance sheet.[4] To illustrate, assume that the liabilities of CareFree Inc. at December 31, 1987, include a note payable for $200,000 due January 15, 1988. The management of CareFree intends to refinance the note by issuing 10-year bonds. The bonds are actually issued before the issuance of the December 31, 1987, balance sheet on February 15, 1988. If the bonds were issued prior to payment of the note, the note should be classified as noncurrent on the December 31, 1987, balance sheet. If payment of the note preceded the sale of the bonds, however, the note should be included in current liabilities.

Normally, classified balance sheets are presented that show a total for "current liabilities." If a short-term obligation is excluded from that category due to refinancing expectations, disclosure should be made in the

---

[3]*Statement of Financial Accounting Standards No. 6*, "Classification of Short-Term Obligations Expected to be Refinanced" (Stamford: Financial Accounting Standards Board, 1975), pars. 10 and 11.

[4]*FASB Interpretation No. 8*, "Classification of a Short-Term Obligation Repaid Prior to Being Replaced by a Long-Term Security" (Stamford: Financial Accounting Standards Board, 1976), par. 3.

notes to the financial statements. The note should include a general description of the refinancing agreement.

Miscellaneous Operating Payables

Many miscellaneous payables arise in the course of a company's operating activities. Three of these are specifically discussed in this section. They are indicative of other specific liabilities that could be reported by a given entity. In general, the points made in discussing the definition of liabilities in the opening section of this chapter apply to these miscellaneous operating liabilities.

Salaries and Bonuses. In an ongoing entity, salaries and wages of officers and other employees accrue daily. Normally, no entry is made for these expenses until payment is made. A liability for unpaid salaries and wages is recorded, however, at the end of an accounting period when a more precise matching of revenues and expenses is desired. An estimate of the amount of unpaid wages and salaries is made, and an adjusting entry is prepared to recognize the amount due. Usually the entire accrued amount is identified as salaries payable with no attempt to identify the withholdings associated with the accrual. When payment is made in the subsequent period, the amount is allocated between the employee and other entities such as government taxing units, unions, and insurance companies.

For example, assume that a company has 15 employees who are paid every two weeks. At December 31, four days of unpaid wages have accrued. Analysis reveals that the 15 employees earn a total of $1,000 a day. Thus the adjusting entry at December 31 would be:

```
Salaries and Wages Expense ....................................    4,000
    Salaries and Wages Payable....................................          4,000
```

This entry may be reversed at the beginning of the next period, or, when payment is made, Salaries and Wages Payable may be debited for $4,000.

Additional compensation in the form of accrued bonuses or commissions should also be recognized. Bonuses are often based on some measure of the employer's income. Employee bonuses, even those viewed as a sharing of profits with employees, are deductible expenses for the purposes of income tax.

An agreement may provide for a bonus computed on the basis of gross revenue or sales, or on the basis of income. When income is used, the computation will depend on several factors. Three possibilities are illustrated here depending on whether the bonus is based on: (1) income before deductions for bonus or income tax, (2) income after deduction for bonus but before deduction for income tax, or (3) net income after deductions for both bonus and income tax. The degree of difficulty in computing a bonus based on income varies with the measure of income used. To illustrate the computations required in each case, assume the following: Photo Graphics Inc. gives the sales managers of its individual stores a bonus of 10% of store earnings. Income for 1987 for store No. 1 before any charges for bonus or income tax was $100,000. The income tax rate is 40%.

$$\text{Let } B = \text{Bonus}$$
$$T = \text{Income Tax}$$

(1) Assuming the bonus is based on income before deductions for bonus or income tax:

$$B = .10 \times \$100,000$$
$$B = \$10,000$$

(2) Assuming the bonus is based on income after deduction for bonus but before deduction for income tax:

$$B = .10 \ (\$100,000 - B)$$
$$B = \$10,000 - .10B$$
$$B + .10B = \$10,000$$
$$1.10B = \$10,000$$
$$B = \$9,090.91$$

Calculation of the bonus may be proved as follows:

Income before bonus and income tax..........................	$100,000.00
Deduct bonus...	9,090.91
Income after bonus but before income tax	$ 90,909.09
Bonus rate	10%
Bonus	$ 9,090.91

(3) Assuming the bonus is based on net income after deductions for bonus and income tax:

$$B = .10 \ (\$100,000 - B - T)$$
$$T = .40 \ (\$100,000 - B)$$

Substituting for T in the first equation and solving for B:

$$B = .10 \ [\$100,000 - B - .40 \ (\$100,000 - B)]$$
$$B = .10 \ (\$100,000 - B - \$40,000 + .40B)$$
$$B = \$10,000 - .1B - \$4,000 + .04B$$
$$B + .1B - .04B = \$10,000 - \$4,000$$
$$1.06B = \$6,000$$
$$B = \$5,660.38$$

Substituting for B in the second equation and solving for T:

$$T = .40 \ (\$100,000 - \$5,660.38)$$
$$T = .40 \times \$94,339.62$$
$$T = \$37,735.85$$

Calculation of the bonus is proved in the following summary:

Income before bonus and income tax......................		$100,000.00
Deduct: Bonus	$ 5,660.38	
Income tax	37,735.85	43,396.23
Net income after bonus and income tax..........		$ 56,603.77
Bonus rate		10%
Bonus		$ 5,660.38

The bonus should be reported on the income statement as an expense before arriving at net income regardless of the method employed in its computation.

Payroll Taxes. Social security and income tax legislation impose four taxes based on payrolls:

1. Federal old-age, survivors, disability and hospital insurance (tax to both employer and employee)
2. Federal unemployment insurance (tax to employer only)
3. State unemployment insurance (tax to employer only)
4. Individual income tax (tax to employee only, but withheld and paid by employer)

Federal Old-Age, Survivors, Disability, and Hospital Insurance. The Federal Insurance Contributions Act (FICA), generally referred to as social security legislation, provides for FICA taxes to both employers and employees to provide funds for federal old-age, survivors, disability, and hospital insurance benefits for certain individuals and members of their families. At one time, only employees were covered by this legislation; however, coverage now includes most individuals who are self-employed.

Provisions of the legislation require an employer of more than one employee, with certain exceptions, to withhold FICA taxes from each employee's wages. The amount of the tax is based on a tax rate and wage base as currently specified in the law. The tax rate and wage base both have increased dramatically over the past several years from less than 1% to over 7% and from less than $3,000 annual earnings to over $42,000. The employer remits the amount withheld for all employees, along with a matching amount, to the federal government. The employer is required to maintain complete records and submit detailed support for the tax remittance. The employer is responsible for the full amount of the tax even if employee contributions are not withheld.

Federal Unemployment Insurance. The Federal Social Security Act and the Federal Unemployment Tax Act provide for the establishment of unemployment insurance plans. Employers with covered workers employed in each of 20 weeks during a calendar year or who pay $1,500 or more in wages during any calendar quarter are affected.

Under present provisions of the law, the federal government taxes eligible employers on the first $7,000 paid to every employee during the calendar year. The rate of tax in effect since 1985 is 6.2%, but the employer is allowed a tax credit limited to 5.4% for taxes paid under state unemployment compensation laws. No tax is levied on the employee. When an employer is subject to a tax of 5.4% or more as a result of state unemployment legislation, the federal unemployment tax, then, is 0.8% of the qualifying wages.

Payment to the federal government is required quarterly. Unemployment benefits are paid by the individual states. Revenues collected by the federal government under the acts are used to meet the cost of administering state and federal unemployment plans as well as to provide supplemental unemployment benefits.

State Unemployment Insurance. State unemployment compensation laws are not the same in all states. In most states, laws provide for tax only on employers; but in a few states, taxes are applicable to both employers and employees. Each state law specifies the classes of exempt employees, the number of employees required or the amount of wages paid before the tax is applicable, and the contributions that are to be made by employers and employees. Exemptions are frequently similar to those under the federal act. Tax payment is generally required on or before the last day of the month following each calendar quarter.

Although the normal tax on employers may be 5.4%, states have merit rating or experience plans providing for lower rates based on employers' individual employment experiences. Employers with stable employment records are taxed at a rate in keeping with the limited amount of benefits required for their former employees; employers with less satisfactory employment records contribute at a rate more nearly approaching 5.4% in view of the greater amount of benefits paid to their former employees. Savings under state merit systems are allowed as credits in the calculation of the federal contribution, so the federal tax does not exceed 0.8% even though payment of less than 5.4% is made by an employer entitled to a lower rate under the merit rating system.

Income Tax. Federal income tax on the wages of an individual are collected in the period in which the wages are paid. The "pay-as-you-go" plan requires employers to withhold income tax from wages paid to their employees. Most states and many local governments also impose income taxes on the earnings of employees that must be withheld and remitted by the employer. Withholding is required not only of employers engaged in a trade or business, but also of religious and charitable organizations, educational institutions, social organizations, and governments of the

United States, the states, the territories, and their agencies, instrumentalities, and political subdivisions. Certain classes of wage payments are exempt from withholding although these are still subject to income tax.

An employer must meet withholding requirements under the law even if wages of only one employee are subject to such withholdings. The amounts to be withheld by the employer are developed from formulas provided by the law or from tax withholding tables made available by the government. Withholding is based on the length of the payroll period, the amount earned, and the number of withholding exemptions claimed by the employee. Taxes required under the Federal Insurance Contributions Act (both employees' and employer's portions) and income tax that has been withheld by the employer are paid to the federal government at the same time. These combined taxes are deposited in an authorized bank quarterly, monthly, or several times each month depending on the amount of the liability. Quarterly and annual statements must also be filed providing a summary of all wages paid by the employer.

Accounting for Payroll Taxes. To illustrate the accounting procedures for payroll taxes, assume that salaries for the month of January for a retail store with 15 employees are $16,000. The state unemployment compensation law provides for a tax on employers of 5.4%. Income tax withholdings for the month are $1,600. Assume FICA rates are 7.15% for employer and employee. Entries for the payroll and the employer's payroll taxes follow:

Salaries Expense	16,000	
FICA Taxes Payable		1,144
Employees Income Taxes Payable		1,600
Cash		13,256
To record payment of payroll and related employee withholdings.		
Payroll Tax Expense	2,136	
FICA Taxes Payable		1,144
State Unemployment Taxes Payable		864
Federal Unemployment Taxes Payable		128
To record the payroll tax liability of the employer.		

Computation:	
Tax under Federal Insurance Contributions Act: 7.15% × $16,000	$1,144
Tax under state unemployment insurance legislation: 5.4% × $16,000	864
Tax under Federal Unemployment Tax Act: 0.8% (6.2% − credit of 5.4%) × $16,000	128
Total payroll taxes expense	$2,136

When tax payments are made to the proper agencies, the tax liability accounts are debited and Cash is credited.

The employer's payroll taxes, as well as the taxes withheld from employees, are based on amounts paid to employees during the period regardless of the basis employed for reporting income. When financial reports are prepared on the accrual basis, the employer will have to recognize both accrued payroll and the employer's payroll taxes relating thereto by adjustments at the end of the accounting period.

For example, assume that the salaries and wages accrued at December 31 were $9,500. Of this amount, $2,000 was subject to unemployment tax and $6,000 to FICA tax. The accrual entry for the employer's payroll taxes would be as follows:

Payroll Tax Expense	553	
FICA Taxes Payable		429
State Unemployment Taxes Payable		108
Federal Unemployment Taxes Payable		16
To accrue the payroll tax liability of the employer.		

Computation:	
Tax under Federal Insurance Contributions Act: 7.15% × $6,000	$429
Tax under state unemployment insurance legislation:	
5.4% × $2,000	108
Tax under Federal Unemployment Tax Act: 0.8% × $2,000	16
	$553

As was true with the accrual entry for the salaries and wages discussed on page 600, the preceding entry may be reversed at the beginning of the new period, or the accrued liabilities may be debited when the payments are made to the taxing authorities.

Agreements with employees may provide for payroll deductions and employer contributions for other items, such as group insurance plans, pension plans, savings bonds purchases, or union dues. Such agreements call for accounting procedures similar to those described for payroll taxes.

Other Tax Liabilities. There are many different types of taxes imposed on business entities. In addition to the several payroll taxes discussed in the previous section, a company usually must pay property taxes, federal and state income taxes on their earnings, and serve as an agent for the collection of sales taxes. Each of these liabilities has some unusual features that can complicate accounting for them.

Property Taxes. Real and personal property taxes are based on the assessed valuation of properties as of a particular date. This has given rise to the view held by courts and others that taxes accrue as of a particular date. Generally, the date of accrual has been held to be the date of property assessment, or **lien date**, and a liability for the full year's property tax can be established at that date. The offset to the liability is a deferred expense since the tax liability is being established in advance of payment and incurrence of the tax expense. The tax expense is generally recognized as a charge against revenue over the fiscal year of the taxing authority for which the taxes are levied. This procedure relates the tax charge to the period in which the taxes provide benefits through government service.

The date for payment of the liability is determined by the taxing authority and is accounted for independently from the monthly recognition of property tax expense.

To illustrate accounting for property taxes, assume that the taxing authority is on a July 1 to June 30 fiscal year, but the entity paying the tax is on a calendar year basis. Property taxes assessed for the period July 1, 1987, to June 30, 1988, are $60,000, and the full year's tax is to be paid on or before November 15, 1987. The following entry is made by the taxpaying entity at the lien date, July 1, 1987, to accrue property taxes for the year:

Deferred Property Taxes	60,000	
Property Taxes Payable		60,000

Each month, the following entry would be made to recognize the expense:

Property Tax Expense	5,000	
Deferred Property Taxes		5,000

The entry to record payment of the property taxes on November 15, 1987, would be:

Property Taxes Payable	60,000	
Cash		60,000

At December 31, 1987, the deferred property tax account would have a debit balance of $30,000, representing the property taxes to be recognized as expenses in 1988. If the tax were due in January, 1988, and no payment had been made as of December 31, 1987, Property Taxes Payable would have a $60,000 credit balance, that would be reported as a current liability on the balance sheet.

Although the preceding approach seems to reflect the current definition of liabilities as established by the FASB, some companies recognize the liability ratably over the year rather than on the assessment or lien date. Under this latter approach a prepaid property tax account is created when the full year's tax is paid before the end of the taxing authority's fiscal year. In the authors' opinion, this practice is not as informative and useful as that illustrated.

Income Taxes. Both federal and state governments raise a large portion of their revenue from income taxes assessed against both individuals and corporations. The taxable income of a business entity is determined by applying the tax rules and regulations to the operations of the business. As indicated in Chapter 4, the income tax rules do not always follow generally accepted accounting principles. Thus, the income reported for tax purposes may differ from that reported on the income statement. This difference can give rise to deferred income taxes, a special liability item discussed more fully in Chapter 20. The actual amount payable for the current year must be determined after all adjusting entries are made at the close of a fiscal period. Federal and some state income tax regulations require companies to estimate their tax liability, and make periodic payments during the year in advance of the final computation and submission of the tax returns. Thus, the amount of income tax liability at year-end is usually much lower than the total tax computed for the year. Because income tax returns are always subject to government audit, a contingent liability exists for any year within the statute of limitations not yet reviewed by the Internal Revenue Service. If an additional liability arises as a result of an audit, the additional assessment should be reported as a liability until the payment is made.

Sales and Use Taxes. With the passage of sales and use tax laws by state and local governments, additional duties are required of a business unit. Laws generally provide that the business unit must act as an agent for the governmental authority in the collection from customers of sales tax on the transfers of tangible personal properties. The buyer is responsible for the payment of sales tax to the seller when both buyer and seller are in the same tax jurisdiction; however, the buyer is responsible for the payment of use tax directly to the tax authority when the seller is outside the jurisdiction of such authority. Provision must be made in the accounts for the liability to the government for the tax collected from customers and the additional tax that the business must absorb.

The sales tax payable is generally a stated percentage of sales. The actual sales total and the sales tax collections are usually recorded separately at the time of sale. Cash or Accounts Receivable is debited; Sales and Sales Tax Payable are credited. The amount of sales tax to be paid to the taxing authority is computed on the recorded sales.

Unearned Revenues

Another category of liabilities that are definite in amount is referred to as **unearned revenues**. Frequently, these liabilities represent an obligation to provide services rather than tangible resources. Examples of unearned revenue include advances from customers, unearned rent, and unearned subscription revenue for publishing companies. Unearned revenue accounts are classified as current or noncurrent liabilities depending on when the revenue will be earned. When the revenue is earned, e.g., when services are performed, the unearned revenue account is debited and an appropriate revenue account is credited. If advances are refunded without providing goods or services, the liability is reduced by the payment, and no revenue is recognized. A full discussion of revenue recognition is presented in Chapter 19.

ESTIMATED LIABILITIES

The amount of an obligation is generally established by contract or accrues at a specified rate. There are instances, however, when an obligation clearly exists on a balance sheet date but the amount ultimately to be paid cannot be definitely determined. Because the amount to be paid is not definite does not mean the liability can be ignored or given a contingent status. The claim must be estimated from whatever data are available. Obligations arising from current operations, for example, the cost of meeting warranties for service and repairs on goods sold, must be estimated when prior experience indicates there is a definite liability. Here, uncertainty as to the amount and timing of expenditures is accompanied by an inability to identify the payees; but the fact that there are charges yet to be absorbed is certain.

Representative of liabilities that are estimated in amount and frequently found on financial statements are the following:

1. Refundable deposits, reporting the estimated amount to be refunded to depositors.
2. Warranties for service and replacements, reporting the estimated future claims by customers as a result of past guarantees of services or products or product part replacements.
3. Customer premium offers, reporting the estimated value of premiums or prizes to be distributed as a result of past sales or sales promotion activities.
4. Tickets, tokens, and gift certificates, reporting the estimated obligations in the form of services or merchandise arising from the receipt of cash in past periods.
5. Compensated absences, reporting the estimated future payments attributable to past services of employees.

Refundable Deposits

Liabilities of a company may include an obligation to refund amounts previously collected from customers as deposits. Refundable deposits may be classified as current or noncurrent liabilities depending on the purpose of the deposit. If deposits are made to protect the company against nonpayment for future services to be rendered, and the services are expected to be provided over a long period, the deposit should be reported as a noncurrent liability. Utility companies characteristically charge certain customers, such as those renting their homes, a deposit that is held until a customer discontinues the service, usually because of a move.

Another type of customer deposit is one made for reusable containers, such as bottles or drums, that hold the product being purchased. When a sale is recorded, a liability is recognized for the deposit. When a container is returned, a refund or credit is given for the deposit made. Periodically, an adjustment to recognize revenue is recorded for containers not expected to be returned. The asset "containers" and the related accumulated depreciation account should be reduced to eliminate the book value of containers not expected to be returned, and any gain or loss is recognized on the "sale" of the containers.

Warranties for Service and Replacements

Many companies agree to provide free service on units failing to perform satisfactorily or to replace defective goods. When these agreements, or warranties, involve only minor costs, such costs may be recognized in the periods incurred. When these agreements involve significant future costs and when experience indicates a definite future obligation exists, estimates of such costs should be made and matched against current revenues. Such estimates are usually recorded by a debit to an expense account and a credit to a liability account. Subsequent costs of fulfilling warranties are debited to the liability account and credited to an appropriate account, e.g., Cash or Inventory.

To illustrate accounting for warranties, consider the following example. MJW Video & Sound sells compact stereo systems with a two-year warranty. Past experience indicates that 10% of all sets sold will need repairs in the first year, and 20% will need repairs in the second year. The average repair cost is $50 per system. The number of systems sold in 1987 and 1988 was 5,000 and 6,000, respectively. Actual repair costs were $12,500 in 1987 and $55,000 in 1988; it is assumed that all repair costs involved cash expenditures.

1987	Warranty Expense		75,000	
	Estimated Liability Under Warranties			75,000
	Estimated warranty expense based on systems sold: 5,000 × .30 × $50 = $75,000.			
	Estimated Liability Under Warranties		12,500	
	Cash			12,500
	Repairs actually made in 1987.			
1988	Warranty Expense		90,000	
	Estimated Liability Under Warranties			90,000
	Estimated warranty expense based on systems sold: 6,000 × .30 × $50 = $90,000.			
	Estimated Liability Under Warranties		55,000	
	Cash			55,000
	Repairs actually made in 1988.			

Periodically, the warranty liability account should be analyzed to see if the actual repairs approximate the estimate. Adjustment to the liability account will be required if experience differs appreciably from the estimates. These adjustments are changes in estimates and are reported in the period of change. If sales and repairs in the preceding example are assumed to occur evenly through the year, analysis of the liability account at the end of 1988 shows the ending balance of $97,500 ($75,000 + $90,000 − $12,500 − $55,000) is reasonably close to the predicted amount of $100,000 based upon the 10% and 20% estimates.

Computation:

1987 sales still under warranty for 6 months: $50 × [5,000 (½ × .20)]......	$ 25,000
1988 sales still under warranty for 18 months: $50 × [6,000 (½ × .10) + 6,000 (.20)]	75,000
Total	$100,000

Assume, however, that warranty costs incurred in 1988 were only $35,000. Then the ending balance of $117,500 would be much higher than the $100,000 estimate. If the $17,500 difference were considered to be material, an adjustment to warranty expense would be made in 1988 as follows:

Estimated Liability Under Warranties	17,500	
Warranty Expense		17,500
Adjustment of estimate for warranty repairs.		

In certain cases, customers are charged special fees for a service or replacement warranty covering a specific period. When fees are collected, an unearned revenue account is credited. The unearned revenue is then recognized as revenue over the warranty period. Costs incurred in meeting the contract requirements are debited to expense; Cash, Inventory, or other appropriate account is credited. The **service contract** is in reality an insurance contract, and the amount charged for the contract is based on the past repair experience of the company for the item sold. The fee usually is set at a rate that will produce a profit margin on the contract if expectations are realized.

To illustrate accounting for service contracts, assume a company sells 3-year service contracts covering its product. During the first year, $50,000 was received on contracts, and expenses incurred for parts and labor in connection with these contracts totaled $5,000. It is estimated from past experience that the pattern of repairs, based on the total dollars spent for repairs, is 25% in the first year of the contract, 30% in the second year, and 45% in the third year. In addition, it is assumed that sales of the contracts are made evenly during the year. The following entries would be made in the first year.

Cash	50,000	
Unearned Revenue from Service Contracts		50,000
Sale of service contracts.		

Unearned Revenue from Service Contracts.........................	6,250	
Revenue from Service Contracts		6,250

Estimated revenue earned from contracts. 12½% (½ of 25%) of $50,000, or $6,250.

Service Contract Expense	5,000	
Inventory		5,000

Repairs actually made during the year.

Based on the above entries, a profit of $1,250 on service contracts would be recognized in the first year. If future expectations change, adjustments will be necessary to the unearned revenue account to reflect the change in estimate.

The accounts Estimated Liability Under Warranties and Unearned Revenue from Service Contracts are classified as current or noncurrent liabilities depending on the period remaining on the warranty. Those warranty costs expected to be incurred within one year or unearned revenues expected to be earned within one year are classified as current; the balance as long-term. In the above illustration, the expected revenue percentage for the second year would be 27½% of the contract price, i.e., 12½% for balance of first year expectations and 15% (½ of 30%) for one-half of the second year expectations, or $13,750. This amount would be classified as current. The remaining 60%, or $30,000, of unearned revenue would be classified as noncurrent.

The method of accounting illustrated above does not recognize any income on the initial sale of the contract, but only as the period of the service contract passes and the actual costs are matched against an estimate of the earned revenue. Alternatively, a company could estimate in advance the cost of the repairs and recognize the difference between the amount of the service contract and the expected repair cost in the period of the contract sale. The choice of which method to use depends on the degree of confidence in the estimated repair cost. As discussed more fully in Chapter 19, revenue recognition varies with the facts involved. When collection is reasonably assured and future costs are known with a high degree of certainty, immediate income recognition is recommended. In the case of service contracts, the uncertainty of future expenses usually dictates use of the illustrated method.

Customer Premium Offers

Many companies offer special premiums to customers to stimulate the regular purchase of certain products. These offers may be open for a limited time or may be of a continuing nature. The premium is normally made available when the customer submits the required number of product labels or other evidence of purchase. In certain instances the premium offer may provide for an optional cash payment.

If a premium offer expires on or before the end of the company's fiscal period, adjustments in the accounts are not required. Premium obligations are fully met and the premium expense account summarizes the full charge for the period. However, when a premium offer is continuing, an adjustment must be made at the end of the period to recognize the liability for future redemptions—Premium Expense is debited and an appropriate liability account is credited. The expense is thus charged to the period benefiting from the premium plan and current liabilities reflect the claim for premiums outstanding. If premium distributions are debited to an expense account, the liability balance may be reversed at the beginning of the new period.

To illustrate the accounting for a premium offer, assume the following: Good Foods offers a set of breakfast bowls upon the receipt of 20 certificates, one certificate being included in each package of the cereal distributed by this company. The cost of each set of bowls to the company is $2. It is estimated that only 40% of the certificates will be redeemed. In 1987, the company purchased 10,000 sets of bowls at $2 per set; 400,000 packages of cereal containing certificates were sold at a price of $1.20 per package. By the end of 1987, 30% of the certificates had been redeemed. Entries for 1987 are as follows:

Transaction	Entry
1987:	
Premium purchases:	Premiums—Bowl Sets.......... 20,000
10,000 sets × $2 = $20,000	Cash....................... 20,000
Sales:	Cash......................... 480,000
400,000 packages × $1.20 = $480,000	Sales...................... 480,000
Premium claim redemptions:	Premium Expense.............. 12,000
120,000 certificates, or 6,000 sets × $2 = $12,000	Premiums—Bowl Sets........ 12,000
December 31, 1987:	
Coupons estimated redeemable in future periods:	Premium Expense.............. 4,000
Total estimated redemptions—	Estimated Premium Claims Out-
40% of 400,000 160,000	standing................... 4,000
Redemptions in 1987 120,000	
Estimated future redemptions 40,000	
Estimated claims outstanding:	
40,000 certificates, or 2,000 sets @ $2.. $ 4,000	
January 1, 1988 (optional):	Estimated Premium Claims Out-
Reversal of accrued liability balance.	standing..................... 4,000
	Premium Expense.......... 4,000

The balance sheet at the end of 1987 will show premiums of $8,000 as a current asset and estimated premium claims outstanding of $4,000 as a current liability; the income statement for 1987 will show premium expense of $16,000 as a selling expense.

Experience indicating a redemption percentage that differs from the assumed rate will call for an appropriate adjustment in the subsequent period and the revision of future redemption estimates.

The estimated cost of the premiums may be shown as a direct reduction of sales by recording the premium claim at the time of the sale. This requires an estimate of the premium cost at the time of the sale. For example, in the previous illustration, the summary entry for sales recorded during the year, employing the sales reduction approach, would be as follows:

Cash..	480,000	
Sales..		464,000
Estimated Premium Claims Outstanding.........................		16,000

The redemption of premium claims would call for debits to the liability account. Either the expense method or the sales reduction method is acceptable, and both are found in practice.

Tickets, Tokens, and Gift Certificates Outstanding

Many companies sell tickets, tokens, and gift certificates that entitle the owner to services or merchandise: for example, airlines issue tickets used for travel; local transit companies issue tokens good for fares; department stores sell gift certificates redeemable in merchandise.

When instruments redeemable in services or merchandise are outstanding at the end of the period, accounts should be adjusted to reflect the obligations under such arrangements. The nature of the adjustment will depend on the entries originally made in recording the sale of the instruments.

Ordinarily, the sale of instruments redeemable in services or merchandise is recorded by a debit to Cash and a credit to a liability account. As instruments are redeemed, the liability balance is debited and Sales or an appropriate revenue account is credited. Certain claims may be rendered void by lapse of time or for some other reason as defined by the sales agreement. In addition, experience may indicate a certain percentage of outstanding claims will never be presented for redemption. These factors must be considered at the end of the period, when the liability balance is reduced to the balance of the claim estimated to be outstanding and a revenue account is credited for the gain indicated from forfeitures. If Sales or a special revenue account is originally credited on the sale of the redemption instrument, the adjustment at the end of the period calls for a debit to the revenue account and a credit to a liability account for the claim still outstanding.

Compensated Absences

Compensated absences include payments by employers for vacation, holiday, illness, or other personal activities. Employees often earn paid absences based on the time employed. Generally, the longer an employee works for a company, the longer the vacation allowed, or the more liberal the time allowed for illnesses. At the end of any given accounting period, a company has a liability for earned but unused compensated absences. The matching principle requires that the estimated amounts earned be charged against current revenue, and a liability established for that amount.[5] The difficult part of this accounting treatment is estimating how much should be accrued. In Statement No. 43, the FASB requires a liability to be recognized for compensated absences that (1) have been earned through services already rendered, (2) vest or can be carried forward to subsequent years, and (3) are estimable and probable.

For example, assume that a company has a vacation pay policy for all employees. If all employees had the same anniversary date for computing time in service, the computations would not be too difficult. However, most plans provide for a flexible employee starting date. In order to compute the liability, a careful inventory of all employees must be made that includes the number of years of service, rate of pay, carryover of unused vacation from prior periods, turnover, and the probability of taking the vacation.

To illustrate the accounting for compensated absences, assume that S&N Corporation has 20 employees that are paid an average of $350 per week. During 1987, a total of 40 vacation weeks were earned by all employees but only 30 weeks of vacation were taken that year. The remaining 10 weeks of vacation were taken in 1988 when the average rate of pay was $400 per week. The entry to record the accrued vacation pay on December 31, 1987, would be:

Wages Expense	3,500	
Vacation Wages Payable		3,500
To record accrued vacation wages ($350 × 10 weeks).		

The above entry assumes that Wages Expense has already been recorded for the 30 weeks of vacation taken during 1987. Therefore, the income statement would reflect the total Wages Expense for the entire

---

[5]*Statement of Financial Accounting Standards No. 43,* "Accounting for Compensated Absences" (Stamford: Financial Accounting Standards Board, 1980), par. 6.

40 weeks of vacation earned during the period. On its December 31, 1987, balance sheet, S&N would report a current liability of $3,500 to reflect the obligation for the 10 weeks of vacation pay that is owed. In 1988, when the additional vacation weeks are taken and the payroll is paid, S&N would make the following entry:

Wages Expense	500	
Vacation Wages Payable	3,500	
Cash		4,000
To record payment at current rates of previously earned vacation time ($400 × 10 weeks).		

Since the vacation weeks are now used, the above entry eliminates the liability. An adjustment to Wages Expense is required because the liability was recorded at the rates of pay in effect during the time the compensation (vacation pay) was earned. However, the cash is being paid at the current rate, which requires an adjustment to Wages Expense. If the rate of pay for the 10 hours of vacation taken in 1988 had remained the same as the rate used to record the accrual on December 31, 1987 there would not have been an adjustment to Wages Expense. The entry to record payment in 1988 would simply be a debit to the payable and a credit to Cash for $3,500.

An exception to the requirement for accrual of compensated absences, such as vacation pay, is made for sick pay. The FASB decided that sick pay should be accrued only if it vests with the employee, i.e., the employee is entitled to compensation for a certain number of "sick days" regardless of whether the employee is actually absent for that period. Upon leaving the firm, the employee would be compensated for any unused sick time. If the sick pay does not vest, it is recorded as an expense only when actually paid.[6]

Although compensated absences are not deductible for income tax purposes until the vacation, holiday, or illness occurs and the payment is made, they are required by GAAP to be recognized as liabilities on the financial statements.

CONTINGENT LIABILITIES

A **contingency** is defined in FASB Statement No. 5 as:

> . . . an existing condition, situation, or set of circumstances involving uncertainty as to possible gain . . . or loss . . . to an enterprise that will ultimately be resolved when one or more future events occur or fail to occur.[7]

---

[6]*Ibid.*, par. 7.

[7]*Statement of Financial Accounting Standards No. 5*, "Accounting for Contingencies" (Stamford: Financial Accounting Standards Board, 1975), par. 1.

As defined, contingencies may relate to either assets or liabilities, and to either a gain or loss. In this chapter, attention is focused on **contingent losses** that might give rise to a liability. As mentioned previously, contingent liabilities are distinguishable from estimated liabilities.

Historically, when liabilities were classified as contingent, they were not recorded on the books, but were disclosed in notes to financial statements. The distinction between a recorded liability and a contingent liability was not always clear. If a legal liability existed and the amount of the obligation was either definite or could be estimated with reasonable certainty, the liability was recorded on the books. If the existence of the obligation depended on the happening of a future event, recording of the liability was deferred until the event occurred. In an attempt to make the distinction more precise, the FASB used three terms in FASB Statement No. 5 to identify the range of possibilities of the event occurring. Different accounting action was recommended for each term. The terms, their definitions, and the accounting actions recommended are as follows:[8]

Term	Definition	Accounting Action
Probable	The future event or events are likely to occur	Record the probable event in the accounts if the amount can be reasonably estimated. If not estimable, disclose facts in note.
Reasonably possible	The chance of the future event or events occurring is more than remote but less than likely	Report the contingency in a note.
Remote	The chance of the future event or events occurring is slight	No recording or reporting unless contingency represents a guarantee. Then note disclosure is required. *parent/subsidiary*

If the happening of an event that would create a liability is **probable**, and if the amount of the obligation can be **reasonably estimated**, the contingency should be recognized as a liability. Some of the liabilities already presented as estimated liabilities may be considered probable contingent liabilities because the existence of the obligation is dependent on some event occurring, e.g., warranties are dependent on the need for repair or service to be given, gift certificates are dependent on the certificate being turned in for redemption, and vacation pay is dependent on a person taking a vacation. These liabilities are not included in this section, however, because historically they have been recognized as recorded liabilities. Other liabilities, such as unsettled litigation claims, self insurance, and loan guarantees have more traditionally been considered as un-

---

[8]*Ibid.*, par. 3.

recorded contingent liabilities, and these will be explored separately in the following pages.

Inasmuch as most liabilities have some element of contingency associated with them, the authors feel that the classification "contingent liability" should be reserved for those items that fit into one of the latter two terms, i.e., **reasonably possible** or **remote.** If the happening of the event is probable and the amount of the obligation can be estimated, the liability is no longer a contingent liability, but a recorded estimated liability. Such liabilities meet the definition for liabilities established by the FASB. This approach avoids having to say that some contingent liabilities are recorded and others are not. By this definition, a contingent liability is never recorded but is either disclosed in a footnote or ignored depending on the degree of remoteness of its expected occurrence.

The FASB statement provided no specific guidelines as to how these three terms should be interpreted in probability percentages. Surveys made of statement preparers and users disclosed a great diversity in the probability interpretations of the terms. It is unlikely, therefore, that FASB Statement No. 5 has greatly reduced the diversity in practice in recording some of these contingent items.

Litigation

An increasing number of lawsuits are being filed against companies and individuals. Lawsuits may result in substantial liabilities to successful plaintiffs. Typically, litigation takes a long time to conclude. Even after a decision has been rendered by a lower court, there are many appeal opportunities available. Thus, both the amount and timing of a loss arising from litigation are generally highly uncertain. Some companies carry insurance to protect them against these losses, so the impact of the losses on the financial statements is minimized. For uninsured risks, however, a decision must be made as to when the liability for litigation becomes probable, and thus a recorded loss.

FASB Statement No. 5 identifies several key factors to consider in making the decision. These include:[9]

1. The nature of the litigation.
2. The period when the cause of action occurred. (Liability is not recognized in any period before the cause of action occurred.)
3. Progress of the case in court, including progress between date of the financial statements and their issuance date.
4. Views of legal counsel as to the probability of loss.

---

[9]*Ibid.,* par. 36.

5. Prior experience with similar cases.

6. Management's intended response to the litigation.

If analysis of these and similar factors results in the judgment that a loss is probable, and the amount of the loss can be reasonably estimated, the liability should be recorded. A settlement after the balance sheet date but before the statements are issued would be evidence that the loss was probable at the year-end, and would result in a reporting of loss in the current financial statements.

Another area of potential liability involves unasserted claims, i.e., a cause of action has occurred but no claim has yet been asserted. For example, a person may be injured on the property of the company, but as of the date the financial statements are issued, no legal action has been taken; or a violation of a government regulation may occur, but no federal action has yet been taken. If it is probable that a claim will be filed, and the amount of the claim can be reasonably estimated, accrual of the liability should be made. If the amount cannot be reasonably estimated, note disclosure is required. If assertion of the claim is not judged to be probable, no accrual or disclosure is necessary.

As a practical matter, it should be noted that a company would be very unlikely to record a loss from unasserted claims or from pending litigation unless negotiations for a settlement had been substantially completed. When that is the case, the loss is no longer a contingency, but an estimated loss.

Some companies do not disclose any information regarding potential liabilities from litigation. Others provide a brief, general description of pending litigation, as illustrated in the following note from the annual report of General Motors Corporation.

NOTE 16. Contingent Liabilities

There are various claims and pending actions against the Corporation and its subsidiaries with respect to commercial matters, including warranties and product liability, governmental regulations including environmental and safety matters, civil rights, antitrust, patent matters, taxes and other matters arising out of the conduct of the business. Certain of these actions purport to be classactions, seeking damages in very large amounts. The amounts of liability on these claims and actions at December 31, 1984 were not determinable but, in the opinion of the management, the ultimate liability resulting will not materially affect the consolidated financial position of the Corporation and its consolidated subsidiaries.

(General Motors)

Sometimes companies provide fairly specific information about pending actions and claims. However, companies must be careful not to increase their chances of losing pending lawsuits, and generally do not disclose dollar amounts of potential losses, which might be interpreted as an admission of guilt and a willingness to pay a certain amount. For example, Union Carbide disclosed the following information in its 1984 annual report in connection with the Bhopal, India plant disaster and the discharge of chemicals at the company's Institute, West Virginia plant.

Numerous lawsuits have been brought against the Corporation and/or Union Carbide India Limited (UCIL), and in two instances the Chairman of the Corporation, in United States District Courts and in state courts in the United States and in Indian courts alleging, among other things, personal injuries or wrongful death from exposure to a release of gas at UCIL's Bhopal, India plant in December 1984. The Corporation owns 50.9% of the stock of UCIL. Some of these actions are purported class actions in which plaintiffs claim to represent large numbers of claimants alleged to have been killed or injured as a result of such exposure. Also, a purported class action has been brought against the Corporation in the United States District Court for the Southern District of West Virginia alleging, among other things, property damage and personal injury from alleged discharges of chemicals at the Corporation's Institute, W.Va. plant which suspended the production of methyl isocyanate following the incident at Bhopal. Plaintiffs purport to represent all persons or entities within a 10-mile radius of the Institute plant. Generally, these actions seek compensatory and punitive damages, either in unspecified amounts or in varying amounts ranging up to billions of dollars. Certain of the actions also seek injunctive relief, including, among other things, restraints on operation of the UCIL plant or the Institute plant and restraints on production of certain chemicals by the Corporation.

While it is impossible at this time to determine with certainty the ultimate outcome of any of the lawsuits described above, in the opinion of management, based in part on the advice of counsel, they will not have a material adverse effect on the consolidated financial position of the Corporation. In the opinion of management, based in part on the advice of counsel, no charge or accrual is required for any liabilities or for any impairment of assets that may result from the lawsuits described above relating to the Bhopal plant or the Institute plant and the Corporation has made adequate provisions for probable losses relating to the other actions referred to in the immediately preceding paragraph. Should any losses be sustained in connection with any of the matters referred to above, in excess of provisions therefore, they will be charged to income in the future.

(Union Carbide)

Self Insurance

Some large companies with widely distributed risks may decide not to purchase insurance for protection against the normal business risks of fire, explosion, flood, or damage to other persons or their property. These companies in effect insure themselves against these risks. The accounting question that arises is whether a liability should be accrued and a loss recognized for the possible occurrence of the uninsured risk. Sometimes companies have recorded as an expense an amount equal to the insurance premium that would have been paid had commercial insurance been carried. The FASB considered this specific subject in Statement No. 5, and concluded that no loss or liability should be recorded until the loss has occurred. Fires, explosions, or other casualties are random in occurrence, and as such, are not accruable. Further, they stated that

> ...unlike an insurance company, which has a contractual obligation under policies in force to reimburse insureds for losses, an enterprise can have no such obligation to itself and, hence, no liability.[10]

Thus, although an exposed condition does exist, it is a future period that must bear any loss that occurs, not a current period.

Loan Guarantees

Enterprises sometimes enter into a contract guaranteeing a loan for another enterprise, frequently a subsidiary company, a supplier, or even a favored customer. These guarantees obligate the entity to make the loan payment if the principal borrower fails to make the payment. A similar contingent obligation exists when the payee of a note receivable discounts it at a bank, but is held contingently liable in the event the maker of the note defaults. Discussion of discounted notes receivable was included in Chapter 8. If the default on the loan or the note is judged to be probable based on the events that have occurred prior to the issuance date of the financial statements, the loss and liability should be accrued in accordance with the general guidelines discussed in this section. Otherwise, note disclosure is required even if the likelihood of making the payment is remote. This exception to not disclosing remote contingencies arose because companies have traditionally disclosed guarantees in notes to the financial statements, and the FASB did not want to reduce this disclosure practice.

BALANCE SHEET PRESENTATION

The liability section of the balance sheet is usually divided between current and noncurrent liabilities as previously discussed. The nature of the detail to be presented for current liabilities depends on the use to be made of the financial statement. A balance sheet prepared for stockholders might report little detail; on the other hand, creditors may insist on full detail concerning current debts.

---

[10]*Ibid.*, par. 28.

Assets are normally recorded in the order of their liquidity, and consistency would suggest that liabilities be reported in the order of their maturity. The latter practice may be followed only to the extent it is practical; observance of this procedure would require an analysis of the different classes of obligations and separate reporting for classes with varying maturity dates.

Liabilities should not be offset by assets to be applied to their liquidation. Disclosure as to future debt liquidation, however, may be provided by an appropriate parenthetical remark or note. Disclosure of liabilities secured by specific assets should also be made by a parenthetical remark or note.

The current liabilities section of a balance sheet prepared on December 31, 1987, might appear as shown below:

Current liabilities:
Notes payable:

Trade creditors	$12,000	
Banks (secured by pledge of accounts receivable)	20,000	
Officers	12,500	$ 44,500
Accounts payable		35,250
Current portion of long-term debt		10,000
Salaries and wages payable		1,250
Income taxes payable		6,000
Real and personal property taxes payable		1,550
Dividends payable		4,500
Other current liabilities:		
Advances from customers	$ 7,500	
Estimated warranty costs	2,500	10,000
Total current liabilities		$113,050

Because most of the noncurrent liabilities are discussed in separate chapters that follow, illustration of the details of the noncurrent liabilities section is deferred until Chapter 17 and illustrated with owners' equity. For a further illustration of a liabilities section of a balance sheet, with related notes, see the General Mills' financial statements reproduced in Appendix A at the end of this book.

QUESTIONS

1. Identify the major elements included in the definition of liabilities established by the FASB.
2. (a) What is meant by an executory contract? (b) Do these contracts fit the definition of liabilities included in this chapter?

3. Distinguish between current and noncurrent liabilities.
4. At what amount should liabilities generally be reported?
5. Under what conditions would debt that will mature within the next year be reported as a noncurrent liability?
6. Distinguish between the following categories: (a) liabilities that are definite in amount, (b) estimated liabilities, and (c) contingent liabilities.
7. The sales manager for Off-Road Enterprises is entitled to a bonus equal to 12% of profits. What difficulties may arise in the interpretation of this profit-sharing agreement?
8. Gross payroll is taxed by both federal and state governments. Identify these taxes and indicate who bears the cost of the tax, the employer or the employee?
9. How should a company account for revenue received in advance for a service contract?
10. Why should a company normally account for product warranties on an accrual basis?
11. What information must a firm accumulate in order to adequately account for estimated liabilities on tickets, tokens, and gift certificates?
12. How should compensated absences be accounted for?
13. How should contingent liabilities that are reasonably possible of becoming liabilities be reported on the financial statements?
14. What factors are important in deciding whether a pending lawsuit should be reported as a liability on the balance sheet?
15. Why does accounting for self-insurance differ from accounting for insurance premiums with outside carriers?

DISCUSSION CASES

CASE 14–1   (How much liability do they have?)

As a consultant for a small CPA firm, you have been asked to provide answers and explanations for each of the following questions:

(a) Under the laws of the state, your client, the Barboza Tile Company, has a choice of methods for paying unemployment insurance contributions. The company may pay a percentage of gross wages or may reimburse the state employment commission directly for actual claims that may arise. Barboza chose the reimbursement of actual claims method. If no claims against the client are filed, may your client record an expense and a liability for future unemployment claims?

(b) Doyle Company franchises distributorships for oxygen inhalator units. The franchises lease the units from Doyle and pay an initial leasing fee for each unit before receipt of the unit. The franchise agreement states that the franchisee is entitled to a refund, upon termination of the franchise agreement and return of the units, of a specified amount of the initial leasing fee depending on the length of time the units were leased out.

When the units are returned, they are generally redistributed without any repair. Should a liability be recorded by Doyle for the return of a portion of the initial leasing fee?

(c) The Juab County Board of Education employed a teacher for the school year, September through June, at an annual salary of $18,000 payable over a 12-month period. The Board's personnel policy states that the annual salary of a teacher is earned evenly over a 10-month period from September through June. The Board withholds an equal amount from each of the ten paychecks to make it possible for teachers to receive their pay in twelve equal installments. What amount, if any, should be reflected on the Board's statements of financial position at June 30 for the $1,500 per month payable to the teacher for July and August?   (AICPA adapted)

CASE 14–2   (Leave my current ratio alone)

Spell Inc., a closely held corporation, has never been audited and is seeking a large bank loan for plant expansion. The bank has requested audited statements. In conference with the president and majority stockholder of Spell, the auditor is informed that the bank looks very closely at the current ratio. The auditor's proposed reclassifications and adjustments include the following:

(a) A note payable issued 4 1/2 years ago matures in six months from the balance sheet date. The auditor wants to reclassify it as a current liability. The controller says no because "we are probably going to refinance this note with other long-term debt."

(b) An accrual for compensated absences. Again the controller objects because the amount of the pay for these absences cannot be estimated. "Some employees quit in the first year and don't get vacation, and it is impossible to predict which employees will be absent for illness or other causes. Without being able to identify the employees, we can't determine the rate of compensation."

How would you as auditor respond to the controller?

CASE 14–3   (When is a loss a loss?)

The following three **independent** sets of facts relate to (a) the possible accrual or (b) the possible disclosure by other means of a loss contingency.

Situation I

A company offers a one-year warranty for the product that it manufactures. A history of warranty claims has been compiled and the probable amount of claims related to sales for a given period can be determined.

Situation II

Subsequent to the date of a set of financial statements, but prior to the issuance of the financial statements, a company enters into a contract which, because of a sudden shift in the economy, will probably result in a significant loss to the company. The amount of the loss can be reasonably estimated.

Situation III

A company has adopted a policy of recording self-insurance for any possible losses resulting from injury to others by the company's vehicles. The premium for an insurance policy for the same risk from an independent insurance company would have an annual cost of $20,000. During the period covered by the financial statements, there were no accidents involving the company's vehicles which resulted in injury to others. Discuss the accrual and/or type of disclosure necessary (if any) and the reason(s) why such disclosure is appropriate for each of the three independent sets of facts above.   (AICPA adapted)

CASE 14–4   (Should a liability be recorded?)

How should the following circumstances affect the presentation of the calendar year-end financial statements for Henderson Corporation? Explain your answer.

(a)   There is a suit pending in federal court against Henderson Corporation. Henderson has been accused of dumping toxic wastes in the Cucamonga River which flows through a residential area. The citizens are seeking both compensatory and punitive damages.

(b)   The Petrochemical Workers Union, which represents 95% of Henderson's employees, is threatening to strike unless Henderson adopts an employee profit-sharing plan. Negotiations are scheduled for November of the following year.

(c)   The Union has pressured Henderson into compensating their employees for a certain number of "sick days" regardless of whether the employee is actually absent for that period.   (AICPA adapted)

CASE 14–5   (Is it really self-insurance?)

The auditors of Data Retrieval Systems are concerned with how to account for the insurance premiums on a liability policy carried with a large insurance company. Premiums on the policy are based on the average loss experience of Data Retrieval Systems over the past five years. In some years, no insured loss occurs; however, the company follows the practice of recognizing expenses for the premiums paid to the insurance company regardless of actual loss. The senior auditor, Gary Wells, has read FASB Statement No. 5 and argues that the premiums paid are really deposits with the insurance company. Since the premiums are based on the losses actually incurred, income should be charged only when the losses occur, not when the premiums are paid. By charging the premiums to expense, an artificial smoothing of income results, something FASB Statement No. 5 was designed to prevent. Barbara Orton, controller, argues that the premiums are arm's-length payments, that FASB Statement No. 5 applies only to self-insurance, and that the policy carried by Data Retrieval Systems is obviously with an outside carrier. Thus, Orton believes the premiums should be recognized as a valid period expense. As audit manager, you are asked to render your opinion on the matter.

EXERCISES

EXERCISE 14–1   (Purchase with non-interest-bearing note)

On September 1, 1987, Bart Manufacturing Co. purchased two new company automobiles from Easy-Terms Auto Sales. The terms of the sale called for Bart to pay $19,992 to Easy-Terms on September 1, 1988. Bart gave the seller a non-interest-bearing note for that amount. At the date of purchase, the interest rate for short-term loans was 12%.

(a) Prepare the journal entries necessary on September 1, 1987, December 31, 1987 (year-end adjusting), and September 1, 1988.

(b) Show how notes payable would be presented in the December 31, 1987 balance sheet.

EXERCISE 14–2   (Calculation of bonus)

Mari Wholesale Company, has an agreement with its sales manager whereby the latter is entitled to 8% of company earnings as a bonus. Company income for a calendar year before bonus and income tax is $350,000. Income tax is 40% of income after bonus. Compute the amount of the bonus under each of the conditions below.

(a) The bonus is calculated on income before deductions for bonus and income tax.

(b) The bonus is calculated on income after deduction for bonus but before deduction for income tax.

(c) The bonus is calculated on net income after deductions for both bonus and income tax.

EXERCISE 14–3   (Calculation of bonus rate)

The Rodriguez Furniture Company provides a special bonus for its executive officers based upon income before bonus or income tax. Income before bonus and income tax for 1988 was $2,500,000. The combined state and federal income tax rate is 55%, and the total income tax liability for 1988 is $1,278,750. What was the bonus rate?

EXERCISE 14–4   (Recording payroll and payroll taxes)

U-Drive Transportation Company paid one week's wages of $10,600 in cash (net pay after all withholdings and deductions) to its 40 employees. Income tax withholdings were equal to 17% of the gross payroll, and the only other deductions were 7.15% for FICA tax and $160 for union dues. Give the entries that should be made on the books of the company to record the payroll and the tax accruals to be recognized by the employer, assuming that the company is subject to unemployment taxes of 5.4% (state) and .8% (federal).

EXERCISE 14–5   (Accounting for property taxes)

On November 20, 1987, Red Rose Floral Shop received a property tax assessment of $144,000 for the fiscal year ending June 30, 1988. No entry was made to record the assessment. Several months later, Red Rose's accountant was preparing the yearly financial statements (based on a February 1 to January 31 fiscal year) and came across the property tax assessment. Give the journal entries to record the tax payment (if any) and any adjusting entries necessary on January 31, assuming:

(a) The full tax of $144,000 had been paid on January 5, 1988.

(b) The full tax of $144,000 had not been paid.

(c) A portion of the tax ($90,500) had been paid on January 20, 1988.

EXERCISE 14–6   (Warranty liability)

In 1987 Daynes Office Supply began selling a new calculator that carried a two-year warranty against defects. Based on the manufacturer's recommendations, Daynes projects that estimated warranty costs (as a percent of dollar sales) as follows:

First year of warranty 4%
Second year of warranty 10%

Sales and actual warranty repairs for 1987 and 1988 are presented below:

	1987	1988
Sales	$250,000	$475,000
Actual warranty repairs.	4,750	26,175

(1) Give the necessary journal entries to record the liability at the end of 1987 and 1988.
(2) Analyze the warranty liability account as of the year ending December 31, 1988, to see if the actual repairs approximate the estimate. Should Daynes revise the manufacturer's warranty estimate? (Assume sales and repairs occur evenly throughout the year).

EXERCISE 14–7   (Warranty liability)

Craig's Appliance Company's accountant has been reviewing the firm's past television sales. For the past two years, Craig's has been offering a special service warranty on all televisions sold. With the purchase of a television, the customer has the right to purchase a three-year service contract for an extra $60. Information concerning past television and warranty contract sales is given below:

Color-All Model II Television

	1987	1988
Television sales in units	460	550
Sales price per unit	$ 400	$ 500
Number of service contracts sold	300	350
Expenses relating to television warranties	$3,350	$9,630

Craig's accountant has estimated from past records that the pattern of repairs has been 40% in the first year after sale, 36% in the second year, and 24% in the third year. Give the necessary journal entries related to the service contracts for 1987 and 1988. In addition, indicate how much profit on service contracts would be recognized in 1988. Assume sales of the contracts are made evenly during the year.

EXERCISE 14–8   (Premium liability)

In an effort to increase sales, Bill Razor Blade Company began a sales promotion campaign on June 30, 1987. Part of this new promotion included placing a special coupon in each package of razor blades sold. Customers were able to redeem 5 coupons for a bottle of shaving lotion. Each premium costs Bill $.50. Bill estimated that 55% of the coupons issued will be redeemed. For the six months ended December 31, 1987, the following information is available:

Packages of razor blades sold	1,800,000
Premiums purchased	135,000
Coupons redeemed	405,000

What is the estimated liability for premium claims outstanding at December 31, 1987?   (AICPA adapted)

EXERCISE 14–9   (Premium liability)

On June 1, 1987, the Happy Pet Company began marketing a new dog food created specifically to meet the nutritional requirements of puppies. As a promotion, Happy was offering a free dog house to all customers returning the weight seals from the purchase of 1,000 pounds of the new dog food. Happy estimates that 30% of the weight seals will be returned. At December 31, 1987, the following information was available:

Sales (1,650,000 pounds × $.40)	$660,000
Dog house purchases (495 × $30)	14,850
Dog house distributed (265 × $30)	7,950

Give the journal entries to record the sales of dog food, purchase of dog house premiums, redemption of weight seals, and the estimated liability for outstanding premium offers as of the end of the year.

EXERCISE 14–10   (Compensated absence — vacation pay)

Rosenbaum Builders Inc. employs five people. Each employee is entitled to two weeks' paid vacation every year the employee works for the company. The conditions of the paid vacation are: (a) for each full year of work, an employee will receive two weeks of paid vacation (no vacation accrues for a portion of a year), (b) each employee will receive the same pay for vacation time as the regular pay in the year taken, and (c) unused vacation pay can be carried forward. The following data were taken from the firm's personnel records:

Employee	Starting Date	Cumulative Vacation Taken as of December 31, 1988	Weekly Salary
Norm Racine	December 21, 1981	11 weeks	$375
Michael Smith	March 6, 1986	2 weeks	500
Phyllis Taylor	August 13, 1987	none	350
Brian Hinsman	December 17, 1986	3 weeks	300
Ann Behan	March 29, 1988	none	400

Compute the liability for vacation pay as of December 31, 1988.

EXERCISE 14–11   (Contingent losses)

Conrad Corporation sells motorcycle helmets. In 1987, Conrad sold 4 million helmets before discovering a significant defect in the helmet's construction. By December 31, 1987, two lawsuits had been filed against Conrad. The first lawsuit, which Conrad has little chance of winning, is expected to settle out of court for $900,000 in January of 1988. The second lawsuit, which is for $400,000, Conrad's attorneys thinks the company has a fifty-fifty chance of winning. What accounting treatment should Conrad give the pending lawsuits in the year-end financial statements? (Include any necessary journal entries.)

EXERCISE 14–12   (Balance sheet classification of liabilities)

Prepare the current liabilities section of the balance sheet for the King Bedding Company on December 31, 1987, from the information appearing below:

(a) Short-term notes payable: arising from purchases of goods, $62,680; arising from loans from banks, $20,000, on which marketable securities valued at $26,100 have been pledged as security; arising from short-term advances by officers, $22,600.
(b) Accounts payable arising from purchase of goods, $59,300.
(c) Employees income taxes payable, $1,584.
(d) First-mortgage serial bonds, $175,000, payable in semiannual installments of $7,000 due on March 1 and September 1 of each year.
(e) Advances received from customers on purchase orders, $4,140.
(f) Estimated expense of meeting warranty for service requirements on merchandise sold, $6,480.

PROBLEMS

PROBLEM 14–1   (Miscellaneous operating payables)

The Marston Corporation closes its books and prepares financial statements on an annual basis. The following information is gathered by the chief accountant to assist in preparing the liability section of the balance sheet:

(a) Property taxes of $45,000 were assessed on the property in May 1987, for the subsequent period of July 1 to June 30. The payment of the taxes is divided into three equal installments, November 1, February 1, and May 1. The November 1 payment was made and charged to Property Tax Expense. No other entries have been made for property taxes relative to the 1987–88 assessment.
(b) The estimated 1987 pretax income for Marston is $629,000. The effective state income tax rate is 10% (applied to pretax income). The effective rate for federal income taxes is estimated at 40% (applied to income after deducting state income taxes). Income tax payments of $280,000 were made by Marston during 1987, including $50,000 as the final payment on 1986 federal income taxes, $20,000 for 1987 state estimated taxes, the balance for 1987 federal estimated taxes.
(c) Taxable sales for 1987 were $7,500,000. The state sales tax rate is 4.5%. Quarterly statements have been filed, and the following tax payments were made with the return.

1st Quarter	$76,000
2nd Quarter	80,000
3rd Quarter	70,000

The balance in the account Sales Tax Payable is $110,800 at December 31, 1987.

Instructions:
(1) Based on the above data, what amounts should be reported on the balance sheet as liabilities at December 31, 1987?
(2) Prepare the necessary adjusting entries to record the liabilities.

PROBLEM 14–2   (Computation of bonus)

Fawn Distributors is considering two different proposals for computing the bonus for its new company president, Brad Berrett. The first plan states that the bonus would be equal to 6% of profits (after the bonus but before taxes have been deducted) exceeding $100,000. The second method bases the bonus on profits after both taxes and the president's bonus have been deducted. It states that the bonus would be 12% of profits above $250,000.

Instructions: Assuming income for 1987 before income tax and bonus of $975,000, and a company tax rate of 40%, compute the bonus under both methods.

PROBLEM 14–3   (Calculation of bonus)

Page Manufacturing Company pays bonuses to its sales manager and two sales agents. The company had income for 1987 of $2,500,000 before bonuses and income tax. Income taxes average 40%.

Instructions: Compute the bonuses assuming:
(1) Sales manager gets 6% and each sales agent gets 5% of income before tax and bonuses.
(2) Each bonus is 12% of net income after income tax and bonuses.
(3) Sales manager gets 12% and each sales agent gets 10% of income after bonuses but before income tax.

PROBLEM 14–4   (Accrued payroll and payroll taxes)

Martina Clothiers' employees are paid on the 10th and 25th of each month for the period ending the previous 5th and 20th respectively. An analysis of the payroll on Thursday, November 5, 1987, revealed the following data:

	Gross Pay	FICA	Federal Income Tax	State Income Tax	Insurance	Net Pay
Office staff salaries .	$11,250	$ 574	$ 1,200	$ 450	$ 270	$ 8,756
Officers' salaries....	28,500	364	5,700	1,500	510	20,426
Sales salaries	18,000	712	3,600	750	390	12,548
Total	$57,750	$1,650	$10,500	$2,700	$1,170	$41,730

It is determined that for the November 5 pay period, no additional employees exceeded the wage base for FICA purposes than had done so in prior pay periods. All of the officers' salaries, 70% of the office staff salaries, and 55% of the sales salaries for the payroll period ending November 5 were paid to employees that had exceeded the wage base for unemployment taxes. Assume the rates in force are as follows: FICA, 7%; federal unemployment tax, .8% and state unemployment tax, 5.4%.

Instructions: Prepare the adjusting entries that would be required at October 31, the end of Martina's fiscal year, to reflect the accrual of the payroll and any related payroll taxes. Separate salary and payroll taxes expense accounts are used for each of the three employee categories: office staff, officers', and sales salaries.

PROBLEM 14–5   (Tax liability)

Mom's Cafe, a new business in town, has asked you for help in calculating and recording its property and sales tax liability. On July 1, 1987, Mom's received notice that property taxes totaling $24,000 were to be paid by October 1, 1987. The property tax was for the period of July 1, 1987 to June 30, 1988. Mom's Cafe had sales of $89,460 in 1987. This amount included sales tax collections. The sales tax rate in the area is 5%. Sales taxes are due on January 31, 1988.

Instructions:
(1) Give the entries to record the accrual, monthly expensing, and payment of property taxes. (Give only one example of the monthly recognition of property tax.) What is the December 31, 1987 balance in the deferred property tax account?
(2) Calculate the amount of sales tax payable as of December 31, 1987. Make the entry needed to record this liability at year end. Also give the entry to record payment of sales tax on January 31, 1988.

PROBLEM 14–6   (Warranty liability)

Darvey Corporation sells stereos under a two-year warranty contract that requires Darvey to replace defective parts and provide free labor on all repairs. During 1987, 850 units were sold at $900 each. In 1988 Darvey sold an additional 900 units at $925. Based on past experience, the estimated two-year warranty costs are $20 for parts and $25 for labor per unit. It is also estimated that 40% of the warranty expenditures will occur in the first year and 60% in the second year.

Actual warranty expenditures were as follows:

	Warranty Costs	
	1988	1989
Stereos sold in 1987	$14,800	$23,000
Stereos sold in 1988	—	16,100

Instructions: Assuming all sales occurred on the last day of the year for both 1987 and 1988, give the necessary journal entries for the years 1987 through 1989. Analyze the warranty liability account for the year ending December 31, 1989 to see if the actual repairs approximate the estimate. Should Darvey revise its warranty estimates?

PROBLEM 14–7   (Warranty liability)

The Rapid Communications Corporation, a client, requests that you compute the appropriate balance for its estimated liability for product warranty account for a statement as of June 30, 1988.

The Rapid Communications Corporation manufactures television tubes and sells them with a six-month warranty under which defective tubes will be replaced without a charge. On December 31, 1987, Estimated Liability for Product

Warranty had a balance of $510,000. By June 30, 1988, this balance had been reduced to $80,250 by debits for estimated net cost of tubes returned that had been sold in 1987.

The company started out in 1988 expecting 8% of the dollar volume of sales to be returned. However, due to the introduction of new models during the year, this estimated percentage of returns was increased to 10% on May 1. It is assumed that no tubes sold during a given month are returned in that month. Each tube is stamped with a date at time of sale so that the warranty may be properly administered. The following table of percentages indicates the likely pattern of sales returns during the six-month period of the warranty, starting with the month following the sale of tubes.

Month Following Sale	Percentage of Total Returns Expected
First	20%
Second	30
Third	20
Fourth through sixth—10% each month	30
	100%

Gross sales of tubes were as follows for the first six months of 1988:

Month	Amount	Month	Amount
January	$3,600,000	April	$2,850,000
February	3,300,000	May	2,000,000
March	4,100,000	June	1,800,000

The company's warranty also covers the payment of freight cost on defective tubes returned and on the new tubes sent out as replacements. This freight cost runs approximately 10% of the sales price of the tubes returned. The manufacturing cost of the tubes is roughly 80% of the sales price, and the salvage value of returned tubes average 15% of their sales price. Returned tubes on hand at December 31, 1987, were thus valued in inventory at 15% of their original sales price.

Instructions: Using the data given, draw up a suitable working-paper schedule for arriving at the balance of the estimated liability for product warranty account and give the proposed adjusting entry.   (AICPA adapted)

PROBLEM 14–8   (Premium liability)

The Cascade Corp. manufactures a special type of low-suds laundry soap. A dish towel is offered as a premium to customers who send in two proof-of-purchase seals from these soap boxes and a remittance of $2. Data for the premium offer are summarized below:

	1987	1988
Soap sales ($2.50 per package)	$2,500,000	$3,125,000
Dish towel purchases ($2.50 per towel)	$130,000	$156,250
Number of dish towels distributed as premiums	40,000	60,000
Number of dish towels expected to be distributed in subsequent periods	7,500	2,000

Mailing costs are $.26 per package.

Instructions:

(1) Give the entries for 1987 and 1988 to record product sales, premium purchases and redemptions, and year-end adjustments.
(2) Present "T" accounts with appropriate amounts as of the end of 1987 and 1988.

PROBLEM 14–9   (Compensated absences)

Hobbs Electronics Inc. has a plan to compensate its employees for certain absences. Each employee can receive five days' sick leave each year plus 10 days' vacation. The benefits carry over for two additional years, after which the provision lapses on a FIFO flow basis. Thus, the maximum accumulation is 45 days. In some cases, the company permits vacations to be taken before they are earned. Payments are made based upon current compensation levels, not on the level in effect when the absence time was earned.

Employee	Days Accrued Jan. 1, 1987	Daily Rate Jan. 1, 1987	Days Earned 1987	Days Taken 1987	Days Accrued Dec. 31, 1987	Daily Rate Dec. 31
A	10	$38	15	10	15	$40
B	--	$44	15	10	5	$50
C	30	$42	7	37	--	Terminated June 15- Rate = $45
D	−5	$36	15	20	−10	$40
E	40	$58	15	5	50	$70
F	Hired July 1- Rate = $40	- - -	8	0	8	$40

Instructions:

(1) How much is the liability for compensated absences at December 31, 1987?
(2) Prepare a summary journal entry to record compensation absence payments during the year and the accrual at the end of the year. Assume the payroll liability account is charged for all payments made during the year for both sickness and vacation leaves. The average rate of compensation for the year may be used to value the hours taken except for Employee C who took leaves at the date of termination. The end-of-year rate should be used to establish the ending liability.

PROBLEM 14–10   (Contingent liabilities)

The Western Supply Co. has several contingent liabilities at December 31, 1987. The following brief description of each liability is obtained by the auditor.

(a) In May 1986, Western Supply became involved in litigation. In December 1987, a judgment for $800,000 was assessed against Western by the court. Western is appealing the amount of the judgment. Attorneys for Western feel it is probable that they can reduce the assessment on appeal by 50%. No entries have been made by Western pending completion of the appeal process, which is expected to take at least a year.

(b) In July 1987, Morgan County brought action against Western for polluting the Jordan River with its waste products. It is reasonably possible that Morgan County will be successful, but the amount of damages Western might have to pay should not exceed $200,000. No entry has been made by Western to reflect the possible loss.

(c) Western Supply has elected to self-insure its fire and casualty risks. At the beginning of the year, the account Reserve for Insurance had a balance of $2,500,000. During 1987, $750,000 was debited to insurance expense and credited to the reserve account. After payment for losses actually sustained in 1987, the reserve account had a balance of $2,800,000 at December 31, 1987. The opening balance was a result of several years of activity similar to 1987.

(d) Western Supply has signed as guarantor for a $50,000 loan by Guaranty Bank to Midwest Parts Inc., a principal supplier to Western. Because of financial problems at Midwest, it is probable that Western Supply will have to pay the $50,000 with only a 40% recovery anticipated from Midwest. No entries have been made to reflect the contingent liability.

Instructions:

(1) What amount should be reported as a liability on the December 31, 1987 balance sheet?

(2) What note disclosure should be included as part of the balance sheet for each of the above items?

(3) Prepare the journal entries necessary to adjust Western's books to reflect your answers in (1) and (2).

PROBLEM 14–11
(Adjusting entries and balance sheet presentation)

The unadjusted trial balance of Herman Company at December 31, 1987, showed the following account balances:

Sales	$427,000
Mortgage Note Payable	80,000
Bank Notes Payable	10,000
Accounts Payable	19,400
Wages Payable	4,000

Additional information:

(a) The Sales account included amounts collected from customers for a 5 percent sales tax. The tax was remitted to the state on January 31, 1988.

(b) The mortgage note is due on March 1, 1988. Interest at 12 percent has been paid through December 31. Herman intended at December 31, 1987, to refinance the note on its due date with a new 5-year mortgage note. In fact, on March 1, 1988, Herman paid $20,000 in cash on the principal balance and refinanced the remaining $60,000.

(c) The bank notes are due over the next four years. The current portion of the notes is $2,500 at December 31, 1987. Interest of $500 has not been accrued. It is to be paid during 1988. *(continued)*

(d) On October 1, 1987, a previous employee filed a suit against Herman, alleging age discrimination and asking for damages of $500,000. At December 31, 1987, Herman's attorney felt that the likelihood of losing the lawsuit was possible but not probable.

(e) During 1987, Herman remitted to the federal government estimated income tax payments of $55,000. The actual taxes for 1987 amounted to $75,000 according to the tax return that was filed in March 1988.

Instructions:

(1) Prepare adjusting journal entries to correct the liability accounts at December 31, 1987. Assume the financial statements will be issued on April 1, 1988.

(2) Prepare the current and noncurrent liability sections of the December 31, 1987 balance sheet.

15

Accounting for Long-Term Debt Securities

The use of long-term debt securities to finance new products, expand operations, acquire other companies, or for a host of other reasons is common practice in today's business environment. This is especially true during periods of low interest rates, allowing companies to use relatively "cheap" money not only for business expansion, but also to retire existing higher-cost debt or, in some cases, to retire equity securities. For example, in 1986, interest rates reached their lowest level in over eight years, resulting in a record number of new corporate bond issues.

In addition to bonds, the **long-term debt** classification includes mortgages, leases, pensions, and other types of long-term obligations. This chapter explains the relative advantages and disadvantages of debt and equity financing, and specifically focuses on how to account for bonds and long-term notes. In discussing bonds, both the liability of the issuer (bonds payable) and the asset of the investor (bond investment) are explained so that the total picture can be seen at one time. Specific issues related to leases and pensions are deferred to Chapters 21 and 22, respectively.

FINANCING WITH LONG-TERM DEBT

The long-term financing of a corporation is accomplished either through the issuance of long-term debt instruments, usually bonds or notes, or through the sale of additional stock. The issuance of bonds or notes instead of stock may be preferred by management and stockholders for the following reasons:

1. Present owners continue in control of the corporation.
2. Interest is a deductible expense in arriving at taxable income, while dividends are not.

3. Current market rates of interest may be favorable relative to stock market prices.
4. The charge against earnings for interest may be less than the amount of dividends that might be expected by shareholders.

There are, however, certain limitations and disadvantages of financing with long-term debt securities. Debt financing is possible only when a company is in satisfactory financial condition and can offer adequate security to creditors. Furthermore, interest must be paid regardless of the company's earnings and financial position. If a company has operating losses and is unable to raise sufficient cash to meet periodic interest payments, debt security holders may take legal action to assume control of company assets.

A complicating factor is that the distinction between debt and equity securities may become fuzzy. Usually, a debt instrument has a fixed interest rate and a definite maturity date when the principal must be repaid. Also, holders of debt instruments generally have no voting privileges. An equity security, on the other hand, has no fixed repayment obligation or maturity date, and dividends on stock become obligations only after being formally declared by the board of directors of a corporation. In addition, common stockholders generally have voting and other ownership privileges. The problem is that certain convertible debt securities have many equity characteristics, and some preferred stocks have many of the characteristics of debt. This makes it important to recognize the distinction between debt and equity and to provide the accounting treatment that is most appropriate under the specific circumstances.

ACCOUNTING FOR BONDS

The main distinction between bonds and long-term notes is the length of time to maturity. Generally, bonds carry a maturity date five years or more after issue, and some bonds do not mature for twenty-five years or more. Long-term notes, however, generally mature in a period of one to five years from the issuance date. Other characteristics of bonds and long-term notes are usually quite similar. Therefore, in the discussion that follows, the accounting and reporting principles relating to bonds can also be applied to long-term notes.

There are three main considerations in accounting for bonds:

1. Recording their issuance or purchase.
2. Recognizing the applicable interest during the life of the bonds.
3. Accounting for the retirement of bonds, either at maturity or prior to the maturity date.

Before these considerations are discussed, the nature of bonds and the determination of bond market prices will be reviewed.

Nature of Bonds

The power of a corporation to create bond indebtedness is found in the corporation laws of a state and may be specifically granted by charter. In some cases formal authorization by a majority of stockholders is required before a board of directors can approve a bond issue.

Borrowing by means of bonds involves the issuance of certificates of indebtedness. **Bond certificates**, commonly referred to simply as "bonds," are frequently issued in denominations of $1,000, referred to as the **face amount, par value**, or **maturity value** of the bond, although in some cases, bonds are issued in varying denominations.

The group contract between the corporation and the bondholders is known as the **bond indenture**. The indenture details the rights and obligations of the contracting parties, indicates the property pledged as well as the protection offered on the loan, and names the bank or trust company that is to represent the bondholders.

Bonds may be sold by the company directly to investors, or they may be underwritten by investment bankers or a syndicate. The underwriters may agree to purchase the entire bond issue or that part of the issue which is not sold by the company, or they may agree simply to manage the sale of the security on a commission basis, often referred to as a "best efforts" basis.

Most companies attempt to sell their bonds to underwriters to avoid incurring a loss after the bonds are placed on the market. An interesting example of this occurred a few years ago when IBM Corporation went to the bond market for the first time and issued a record $1 billion worth of bonds and long-term notes. After the issue was released by IBM to the underwriters, interest rates soared as the Federal Reserve Bank sharply increased its rediscount rate. The market price of the IBM securities fell, and the brokerage houses and investment bankers participating in the underwriting incurred a loss in excess of $50 million on the sale of the securities to investors.

Issuers of Bonds. Bonds and similar debt instruments are issued by private corporations, the United States Government, state, county and local governments, school districts, and government sponsored organizations such as the Federal Home Loan Bank and the Federal National Mortgage Association. The total amount of debt issued by these organizations is now well in excess of $1 trillion.

The U.S. debt includes not only Treasury bonds, but also Treasury bills, which are notes with less than one year to maturity date, and Treasury notes, which mature in one to seven years. Both Treasury bills and Treasury notes are in demand in the marketplace, perhaps even more so in recent years than Treasury bonds.

Debt securities issued by state, county, and local governments and their agencies are collectively referred to as **municipal debt.** A unique feature of municipal debt is that the interest received by investors from such securities is exempt from federal income tax. Because of this tax advantage, "municipals" generally carry lower interest rates than debt securities of other issuers, enabling these governmental units to borrow at favorable interest rates. The tax exemption is in reality a subsidy granted by the federal government to encourage capital investment in state and local governments.

Types of Bonds. Bonds may be categorized in many different ways, depending on the characteristics of a particular bond issue. The major distinguishing features of bonds are identified and discussed in the following sections.

Term Versus Serial Bonds. Bonds that mature on a single date are called **term bonds.** When bonds mature in installments, they are referred to as **serial bonds.** Serial bonds are less common than term bonds, and the special considerations in accounting for serial bonds are covered in the appendix to this chapter.

Secured Versus Unsecured Bonds. Bonds issued by private corporations may be either secured or unsecured. **Secured bonds** offer protection to investors by providing some form of security, such as a mortgage on real estate or a pledge of other collateral. A **first-mortgage bond** represents a first claim against the property of a corporation in the event of the company's inability to meet bond interest and principal payments. A **second-mortgage bond** is a secondary claim ranking only after the claim of the first-mortgage bonds or senior issue has been completely satisfied. A **collateral trust bond** is usually secured by stocks and bonds of other corporations owned by the issuing company. Such securities are generally transferred to a trustee who holds them as collateral on behalf of the bondholders and, if necessary, will sell them to satisfy the bondholders' claim.

Unsecured bonds are not protected by the pledge of any specific assets and are frequently termed **debenture bonds,** or **debentures.** Holders of debenture bonds simply rank as general creditors along with other unsecured parties. The risk involved in these securities varies with the financial strength of the debtor. Debentures issued by a strong company may involve little risk; debentures issued by a weak company whose properties are already heavily mortgaged may involve considerable risk. Quality ratings for bonds are published by both Moody's and Standard and Poor's investment services companies. For example, Moody's bond ratings range from prime, or highest quality (Aaa) to default (C) for a very high risk bond. Standard and Poor's range is from AAA to D.

Registered Versus Bearer (Coupon) Bonds. **Registered bonds** call for the registry of the owner's name on the corporation books. Transfer of bond ownership is similar to that for stock. When a bond is sold, the corporate transfer agent cancels the bond certificate surrendered by the seller and issues a new certificate to the buyer. Interest checks are mailed periodically to the bondholders of record. **Bearer or coupon bonds** are not recorded in the name of the owner, title to such bonds passing with delivery. Each bond is accompanied by coupons for individual interest payments covering the life of the issue. Coupons are clipped by the owner of the bond and presented to a bank for deposit or collection. The issue of bearer bonds eliminates the need for recording bond ownership changes and preparing and mailing periodic interest checks. But coupon bonds fail to offer the bondholder the protection found in registered bonds in the event the bonds are lost or stolen. In some cases, bonds provide interest coupons but require registry as to principal. Here, ownership safeguards are provided, while the time-consuming routines involved in making interest payments are avoided. Most bonds of recent issue are registered.

Zero-Interest Bonds and Bonds with Floating Interest Rates. In recent years, some companies have issued long-term debt securities that do not bear interest. Instead, these securities sell at a significant discount that provides an investor with a total interest payoff at maturity. These bonds are known as **zero-interest bonds** or **deep-discount bonds**. On the other hand, some bonds and long-term notes have been issued recently with **floating interest rates**. Because of the wide fluctuations in interest rates that have occurred in the past few years, a floating interest rate security reduces the risk to the investor when interest rates are rising and to the issuer when interest rates are falling.

Convertible and Commodity-Backed Bonds. Bonds may provide for their conversion into some other security at the option of the bondholder. Such bonds are known as **convertible bonds**. The conversion feature generally permits the owner of bonds to exchange them for common stock. The bondholder is thus able to convert the claim into an ownership interest if corporate operations prove successful and conversion becomes attractive; in the meantime the special rights of a creditor are maintained. Bonds may also be redeemable in terms of commodities, such as oil or precious metals. These types of bonds are sometimes referred to as **commodity-backed bonds** or **asset-linked bonds**.

Callable Bonds. Bond indentures frequently give the issuing company the right to call and retire the bonds prior to their maturity. Such bonds are termed **callable bonds**. When a corporation wishes to reduce its outstanding indebtedness, bondholders are notified of the portion of the issue to be surrendered, and they are paid in accordance with call provisions. Interest does not accrue after the call date.

Market Price of Bonds

The market price of bonds varies with the safety of the investment and the current market interest rate for similar instruments. When the financial condition and earnings of a corporation are such that payment of interest and principal on bond indebtedness is virtually assured, the interest rate a company must offer to dispose of a bond issue is relatively low. As the risk factor increases, a higher interest return is necessary to attract investors. The amount of interest paid on bonds is a specified percentage of the face value. This percentage is termed the **stated or contract rate**. This rate, however, may not be the same as the prevailing or **market rate** for bonds of similar quality and length of time to maturity at the time the issue is sold. Furthermore, the market rate constantly fluctuates. These factors often result in a difference between bond face values and the prices at which the bonds actually sell on the market.

The purchase of bonds at face value implies agreement between the bond stated rate of interest and the prevailing market rate of interest. If the stated rate exceeds the market rate, the bonds will sell at a **premium**; if the stated rate is less than the market rate, the bonds will sell at a **discount**. The premium or the discount is the amount needed to adjust the stated rate of interest to the actual market rate of interest for that particular bond. Thus, the stated rate adjusted for the premium or the discount on the purchase gives the actual rate of return on the bonds, known as the **yield** or **effective interest rate**. A declining market rate of interest subsequent to issuance of the bonds results in an increase in the market value of the bonds; a rising market rate of interest results in a decrease in their market value.

Bonds are quoted on the market as a percentage of face value. Thus, a bond quotation of 96.5 means the market price is 96.5% of face value, or at a discount; a bond quotation of 104 means the market price is 104% of face value, or at a premium. U.S. Government note and bond quotations are made in 32's rather than 100's. Thus a Government bond selling at 98.16 is selling at 98 $\frac{16}{32}$, or in terms of decimal equivalents, 98.5%.

The market price of a bond at any date can be determined by discounting the maturity value of the bond and each remaining interest payment at the yield or effective rate of interest for similar debt on that date.

The present value tables in Chapter 6 can be used for computing bond market price.

To illustrate the computation of a bond market price from the tables, assume 10-year, 8% bonds of $100,000 are to be sold on the bond issue date. Further assume that the market interest rate for bonds of similar quality and maturity is 10%, compounded semiannually.

The computation of the market price of the bonds may be divided into two parts:

(1) Present value of principal (maturity value)

Maturity value of bonds after 10 years or 20 semiannual periods = $100,000
Effective interest rate = 10% per year, or 5% per semiannual period
Present value of $100,000 discounted at 5% for 20 periods:

$\quad$ PV = R (PVF$_{\overline{n}|i}$) = $100,000 (Table II$_{\overline{20}|5}$) = $100,000 (.3769) = $\qquad$ $37,690

(2) Present value of 20 interest payments

Semiannual payment, 4% of $100,000 = $4,000
Effective interest rate, 10% per year, or 5% per semiannual period
Present value of 20, $4,000 payments, discounted at 5%:

$\quad$ PV = R (PVAF$_{\overline{n}|i}$) = $4,000 (Table IV$_{\overline{20}|5}$) = $4,000 (12.4622) = $\qquad$ $\underline{49,849}$

Total present value (market price) of bond .... $\underline{\underline{\$87,539}}$

The market price for the bonds would be $87,539, the sum of the present values of the two parts. Because the effective interest rate is higher than the stated interest rate, the bonds would sell at a $12,461 discount at the issuance date. It should be noted that if the effective interest rate on these bonds were 8% instead of 10%, the sum of the present values of the two parts would be $100,000, meaning that the bonds would sell at their face amount, or at par. If the effective interest rate were less than 8%, the market price of the bonds would be more than $100,000, and the bonds would sell at a premium.

Specially adapted present value tables are available to determine directly the price to be paid for bonds if they are to provide a certain return. A portion of such a bond table is illustrated on page 642.

Note that the market price from the bond table for 8% bonds to yield 10% in 10 years is $87,539, the same amount as computed using present value tables. Also, the bond table shows that if the effective interest rate were 8%, the bonds would sell at par, $100,000. If the effective rate were 7.5%, the market price would be $103,476.

The bond table can also be used to determine the effective rate of interest on a bond acquired at a certain price. To illustrate, assume that a $1,000, 8% bond due in 10 years is selling at $951. Reference to the column

"10 years" for $95,070 shows an annual return of 8.75% is provided on an investment of $950.70.

Bond Table
Values to the Nearest Dollar of 8% Bond for $100,000
Interest Payable Semiannually

Yield	8 years	8½ years	9 years	9½ years	10 years
7.00	$106,046	$106,325	$106,595	$106,855	$107,107
7.25	104,495	104,699	104,896	105,090	105,272
7.50	102,971	103,100	103,232	103,360	103,476
7.75	101,472	101,537	101,595	101,658	101,718
8.00	100,000	100,000	100,000	100,000	100,000
8.25	98,552	98,494	98,437	98,372	98,325
8.50	97,141	97,012	96,893	96,787	96,678
8.75	95,746	95,568	95,398	95,232	95,070
9.00	94,383	94,147	93,920	93,703	93,496
9.25	93,042	92,757	92,480	92,214	91,953
9.50	91,723	91,380	91,055	90,751	90,452
9.75	90,350	89,960	89,588	89,238	88,902
10.00	89,162	88,726	88,310	87,914	87,539

Issuance of Bonds

Bonds may be sold directly to investors by the issuer or they may be sold on the open market through securities exchanges or through investment bankers. Over 50% of bond issues are privately placed with large investors. Regardless of how placed, when bonds are issued (sold), the issuer must record the receipt of cash and recognize the long-term liability. The purchaser must record the payment of cash and the bond investment.

An issuer normally records bonds at their face value—the amount that the company must pay at maturity. Hence, when bonds are issued at an amount other than face value, a bond discount or premium account is established for the difference between the cash received and the bond face value. The premium is added to or the discount is subtracted from the bond face value to report the bonds at their present value. Although an investor could also record the investment in bonds at their face value by using a premium or discount account, traditionally investors record their bond investments at cost, that is, the face value net of any premium or discount. Cost includes brokerage fees and any other costs incident to the purchase.

Bonds issued or acquired in exchange for noncash assets or services are recorded at the fair market value of the bonds, unless the value of the exchanged assets or services is more clearly determinable. A difference between the face value of the bonds and the cash value of the bonds or the value of the property acquired is recognized as bond discount or bond premium. When bonds and other securities are acquired for a lump sum, an apportionment of such cost among the securities is required.

As indicated earlier, bonds may be issued at par, at a discount, or at a premium. They may be issued on an interest payment date or between interest dates, which calls for the recognition of accrued interest. Each of these situations will be illustrated using the following data: $100,000, 8%, 10-year bonds are issued. Semiannual interest of $4,000 ($100,000 × .08 × $6/12$) is payable on January 1 and July 1.

Bonds Issued at Par on Interest Date. When bonds are issued at par, or face value, on an interest date, there is no premium or discount to be recognized nor any accrued interest at the date of issuance. The appropriate entries for the first year, on the issuer's books and on the investor's books, assuming the data in the preceding paragraph and issuance on January 1 at par value, would be:

		Issuer's Books			Investor's Books		
Jan.	1	Cash....................	100,000		Bond Investment...........	100,000	
		Bonds Payable.........		100,000	Cash		100,000
July	1	Interest Expense	4,000		Cash	4,000	
		Cash.................		4,000	Interest Revenue........		4,000
Dec. 31		Interest Expense	4,000		Interest Receivable.........	4,000	
		Interest Payable........		4,000	Interest Revenue.........		4,000

Bonds Issued at Discount on Interest Date. Now assume that the bonds were issued on January 1 but that the effective or market rate of interest was 10%, requiring recognition of a discount of $12,461 ($100,000 − $87,539). The appropriate entries on January 1 are shown below. The interest entries on July 1 and December 31 are illustrated in a later section that discusses the amortization of discounts and premiums.

		Issuer's Books			Investor's Books		
Jan.	1	Cash....................	87,539		Bond Investment...........	87,539	
		Bond Discount	12,461		Cash		87,539
		Bonds Payable.........		100,000			

Bonds Issued at Premium on Interest Date. Again using the data above, assume that the bonds were sold at an effective interest rate of 7%, resulting in a premium of $7,107. In this case the entries on January 1 would be:

	Issuer's Books			Investor's Books		
Cash....................	107,107		Bond Investment...........	107,107	
Bond Premium		7,107	Cash		107,107
Bonds Payable.........		100,000			

Bonds Issued at Par Between Interest Dates. When bonds are issued or sold between interest dates, an adjustment is made for the interest accrued between the last interest payment date and the date of the transaction. A buyer of the bonds pays the amount of accrued interest along with the purchase price and then receives the accrued interest plus interest earned subsequent to the purchase date when the next interest payment is made. This practice avoids the problem an issuer of bonds would have in trying to split interest payments for a given period between two or more owners of the securities. To illustrate, if the bonds in the previous example were issued at par on March 1, the appropriate entries would be:

	Issuer's Books			Investor's Books		
Mar. 1	Cash....................	101,333		Bond Investment...........	100,000	
	Bonds Payable.........		100,000	Interest Receivable.........	1,333	
	Interest Payable........		1,333*	Cash		101,333
	*($100,000 × .08 × 2/12)					
July 1	Interest Expense	2,667*		Cash	4,000	
	Interest Payable..........	1,333		Interest Receivable.......		1,333
	Cash...................		4,000	Interest Revenue.........		2,667
	*($100,000 × .08 × 4/12)					

Alternatively, as illustrated below, the accrued interest could be initially credited to Interest Expense by the issuer and debited to Interest Revenue by the investor. Then when the full interest payment is made, the proper amount of interest will be recognized.

	Issuer's Books			Investor's Books		
Mar. 1	Cash....................	101,333		Bond Investment...........	100,000	
	Bonds Payable.........		100,000	Interest Revenue...........	1,333	
	Interest Expense		1,333	Cash		101,333
July 1	Interest Expense	4,000		Cash	4,000	
	Cash..................		4,000	Interest Revenue.........		4,000

Bond Issuance Costs. The issuance of bonds normally involves costs to the issuer for legal services, printing and engraving, taxes and underwriting. Traditionally, these costs have been either (1) summarized separately as **bond issuance costs**, classified as deferred charges, and charged to expense over the life of the bond issue, or (2) offset against any premium or added to any discount arising on the issuance and thus netted against the face value of the bonds. The Accounting Principles Board in Opinion No. 21 recommended that these costs be reported on the balance sheet as deferred charges.[1] However, in Statement of Concepts No. 3, the FASB stated that such costs fail to meet the definition of assets adopted by the Board.[2] The authors agree with the position of the FASB, and favor netting the issuance costs against the bonds payable as part of the premium or discount on the

---

[1]*Opinions of the Accounting Principles Board, No. 21,* "Interest on Receivables and Payables" (New York: American Institute of Certified Public Accountants, 1971), par. 16.

[2]*Statement of Financial Accounting Concepts No. 3,* "Elements of Financial Statements of Business Enterprises" (Stamford: Financial Accounting Standards Board, December 1980), par. 161.

bonds. Concepts Statements do not establish GAAP, however, and until such time as the FASB addresses the issue, the APB Opinion governs generally accepted practice.

Accounting for Bond Interest

With coupon bonds, cash is paid by the issuing company in exchange for interest coupons on the interest dates. Payments on coupons may be made by the company directly to bondholders, or payments may be cleared through a bank or other disbursing agent. Subsidiary records with bond-holders are not maintained since coupons are redeemable by bearers. In the case of registered bonds, interest checks are mailed either by the company or its agent. When bonds are registered, the bonds account requires subsidiary ledger support. The subsidiary ledger shows holdings by individuals and changes in such holdings. Checks are sent to bond-holders of record as of the interest payment dates.

When bonds are issued at a premium or discount, the market acts to adjust the stated interest rate to a market or effective interest rate. Because of the initial premium or discount, the periodic interest payments made over the bond life by the issuer to the investors do not represent the complete revenue and expense for the periods involved. An adjustment to the cash transfer for the periodic write-off of the premium or discount is necessary to reflect the effective interest rate being incurred or earned on the bonds. This adjustment is referred to as **bond premium** or **discount amortization.** The periodic adjustment of bonds results in a gradual adjust-ment of the carrying value toward the bond's face value.

A premium on issued bonds recognizes that the stated interest rate is higher than the market interest rate. Amortization of the premium reduces the interest revenue or expense below the amount of cash trans-ferred. A discount on issued bonds recognizes that the stated interest rate is lower than the market interest rate. Amortization of the discount increases the amount of interest revenue or expense above the amount of cash transferred.

Two principal methods are used to amortize the premium or discount: (1) the straight-line method and (2) the effective-interest method.

Straight-Line Method. The **straight-line method** provides for the recog-nition of an equal amount of premium or discount amortization each period. The amount of monthly amortization is determined by dividing the pre-mium or discount at purchase or issuance by the number of months remain-ing to the bond maturity date. For example, if a 10-year, 10% bond issue with a maturity value of $200,000 was sold on the issuance date at 103, the $6,000 premium would be amortized evenly over the 120 months until maturity, or at a rate of $50 per month, ($6,000 ÷ 120). If the bonds were sold three months after the issuance date, the $6,000 premium would be amortized evenly over 117 months, or a rate of $51.28 per month, ($6,000 ÷ 117). The amortization period is always the time from original sale to maturity. The premium amortization would reduce both interest expense on the issuer's books and interest revenue on the investor's books. A discount amortization would have the opposite results: both accounts would be increased.

To illustrate the accounting for bond interest using straight-line amortization, consider again the earlier example of the $100,000, 8%, 10-year bonds issued on January 1. When sold at a $12,461 discount, the appropriate entries to record interest on July 1 and Dec. 31 would be as follows:

	Issuer's Books			Investor's Books		
July 1	Interest Expense	4,623		Cash	4,000	
	Bond Discount		623	Bond Investment	623	
	Cash		4,000	Interest Revenue		4,623

($100,000 × .08 × 6/12 = $4,000 cash;
$12,461 ÷ 120 × 6 months = $623 (rounded) discount amortization)

	Issuer's Books			Investor's Books		
Dec. 31	Interest Expense	4,623		Interest Receivable	4,000	
	Bond Discount	623		Bond Investment	623	
	Interest Payable		4,000	Interest Revenue		4,623

Note that the discount amortization has the effect of increasing the effective interest rate from the 8% stated rate to the 10% market rate of interest that the bonds were sold to yield. Over the life of the bond, the $12,461 discount will be charged to interest expense for the issuer and will be recognized as interest revenue by the investor.

Also note that the amortization of premium or discount may be recognized only once a year prior to preparing financial statements instead of with each interest payment. If this were the case in the preceding illustration, the entries would be:

	Issuer's Books			Investor's Books		
July 1	Interest Expense	4,000		Cash	4,000	
	Cash		4,000	Interest Revenue		4,000
Dec. 31	Interest Expense	5,246		Interest Receivable	4,000	
	Bond Discount		1,246	Bond Investment	1,246	
	Interest Payable		4,000	Interest Revenue		5,246

($12,461 ÷ 120 × 12 months = $1,246 (rounded) discount amortization for year)

Because the results are identical, many companies only make the amortization entry once a year.

To illustrate the entries that would be required to amortize a bond premium, consider again the situation where the 8% bonds were sold to yield 7%, or $107,107. The $7,107 premium would be amortized on a straight-line basis, at year-end, as follows:

	Issuer's Books			Investor's Books		
July 1	Interest Expense	4,000		Cash	4,000	
	Cash		4,000	Interest Revenue		4,000
Dec. 31	Interest Expense	3,289		Interest Receivable	4,000	
	Bond Premium	711		Bond Investment		711
	Interest Payable		4,000	Interest Revenue		3,289

($7,107 ÷ 120 × 12 months = $711 (rounded) premium amortization for year)

The amortization of the premium has the effect of reducing the amount of interest expense or interest revenue to the actual yield or market rate of the bonds, 7%.

Effective-Interest Method. The **effective-interest method** of amortization uses a uniform interest rate based on a changing investment balance and provides for an increasing premium or discount amortization each period. In order to use this method, the effective interest rate for the bonds must be known. This is the rate of interest at bond issuance that discounts the maturity value of the bonds and the periodic interest payments to the market price of the bonds. This rate is used to determine the effective revenue or expense to be recorded on the books.

[handwritten margin note: Compute amount of interest exp. — force amount of amortization]

To illustrate the amortization of a bond discount using the effective-interest method, consider once again the $100,000, 8%, 10-year bonds sold for $87,539, based on an effective interest rate of 10%.

The discount amortization for the first six months using the effective-interest method would be computed as follows:

Investment balance at beginning of first period	$87,539
Effective rate per semiannual period	5%
Stated rate per semiannual period	4%
Interest amount based on effective rate ($87,539 × .05)	$ 4,377
Interest payment based on stated rate ($100,000 × .04)	4,000
Discount amortization—difference between interest based on effective rate and stated rate	$ 377

This difference is the discount amortization for the first period using the interest method. For the second semiannual period, the bond carrying value increases by the discount amortization. The amortization for the second semiannual period would be computed as follows:

Investment balance at beginning of second period ($87,539 + $377)	$87,916
Interest amount based on effective rate ($87,916 × .05)	$ 4,396
Interest payment based on stated rate ($100,000 × .04)	4,000
Discount amortization—difference between interest based on effective rate and stated rate	$ 396

The amount of interest to be recognized each period is computed at a uniform rate on an increasing balance. This results in an increasing discount amortization over the life of the bonds, which is graphically demonstrated and compared with straight-line amortization below.

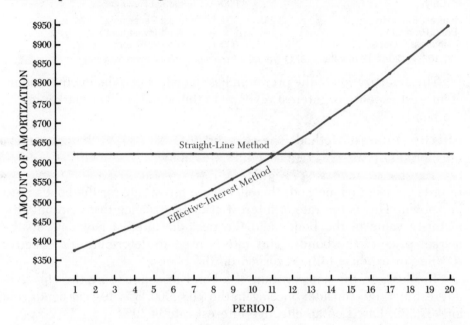

The entries for amortizing the discount would be the same as those shown for straight-line amortization; only the amounts would be different.

Premium amortization would be computed in a similar way except that the interest payment based on the stated interest rate would be higher than the interest amount based on the effective rate. For example, assume that the $100,000, 8%, 10-year bonds were sold on the issuance date for $107,107, thus providing an effective interest rate of 7%. The premium amortization for the first and second six-month periods would be computed as follows (amounts are rounded to the nearest dollar):

Investment balance at beginning of first period...........................	$107,107
Effective rate per semiannual period......................................	3.5%
Stated rate per semiannual period.......................................	4.0%
Interest payment based on stated rate ($100,000 × .04)....................	$ 4,000
Interest amount based on effective rate ($107,107 × .035).................	3,749
Premium amortization—difference between interest based on stated rate and effective rate...	$ 251
Investment balance at beginning of second period ($107,107 − $251)........	$106,856
Interest payment based on stated rate ($100,000 × .04)....................	$ 4,000
Interest amount based on effective rate ($106,856 × .035).................	3,740
Premium amortization—difference between interest based on stated rate and effective rate...	$ 260

As illustrated, as the investment or liability balance is reduced by the premium amortization, the interest, based on the effective rate, also decreases. The difference between the interest payment and the effective interest amount increases in a manner similar to discount amortization. Bond amortization tables may be prepared to determine the periodic adjustments to the bond carrying value, i.e., the present value of the bond. A partial bond amortization table is illustrated below.

Amortization of Bond Premium — Effective-Interest Method
$100,000, 10-Year Bonds, Interest at 8% Payable Semiannually,
Sold at $107,107 to Yield 7%

Interest Payment	A Interest Paid (.04 × $100,000)	B Interest Expense (.035 × Bond Carrying Value)	C Premium Amortization (A − B)	D Unamortized Premium (D − C)	E Bond Carrying Value ($100,000 + D)
				$7,107	$107,107
1	$4,000	$3,749 (.035 × $107,107)	$251	6,856	106,856
2	4,000	3,740 (.035 × $106,856)	260	6,596	106,596
3	4,000	3,731 (.035 × $106,596)	269	6,327	106,327
4	4,000	3,721 (.035 × $106,327)	279	6,048	106,048
5	4,000	3,712 (.035 × $106,048)	288	5,760	105,760

Because the effective-interest method adjusts the stated interest rate to an effective interest rate, it is theoretically more accurate as an amortization method than is the straight-line method. Note that the total amortization is the same under either method; only the interim amounts differ. Since the issuance of APB Opinion No. 21, the effective-interest method is the recommended amortization method. However, the straight-line method may be used by a company if the interim results of using it do not differ materially from the amortization using the effective-interest method.[3]

Retirement of Bonds at Maturity

Bonds always include a specified termination or maturity date. At that time, the issuer must pay the current investors the maturity or face value of the bonds. When bond discount or premium and issuance costs have been properly amortized over the life of the bonds, bond retirement simply calls for elimination of the liability or the investment by a cash transaction, illustrated as follows.

Issuer's Books			Investor's Books		
Bonds Payable.....................	100,000		Cash......................	100,000	
Cash............................		100,000	Bond Investment.........		100,000

[3]*APB Opinion No. 21*, par. 15.

There is no recognition of any gain or loss on retirement since the carrying value is equal to the maturity value, which is also equal to the market value of the bonds at that point in time.

Any bonds not presented for payment at their maturity date should be removed from the bonds payable balance on the issuer's books and reported separately as Matured Bonds Payable; these are reported as a current liability except when they are to be paid out of a bond retirement fund. Interest does not accrue on matured bonds not presented for payment. If a bond retirement fund is used to pay off a bond issue, any cash remaining in the fund may be returned to the cash account.

Extinguishment of Debt Prior to Maturity

When debt is retired prior to the maturity date of the obligation, a gain or loss must be recognized for the difference between the carrying value of the debt security and the amount paid.[4] This gain or loss is classified as an **early extinguishment of debt** and, according to FASB Statement No. 4, is to be reported as an extraordinary item on the income statement.[5]

The problems that arise in retiring bonds or other forms of long-term debt prior to maturity are described in the following sections. Bonds may be retired prior to maturity in one of the following ways:

1. Bonds may be **redeemed** by the issuer by purchasing the bonds on the open market or by exercising the call provision that is frequently included in bond indentures;
2. Bonds may be **converted**, i.e., exchanged for other securities; or
3. Bonds may be **refinanced** (sometimes called "refunded") by using the proceeds from the sale of a new bond issue to retire outstanding bonds.

Another form of early extinguishment of debt, called **in-substance defeasance**, will also be discussed. Unlike redemption, conversion, and refinancing, in-substance defeasance does not involve the actual retirement of bonds.

Redemption by Purchase of Bonds on the Market. Corporations frequently purchase their own bonds on the market when prices or other

---

[4]*Opinions of the Accounting Principles Board, No. 26*, "Early Extinguishment of Debt" (New York: American Institute of Certified Public Accountants, 1972), par. 20.

[5]*Statement of Financial Accounting Standards No. 4*, "Reporting Gains and Losses from Extinguishment of Debt" (Stamford: Financial Accounting Standards Board, 1975), par. 8. Note that an exception to the extraordinary classification is made if the early termination is necessary to satisfy bond retirement (sinking) fund requirements within a one-year period; see *Statement of Financial Accounting Standards No. 64*, "Extinguishment of Debt Made to Satisfy Sinking-Fund Requirements" (Stamford: Financial Accounting Standards Board, 1982), par. 3.

factors make such actions desirable. When bonds are purchased, amortization of bond premium or discount and issue costs should be brought up to date. Purchase by the issuer calls for the cancellation of the bond face value together with any related premium, discount, or issue costs as of the purchase date.

To illustrate a bond purchase prior to maturity, assume that $100,000, 8% bonds of Triad Inc. are not held until maturity, but are sold back to the issuer on February 1, 1988, at 97 plus accrued interest. The book value of the bonds on both the issuer's and investor's books is $97,700 as of January 1. Discount amortization has been recorded at $50 a month using the straight-line method. Interest payment dates on the bonds are November 1 and May 1; accrued interest adjustments are reversed. Entries on both the issuer's and investor's books at the time of purchase would be as follows:

Issuer's Books

Feb. 1	Interest Expense..		50	
	Discount on Bonds Payable.............................			50
	To record discount amortization for January, 1988.			
1	Bonds Payable (or Treasury Bonds)		100,000	
	Interest Expense...		2,000	
	Discount on Bonds Payable.............................			2,250
	Cash...			99,000
	Gain on Bond Reacquisition.............................			750
	To record purchase of bonds and payment of three months' interest.			

Computation:

Book value of bonds, January 1, 1988....................	$97,700
Discount amortization for January........................	50
Book value of bonds, February 1, 1988...................	$97,750
Purchase price	97,000
Gain on purchase.......................................	$ 750

Interest expense for 3 months:
$100,000 × .08 × ¼ = $2,000

Investor's Books

Feb. 1	Investment in Triad Inc. Bonds		50	
	Interest Revenue			50
	To record discount amortization for January, 1988.			
1	Cash..		99,000	
	Loss on Sale of Bonds		750	
	Investment in Triad Inc. Bonds			97,750
	Interest Revenue			2,000
	To record sale of bonds and receipt of three months' interest.			

Redemption by Exercise of Call Provision. A call provision gives the issuer the option of retiring bonds prior to maturity. Frequently the call must be made on an interest payment date, and no further interest accrues on the bonds not presented at this time. When only a part of an issue is to be redeemed, the bonds called may be determined by lot.

The inclusion of call provisions in a bond agreement is a feature favoring the issuer. The company is in a position to terminate the bond agreement and eliminate future interest charges whenever its financial position makes such action feasible. Furthermore, the company is protected in the event of a fall in the market interest rate by being able to retire the old issue from proceeds of a new issue paying a lower rate of interest. A bond contract normally requires payment of a premium if bonds are called. A bondholder is thus offered special compensation if the investment is terminated early.

When bonds are called, the difference between the amount paid and the bond carrying value is reported as a gain or a loss on both the issuer's and investor's books. Any interest paid at the time of the call is recorded as a debit to Interest Expense on the issuer's books and a credit to Interest Revenue on the investor's books. The entries to be made are the same as illustrated previously for the purchase of bonds by the issuer.

Convertible Bonds. The issuance of **convertible debt securities**, most frequently bonds, has become increasingly popular.[6] These securities raise specific questions as to the nature of the securities, i.e., whether they should be considered debt or equity securities, the valuation of the conversion feature, and the treatment of any gain or loss on conversion.

Convertible debt securities usually have the following features:[7]

1. An interest rate lower than the issuer could establish for nonconvertible debt.
2. An initial conversion price higher than the market value of the common stock at time of issuance.
3. A call option retained by the issuer.

The popularity of these securities may be attributed to the advantages to both an issuer and a holder. An issuer is able to obtain financing at a lower interest rate because of the value of the conversion feature to the holder. Because of the call provision, an issuer is in a position to exert influence upon the holders to exchange the debt for equity securities if stock values increase; the issuer has had the use of relatively low interest rate financing if stock values do not increase. On the other hand, the holder has a debt instrument that, barring default, assures the return of invest-

---

[6]See Leslie Pittel, "Playing Safe—and Sporty, Too," *Forbes* (Oct. 22, 1984), pp. 248–252.

[7]*Opinions of the Accounting Principles Board, No. 14,* "Accounting for Convertible Debt and Debt Issued with Stock Purchase Warrants" (New York: American Institute of Certified Public Accountants, 1969), par. 3.

ment plus a fixed return, and at the same time offers an option to transfer his or her interest to equity capital should such transfer become attractive.

Many convertible bond issues place no restriction on when an issuer can call in bonds, and interest accrued on such bonds is sometimes absorbed in a conversion and not paid to the investor. Thus, a company can have the use of interest-free money as a result of calling in bonds prior to the first interest payment. Widespread use of early call provisions in the early 1980s led some investors to demand a provision restricting exercise of the call provision for a specified time period.[8]

Differences of opinion exist as to whether convertible debt securities should be treated by an issuer solely as debt, or whether part of the proceeds received from the issuance of debt should be recognized as equity capital. One view holds that the debt and the conversion privilege are inseparably connected, and therefore the debt and equity portions of a security should not be separately valued. A holder cannot sell part of the instrument and retain the other. An alternate view holds that there are two distinct elements in these securities and that each should be recognized in the accounts: that portion of the issuance price attributable to the conversion privilege should be recorded as a credit to Paid-In Capital; the balance of the issuance price should be assigned to the debt. This would decrease the premium otherwise recognized in the debt or perhaps result in a discount.

These views are compared in the illustration that follows. Assume that 500 ten-year bonds, face value $1,000, are sold at 105. The bonds contain a conversion privilege that provides for exchange of a $1,000 bond for 20 shares of stock, par value $40. The interest rate on the bonds is 8%. It is estimated that without the conversion privilege, the bonds would sell at 96. The journal entries to record the issuance on the issuer's books under the two approaches follow.

Debt and Equity Not Separated

Cash	525,000	
Bonds Payable		500,000
Premium on Bonds Payable		25,000

Debt and Equity Separated

Cash	525,000	
Discount on Bonds Payable	20,000	
Bonds Payable		500,000
Paid-In Capital Arising from Bond Conversion Privilege		45,000

The periodic charge for interest will differ depending on which method is employed. To illustrate the computation of interest charges, assume that

---

[8]*See* Ben Weberman, "The Convertible Bond Scam," *Forbes* (January 19, 1981), p. 92.

the straight-line method is used to amortize bond premium or discount. Under the first approach, the annual interest charge would be $37,500 ($40,000 paid less $2,500 premium amortization). Under the second approach, the annual interest charge would be $42,000 ($40,000 paid plus $2,000 discount amortization).

The Accounting Principles Board stated that when convertible debt is sold at a price or with a value at issuance not significantly in excess of the face amount, ". . . no portion of the proceeds from the issuance . . . should be accounted for as attributable to the conversion feature."[9]

The APB stated that greater weight for this decision was placed on the inseparability of the debt and the conversion option than upon the practical problems of valuing the separate parts. However, the practical problems are considerable. Separate valuation requires asking the question: How much would the security sell for without the conversion feature? In many instances this question would appear to be unanswerable. Investment banks responsible for selling these issues are frequently unable to separate the two features for valuation purposes; they contend that the cash required simply could not be raised without the conversion privilege.

There would seem to be strong theoretical support for separating the debt and equity portions of the proceeds from the issuance of convertible debt on the issuer's books. Despite these theoretical arguments, current practice follows APB Opinion No. 14, and no separation is usually made between debt and equity. This is true even when separate values are determinable.

When conversion takes place, a special valuation question must be answered. Should the market value of the securities be used to compute a gain or loss on the transaction? If the security is viewed as debt, then the conversion to equity would seem to be a significant economic transaction and a gain or loss would be recognized. If, however, the security is viewed as equity, the conversion is really an exchange of one type of equity capital for another, and the historical cost principle would seem to indicate that no gain or loss would be recognized. In practice, the latter approach seems to be most commonly followed by both the issuer and investor of the bonds. No gain or loss is recognized either for book or tax purposes. The book value of the bonds is transferred to become the book value of the stock issued. However, this treatment seems inconsistent with APB Opinion No. 14 in which convertible debt is considered to be debt rather than equity.

If an investor views the security as debt, conversion of the debt could be viewed as an exchange of one asset for another. The general rule for the

---

[9]*APB Opinion No. 14*, par. 12.

exchange of nonmonetary assets is that the market value of the asset exchanged should be used to measure any gain or loss on the transaction.[10] If there is no market value of the asset surrendered or if its value is undeterminable, the market value of the asset received should be used. The market value of convertible bonds should reflect the market value of the stock to be issued on the conversion, and thus the market value of the two securities should be similar.

To illustrate bond conversion for the investor recognizing a gain or loss on conversion, assume HiTec Co. offers bondholders 40 shares of HiTec Co. common stock, $25 par, in exchange for each $1,000, 8% bond held. An investor exchanges bonds of $10,000 (book value as brought up to date, $9,850) for 400 shares of common stock having a market price at the time of the exchange of $26 per share. The exchange is completed at the interest payment date. The exchange is recorded as follows:

Investment in HiTec Co. Common Stock.............................	10,400	
Investment in HiTec Co. Bonds..................................		9,850
Gain on Conversion of HiTec Co. Bonds		550

If the investor chose not to recognize a gain or loss, the journal entry would be as follows:

Investment in HiTec Co. Common Stock.............................	9,850	
Investment in HiTec Co. Bonds..................................		9,850

Similar differences would occur on the issuer's books depending on the viewpoint assumed. If the issuer desired to recognize the conversion of the convertible debt as a significant culminating transaction, the market value of the securities would be used to record the conversion. To illustrate the journal entries for the issuer using this reasoning, assume 100 bonds, face value $1,000, are exchanged for 2,000 shares of common stock, $40 par value, $55 market value. At the time of the conversion, there is an unamortized premium on the bond issue of $3,000. The conversion would be recorded as follows:

Bonds Payable...	100,000	
Premium on Bonds Payable	3,000	
Loss on Conversion of Bonds................................	7,000	
Common Stock...		80,000
Paid-In Capital in Excess of Par............................		30,000

Computation:		
Market value of stock issued (2,000 shares at $55)..............		$110,000
Face value of bonds payable................................	$100,000	
Plus unamortized premium..................................	3,000	103,000
Loss to company on conversion of bonds.....................		$ 7,000

[10]*Opinions of the Accounting Principles Board, No. 29*, "Accounting for Nonmonetary Transactions" (New York: American Institute of Certified Public Accountants, 1973), par. 18.

If the issuer did not consider the conversion as a culminating transaction, no gain or loss would be recognized. The bond carrying value would be transferred to the capital stock account on the theory that the company upon issuing the bonds is aware of the fact that bond proceeds may ultimately represent the consideration identified with stock. Thus, when bondholders exercise their conversion privileges, the value identified with the obligation is transferred to the security that replaces it. Under this assumption, the conversion would be recorded as follows:

Bonds Payable	100,000	
Premium on Bonds Payable	3,000	
Common Stock, $40 par		80,000
Paid-In Capital in Excess of Par		23,000

The profession has not resolved the accounting issues surrounding convertible debt. Although the practice of not recognizing gain or loss on either the issuer's or the investor's books is widespread, it seems inconsistent with the treatment of other items that are transferred by an entity. The economic reality of the transaction would seem to require a recognition of the change in value at least at the time conversion takes place.

Bond Refinancing. Cash for the retirement of a bond issue is frequently raised through the sale of a new issue and is referred to as **bond refinancing, or refunding.** Bond refinancing may take place when an issue matures, or bonds may be refinanced prior to their maturity when the interest rate has dropped and the interest savings on a new issue will more than offset the cost of retiring the old issue. To illustrate, assume that a corporation has outstanding 12% bonds of $1,000,000 callable at 102 and with a remaining 10-year term, and similar 10-year bonds can be marketed currently at an interest rate of only 10%. Under these circumstances it would be advantageous to retire the old issue with the proceeds from a new 10% issue since the future savings in interest will exceed by a considerable amount the premium to be paid on the call of the old issue.

The desirability of refinancing may not be so obvious as in the preceding example. In determining whether refinancing is warranted in marginal cases, careful consideration must be given to such factors as the different maturity dates of the two issues, possible future changes in interest rates, changed loan requirements, different indenture provisions, income tax effects of refinancing, and legal fees, printing costs, and marketing costs involved in refinancing.

When refinancing takes place before the maturity date of the old issue, the problem arises as to how to dispose of the call premium and unamortized discount and issue costs of the original bonds. Three positions have been taken with respect to disposition of these items:

1. Such charges are considered a loss on bond retirement.
2. Such charges are considered deferrable and to be amortized systematically over the remaining life of the original issue.
3. Such charges are considered deferrable and to be amortized systematically over the life of the new issue.

Although arguments can be presented supporting each of these alternatives, the Accounting Principles Board concluded that "all extinguishments of debt before scheduled maturities are fundamentally alike. The accounting for such transactions should be the same regardless of the means used to achieve the extinguishment."[11] The first position, immediate recognition of the gain or loss, was selected by the Board for all early extinguishment of debt. The Financial Accounting Standards Board considered the nature of this gain or loss and defined it as being an extraordinary item requiring separate income statement disclosure, as indicated earlier.

In-Substance Defeasance. Another form of early extinguishment of debt is referred to as **in-substance defeasance**, or economic defeasance. This is a technique used by companies to reduce the amount of long-term debt reported on the balance sheet. In-substance defeasance is a process of transferring assets, generally cash and securities, to an irrevocable trust, and using the assets and earnings therefrom to satisfy the long-term obligations as they come due. The transfer of the assets is treated as an extinguishment of debt, and a gain may be recognized on the early retirement, even though the debt has not actually been paid at that point. In some instances, the debt holders are not even aware of these transactions, and continue to rely on the issuer of the debt for settlement of the obligation. In other words, there has been no "legal defeasance" or release of the debtor from the legal liability.

To illustrate the effects of in-substance defeasance and the practical problems associated with these arrangements, assume that Tenax Corporation transfers $350,000 cash to a trust established solely for the retirement of $400,000 of Tenax bonds outstanding. The trust purchases government securities for $350,000. Interest and proceeds from the eventual sale or maturity of the government securities will be used to pay off the principal and interest of the bond indebtedness. Tenax removes the bonds from its balance sheet and recognizes an extraordinary gain of $50,000 on the extinguishment, i.e., the difference between the $400,000 liability to bondholders and the $350,000 cash transferred to the trust. The results of Tenax Corporation's in-substance defeasance are illustrated in the condensed financial statements on page 658.

---

[11]*Opinions of the Accounting Principles Board, No. 26,* par. 19.

Before In-Substance Defeasance

Tenax Corporation
Balance Sheet

Assets		Liabilities and Equity	
Cash	$ 400,000	Current liabilities	$ 200,000
Other assets	6,000,000	Bonds payable	400,000
Total assets	$6,400,000	Other long-term liabilities	1,200,000
		Equity (400,000 common shares outstanding)	4,600,000
		Total liabilities & equity	$6,400,000

Income Statement

Revenues	$8,000,000
Expenses	(6,000,000)
Net income	$2,000,000

Earnings per share ($2,000,000 ÷ 400,000 shares)............................ $5.00
Debt-to-equity ratio (total liabilities ÷ equity = $1,800,000 ÷ $4,600,000)........ .39
Return on assets (net income ÷ total assets = $2,000,000 ÷ $6,400,000)....... .31

After In-Substance Defeasance

Tenax Corporation
Balance Sheet

Assets		Liabilities and Equity	
Cash	$ 50,000	Current liabilities	$ 200,000
Other assets	6,000,000	Other long-term liabilities	1,200,000
Total assets	6,050,000	Equity	4,650,000
		Total liabilities & equity	$6,050,000

Income Statement

Revenues	$8,000,000
Gain ($400,000 − $350,000)	50,000
Expenses	(6,000,000)
Net income	$2,050,000

Earnings per share ($2,050,000 ÷ 400,000 shares)............................ $5.13
Debt-to-equity ratio ($1,400,000 ÷ $4,650,000) .... .30
Return on assets ($2,050,000 ÷ $6,050,000) .... .34

As the statements show, the transaction improves both the earnings per share and key financial ratios of Tenax. Earnings are increased by the amount of gain recognized by Tenax, $50,000 or $.13 per share. The debt is removed from the balance sheet, without actually being retired, thereby decreasing the debt-to-equity ratio and increasing the return on assets. In many in-substance defeasance cases, the actual retirement of debt may not be desirable due to market conditions, or may be too costly due to significant call premiums.

To deal with the potential problems of overstating earnings or manipulating financial position, the FASB issued Statement No. 76 as a guideline for in-substance defeasance transactions. For a transaction to qualify as an extinguishment of debt, and therefore for removal of the debt from the balance sheet, the debtor must place cash or risk-free securities (those backed by the U.S. Government) in an irrevocable trust for the sole purpose of retiring the debt principal and interest obligations. In addition, the possibility that the debtor will be required to make further payments on that particular debt security must be remote.[12]

Not all accountants agree with the conclusions of FASB Statement No. 76. Some argue that until a debt is actually retired, it should not be removed from the balance sheet under any conditions. Others are skeptical of recognizing a gain or loss on a transaction where the debtor is not legally released from the primary obligation of the debt. On the other hand, supporters of the FASB position claim that the economic reality of in-substance defeasance transactions is essentially the same as a cash settlement. They further maintain that the strict guidelines of having risk-free securities placed in an irrevocable trust and having the probability of additional payments being remote are sufficient to recognize the transaction as an extinguishment of debt. Regardless of individual viewpoints, since FASB Statement No. 76 is generally accepted, transactions that qualify as in-substance defeasance are treated in the same manner as other forms of early retirement. Regardless of the reasons for extinguishment or the means used to accomplish the early retirement, a gain or loss should be recognized as an extraordinary item of that period.

---

[12]*Statement of Financial Accounting Standards No. 76*, "Extinguishment of Debt" (Stamford: Financial Accounting Standards Board, 1983), p. 5. It should be noted that current accounting practice does not allow extinguishment of debt through *instantaneous* in-substance defeasance, which means newly issued debt is immediately "retired" by having assets placed in trust to meet the interest and principal obligations as they come due. Instantaneous defeasance must be accounted for as a borrowing and as an investment, not as an extinguishment. See also *FASB Technical Bulletin No. 84-4*, "In-Substance Defeasance of Debt" (Stamford: Financial Accounting Standards Board, 1984).

TROUBLED DEBT RESTRUCTURING

Another significant accounting problem is created when economic conditions make it difficult for an issuer of long-term debt to make the cash payments required under the terms of the debt instrument. These payments include interest payments, principal payments on installment obligations, periodic payments to bond retirement funds, or even payments to retire debt at maturity. To avoid bankruptcy proceedings or foreclosure on the debt, investors in such situations may agree to make concessions and revise the original terms of the debt to permit the issuer to recover from financial problems. The restructuring may take many different forms. For example, there may be a suspension of interest payments for a period of time, a reduction in the interest rate, an extension of the maturity date of the debt, or even an exchange of assets or equity securities for the debt. The principal accounting question in these cases, on both the books of the issuer and the investor, is whether a gain or loss should be recognized upon the restructuring of the debt.

The issue became critical in the mid 1970's when several issues of municipal bonds, notably New York City bonds, were restructured due to the financial difficulties of the issuing organizations. Investors in the bonds were faced with interest and fund payments in arrears, and a near bankrupt situation for New York City. Most investors felt the decline was only temporary, and so did not recognize any loss on the books. After considerable negotiation, the terms of the bonds were restructured. Changes included a moratorium on interest and fund payments and extended maturity dates. Other municipalities and private companies such as Chrysler and Massey-Ferguson have experienced similar restructuring needs.

The Financial Accounting Standards Board considered this area carefully, and issued Statement No. 15 in 1977. In this statement the Board defined **troubled debt restructuring** as a situation where "the creditor for economic or legal reasons related to the debtor's financial difficulties grants a concession to the debtor that it would not otherwise consider. That concession either stems from an agreement between the creditor and the debtor or is imposed by law or a court."[13] The key word in this definition is *concession*. If a concession is not made by creditors, accounting for the restructuring follows the procedures discussed for extinguishment of debt prior to maturity.

---

[13]*Statement of Financial Accounting Standards No. 15,* "Accounting by Debtors and Creditors for Troubled Debt Restructuring" (Stamford: Financial Accounting Standards Board, 1977), par. 2.

The major issue addressed by the FASB in Statement No. 15 is whether a troubled debt restructuring agreement should be viewed as a significant economic transaction. It was decided that if it is considered to be a significant economic transaction, entries should be made on both the issuer's and the investor's books to reflect the gain or loss. If the restructuring is not considered to be a significant economic transaction, no entries are required. The accounting treatment thus depends on the nature of the restructuring. The FASB conclusions are summarized in the following table.

Accounting for Different Types of Troubled Debt Restructuring

Type	Restructuring Considered Significant Economic Transaction: Gain or Loss Recognized	Restructuring Not Considered Significant Economic Transaction: No Gain or Loss Recognized
Transfer of assets in full settlement (asset swap)	X	
Grant of equity interest in full settlement (equity swap)	X	
Modification of terms: total payment under new structure exceeds debt carrying value		X
Modification of terms: total payment under new structure is less than debt carrying value	X	

Each type of restructuring is discussed and illustrated in the following sections.

Transfer of Assets in Full Settlement (Asset Swap)

A debtor that transfers assets, such as real estate, inventories, receivables, or investments, to a creditor to fully settle a payable usually will recognize two types of gains or losses: (1) **a gain or loss on disposal of the asset,** and (2) **a gain arising from the concession** granted in the restructuring of the debt. The computation of these gains and/or losses is made as follows:

Carrying value of assets being transferred . . . .

Difference represents gain or loss on disposal

Market value of asset being transferred . . . .

Difference represents gain on restructuring

Carrying value of debt being liquidated . . . .

The gain or loss on disposal of an asset is usually reported as an ordinary income item unless it meets criteria for reporting it is an unusual or irregular item. However, the gain on restructuring is considered to arise from an early extinguishment of debt and must be reported as an extraordinary item.[14] An investor always recognizes **a loss on the restructuring** due to the concession granted unless the investment has already been written down in anticipation of the loss. The computation of the loss is made as follows:

Carrying value of investment liquidated. . . . .
┌───┐
│ Difference represents loss on restruc-   │
│ turing   │
└───┘
Market value of asset being transferred . . . .

The classification of this loss depends on the criteria being used to recognize irregular or extraordinary items. However, usually the loss is anticipated as market values of the investment decline, and it is recognized as an ordinary loss, either prior to the restructuring or as part of the restructuring.

To illustrate these points, assume that Stanton Industries is behind in its interest payments on outstanding bonds of $500,000, and is threatened with bankruptcy proceedings. The carrying value of the bonds on Stanton's books is $545,000 after deducting the unamortized discount of $5,000 and adding unpaid interest of $50,000. To settle the debt, Stanton transfers long-term investments it holds in Worth common stock with a carrying value of $350,000 and a current market value of $400,000, to all investors on a prorata basis. Assume Realty Inc. holds $40,000 face value of bonds. Because of the troubled financial condition of Stanton Industries, Realty Inc. has previously recognized as a loss a $5,000 decline in the value of the debt, and is carrying the investment at $35,000 on its books plus interest receivable of $4,000. The entries to record the asset transfer would be as follows:

Stanton Industries (Issuer)

Interest Payable	50,000	
Bonds Payable	500,000	
Discount on Bonds.		5,000
Long-Term Investments — Worth Common.		350,000
Gain on Disposal of Worth Common		50,000
Gain on Restructuring of Debt.		145,000

Computation:

Carrying value of Worth Common.	$350,000	
		>$50,000 gain on disposal
Market value of Worth Common	400,000	
		>$145,000 gain from restructuring
Carrying value of debt liquidated	545,000	

---
[14]*Ibid.*, par. 21.

Realty Inc. (Investor)

Long-Term Investments—Worth Common........................	32,000	
Loss on Restructuring of Debt....................................	7,000	
Long-Term Investments—Stanton Bonds.......................		35,000
Interest Receivable		4,000

Computation:
Percentage of debt held by Realty Inc.: $40,000/$500,000 = 8%
Market value of long-term investment received in settlement of debt:
  8% × $400,000 = $32,000

If an active market does not exist for the assets being transferred, estimates of the value should be made based on transfer of similar assets or by analyzing future cash flows from the assets.[15]

Grant of Equity Interest (Equity Swap)

A debtor that grants an equity interest to the investor as a substitute for a liability must recognize an extraordinary gain equal to the difference between the fair market value of the equity interest and the carrying value of the liquidated liability. A creditor (investor) must recognize a loss equal to the difference between the same fair market value of the equity interest and the carrying value of the debt as an investment. For example, assume that Stanton Industries transferred 20,000 shares of common stock to satisfy the $500,000 face value of bonds. The par value of the common stock per share is $15 and the market value at the date of the restructuring is $20 per share. Assume the other facts described in the illustration of an asset swap on page 662 are unchanged. The entries to record the grant of the equity interest on both sets of books would be as follows:

Stanton Industries (Issuer)

Interest Payable...	50,000	
Bonds Payable..	500,000	
Discount on Bonds...		5,000
Common Stock..		300,000
Paid-In Capital in Excess of Par...............................		100,000
Gain on Restructuring of Debt................................		145,000

Computation:
Market value of common stock......... $400,000
                                    $145,000 gain from restructuring
Carrying value of debt liquidated $545,000

Realty Inc. (Investor)

Long-Term Investments—Stanton Common Stock	32,000	
Loss on Restructuring of Debt....................................	7,000	
Long-Term Investment—Stanton Bonds.......................		35,000
Interest Receivable		4,000

---

[15]*Ibid.*, par. 13.

The entry on Stanton's books for an equity swap differs from that made for the asset swap because there can be no gain or loss on disposal of a company's own stock. However, the entry on Realty's books for an equity swap is identical with that for an asset swap except that the investment is in Stanton common stock.

Modification of Debt Terms

There are many ways debt terms may be modified to aid a troubled debtor. Modification may involve either the interest, the maturity value, or both. Interest concessions may involve a reduction of the interest rate, forgiveness of unpaid interest, or a moratorium on interest payments for a period of time. Maturity value concessions may involve an extension of the maturity date or a reduction in the amount to be repaid at maturity. Basically, the FASB decided that most modifications of debt did not result in a significant economic transaction, and thus did not give rise to a gain or loss at the date of restructuring. They argued that the new terms were merely an extension of an existing debt and that the modifications should be reflected in future periods through modified interest charges based on computed implicit interest rates. The only exception to this general rule occurs if the total payments to be made under the new structure, including all future interest payments, are less than the carrying value of the debt or the investment at the time of restructuring. Under this exception, the difference between the total future cash payments required and the carrying value of the debt or investment is recognized as a gain on the debtor's books and a loss on the creditor's books.

To illustrate the accounting for this type of restructuring, assume the interest rate on the Stanton Industries bonds (see page 662) is reduced from 10% to 7%, the maturity date is extended from 3 to 5 years from the restructuring date, and the past interest due of $50,000 is forgiven. The total future payments to be made after this restructuring are as follows:

Maturity value of bonds.	$500,000
Interest — 7% × $500,000 × 5 years	175,000
Total payments to be made after restructuring.	$675,000

Since the $675,000 exceeds the carrying value of $545,000, no gain is recognized on the books of Stanton Industries at the time of restructuring. A similar computation for Realty Inc. results in total future payments of $54,000 [$40,000 + ($2,800 × 5)] as compared with a carrying value of $39,000. Thus, no further loss is recognized on Realty Inc. books at the time of restructure.

However, if in addition to the preceding changes, $200,000 of maturity value is forgiven, the future payments would be reduced as follows:

Maturity value of bonds..	$300,000
Interest—7% × $300,000 × 5 years	105,000
Total payments to be made after restructuring............................	$405,000

Now the carrying value exceeds the future payments by $140,000, and this gain would be recognized by Stanton as follows:

Interest Payable...	50,000	
Bonds Payable..	500,000	
Discount on Bonds...		5,000
Restructured Debt		405,000
Gain on Restructuring of Debt................................		140,000
To reclassify restructured debt and recognize a gain of $140,000 on restructuring.		

Similar computations could be made on Realty's books assuming 40% of the debt is cancelled ($200,000/$500,000 = 40%).

Maturity value—($40,000 × 60%)...	$24,000
Interest—7% × $24,000 × 5 years	8,400
Total receipts after restructuring	$32,400
Carrying value of investment...	39,000
Loss on restructuring..	$ 6,600

The entry to record the loss on Realty's books would be as follows:

Loss on Restructuring of Debt...................................	6,600	
Investment in Stanton Bonds...................................		2,600
Interest Receivable		4,000
To recognize a loss of $6,600 on restructuring.		

When terms are modified, the amount recognized as interest expense or interest revenue in the remaining periods of the debt instrument's life is based on a computed implicit interest rate. The implicit interest rate is the rate that equates the present value of all future debt payments to the present carrying value of the debt or investment. The interest expense or interest revenue for each period is equal to the carrying value of the debt for the period involved times the implicit interest rate. The computation of the implicit interest rate can be complex, and usually requires the use of a computer program. However, approximations can be made by using a trial and error approach from the present value tables in Chapter 6.

To illustrate the computation of an implicit interest rate, the restructuring of Stanton Industries described on page 664 will be used. The question to be answered is what rate of interest will equate the total payments of $675,000 to the present carrying value of $545,000. Trial and error use of Tables II and IV in Chapter 6 shows that the rate is between 4% and 6% per year. The computations are as follows:

	Interest Rate 6% (3% per Semiannual Period)	Interest Rate 4% (2% per Semiannual Period)
Present value of maturity value due in five years (ten semiannual periods) .	.7441 × $500,000 = $372,050	.8203 × $500,000 = $410,150
Present value of $17,500 interest payments for ten semiannual payments....	8.5302 × $17,500 = 149,279	8.9826 × $17,500 = 157,196
Total present value	$521,329	$567,346

Interpolation indicates that the present value of $545,000 lies almost exactly midway between the present values computed at 6% and 4%; therefore, the approximate interest rate is 5%. For purposes of the illustration, the 5% rate will be used, or 2½% per semiannual payment period.

Using this rate, the recorded interest expense for the first six months would be $13,625, or 2½% of $545,000. Since the actual cash payment for interest is $17,500, the carrying value of the debt will decline by $3,875 ($17,500 − $13,625). The interest expense for the second semiannual period will be less than for the first period because of the decrease in the carrying value of the debt [($545,000 − $3,875) × 2.5% = $13,528 interest expense]. These computations are the same as those required in applying the effective-interest method of amortization described on pages 647–649. If the exact implicit interest rate were used, continuation of the procedure for the 10 periods would leave a balance of $500,000, the maturity value, in the liability account of Stanton Industries. The entries to record the restructuring on Stanton's books and the first two interest payments would be as follows:

Bonds Payable...	500,000	
Interest Payable...	50,000	
Discount on Bonds..		5,000
Restructured Debt..		545,000
To reclassify debt into one account.		
Interest Expense	13,625	
Restructured Debt..	3,875	
Cash..		17,500
Payment of first semiannual interest after restructuring.		
Interest Expense	13,528	
Restructured Debt..	3,972	
Cash..		17,500
Payment of second semiannual interest after restructuring.		

A similar computation of an implicit interest rate could be made for Realty based on future receipts of $54,000 [$40,000 + ($2,800 × 5)], and the present carrying value of the investment of $39,000. Use of this rate would increase the investment account to $40,000 at the end of the 10 periods, or the maturity value of the investment held.

The preceding discussion covers all situations when bond restructuring reflects a modification of terms except when the cash to be received after the restructuring is less than the carrying value of the debt or investment. Under these conditions the implicit interest rate is negative. In order to raise the rate to zero, the carrying value must be reduced to the cash to be realized and a gain or loss recognized for the difference. All interest payments or receipts in the future are offset directly to the debt or investment account. No interest expense or revenue will be earned or incurred in the future because of the extreme concessions made in the restructuring. By charging or crediting all interest payments to the debt or investment account, the balance remaining at the maturity date will be the maturity value of the debt.

Any combination of these methods of bond restructuring may be employed. Accounting for these multiple restructurings can become very complex, and must be carefully evaluated.

OFF-BALANCE-SHEET FINANCING

A major issue facing the accounting profession today is how to deal with companies that do not disclose all their debt in order to make their financial position look stronger. This is often referred to as **off-balance-sheet financing**. Among the most common techniques used to borrow money while keeping the debt off the balance sheet are:

1. Sale of receivables with recourse
2. Captive finance companies and other unconsolidated entities
3. Research and development arrangements
4. Project financing arrangements

Sale of Receivables with Recourse

In Chapter 8, the transfer of receivables was identified as a source of financing. It was noted that the transfer of receivables is no longer a "last-ditch" method to prevent bankruptcy, but is a method commonly used by companies to raise needed funds or to avoid the collection and management problems associated with receivables. When receivables are transferred with recourse, and the transaction qualifies as a sale under FASB Statement No. 77, no liability need be recorded on the balance sheet. However, companies are required to disclose the sale of receivables with recourse in notes accompanying the statements. For example, Allied Products Corporation included the following information in a note to the 1984 financial statements:

At December 31, 1984, the Company was contingently liable for approximately $10,920,000 relating to outstanding letters of credit and the sale of notes and accounts receivable with recourse (including the recourse portion of the notes and accounts receivable sold to one of its wholly-owned finance subsidiaries—see Note 4).

Captive Finance Companies and Other Unconsolidated Entities

Several major companies have created wholly owned subsidiaries to assist in the financing of the parent company. These are often called **captive finance companies**. Examples include IBM Credit Corporation, Chrysler Finance Corporation, General Motors Acceptance Corporation, and Sears Roebuck Acceptance Corporation. The accounting question is whether these finance companies should be consolidated with the parent company. Traditionally, generally accepted accounting principles have not required consolidation of these wholly owned finance subsidiaries. Therefore, any debt that may be incurred by these finance companies does not get reported on the parent company's balance sheet.

To illustrate this point in a slightly broader context, consider Avis Rent-A-Car, which in 1980 was a subsidiary of Norton Simon, Inc. Avis set up a trust to borrow money for the purchase of automobiles, which were leased to Avis for its rental fleet. Since the trust was separate from both Avis and Norton Simon, the debt incurred by the trust was not shown on the balance sheet of either of the other companies. As a result, Norton Simon kept $400 million of liabilities off its balance sheet.

The FASB has not yet provided definitive guidelines that deal with the consolidation of captive finance companies. At present, the Board is reconsidering the overall accounting and reporting standards for consolidation of subsidiaries.

Research and Development Arrangements

Another way a company may obtain off-balance-sheet financing is with **research and development arrangements**. These involve situations where an enterprise obtains the results of research and development activities funded partially or entirely by others. The main accounting issue is whether the arrangement is, in essence, a means of borrowing to fund research and development or if it is simply a contract to do research for others.[16] In deciding on the appropriate accounting treatment, a major consideration is whether the enterprise is obligated to repay the funds provided by the

---

[16]*Statement of Financial Accounting Standards No. 68,* "Research and Development Arrangements" (Stamford: Financial Accounting Standards Board, 1982).

other parties regardless of the outcome of the research and development activities. If there is an obligation to repay, then the enterprise should estimate and recognize that liability and record the research and development expenses in the current year in accordance with FASB Statement No. 2. If the financial risk associated with the research and development is transferred from the enterprise to other parties and there is no obligation to them, then the liability need not be reported by the enterprise.

Research and development arrangements may take a variety of forms, including a limited partnership. For example, assume Kincher Company formed a limited partnership for the purpose of conducting research and development. Kincher is the general partner and manages the activities of the partnership. The limited partners are strictly investors. The question is—should Kincher record the research and development expenses and the obligation to the investors on its books? The answer depends on an assessment of who is at risk and if Kincher is obligated to repay the limited partners regardless of the results of the research and development. If the limited partners are at risk and have no guarantee or claim against Kincher Company for any of the funds contributed, the debt and related expenses need not be reported on Kincher's books.

Project Financing Arrangements

At times, companies become involved in long-term commitments that are related to **project financing arrangements**. As an example, assume that two oil- and gas-producing companies, Striker Corporation and Jetco, Inc., agree to a joint venture. They form a separate company to construct a refinery in Alaska that both will use. The new company borrows funds for the construction and plans to repay the debt from the proceeds of the project. Striker and Jetco guarantee the repayment of the debt by the new company. The advantage to Striker and Jetco under such an arrangement is that neither of them shows the liability from the borrowing on its balance sheet. Each would report a contingency related to the guarantee of debt repayment in a note to the financial statements. This type of arrangement is another form of off-balance-sheet financing.[17]

Reasons for Off-Balance-Sheet Financing

There are several reasons why companies might use one of the preceding or other techniques to avoid including debt on the balance sheet. It may allow a company to borrow more than it otherwise could due to

---

[17]See *Statement of Financial Accounting Standards, No. 47.* "Disclosure of Long-Term Obligations" (Stamford: Financial Accounting Standards Board, 1981).

debt-limit restrictions. Also, if a company's financial position looks stronger, it will usually be able to borrow at a lower cost. Another reason may be that inflation tends to understate assets and so companies seek ways to understate liabilities.

Whatever the reasons, the problems of off-balance-sheet financing are serious. Many investors and lenders aren't sophisticated enough to see through the off-balance-sheet borrowing tactics, and so make ill-informed decisions. For example, in periods of economic downturn, a company with hidden debt may find it is not able to meet its obligations, and as a result may suffer severe financial distress or, in extreme cases, business failure. In turn, unsuspecting creditors and investors may sustain substantial losses that could have been avoided had they known the true extent of the company's debt.

The FASB and the accounting profession will no doubt continue to deal with the potentially serious problems of off-balance-sheet financing.[18] As the techniques become more complex and widely used, there is growing concern that the amount of total corporate debt is reaching unhealthy proportions.

VALUATION AND REPORTING OF LONG-TERM DEBT SECURITIES ON THE BALANCE SHEET

Thus far, no reference has been made in this chapter to adjusting investments and liabilities when the debt or investment valuation differs from cost. In Chapter 13, accounting for declines in value of long-term equity securities was presented. There it was noted that temporary declines in the market value of equity securities are recognized on the books of the investor by a debit to a contra equity account and by a credit to an allowance account. Permanent declines are recognized by a debit to a recognized loss account on the income statement and a credit to the Investment account. Debt instruments were not explicitly included in FASB Statement No. 12. However, if a market decline in debt securities is deemed to be permanent, and it is probable that the maturity value will not be paid when due, entries similar to those made for permanent declines in equity securities are normally made on the investor's books. If the market declines are considered temporary, no accounting entries are usually made, but the decline in value is recognized in a note to the financial statements.

---

[18]See John E. Stewart and Benjamin S. Neuhausen, "Financial Instruments and Transactions: The CPA's Newest Challenge," *Journal of Accountancy* (August 1986), pp. 102–110.

Entries likewise are not made to reflect increases in the market values of bond investments. Changes in the market value of the liability are ignored by the issuer unless a troubled debt restructuring takes place.

Long-term debt securities are frequently very significant items on the balance sheet of both the investor and the issuer. The valuation and reporting problems for the investor and issuer will be considered separately.

Reporting Bonds and Long-Term Notes as Investments

The market value of long-term debt varies with changes in the financial strength of the issuing company, changes in the level of interest rates, and shrinkage in the remaining life of the issue. In the absence of material price declines, bonds held as long-term investments are reported on the balance sheet at book value. This book value approaches maturity value as the bonds move closer to maturity. To this extent, then, the accounting can be considered to follow a similar change that is taking place on the market as the bond life is reduced and a correspondingly lower valuation is attached to the difference between the actual rate and the market rate of remaining interest payments. Although investments are usually reported at book value, parenthetical disclosure of the aggregate market value of the securities makes the financial statements more informative.

Data relative to long-term note and bond investments might be reported as follows:

Long-term investments:
Investment in Golden Corp. Long-Term Note, 11%, $50,000 face value, due
July 1, 1989. (Market value, $48,500 at December 31, 1987) .... $ 50,000
Investment in Wilkins Co. Bonds; 9%, $1,000,000 face value, due July 1, 1995
(reported at cost as adjusted for amortized discount).................... 982,500

Reporting Bonds and Long-Term Notes as Liabilities

In reporting long-term debt on the balance sheet, the nature of the liabilities, maturity dates, interest rates, methods of liquidation, conversion privileges, sinking fund requirements, borrowing restrictions, assets pledged, dividend limitations, and other significant matters should be indicated. The portion of long-term debt coming due in the current period should also be disclosed.

Bond liabilities are often combined with other long-term debt for balance sheet presentation, with supporting detail disclosed in a note. An example adapted from the 1985 annual report of United States Steel is presented on page 672. For another example of disclosure of long-term debt, see Note Eight to General Mills' financial statements in Appendix A at the end of this text.

Consolidated Balance Sheet

Current liabilities:

Long-term debt due within one year *(Note 18, page 39)*	**165**	220
Long-term debt, less unamortized discount *(Note 18, page 39)*	**5,348**	6,261

Notes to Consolidated Financial Statements (continued)

18. Long-Term Debt

(In millions)	Interest Rates — %	Maturity	December 31 1985	1984
United States Steel Corporation:				
Sinking Fund Debentures (callable)[a]	4½	1986	$ 15	$ 25
Sinking Fund Debentures (callable)[a]	7¾	2001	—	50
Sinking Fund Subordinated Debentures (callable)[a]	4⅝	1996	—	178
Convertible Subordinated Debentures (callable)[a][b]	5¾	2001	254	254
Obligations relating to Industrial Development and Environmental Improvement Bonds and Notes[a][c]	4¾–7⅝	1986–2012	616	780
Notes payable to banks	8½	1986–1988	6	11
Notes payable to others[d]	7⅜–9¾	1986–1995	246	301
Commercial paper[e]	8¼	(e)	1,039	1,362
Other long-term debt			4,031	4,265
Total[i]			6,207	7,226
Less unamortized discount[j]			694	745
			5,513	6,481
Less amount due within one year			165	220
Long-term debt due after one year			$5,348	$6,261

APPENDIX

ACCOUNTING FOR SERIAL BONDS

As noted in the chapter, serial bonds mature in installments at various dates. Usually, each bond indicates when it will mature. Because of the difference in time to maturity, the interest rate often varies depending on the due date. In some instances, the stated interest rate remains constant for all maturity dates, but the effective interest rate differs as the selling prices for the different maturity dates vary to reflect the added risk. When serial bonds are issued at other than par, the premium or discount could be related to the bonds maturing on each specific date, and the amortization of the premium or discount could be made as though each maturity date was a separate bond issue. No new problems related to accounting for interest arise under this approach.

However, an entire serial bond issue is sometimes sold directly to underwriters at a lump-sum price that differs from the total face value of the issue. When this occurs, the issue price usually cannot be identified with each maturity date. Under these circumstances, the premium or discount on the entire serial bond issue must be amortized as a unit. This requires that either an average effective rate be determined for the entire issue, and the effective-interest method used to determine the amortization; or that a variation of the straight-line method known as the **bonds outstanding** method be applied. Both methods provide for decreases in the amortization schedule as the principal amounts of the serial bonds mature.

Bonds-Outstanding Method

Amortization by the bonds-outstanding method is illustrated in the example that follows. Assume that bonds with a face value of $100,000, dated January 1, 1987, are issued on this date for a lump-sum price of $101,260. Bonds of $20,000 mature at the end of each year starting on December 31, 1987. The bonds pay interest of 8% annually. The company's accounting period ends on December 31; the accounting period and the bond year thus coincide. A table showing the premium to be amortized each year is developed as shown in the schedule at the top of page 674.

The annual premium amortization is found by multiplying the premium by a fraction whose numerator is the number of bond dollars outstanding in that year and whose denominator is the total number of bond dollars outstanding for the life of the bond issue. As bonds are retired, the amounts of premium amortization decline accordingly.

Amortization Schedule — Bonds-Outstanding Method

Year	Bonds Outstanding	Fraction of Premium to be Amortized	Annual Premium Amortization (Fraction × $1,260)
1987	$100,000	100,000/300,000 (or 10/30)	$ 420
1988	80,000	80,000/300,000 (or 8/30)	336
1989	60,000	60,000/300,000 (or 6/30)	252
1990	40,000	40,000/300,000 (or 4/30)	168
1991	20,000	20,000/300,000 (or 2/30)	84
	$300,000	300,000/300,000 (or 30/30)	$1,260

An alternative computation can be made by computing the amount of amortization related to each $1,000 of outstanding bonds. In the preceding example, this would be $4.20 per 1,000 bond ($1,260 ÷ 300). Applying this amount to the number of $1,000 bonds outstanding each year would result in the same amortization shown in the table; e.g., for 1988, 80 × $4.20, or $336. The use of this alternative method of computing the amortization is especially useful when computing the unamortized premium or discount on serial bonds retired early.

Periodic amortization may be incorporated in a table summarizing the interest charges and changes in bond carrying values as follows:

Amortization of Premium — Serial Bonds Bonds-Outstanding Method

Date	A Interest Payment (8% of Face Value)	B Premium Amortization	C Interest Expense (A − B)	D Principal Payment	E Bond Carrying Value Decrease (B + D)	F Bond Carrying Value (F − E)
Jan. 1, 1987						$101,260
Dec. 31, 1987	$8,000	$420	$7,580	$20,000	$20,420	80,840
Dec. 31, 1988	6,400	336	6,064	20,000	20,336	60,504
Dec. 31, 1989	4,800	252	4,548	20,000	20,252	40,252
Dec. 31, 1990	3,200	168	3,032	20,000	20,168	20,084
Dec. 31, 1991	1,600	84	1,516	20,000	20,084	—

Effective-Interest Method

Tables show that the bonds discussed on the preceding page were sold to return approximately 7½%. Use of this rate results in the following interest charges and premium amortization using the effective-interest method:

Amortization of Premium — Serial Bonds
Effective-Interest Method

Date	A Interest Payment (8% of Face Value)	B Interest Expense (7½% of Bond Carrying Value)	C Premium Amortiza- tion (A − B)	D Principal Payment	E Bond Carry- ing Value Decrease (C + D)	F Bond Carrying Value (F − E)
Jan. 1, 1987						$101,260
Dec. 31, 1987	$8,000	$7,595	$405	$20,000	$20,405	80,855
Dec. 31, 1988	6,400	6,064	336	20,000	20,336	60,519
Dec. 31, 1989	4,800	4,539	261	20,000	20,261	40,258
Dec. 31, 1990	3,200	3,019	181	20,000	20,181	20,077
Dec. 31, 1991	1,600	1,523*	77*	20,000	20,077	—

*The last payment is adjusted because the effective rate was not exactly 7½%. On the final payment the premium balance is closed and interest expense is reduced by this amount.

The bonds-outstanding method of amortization provides for the recognition of uniform amounts of amortization in terms of the par value of bonds outstanding. The effective-interest method provides for the recognition of interest at a uniform rate on the declining debt balance.

Bond Redemption Prior to Maturity — Serial Bonds

When serial bonds are redeemed prior to their maturities, it is necessary to cancel the unamortized premium or discount relating to that part of the bond issue that is liquidated. For example, assume the issuance of serial bonds previously described on page 673 and amortization of the premium by the bonds-outstanding method as given on that page. On April 1, 1988, $10,000 of bonds due December 31, 1989, and $10,000 of bonds due December 31, 1990, are redeemed at 100½ plus accrued interest. The premium for the period January 1–April 1, 1988, relating to redeemed bonds affects bond interest for the current period and will be written off as an adjustment to expense. The balance of the premium from the redemption date to the respective maturity dates of the series redeemed must be canceled. The premium balance relating to redeemed bonds is calculated as follows:

Premium identified with 1988: 20,000/80,000 × $336 × 9/12	= $ 63
Premium identified with 1989: 20,000/60,000 × 252	= 84
Premium identified with 1990: 10,000/40,000 × 168	= 42
Premium identified with redeemed bonds	$189

Instead of the foregoing procedure, the premium amortization per year on each $1,000 bond may be applied to bonds of each period that are redeemed. As shown on page 674, the annual amortization per $1,000 bond is $4.20.

The premium to be canceled may now be determined as follows:

Year	Number of $1,000 Bonds	Annual Premium Amortization per $1,000 Bond	Fractional Part of Year	Total Premium Cancellation
1988	20	$4.20	9/12	$ 63
1989	20	4.20		84
1990	10	4.20		42
Premium identified with redeemed bonds				$189

Bonds, carrying value $20,189, are redeemed at a cost of $20,100 resulting in a gain of $89. Payment is also made for interest on bonds of $20,000 for three months at 8%, or $400. The entry to record the redemption of bonds and the payment of interest on the series retired follows:

Bonds Payable...	20,000	
Premium on Bonds Payable	189	
Interest Expense	400	
Cash..		20,500
Gain on Bond Redemption.......................................		89

The following is a revised schedule for the amortization of bond premium.

Amortization Schedule — Bonds-Outstanding Method
Revised for Bond Retirement

Year	Annual Premium Amortization per Original Schedule	Premium Cancellation on Bond Retirement	Annual Premium Amortization Adjusted for Bond Retirement
1987	$ 420		$ 420
1988	336	$ 63	273
1989	252	84	168
1990	168	42	126
1991	84		84
	$1,260	$189	$1,071

QUESTIONS

1. What factors should be considered in determining whether cash should be raised by the issue of bonds or by the sale of additional stock?

2. Distinguish between (a) secured and unsecured bonds, (b) collateral trust and debenture bonds, (c) convertible bonds and callable bonds, (d) coupon bonds and registered bonds, (e) municipal bonds and corporate bonds, and (f) term and serial bonds.

3. What is meant by market rate of interest, stated or contract rate, and effective or yield rate? Which of these rates changes during the lifetime of the bond issue?

4. An investor purchases bonds with a face value of $100,000. Payment for the bonds includes (a) a premium, (b) accrued interest, and (c) brokerage fees. How would each of these charges be recorded and what disposition would ultimately be made of each of these charges?

5. How should bond issuance costs be accounted for on the issuer's books?

6. What amortization method for premiums and discounts on bonds is recommended by APB Opinion No. 21? Why? When can the alternative method be used?

7. Under what conditions would the following statement be true? "The effective-interest method of bond premium or discount amortization for the issuer results in higher net income than would be reported using straight-line amortization."

8. List three ways that bonds are commonly retired prior to maturity. How should the early extinguishment of debt be presented on the income statement?

9. What purpose is served by issuing callable bonds?

10. What are the distinguishing features of convertible debt securities? What questions relate to the nature of this type of security?

11. The conversion of convertible bonds to common stock by an investor may be viewed as an exchange involving no gain or loss, or as a transaction for which market values should be recognized and a gain or loss reported. What arguments support each of these views for the investor and for the issuer?

12. Why do companies find the issuance of convertible bonds a desirable method of financing?

13. What is meant by refinancing or refunding a bond issue? When may refinancing be advisable?

14. What is in-substance defeasance, and what action must the debtor take for it to qualify as an early extinguishment of debt?

15. What distinguishes a troubled debt restructuring from other debt restructurings?

16. What is the recommended accounting treatment for bond restructurings effected as:
    a. An asset swap?
    b. An equity swap?
    c. A modification of terms?

17. Why is off-balance-sheet financing popular with many companies? What problems are associated with the use of this method of financing?

18. How should long-term investments in bonds be recorded and adjusted for significant price changes in periods subsequent to their purchase so that their valuation will be in accordance with GAAP?

19. * (a) Describe the bonds-outstanding method for premium or discount amortization for serial bonds. (b) How does this method differ from the effective-interest method of amortization?

*Relates to Appendix

DISCUSSION CASES

CASE 15–1   (Debt or equity financing)

Assume you are a member of the board of directors of Intec Enterprises, a relatively new company in the computer industry. You have just listened to a presentation of the treasurer and an extended discussion among the other board members. The issue is how to raise $13 million of additional funds for company expansion. You must now vote on whether to authorize debt financing through a bond issue or to seek equity financing through additional stock sales. What are the advantages and disadvantages of debt financing versus equity financing? As a member of the board, how would you vote and why?

CASE 15–2   (Is there a loss on conversion?)

Holton Co. recently issued $1,000,000 face value, 8%, 30-year subordinated debentures at 97. The debentures are redeemable at 103 on demand by the issuer at any date upon 30 days notice 10 years after issue. The debentures are convertible into $10 par value common stock of the company at the conversion price of $12.50 per share for each $500 or multiple thereof of the principal amount of the debentures. ($500 ÷ $12.50 = 40 shares for each $500 of face value.)

Assume that no value is assigned to the conversion feature at date of issue of the debentures. Assume further that 5 years after issue, debentures with a face value of $100,000 and book value of $97,500 are tendered for conversion on an interest payment date when the market price of the debentures is 104 and the common stock is selling at $14 per share and that J. K. Biggs, the company accountant, records the conversion as follows:

Bonds Payable	100,000	
Discount on Bonds Payable		2,500
Common Stock		80,000
Paid-In Capital in Excess of Par		17,500

Julie Robinson, staff auditor for the CPA firm, reviews the transaction and feels the conversion entry should reflect the market value of the stock. According to Robinson's analysis, a loss on the bond conversion of $14,500 should be recognized. Biggs objects to recognizing a loss, so Robinson discusses the problem with the audit manager, K. Ashworth. Ashworth has a different view and recommends using the market value of the debentures as a basis for recording the conversion and recognizing a loss of only $6,500.

Evaluate the various positions. Include in your evaluation the substitute entries that would be made under both Robinson's and Ashworth's proposals.

CASE 15–3   (Do we really have income?)

The Jefferson Corporation has $20,000,000 of 10% bonds outstanding. Because of cash flow problems, the company is behind in interest payments and in contributions to its bond retirement fund. The market value of the bonds has declined until it is currently only 50% of the face value of the bonds. After lengthy negotiations, the principal bondholders have agreed to exchange their bonds for preferred stock that has a current market value of $10,000,000. The accountant for Jefferson Corporation recorded the transaction by charging the bond liability for the entire $20,000,000, and crediting Preferred Stock for the same amount. This entry thus transfers the amount received by the company from debt to equity.

The CPA firm performing the annual audit, however, does not agree with this treatment. The auditors argue that this transfer represents a troubled debt restructuring due to the significant concessions made by the bondholders, and under these conditions, the FASB requires Jefferson to use the market value of the preferred stock as its recorded value. The difference between the $20,000,000 face value of the bonds and the $10,000,000 market value of the preferred stock is a reportable gain.

The controller of Jefferson, L. Rogers, is flabbergasted. "Here we are, almost bankrupt, and you tell us we must report the $10,000,000 as a gain. I don't care what the FSAB or whatever it is says, that's a ridiculous situation. You can't be serious." But the auditor in charge of the engagements is adamant. "We really have no choice. You have had a forgiveness of debt for $10,000,000. You had use of the money, and based on current conditions, you won't have to pay it back. That situation looks like a gain to me."

What position do you think should be taken? Consider the external users of the statement and their needs in your discussion.

CASE 15–4   (Can we take a loss today for a gain in the future?)

Western Investment Group follows the policy of borrowing money for relatively long periods of time and lending the money to newly formed companies on a medium-term basis. At December 31, 1987, Western has several loans outstanding, and all but one are current in their interest payments and are living up to the covenant agreements made in conjunction with the loan. However, one loan to Digitec Corporation for $10,000,000 made at 14% interest is of much concern to Western. The company has not been successful in generating a steady cash flow, and thus has fallen behind in its interest payments. The current position of the company is also far below the amount specified in the loan agreement. The president of Digitec has asked Western for help and suggests a two-year suspension of interest payments followed by a new rate of 4% on the debt. The owners of Western initially refuse, saying that for the risk now involved, the going interest rate would really be more like 20%. After a somewhat bitter discussion, the president of Digitec says that Western leaves them no alternative; they must declare bankruptcy. After renewed discussion, the new terms requested are agreed upon and the past accrued interest is removed from the books by crediting accrued interest expense.

After reviewing the situation, Western's auditor argues that present value accounting for debt requires Western to restate the loan so that it would reflect the present value of the future payments at the 20% effective interest rate. This means that the present value of the $10,000,000 investment would be significantly reduced and the loss recognized in the current year. Future income would then reflect interest revenue at the 20% rate rather than the greatly reduced 4% rate. Now Western's partners are really upset. "Must we take a loss now just to report an increased profit in the future? That is ridiculous accounting!"

Before agreement is reached, the Financial Accounting Standards Board issues its Statement No. 15 that supports Western's position. But their auditors are still concerned. How can we argue for present value accounting and ignore the impact of the changed terms on the indebtedness? The FASB has abandoned the conceptual basis for expediency.

How would you evaluate the situation?

EXERCISES

EXERCISE 15–1   (Raising capital with bonds or stock)

The Marta Company must raise $600,000 for additional working capital. Management wants to choose the method of financing that will result in the highest return per share to the original shareholders. 10,000 shares of $60 par common stock have already been issued. Assume the company can sell an additional 7,500 shares at $80 or it can issue $600,000 in 8% bonds. Earnings before income taxes have historically been approximately $100,000 annually, and it is expected that they will increase by 15% (before additional interest charges) as a result of the additional funds. Assuming an income tax rate of 40%, which method of financing would you recommend? Why? (Show computations.)

EXERCISE 15–2   (Computation of market values of bond issues)

What is the market value of each of the following bond issues? (Round to the nearest dollar.)
(a) 10% bonds of $60,000 sold on bond issue date; 10-year life; interest payable semiannually; effective rate, 12%.
(b) 9% bonds of $200,000 sold on bond issue date; 20-year life; interest payable semiannually; effective rate, 8%.
(c) 6% bonds of $150,000 sold 30 months after bond issue date; 15-year life; interest payable semiannually; effective rate, 10%.

EXERCISE 15–3   (Issuance and reacquisition of bonds)

On December 1, 1986, the Taylor Company issued 10-year bonds of $300,000 at 103. Interest is payable on December 1 and June 1 at 10%. On April 1, 1988, the Taylor Company reacquires and retires 50 of its own $1,000 bonds at 98 plus accrued interest. The fiscal period for the Taylor Company is the calendar year.

[Handwritten notes in top margin: 80,000 × 90% = 72,000 − 80,000 = 8000; 8,000 / 120 = 66.67 × 12 = $800/yr; (A) 12 mos × 10 yrs.]

Prepare entries to record (a) the issuance of the bonds, (b) the interest payments and adjustments relating to the debt in 1987, (c) the reacquisition and retirement of bonds in 1988, and (d) the interest payments and adjustments relating to the debt in 1988. Assume the premium is amortized at year-end on a straight-line basis. (Round to the nearest dollar.)

[Handwritten notes in right margin: (B) 80,000 × 6% = 4800; Int. Exp → 72,000 × 7% = 5040; Amort $240; Int. Exp. 5040 / Disc on Bonds 240 / Cash 4800]

EXERCISE 15–4 (Amortization of bond discount)

On January 1, 1987, Spifco sold $80,000 of 10-year, 6% bonds at 90, an effective rate of 7%. Interest is to be paid on July 1 and December 31. Compute the discount to be amortized in 1987 and 1988 using (a) the straight-line method and (b) the effective-interest method. Make the journal entries to record the amortization when the effective-interest method is used. *(debit Premium)*

EXERCISE 15–5 (Bond interest and discount amortization)

Assume that $100,000 Baker School District 6% bonds are sold on the bond issue date for $92,894. Interest is payable semiannually and the bonds mature in 10 years. The purchase price provides a return of 7% on the investment.

1. What entries would be made on the investor's books for the receipt of the first two interest payments, assuming discount amortization on each interest date by (a) the straight-line method and (b) the effective-interest method? (Round to the nearest dollar.)
2. What entries would be made on Baker School District's books to record the first two interest payments, assuming discount amortization on each interest date by (a) the straight-line method and (b) the effective-interest method? (Round to the nearest dollar.)

EXERCISE 15–6 (Discount and premium amortization)

The Randolf Corporation issued $200,000 of 8% debenture bonds to yield 10%, receiving $184,556. Interest is payable semiannually and the bonds mature in 5 years.

1. What entries would be made by Randolf for the first two interest payments, assuming discount amortization on interest dates by (a) the straight-line method and (b) the effective-interest method? (Round to nearest dollar.)
2. Assuming the situation in (1) above, what entries would be made on the books of the investor for the first two interest receipts assuming one party obtained all the bonds and the straight-line method of amortization was used? (Round to the nearest dollar.)
3. If the sale is made to yield 6%, $217,062 being received, what entries would be made by Randolf for the first two interest payments, assuming premium amortization on interest dates by (a) the straight-line method and (b) the effective-interest method? (Round to nearest dollar.)

EXERCISE 15–7 (Sale of bond investment)

E. Hensen acquired $100,000 of Bedrock Corp. 9% bonds on July 1, 1985. The bonds were acquired at 92; interest is paid semiannually on March 1 and September 1. The bonds mature September 1, 1992. Hensen's books are kept on a calendar-year basis. On February 1, 1988, Hensen sold the bonds for 97 plus accrued interest. Assuming straight-line discount amortization recorded on a calendar-year basis, give the entry to record the sale of the bonds on February 1. (Round to the nearest dollar.)

EXERCISE 15–8 (Retirement of debt before maturity)

The long-term debt section of Viking Company's balance sheet as of December 31, 1987, included 9% bonds payable of $100,000 less unamortized discount of $8,000. Further examination revealed that these bonds were issued to yield 10%. The amortization of the bond discount was recorded using the effective-interest method. Interest was paid on January 1 and July 1 of each year. On July 1, 1988, Viking retired the bonds at 102 before maturity. Prepare the journal entries to record the July 1, 1988, payment of interest, the amortization of the discount since December 31, 1987, and the early retirement on the books of Viking Company.

EXERCISE 15–9 (Retirement of bonds)

The December 31, 1987, balance sheet of Baylor Company includes the following items:

9% bonds payable due December 31, 1996. . . . . $400,000
Premium on bonds payable 10,800

The bonds were issued on December 31, 1986, at 103, with interest payable on June 30 and December 31 of each year. The straight-line method is used for premium amortization.

On March 1, 1988, Baylor retired $200,000 of these bonds at 98, plus accrued interest. Prepare the journal entries to record retirement of the bonds, including accrual of interest since the last payment and amortization of the premium.

EXERCISE 15–10 (Retirement and refinancing of bonds)

Joplin Corporation has $300,000 of 12% bonds, callable at 102, with a remaining 10-year term, and interest payable semiannually. The bonds are currently valued on the books at $290,000 and the company has just made the interest payment and adjustments for amortization of the discount. Similar bonds can be marketed currently at 10% and would sell at par.
1. Give the journal entries to retire the old debt and issue $300,000 of new 10% bonds at par.
2. In what year will the reduction in interest offset the cost of refinancing the bond issue?

EXERCISE 15–11 (Issuance of convertible bonds)

Wright Insurance decides to finance expansion of its physical facilities by issuing convertible debenture bonds. The terms of the bonds are: maturity date 20 years after May 1, 1987, the date of issuance; conversion at option of holder after 2 years; 40 shares of $30 par value stock for each $1,000 bond held; interest rate of 12% and call provision on the bonds of 103. The bonds were sold at 101.
1. Give the entry of Wright's books to record the sale of $1,000,000 of bonds on July 1, 1987; interest payment dates are May 1 and November 1.
2. Assume the same condition as in (1) except that the sale of the bonds is to be recorded in a manner that will recognize a value related to the conversion

privilege. The estimated sales price of the bonds without the conversion privilege is 97.

EXERCISE 15–12   (Convertible bonds)

Lewis Inc. issued $1,000,000 of convertible 10-year 11% bonds on July 1, 1987. The interest is payable semiannually on January 1 and July 1. The discount in connection with the issue was $8,500, which is amortized monthly using the straight-line basis. The debentures are convertible after 1 year into 5 shares of the company's $50 par common stock for each $1,000 of bonds.

On August 1, 1988, $100,000 of the bonds were converted. Interest has been accrued monthly and paid as due. Any interest accrued at the time of conversion of the bonds is paid in cash.

Prepare the journal entries to record the conversion, amortization, and interest on the bonds as of August 1 and August 31, 1988.

EXERCISE 15–13   (Troubled-debt restructuring-asset swap)

The Buck Machine Company has outstanding a $150,000 note payable to the Ontario Investment Corporation. Because of financial difficulties, Buck negotiates with Ontario to exchange inventory of machine parts to satisfy the debt. The cost of the inventory transferred is carried on Buck's books at $90,000. The estimated retail value of the inventory is $120,000. Buck uses a perpetual inventory system. The note receivable is carried on Ontario's books at $150,000. Prepare journal entries for the exchange on the books of both Buck Machine Company and Ontario Investment Corporation according to the requirements of FASB Statement No. 15.

EXERCISE 15–14   (Troubled-debt restructuring-equity swap)

Lucky Enterprises is threatened with bankruptcy due to its inability to meet interest payments and fund requirements to retire $10,000,000 of long-term notes. The notes are all held by Fidelity Insurance Company. In order to prevent bankruptcy, Lucky has entered into an agreement with Fidelity to exchange equity securities for the debt. The terms of the exchange are as follows: 500,000 shares of $5 par common stock, current market value $8 per share, and 40,000 shares of $10 par preferred stock, current market value $70 per share. Fidelity has previously written down its investment in Lucky by 20%. Prepare journal entries for the exchange on the books of both Fidelity Insurance Company and Lucky Enterprises according to the requirements of FASB Statement No. 15.

EXERCISE 15–15   (Valuation of bonds used as investment)

Several years ago, Buffalo Life Insurance Company bought $1,000,000 of Markland City 6% bonds at par. The bonds are currently selling at 78. Because of recent trouble the bond issuer has had in meeting bond payments, the bondholder has decided to write down the market decline as a permanent decline. It is felt that only 80% of the original bond value will be recovered. Buffalo Life Insurance Company also holds $500,000 of Picto City 8% bonds that were bought at par but are selling at 96. They perceive this to be a temporary decline.
1. What journal entries would you make to record the decisions?
2. What disclosure would you make in the financial statements?

EXERCISE 15–16   (Disclosure of bonds)

For the Ribsey Corporation, arrange the following information as you would present it on the balance sheet dated December 31, 1988.

(a) Items in the possession of a bond retirement fund trustee for the first-mortgage bonds in (c): Cash of $8,000 and stocks of $84,000 (market value $94,500).

(b) Investment in Holder Company 10% bonds, $100,000 face value, due July 1, 1993, (cost as adjusted for unamortized premium $103,000) currently selling at 99.

(c) 20-year, 9% Ribsey Corp. first-mortgage bonds, $500,000 face value, due January 1, 2006 (cost as adjusted for unamortized discount $493,000).

(d) Investment in Stahman Corporation long-term notes, 12%, $60,000 face value, due September 1, 1995 (market value $63,000).

*EXERCISE 15–17   (Issuance of serial bonds)

On January 1, 1986, JVJ Corporation issued and sold $1,000,000 in five-year, 10% serial bonds to be repaid in the amount of $200,000 on January 1 of 1987, 1988, 1989, 1990, and 1991. Interest is payable at the end of each year. The bonds were sold to yield a rate of 12%. Prepare the entry to record the issuance of the serial bonds on the books of JVJ Corporation.

*Relates to Appendix

*EXERCISE 15–18   (Bonds-outstanding table)

Badger Corporation purchased 9% serial bonds on April 1, 1986, face value $2,000,000. The bonds mature in $400,000 lots on April 1 of each of the following years. Interest is payable semiannually; the issue has an overall discount of $50,000. Assuming that Badger reports on a calendar year, prepare a table summarizing interest charges and bond carrying values by the bonds-outstanding method.

*Relates to Appendix

PROBLEMS

PROBLEM 15–1   (Bond issuance and adjusting entries)

On January 1, 1987, Higgins Company issued bonds with a face value of $500,000 and a maturity date of December 31, 1996. The bonds have a stated interest rate of 10%, payable on January 1 and July 1. They were sold to Magnum Company for $442,648, a yield of 12%. It cost Higgins $30,000 to issue the bonds. This amount was deferred and amortized over the life of the issue using the straight-line method. Assume that both companies have December 31 year-ends and that Higgins uses the effective-interest method to amortize the discount and Magnum uses the straight-line method.

Instructions:

(1)   Make all entries necessary to record the sale and purchase of the bonds on the two companies' books.

(2)   Prepare the adjusting entries as of December 31, 1987, for both companies. Assume adjusting entries for amortization are made only once each year and that Magnum is carrying the bonds as a long-term investment.

PROBLEM 15–2
(Computation of bond market price and amortization of discount)

Simon Products decided to issue $1,500,000 of 10-year bonds. The interest rate on the bonds is stated at 7%, payable semiannually. At the time the bonds were sold, the market rate had increased to 8%.

Instructions:

(1)   Determine the maximum amount an investor should pay for these bonds. (Round to the nearest dollar.)

(2)   Assuming that the amount in (1) is paid, compute the amount at which the bonds would be reported after being held for one year. Use two recognized methods of handling amortization of the difference in cost and maturity value of the bonds, and give support to the method you prefer. (Round to the nearest dollar.)

PROBLEM 15–3   (Premium amortization table)

The Young Co. acquired $20,000 of Mexico Sales Co. 7% bonds, interest payable semiannually, bonds maturing in 5 years. The bonds were acquired at $20,850, a price to return approximately 6%. → *2x year = 10*

Prem = 850

Instructions: *Int. Rec = 20,000 x 7% x 6/12*

(1)   Prepare tables to show the periodic adjustments to the investment account and the annual bond earnings, assuming adjustment by each of the following methods: (a) the straight-line method, and (b) the effective-interest method. Round to the nearest dollar. → *Prem Amort = Int. Rec − Int. Exp*

(2)   Assuming use of the effective-interest method, give entries for the first year on the books of both companies. *Carrying value = face − Prem Amort.*

b) Int. exp = carrying value x 6% x 1/2

a) Prem. Amort = 850/10

$85

exp = 700 − 85 =

$615

Always!

PROBLEM 15–4   (Bond entries-issuer)

On April 1, 1977, the Box Company issued $8 million of 7% convertible bonds with interest payment dates of April 1 and October 1. The bonds were sold on July 1, 1977, and mature on April 1, 1997. The bond discount totaled $426,600. The bond contract entitles the bondholders to receive 25 shares of $15 par value common stock in exchange for each $1,000 bond. On April 1, 1987, the holders of bonds with total face value of $1,000,000 exercised their conversion privilege. On July 1, 1987, the Box Company reacquired bonds, face value $500,000, on the open market. The balances in the capital accounts as of December 31, 1986, were:

Common Stock, $15 par, authorized 3 million shares, issued and
  outstanding, 250,000 shares $3,750,000
Paid-in capital in excess of par   2,500,000

Market values of the common stock and bonds were as follows:

Date	Bonds (per $1,000)	Common Stock (per share)
April 1, 1987	$1,220	$47
July 1, 1987	1,250	51

Instructions: Prepare journal entries on the issuer's books for each of the following transactions. (Use straight-line amortization for the bond discount.)

(1) Sale of the bonds on July 1, 1977.
(2) Interest payment on October 1, 1977.
(3) Interest accrual on December 31, 1977, including bond discount amortization.
(4) Conversion of bonds on April 1, 1987. (Assume that interest and discount amortization are correctly shown as of April 1, 1987. No gain or loss on conversion is recognized.)
(5) Reacquisition and retirement of bonds on July 1, 1987. (Assume that interest and discount amortization are correctly reported as of July 1, 1987.)

PROBLEM 15–5   (Bond entries-issuer)

The Douglas Company sold $3,000,000 of 9% first-mortgage bonds on October 1, 1979, at $2,873,640 plus accrued interest. The bonds were dated July 1, 1979, (issue date); interest payable semiannually on January 1 and July 1; redeemable after June 30, 1984, and to June 30, 1986, at 101, and thereafter until maturity at 100; and convertible into $100 par value common stock as follows:

Until June 30, 1984, at the rate of 6 shares for each $1,000 bond.
From July 1, 1984 to June 30, 1987, at the rate of 5 shares for each $1,000 bond.
After June 30, 1987, at the rate of 4 shares for each $1,000 bond.

The bonds mature in 10 years from their issue date. The company adjusts its books monthly and closes its books as of December 31 each year. It follows the practice of writing off all unamortized bond discount in the period of bond retirement.

The following transactions occur in connection with the bonds:

1985
July   1 $1,000,000 of bonds were converted into stock.
1986
Dec. 31 $500,000 face amount of bonds were reacquired at 99¼ plus accrued interest. These were immediately retired.
1987
July   1   The remaining bonds were called for redemption. For purposes of obtaining funds for redemption and business expansion, a $4,000,000 issue of 7% bonds was sold at 97. These bonds are dated July 1, 1987, and are due in 20 years.

Instructions: Prepare in journal form the entries necessary for Douglas Company in connection with the preceding transactions, including monthly adjustments where appropriate, as of the following dates. (Round to nearest dollar.)

(1)   October 1, 1979
(2)   December 31, 1979
(3)   July 1, 1985

(4)   December 31, 1986
(5)   July 1, 1987

(AICPA adapted)

PROBLEM 15–6   (Bond entries-investor)

On June 1, 1987, Warner Inc. purchased as a long-term investment 800 of the $1,000 face value, 8% bonds of Universal Corporation for $738,300. The bonds were purchased to yield 10% interest. Interest is payable semiannually on December 1 and June 1. The bonds mature on June 1, 1992. Warner uses the effective-interest method of amortization. On November 1, 1988, Warner sold the bonds for $785,000. This amount includes the appropriate accrued interest.

Instructions: Prepare a schedule showing the income or loss before income taxes from the bond investment that Warner should record for the year ended December 31, 1987, and 1988.

(AICPA adapted)

PROBLEM 15–7   (Bond entries-investor)

On May 1, 1984, the Timp Co. acquired $40,000 of XYZ Corp. 9% bonds at 97 plus accrued interest. Interest on bonds is payable semiannually on March 1 and September 1, and bonds mature on September 1, 1987.

On May 1, 1985, the Timp Co. sold bonds of $12,000 for 103 plus accrued interest. On July 1, 1986, bonds of $16,000 were exchanged for 2,250 shares of XYZ Corp. no-par common, quoted on the market on this date at $8. Interest was received on bonds to date of exchange.

On September 1, 1987, remaining bonds were redeemed.

Instructions: Give journal entries for 1984–1987 to record the foregoing transactions on the books for the Timp Co., including any adjustments that are required at the end of each fiscal year ending on December 31. Assume bond discount amortization by the straight-line method.

PROBLEM 15–8   (Note payable entries-investor and issuer)

White Inc. issued $750,000 of 8-year, 11% notes payable dated April 1, 1987. Interest on the notes is payable semiannually on April 1 and October 1. The notes were sold on April 1, 1987, to an underwriter for $720,000 net of issuance costs. The notes were then offered for sale by the underwriter, and on July 1, 1987, J. Farmer purchased the entire issue as a long-term investment. Farmer paid 101 plus accrued interest for the notes. On June 1, 1990, Farmer sold the investment in White notes to M. Barney as a short-term investment. Barney paid 96 plus accrued interest for the notes as well as $1,500 for brokerage fees. Farmer paid $1,000 broker's fees to sell the notes. Barney held the investment until April 1, 1991, when the notes were called at 102 by White.

Instructions: Prepare all journal entries required on the books of White Inc. for 1987 and 1991; on the books of Farmer for 1987 and 1990; and on the books of Barney for 1990 and 1991. Assume each entity uses the calendar year for reporting purposes and that issue costs are netted against the note proceeds by White. Any required amortization is made using the straight-line method at the end of each calendar year or when the notes are transferred.

PROBLEM 15–9   (Adjustment of bond investment account)

In auditing the books for the Chemical Corporation as of December 31, 1987, before the accounts are closed, you find the following long-term investment account balance:

Account   **Investment in Big Oil 9% Bonds (Maturity date, June 1, 1991)**

Date		Item	Debit	Credit	Balance Debit	Balance Credit
					Debit	Credit
1987 Jan.	21	Bonds, $200,000 par, acquired at 102 plus accrued interest	206,550		206,550	
Mar.	1	Proceeds from sale of bonds, $100,000 par and accrued interest		106,000	100,550	
June	1	Interest received		4,500	96,050	
Nov.	1	Amount received on call of bonds, $40,000 par, at 101 and accrued interest		41,900	54,150	
Dec.	1	Interest received		2,700	51,450	

Instructions:
(1)   Give the entries that should have been made relative to the investment bonds, including any adjusting entries that would be made on December 31, the end of the fiscal year. (Assume bond premium amortization by the straight-line method.)
(2)   Give the journal entries required at the end of 1987 to correct and bring the accounts up to date in view of the entries actually made.

PROBLEM 15–10   (Reacquisition of bonds)

Wagstaff Company issued $1,000,000 of 12%, 10-year debentures on January 1, 1982. Interest is payable on January 1 and July 1. The entire issue was sold on April 1, 1982, at 103 plus accrued interest. On April 1, 1987, $500,000 of the bond issue was reacquired and retired at 98 plus accrued interest. On June 30, 1987, the remaining bonds were reacquired at 97 plus accrued interest and refunded with $400,000, 9% bonds issue sold at 100.

Instructions: Give the journal entries for 1982 and 1987 (through June 30) on the Wagstaff Company books. The company's books are kept on a calendar-year basis. (Round to nearest dollar. Assume straight-line amortization of premium.)

PROBLEM 15–11   (Convertible bonds)

The Beck Co. issued $1,000,000 of convertible 10-year debentures on July 1, 1986. The debentures provide for 9% interest payable semiannually on January 1 and July 1. The discount in connection with the issue was $19,500, which is being amortized monthly on a straight-line basis.

The debentures are convertible after 1 year into 7 shares of the Beck Co.'s $100 par value common stock for each $1,000 of debentures.

On August 1, 1987, $100,000 of debentures were turned in for conversion into common. Interest has been accrued monthly and paid as due. Accrued interest on debentures is paid in cash upon conversion.

Instructions: Prepare the journal entries to record the conversion, amortization, and interest in connection with the debentures as of: August 1, 1987, August 31, 1987, and December 31, 1987—including closing entries for end of year. No gain or loss is to be recognized on the conversion. (Round to nearest dollar)

(AICPA adapted)

PROBLEM 15–12
(Troubled-debt restructuring—modification of terms)

Carthage Company, after having experienced financial difficulties in 1987, negotiated with two major creditors and arrived at an agreement to restructure their debts on December 31, 1987. The two creditors were M. Barboza and R. Janeiro. Barboza was owed principal of $300,000 and interest of $60,000 but agreed to accept equipment worth $60,000 and notes receivable from Carthage Company's customers worth $250,000. The equipment had an original cost of $80,000 and accumulated depreciation of $30,000. Janeiro was owed $500,000 and agreed to extend the terms and to accept immediate payment of $100,000 and the remaining balance of $424,360 to be paid on December 31, 1989. All payments were made according to schedule.

Instructions: Prepare journal entries to record the restructuring on December 31, 1987, and the entries necessary to make the adjustments and record payments on December 31, 1988, and 1989. (Assume a reasonable interest rate for Carthage is 15%.)

PROBLEM 15–13
(Troubled debt restructuring—modification of terms)

In the latter part of 1988, Belvue Air Company experienced severe financial pressure and is in default in meeting interest payments on long-term notes of $6,000,000 due on December 31, 1993. The interest rate on the debt is 11% payable semiannually on June 30 and December 31. In an agreement with Iowa Investment Corporation, Belvue obtained acceptance of a change in principal and interest terms for the remaining 5-year life of the notes. The changes in terms are as follows:
  (a) A reduction of principal of $600,000.
  (b) A reduction in the interest rate to 8%.
  (c) Belvue agreed to pay on December 31, 1988, both the $660,000 of interest in arrears and the normal interest payment under the old terms.

Instructions:
(1) What is the total dollar difference in cash payments by Belvue over the five-year period as a result of the restatement of terms?
(2) What journal entries for the restructuring of the debt, payment of interest under the old terms, and the first two interest payments under the new terms would Belvue make? (Assume an implicit interest rate of 6%).
(3) What journal entries would Iowa Investment make in 1988 and 1989?

*PROBLEM 15–14   (Serial bonds—amortization of discount)

A serial bond issue in the amount of $2,000,000, dated January 1, 1987, bearing 8% interest payable at December 31 each year, is sold by Phillips Farm Co. to yield 9% per year. The bonds mature in the amount of $400,000 on January 1 of each year starting in 1988.

Instructions:
(1) Compute the bond price and discount.
(2) Prepare an amortization schedule using the bonds outstanding method.
Relates to Appendix

*PROBLEM 15–15   (Bonds-outstanding tables)

The Macy Manufacturing Company issued $2,000,000 of 8% serial bonds on January 1, 1980, at 98. The bonds mature in units of $250,000 beginning January 1, 1985, with interest payable semiannually on January 1 and July 1. On June 1, 1988, Macy reacquired at 101 plus accrued interest, $200,000 of the bonds due January 1, 1990, and $100,000 due January 1, 1991.

Instructions:
(1) Assuming discount amortization by the bonds-outstanding method and bond retirements as scheduled, prepare a table summarizing interest charges and bond carrying values for the bond life, supported by a schedule showing the calculation of amortization amounts. (Round to the nearest dollar.)
(2) Prepare a similar table summarizing interest charges and bond carrying values for the bond life taking into consideration bond redemptions in advance of maturity dates as indicated. (Round to nearest dollar.)
(3) Record in general journal form the retirement of bonds on June 1, 1988.
Relates to Appendix

Effective Interest Rate:

DISC

15,444	1228
4216	1289

Bonds 200,000 @ 8% yield 10%
Interest 8,000

200,000 − 15,444 = 184,556 × 10% × 6/12 = 9228
−8000
1228

200,000 − 14,216 = 185,784 × 10% × 6/12 = 9289
−8000
1289

16
Owners' Equity—Contributed Capital

In analyzing the financial position of a company, it is important to understand certain key relationships. For example, the basic accounting equation — **Assets = Liabilities + Owners' Equity** — shows that the assets of an enterprise have been provided by creditors and owners. Assets represent entity resources, while liabilities reflect the creditor claims against those resources. Since the difference between assets and liabilities is owners' equity or capital, the owners' equity of an entity represents the residual interest of the owners in the net assets (total assets less total liabilities) of the enterprise.

The capital of a business originates from two primary sources — investments by owners and business earnings. Reductions in capital result primarily from distributions to owners and business losses. In a **proprietorship**, the entire owner's equity resulting from investments, withdrawals, and earnings or losses is reflected in a single capital account. Similarly, in a **partnership**, a single capital account for each partner reports the partner's equity resulting from investments, withdrawals, and earnings or losses. In reporting **corporate capital**, however, a distinction is made between (1) investments by owners, called **contributed capital** or **paid-in capital** and (2) increases in net assets arising from earnings, designated as **retained earnings**. The issues surrounding contributed capital are discussed in this chapter, while those relating to retained earnings are considered in Chapter 17. Accounting for corporations is emphasized because they are the dominant form of organization in today's economy. Not only are corporations the major source of our national output, but they also provide the majority of employment opportunities. Millions of people hold equity securities (capital stock) in corporations throughout the world.

691

NATURE AND CLASSIFICATIONS OF CAPITAL STOCK

A corporation is an artificial entity created by law that has an existence separate from its owners and may engage in business within prescribed limits just as a natural person. Unless the life of a corporation is limited by law, it has perpetual existence. The modern corporation makes it possible for large amounts of resources to be assembled under one management. These resources are transferred to the corporation by individual owners because they believe they can earn a greater rate of return through the corporation's efficient use of the resources than would be possible from alternative investments. In exchange for these resources, the corporation issues **stock certificates** evidencing ownership interests. Directors elected by stockholders delegate to management responsibility for supervising the use, operation, and disposition of corporate resources.

Business corporations may be created under the incorporating laws of any one of the fifty states or of the federal government. Since the states do not follow a uniform incorporating act, the conditions under which corporations may be created and under which they may operate are somewhat varied.

In most states at least three individuals must join in applying for a corporate charter. Application is made by submitting **articles of incorporation** to the secretary of state or other appropriate official. The articles must set forth the name of the corporation, its purpose and nature, the stock to be issued, those persons who are to act as first directors, and other data required by law. If the articles conform to the state's laws governing corporate formation, they are approved and are recognized as the **charter** for the new corporate entity. When stock of a corporation is to be offered or distributed outside the state in which it is incorporated, registration with the Securities and Exchange Commission may be required. The objective of such registration is to insure that all facts relative to the business and its securities will be adequately and honestly disclosed. A stockholders' meeting is called at which a code of rules or **bylaws** governing meetings, voting procedures, and other internal operations are adopted; a **board of directors** is elected; and the board appoints company administrative officers. Corporate activities may now proceed in conformance with laws of the state of incorporation and charter authorization. A complete record of the proceedings of both the stockholders' and the directors' meetings should be maintained in a minutes book.

When a corporation is formed, a single class of stock, known as **common stock**, is usually issued. Corporations may later find that there are advantages to issuing one or more additional classes of stock with varying rights and priorities. Stock with certain preferences (rights) over the common stock is called **preferred stock**. All shares within a particular class of stock are identical in terms of ownership rights represented.

Rights of Ownership

Unless restricted or withheld by terms of the articles of incorporation or bylaws, certain basic rights are held by each stockholder. These rights are as follows:

1. To share in distributions of corporate earnings.
2. To vote in the election of directors and in the determination of certain corporate policies.
3. To maintain one's proportional interest in the corporation through purchase of additional capital stock if issued, known as the *preemptive right*. (In recent years, some states have eliminated this right.)
4. To share in distributions of cash or other properties upon liquidation of the corporation.

If both preferred and common stock are issued, the special features of each class of stock are stated in the articles of incorporation or in the corporation bylaws and become a part of the contract between the corporation and its stockholders. One must be familiar with the overall capital structure to understand fully the nature of the equity found in any single class of stock. Frequently, the stock certificate describes the rights and restrictions relative to the ownership interest it represents together with those pertaining to other securities issued. Shares of stock represent personal property and may be freely transferred by their owners in the absence of special restrictions.

Par or Stated Value of Stock

As indicated, the capital of a corporation is divided between contributed capital and retained earnings. This is an important distinction because readers of financial statements need to know the portion of equity derived from investments by owners as contrasted with the portion of equity that has been earned and retained by the business. The invested or contributed capital may be further classified into (a) an amount forming the corporate **legal capital**, and (b) the balance, if any, in excess of legal capital. The amount of the investment representing the legal capital is reported as **capital stock**. The remaining balance is recognized as **additional paid-in capital**. As discussed in this chapter, and elsewhere in the text, additional paid-in capital may arise from several sources, including the sale of stock at more than par or stated value, treasury stock transactions, and donations of assets. Additional paid-in capital includes all sources of contributed capital other than, or in excess of, legal capital.

The major components of owners' equity are shown below. It should be recognized, however, that the definitions and classifications of legal and other capital categories may vary according to state statutes.

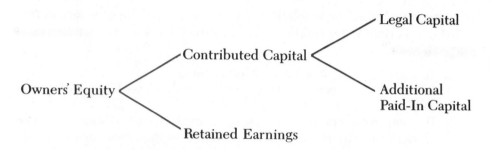

Elements of Owners' Equity for a Corporation

The significance of legal capital is that most state incorporation laws provide that dividends cannot reduce corporate capital below an amount designated as legal capital. Modern corporation laws normally go beyond these limitations and add that legal capital cannot be impaired by the reacquisition of capital stock. Creditors of a corporation cannot hold individual stockholders liable for claims against the company. But with a portion of the corporate capital restricted as to distribution, creditors can rely on the absorption by the ownership group of losses equal to the legal capital before losses are applied to the creditors' equity. As a practical matter, the legal capital of a corporation is generally small in comparison to total capital and does not strongly influence dividend policy nor provide significant creditor protection.

When a value is assigned to each share of stock, whether common or preferred, and is reported on the stock certificate, the stock is said to have a **par value**; stock without such an assigned value is called **no-par** stock. When shares have a par value, the legal capital is normally the aggregate par value of all shares issued and subscribed. When a corporation is authorized to issue stock with a par value, the incorporation laws of most states permit such issue only for an amount equal to or in excess of par. Par value may be any amount, for example, $100, $5, or 25 cents. An amount received on the sale of stock in excess of its par value is recorded in a separate account, such as Paid-In Capital in Excess of Par. The balance in this account is added to capital stock at par in reporting total contributed capital.

When shares are no-par, laws of certain states require that the total consideration received for the shares, even when they are sold at different prices, be recognized as legal capital. Laws of a number of states, however, permit the corporate directors to establish legal capital by assigning an arbitrary value to each share regardless of issue price, although in some instances the value cannot be less than a certain minimum amount. The value fixed by the board of directors or the minimum value required by law is known as the share's **stated value**, and an amount received in excess of stated value is reported in the same manner as an excess over par value, using an appropriate account title, e.g., Paid-In Capital in Excess of Stated Value.

Prior to 1912, corporations were permitted to issue only stock with a par value. In 1912, however, New York state changed its corporation laws to permit the issuance of stock without a par value, and since that time all other states have followed with similar statutory provisions. Today many of the common stocks, as well as some of the preferred stocks, listed on the major securities exchanges are no-par. Usually, no-par stock must have a stated value for reporting purposes. This makes it very similar to par stock and defines a separation of the stock proceeds between stated value and additional paid-in capital.

Preferred Stock

When a corporation issues both preferred and common stock, the preference rights attaching to preferred stock normally consist of prior claims to dividends. A dividend preference does not assure stockholders of dividends on the preferred issue but simply means that dividend requirements must be met on preferred stock before anything may be paid on common stock. Dividends do not legally accrue; a dividend on preferred stock, as on common stock, requires the ability on the part of the company to make such a distribution as well as appropriate action by the board of directors. When the board of directors fails to declare a dividend on preferred stock at the time such action would be called for, the dividend is said to be "passed." Although preferred stockholders have a prior claim on dividends, such preference is usually accompanied by limitations on the amount of dividends they may receive.

Preferred stock is generally issued with a par value. When preferred stock has a par value, the dividend is stated in terms of a percentage of par value. When preferred stock is no-par, the dividend must be stated in terms of dollars and cents. Thus, holders of 5% preferred stock with a $50 par value are entitled to an annual dividend of $2.50 per share before any distribution is made to common stockholders; holders of $5 no-par preferred stock are entitled to an annual dividend of $5 per share before dividends are paid to common stockholders.

A corporation may issue more than one class of preferred stock. For example, preferred issues may be designated first preferred or second preferred with the first preferred issue having a first claim on earnings and the second preferred having a second claim on earnings. In other instances the claim to earnings on the part of several preferred issues may have equal priority, but dividend rates or other preferences may vary. Holders of the common stock may receive dividends only after the satisfaction of all preferred dividend requirements.

Other characteristics and conditions are frequently added to preferred stock in the extension of certain advantages or in the limitation of certain rights. For example, preferred stock may be cumulative, convertible, callable, or redeemable. More than one of these characteristics may be applicable to a specific issue of preferred stock.

Cumulative and Noncumulative Preferred Stock. When a corporation fails to declare dividends on **cumulative preferred stock**, such dividends accumulate and require payment in the future before any dividends may be paid to common stockholders.

For example, assume that Blue Bell Corporation has outstanding 100,000 shares of 9% cumulative preferred stock, $10 par. Dividends were last paid in 1984. Total dividends of $300,000 are declared in 1987 by the board of directors. The majority of this amount will be paid to the preferred shareholders as follows:

	Dividends to Preferred Shareholders	Dividends to Common Shareholders	Total Dividends
Cumulative dividend for 1985..	$ 90,000	0	$ 90,000
Cumulative dividend for 1986..	90,000	0	90,000
Dividends for 1987	90,000	$30,000	120,000
Totals.	$270,000	$30,000	$300,000

Dividends on cumulative preferred stock that are passed are referred to as **dividends in arrears**. Although these dividends are not a liability until declared by the board of directors, this information is of importance to stockholders and other users of the financial statements. Disclosure of the amount of dividends in arrears is made by special note on the balance sheet.

If preferred stock is **noncumulative**, it is not necessary to provide for passed dividends. A dividend omission on preferred stock in any one year means it is irretrievably lost. Dividends may be declared on common stock as long as the preferred stock receives the preferred rate for the current period. Thus, in the previous example, if the preferred stock were noncumulative, the 1987 dividends would be distributed as follows:

	Dividends to Preferred Shareholders	Dividends to Common Shareholders	Total Dividends
Dividend passed in 1985......	0	0	0
Dividend passed in 1986......	0	0	0
Dividends for 1987	$90,000	$210,000	$300,000
Totals....................	$90,000	$210,000	$300,000

Preferred stock contracts normally provide for cumulative dividends. Also, courts have generally held that dividend rights on preferred stock are cumulative in the absence of specific provisions to the contrary.

Convertible Preferred Stock. Preferred stock is **convertible** when terms of the issue provide that it can be exchanged by its owner for some other security of the issuing corporation. Conversion rights generally provide for the exchange of preferred stock into common stock. Since preferred stock normally has a prior but limited right to earnings, large earnings resulting from successful operations accrue to the common stockholders. The conversion privilege gives the preferred stockholders the opportunity to exchange their holdings for stock in which the rights to earnings are not limited. In some instances, preferred stock may be convertible into bonds, thus allowing investors the option of changing their positions from stockholders to creditors. Convertible preferred issues have become increasingly popular in recent years, as indicated by the following excerpt from an article that appeared in the November 11, 1985, issue of *Barron's*.

> In recent years, a growing number of blue-chip companies have turned to convertibles as a source of cheaper cash than straight debt, and when IBM issued $1.3 billion worth last year to finance its acquisition of Rolm Corp., it symbolized a rite of passage for these securities.
>   This year, both volume and demand have continued to soar. Some $6.55 billion worth of convertibles was issued by mid-July, more than the $5.05 billion for all of 1984.[1]

Callable Preferred Stock. Preferred stock is **callable** when it can be called or redeemed at the option of the corporation. Many preferred issues are callable. The **call price** is usually specified in the original agreement and provides for payment of dividends in arrears as part of the repurchase price. When convertible stock has a call provision, the holders of the stock, at the time of the call, are frequently given the option of converting their holdings into common stock rather than accepting the call price. The decision made by the investor will be based on the market price of the common stock.

---

[1] Jaye Scholl, "Convertibles Come Into Their Own," *Barron's* (November 11, 1985), p. 68.

Redeemable Preferred Stock. Preferred stock is sometimes subject to mandatory redemption requirements or other redemption provisions that give the security overlapping debt and equity characteristics. This type of stock is referred to as **redeemable preferred stock** and is defined as preferred stock that is redeemable at the option of the holder, or at a fixed or determinable price on a specific date, or upon other conditions not solely within the control of the issuer (e.g., redemption upon reaching a certain level of earnings). The FASB currently requires disclosure of long-term obligations, including the extent of redemption requirements for all issues of capital stock that are redeemable at fixed or determinable prices on fixed or determinable dates. Redemption requirements may be disclosed separately for each issue or for all issues combined.[2]

Asset and Dividend Preferences upon Corporation Liquidation. Preferred stock is generally preferred over common stock as to assets distributed upon corporate liquidation. Such a preference, however, cannot be assumed but must be specifically stated in the preferred stock contract. The asset preference for stock with a par value is an amount equal to par, or par plus any amount paid in excess of par; in the absence of a par value, the preference is a stated amount. Terms of the preferred contract may also provide for the full payment of any dividends in arrears upon liquidation, regardless of the retained earnings balance reported by the company. When this is the case and there are insufficient retained earnings, i.e., a deficit, such dividend priorities must be met from paid-in capital of the common stock; the common stockholders receive whatever assets remain after settlement with the preferred group.

Common Stock

Strictly speaking, there should be but one kind of common stock, representing the residual ownership equity of a company. In recent years, however, a few companies have begun to issue different classes of common stock with different ownership rights. General Motors, for example, has three classes of common stock to appeal to different types of investors. In many ways, these classes of common stock are similar in nature and purpose to preferred stock. For most companies, there is but one class of common stock.

Common stock carries the greatest risk since common shareholders receive dividends only after preferred dividends are paid. In return for this risk, common stock ordinarily shares in earnings to the greatest extent if

---

[2]*Statement of Financial Accounting Standards No. 47,* "Disclosure of Long-Term Obligations" (Stamford: Financial Accounting Standards Board, 1981), par. 10c.

the corporation is successful. There is no inherent distinction in voting rights between preferred and common stocks; however, voting rights are frequently given exclusively to common stockholders as long as dividends are paid regularly on preferred stock. Upon failure to meet preferred dividend requirements, special voting rights may be granted to preferred stockholders, thus affording this group a more prominent role in the management. In some states, voting rights cannot be withheld on any class of stock.

ISSUANCE OF CAPITAL STOCK

In accounting for capital stock, it should be recognized that stock may be:

1. Authorized but unissued;
2. Subscribed for and held for issuance pending receipt of cash for the full amount of the subscription price;
3. Outstanding in the hands of stockholders;
4. Reacquired and held by the corporation for subsequent reissuance; or
5. Canceled by appropriate corporate action.

Thus, an accurate record of all transactions involving capital stock must be maintained by a corporation. Separate general ledger accounts are required for each source of capital including each class of stock. In addition, subsidiary records are needed to keep track of individual stockholders and stock certificates.

Capital Stock Issued for Cash

The issuance of stock for cash is recorded by a debit to Cash and a credit to Capital Stock for the par or stated value.[3] When the amount of cash received from the sale of stock is greater than the par or stated value, the excess is recorded separately as a credit to an additional paid-in capital account. This account is carried on the books as long as the stock to which it relates is outstanding. When stock is retired, the capital stock balance as well as any related paid-in-capital balance is generally canceled.

To illustrate, assume the Kling Corporation is authorized to issue 10,000 shares of $10 par common stock. On April 1, 1987, 4,000 shares are sold for $45,000 cash. The entry to record the transaction is:

---

[3]The term *Capital Stock* is used in account titles in the text when the class of stock is not specifically designated. When preferred and common designations are given, these are used in the account titles.

```
1987
April 1   Cash ...................................................   45,000
               Common Stock ........................................        40,000
               Paid-In Capital in Excess of Par .........................         5,000
                    To record the issuance of 4,000 shares of $10 par com-
                    mon stock for $45,000.
```

If, in the example, the common stock were no-par stock but with a $10 stated value, the entry would be the same except the $5,000 would be designated Paid-In Capital in Excess of Stated Value. Generally, stock is assigned a par or a stated value. However, if there is no such value assigned, the entire amount of cash received on the sale of stock is credited to the capital stock account and there is no additional paid-in capital account associated with the stock. Assuming Kling Corporation's stock were no-par common without a stated value, the entry to record the sale of 4,000 shares for $45,000 would be:

```
1987
April 1   Cash ...................................................   45,000
               Common Stock ........................................        45,000
                    To record the issuance of 4,000 shares of no-par, no
                    stated-value common stock for $45,000.
```

Capital Stock Sold on Subscription

Capital stock may be issued on a subscription basis. **A subscription** is a legally binding contract between the subscriber (purchaser of stock) and the corporation (issuer of stock). The contract states the number of shares subscribed, the subscription price, the terms of payment, and other conditions of the transaction. A subscription, while giving the corporation a legal claim for the contract price, also gives the subscriber the legal status of a stockholder unless certain rights as a stockholder are specifically withheld by law or by terms of the contract. Ordinarily, stock certificates evidencing share ownership are not issued until the full subscription price has been received by the corporation.

When stock is subscribed for, Capital Stock Subscriptions Receivable is debited for the subscription price, Capital Stock Subscribed is credited for the amount to be recognized as capital stock when subscriptions have been collected, and a paid-in capital account is credited for the amount of the subscription price in excess of par or stated value.

Capital Stock Subscriptions Receivable is a control account, individual subscriptions being reported in the subsidiary **subscribers ledger**. A special **subscribers journal** may be used in recording capital stock subscriptions. Subscriptions Receivable is regarded as a current asset when the corporation expects to collect the balance within one year, which is the usual situation. Capital Stock Subscribed and any related paid-in capital accounts are reported in the stockholders' equity section of the balance sheet.

Subscriptions may be collected in cash or in other assets accepted by the corporation. When collections are made, the appropriate asset account is debited and the receivable account is credited. Credits are also made to subscribers' accounts in the subsidiary ledger.

The actual issuance of stock is recorded by a debit to Capital Stock Subscribed and a credit to Capital Stock. The following entries illustrate the recording and issuance of capital stock sold on subscription. It is assumed that the Thalman Corporation is authorized to issue 10,000 shares of $10 par value common stock.

Recording and Issuance of Capital Stock Sold on Subscription

November 1–30: Received subscriptions for 5,000 shares of $10 par common at $12.50 per share with 50% down, balance due in 60 days.

Common Stock Subscriptions Receivable	62,500	
Common Stock Subscribed		50,000
Paid-In Capital in Excess of Par		12,500
Cash	31,250	
Common Stock Subscriptions Receivable		31,250

December 1–31: Received balance due on one half of subscriptions and issued stock to the fully paid subscribers, 2,500 shares.

Cash	15,625	
Common Stock Subscriptions Receivable		15,625
Common Stock Subscribed	25,000	
Common Stock		25,000

As a result of the preceding transactions, current assets in the December 31 balance sheet would include subscriptions receivable of $15,625. The stockholders' equity section of the balance sheet would appear as follows:

Stockholders' Equity

Contributed capital:	
Common stock, $10 par, 10,000 shares authorized, 2,500 shares issued and outstanding	$25,000
Common stock subscribed, 2,500 shares	25,000
Paid-in capital in excess of par	12,500
Total stockholders' equity	$62,500

Subscription Defaults

If a subscriber defaults on a subscription by failing to make a payment when it is due, a corporation may (1) return to the subscriber the amount paid, (2) return to the subscriber the amount paid less any reduction in price or expense incurred on the resale of the stock, (3) declare the amount paid by the subscriber as forfeited, or (4) issue to the subscriber shares equal to the number paid for in full. The practice followed will depend on the policy adopted by the corporation within the legal limitations set by the state in which it is incorporated.

To illustrate the entries under these different circumstances, assume in the Thalman Corporation example described earlier (with subscriptions at $12.50 per share) that one subscriber for 100 shares defaults after making the 50% down payment. Defaulted shares are subsequently resold at $11. The entries to record the default by the subscriber and the subsequent resale of the defaulted shares would be as follows: *Variations not options*

1. Assuming the amount paid in is returned to the subscriber:

Best for Stockholder

Common Stock Subscribed	1,000	
Paid-In Capital in Excess of Par	250	
Common Stock Subscriptions Receivable		625
Cash		625
Cash	1,100	
Common Stock		1,000
Paid-In Capital in Excess of Par		100

2. Assuming the amount paid in less the price reduction on the resale is returned to the subscriber:

Company can resell

Middle-ground

Common Stock Subscribed	1,000	
Paid-In Capital in Excess of Par	250	
Common Stock Subscriptions Receivable		625
Payable to Defaulting Subscriber *(payment withheld pending stock resale)*		625
Cash	1,100	
Payable to Defaulting Subscriber	150	
Common Stock		1,000
Paid-In Capital in Excess of Par		250
Payable to Defaulting Subscriber	475	
Cash		475

3. Assuming the full amount paid in is declared to be forfeited:

Best for Company

Common Stock Subscribed	1,000	
Paid-In Capital in Excess of Par	250	
Common Stock Subscriptions Receivable		625
Paid-In Capital from Forfeited Stock Subscriptions		625
Cash	1,100	
Common Stock		1,000
Paid-In Capital in Excess of Par		100

4. Assuming shares equal to the number paid for in full are issued:

Middleground

Common Stock Subscribed	1,000	
Paid-In Capital in Excess of Par	125	
Common Stock		500
Common Stock Subscriptions Receivable		625
Cash	550	
Common Stock		500
Paid-In Capital in Excess of Par		50

Capital Stock Issued for Consideration Other Than Cash

When capital stock is issued for consideration in the form of property other than cash or for services received, the fair market value of the stock or the value of the property or services is used to record the transaction. If a quoted market price for the stock is available, that amount can be used as a basis for recording the exchange. Otherwise, it may be possible to determine the fair market value of the property or services received, e.g., through appraisal by a competent outside party.

To illustrate, assume that Z Company issues 200 shares of $100 par value common stock in return for land with a fair market value of $30,000. The entry on Z Company's books would be:

Land	30,000	
Common Stock		20,000
Paid-In Capital in Excess of Par		10,000

If, on the other hand, the land had no readily determinable market price but Z Company's common stock was currently selling for $125 per share, the transaction would be recorded as follows:

Land	25,000	
Common Stock		20,000
Paid-In Capital in Excess of Par		5,000

If an objective value cannot be established for either the stock or the property or services received, the board of directors normally has the right to assign values to the securities issued and the assets or services received. These values will stand for all legal purposes in the absence of proof that fraud was involved. However, the assignment of values by the board of directors should be subject to particularly careful scrutiny. There have been cases where directors have assigned excessive values to the consideration received for stock to improve the company's reported financial position. When the value of the consideration cannot be clearly established and the directors' valuations are used in reporting assets and invested capital, the source of the valuations should be disclosed on the balance sheet. When there is evidence that improper values have been assigned to the consideration received for stock, such values should be restated. Stock is said to be **watered** when assets are overstated and capital items are correspondingly overstated. On the other hand, the balance sheet is said to contain **secret reserves** when there is an understatement of assets or an overstatement of liabilities accompanied by a corresponding understatement of capital.

Issuance of Capital Stock in Exchange for a Business

A corporation, upon its formation or at some later date, may be combined with another ongoing business, issuing capital stock in exchange for the net assets acquired. This is referred to as a **business combination**. In determining the amount of stock to be issued, the fair market value of the stock, as well as the values of the net assets acquired, must be considered.

Frequently the value of the stock transferred by a corporation will exceed the value of the identifiable assets acquired because of a favorable earnings record of the business acquired. If the exchange is accounted for as a **purchase**, the value of the stock in excess of the values assigned to identifiable assets is recognized as goodwill. Under this approach, the retained earnings of the company acquired *do not* become part of the combined retained earnings. On the other hand, if the exchange is treated as a **pooling of interest**, neither the revaluation of assets nor the recognition of goodwill is recorded. Assets are stated at the amounts previously reported; the retained earnings accounts of the two companies are added together and become the amount of retained earnings for the combined entity. The purchase method assumes that one of the companies is dominant and is acquiring the other company. The pooling of interests method assumes equal status and continuity of common ownership. The accounting for business combinations is dealt with in APB Opinion No. 16, and is discussed in detail in advanced accounting texts.

CAPITAL STOCK REACQUISITION

For a variety of reasons, a company may find it desirable to reacquire shares of its own stock. In 1986, for example, General Motors Corporation bought back almost 10 million shares of its three classes of common stock at a cost of almost $2 billion. These shares were repurchased for use in acquisitions and for incentive compensation and employee savings plans. Other companies have repurchased their stock to:

1. Improve per-share earnings by reducing the number of shares outstanding.
2. Support the market price of the stock.
3. Increase the ratio of debt to equity.
4. Obtain shares for conversion of other securities.
5. Invest excess cash temporarily.

Whatever the reason, a company's stock may be reacquired by exercise of call or redemption provisions, by repurchase of the stock on the open market, or by donation from stockholders. In reacquiring stock, a company must comply with applicable state laws, which can have a significant impact on transactions involving a company's stock. For example, state laws normally provide that the reacquisition of stock must serve a legitimate corporate purpose and must be made without injury or prejudice to the creditors or to the remaining stockholders. Another general restriction relates to the preserving of sufficient legal capital of the corporation.

In accounting for the reacquisition of stock, it should be emphasized that *reacquisitions do not give rise to income or loss*. A company issues stock to raise capital, which it intends to employ profitably; in reacquiring shares of its stock, the company reduces the capital to be employed in subsequent operations. Income or loss arises from the operating and investing activities of the business, not from transactions with its shareholders.

A company's stock may be reacquired for immediate retirement or reacquired and held as treasury stock for subsequent disposition, either eventual retirement or reissuance. Accounting for immediate retirements will be discussed first, followed by accounting for treasury stock transactions.

Stock Reacquired for Immediate Retirement

If shares of stock are reacquired at par or stated value and then retired, the capital stock account is debited and Cash is credited. However, if the purchase price of the stock exceeds the par or stated value, the excess amount may be: (1) charged to any paid-in capital balances applicable to that class of stock, (2) allocated between paid-in capital and retained earnings, or (3) charged entirely to retained earnings.[4] The alternative used depends on the existence of previously established paid-in capital amounts and on management's preference. To illustrate the application of the alternatives, assume that Sparks Corporation reports the following balances related to an issue of preferred stock:

Preferred Stock (par $10, 10,000 shares outstanding)...................... $100,000
Paid-In Capital in Excess of Par... 10,000

Assume Sparks redeems and retires 2,000 shares, or 20%, of the preferred stock at $12.50 per share, or a total purchase price of $25,000. Reductions are made in the preferred stock account for $20,000 (2,000 shares at par of $10) and in the related paid-in capital account for a pro rata share, 20% of $10,000, or $2,000. The remainder of the purchase price, $3,000, is charged to Retained Earnings. The journal entry would be:

---

[4]*Opinions of the Accounting Principles Board, No. 6*, "Status of Accounting Research Bulletins" (New York: American Institute of Certified Public Accountants, 1965), par. 12a.

```
Preferred Stock..................................................    20,000
Paid-In Capital in Excess of Par..................................     2,000
Retained Earnings...............................................     3,000
    Cash......................................................              25,000
```

Alternatively, the entire amount paid over par or stated value of the retired shares can be debited to Retained Earnings. In the example, the entry would be:

```
Preferred Stock..................................................    20,000
Retained Earnings...............................................     5,000
    Cash......................................................              25,000
```

When a corporation reacquires stock at a price that is less than par or stated value, the difference is credited to a paid-in capital account, not to Retained Earnings. To illustrate, assume Sparks Corporation redeems the 2,000 shares of preferred stock at only $9 per share, or a total of $18,000. The preferred stock account is reduced by the par value of the shares, $20,000, and the difference between the debit to Preferred Stock and the amount paid is credited to a paid-in capital account, as illustrated in the following entry:

```
Preferred Stock..................................................    20,000
    Cash......................................................              18,000
    Paid-In Capital from Preferred Stock Reacquisition ................       2,000
```

If additional shares of preferred stock are subsequently reacquired at amounts in excess of par, the excess can be debited to Paid-In Capital in Excess of Par, Paid-In Capital from Preferred Stock Reacquisition, and/or Retained Earnings.

The preceding discussion and illustrations dealt only with the corporation's books. From the investor's perspective, a stock redemption is recorded by a debit to Cash for the call price received and a credit to the investment account at cost; the difference, if any, is recorded as a gain or loss. Generally, a gain is recognized, since the call price is usually higher than the cost of the investment. Using the first example given for the Sparks Corporation (reacquisition price of $12.50 per share) and assuming only one investor held the 2,000 shares of preferred stock at a cost of $22,000, the entry for the stockholder would be:

```
Cash..........................................................    25,000
    Gain on Redemption of Sparks Corporation Preferred Stock.........       3,000
    Investment in Sparks Corporation Preferred Stock..................      22,000
```

Treasury Stock

When a company's own stock is reacquired and held in the name of the company rather than formally retired, it is referred to as **treasury stock**. Treasury shares may subsequently be reissued or formally retired. Before discussing how to account for treasury stock, several important features should be noted.

First, treasury stock should not be viewed as an asset; instead, it should be reported as a reduction in total owners' equity. A company cannot have an ownership interest in itself. Furthermore, treasury stock does not confer upon the corporation stockholder rights, e.g., dividend or voting rights, as would generally be the case with an investment in the securities of another company. Second, there is no effect on legal capital from the acquisition or reissuance of treasury stock. The acquisition of treasury stock decreases the number of shares outstanding, while reissuance increases the number of shares outstanding, but the legal capital is not changed by either the reacquisition or the subsequent reissuance. Third, as noted earlier, there is no income or loss on the reacquisition, reissuance, or retirement of treasury stock. Finally, as illustrated in the next section, Retained Earnings can be decreased by treasury stock transactions, but is never increased by such transactions.

Accounting for Treasury Stock. Two methods for recording treasury stock transactions are generally accepted: (1) the **cost method**, where the purchase of treasury stock is viewed as giving rise to a capital element whose ultimate disposition remains to be determined; and (2) the **par (or stated) value method**, where the purchase of treasury stock is viewed as effective or "constructive" retirement of outstanding stock.

Cost Method. Under the cost method, the purchase of treasury stock is recorded by debiting a treasury stock account for the cost of the purchase and crediting Cash. The cost is determined by the current market price of the stock and is not necessarily tied to the original stock issue price. The balance in the treasury stock account is reported as a deduction from total stockholders' equity on the balance sheet. If treasury stock is subsequently retired, the debit balance in the treasury stock account is eliminated by allocating proportionate amounts to the appropriate capital stock, paid-in capital, and retained earnings accounts, as noted previously. If treasury stock is subsequently sold, the difference between the acquisition cost and the selling price is reported as an increase or decrease in stockholders' equity. If stockholders' equity is increased by the sale of treasury stock, a paid-in capital account, such as Paid-In Capital from Treasury Stock, is credited. If stockholders' equity is decreased, paid-in capital accounts established from previous treasury stock transactions may be debited, or the entire amount may be debited to Retained Earnings.

The cost method of accounting for treasury stock transactions is illustrated in the following example.

Cost Method of Accounting for Treasury Stock

1987 Newly organized corporation issued 10,000 shares of common stock, $10 par, at $15:

Cash	150,000	
Common Stock		100,000
Paid-In Capital in Excess of Par		50,000

Net income for first year of business, $30,000:

Income Summary	30,000	
Retained Earnings		30,000

1988 Reacquired 1,000 shares of common stock at $16 per share:

Treasury Stock	16,000	
Cash		16,000

Sold 200 shares of treasury stock at $20 per share:

Cash	4,000	
Treasury Stock		3,200
Paid-In Capital from Treasury Stock		800

Sold 500 shares of treasury stock at $14 per share:

Cash	7,000	
Paid-In Capital from Treasury Stock	800	
Retained Earnings	200	
Treasury Stock		8,000

Retired 300 shares of treasury stock (3% of original issue of 10,000 shares):

Common Stock	3,000	
Paid-In Capital in Excess of Par	1,500*	
Retained Earnings	300*	
Treasury Stock		4,800

*As indicated earlier, the entire $1,800 difference between the debit to Common Stock and the cost to acquire the treasury stock may be debited to Retained Earnings.

In the preceding example, if a balance sheet were prepared after the acquisition of the treasury stock but prior to the reissuance and retirement of the stock, the stockholders' equity section would appear as follows:

Contributed capital:	
Common stock	$100,000
Paid-in capital in excess of par	50,000
Retained earnings	30,000
Total	$180,000
Less treasury stock at cost	16,000
Total stockholders' equity	$164,000

It should be noted that in the example, all treasury stock was acquired at $16 per share. If several acquisitions of treasury stock are made at different prices, the resale or retirement of treasury shares must be recorded using the actual cost to reacquire the shares being sold or retired (specific identification) or on the basis of a cost-flow assumption, such as FIFO or average cost.

Par (or Stated) Value Method. If the par (or stated) value method is used, the purchase of treasury stock is regarded as a withdrawal of a group of stockholders. Similarly, the sale or reissuance of treasury stock, under this approach, is viewed as the admission of a new group of stockholders, requiring entries giving effect to the investment by this group. Thus, the purchase and sale are viewed as two separate and unrelated transactions.

Using the data given for the cost method illustration, the following entries would be made for 1988 under the par value method.

Par Value Method of Accounting for Treasury Stock

1988 Reacquired 1,000 shares of common stock at $16 per share:

Treasury Stock	10,000	
Paid-In Capital in Excess of Par	5,000	
Retained Earnings	1,000	
Cash		16,000

Sold 200 shares of treasury stock at $20 per share:

Cash...	4,000	
Treasury Stock		2,000
Paid-In Capital in Excess of Par		2,000

Sold 500 shares of treasury stock at $14 per share:

Cash...	7,000	
Treasury Stock		5,000
Paid-In Capital in Excess of Par		2,000

Retired 300 shares of treasury stock:

Common Stock.....................................	3,000	
Treasury Stock		3,000

Prior to the reissuance of treasury stock in the example using the par value method, the stockholders' equity section would show:

Stockholders' Equity

Contributed capital:		
Common stock..............................	$100,000	
Less treasury stock at par value	10,000	
	$ 90,000	
Paid-in capital in excess of par................	45,000	$135,000
Retained earnings.............................		29,000
Total stockholders' equity......................		$164,000

Evaluating the Cost and Par Value Methods. Neither the AICPA through the Accounting Principles Board, nor the FASB has expressed a preference between the two methods of accounting for treasury stock transactions.

Although there is theoretical support for each approach, in practice the cost method is favored because of its simplicity.

The following comparison shows the impact on stockholders' equity of the two approaches after all treasury stock transactions have occurred in the illustrative example. Note that total stockholders' equity is the same regardless of which method is used. As shown by the example, however, there may be differences in the relative amounts of contributed capital and Retained Earnings reported. Note again that Retained Earnings may be decreased by treasury stock transactions, but can never be increased by buying and selling treasury stock.

Comparison of Stockholders' Equity

	Cost Method	Par Value Method
Contributed capital:		
Common stock	$ 97,000	$ 97,000
Paid-in capital in excess of par	48,500	49,000
Retained earnings	29,500	29,000
Total	$175,000	$175,000
Less treasury stock	-0-	-0-
Total stockholders' equity	$175,000	$175,000

Donated Treasury Stock

Treasury stock is occasionally acquired by donation from stockholders. Shares may be donated to enable the company to raise capital by reselling the shares. In other cases, shares may be donated to eliminate a deficit. Ordinarily, all stockholders participate in the donation on a pro rata basis, each party donating a certain percentage of holdings so that relative interests in the corporation remain unchanged.

When treasury stock is donated and the market value of the stock is known, the transaction would be recorded normally, using either the cost or the par value method. Instead of a credit to cash, however, the credit entry would be to a paid-in capital account, e.g., Paid-In Capital from Donations.

In the absence of an objective basis for valuation, the acquisition of treasury stock by donation may be reported on a corporation's books by a memorandum entry. Upon sale of the donated stock, the entry would be recorded by a debit to Cash and a credit to a paid-in capital account.

STOCK RIGHTS, WARRANTS, AND OPTIONS

A corporation may issue rights, warrants, or options that permit the purchase of the company's stock for a specified period (the **exercise period**) at a certain price (the **exercise price**). Although the terms *rights, warrants,* and *options* are sometimes used interchangeably, a distinction may be made as follows:

1. **Stock rights**—issued to existing shareholders to permit them to maintain their proportionate ownership interests when new shares are to be issued. (Some state laws require this preemptive right.)
2. **Stock warrants**—sold by the corporation for cash, generally in conjunction with another security.
3. **Stock options**—granted to officers or employees, sometimes as part of a compensation plan.

A company may offer rights, warrants, or options: (1) to raise additional capital, (2) to encourage the sale of a particular class of securities, or (3) as compensation for services received. The exercise period is generally longer for warrants and options than for rights. Warrants and rights may be traded independently among investors, whereas options generally are restricted to a particular person or specified group to whom the options are granted. The accounting considerations relating to stock rights, warrants, and options are described in the following sections.

Stock Rights

When announcing rights to purchase additional shares of stock, the directors of a corporation specify a date on which the rights will be issued. All stockholders of record on the issue date are entitled to receive the rights. Thus, between the announcement date and the issue date, the stock is said to sell *rights-on*. After the rights are issued, the stock sells *ex-rights*, and the rights may be sold separately by those receiving them from the corporation. An expiration date is also designated when the rights are announced, and rights not exercised by this date are worthless.

Accounting for Stock Rights by the Issuer. When rights are issued to stockholders, only a memorandum entry is made on the issuing company's books stating the number of shares that may be claimed under the outstanding rights. This information is required so the corporation may retain sufficient unissued or reacquired stock to meet the exercise of the rights. Upon surrender of the rights and the receipt of payments as specified by the rights, the stock is issued. At this time a memorandum entry is made to record the decrease in the number of rights outstanding accompanied by an entry to record the stock sale. The entry for the sale is recorded the same as any other issue of stock, with appropriate recognition of the cash received, the par or stated value of the stock issued, and any additional paid-in capital.

Information concerning outstanding rights should be reported with the corporation's balance sheet so that the effects of the future exercise of remaining rights may be determined.

Accounting for Stock Rights by the Investor. The receipt of stock rights by a stockholder is comparable to the receipt of a stock dividend (to be discussed fully in Chapter 17). The corporation has made no asset distribution and stockholders' equity remains unchanged. However, a stockholders' investment is now evidenced by shares of stock previously acquired and by rights that have a value of their own when they permit the purchase of shares at less than the market price. These circumstances call for an **allocation of cost** between the shares of stock and the rights. Since the shares and the rights have different values, an apportionment should be made in terms of the relative market values as of the date the rights are issued. Subsequently, the stock and the rights are accounted for separately. Accounting for stock rights by the shareholder is illustrated in the following example.

Assume that in 1987, Western Sales Co. acquired 100 shares of Agri Inc.'s common stock at $180 per share. In 1988, the corporation issues rights to purchase 1 share of common at $110 for every 5 shares owned. Western Sales Co. thus receives 100 rights—1 right for each share owned. However, since 5 rights are required for the acquisition of a single share, the 100 rights enable Western to subscribe for only 20 new shares. Western's original investment cost of $18,000 now applies to 2 assets, the shares and the rights. This cost is apportioned on the basis of the relative market values of each security as of the date that the rights are issued to the stockholders. The cost allocation may be expressed as follows:

Cost assigned to rights:
$$\frac{\text{Market Value of Rights}}{\text{Market Value of Stock Ex-rights} + \text{Market Value of Rights}} \times \begin{array}{c}\text{Original}\\\text{Cost of}\\\text{Stock}\end{array}$$

Cost assigned to stock:
$$\frac{\text{Market Value of Stock Ex-rights}}{\text{Market Value of Stock Ex-rights} + \text{Market Value of Rights}} \times \begin{array}{c}\text{Original}\\\text{Cost of}\\\text{Stock}\end{array}$$

Assume that Agri Inc.'s common stock is selling ex-rights at $131 per share, and rights are selling at $4 each. The cost allocation would be made as follows:

To rights: $\frac{\$4}{\$131 + \$4} \times \$18,000 = \$533$ (rounded) ($533 ÷ 100 = $5.33, cost per right)

To stock: $18,000 − $533 = $17,467 ($17,467 ÷ 100 = $174.67, cost per share)

The following entry may be made to record the allocation:

```
Investment in Agri Inc. Stock Rights ......................................    533
    Investment in Agri Inc. Common Stock................................        533
        Received 100 rights permitting the purchase of 20 shares at $110.
```

The cost apportioned to the rights is used in determining any gain or loss arising from the sale of rights. Assume that the rights in the preceding example are sold for $4.50 each. The following entry would be made:

```
Cash........................................................................    450
Loss on Sale of Agri Inc. Stock Rights ....................................     83
    Investment in Agri Inc. Stock Rights ...................................        533
        Sold 100 rights at $4.50.
```

If the rights are exercised rather than sold, the cost of the new shares acquired consists of the cost assigned to the rights plus the cash that is paid on the exercise of rights. Assume that, instead of selling the rights, Western Sales Co. exercises its rights to purchase 20 additional shares at $110. The following entry would be made:

```
Investment in Agri Inc. Common Stock ...............................    2,733
    Investment in Agri Inc. Stock Rights ...............................        533
    Cash...............................................................        2,200
        Exercised rights, acquiring 20 shares at $110.
```

Upon exercising the rights, Western's records show an investment balance of $20,200 consisting of two lots of stock as follows:

```
Lot 1 (1987 acquisition) 100 shares: ($17,467 ÷ 100 = $174.67, cost per share,
    adjusted for stock rights) ............................................    $17,467
Lot 2 (1988 acquisition) 20 shares: ($2,733 ÷ 20 = $136.65, cost per share,
    acquire through stock rights) .........................................      2,733
Total ....................................................................    $20,200
```

These costs provide the basis for calculating gain or loss on subsequent sale of the stock.

Frequently the receipt of rights includes 1 or more rights that cannot be used in the purchase of a whole share. For example, assume that the owner of 100 shares receives 100 rights; 6 rights are required for the purchase of 1 share. Here the holder uses 96 rights in purchasing 16 shares. Several alternatives are available to the holder: allow the remaining 4 rights to lapse; sell the rights and report a gain or a loss on such sale; or supplement the rights held by the purchase of 2 more rights making possible the purchase of an additional share of stock.

If the owner of valuable rights allows them to lapse, it would appear that the cost assigned to such rights should be written off as a loss. This can be supported on the theory that the issuance of stock by the corporation at less than current market price results in a dilution in the equities identified with original holdings. However, when changes in the market price of the stock make the exercise of rights unattractive to all investors and none of the rights can be sold, no dilution has occurred and any cost of rights reported separately should be returned to the investment account.

Stock Warrants

As noted previously, warrants may be sold in conjunction with other securities as a "sweetener" to make the purchase of the securities more attractive. For example, warrants to purchase shares of a corporation's common stock may be issued with bonds to encourage investors to purchase the bonds. A warrant has value when the exercise price is less than the market value, either present or potential, of the security that can be purchased with the warrants. Warrants issued with other securities may be detachable or nondetachable. **Detachable warrants** are similar to stock rights because they can be traded separately from the security with which they were originally issued. **Nondetachable warrants** cannot be separated from the security they were issued with.

As described in Chapter 15, the Accounting Principles Board in Opinion No. 14 recommended assigning part of the issuance price of debt securities to any detachable stock warrants and classifying it as part of owners' equity.[5] The value assigned to the warrant is determined by a procedure similar to that described for stock rights and is expressed in the following equation:

$$\text{Value assigned to warrants} = \text{Total issue price} \times \frac{\text{Fair market value of warrant}}{\begin{array}{c}\text{Fair market value} \\ \text{of security} \\ \text{without warrant}\end{array} + \begin{array}{c}\text{Fair market} \\ \text{value} \\ \text{of warrant}\end{array}}$$

Although Opinion No. 14 is directed only to warrants attached to debt, it appears logical to extend the conclusions of that Opinion to warrants attached to preferred stock. Thus, if a market value exists for the warrants at the issuance date, a separate equity account is credited with that portion of the issuance price assigned to the warrants. If the warrants are exercised, the value assigned to the common stock is the value allocated to the warrants plus the cash proceeds from the issuance of the common stock. If the warrants are allowed to expire, the value assigned to the warrants may be transferred to a permanent paid-in capital account.

Accounting for detachable warrants attached to a preferred stock issue is illustrated as follows: assume the Randall Co. sells 1,000 shares of $50 par preferred stock for $58 per share. As an incentive to purchase the stock, Randall Co. gives the purchaser detachable warrants enabling holders to subscribe to 1,000 shares of $20 par common stock for $25 per share. The

[5]*Opinions of the Accounting Principles Board, No. 14,* "Accounting for Convertible Debt and Debt Issued with Stock Purchase Warrants" (New York: American Institute of Certified Public Accountants, 1969), par. 16.

warrants expire after one year. Immediately following the issuance of the preferred stock, the warrants are selling at $3, and the fair market value of the preferred stock without the warrant attached is $57. The proceeds of $60,000 should be allocated by the Randall Co. as follows:

$$\text{Value assigned to the warrants} = \frac{\$3}{\$57 + \$3} \times \$58,000 = \$2,900$$

A similar allocation would be made by the investor, and the warrants would subsequently be accounted for in the same manner as stock rights.

The entry on Randall's books to record the sale of the preferred stock with detachable warrants is as follows:

Cash..	58,000	
Preferred Stock, $50 par		50,000
Paid-In Capital in Excess of Par—Preferred Stock		5,100
Common Stock Warrants		2,900

If the warrants are exercised, the entry to record the issuance of common stock would be as follows:

Common Stock Warrants	2,900	
Cash..	25,000	
Common Stock, $20 par...		20,000
Paid-In Capital in Excess of Par—Common Stock		7,900

This entry would be the same regardless of the market price of the common stock at the issuance date.

If the warrants in the example were allowed to expire, the following entry would be made.

Common Stock Warrants	2,900	
Paid-In Capital from Expired Warrants............................		2,900

If warrants are nondetachable, the securities are considered inseparable, and no allocation is made to recognize the value of the warrant. The entire proceeds are assigned to the security to which the warrant is attached. Thus, for nondetachable warrants, the accounting treatment is similar to that for convertible securities, such as convertible bonds. Some accountants feel this inconsistency is not justified since the economic value of a warrant exists, even if the warrant cannot be traded separately or "detached." This is essentially the same argument made for recognizing the conversion feature of a convertible security. Notwithstanding this argument, a separate instrument does not exist for a nondetachable warrant, and current practice does not require a separate value to be assigned to these warrants.

Stock Options Issued to Employees

Many corporations have adopted various types of stock option plans giving executives and other employees the opportunity to purchase stock in the employer company. Often these plans are intended as a form of compensation, especially when directed toward or restricted to the executives of a company. These plans are referred to as **compensatory plans**, as contrasted to **noncompensatory plans** that are offered to all full-time employees on an equal basis. Noncompensatory plans generally provide for the purchase of stock at a relatively small discount from the market price of the stock. For example, all employees of IBM Corporation are allowed to purchase IBM stock at a 15% discount.

No special accounting problems arise for noncompensatory stock option plans. Stock issued upon the exercise of the options is recorded normally, as an increase in common or preferred stock including any applicable paid-in capital in excess of par or stated value. The issue price is the amount of cash received, i.e., the exercise price.

The major accounting questions associated with compensatory plans include:

1. What amount of compensation expense, if any, should be recognized?
2. When should the compensation expense be recognized, i.e., what period should be charged with the cost?
3. What information should be disclosed relative to stock option plans?

Measuring Compensation Expense. For a number of years, the accounting standard in this area has been APB Opinion No. 25, "Accounting for Stock Issued to Employees."[6] Even though APB Opinion No. 25 has been generally accepted for some time, its guidelines have been questioned perhaps because of perceived inconsistencies in the treatment of various types of stock option plans. Consequently, this is a topic that is currently being considered by the FASB.

One of the key issues regarding compensatory stock option plans concerns an appropriate **measurement date**, i.e., the date on which the value of stock options should be determined. Several possibilities exist: (1) the date of adoption of a plan (**plan date**); (2) the date an option is granted to a specific individual grantee (**grant date**); (3) the date on which the grantee may first exercise an option (**exercisable date**); (4) the date the grantee actually exercises an option (**exercise date**); (5) the date the grantee disposes of the stock acquired (**disposal date**); or (6) when variable factors are involved, the date at which both the number of shares and the option price are first known. These dates are not necessarily mutually exclusive. In some cases, for example, the exercisable date may coincide with the exercise date.

---

[6]*Opinions of the Accounting Principles Board, No. 25,* "Accounting for Stock Issued to Employees" (New York: American Institute of Certified Public Accountants, 1972), par. 7.

The Accounting Principles Board defined the proper measurement date as the first date on which the following are both known: (1) the number of shares that an individual employee is entitled to receive, and (2) the option or exercise price, if any.[7] For "fixed plans," i.e., plans in which the number of shares and the exercise price are set at the date of grant, the measurement date is generally the date of grant. Plans with variable terms, however, normally use a later measurement date, often the exercisable or exercise date.

The amount of compensation expense to be recognized for a compensatory plan is the amount by which the market price of the stock at the measurement date exceeds the exercise price. Thus, an employer will recognize compensation expense only if the exercise price is less than the market price at the measurement date.

If compensation expense is to be recognized and the amount has been determined, the remaining accounting problem is determining when the compensation expense should be recognized. Generally, the compensation should be charged to the current and future periods in which the employees perform the services for which the options were granted. Past periods should not be adjusted. The grant may specify the period or periods during which the service is to be performed, or it may be inferred from the past patterns of grants or awards. When several periods of employment are involved before the stock is issued, the employer corporation should accrue compensation expense in each period involved. If the measurement date is later than the grant date, the compensation expense for each period prior to the measurement date must be estimated based on the quoted market price of the stock at the end of each period.[8]

As noted earlier, the FASB is currently studying the issues surrounding accounting and reporting for stock option plans. As a result, accounting for these plans is in a state of uncertainty. This uncertainty is compounded by frequent changes in the tax laws, some of which make certain types of stock option plans less attractive as a form of compensation. At present, however, the accounting and reporting requirements for stock option plans are those in APB Opinion No. 25. These requirements are illustrated in the following sections. Fixed stock option plans are presented first, followed by variable plans.

Recording Compensatory Stock Options—Fixed Plans. To illustrate accounting for compensatory stock options under a fixed plan, assume that on December 31, 1985, the board of directors of the Duncan Co. authorized the grant of stock options to supplement the salaries of certain execu-

---

[7]*Ibid.*, par. 10b.
[8]*Ibid.*, par. 13.

tives. The options permit the purchase of 10,000 shares of $10 par common stock at a price of $47.50. The market price of the stock at the grant date was $50. Options can be exercised beginning January 1, 1988, but only by executives that are still in the employ of the company; the options expire at the end of 1989. All options are exercised on December 31, 1988, when the $10 par common stock is quoted on the market at $60.

The value of the stock options at the date of the grant (compensation expense) is determined as follows:

Market value of common stock on December 31, 1985, 10,000 shares at $50..	$500,000
Option price, 10,000 shares at $47.50...................................	475,000
Value of stock options (compensation expense)	$ 25,000

The terms of the grant indicate that the options relate to services to be performed for the period from the grant date to the exercisable date, or for 1986 and 1987.

The following entries are made by the corporation to record the grant of the options, the annual accrual of option rights, and the exercise of the options.

Transaction	Entry		
December 31, 1985 Grant of compensatory stock options.	(Memorandum entry) Granted options to executives for the purchase of 10,000 shares of common stock at $47.50. Options are exercisable beginning January 1, 1988, providing officers are in the employ of the company on that date. Options expire on December 31, 1989. Value of options on December 31, 1985, is $25,000 (market value of stock, $500,000; option price, $475,000).		

December 31, 1986
To record compensation and stock option credit accrual for 1986. Value of stock options, $25,000; period of service covered by plan, 1986 and 1987; cost assigned to 1986: ½ × $25,000 = $12,500.
	Executive Compensation Expense..
	    Credit Under Stock Option
	      Plan......................
		12,500	12,500

December 31, 1987
To record compensation and stock option credit accrual for 1987: ½ × $25,000 = $12,500.
	Executive Compensation Expense..
	    Credit Under Stock Option
	      Plan......................
		12,500	12,500

December 31, 1988
To record exercise of stock options: cash received for stock, 10,000 shares at $47.50, or $475,000; par value of stock issued, 10,000 shares at $10, or $100,000.
	Cash.............................
	Credit Under Stock Option Plan ....
	    Common Stock...............
	    Paid-In Capital in Excess of
	      Par ....
		475,000
		25,000
			100,000
			
			400,000

The accrued compensation reported in Credit Under Stock Option Plan is properly reported as a part of paid-in capital because it represents investments of services made by employees that are expected to be paid for by the issuance of capital stock at a reduced price. If options expire through a failure of employees to meet the conditions of the option or through changes in the price of the stock making exercise of options unattractive, the balance of the account should be eliminated by decreasing compensation expense in the period of forfeiture.[9]

Recording Compensatory Stock Options—Variable Plans. As noted previously, stock option plans with variable terms generally use the exercisable or exercise date as the measurement date instead of the grant date, since this is usually the earliest date that both the number of shares and the option price can be determined. This presents a problem in recording the compensation expense during the period between the grant date and the exercise date. FASB Interpretation No. 28 addressed this problem and requires the accrual of compensation expense for variable plans in the appropriate service periods.[10] The Interpretation indicates that changes in the market value, either up or down, between the grant date and the measurement date result in a change in the measurement of compensation associated with the options. If a quoted market price is not available, the best estimate of the market value should be used. A catch-up adjustment for the changes in values is to be reflected in the period when the change occurs and the new balance spread over current and future periods.

To illustrate, if the grant provisions offered by Duncan Co. were variable and the measurement date occurred after the grant date, different entries would be required than those shown on page 718. Assume that on December 31, 1985, the executives of Duncan Co. are given the right to purchase 10,000 shares of $10 par stock at 80% of the market price on December 31, 1987, two years after the grant date. December 31, 1987, is the measurement date in this case, since it is the earliest date that the option price is known. To be eligible for the stock, the executives must remain with the company until the exercisable date, December 31, 1988. The market price for the stock is as follows: December 31, 1985, date of grant, $50; December 31, 1986, end of first year of service period, $60; December 31, 1987, end of second year of service period, $65; and December 31, 1988, exercise date, $80.

---

[9]*Ibid.*, par. 15.

[10]*FASB Interpretation No. 28*, "Accounting for Stock Appreciation Rights and Other Variable Stock Option or Award Plans" (Stamford: Financial Accounting Standards Board, 1978).

The following entries and computations would be made to record the annual accruals of option rights and the exercise of the options for the variable stock option plan.

Transaction	Entry

December 31, 1986
To record estimate of compensation expense accrual for 1986, market price of stock, December 31, 1986, $60; estimated option price, 80% of $60, or $48; estimated value of option per share, $12 ($60 − $48); total compensation, $120,000 ($12 × 10,000). Period of services rendered, three years or $40,000 each year.
	Executive Compensation Expense.. 40,000
	  Credit Under Stock Option
	    Plan...................... 40,000

December 31, 1987
To record estimate of compensation expense accrual for 1987; market price of stock, December 31, 1987, $65; estimated option price, 80% of $65, or $52; estimated value of option per share, $13 ($65 − $52); total compensation, $130,000 ($13 × 10,000). Compensation recognized 1986, $40,000. Compensation as adjusted for changes in market values, to be recognized in 1987, $46,667 = ($130,000 ÷ 3 = $43,333) plus $3,334 catch-up from 1986.
	Executive Compensation Expense.. 46,667
	  Credit Under Stock Option
	    Plan...................... 46,667

December 31, 1988
To record compensation expense for 1988, as adjusted, and issuance of stock. (See computations.)
	Executive Compensation Expense .. 43,333
	  Credit Under Stock Option
	    Plan...................... 43,333
	
	Cash........................... 520,000
	Credit Under Stock Option Plan 130,000
	  Common Stock.............. 100,000
	  Paid-In Capital in Excess of
	    Par 550,000

Computations:

Date	Market Price	Per Share	Compensation Aggregate	Percentage Accrued	Accrued to Date	Accrual of Expense by Year 1986	1987	1988
12/31/86	$60	$12	$120,000	33⅓%	$ 40,000	$40,000		
					46,667		$46,667	
12/31/87	$65*	$13	$130,000	66⅔%	$ 86,667			
					43,333			$43,333
12/31/88	$65*	$13	$130,000	100%	$130,000			

*Measurement date value

It should be noted in the example that the compensation expense accrual of $46,667 recognizes the "catch-up" adjustment for changes in market value in 1987, which is in accordance with Interpretation No. 28. Recall that changes in accounting estimates are generally reflected in the current period or "spread" over current and future periods and that no cumulative effect or "catch-up" adjustment is required per APB Opinion No. 20. If the $10,000 change in estimate in the example had been spread only over the current and future periods, the compensation expense entry for 1987 and 1988 would have been $45,000 in each year ($130,000 − $40,000 = $90,000; $90,000 ÷ 2 = $45,000). Because the example deals with a variable stock option plan and falls specifically under Interpretation No. 28, a catch-up adjustment must be made to the current period, that is, in the period when the change was first determined.

Disclosure of Stock Options

When stock option plans are in existence, disclosure should be made as to the status of the option or plan at the end of the reporting period, including the number of shares under option, the option (exercise) price, and the number of shares that were exercisable. Information on options exercised should also be provided, including the number of options exercised and the option price. Note Eight to the financial statements of General Mills, Inc., reproduced in Appendix A, provides an illustration of disclosures for stock options.

STOCK CONVERSIONS

Stockholders may be permitted by the terms of their stock agreement or by special action of the corporation to exchange their holdings for stock of other classes. No gain or loss is recognized by the issuer on these conversions because it is an exchange of one form of equity for another. In certain instances, the exchanges may affect only corporate contributed capital accounts; in other instances, the exchanges may affect both capital and retained earnings accounts.

To illustrate the different conditions, assume that the capital of the Ellis Corporation on December 31, 1987 is as follows:

Preferred stock, $100 par, 10,000 shares	$1,000,000
Paid-in capital in excess of par	100,000
Common stock, $25 stated value, 100,000 shares	2,500,000
Paid-in capital in excess of stated value	500,000
Retained earnings	1,000,000

Preferred shares are convertible into common shares at any time at the option of the shareholder.

Case 1 — Assume the terms of conversion permit the exchange of one share of preferred for 4 shares of common. On December 31, 1987, 1,000 shares of preferred stock are exchanged for 4,000 shares of common. The amount originally paid for the preferred, $110,000, is now the consideration identified with 4,000 shares of common stock with a total stated value of $100,000. The conversion is recorded by the issuer as follows:

Preferred Stock, $100 par	100,000	
Paid-In Capital in Excess of Par.........................	10,000	
Common Stock, $25 stated value......................		100,000
Paid-In Capital in Excess of Stated Value................		10,000

Case 2 — Assume terms of conversion permit the exchange of one share of preferred for 5 shares of common. In converting 1,000 shares of preferred for 5,000 shares of common, an increase in common stock of $125,000 must be recognized, although it is accompanied by a decrease in the preferred equity of only $110,000; the increase in the legal capital related to the issue of common stock is generally accomplished by a debit to Retained Earnings. The conversion, then, is recorded as follows:

Preferred Stock, $100 par	100,000	
Paid-In Capital in Excess of Par.........................	10,000	
Retained Earnings	15,000	
Common Stock, $25 stated value......................		125,000

The problems relating to the conversion of bonds for capital stock were described in Chapter 15. When either stocks or bonds have conversion rights, the company must be in a position to issue securities of the required class. Unissued or reacquired securities may be maintained by the company for this purpose. Detailed information should be given on the balance sheet or in notes to the financial statements relative to security conversion features as well as the means for meeting conversion requirements.

STOCK SPLITS AND REVERSE STOCK SPLITS

When the market price of shares is relatively high and it is felt that a lower price will result in more active trading and a wider distribution of ownership, a corporation may authorize the shares outstanding to be replaced by a larger number of shares. For example, 100,000 shares of stock, par value $100, are exchanged for 500,000 shares of stock, par value $20. Each stockholder receives 5 new shares for each share owned. The increase in shares outstanding in this manner is known as a **stock split** or **stock split-up**. The reverse procedure, replacement of shares outstanding by a smaller number of shares, may be desirable when the price of shares is low and it is felt there may be certain advantages in having a higher price for shares. The reduction of shares outstanding by combining shares is referred to as a **reverse stock split** or a **stock split-down**.

After a stock split or reverse stock split, the capital stock balance remains the same; however, the change in the number of shares of stock outstanding is accompanied by a change in the par or stated value of the stock. The change in the number of shares outstanding, as well as the change in the par or stated value, may be recorded by means of a memorandum entry.

Stock splits are sometimes effected by issuing a large stock dividend. In this case, the par value of the stock is not changed, and an amount equal to the par value of the newly issued shares is transferred to the capital stock account from either additional paid-in capital or from retained earnings. A further discussion of this type of stock split is included in Chapter 17.

BALANCE SHEET DISCLOSURE OF CONTRIBUTED CAPITAL

Contributed capital and its components should be disclosed separately from Retained Earnings in the balance sheet. Within the contributed capital section, it is important to identify the major classes of stock with their related additional paid-in capital accounts. Although it is common practice to report a single amount for additional paid-in capital for each class of stock, separate accounts should be provided in the ledger to identify the individual sources of additional paid-in capital, e.g., paid-in capital in excess of par or stated value, paid-in capital from treasury stock, from forfeited stock subscriptions, or from donations by stockholders.

For each class of stock, a description of the major features should be disclosed, such as par or stated value, dividend preference, or conversion terms. The number of shares authorized, issued, and outstanding should also be disclosed. The balance sheet for General Mills, Inc. in Appendix A illustrates many of these points.

QUESTIONS

1. What are the basic rights inherent in the ownership of capital stock? What modifications of these basic rights are usually found in preferred stock?
2. What are the two major classifications of contributed capital?
3. Distinguish between cumulative preferred stock and noncumulative preferred stock. If a company with cumulative preferred stock outstanding fails to

declare dividends during the year, what disclosure should be made in the financial statements?

4. What is callable preferred stock? Redeemable preferred stock? Convertible preferred stock?

5. The Meat Co. treats proceeds from capital stock subscription defaults as miscellaneous revenue. (a) Would you approve of this practice? Explain. (b) What alternatives would the Meat Co. have when dealing with subscription defaults? (c) What limits the choice between the alternatives in (b)?

6. Explain the accounting principle followed in recording the issuance of capital stock in exchange for nonmonetary assets or services.

7. Why might a company purchase its own stock?

8. The Sun Co. reports treasury stock as a current asset, explaining that it intends to sell the stock soon to acquire working capital. Do you approve of this reporting?

9. (a) What is the basic difference between the cost method and the par value method of accounting for treasury stock?
(b) How will total stockholders' equity differ, if at all, under the two methods?

10. There is frequently a difference between the purchase price and the selling price of treasury stock. Why isn't this difference properly shown as an income statement item, especially in view of accounting pronouncements that restrict entries to Retained Earnings?

11. (a) What entries should be made on both the issuer's books and the investor's books when stock rights are issued to stockholders? (b) What entries should be made by both issuer and investor when stock is issued on the exercise of rights? (c) What information, if any, should appear on the company's balance sheet relative to outstanding rights?

12. Distinguish between a compensatory stock option plan and a noncompensatory stock option plan.

13. What determines the measurement date for purposes of a stock option plan valuation?

14. Preferred stockholders of the Light Corporation exchange their holdings for no-par common stock in accordance with terms of the preferred stock issue. How should this conversion be reported on the corporation books?

15. The controller of Upright Company contends that the redemption of preferred stock at less than its issuance price should be reported as an increase in Retained Earnings, since redemption at more than issuance price calls for a decrease in Retained Earnings. How would you answer the controller's argument?

16. Define a stock split and identify the major objectives of this corporate action.

DISCUSSION CASES

CASE 16-1
(Should par value be used to determine
the amount of contributed capital?)

The Boca Company, in payment for services, issues 5,000 shares of common stock to persons organizing and promoting the company, and another 20,000 shares in exchange for properties believed to have valuable mineral rights. The par value of the stock, $10 per share, is used in recording the consideration for the shares. Shortly after organization, the company decides to sell the properties and use the proceeds for another venture. The properties are sold for $265,000. What accounting issues are involved? How would you record the sale of properties and why?

CASE 16–2 (Giving something for nothing?)

Excerpts from an article appearing in the May 1, 1979, *Wall Street Journal* are presented as follows:

Dividend News

**IBM Holders Vote
4-for-1 Stock Split,
Effective May 10**

By a *Wall Street Journal* Staff Reporter

SAN DIEGO—International Business Machines Corp. shareholders as expected, authorized a four-for-one split of the company's stock, effective May 10.

At a quiet annual meeting attended by an estimated 1,400 of the computer giant's more than 600,000 shareholders, the split was opposed by less than 1% of the votes cast.

The split which is expected to make IBM's shares more attractive to small investors, will increase the number of authorized shares to 650 million from 162.5 million. About 583 million shares are expected to be outstanding after the split.

IBM has made numerous stock distributions in recent years so that 100 shares from 1958 ballooned to 1,135 shares at the annual meeting, but the forthcoming split is the first distribution since 1958 that will result in a change in the par value of IBM's shares. The par value will be reduced to $1.25 a share, from $5.00.

Regarding the mechanics of the split, IBM said that current stock certificates will remain in effect. Each shareholder of record May 10 will receive new certificates representing three shares for each held. The new certificates will be mailed around May 31.

Why did IBM propose the 4-for-1 stock split and why were the stockholders not opposed to the split? What will the impact be on the owners' equity section of IBM's balance sheet?

CASE 16–3 (Conversion of preferred stock)

Kenny Corporation suspended dividend payments on all four classes of capital stock outstanding because of a downturn in the economy. The four classes of stock include: 7% preferred stock, cumulative, $50 par; 5% preferred stock, noncumulative, convertible, $35 par; 9% preferred stock, noncumulative, $80 par; and common stock. Fifteen thousand shares of each class of stock were outstanding.

Dividends had been paid through 1984. Kenny did not pay dividends in 1985 or 1986. In 1987, the economy improved and a proposal to pay a dividend of $1.50 per share of common stock was made.

You own 100 shares of the 5%, noncumulative, convertible preferred stock and have been thinking of converting those 100 shares to common stock at the existing conversion rate of 3 to 1 (3 shares of common for 1 share of preferred). The rate is scheduled to drop to 2 to 1 at the end of 1987. Because the price of common stock has been rising rapidly, you are trying to decide between retaining your preferred stock or converting to common stock before the price goes higher and the ratio is lowered.

Assuming there is no conversion of preferred stock, how much cash does Kenny need to pay the proposed dividend? What are the merits of converting your stock at this time as opposed to waiting until after the dividend is paid and the conversion ratio decreases. Explain the issues involved.

IF no stated value or par, sell at purchase price

EXERCISES

EXERCISE 16–1   (Issuance of common stock)

The Rogers Company is authorized to issue 50,000 shares of $30 par value common stock. Record the following transactions in journal entry form.
(a) Issued 10,000 shares at par value; received cash.
(b) Issued 250 shares to attorneys for services in securing the corporate charter and for preliminary legal costs of organizing the corporation. The value of the services was $9,000.
(c) Issued 300 shares, valued objectively at $10,000, to the corporate promoters.
(d) Issued 8,500 shares of stock in exchange for buildings valued at $175,000 and land valued at $80,000.
(e) Received cash for 6,500 shares of stock sold at $38 per share.
(f) Issued 4,000 shares at $45 per share; received cash.

EXERCISE 16–2   (Par and stated values)

At the time of formation, the Dimension Corporation was authorized to issue 100,000 shares of common stock. Dimension later received cash from the issuance of 30,000 shares at $24.50 per share. Record the entries for the issuance of the common stock under each of the following assumptions. (Consider each assumption independently.)
(a) Stock has a par value of $22 per share.
(b) Stock has a stated value of $20 per share.
(c) Stock has no par or stated value.

EXERCISE 16–3
(Dividends per share; cumulative and noncumulative features)

The Lowell Company paid dividends at the end of each year as follows: 1985, $150,000; 1986, $240,000; 1987, $560,000. Determine the amount of dividends per

[Margin handwritten notes:]

c) Cash   735,000
*   C.S.   735,000*
*   (30,000 × 24.50)*

b) Cash   735,000
*   C.S.   600,000*
*   Pd-In Cap.   135,000*
*   (20 × 30,000)*

a) Cash   735,000
*   C.S. PAR   660,000*
*   Pd-In Cap   75,000*

share paid on common and preferred stock for each year, assuming independent capital structures as follows:

(a)   300,000 shares of no-par common; 10,000 shares of $100 par, 9% noncumulative preferred.

(b)   250,000 shares of no-par common; 20,000 shares of $100 par, 9% noncumulative preferred.

(c)   250,000 shares of no-par common; 20,000 shares of $100 par, 9% cumulative preferred.

(d)   250,000 shares of $10 par common; 30,000 shares of $100 par, 9% cumulative preferred.

EXERCISE 16–4   (Computing liquidation amounts)

The stockholders' equity for the Bigler Company on July 1, 1987, is given below.

Contributed capital:

Preferred stock, cumulative, $10 stated value, 37,000 shares outstanding, entitled upon involuntary liquidation to $12 per share plus dividends in arrears amounting to $4 per share on July 1, 1987	$370,000
Common stock, $2 stated value, 90,000 shares outstanding	180,000
Paid-in capital from sale of common stock at more than stated value	200,000
Retained Earnings	56,000
Total stockholders' equity	$806,000

Determine the amounts that would be paid to each class of stockholders if the company is liquidated on this date, assuming cash available for stockholders after meeting all of the creditors' claims is (a) $300,000; (b) $500,000; (c) $640,000.

EXERCISE 16–5   (Issuance of capital stock)

The Riverbottom Company was incorporated on January 1, 1987, with the following authorized capitalization:

20,000 shares of common stock, stated value $50 per share.
5,000 shares of 7% cumulative preferred stock, par value $15 per share.

Give the entries required for each of the following transactions:

(a)   Issued 12,000 shares of common stock for a total of $648,000 and 3,000 shares of preferred stock at $18 per share.

(b)   Subscriptions were received for 2,500 shares of common stock at a price of $52. A 30% down payment is received.

(c)   One subscriber defaults for 300 shares of common and the down payment is retained pending sale of these shares.

(d)   The 300 shares of common are sold at $51 per share. Loss on resale is charged against the account of the defaulting subscriber, and the down payment less the loss is returned to the subscriber.

(e)   Collected the remaining amount owed on the stock subscriptions and issued the stock.

(f)   The remaining authorized shares of common stock are sold at $58 per share.

EXERCISE 16–6 (Accounting for defaulted subscriptions)

On January 1, 1987, Cantor Corporation received authorization to issue 100,000 shares of common stock with a par value of $22 per share. The stock was offered at a subscription price of $40 per share, and subscriptions were received for 20,000 shares. Subscriptions were recorded by a debit to Common Stock Subscriptions Receivable and credits to Common Stock Subscribed and to a paid-in capital account. Subsequently, a subscriber who had contracted to purchase 1,500 shares defaulted after paying 40% of the subscription price. Identify four methods of accounting for the default, and give the journal entry to record the default under each method.

EXERCISE 16–7 (Acquisition and retirement of stock)

The Mathis Company reported the following balances related to common stock as of December 31, 1987:

Common Stock, $20 par, 100,000 shares issued and outstanding .. $2,000,000
Paid-in capital in excess of par 100,000

The company purchased and immediately retired 5,000 shares at $26 on June 1, 1988, and 12,000 shares at $18 on December 31, 1988. Give the entries to record the acquisition and retirement of the common stock. (Assume all shares were originally sold at the same price.)

EXERCISE 16–8 (Treasury stock; par value and cost methods)

The stockholders' equity of the Crawford Company as of December 31, 1987 was as follows:

Common stock, $15 par, authorized 275,000 shares; issued and
    outstanding 240,000 shares $3,600,000
Paid-in capital in excess of par 480,000
Retained earnings. 900,000

On June 1, 1988, Crawford reacquired 15,000 shares of its common stock at $16. The following transactions occurred in 1988 with regard to these shares.
    July 1   Sold 5,000 shares at $20.
    Aug. 1   Sold 8,000 shares at $14.
    Sept. 1   Retired 1,000 shares.
  (1) Using the *cost method* to account for treasury stock:
    (a) Prepare the journal entries to record all treasury stock transactions in 1988.
    (b) Prepare the stockholders' equity section of the balance sheet at December 31, 1988, assuming retained earnings of $1,005,000.
  (2) Using the *par value method* to account for treasury stock:
    (a) Prepare the journal entries to record all treasury stock transactions in 1988.
    (b) Prepare the stockholders' equity section of the balance sheet at December 31, 1988, assuming retained earnings of $1,005,000.

EXERCISE 16–9   (Stock rights)

P. Falcon bought 2,000 shares of Maltese Mining Co. common stock for $15 per share, on April 3, 1987. On June 22, 1988, Maltese Mining Co. issued stock rights to its holders of common stock, one right for each share owned. The terms of the exercise required 4 rights plus $15 for each share purchased. Maltese stock was selling ex-rights for $19 per share, and the rights have a market value of $1 each. On September 1, 1988, Falcon exercises 1,000 rights, and on October 15, 1988, sold the remaining rights at $1.40 each. What entries would be required to reflect the stock rights transactions in Falcon's accounting records?

EXERCISE 16–10   (Stock rights)

The Murray Co. holds stock of Hales Inc. acquired as follows:

	Shares	Total Cost
Lot A, 1986	75	$ 6,000
Lot B, 1987	125	11,000

In 1988, Murray Co. receives 200 rights to purchase Hales Inc. stock at $75 per share. Five rights are required to purchase one share. At issue date, rights had a market value of $4 each and stock was selling ex-rights at $96. Murray Co. used rights to purchase 30 additional shares of Hales Inc. Subsequently, the market price of the stock fell to $92, and Murray Co. allowed the unexercised rights to lapse. Assume use of the first-in, first-out method of identifying stock rights exercised. What entries are required to record the preceding events in Murray's accounting records?

EXERCISE 16–11   (Accounting for stock warrants)

The Long Company wants to raise additional equity capital. After analysis of the available options, the company decides to issue 1,000 shares of $80 par preferred stock with detachable warrants. The package of the stock and warrants sells for $92. The warrants enable the holder to purchase 1,000 shares of $25 par common stock at $30 per share. Immediately following the issuance of the stock, the stock warrants are selling at $9 per share. The market value of the preferred stock without the warrants is $85.

(1)   Prepare a journal entry for Long Company to record the issuance of the preferred stock and the attached warrants.
(2)   Assuming that all the warrants are exercised, prepare a journal entry for Long to record the exercise of the warrants.
(3)   Assuming that only 80% of the warrants are exercised, prepare a journal entry for Long to record the exercise and expiration of the warrants.

EXERCISE 16–12   (Accounting for compensatory stock options)

The stockholders of the Dear Co. on December 24, 1980, approved a plan granting certain officers of the company nontransferable options to buy 100,000 shares of no-par common stock at $32 per share. Stock was selling at this time at $40 per share. The option plan provides that the officers must be employed by the company for the next five years, that options can be exercised after January 1,

1986, and that options will expire at the end of 1987. One of the officers who had been granted options for 20,000 shares left the company at the beginning of 1984; remaining officers exercised their rights under the option plan at the end of 1987. Give the entries that should be made on the books of the corporation at the end of each year for 1980–1987 inclusive. The market price of the stock at January 1, 1986, was $60 per share.

EXERCISE 16–13   (Accounting for variable stock option plans)

On March 31, 1985, the Board of Directors of Allen Industries approved a stock option plan for its twenty executives to purchase 500 shares of $25 par common stock each. The plan further indicated that the twenty executives must remain with the company until March 31, 1988, at which time they could exercise their options. The exercise price is 90% of the market price of the stock on December 31, 1987. All outstanding options expire on December 31, 1989. Assuming the following stock prices and that all options are exercised on June 27, 1988, give the journal entries for the company for its calendar years 1985, 1986, 1987, and 1988.

Date	Stock Price
March 31, 1985	$30
December 31, 1985	35
December 31, 1986	45
December 31, 1987	42
March 31, 1988	45
June 27, 1988	46

exercise price

irrelevant

EXERCISE 16–14   (Convertible preferred stock)

Stockholders' equity for the Dome Co. on December 31 was as follows:

Preferred stock, $20 par, 30,000 shares issued and outstanding	$ 600,000
Paid-in capital in excess of par — preferred stock	90,000
Common stock, $10 par, 150,000 shares issued and outstanding	1,500,000
Paid-in capital in excess of par — common stock	450,000
Retained earnings	1,450,000

Preferred stock is convertible into common stock. Give the entry made on the corporation books assuming 1,800 shares of preferred are converted under each assumption listed:
  (a)   Preferred shares are convertible into common on a share-for-share basis.
  (b)   Each share of preferred stock is convertible into 4 shares of common.
  (c)   Each share of preferred stock is convertible into 2 shares of common.

EXERCISE 16–15   (Analysis of owners' equity)

From the following information, reconstruct the journal entries that were made by the Riverboat Corporation during 1987.

	December 31, 1987		December 31, 1986	
	Amount	Shares	Amount	Shares
Common stock	$175,000	7,000	$150,000	6,000
Paid-in capital in excess of par	54,250		36,000	
Paid-in capital from treasury stock ..	1,000	200	—	—
Retained earnings	76,500*	—	49,000	—
Treasury stock..................	15,000	300	—	—

*Includes net income for 1987 of $40,000. There were no dividends.

2,500 shares of common stock issued when the company was formed were purchased at the beginning of 1987 and were retired later in the year. The cost method is used to record treasury stock transactions.

PROBLEMS

PROBLEM 16–1   (Journalizing stock transactions)

Barclay Company began operations on January 1. 20,000 shares of $10 par value common stock and 4,000 shares of $100 par value convertible preferred stock were authorized. The following transactions involving stockholders' equity occurred during the first year of operations.

Jan.   1   Issued 500 shares of common stock to the corporation promoters in exchange for property valued at $13,000 and services valued at $5,000. The property had cost the promoters $9,000 three years previously and was carried on the promoters' books at $5,000.

Feb. 23   Issued 500 shares of convertible preferred stock with a par value of $100 per share. Each share can be converted to 5 shares of common stock. The stock was issued at a price of $150 per share, and the company paid $3,000 to an agent for selling the shares.

Mar. 10   Sold 3,000 shares of the common stock for $39 per share. Issue costs were $2,500.

Apr. 10   4,000 shares of common stock were sold under stock subscriptions at $45 per share. No shares are issued until a subscription contract is paid in full. No cash was received.

July 14   Exchanged 700 shares of common stock and 140 shares of preferred stock for a building with a fair value of $51,000. In addition, 600 shares of common stock were sold for $24,000 in cash.

Aug.   3   Received payments in full for half of the stock subscriptions, and payments on account on the rest of the subscriptions. Total cash received was $140,000. Shares of stock were issued for the subscriptions paid in full.

Sept. 28   Received 10 acres of land from the city of Riverton to be used for construction of a new factory. Total cost for Barclay was legal fees of $4,000, but the estimated fair value of the land was $75,000.

Dec.   1   Declared a cash dividend of $10 per share on preferred stock, payable on December 31 to stockholders of record on December 15, and a $2 per share dividend on common stock, payable on January 5 of the following year to stockholders of record on December 15. No dividends are paid on unissued subscribed stock.

Dec. 31   Received notice from holders of stock subscriptions for 800 shares that they would not pay further on the subscriptions since the price of the stock had fallen to $25 per share and the amount still due on those contracts was $30,000. Amounts previously paid on the contracts are forfeited according to the agreements.

Net income for the first year of operations was $60,000.

Instructions:

(1) Prepare journal entries to record the preceding transactions.

(2) Prepare the stockholders' equity section of the balance sheet at December 31.

PROBLEM 16–2
(Stockholders' equity transactions and balance sheet presentation)

The Riley Corporation was organized on September 1, 1987, with authorized capital stock of 200,000 shares of 9% cumulative preferred with a $40 par value and 1,000,000 shares of no-par common stock with a $30 stated value. During the balance of the year, the following transactions relating to capital stock were completed:

Oct.   1   Subscriptions were received for 300,000 shares of common stock at $42, payable $22 down and the balance in two equal installments due November 1 and December 1. On the same date 16,500 shares of common stock were issued to Jim Williams in exchange for his business. Assets transferred to the corporation were valued as follows: land, $210,000; buildings, $250,000; equipment, $50,000; merchandise, $110,000. Liabilities of the business assumed by the corporation were: mortgage payable, $41,000; accounts payable, $11,000; accrued interest on mortgage, $550. No goodwill is recognized in recording the issuance of the stock for net assets.

Oct.   3   Subscriptions were received for 120,000 shares of preferred stock at $45, payable $15 down and the balance in two equal installments due November 1, and December 1.

Nov.   1   Amounts due on this date were collected from all common and preferred stock subscribers.

Nov. 12   Subscriptions were received for 480,000 shares of common stock at $44, payable $22 down and the balance in two equal installments due December 1, and January 1.

Dec.   1   Amounts due on this date were collected from all common stock subscribers and stock fully paid for was issued. The final installment on preferred stock subscriptions was received from all subscribers except one whose installment due on this date was $9,000. State corporation laws provide that the company is liable for the return to the subscriber of the amount received less the loss on the subsequent resale of the stock. Preferred stock fully paid for was issued.

Dec.   6   Preferred stock defaulted on December 1 was issued for cash at $36. Stock was issued, and settlement was made with the defaulting subscriber.

Instructions:
(1) Prepare journal entries to record the foregoing transactions.
(2) Prepare the contributed capital section of stockholders' equity for the corporation as of December 31.

PROBLEM 16–3   (Reconstruction of equity transactions)

The Flaxin Company had the following account balances in its balance sheet at December 31, 1987, the end of its first year of operations. All stock was issued on a subscription basis, and the state laws permit the company to retain all partial subscriptions paid by defaulting subscribers.

Common Stock Subscriptions Receivable	$150,000
Common Stock, $25 par	75,000
Common Stock Subscribed	225,000
Paid-In Capital in Excess of Par — Common Stock	40,000
8% Preferred Stock, $100 par	100,000
Paid-In Capital in Excess of Par — 8% Preferred Stock	50,000
Paid-In Capital from Default on 8% Preferred Stock Subscriptions (200 Shares)	10,000
10% Preferred Stock, $50 par	25,000
Retained Earnings	20,000

The reported net income for 1987 was $55,000.

Instructions: From the data given, reconstruct in summary form the journal entries to record all transactions involving the company's stockholders. Indicate the amount of dividends distributed on each class of stock.

PROBLEM 16–4
(Comprehensive analysis and reporting of stockholders' equity)

The Grimmer Company has two classes of capital stock outstanding: 9%, $20 par preferred and $70 par common. During the fiscal year ending November 30, 1988, the company was active in transactions affecting the stockholders' equity. The following summarizes these transactions:

Type of Transaction	Number of Shares	Price per Share
(a) Issue of preferred stock	10,000	$28
(b) Issue of common stock	35,000	70
(c) Reacquisition and retirement of preferred stock	2,000	30
(d) Purchase of treasury stock — common (reported at cost)	5,000	80
(e) Stock split — common (par value reduced to $35)	2 for 1	
(f) Reissue of treasury stock — common	5,000	52

Balances of the accounts in the stockholders' equity section of the November 30, 1987, balance sheet were:

Preferred Stock, 50,000 shares	$1,000,000
Common Stock, 100,000 shares	7,000,000
Paid-In Capital in Excess of Par — Preferred	400,000
Paid-In Capital in Excess of Par — Common	1,200,000
Retained Earnings	550,000

Dividends were paid at the end of the fiscal year on the common stock at $1.20 per share, and on the preferred stock at the preferred rate. Net income for the year was $850,000.

Instructions: Based on the preceding data, prepare the stockholders' equity section of the balance sheet as of November 30, 1988. (Note: A work sheet beginning with November 30, 1987 balances and providing for transactions for the current year will facilitate the preparation of this section of the balance sheet.)

PROBLEM 16–5   (Accounting for various capital stock transactions)

The stockholders' equity section of Maverick Inc. showed the following data on December 31, 1986: common stock, $30 par, 300,000 shares authorized, 250,000 shares issued and outstanding, $7,500,000; paid in capital on common stock, $300,000; credit under stock option plan, $150,000; retained earnings, $580,000. The stock options were granted to key executives and provided them the right to acquire 30,000 shares of common stock at $35 per share. The stock was selling at $40 at the time the options were granted.

The following transactions occurred during 1987:

Mar. 31   4,500 options outstanding at December 31, 1986 were exercised. The market price per share was $44 at this time.

Apr.   1   The company issued bonds of $2,000,000 at par, giving each $1,000 bond a detachable warrant enabling the holder to purchase 2 shares of stock at $40 for a 1-year period. The stock was selling for $41 per share at that date.

June 30   The company issued rights to stockholders (1 right on each share) permitting holders to acquire for a 30-day period 1 share at $40 with every 10 rights submitted. Shares were selling for $43 at this time. All but 6,000 rights were exercised on July 31, and the additional stock was issued.

Sept. 30   All shares were issued in connection with rights issued on the sale of bonds.

Nov. 30   The market price per share dropped to $32 and options came due. Since the market price was below the option price, no remaining options were exercised.

Instructions:
(1) Give entries to record the foregoing transactions.
(2) Prepare the stockholders' equity section of the balance sheet as of December 31, 1987, (assume net income of $210,000 for 1987).

PROBLEM 16–6   (Accounting for various capital stock transactions)

The Weber Co., organized on June 1, 1987, was authorized to issue stock as follows:

80,000 shares of preferred 9% stock, convertible, $100 par
250,000 shares of common stock, $25 stated value

During the remainder of the Weber Co.'s fiscal year ending May 31, 1988 the following transactions were completed in the order given.

(a) 30,000 shares of preferred stock were subscribed for at $103 and 80,000 shares of the common stock were subscribed for at $28. Both subscriptions were payable 30% upon subscription, the balance in one payment.

(b) The second subscription payment was received, except one subscriber for 6,000 shares of common stock defaulted on payment. The full amount paid by this subscriber was returned, and all of the fully paid stock was issued.

(c) 15,000 shares of common stock were reacquired by purchase at $18. (Treasury stock is recorded at cost.)

(d) Each share of preferred stock was converted into 4 shares of common stock.

(e) The treasury stock was exchanged for machinery with a fair market value of $280,000.

(f) There was a 2:1 stock split and the stated value of the new common stock is $12.50.

(g) A major stockholder donated 100,000 shares of common stock to the company when the market value was $20 per share.

(h) Net income was $123,000.

Instructions:

(1) Give the journal entries to record the foregoing transactions. (For net income, give the entry to close the income summary account to Retained Earnings.)

(2) Prepare the stockholders' equity section as of May 31, 1988.

PROBLEM 16–7   (Issuance, reacquisition, and resale of capital stock)

Deseret Diamond Company had the following transactions occur during 1987:

(a) 8,000 shares of common stock are issued to the founders for land valued at $450,000. Par value of the common stock is $30 per share.

(b) 3,000 shares of $100 par preferred stock were issued for cash at 110.

(c) 500 shares of common stock were sold to the company president for $60 per share.

(d) 300 shares of outstanding preferred stock were purchased for cash at par.

(e) 500 shares of the outstanding common stock issued in (a) were purchased for $55 per share.

(f) 150 shares of repurchased preferred stock were reissued at 102.

(g) 300 shares of reacquired common stock was reissued for $57 per share.

(h) 100 shares of the common stock sold in (g) were repurchased for $53 per share.

Instructions:

(1) Prepare the necessary entries to record the preceding transactions involving Deseret Diamond's preferred stock. Assume that the par value method is used for recording treasury stock.

(2) Prepare the necessary entries for the common stock transactions assuming that the cost method is used for recording treasury stock.

PROBLEM 16–8   (Treasury stock transactions)

Transactions of the Excellsor Company during 1987, the first year of operations, that affected its stockholders' equity are given below.

(a) Issued 30,000 shares of 9% preferred stock, $20 par, at $26.

(b) Issued 50,000 shares of $30 par common stock at $33.
(c) Purchased and immediately retired 4,000 shares of preferred stock at $28.
(d) Purchased 6,000 shares of its own common stock at $35.
(e) Reissued 1,000 shares of treasury stock at $37.
(f) Stockholders donated to the company 4,000 shares of common when shares had a market price of $36. One half of these shares were sold for $38.

No dividends were declared in 1987 and net income for 1987 was $185,000.

Instructions:
(1) Record each of the transactions. Assume treasury stock acquisitions are recorded at cost.
(2) Prepare the stockholders' equity section of the balance sheet, assuming treasury stock is recorded at cost.

PROBLEM 16–9   (Accounting for stock options)

The board of directors of the Marlin Company adopted a stock option plan to supplement the salaries of certain executives of the company. Options to buy common stock were granted as follows:

	Number of Shares	Option Price	Price of Shares at Date of Grant
Jan. 10, 1985.........Q. L. Peck......	75,000	20	21
June 30, 1985.........A. G. Byrd......	50,000	25	26
June 30, 1985.........K. C. Nelson....	20,000	25	26

Options are nontransferable and can be exercised 3 years after date of grant providing the executive is still in the employ of the company. Options expire 2 years after the date they can first be exercised.

Nelson left the employ of the company at the beginning of 1987.

Stock options were exercised as follows:

	Number of Shares	Price of Shares at Date of Exercise
Jan. 15, 1988 .... Q. L. Peck..........	60,000	45
Dec. 20, 1988 .... Q. L. Peck..........	15,000	36
Dec. 22, 1988 .... A. G. Byrd..........	50,000	32

Stock of the company has a $14 par value. The accounting period for the company is the calendar year.

Instructions: Give all entries that would be made on the books of the company relative to the stock option agreement for the period 1985 to 1988 inclusive.

PROBLEM 16–10   (Variable stock options)

The Denver Distributing Company adopted an executive stock option plan on January 1, 1986. The plan states that all executives remaining with the firm until the exercisable date would be eligible for the stock. The options are exercisable beginning January 1, 1989, and will expire on December 31, 1989. The option price is to be 75% of the market price on January 1, 1988. The stock price on December 31, 1986, was 90 and on December 31, 1988, was 120. The following information was given for 1989:

Change in common stock (par $30) from options exercised	$180,000
Change in paid-in capital on common stock from options exercised . .	450,000
Balance remaining in Credit Under Stock Option Plan	78,750

Instructions:
(1) Compute the following:
   (a) The stock price at December 31, 1987, (b) cash received on options exercised, (c) the total number of shares optioned to the executives, and (d) the executive compensation expense for 1986, 1987, and 1988.
(2) Give the journal entries for 1989.

PROBLEM 16–11   (Analysis of stock transactions)

You have been asked to audit the Jamestown Company. During the course of your audit, you are asked to prepare comparative data from the company's inception to the present. You have determined the following:
   (a) Jamestown Company's charter became effective on January 2, 1984, when 2,000 shares of no-par common and 1,000 shares of 7% cumulative, non-participating, preferred stock were issued. The no-par common stock had no stated value and was sold at $120 per share, and the preferred stock was sold at its par value of $100 per share.
   (b) Jamestown was unable to pay preferred dividends at the end of its first year. The owners of the preferred stock agreed to accept 2 shares of common stock for every 50 shares of preferred stock owned in discharge of the preferred dividends due on December 31, 1984. The shares were issued on January 2, 1985, which was also the declaration date. The fair market value was $100 per share for common on the date of issue.
   (c) Jamestown Company acquired all of the outstanding stock of Booth Corporation on May 1, 1986, in exchange for 1,000 shares of Jamestown common stock.
   (d) Jamestown split its common stock 3 for 2 on January 1, 1987, and 2 for 1 on January 1, 1988.
   (e) Jamestown offered to convert 20% of the preferred stock to common stock on the basis of 2 shares of common for 1 share of preferred. The offer was accepted, and the conversion was made on July 1, 1988.
   (f) No cash dividends were declared on common stock until December 31, 1986. Cash dividends per share of common stock were declared as follows:

	June 30	Dec 31
1986.		$3.19
1987.	$1.75	2.75
1988.	1.25	1.25

Instructions: Prepare schedules that show the computation of:
(1) The number of shares of each class of stock outstanding on the last day of each year from 1984 through 1988.

(continued)

(2) Total cash dividends applicable to common stock for each year from 1986 through 1988.   (AICPA adapted)

PROBLEM 16–12   (Auditing stockholders' equity)

You have been assigned to the audit of Baylor Inc., a manufacturing company. You have been asked to summarize the transactions for the year ended December 31, 1987, affecting stockholders' equity and other related accounts. The stockholders' equity section of Baylor's December 31, 1987, balance sheet follows:

Stockholders' Equity

Paid-in capital:		
Common stock, $20 par value, 500,000 shares authorized, 90,000 shares issued...................	$1,800,000	
Paid-in capital from treasury stock...................	22,500	
Paid-in capital in excess of par......................	200,000	$2,022,500
Retained earnings		324,689
Total		$2,347,189
Less cost of 1,210 shares of common stock in treasury		72,600
Total stockholders' equity...........................		$2,274,589

You have extracted the following information from the accounting records and audit working papers.

1988

Jan. 15   Six hundred fifty shares of treasury stock were reissued for $40 per share. The 1,210 shares of treasury stock on hand at December 31, 1987, were purchased in one block in 1987. Baylor used the cost method for recording the treasury shares purchased.

Feb. 2   Ninety, $1,000, 9% bonds due February 1, 1991, were sold at 103 with one detachable stock purchase warrant attached to each bond. Interest is payable annually on February 1. The fair value of the bonds without the stock warrants is 97. The detached warrants have a fair value of $60 each and expire on February 1, 1989. Each warrant entitles the holder to purchase 10 shares of common stock at $40 per share.

Mar. 6   Subscriptions for 1,400 shares of common stock were issued at $44 per share, payable 40% down and the balance by March 20.

Mar. 20   The balance due on 1,200 shares was received and those shares were issued. The subscriber who defaulted on the 200 remaining shares forfeited the down payment in accordance with the subscription agreement.

Nov. 1   Fifty-five stock warrants detached from the bonds were exercised.

Instructions: Give journal entries required to summarize the above transactions.
(AICPA adapted)

17
Owners' Equity — Retained Earnings

In the previous chapter, owners' equity was defined as the residual ownership interest in the net assets (total assets minus total liabilities) of a business. Owners' equity was further classified into that portion of capital that is contributed by owners and the amount of earnings generated and retained by the enterprise. Chapter 16 discussed the accounting issues associated with contributed capital; the purpose of this chapter is to identify and explain the different types of transactions and events that directly affect **Retained Earnings**.

The nature of retained earnings is frequently misunderstood, and this misunderstanding may lead to incorrect impressions in reading and interpreting financial statements. The retained earnings account is essentially the meeting place of the balance sheet accounts and the income statement accounts. In successive periods, retained earnings are increased by income and decreased by losses and dividends. As a result, the retained earnings balance represents the net accumulated earnings of a corporation. If the retained earnings account were affected only by income (losses) and dividends, there would be little confusion in its interpretation. A number of other factors, however, can affect retained earnings.

FACTORS AFFECTING RETAINED EARNINGS

In addition to earnings or losses and dividends, factors that affect Retained Earnings include: prior period adjustments for corrections of errors, quasi-reorganizations, and treasury stock transactions (discussed in Chapter 16). The transactions and events that increase or decrease Retained Earnings may be summarized as follows:

Retained Earnings

Decreases	Increases
Prior period adjustments for overstatements of past earnings	Prior period adjustments for understatements of past earnings
Current net loss	Current net income
Dividends	Quasi-reorganizations
Treasury stock transactions	

Prior Period Adjustments

In some situations, errors made in past years are discovered and corrected in the current year by an adjustment to Retained Earnings, referred to as a **prior period adjustment**. There are several types of errors that may occur in measuring the results of operations and the financial status of an enterprise. Accounting errors can result from mathematical mistakes, a failure to apply appropriate accounting procedures, or a misstatement or omission of certain information. In addition, a change from an accounting principle that is not generally accepted to one that is accepted is considered a correction of an error.[1]

Fortunately, most errors are discovered during the accounting period, prior to closing the books. When this is the case, corrections can be made by adjusting entries directly to the accounts. The corrected balances are then shown on the balance sheet and on the income statement.

Sometimes errors go undetected during the current period, but they are offset by an equal misstatement in the subsequent period; that is, they are **counterbalanced**. When this happens, the under- or overstatement of income in one period is counterbalanced by an equal over- or understatement of income in the next period, and after the closing process is completed for the second year, Retained Earnings is correctly stated. If a counterbalancing error is discovered during the second year, however, it should be corrected at that time.

When errors of past periods are not counterbalancing, Retained Earnings will be misstated until a correction is made in the accounting records. If the error is material, a prior period adjustment should be made directly to the retained earnings account.[2] If an error resulted in an understatement of income in previous periods, a correcting entry would be needed to increase retained earnings; if an error overstated income in prior periods, then retained earnings would have to be decreased. These adjustments for corrections in net income of prior periods would typically be shown as a part of the total change in retained earnings as follows:

---

[1]*Opinions of the Accounting Principles Board, No. 20,* "Accounting Changes" (New York: American Institute of Certified Public Accountants, 1971) par. 13.

[2]*Ibid.*, par. 36.

Retained Earnings, unadjusted beginning balance	$xxx
Add or deduct prior period adjustments	xx
Retained Earnings, adjusted beginning balance.............................	$xxx
Add current year's net income or deduct current year's net loss..............	xx
	$xxx
Deduct dividends..	xx
Retained Earnings, ending balance.......................................	$xxx

When errors are discovered, the accountant must be able to analyze the situation and determine what action is appropriate under the circumstances. This calls for an understanding of accounting standards as well as good judgment. Chapter 23 covers in detail the techniques for analyzing and correcting errors.

Earnings

The primary source of retained earnings is the net income generated by a business. The retained earnings account is increased by net income and is reduced by net losses from business activities. When operating losses or other debits to Retained Earnings produce a debit balance in this account, the debit balance is referred to as a **deficit**.

Corporate earnings originate from transactions with individuals or businesses outside the company. No earnings are recognized for the construction of buildings or other plant assets for a company's own use, even though the cost of such construction is below the market price for similar assets; self-construction at less than the asset purchase price is regarded simply as a savings in cost. No increases in retained earnings are recognized from transactions with stockholders involving treasury stock; however, as indicated in Chapter 16, decreases may be recognized. The receipt of assets through donation is not recognized as earnings, but as paid-in capital. The earnings of a corporation may be distributed to the stockholders or retained to provide for expanding operations.

Dividends

Dividends are distributions to the stockholders of a corporation in proportion to the number of shares held by the respective owners. Distributions may take the form of (1) cash, (2) other assets, (3) notes or other evidence of corporate indebtedness, in effect, deferred cash dividends, and (4) stock dividends, i.e., shares of a company's own stock. Most dividends involve reductions in retained earnings. Exceptions include (1) some stock dividends issued in the form of stock splits, which involve a transfer from additional paid-in capital to legal capital, and (2) dividends in corporate liquidation, which represent a return to stockholders of a portion or all of their investment and call for reductions in contributed capital.

Use of the term *dividend* without qualification normally implies the distribution of cash. Dividends in a form other than cash, such as property or stock dividends, should be designated by their special form. Distributions from a capital source other than retained earnings should carry a description of their special origin, e.g., *liquidating dividend* or *dividend distribution of paid-in capital*.

"Dividends paid out of retained earnings" is an expression frequently encountered. Accuracy, however, requires recognition that dividends are paid out of cash, which serves to reduce retained earnings. Earnings of the corporation increase net assets or stockholders' equity. Dividend distributions represent no more than asset withdrawals that reduce net assets. The nature and types of dividends are covered in depth later in the chapter.

Other Changes in Retained Earnings

The most common changes in Retained Earnings result from earnings (or losses) and dividends. Other changes may occur, however, resulting from treasury stock transactions or from a quasi-reorganization, which is effected only under special circumstances where a business seeks a "fresh start."

The remainder of this chapter focuses on accounting for dividends, followed by a discussion of quasi-reorganizations.

ACCOUNTING FOR DIVIDENDS

Among the powers delegated by the stockholders to the board of directors is the power to control the dividend policy. Whether dividends shall or shall not be paid, as well as the nature and the amount of dividends, are matters that the board determines. In setting dividend policy, the board of directors must answer two questions:

1. Do we have the legal right to declare a dividend?
2. Is a dividend distribution financially advisable?

In answering the first question, the board of directors must observe the legal requirements governing the maintenance of legal capital. The laws of different states range from those making any part of capital other than legal capital available for dividends to those permitting dividends only to the extent of retained earnings and under specified conditions. In most states dividends cannot be declared in the event of a deficit; in a few states, however, dividends equal to current earnings may be distributed despite a previously accumulated deficit. The availability of capital as a basis for dividends is a determination to be made by the legal counsel and not by the accountant. The accountant must report accurately the sources of each capital increase or decrease; the legal counsel investigates the availability of such sources as bases for dividend distributions.

The board of directors must also consider the second question, i.e., the financial aspect of dividend distributions. The company's cash position relative to present and future cash requirements is a key factor. For example, a corporation may have retained earnings of $500,000. If it has cash of only $150,000, however, cash dividends must be limited to this amount unless it converts certain assets into cash or borrows cash. If the cash required for regular operations is $100,000, the cash available for dividends is then only $50,000. Although legally able to declare dividends of $500,000, the company would be able to distribute no more than one tenth of that amount at this time. Generally, companies pay dividends that are significantly less than the legal amount allowed or the amount of cash on hand.

When a dividend is legally declared and announced, it cannot be revoked. In the event of corporate insolvency after declaration but prior to payment of the dividend, stockholders have claims as a creditor group to the dividend, and as an ownership group to any assets remaining after all corporate liabilities have been paid. A dividend that was illegally declared, however, is revocable; in the event of insolvency at the time of declaration, such action is nullified and stockholders participate in asset distributions only after creditors have been paid in full.

Restrictions on Retained Earnings

Although state laws generally permit the distribution of dividends to the extent of retained earnings, other factors may limit the amount of dividends that can be declared. For example, a portion of retained earnings may be restricted as a result of contractual requirements, such as agreements with creditors that provide for the retention of earnings to ensure repayment of debt at maturity. Retained earnings may also be restricted at the discretion of the board of directors. For example, the board may designate a portion of retained earnings as restricted for a particular purpose, such as expansion of plant facilities.

If restrictions on retained earnings are material, they are generally disclosed in a note to the financial statements. Sometimes, however, the restricted portion of retained earnings is reported on the balance sheet separately from the unrestricted amount that is available for dividends. The restricted portion may be designated as **appropriated retained earnings** and the unrestricted portion as **unappropriated** (or **free**) **retained earnings**. When the restrictions are recognized in the accounts, the entry is a debit to the regular retained earnings account and a credit to a special appropriated retained earnings account.

As an example, assume Hanover Company restricted $100,000 of its $600,000 retained earnings balance for possible plant expansion by making the following entry on January 1, 1987.

Jan. 1, 1987	Retained Earnings..	100,000	
	Appropriated Retained Earnings............................		100,000
	To restrict retained earnings for possible plant expansion.		

The balance sheet subsequent to this entry would reflect both retained earnings accounts.

Appropriated retained earnings	$100,000
Unappropriated retained earnings....................	500,000
Total retained earnings	$600,000

Once the purpose of the appropriation has been served, the original entry creating the appropriated retained earnings balance is reversed. To illustrate, assume that on June 15, the Hanover Company decided not to expand its plant and to eliminate the appropriated retained earnings balance. The applicable entry would be

Appropriated Retained Earnings.................................	100,000	
Retained Earnings		100,000
To discontinue the appropriation of retained earnings for plant expansion.		

Note that there is no segregation of funds and no gain or loss involved in the restriction of retained earnings. Whatever the form of disclosure, the main idea behind restrictions on retained earnings is to alert stockholders that some of the assets that might otherwise be available for dividend distribution are being retained within the business for specific purposes. Because the amount of dividends actually paid is usually much less than the retained earnings balance, this is generally not a significant issue.

Recognition and Payment of Dividends

Three dates are essential in the recognition and payment of dividends: (1) date of declaration, (2) date of record, and (3) date of payment. Dividends are made payable to stockholders of record as of a date following the date of declaration and preceding the date of payment. The liability for dividends payable is recorded on the declaration date and is canceled on the payment date. No entry is required on the record date, but a list of the stockholders is made as of the close of business on this date. These are the persons who receive dividends on the payment date. For example, on April 1, 1986, Ford Motor Co. declared a cash dividend payable on June 2 to stockholders of record on May 2.

Stockholders become aware of a forthcoming dividend upon its declaration and announcement. If stock is sold and a new owner is recognized by the corporation prior to the record date, the dividend is paid to the new owner. If a stock transfer is not recognized by the corporation until after the record date, the dividend will be paid to the former owner, i.e., the shareholder of record. After the record date, stock no longer carries a right to dividends and sells at a lower price or **ex-dividend**.[3] Accordingly, a stockholder is justified in recognizing the corporate dividend action on the record date by debiting a receivable and crediting Dividend Revenue. Upon receipt of the dividend, Cash is debited and the receivable is eliminated. In practice, however, the accrual is frequently omitted, and dividend revenue is recognized when the cash is received.

Cash Dividends

The most common type of dividend is a **cash dividend**. For the corporation, these dividends involve a reduction in retained earnings and in cash. For the investor, a cash dividend generates cash and is recognized as dividend revenue. Entries to record the declaration and the payment of a cash dividend by a corporation follow:

Retained Earnings	100,000	
Dividends Payable		100,000
Dividends Payable	100,000	
Cash		100,000

Property Dividends

A distribution to stockholders that is payable in some asset other than cash is generally referred to as a **property dividend**. Frequently the assets to be distributed are securities of other companies owned by the corporation. The corporation thus transfers to its stockholders its ownership interest in such securities. Property dividends occur most frequently in closely held corporations.

This type of transfer is sometimes referred to as a **nonreciprocal transfer to owners** inasmuch as nothing is received by the company in return for its distribution to the stockholders. These transfers should be recorded using the fair market value (as of the day of declaration) of the assets distributed, and a gain or loss recognized for the difference between the carrying value on the books of the issuing company and the fair market

---

[3]Stock on the New York Stock Exchange is normally quoted ex-dividend (or ex-rights) four full trading days prior to the record date because of the time required to deliver the stock and to record the stock transfers.

value of the assets.[4] Property dividends are valued at carrying value if the fair market value is not determinable.

To illustrate the entries for a property dividend, assume that the Bingo Corporation owns 100,000 shares in the Tri-State Oil Co., cost $2,000,000, fair market value $3,000,000, which it wishes to distribute to its stockholders. There are 1,000,000 shares of Bingo Corporation stock outstanding. Accordingly, a dividend of 1/10 of a share of Tri-State Oil Co. stock is declared on each share of Bingo Corporation stock outstanding. The entries for the dividend declaration and payment are:

Retained Earnings	3,000,000	
Property Dividends Payable		3,000,000
Property Dividends Payable	3,000,000	
Investment in Tri-State Oil Co. Stock		2,000,000
Gain on Distribution of Property Dividends		1,000,000

Stock Dividends

A corporation may distribute to stockholders additional shares of the company's own stock as a **stock dividend**. A stock dividend permits the corporation to retain within the business net assets produced by earnings while at the same time offering stockholders additional ownership shares.

Accounting for Stock Dividends by the Issuer. A stock dividend usually involves (1) the capitalization of retained earnings, and (2) a distribution of common stock to common stockholders. These distributions are sometimes referred to as "ordinary stock dividends." In other instances, common stock is issued to holders of preferred stock or preferred stock is issued to holders of common stock. These distributions are sometimes referred to as "special stock dividends."

A stock dividend decreases retained earnings while increasing the legal capital of a corporation. In recording the dividend, a debit is made to Retained Earnings and credits are made to appropriate paid-in capital balances. A stock dividend has the same effect as the payment by the corporation of a cash dividend and a subsequent return of the cash to the corporation in exchange for capital stock, as illustrated in a subsequent section.

In distributing stock as a dividend, the issuing corporation must meet legal requirements relative to the minimum amounts to be capitalized. If stock has a par or a stated value, an amount equal to the par or stated value of the shares issued will have to be transferred to capital stock; if stock has

---

[4]*Opinions of the Accounting Principles Board, No. 29,* "Accounting for Nonmonetary Transactions" (New York: American Institute of Certified Public Accountants, 1973), par. 18.

no par value and no stated value, the laws of the state of incorporation may provide specific requirements as to the amounts to be transferred, or they may leave such determinations to the corporate directors.

Accounting for Stock Dividends by the Investor. From the shareholders' point of view, a stock dividend does not change the proportional ownership interests. Although the number of shares held by each individual stockholder has gone up, there are now a greater total number of shares outstanding, and proportionate interests remain unchanged. This division of equities into a greater number of parts should not be regarded as giving rise to revenue. To illustrate, assume the following for JNS Corporation and a shareholder owning 10 shares of stock.

	Prior to 10% Stock Dividend	After 10% Stock Dividend
Common stock outstanding............	10,000 shares	11,000 shares
Total stockholders' equity	$330,000	$330,000
Company book value per share........	$33	$30
Individual stockholder book value	$330	$330
	(10 shares × $33)	(11 shares × $30)

The market value of the stock may or may not react in a similar manner. Theoretically, the same relative decrease should occur in the market price as occurred in the book value; however, there are many variables that influence the market price of securities. If the percentage of the stock dividend is comparatively low, there is generally less than a pro rata immediate effect on the market price of the stock. This has led the profession to treat small stock dividends somewhat differently than large stock dividends, as explained in the next section. In any event, since there is no effect on the underlying book value of the investment, the investor need only make a memorandum entry noting the receipt of additional shares and the new, lower per-share cost basis of the investment.

Small vs. Large Stock Dividends. In accounting for stock dividends, a distinction is made between a small and a large stock dividend.[5] **A small stock dividend** is one in which the number of shares issued is so small in comparison to the number of shares outstanding that it has little or no impact on the market price per share; therefore, the market value of the shares previously held remains substantially unchanged. As a general guideline, a stock dividend of less than 20–25% of the number of shares

---

[5]See *Accounting Research and Terminology Bulletins—Final Edition. No. 43*, "Restatement and Revision of Accounting Research Bulletins," (New York: American Institute of Certified Public Accountants, 1961), Ch. 7, Sec. B.

previously outstanding is considered a small stock dividend. Stock dividends involving the issuance of more than 20–25% are considered large stock dividends.

With a small stock dividend, which is the normal situation, the accounting profession recommends transferring from Retained Earnings to legal and additional paid-in capital an amount equal to the fair value of the additional shares at the declaration date. Such a transfer is consistent with the general public's view of a stock dividend as a distribution of corporate earnings at an amount equivalent to the fair value of the shares received. When a large stock dividend is involved, however, the transfer from Retained Earnings to contributed capital is made at the stock's par value, stated value, or other value as required by law. The following examples illustrate the entries for the declaration and issuance of stock dividends.

Assume that stockholders' equity for the Wong Company on July 1 is as follows:

Common stock, $10 par, 100,000 shares outstanding	$1,000,000
Paid-in capital in excess of par	1,100,000
Retained earnings..	750,000

The company declares a 10% stock dividend, or a dividend of 1 share of common for every 10 shares held. The stock is selling on the market on this date at $16 per share. The stock dividend is to be recorded at the market value of the shares issued, or $160,000 (10,000 shares at $16). The entries to record the declaration of the dividend and the issue of stock are:

Retained Earnings..	160,000	
Stock Dividends Distributable		100,000
Paid-In Capital in Excess of Par................................		60,000
Stock Dividends Distributable	100,000	
Common Stock, $10 par..		100,000

Assume, however, that the company declares a large stock dividend of 50%, or a dividend of 1 share for every 2 held. Legal requirements call for the transfer to capital stock of an amount equal to the par value of the shares issued. Entries for the declaration of the dividend and the issue of stock follow:

Retained Earnings..	500,000	
Stock Dividends Distributable		500,000
Stock Dividends Distributable	500,000	
Common Stock, $10 par..		500,000

Fractional Share Warrants. When stock dividends are issued by a company, it may be necessary to issue **fractional share warrants** to certain stockholders. For example, when a 10% stock dividend is issued, a stockholder owning 25 shares can be given no more than 2 full shares; however, the holdings in excess of an even multiple of 10 shares are recognized by the issue of a fractional share warrant for one-half share. The warrant for one-half share may be sold, or a warrant for an additional half share may be purchased so that a full share may be claimed from the company. In some instances, the corporation may arrange for the payment of cash in lieu of fractional warrants or it may issue a full share of stock in exchange for warrants accompanied by cash for the fractional share deficiency.

Assume that the Wong Company in distributing a stock dividend issues fractional share warrants equivalent to 500 shares of $10 par common. The entry for the fractional share warrants issued would be as follows:

Stock Dividends Distributable	5,000	
Fractional Share Warrants Issued		5,000

Assuming 80% of the warrants are ultimately turned in for shares and the remaining warrants expire, the following entry would be made:

Fractional Share Warrants Issued	5,000	
Common Stock, $10 par		4,000
Paid-In Capital from Forfeitures of Fractional Share Warrants		1,000

Stock Dividends vs. Stock Splits. As noted in Chapter 16, a corporation may effect a **stock split** by reducing the par or stated value of capital stock and increasing accordingly the number of shares outstanding. For example, a corporation with 1,000,000 shares outstanding may split the stock on a 3-for-1 basis. After the split, the corporation will have 3,000,000 total shares outstanding and each stockholder will have 3 shares for every 1 previously held. However, each share now represents only one third of the capital interest it previously represented; furthermore, each share of stock can be expected to sell for approximately one-third of its previous market price. From an investor's perspective, therefore, a stock split can be viewed the same as a stock dividend. In fact, the accounting for the investor is the same for stock splits as for stock dividends. With an increase in the number of shares, each share is assigned a portion of the original cost.

Although a stock dividend can be compared to a stock split from the investors' point of view, its effects on corporate capital differ from those of a stock split. **A stock dividend** results in not only an increase in the number of shares outstanding, but also an increase in the capital stock balance, with no change in the value assigned to each share of stock on the company records; the increase in capital stock outstanding is effected by a transfer from the retained earnings balance, retained earnings available for dividends being permanently reduced by this transfer. **A stock split** merely divides the existing capital stock balance into more parts, with a reduction in the stated or legal value related to each share; there is no change in the retained earnings balance or the capital stock balance.

Stock Dividends on the Balance Sheet. Special disclosure should be provided on the balance sheet when retained earnings have been reclassified as paid-in capital as a result of stock dividends, recapitalizations, or other actions. Information concerning the amount of retained earnings transferred to paid-in capital will contribute to an understanding of the extent to which business growth has been financed through corporate earnings. For example, assume the information for the Wong Company on page 748 and the transfer to paid-in capital of $500,000 as a result of the 50% stock dividend. The stockholders' equity may be presented as illustrated below.

Contributed capital:		
Common stock, $10 par, 150,000 shares	$1,500,000	
Paid-in capital in excess of par......................	1,100,000	$2,600,000
Retained earnings	$ 750,000	
Less amount transferred to paid-in capital by stock		
dividend	500,000	250,000
Total stockholders' equity..............................		$2,850,000

If a balance sheet is prepared after the declaration of a stock dividend but before issue of the shares, Stock Dividends Distributable is reported in the stockholders' equity section as an addition to capital stock outstanding. Through stock dividends, the corporation reduces its retained earnings balance and increases its capital stock.

Liquidating Dividends

A liquidating dividend is a distribution representing a return to stockholders of a portion of contributed capital. Whereas a normal cash dividend provides a return *on* investment, and is accounted for by reducing Retained Earnings, a liquidating dividend provides a return *of* investment. A liquidating dividend is accounted for by reducing paid-in capital.

To illustrate, assume the Carefree Corporation declared and paid a cash dividend and a partial liquidating dividend amounting to $150,000. Of this amount, $100,000 represents a regular $10 cash dividend on 10,000 shares of common stock. The balance is to be recorded as a reduction to Paid-in Capital in Excess of Par. The entry would be:

Retained Earnings..	100,000	
Paid-in Capital in Excess of Par.................................	50,000	
Cash...		150,000
Paid a $10 per share cash dividend on 10,000 shares and a partial liquidating dividend of $50,000.		

Stockholders should be notified as to the allocation of the total dividend payment so they can determine the amount that represents revenue and the amount that represents a return of investment.

QUASI-REORGANIZATIONS

As noted earlier, a debit balance in the Retained Earnings account is called a deficit. It may be the result of accumulated losses over a number of years or other significant debits to Retained Earnings. Sometimes a company with a large deficit is forced to discontinue operations and/or enter into bankruptcy proceedings. In some cases, however, where state laws permit, a company may eliminate a deficit through a restatement of invested capital balances, providing, in effect, a fresh start in the form of a zero Retained Earnings balance. This is known as a **quasi-reorganization**. The advantage of a quasi-reorganization is that the procedure does not require recourse to the courts as in a formal reorganization or bankruptcy, and there is no change in the legal corporate entity or interruption of business activity.

Quasi-reorganizations are not common, but may be appropriate for a company operating under circumstances that are quite different from those of the past, e.g., a company with new management. Even if operated profitably, the company may take years to eliminate the deficit which was created under a prior management. In the meantime, the corporation generally cannot pay dividends to stockholders. With a quasi-reorganization, however, the accumulated deficit is eliminated. Performance from the reorganization date forward can then be measured and reported without having past mistakes and negative results reflecting unfavorably on the "new" company.

Normally in a quasi-reorganization, assets are revalued to reflect their current market values. This may require significant write-downs of assets against Retained Earnings, thus increasing the deficit. The total deficit is then written off (Retained Earnings is adjusted to a zero balance) against paid-in capital balances, giving the company a new capital structure.

To illustrate the nature of a quasi-reorganization, assume Stanley Corporation has suffered operating losses for some time, but is now operating profitably and expects to continue to do so. Current and projected income, however, will not be sufficient to eliminate the deficit in the near term. It also appears that plant assets are overstated considering current prices and economic conditions. After receiving permission from state authorities and approval from the shareholders, the board of directors of Stanley Corporation decides to restate company assets and paid-in capital balances in order to remove the deficit and make possible the declaration of dividends from profitable operations. A balance sheet for the company just prior to this action is presented below.

Stanley Corporation Balance Sheet June 30, 1987					
Assets			**Liabilities and Stockholders' Equity**		
Current assets..........		$ 250,000	Liabilities		$ 300,000
Land, buildings, and			Common stock, $10 par,		
equipment...........	$1,500,000		100,000 shares........	$1,000,000	
Less accumulated			Less deficit	150,000	850,000
depreciation	600,000	900,000	Total liabilities and		
Total assets		$1,150,000	stockholders' equity....		$1,150,000

The quasi-reorganization is to be accomplished as follows:

1. Land, buildings, and equipment are to be reduced to their present fair market value of $600,000 by reductions in the asset and accumulated depreciation balances of 33⅓%.
2. Common stock is to be reduced to a par value of $5, $500,000 in capital stock thus being converted into "additional paid-in capital."
3. The deficit of $450,000 ($150,000 as reported on the balance sheet increased by $300,000 arising from the write-down of land, buildings, and equipment) is to be applied against the capital from the reduction of the par value of stock.

Entries to record the changes follow:

Transaction	Entry		
(1) To write down land, buildings, and equipment and accumulated depreciation balances by 33⅓%.	Retained Earnings............ Accumulated Depreciation..... Land, Buildings, and Equipment....................	300,000 200,000	 500,000
(2) To reduce the common stock balance from $10 par to $5 par and to establish paid-in capital from reduction in stock par value.	Common Stock, $10 par....... Common Stock, $5 par...... Paid-In Capital from Reduction in Stock Par Value....	1,000,000	500,000 500,000
(3) To apply the deficit after asset devaluation against paid-in capital from reduction in stock par value.	Paid-In Capital from Reduction in Stock Par Value.......... Retained Earnings........	450,000	 450,000

The balance sheet after the quasi-reorganization is shown below.

Stanley Corporation Balance Sheet June 30, 1987					

Assets			Liabilities and Stockholders' Equity	
Current assets		$250,000	Liabilities..............................	$300,000
Land, buildings, and			Common stock, $5 par, 100,000 shares.	500,000
equipment..............	$1,000,000		Paid-in capital from reduction in stock	
Less accumulated			par value..........................	50,000
depreciation	400,000	600,000	Total liabilities and	
Total assets..............		$850,000	stockholders' equity	$850,000

Following the quasi-reorganization, the accounting for the company's operations is similar to that for a new company. Earnings subsequent to the quasi-reorganization, however, should be accumulated in a **dated retained earnings account**. On future balance sheets, retained earnings dated as of the time of account readjustment will inform readers of the date of such action and of the fresh start in earnings accumulation.

REPORTING STOCKHOLDERS' EQUITY

In reporting stockholders' equity, it is important to provide readers with information concerning:

1. The sources of stockholders' equity, especially the amount paid in by stockholders (contributed capital) and the amount representing earnings retained in the business (retained earnings).
2. The classes of capital stock, including par or stated values; number of shares authorized, issued, and outstanding; number of shares of treasury stock.
3. Any restrictions on retained earnings.

In addition to the preceding information, the cost (or par value) of treasury stock should be deducted from stockholders' equity. Similarly, any unrealized loss on noncurrent marketable equity securities is to be reported as a contra-equity item and deducted in determining total stockholders' equity.

As an illustration, the stockholders' equity section of the balance sheet of Terry Corporation as of December 31, 1987, is presented. Many companies do not provide as much detail in the balance sheet as is illustrated for Terry Corporation. A typical presentation is made in the actual financial statements of General Mills, Inc. in Appendix A.

Stockholders' Equity

Contributed capital:		
6% Preferred stock, $100 par, cumulative, callable, 5,000 shares authorized and issued ..	$500,000	
Common stock, $5 stated value, 100,000 shares authorized, 60,000 shares issued; treasury stock, 5,000 shares—deducted below	300,000	$ 800,000
Paid-in capital in excess of stated value......	$260,000	
Paid-in capital from treasury stock...........	16,000	276,000
Total contributed capital		$1,076,000
Retained earnings:		
Appropriated for contingencies (Note X)......	$125,000	
Unappropriated...........................	225,000	
Total retained earnings...................		350,000
Total contributed capital and retained earnings....................		$1,426,000
Deduct: Common treasury stock, at cost (5,000 shares acquired at $8)................	$ 40,000	
Net unrealized loss on noncurrent marketable equity securities.........	24,000	64,000
Total stockholders' equity.....................		$1,362,000

Readers of financial statements should be provided with an explanation of the changes during the period in individual equity balances. Frequently, such explanation is provided in notes to the financial statements. When stockholders' equity is composed of numerous accounts, as in the preceding example, a **statement of changes in stockholders' equity** is sometimes presented. An illustrative statement for the Terry Corporation is shown on the following page.

The net ownership equity of a business is an important element. Analyses of the amounts and sources of contributed capital compared to those generated and retained by the company provide useful information for assessing the long-term profitability and solvency of a business. The techniques for analyzing financial statements are discussed in Chapter 26.

QUESTIONS

1. What is the impact of each of the following transactions or events on Retained Earnings or total stockholders' equity?
   (a) Operating profits.
   (b) Discovery of an understatement of income in a previous period.

(continued)

Terry Corporation
Statement of Changes in Stockholders' Equity
For the Year Ended December 31, 1987

	Preferred Stock	Common Stock	Paid-In Capital	Appropriated Retained Earnings for Contingencies	Unappropriated Retained Earnings	Contra-Equity Balances	Total
Balances, December 31, 1986	$300,000	$300,000	$260,000*	$ 90,000	$222,500	$ –0–	$1,172,500
Prior period adjustment—correction of 1985 error, net of tax					(25,000)		(25,000)
Adjusted balances, December 31, 1986	$300,000	$300,000	$260,000	$ 90,000	$197,500	$ –0–	$1,147,500
Increase from sale of 1,000 shares of preferred stock in January, 1987, at par value	200,000						200,000
Increase from sale of 25,000 shares of treasury stock, common, in January, 1987, cost $20,000, for $36,000			16,000				16,000
Net income for 1987					120,000		120,000
Cash dividends:							
Preferred stock, $6 on 5,000 shares, $30,000					(57,500)		(57,500)
Common stock 50¢ on 55,000 shares, $27,500							
Retained earnings appropriated for contingencies				35,000	(35,000)		
Purchase of 5,000 shares of common treasury stock @ cost, $8						(40,000)	(40,000)
Net unrealized loss on non-current marketable equity securities						(24,000)	(24,000)
Balances, December 31, 1987	$500,000	$300,000	$276,000	$125,000	$225,000	$(64,000)	$1,362,000

*From sale of common stock at more than stated value.

   (c) Release of Retained Earnings Appropriated for Purchase of Treasury Stock upon the sale of treasury stock.

   (d) Issue of bonds at a premium.

   (e) Purchase of a corporation's own capital stock.

   (f) Increase in the company's earning capacity, assumed to be evidence of considerable goodwill.

   (g) Construction of equipment for the company's own use at a cost less than the prevailing market price of identical equipment.

   (h) Donation to the corporation of its own stock.

   (i) Sale of land, buildings, and equipment at a gain.

   (j) Gain on bond retirement.

   (k) Conversion of bonds into common stock.

   (l) Conversion of preferred stock into common stock.

2. What are the two major considerations of a board of directors in making decisions involving dividend declarations?

3. Very few companies pay dividends in amounts equal to their retained earnings. Why?

4. The following announcement appeared on the financial page of a newspaper.

> The Board of Directors of Benton Co., at their meeting on June 15, 1987, declared the regular quarterly dividend on outstanding common stock of $1.40 per share, payable on July 10, 1987, to the stockholders of record at the close of business June 30, 1987.

   (a) What is the purpose of each of the three dates given in the announcement?

   (b) When would the common stock of Benton Co. normally trade "ex-dividend"?

5. Dividends are sometimes said to have been paid "out of retained earnings." What is wrong with such a statement?

6. The directors of The Fern Shoppe are considering issuance of a stock dividend. They have asked you to answer the following questions regarding the proposed action:

   (a) How is a stock dividend different from a stock split?

   (b) How are stock dividends accounted for: (1) by the issuing corporation? (2) by the stockholder?

7. Often, when a company declares a stock dividend, fractional share warrants are issued to certain stockholders. (a) What is a fractional share warrant? (b) What can the stockholder do with fractional share warrants? (c) If the company does not want to issue fractional share warrants, what alternatives are available?

8. At a regular meeting of the board of directors of the Lawton Corporation, a dividend payable in the stock of the Colter Corporation is to be declared. The stock of the Colter Corporation is recorded on the books of the Lawton Corporation at $190,000; the market value of the stock is $230,000. The question is raised whether the amount to be recorded for the dividend payable should be the book value or the market value. What is the proper accounting treatment?

9. (a) What is a liquidating dividend? (b) Under what circumstances are such distributions made?

10. (a) Why might a company seek a quasi-reorganization? (b) What are the steps in a quasi-reorganization?

11. In reviewing the financial statements of Barker Inc., a stockholder does not understand the purpose of Appropriation of Retained Earnings for Bond Redemption Fund that has been set up by periodic debits to Retained Earnings. The stockholder is told that this balance will not be used to redeem the bonds at their maturity. (a) What account will be reduced by the payment of the bonds? (b) What purpose is accomplished by the Appropriation of Retained Earnings for Bond Redemption Fund? (c) What disposition is made of the appropriation after the bonds are retired?

DISCUSSION CASES

CASE 17–1   (Small stock dividends)

The president of James Company suggests including the following statement in this year's annual report.

> On December 18, a 10% common stock dividend was distributed to stockholders, resulting in a transfer of $1,536,000 from Retained Earnings to Common Stock and Capital in Excess of Par. While the percentage of the stock dividend was the same as the previous year, the sum transferred to stockholders' equity was nearly $80,000 less.
> The seeming inconsistency is the result of the requirement of regulatory authorities that the value of stock dividends on the company's books be related to the market value of the stock. As a result, the present year's dividend was valued at $65 per share as compared to $74 per share for last year's stock dividend.

The president feels that this statement would help clarify the apparent inconsistency in the company's dividend policy. As partner for the accounting firm that is performing the annual audit of James Company, you feel that the president's statement may mislead the readers of the report even though the figures are correct.

State how the stock dividends should be accounted for in a situation such as this one, explaining your reasoning. What criticism, if any, do you have of the terminology used by the president? Explain.

CASE 17–2   (How much should our dividend be?)

Allenon Stone Corp. has paid quarterly dividends of $.70 per share for the last three years and is trying to continue this tradition. Allenon's balance sheet is as follows:

Allenon Stone Corp.
Balance Sheet
December 31, 1987

Assets		Liabilities	
Current assets:		Current liabilities:	
Cash...................	$ 50,000	Accounts payable......	$ 520,000
Accounts receivable.....	450,000	Taxes payable.........	100,000
Inventory	1,200,000	Accrued liabilities	90,000
Total current assets...	$1,700,000	Total current liabilities	$ 710,000
		Bonds payable........	1,500,000
Investments...........	500,000	Total liabilities	$2,210,000
Land, buildings, and			
equipment (net)	1,600,000	Stockholders' Equity	
		Common stock ($10 par, 69,000 shares outstanding)............	$ 690,000
		Retained earnings......	900,000
		Total stockholders' equity..............	$1,590,000
Total assets...........	$3,800,000	Total liabilities and stockholders' equity ..	$3,800,000

Discuss Allenon's possibilities concerning the issuance of dividends.

CASE 17–3   (Cash or stock dividend?)

Mountain Ski Manufacturer is considering offering a 10% stock dividend rather than its normal cash dividend of $1 per share in the first quarter of 1987. However, some of Mountain's stockholders have expressed displeasure at the idea and say they strongly prefer cash dividends.

Discuss the issue of a stock dividend as opposed to a cash dividend from the points of view of (a) a stockholder and (b) the board of directors.

CASE 17–4   (Stock splits and stock dividends)

Flick Corporation has been one of the more popular growth stocks during the past several years. In 1987, its $20 par common stock was selling in the range of $200–$230, with about 146,000 shares outstanding. On May 1, 1987, Flick announced that, effective May 10, 1987, its stock would be split 4-for-1. This was the first time since 1967 that Flick's stock had been split, although several stock dividends had been issued during the past 20 years. (a) What are the differences between a stock dividend and a stock split both from the standpoint of the investor and the company? (b) What are some possible reasons for Flick issuing stock dividends prior to 1987? |EX 17–1|

(handwritten annotations):

9/30 R|E   60,000
    C.S.   30,000
    Prem -C.S.   30,000

$\frac{6000}{40,000}$ = .15 < 20% use market
6000 × 10 = 60,000

12/30 DIV.   138,000
    Div Pay   138,000   ($3 × 46,000)

1/5 Div Pay   138,000
    Cash   138,000

USE MARKET : < 20-25%
USE PAR : > 20-25%

EXERCISES

EXERCISE 17–1   (Cash and stock dividends)

On September 30, 1987, Grey Company issued 6,000 shares of its $5 par common stock in connection with a stock dividend. No entry was made on the stock dividend declaration date. The market value per share on the date of declaration was $10 per share. The stockholders' equity accounts of Grey Company immediately before issuance of the stock dividend shares were as follows:

Common stock, $5 par; 100,000 shares authorized; 40,000 shares outstanding.	$200,000
Additional paid-in capital.	300,000
Retained earnings	350,000

On December 30, 1987, Grey Company declared a cash dividend of $3 per share payable January 5, 1988. Give the necessary entries to record the declaration and payment or issuance of the dividends.   (AICPA adapted)

EXERCISE 17–2   (Property dividends)

Best Company distributed the following dividends to its stockholders:

(a) 400,000 shares of Snell Corporation stock, carrying value of investment $1,200,000, fair market value $2,300,000.
(b) 230,000 shares of Newbold Company stock, a closely held corporation. The shares were purchased by Best 3 years ago at $5.60 per share, but no current market price is available.

Give the journal entries to account for the declaration and the payment of the dividends.

EXERCISE 17–3   (Dividend computation)

Stone Company has been paying regular quarterly dividends of $1.50 and wants to pay the same amount in the third quarter of 1988. Given the following information, what is the total amount that Stone will have to pay in dividends in the third quarter in order to pay $1.50 per share?

1988
Jan.   1   Shares outstanding, 800,000; $8 par (1,500,000 shares authorized)
Feb. 15   Issued 50,000 new shares at $10.50
Mar. 31   Paid quarterly dividends of $1.50 per share
May 12 $1,000,000 of $1,000 bonds were converted to common stock at the rate
                of 100 shares of stock per $1,000 bond.
June 15   Issued a 15% stock dividend.
        30   Paid quarterly dividends of $1.50 per share.

EXERCISE 17–4   (Stock dividends)

The balance sheet of the Rubios Corporation shows the following:

Common stock, $5 stated value, 80,000 shares issued and
    outstanding. $400,000
Paid-in capital in excess of stated value   800,000
Retained earnings.   350,000

A 25% stock dividend is declared, the board of directors authorizing a transfer from Retained Earnings to Common Stock at the stated value of the shares.
(a) Give entries to record the declaration and issuance of the stock dividend.
(b) What was the effect of the issue of the stock dividend on the ownership equity of each stockholder in the corporation?
(c) Give entries to record the declaration and issuance of the dividend if the board of directors had elected to transfer amounts from Retained Earnings to Common Stock equal to the market value of the stock ($10 per share).

EXERCISE 17–5   (Stock dividends and stock splits)

The capital accounts for Day's Market on June 30, 1988, are as follows:

Common stock, $15 par, 40,000 shares. . . . . $ 600,000
Paid-in capital in excess of par   435,000
Retained earnings.   2,160,000

Shares of the company's stock are selling at this time at $25. What entries would you make in each of the following cases?
(a) A 15% stock dividend is declared and issued.
(b) A 100% stock dividend is declared and issued.
(c) A 3-for-1 stock split is declared and issued.

EXERCISE 17–6   (Stock dividend computation)

The directors of Granite Supplies Inc., whose $80 par value common stock is currently selling at $100 per share, have decided to issue a stock dividend. Granite has authorization for 400,000 shares of common, has issued 220,000 shares of which 20,000 shares are now held as treasury stock, and desires to capitalize $2,400,000 of the retained earnings account balance. What percent stock dividend should be issued to accomplish this goal?

EXERCISE 17–7   (Accounting for dividends)

The following information has been taken from the balance sheet of Able Company.

Current assets..	$371,250
Investments	431,400
Common stock (par value $20)	337,000
Paid-in capital in excess of par	200,000
Retained earnings.......................................	385,000

Prepare the journal entries for the following unrelated items:
- (a) A 30% stock dividend is declared and distributed when the market value of the stock is $23 per share.
- (b) Par value of the common stock is reduced to $5, and the stock is split 4-for-1.
- (c) A dividend of 1 share of Midwest Co. common stock for every share of Able Company stock is declared and distributed. Midwest Co. common stock is carried on the books of Able Co. at a cost of $.80 per share, and the market value is $1.10 per share.

EXERCISE 17–8   (Restricting retained earnings)

On January 1, 1986, Southeast Manufacturing Corporation issued $20,000,000 of bonds payable. The bond issue agreement with the underwriters required Southeast Manufacturing to appropriate earnings of $1,250,000 at the end of each year until the bonds are retired. During their June, 1988, board meeting, the directors decided to change the company's financial structure to include only short-term debt and equity, and to drop their present insurance policy in favor of a self-insurance plan. On July 1, 1988, the company retired the bond issue and set up the first annual appropriation for self-insurance for $28,000.
- (1) Give the entries to record the periodic appropriations under the bond issue agreement for 1986 and 1987 and their cancellation in 1988.
- (2) Give the entry to record the appropriation for self-insurance.

EXERCISE 17–9   (Computation of retained earnings)

The following information has been taken from the accounts of Decker Corporation:

Total net income reported since incorporation	$400,000
Total cash dividends paid	100,000
Proceeds from sale of donated stock.......................	100,000
Capitalized value of stock dividends distributed..............	70,000
Paid-in capital from treasury stock	35,000
Unamortized discount on bonds payable....................	75,000
Appropriation for plant expansion	100,000

Determine the current balance of unappropriated retained earnings.

EXERCISE 17–10   (Correcting the retained earnings account)

The retained earnings account for Nixon Corp. shows the following debits and credits. Give all entries required to correct the account.

Account   Retained Earnings

Date		Item	Debit	Credit	Balance Debit	Balance Credit
Jan.	1	Balance......................				263,200
(a)		Loss from fire.................	2,625			260,575
(b)		Write-off of goodwill	26,250			234,325
(c)		Stock dividend................	70,000			164,325
(d)		Loss on sale of equipment	24,150			140,175
(e)		Officers compensation related to income of prior periods— accrual overlooked	162,750		22,575	
(f)		Loss on retirement of preferred shares at more than issuance price......................	35,000		57,575	
(g)		Paid-in capital in excess of par ..		64,750		7,175
(h)		Stock subscription defaults		4,235		11,410
(i)		Gain on retirement of preferred stock at less than issuance price......................		12,950		24,360
(j)		Gain on early retirement of bonds at less than book value		7,525		31,885
(k)		Gain on life insurance policy settlement...................		5,250		37,135
(l)		Correction of prior period error...		25,025		62,160

EXERCISE 17–11   (Multiple choice)

(1) Rae Corporation owned 1,800 shares of Sun Corporation common stock. These shares were purchased in 1984 for $18,000. On September 15, 1987, Rae declared a property dividend of 1 share of Sun for every 10 shares of Rae common stock held by stockholders. On that date, when the market price of Sun was $28 per share, there were 18,000 shares of Rae common stock outstanding. What amount of gain and net reduction in Retained Earnings would result from this property dividend?

	Gain	Net reduction in Retained Earnings
a.	$ 0	$32,400
b.	0	50,400
c.	18,000	14,400
d.	32,400	18,000

(2) Effective April 27, 1987, the stockholders of Walker Corporation approved a 2-for-1 split of the company's common stock, and an increase in authorized common shares from 100,000 shares (par value $20 per share) to

200,000 shares (par value $10 per share). Walker's stockholders' equity accounts immediately before issuance of the stock split shares were as follows:

Common stock, par value $20; 100,000 shares authorized;
  50,000 shares outstanding............................... $1,000,000
Additional paid-in capital ($3 per share on issuance of common
  stock) 150,000
Retained earnings 1,350,000

What should be the balances in Walker's additional paid-in capital and retained earnings accounts immediately after the stock split?

	Additional Paid-in Capital	Retained Earnings
a.	$ 0	$ 500,000
b.	150,000	350,000
c.	150,000	1,350,000
d.	1,150,000	350,000

(3) The following information pertains to a property dividend of marketable securities, declared by Rolfe Corp.:

	Fair Value
Declaration date, Dec. 20, 1987	$300,000
Record date, Jan. 10, 1988	310,000
Distribution date, Jan. 28, 1988......................	305,000

The carrying value of the securities on Rolfe's books was $200,000. How much gain should Rolfe recognize in 1987 as a result of this property dividend?

a. $ 0
b. 100,000
c. 105,000
d. 110,000

(4) A clearly identified appropriation of retained earnings for reasonably possible loss contingencies should be:

a. Charged with all losses related to that contingency.
b. Transferred to income as losses are realized.
c. Classified in the liability section of the balance sheet.
d. Shown within the stockholders' equity section of the balance sheet.

(AICPA adapted)

EXERCISE 17–12 (Quasi-reorganization)

Brownstone Corporation has incurred losses from operations for many years. At the recommendation of the newly hired president, the board of directors voted to implement a quasi-reorganization, subject to stockholders' approval. Immediately prior to the quasi-reorganization, on June 30, 1988, Brownstone's balance sheet was as follows:

Current assets...	$ 275,000
Property, plant, and equipment (net)........................	675,000
Other assets	100,000
	$1,050,000
Total liabilities	$ 300,000
Common stock	800,000
Additional paid-in capital.................................	150,000
Retained earnings..	(200,000)
	$1,050,000

The stockholders approved the quasi-reorganization effective July 1, 1988, to be accomplished by a reduction in property, plant, and equipment (net) of $175,000, a reduction in other assets of $75,000, and appropriate adjustment to the capital structure.

(1) Prepare the journal entries to record the quasi-reorganization on July 1, 1988.

(2) Prepare a new balance sheet after the quasi-reorganization.

(AICPA adapted)

PROBLEMS

PROBLEM 17–1   (Accounting for stock transactions)

Trump Corporation is publicly owned and its shares are traded on a national stock exchange. Trump has 16,000 shares of $25 stated value common stock authorized. Only 75% of these shares have been issued, and, of the shares issued, only 11,000 are outstanding. On December 31, 1987, the stockholders' equity section revealed that the balance in Paid-In Capital in Excess of Stated Value was $140,000, and the Retained Earnings balance was $110,000. Treasury stock was purchased at a cost of $37.50 per share. Net income for 1987 was $50,000.

During 1988, Trump had the following transactions:

Jan. 15 Trump issued, at $60 per share, 800 shares of $50 par, 5% cumulative preferred stock.

Feb.   1 Trump sold 1,500 shares of newly issued $25 stated value common stock at $42 per share.

Mar. 15 Trump declared a cash dividend on common stock of $.15 per share payable on April 30 to all stockholders of record on April 1.
          Trump reacquired 200 shares of its common stock for $43 per share. Trump uses the cost method to account for treasury stock.

Apr. 30 Employees exercised 1,000 options granted in 1986 under a noncompensatory stock option plan. When the options were granted, each option entitled the employee to purchase 1 share of common stock for $50 per share. On April 30, when the market price was $55 per share, Trump issued new shares to the employees.

May   1 Trump declared a 5% stock dividend to be distributed on June 1 to stockholders of record on May 7. The market price of the common stock was $50 per share on May 1.

May 31 Trump sold 150 treasury shares reacquired on March 15 and an additional 200 shares costing $7,500 that had been on hand since the beginning of the year. The selling price was $57 per share.

Sept. 15 The semiannual cash dividend on common stock was declared amounting to $.15 per share. Trump also declared the yearly dividend on preferred stock. Both are payable on October 15 to stockholders of record on October 1.

Instructions:
(1) Compute the number of shares and dollar amount of treasury stock at the beginning of 1988.
(2) Make the necessary journal entries to record the transactions in 1988 relating to stockholders' equity.
(3) Prepare the stockholders' equity section of Trump Corporation's December 31, 1988, balance sheet.

PROBLEM 17–2   (Accounting for stock transactions)

Williams Corporation was organized on June 30, 1985. After two and one-half years of profitable operations, the equity section of Williams' balance sheet was as follows:

Contributed capital:	
Common stock, $30 par, 600,000 shares authorized, 200,000	
shares issued and outstanding	$6,000,000
Paid-in capital in excess of par	600,000
Retained earnings	2,800,000
Total stockholders' equity	$9,400,000

During 1988, the following transactions affected the stockholders' equity:

Jan. 31 15,000 shares of common stock were reacquired at $32; treasury stock is recorded at cost.

Apr. 1 The company declared a 35% stock dividend. (Applies to all issued stock.)

30 The company declared a $.60 cash dividend. (Applies only to outstanding stock.)

June 1 The stock dividend was issued, and the cash dividend was paid.

Aug. 31 The treasury stock was sold at $35.

Instructions: Give journal entries to record the stock transactions.

PROBLEM 17–3   (Stockholders' equity transactions)

The stockholders' equity of the Plank Lumber Co. on June 30, 1988, was as follows:

Contributed capital:		
5% Preferred stock, $50 par, cumulative, 30,000 shares issued,		
dividends 5 years in arrears		$1,500,000
Common stock, $30 par, 100,000 shares issued		3,000,000
		$4,500,000
Deficit from operations		(600,000)
Total stockholders' equity		$3,900,000

On this date the following action was taken:

    (a) Common stockholders turned in their old common stock and received in exchange new common stock, 1 share of the new stock being exchanged for every 4 shares of the old. New common stock was given a stated value of $60 per share.

    (b) One-half share of the new common stock was issued on each share of preferred stock outstanding in liquidation of dividends in arrears on preferred stock.

    (c) The deficit from operations was applied against the paid-in capital arising from the common stock restatement.

Transactions for the remainder of 1988 affecting the stockholders' equity were as follows:

Oct.   1   10,000 shares of preferred stock were called at $55 plus dividends for 3 months at 5%. Stock was formally retired.

Nov. 10   60,000 shares of new common stock were sold at $65.

Dec. 31   Net income for the 6 months ended on this date was $400,000. (Debit Income Summary.) The semiannual dividend was declared on preferred shares and a $.75 dividend was declared on common shares, dividends being payable January 20, 1989.

Instructions:

(1) Record in journal form the foregoing transactions.

(2) Prepare the stockholders' equity section of the balance sheet as of December 31, 1988.

PROBLEM 17-4   (Stockholders' equity transactions)

Crazy Horse Inc. was organized on January 2, 1987, with authorized capital stock consisting of 50,000 shares of 10%, $200 par preferred, and 200,000 shares of no-par, no-stated value common. During the first 2 years of the company's existence, the following selected transactions took place:

1987

Jan.   2   Sold 10,000 shares of common stock at 16.

       2   Sold 3,000 shares of preferred stock at 216.

Mar. 2   Sold common stock as follows: 10,800 shares at 22; 2,700 shares at 25.

July 10   A nearby piece of land, appraised at $400,000 was acquired for 600 shares of preferred stock and 27,000 shares of common. (Preferred stock was recorded at $216, the balance being assigned to common.)

Dec. 16   The regular preferred and a $1.50 common dividend were declared.

     28   Dividends declared on December 16 were paid.

     31   The income summary account showed a credit balance of 450,000, which was transferred to retained earnings.

1988

Feb. 27   The corporation reacquired 12,000 shares of common stock at 19. The treasury stock is carried at cost. (State law required that an appropriation of retained earnings be made for the purchase price of treasury stock. Appropriations are to be returned to retained earnings upon resale of the stock).

June 17 Resold 10,000 shares of the treasury stock at 23.
July 31 Resold all of the remaining treasury stock at 20.
Sept. 30 The corporation sold 11,000 additional shares of common stock at 21.
Dec. 16 The regular preferred dividend and an $.80 common dividend were declared.
     28 Dividends declared on December 16 were paid.
     31 The income summary account showed a credit balance of $425,000 which was transferred to retained earnings.

Instructions:
(1) Give the journal entries to record the foregoing transactions.
(2) Prepare the stockholders' equity section of the balance sheet as of December 31, 1988.

PROBLEM 17–5   (Accounting for stockholders' equity)

A condensed balance sheet for Tax Facts Inc. as of December 31, 1985, appears below:

Tax Facts Inc.
Condensed Balance Sheet
December 31, 1985

Assets		Liabilities and Stockholders' Equity	
Assets....................	$525,000	Liabilities.................	$120,000
		8% Preferred stock, $100 par......................	75,000
		Common stock, $50 par	150,000
		Paid-in capital in excess of par...................	30,000
		Retained earnings	150,000
		Total liabilities and	
Total assets..............	$525,000	stockholders' equity	$525,000

Capital stock authorized consists of: 750 shares of 8%, cumulative preferred stock, and 15,000 shares of common stock.

Information relating to operations of the succeeding 3 years follows:

	1986	1987	1988
Dividends declared on Dec. 20, payable on Jan. 10 of the following year:			
Preferred stock......................	8% cash	8% cash	8% cash
Common stock	$1.00 cash	$1.25 cash	$1.00 cash
	50% stock*		
Net income for year......................	$67,500	$39,000	$51,000

*Retained earnings is reduced by the par value of the stock dividend.
   1987
   Feb. 12 Accumulated depreciation was reduced by $72,000 following an income tax investigation. (Assume that this was an error that quali-

		fied as a prior period adjustment.) Additional income tax of $22,500 for prior years was paid.
Mar.	3	300 shares of common stock were purchased by the corporation at $54 per share; treasury stock is recorded at cost, and retained earnings are appropriated equal to such costs.
1988		
Aug.	10	All the treasury stock was resold at $59 per share and the retained earnings appropriation was canceled.
Sept.	12	By vote of the stockholders, each share of the common stock was exchanged by the corporation for 4 shares of no-par common stock with a stated value of $15.

Instructions:

(1) Give the journal entries to record the foregoing transactions for the 3-year period ended December 31, 1988.

(2) Prepare the stockholders' equity section of the balance sheet as it would appear at the end of 1986, 1987, and 1988.

PROBLEM 17–6 (Adjustments to Retained Earnings)

On March 31, 1988, the retained earnings account of State Wrecking Service showed a balance of $19,000,000. The board of directors of State made the following decisions during the remainder of 1988 that possibly affect the retained earnings account.

Apr.	1	State decided to assume the risk for workers' compensation insurance. The estimated liability for 1988 is $120,000. Also, a fund was set up to cover the estimated liability.
	30	State has not experienced even a small fire since 1946; therefore, the board of directors decided to start a self-insurance plan. They decided to start with a $400,000 appropriation.
May	15	A fire did considerable damage to the outside warehouse. It cost $360,000 to repair the warehouse.
Aug.	20	The board of directors received a report from the plant engineer indicating that the company is possibly in violation of pollution control standards. The fine for such a violation is $800,000. As a result of the engineer's report, the board decided to set up a general contingency appropriation for $800,000.
Sept.	1	The company reacquired 80,000 shares of its own stock at $29; treasury stock is recorded at cost. Due to legal restrictions, State has to set up an appropriation to cover the cost of the treasury stock.
Dec.	31	The company had to pay an $800,000 fine for pollution control violations and the treasury stock was sold at $31. No workers' compensation was paid during the year.

Instructions: Prepare all of the necessary entries to record the transactions.

PROBLEM 17–7 (Reporting stockholders' equity)

Accounts of Alpine Ranch on December 31, 1988, show the following balances:

	Debits	Credits
Accumulated Depreciation—Buildings		$ 255,000
Allowance for Purchase Discounts.....................	$ 4,200	
Bonds Payable......................................		325,000
Bond Retirement Fund	138,000	
Buildings	1,150,000	
Common Stock, $10 par (80,000 shares authorized, 63,200 shares issued and outstanding)...............		632,000
Common Stock Subscribed (4,000 shares)		40,000
Current Assets	786,000	
Current Liabilities—Other		270,000
Customers Deposits		17,000
Dividends Payable—Cash............................		16,000
Income Taxes Payable		43,000
Paid-In Capital from Treasury Stock....................		32,000
Paid-In Capital in Excess of Par......................		24,000
Retained Earnings Appropriated for Contingencies........		100,000
Retained Earnings Appropriated for Bond Retirement Fund..		138,000
Retained Earnings Appropriated for Purchase of Treasury Stock...		56,000
Stock Dividends Distributable (5,040 shares).............		50,400
Treasury Stock (4,800 shares at cost)..................	56,000	
Unappropriated Retained Earnings.....................		135,800
	$2,134,200	$2,134,200

Instructions: From these data prepare the stockholders' equity section as it would appear on the balance sheet.

PROBLEM 17–8   (Quasi-reorganization)

Darton Magnesium Works has experienced several loss years and has plant assets on its books that are overvalued. Darton plans to revalue its assets downward and eliminate the deficit. At December 31, 1988, the company owns the following plant assets:

	Cost	Accumulated Depreciation	Book Value	Current Value
Land..............	$ 600,000	—	$ 600,000	$300,000
Buildings	850,000	$350,000	500,000	250,000
Machinery and Equipment.......	450,000	250,000	200,000	150,000
	$1,900,000	$600,000	$1,300,000	$700,000

The balance sheet on December 31, 1988, reported the following balances in the stockholders' equity section:

Common stock, $25 par, 70,000 shares	$1,750,000
Paid-in capital in excess of par...........................	300,000
Retained earnings (deficit)	(350,000)
Total	$1,700,000

As part of the reorganization, the common stock is to be canceled and reissued at $10 par.

Instructions:
(1) Prepare the journal entries to record the quasi-reorganization.
(2) Give the plant asset section and stockholders' equity section of the company's balance sheet as they would appear after the entries are posted.

PROBLEM 17–9 (Balance sheet preparation)

The following trial balance was taken from the books of Peachtree Inc., a calendar-year corporation, as of April 30, 1988:

Peachtree Inc.
Trial Balance
April 30, 1988

Cash	310,000	
Accounts Receivable	800,000	
Finished Goods	500,000	
Goods in Process	100,000	
Raw Materials	750,000	
Land, Buildings, and Equipment	1,460,000	
Prepaid Expenses	5,400	
Sales Returns and Allowances	25,000	
Administrative Salaries	65,000	
Cost of Goods Sold	2,350,000	
Travel Expense	30,030	
Interest Expense	10,570	
Accounts Payable		175,000
Notes Payable		100,000
Payroll Payable		6,000
Interest Payable on 6% Bonds		10,000
6% Preferred Stock, $50 par		1,000,000
Common Stock, $100 par		1,416,000
6% Bonds Payable (due June 30, 1996)		500,000
Sales		2,500,000
Retained Earnings, December 31, 1987		520
Paid-In Capital		698,480
	6,406,000	6,406,000

The following transactions have been completed by the company:
(a) The company has purchased various lots of its $100 par value common stock, aggregating 840 shares, at an average price of $65.50 per share, for $55,020. In recording these transactions, the company has canceled the stock certificates and debited the common stock account with the par value of $84,000 and credited the paid-in capital account with the difference of $28,980 between par and the cash paid.
(b) Paid-In Capital was previously credited for $20 per share on the sale of 15,000 shares of common stock at $120.
(c) 6% bonds with a total face amount of $250,000 falling due on December 31, 1994, were issued on January 1, 1970, at a 10% discount. To

June 30, 1986, $16,500 of this discount had been charged against revenues and as of this date the entire issue of these bonds was retired at par and the unamortized discount debited to Additional Paid-In Capital.

(d) A new issue of $500,000, 6% 10-year bonds was sold at par on July 1, 1986. Expenses incurred with respect to this issue in the amount of $20,000 were debited to Paid-In Capital.

Instructions: Prepare a balance sheet as of April 30, 1988, making any corrections necessary in view of the company's treatment of the preceding transactions.

(AICPA adapted)

PROBLEM 17–10
(Dividends and stock rights—entries for company and investor)

On April 1, 1987, Bart Co. purchased 1,000 shares of Thomas Co. common stock, par $10, at $20. On June 1, when the stock is selling for $22 on the open market, Bart Co. received a 10% stock dividend from Thomas Co. On October 26, Thomas Co. paid Bart Co. a dividend of $.75 on the stock and granted a stock right to purchase 1 share at $15 for every 5 shares held. On this date stock had a market value ex-rights of $22.50 and each right had a value of $1.70; the stock cost was allocated on this basis. On November 15, Bart sold 120 rights at $1.25 and exercised the remaining rights. On March 3, 1988, Bart received a cash dividend from Thomas Co. of $1.50 per share. On October 13, Thomas Co. declared a 2-for-1 stock split and on October 31 declared dividends of $.40 per share. On December 31, Bart sold all of its shares in Thomas Co. for $11.50.

Instructions: Prepare all entries for the preceding transactions on the books of (a) Bart Co. and (b) Thomas Co. Omit explanations but show computations. Assume these are the only equity transactions for Thomas Co.

18
Earnings per Share

Investors are among the principal external users of corporate financial statements. As indicated in Chapter 1, a primary concern of investors is how profitable a company is relative to their investment in the company. When evaluating a company, it is not enough to know that income is increasing. The investor is concerned with how net income relates to shares held and to the market price of the stock. Total amounts can often, on the surface, give misleading impressions. Only by converting the total amounts to per share data can a meaningful evaluation be made.

Earnings per share is thus a useful measurement for comparing earnings of different entities and for comparing earnings of a single entity over time when changes occur in the capital structure. As a successful company grows, net income will naturally increase. But an investor is interested in determining if net income is growing relative to the size of the company's capital structure. Investors use earnings per share figures to evaluate the results of operations of a business in order to make investment decisions. For example, by dividing the earnings per share figure into the market price per share, a **price-earnings ratio** may be computed and compared among different companies. Thus, if Company A earns $3 per share on common stock with a $21 per share market price, and Company B earns $6 per share on common stock with a $54 per share market value, an investor can state that Company A stock is selling at seven times earnings and Company B stock is selling at nine times earnings. Other things being equal between these two companies, Company A's stock would be the better buy since its market price is lower in relation to earnings than is the price of Company B's stock.

Investors are also interested in dividends and can use earnings per share data to compute a **dividend payout percentage** or **payout rate**. This rate is computed by dividing earnings per share into dividends per share.

Thus, if Company A in the previous example pays a dividend of $2 per share, and Company B pays $3 per share, the payout percentage would be 66⅔% for Company A and 50% for Company B.

Earnings per share data receive wide recognition in the annual reports issued by companies, in the press, and in financial reporting publications. This measurement is frequently regarded as an important determinant of the market price of common stock.

EVOLUTION OF REQUIREMENTS FOR EARNINGS PER SHARE DISCLOSURE

Earnings per share figures were historically computed and used primarily by financial analysts. Sometimes the computation was disclosed in the unaudited section of the annual report along with a message from the company's president. However, because this measurement was not audited, figures used to develop earnings per share were often different from those attested to by the auditor. The situation became more complex when some companies and analysts began computing earnings per share not only on the basis of common shares actually outstanding, but also on the basis of what shares would be outstanding if certain convertible securities were converted and if certain stock options were exercised. Usually, the conversion or exercise terms were very favorable to the holders of these securities, and earnings per share would decline if common stock were issued upon conversion or exercise. This result, a reduced earnings per share, is referred to as a **dilution of earnings**. In some cases, however, the exercise of options or conversion of securities might result in an increased earnings per share. This result is referred to as an **antidilution of earnings**. Securities that would lead to dilution are referred to as **dilutive securities**, and those that would lead to antidilution are referred to as **antidilutive securities**. Rational investors would not convert or exercise antidilutive securities because they could do better by purchasing common stock in the market place.

These forward-looking computations of earnings per share attempted to provide information as to what future earnings per share *might* be assuming conversions and exercises took place. Because these "as if" conditions were based on assumptions, they could be computed in several ways. Recognizing the diversity of reporting practices, the Accounting Principles Board became involved in establishing guidelines for the computation and disclosure of earnings per share figures. The result was the issuance in 1969 of APB Opinion No. 15, "Earnings per Share," which concluded:

The Board believes that the significance attached by investors and others to earnings per share data, together with the importance of evaluating the data in conjunction with the financial statements, requires that such data be presented prominently in the financial statements. The Board has therefore concluded that earnings per share or net loss per share data should be shown on the face of the income statement. The extent of the data to be presented and the captions used will vary with the complexity of the company's capital structure. . . .[1]

For the first few years after Opinion No. 15 was issued, all business entities were required to include earnings per share data in their income statements. However, in 1978, the FASB issued Statement No. 21, which eliminated this requirement for nonpublic entities. A nonpublic company is defined as any enterprise other than "one (a) whose debt or equity securities trade in a public market on a foreign or domestic stock exchange or in the over-the-counter market, . . . or (b) that is required to file financial statements with the Securities and Exchange Commission."[2]

In the process of establishing rules for computing earnings per share, the Accounting Principles Board felt it necessary to be very specific about how future-oriented "as if" figures were to be computed. Many interpretations and amendments were issued with the intent to clarify the computations for a variety of securities and under varied circumstances. In some areas the rules became arbitrary and complex, and the resulting earnings per share computations have received much criticism as to their usefulness. Indeed, for companies with complex capital structures, the **historical** or **simple earnings per share** figure based on actual shares of common stock outstanding may not even be reported. In its place the APB substituted two earnings per share amounts: (1) **primary earnings per share** based on the assumed conversion or exercise of certain securities identified as common stock equivalents and (2) **fully diluted earnings per share** based on the assumed conversion of all convertible securities or exercise of all stock options that would reduce or dilute primary earnings per share.

Although almost twenty years have passed since APB Opinion No. 15 was issued, there has been little evidence to support the usefulness of these forward-type earnings per share figures. Shortly after APB Opinion No. 15 was issued, in fact, the Canadian Institute of Chartered Accountants

[1]*Opinions of the Accounting Principles Board, No. 15*, "Earnings per Share" (New York: American Institute of Certified Public Accountants, 1969), par. 12.

[2]*Statement of Financial Accounting Standards No. 21*, "Suspension of the Reporting of Earnings Per Share and Segment Information by Nonpublic Enterprises" (Stamford: Financial Accounting Standards Board, 1978), par. 13.

reviewed what the APB had done, and concluded that only a historical earnings per share and a fully diluted earnings per share had potential value. They rejected the attempt to define an intermediary figure that was intended to measure the probability of conversion or exercise.[3] A United States survey of investors in 1980 indicated that various return on investment figures are becoming more popular than earnings per share as a measure of profitability.[4] Of those corporate, government, and accounting executives surveyed, 66% listed return on investment as highly important, while only 49% listed earnings per share as highly important. A majority of 3 to 1 felt that return on investment was a better or more desirable measure of corporate performance than earnings per share. However, because earnings per share figures are presently required for all public companies, accountants must understand how they are computed and the rationale for the computations. Only the basic recommendations can be presented here. When Opinion No. 15 fails to state the specific procedures to be followed under special circumstances, the accountant must exercise judgment in developing supportable presentations within the recommended framework.

SIMPLE AND COMPLEX CAPITAL STRUCTURES

The capital structure of a company may be classified as simple or complex. If a company has only common stock outstanding and there are no convertible securities, stock options, warrants, or other rights outstanding, it is classified as a company with a **simple capital structure**. Earnings per share is computed by dividing the net income for the period by the weighted average number of common shares outstanding for the period. No future-oriented "as if" conditions need to be considered. If net income includes extraordinary gains or losses or other below-the-line items as discussed in Chapter 4, a separate earnings per share figure is required for each major component of income, as well as for net income.

Even if convertible securities, stock options, warrants or other rights do exist, the capital structure may be classified as simple if there is no potential material dilution to earnings per share from the conversion or exercise of these items. Potential earnings per share dilution exists if the earnings per share would decrease or the loss per share would increase

---

[3]*CICA Handbook, Section 3500,* "Earnings per Share" (Toronto: The Canadian Institute of Chartered Accountants, February 1970).

[4]As reported by a Lou Harris survey for the Financial Accounting Foundation in the Alexander Grant Newsletter, July 1980.

as a result of the conversion of securities or exercise of stock options, warrants, or other rights based on the conditions existing at the financial statement date. The Accounting Principles Board defined **material dilution** as being a decrease of 3% or more in the simple earnings per share. If a company's capital structure does not qualify as simple, it is classified as a **complex capital structure**, and the two figures identified previously— primary and fully diluted earnings per share—are required if either is materially dilutive.

The Simple Capital Structure—Computational Guidelines

The earnings per share computation presents no problem when only common stock has been issued and the number of shares outstanding has remained the same for the entire period. The numerator is the net income (loss), and the denominator is the number of shares outstanding for the entire period. Frequently, however, either the numerator, the denominator, or both must be adjusted because of the following conditions:

(1) When common shares have been issued or have been reacquired by a company during a period, the resources available to the company have changed and this change should affect earnings. Under these circumstances, a weighted average for shares outstanding should be computed.

The weighted average number of shares may be computed by determining month-shares of outstanding stock and dividing by 12 to obtain the weighted average for the year. For example, if a company has 10,000 shares outstanding at the beginning of the year, issues 5,000 more shares on May 1, and reacquires 2,000 shares on November 1, the weighted average number of shares would be computed as illustrated below. Note that a separate period computation is required each time stock is sold or reacquired.

		Month-Shares
Jan. 1 to May 1	10,000 × 4 months	40,000
May 1 to Nov. 1	15,000 × 6 months	90,000
Nov. 1 to Dec. 31	13,000 × 2 months	26,000
Total month-shares		156,000
Weighted average number of shares: 156,000 ÷ 12		13,000

The same answer can be obtained by applying a weight to each period equivalent to the portion of the year since the last change in shares outstanding, as follows:

Jan. 1 to May 1	10,000 × 4/12 year	3,333
May 1 to Nov. 1	15,000 × 6/12 year	7,500
Nov. 1 to Dec. 31	13,000 × 2/12 year	2,167
Weighted average number of shares		13,000

(2) When the number of common shares outstanding has changed during a period as a result of a stock dividend, a stock split, or a reverse split, a retroactive recognition of this change must be made in arriving at the amount of earnings per share. To illustrate, assume that in the preceding example a 2-for-1 stock split occurred on October 1. The computation of the weighted average number of shares would be changed as follows:

Jan. 1 to May 1—10,000 × 200% (two-for-one stock split) × 4/12 year   6,667
May 1 to Nov. 1—15,000 × 200% (two-for-one stock split) × 6/12 year   15,000
Nov. 1 to Dec. 31—28,000* × 2/12 year................................   4,667

Weighted average number of shares   26,334

*30,000 outstanding − 2,000 reacquired = 28,000 shares outstanding

Note that a separate period computation is not required for the issuance of a stock dividend or a stock split.

In reporting comparative data, recognition of the stock dividend or split in the common stock of all prior periods included in the statements is necessary. Only with the retroactive recognition of changes in the number of shares can earnings per share presentations for prior periods be stated on a basis comparable with the earnings per share presentation for the current period. Similar retroactive adjustments must be made even if a stock dividend or stock split occurs after the end of the period but before the financial statements are prepared; disclosure of this situation should be made in a note to the financial statements.

(3) Earnings per share reflects only income available to common stockholders, and does not include preferred stock. It would be inappropriate to report earnings per share on preferred stock in view of the limited dividend rights of such stock. When a capital structure includes preferred stock, dividends on preferred stock should be deducted from net income and also from income before extraordinary or other special items, when such items appear on the income statement, in arriving at the earnings related to common shares. If preferred dividends are not cumulative, only the dividends declared on preferred stock during the period are deducted. If preferred dividends are cumulative, the full amount of dividends on preferred stock for the period, whether declared or not, should be deducted from income before extraordinary or other special items and from net income in arriving at the earnings or loss balance related to the common stock. If there is a loss for the period, preferred dividends for the period, including any undeclared dividends on cumulative preferred stock, are added to the loss in arriving at the full loss related to the common stock.

To illustrate the computation of earnings per share at December 31, 1988, for a company with a simple capital structure for a comparative two-year period, assume the following data:

Summary of changes in capital balances:

	8% Cumulative Preferred Stock $100 Par		Common Stock No Par		Retained Earnings
	Shares	Amount	Shares	Amount	
December 31, 1986 balances	10,000	$1,000,000	200,000	$1,000,000	$4,000,000
June 30, 1987 issuance of 100,000 shares of common stock			100,000	600,000	
June 30, 1987 dividend on preferred stock, 8%					(80,000)
June 30, 1987 dividend on common stock, $.30					(90,000)
December 31, 1987 net income for year, including extraordinary gain of $75,000					380,000
December 31, 1987 balances	10,000	$1,000,000	300,000	$1,600,000	$4,210,000
May 1, 1988 50% stock dividend on common stock . . .			150,000	800,000	(800,000)
December 31, 1988 net loss for year					(55,000)
	10,000	$1,000,000	450,000	$2,400,000	$3,355,000

Because comparative statements are desired, the denominator of weighted shares outstanding must be adjusted for the 50% stock dividend issued in 1988 as follows:

1987: January 1–June 30	—200,000 × 150% (50% stock dividend in 1988) × 6/12 year	150,000	
July 1–December 31	—200,000 + 100,000 (issuance of stock in 1987) × 150% (50% stock dividend in 1988) × 6/12 year	225,000	375,000
1988: January 1–December 31	—300,000 × 150% (50% stock dividend in 1988) × 1 year		450,000

Continuing the example, earnings per share for 1987 must be shown separately for income from continuing operations, the extraordinary gain, and net income. The preferred dividends must be deducted from both income from continuing operations and net income in computing earnings per share for these income components. For 1988, the reported net loss must be increased by the full amount of the preferred dividend even though the dividend was not declared. If the preferred stock were non-cumulative, no adjustment for the undeclared preferred dividend would be necessary in 1988. The adjusted income (loss) figures for computing earnings per share are determined as follows:

1987:	Income from continuing operations ($380,000 net income − $75,000 extraordinary gain)	$305,000
	Less preferred dividend	80,000
	Income from continuing operations identified with common stock . . .	$225,000
	Net income	$380,000
	Less preferred dividend	80,000
	Net income identified with common stock	$300,000
1988:	Net loss	$ 55,000
	Add preferred dividend	80,000
	Net loss identified with common stock	$135,000

The earnings per share amounts can now be computed as follows:

1987: Earnings per common share from continuing operations ($225,000 ÷
         375,000) .... $.60
       Extraordinary gain ($75,000 ÷ 375,000) .... .20
       Net income per share ($300,000 ÷ 375,000) .... $.80
1988: Loss per share ($135,000 ÷ 450,000) .... $.30

The Complex Capital Structure — Computational Guidelines

As discussed earlier, complex capital structures call for a dual
presentation of earnings per share data on the face of the income statement:
(1) primary earnings per share — a presentation based on the number of
common shares outstanding plus the shares represented by common
stock equivalents that have a dilutive effect on earnings per share; (2) fully
diluted earnings per share — a second presentation based on the assumption that all of the contingent issuances of shares of common stock that
would dilute earnings per share had taken place. In computing both primary and fully diluted earnings per share, any securities whose exercise or
conversion would increase earnings per share or reduce loss per share are
referred to as **antidilutive** securities. In general, these securities are not
included in the computation of either earnings per share figure.

Computation of dual earnings per share requires application of the
procedures for the simple structure previously described as well as special
analyses and additional computations described in the following sections.
The first section describes the computation of primary earnings per share;
the second section describes the computation of fully diluted earnings per
share.

PRIMARY EARNINGS PER SHARE

The computation of primary earnings per share requires an identification of those securities qualifying as common stock equivalents. **A common
stock equivalent** is a security that is in substance equivalent to common
stock due to its terms or the circumstances under which it was issued.[5]
Holders of these securities can expect to participate in the appreciation
of the value of common stock resulting primarily from present and potential earnings of the issuing company. A security identified as a common
stock equivalent enters into the computation of primary earnings per share
only if it is dilutive. Once a security is recognized as a common stock

---

[5] *Opinions of the Accounting Principles Board No. 15,* Appendix D.

equivalent, the Accounting Principles Board indicated that it retains this status. However, depending on its dilutive effect, it could enter into the computation of primary earnings per share in one period and not in another. Common stock equivalents are composed of the securities described in the following paragraphs.

Stock Options, Warrants, and Rights

As explained in Chapter 16, stock options, warrants, and rights provide no cash yield to investors, but have value because they permit the acquisition of common stock at specified prices for a certain period of time. By definition of the APB, these items are always regarded as common stock equivalents. However, options, warrants, and rights are included in the computation of primary earnings per share for a particular period only if they are dilutive and if they are exercisable within five years from the date of the financial statements. If the price for which stock can be acquired (exercise price) is lower than the current market price, the options, warrants, or rights would probably be exercised and their effect would be dilutive. If the exercise price is higher than the current market price, no exercise would take place; thus, there is no potential dilution from these securities.[6]

If it is assumed that exercise of options, warrants, or rights takes place as of the beginning of the year or at the date they are issued, whichever comes later, additional cash resources would have been available for the company's use. In order to compute primary earnings per share when these types of securities exist, either net income must be increased to take into consideration the increase in revenue such additional resources would produce, or the cash must be assumed to be used for some nonrevenue producing purpose. The latter approach was selected by the APB, and they recommended it be assumed that the cash proceeds from the exercise of options, warrants, or rights be used to purchase common stock on the market (treasury stock) at the **average market price** for the period involved. It is further assumed that the shares of treasury stock are issued to those exercising their options, warrants, or rights, and the remaining shares required to be issued will be added to the actual number of shares outstanding to compute primary earnings per share. This method is known as the **treasury stock method**.

---

[6]The Board stated that, as a practical matter, no assumption of exercise is necessary until the market price has exceeded the exercise price for substantially all of three consecutive months ending with the last month to which earnings per share relate. "Substantially all" has been defined as 11 of the 13 weeks. This is a one-time test. Once the requirement is met, future computations of primary earnings per share will include the options, warrants, or rights unless they are antidilutive. See APB Opinion No. 15, par. 36.

To illustrate, assume that at the beginning of the current year, employees were granted options to acquire 5,000 shares of common stock at $40 per share. The year-end market price of the stock is $50, so exercise would be assumed and the effect will be dilutive. The proceeds received by the corporation from the issuance of stock to the employees would be $200,000 (5,000 shares × $40 exercise price). Assuming the average market price of the stock for the year was also $50, these proceeds would purchase 4,000 shares of treasury stock ($200,000 ÷ $50). If it is assumed that these 4,000 shares are issued to the employees, an additional 1,000 shares would have to be issued, and the number of shares of stock for computing primary earnings per share would be increased by 1,000 shares.[7] The interpretations of Opinion No. 15 refer to these shares as **incremental shares**.[8]

Illustration of Primary EPS with Stock Options. The use of the treasury stock method in computing primary earnings per share is illustrated with the following data for the Tring Corporation:

Summary of relevant information:

Net income for the year	$92,800
Common shares outstanding (no change during year)	100,000
Options outstanding to purchase equivalent shares	20,000
Exercise price per share on options	$ 6
Average market price for common shares	$10

Earnings per share without common stock equivalents (simple EPS):

Net income for the year	$92,800
Actual number of shares outstanding	100,000
Simple earnings per share ($92,800 ÷ 100,000)	$.93

Application of proceeds from assumed exercise of options outstanding to purchase treasury stock:

Proceeds from assumed exercise of options outstanding (20,000 × $6)	$120,000
Number of outstanding shares assumed to be repurchased with proceeds from options ($120,000 ÷ $10)	12,000

---

[7]The computation of incremental shares may be expressed in the form of a formula as follows:

$$I = N(M - E)/M$$

where: I = incremental shares
N = number of exercisable shares
M = market value of share of stock
E = exercise price of option

Using the assumed figures from the example, the number of incremental shares is computed as follows:

$$I = 5,000 \times \frac{(\$50 - \$40)}{\$50} = 1,000 \text{ shares}$$

[8]*Accounting Interpretations of APB Opinion No. 15, Interpretation 51,* "Computing Earnings Per Share" (New York: American Institute of Certified Public Accountants, 1970).

Number of shares to be used in computing primary earnings per share:

Actual number of shares outstanding...		100,000
Incremental shares:		
Issued on assumed exercise of options	20,000	
Less assumed repurchase of shares from proceeds of options...........	12,000	8,000
Total		108,000
Primary earnings per share ($92,800 ÷ 108,000).........................		$.86

Percentage dilution: $.93 − $.86 = $.07; $.07 ÷ $.93 = 7.5% (rounded)

The materiality test of dilution is applied after all dilutive common stock equivalents have been included. In this illustration, there is only one such security; therefore, the test is applied after its inclusion. The dilution of approximately 7.5% exceeds the materiality standard (3% or more), so the common stock equivalent would be used in computing primary earnings per share.

Limitation on Use of Treasury Stock Method. If the number of common shares of stock involved in exercising options, warrants, or rights is large, the market price of the shares may not be a reliable figure, because any attempt to purchase a large block of stock would drive the stock price upward. The Accounting Principles Board recognized this possibility, and declared the treasury stock method inappropriate for proceeds in excess of those required to purchase 20% of the shares outstanding at the end of the year. Proceeds beyond that required to purchase 20% of the common stock are assumed to be applied first to reduce any short-term or long-term borrowings, and any remaining proceeds are assumed to be invested in U.S. Government securities or commercial paper, with appropriate recognition of any income effect, net of tax.

To illustrate the computation of primary earnings per share under these circumstances, assume the following data for the Valtek Corporation:

Summary of relevant information:

Net income for the year	$4,000,000
Common shares outstanding (no change during year)........................	3,000,000
8% Bonds payable...	$5,000,000
Options outstanding to purchase equivalent shares	1,000,000
Limitation on assumed repurchase of shares (3,000,000 × 20%)...............	600,000
Exercise price per share on options......................................	$15
Average market price for common shares	$20
Income tax rate	40%

Earnings per share without common stock equivalents (simple EPS):

Net income for the year	$4,000,000
Actual number of shares outstanding......................................	3,000,000
Simple earnings per share ($4,000,000 ÷ 3,000,000)	$1.33

Application of proceeds from assumed exercise of options outstanding:

Proceeds from assumed exercise of options outstanding (1,000,000 × $15)	$15,000,000
Maximum applied toward repurchase of outstanding shares (600,000 × $20)	12,000,000
Balance of proceeds applied to retirement of 8% bonds	$ 3,000,000

Net income to be used in computing primary earnings per share:

Net income		$4,000,000
Add interest on 8% bonds assumed retired, net of income tax:		
Interest ($3,000,000 × 8%)	$240,000	
Less income tax savings ($240,000 × 40%)	96,000	144,000
Adjusted net income		$4,144,000

Number of shares to be used in computing primary earnings per share:

Actual number of shares outstanding.		3,000,000
Incremental shares:		
Issued on assumed exercise of options	1,000,000	
Less assumed repurchase of shares from proceeds of options	600,000	400,000
Total		3,400,000
Primary earnings per share ($4,144,000 ÷ 3,400,000)		$1.22

Percentage dilution: $1.33 − $1.22 = $.11; $.11 ÷ $1.33 = 8.3% (rounded)

The dilution again is considered material, and the options would be included.

Partially paid stock subscriptions are to be considered the equivalent of warrants for purposes of computing earnings per share amounts. The unpaid balance is assumed to be the proceeds used to purchase stock under the treasury stock method. The number of incremental shares for partially paid stock subscriptions is the difference between the number of shares subscribed and the number of shares assumed to be purchased under the treasury stock method.[9]

Convertible Securities

A convertible security, whether bonds or preferred stock, that at the time of its issuance has terms indicating the purchaser is placing a premium on the conversion feature, and whose terms permit conversion within the succeeding 5 years, is recognized as a common stock equivalent. The Accounting Principles Board indicated that if the cash yield of the convertible security at the time of its issuance is significantly less than a comparable security without the conversion option, it is a common stock equivalent. Cash yield as used in Opinion No. 15 is the cash to be received annually expressed as a percentage of the market value of the security at the specified date. For example, a $1,000 bond paying interest at 9% and

---

[9]*Accounting Interpretations of APB Opinion No. 15, Interpretation No. 83,* "Stock Subscriptions Are Warrants" (New York: American Institute of Certified Public Accountants, 1970).

selling for 90 would have a cash yield of 10% ($90/$900). To make the determination both simple and objective, the APB, after considering a number of alternatives, concluded that a convertible security should be recognized as a common stock equivalent if it had a cash yield based on its market price of less than 66⅔% of the bank prime interest rate for short-term loans at the time of its issuance. Because the bank prime interest rate began to fluctuate widely in the late 1970s and early 1980s, the FASB changed the base measure for convertible securities issued after February 28, 1982, to the average Aa corporate bond yield.[10] This designation is widely used in the financial community and refers to bonds of equal quality to those rated Aa by either Moody's or Standard and Poor's investment services. The identification of a convertible security as a common stock equivalent is made at the time of its issuance, and it **retains this identity** as long as it remains outstanding, regardless of changes in the interest rate. Convertible securities are included in primary earnings per share only if they are dilutive.

For example, assume at December 31, 1987, the Aa corporate bond yield is 11%. A $1,000, 20-year, convertible bond with a stated interest rate of 7% is sold at 109 providing a cash yield of 6.42% ($70/$1,090). Since the yield is less than 66⅔% of the Aa corporate bond yield of 11%, or 7⅓%, the bond is recognized as a common stock equivalent. The bond will retain this classification even though future bond interest rates fall and the cash yield exceeds 66⅔% of the Aa yield.

In order to compute primary earnings per share when convertible securities exist, adjustments must be made **both** to net income and to the number of shares of common stock outstanding. These adjustments must reflect what these amounts would have been if the conversion had taken place at the beginning of the current year or at the date of issuance of the convertible securities, whichever comes later. This is referred to as the **if-converted method**. If the securities are bonds, net income is adjusted by adding back the interest expense, net of tax, to net income; the number of shares of common stock outstanding is increased by the number of shares that would have been issued on conversion.[11] Any amortization of initial premium or discount is included in the interest expense added back. If the convertible securities are shares of preferred stock, no reduction is made

---

[10]*Statement of Financial Accounting Standards No. 55*, "Determining Whether a Convertible Security Is a Common Stock Equivalent" (Stamford: Financial Accounting Standards Board, 1982).

[11]In addition to adjustments for interest, adjustments to net income for nondiscretionary or indirect items would have to be made in many situations. These items would include profit-sharing bonuses and other payments whose amount is determined by the net income reported. For simplicity, no indirect effects are illustrated in this chapter. See Chapter 23 for impact of such effects on accounting changes.

from net income for preferred dividends, as is done with the computation of earnings per share in a simple capital structure; the number of shares of common stock outstanding is increased by the number of shares that would have been issued upon conversion. If the convertible securities were issued during the year, adjustments would be made for only the portion of the year since the issuance date.

In order to test for dilution, each convertible security that qualifies as a common stock equivalent must be evaluated individually. If there is only one such security, comparison is made between earnings per share before considering the convertible security with the earnings per share after including it. As indicated earlier, if the earnings per share decreases or the loss per share increases, the convertible security is defined as dilutive. Antidilutive securities are excluded from the computation of primary earnings per share. The 3% materiality test for dilution is applied by comparing the primary earnings per share after considering all dilutive common stock equivalents with the simple earnings per share. A simplified procedure for considering multiple common stock equivalents is included in the appendix to this chapter.

Illustration of Primary EPS with Convertible Securities. The following examples for the Ramage Corporation illustrate the computation of primary earnings per share when convertible securities qualifying as common stock equivalents exist.

Summary of relevant information:

8% convertible bonds issued at par	$500,000
Net income for the year	$ 83,000
Common shares outstanding (no change during year)	100,000
Conversion terms of convertible bonds	80 shares for each $1,000 bond
Assumed tax rate	40%

Earnings per share without common stock equivalents (simple EPS):

Net income	$ 83,000
Actual number of shares outstanding	100,000
Simple earnings per share ($83,000 ÷ 100,000)	$.83

Primary earnings per share including common stock equivalents:

Net income		$ 83,000
Add interest on convertible bonds, net of income tax:		
Interest ($500,000 × 8%)	$40,000	
Less income tax savings ($40,000 × 40%)	16,000	24,000
Adjusted net income		$107,000
Actual number of shares outstanding		100,000
Additional shares issued on assumed conversion of bonds (500 × 80)		40,000
Adjusted number of shares		140,000
Primary earnings per share ($107,000 ÷ 140,000)		$.76

Percentage dilution: $.83 − $.76 = $.07; $.07 ÷ $.83 = 8.4% (rounded)

Computation of Primary EPS for Partial Year. If the convertible bonds had been issued by Ramage Corporation on March 31 of the current year, the adjustment would be made to reflect only the period subsequent to the issuance date, or ¾ of a year.

Primary earnings per share including common stock equivalents (¾ year):

Net income		$ 83,000
Add interest on convertible bonds, net of income tax:		
Interest ($500,000 × 8% × ¾ year)	$30,000	
Less income tax ($30,000 × 40%)	12,000	18,000
Adjusted net income		$101,000
Actual number of shares outstanding		100,000
Additional shares issued on assumed conversion of bonds (500 × 80 × ¾)		30,000
Adjusted number of shares		130,000
Primary earnings per share ($101,000 ÷ 130,000)		$.78

Percentage dilution: $.83 − $.78 = $.05; $.05 ÷ $.83 = 6% (rounded)

Convertible preferred stock is treated in the same manner as convertible debt securities (bonds). To illustrate application of the "if-converted" method to preferred stock, assume the same facts as given for the bond example for Ramage Corporation on page 785, except that instead of 8% convertible bonds, the company has 8% preferred stock outstanding, par value $500,000, convertible into 40,000 shares of common stock. The preferred stock was outstanding for the entire year and qualifies as a common stock equivalent.

Earnings per share without common stock equivalents (simple EPS):

Net income, without the deduction for interest on bonds (as computed on page 785)	$107,000
Less preferred dividends	40,000
Net income identified with common stock	$ 67,000
Actual number of shares outstanding	100,000
Simple earnings per share ($67,000 ÷ 100,000)	$.67

Primary earnings per share including common stock equivalents:

Net income assuming no payment of preferred dividends	$107,000
Actual number of shares outstanding	100,000
Additional shares issued on assumed conversion of preferred stock	40,000
Adjusted number of shares	140,000
Primary earnings per share ($107,000 ÷ 140,000)	$.76

In this example, primary earnings per share ($.76) is greater than simple earnings per share ($.67). Thus the convertible preferred stock is antidilutive and would not be considered in the computation of earnings per share. Assuming the corporation had no other potentially dilutive securities outstanding, only simple earnings per share would be presented on the income statement.

Short-Cut Test for Antidilution. It is possible to determine if a convertible security is antidilutive without actually computing primary or fully diluted earnings per share assuming conversion. If a company has net income rather than losses, the antidilutive test is performed by computing what the conversion contributes to per share earnings. For example, if the 8% bonds are converted, net income to the common shareholders will increase by $24,000 (see page 786) and the number of common shares outstanding will increase by 40,000 shares. The contribution of this conversion to earnings is $.60 per share, ($24,000 ÷ 40,000). Since this amount is less than the preconversion simple earnings per share of $.83, the bonds are dilutive. On the other hand, if the preferred stock is converted, the preferred dividends of $40,000 would no longer be deducted from net income in computing earnings per share, and the number of common shares outstanding will increase by 40,000 shares. The contribution of this conversion to earnings is $1.00 per share, ($40,000 ÷ 40,000). Since the preferred stock conversion contributes more per share than preconversion simple earnings of $.67, the preferred stock is antidilutive.

Multiple Potentially Dilutive Securities

When several potentially dilutive securities exist, the combination of convertible securities and options, warrants, and other rights that produce the lowest primary earnings per share should be determined and reported. This lowest figure is found by computing earnings per share for all possible combinations of potentially dilutive securities that are not antidilutive, and identifying the lowest figure. The use of computers assists greatly in testing for the lowest combination figure. A comprehensive illustration that includes multiple dilutive securities is included in the Appendix to this chapter.

FULLY DILUTED EARNINGS PER SHARE

In calculating fully diluted earnings in the dual presentation of earnings per share, it is necessary to consider not only all dilutive common stock equivalents, but all other potentially dilutive securities even though they do not qualify as common stock equivalents. For example, fully diluted earnings per share would include convertible securities whose cash yield equaled or exceeded 66⅔% of the Aa corporate bond yield at the issuance date that were exercisable or convertible within 10 years, and that were dilutive. As with common stock equivalents, conversion is assumed to have taken place at the beginning of the period or at the time the convertible security was issued, if later. The maximum potential dilution of current earnings per share on a prospective basis is thus determined.

When primary earnings are diluted as a result of the inclusion of outstanding options and warrants, a modification in the application of the treasury stock method may be necessary for purposes of calculating the fully diluted earnings per share. To reflect maximum potential dilution, the market price of the common stock at the close of the period is used in computing the number of shares assumed to be reacquired if the ending market price is higher than the average price used in computing primary earnings per share.

As is the case for primary earnings per share, the computation of fully diluted earnings per share should include only dilutive securities. Also, only those securities that are exercisable or convertible within 10 years from the date of the financial statements are included in fully diluted earnings per share.

Illustration of Fully Diluted Earnings Per Share

To illustrate fully diluted earnings per share, assume the following additional facts for the Tring Corporation as presented on page 781:

Additional relevant information:

Ending market price for common shares...	$16
9% convertible bonds not qualifying as common stock equivalents	$60,000
Conversion terms for 9% bonds.........................	100 shares for each $1,000 bond

Test for dilution of 9% bonds:

$$\frac{\text{Interest, net of tax}}{\text{Additional shares}} = \frac{(\$60,000 \times .09 \times .60)}{100 \times 60} = \$.54 \text{ per share}$$

Because the contribution of $.54 is less than the primary earnings per share of $.86 (see page 782), the convertible bonds are potentially dilutive and will be used in computing fully diluted earnings per share.

Net income to be used in computing fully diluted earnings per share:

Net income		$ 92,800
Add interest on convertible bonds net of income tax:		
Interest ($60,000 × 9%)..	$5,400	
Less income tax savings ($5,400 × 40%)	2,160	3,240
Adjusted net income		$ 96,040

Application of proceeds from assumed exercise of options outstanding to purchase treasury stock:

Proceeds from assumed exercise of options outstanding (20,000 × $6).............	$120,000
Number of outstanding shares assumed to be repurchased with proceeds from options ($120,000 ÷ $16)...	7,500

Number of shares to be used in computing fully diluted earnings per share:

Actual number of shares outstanding..................................		100,000
Incremental shares:		
Issued on assumed exercise of options	20,000	
Less assumed repurchase of shares from proceeds of options.........	7,500	12,500
Additional shares issued on assumed conversion of 9% bonds (100 × 60)		6,000
Total		118,500
Fully diluted earnings per share ($96,040 ÷ 118,500)..................		$.81

Primary and fully diluted earnings in the example would be reported on the income statement as shown below. This presentation would be accompanied by notes explaining the nature of the calculations.

Primary earnings per share......................	$.86
Fully diluted earnings per share..................	$.81

Effect of Actual Exercise or Conversion

If exercise or conversion actually takes place during the year, the weighted average number of shares issued will be included in all earnings per share computations. In addition, however, an adjustment is made to reflect what the earnings per share would have been if conversion or exercise had taken place at the beginning of the period or issuance° date whichever comes later. This adjustment is required for all securities actually converted or exercised during the period for computing fully diluted earnings per share whether dilutive or not. However, for computing primary earnings per share, the adjustment is required only if the results are dilutive.

When options or warrants are exercised, the adjustment for the period before exercise for primary earnings per share uses the average market price for the pre-exercise period; the adjustment for fully diluted earnings per share uses the market price at exercise date, regardless of whether it is higher than the average price.

To illustrate the computation of primary and fully diluted earnings per share when stock options are exercised during the year, assume the data that follow for Weatherby, Inc.

Summary of relevant information:

Net income for the year	$2,300,000
Common shares outstanding at beginning of year	400,000
Options outstanding at beginning of year to purchase equivalent shares ..	100,000
Exercise price per share on options...................................	$9.00
Proceeds from actual exercise of options on October 1 of current year...	$900,000
Market prices of common stock during year:	
Average for 9 months ending September 30	$12.50
Market price at exercise date, October 1	$15.00

Number of shares to be used in computing simple earnings per share:

Actual number of shares outstanding for full year......................	400,000
Weighted shares issued on October 1 (100,000 × ¼ year)	25,000
Weighted average number of shares for simple earnings per share......	425,000
Simple earnings per share ($2,300,000 ÷ 425,000)....................	$5.41

Number of shares to be used in computing primary earnings per share:

Weighted average number of shares for simple earnings per share......		425,000
Incremental shares if options had been exercised on January 1 (options are dilutive since average market price of stock exceeds the exercise price):		
Issued on assumed exercise of options	100,000	
Less assumed repurchase of shares with proceeds ($900,000 ÷ $12.50)...	72,000	
Incremental shares assumed to be issued......................	28,000	
Weighted average of incremental shares assumed to be issued (28,000 × ¾ year)...		21,000
Weighted average number of shares for primary earnings per share.....		446,000
Primary earnings per share ($2,300,000 ÷ 446,000)..................		$5.16

Percentage dilution: $5.41 − $5.16 = $.25; $.25 ÷ $5.41 = 4.6%

Number of shares to be used in computing fully diluted earnings per share:

Weighted average number of shares for simple earnings per share......		425,000
Incremental shares if options had been exercised on January 1 (included whether dilutive or not):		
Issued on assumed exercise of options	100,000	
Less assumed repurchase of shares with proceeds ($900,000 ÷ $15)..	60,000	
Incremental shares assumed to be issued......................	40,000	
Weighted average of incremental shares assumed to be issued (40,000 × ¾ year)...		30,000
Weighted average number of shares for fully diluted earnings per share..		455,000
Fully diluted earnings per share ($2,300,000 ÷ 455,000)..............		$5.05

EFFECT OF NET LOSSES

If a company has a net loss, no dual computation of earnings per share is necessary since inclusion of stock options or convertible securities would decrease the loss per share and thus always be antidilutive. To illustrate this situation, assume the following data for the Boggs Co.

Summary of relevant information:

Net loss for the year	($50,000)
Number of shares of stock outstanding—full year.............................	100,000
Number of shares of convertible preferred stock.............................	10,000
Conversion terms........................... 2 shares of common for 1 share of preferred	
Dividends on preferred stock..	$8,000

The computation of simple and primary earnings per share would be as follows:

Loss per share without common stock equivalents (simple):

Net loss	($50,000)
Dividends on preferred stock	(8,000)
Total loss to common shareholders	($58,000)
Actual number of shares outstanding	100,000
Loss per share ($58,000 ÷ 100,000)	($.58)

Primary loss per share including common stock equivalents:

Net loss	($50,000)
Actual number of shares outstanding	100,000
Incremental shares on assumed conversion of preferred stock	20,000
Adjusted number of shares	120,000
Primary loss per share ($50,000 ÷ 120,000)	($.42)

Because the primary loss per share is less than the simple loss per share, only the simple loss per share would be reported on the income statement.

If a company has an operating loss, but a positive net income because of net nonrecurring gains, or a negative net income but a positive operating income, the dilutive effect must be computed for each income figure. If inclusion of stock options or convertible securities results in dilution of any one income figure (i.e., operating income, extraordinary gains, gain from discontinued operations, etc.), the securities are included in all earnings per share calculations.

SUMMARY OF EARNINGS PER SHARE COMPUTATIONS

The discussion and illustration of earnings per share computations included in this chapter present only a few of the many provisions included in the accounting standards and their interpretations. The existence of various kinds of dilutive securities has made the accounting standard and its application very complex. Elaborate computer programs have been designed to assist companies and their auditors in computing the various earnings per share figures required. In some instances, the rules appear arbitrary and inconsistent with the objective of showing the most dilutive position. Exhibit 18–1 summarizes the rules for the inclusion of stock options, warrants, rights, and convertible securities in computing primary and fully diluted earnings per share.

APB Opinion No. 15 is frequently cited by accountants who argue that there is an accounting standards overload, and that the standards have become too detailed. Because of the complexity involved in applying the provisions of the opinion, in 1978 the FASB suspended the requirement of reporting earnings per share data for nonpublic companies.[12]

Exhibit 18–1   Summary of Earnings Per Share Components

Type of Securities	Simple EPS	Primary EPS	Fully Diluted EPS
Stock Options, Warrants, and Rights	Exclude	Always common stock equivalent. Include if dilutive and if exercisable within 5 years.	Include if dilutive and exercisable within 10 years.
Convertible Securities (Bonds and Preferred Stocks)	Exclude	Include if common stock equivalent, (cash yield at time of issue is less than 66⅔% of the Aa bond rate), if dilutive, and if convertible within 5 years.	Include if dilutive and convertible within 10 years.

FINANCIAL STATEMENT PRESENTATION

When earnings of a period include extraordinary items, income or loss from discontinued operations, or a cumulative effect of a change in accounting principle, earnings per share amounts should be presented for amounts before these special items, for each of these significant items, and for net income. For a complex capital structure, each of these items should be presented on both a primary and a fully diluted basis.

A schedule or note should be provided for a dual presentation explaining how primary and fully diluted earnings are calculated. Those securities included as common stock equivalents in arriving at primary earnings per share, as well as those included in the computation of fully diluted earnings per share, should be identified. All assumptions made and the resulting adjustments required in developing the earnings per share data should be disclosed. Additional disclosures should be made of the number of shares of common stock issued upon conversion, exercise, or satisfaction of required conditions for at least the most recent annual fiscal period. To illustrate, pertinent sections of the 1985 financial statements of Republic Airlines and United States Steel are reproduced on pages 793–795.

---

[12]*Statement of Financial Accounting Standards No. 21.*

Republic AiRlines

NET EARNINGS (LOSS) PER COMMON SHARE—	Year Ended December 31		
PRIMARY	1985	1984	1983
Before extraordinary items	$1.80	$.30	$(4.28)
Extraordinary items	2.94	.46	—
Net earnings (loss).	$4.74	$.76	$(4.28)
NET EARNINGS (LOSS) PER COMMON SHARE—			
FULLY DILUTED			
Before extraordinary items	$1.53	$.29	$(4.28)
Extraordinary items	2.45	.46	—
Net earnings (loss).	$3.98	$.75	$(4.28)

Note J—Net Earnings (Loss) Per Common Share—Primary earnings per common share for 1985, 1984 and 1983 were based on the weighted average number of common and common equivalent shares outstanding of 36,697,852; 34,139,472; and 26,720,591; respectively. In 1985 and 1984, common shares outstanding included 5,529,195 shares relating to employee stock agreements, of which 2,600,000 shares were issued in 1985 (see Note I). Common equivalent shares included 261,638 shares in 1985 and 46,220 shares in 1984 from the assumed exercise of stock options and warrants.

In 1985, fully diluted earnings per common share assumed conversion of the 10-1/8% convertible senior subordinated debentures into 7,499,992 shares, the 13% convertible subordinated debentures into 1,114,126 shares, and included 414,716 additional common shares from the assumed exercise of stock options and warrants. Fully diluted earnings per common share in 1984 included the assumed issuance of 228,975 additional common shares relating to the stock bonus plan for pilots and conversion of stock op-

tions. In 1983, fully diluted loss per common share was the same as primary, as the assumed conversion of convertible debentures and exercise of stock options and warrants were antidilutive.

Net earnings were reduced or net loss increased by preferred dividend requirements of $3,147,000 in 1985, $3,640,000 in 1984, and $3,337,000 in 1983 prior to computing the per common share amounts. In the fully diluted calculation for 1985, net earnings were adjusted for interest relating to the convertible debentures, net of income tax and profit-sharing effect. This amounted to $4,137,000 for net earnings per common share before extraordinary items, and $4,221,000 for net earnings per common share for the extraordinary items.

In January 1986 the Company's 10-1/8% convertible senior subordinated debentures were called for redemption (see Notes C and M). If these debentures had been converted into common stock as of January 1, 1985, primary earnings per share would have been $1.57 in 1985 before extraordinary items and $4.09 for net earnings.

(UsS) United States Steel

	1985	1984	1983
Income per common share			
Primary:			
Total income (loss) before extraordinary gain, cumulative effect of a change in accounting principle and preferred stock dividends	$ 2.79	$ 3.90	$(11.24)
Extraordinary gain	.45	.74	—
Cumulative effect of a change in accounting principle	.40	—	—
Dividends on preferred stock	(1.08)	(1.12)	(.83)
Net income (loss) per common share *(Note 10)*	**$ 2.56**	**$ 3.52**	**$(12.07)**
Fully diluted:			
Total income (loss) before extraordinary gain, cumulative effect of a change in accounting principle and preferred stock dividends	$ 2.53	$ 3.19	$(11.24)
Extraordinary gain	.40	.59	—
Cumulative effect of a change in accounting principle	.35	—	—
Dividends on preferred stock	(.72)	(.40)	(.83)
Net income (loss) per common share *(Note 10)*	**$ 2.56**	**$ 3.38**	**$(12.07)**

10. Income Per Common Share

Primary net income per share is calculated by adjusting net income for the dividend requirements of preferred stock and is based on the weighted average number of common shares outstanding plus common stock equivalents, provided they are not antidilutive. Common stock equivalents result from the assumed surrender of stock appreciation rights (50% stock—50% cash) associated with the 1976 Stock Option Incentive Plan at the average market price of the Corporation's common stock during the period.

Fully diluted net income per share assumes full conversion of the 5¾% Convertible Subordinated Debentures and convertible preferred stock for the applicable periods outstanding and assumes stock appreciation rights were surrendered (50% stock—50% cash) at the higher of the closing market price at year-end or the year's average market price of the Corporation's common stock, provided the effect is not antidilutive. The following preferred issues were antidilutive for the years indicated: 1985—$2.25 convertible exchangeable and $10.75 exchangeable convertible; 1984—$10.75 exchangeable convertible; and 1983—all convertible issues. In 1985, the $12.75 convertible preference stock was antidilutive, but was included in fully diluted calculations because it was converted. In the calculation of fully diluted net income per share, net income was adjusted for interest and other related costs of the convertible subordinated debentures and dividends on nonconvertible preferred stock.

The weighted average common shares are as follows:

(In thousands)	1985	1984	1983
Primary	**112,346**	106,147	103,277
Fully diluted	**126,953**	133,921	103,277

A common stock equivalent or other dilutive security may dilute one of the several per share amounts required to be disclosed on the face of the income statement, while increasing another amount. In such a case, the common stock equivalent or other dilutive securities should be recognized for all computations even though they have an antidilutive effect on one or more of the per share amounts.[13]

Earnings per share data should be presented for all periods covered by the income statement. If potential dilution exists in any of the periods presented, the dual presentation of primary and fully diluted earnings per share should be made for all periods presented.[14] Whenever net income of prior periods has been restated as a result of a prior period adjustment, the earnings per share for these prior periods should be restated and the effect of the restatements disclosed in the current year.[15]

It is important that great care be exercised in interpreting earnings per share data regardless of the degree of refinement applied in the development of the data. These values are the products of the principles and practices employed in the accounting process and are subject to the same limitations as found in the net income measurement reported on the income statement.

APPENDIX

COMPREHENSIVE ILLUSTRATION USING MULTIPLE POTENTIALLY DILUTIVE SECURITIES

The illustrations in the chapter dealt primarily with one type of potentially dilutive security at a time. For a company having several different

---

[13]*Opinions of the Accounting Principles Board, No. 15,* par. 30.
[14]*Ibid.,* par. 17.
[15]*Ibid.,* par. 18.

issues of convertible securities and/or stock options and warrants, the APB requires selection of the combination of securities producing the lowest possible earnings per share figure. To avoid having to test a large number of different combinations to find the lowest one, companies can compute the individual impact on earnings per share for each potentially dilutive security, rank them in order from the smallest to the largest in terms of impact on EPS, and introduce each security into the computation until the earnings per share is lower than the next security's individual impact. At that point, all remaining securities in the list would be antidilutive.

To illustrate, assume a company had four convertible securities that would have the following effects on fully diluted earnings per share if each were considered separately.

	Effects of Assumed Conversion		
	Increase in Net Income	Increase in No. of Shares	Individual Impact on EPS
Convertible Security A	$ 75,000	50,000	$1.50
Convertible Security B	150,000	60,000	2.50
Convertible Security C	110,000	20,000	5.50
Convertible Security D	600,000	100,000	6.00

Assume further that simple earnings per share was $6.50 ($2,275,000 income divided by 350,000 outstanding shares). Each of the four securities considered separately results in an earnings per share figure lower than simple earnings per share and would thus be dilutive. However, when considering all four securities together, only the first two (A and B) would be dilutive and therefore included in fully diluted earnings per share. This is determined by adding one security at a time to the simple earnings per share figure as follows:

	Net Income (adjusted)	Number of Shares (adjusted)	Fully Diluted EPS
Simple capital structure	$2,275,000	350,000	$6.50
Convertible Security A	75,000	50,000	
	$2,350,000	400,000	$5.87
Convertible Security B	150,000	60,000	
	$2,500,000	460,000	$5.43
Convertible Security C	110,000	20,000	
	$2,610,000	480,000	$5.44
Convertible Security D	600,000	100,000	
	$3,210,000	580,000	$5.53

It would not be necessary to continue the computation beyond Security B since the EPS at that point ($5.43), is lower than the EPS impact of Security C ($5.50). Inclusion of Securities C and D would be antidilutive as the computations show.

This approach to multiple securities will be used in the comprehensive problem that follows.

The Circle West Transportation Co. has the following outstanding stocks and bonds at January 1, 1988. All securities had been sold at par or face value.

Date of Issue	Type of Security	Par or Face Value	Number of Shares or Total Face Value	Conversion Terms	Aa Bond Rate at Date of Issue
1976–1987	Common stock	$25	200,000	none	
May 1, 1982	12% debentures	$1,000	$750,000	none	9%
Jan. 1, 1986	6% cumulative preferred stock	$100	40,000	4 shares of common for each preferred share	14%
Jan. 1, 1987	8% debentures	$1,000	$1,000,000	15 shares of common for each $1,000 debenture	13%
June 30, 1987	10% debentures	$1,000	$600,000	30 shares of common for each $1,000 debenture	12%
Dec. 31, 1987	8% cumulative preferred stock	$50	12,500	none	11%

Circle West also had stock options outstanding at January 1, 1988, for the purchase of 20,000 shares of common. During 1988, options were granted for an additional 40,000 shares. The terms of these stock options are as follows:

Date of Issue	Exercisable Date	Exercise Price	Number of Options
Jan. 1, 1985	June 30, 1988	$30	20,000
June 30, 1988	June 30, 1990	$62	40,000

Common stock market prices for 1988 were as follows:

Average for year	$60
Average for first ¾ of year	$58
Average for last half of year	$61
October 1 price	$62
December 31 price	$65

(Market price exceeded October 1 price for entire fourth quarter)

During 1988, Circle West issued the following common stock:

Apr. 1   30,000 shares sold at $56
Oct. 1   20,000 shares issued from exercise of Jan. 1, 1985, options

On December 1, 1988, Circle West paid a full year's dividend on the 6% preferred stock and on the 8% preferred stock. Assume that the company had net income of $1,026,000 in 1988, all of which was income from continuing operations. The income tax rate is 40%.

When a company has multiple potentially dilutive convertible securities an orderly approach to computing earnings per share is necessary. The following steps should prove helpful in understanding this illustration and in solving complex earnings per share problems.

1. Compute simple earnings per share using a weighted average number of shares for common stock outstanding during the year.

2. Identify common stock equivalents:
   (a) All stock options, warrants, and rights.
   (b) Convertible securities with a cash yield less than ⅔ of the Aa bond rate at the time the securities were issued.

3. Determine whether common stock equivalents are dilutive.
   (a) Stock options, warrants, and rights: If the exercise price is less than average market price for primary; or ending market price, if higher than average, for fully diluted.
   (b) Convertible securities: Compute impact of assumed conversion on earnings per share for each security individually. Those with an impact greater than simple earnings per share are antidilutive and are excluded.

4. Compute primary earnings per share:
   (a) Include dilutive stock options, warrants, and rights first. Use the average market price for the period they were outstanding to compute incremental shares under the treasury stock method.
   (b) Include dilutive common stock equivalent convertible securities one at a time beginning with the security that has the smallest EPS impact. Compute new earnings per share. Continue until the next security in the list has an impact on earnings per share greater than the last computed earnings per share. Discontinue the process at that point. All other securities in the list are antidilutive for purposes of computing the lowest possible primary earnings per share figure.
   (c) Test for materiality. If primary earnings per share is 3% or more dilutive when compared with simple earnings per share, primary earnings per share is reported and dual presentation is required.

5. Determine whether convertible securities that are not common stock equivalents are individually dilutive. Rank all dilutive convertible securities, both common stock equivalents and non-common-stock equivalents, in order from lowest to highest impact on earnings per share.

6. Compute fully diluted earnings per share:
   (a) Stock options, warrants, and rights: Include all dilutive securities as identified in step 3a. Use ending common stock market price, if higher than average price, to compute incremental shares under the treasury stock method.

(b) Convertible securities: Include convertible securities one at a time, following the same process described in step 4b.

(c) Test for materiality. The 3% materiality test is applied to both primary and fully diluted earnings per share. If either of these earnings per share figures meets the test, dual presentation is required.

These steps will be applied to the data for Circle West Transportation Company to compute the various earnings per share amounts.

Step 1. Compute simple earnings per share.

Net income......................................		$1,026,000
Less preferred dividends:		
6% stock (40,000 × $100 × .06)................	$240,000	
8% stock (12,500 × $50 × .08).................	50,000	290,000
Net income identified with common stock		$ 736,000

Weighted average number of shares:

Jan. 1 to Apr. 1	200,000 × ¼.............	50,000
Apr. 1 to Oct. 1	230,000 × ½.............	115,000
Oct. 1 to Dec. 31...........	250,000 × ¼.............	62,500
Total weighted average number of shares..............		227,500
Simple earnings per share ($736,000 ÷ 227,500).........		$3.24

Step 2. Identify common stock equivalents.

Both stock options are common stock equivalents. Circle West has 3 convertible securities. The 6% preferred stock and the 8% debentures both qualify as common stock equivalents, since the 6% dividend rate and 8% interest rate are less than ⅔ of the Aa bond rate at the date of issuance (14% and 13% respectively). The 10% debentures do not qualify as common stock equivalents, since the 10% rate is more than ⅔ of the Aa bond rate of 12%. The 8% preferred stock and 12% debentures are not potentially dilutive securities because they are not convertible.

Step 3. Determine whether common stock equivalents are dilutive.

(a) Stock options—The options issued on January 1, 1985, are dilutive since the exercise price ($30) is less than the average price for the period in which the options were outstanding ($58). The options issued June 30, 1988 are antidilutive since the exercise price ($62) is more than the average price for the last half of 1988 ($61).

(b) Common stock equivalent convertible securities:

	Net Income Impact	Number of shares	EPS Impact
6% Preferred stock......................	$240,000*	160,000	$1.50
8% Debentures	$48,000**	15,000	$3.20

*40,000 × $100 × .06
**$1,000,000 × .08 × .60 (1-tax rate)

Each security is potentially dilutive, since its impact on EPS is less than the $3.24 simple earnings per share. The 6% preferred stock has a lower impact on earnings per share than the 8% debentures; therefore, it will be used first in computing primary earnings per share.

Step 4.   Compute primary earnings per share.

Description	Net Income	Number of Shares	Part of Year	Weighted Average	EPS
Simple earnings per share............	$736,000			227,500	$3.24
Jan. 1, 1985, options–exercised Oct. 1, as if exercised Jan. 1, 1988 Number of shares assumed issued........................		20,000	¾	15,000	
Number of treasury shares assumed repurchased [(20,000 × $30) ÷ $58 (average for ¾ year)]		(10,345)	¾	(7,759)	
	$736,000			234,741	$3.14
6% preferred stock..................	240,000	160,000	1	160,000	
Primary earnings per share	$976,000			394,741	$2.47

Percentage dilution: $3.24 − $2.47 = $.77; $.77 ÷ $3.24 = 24%
8% debentures: Because impact value of $3.20 exceeds latest EPS of $2.47, the debentures are antidilutive and not included in primary EPS.

Step 5.   Determine whether options and convertible securities that are not common stock equivalents are dilutive for computing fully diluted earnings per share.

(a) Stock options: Both stock options are dilutive since the exercise prices ($30 and $62) are less than the applicable ending market prices ($62 on October 1 for the exercised options and $65 at year-end for the unexercised options).

(b) Convertible securities:

	Net Income Impact	Number of Shares	EPS Impact
6% Preferred stock......................	$240,000	160,000	$1.50
10% Debentures	$36,000*	18,000	$2.00
8% Debentures	$48,000	15,000	$3.20

*$600,000 × .10 × .60 (1-tax rate)

All three convertible securities are potentially dilutive since their impact on earnings per share is less than the $3.24 simple earnings per share.

Step 6.   Compute fully diluted earnings per share

Description	Net Income	Number of Shares	Part of Year	Weighted Average	EPS
Simple earnings per share..........	$ 736,000			227,500	$3.24
Jan. 1, 1985 options–exercised Oct. 1, as if exercised Jan. 1, 1988					
Number of shares assumed issued.....................		20,000	¾	15,000	
Number of treasury shares assumed repurchased [(20,000 × $30) ÷ $62 (price at exercise date)]		(9,677)	¾	(7,258)	
June 30, 1988 options					
Number of shares assumed issued.....................		40,000	½	20,000	
Number of treasury shares assumed repurchased [(40,000 × $62) ÷ $65 (price at year-end)]		(38,154)	½	(19,077)	
	$ 736,000			236,165	$3.12
6% preferred stock...............	240,000	160,000	1	160,000	
	$ 976,000			396,165	$2.46
10% debentures..................	36,000			18,000	
Fully diluted earnings per share	$1,012,000			414,165	$2.44

Percentage dilution: Since primary EPS was materially dilutive, and fully diluted EPS is lower, a dual presentation would be required.
8% debentures: Because impact value of $3.20 exceeds latest EPS of $2.44, the debentures are antidilutive and not included in fully diluted EPS.

QUESTIONS

1. Earnings per share computations have received increased prominence on the income statement. How would an investor use such information in making investment decisions?
2. Why are earnings per share figures computed on the basis of common stock transactions that have not yet happened rather than on the basis of strictly historical common stock data?
3. What is meant by "dilution of earnings per share"?
4. What is an antidilutive security? Why are such securities generally excluded from the computation of earnings per share?
5. What distinguishes a simple from a complex capital structure?
6. A dual presentation of earnings per share is required only if the effects of including dilutive securities is material. How does the profession define materiality in this case?

7.   What constitutes a common stock equivalent for calculating primary earnings per share?

8.   Why are earnings per share figures adjusted retroactively for stock dividends, stock splits, and reverse stock splits?

9.   (a) Under what conditions are stock options and warrants recognized as common stock equivalents? (b) Under what conditions is a convertible security recognized as a common stock equivalent?

10.   What is the treasury stock method of accounting for outstanding stock options and warrants in computing primary earnings?

11.   What modification to the treasury stock method is required if the number of shares obtainable from the exercise of outstanding options and warrants exceeds 20% of the number of shares outstanding?

12.   Compare the concept of primary earnings per share with the concept of fully diluted earnings per share.

13.   If stock options are actually exercised during the year, how is fully diluted earnings per share affected?

14.   How is the treasury stock method for stock options and warrants modified in computing fully diluted earnings per share as compared with computing primary earnings per share?

15.   When convertible debentures are not considered common stock equivalents, how are they handled for purposes of earnings per share computations?

16.   Why are all convertible securities and options antidilutive when a company is operating at a loss?

17.   What limitations should be recognized in using earnings per share data?

*18.   If a company has multiple potentially dilutive securities, how are the computations made to assure obtaining the lowest earnings per share figure?

*Relates to Appendix.

DISCUSSION CASES

CASE 18–1   (How does a complex capital structure affect EPS?)

Big Mountain Construction Company has gradually grown in size since its inception in 1919. The third generation of Clarksons who now manage the enterprise are considering selling a large block of stock to raise capital for new equipment purchases and to help finance several big projects. The Clarksons are concerned about how the earnings per share information should be presented on the income statement and have many questions concerning the nature of EPS.

(1) Discuss the EPS presentation that would be required if Big Mountain Construction has (a) a simple capital structure; (b) a complex capital structure. What factors determine whether a capital structure is simple or complex?

(2) Are primary earnings per share for a complex structure with common stock equivalents the same as earnings per share for a simple structure? Discuss

why APB Opinion No. 15 does not provide for a simple earnings per share for a complex capital structure.

(3) Assume Big Mountain Construction Company has a complex capital structure. Discuss the effect, if any, of each of the following transactions on the computation of earnings per share:

(a) The firm acquires some of its outstanding common stock to hold as treasury stock.

(b) The firm pays a dividend of 50¢ per common stock share.

(c) The firm declares a dividend of 75¢ per share on cumulative preferred stock.

(d) A 3-for-1 common stock split occurs during the year.

(e) Retained earnings are appropriated for a disputed construction contract that may be litigated.

CASE 18–2   (Are we in trouble or not?)

Inman Yacht Company has just completed its determination of earnings per share for the year. As a result of issuing convertible securities during the year, the capital structure of Inman is now defined as being complex. The primary earnings per share for this year is $2.90, but the fully diluted earnings per share is only $2.50, both figures down from the prior year's $3.25 simple earnings per share figure.

Richard Pearce and Linda Connell, two stockholders, have received their financial statements from Inman, and are discussing the earnings per share figures over lunch. The following dialogue ensues:

Pearce: I guess Inman must be having trouble. I see their earnings per share is down significantly.

Connell: Maybe so, but this year there are two figures where before there was only one.

Pearce: Something to do with the convertible bonds and preferred stock they issued during the year making it a complex capital structure. But both of the earnings per share figures are lower than the single figure the year before.

Connell: That's true. But income for the current year is higher than last year. I'm confused.

Enlighten the stockholders.

CASE 18–3   (When should common stock equivalency be determined?)

Frank Smith and Kim Morse are discussing the concept of common stock equivalents for convertible securities as defined by APB Opinion No. 15. Smith believes the status of a convertible security should be determined (using the cash yield test) not only at the time of issuance but from time to time thereafter because convertible securities are designed to react to changes in the earnings or earnings potential just as does common stock. Furthermore, although many convertible securities are issued under market and yield conditions that do not emphasize their common stock characteristics, both the issuer and the holder recognize the possibility of these characteristics becoming more significant as the value of the underlying common stock increases. But limiting determination of the common stock equivalent status to "at issuance only" disregards these factors.

Morse believes that for practical simplicity, common stock equivalent status should be determined only by the conditions that exist at time of issuance and that fully diluted earnings per share adequately disclose the potential dilution that may exist.

You are asked to give a third opinion. Which argument is more valid?

CASE 18–4   (But let's maintain earnings per share)

On January 1, 1985, Farnsworth Company had 1,000,000 shares of common stock and 100,000 shares of $8 cumulative preferred stock issued and outstanding. A principal goal of Farnsworth's management is to maintain or increase earnings per share.

On January 1, 1986, Farnsworth Company retired 50,000 shares of the preferred stock with excess cash and additional funds provided from the sale of a subsidiary.

At the beginning of 1987, the company borrowed $5,000,000 at 10% and used the proceeds to retire 200,000 shares of common stock. Operating income, before interest and income taxes (income tax rate is 40%), is as follows:

	1987	1986	1985
Operating income	$6,500,000	$7,000,000	$7,500,000

Did Farnsworth Company maintain its earnings per share even though income declined? What was the impact of the preferred and common stock transactions on earnings per share?

EXERCISES

EXERCISE 18–1   (Weighted average number of shares)

Compute the weighted average number of shares outstanding for Marvell Company, which has a simple capital structure, assuming the following transactions in common stock occurred during the year:

Date	Transactions in Common Stock	Number of Shares $10 Par Value
Jan. 1	Shares outstanding.........................	40,000
Feb. 1	Issued for cash	8,000
May 1	Acquisition of treasury stock..................	(6,000)
July 1	Resold part of treasury stock shares..........	3,200
Sept. 1	50% stock dividend.........................	50% of shares outstanding
Dec. 1	Issued in exchange for property..............	12,800

EXERCISE 18–2   (Weighted average number of shares)

Transactions involving the common stock account of the Nocturnal Gas Company during the 2-year period, 1987 and 1988 were as follows:

<u>1987</u>

Jan. 1   Balance 200,000 shares of $10 par common stock.

Apr. 1 $2,500,000 of convertible bonds were converted with 50 shares issued for each $1,000 bond.

July 1   A 10% stock dividend was declared.

Oct. 1   Option to purchase 6,125 shares for $20 a share was exercised.

<u>1988</u>

Apr. 1   A 2-for-1 stock split was declared.

Oct. 1   100,000 shares were sold for $30 a share.

From the information given, compute the comparative number of weighted average shares outstanding for 1987 and 1988 to be used for earnings per share computations at the end of 1988. Assume that conversion of bonds and exercise of options at January 1, 1987, would not have resulted in material dilution, and there are no other convertible securities or options outstanding. Thus, only a simple earnings per share is required.

EXERCISE 18–3   (Weighted average number of shares)

Assume the following transactions affected owners' equity for Judy Inc. during 1988.

Feb. 1   10,000 shares of common stock were sold in the market.

Apr. 1   Purchased 5,000 shares of common stock to be held as treasury stock. Paid cash dividends of $.50 per share.

May 1   Split common stock 3-for-1.

July 1   35,000 shares of common stock sold.

Oct. 1   A 5% stock dividend was issued.

Dec. 31   Paid a cash dividend of $.75 per share. The total amound paid for dividends on December 31 was $511,875.

Compute the weighted average number of shares to be used in computing earnings per share for 1988. Because no beginning share figures are available, you must work backwards from December 31, 1988, to compute shares outstanding.

EXERCISE 18–4   (Earnings per share — simple capital structure)

At December 31, 1987, the Bryner Corporation had 50,000 shares of common stock issued and outstanding, 30,000 of which had been issued and outstanding throughout the year and 20,000 of which had been issued on October 1, 1987. Operating income before income taxes for the year ended December 31, 1987, was $703,200. In 1987 and 1988, a dividend of $60,000 was paid on 60,000 shares of 10% cumulative preferred stock, $10 par.

On April 1, 1988, 30,000 additional shares were issued. Total income before income taxes for 1988 was $477,000, which included an extraordinary gain before income taxes of $37,000. Assuming a 40% tax rate, what is Bryner's earnings per common share for 1987 and for 1988, rounded to the nearest cent? Show computations in good form.

EXERCISE 18–5   (Earnings per share — simple capital structure)

The income statement for the Sanders Co. for the year ended December 31, 1988, reported the following:

Income from continuing operations before income taxes...........	$330,000
Income taxes...	132,000
Income from continuing operations.............................	$198,000
Loss from disposal of segment (net of income taxes)..............	(40,000)
Net income...	$158,000

Compute earnings per share amounts for 1988 under each of the following assumptions:
  (a) The company has only one class of common stock with 150,000 shares outstanding.
  (b) The company has shares outstanding as follows: preferred 8% stock, $50 par, cumulative, 30,000 shares; common, $25 par, 150,000 shares. Only the current year's preferred dividends are unpaid.
  (c) Same as (b) except Sanders Co. *also* has preferred 7% stock, $40 par, noncumulative, 20,000 shares. Only $30,000 in dividends on the non-cumulative preferred have been declared.

EXERCISE 18–6   (Common stock equivalents)

Which of the following securities would qualify as common stock equivalents? If a common stock equivalent, would it be used in computing primary earnings per share? Give reasons supporting each answer.
  (a) Employee stock options to purchase 1,000 shares of common stock in 6 years at $40 are outstanding. The market price of the common stock has been in excess of $45 for the past three months.
  (b) Warrants to purchase 2,000 shares at $30 are issued. The current market price is $27.
  (c) 8%, $1,000 convertible bonds are sold: sales price, 120. The Aa corporate bond yield is 11½%.
  (d) Preferred stock, 7%, convertible, is sold at par. The Aa corporate bond yield is 10¼%.

EXERCISE 18–7   (Primary earnings per share — convertible bonds)

On January 2, 1988, Yewdall Co. issued at par $30,000 of 8% bonds convertible in total into 1,500 shares of Yewdall's common stock. These bonds are common stock equivalents for purposes of computing earnings per share. No bonds were converted during 1988.

Throughout 1988, Yewdall had 5,000 shares of common stock outstanding. Yewdall's 1988 net income was $45,000. Yewdall's tax rate is 40%.

No other potentially dilutive securities other than the convertible bonds were outstanding during 1988. For 1988, compute Yewdall's primary earnings per share.

EXERCISE 18–8   (Dilutive securities)

The Stepp Corporation has earnings per common share of $2.09 for the period ended December 31, 1987. For each of the following examples, decide whether the convertible security would be dilutive or antidilutive in computing primary earnings per share. Consider each example individually. All are common stock equivalents. The tax rate is 40%.

(a) 8½% debentures, $1,000,000 face value, are convertible into common stock at the rate of 40 shares for each $1,000 bond.

(b) $5 preferred stock is convertible into common stock at the rate of 2 shares of common for 1 share of preferred. There are 50,000 shares of preferred stock outstanding.

(c) Options to purchase 200,000 shares of common stock are outstanding. The exercise price is $25 per share. Current market price is $20 per share.

(d) $400,000 of 8% debentures are convertible at the rate of 25 shares of common stock per each $1,000 bond.

(e) Preferred 7% stock, $100 par, 5,000 shares outstanding, convertible into 3 shares of common stock for each 1 share of preferred.

EXERCISE 18–9   (Primary earnings per share—convertible bonds)

The Benton Manufacturing Company reports long-term liabilities and stockholders' equity balances at December 31, 1987, as follows:

Convertible 6% bonds (sold at par)	$ 500,000
Common stock, $25 par, 90,000 shares issued and outstanding ..	2,250,000

Additional information is determined as follows:

Conversion terms of bonds .... 80 shares for each $1,000 bond	
Income before extraordinary gain—1987.......................	$200,000
Extraordinary gain (net of tax).................................	40,000
Net income—1987	$240,000

What are the primary earnings per share for the company for 1987, assuming that the income tax rate is 40% and the Aa corporate bond yield at the date the bonds were sold was 9½%? No changes occurred in the debt and equity balances during 1987.

EXERCISE 18–10   (Number of shares—stock options)

On January 1, 1988, McCarty Corporation had 56,000 shares of outstanding common stock which did not change during 1988. In 1987 McCarty Corporation granted options to certain executives to purchase 9,000 shares of its common stock at $7 each. The market price of common was $10.50 per share on December 31, 1988, and averaged $9 per share during the year. Compute the number of shares to be used in computing primary and fully diluted earnings per share for 1988.

EXERCISE 18–11   (Number of shares—stock options)

Alkema Company has employee stock options outstanding to purchase 40,000 common shares at $10 per share. All options were outstanding during the entire year and are presently exercisable or will become exercisable within 4 years. The average market price of the company's common stock during the year was $20 and the price of the stock at the end of the year was $25. Compute the common stock equivalent incremental shares that would be used in arriving at (1) primary earnings per share, and (2) fully diluted earnings per share. Alkema has 80,000 shares outstanding at the date the option is granted.

EXERCISE 18–12   (Earnings per share — convertible bonds)

At December 31, 1988, the books of Wyatt Corporation include the following balances:

Long-term liabilities:	
Bonds payable, 8%, each $1,000 bond is convertible into 50 shares of common stock; bonds sold at par and were issued November 3, 1987	$ 500,000
Stockholders' equity:	
Preferred stock, 7%, par $50, cumulative, nonconvertible, 10,000 shares outstanding..	500,000
Paid-in capital in excess of par, preferred stock............................	300,000
Common stock, par $10, authorized 300,000 shares; 199,500 outstanding	1,995,000
Paid-in capital in excess of par, common stock	450,000
Retained earnings..	519,000

The records of Wyatt reveal the following additional information:
(a) 150,000 shares of common stock were outstanding January 1, 1988.
(b) 40,000 shares of common stock were sold for cash on April 30, 1988.
(c) Issued 5% stock dividend on July 2, 1988.
(d) Aa corporate bond yield was 12% when bonds were issued.
(e) Operating income before extraordinary items (after tax) was $629,000.
(f) Extraordinary loss (net of tax), $16,000.
(g) Income tax rate, 40%.
(h) Bond indenture does not provide for increase in shares at conversion due to stock dividends declared subsequent to the bond issue date.

(1) Is this a simple or complex capital structure?
(2) How should earnings per share data be presented?

EXERCISE 18–13
(Earnings and loss per share — convertible preferred stock, net loss)

During all of 1987, Athens Inc. had outstanding 100,000 shares of common stock and 5,000 shares of $7 preferred stock. Each share of the preferred stock, which is classified as a common stock equivalent, is convertible into 3 shares of common stock. For 1987, Athens had $230,000 income from operations and $575,000 extraordinary losses, net of income tax effect; no dividends were paid or declared.

Compute the required earnings (loss) per share for income (loss) before extraordinary items and for net income (loss) assuming:
(a) The preferred stock is noncumulative.
(b) The preferred stock is cumulative.

*EXERCISE 18–14   (Earnings per share — convertible securities)

Information relating to the capital structure of the Rogers Corporation at December 31, 1986 and 1987, is as follows:

	Outstanding
Common stock....................................	90,000 shares
Convertible preferred stock noncumulative	
(issued in 1985).................................	10,000 shares
9% convertible bonds (issued in 1986)................	$1,000,000

Rogers Corporation paid dividends of $4 per share on its preferred stock. The preferred stock is convertible into 30,000 shares of common stock and is considered a common stock equivalent. The 9% convertible bonds are convertible into 25,000 shares of common stock, but are *not* considered to be common stock equivalents. The net income for the year ended December 31, 1987, is $625,000. Assume that the income tax rate is 40%. Compute (1) simple earnings per share, (2) primary earnings per share, and (3) fully diluted earnings per share for the year ended December 31, 1987.

Relates to appendix.

PROBLEMS

PROBLEM 18–1   (Weighted average number of shares)

Keller's Wholesale Products Inc. had 75,000 shares of common stock outstanding at the end of 1986. During 1987 and 1988, the following transactions took place.

1987

Mar. 31	Sold 5,000 shares at $27.
Apr. 26	Paid cash dividend of 50¢ per share.
July 31	Paid cash dividend of 25¢ per share, and issued a 10% stock dividend.
Nov. 1	Sold 7,000 shares at $30.

1988

Feb. 28	Purchased 5,000 shares of common stock to be held in treasury.
Mar. 1	Paid cash dividend of 50¢ per share.
Apr. 30	Issued 3-for-1 stock split.
Nov. 1	Sold 6,000 shares of treasury stock.
Dec. 20	Declared cash dividend of 25¢ per share.

Keller's Wholesale Products Inc. has a simple capital structure.

Instructions: Compute the weighted average number of shares for 1987 and 1988 to be used in the earnings per share computation at the end of 1988.

PROBLEM 18–2   (Earnings per share — simple capital structure)

The following condensed financial statements for the Fowler Corporation were prepared by the accounting department:

Fowler Corporation
Income Statement
For Year Ended December 31, 1988

Sales.		$10,000,000
Cost of goods sold.		8,000,000
Gross profit on sales.		$ 2,000,000
Expenses:		
Selling expense	$405,000	
Administrative expense.	500,000	
Interest expense.	29,000	934,000
Income from continuing operations before income taxes. . .		$ 1,066,000
Income taxes.		426,400
Income from continuing operations.		$ 639,600
Extraordinary gain, net of tax.		30,000
Net income		$ 669,600

Fowler Corporation
Balance Sheet
December 31, 1988

Assets.	$4,500,000
Current liabilities.	$1,000,000
8% Bonds, due December 31, 1995	600,000
Stockholders' equity:	
Common stock, $5 par, 250,000 shares authorized, issued and	
outstanding	1,250,000
Additional paid-in capital.	400,000
Retained earnings	1,250,000
	$4,500,000

Instructions: Compute the earnings per share under each of the following separate assumptions (the company has a simple capital structure):
(1) No change in the capital structure occurred in 1988.
(2) On December 31, 1987, there were 150,000 shares outstanding. On April 1, 1988, 80,000 shares were sold at par and on October 1, 1988, 20,000 shares were sold at par.
(3) On December 31, 1987, there were 187,500 shares outstanding. On July 1, 1988, the company issued a 33⅓% stock dividend.

PROBLEM 18–3   (Earnings per share — simple capital structure)

Great Western Inc. reported the following comparative information in the stockholders' equity section of its 1988 balance sheet.

	Dec. 31 1988	Dec. 31 1987	Dec. 31 1986
12% Preferred stock, $50 par............	$ 82,500	$ 67,500	$ 50,000
Paid-in capital in excess of par—			
preferred........................	13,400	9,200	5,000
Common stock, $10 par	410,600	399,600	325,000
Paid-in capital in excess of par—			
common	64,300	58,800	35,000
Paid-in capital from treasury stock	1,800	800	800
Retained earnings.....................	471,200	396,460	290,200
Total Stockholders' Equity..............	$1,043,800	$932,360	$706,000

In addition, company records show that the following transactions involving stockholders' equity were recorded in 1987 and 1988:

1987

Apr. 2	Sold 4,500 shares of common stock for $12, par value $10.
June 30	Sold 350 shares of preferred stock for $62, par value $50.
Aug. 1	Issued an 8% stock dividend on common stock. The market price of the stock was $15.
Sept. 1	Declared cash dividends of 12% on preferred stock and $1.50 on common stock.
Dec. 31	Income from operations for the year totaled $228,500. In addition, Great Western had an extraordinary loss of $9,800, net of tax savings.

1988

Jan. 31	Sold 1,100 shares of common stock for $15.
May 1	Sold 300 shares of preferred stock for $64.
June 1	Issued a 2-for-1 split of common stock.
Sept. 1	Purchased 500 shares of common stock for $9 to be held as treasury stock.
Oct. 1	Declared cash dividends of 12% on preferred stock and $1 on common stock.
Nov. 1	Sold 500 shares of treasury stock for $11.
Dec. 31	Net income for the year included an extraordinary gain net of income tax of $5,000.

Instructions: Compute the earnings per share amounts for 1987 and 1988 to be presented in the income statement for 1988.

PROBLEM 18–4   (Earnings per share — stock options)

The records of Mountain View Company reveal the following capital structure as of December 31, 1987:

$8 Preferred stock, $80 par, 7,500 shares issued and outstanding.......	$ 600,000
Additional paid-in capital on preferred stock.........................	60,000
Common stock, $20 par, 100,000 shares issued and outstanding........	2,000,000
Additional paid-in capital on common stock	350,000
Retained earnings	886,000

To stimulate work incentive and to bolster trade relations, Mountain View on May 1, 1988 issued stock options to select executives, creditors, and others allowing the purchase of 26,000 shares of common stock for $30 a share. Market prices for the stock at various times during the year were:

Option issuance date	$25
Year-end	75
Average for the year...........	50

A dividend on preferred stock was paid during the year, and there are no dividends in arrears at year-end. There are no other capital transactions during the year. Net income for 1988 was $500,000.

Instructions: Compute the earnings per share data required to satisfy generally accepted accounting principles.

PROBLEM 18–5   (Earnings per share — conversion of debentures)

The following is a partial balance sheet for Interwest Incorporated for the year ended December 31, 1987:

8% Convertible debentures	$ 800,000
Common stock, $12 par, 80,000 shares issued and outstanding..	$ 960,000
Retained earnings	882,000
Total stockholders' equity.................................	$1,842,000

(a) The convertible debentures include terms stating that each $1,000 bond can be converted into 55 shares of common stock. The Aa bond interest rate at date of issuance was 13%.

(b) On July 31, 1988, the complete issue of convertible debentures was converted into common stock.

(c) Interwest reported net income of $665,000 in 1988. The company's income tax rate was 40%.

(d) No other common stock transactions took place during the year other than the debenture conversion.

Instructions:

(1) Compute earnings per share for Interwest for the year ended December 31, 1988.

(2) Assume Interwest had a net loss of $250,000. Show why the convertible debentures are antidilutive under loss conditions.

PROBLEM 18–6   (Earnings per share — stock options)

The Craft Hardware Co. provides the following data at December 31, 1988:

Operating revenue......................................	$875,000
Operating expenses.....................................	$450,000
Income tax rate	40%
Common stock outstanding during the entire year	22,000 shares

On January 1, 1988, there were options outstanding to purchase 10,000 shares of common stock at $20 per share. During 1988, the average price per share was $25 but at December 31, 1988, the market price had risen to $30 per share. The balance sheet reports $200,000 of 8% nonconvertible bonds at December 31, 1988. (Interest expense is included in operating expenses.)

Instructions: Compute for 1988:
(1) Primary earnings per share.
(2) Fully diluted earnings per share.

PROBLEM 18–7   (Earnings per share with exercise of stock options)

As of January 1, 1988, the Motion Corporation had 25,000 shares of $5 par common stock outstanding. The company had issued stock options in 1986 to its management personnel permitting them to acquire 6,000 shares of common stock at $8 per share. At the time of the issuance, common stock was selling for $8 per share. The average price of common stock for the year 1988 was $21. The market price was $23 on September 1, 1988, and $25 on December 31, 1988. The average price for the first eight months of the year was $20. Income from operations for 1988 is $76,800. The company also had an extraordinary gain of $36,000, net of taxes. Terms of the options make them currently exercisable. On September 1, 1988, options to acquire 2,000 shares were exercised. The other 4,000 options are still outstanding at December 31, 1988.

Instructions: Compute primary and fully diluted earnings per share to be reported on the income statement for the year ended December 31, 1988.

PROBLEM 18–8   (Earnings per share—complex capital structure)

The "Stockholders' equity" section of Gunn Company's balance sheet as of December 31, 1988, contains the following:

$1 cumulative preferred stock, $25 par, convertible, 1,600,000 shares authorized, 1,400,000 shares issued, 750,000 converted to common, 650,000 shares outstanding	$16,250,000
Common stock, $.25 par, 15,000,000 shares authorized, 8,800,000 shares issued and outstanding.	2,200,000
Additional paid-in capital	32,750,000
Retained earnings.	40,595,000
Total stockholders' equity.	$91,795,000

Included in the liabilities of Gunn Company are 8½% convertible subordinated debentures issued at their face value of $20,000,000 in 1987. The debentures are due in 2000 and until then are convertible into the common stock of Gunn Company at the rate of 5 shares of common stock for each $100 debenture. To date none of these have been converted.

On April 2, 1988, Gunn Company issued 1,400,000 shares of convertible preferred stock at $40 per share. Quarterly dividends to December 31, 1988, have been paid on these shares. The preferred stock is convertible into common stock at the rate of 2 shares of common for each share of preferred. On October 1, 1988, 150,000 shares and on November 1, 1988, 600,000 shares of the preferred stock were converted into common stock.

During July 1987, Gunn Company granted options to its officers and key employees to purchase 500,000 shares of the company's common stock at a price of $20 a share. The options do not become exercisable until 1989.

During 1988 dividend payments and average market prices of the Gunn common stock were as follows:

	Dividend per Share	Average Market Price per Share
First quarter	$.10	$20
Second quarter	.15	25
Third quarter	.10	30
Fourth quarter	.15	25
Average for the year		25

The December 31, 1988, closing price of the common stock was $25 a share.

Assume that the Aa corporate bond yield was 12% throughout 1987 and 1988. Gunn Company's net income for the year ended December 31, 1988, was $9,200,000. The provision for income tax was computed at a rate of 40%.

Instructions:

(1) Prepare a schedule that shows the evaluation of the common stock equivalency status of the (a) convertible debentures, (b) convertible preferred stock, and (c) employee stock options.
(2) Compute simple earnings per share and test any common stock equivalents for dilution.
(3) Compute primary earnings per share.
(4) Compute fully diluted earnings per share.   (AICPA adapted)

PROBLEM 18–9   (Earnings per share — complex capital structure)

Mason Corporation's capital structure is as follows:

	December 31 1988	December 31 1987
Outstanding shares of:		
Common stock	336,000	300,000
Nonconvertible, noncumulative preferred stock	10,000	10,000
8% convertible bonds	$1,000,000	$1,000,000

The following additional information is available:
(a) On September 1, 1988, Mason sold 36,000 additional shares of common stock.
(b) Net income for the year ended December 31, 1988, was $750,000.
(c) During 1988 Mason declared and paid dividends of $3 per share on its preferred stock.
(d) The 8% bonds are convertible into 40 shares of common stock for each $1,000 bond, and were not considered common stock equivalents at the date of issuance.

(e) Unexercised options to purchase 30,000 shares of common stock at $22.50 per share were outstanding at the beginning and end of 1988. The average market price of Mason's common stock was $36 per share during 1988. The market price was $33 per share at December 31, 1988.

(f) Warrants to purchase 20,000 shares of common stock at $38 per share were attached to the preferred stock at the time of issuance. The warrants, which expire on December 31, 1993, were outstanding at December 31, 1988.

(g) Mason's effective income tax rate was 40% for 1987 and 1988.

Instructions: Compute the following earnings per share amount as of December 31, 1988:
(1) Simple
(2) Primary
(3) Fully diluted   (AICPA adapted)

*PROBLEM 18–10   (Earnings per share — complex capital structure)

At December 31, 1987, the Jay Jensen Company had 400,000 shares of common stock outstanding. Jensen sold 100,000 shares on October 1, 1988. Net income for 1988 was $2,565,000; the income tax rate was 40%. In addition, Jensen had the following debt and equity securities on its books at December 31, 1987.

(a) 20,000 shares of $100 par 10% cumulative preferred stock. Aa corporate bond yield was 11% at time of sale. Stock was sold at 102.

(b) 30,000 shares of 8% convertible cumulative preferred stock, par $100, sold at 110 when Aa corporate bond yield was 11%. Each share of preferred stock is convertible into two shares of common.

(c) $2,000,000 face value of 8% bonds sold at par when Aa corporate bond yield was 10%.

(d) $3,000,000 face value of 6% convertible bonds sold at par when Aa corporate bond yield was 8%. Each $1,000 bond is convertible into 20 shares of common.

Also, options to purchase 10,000 shares were issued May 1, 1988. Exercise price is $30 per share; market value at date of option was $29; market value at end of year, $40; average market value May 1 to December 31, 1988, $35.

Instructions:
For the year ended December 31, 1988.
(1) Compute simple earnings per share.
(2) Compute primary earnings per share.
(3) Compute fully-diluted earnings per share.

Relates to appendix.

*PROBLEM 18–11
(Earnings per share — multiple convertible securities)

Data for the Cooley Powder Company at the end of 1988 are listed below. All bonds are convertible as indicated and were issued at their face amounts.

Description of Bonds	Amount	Date Issued	Aa Corporate Bond Yield on Date Issued	Conversion Terms
10-year, 6½% Convertible bonds.........	$ 700,000	1/1/82	9½%	100 shares of common for each $1,000 bond
20-year, 7% Convertible bonds...........	1,000,000	1/1/83	11%	50 shares of common for each $1,000 bond
25-year, 9½% Convertible bonds.........	1,600,000	6/30/87	14¼%	32 shares of common for each $1,000 bond
Common shares outstanding at December 31, 1987				700,000
Net income for 1988				$1,275,000
Income tax rate...				40%

Instructions:

(1) Compute primary earnings per share for 1988, assuming that no additional shares of common stock were issued during the year.

(2) Compute fully diluted earnings per share for 1988, assuming that no additional shares of common stock were issued during the year.

(3) Compute both primary and fully diluted earnings per share assuming that the 10-year bonds were converted on July 1, 1988, and that net income for the year was $1,288,650 (reflects reduction in interest due to bond conversion).

Relates to appendix.

PART FOUR

SPECIAL PROBLEMS IN INCOME
DETERMINATION AND REPORTING

19   Revenue Recognition

20   Accounting for Income Taxes

21   Accounting for Leases

22   Accounting for Pensions

23   Accounting Changes and Error Corrections

19
Revenue Recognition

As discussed and illustrated in Chapter 4, both internal and external users of financial information focus considerable attention on how business activities affect the income statement. The application of the transaction approach to income measurement has required standard-setting bodies to focus on revenue recognition, that is, at what point in the operating cycle should an enterprise recognize revenue. The FASB's two criteria for recognizing revenues and gains were listed in Chapter 4, and are repeated here for added emphasis.

Revenues and gains are generally recognized when:

1. they are realized or realizable and
2. they have been earned through substantial completion of the activities involved in the earnings process.

While the "point-of-sale" rule has dominated the interpretation of revenue recognition, there have been notable variations to this rule, especially in specific industries such as construction, real estate, and franchising. Special committees of the AICPA, and later the FASB, have studied these and other areas. For several years, these special studies were conducted under the direction of the AICPA, and publications of the committees' results appeared in the form of **Industry Accounting Guides, Industry Audit Guides,** or **Statements of Position (SOP's)**. These publications have been studied by the FASB, and where deemed desirable, have been incorporated in the literature as Statements of Financial Accounting Standards.[1]

---

[1] In the early 1980's, the FASB issued three research reports dealing with revenue recognition. These reports were used by the FASB in its deliberations leading to Concepts Statement No. 5 and several of the special industry standards. The reports were: (1) Yuji Ijiri, *Recognition of Contractual Rights and Obligations* (Stamford: Financial Accounting Standards Board, 1980); (2) Henry R. Jaenicke, *Survey of Present Practice in Recognizing Revenues, Expenses, Gains and Losses* (Stamford: Financial Accounting Standards Board, 1981); (3) L. Todd Johnson and Reed K. Storey, *Recognition in Financial Statements: Underlying Concepts and Practical Conventions* (Stamford: Financial Accounting Standards Board, 1982).

This chapter will explore some of the variations in revenue recognition that have arisen through these special industry studies. The focus of the presentation will be upon the revenue recognition variations and not on the detailed accounting procedures for a specific industry. The discussion focuses first on revenue recognition **prior to delivery** of goods or performance of services; second on revenue recognition **after delivery** of goods or performance of services; and finally upon methods of accounting before revenue recognition occurs. The special industries referred to are construction, real estate, service, and franchising.

REVENUE RECOGNITION PRIOR TO DELIVERY OF GOODS OR PERFORMANCE OF SERVICES

Under some circumstances, revenue can be meaningfully reported prior to the delivery of the finished product or completion of a service contract. Usually this occurs when the construction period of the asset being sold or the period of service performance is relatively long; that is, more than one year. If a company waits until the production or service period is complete to recognize revenue, the income statement may not meaningfully report the periodic achievement of the company. All income from the contract will be related to the year of completion, even though only a small part of the earnings may be attributable to effort in that period. Previous periods receive no credit for their efforts; in fact, they may be penalized through the absorption of selling, general and administrative, and other overhead costs relating to the contract but not considered part of the inventory cost.

Percentage-of-completion accounting, an alternative to the **completed-contract** method, was developed to relate recognition of revenue on long-term construction-type contracts to the activities of a firm in fulfilling these contracts. Similarly, the **proportional performance method** has been developed to reflect revenue earned on service contracts under which many acts of service are to be performed before the contract is completed. Examples include contracts covering maintenance on electronic office equipment, correspondence schools, trustee services, health clubs, professional services such as those offered by attorneys and accountants, and servicing of mortgage loans by mortgage bankers. Percentage-of-completion accounting and proportional performance accounting are similar in their application. However, some special problems arise in accounting for service contracts. The discussion and examples in the following sections relate first to long-term construction contracts, then to the special problems encountered with service contracts.

General Concepts of Percentage-of-Completion Accounting

Under the percentage-of-completion method, a company recognizes revenues and costs on a contract as it progresses toward completion rather than deferring recognition of these items until the contract is completed. The amount of revenue to be recognized is based on some measure of progress toward completion. This requires an estimate of costs yet to be incurred. Changes in estimates of future costs arise normally, and the necessary adjustments are made in the year the estimates are revised. Thus, the revenues and costs to be recognized in a given year are affected by the revenues and costs already recognized. The actual costs incurred and the profit being recognized during the construction period are charged to inventory. If a company projects a loss on the contract prior to completion, the full amount of the loss is recognized immediately.

Necessary Conditions to Use Percentage-of-Completion Accounting

Most long-term construction-type contracts should be reported using the percentage-of-completion method. The guidelines presently in force, however, are not specific as to when a company must use percentage-of-completion and when it must use the alternative completed-contract method. The accounting standards that still govern this area were issued by the Committee on Accounting procedure in 1955.[2] In January 1981, the Construction Contractor Guide Committee of the Accounting Standards Division of the AICPA issued Statement of Position 81-1, "Accounting for Performance of Construction-Type and Certain Production-Type Contracts." In this SOP, the committee strongly recommended which of the two common methods of accounting for these types of contracts should be required, depending on the specific circumstances involved. They further stated that the two methods should not be viewed as acceptable alternatives for the same circumstances. The committee identified several elements that should be present if percentage-of-completion accounting is to be used.[3]

1. Dependable estimates can be made of the extent of progress towards completion, contract revenues, and contract costs.

---

[2] Committee on Accounting Procedure, *Accounting Research Bulletin No. 45*, "Long-Term Construction-Type Contracts" (New York: American Institute of Certified Public Accountants, 1955).

[3] Construction Contractor Guide Committee of the Accounting Standards Division, AICPA, *Statement of Position 81-1*, "Accounting for Performance of Construction-Type and Certain Production-Type Contracts" (New York: American Institute of Certified Public Accountants, 1981), par. 23.

2. The contract clearly specifies the enforceable rights regarding goods or services to be provided and received by the parties, the consideration to be exchanged, and the manner and terms of settlement.
3. The buyer can be expected to satisfy obligations under the contract.
4. The contractor can be expected to perform the contractual obligation.

The completed-contract method should be used only when an entity has primarily short-term contracts, when the conditions for using the percentage-of-completion accounting are not met, or when there are inherent uncertainties in the contract beyond the normal business risks.

In February 1982, the FASB issued Statement No. 56 designating the accounting and reporting principles and practices contained in SOP 81-1 and in the *AICPA Audit and Accounting Guide for Construction Contractors* as preferable accounting principles.[4] The Board indicated that they would consider adopting these principles as FASB standards after allowing sufficient time for the principles to be used in practice so that a basis can be provided for determining their usefulness. A critical issue involved in this area is the clear preference in the SOP for using the percentage-of-completion method of accounting.

Measuring the Percentage of Completion

Various methods are currently used in practice to measure progress on a contract. They can be conveniently grouped in two categories: input and output measures.

Input Measures. Input measures are made in relation to the costs or efforts devoted to a contract. They are based on an established or assumed relationship between a unit of input and productivity. They include the widely used cost-to-cost method and several variations of efforts-expended methods.

Cost-to-Cost Method. Perhaps the most popular of the input measures is the **cost-to-cost method**. Under this method, the degree of completion is determined by comparing costs already incurred with the most recent estimates of total expected costs to complete the project. The percentage that costs incurred bear to total expected costs is applied to the expected net income on the project in arriving at earnings to date. Some of the costs

---

[4] *Statement of Financial Accounting Standards No. 56*, "Designation of AICPA Guide and Statement of Position (SOP) 81-1 on Contractor Accounting and SOP 81-2 Concerning Hospital-Related Organizations as Preferable for Purposes of Applying APB Opinion 20" (Stamford: Financial Accounting Standards Board, 1982).

incurred, particularly in the early stages of the contract, should be disregarded in applying this method because they do not directly relate to effort expended on the contract. These include such items as subcontract costs for work that has yet to be performed and standard fabricated materials that have not yet been installed. One of the most difficult problems in using this method is estimating the costs yet to be incurred. However, this estimation is required in reporting income, regardless of how the percentage of completion is computed.

To illustrate, assume that in January, 1986, Jiffy Construction Company was awarded a contract with a total price of $3,000,000. Jiffy expected to earn $400,000 profit on the contract or, in other words, total costs on the contract were estimated to be $2,600,000. The construction was completed over a 3-year period, and the following cost data and cost percentages were compiled during that time:

	(1) Actual Costs Incurred	(2) Estimated Cost to Complete	(3) Total Cost (1) + (2)	(4) Cost Percentage (1) ÷ (3)
1986.	$1,092,000	$1,508,000	$2,600,000*	42%
1987.	832,000			
Total.	$1,924,000	676,000	2,600,000*	74%
1988.	700,000			
Total.	$2,624,000	–0–	2,624,000**	100%

*Estimated total contract cost
**Actual total contract cost

Note that the cost percentage is computed by dividing cumulative actual costs incurred by total cost, the amount of which is estimated for the first two years.

Efforts-Expended Methods. The **efforts-expended methods** are based on some measure of work performed. They include labor hours, labor dollars, machine hours, or material quantities. In each case, the degree of completion is measured in a way similar to that used in the cost-to-cost approach: the ratio of the efforts expended to date to the estimated total efforts to be expended on the entire contract. For example, if the measure of work performed is labor hours, the ratio of hours worked to date to the total estimated hours would produce the percentage for use in measuring income earned.

Output Measures. Output measures are made in terms of results achieved. Included in this category are methods based on units produced, contract milestones reached, and values added. For example, if the contract calls for units of output, such as miles of roadway, a measure of completion would be a ratio of the miles completed to the total miles in the contract. Architects or engineers are sometimes asked to evaluate jobs and estimate what percentage of a job is complete. These estimates are in reality output measures and are usually based on the physical progress made on a contract.

Accounting for Long-Term Construction-Type Contracts

There are relatively few differences in accounting for long-term construction-type contracts under either the percentage-of-completion or completed-contract methods. Only the timing of revenue recognition and the recognition of matching costs is different. All direct and allocable indirect costs of the contracts are charged to an inventory account, Construction in Progress, as they accrue. The inventory account is also increased by the profit recognized during the construction period. Usually, contracts require progress billings by the contractor and payments by the customer on these billings. The amount of these billings is usually specified by the contract terms, and may be related to the costs actually incurred. Generally, these contracts require inspection before final settlement is made. As a protection for the customer, the contract frequently provides for an amount to be held out from the progress payment. This retention is usually a percentage of the progress billings, 10–20%, and is paid upon final acceptance of the construction. The billings, including any amount to be retained, are debited to Accounts Receivable and credited to a deferred credit account, Progress Billings on Construction Contracts, that serves as an offset to the inventory account, Construction in Progress. The billing of the contract thus in reality transfers the asset value from inventory to receivables, but because of the long-term nature of the contract, the construction costs continue to be reflected in the accounts.

To illustrate accounting for a long-term construction contract, assume that a dam was constructed over a two-year period commencing in September 1986, at a contract price of $5,000,000. The direct and allocable indirect costs, billings, and collections for 1986, 1987, and 1988 were as follows:

Year	Direct and Allocable Indirect Costs	Billings Including 10% Retention	Collections
1986....................	$1,125,000	$1,000,000	$ 800,000
1987....................	2,250,000	2,300,000	1,900,000
1988....................	1,125,000	1,700,000	2,300,000

The following entries for the three years would be made on the contractor's books under either the percentage-of-completion or the completed-contract methods.

	1986		1987		1988	
Construction in Progress..........	1,125,000		2,250,000		1,125,000	
Materials, Cash etc.............		1,125,000		2,250,000		1,125,000
Accounts Receivable.............	1,000,000		2,300,000		1,700,000	
Progress Billings on Construction Contracts..................		1,000,000		2,300,000		1,700,000
Cash..........................	800,000		1,900,000		2,300,000	
Accounts Receivable..........		800,000		1,900,000		2,300,000

No other entries would be required in 1986 and 1987 under the completed-contract method. In both years, the balance of the construction in progress account exceeds the amount in Progress Billings on Construction Contracts, thus the latter account would be offset against the inventory account in the balance sheet. Because the operating cycle of a company that emphasizes long-term contracts is usually more than one year, all of the above balance sheet accounts would be classified as current. The balance sheet at the end of 1987 would disclose the following balances related to the dam construction contract.

Current assets:
Accounts receivable, including 10% retention fee of
$330,000... $600,000
Construction in progress $3,375,000
Less progress billings on construction contracts 3,300,000   75,000

If the billings exceeded the construction costs, the excess would be reported in the current liability section of the balance sheet.

At the completion of the contract, the following entries would be made under the completed-contract method to recognize revenue and costs and to close out the inventory and billings accounts.

Progress Billings on Construction Contracts 5,000,000
  Revenue from Long-Term Construction Contracts.......... 5,000,000

Cost of Long-Term Construction Contracts 4,500,000
  Construction in Progress................................ 4,500,000

The income statement for 1988 would report the gross revenues and the matched costs, thus recognizing the entire $500,000 profit in one year.

Using Percentage-of-Completion—Cost-to-Cost Method. If the company used the percentage-of-completion method of accounting, the $500,000 profit would be spread over all three years of construction according to the estimated percentage of completion for each year. Assume that the estimated cost from the beginning of construction was $4,500,000, and that the estimate did not change over the three years. Also, assume that the cost-to-cost method of determining percentage of completion is used. The percentage for each year would be calculated as follows:

	1986	1987	1988
(1) Cost incurred to date..................	$1,125,000	$3,375,000	$4,500,000
(2) Estimated cost to complete	3,375,000	1,125,000	—0—
(3) Total estimated cost..................	$4,500,000	$4,500,000	$4,500,000
Percentage of completion to date [(1) ÷ (3)]...........................	25%	75%	100%

These percentages may be used directly to determine the gross profit that should be recognized on the income statement. Preferably, however, they should be used to determine both revenues and cost. The income statement will then disclose the gross profit as the difference between these elements, a method more consistent with normal income statement reporting. The AICPA Audit and Accounting Guide for Construction Contractors recommended following this procedure, and the presentations in this chapter will follow their recommendations.[5]

Thus, for 1986, 25% of the fixed contract price of $5,000,000 would be recognized as revenue and 25% of the expected total cost of $4,500,000 would be reported as cost. Since the cost-to-cost method is being used, this will always result in the same amount as the costs actually incurred. The following revenue recognition entries would be made for each of the three years of the contract.

	1986	1987	1988
Cost of Long-Term Construction Contracts....................	1,125,000	2,250,000	1,125,000
Construction in Progress.........	125,000	250,000	125,000
Revenue from Long-Term Con- struction Contracts	1,250,000	2,500,000	1,250,000

The gross profit recognized each year is added to the construction in progress account. This changes the valuation base for this account from cost to a measure of net realizable value. At the conclusion of the construction, the balance in Construction in Progress will be exactly equal to the amount in Progress Billings on Construction Contracts, and the following closing entry would complete the accounting process.

| Progress Billings on Construction Contracts .... | 5,000,000 | |
| Construction in Progress............................... | | 5,000,000 |

Using Percentage-of-Completion—Other Methods. If the cost-to-cost method is not used to measure progress on the contract, the amount of costs recognized under this method may not be equal to the costs incurred.

---

[5]Construction Contractor Guide Committee of the Accounting Standards Division, AICPA, *Audit and Accounting Guide for Construction Contractors* (New York: American Institute of Certified Public Accountants, 1980), p. 44.

For example, assume in 1986 that an engineering estimate measure was used, and 20% of the contract was assumed to be completed. The gross profit recognized would therefore be computed and reported as follows:

Earned revenue (20% of $5,000,000)....................	$1,000,000
Cost of earned revenue (20% of $4,500,000).............	900,000
Gross profit (20% of $500,000)	$ 100,000

This approach is labeled Alternative A in SOP 81-1.

Because some accountants felt that the amount of cost recognized should be equal to the costs actually incurred, an alternative to the preceding approach was included in the SOP.[6] Under this approach, labeled Alternative B in the SOP, revenue is defined as the costs incurred on the contract plus the gross profit earned for the period on the contract. Using the data from the previous example, the revenue and costs to be reported on the 1986 income statement would be as follows:

Costs incurred to date	$1,125,000
Gross profit (20% of $500,000)	100,000
Earned revenue.......................................	$1,225,000

This contrasts with the $1,000,000 revenue using Alternative A.

In a footnote to this discussion in the SOP, the Committee made it clear that Alternatives A and B are equally acceptable. However, because Alternative B results in a varying gross profit percentage from period to period whenever the measurement of completion differs from that which would occur if the cost-to-cost method were used, the authors feel that Alternative A is preferable. Unless a different method is explicitly stated, examples and end-of-chapter material will assume the use of Alternative A.

Revision of Estimates. In the example, it was assumed that the estimated cost did not vary from the beginning of the contract. This would rarely be true. As estimates change, cumulative catch-up adjustments are made in the year of the change. To illustrate the impact of changing estimates, assume that at the end of 1987 it was estimated that the remaining cost to complete the contract would be $1,225,000, making a total estimated cost of $4,600,000. Since costs of $3,375,000 had been incurred by the end of 1987, the estimated percentage of completion for 1987 using the cost-to-cost method would be 73.37% ($3,375,000 ÷ $4,600,000).

The following analysis would be made to compute revenues and expenses for the three years of the contract under the change in estimate, assuming actual costs of $1,175,000 were incurred in 1988.

---

[6] *SOP 81-1,* par. 80 and 81.

	(A) To Date	(B) Recognized in Prior Years	(C) Recognized in Current Year (A)—(B)
1986—(25% completed)			
Earned revenue ($5,000,000 × .25)	$1,250,000		$1,250,000
Cost of earned revenue ($4,500,000 × .25)..	1,125,000		1,125,000
Gross profit	$ 125,000		$ 125,000
Gross profit rate........................	10%		10%
1987—(73.37% completed)			
Earned revenue ($5,000,000 × .7337)	$3,668,500	$1,250,000	$2,418,500
Cost of earned revenue ($4,600,000 ×			
.7337)................................	3,375,000*	1,125,000	2,250,000
Gross profit	$ 293,500	$ 125,000	$ 168,500
Gross profit rate........................	8%	10%	6.97%
1988—(100% completed)			
Earned revenue	$5,000,000	$3,668,500	$1,331,500
Cost of earned revenue	4,550,000	3,375,000	1,175,000
Gross profit	$ 450,000	$ 293,500	$ 156,500
Gross profit rate........................	9%	8%	11.75%

*Made equal to cost incurred, difference due to rounding of completion percentage.

The entries to record revenue and expense for the three years given the assumed estimate revision would be as follows:

	1986	1987	1988
Cost of Long-Term Construction Contracts....................	1,125,000	2,250,000	1,175,000
Construction in Progress........	125,000	168,500	156,500
Revenue from Long-Term Construction Contracts	1,250,000	2,418,500	1,331,500

The computation of gross profit rates shows how sensitive the reporting is to revisions in estimated costs, and why great care is required in making these estimates.

Reporting Anticipated Contract Losses. The examples thus far have assumed a profit is expected to be realized. If a loss on the total contract is anticipated, however, generally accepted accounting principles require reporting the loss *in its entirety* in the period when the loss is first anticipated. This is true under either the completed-contract or the percentage-of-completion methods. For example, assume that in the earlier dam construction example the estimated cost to complete the contract at the end of 1987 was $1,725,000. This would mean the total estimated cost of the contract would be $5,100,000 or $100,000 more than the contract price. If the completed-contract method were being used, the following entry would be required at the end of 1987.

Anticipated Loss on Long-Term Construction Contracts	100,000	
Construction in Progress		100,000

The inventory account, Construction in Progress, is thus reduced by the anticipated loss.

Accounting for such an anticipated loss is more complicated under the percentage-of-completion method because of the impact of prior years on the current year. Again referring to the dam construction example, the percentage of completion under the cost-to-cost method would be 66.18% under the changed assumptions ($3,375,000 ÷ $5,100,000). Cumulative earned revenue would be computed as before, 66.18% × $5,000,000, or $3,309,000. However, construction costs for the current period would be computed by adding the anticipated loss to the earned revenue, thus resulting in cumulative recognized costs of $3,409,000. The loss to be recognized in 1987 would thus be not only the $100,000 loss anticipated on the entire contract but also an additional loss of $125,000 to adjust for the 1986 recognized profit that is now not expected to be realized. These computations can be illustrated by reconstructing part of the earlier table as follows:

	(A) To Date	(B) Recognized in Prior Year	(C) Recognized in Current Year (A)—(B)
1987—(66.18% completed)			
Earned revenue ($5,000,000 × .6618)	$3,309,000	$1,250,000	$2,059,000
Cost of earned revenue ($3,309,000 + $100,000).............................	3,409,000	1,125,000	2,284,000
Gross profit (loss).......................	($ 100,000)	$ 125,000	($ 225,000)

The entry to record the revenue, costs, and adjustments to Construction in Progress for the loss would be as follows:

Cost of Long-Term Construction Contracts.....................	2,284,000	
Revenue from Long-Term Construction Contracts		2,059,000
Construction in Progress		225,000

The construction in progress account under both methods would have a balance of $3,275,000 computed as follows:

Completed-contract method:

Construction in Progress

1986 cost	1,125,000	1987 loss	100,000
1987 cost	2,250,000		
Bal.	3,275,000		

Percentage-of-completion method:

Construction in Progress

1986 cost	1,125,000	1987 loss	225,000
1986 gross profit	125,000		
1987 cost	2,250,000		
Bal.	3,275,000		

Accounting for Contract Change Orders. Long-term construction contracts are seldom completed without change orders that affect both the contract price and the cost of performance. **Change orders** are modifications of an original contract that effectively change the provisions of the contract. They may be initiated by the contractor or the customer, and include changes in specifications or design, method or manner of performance, facilities, equipment, materials, location, site, etc. If the contract price is changed as a result of a change order, future computations are made with the revised expected revenue and any anticipated cost changes that will arise because of the change order. Change orders are often unpriced, that is, the work to be performed is defined, but the adjustment to the contract price is to be negotiated later. If it is probable that a contract price change will be negotiated to at least recover the increased costs, the increased costs may be included with the incurred costs of the period and the revenue may be increased by the same amount.

Income Tax Considerations

When a building, installation, or construction contract covers more than one year, federal income tax regulations permit the taxpayer to recognize income on a percentage-of-completion basis over the life of the project or in the year when the project is completed and accepted. General and administrative salaries, taxes, and other expenses that are not directly attributable to specific contracts have previously been expensed in the year incurred under either the completed contract or the percentage of completion method. The Tax Equity and Fiscal Responsibility Act of 1982 identified many of these costs as being more properly allocated to existing contracts, especially if the contracts have a construction period in excess of two years. The effect of this regulation is to make the completed contract method less favorable for tax deferral purposes. The Income Tax Reform Act of 1986 further discourages the use of the completed-contract method.

Consistent application of the method of accounting chosen is required for tax purposes; a change from the percentage-of-completion method to the completed-contract method, or a change from the completed-contract method to the percentage-of-completion method, requires special permission. The use of different methods for financial statements and for income tax purposes will require the application of interperiod tax allocation procedures, which will be discussed in Chapter 20.

Accounting for Long-Term Service Contracts — the Proportional Performance Method

Thus far, the discussion in this chapter has focused on long-term construction contracts. As indicated earlier, another type of contract that frequently extends over a long period of time is a **service contract**. An increasing percentage of sales in our economy are classified as sales of services as opposed to sales of goods. When the service to be performed is completed as a single act or over a relatively short period of time, no revenue recognition problems arise. The revenue recognition criteria previously defined apply, and all direct and indirect costs related to the service are charged to expense in the period the revenue is recognized. However, when several acts over a period of time are involved, the same revenue recognition problems illustrated for long-term construction contracts arise. Although the FASB has not issued a standard dealing with these contracts, the Board did issue an Invitation to Comment on a proposed Statement of Position that had been issued by the AICPA's Accounting Standards Division.[7] The discussion in the following pages reflects the recommendations made by the Accounting Standards Division.

The Division recommends that unless the final act of service to be performed is so vital to the contract that earlier acts are relatively insignificant, e.g., the packaging, loading, and final delivery of goods in a delivery contract, revenue should be recognized under the **proportional performance method**.[8] Both input and output measures are identified as possible ways of measuring progress on a service contract. If a contract involves a specified number of identical or similar acts, e.g., the processing of monthly mortgage payments by a mortgage banker, an output measure derived by relating the number of acts performed to the total number of acts to be performed over the contract life is recommended. If a contract involves a specified number of defined but not identical acts, e.g., a correspondence school that provides evaluation, lessons, examinations, and grading, a cost-to-cost input measurement percentage would be applicable. If future costs are not objectively determinable, output measures such as relating sales value of the individual acts to the total sales value of the service contract may be used. If no pattern of performance can be determined, or if a service contract involves an unspecified number of similar or identical acts with a fixed period for performance, e.g., a maintenance contract for electronic office equipment, the Division recommends the use of the straight-line method, i.e., equally over the periods of performance.

These measures are used to determine what portion of the service contract fee should be recognized as revenue. Generally, the measures are only indirectly related to the pattern of cash collection; however, they are applicable only if cash collection is reasonably assured and if losses from nonpayment can be objectively determined.

The cost recognition problems of service contracts are somewhat different from long-term construction contracts. Most service contracts involve

---

[7] *FASB Invitation to Comment*, "Accounting for Certain Service Transactions," (Stamford: Financial Accounting Standards Board, 1978).
   [8] *Ibid*, pp. 12–13.

three different types of costs: (1) initial direct costs related to obtaining and performing initial services on the contract, such as commissions, legal fees, credit investigations, and paper processing; (2) direct costs related to performing the various acts of service; and (3) indirect costs related to maintaining the organization to service the contract, e.g., general and administrative expenses. Initial direct costs are generally charged against revenue using the same input or output measure used for revenue recognition. If the cost-to-cost method of input measurement is used, initial direct costs should be excluded from the cost incurred to date in computing the measure. Only direct costs related to the acts of service are relevant. Direct costs are usually charged to expense as incurred because they are felt to relate directly to the acts for which revenue is recognized. Similarly, all indirect costs should be charged to expense as incurred. As is true for long-term construction contracts, any indicated loss on completion of the service contract is to be charged to the period in which the loss is first indicated. If collection of a service contract is highly uncertain, revenue recognition should not be related to performance but to the collection of the receivable using one of the methods described in the latter part of this chapter.

To illustrate accounting for a service contract using the proportional performance method, assume a correspondence school enters into one hundred contracts with students for an extended writing course. The fee for each contract is $500 payable in advance. This fee includes many different services such as providing the text material, evaluations of writing, examinations, and awarding of a certificate. The total initial direct costs related to the contracts are $5,000. Direct costs for the lessons actually completed during the period are $12,000. It is estimated that the total direct costs of these contracts will be $30,000. The facts of this case suggest that the cost-to-cost method is applicable, and the following entries would be made to record these transactions:

Cash	50,000	
Deferred Course Revenue		50,000
Deferred Initial Costs	5,000	
Cash		5,000
Contract Costs	12,000	
Cash		12,000
Deferred Course Revenue	20,000[1]	
Recognized Course Revenue		20,000
Contract Costs	2,000[2]	
Deferred Initial Costs		2,000

Computations:
[1] Cost-to-cost percentage: $12,000 ÷ $30,000 = 40%; $50,000 × .40 = $20,000
[2] $5,000 × .40 = $2,000

The gross profit reported on these contracts for the period would be $6,000 ($20,000 − $12,000 − $2,000). The deferred initial cost and deferred course revenues would normally be reported as current balance sheet deferrals because the operating cycle of a correspondence school would be equal to the average time to complete a contract or one year, whichever is longer.

Many companies use the straight-line computation for unearned service revenue because of the difficulties encountered in applying the proportional performance method. The Harris Corporation note to their financial statements illustrates this condition.

HARRIS CORPORATION

	1984	1983
	($000)	
Current Liabilities		
Short-term debt	$ 11,716	$ 11,260
Trade accounts payable	128,590	98,127
Compensation and benefits	93,933	106,394
Other accrued items	59,153	62,701
Advance payments by customers	71,921	46,896
Unearned leasing and service income	57,201	52,422
Income taxes	134,149	115,755
Total Current Liabilities	$556,663	$493,555

NOTES TO FINANCIAL STATEMENTS

Significant Accounting Policies (In Part)

Revenue Recognition—Revenue is recognized from sales other than on long-term contracts when a product is shipped, from rentals as they accrue, and from services when performed. Revenue on long-term contracts is accounted for principally by the percentage-of-completion method whereby income is recognized based on the estimated stage of completion of individual contracts. Unearned income on service contracts is amortized by the straight-line method over the life of the contracts.

Evaluation of Proportional Performance Method

The FASB has not issued a standard on service industries. While the proportional performance method has theoretical support for its adoption, it tends to be extremely conservative, especially during a period of rapid growth in a company's revenues. This situation is often encountered with new companies, such as those in the rapidly expanding health-spa industry. Since no income is recognized until performance of the service is begun, the proportional performance method recognizes no income at the critical point of signing a service contract. Thus, in the growing years of a company, use of the proportional performance method will result in large losses being reported even though the operation might be very profitable over time. This can lead to the questionable conclusion that a company is no better off after service contracts are sold than it was before.

An alternative method of recognizing revenue for service contracts would be to recognize part of the income upon the signing of the contract, and then spread the balance of the income over the contract life using the proportional performance concept. The decision as to how much income should be recognized at the beginning of the contract would depend on the nature and terms of the contract, including any forfeiture or cancellation provisions.

REVENUE RECOGNITION AFTER DELIVERY OF GOODS OR PERFORMANCE OF SERVICES

One of the FASB's two revenue recognition criteria, listed at the beginning of this chapter, states that revenue should not be recognized until the earnings process is substantially complete. Normally, the earnings process is substantially completed by the delivery of goods or performance of services. Collection of receivables is usually routine, and any future warranty costs can be reasonably estimated. In some cases, however, the circumstances surrounding a revenue transaction are such that considerable uncertainty exists as to whether payments will indeed be received. This can occur if the sales transaction is unusual in nature and involves a customer in such a way that default carries little cost or penalty. Under these circumstances, the uncertainty of cash collection suggests that revenue recognition should await the actual receipt of cash. There are at least three different approaches to revenue recognition that depend on the receipt of cash: **installment sales, cost recovery,** and **cash.** These methods differ as to the treatment of costs incurred and the timing of revenue recognition. They are summarized and contrasted with the full accrual method in the table at the top of page 834.

These methods are really not alternatives to each other; however, the guidelines for applying them are not well defined. As the uncertainty of the environment increases, generally accepted accounting principles would require moving from the full accrual method to installment sales, cost recovery and finally, a strict cash approach. The cash method is the most conservative approach because it would not permit the deferral of any costs, but would charge them to expense as incurred. In the following pages, each of these revenue recognition methods will be discussed and illustrated.

Method	Treatment of Product Costs or Initial Costs Under Service Contracts	Timing of Revenue and/or Income Recognition
Full accrual	Charge against revenue at time of sale or rendering of service.	At point of sale.
Installment sales	Defer to be matched against part of each cash collection. Usually done by deferring the estimated profit.	At collection of cash. Usually a portion of the cash payment is recognized as income.
Cost recovery	Defer to be matched against total cash collected.	At collection of cash, but only after all costs are recovered.
Cash	Charge to expense as incurred.	At collection of cash.

Installment Sales Method

Traditionally, the most commonly applied method for dealing with the uncertainty of cash collections has been the **installment sales method**. Under this method, income is recognized as cash is collected rather than at the time of sale. This method of accounting was developed after World War II in response to an increasing number of sales contracts that extended the time of payment over several years, with full title to the "sold" property being transferred only at the time of final collection. Consumer goods such as electrical appliances, jewelry, automobiles, and recreational equipment were commonly purchased and accounted for in this way. As this method of sales became more popular, and as credit rating evaluations became more sophisticated, the probability of collection on these contracts became more certain. The collection of cash was no longer the critical event, but the point of sale essentially completed the earnings process. Collection costs and the cost of uncollectible accounts could be estimated at the time of sale. Additional protection was afforded the seller because most contracts included a right of repossession. For these reasons, the Accounting Principles Board concluded in 1966 that, except for special circumstances, the installment method of recognizing revenue is not acceptable for reporting purposes.[9] The installment method continues to be widely used for income

---

[9] *Opinions of the Accounting Principles Board, No. 10,* "Omnibus Opinion — 1966" (New York: American Institute of Certified Public Accountants, 1967), par. 12.

tax purposes because it permits the deferral of tax payments until cash is collected.

In more recent years, sales of other types of property, such as developed real estate and undeveloped land, have also been made with greatly extended terms. Commonly, these contracts involve little or no down payment, the payments are spread over ten to thirty or forty years, and the probability of default in the early years is high because of a small investment by the buyer in the contract and because the market prices of the property are often unstable. Application of the accrual method to these contracts frequently overstates income in the early years due to the failure to realistically provide for future costs related to the contract, including losses from contract defaults. The FASB considered these types of sales, and concluded that accrual accounting applied in these circumstances often results in "front-end loading," i.e., a recognition of all revenue at the time of the sales contract with improper matching of related costs. Thus, the Board has established criteria that must be met before real estate and retail land sales can be recorded using the full accrual method of revenue recognition. If the criteria are not fully met, then the use of the installment sales method, or in some cases the cost recovery or deposit methods, is recommended to reflect the conditions of the sale more accurately.[10] Because the installment sales method is often recommended in new sales environments, and because it is a popularly recognized income tax method, it is important for accountants to understand its application.

Accounting for installment sales using the deferred gross profit approach requires determining a gross profit rate for the sales of each year, and establishing an accounts receivable and a deferred revenue account identified by the year of the sale. As collections are made of a given year's receivables, a portion of the deferred revenue equal to the gross profit rate times the collections made is recognized as income. The most common application of this method has been for the sale of merchandise. However, any sale of property or services may be recorded using the concept. The following examples of transactions and journal entries will illustrate this method of recognizing revenue.

Installment Sales of Merchandise. Assume that the Riding Corporation sells merchandise on the installment basis, and that the uncertainties of cash collection make the use of the installment sales method acceptable. The following data relate to three years of operations. To simplify the presentation, interest charges are excluded from the example.

---

[10] *Statement of Financial Accounting Standards No. 66,* "Accounting for Sales of Real Estate" (Stamford: Financial Accounting Standards Board, October, 1982).

	1987	1988	1989
Installment sales	$150,000	$200,000	$300,000
Cost of installment sales	100,000	140,000	204,000
Gross profit	$ 50,000	$ 60,000	$ 96,000
Gross profit percentage	33.3%	30%	32%
Cash collections:			
1987 Sales	$ 30,000	$ 75,000	$ 30,000
1988 Sales		70,000	80,000
1989 Sales			100,000

The entries to record the transactions for 1987 would be as follows:

Installment Accounts Receivable—1987	150,000	
Installment Sales		150,000
Cost of Installment Sales	100,000	
Inventory		100,000
Cash	30,000	
Installment Accounts Receivable—1987		30,000
Installment Sales	150,000	
Cost of Installment Sales		100,000
Deferred Gross Profit—1987		50,000
Deferred Gross Profit—1987	10,000*	
Realized Gross Profit on Installment Sales		10,000

*$30,000 × 33.3%

The sales and costs related to sales are recorded in a manner identical with the accounting for sales discussed in Chapter 8. At the end of the year, however, the sales and cost of sales accounts are closed to a deferred gross profit account rather than to Income Summary. The realized gross profit is then recognized by applying the gross profit percentage to cash collections. All other general and administrative expenses are normally written off in the period incurred.

Entries for the next two years are summarized in the schedule at the top of page 837.

Although this method of recording installment sales is the one most commonly followed, it would also be possible to defer both the gross revenue and the gross costs rather than just the net difference. If this approach is followed, the resulting entries would be more similar to those illustrated for percentage-of-completion accounting. Each year a portion of the gross revenue and gross costs would be recognized with the difference being the realized gross profit. Both methods produce the same net income.

If a company is heavily involved in installment sales, the operating cycle of the business is normally the period of the average installment contract. Thus, the currently accepted definition of current assets and current liabilities requires the receivables and their related deferred gross profit accounts to be reported in the current asset section of classified

	1988		1989	
Installment Accounts Receivable—1988	200,000			
Installment Accounts Receivable—1989			300,000	
Installment Sales		200,000		300,000
Cost of Installment Sales	140,000		204,000	
Inventory		140,000		204,000
Cash....................................	145,000		210,000	
Installment Accounts Receivable—1987		75,000		30,000
Installment Accounts Receivable—1988		70,000		80,000
Installment Accounts Receivable—1989				100,000
Installment Sales	200,000		300,000	
Cost of Installment Sales		140,000		204,000
Deferred Gross Profit—1988		60,000		
Deferred Gross Profit—1989				96,000
Deferred Gross Profit—1987	25,000[1]		10,000[3]	
Deferred Gross Profit—1988	21,000[2]		24,000[4]	
Deferred Gross Profit—1989			32,000[5]	
Realized Gross Profit on Installment Sales.......		46,000		66,000

Computations:
[1] $ 75,000 × .333 = $25,000
[2] $ 70,000 × .30 = $21,000
[3] $ 30,000 × .333 = $10,000
[4] $ 80,000 × .30 = $24,000
[5] $100,000 × .32 = $32,000

balance sheets. The deferred gross profit accounts should be reported as an offset to the related accounts receivable. Thus, at the end of 1987 the current asset section would include the following accounts:

| Installment accounts receivable .... | $120,000 | |
| Less deferred gross profit................................. | 40,000 | $80,000 |

Complexities of Installment Sales of Merchandise. In the previous example, no provision was made for interest. In reality, however, installment sales contracts always include interest, either expressed or implied. The interest portion of the payments is recognized as income in the period accrued, and the balance of the payment is treated as a collection on the installment sale. Thus, if in the example on pages 835–836 the $75,000 collection of 1987 sales in 1988 included interest of $40,000, only $35,000 would be used to compute the realized gross profit from 1987 sales. A complete example involving interest is illustrated in the next section dealing with real estate installment sales.

Additional complexities can arise in installment sales accounting in providing for uncollectible accounts. Because of the right to repossess merchandise in the event of nonpayment, the provision for uncollectible accounts can be less than might be expected. Only the amount of the receivable in excess of the current value of the repossessed merchandise is a potential loss. Accounting for repossessions was discussed in Chapter 10.

Theoretically, a proper matching of estimated losses against revenues would require allocating the expected losses over the years of collection. Practically, however, the provision is made and charged against income in the period of the sale. Thus, the accounting entries for handling estimated uncollectible accounts are the same as illustrated in Chapter 8.

Installment Sales of Real Estate. The installment sales method of accounting is often used for sales of real estate on a long-term contract basis. These sales are frequently characterized by small down payments with long payout periods on the balance. Usually the seller retains title to the real estate until the final payment is made, thus giving the seller the right of repossession. In an inflationary economy, this right is valuable and in most cases means that ultimate collection of the debt, either through payment or repossession, is virtually assured. However, if circumstances reduce the probability of collection or if the market value of the property is unstable, then the installment sales method may be applied, or in extreme cases, the cost recovery method may be required.

To illustrate the accounting for real estate sales using the installment method, assume that Carbon Industries Inc. sells land and buildings on January 1, 1987, for $4,000,000. Carbon receives a down payment of $300,000 and a promissory note for the remaining $3,700,000 plus interest at 12% to be paid in equal installments of $471,752 at the end of each of the next 25 years. The land has a carrying value on Carbon's books at the time of sale of $200,000, and the buildings have a carrying value of $2,000,000. The sale does not meet the FASB's criteria for the full accrual method of revenue recognition, and the installment method of accounting is assumed to be appropriate. The following entries would be made to record the initial transaction:

1987			
Jan. 1	Cash	300,000	
	Notes Receivable	11,793,800[1]	
	Discount on Notes Receivable		8,093,800[2]
	Real Estate Sales		4,000,000
	Cost of Real Estate Sales	2,200,000	
	Land		200,000
	Building (net of accumulated depreciation)		2,000,000
	Real Estate Sales	4,000,000	
	Cost of Real Estate Sales		2,200,000
	Deferred Gross Profit on Real Estate Sales		1,800,000

Computations:
[1] $471,752 \times 25 = \$11,793,800$
[2] $\$11,793,800 - \$3,700,000 = \$8,093,800$

The gross profit percentage for this sale is 45% ($1,800,000 ÷ $4,000,000). This percentage is applied to each cash collection reduced by the amount of interest included in the cash receipt. Thus, $135,000 would be recognized immediately upon receipt of the $300,000 down payment (.45 × $300,000) and the following entry would be made to recognize this profit.

```
1987
Jan.  1   Deferred Gross Profit on Real Estate Sales.............   135,000
          Realized Gross Profit on Real Estate Sales...........              135,000
```

At the end of the first year, cash of $471,752 will be collected in accordance with the contract terms. Included in this amount is interest earned of $444,000 (.12 × $3,700,000). The remainder of the cash collected, $27,752, is payment on the principal amount of the debt; 45% of this portion of the payment, or $12,488 (.45 × $27,752), would also be recognized as realized gross profit in the first year.

```
1987
Dec. 31   Cash...............................................   471,752
          Discount on Notes Receivable ......................   444,000
               Notes Receivable.................................              471,752
               Interest Revenue .................................              444,000

          Deferred Gross Profit on Real Estate Sales.............   12,488
          Realized Gross Profit on Real Estate Sales...........               12,488
```

The following T-accounts summarize these transactions for the first year before closing entries.

Notes Receivable	
11,793,800	471,752
Bal. 11,322,048	

Land	
200,000	200,000

Discount on Notes Receivable	
444,000	8,093,800
	Bal. 7,649,800

Buildings (net of accumulated depreciation)	
2,000,000	2,000,000

Real Estate Sales	
4,000,000	4,000,000

Deferred Gross Profit on Real Estate Sales	
135,000	1,800,000
12,488	
	Bal. 1,652,512

Cost of Real Estate Sales	
2,200,000	2,200,000

Interest Revenue	
	444,000

Realized Gross Profit on Real Estate Sales	
	135,000
	12,488
	Bal. 147,488

Cash collections in subsequent years would be divided between interest and principal in the same manner, and a portion of the deferred profit would be recognized each year. Because the collections are constant, and the interest revenue is declining as the carrying value of the receivable declines, the gross profit recognized would increase each year.

Care must be taken in evaluating a sale of real estate. In some cases, the contract may be in reality a financial arrangement or an operating lease, or it may be a deposit on a possible future sale. Revenue should be recognized only after careful evaluation of the contractual arrangements and application of the criteria in FASB Statement No. 66.

Cost Recovery Method

Under the cost recovery method, no income is recognized on a sale until the cost of the item sold is recovered through cash receipts. Then, all subsequent receipts are reported as revenue. Because all costs have been recovered, the recognized revenue after cost recovery represents income. This method is used only when the circumstances surrounding a sale are so uncertain that earlier recognition is impossible.

To illustrate the accounting entries required under this method, assume that collection on the real estate sales contract for Carbon Industries Inc. is felt to be so uncertain that the cost recovery method should be used. Under this method, the $2,200,000 carrying value of the real estate must be collected before any revenue or income is recognized, including any recognition of interest revenue on the contract. The same entries would be made to record the sale, the cost of the sale, and the deferred gross profit as was done under the installment sales method. The difference between the book value of the property and the down payment received equals the unrecovered cost of $1,900,000 ($2,200,000 − $300,000). Unrecovered cost may also be computed as follows:

Notes receivable		$11,793,800
Less:		
Discount on notes receivable	$8,093,800	
Deferred gross profit	1,800,000	9,893,800
		$ 1,900,000

When the first annual payment of $471,752 is collected, the following entry would be made:

1987			
Dec. 31	Cash	471,752	
	Discount on Notes Receivable	444,000	
	Notes Receivable		471,752
	Deferred Gross Profit on Real Estate Sales		444,000

The unrecovered cost would be $1,428,248 ($1,900,000 − $471,752). This agrees with the balance to be reported on the balance sheet as follows:

Notes receivable..		$11,322,048
Less:		
Discount on notes receivable............................	$7,649,800	
Deferred gross profit.....................................	2,244,000	9,893,800
		$ 1,428,248

Note that the deferred gross profit account includes both gross profit and interest revenue that will not be recognized until the cost is recovered.

At the end of 1990, the difference between the receivable and the two offset accounts would be $12,992. The 1991 collection would result in a cost recovery of $12,992 and a recognition of $458,760 revenue. In each of the remaining collection years, the total cash receipt will be recognized as revenue.

The selection of a revenue recognition method has a great impact on revenue and income, especially in the first year of a sales contract. The following summary shows how income would vary on the real estate sale of Carbon Industries Inc. depending on which revenue recognition method is used.

Revenue Recognition Method	Income for 1987
Full Accrual	$2,244,000[1]
Installment Sales	591,488[2]
Cost Recovery	–0–

Computations:
[1] $1,800,000 gross profit + $444,000 interest revenue = $2,244,000
[2] $147,488 gross profit + $444,000 interest revenue = $591,488

In subsequent years, only interest revenue is recognized as revenue under the full accrual method, but interest revenue plus a portion of the payment on the principal is recognized under the installment sales method. After four years, all the cash collected is recognized as revenue under the cost recovery method. The graph on the following page illustrates how revenue for the real estate sale would be recognized over the twenty-five years assuming all payments were made as scheduled.

Cash Method

If the probability of recovering product or service costs is remote, the cash method of accounting could be used. Seldom would this method be applicable for sales of merchandise or real estate because the right of repossession would leave considerable value to the seller. However, the cash method might be appropriate for service contracts with high initial costs and considerable uncertainty as to the ultimate collection of the contract price. Under this method, all costs are charged to expense as

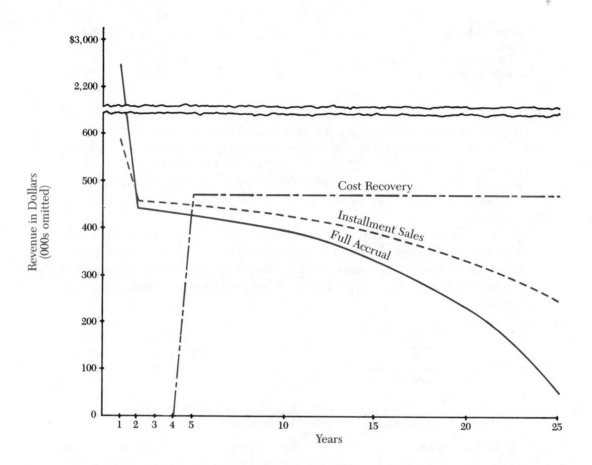

Comparison of Revenue Recognition Methods

incurred, and revenue is recognized as collections are made. This extreme method of revenue and expense recognition would be appropriate only when the potential losses on a contract cannot be estimated with any degree of certainty.

METHODS OF ACCOUNTING BEFORE REVENUE RECOGNITION

In addition to the revenue recognition methods discussed in this chapter, some sales arrangements involve an exchange of either goods or monetary assets such as cash and notes receivable prior to the point where the earnings process has been completed sufficiently to recognize revenue.

Under these circumstances, special accounting procedures must be applied pending the finalization of the sale and subsequent application of one of the methods of revenue recognition. If monetary assets are received prior to finalization of a sale, the deposit method of accounting should be used. If inventory is exchanged in advance of a sale, consignment accounting procedures should be applied. Each of these methods will be discussed briefly.

Deposit Method — General

In some cases, cash is collected before a sales contract is sufficiently defined to recognize revenue. This situation frequently arises in real estate sales contracts. For these cases, a method of accounting referred to as the **deposit method** has been developed.[11] Pending recognition of a sale, the cash received from a buyer is reported as a deposit on the contract and classified among the liabilities on the balance sheet. The property continues to be shown as an asset of the seller, and any related debt on the property continues to be reported as debt of the seller. No revenue or income should be recognized until the sales contract is finalized. At that time, one of the revenue recognition methods illustrated in this chapter may be used, and the deposit account would be closed. If the deposit is forfeited, it should be credited to income.

Deposit Method — Franchising Industry

A special application of the deposit method is found in the franchising industry, one of the fastest growing retail industries of recent years. Franchisors create faster growth by selling various rights to use a name and/or a product to operators (franchisees) who manage independent units as separate entrepreneurs from the franchisor.

Sales of franchises usually include several different services, products, and/or plant assets including: (1) intangible rights to use a trademark or name, (2) property owned by the franchisor, (3) pre-opening services such as helping locate suitable business sites, constructing a building, and training employees, and (4) ongoing services, products, and processes as the operations are carried out. Many revenue recognition problems are present in typical franchises, however, most of them may be solved if the elements are separately identified and accounted for in the same manner as they would be if the sale were a separate transaction. The most troublesome revenue recognition problem has been the initial fee. Typically, the franchisor charges a substantial amount for the right to use the

---

[11] *Statement of Financial Accounting Standards No. 66,* par. 65–67.

franchise name and to provide for pre-opening services. Sometimes these are payable immediately in cash, but typically they include a long-term note receivable. Frequently liberal refund provisions are included in the agreement, especially in the period prior to opening.

In the early days of franchising agreements, franchisors often reported the initial fee as revenue when the monetary assets were received. Future estimated costs were provided as offsets to the revenue. However, this treatment often resulted in questionable front-end loading of revenue similar to that occurring in the real estate and retail land sale industries. As a result, the AICPA issued an Industry Accounting Guide in 1973 that established revenue recognition guidelines for the franchising industry.[12] The essentials of this guide were later incorporated into FASB Statement No. 45.[13] This standard specifies that no revenue be recognized prior to **substantial performance** of the services covered by the initial fee. Until that time, any monetary assets received should be offset by a deposit or deferred credit account, and any costs related to the services rendered should be deferred until revenue is recognized, except that such deferred costs shall not exceed anticipated revenue less estimated additional related costs. Once substantial performance is achieved, revenue should be recognized using the method that best reflects the probability of cash collection, i.e., accrual, installment sales, or cost recovery method. The latter two methods "shall be used to account for franchise fee revenue only in those exceptional cases when revenue is collectible over an extended period and no reasonable basis exists for estimating collectibility."[14]

To illustrate, assume that a franchisor charges new franchisees an initial fee of $25,000. Of this amount $10,000 is payable in cash when the agreement is signed, and the remainder is to be paid in four annual installments of $3,750 each. The agreement provides that the franchisor will assist in locating the site for a building, conduct a market survey to estimate potential income, supervise the construction of a building, and provide initial training to employees. Assume that the franchisee could borrow money at 10%. Thus, the present value of the four $3,750 payments would be $11,887 ($3,750 × 3.1699). The discount of $3,113 represents interest to be earned over the payment period.

---

[12] Committee on Franchise Accounting and Auditing, AICPA, *Industry Accounting Guide*, "Accounting for Franchise Fee Revenue" (New York: American Institute of Certified Public Accountants, 1973).

[13] *Statement of Financial Accounting Standards No. 45*, "Accounting for Franchise Fee Revenue" (Stamford: Financial Accounting Standards Board, March, 1981).

[14] *Ibid*, par 6.

If the down payment is refundable, and no services have been rendered at the time the arrangement is made, the deposit method would be used as long as collection on the note is reasonably certain. The following entry would be made to record the transaction:

Cash..	10,000	
Notes Receivable...	15,000	
Discount on Notes Receivable		3,113
Deposit on Franchise (or Unearned Franchise Fee).................		21,887

When the initial services are determined to be substantially performed, the revenue recognition method to be used and the resulting journal entries depend on the probability of future cash collection. If the collection of the note is reasonably assured, the full accrual method would be used. Assume that substantial performance of the initial services costs $15,000. The entries to record this event using the full accrual method would be as follows:

Cost of Franchise Fee Revenue...................................	15,000	
Cash..		15,000
Deposit on Franchise (or Unearned Franchise Fee).................	21,887	
Franchise Fee Revenue		21,887

If the collection of the note is doubtful, the installment sales method could be used. The following additional entries to those of the full accrual method would be required.

Franchise Fee Revenue	21,887	
Cost of Franchise Fee Revenue.................................		15,000
Deferred Gross Profit on Franchise		6,887
Deferred Gross Profit on Franchise	3,147*	
Realized Gross Profit on Franchise		3,147

*Computation:
$6,887 ÷ $21,887 = 31.47% gross profit percentage
.3147 × $10,000 = $3,147

Consignment Sales

Another method of accounting has developed when property is exchanged without a transfer of title and without a sales contract being completed. This type of arrangement is referred to as a **consignment**. Under a consignment, the potential seller, the **consignor**, ships merchandise to another party, the **consignee**, who then acts as an *agent* for the consignor to sell the goods. Title to the merchandise continues to be held by the consignor until a sale is made, at which time title passes to the ultimate purchaser. The consignee is usually entitled to reimbursement for expenses incurred in relation to this arrangement, and is also entitled to a commission if a sale is successfully made.

Because title to the merchandise is held by the consignor, but physical possession is held by the consignee, special accounting records must be maintained by the consignor for control purposes. No revenue is recognized until a sale is made by the consignee. Upon shipment of the merchandise by the consignor, a special inventory account is established on the consignor's books to identify the consigned merchandise. Any consignment expenses paid by the consignor are added to the inventory balance as added costs. The consignee does not make an entry for receipt of the inventory in the general ledger; however, memorandum control records are usually kept. Any reimbursable expense paid by the consignee is charged to a receivable account by the consignee and added to the inventory balance by the consignor. When a sale is made, the consignor recognizes the sale as revenue according to one of the revenue recognition methods, and the consigned inventory cost is matched against revenue when it is recognized. The consignee recognizes the commission as revenue on the transaction.

To illustrate consignment accounting entries, assume that Harrison Products Inc. sends $500,000 worth of goods on consignment to Benson Industries. Shipping costs of $5,000 are paid by Harrison, and reimbursable advertising costs of $20,000 are paid by Benson Industries. By the end of the year, one half of the goods on consignment are sold for $400,000 cash. A 10% commission is earned by Benson Industries according to the terms of the consignment. The journal entries shown in page 847 would be made on the consignor's and consignee's books.

If the sale by Benson Industries had been on the installment basis, the installment sales entries illustrated earlier in this chapter could have been used in place of the accrual entries illustrated.

CONCLUDING COMMENTS

This chapter has explored some special problems that arise in recognizing revenue. Some industries such as franchising, construction, and real estate, have been used as illustrative of the types of problems that exist in applying the revenue recognition criteria included in currently accepted accounting standards. The importance of revenue recognition is based on the traditional revenue/expense approach to measuring income. Under this approach, revenue recognition is the key and most critical decision. Under the alternative method of income measurement, the asset/liability view, the emphasis shifts to definition of the elements such as assets and liabilities.

Transaction	Entries on Consignor's Books (Harrison Products Inc.)		Entries on Consignee's Books (Benson Industries)	
(1) Shipment of goods on consignment.	Inventory on Consignment . . . . 500,000 Finished Goods Inventory	500,000	No entry (memorandum control record)	
(2) Payment of expenses by consignor.	Inventory on Consignment . . . . 5,000 Cash	5,000	No entry	
(3) Payment of expenses by consignee.	Inventory on Consignment . . . . 20,000 Consignee Payable	20,000	Consignor Receivable . 20,000 Cash	20,000
(4) Sale of merchandise.	No entry		Cash . . . . 400,000 Consignor Payable . .	400,000
(5) Notification of sale to consignor and payment of cash due.	Commission Expense . . . . 40,000 Cash . . . . 340,000 Consignee Payable . . 20,000 Consignment Sales Revenue	400,000	Consignor Payable . . . . 400,000 Cash . . . . Commission Revenue . . . . Consignor Receivable	340,000 40,000 20,000
	Cost of Goods Sold . . 262,500* Inventory on Consignment	262,500		
	*Computation: ½($500,000 + $25,000) = $262,500			

QUESTIONS

1. Under what conditions is percentage-of-completion accounting recommended for construction contractors?
2. Distinguish between the cost-to-cost method and efforts-expended methods of measuring the percentage of completion.
3. Output measures of percentage of completion are sometimes used in preference to input measures. What are some examples of commonly used output measures?

4. What is the relationship between the construction in progress account and the progress billings on construction contracts account? How should these accounts be reported on the balance sheet?

5. When a measure of percentage of completion other than cost-to-cost is used, the amount of cost charged against revenue using the percentage of completion will usually be different from the costs incurred. How do some AICPA committee members recommend handling this situation so that the costs charged against revenue are equal to the costs incurred?

6. The construction in progress account is used to accumulate all costs of construction. What additional item is included in this account when percentage-of-completion accounting is followed?

7. The gross profit percentage reported on long-term construction contracts often varies from year to year. What is the major reason for this variation?

8. How are anticipated contract losses treated under the completed-contract and percentage-of-completion methods?

9. What input and output measures are usually applicable to the proportional performance method for long-term service contracts?

10. The proportional performance method spreads the profit over the periods in which services are being performed. What arguments could be made against this method of revenue recognition for newly formed service oriented companies?

11. Distinguish among the three different approaches to revenue recognition that await the receipt of cash. How does the treatment of costs incurred vary depending on the approach used?

12. Under what general conditions is the installment sales method of accounting preferred to the full accrual method?

13. The normal accounting entries for installment sales require keeping a separate record by year of receivables, collections on receivables, and the deferred gross profit percentage. Why are these separate records necessary?

14. Installment sales contracts generally include interest. Contrast the method of recognizing interest revenue from the method used to recognize the gross profit on the sale.

15. Under what conditions would the cash method of recognizing revenue be acceptable for reporting purposes?

16. What special recognition problems arise in accounting for franchise fees?

17. Consignment accounting is primarily a method of accounting for transfers of inventory prior to the point of revenue recognition. Describe the essential elements of this method from the standpoint of (a) the consignor and (b) the consignee.

DISCUSSION CASES

CASE 19–1
(Recognizing revenue on a percentage-of-completion basis)

As the new controller for Sumsion Construction Company, you have been advised that your predecessor classified all revenues and expenses by project, each project being considered a separate venture. All revenues from uncompleted projects were treated as unearned revenue, and all expenses applicable to each uncompleted project were treated as "work in process" inventory. Thus, the income statement for the current year included only the revenues and expenses related to projects completed during that year. What do you think about the use of the completed-contract method by the previous controller? What alternative approach might you suggest to company management?

CASE 19–2   (Let's spread our losses too!)

The Clyde Construction Company has several contracts to build sections of freeways, bridges, and dams. Because most of these contracts require more than one year to complete, the accountant, James Gregson, has recommended use of the percentage-of-completion method to recognize revenue and income on these contracts. The president, Gretta Dunn, isn't quite sure how it works, and indicates concern about the impact of this decision on income taxes. Dunn also inquires as to what happens when a contract results in a loss. When told by Gregson that any estimated loss must be recognized when it is first identified, Dunn becomes upset. "If it is a percentage-of-completion method, and we are recognizing profits as production is finished, why shouldn't we be able to do the same for losses?" How would you as the accountant answer Dunn's concerns?

CASE 19–3
(What is the difference between completed-contract and percentage-of-completion accounting?)

In accounting for long-term contracts (those taking longer than one year to complete), the two methods commonly followed are the percentage-of-completion method and the completed-contract method.
  (1) Discuss how earnings on long-term contracts are recognized and computed under these two methods.
  (2) Under what circumstances is it preferable to use one method over the other?
  (3) Why is earnings recognition as measured by interim billings not generally accepted for long-term contracts?

(AICPA adapted)

CASE 19–4   (When is the membership fee earned?)

The Fitness Health Studio has been operating for 5 years but is presently for sale. It has opened 50 salons in various cities in the United States. The normal pattern for a new opening is to advertise heavily and sell different types of memberships: 1-year, 3-year, and 5-year. For the initial membership fee, members may use the pool, exercise rooms, sauna, and other recreational facilities without charge. If special courses or programs are taken, additional fees are charged; however, members are granted certain priorities and the fees are less than those charged to outsiders. In addition, a minimal $10 a month dues charge is made to all members. Non-members may use the facilities; however, they must pay a substantial daily charge for services they receive.

Your client, Getty Inc., is considering purchasing the chain of health studios, and asks you to give your opinion on its operations. You are provided with financial statements that show a growing revenue and income pattern over the 5-year period. The balance sheet shows that the physical facilities are apparently owned rather than leased. But you are aware that health studios, like all service institutions, have some challenging revenue recognition problems. What questions would you want answered in preparing your report for Getty?

CASE 19–5   (When is it income?)

Ekins Advertising Agency handles advertising for clients under contracts that require the agency to develop advertising copy and layouts, and place ads in various media, charging clients a commission of 15% of the media cost as its fee. The agency makes advance billings to its clients of estimated media cost plus its 15% commission. Adjustments to these advances are usually small. Frequently both the billings and receipt of cash from these billings occur before the period in which the advertising actually appears in the media.

A conference meeting is held between officers of the agency and the new firm of CPAs recently engaged to perform annual audits. In this meeting, consideration is given to 4 possible points for measuring income: (1) at the time the advanced billing is made, (2) when payment is received from the client, (3) in the month when the advertising appears in the media, and (4) when the bill for advertising is received from the media, generally in the month following its appearance. The agency has been following the first method for the past several years on the basis that a definite contract exists and the income is earned when billed. When the billing is made, an entry is prepared to record the estimated receivable and liability to the media. Estimated expenses related to the contract are also recorded. Adjusting entries are later made for any differences between the estimated and actual amounts.

As a member of the CPA firm attending this meeting, how would you react to the agency's method of recognizing income? Discuss the strengths and weaknesses of each of the 4 methods of income recognition and indicate which one you would recommend the agency follow.

CASE 19–6   (When is the initial franchise fee really earned?)

Cottontree Inn sells franchises to independent operators throughout the western part of the United States. The contract with the franchisee includes the following provisions:

(a) The franchisee is charged an initial fee of $25,000. Of this amount $5,000 is payable when the agreement is signed and a $4,000 non-interest-bearing note is payable at the end of each of the 5 subsequent years.

(b) All the initial franchise fee collected by Cottontree Inn is to be refunded and the remaining obligation canceled if, for any reason, the franchisee fails to open the franchise.

(c) In return for the initial franchise fee, Cottontree agrees to: assist the franchisee in selecting the location for the business; negotiate the lease for the land; obtain financing and assist with building design; supervise construction; establish accounting and tax records; and, provide expert advice over a 5-year period relating to such matters as employee and management training, quality control, and promotion.

(d) In addition to the initial franchise fee, the franchisee is required to pay to Cottontree Inn a monthly fee of 2% of sales for recipe innovations, and the privilege of purchasing ingredients from Cottontree Inn at or below prevailing market prices.

Management of Cottontree Inn estimates that the value of the services rendered to the franchisee at the time the contract is signed amounts to at least $5,000. All franchisees to date have opened their locations at the scheduled time and none has defaulted on any of the notes receivable.

The credit ratings of all franchisees would entitle them to borrow at the current interest rate of 10%.

Given the nature of Cottontree's agreement with its franchisees, when should revenue be recognized? Discuss the question of revenue recognition for both the initial franchise fee and the additional monthly fee of 2% of sales and give illustrative entries for both types of revenue.   (AICPA adapted)

CASE 19–7   (I think they're sales!)

The Rain-Soft Water Company distributes its water softeners to dealers upon their request. The contract agreement with the dealers is that they may have 90 days to sell and pay for the softeners. Until the 90-day period is over, any softeners may be returned at the dealer's expense and with no further obligation on the dealer's part. Full payment by the dealer is required after 90 days has elapsed, whether the softeners are sold or not. Past experience indicates that 75% of all softeners distributed on this basis are sold by the dealer. In June, 100 units are delivered to dealers at an average billed price of $800 each. The average cost of the softeners to Rain-Soft is $600. Based on the expected sales, Rain-Soft reports profit of $15,000 [$200 × .75(100)]. You are asked to evaluate the income statement for its compliance with GAAP. What recommendations would you make?

EXERCISES

EXERCISE 19–1   (Completed-contract method)

On December 1, 1987, bids were submitted for a construction project to build a new municipal building and fire station. The lowest bid was $3,980,000 submitted by the Yancey Construction Company, and they were awarded the contract. Yancey uses the completed-contract method to report gross profit. The following data are given to summarize the activities on this contract for 1987 and 1988. Give the entries to record these transactions using the completed-contract method.

Year	Cost Incurred	Estimated Cost to Complete	Billings on Contract	Collections of Billings
1987	$1,620,000	$2,060,000	$1,350,000	$1,230,000
1988	2,020,000	-0-	2,630,000	2,750,000

EXERCISE 19–2　(Percentage-of-completion analysis)

Fanelli Construction Co. has used the cost-to-cost percentage-of-completion method of recognizing profits. Tony Fanelli assumed leadership of the business after the recent death of his father, Rudy. In reviewing the records, Fanelli finds the following information regarding a recently completed building project for which the total contract was $2,000,000.

	1986	1987	1988
Gross profit (loss)............	$ 40,000	$140,000	$ (20,000)
Cost incurred to date........	360,000	?	820,000

Fanelli wants to know how effectively the company operated during the last 3 years on this project and, since the information is not complete, has asked you to help by answering the following questions.
(1) How much cost was incurred in 1987?
(2) What percentage of the project was completed by the end of 1987?
(3) What was the total estimated gross profit on the project by the end of 1987?
(4) What was the estimated cost to complete the project at the end of 1987?

EXERCISE 19–3
(Percentage of completion using architect's estimates)

Central Utah Builders Inc. entered into a contract to construct an office building and plaza at a contract price of $10,000,000. Income is to be reported using the percentage-of-completion method as determined by estimates made by the architect. The data below summarize the activities on the construction for the years 1987 through 1989. What entries are required to record this information, assuming the architect's estimate of the percentage completed is used to determine revenue?

Year	Actual Cost Incurred	Estimated Cost to Complete	Percentage Complete— Architect's Estimate	Project Billings	Collections on Billings
1987	$3,200,000	$5,800,000	25%	$3,300,000	$3,100,000
1988	4,100,000	1,200,000	75	4,200,000	4,000,000
1989	1,300,000	0	100	2,500,000	2,900,000

EXERCISE 19–4　(Percentage-of-completion analysis)

Cascade International Inc. recently acquired the Despain Builders Company. Despain has incomplete accounting records. On one particular project, only the information below is given. Because the information is incomplete, you are asked the following questions assuming the percentage-of-completion method is used and an output measure is used to estimate the percentage completed, and revenue is recorded using the costs actually incurred (Alternative B).

	1986	1987	1988
Costs incurred during year	$200,000	$250,000	?
Estimated cost to complete	450,000	190,000	-0-
Contract revenue	250,000	?	?
Gross profit on contract.................	?	10,000	$(20,000)
Contract price	700,000		

(1) How much gross profit should be reported in 1986?
(2) How much revenue should be reported in 1987?
(3) How much revenue should be reported in 1988?
(4) How much cost was incurred in 1988?
(5) What are the total costs on the contract?
(6) What would the gross profit be for 1987 if the cost-to-cost percentage-of-completion method were used? Ignore the revenue amount shown for 1986 and gross profit amount reported for 1987.

EXERCISE 19–5   (Reporting construction contracts)

Dean Builders Inc. is building a new home for Gaylin Lytle at a contracted price of $120,000. The estimated cost at the time the contract is signed (January 2, 1988) is $97,000. At December 31, 1988, the total cost incurred is $64,000 with estimated costs to complete of $36,000. Dean has billed $70,000 on the job and has received a $60,000 payment. This is the only contract in process at year end. Prepare the sections of the balance sheet and the income statement of Dean Builders Inc. affected by these events assuming use of (a) the percentage-of-completion method and (b) the completed-contract method.

EXERCISE 19–6   (Completed-contract method)

On January 1, 1987, the Build Rite Construction Company entered into a 3-year contract to build a dam. The original contract price for the construction was $18,000,000 and the estimated cost was $16,100,000. The following cost data relate to the construction period.

Year	Cost Incurred in Year	Estimated Cost to Complete	Billings	Cash Collected
1987	$6,000,000	$10,000,000	$6,300,000	$6,000,000
1988	5,100,000	7,400,000	5,700,000	5,200,000
1989	7,650,000	-0-	6,000,000	6,800,000

Prepare the required journal entries for the 3 years of the contract, assuming Build Rite uses the completed-contract method.

EXERCISE 19–7
(Percentage-of-completion method with change orders)

The High-Tower Construction Company enters into a contract on January 1, 1988, to construct a 20-story office building for $40,000,000. During the construction period, many change orders are made to the original contract. The following schedule summarizes these changes made in 1988.

	Cost Incurred 1988	Estimated Cost to Complete	Contract Price
Basic contract..............	$8,000,000	$28,000,000	$40,000,000
Change Order #1	50,000	50,000	125,000
Change Order #2	—	50,000	-0-
Change Order #3	100,000	100,000	Still to be negotiated. At least cost.
Change Order #4	125,000	-0-	100,000

Compute the revenue, costs, and gross profit to be recognized in 1988, assuming use of the cost-to-cost method to determine the percentage completed. Round percentage to two decimal places.

EXERCISE 19–8   (Service industry accounting)

The Olympia Health Spa charges an annual membership fee of $400 for its services. For this fee, each member receives a fitness evaluation (value $100), a monthly magazine (value $32), and 2-hour's use of the equipment each week. The initial direct costs to obtain the membership are estimated to be $80. The direct cost of the fitness evaluation is $50, and the monthly direct costs to provide the services are estimated to be $15 per person. In addition, the monthly indirect costs are estimated to average $6 per person. Give the journal entries to record the transactions in 1988 relative to a membership sold on July 1, 1988. The fitness evaluation is given in the first month of the membership, and the initial direct cost is to be spread over all direct costs using the proportional performance method. (Round percentage of performance to two decimal places and journal entries to nearest dollar.)

EXERCISE 19–9   (Installment sales accounting—real estate)

On January 1, 1988, the Susannah Realty Company sold property carried in inventory at a cost of $75,000 for $120,000 to be paid 10% down and the balance in annual installments over a 10-year period at 12% interest. Installment payments are to be made at the end of each year.

(1) What is the equal annual payment necessary to pay for this property under the stated terms. (Round to nearest dollar.)
(2) Give the entries for the first year assuming the installment sales method is used.

EXERCISE 19–10   (Installment sales accounting)

McDermott Corporation had sales in 1987 of $210,000, in 1988 of $270,000, and in 1989 of $320,000. The gross profit percentage of each year, in order, is 28%, 29%, and 26%. Past history has shown that 10% of total sales are collected in the first year, 40% in the second year, and 30% in the third year. Assuming these collections are made as projected, give the journal entries for 1987, 1988, and 1989, assuming use of the installment sales method. Ignore provisions for doubtful accounts and interest.

EXERCISE 19–11   (Installment sales analysis)

Complete the following table:

	1986	1987	1988
Installment sales..............................	$50,000	$80,000	(7)
Cost of installment sales......................	(1)	(5)	91,800
Gross profit	(2)	(6)	28,200
Gross profit percentage.......................	(3)	25%	(8)
Cash collections:			
1986	(4)	25,000	10,000
1987		20,000	50,000
1988			45,000
Realized gross profit on installment sales.......	1,100	10,500	(9)

EXERCISE 19–12   (Cost recovery method)

Indianola Inc. is a land development company. It has acquired 1,000 acres of choice recreational property for $1,200 per acre, and is selling developed recreational building lots for $5,000 per acre. The improvement costs amount to $1,200 per acre. The land cost is carried on Indianola's books as inventory. In the first year, Indianola sold 20 one-acre lots, 10% down, the balance to be paid over 10 years in annual installments at an interest rate of 10%. Assume the lots are sold on January 1, 1987.

(1) Give the entries required for 1987 and 1988 if the cost recovery method is used to recognize revenue.

(2) Prove that the balance reported on the December 31, 1988 balance sheet is equal to the unrecovered cost of the land.

EXERCISE 19–13   (Franchise accounting)

On September 1, 1988, Bulletin Company entered into franchise agreements with three franchisees. The agreement required an initial fee payment of $7,000 plus four $3,000 payments due every 4 months, the first payment due December 31, 1988. The interest rate is 12%. The initial deposit is refundable until substantial performance has been completed. The following table describes each agreement.

Franchisee	Probability of Full Collection	Services Performed by Franchisor at December 31, 1988	Total Cost Incurred to December 31, 1988
A	Likely	Substantial	$ 7,000
B	Doubtful	25%	2,000
C	Doubtful	Substantial	10,000

For each franchisee, identify the revenue recognition method that you would recommend considering the circumstances. What amount of revenue and income would be reported in 1988 for the method selected? Assume $10,000 was received from each franchisee during the year.

EXERCISE 19–14   (Franchise accounting)

Sunshine Pizza's franchises its name to different people across the country. The franchise agreement requires the franchisee to make an initial payment of $12,000 on the agreement date and 4 annual payments of $6,000 each beginning one year from the agreement date. The initial payment is refundable until the date of opening. Interest rates are assumed to be 10%. The franchisor agrees to make market studies, find a location, train the employees, and a few other relatively minor services. The following transactions describe the relationship with Reed Howard, a franchisee.

July 1, 1987 — Entered into a franchise agreement.
September 1, 1987 — Completed a market study at cost of $4,000.
November 15, 1987 — Found suitable location. Service cost $3,000.
January 10, 1988 — Completed training program for employees, cost $5,000.
January 15, 1988 — Franchise outlet opened.

Give the journal entries in 1987–1988 to record these transactions, including any adjusting entries at December 31, 1987.

EXERCISE 19–15   (Consignment accounting)

In 1987, Kranenburg Wholesalers transferred goods to a retailer on consignment. The transaction was recorded as a sale by Kranenburg. The goods cost $40,000 and were sold at a 30% markup. In 1988, $12,000 (cost) of the merchandise was sold by the retailer at the normal markup, and the balance of the merchandise was returned to Kranenburg. The retailer withheld a 10% commission from payment. Prepare the journal entry in 1988 to correct the books for 1987, and prepare the correct entries relative to the consignment sale in 1988.

PROBLEMS

PROBLEM 19–1   (Construction accounting)

Shimizu's Construction Company reports its income for tax purposes on a completed-contract basis and income for financial statement purposes on a percentage-of-completion basis. A record of construction activities for 1987 and 1988 follows:

		1987			1988	
	Contract Price	Cost Incurred 1987	Estimated Cost to Complete	Cost Incurred 1988	Estimated Cost to Complete
Project A	$1,450,000	$910,000	$490,000	$410,000	-0-
Project B	1,700,000	720,000	880,000	340,000	$650,000
Project C	850,000	160,000	480,000	431,500	58,500
Project D	1,000,000			280,000	520,000

General and administrative expenses for 1987 and 1988 were $60,000 for each year and are to be recorded as a period cost.

Instructions:
(1) Calculate the income for 1987 and 1988 that should be reported for financial statement purposes.
(2) Calculate the income for 1988 to be reported on a completed-contract basis.

PROBLEM 19–2   (Construction accounting)

The S. P. Penrose Construction Company obtained a construction contract to build a highway and bridge over the Missouri River. It is estimated at the beginning of the contract that it would take 3 years to complete the project at an expected cost of $50,000,000. The contract price was $60,000,000. The project actually took 4 years, being accepted as completed late in 1988. The following information describes the status of the job at the close of production each year.

	1985	1986	1987	1988	1989
Annual costs incurred	$12,000,000	$15,000,000	$18,000,000	$10,000,000	
Estimated cost to complete	38,000,000	29,250,000	10,555,555		
Collections on contract ...	12,000,000	13,500,000	15,000,000	15,000,000	$4,500,000
Billings on contract.......	13,000,000	15,500,000	17,000,000	14,500,000	

Instructions:
(1) What is the revenue, cost, and gross profit recognized for each of the years 1985–1989 under (a) the percentage-of-completion method, (b) the completed-contract method?
(2) Give the journal entries for each year assuming that the percentage-of-completion method is used.

PROBLEM 19–3   (Construction accounting)

The Urban Construction Company commenced doing business in January 1988. Construction activities for the year 1988 are summarized as follows:

Project	Total Contract Price	Contract Expenditures to December 31, 1988	Estimated Additional Costs to Complete Contracts	Cash Collections to December 31, 1988	Billings to December 31, 1988
A	$ 310,000	$187,500	$ 12,500	$155,000	$155,000
B	415,000	195,000	255,000	210,000	249,000
C	350,000	310,000	—	300,000	350,000
D	300,000	16,500	183,500	—	4,000
	$1,375,000	$709,000	$451,000	$665,000	$758,000

The company is your client. The president has asked you to compute the amounts of revenue for the year ended December 31, 1988, that would be reported under the completed-contract method and the percentage-of-completion method of accounting for long-term contracts.

The following information is available:

(a) Each contract is with a different customer.

(b) Any work remaining to be done on the contracts is expected to be completed in 1989.

(c) The company's accounts have been maintained on the completed-contract method.

Instructions:

(1) Prepare a schedule computing the amount of revenue, cost, and gross profit (loss) by project for the year ended December 31, 1988, to be reported under (a) the percentage-of-completion method, and (b) the completed-contract method.(Round to two decimal places on percentages.)

(2) Prepare a schedule under the completed-contract method, computing the amount that would appear in the company's balance sheet at December 31, 1988, for (a) costs in excess of billings, and (b) billings in excess of costs.

(3) Prepare a schedule under the percentage-of-completion method that would appear in the company's balance sheet at December 31, 1988, for (a) costs and estimated earnings in excess of billings, and (b) billings in excess of costs and estimated earnings.   (AICPA adapted)

PROBLEM 19–4   (Construction accounting)

The Holbrook Construction Corporation contracted with the City of Port Huron to construct a dam on the Erie River at a price of $16,000,000. The Holbrook Corporation expects to earn $1,360,000 on the contract. The percentage-of-completion method is to be used and the completion stage is to be determined by estimates made by the engineer. The following schedule summarizes the activities of the contract for the years 1986–1988.

Year	Cost Incurred	Estimated Cost to Complete	Engineer's Estimate of Completion	Billings on Contract	Collection on Billings
1986	$5,000,000	$9,640,000	31%	$5,000,000	$4,500,000*
1987	4,500,000	5,100,000	61%	6,000,000	5,400,000*
1988	5,250,000	-0-	100%	5,000,000	6,100,000

*A 10% retainer accounts for the difference between billings and collections.

Instructions:

(1) Prepare a schedule showing the revenue, costs, and the gross profit earned each year under the percentage-of-completion method, using the engineer's estimate as the measure of completion to be applied to revenues and costs.

(2) Prepare all journal entries required to reflect the contract.

(3) Prepare journal entries for 1988, assuming the completed-contract method is used.

(4) How would the journal entries in (2) differ if the actual costs incurred were used to calculate cost for the period instead of the engineer's estimate. (Alternative B.)

PROBLEM 19–5   (Construction accounting)

Laura Sill is a contractor for the construction of large office buildings. At the beginning of 1988, 3 buildings were in progress. The following data describe the status of these buildings at the beginning of the year:

	Contract Price	Costs Incurred to 1/1/88	Estimated Cost To Complete 1/1/88
Building 1	$ 4,000,000	$2,070,000	$1,380,000
Building 2	9,000,000	6,318,000	1,782,000
Building 3	13,150,000	3,000,000	9,000,000

During 1988 the following costs were incurred:

Building 1—$930,000 (estimated cost to complete as of 12/31/88, $750,000)
Building 2—$1,800,000 (job completed)
Building 3—$7,400,000 (estimated cost to complete as of 12/31/88, $2,800,000)
Building 4—$800,000 (contract price, $2,500,000; estimated cost to complete as of 12/31/88, $1,200,000)

Instructions:
(1) Compute the total revenue, costs, and gross profit in 1988. Assume that Sill uses the cost-to-cost percentage-of-completion method. (Round to the nearest two decimal places for percentage completed.)
(2) Compute the gross profit for 1988 if Sill uses the completed-contract method.

PROBLEM 19–6   (Installment sales accounting)

Primary Corporation has been using the cash method to account for income since its first year of operation in 1987. All sales are made on credit with notes receivable given by the customer. The income statements for 1987 and 1988 included the following amounts:

	1987	1988
Revenues—collection on principal.	$32,000	$50,000
Revenues—interest	3,600	5,500
Cost of goods purchased*	50,140	52,020

*Includes increase in inventory of goods on hand of $5,000 in 1987 and $8,000 in 1988

The balance due on the notes at the end of each year were as follows:

	1987	1988
Notes receivable 1987	$54,000	$36,000
Notes receivable 1988		60,000
Discount on notes receivable—1987	7,167	5,579
Discount on notes receivable—1988		8,043

Instructions: Give the journal entries for 1987 and 1988 assuming the installment sales method was used rather than the cash method.

PROBLEM 19–7   (Cost recovery accounting)

After a 2-year search for a buyer, Hallen Inc. sold its idle plant facility to Booth Company for $800,000 on January 1, 1984. On this date the plant had a depreciated cost on Hallen's books of $550,000. Under the agreement, Booth paid $200,000 cash on January 1, 1984, and signed a $600,000 note bearing interest at 10%. The note was payable in installments of $100,000, $200,000, and $300,000 on January 1, 1985, 1986, and 1987, respectively. The note was secured by a mortgage on the property sold. Hallen appropriately accounted for the sale under the cost recovery method since there was no reasonable basis for estimating the degree of collectibility of the note receivable. Booth repaid the note with 3 late installment payments, which were accepted by Hallen, as follows:

Date of payment	Principal	Interest
July 1, 1985	$100,000	$90,000
December 31, 1986	200,000	75,000
February 1, 1988	300,000	32,500

Instructions: Prepare the journal entries required for the years 1984–1988 for the sale and subsequent collections.   (AICPA adapted)

PROBLEM 19–8   (Consignment accounting)

Cleghorn Industries sells merchandise on a consignment basis to dealers. Shipping costs are chargeable to Cleghorn, although in some cases, the dealer pays them. The selling price of the merchandise averages 25% above cost. The dealer is paid a 10% commission on the sales price for all sales made. All dealer sales are made on a cash basis. The following consignment sales activities occurred during 1988.

Manufacturing cost of goods shipped on consignment....		$200,000
Freight costs incurred:		
Paid by Cleghorn Industries........................	$15,000	
Paid by dealer.....................................	5,000	20,000
Sales price of merchandise sold by dealers.............		176,000
Payments made by dealers after deducting commission		
and freight costs..................................		114,000

Instructions:
(1) Prepare summary entries on the books of the consignor for these consignment sales transactions.
(2) Prepare summary entries on the books of the dealer consignee assuming there is only one dealer involved.
(3) Prepare the parts of Cleghorn Industries financial statements at December 31, 1988, that relate to these consignment sales.

PROBLEM 19–9   (Revenue recognition analysis)

The Juab Construction Company entered into a $3,000,000 contract in early 1988 to construct a multipurpose recreational facility for the City of Nephi. Construction time extended over a 2-year period. The table below describes the pattern of progress payments made by the City of Nephi and costs incurred by Juab

Construction by semiannual periods. Estimated costs of $2,400,000 were incurred as expected.

Period	Progress Payments for Period	Progress Cost for Period
(1) (January 1–June 30, 1988)...............	$ 500,000	$ 600,000
(2) (July 1–December 31, 1988)	700,000	800,000
(3) (January 1–June 30, 1989)...............	1,300,000	720,000
(4) (July 1–December 31, 1989)	500,000	280,000
Total................................	$3,000,000	$2,400,000

The Juab Company prepares financial statements twice each year, June 30 and December 31.

Instructions:

(1) Based on the foregoing data, compute the amount of revenue, costs, and gross profit for the 4 semiannual periods under each of the following methods of revenue recognition:
  (a) Percentage of completion.
  (b) Completed contract.
  (c) Installment sales (gross profit only).
  (d) Cost recovery (gross profit only).
(2) Which method do you feel best measures the performance of Juab on this contract?

20

Accounting For Income Taxes

Income taxes are a necessary cost of doing business in our society, and income tax expense is usually a material item on corporate income statements. Although the federal income tax represents the major portion of the income tax liability in most cases, state and local income taxes are also generally a significant expense.

If the income taxes payable and the income tax expense reported on the income statement were the same amount each year, there would be very few tax issues to present in an intermediate accounting textbook. However, as emphasized in Chapter 1, taxable income and financial or book income are not necessarily the same in any given period. The amount of income taxes payable is based on the laws of the various governmental bodies imposing a tax, not on generally accepted accounting principles. As these laws have become increasingly complex, accounting for income taxes has also become a very complex area. Even when tax simplification goals are pursued, as was true of the Tax Reform Act of 1986, the end result is often even more complex provisions.

The purpose of this chapter is not to discuss the income tax laws specifically, except as they affect financial accounting and reporting. The major issues in accounting for and reporting income taxes include:

1. Intraperiod income tax allocation.
2. Interperiod income tax allocation.
3. Operating loss carrybacks and carryforwards.
4. The investment tax credit.
5. Financial presentation and disclosure.

Each of these areas is discussed in this chapter. Although the emphasis is on the federal income tax, many state and local governments pattern their income tax laws after those of the federal government. As a result, state and local income taxes are accounted for in the same manner as the federal income tax, with variations depending on the particular state and local laws involved.

INTRAPERIOD INCOME TAX ALLOCATION

Because income tax is related specifically to revenue and expense items, the reporting of income tax should be directly related to the items involved. As illustrated in Chapter 4, if all current revenues and expenses are directly related to continuing operations, the total income tax expense for the period is reported as a single amount and deducted from "Income from continuing operations before income taxes." However, the income statement may also include nonoperating components, such as income from discontinued operations, extraordinary items, and cumulative effects of accounting changes. Each of these items is usually included in the computation of taxable income, either as an addition or deduction. Intraperiod income tax allocation requires the allocation of total income tax expense for the period among the various components of income.

To review the concept of intraperiod tax allocation, assume that Springer, Inc. has a $70,000 gain on the early retirement of long-term debt, which must be reported as an extraordinary item according to generally accepted accounting principles. The gain would also be reported as income for income tax purposes. The intraperiod tax allocation principle requires that the gain and the amount of income tax related to the gain be reported together in the income statement. If the tax rate were 40%, the disclosure might be shown as follows:

Extraordinary gain from early retirement of debt	$70,000	
Less income taxes on gain	28,000	$42,000

An alternative method of disclosure shows the amount of tax parenthetically as follows:

Extraordinary gain (net of income taxes of $28,000)	$42,000

In either case, the income tax on continuing operations would not include the tax on the extraordinary gain.

If the special item is a loss that must be disclosed separately, such as a loss from discontinued operations, the income tax savings arising from the loss is applied to reduce the reported loss. Thus, if the tax rate were 40% and the loss on the sale of a discontinued division were $40,000, the special item might be disclosed as follows:

Loss from discontinued operations (net of $16,000 income tax savings)	$24,000

When a prior period adjustment is reported as a direct adjustment to Retained Earnings, the related tax effect should be disclosed in the statement of retained earnings. To illustrate, assume that a company discovers in 1988 that depreciation for 1986 was overstated by $30,000, and the related increase in income tax is 40% or $12,000. The adjustment could be presented in the statement of retained earnings as follows:

Retained earnings, January 1, 1988, as previously reported..............	$210,000
Add prior period adjustment for overstatement of depreciation expense for 1986 (net of $12,000 increase in income taxes payable)	18,000
Adjusted retained earnings, January 1, 1988	$228,000

INTERPERIOD INCOME TAX ALLOCATION

Perhaps the most complex area involving accounting for income taxes is the adjustment necessary to apply the accrual concept to income tax expense. **Taxable income** is defined by laws enacted by Congress and by regulations issued by the Internal Revenue Service. The objectives of Congress and the IRS are not the same as those of accounting bodies, such as the Financial Accounting Standards Board, that establish generally accepted accounting principles to determine **financial income** (sometimes referred to as accounting or book income). Income taxes are sometimes used to regulate the economy, to encourage additional investment, or to favor specific industries. Generally, Congress is not concerned with measuring income as a basis for assessing enterprise performance, but as a basis for determining the ability of an enterprise to pay taxes. For example, revenues received in advance for goods or services are taxed in the period received, while such revenues are not recognized on the books until they are earned.

Differences between tax and financial income may be permanent or temporary. **Permanent differences** arise from: (1) items that are included in the computation of taxable income, but are never recognized for financial accounting purposes and (2) items that are recognized for financial accounting purposes but are never included in the computation of taxable income. **Temporary or timing differences** arise from revenue and expense items that are recognized for financial accounting purposes in a period preceding or subsequent to the period in which they are included in the computation of taxable income. These timing differences have created the need for **interperiod income tax allocation**. This allocation and its ramifications have created some challenging problems in accounting for income taxes.

The Accounting Principles Board spent considerable time in studying the issues surrounding income taxes, expecially interperiod income tax allocation and the investment tax credit. In 1967, the APB issued Opinion No. 11, which resulted in greater uniformity in the reporting of corporate income taxes, and required that interperiod income tax allocation be followed.[1] The Financial Accounting Standards Board found many conceptual problems with APB Opinion No. 11 and subsequent pronouncements dealing with income taxes. Accounting for income taxes was added to the Board's agenda in 1982, and in late 1986, a new proposed statement was issued as an exposure draft that recommended several significant changes to the previous standards.[2] The discussion in the following pages includes, where pertinent, recommendations included in the FASB exposure draft.

Permanent Differences

As the name implies, permanent differences are defined as:

> Differences between taxable income and pretax accounting income arising from transactions that, under applicable tax laws and regulations, will not be offset by corresponding differences or "turn around" in other periods.[3]

Most permanent differences can be classified as revenues exempt from income tax or expenses not deductible in determining taxable income. Examples of **nontaxable revenues** include:

1. Interest revenue on municipal bonds.
2. Life insurance proceeds on officers' lives.
3. 80% of dividends received from other corporations (100% of dividends from wholly owned subsidiaries).

Examples of **nondeductible expenses** include:

1. Fines and expenses arising from violation of laws.
2. Life insurance premiums paid on lives of a corporation's officers or employees if the corporation is the beneficiary.
3. Interest on indebtedness incurred to purchase tax-exempt municipal securities.
4. Goodwill amortization.

Expenses recognized for tax purposes but not recognized as expenses on the books are rarely encountered. An example of this type of permanent

---

[1] *Opinions of the Accounting Principles Board, No. 11,* "Accounting for Income Taxes" (New York: American Institute of Certified Public Accountants, 1967).

[2] *Exposure Draft of Proposed Statement of Financial Accounting Standards,* "Accounting for Income Taxes" (Stamford: Financial Accounting Standards Board, 1986).

[3] *Opinions of the Accounting Principles Board, No. 11,* par. 13.

difference would be percentage depletion in excess of actual cost depletion. Although theoretically there could be revenue recognized on the tax return that is never recognized on the books, there are no common examples of such items.

Timing Differences

Most differences between pretax financial income and taxable income are temporary in nature. **Temporary differences** include: (1) timing differences that arise from recognizing revenue and expense items in different periods for financial reporting purposes and for the tax return and (2) other differences that may arise from a reduction in the tax basis of depreciable assets because of specific income tax laws.[4] Because these latter temporary differences relate to detailed and complex provisions of the income tax laws, only timing differences are illustrated in this chapter.

Timing differences may be classified into the following categories. Examples of items fitting into each category are also included.

1. Pretax financial income is more than taxable income.
   (a) Revenues or gains are taxable in periods after they are recognized for financial reporting purposes.
      - Installment sales method used for tax purposes, but accrual method of recognizing sales revenue used for financial reporting purposes.
      - Completed-contract method of recognizing construction revenue used for tax purposes, but percentage-of-completion method used for financial reporting purposes.
   (b) Expenses or losses are deductible for tax purposes in the current period, but are deductible for financial reporting purposes in some future period.
      - ACRS used for tax purposes, but straight-line method used for financial reporting purposes.
      - Intangible drilling costs for extractive industry written off as incurred for tax purposes, but capitalized and deferred for financial reporting purposes.
2. Pretax financial income is less than taxable income.
   (a) Revenues or gains are taxable in the current period, but are deferred and recognized in future periods for financial reporting purposes.
      - Rent revenue received in advance of period earned recognized as revenue for tax purposes, but deferred to be recognized in future periods for financial reporting purposes.
      - Subscription revenue received in advance of period earned recognized as revenue for tax purposes, but deferred to be recognized in future periods for financial reporting purposes.

---

[4] *Exposure Draft*, "Accounting for Income Taxes," par. 8–11.

(b) Expenses or losses are deductible for tax purposes in a future period, but are deductible in the current period for financial reporting purposes.
- Warranty expense deductible for tax purposes only when actually incurred, but accrued in advance for financial reporting purposes.
- Marketable securities valued at cost for tax purposes, but valued at lower of cost or market for financial reporting purposes.

The Tax Reform Act of 1986 created some additional timing differences between financial and taxable income. For example, the Act limits the use of the allowance method for bad debts for corporations and requires capitalization of some general and administrative expenses in inventory. Neither of these changes is likely to be incorporated into GAAP.

Computation of Income Tax Expense and Income Taxes Payable

To illustrate interperiod income tax allocation and the effect of permanent and timing differences on the computation of income taxes, assume that for the year ending December 31, 1988, the Monroe Corporation reported pretax financial income of $420,000. This amount includes $20,000 of tax-exempt income and $5,000 of nondeductible expenses. Depreciation expense in the current year for tax purposes exceeds that recognized for financial reporting purposes by $30,000, and rent revenue in the current year for tax purposes exceeds that recognized for financial reporting purposes by $14,000. Assuming a tax rate of 40%, the income tax expense for financial reporting purposes and the income taxes payable in the current period would be computed as follows:

Pretax financial income		$420,000
Add (deduct) permanent differences:		
Nondeductible expenses	$ 5,000	
Tax-exempt income	(20,000)	(15,000)
Financial income subject to tax		$405,000
Add (deduct) timing differences:		
Excess of tax depreciation over book depreciation		(30,000)
Excess of tax rent revenue over book rent revenue		14,000
Taxable income		$389,000
Tax on financial income (income tax expense): $405,000 × .40		$162,000
Tax on taxable income (income taxes payable): $389,000 × .40		155,600
Difference between income tax expense and income taxes payable		$ 6,400

The $6,400 net difference between the income taxes currently payable of $155,600 and the reported income tax expense of $162,000 is attributable to the timing differences. As illustrated, the permanent differences are not included in the computation of either the income tax expense or the income taxes payable, and thus do not require income tax allocation. The depreciation timing difference results in a deferral in the payment of income taxes until a later period, while the rent revenue timing difference results in a payment of income taxes prior to the recognition of rent revenue in financial income. These differences are usually netted, and the net difference is recorded as a debit or credit to a **deferred income taxes account**. The journal entry to record income taxes for the Monroe Corporation is as follows:

Income Tax Expense.	162,000	
Income Taxes Payable		155,600
Deferred Income Taxes.		6,400

The balance in Deferred Income Taxes is generally reported on the balance sheet either with the assets (debit balance) or with the liabilities (credit balance). The nature, classification, and reporting of deferred income taxes are discussed and illustrated later in the chapter.

This simple example, for a single year, illustrates the manner in which permanent and timing differences affect the computation and recording of income taxes. The following section discusses and illustrates the impact of interperiod income tax allocation on the financial statements over several years.

Impact of Interperiod Income Tax Allocation

The objective of accounting for income taxes on an accrual basis is to recognize the tax consequences of an event in the same year the event is recognized in the financial statements.[5] The accrual basis assumes that income taxes are necessary expenses of doing business and should be accounted for in the same manner as other expenses. If the income tax expense is recognized on a cash basis, reported income amounts could be misleading when one year is compared with another.

To illustrate, assume that Horizon Limited, Inc. acquired a machine costing $100,000 on January 2, 1986. At the time of purchase, it was estimated that the asset would have a 5-year useful life with no residual value. For income tax purposes, the company uses the 3-year ACRS method of cost allocation, but for financial accounting purposes, the company uses straight-line depreciation. From 1986 through 1990, Horizon reported revenues of $200,000 for each year and operating expenses other than depreciation of $125,000. The income tax rate is 40%.

---

[5] *Exposure Draft*, "Accounting for Income Taxes," par. 7.

The schedules on page 870 illustrate the computation of net income with and without interperiod income tax allocation. Note that *without* interperiod income tax allocation, income tax expense is equal to the amount of taxes paid each year, and net income varies from a low of $25,000 to a high of $40,200. *With* interperiod income tax allocation, however, the net income is a constant $33,000. Since the underlying activity of the company is the same each year, the income should be constant over the years if income taxes are properly matched with pretax financial income. Thus, interperiod income tax allocation helps meet the qualitative characteristic of representational faithfulness and increases the usefulness of the financial statements.

The journal entries for Horizons Limited, Inc., using interperiod income tax allocation for the 5-year period, are summarized in the schedule on page 870. Note that for the first 3 years, the income tax expense exceeds the income taxes payable. These differences are referred to as **originating differences**, because each year additional amounts are added to the Deferred Income Taxes credit balance. For the last 2 years, the amount of income taxes payable exceeds the reported income tax expense. These differences are referred to as **reversing differences** as the accumulated amount of originating differences is reversed. After the fifth year, there is no deferred income taxes balance, and the total income tax expense and total income taxes paid for the 5-year period are the same. All timing differences eventually reverse as shown in this example involving only one asset. In the normal situation, however, many assets are being purchased and retired each year. Because of the differing stages of life of the assets, originating and reversing differences are occurring simultaneously. The same is true for other types of timing differences as well as depreciation. This condition is illustrated in the comprehensive example that follows.

Comprehensive Illustration of Interperiod Income Tax Allocation

A comprehensive illustration of interperiod income tax allocation is presented using the following information for Coronado Publishing Inc., a publisher of sports and fitness periodicals which began operations in 1987.

1. Subscriptions are sold on either a 1-year or a 2-year basis, and all subscriptions are collected in advance. For income tax purposes, subscription revenues are taxable in the year received, but for financial reporting purposes, revenues are recognized when they are earned.
2. Depreciation is determined on a straight-line basis for financial reporting purposes, while for income tax purposes, ACRS is used.
3. The corporate tax rate to be used is 40%.

Horizons Limited, Inc.
Computation of Net Income With and Without
Interperiod Income Tax Allocation

Computation of Income Taxes Payable

	1986	1987	1988	1989	1990
Revenues...................	$200,000	$200,000	$200,000	$200,000	$200,000
Operating expenses:					
Depreciation—ACRS	(25,000)	(38,000)	(37,000)	-0-	-0-
Other than depreciation	(125,000)	(125,000)	(125,000)	(125,000)	(125,000)
Taxable income	$ 50,000	$ 37,000	$ 38,000	$ 75,000	$ 75,000
Income taxes payable (40%)...	$ 20,000	$ 14,800	$ 15,200	$ 30,000	$ 30,000

Income Statement Without Income Tax Allocation

	1986	1987	1988	1989	1990	Total
Revenues...................	$200,000	$200,000	$200,000	$200,000	$200,000	$1,000,000
Operating expenses:						
Depreciation—straight line ..	(20,000)	(20,000)	(20,000)	(20,000)	(20,000)	(100,000)
Other than depreciation	(125,000)	(125,000)	(125,000)	(125,000)	(125,000)	(625,000)
Pretax financial income........	$ 55,000	$ 55,000	$ 55,000	$ 55,000	$ 55,000	$ 275,000
Income tax expense*.........	20,000	14,800	15,200	30,000	30,000	110,000
Net income	$ 35,000	$ 40,200	$ 39,800	$ 25,000	$ 25,000	$ 165,000

*Without interperiod income tax allocation, income tax expense equals income taxes payable.

Income Statement With Income Tax Allocation

	1986	1987	1988	1989	1990	Total
Revenues...................	$200,000	$200,000	$200,000	$200,000	$200,000	$1,000,000
Operating expenses:						
Depreciation—straight line ..	(20,000)	(20,000)	(20,000)	(20,000)	(20,000)	(100,000)
Other than depreciation	(125,000)	(125,000)	(125,000)	(125,000)	(125,000)	(625,000)
Pretax financial income........	$ 55,000	$ 55,000	$ 55,000	$ 55,000	$ 55,000	$ 275,000
Income tax expense (40%)	22,000	22,000	22,000	22,000	22,000	110,000
Net income	$ 33,000	$ 33,000	$ 33,000	$ 33,000	$ 33,000	$ 165,000

Horizons Limited, Inc.
Summary of Journal Entries
With Interperiod Income Tax Allocation

Year	Income Tax Expense Dr.	Income Taxes Payable (Cr.)	Deferred Income Taxes Dr. (Cr.)
1986........................	$ 22,000	($ 20,000)	($2,000)
1987........................	22,000	(14,800)	(7,200)
1988........................	22,000	(15,200)	(6,800)
1989........................	22,000	(30,000)	8,000
1990........................	22,000	(30,000)	8,000
Totals......................	$110,000	($110,000)	-0-

4. For each of the years 1987 through 1989, Coronado reported interest revenue from investments in municipal bonds of $8,000, which is not includable in taxable income. In 1988, Coronado paid a $5,500 fine for violation of a local zoning ordinance. The fine is not deductible for income tax purposes.

Additional data for 1987–1989 follow:

		Timing Differences			
	Pretax Financial	Excess of ACRS over Straight-Line Depreciation		Excess of Subscription Revenue Received in Advance over Subscription Revenue Earned	
Year	Income	Originating	Reversing	Originating	Reversing
1987	$100,000	$25,000	-0-	$15,000	-0-
1988	130,000	40,000	$ 5,000	20,000	$12,000
1989	175,000	20,000	25,000	19,000	15,000

Coronado Publishing Inc.
Computation of Income Tax Expense,
Income Taxes Payable, and Deferred Income Taxes

	1987	1988	1989
Pretax financial income..................	$100,000	$130,000	$175,000
Permanent differences:			
Nontaxable interest revenue	(8,000)	(8,000)	(8,000)
Nondeductible expense (fines)		5,500	
Financial income subject to tax..........	$ 92,000	$127,500	$167,000
Income tax rate........................	.40	.40	.40
Income tax expense	$ 36,800 dr.	$ 51,000 dr.	$ 66,800 dr.
Financial income subject to tax..........	$ 92,000	$127,500	$167,000
Timing differences:			
Depreciation—originating	(25,000)	(40,000)	(20,000)
reversing		5,000	25,000
Subscription revenue—originating......	15,000	20,000	19,000
reversing.......		(12,000)	(15,000)
Taxable income	$ 82,000	$100,500	$176,000
Income tax rate.......................	.40	.40	.40
Income taxes payable..................	$ 32,800 cr.	$ 40,200 cr.	$ 70,400 cr.
Deferred income taxes (difference)	$ 4,000 cr.	$ 10,800 cr.	$ 3,600 dr.

In this example, the permanent differences are deducted first, and the income tax expense is computed without them. The income tax liability is computed after adjusting pretax financial income for timing differences, both originating and reversing. The example includes two timing differences:

1. ACRS depreciation exceeds straight-line depreciation in the early years of an asset's life, so the amount of income taxes payable in those years is lower than would be true if the taxes were computed using straight-line

depreciation. As demonstrated earlier, these originating differences reverse themselves in the later years of an asset's life.

2. Subscription receipts exceed revenues earned on subscriptions in the first year of a subscription. Because subscription revenue is reported for income tax purposes when the subscriptions are received and not when they are earned, the amount of income taxes payable is greater in the first years than income tax expense.

These originating differences will also reverse in subsequent years. Although separate accounts could be maintained in the general ledger for each type of timing difference, it is more common to combine all timing differences for purposes of making the journal entries. Detailed schedules and working papers are usually maintained, however, for classification and reporting purposes.

The journal entries for the three years can be summarized as follows:

Coronado Publishing Inc.
Summary of Journal Entries for
Recording Income Taxes

Year	Income Tax Expense Dr.	Income Taxes Payable (Cr.)	Deferred Income Taxes Dr. (Cr.)
1987	36,800	(32,800)	(4,000)
1988	51,000	(40,200)	(10,800)
1989	66,800	(70,400)	3,600

In 1987 and 1988, the deferred income taxes account was credited since the net timing differences resulted in more income tax expense than income taxes payable. In 1989, however, a decrease in the credit balance occurs since income tax expense is lower than income taxes payable.

Interperiod Income Tax Allocation with Changing Income Tax Rates

The preceding examples assumed a single income tax rate that remained constant over time. In reality, however, both corporate and individual tax rates are graduated and, further, the rates have changed frequently in recent years. The Tax Reform Act of 1986, for example, revised the corporate rate structure from a 5-step graduated structure to a 3-step structure with rates of 15%, 25%, and 34%. The highest rate beginning in 1988 will be 34%, down from 46% in 1986. Because interperiod income tax allocation requires use of specific income tax rates, the existence of graduated rates can lead to complications in deciding which rate to apply to timing differences. The application of graduated tax rates is a computational, rather than conceptual, problem that is greatly simplified by the use of computers. This complexity will not be an issue for larger companies under the Tax Reform Act of 1986, because the graduated rates do not apply to companies with income over \$335,000; all income, including the first \$335,000, is taxed at the maximum rate.

There has been considerable debate within the accounting profession and the business community as to how **changing tax rates** should be treated for purposes of interperiod income tax allocation. Conceptually, there are two basic approaches that can be taken to interperiod income tax allocation, the deferred concept and the liability concept.[6]

The **deferred concept** was adopted by the Accounting Principles Board in 1967 when it issued APB Opinion No. 11. Under this concept, the income tax rate in effect when the timing difference originates is used to determine the amount of deferred income taxes. No immediate adjustment is made to the deferred amounts if rates change, and any gain or loss arising from the rate change is recognized when timing differences reverse. The emphasis under the deferred concept is on the income statement. The deferred charge or credit is looked upon as an amount that will be allocated in future periods as timing differences reverse.

While working on the conceptual framework, the FASB found that its definitions of assets and liabilities did not seem to include the deferred income taxes account. The Board also perceived other conceptual difficulties with the reporting of deferred taxes which, in many cases, are very significant amounts on the financial statements. As noted previously, in 1982, the Board added accounting for income taxes to its agenda, and in late 1986, an exposure draft of a proposed new standard was issued. If the FASB's proposal is adopted, the **liability concept** will become the generally accepted standard for interperiod tax allocation. Under this concept, the emphasis is on the balance sheet and the amount of the liability for taxes that must be paid in the future when timing differences reverse. If the deferred income taxes account has a debit balance, that amount is viewed under the liability concept as a receivable due from the taxing authority. Because the emphasis is on the amount of a specific asset or liability, a change in income tax rates is reflected in the accounting records when the rate change occurs. Adjustments are required based on the expected reversal dates. The application of both the deferred and liability methods when tax rates change is illustrated for Coronado Publishing Inc.

Deferred Concept. Under the deferred concept, rate changes may be accounted for by either the gross change or the net change method. Under the **gross change method**, the tax effects of timing differences originating

---

[6]Homer A. Black, *Accounting Research Study No. 9*, "Interperiod Allocation of Corporate Income Taxes" (New York: American Institute of Certified Public Accountants, 1966), Ch. 2.

in the current period are determined using the current income tax rates, and the tax effects of reversing differences are determined by applying the income tax rate reflected in the accounts at the beginning of the current period. This may be done using either a weighted average rate, or a specified rate based on a FIFO flow assumption. The gain or loss on the rate change is reflected in the income tax expense for the current period. Under the **net change method**, the current income tax rate is applied to the net change in timing differences for the current period, and no gain or loss on rate changes is recognized currently. A gain or loss is recognized under the net change method only when a particular type of timing difference has almost completely reversed and there are no new originating differences of this type. Once one of these alternative methods is adopted by a company, it should be consistently applied.

To illustrate, assume that the tax rates for Coronado changed in 1989 to 34%. Assume further that the 1989 rate reduction from 40% to 34% resulted from tax legislation enacted in 1987. Under the deferred concept, the rate change would not be reflected until 1989 even though it was enacted in 1987. Thus the income tax amounts for Coronado Publishing for 1987 and 1988 would be the same as illustrated on page 871. The computations for 1989, using both the gross change and net change methods, are shown in the following schedule.

Coronado Publishing Inc.
Interperiod Income Tax Allocation with
Changing Tax Rates—Deferred Concept

	1989 Gross Change Method	1989 Net Change Method
Taxable income (from page 871)	$176,000	$176,000
Income tax rate.......................................	.34	.34
Income taxes payable...............................	$ 59,840 cr.	$ 59,840 cr.
Tax effects of timing differences:		
Depreciation—originating $20,000 × .34.............	$ 6,800 cr.	
reversing 25,000 × .40.............	10,000 dr.	
net $ 5,000 × .34		$ 1,700 dr.
Subscription revenue—originating $19,000 × .34	6,460 dr.	
reversing 15,000 × .40	6,000 cr.	
net $ 4,000 × .34		1,360 dr.
Deferred income taxes	$ 3,660 dr.	$ 3,060 dr.
Income tax expense (balancing amount)...............	$ 56,180 dr.	$ 56,780 dr.

As illustrated, under the gross change method, the timing differences that reverse are removed from the deferred income taxes account at the tax rate in effect when the items originated, while the current tax rate is used for reversal under the net method. Even though the reversing depreciation timing differences in 1989 were greater than the originating depreciation timing differences, there was still a large deferred credit balance for depreciation from 1987 and 1988 and thus no gain from the reduction in tax rates would be recognized in 1989 under the net method.

The gross change method is conceptually superior to the net method because of its separate recognition of originating and reversing timing differences. However, the net change method is most commonly followed in practice because of its simplicity.

Liability Concept. Under the liability concept, the tax rate to be used to compute deferred income taxes is the **rate expected to be in effect** when the timing differences reverse. Thus, when tax legislation provides for rate changes at a future date, an estimate of when timing differences will reverse must be made. Assume in the Coronado example that the 1989 tax rate reduction from 40% to 34% resulted from tax legislation enacted in 1987. Further, assume that the expected reversals of 1987 and 1988 originating timing differences are as follows:

Timing Differences			
Originating		Reversing	
Year	Amount	Year	Amount
Depreciation:			
1987	$25,000	1988	$ 5,000
		1989 and beyond	$20,000
1988	$40,000	1989 and beyond	$40,000
Subscription Revenue:			
1987	$15,000	1988	$12,000
		1989 and beyond	$ 3,000
1988	$19,000	1989 and beyond	$19,000

Using these assumptions, deferred taxes in 1987 under the liability concept would be computed as follows:

Depreciation:	$ 5,000	×	.40	=	$2,000 cr.
	$20,000	×	.34	=	6,800 cr.
Subscription revenue:	$12,000	×	.40	=	4,800 dr.
	$ 3,000	×	.34	=	1,020 dr.
Net deferred income taxes credit					$2,980 cr.

The $2,980 credit balance at the end of 1987 under the liability concept is $1,020 less than the $4,000 credit balance under the deferred concept as shown on page 871. Thus, the legislated change in rates is immediately reflected in the deferred accounts under the liability concept. In 1988, all originating timing differences will reverse in 1989 or beyond. Unless additional tax rate changes have been legislated, the 1989 tax rate of 34% will be used to compute deferred income taxes for 1988 as follows:

Depreciation timing differences not reversed by end of 1988:

From 1987	$20,000	
From 1988	40,000	
	$60,000 × .34................	$20,400 cr.

Subscription revenue timing differences not reversed by end of 1988:

From 1987	$ 3,000	
From 1988	19,000	
	$22,000 × .34................	7,480 dr.
Net deferred income taxes balance at end of 1988..................		$12,920 cr.
Less deferred income taxes balance at end of 1987.................		2,980 cr.
Increase in deferred income taxes—1988		$ 9,940 cr.

Because the 1988 income taxes payable would be the same as computed on page 871, or $40,200, the amount charged to income tax expense for 1988 would be $50,140 ($40,200 + $9,940) as opposed to $51,000 under the deferred concept. The $860 difference represents the tax savings to be realized in 1988 from the future reduction in tax rates. Each subsequent year's computation of income tax expense and the change in deferred income taxes would be made in the same way, i.e., calculate the liability for future taxes at the income tax rates expected to be in effect when reversals occur and adjust the deferred income taxes account to the computed balance.

In the preceding example, the rate change was enacted in the first year of the company's operations. Thus, there was no deferred income tax balance from prior years. Under the liability concept, any existing balances must be adjusted to reflect enacted rate changes. To illustrate, assume that Toliver Corporation reported a credit balance in Deferred Income Taxes of $80,000 as of December 31, 1987. This balance reflected a tax rate of 40% applied to net timing differences of $200,000. Assume further that in 1988, a rate change was enacted, reducing the corporate tax rate from 40% to 36%, effective for 1988 and subsequent years. Under the liability concept, the existing balance in Deferred Income Taxes would be adjusted immediately to reflect the enacted rate change. The entry to record the adjustment would be as follows:

Deferred Income Taxes...	8,000	
Income Tax Expense...		8,000

In effect, this entry recognizes a gain of $8,000 from the 4% reduction in the tax rate ($200,000 × .04 = $8,000). The gain is reflected as a reduction of the income tax expense to be reported for 1988.

Classification and Reporting of Deferred Income Taxes. Throughout the discussion of interperiod income tax allocation, the tax effects of timing differences were netted and recorded in a single deferred taxes account. For reporting purposes, however, netting is permitted only for similarly classified items, i.e., a net amount is reported for current deferred taxes and a net amount is reported for noncurrent deferred taxes. The classification of current and noncurrent amounts is related to the concept adopted.

Under the deferred concept, timing differences are classified as current or noncurrent differences according to the accounts to which they relate. Thus, since depreciation timing differences relate to plant assets, deferred income taxes relating to depreciation are classified as noncurrent. On the other hand, timing differences arising from installment receivables that are classified as current assets are classified as current. Timing differences that are not related to a specific asset or liability account are classified according to their expected reversal dates. Thus, differences expected to reverse within one year are classified as current; otherwise, they are classified as noncurrent. As discussed previously, if the net current or net noncurrent amount of deferred taxes is a debit, that amount is reported with the assets on the balance sheet. A credit balance is reported with the liabilities.

Under the liability concept, all timing differences are classified according to their expected reversal dates. This results from the underlying assumption that deferred income tax balances represent specific assets (receivables) or liabilities (taxes payable in the future).

As long as the deferred income taxes account has a credit balance, it is reported as a liability that must be paid in the future. However, if the net balance is a debit, it can be reported as an asset under the liability concept only if there is future benefit to be realized from the asset. Benefit is realized by offsetting the asset against future income tax liabilities. If a company does not earn income in future periods, any benefit is limited to the amount of loss carryback permitted under the income tax laws. The FASB has proposed that any debit balance be reported as an asset only to the extent it can be recovered through the net operating loss carryback provision. This avoids the situation of reporting an asset that depends on future income for its realization. This differs from the deferred concept, under which debit balances in deferred income taxes are reported as assets in the same manner as credit balances are reported as liabilities.

Evaluation of Deferred and Liability Concepts. Although the principal difference between the deferred and liability concepts relates to tax rate changes, the liability concept is more consistent with the conceptual framework developed by the FASB. In the summary to its exposure draft on income taxes, the FASB recognized that APB Opinion No. 11 has been criticized "(a) for the complexity of mechanical calculations based on ambiguous and inconsistent requirements and (b) for producing balance sheet amounts that can be described only in terms of the product of a mechanical process."[7] The Board concludes that the requirements of the proposed statement "(a) are understandable and internally consistent and (b) produce more relevant and useful information than present accounting requirements." The authors agree with this position, and feel that the proposed standard addresses many of the troublesome issues in accounting for income taxes. However, the Board did not address the need to discount the future deferred tax liability to take into consideration the impact of time on the obligation. The authors believe this is a serious weakness in accounting for income taxes, and that noncurrent deferred income tax balances, like other long-term liabilities, should be reported on the balance sheet at their present values.[8]

Partial vs. Comprehensive Income Tax Allocation

Some accountants have argued that only certain types of timing differences should give rise to deferred income taxes. Many timing differences are recurring in nature; that is, as reversals take place, new originating differences occur. This is true, for example, for the depreciation and subscription revenue timing differences included in the previous examples. As long as a company is growing and its plant assets and subscription revenues are increasing, the originating differences will exceed the reversing differences, and the deferred income tax balance will continue to increase. Since, in total, the deferred income tax liability will never have to be paid, so the argument goes, only a **partial allocation** for nonrecurring timing differences is necessary.

Although this argument was used prior to 1967 by many companies to justify ignoring interperiod income tax allocation, the APB rejected it in Opinion No. 11.[9] The Board reasoned that although the balance of a timing difference may increase each year, the individual timing differences do reverse in time, and therefore a **comprehensive allocation** of all timing differences should be followed. A few exceptions to this general rule were identified in APB Opinion No. 23 for specific types of timing differences.[10] They included undistributed profits from foreign subsidiaries and life insurance special reserves. The FASB reconsidered these exceptions, and,

---

[7]*Exposure Draft*, "Accounting for Income Taxes," summary.

[8]For a discussion of arguments for and against discounting, see Homer A. Black, *Accounting Research Study No. 9*, "Interperiod Allocation of Corporate Income Taxes," pp. 82–84.

[9]*Opinions of the Accounting Principles Board, No. 11*, par. 34.

[10]*Opinions of the Accounting Principles Board, No. 23*, "Accounting for Income Taxes — Special Areas" (New York: American Institute of Certified Public Accountants, 1972), par. 12.

in its 1986 exposure draft, recommended that the exceptions be terminated, and that comprehensive income tax allocation be followed for all temporary differences.

ACCOUNTING FOR NET OPERATING LOSSES (NOL's)

Since income tax is based on the amount of income earned, no tax is payable if a company experiences an operating loss. As an incentive to those businesses that experience alternate periods of income and losses, the income tax regulations provide a way to ease the risk of loss years. This is done through a carryback and carryforward provision that permits a company to apply a net operating loss occurring in one year against income of other years. The number of years the loss can be carried backward and forward has varied over time. The tax code currently provides for a three-year carryback and a fifteen-year carryforward for most operating losses.

Net Operating Loss Carryback

A company has a choice for any given year's net operating loss as to whether or not it desires to use the carryback provision. It may choose only to go forward. If it chooses to go backward, a company experiencing an operating loss for the current year first applies the loss to the income of the third previous year and an income tax refund claim is filed. If the income in the third previous year is not sufficient to use all the operating loss, the remainder is carried back two years; then one year. Net operating loss carrybacks result in an entry establishing a receivable for the refund claim and reducing the operating loss for the current year reflecting the tax savings arising from recovery of the prior years' income taxes.

To illustrate, assume that the Prairie Company had the following pattern of income and losses for the years 1985–1988. For simplicity, complicating factors, such as capital gains, investment credit, and timing differences are not included as part of this example.

Year	Income (Loss)	Income Tax at 40%
1985	$15,000	$6,000
1986	10,000	4,000
1987	14,000	5,600
1988	(29,000)	0

The $29,000 net operating loss would be carried back to 1985 first, then to 1986, and finally, $4,000 to 1987. The income tax rate for these former years was 40%. Therefore, an income tax refund claim of $11,600 would be filed for the 3 years ($29,000 × .40). The entry to record the income tax receivable would be as follows:

```
Income Tax Refund Receivable ....................................  11,600
    Refund of Income Tax from Net Operating Loss Carryback .........          11,600
    Refund from applying net operating loss carryback.
```

The refund will be reflected on the income statement as a reduction of the operating loss as follows:

```
Net operating loss before refundable income tax ...........................  $29,000
Refund of prior years' income tax arising from carryback of operating loss......   11,600
Net loss ....................................................................  $17,400
```

The preceding example assumed there were no deferred tax credits or charges involved. Frequently a company has timing differences, and these are affected by the carryback of an operating loss. The amount of the carryback for financial reporting purposes should be based on pretax financial income rather than on the taxable income, and the difference between the amounts actually refundable and the amount computed on pretax financial income should be added or deducted from any deferred income taxes amount on the balance sheet.

To illustrate this interaction, assume that the following history relates to the Carter Corporation.

Year	Pretax Financial Income	Taxable Income	Income Tax Expense Current	Income Tax Expense Deferred	Cumulative Deferred Taxes Credit
1986	$15,000	$ 5,000	$2,000	$4,000	$ 4,000
1987	15,000	5,000	2,000	4,000	8,000
1988	15,000	5,000	2,000	4,000	12,000
1989	(35,000)	(45,000)	(6,000)	(8,000)	4,000

For each of the first 3 years, the pretax financial income exceeded the taxable income by $10,000 due to timing differences, and the deferred income taxes credit at a 40% tax rate was $4,000 each year. In year 4, or 1989, Carter Corporation had a reported operating loss for book purposes of $35,000 and a loss for tax purposes of $45,000. Again, the difference in 1989 between the operating losses was caused by timing differences. The taxable operating loss carryback of $45,000 exceeded the sum of the taxable income for the preceding 3 years, therefore all $6,000 paid is recoverable. The accounting operating loss of $35,000 would be applied in full to the years 1986 and 1987, and the remaining $5,000 to 1988. Based on financial income, the operating loss carryback resulted in a computed recovery of $14,000 ($35,000 × .40). The $8,000 difference between the actual refund of $6,000 and the computed recovery of $14,000, based on financial income, reduces the amount of deferred taxes credit. The entry to record the carryback would be as follows:

```
Income Tax Refund Receivable ...................................   6,000
Deferred Income Taxes...........................................   8,000
   Adjustment to Net Income from Application of Operating Loss
   Carryback ..................................................              14,000
```

Operating Loss Carryforward

As indicated previously, any unused operating loss may be applied against net income earned over the future fifteen years. In the example on page 879, the Prairie Company had $10,000 of income left against which operating losses could be applied. Assume that in 1989, another operating loss of $40,000 was incurred. After applying $10,000 to the 1987 income, $30,000 is left to carry forward. Because the ability to earn income in the future is generally not assured, the Accounting Principles Board recommended that carryforward of operating losses be reflected in the accounts only when future earnings are assured beyond reasonable doubt. This will exist only if both of the following conditions exist, "(a) the loss results from an identifiable, isolated, and nonrecurring cause and the company either has been continuously profitable over a long period or has suffered occasional losses that were more than offset by taxable income in subsequent years, and (b) future taxable income is virtually certain to be large enough to offset the loss carry*forward* and will occur soon enough to provide realization during the carry*forward* period."[11] The Securities and Exchange Commission has given further guidelines to the virtual certainty test in its Staff Accounting Bulletin No. 8. Virtual certainty requires meeting the following conditions:

1. The company has a strong earnings history.
2. The loss was not caused by a general economic or industry decline.
3. The company has reasonable alternative tax strategies available.
4. A forecast based on reasonable assumptions indicates more than enough future income to offset the carryforward.[12]

When these requirements are met, the carryforward may be recognized in the loss period in a similar manner as was done for loss carrybacks.

When this assurance of future earnings does not exist, no entry is made in the loss period. When the carryforward benefit can be applied against subsequent income, the income tax benefit should be reported as an

[11] *Opinions of the Accounting Principles Board, No. 11,* par. 47.

[12] Securities and Exchange Commission, *Staff Accounting Bulletin No. 8,* "Corrections or Changes to Bulletin No. 1 — New Interpretations" (Washington, D.C.: U.S. Government Printing Office, 1976).

extraordinary gain in the year of realization.[13] The FASB has proposed that the virtual certainty test be eliminated, and under no conditions should an asset be reported for unused operating loss carryforwards. The Board has also proposed that the income tax benefit of an operating loss carryforward be reported as an ordinary adjustment to income tax expense, rather than an extraordinary item.

Assume a company had used up its income in carryback years, but had a $40,000 carryforward in the current year. In the subsequent year, income before taxes is $50,000, and income tax without the carryforward would have been $20,000 or 40% of $50,000. The carryforward benefit would reduce the income tax liability by $16,000, or 40% of $40,000. The following entries would be required to record the tax provision:

```
Income Tax Expense...........................................  20,000
    Income Taxes Payable .....................................            20,000
        Income tax liability assuming no carryforward.
Income Taxes Payable .........................................  16,000
    Gain from Use of Operating Loss Carryforward....................            16,000
        Application of carryforward provision against current year's income
        tax.
```

INVESTMENT TAX CREDIT

In order to encourage investment in productive assets, the Revenue Act of 1962 permitted taxpayers to reduce their federal income tax by an **investment tax credit (ITC)** equal to a specified percentage of the cost of certain depreciable assets acquired after December 31, 1961. Since this provision was first included in the tax code, there have been many modifications of the investment tax credit, including its temporary suspension. Whenever the economy has needed a stimulus, however, Congress has returned to the ITC as a way of encouraging business to invest in new productive assets and thus increase the gross national product. As part of the Tax Reform Act of 1986, Congress repealed the investment tax credit for property placed in service after December 31, 1985.

Although the investment tax credit was suspended by the 1986 Act, history suggests that it could be reinstated at any future time. With this in mind, a brief discussion of the accounting implications of the credit is warranted.

Accounting for the Investment Tax Credit

Essentially, there are two methods that can be used to record the tax reduction resulting from the ITC: (1) the credit can be used to reduce the

---

[13] *Opinions of the Accounting Principles Board, No. 11.*

income tax expense for the year in which it is received, commonly referred to as the **flow-through method**, or (2) the credit can be deferred and reflected as a reduction of tax expense over the period during which the asset is depreciated, commonly referred to as the **deferred method**.

Flow-Through Method. Using the flow-through method, the investment tax credit is treated as a reduction of income tax expense in the year the credit is allowed. To illustrate, assume that a business acquired machinery in 1987 for $100,000, and the applicable investment tax credit rate was 10%. The federal income tax for 1987 is $75,000 reduced by an investment tax credit of $10,000 (10% of $100,000). The entry to record the federal income tax for 1987 would be:

```
Income Tax Expense...........................................  65,000
   Income Taxes Payable ......................................           65,000
      Recognition of income tax of $75,000 less investment tax credit
      of $10,000.
```

Deferred Method. Under the deferred method of accounting for the investment tax credit, the credit is viewed as a reduction of income tax expense over the life of the asset rather than in the year the credit is applied to the tax liability. Using the information in the previous example, the entry to record income tax in 1987 under the deferred method would be:

```
Income Tax Expense...........................................  75,000
   Deferred Investment Tax Credit ...............................           10,000
   Income Taxes Payable ......................................           65,000
```

The following entry would be made each year to amortize the investment tax credit over the 5-year life of the asset.

```
Deferred Investment Tax Credit ...................................  2,000
   Income Tax Expense............................................           2,000
```

Evaluation of Accounting Treatment of Investment Tax Credit

The Accounting Principles Board favored the deferred method and approved it in Opinion No. 2. Lack of support for this view among many prominent accountants led to the issuance in 1964 of Opinion No. 4 in which the Board accepted both methods, although still stating a preference for the deferred method. In 1968, a further attempt was made by the Accounting Principles Board to restore the deferred method as a single uniform method. Again, differences of opinion resulted in failure to adopt the original conclusions. In 1971, the Board once again made serious effort to restore the deferred method. However, they had to postpone such effort as a result of congressional action permitting the taxpayer to choose the method to be used in recognizing the benefit arising from the credit.

Good theoretical arguments can be presented for either of the methods. Those who advocate using the deferred method argue that the cost of the asset is effectively reduced by the investment credit, and the tax benefit should be spread over the acquired asset's useful life. Those who advocate using the flow-through method argue that the tax credit is in reality a tax reduction in the current period. They argue that tax regulations establish the tax liability each year, and that amount is the proper expense to match against current revenues. This latter treatment affects current income more and is favored by political leaders when the investment tax credit is being used to stimulate a sluggish economy.

It is unfortunate that this issue has become such a political item. It is an example of an area where there seems to be no justification for having two methods. It is difficult to see how different economic circumstances among companies would justify dual treatment. If the investment tax credit is reinstated by Congress, the authors believe that a uniform accounting method for its treatment should be adopted by the accounting profession.

DISCLOSURE OF INCOME TAXES

Income tax expense as reported on the income statement is separated between ordinary operations and unusual and nonrecurring items as required by intraperiod income tax allocation. Deferred income taxes are reported on the balance sheet as discussed earlier in the chapter. A note to the financial statements should identify (1) the taxes currently payable, (2) the tax effects of timing differences, and (3) the tax effect of any operating losses.[14] In addition, the SEC requires a reconciliation of the differences between the statutory income tax rate and the effective rate actually paid by the company. Frequently, there is a considerable difference between the two because of such items as permanent differences, investment credit, and operating loss carrybacks and carryforwards.

An illustration of the information necessary for adequate disclosure of income taxes is presented on pages 885 and 886 for General Electric Company. Another example of disclosure for income taxes is included in Note Thirteen to the General Mills statements reproduced in Appendix A.

CONCLUDING COMMENTS

Accounting for income taxes has been, and will continue to be, a complex financial accounting issue. Users of financial statements are

---

[14] *Opinions of the Accounting Principles Board No. 11,* par. 60.

GENERAL ELECTRIC COMPANY

Note 8 (in part)

Provision for income taxes (In millions)	1985	1984	1983
U.S. federal income taxes:			
Estimated amount payable	$ 842	$1,051	$657
Effect of timing differences	139	(129)	(5)
Investment credit deferred—net	35	41	5
	1,016	963	657
Foreign income taxes:			
Estimated amount payable	135	143	263
Effect of timing differences	(4)	(85)	10
	131	58	273
Other (principally state and local income taxes)	45	44	45
	$1,192	$1,065	$975

● Some items are reported in financial statements in different years than they are included in tax returns. Deferred taxes are provided on these timing differences as summarized below.

Effect of timing differences on U.S. federal income taxes

Increase (decrease) in provision for income taxes (In millions)	1985	1984	1983
Tax over book depreciation	$124	$ 168	$54
Margin on installment sales	48	28	(8)
Provision for warranties	23	24	(5)
Provision for pensions	(171)	(47)	12
Other—net	115	(302)	(58)
	$139	$(129)	$ (5)

● Other—net reflects a number of individual timing differences, including those related to various portions of transactions involving business dispositions, restructuring expense provisions and reductions of intangibles.
● Investment tax credit amounted to $111 million in 1985, compared with $110 million in 1984 and $72 million in 1983. In 1985, $76 million was included in net earnings, compared with

$69 million in 1984 and $67 million in 1983. At the end of 1985, the amount deferred which will be included in net earnings in future years was $414 million.

Reconciliation from statutory to effective income tax rates	1985	1984	1983
U.S. federal statutory rate	46.0%	46.0%	46.0%
Reduction in taxes resulting from:			
Varying tax rates of consolidated affiliates (including DISC and FSC)	(3.6)	(3.8)	(5.9)
Inclusion of GEFS earnings in before-tax income on an after-tax basis	(5.3)	(4.5)	(4.1)
Investment credit	(2.1)	(2.1)	(2.2)
Unusual items (varying tax rates)	(0.5)	(2.3)	(0.6)
Income tax at capital gains rate	(0.2)	(0.3)	(0.6)
Other—net	(0.6)	(1.3)	(0.5)
Effective tax rate	33.7%	31.7%	32.1%

frequently confused by such items as deferred income tax accounts and investment tax credits. This chapter has only introduced some of these complex areas. Reference to the underlying accounting standards is required to deal with the many specialized issues that surround income taxes. A basic cause of the difficulty has been conceptual. The proposed statement by the FASB addresses some of these conceptual questions, and its adoption would bring increased understanding of deferred income taxes within the financial community. However, as the income tax laws change, the pervasive impact of income taxes on the financial statements will continue to require careful analysis of the statements by preparers and users.

QUESTIONS

1. Distinguish between intraperiod and interperiod income tax allocation.
2. Accounting methods used by a company to determine income for reporting purposes frequently differ from those used to determine taxable income. What is the justification for these differences?

3. Distinguish between a timing difference and a permanent difference.
4. In accounting for timing differences between pretax financial and taxable income, what entries are made when (a) pretax financial income is less than taxable income, and (b) pretax financial income is more than taxable income? (c) What timing differences are most commonly found?
5. Under what circumstances will a Deferred Income Taxes credit balance be reduced to zero? Why do most companies report an increasing balance in this account?
6. Why was the deferred method of income tax allocation adopted by the Accounting Principles Board?
7. The net change method of accounting for interperiod tax allocation under the deferred concept is more commonly used than the gross change method. Since both were recognized as acceptable methods by the Accounting Principles Board, why has this preference developed?
8. How would the balance sheet account for deferred income taxes differ if a company used the liability concept of interperiod income tax allocation as opposed to the deferred concept?
9. Why has the FASB recommended changing the recording and reporting of deferred income taxes from the deferred concept to the liability concept?
10. What is the principal argument used by those favoring partial income tax allocation?
11. In applying the net operating loss carryback and carryforward provisions, what order of application must be followed?
12. Two methods of accounting for investment tax credits are acceptable. Identify and briefly describe the two methods.
13. How should deferred income taxes be classified and reported on the balance sheet?
14. What financial statement disclosures are required concerning income taxes?

DISCUSSION CASES

CASE 20–1   (What are deferred income taxes?)

Hurst Inc. is a new corporation that has just completed a highly successful first year of operation. Hurst is a privately held corporation, but its president, Bruce Hurst, has indicated that if the company continues to do as well for the next 4 or 5 years, it will go public. By all indications, the company should continue to be highly profitable on both a short-term and long-term basis.

The controller of the new company, Lori James, plans on using the ACRS method of depreciating Hurst's assets and using the installment sales method of recognizing income for tax purposes. For financial statement presentation, straight-line depreciation will be used and all sales will be fully recognized in the year of sale. There are no other differences between book and taxable income.

Hurst has hired your firm to prepare its financial statements. You are now preparing the income statement. The controller wants to show, as "income tax expense," the amount of the tax liability actually due. "After all," James reasons, "that's the amount we'll actually pay, and in light of our plans for continued expansion, it's highly unlikely that the timing differences will ever reverse."

Draft a memo to the controller outlining your reaction to the plan. Give reasons in support of your decision.

CASE 20–2 (Should health of the economy govern GAAP?)

Perhaps no issue has created more controversy and discussion in the accounting profession, business, and government than the investment tax credit. The government's involvement has been an intriguing one. The purpose of the investment tax credit has been to stimulate investment in new business property and thus promote a steady growth in the Gross National Product and avoid severe recession or depression. In order to have the most significant impact possible on a company's income, legislative officials who enacted the investment tax credit legislation indicated a preference for the flow-through method of accounting. Many people in the business community agree with this approach because of its favorable impact on reported income. Accounting theorists, on the other hand, argue that the deferred method of accounting for the credit is preferable because it reflects more clearly the economic reality of the credit. Evaluate these two positions. What role, if any, should public policy and the impact of accounting principles on the economy have upon the establishment of GAAP?

CASE 20–3   (How do deferred taxes work?)

The Primrose Company appropriately uses the deferred method for interperiod income tax allocation.

Primrose reports depreciation expense for certain machinery purchased this year using the accelerated cost recovery system (ACRS) for income tax purposes and the straight-line basis for accounting purposes. The tax deduction is the larger amount this year.

Primrose received rent revenues in advance this year. These revenues are included in this year's taxable income. However, for accounting purposes, these revenues are reported as unearned revenues, a current liability.

(1) What is the theoretical basis for deferred income taxes under the deferred concept?
(2) How would Primrose determine and account for the income tax effect for the depreciation and rent? Why?
(3) How should Primrose classify the income tax effect of the depreciation and rent on its balance sheet and income statement? Why?
(4) How would your answers to these questions differ under the liability concept? (AICPA adapted)

EXERCISES

EXERCISE 20–1   (Identification of permanent and timing differences)

Indicate whether each of the following items is a timing difference or a permanent difference. For each timing difference, indicate whether it is a debit or a credit to Deferred Income Taxes.

(a) Tax depreciation in excess of book depreciation, $150,000.
(b) Excess of income on installment sales over income reportable for tax purposes, $130,000.
(c) Premium payment for insurance policy on life of president, $35,000.
(d) Earnings of foreign subsidiary received and taxed in the current year but recorded on the books in a previous year, $150,000.
(e) Amortization of goodwill, $60,000.
(f) Rent collected in advance of period earned, $75,000.
(g) Actual expense for warranty repairs in excess of warranty provision for year, $50,000.
(h) Interest revenue received on municipal bonds, $30,000.

EXERCISE 20–2   (Interperiod income tax allocation)

Using the information given in Exercise 1, and assuming pretax financial income of $2,060,000 and an income tax rate of 40%, calculate taxable income and give the entry to record income tax for the year. Your entry may "net" the various deferred income tax accounts into one account.

EXERCISE 20–3   (Interperiod income tax allocation)

Energizer Manufacturing Corporation reports taxable income of $829,000 on its income tax return for the year ended December 31, 1987. Timing differences between pretax financial income and taxable income for the year are:

Book depreciation in excess of tax depreciation.....................	$ 80,000
Accrual for product liability claims in excess of actual claims	125,000
Reported installment sales income in excess of taxable installment sales income...	265,000

Assuming an income tax rate of 40%, compute the income tax expense, deferred income tax, and income tax payable balances to be recorded on Energizer's books. Give the necessary journal entry to record these amounts. Use one deferred income tax account.

EXERCISE 20–4   (Interperiod income tax allocation)

The Parker Co. shows pretax financial income and taxable income for 1987 and 1988 as follows:

	Pretax Financial Income	Taxable Income
1987.................................	$140,600	$212,000
1988.................................	$257,000	240,200

The differences arose because the company, organized on April 1, 1987, wrote off against revenue of that year organization costs totaling $84,000. For federal income tax purposes, however, the organization costs can be written off ratably over a period of not less than 60 months. For income tax purposes, then, the company deducted $\frac{9}{60}$ of the costs in 1987 and $\frac{12}{60}$ of the costs in 1988. Income tax is to be calculated at 40% of taxable income.

Give the entries that would be made on the books of the company at the end of 1987 and 1988 to recognize the income tax liability and to provide for a proper allocation of income tax in view of the differences in financial and income tax reporting.

EXERCISE 20–5 (Interperiod income tax allocation)

The McCall Exploration Company reported pretax financial income of $596,500 for the calendar year 1987. Included in the "Other income" section of the income statement was $86,000 of interest revenue from municipal bonds held by the company. The income statement also included depreciation expense of $610,000 for a machine that cost $4,000,000. The income tax return reported $800,000 as ACRS depreciation on the machine.

Prepare the journal entry necessary to record income tax for the year, assuming an income tax rate of 40%.

EXERCISE 20–6 (Interperiod income tax allocation—changing rates)

The following historical information for the Golightly Corporation shows timing differences for the past 3 years along with their effects on deferred income taxes.

Year	Originating Timing Differences— Depreciation	Tax Rate	Deferred Income Taxes (Credit)
1985	$ 40,000	45%	$18,000
1986	70,000	40%	28,000
1987	80,000	37%	29,600
	$190,000		$75,600

Pretax financial income for 1988 was $714,000. Timing differences for 1988 were as follows:

Originating timing difference—tax depreciation in excess
  of book depreciation $160,000
Reversing timing difference—book depreciation in excess
  of tax depreciation .... $ 70,000

The income tax rate for 1988 and beyond is expected to be 34%.
  (1) Determine the change in deferred income taxes for 1988 under the following 3 methods:
    (a) The gross change method, FIFO flow
    (b) The gross change method, average flow
    (c) The net change method
  (2) Assume the 1988 tax rate change was legislated in 1988 and that the liability concept of interperiod tax allocation is followed. Prepare the adjusting entry necessary to reflect the change in rates.

EXERCISE 20–7 (Interperiod income tax allocation—changing rates)

The books of Cosby Company for the year ended December 31, 1987, showed a pretax financial income of $260,000. In computing the year's taxable income for federal income tax purposes, the following timing differences were taken into account:

Originating timing differences:
(1) Tax depreciation in excess of book depreciation, $26,000.
(2) Installment sales income recognized in excess of income reported for tax purposes, $6,000.
Reversing timing differences:
(1) Book depreciation in excess of tax depreciation, $16,000.
(2) Installment sales income reportable for tax purposes in excess of income recognized on the books, $10,500.

The income tax rate was reduced on January 1, 1987, from 44% to 36%. Prior to that date it was 44%, which was the rate in effect when the Cosby Company was organized.

Calculate income taxes payable, the change in the deferred income taxes account, and income tax expense, using: (a) the gross change method and (b) the net change method.

EXERCISE 20–8   (Net operating loss carryback)

The following historical financial data are available for the Bradshaw Manufacturing Company.

Year	Income	Tax Rate	Tax Paid
1985	$175,000	46%	$ 80,500
1986	230,000	42%	96,600
1987	310,000	35%	108,500

In 1988, the Bradshaw Company suffered a $750,000 net operating loss due to an economic recession. The company elects to use the carryback provision in the tax law.
(1) Using the information given, calculate the refund due arising from the loss carryback and the amount of the loss available to carryforward to future periods. Assume a 1988 tax rate of 34%. Also, assume that no adjustments need to be made to prior years' net income for purposes of the loss carryback and that there is no guarantee that future periods will be profitable.
(2) Give the entry necessary to record the refund due and the loss reduction.
(3) Using the answer from (1), prepare the bottom portion of the income statement reflecting the effect of the loss carryback on the 1988 statement.

EXERCISE 20–9   (Investment tax credit)

Brossard Electric Company purchased a new machine on January 1, 1986, for $350,000. The machine had a 10-year life and was depreciated by the straight-line method. Assuming a 10% investment tax credit, give the entries to record the recognition of income taxes for the first 2 years under (a) the flow-through method and (b) the deferred method. (Income tax before the credit in 1986 and 1987 was $217,500 and $312,000 respectively.)

EXERCISE 20–10   (Investment tax credit)

The Ferre Corporation purchased a stamping press for $1,360,000 on January 1, 1988. The press had an estimated useful life of 12 years and no salvage value. The corporation uses the straight-line method of depreciation. Assuming an income tax liability for the current year of $476,000 before an eligible investment tax credit of 6%, give the entries to record income tax for 1988 using (a) the flow-through method and (b) the deferred method.

PROBLEMS

PROBLEM 20–1   (Intraperiod income tax allocation)

Art Associates completed its fiscal year on October 31, and prepared annual financial statements. Included in company taxable income was a gain properly classified as extraordinary. Also included in taxable income was a loss from the disposal of the scale models division, a complete business segment. The loss is deductible from ordinary income under applicable tax law. Company records provide the following information.

Amounts for the year ended October 31, 1987	
Reported taxable income	$845,000
Ordinary income tax rates	40%
Extraordinary gain	110,000
Tax rate on extraordinary gain	40%
Loss on segment disposal	121,000

The annual audit disclosed an overstatement of income from the previous year. Art Associates, on the advice of their tax accountant, decided to file an amended tax return for a refund of taxes paid.

Amount of the overstatement	$80,000
Income tax rate on the refund	42%

Instructions:
(1) Prepare a partial income statement for the fiscal year ending on October 31, 1987, beginning with income from continuing operations before income taxes.
(2) How would the overstatement of the prior year's income be reported in the financial statements at October 31, 1987?

PROBLEM 20–2
(Interperiod income tax allocation — no change in rates)

A. J. Johnson & Co. recorded certain revenues on its books in 1985 and 1986 of $15,400 and $16,600 respectively. However, such revenue was not subject to income taxation until 1987. Company records reveal pretax financial income and taxable income for the 3-year period as follows:

	Pretax Financial Income	Taxable Income
1985	$44,200	$28,800
1986	38,200	21,600
1987	21,100	32,400

Assume Johnson's tax rate is 40% in each year.

Instructions: Give the entries that would be made at the end of each year to recognize the income tax liability and to provide for a proper allocation of income tax in view of the differences between pretax financial income and taxable income.

PROBLEM 20–3   (Intraperiod income tax)

The Hughes Enterprise Company paid $360,000 income taxes for the year ended December 31, 1987. $20,000 of these taxes related to an extraordinary gain that was taxed at 25%. Hughes discontinued one of their segments during 1987, and had a tax savings of $50,000 resulting from the loss on disposition of the segment. The loss was treated for tax purposes as an ordinary loss, and was deducted from ordinary income that was taxed at 40%. Included in the $360,000 tax payment was $10,000 resulting from a gain on the sale of equipment. The tax rate on the gain was 25%. All other income items were from normal operations and were taxed at 40%. Hughes had 40,000 shares of common stock outstanding.

Instructions: Prepare the income statement for Hughes Enterprise beginning with "Income from continuing operations before income taxes." Include intraperiod tax allocation procedures as appropriate.

PROBLEM 20–4   (Interperiod income tax allocation)

Killpack Manufacturing began its operations five years ago. A 5-year summary of income is as follows:

	1984	1985	1986	1987	1988
Sales	$1,000,000	$1,040,000	$1,120,000	$1,120,000	$1,200,000
Cost of goods sold	600,000	624,000	656,000	672,000	720,000
Gross profit on sales	$ 400,000	$ 416,000	$ 464,000	$ 448,000	$ 480,000
Operating expenses	160,000	168,000	184,000	176,000	192,000
Income before taxes	$ 240,000	$ 248,000	$ 280,000	$ 272,000	$ 288,000

Killpack's cost of goods sold includes depreciation on buildings and equipment calculated using the straight-line method. For tax purposes, Killpack elected to use the accelerated depreciation method allowed by the Internal Revenue Service. A schedule showing comparisons between book depreciation charges and income tax allowances is as follows:

	1984	1985	1986	1987	1988
Depreciation per books	132,000	136,000	136,000	140,000	140,000
Accelerated depreciation per tax return	216,000	180,800	144,000	124,000	100,000

All company revenue is taxable income and all of the expenses are deductible for income tax purposes. Income tax rates in each year were 40%.

Instructions:

(1) Prepare comparative income statements for Killpack Manufacturing for the 5-year period assuming the use of interperiod income tax allocation procedures.

(2) Prepare comparative income statements for Killpack Manufacturing for the 5-year period assuming the interperiod income tax allocation procedures were not used and charges for income tax were recognized at the amounts actually becoming payable each year.

(3) Give the entries that would be made by the company for each year during the 5-year period to record the accrual of income taxes.

PROBLEM 20–5 (Interperiod income tax allocation with permanent and timing differences)

Tristar Corporation reported taxable income of $1,996,000 for the year ended December 31, 1987. The controller is unfamiliar with the required treatment of timing and permanent differences in reconciling taxable income to financial income, and has contacted your firm for advice. You are given company records that list the following differences:

Book depreciation in excess of tax depreciation	$275,000
Proceeds from life insurance policy upon death of officer	125,000
Interest revenue on municipal bonds	98,000

Instructions:

(1) Compute pretax financial income.

(2) Given an income tax rate of 40%, prepare the journal entry to record income taxes for the year.

(3) Prepare a partial income statement beginning with "income from continuing operations before income taxes."

PROBLEM 20–6 (Journal entries—interperiod income tax allocation)

Dynametric Manufacturing prepared the following reconciliation between taxable income and pretax financial income for 1987:

Income per tax return	$6,500,000
Add excess depreciation deducted on tax return but not allowed for book purposes	450,500
	$6,950,500
Deduct: Extraordinary gain on early extinguishment of debt	(199,000)
Estimated future warranty expenses not allowable for tax purposes until expenses are actually incurred...........	(145,000)
Advance rent revenue taxable in period of receipt	(66,800)
Book income before taxes and extraordinary items	$6,539,700

Dynametric's accountants made a prior period adjustment of $300,000 for the correction of an error. This amount was debited directly to Retained Earnings. An income tax refund claim was filed to reflect this adjustment. Ordinary income rates apply to all items.

Instructions:

(1) Given an income tax rate of 40%, prepare the journal entry to record the income tax liability at December 31, 1987.

(2) Prepare a partial income statement beginning with "income from continuing operations before income taxes."

PROBLEM 20–7 (Interperiod income tax allocation — changing rates)

You have been asked by Nizar Corp. to review the company's books and indicate what effect income tax allocation procedures will have on the financial statements. The following information regarding financial and taxable income is made available to you.

	1986	1987	1988
Pretax financial income	$180,000	$270,000	$360,000
Nondeductible fine		60,000	
Net warranty expenses not deductible on tax return until paid....................	40,000	42,000	20,000
Net excess of ACRS depreciation over straight-line depreciation	36,000	21,000	(35,000)
Net excess of installment sales profit reported in financial income..............	46,000	54,000	48,000

Instructions:
(1) Assume tax rates are 40% on taxable income for all years. Prepare a schedule similar to that on page 871 showing income tax expense, income taxes payable, and deferred income taxes.
(2) Assume the tax rate changed in 1988 to 34%. Prepare the journal entry to record the tax liability for 1988 under the deferred concept using the net change method.
(3) Assume the rate change in (2) was enacted in 1988. Prepare the entry to adjust the balance in deferred income taxes at January 1, 1988, under the liability concept.

PROBLEM 20–8 (Interperiod income tax allocation — changing rates)

The financial records of Shimizu Manufacturing Company disclosed the following historical information:

Year	Warranty Expense Accrual in Excess of Actual Expenditures	Tax Depreciation in Excess of Book Depreciation	Tax Rate	Deferred Taxes — Credit
1985	$ 80,000	$200,000	42%	$ 50,400
1986	71,500	175,000	38%	39,330
1987	36,000	425,000	36%	140,040
	$187,500	$800,000		$229,770

In 1988, pretax financial income was $2,265,100. The timing differences for 1988 were as follows:

Originating timing differences:
    Tax depreciation in excess of book depreciation ... $360,000
    Warranty expense accrued 92,000
Reversing timing differences:
    Book depreciation in excess of tax depreciation.... $195,000
    Actual warranty expense 105,000

The income tax rate for 1988 and beyond is expected to be 34%.

Instructions:

(1) Determine the change in deferred income taxes for 1988 under the following three methods:
    (a) Gross change method, FIFO flow
    (b) Gross change method, average flow
    (c) Net change method
(2) Assume the 1988 tax rate change was legislated in 1988 and that the liability concept is followed. Prepare the adjusting entry necessary to reflect the change in rates.

PROBLEM 20–9   (Operating loss carryback and carryforward)

The following information is taken from the financial statements of Columbia Enterprises:

Year	Taxable and Pretax Financial Income	Income Tax Rate	Income Tax Paid
1983	$24,000	40%	$ 9,600
1984	27,400	40%	10,960
1985	31,500	44%	13,860
1986	21,240	46%	9,770
1987	(86,000)	44%	0

The company elects to use the carryback provisions in the tax law.

Instructions:

(1) Given the information from the financial statements, compute the amount of income tax refund due as a result of the operating loss.
(2) What is the amount, if any, of the operating loss carryforward?
(3) (a) Assume the foregoing information except that the loss in 1987 was $61,000. Calculate the refund due and prepare the journal entry to record the claim for income tax refund.
    (b) Assume that in addition to (a), there was a loss in 1988 of $24,000. How much could be carried back and how much could be carried forward?

PROBLEM 20–10   (Net operating loss carryback and carryforward)

The following financial history shows the income and losses for Steele and Associates for the 10-year period 1978–1987:

Year	Taxable and Pretax Financial Income (Before NOL)	Income Tax Rate	Income Tax Paid
1978	$ 8,800	50%	$ 4,400
1979	12,300	50%	6,150
1980	14,800	44%	6,512
1981	(29,250)	44%	0
1982	7,200	44%	3,168
1983	(21,750)	46%	0
1984	16,600	46%	?
1985	32,000	40%	12,800
1986	(58,700)	40%	0
1987	65,000	40%	?

Assume that no adjustments to taxable income are necessary for purposes of the net operating loss carryback and the company elects to use the carryback provisions of the tax code. (Assume the income tax provisions described in the text are in effect for all years.)

Instructions:
(1) Given the foregoing information, compute the amount of income tax refund for each year as a result of each loss carryback and the amount of the carryforward (if any).
(2) Calculate the amount of income tax paid, showing the benefit of the loss carryforward, for the years 1984 and 1987.
(3) For 1987, give the entry to record the income tax liability.

PROBLEM 20–11   (Operating loss carryback)

Kinateder Company records reveal the following amounts for financial and taxable income for 5 years. Kinateder's effective income tax rate is 40%.

Year	Pretax Financial Income	Taxable Income	Income Taxes Payable	Deferred Income Taxes	Cumulative Deferred Taxes
1984	$228,000	$215,000	$86,000	$ 5,200	$ 5,200
1985	255,000	212,000	84,800	17,200	22,400
1986	175,000	188,000	75,200	(5,200)	17,200
1987	(350,000)	(440,000)			
1988	(232,000)	(260,000)			

Instructions:
(1) Given the foregoing information, compute the amount of income tax refunds available in each loss year for taxes paid in the other profitable years. Assume the operating losses are 100% available to offset taxable and book income.
(2) Prepare the journal entries required at December 31 (year end) in each loss year to record the refund receivable and any necessary adjustment to the deferred income taxes account.

PROBLEM 20–12   (Investment tax credit)

Granite Sand and Gravel purchased a gravel sifting machine from Steelco Fabrications in 1987. Granite also purchased from Steelco the patent on the machine. In conjunction with the acquisition, Granite hired an independent appraiser to assess the fair market values of the machine and the patent at the purchase date. Company records revealed the following information:

Machine and patent purchase price	$ 530,000
Fair market value of the machine	425,000
Fair market value of the patent	125,000
Useful life of the machine	10 years
Useful life of the patent	15 years
Precredit tax liability: 1987	650,800
1988	1,180,200

Assume that an investment tax credit of 10% is allowable in 1987.

Instructions: Give the journal entries to record the acquisition of the machine and the patent, the recognition of income taxes in 1987 and 1988, and any amortization of deferred investment tax credits under both (1) the flow-through method and (2) the deferred method (assume the company records depreciation for a full year in the year of acquisition).

PROBLEM 20–13   (Comprehensive income tax problem)

As the financial advisor for Centon Company, you have been provided the following information regarding the company's 1987 income tax expense for financial statement reporting. Centon Company keeps its books on a calendar-year basis.

(a) The provision for current income taxes (exclusive of investment tax credit) is $800,000 for the year ended December 31, 1987. Centon is required to make estimated tax payments during the year. These payments totaled $620,000 for 1987.

(b) Assume an investment tax credit is allowable in 1987, and Centon Company placed into service during the year plant assets that generated total credits of $225,000. These credits were utilized for income tax reporting in 1987. Company officials adopted the deferred method of accounting for investment tax credits and they desire to continue this practice. Unamortized deferred investment tax credits amounted to the following amounts:

    December 31, 1987................................. $500,000
    December 31, 1986................................. $440,000

(c) Centon depreciates plant assets using the straight-line method for financial reporting purposes and the ACRS method for income tax purposes. The amounts calculated for each are as follows:

    Financial statement depreciation........................ $875,000
    Income tax depreciation $940,000

In addition, commitments for the purchase of plant assets amounted to $300,000 at December 31, 1987. Such plant assets will be subject to an investment credit of 10%.

(d) For financial statement reporting, Centon has accrued estimated losses from product warranty contracts prior to their occurrence. For income tax reporting, no deduction is taken until payments are made. At December 31, 1986, accrued estimated losses of $310,000 were included in the liability section of Centon's balance sheet. Using recent information, Centon now believes that the estimate should be revised to reflect an amount that is 30% higher at December 31, 1987. Payments of $350,000 were made in 1987.

(e) In 1982, Centon acquired another company for cash. Goodwill resulting from this transaction totaled $780,000 and is being amortized over 30 years for financial reporting purposes. The tax laws do not allow any goodwill amortization in calculating taxable income.

(f) Premiums paid on officers' life insurance amounted to $75,000 in 1987. These premiums are not deductible for income tax reporting.

(g) Assume that the United States income tax rate is 46%.

Instructions:
(1) Prepare a schedule in good form that computes the amount of income tax expense to be reported on Centon's 1987 income statement. The schedule should clearly show the following items:
  (a) Investment tax credits recognized in 1987 as a reduction of Centon's 1987 income tax expense.
  (b) Effect of deferred income taxes on 1987 income tax expense.
  Show the supporting computations in good form.
(2) Identify any information in the fact situation which was not used to determine the answer to (1) and explain why this information was not used.

(AICPA adapted)

PROBLEM 20–14   (Disclosure of income taxes)

Before closing the books for the year ended December 31, 1987, Glenn Corporation, a Kansas corporation, prepared the following adjusted trial balance:

Adjusted Trial Balance
December 31, 1987

Cash	$ 550,000	
Accounts receivable, net......................	1,650,000	
Inventory....................................	2,750,000	
Property, plant and equipment.................	13,550,000	
Accumulated depreciation.....................		$ 4,400,000
Cash surrender value on officers' life insurance...	65,000	
Accounts payable and accrued expenses........		1,550,000
Income tax payable		200,000
Deferred income tax..........................		150,000
Notes payable...............................		1,500,000
Common stock		2,500,000
Additional paid-in capital......................		4,375,000
Retained earnings, 1/1/87.....................		3,300,000
Net sales		12,500,000
Cost of sales	7,500,000	
Selling and administrative expenses.............	2,425,000	
Interest expense.............................	245,000	
Gain on sale of long-term investments..........		260,000
Income tax expense..........................	600,000	
Loss on litigation settlement...................	450,000	
Loss due to earthquake damage...............	950,000	
	$30,735,000	$30,735,000

Other financial data for the year ended December 31, 1987:

Federal income tax

Estimated tax payments	$400,000
Accrued tax expense......................................	200,000
Total charged to income tax expense (estimated)............	$600,000*
Tax rate on all types of taxable income......................	40%

*Does not properly reflect current or deferred income tax expense or intraperiod income tax allocation for income statement purposes.

Timing difference

Depreciation per tax return...............................	$760,000
Depreciation per books..................................	580,000

Permanent difference

Premiums on officers' life insurance........................	$140,000

Capital structure   Shares

Common stock, par value $10 per share, traded on a national exchange:

Number of shares outstanding at 1/1/87	200,000
Number of shares issued on 3/30/87 as a 10% stock dividend	20,000
Number of shares sold for $25 per share on 6/30/87	30,000
Number of shares outstanding at 12/31/87	250,000

Instructions:

(1) Using the multiple-step format, prepare a formal income statement for Glenn for the year ended December 31, 1987. All components of income tax expense should be appropriately shown.

(2) Prepare a schedule to reconcile net income to taxable income reportable on Glenn's tax return for 1987.   (AICPA adapted)

21
Accounting for Leases

A **lease** is a contract specifying the terms under which the owner of property, the **lessor**, transfers the right to use the property to a **lessee**. Leasing is widely used in our economy as a method of obtaining various kinds of assets. Individuals may lease houses, apartments, automobiles, televisions, appliances, furniture, and almost any other consumer good on the market. Business enterprises lease land, buildings, and almost any type of equipment. For example, Farmland Industries in its 1985 financial statements reported leased assets including "railroad cars, automobiles, . . . three fertilizer manufacturing facilities, electronic data processing equipment, and other manufacturing facilities." Indeed, almost any asset that can be acquired through purchase can be obtained through leasing. Of the 600 companies surveyed in the annual AICPA publication, *Accounting Trends and Techniques*, 542 companies, or approximately 90%, reported some form of lease arrangement.[1]

Some leases are simple rental agreements, while others closely resemble a debt-financed purchase of property. A major issue for the accounting profession has been whether this type of lease should be accounted for as a rental agreement in accordance with its legal form, or as a purchase of property that reflects the economic substance of the transaction. To illustrate the issue, assume that Tolbin Co. decides to acquire equipment costing $10,000. The equipment has a useful life of 5 years, with no expected residual value. Tolbin Co. can purchase the equipment by issuing a 5-year, 10%, $10,000 note with principal and interest to be paid in 5 equal installments of $2,368. Alternatively, Tolbin Co. can lease the asset for 5 years, making 5 annual "rental" payments of $2,368. In sub-

---

[1] *Accounting Trends and Techniques, 1985* (New York: American Institute of Certified Public Accountants, 1985), p. 188.

stance, the lease is equivalent to purchasing the asset, the only difference being the legal form of the transaction. However, if the lease is accounted for as a simple rental agreement, Tolbin Co. will not report the equipment as an asset nor the obligation to the lessor as a liability. Under conditions such as these, recording the transaction as a rental agreement does not reflect the underlying economic substance of acquiring and using the equipment.

As illustrated by this simple example, leasing can be used to avoid reporting a liability on the balance sheet. As discussed in Chapter 15, "off-balance-sheet financing" continues to be a perplexing problem for the accounting profession, and leasing is probably the oldest and most widely used means of keeping debt off the balance sheet. The FASB has attempted to eliminate this practice by requiring leases which meet certain criteria to be treated as **capital leases**—in effect, purchases of property.

ECONOMIC ADVANTAGES OF LEASING

It would be unfair and incorrect to imply that the only reason companies lease property is to avoid reporting the lease obligation in the financial statements. While the accounting issue is one factor, other financial and tax considerations also play an important role in the leasing decision. While every situation is different, there are two primary advantages to the lessee of leasing over purchasing.

(1) **No down payment**. Most debt-financed purchases of property require a portion of the purchase price to be paid immediately by the borrower. This provides added protection to the lender in the event of default and repossession. Lease agreements, in contrast, are frequently structured so that 100% of the value of the property is financed through the lease. This aspect of leasing makes it an attractive alternative to a company that does not have sufficient cash for a down payment or wishes to use available capital for other operating or investing purposes.

(2) **Avoids risks of ownership**. There are many risks accompanying the ownership of property. They include casualty loss, obsolescence, changing economic conditions, and physical deterioration. The lessee may terminate a lease, although usually with a certain penalty, and thus avoid assuming the risk of these events. This flexibility is especially important in businesses where innovation and technological change make the future usefulness of particular equipment or facilities highly uncertain. A prime example of this condition in recent years has been the electronics industry with its rapid change in areas such as computer technology, robotics, and telecommunication.

The lessor also may find benefits to leasing its property rather than selling it. Advantages of the lease to the lessor include the following:

(1) **Increased sales.** By offering potential customers the option of leasing its products, a manufacturer or dealer may significantly increase its sales volume. For the reasons suggested in the preceding paragraphs, customers may be unwilling or unable to purchase property.

(2) **Tax benefits**. Many tax provisions grant benefits to owners of property. For example, prior to the 1986 Tax Reform Act, tax laws provided for investment tax credits that allowed owners of property a direct credit against income taxes payable, either in the current period or in future periods through carryover provisions. If a lessor sells the asset, the benefits go with the property, but lease agreements can specify who gets the benefits. This flexibility made it possible for the tax credits to be a significant element in lease negotiations.

(3) **Ongoing business relationship with lessee**. When property is sold, the purchaser frequently has no more dealings with the seller of the property. In leasing situations, however, the lessor and lessee maintain contact over a period of time, and long-term business relationships can often be established through leasing.

(4) **Residual value retained**. In many lease arrangements, title to the leased property never passes to the lessee. The lessor benefits from economic conditions that may result in a significant residual value at the end of the lease term. The lessor may lease the asset to another lessee or sell the property and realize an immediate gain. Many lessors have realized significant profits from unexpected increases in residual values.

HISTORICAL DEVELOPMENT OF LEASE ACCOUNTING

The earliest accounting recognition of the importance of leasing as a financing device occurred in 1949 when the Committee on Accounting Procedures issued Accounting Research Bulletin No. 38, "Disclosure of Long-Term Leases in Financial Statements of Lessees." When the Accounting Principles Board was formed in 1959, the topic of leases was one of the initial ones to be considered. The Board issued four opinions on the subject of leasing during its fourteen-year history. Two of the opinions dealt with accounting by lessees, the other two with accounting by lessors. But the profession was not satisfied with the results of these opinions. Inconsistencies developed between accounting by lessees and lessors, and much of the opinions dealt with note disclosure rather than the accounting procedures themselves. Criteria for capitalization of leases were vague, and few lessees actually reported leases as assets with the accompanying liabilities.

Leasing was one of the topics on the original agenda of the FASB, and in 1976 the Board issued Statement No. 13, "Accounting for Leases." The objective of the FASB in issuing Statement No. 13 was to reflect the economic reality of leasing by requiring that the majority of long-term leases be accounted for as capital acquisitions by the lessee and as sales by the lessor. However, comparatively few leases have been capitalized as a result of the statement because of the liberal interpretations applied to the criteria used to define a capital lease.[2] An example of the broad interpretation of Statement No. 13 can be observed in the financial statements of General Mills, Inc. reproduced in Appendix A. Note fourteen refers to the company's existing leases, all of which are apparently reported as rental agreements rather than capitalized, even though they are labeled noncancellable, and require future rental payments totaling $182 million.

The failure of Statement No. 13 to achieve the desired objective forced the FASB to issue additional pronouncements in the area of leasing. By 1980, several Interpretations of Statement No. 13 and seven new statements had been issued in an attempt to achieve the original goal of increased lease capitalization. In May 1980, the FASB issued an integrated revision of Statement No. 13 and its amendments and interpretations.[3] Since 1980, there have not been any further statements issued involving leases, although new technical bulletins continue to be issued.

NATURE OF LEASES

Leases vary widely in their contractual provisions. Variables include cancellation provisions and penalties, lease term, bargain renewal and purchase options, economic life of assets, residual asset values, minimum lease payments, interest rates implicit in the lease agreement, and the degree of risk assumed by the lessee, including payments of certain costs such as maintenance, insurance, and taxes. These and other relevant facts must be considered in determining the appropriate accounting treatment of a lease.

The many variables affecting lease capitalization have been given precise definitions which must be understood in order to account for the

---

[2] For an interesting analysis of these problems, see Richard Dieter, "Is Lessee Accounting Working?" *CPA Journal* (August 1979), pp. 13–19.

[3] *Statement of Financial Accounting Standards No. 13,* "Accounting for Leases" (Stamford: Financial Accounting Standards Board, 1976), as amended and interpreted through May 1980 incorporating Statements 13, 17, 22, 23, 26, 27, 28, & 29, and Interpretations 19, 21, 23, 24, 26, & 27.

various types of leases found in practice. Each of these variables is defined and briefly discussed below.

Cancellation Provisions. Noncancellable refers to those lease contracts whose cancellation provisions and penalties are so costly for the lessee to invoke that in all likelihood, cancellation will not occur. Only noncancellable leases are subject to capitalization.

Lease Term. An important variable in lease agreements is the **lease term**; that is, the time period from the beginning to the end of the lease. The **inception of the lease** is defined as the date of the lease agreement, or date of an earlier written commitment if all the principal provisions have been negotiated. The **beginning of the lease term** occurs when the lease agreement takes effect, i.e., when the leased property is transferred to the lessee.

The date of the beginning of the lease term may coincide with the date of the inception of the lease. In many cases, however, a considerable amount of time may elapse between the inception date and the beginning of the lease term. For example, property may be constructed by the lessor to the lessee's specifications following the execution of a written agreement specifying all the major provisions for leasing the property to the lessee when the construction is complete. The inception of the lease is the date of the agreement to construct the property, but the beginning of the lease term is after the construction is completed and the property is turned over to the lessee.

The **end of the lease term** is the end of the fixed noncancellable period of the lease plus all periods, if any, covered by **bargain renewal options**, or other provisions that, at the inception of the lease strongly indicate that the lease will be renewed. If a bargain purchase option, as defined in the next section, is included in the lease contract, the lease term includes any renewal periods preceding the date of the bargain purchase option. In no case does the lease term extend beyond the date of a bargain purchase option.

Bargain Purchase Option. Leases often include a provision giving the lessee the right to purchase leased property at some future date. A definite purchase or option price may be specified, although in some cases the price is expressed as the fair market value at the date the option is exercised. If the specified option price is expected to be considerably less than the fair market value at the date the purchase option may be exercised, a **bargain purchase option** is indicated.

Residual Value. The market value of the leased property at the end of the lease term is referred to as its **residual value**. In some leases, the lease term extends over the entire **economic life of the asset**, or the period in which the asset continues to be productive, and there is little if any residual value. In other leases, the lease term is shorter, and a residual value does exist. If the lessee can purchase the asset at the end of the lease term at a materially reduced price from its residual value, a bargain purchase option is present and it can be assumed that the lessee would exercise the option and purchase the asset.

Some lease contracts require the lessee, or a designated third party, to guarantee a minimum residual value. If the market value at the end of the lease term falls below the **guaranteed residual value**, the lessee or third party must pay the difference. This provision protects the lessor from loss due to unexpected declines in the market value of the asset. For example, assume a piece of equipment is expected to have a $25,000 residual value at the end of the lease term, and the lessee guarantees that amount. However, at the end of the lease term, the residual value is only $15,000. The lessee is obligated to pay the $10,000 differential to the lessor so that the lessor is in effect guaranteed the full amount of the residual value that was estimated at the beginning of the lease. The lessee or the third party may buy the property for the $25,000 guaranteed amount, but the terms do not require the purchase. As will be demonstrated later in the chapter, a guarantee of residual value by a third party requires lessees to account for leases differently than would be true if the lessee were making the guarantee.

If there is no bargain purchase option or guarantee of the residual value, the lessor reacquires the property and may offer to renew the lease, lease the asset to another lessee, or sell the property. The actual amount of the residual value is unknown until the end of the lease term; however, it must be estimated at the inception of the lease. The residual value under these circumstances is referred to as the **unguaranteed residual value**.

Minimum Lease Payments. The rental payments required over the lease term plus any amount to be paid for the residual value either through a bargain purchase option or a guarantee of the residual value are referred to as the **minimum lease payments**. If these payments are all made by the lessee, the minimum lease payments are the same for the lessee and the lessor. However, if a third party guarantees the residual value, the lessee would not include the guarantee as part of the minimum lease payments, but the lessor would.

Rental payments sometimes include charges for such items as insurance, maintenance, and taxes incurred for the leased property. These are referred to as **executory costs**, and are not included as part of the minimum lease payments. If the lessor includes a charge for profit on these costs, the profit is also considered an executory cost.

To illustrate the computation of minimum lease payments, assume that Olaf Leasing Co. leases road equipment for 3 years at $3,000 per month. Included in the rental payment is $500 per month for executory costs to insure and maintain the equipment. At the end of the 3-year period, Olaf is guaranteed a residual value of $10,000 by the lessee.

Minimum lease payments:	
Rental payments exclusive of executory costs ($2,500 × 36).....	$ 90,000
Guaranteed residual value	10,000
Total minimum lease payments	$100,000

Because the minimum lease payments are to be made in future periods, the present value of these payments is needed to account for capitalized leases. Two different discount rates must be considered in computing the present value of minimum lease payments: the lessee's incremental borrowing rate and the implicit interest rate. The **incremental borrowing rate** is the rate at which the lessee could borrow the amount of money necessary to purchase the leased asset, taking into consideration the lessee's financial situation and the current conditions in the marketplace. The **implicit interest rate** is that rate which would discount the minimum lease payments to the fair market value of the asset at the inception of the lease. The lessor uses the implicit interest rate in determining the present value of the minimum lease payments. The lessee, however, uses either the implicit rate or the incremental borrowing rate, whichever is lower. If the lessee does not know the implicit rate, the incremental borrowing rate is used.

To illustrate using the Olaf Leasing Co. example, assume that the $3,000 rental payments to Olaf are made at the beginning of each month, the implicit interest rate in the lease contract is 12% per year, and the lessee's incremental borrowing rate is 14%. Assuming the lessee knows the implicit rate, both the lessor and lessee would discount the minimum lease payments using the 12% rate. The present value of the $100,000 minimum lease payments would be:

Present value of 36 payments of $2,500 ($3,000 less executory costs of $500)	$76,022
Present value of $10,000 guaranteed residual value at the end of 3 years......	7,118
Present value of minimum lease payments	$83,140

The present value of $83,140 would be the selling price or fair market value of the asset at the inception of the lease. The use of present value formulas and tables in discounting minimum lease payments is illustrated later in the chapter.

LEASE CLASSIFICATION CRITERIA

As indicated earlier, FASB Statement No. 13 identified criteria to determine whether a lease is merely a rental contract, or operating lease, or in substance a purchase of property, or capital lease. In considering this issue, the FASB was concerned with the fact that, under the APB pronouncements, leases were often reported differently by the lessee and the lessor. The Board felt that in most cases, there should be consistent treatment between the two parties; i.e., if the lessee treated the agreement as a purchase of property, the lessor should treat it as a sale of property. For this reason, the Board specified four criteria that apply to both the lessee and the lessor, any one of which would identify the lease agreement as a purchase and sale of property, or in other words, a **capital lease**. Two additional criteria were specified for lessors, both of which must be met before the lease can be treated as a sale by the lessor.

Although an increase in lease capitalization occurred as a result of FASB Statement No. 13 and related pronouncements, the goals of the FASB have not been fully realized. The terms of lease agreements have been written and variables have been measured according to whether the lessee or lessor desired to account for the lease as a capital lease or not. Inconsistent treatment between the lessee and the lessor has often occurred because of guarantees of residual values by third parties. Some accountants have suggested that the criteria specified by the FASB are too flexible, and that a direct requirement to capitalize all noncancellable leases with terms exceeding a specific number of years should be adopted for both lessees and lessors. While the lease issue will undoubtedly be addressed again in the future by the FASB, for now the following criteria govern the treatment of leases.

Lease Classification Criteria. The following four criteria apply to both the lessee and the lessor.[4] If a lease meets any one of the criteria, it is classified as a capital lease by the lessee and by the lessor, assuming the other two criteria for lessors are met.

Criteria applicable to both the lessee and the lessor:

1. The lease transfers ownership of the property to the lessee by the end of the lease term.
2. The lease contains a bargain purchase option.
3. The lease term is equal to 75% or more of the estimated economic life of the leased property.

Applied in this order

economic life

---

[4]*Ibid.*, par. 7.

for amortization

↓

lease term } *if shorter economic life*

4. The present value of the minimum lease payments excluding that portion representing executory costs equals or exceeds 90% of the fair market value of the property.

Additional criteria applicable to lessors:

1. Collectibility of the minimum lease payments is reasonably predictable.
2. No important uncertainties surround the amount of unreimbursable costs yet to be incurred by the lessor. This test is to be applied at the date construction of the leased asset is completed or when the property is acquired if these dates are after the inception of the lease.[5]

Classification Criteria—Lessee and Lessor. The four general criteria that apply to all leases for both the lessee and lessor relate to transfer of ownership, bargain purchase options, economic life, and investment recovery. Each of these criteria will be discussed in more depth.

(1) Transfer of ownership. The lease includes a clause that transfers full ownership of the property to the lessee by the end of the lease term.

(2) Bargain purchase option. The lease contains a bargain purchase option that makes it reasonably assured that the property will be purchased by the lessee at some future date. This criterion is more difficult to apply than the first criterion because the future fair market value of the leased property must be estimated at the inception of the lease and compared with the purchase option price to determine if a bargain purchase is indeed indicated.

(3) Economic life. The lease term is equal to 75% or more of the estimated economic life of the leased property. As defined earlier, the lease term includes renewal periods if renewal seems assured. This criterion is difficult to apply objectively because of the uncertainty of an asset's economic life. It can also be easily manipulated to achieve whatever result is desired. An exception to the economic life criterion was made for certain used property. The Board recognized that used property may be leased near the end of the property's economic life, and this criterion would result in capitalization of all such leases. The Board provided that this criterion would not be applicable to leases occurring in the last 25% of the leased property's economic life. It should also be recognized that this criterion cannot apply to land leases, since land has an unlimited life.

(4) Investment Recovery. The present value at the beginning of the lease term of the minimum lease payments, excluding that portion repre-

---

[5] *Statement of Financial Accounting Standards No. 23,* "Inception of the Lease" (Stamford: Financial Accounting Standards Board, 1978), par. 7.

senting executory costs, equals or exceeds 90% of the fair market value of the property. This criterion was intended to be the key factor in determining the existence of a capital lease.[6] If the lessee is obligated to pay, in present value terms, almost all of the fair market value of the leased property, the lease is in substance a purchase of the property. But the application of this criterion has also been difficult and subject to manipulation by lessees and lessors. The key variable in this criterion is the discounted minimum lease payments exclusive of executory costs.

Since larger minimum lease payments cause the investment recovery criteria to be met, the use of third parties to guarantee residual values has led to a lack of consistency between lessees and lessors in many lease arrangements. Many lessors want to report the lease as a sale and thus recognize income at the inception of the lease. However, lessees generally want to report the lease as a rental contract and gain the advantage of off-balance-sheet financing. Since third-party guarantees are considered minimum lease payments to the lessor but not to the lessee, a careful structuring of the lease terms can allow both parties to achieve their goals.

This variable, more than any other, has been used in lease arrangements to avoid the intent of the FASB to achieve increased consistency in reporting. In fact, a new industry of third-party financing has arisen to take advantage of this difference in defining minimum lease payments between the lessee and the lessor. This phenomenon will be illustrated later in the chapter.

The rate used to discount the future minimum lease payments is critical in determining whether the investment recovery criterion is met. The lower the discount rate used, the higher the present value of the minimum lease payments and the greater the likelihood that the investment recovery criterion of 90% will be met. As explained earlier in the chapter, the FASB specified that the lessor should use the implicit interest rate of the lease agreement, including consideration of residual values. The lessee also uses the lessor's implicit interest rate if it is known and if it is lower than the lessee's incremental borrowing rate. If the lessee cannot determine the lessor's implicit interest rate, the lessee must use its incremental borrowing rate.

Because incremental borrowing rates are often higher than the implicit interest rates, and because lessees do not generally want to capitalize leases, many lessees use the borrowing rate and do not attempt to estimate

---

[6] For an interesting analysis that demonstrates that the first three criteria are in reality redundant and are incorporated in the fourth criterion for the lessor and, in most cases, for the lessee, see John W. Coughlan, "Regulations, Rents, and Residuals," *Journal of Accountancy* (February 1980), pp. 58–66.

the implicit rate. If there is no residual value, the lessee can usually determine the implicit rate because the market value of the leased asset is usually known. If a residual value exists, however, the lessee must obtain knowledge of these values from the lessor.

The use of different discount rates between lessees and lessors is another cause of inconsistent accounting treatment between lessees and lessors.

Additional Classification Criteria — Lessor. In addition to meeting one of the four preceding criteria, lessors must meet two additional criteria in order to report leases as capital leases.[7] These are as follows:

1. **Collectibility**. Collection of the minimum lease payments is reasonably predictable, whether from the lessee or from a third party guarantor.
2. **Substantial completion**. No important uncertainties surround the amount of unreimbursable costs yet to be incurred by the lessor under the lease.

These two additional criteria are designed to add assurance that revenue recognition for the lessor is warranted. If there is considerable uncertainty as to the ability of the lessor to collect the minimum lease payments, or as to costs yet to be incurred by the lessor, no sale should be recorded.

Application of Lease Classification Criteria

To illustrate the application of the classification criteria specified in FASB Statement No. 13, four different leasing situations are presented in Exhibit 21–1 on page 912. A summary analysis of each lease is also presented in the exhibit. Following is a brief explanation of the analysis for each of the four leases.

Lease #1 will be treated as an operating lease by the lessee but as a capital lease by the lessor. Since the lessee does not know the implicit rate of the lessor, the incremental borrowing rate is used to test for criteria 4. The incremental borrowing rate is higher than the implicit rate, and the present value of the minimum lease payments is less than 90% of the fair market value of the property; thus criteria 4 is not met for the lessee. The lessor will use the implicit rate, and criteria 4 is met.

Lease #2 will be treated as a capital lease by both the lessee and the lessor, because title passes to the lessee at the end of the lease term. Because there is a third-party guaranteed residual value, the minimum lease payments are higher for the lessor than the lessee, and criteria 4 is met by the lessor but not by the lessee. Thus, if title had not passed,

---

[7] *Statement of Financial Accounting Standards No. 13*, par. 16a.

Exhibit 21–1
Application of FASB Statement No. 13 Criteria to Lease Situations

Lease provisions	Lease #1	Lease #2	Lease #3	Lease #4
Cancellable.........................	No	No	No	Yes
Title passes to lessee.................	No	Yes	No	Yes
Bargain purchase option...............	No	No	Yes	No
Lease term	10 years	10 years	8 years	10 years
Economic life of asset.................	14 years	15 years	13 years	12 years
Present value of minimum lease payments as a percentage of fair market value— incremental rate	80%	79%	95%	76%
Present value of minimum lease payments as a percentage of fair market value— implicit rate	92%	91%	92%	82%
Lessee knows implicit rate..............	No	No	Yes	Yes
Unguaranteed residual value...........	Yes	No	No	No
Residual value guaranteed by third party................................	No	Yes	No	No
Present value of minimum lease payments exclusive of third-party guaranteed residual value as a percentage of fair market value—implicit rate..............	92%	80%	92%	82%
Rental payments collectible and lessor costs certain............................	Yes	Yes	No	Yes
Analysis of Leases:				
Lessee				
Treat as capital lease	No	Yes	Yes	No
Criteria met.......................	None	1	2 and 4	must be non-
Use incremental borrowing rate	NA	Yes	No	cancellable
Amortization period	NA	15 years	13 years	
Lessor				
Treat as capital lease	Yes	Yes	No	No
First four criteria met.................	4	1 and 4	2 and 4	must be non-
Lessor criteria met..................	Yes	Yes	No	cancellable

Lease #2 would be treated as an operating lease by the lessee but a capital lease by the lessor. Since title passes to the lessee, the economic life of the lease will be used as the amortization period.

Lease #3 will be treated as a capital lease by the lessee, but as an operating lease by the lessor. The difference is caused by the lease failing to meet the lessor criteria. The bargain purchase option meets criteria 2 and, since the lessee knows the implicit rate, both the lessee and lessor computations meet criteria 4. Because of the bargain purchase option, the economic life of the lease will be used as the amortization period.

Lease #4 will be treated as an operating lease by both the lessee and the lessor. The lease is a cancellable lease, and even though title passes to the lessee at the end of the lease, it would be classified as a rental agreement.

ACCOUNTING FOR LEASES — LESSEE

All leases as viewed by the lessee may be divided into two types: **operating leases** and **capital leases**. If a lease meets any one of the four classification criteria discussed previously, it is treated as a capital lease. Otherwise, it is accounted for as an operating lease.

Accounting for operating leases involves the recognition of rent expense over the term of the lease. The leased property is not reported as an asset on the lessee's balance sheet nor is a liability recognized for the obligation to make future payments for use of the property. Information concerning the lease is limited to disclosure in notes to the financial statements. Accounting for a capital lease essentially requires the lessee to report on the balance sheet the present value of the future lease payments, both as an asset and a liability. The asset is depreciated as though it had been purchased by the lessee. The liability is accounted for in the same manner as would be a mortgage on the property. The difference in the impact of these two methods on the financial statements is frequently significant.

Accounting for Operating Leases — Lessee

Operating leases are considered to be simple rental agreements with debits being made to an expense account as the payments are made. For example, assume the lease terms for manufacturing equipment were $40,000 a year on a year-to-year basis. The entry to record the payment for a year's rent would be as follows:

Rent Expense	40,000	
Cash		40,000

Rent payments are frequently made in advance. In this event, if the lease period does not coincide with the lessee's fiscal year, or if the lessee prepares interim reports, a prepaid rent account would be required to record the unexpired portion of rent at the end of the accounting period involved. The prepaid rent account should be adjusted at the end of each period.

Operating Leases with Varying Rental Payments. Some operating leases specify rental terms that provide for varying rental payments over the lease term. Most commonly, these types of agreements call for lower initial payments and scheduled rent increases later in the life of the lease. They may even provide an inducement to prospective lessees in the form of a "rent holiday" (free rent). In some cases, however, the lease may provide for higher initial rentals. FASB Statement No. 13 requires that when rental payments vary over the lease term, rental expense be recognized on a straight-line basis "unless another systematic and rational basis is more representative of the time pattern in which use benefit is derived from the leased property, in which case that basis shall be used."[8]

When recording rent expense under these agreements, differences between the actual payments and the debit to expense would be reported as Rent Payable or Prepaid Rent, depending on whether the payments were accelerating or declining. For example, assume the terms of the lease for an aircraft by International Airlines provide for payments of $150,000 a year for the first 2 years of the lease and $250,000 for the next 3 years. The total lease payments for the 5 years would be $1,050,000, or $210,000 a year on a straight-line basis. The required entries in the first 2 years would be as follows:

Rent Expense	210,000	
Cash		150,000
Rent Payable		60,000

The entries for each of the last 3 years would be as follows:

Rent Expense	210,000	
Rent Payable	40,000	
Cash		250,000

The portion of Rent Payable due in the subsequent year would be classified as a current liability.

Accounting for Capital Leases—Lessee

Capital leases are considered to be more like a purchase of property than a rental. Consequently, accounting for capital leases by lessees requires entries similar to those required for the purchase of an asset with long-term credit terms. The amount to be recorded as an asset and as a liability is the **present value of the future minimum lease payments** as previously defined. The discount rates used by lessees to record capital leases are the same as those used to apply the classification criteria previously discussed, e.g., the lower of the implicit interest rate (if known) and the incremental borrowing rate. The minimum lease payments consist of the total rental payments, bargain purchase options, and lessee-guaranteed residual values.

---

[8] *Ibid.*, par. 15.

An important exception to the use of the present value of future minimum lease payments as a basis for recording a capital lease was included by the FASB in Statement No. 13 as follows:

> However, if the amount so determined exceeds the fair value of the leased property at the inception of the lease, the amount recorded as the asset and obligation shall be the fair value.[9]

This means that if the leased asset has a determinable sales price, the present value of the future minimum lease payments should be compared with that price. If the sales price is lower, it should be used as the capitalized value of the lease, and an implicit interest rate would have to be computed using the sales price as the capitalized value of the asset.

Illustrative Entries for Capital Leases. Assume that Vincent Corporation leases equipment from Universal Leasing Company with the following terms:

> Lease period: 5 years, beginning January 1, 1988. Noncancellable.
> Rental amount: $65,000 per year payable annually in advance; includes
> $5,000 to cover executory costs.
> Estimated economic life of equipment: 5 years.
> Expected residual value of equipment at end of lease period: None.

Because the rental payments are payable in advance, the formula to find the present value of the lease is the annuity-due formula described in Chapter 6. Assuming the Vincent Corporation's incremental borrowing rate is 10% and that rate is equal to or less than the implicit rate, the present value for the lease would be $250,194 computed as follows:[10]

$$PV_n = R(PVAF_{\overline{n-1}|i} + 1)$$
$$PV_n = \$60,000 \text{ (Table IV}_{\overline{4}|10\%} + 1)$$
$$PV_n = \$60,000 \text{ (3.1699} + 1)$$
$$PV_n = \$250,194$$

$\boxed{p.233}$

The journal entry to record the lease at the beginning of the lease term would be as follows:

```
1988
Jan. 1  Lease Expense .........................................    5,000
        Leased Equipment .....................................  250,194
            Obligations Under Capital Leases....................             190,194[11]
            Cash .............................................              65,000
```

---

[9] *Ibid.*, par. 10.

[10] All computations of present value in this chapter will be rounded to the nearest dollar. This will require some adjustment at times to the final figures in the tables to balance the amounts.

[11] It is also possible to record the liability at the gross amount of the payments (300,000) and offset it with a discount account — Discount on Lease Contract. The net method is more common in accounting for leases by the lessee and will be used in this chapter.

The asset value is amortized in accordance with the lessee's normal method of depreciation. The amortization period to be used depends on which of the criteria was used to qualify the lease as a capital lease. If the lease qualified under either of the first two criteria, ownership transfer or bargain purchase option, the economic life of the asset should be used. If the lease qualified under either of the last two criteria, economic life or investment recovery, and the lease term is shorter than the estimated life of the asset, the lease term should be used for amortization purposes. In the preceding example, the lease qualifies under the third criterion and presumably the fourth since the lessor would not lease the asset over its entire economic life if the present value of the lease payments were less than the fair market value of the asset at the inception of the lease. The liability should be reduced each period so as to produce a constant rate of interest expense on the remaining balance of the obligation. The lessee's incremental borrowing rate, or the lessor's implicit rate if lower, is the constant interest rate for the lessee under the provisions of FASB Statement No. 13. Table 1 shows how the $60,000 payments (excluding executory costs) would be allocated between payment on the obligation and interest expense. To simplify the schedule, it is assumed that all lease payments after the first payment are made on December 31 of each year. If the payments were made in January, an accrual of interest at December 31 would be required.

TABLE 1
Schedule of Lease Payments
[Five-Year Lease, $60,000 Annual Payments (Net of Executory Costs) 10% Interest]

Date	Description	Lease Payment Amount	Interest Expense*	Principal	Lease Obligation
1- 1-88	Initial balance				$250,194
1- 1-88	Payment	$60,000		$60,000	190,194
12-31-88	Payment	60,000	$19,019	40,981	149,213
12-31-89	Payment	60,000	14,921	45,079	104,134
12-31-90	Payment	60,000	10,413	49,587	54,547
12-31-91	Payment	60,000	5,453	54,547	0

*Preceding lease obligation × 10%.

If the normal company depreciation policy for this type of equipment is straight-line, the required entry at December 31, 1988, for amortization of the asset would be as follows:

```
1988
Dec. 31 Amortization Expense on Leased Equipment............... 50,039
            Accumulated Amortization on Leased Equipment..........         50,039

        Computation:
        $250,194 ÷ 5 = $50,039
```

Similar entries would be made for each of the remaining 4 years. Although the credit could be made directly to the asset account, the use of a contra asset account provides the necessary disclosure information about the original lease value and accumulated amortization to date.

Another entry is required at December 31, 1988, to record the second lease payment, including a prepayment of next year's executory costs. As indicated in Table 1, the interest expense for 1988 would be computed by multiplying the incremental borrowing rate of 10% by the initial present value of the obligation less the immediate $60,000 first payment, or ($250,194 − $60,000) × .10 = $19,019.

```
1988
Dec. 31 Prepaid Executory Costs ................................. 5,000
        Obligations Under Capital Leases ........................ 40,981
        Interest Expense ....................................... 19,019
            Cash.................................................         65,000
```

Because of the assumption that all lease payments after the first payment are made on December 31, the portion of each payment that represents executory costs must be recorded as a prepayment and charged to lease expense in the following year.

The December 31, 1988, balance sheet of Vincent Corporation would include information concerning the leased equipment and related obligation as illustrated below:

Vincent Corporation
Balance Sheet (Partial)
December 31, 1988

Assets		Liabilities	
Land, buildings, and equipment:		Current liabilities:	
Leased equipment	$250,194	Obligations under capital leases, current portion..............	$ 45,079
Less accumulated amortization............	50,039	Noncurrent liabilities:	
Net value	$200,155	Obligations under capital leases, exclusive of $45,079 included in current liabilities	104,134

Note that the principal portion of the December 31, 1989, payment is reported as a current liability.[12]

The income statement would include the amortization on leased property of $50,039, interest expense of $19,019, and executory costs of $5,000 as expenses for the period. The total expense of $74,058 exceeds the $65,000 rental payment made in the first year. As the amount of interest expense declines each period, the total expense will be reduced and, for the last 2 years, will be less than the $65,000 payments (Table 2). The total amount debited to expense over the life of the lease will, of course, be the same regardless of whether the lease is accounted for as an operating lease or as a capital lease. If a declining-balance method of amortization is used, the difference in the early years between the expense and the payment would be even larger. In addition to this statement disclosure, a note to the financial statements would be necessary to explain the terms of the lease and future rental payments in more detail.

TABLE 2
Schedule of Expenses Recognized— Capital and Operating Leases Compared

| Year | Expenses Recognized—Capital Lease | | | | Expenses Recognized— Operating Lease | Difference |
	Interest	Executory Costs	Amorti- zation	Total		
1988	$19,019	$ 5,000	$ 50,039	$ 74,058	$ 65,000	$9,058
1989	14,921	5,000	50,039	69,960	65,000	4,960
1990	10,413	5,000	50,039	65,452	65,000	452
1991	5,453	5,000	50,039	60,492	65,000	(4,508)
1992	—	5,000	50,038	55,038	65,000	(9,962)
	$49,806	$25,000	$250,194	$325,000	$325,000	$ 0

If in this example, the fair market value of the leased asset had been less than $250,194, the exception discussed previously would be applied, and

---

[12] There have been some theoretical arguments advanced against this method of allocating lease obligations between current and noncurrent liabilities. See Robert J. Swierenga, "When Current is Noncurrent and Vice Versa," *Accounting Review* (January 1984), pp. 123–130. Professor Swierenga identifies two methods of making the allocation: the "change in present value" (CPV) approach that is used in the example, and the "present value of the next year's payment" (PVNYP) approach that allocates a larger portion of the liability to the current category. A later study shows that the CPV method is almost universally followed in practice. A. W. Richardson, "The Measurement of the Current Portion of Long-Term Lease Obligations—Some Evidence from Practice," *Accounting Review* (October 1985), pp. 744–752. While there is theoretical support for both positions, this text uses CPV in chapter examples and problem materials.

the lower fair market value would be used for the capitalized value of the lease. For example, assume the fair market value, or sales price, of the leased asset is $242,250. By using the present value tables and the method illustrated in Chapter 6, the implicit interest rate of the lease can be computed as being approximately 12%. A table similar to Table 1 may now be constructed using $242,250 as the initial balance and 12% as the interest rate. For complex lease situations involving something other than equal annual lease payments, computation of the implicit rate of interest must be done from the present value formulas themselves. This computation is facilitated by use of a computer.

Accounting for Lease with Bargain Purchase Option. Frequently, the lessee is given the option of purchasing the property at some future date at a bargain price. As discussed previously, the present value of the bargain purchase option should be included in the capitalized value of the lease. Assume in the preceding example that there was a bargain purchase option of $75,000 exercisable after 5 years, and the economic life of the equipment was expected to be 10 years. The other lease terms remain the same. The present value of the minimum lease payments would be increased by the present value of the bargain purchase amount of $75,000 or $46,568 computed as follows:

$$PV = A(PVF_{\overline{n}|i})$$
$$PV = \$75,000(\text{Table II}_{\overline{5}|10\%})$$
$$PV = \$75,000 \ (.6209)$$
$$PV = \$46,568$$

The total present value of the lease is $296,762 ($250,194 + $46,568). This amount will be used to record the initial asset and liability. The asset balance of $296,762 will be amortized over the asset life of 10 years because of the existence of the bargain purchase option, which makes the transaction in reality a sale. The liability balance will be reduced as shown in Table 3 at the top of page 920.

At the date of exercising the option, the net balance in the asset account, Leased Equipment, and its related accumulated amortization account would be transferred to the regular equipment account. The entries at the exercise of the option would be as follows:

Obligations Under Capital Leases	68,183	
Interest Expense	6,817	
Cash		75,000
To record exercise of bargain purchase option.		

TABLE 3
Schedule of Lease Payments
[Five-Year Lease with Bargain Purchase Option of $75,000 after Five Years, $60,000 Annual Payments (Net of Executory Costs) 10% Interest]

Date	Description	Lease Payment Amount	− Interest Expense =	Principal	Lease Obligation
1- 1-88	Initial balance				$296,762
1- 1-88	Payment	$60,000		$60,000	236,762
12-31-88	Payment	60,000	$23,676	36,324	200,438
12-31-89	Payment	60,000	20,044	39,956	160,482
12-31-90	Payment	60,000	16,048	43,952	116,530
12-31-91	Payment	60,000	11,653	48,347	68,183
12-31-92	Payment	75,000	6,817	68,183	0

Equipment...	148,381	
Accumulated Amortization on Leased Equipment.................	148,381	
Leased Equipment..		296,762

To transfer remaining balance in leased asset account to equipment account.

Computation:
Accumulated amortization:
One-half amortized after 5 years of a 10-year life: $296,762 ÷ 2 = $148,381

If the equipment is not purchased and the lease is permitted to lapse, a loss in the amount of the net remaining balance in the asset account, less any remaining liabilities, would have to be recognized by the following entry:

Loss from Failure to Exercise Bargain Purchase Option............	73,381	
Obligations Under Capital Leases	68,183	
Interest Expense	6,817	
Accumulated Amortization on Leased Equipment.................	148,381	
Leased Equipment..		296,762

Accounting for Lease with Lessee Guaranteed Residual Value. If the lease terms require the lessee to guarantee a residual value, the present value of the guaranty is included as part of the capitalized value of the lease. At the expiration of the lease term, the amount of the guaranty will be reported as a liability under the lease. If the lessee is required to pay the guaranteed amount, the liability will be reduced accordingly. If only part of the guaranteed amount is paid, the difference can be reflected as an adjustment to the current lease expense.

Accounting for Purchase of Asset During Lease Term. When a lease does not provide for a transfer of ownership or a purchase option, it is still possible that a lessee may purchase leased property during the term of the lease. Usually the purchase price will differ from the recorded lease obligation at the purchase date. The FASB issued Interpretation No. 26 to cover this situation. The Board decided that no gain or loss should be recorded on the purchase, but the difference between the purchase price and the obligation still on the books should be charged or credited to the acquired asset's carrying value.[13]

To illustrate, assume that on December 31, 1990, rather than making the lease payment due on that date the lessee purchased the leased property described on page 915 for $120,000. At that date, the remaining liability recorded on the lessee's books is $114,547 ($104,134 + $10,413), and the net book value of the recorded leased asset is $100,077, the original capitalized value of $250,194 less $150,117 amortization ($50,039 × 3). The entry to record the purchase on the lessee's books would be as follows:

Interest Expense	10,413	
Obligations Under Capital Leases	104,134	
Equipment	105,530	
Accumulated Amortization on Leased Equipment	150,117	
Leased Equipment		250,194
Cash		120,000

The purchased equipment is capitalized at $105,530, which is the book value of the leased asset, $100,077, plus $5,453, the excess of the purchase price over the carrying value of the lease obligation ($120,000 − $114,547).

ACCOUNTING FOR LEASES—LESSOR

The lessor in a lease transaction gives up the physical possession of the property to the lessee. If the transfer of the property is considered temporary in nature, the lessor will continue to carry the leased asset as an owned asset on the balance sheet, and the revenue from the lease will be reported as it is earned. Depreciation of the leased asset will be matched against the revenue. This type of lease is described as an **operating lease** and is similar to the operating lease described for the lessee. However, if a lease has terms that make the transaction similar in substance to a sale or a permanent transfer of the asset to the lessee, the lessor should no longer report the asset as though it were owned, but should reflect the transfer to the lessee.

As indicated on page 908, if a lease meets one of the four criteria that apply to both lessees and lessors, plus both of the lessor conditions, collectibility and substantial completion, it is classified by the lessor as a capital lease and recorded as either a direct financing lease or a sales-type lease.

---

[13] *FASB Interpretation No. 26,* "Accounting for Purchase of a Leased Asset by the Lessee during the Term of the Lease" (Stamford: Financial Accounting Standards Board, 1978), par. 5.

Direct financing leases involve a lessor who is primarily engaged in financial activities, such as a bank or finance company. The lessor views the lease as an investment. The revenue generated by this type of lease is interest revenue. **Sales-type leases,** on the other hand, involve manufacturers or dealers who use leases as a means of facilitating the marketing of their products. Thus, there are really two different types of revenue generated by this type of lease: (1) an immediate profit or loss which is the difference between the cost of the property being leased and its sales price, or fair value, at the inception of the lease, and (2) interest revenue to compensate for the deferred payment provisions.

The three types of leases from the lessor's standpoint: operating leases, direct financing leases, and sales-type leases are discussed in the following sections.

A lessor may incur certain costs, referred to as **initial direct costs,** in connection with obtaining a lease. These costs, originally defined in FASB Statement No. 13 and subsequently redefined in Statement No. 91, include:[14]

1. Costs to originate a lease that result directly from and are essential to acquire that lease and would not have been incurred if that leasing transaction had not occurred.
2. Certain costs directly related to the following specified activities performed by the lessor for that lease: evaluating the prospective lessee's financial condition; evaluating and recording guarantees, collateral, and other security arrangements; negotiating lease terms; preparing and processing lease documents; and closing the transaction.

Initial direct costs are accounted for differently depending on which of the three types of leases is involved. Exhibit 21–2 summarizes the accounting treatment of initial direct costs. These costs will be discussed further as each type of lease is presented.

Exhibit 21–2 Accounting for Initial Direct Costs

Type of Lease	Accounting Treatment of Costs
Operating	Amortized over lease term
Direct financing	Added to gross investment in leased asset. In effect recognized over lease term through reduced interest revenue.
Sales-type	Immediately recognized as reduction in manufacturer's profit.

---

[14] *Statement of Financial Accounting Standards No. 91,* "Accounting for Nonrefundable Fees and Costs Associated with Originating or Acquiring Loans and Initial Direct Costs of Leases" (Stamford: Financial Accounting Standards Board, 1986), par. 24.

Accounting for Operating Leases — Lessor

Accounting for operating leases for the lessor is very similar to that described for the lessee. The lessor recognizes revenue as the payments are received. If there are significant variations in the payment terms, entries will be necessary to reflect a straight-line pattern of revenue recognition. Initial direct costs incurred in connection with an operating lease are deferred and amortized on a straight-line basis over the term of the lease, thus matching them against rent revenue.

To illustrate accounting for an operating lease on the lessor's books, assume that the equipment leased for 5 years by Vincent Corporation for $65,000 a year including executory costs of $5,000 per year had a cost of $400,000 to the lessor. Initial direct costs of $15,000 were incurred to obtain the lease. The equipment has an estimated life of 10 years, with no residual value. Assuming no purchase or renewal options or guarantees by the lessee, the lease does not meet any of the four general classification criteria and would be treated as an operating lease. The entries to record the payment of the initial direct costs and the receipt of rent would be as follows:

```
1988
Jan. 1 Deferred Initial Direct Costs .............................   15,000
          Cash ...............................................               15,000

       1 Cash ...............................................   65,000
          Rent Revenue .......................................               65,000
```

Assuming the lessor depreciates the equipment on a straight-line basis over its expected life of 10 years and amortizes the initial direct costs on a straight-line basis over the 5-year lease term, the depreciation and amortization entries at the end of the first year would be:

```
1988
Dec. 31 Amortization of Initial Direct Costs .......................   3,000
           Deferred Initial Direct Costs............................            3,000

       31 Depreciation Expense on Leased Equipment................  40,000
           Accumulated Depreciation on Leased Equipment..........           40,000
```

Executory costs would be recognized as expense when paid or accrued. If the rental period and the lessor's fiscal year do not coincide, or if the lessor prepares interim reports, an adjustment would be required to record the unearned rent revenue at the end of the accounting period. Amortization of the initial direct costs would be adjusted to reflect a partial year.

Accounting for Direct Financing Leases

Accounting for direct financing leases for lessors is very similar to that used for capital leases by lessees, but with the entries reversed to provide for interest revenue rather than interest expense and reduction of an asset rather than a liability. In practice, the receivable is usually recorded by the lessor at the gross amount of the minimum lease payments with an off-setting valuation account for the unearned interest revenue, rather than at a net figure which is true for lessee accounting.

Illustrative Entries for Direct Financing Leases. Referring to the lessee example on page 915, assume that the cost of the equipment to the Universal Leasing Company was the same as its fair market value, $250,194, and the purchase by the lessor had been entered into the account Equipment Purchased for Lease. The entry to record the initial lease would be as follows:

Cash...	65,000	
Minimum Lease Payments Receivable	240,000	
Equipment Purchased for Lease..............................		250,194
Unearned Interest Revenue..................................		49,806
Executory Costs Payable....................................		5,000

The lessor is paying the executory costs, but charging them to the lessee. The lessor can record the receipt of the executory costs by debiting cash and crediting Executory Costs Payable. As the lessor pays the costs, the liability account is decreased. The lessor is serving as a conduit for these costs to the lessee, and will have an expense only if the lessee fails to make the payments.

Interest revenue will be recognized over the lease term as shown in Table 4.

TABLE 4
Schedule of Lease Receipts and Interest Revenue
[Five-Year Lease, $60,000 Annual Payments
(Exclusive of Executory Costs) 10% Interest]

Date	Description	Interest Revenue*	Lease Receipt	Lease Payments Receivable	Unearned Interest Revenue
1- 1-88	Initial balance			$300,000	$49,806
1- 1-88	Receipt		$60,000	240,000	49,806
12-31-88	Receipt	$19,019	60,000	180,000	30,787
12-31-89	Receipt	14,921	60,000	120,000	15,866
12-31-90	Receipt	10,413	60,000	60,000	5,453
12-31-91	Receipt	5,453	60,000	0	0

*Preceding lease payment receivable less unearned interest revenue × 10%.

At the end of the first year, the following entries would be made to record receipt of the second lease payment and to recognize interest revenue for 1988.

```
1988
Dec. 31  Cash.................................................   65,000
               Minimum Lease Payments Receivable ..................           60,000
               Executory Costs Payable ..............................            5,000

       31  Unearned Interest Revenue............................   19,019
               Interest Revenue ......................................           19,019
```

The balance sheet of the lessor at December 31, 1988, will report the lease receivable less the unearned interest revenue as follows:

Universal Leasing Company		
Balance Sheet (Partial)		
December 31, 1988		
Assets		
Current assets:		
Minimum lease payments receivable	$ 60,000	
Less unearned interest revenue	14,921	$ 45,079
Noncurrent assets:		
Minimum lease payments receivable (exclusive of		
$60,000 included in current assets)	$120,000	
Less unearned interest revenue	15,866	104,134

If a direct financing lease contains a bargain purchase option, the amount of the option is added to the receivable and the interest included in the option amount is added to the unearned interest revenue account. The periodic entries and computations are made as though the bargain purchase amount was an additional rental payment.

Lessor Accounting for Direct Financing Lease with Residual Value. If leased property is expected to have residual value, the gross amount of the expected residual value is added to the receivable account. It does not matter whether the residual value is guaranteed or unguaranteed. If guaranteed, it is treated in the accounts exactly like a bargain purchase option. If unguaranteed, the lessor is expected to have an asset equal in value to the residual amount at the end of the lease term. The estimated residual value is added to the asset account and the interest attributable to the unguaranteed residual value is added to the unearned interest revenue account. Because there is no existing receivable for the residual value, a more descriptive term may be used for the asset, Gross Investment in Leased Assets.

To illustrate the recording of residual values, assume the same facts for the Universal Leasing Company as the example on page 915 except that the asset has a residual value at the end of the 5-year lease term of $75,000 (either guaranteed or unguaranteed). Assume this additional value increased the cost of the equipment to Universal by $46,568, the present value at 10% of the expected residual value.

The entries to record this lease would be as follows:

Cash	65,000	
Gross Investment in Leased Assets	$315,000	
Equipment Purchased for Lease		296,762
Unearned Interest Revenue		78,238
Executory Costs Payable		5,000

Note that as compared with the entry on page 924 when there was no residual value, the asset value is increased by $75,000, the cost of the equipment to Universal is increased by $46,568, and Unearned Interest Revenue is increased by $28,432, the difference between the $75,000 residual value and the $46,568 present value of the residual amount.

Interest revenue would be recognized in accordance with Table 3, page 920. At the end of the first year, for example, the lessor would make the following entries:

Cash	65,000	
Gross Investment in Leased Assets		60,000
Executory Costs Payable		5,000
Unearned Interest Revenue	23,676	
Interest Revenue		23,676

At the end of the lease term, the lessor would make the following entry to record the recovery of the leased asset assuming the residual value was the same as originally estimated:

Equipment	75,000	
Unearned Interest Revenue	6,817	
Gross Investment in Leased Assets		75,000
Interest Revenue		6,817

The unguaranteed residual value should be reviewed at least annually by the lessor and adjusted for any decline that is considered other than temporary. Such adjustment is accounted for as a change in estimate.

Initial Direct Costs Related to Direct Financing Lease. If the lessor incurs any initial direct costs in connection with a direct financing lease, those costs are to be added to the gross investment in leased assets.[15] The effective interest rate used for amortization of the unearned revenue will be lowered because of the higher gross investment. In effect, the initial direct costs will be amortized as a reduction of interest revenue over the lease term.

---

[15] *Statement of Financial Accounting Standards No. 91*, par. 25.

To illustrate, assume that the lessor in the preceding example incurred initial direct costs of $15,000. The entry relating to these costs would be as follows:

Gross Investment in Leased Assets.............................. 15,000
    Cash..   15,000
        To record payment of initial direct costs.

Accounting for Sales-Type Leases

Accounting for sales-type leases adds one more dimension to the lessor's revenue, an immediate profit or loss arising from the difference between the sales price of the leased property and the lessor's cost to manufacture or purchase the asset. If there is no difference between the sales price and the lessor's cost, the lease is not a sales-type lease. The lessor also will recognize interest revenue over the lease term for the difference between the sales price and the gross amount of the minimum lease payments. The three values that must be identified to determine these income elements, therefore, can be summarized as follows:

1. The minimum lease payments as defined previously for the lessee, i.e., rental payments over the lease term net of any executory costs included therein plus the amount to be paid under a bargain purchase option or guarantee of the residual value.
2. The fair market value of the asset.
3. The cost or carrying value of the asset to the lessor increased by any initial direct costs to lease the asset.

The manufacturer's or dealer's profit is the difference between the fair market value of the asset [(2) above] and the cost or carrying value of the asset to the lessor [(3) above]. If cost exceeds the fair market value, a loss will be reported. The difference between the gross rentals [(1) above] and the fair market value of the asset [(2) above] is interest revenue and arises because of the time delay in paying for the asset as described by the lease terms. The relationship between these three values can be demonstrated as follows:

(1) Minimum lease payments ....
                Financial Revenue (Interest)

(2) Fair market value of leased asset ....
                Manufacturer's or Dealer's Profit (Loss)

(3) Cost or carrying value of leased asset to lessor...........

To illustrate this type of lease, assume the lessor for the equipment described on page 915 is American Manufacturing Company. The fair market value of the equipment is equal to its present value (the future lease payments discounted at 10%), or $250,194. Assume the equipment cost American $160,000 and initial direct costs of $15,000 were incurred. The three values and their related revenue amounts would be as follows:

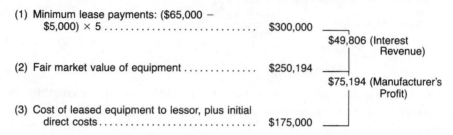

(1) Minimum lease payments: ($65,000 −
   $5,000) × 5 . . . . $300,000
                                                                                    $49,806 (Interest
                                                                                             Revenue)
(2) Fair market value of equipment $250,194
                                                                                    $75,194 (Manufacturer's
                                                                                             Profit)
(3) Cost of leased equipment to lessor, plus initial
   direct costs $175,000

Illustrative Entries for Sales-Type Leases. The interest revenue ($49,806) is the same as that illustrated for a direct financing lease on page 924, and it is recognized over the lease term by the same entries and according to Table 4. The manufacturer's profit is recognized as revenue immediately in the current period by including the fair market value of the asset as a sale and debiting the cost of the equipment carried in the finished goods inventory to Cost of Goods Sold. The initial direct costs previously deferred are recognized as an expense immediately by increasing Cost of Goods Sold by the amount expended for these costs. This reduces the amount of immediate profit to be recognized. The reimbursement of executory costs is treated in the same way as illustrated for direct financing leases.

The entries to record this information on American Manufacturing Company's books at the beginning of the lease term would be as follows:

```
1988
Jan. 1  Cash . . . . . . . . . . . . . . . . . . . . . . . . . . . . . . . . . . . . . . . . . . . . . . . . . . .    65,000
        Minimum Lease Payments Receivable. . . . . . . . . . . . . . . . . . . .   240,000
        Cost of Goods Sold . . . . . . . . . . . . . . . . . . . . . . . . . . . . . . . . . . . .   175,000
            Finished Goods Inventory . . . . . . . . . . . . . . . . . . . . . . . . . . . . . .                160,000
            Unearned Interest Revenue . . . . . . . . . . . . . . . . . . . . . . . . . . . .                 49,806
            Sales . . . . . . . . . . . . . . . . . . . . . . . . . . . . . . . . . . . . . . . . . . . . . . .               250,194
            Deferred Initial Direct Costs . . . . . . . . . . . . . . . . . . . . . . . . . . . .                 15,000
            Executory Costs Payable . . . . . . . . . . . . . . . . . . . . . . . . . . . . .                  5,000
```

The 1988 income statement would include the sales and cost of sales amounts yielding the manufacturer's profit of $75,194, and interest revenue of $19,019. A note to the statements would describe in more detail the nature of the lease and its terms.

In the preceding example, it was implied that the fair market value of the leased equipment was determined by discounting the minimum lease payments at a rate of 10%. Normally, however, the fair market value is known, and the minimum lease payments are set at an amount that will yield the desired rate of return to the lessor.

Accounting for Sales-Type Lease with Bargain Purchase Option or Guarantee of Residual Value. If the lease terms provide for the lessor to receive a lump-sum payment at the end of the lease term in the form of a bargain purchase option or a guarantee of residual value, the minimum lease payments include these amounts. The receivable is thus increased by the gross amount of the future payment, the unearned interest revenue account is increased by the interest on the end-of-lease payment, and sales are increased by the present value of the additional amount. Because of the additional payment, the fair market value of the leased item would tend to increase by the present value of the additional payment.

Continuing the example for American Manufacturing Company, the initial entry when either a bargain purchase option or a guarantee of residual value of $75,000 is payable at the end of the 5-year lease term would be as follows:

```
1988
Jan. 1  Cash .............................................    65,000
        Gross Investment in Leased Assets ......................   315,000
        Cost of Goods Sold ...................................   175,000
            Finished Goods Inventory..............................          160,000
            Unearned Interest Revenue ...........................           78,238
            Sales................................................          296,762
            Deferred Initial Direct Costs ...........................           15,000
            Executory Costs Payable ............................            5,000
```

Note that as compared with the entry on page 928 when there was no bargain purchase option or guaranteed residual value, Minimum Lease Payments Receivable is increased by $75,000; Sales is increased by $46,568, the present value for 5 years at 10% interest; and Unearned Interest Revenue is increased by $28,432, the difference between the $75,000 payment and the $46,568 present value of the final payment.

Accounting for Sales-Type Leases with Unguaranteed Residual Value. When a sales-type lease does not contain a bargain purchase option or a guaranteed residual value, but the economic life of the leased asset exceeds the lease term, the residual value of the property will remain with the lessor. As indicated earlier, this is called an unguaranteed residual value. The only difference between accounting for an unguaranteed residual value and a guaranteed residual value or bargain purchase option is that rather than increasing Sales by the present value of the residual value as was illustrated above, the present value is deducted from the cost of the leased equipment. The entries to record the lease with an unguaranteed residual value, therefore, would be as follows:

Jan. 1	Cash	65,000	
	Gross Investment in Leased Assets	315,000	
	Cost of Goods Sold	128,432	
	Finished Goods Inventory		160,000
	Unearned Interest Revenue		78,238
	Sales		250,194
	Deferred Initial Direct Costs		15,000
	Executory Costs Payable		5,000

Note that the gross profit on the transaction is the same regardless of whether the residual value is guaranteed or unguaranteed as demonstrated below:

	Guaranteed Residual Value	Unguaranteed Residual Value
Sales	$296,762	$250,194
Cost of goods sold	175,000	128,432
Gross Profit	$121,762	$121,762

Sale of Asset During Lease Term

If the lessor sells an asset to the lessee during the lease term, a gain or loss is recognized on the difference between the receivable balance, after deducting any unearned finance charges, and the selling price of the asset. Thus, if the leased asset described in Table 4, page 924, is sold on December 31, 1990, for $140,000 before the $60,000 rental payment is made, a gain of $25,453 would be reported. ($140,000 − $120,000 + $15,866 − $10,413). The following journal entry would be made to record the sale.

Unearned Interest Revenue	15,866	
Cash	140,000	
Interest Revenue		10,413
Minimum Lease Payments Receivable		120,000
Gain on Sale of Leased Asset		25,453

It should be remembered that although the lessor does recognize a gain or loss on the sale, the lessee defers any gain or loss in the value placed on the purchased asset.

DISCLOSURE REQUIREMENTS FOR LEASES

The Financial Accounting Standards Board has established specific disclosure requirements for all leases, regardless of whether they are classified as operating or capital leases. The required information supplements the disclosures required in the financial statements, and is usually included in a single note to the financial statements. For example, General Mills,

Inc. reports information concerning its operating leases in Note Fourteen (see Appendix A at the end of the text).

The following information is required for all leases that have initial or remaining noncancellable lease terms in excess of one year:

Lessee

1. Gross amount of assets recorded as capital leases and related accumulated depreciation as of the date of each balance sheet presented by major classes according to the nature of the function.
2. Future minimum rental payments required as of the date of the latest balance sheet presented in the aggregate and for each of the five succeeding fiscal years. These payments should be separated between operating and capital leases. For capital leases, executory costs should be excluded.
3. Rental expense for each period for which an income statement is presented. Additional information concerning minimum rentals, contingent rentals, and sublease rentals is required for the same periods.
4. A general description of the lease contract including information about restrictions on such items as dividends, additional debt, and further leasing.
5. For capital leases the amount of imputed interest necessary to reduce the lease payments to present value.

A note accompanying the 1984 financial statements of Uniroyal, Inc., reproduced on the next page, illustrates the required lessee disclosures for both operating and capital leases.

Lessor

1. The following components of the net investment in sales-type and direct financing leases as of the date of each balance sheet presented:
   (a) future minimum lease payments receivable with separate deductions for amounts representing executory costs and the accumulated allowance for uncollectible minimum lease payments receivable.
   (b) unguaranteed residual values accruing to the benefit of the lessor.
   (c) unearned revenue.
   (d) for direct financing leases only, initial direct costs.
2. Future minimum lease payments to be received for each of the five succeeding fiscal years as of the date of the latest balance sheet presented, including information on contingent rentals.
3. The amount of unearned revenue included in income to offset initial direct costs for each year for which an income statement is prepared.
4. For operating leases, the cost of assets leased to others and the accumulated depreciation related to these assets.
5. A general description of the lessor's leasing arrangements.

An example of lessor disclosure of sales-type leases for Sperry Corporation is shown on page 933.

UNIROYAL, INC.

Leases

The company leases certain manufacturing, administrative, warehousing, transportation, and other facilities and equipment. The leases generally provide that the company pay the taxes, insurance and maintenance expenses related to the leased assets.

An analysis of assets under capital leases follows:

In millions	1984	1983
Real estate	$ 84	84
Machinery and equipment	103	105
	187	189
Less accumulated amortization	134	129
Net	$ 53	60
Lease obligations	$ 92	104

A schedule of future minimum lease payments at year-end 1984 follows:

In millions	Operating	Capital
For the year:		
1985	$ 17	12
1986	15	11
1987	12	14
1988	10	13
1989	7	13
Later years	17	74
Total minimum lease payments	$ 78	137
Less amount representing interest		45
Present value of net minimum lease payments		$ 92

Sublease rental income totaling $20 million under operating leases and $3 million under capital leases is not reflected in the above totals.
Rental expense for all operating leases charged to operations was as follows:

In millions	1984	1983	1982
Gross rentals	$25	24	24
Sublease rentals	7	7	6
Rental expense	$18	17	18

Contingent rentals included in rental expense amounted to $2 million for each of the years 1984, 1983 and 1982.

ACCOUNTING FOR SALE-LEASEBACK TRANSACTIONS

A common type of lease arrangement is referred to as a **sale-leaseback** transaction. Typical of this type of lease is an arrangement whereby one

SPERRY CORPORATION

	1984	1983
	(In millions of dollars)	
Total Current Assets	$2,639.1	$2,480.8
Long-Term Receivables (Note 7)		
Sales-type leases, less allowance for unearned income:		
1984, $226.0; 1983, $259.4	1,225.5	1,354.5
Due from wholly-owned finance company...............	110.0	110.0
Other, less allowance for doubtful accounts: 1984, $1.7;		
1983, $1.9	80.3	65.1
	1,415.8	1,529.6
Investments at Equity		
Wholly-owned finance and insurance companies	345.6	325.1
Other companies	81.8	71.5
Rental machines, at cost	682.4	659.8
Less allowance for depreciation and obsolescence	468.0	451.4
	214.4	208.4

NOTES TO FINANCIAL STATEMENTS
1 (In part): Summary of Significant Accounting Policies

Revenue and Related Costs

Revenue is derived from product sales, rentals of leased equipment, and services rendered.

Revenue under U.S. Government cost-type contracts is recognized when costs are incurred, and under fixed price contracts when products or services are accepted and billings can be made. General and administrative expenses are charged to income as incurred. Cost of revenue under long-term U.S. Government contracts is charged based on current estimated total costs. When estimates indicate a loss under a contract, cost of revenue is charged with a provision for such loss.

Noncancellable full payout lease contracts, generally covering five years, are accounted for as sales-type leases. Accordingly, the present value of all payments due under the lease contract is recorded as revenue from product sales at the time the equipment is accepted by the customer, and interest is recorded as service revenue over the lease term.

Cost of revenue is charged with the book value of the equipment plus installation costs and provisions for other costs to be incurred over the lease term. The lease term covers the estimated economic life of the equipment; accordingly, no consideration is given to any residual value of the equipment which remains with the Company. Rentals for equipment under other leases are accounted for under the operating method and are included in revenue as earned over the lease term; related cost consists mainly of depreciation.

7. Long-Term Receivables and Operating Leases

At March 31, 1984 long-term receivables under sales-type leases before allowance for unearned income were collectible by fiscal years as follows: 1986, $548.4 million; 1987, $430.9 million; 1988, $285.4 million; 1989, $146.1 million; thereafter, $40.7 million. Interest rates on all long-term receivables ranged from 9% to 22% per annum.

Rental income to be received under noncancellable operating leases was as follows: 1985, $106.6 million; 1986, $60.3 million; 1987, $37.8 million; 1988, $21.6 million; 1989, $7.2 million.

party sells the property to a second party, and then the first party leases the property back. Thus, the seller becomes a seller-lessee and the purchaser a purchaser-lessor. The accounting problem raised by this transaction is whether the seller-lessee should recognize the profit from the original sale immediately, or defer it over the lease term. The Financial Accounting Standards Board has recommended that if the initial sale produces a profit, it should be deferred and amortized in proportion to the amortization of the leased asset if it is a capital lease or in proportion to the rental payments if it is an operating lease. If the transaction produces a loss because the fair market value of the asset is less than the undepreciated cost, an immediate loss should be recognized.[16]

To illustrate the accounting treatment for a sale at a gain, assume that on January 1, 1988, Hopkins Inc. sells a warehouse having a carrying value of $5,500,000 on its books to Ashcroft Co. for $7,500,000 and immediately leases the warehouse back. The following conditions are established to govern the transaction.

1. The land value is less than 25% of the total fair market value.
2. The term of the lease is 10 years, noncancellable. Equal rental payments of $1,071,082 are paid at the beginning of each year.
3. The warehouse has a fair value of $7,500,000 on January 1, 1988, and an estimated economic life of 20 years. Straight-line depreciation is used on all owned assets.
4. The lessee has an option to renew the lease for $100,000 per year for 10 years, the rest of its economic life.

Analysis of this lease shows that it qualifies as a capital lease under both the third and fourth criteria. Since the land value is less than 25% of the total fair value, the lease is treated as a single depreciable unit. It meets the third "75% of economic life" criterion because of the bargain renewal option which makes both the lease term and the economic life of the warehouse 20 years. It meets the fourth "90% of fair market value" criterion, because the present value of the rental payments is equal to the fair market value of the warehouse ($7,500,000).[17] The entries for recording

---

[16] *Ibid.*, par. 32–33.

[17] *Computation of present value of lease:*

(a) Present value of 10 years' rentals:
   $R(PVAF_{\overline{10-1}|10\%} + 1) = \$1,071,082 \times 6.7590 = \$7,239,443.$

(b) Present value of second 10 years' rentals:
   $R(PVAF_{\overline{10-1}|10\%} + 1) = \$100,000 \times 6.7590 = \$675,900$, present value at beginning of second 10 years' lease period.
   Present value at beginning of lease, 10 years earlier:
   $A(PVF_{\overline{10}|10\%}) = \$675,900 \times .3855 = \$260,559.$

(c) Total present value, $\$7,239,443 + \$260,559 = \$7,500,000$ (rounded).

the sale and the leaseback on both the seller-lessee's books and the purchaser-lessor's books for the first year of the lease are as follows:

Hopkins Inc. (Seller-Lessee)

1988
Jan. 1 Cash.. 7,500,000
      Warehouse   5,500,000
      Unearned Profit on Sale-Leaseback...............   2,000,000
      Original sale of warehouse.

    1 Leased Warehouse 7,500,000
      Obligations Under Capital Lease   6,428,918
      Cash...   1,071,082
      Lease of warehouse, including first payment.

Dec. 31 Amortization Expense on Leased Warehouse 375,000
      Accumulated Amortization on Leased Warehouse ..   375,000
      Amortization of warehouse over 20 year period
      ($7,500,000 ÷ 20).

    31 Interest Expense 642,892
      Obligations Under Capital Lease 428,190
      Cash...   1,071,082
      Second lease payment. Interest expense:
      $6,428,918 × 10% = $642,892.

    31 Unearned Profit on Sale-Leaseback................ 100,000
      Revenue Earned on Sale-Leaseback.............   100,000
      Recognition of revenue over 20-year life in propor-
      tion to the amortization of the leased asset.

Ashcroft Co. (Purchaser-Lessor)

1988
Jan. 1 Warehouse 7,500,000
      Cash...   7,500,000
      Purchase of warehouse.

    1 Cash.. 1,071,082
      Minimum Lease Payments Receivable 10,639,738
      Warehouse   7,500,000
      Unearned Interest Revenue......................   4,210,820
      Direct financing leaseback to Hopkins Inc.
      Total receivable = (10 × $1,071,082) + (10 ×
      $100,000) = $11,710,820; $11,710,820 −
      $1,071,082 = $10,639,738.

Dec. 31 Cash.. 1,071,082
      Unearned Interest Revenue...................... 642,892
      Lease Payments Receivable.....................   1,071,082
      Interest Revenue   642,892
      Receipt of second lease payment. See computa-
      tions under Hopkins Inc.

The amortization entries and recognition of the deferred gain on the sale for Hopkins Inc. would be the same each year for the 20-year lease term. The interest expense and interest revenue amounts would decline each year using the interest method of computation.

If the lease had not met criteria three or four, it would have been recorded as an operating lease. The gain on the sale would have been deferred and recognized in proportion to the lease payments. If the initial sale had been at a loss, an immediate recognition of the loss would have been recorded.

CONCLUDING COMMENT

This chapter has discussed the basics of accounting for leases. Special considerations applicable to real estate leases and leveraged leases are discussed in Appendix A and B, respectively, at the end of the chapter. **Leveraged leases** are often very complex arrangements involving third parties who assist in financing lease transactions.

As indicated at the beginning of this chapter, the Board is convinced that more leases should be reported as capital items. Until such time as companies respond, more statements and interpretations from the Board on leases can be expected. In the meantime, full disclosure of lease arrangements seems to be a minimum requirement to meet the spirit of Statement No. 13.

APPENDIX A

CRITERIA FOR CAPITALIZATION OF REAL ESTATE LEASES

A significant percentage of leases involve real estate. If the real estate includes both nondepreciable land and depreciable buildings and equipment, special problems arise in determining how the lease should be treated. Some of the criteria used to evaluate a lease do not apply to leases of land. The FASB treated leases of real estate separately in Statement No. 13. This treatment is summarized in the flowchart on page 937 and in subsequent sections.

Leases Involving Land Only or Buildings Only

Leases of land should be capitalized only if title to the land is certain to be transferred in the future or if transfer is reasonably assured based on the existence of a bargain purchase option. Thus, only the first two general criteria listed on page 908 apply to the leasing of land. The third criterion

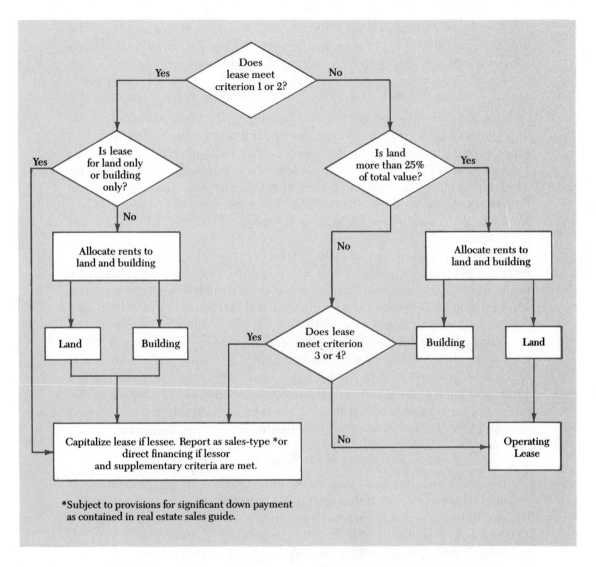

*Subject to provisions for significant down payment
as contained in real estate sales guide.

cannot apply because land has an unlimited life. The fourth criterion was
not felt to be applicable, because under this criterion no actual ownership
transfer is contemplated. Ownership transfer is an important consideration, because the residual value of the land to the lessor would be material
since there is no depreciation on land. Leases of land that meet either of
the first two general criteria are capitalized on the lessee's books and
treated as sales-type or direct financing leases on the lessor's books if both
of the lessor's supplementary criteria are also met. Other leases of land are
treated as operating leases.

No special problems arise when a lease involves only the building. The four general criteria for lessees and lessors and the two additional criteria for the lessor can be applied as discussed previously.

Leases Involving Land and Buildings

If a lease involves both land and buildings, the accounting treatment depends on which criteria the lease meets. If it meets either of the first two criteria, both the land and the buildings should be capitalized using the fair market values of the properties to allocate the capital value between them. The building lease portion will be amortized by the lessee and the land will be left at originally allocated cost. The lessor treats the lease as a sale of a single unit and accounts for it as a sales-type or direct financing lease depending on the circumstances.

If the lease does not meet either of the first two criteria, then additional tests are prescribed by the FASB to determine if any portion should be capitalized. If the land fair market value is less than 25% of the total fair value, the lease is treated as a single unit and the third and fourth criteria are applied to the single unit to determine if it should be treated as an operating or a capital lease. The estimated economic life of the building is used in applying the third classification criterion. If the fair market value of the land exceeds 25% of the total fair value, the land portion is treated as an operating lease and the third and fourth criteria are applied to the building as a separate unit. If the test is met for the building, the building portion is capitalized; otherwise it is treated as an operating lease.

Leases Involving Real Estate and Equipment

If a lease includes both real estate and equipment, the equipment is considered separately in determining the appropriate classification by the lessee and lessor and is accounted for separately over the term of the lease. The real estate portion of the lease is then classified and accounted for in accordance with the criteria applicable to leases of real estate.

Profit Recognition on Sales-Type Real Estate Leases

The provisions of profit recognition on sales of real estate (see Chapter 19) have an impact on the lessor's classification of real estate leases. Under the guidelines for sales of real estate, a substantial down payment (approximately 25%) must be made before the profit on the sale can be recognized in full. The FASB amended Statement No. 13 to specify that leases that fail to meet the criteria for full and immediate profit recognition if the real estate had been sold should be classified as operating leases, and no immediate profit recognized. This amendment does not apply to direct financing leases, or sales-type leases where a loss is indicated.

APPENDIX B

LEVERAGED LEASES

As indicated in the chapter, there are several potential economic advantages to a lessor in leasing property to others. A lessor who wishes to maximize its ability to lease often has to obtain outside financing for the investment in leased assets. A popular type of lease that has developed over the past twenty-five years to accommodate this type of situation is the **leveraged lease**. There are generally three parties in a leveraged lease: the **lessee**; the **owner-lessor**, or equity participant; and the **third-party long-term creditor**, or debt participant. Only direct financing leases are treated as leveraged leases.

A leveraged lease generally requires a down payment by the owner-lessor equivalent to 20–30% of the purchase price. The rest of the financing is provided by the debt participant as a nonrecourse loan on the general credit of the lessor. The interest rate charged on the loan is dependent on the credit rating of the owner-lessor. The owner-lessor enters into the lease arrangement with the lessee, receives rental payments, makes required principal and interest payments on the debt, and recognizes the difference as income. No special accounting is required by the lessee. The lessor records the investment in the leveraged lease net of the nonrecourse debt. The interaction of deferred income taxes, rental payments, and debt-related costs can result in complex accounting entries for the lessor. These complexities are not treated in this text.[18]

---

[18] For additional discussion and illustrations concerning leveraged leases, see *Statement of Financial Accounting Standards No. 13*, Appendix E, par. 123.

QUESTIONS

1. What are the principal advantages to a lessee in leasing rather than purchasing property?
2. What are the principal advantages to a lessor in leasing rather than selling property?
3. Why is the concept of residual value an important one in capital leases?
4. How is the lease term measured?
5. What criteria must be met before a lease can be properly accounted for as a capital lease on the books of the lessee?
6. The third and fourth criteria for classifying a lease as a capital transaction are not as restrictive as originally intended. Explain how each of these criteria can be circumvented.
7. In determining the classification of a lease, a lessor uses the criteria of the lessee plus two additional criteria. What are these additional criteria and why are they included in the classification of leases by lessors?
8. Under what circumstances are the minimum lease payments for the lessee different from that of the lessor?
9. (a) What discount rate is used to determine the present value of a lease by the lessee? (b) by the lessor?
10. What is the basic difference between an operating lease and a capital lease from the viewpoint of the lessee?
11. If an operating lease requires the payment of uneven rental amounts over its life, how should the lessee recognize rental expense?
12. What amount should be recorded as an asset and a liability for capital leases on the books of the lessee?
13. The FASB has identified a situation in which the present value of future minimum payments would not be used as the amount for the initial recording of an asset and liability for lessees under capital leases. Describe this situation and how an interest rate would be calculated for determining interest expense.
14. Why do asset and liability balances for capital leases usually differ after the first year?
15. A capitalized lease should be amortized in accordance with the lessee's normal depreciation policy. What life should be used for lease amortization?
16. The use of the capital lease method for a given lease will always result in a lower net income than the operating lease method. Do you agree? Explain fully.
17. If a lease contains a bargain purchase option, what entries are required on the books of the lessee under each of the following conditions?
    (a) The bargain purchase option is exercised.
    (b) The bargain purchase option is not exercised and no renewal of the lease is made.
    (c) The bargain purchase option is not exercised, but a renewal of the lease is obtained.
18. Distinguish a sales-type lease from a direct financing lease.

19. Under what circumstances would a lessor recognize as interest revenue over the lease term an amount greater than the difference between the gross amount of lease receivables and the cost of the asset to the lessor?

20. Terms of leases may provide for guaranteed residual values by third parties. Why have such agreements been popular in many leasing situations?

21. Unguaranteed residual values may accrue to the lessor at the expiration of the lease. How are these values treated in a sales-type lease?

22. Describe the specific disclosure requirements for lessees under leases.

23. What disclosure is required by the FASB for lessors under sales-type and direct financing leases?

24. When should the profit or loss be recognized by the seller-lessee in a sale-leaseback arrangement?

*25. Real estate leases can include land and/or buildings. Explain how the four criteria for determining lease capitalization are applied to the following:
   (a) Leases involving land only.
   (b) Leases involving land and buildings.
   (c) Leases involving buildings only.

**26. What characteristics are unique to a leveraged lease?

*Relates to Appendix A
**Relates to Appendix B

DISCUSSION CASES

CASE 21–1   (How should the lease be recorded?)

Milton Corporation entered into a lease arrangement with James Leasing Corporation for a certain machine. James's primary business is leasing and it is not a manufacturer or dealer. Milton will lease the machine for a period of 3 years, which is 50% of the machine's economic life. James will take possession of the machine at the end of the initial 3-year lease and lease it to another smaller company that does not need the most current version of the machine. Milton does not guarantee any residual value for the machine and will not purchase the machine at the end of the lease term.

Milton's incremental borrowing rate is 10% and the implicit rate in the lease is 8½%. Milton has no way of knowing the implicit rate used by James. Using either rate, the present value of the minimum lease payments is between 90% and 100% of the fair value of the machine at the date of the lease agreement.

Milton has agreed to pay all executory costs directly and no allowance for these costs is included in the lease payments.

James is reasonably certain that Milton will pay all lease payments, and, because Milton has agreed to pay all executory costs, there are no important uncertainties regarding costs to be incurred by James.

(a) With respect to Milton (the lessee) answer the following:
   (1) What type of lease has been entered into? Explain the reason for your answer.

(2) How should Milton compute the appropriate amount to be recorded for the lease or asset acquired?

(3) What accounts will be created or affected by this transaction and how will the lease or asset and other costs related to the transaction be matched with earnings?

(4) What disclosures must Milton make regarding this lease or asset?

(b) With respect to James (the lessor) answer the following:

(1) What type of leasing arrangement has been entered into? Explain the reason for your answer.

(2) How should this lease be recorded by James and how are the appropriate amounts determined?

(3) How should James determine the appropriate amount of earnings to be recognized from each lease payment?

(4) What disclosures must James make regarding this lease?

(AICPA adapted)

CASE 21–2   (Leasing isn't as risky.)

The Pueblo Machine and Die Company has learned that a sophisticated piece of computer-operated machinery is available to either buy or rent. The machinery will result in 3 employees being replaced, and the quality of the output has been tested to be superior in every demonstration. There is no doubt that this machinery represents the latest in technology; however, new inventions and research make it difficult to estimate when the machinery will be made obsolete by new technology. The physical life expectancy of the machine is 10 years; however, the estimated economic life is between 2 and 5 years.

Pueblo has a debt-to-equity ratio of .75. If the machine is purchased, and the minimum down payment is made, the debt-to-equity ratio will increase to 1.1. The monthly payments if the machine is purchased are 20% lower than the rental payments if it is leased. The incremental borrowing rate for Pueblo is 11%. The rate implicit in the lease is 12%. What factors should Pueblo consider in deciding how to finance the acquisition of the machine?

CASE 21–3   (How should the leases be classified and accounted for?)

On January 1, Borman Company, a lessee, entered into three noncancellable leases for brand new equipment, Lease J, Lease K, and Lease L. None of the three leases transfers ownership of the equipment to Borman at the end of the lease term. For each of the three leases, the present value at the beginning of the lease term of the minimum lease payments, excluding that portion of the payments representing executory costs such as insurance, maintenance, and taxes to be paid by the lessor, including any profit thereon, is 75% of the fair value of the equipment to the lessor at the inception of the lease.

The following information is peculiar to each lease:

(a) Lease J does not contain a bargain purchase option; the lease term is equal to 80% of the estimated economic life of the equipment.

(b) Lease K contains a bargain purchase option; the lease term is equal to 50% of the estimated economic life of the equipment.

(c) Lease L does not contain a bargain purchase option; the lease term is equal to 50% of the estimated economic life of the equipment.

(1) How should Borman Company classify each of the 3 leases and why? Discuss the rationale for your answer.

(2) What amount, if any, should Borman record as a liability at the inception of the lease for each of the 3 leases?

(3) Assuming that the minimum lease payments are made on a straight-line basis, how should Borman record each minimum lease payment for each of the 3 leases?   (AICPA adapted)

CASE 21-4   (More leases mean lower profits.)

Ultrasound, Inc. has introduced a new line of equipment that may revolutionize the medical profession. Because of the new technology involved, potential users of the equipment are reluctant to purchase the equipment, but they are willing to enter into a lease arrangement as long as they can classify the lease as an operating lease. The new equipment will replace equipment that Ultrasound has been selling in the past. It is estimated that a 25% loss of actual equipment sales will occur as a result of the leasing policy for the new equipment.

Management must decide how to structure the leases so that the lessees can treat them as operating leases. Some members of management want to structure the leases so that Ultrasound, as lessor, can classify the lease as a sales-type lease and thus avoid a further reduction of income. Others feel they should treat the leases as operating leases and minimize the income tax liability in the short term. They are uncertain, however, as to how the financial statements would be affected under these two different approaches. They also are uncertain as to how leases could be structured to permit the lessee to treat the lease as an operating lease and the lessor to treat it as a sales-type lease. You are asked to respond to their questions.

EXERCISES

EXERCISE 21-1   (Criteria for capitalizing leases)

Missile Supply Co. leases its equipment from Joyner's Leasing Company. In each of the following cases, assuming none of the other criteria for capitalizing leases is met, determine whether the lease would be a capital lease or an operating lease under FASB Statement No. 13 on leases. Your decision is to be based only on the terms presented, considering each case independently of the others.

(a) At the end of the lease term, the market value of the equipment is expected to be $20,000. Missile has the option of purchasing it for $5,000.

(b) The fair market value of the equipment is $75,000. The present value of the lease payments is $71,000 (excluding any executory costs).

(c) Ownership of the property automatically passes to Missile at the end of the lease term.

(d) The economic life of the equipment is 15 years. The lease term is for 12 years.

(e) The lease requires payments of $9,000 per year in advance, plus executory costs of $500 per year. The lease period is for 3 years, and Missile's

incremental borrowing rate is 12%. The fair market value of the equipment is $28,000.

(f) The lease requires payments of $6,000 per year in advance which includes executory costs of $500 per year. The lease period is for 3 years, and Missile's incremental borrowing rate is 10%. The fair market value of the equipment is $16,650.

EXERCISE 21–2   (Entries for operating lease—lessor and lessee)

The Diane Company purchased a machine on January 1, 1987, for $1,250,000 for the express purpose of leasing it. The machine was expected to have a 6-year life from January 1, 1987, no salvage value, and be depreciated on a straight-line basis. On March 1, 1987, Diane leased the machine to Melton Company for $300,000 a year for a 4-year period ending February 28, 1991. Diane paid a total of $15,000 for maintenance, insurance, and property taxes on the machinery for the year ended December 31, 1987. Melton paid $300,000 to Diane on March 1, 1987. Give all the 1987 entries relating to the lease on (a) Diane Company's books, (b) Melton Company's books. Assume both sets of books are maintained on the calendar-year basis.   (AICPA adapted)

EXERCISE 21–3   (Entries for operating lease—lessee)

Hirsch Inc. leases equipment on a 5-year lease. The lease payments are to be made in advance as shown below.

January 1, 1987	$100,000
January 1, 1988	100,000
January 1, 1989	130,000
January 1, 1990	150,000
January 1, 1991	200,000
Total	$680,000

The equipment is to be used evenly over the 5-year period. For each of the 5 years, give the entry that should be made at the time the lease payment is made to allocate the proper share of rent expense to each period. The lease is classified as an operating lease by Hirsch Inc.

EXERCISE 21–4   (Entries for capital lease—lessee)

Ironton Smelting Company entered into a 15-year old noncancellable lease beginning January 1, 1988, for equipment to use in its smelting operations. The term of the lease is the same as the expected economic life of the equipment. Ironton uses straight-line depreciation for all plant assets. The provisions of the lease call for annual payments of $325,000 in advance plus $30,000 per year to cover executory costs, such as taxes and insurance, for the 15-year period of the lease. At the end of the 15 years, the equipment is expected to be scrapped. The incremental borrowing rate of Ironton is 10%. The lessor's computed implicit interest rate is unknown to Ironton.

Record the lease on the books of Ironton and give all the entries necessary to record the lease for its first year plus the entry to record the second lease payment on December 31, 1988. (Round to the nearest dollar.)

EXERCISE 21–5   (Entries for capital lease — lessee)

On January 2, 1987, the Southwest Company entered into a noncancellable lease for a new warehouse. The warehouse was built to the Southwest Company's specifications and is in an area where rental to another lessee would be difficult. Rental payments are $250,000 a year for 10 years, payable in advance. The warehouse has an estimated economic life of 20 years. The taxes, maintenance, and insurance are to be paid directly by the Southwest Company, and the title to the warehouse is to be transferred to Southwest at the end of the lease term. Assume the cost of borrowing funds for this type of an asset by Southwest Company is 12%.

(1) Give the entry on Southwest's books that should be made at the inception of the lease.
(2) Give the entries for 1987 and 1988 assuming the second payment and subsequent payments are made on December 31 and assuming straight-line amortization.

EXERCISE 21–6   (Schedule of lease payments)

Monroe Construction Co. is leasing equipment from Siminetti Inc. The lease calls for payments of $50,000 a year plus $5,000 a year executory costs for 5 years. The first payment is due on January 1, 1988, when the lease is signed, with the other 4 payments due on December 31 of each year. Monroe has also been given the option of purchasing the equipment at the end of the lease at a bargain price of $100,000. Monroe has an incremental borrowing rate of 10%, the same as the implicit interest rate of Siminetti. Monroe has hired you as an accountant and asks for a schedule of its obligations under the lease contract. Prepare a schedule that shows all of the lessee's obligations.

EXERCISE 21–7   (Entry for purchase by lessee)

The Pavlock Enterprise Company leases many of its assets and capitalizes most of the leased assets. At December 31, the company had the following balances on its books in relation to a piece of specialized equipment.

Leased Equipment..	$62,000
Accumulated Amortization — Leased Equipment.................	49,300
Obligation Under Capital Leases	22,500

Amortization has been recorded up to the end of the year, and no accrued interest is involved. At December 31, Pavlock decided to purchase the equipment for $27,500, and paid cash to complete the purchase. Give the entry required on Pavlock's books to record the purchase.

EXERCISE 21–8   (Computation of implicit interest rate)

Morgan Leasing leases equipment to Belnap Manufacturing. The fair market value of the equipment is $442,974. Lease payments, excluding executory costs, are $70,000 per year, payable in advance, for 10 years. What is the implicit rate of interest Morgan Leasing should use to record this capital lease on its books?

EXERCISE 21-9   (Direct financing lease — lessor)

The Western Finance Company purchased a printing press to lease to the Donaldson Printing Company. The lease was structured so that at the end of the lease period of 15 years Donaldson would own the printing press. Lease payments required in this lease were $230,000 (excluding executory costs) per year, payable in advance. The cost of the press to Western was $1,924,341, which is also its fair market value at the time of the lease.

(1) Why is this a direct financing lease?
(2) Give the entry to record the lease transaction on the books of Western Finance Company.
(3) Give the entry at the end of the first year on Western Finance Company's books to recognize interest revenue.   *10 %*

EXERCISE 21-10   (Direct financing lease with residual value)

The Mountain West Insurance Company has decided to enter the leasing business. It acquires a specialized packaging machine for $300,000 cash and leases it for a period of 6 years after which the machine is returned to the insurance company for disposition. The expected unguaranteed residual value of the machine is $20,000. The lease terms are arranged so that a return of 12% is earned by the insurance company.

(1) Calculate the annual rent, payable in advance, required to yield the desired return.
(2) Prepare entries for the lessor for the first year of the lease assuming the machine is acquired and the lease is recorded on January 1, 1987. The first lease payment is made on January 1, 1987, and subsequent payments are made each December 31.
(3) Assuming the packaging machine is sold by Mountain West at the end of the 6 years for $35,000, give the required entry to record the sale.

EXERCISE 21-11   (Table for direct financing lease — lessor)

The Driggs Savings and Loan Company acquires a piece of specialized hospital equipment for $1,500,000 that it leases on January 1, 1987, to a local hospital for $391,006 per year, payable in advance. Because of rapid technological developments, the equipment is expected to be replaced after 4 years. It is expected that the machine will have a residual value of $200,000 to Driggs Savings at the end of the lease term. The implicit rate of interest in the lease is 10%.

(1) Prepare a 4-year table for Driggs Savings and Loan similar to Table 4 on page 924, but with a Gross Investment column replacing Lease Payments Receivable.
(2) How would the table differ if the local hospital guaranteed the residual value to Driggs?

EXERCISE 21-12   (Direct financing lease with residual value)

The Wagstaff Automobile Company leases automobiles under the following terms: A 3-year lease agreement is signed in which the lessor receives annual rental of $5,000 (in advance). At the end of the 3 years, the lessee agrees to make up any deficiency in residual value below $4,800. The cash price of the automobile is $16,866. The implicit interest rate is 12%, which is known to the lessee, and the lessee's incremental borrowing rate is 13½%. The lessee estimates the residual value at the end of 3 years to be $5,400 and depreciates its automobiles on a straight-line basis.

(1) Give the entries on the lessee's books required in the first year of the lease including the second payment on April 30, 1988. Assume the lease begins May 1, 1987, the beginning of the lessee's fiscal year.
(2) What balances relative to the lease would appear on the lessee's balance sheet at the end of year 3?
(3) Assume the automobile is sold by the lessee for $4,000. Prepare the entries to record the sale and settlement with the lessor.

EXERCISE 21–13   (Sales-type lease — lessor)

Collins Co. leased equipment to Afton Inc. on April 1, 1987. The lease is appropriately recorded as a sale by Collins. The lease is for an 8-year period ending March 31, 1995. The first of 8 equal annual payments of $175,000 (excluding executory costs) was made on April 1, 1987. The cost of the equipment to Collins is $975,000. The equipment has an estimated useful life of 8 years with no residual value expected. Collins uses straight-line depreciation and takes a full year's depreciation in the year of purchase. The cash selling price of the equipment is $1,026,900.

(1) Give the entry required to record the lease on Collins' books.
(2) How much interest revenue will Collins recognize in 1987?

EXERCISE 21–14   (Sales-type lease — lessor)

The Bullfrog Leasing and Manufacturing Company uses leases as a means of financing sales of its equipment. Bullfrog leased a machine to Sunscreen Awning for $15,000 per year, payable in advance, for a 10-year period. The cost of the machine to Bullfrog was $90,000. The fair market value at the date of the lease was $97,500. Assume a residual value of zero at the end of the lease.

(1) Give the entry required to record the lease on Bullfrog's books.
(2) How much profit will Bullfrog recognize initially on the lease, excluding any interest revenue?
(3) How much interest revenue would be recognized in the first year?

EXERCISE 21–15
(Effect of lease on reported income — lessee and lessor)

On February 20, 1987, Riley, Inc. purchased a machine for $1,200,000 for the purpose of leasing it. The machine is expected to have a 10-year life, no residual value, and will be depreciated on the straight-line basis. The machine was leased to Sutter Company on March 1, 1987, for a 4-year period at a monthly rental of $18,000. There is no provision for the renewal of the lease or purchase of the machine by the lessee at the expiration of the lease term. Riley paid $60,000 of commissions associated with negotiating the lease in February 1987.

(1) What expense should Sutter record as a result of the lease transaction for the year ended December 31, 1987? Show supporting computations in good form.

(2) What income or loss before income taxes should Riley record as a result of the lease transaction for the year ended December 31, 1987? Show supporting computations in good form.   (AICPA adapted)

EXERCISE 21-16   (Lease disclosures—lessee)

The following lease information was obtained by a staff auditor for a client, Schreiber, Inc. at December 31, 1988. Indicate how this information should be presented in Schreiber's 2-year comparative financial statements. Include any notes to the statements required to meet generally accepted accounting principles. Lease payments are made on January 1 of each year.

Leased building; minimum lease payments per year; 10 years remaining life..	$ 36,200
Executory costs per year (included in the minimum lease payments)..	1,200
Capitalized lease value, 12% interest............................	266,987
Accumulated amortization of leased building at December 31, 1988..	88,995
Amortization expense for 1988....................................	17,799
Obligations under capital leases; balance at December 31, 1988 ...	221,487
Obligations under capital leases; balance at December 31, 1987 ...	232,757

EXERCISE 21-17   (Sale-leaseback accounting)

On July 1, 1987, Higginson Corporation sold equipment it had recently purchased to an unaffiliated company for $600,000. The equipment had a book value on Higginson's books of $450,000 and a remaining life of 6 years. On that same day, Higginson leased back the equipment at $125,000 per year, payable in advance, for a 5-year period. Higginson's incremental borrowing rate is 10%, and it does not know the lessor's implicit interest rate. What entries are required for Higginson to record the transactions involving the equipment during the first full year assuming the second lease payment is made on June 30, 1988? Ignore consideration of the lessee's fiscal year. The lessee uses the double-declining balance method of depreciation for similar assets it owns outright.

*EXERCISE 21-18
(Entries for real estate lease with residual value—lessee)

Oceanic Corporation leases its land and building from an investment company. The terms of the lease are as follows:

(a) Lease term is 20 years, after which title to the property can be acquired for 25% of the market value at that date. The estimated remaining life of the building is 30 years.

(b) Annual lease payments payable in advance are $250,000 (excluding executory costs). Expected residual value of the property in 20 years is $800,000.

(c) Assume the current market value of the combined land and buildings is $2,370,945, of which the market value of the land is $350,000. The implicit interest rate of the lease is 10%.

What entries would be required on Oceanic Corporation's books for the first year of the lease? Assume the second lease payment is made on the last day of the first year.

*Relates to Appendix A

*EXERCISE 21–19   (Lease of real estate — lessee)

Murdock Entertainment Company leased its land and buildings on a 10-year lease from M. L. Tenneysen. The property includes 10 acres of land that is used for parking and an amusement area. The market value of the leased land is $500,000, and the market value of the leased buildings is $1,000,000. The annual rent for the property payable in advance is $221,926. There is no provision in the lease for Murdock to purchase the property at the conclusion of the lease. The buildings are estimated to have a 12-year remaining life, and are depreciated on a straight-line basis.

   (1) Does the lease of Murdock Entertainment Company qualify as a capital lease? If yes, what criteria apply?
   (2) Record the lease on Murdock's books and give the entries for the first full year of the lease assuming the first payment is made on January 1, 1987, and the second payment is made on December 31, 1987.

*Relates to Appendix A

PROBLEMS

PROBLEM 21–1   (Entries for capital lease — lessee; lease criteria)

The Bartell Company leased a machine on July 1, 1987, under a 10-year lease. The economic life of the machine is estimated to be 15 years. Title to the machine passes to Bartell Company at the expiration of the lease and thus the lease is a capital lease. The lease payments are $73,000 per year, including executory costs of $3,000 per year, all payable in advance annually. The incremental borrowing rate of the company is 10% and the lessor's implicit interest rate is unknown. The Bartell Company uses the straight-line method of depreciation and uses the calendar year as its fiscal year.

Instructions:
(1) Give all entries on the books of the lessee relating to the lease for 1987.
(2) Assume the lessor retains title to the machine at the expiration of the lease, there is no bargain renewal or purchase option, and that the fair market value of the equipment was $500,000 as of the lease date. Using the criteria for distinguishing between operating and capital leases according to FASB Statement No. 13, what would be the amortization or depreciation expense for 1987?

PROBLEM 21–2 (Operating lease—lessee and lessor)

Fraelick Industries leases a large specialized machine to the Humbolt Company at a total rental of $1,800,000, payable in 5 annual installments in the following declining pattern: 25% for first 2 years, 22% in the third year, and 14% in each of the last 2 years. The lease begins January 1, 1988, with annual renewal for $150,000 available after that time. In addition to the rent, Humbolt is required to pay annual executory costs of $20,000 to cover unusual repairs and insurance. The lease does not qualify as a capital lease for reporting purposes. Fraelick incurred initial direct costs of $15,000 in obtaining the lease. The machine cost Fraelick $2,100,000 to construct and has an estimated life of 10 years with an estimated residual value of $100,000 at that time. Fraelick uses the straight-line depreciation method on its equipment. Both companies' fiscal year is the calendar year.

Instructions:

(1) Prepare the journal entries on Fraelick's books for 1988 and 1992 related to the lease.
(2) Prepare the journal entries on Humbolt's books for 1988 and 1992 related to the lease.

PROBLEM 21–3 (Entries for capital lease—lessee)

Hughes Enterprises has a long standing policy of acquiring company equipment by leasing. Early in 1987, the company entered into a lease for a new milling machine. The lease stipulates that annual payments will be made for 5 years. The payments are to be made in advance on December 31 of each year. At the end of the 5-year period, Hughes may purchase the machine. Company financial records show the incremental borrowing rate to be less than the implicit interest rate. The estimated economic life of the equipment is 12 years. Hughes has a calendar year for reporting purposes and uses straight-line depreciation for other equipment. In addition, the following information about the lease is also available.

[handwritten margin note: Makes lease capital instead of operating]

Original cost of machine	$255,000
Annual lease payments..........................	$ 50,000
Purchase option price	$ 25,000
Estimated fair market value of machine after 5 years	$ 75,000
Incremental borrowing rate......................	10%
Date of first lease payment......................	January 1, 1987

Instructions:

(1) Compute the amount to be capitalized as an asset for the lease of the milling machine.
(2) Prepare a table similar to Table 3, page 920, that shows the computation of the interest expense for each period.
(3) Give the journal entries that would be made on Hughes' books for the first 2 years of the lease.
(4) Assume that the purchase option is exercised at the end of the lease. Give the Hughes journal entry necessary to record the exercise of the option.

PROBLEM 21–4
(Entries for capital lease—lessee; guaranteed residual value)

For some time, Red E Mix has maintained a policy of acquiring company equipment by leasing. On January 1, 1988, Red E Mix entered into a lease with HV Equipment Fabricators for a new concrete truck that had a selling price of $265,000. The lease stipulates that annual payments of $52,500 will be made for 6 years. The first lease payment is made on January 1, 1988, and subsequent payments are made on December 31 of each year. At the end of the 6-year period, Red E Mix guarantees a residual value of $45,890. Red E Mix has an incremental borrowing rate of 13%, and the implicit interest rate to HV Equipment is 12% after considering the guaranteed residual value. The economic life of the truck is 9 years. Red E Mix uses the calendar year for reporting purposes, and uses straight-line depreciation to depreciate other equipment.

Instructions:
(1) Compute the amount to be capitalized as an asset on the lessee's books for the concrete truck.
(2) Prepare a table showing the reduction of the liability by the annual payments after considering the interest charges. (See Table 1 as an example.)
(3) Give the journal entries that would be made on Red E Mix's books for the first 2 years of the lease.
(4) Assume that the lessor sells the truck for $35,000 at the end of the 6-year period to a third party. Give the Red E Mix journal entries necessary to record the payment to satisfy the residual guaranty and to write off the leased equipment accounts. Write off any remaining liability to lease expense—adjustment.

PROBLEM 21–5
(Accounting for direct financing lease—lessee and lessor)

The Winfield Leasing Company buys equipment for leasing to various manufacturing companies. On October 1, 1986, Winfield leases a strap press to the Fullmer Shoe Company. The cost of the machine to Winfield, which approximated its fair market value on the lease date, was $163,425. The lease payments stipulated in the lease are $27,500 per year in advance for the 10-year period of the lease. The payments include executory costs of $2,500 per year. The expected economic life of the equipment is also 10 years. The title to the equipment remains in the hands of Winfield Leasing Company at the end of the lease term, although only nominal residual value is expected at that time. Fullmer's incremental borrowing rate is 10% and it uses the straight-line method of depreciation on all owned equipment. Both Fullmer and Winfield have a fiscal year end of September 30 and lease payments are made on September 30.

Instructions:
(1) Prepare the entries to record the lease on the books of the lessor and lessee assuming the lease meets the criteria of a direct-financing lease for the lessor and a capital lease for the lessee.
(2) Compute the implicit rate of interest of the lessor.
(3) Give all entries required to account for the lease on both the lessee's and lessor's books for the fiscal years 1987, 1988, and 1989 [exclusive of the initial entry required in (1)].

PROBLEM 21–6   (Lease computations — lessee and lessor)

Electronix Corporation is in the business of leasing new sophisticated computer systems. As a lessor of computers, Electronix purchased a new system on December 31, 1987. The system was delivered the same day (by prior arrangement) to Ericsson Investment Company, the lessee. The company accountant revealed the following information relating to the lease transaction:

Cost of system to Electronix.....................	$550,000
Estimated useful life and lease term............	8 years
Expected residual value (unguaranteed)........	$ 40,000
Electronix implicit rate of interest...............	12%
Ericsson's incremental borrowing rate	14%
Date of first lease payment....................	December 31, 1987

Additional information follows:

(a) At the end of the lease, the system will revert to Electronix.
(b) Ericsson is aware of Electronix's rate of implicit interest.
(c) The lease rental consists of equal annual payments.
(d) Electronix accounts for leases using the direct financing method. Ericsson intends to record the lease as a capital lease. Both the lessee and the lessor are calendar-year corporations and elect to depreciate all assets on the straight-line bases.

Instructions:

(1) Compute the annual rental under the lease. (Round to the nearest dollar.)
(2) Compute the amounts of the minimum lease payments receivable and the unearned interest revenue that Electronix should disclose at the inception of the lease.
(3) What total lease expense should Ericsson record for the year ended December 31, 1988?

PROBLEM 21–7   (Sales type lease — lessor)

Aquatech Incorporated uses leases as a method of selling its products. In early 1987, the company completed construction of a passenger ferry for use on the Upper New York Bay between Manhattan and Staten Island. On April 1, 1987, the ferry was leased to the New York Ferry Line on a contract specifying that ownership of the ferry will revert to the lessee at the end of the lease period. Annual lease payments do not include executory costs. Other terms of the agreement are as follows:

Original cost of the ferry	$1,294,855
Fair market value of ferry at lease date..............	$1,766,220
Lease payments (paid in advance)..................	$ 188,600
Estimated residual value..........................	$ 66,500
Incremental borrowing rate — lessor.................	10%
Date of first lease payment........................	April 1, 1987
Lease period	20 years

Instructions:
(1) Compute the amount of financial revenue that will be earned over the lease term and the manufacturer's profit that will be earned immediately by Aquatech.
(2) Give the entries to record the lease on Aquatech's books. Compute the implicit rate of interest on the lease.
(3) Give the journal entries necessary to record the operating of the lease for the first 3 years exclusive of the initial entry. Aquatech's accounting period is the calendar year.
(4) Indicate the balance of each of the following accounts at December 31, 1989:
  Unearned Interest Revenue
  Minimum Lease Payments Receivable

PROBLEM 21–8   (Sales type lease — lessor)

Aerotech Enterprises adopted the policy of leasing as the primary method of selling its products. The company's main product is a small jet airplane that is very popular among corporate executives. Aerotech constructed such a jet for Executive Transport Services (ETS) at a cost of $8,329,784. Financing of the construction was accomplished through borrowings at a 13% rate. The terms of the lease provided for annual advance payments of $1,331,225 to be paid over 20 years with the ownership of the airplane transferring to ETS at the end of the lease period. It is estimated that the plane will have a residual value of $800,000 at that date. The lease payments began on October 1, 1988. Aerotech incurred initial direct costs of $150,000 in finalizing the lease agreement with ETS. The sales price of similar airplanes is $11,136,734.

Instructions:
(1) Compute the amount of manufacturer's profit that will be earned immediately by Aerotech.
(2) Prepare the journal entries to record the lease on Aerotech's books at October 1, 1988.
(3) Prepare the journal entries to record the lease for the years 1988–1990 exclusive of the initial entry. Aerotech's accounting period is the calendar year.
(4) How much revenue did Aerotech earn from this lease for each of the first 3 years of the lease?

PROBLEM 21–9   (Entries for capital lease — lessee and lessor)

The Alpina Corporation entered into an agreement with Multilaminar Company to lease equipment for use in its ski manufacturing facility. The lease is appropriately recorded as a purchase by Alpina and as a sale by Multilaminar. The agreement specifies that lease payments will be made on an annual basis. The cost of the machine is reported as inventory on Multilaminar's accounting records. Because of extensive changes in ski manufacturing technology, the machine is not expected to have residual value. Alpina uses straight-line depreciation and computes depreciation to the nearest month. After 3 years, Alpina purchased the machine from Multilaminar.

Annual lease payments will not include executory costs. Other terms of the agreement are as follows:

Machine cost recorded in inventory	$4,400,000
Price at purchase option date	$3,250,000
Lease payments (paid in advance)	$ 620,000
Contract interest rate	10%
Contract date/first lease payment	October 1, 1987
Date of Alpina purchase	October 1, 1990
Lease period	8 years

Instructions: Prepare journal entries on the books of both the lessee and the lessor as follows:

(1) Entries in 1987 to record the lease, including adjustments necessary at December 31, the end of each company's fiscal year.
(2) All entries required in 1988. The companies do not make reversing entries.
(3) Entry in 1990 to record (on that date) the sale and purchase assuming no previous entries have been made during the year in connection with the lease.

PROBLEM 21–10 (Accounting for capital lease—lessee and lessor)

The Gunnell Equipment Company both leases and sells its equipment to its customers. The most popular line of equipment includes a machine that costs $340,000 to manufacture. The standard lease terms provide for 5 annual payments of $130,000 each (excluding executory costs), with the first payment due when the lease is signed and subsequent payments due on December 31 of each year. The implicit rate of interest in the contract is 10% per year. Rigby Tool Co. leases one of these machines on January 2, 1988. Initial direct costs of $17,000 are incurred by Gunnell on January 2, 1988, to obtain the lease. Rigby's incremental borrowing rate is determined to be 12%. The equipment is very specialized, and it is assumed it will have no salvage value after 5 years. Assume the lease qualifies as a capital lease and a sales-type lease for lessee and lessor respectively. Also assume that both the lessee and the lessor are on a calendar-year basis and that the lessee is aware of the lessor's implicit interest rate.

Instructions:

(1) Give all entries required on the books of Rigby Tool Co. to record the lease of equipment from Gunnell Equipment Company for the year 1988. The depreciation on owned equipment is computed once a year on the straight-line basis.
(2) Give entries required on the books of Gunnell Equipment Company to record the lease of equipment to Rigby Tool Co. for the year 1988.
(3) Prepare the balance sheet section involving lease balances for both the lessee's and lessor's financial statements at December 31, 1988.
(4) Determine the amount of expense Rigby Tool Co. will report relative to the lease for 1988 and the amount of revenue Gunnell Equipment Company will report for the same period.

PROBLEM 21–11 (Accounting for sales-type lease—lessee and lessor)

Pinnock Manufacturing Company manufactures and leases a variety of items. On January 2, 1988, Pinnock leased a piece of equipment to Warren Industries Co. The lease is for 6 years with an annual amount of $38,000 payable annually in advance. The equipment has an estimated useful life of 9 years, and was manufactured by Pinnock at a cost of $130,000. The lease payment includes executory costs of $1,500 per year. It is estimated that the equipment will have a residual value of $50,000 at the end of the 6-year lease term. There is no guarantee by the lessee of this amount, nor is there any provision for purchase or renewal by Warren at the end of the lease term. The equipment has a fair market value at the lease inception of $203,089. The implicit rate of interest in the contract is 10%, the same rate at which Warren Industries Co. can borrow money at their bank. Warren depreciates assets on a straight-line basis. All lease payments after the first one are made on December 31 of each year.

Instructions:
(1) Give the entries required on the books of the lessor and lessee to record the incurrence of the lease and its operation for the first year.
(2) Show how the lease would appear on the balance sheet of Pinnock Manufacturing Company and Warren Industries Co. (if applicable) as of December 31, 1988.
(3) Assume Pinnock Manufacturing Co. sold the equipment at the end of the 6-year lease for $60,000. Give the entry to record the sale assuming all lease entries have been properly made.
(4) Assume that a third party has guaranteed the residual value of $50,000. Give the entry required on the books of the lessor for the first year.

PROBLEM 21–12   (Disclosure requirements — operating leases)

Aztec Mining and Manufacturing Company leases from Granite Leasing Company three machines under the following terms:

    Machine #1 Lease Period — 10 years, beginning April 1, 1982.
                Lease Payment — $18,000 per year, payable in advance.
    Machine #2 Lease Period — 10 years, beginning July 1, 1986.
                Lease Payment — $30,000 per year, payable in advance.
    Machine #3 Lease Period — 15 years, beginning January 1, 1987.
                Lease Payment — $12,500 per year, payable in advance.

All of the leases are classified as operating leases.

Instructions: Prepare the note to the 1988 financial statements that would be required to disclose the lease commitments of Aztec Mining and Manufacturing Company. Aztec uses the calendar year as its accounting period.

22
Accounting For Pensions

A widely recognized phenomenon of the 20th Century has been the increasing life expectancy of people in almost all countries of the world. For example, in 1900, the average life expectancy of people in the United States was 49 years; by 1983 it had increased to 74.5 years.[1] As people live longer, they must deal with the problem of financing their extended retirement years. The magnitude of the problem in the United States will increase in the next 15 to 20 years as the "baby-boomer" population of the 1940's and 50's moves into retirement.

PENSION PLANS IN OUR ECONOMY

The financing of the retirement years is accomplished by establishing some type of **pension plan** that sets aside funds during an employee's working years so that at retirement the funds and earnings from investment of the funds may be returned to the employee in lieu of earned wages. The primary responsibility for setting funds aside has varied over time and with the economic environment. In some societies and times, the emphasis has been placed on individuals assuming the responsibility for setting funds aside for future use, through prudent investment of a portion of current earnings. In other societies and times, the individual responsibility has been shared with the employer and/or government. This latter condition has become prominent in the United States, especially in the mid and late twentieth century. Three basic types of pension plans have emerged:

1. Government plans, primarily social security
2. Employer plans, either with or without employee contributions
3. Individual plans, including IRAs and Keoghs

---

[1]*The World Almanac*, 1986, (New York: Newspaper Enterprise Association, Inc., 1986), p. 783.

The United States Government introduced the social security system in the 1930s to help deal with the problems of the aged. This was accompanied by increased union demands on employers to initiate company pension plans to supplement the social security benefits. A majority of companies responded to these demands, and various types of private employer pension plans arose. Individuals, including employees and self-employed persons, have been encouraged by the tax laws to establish their own retirement plans, referred to as **Individual Retirement Accounts, or IRAs**, in the case of employees, and **Keogh plans**, in the case of self-employed individuals. Individual plans became increasingly popular in the 1980s, and by the end of 1985, in excess of $220 billion had been invested in these plans.[2]

As private pension plans have grown in number and size, the investment of the funds has become an important financial issue. For example, the General Electric Company reported almost $11 billion in its Pension Trust as of the end of 1985, and it was estimated that in the same year, the assets of all pension plans exceeded $600 billion. Investment of these large sums in the stock market has led pension plans to a prominent place in the growth of our economy and in the wide fluctuations of the investment markets.

Accounting for pension costs has been the subject of considerable discussion by accounting standard-setting bodies. FASB Statement No. 87, "Employers' Accounting for Pensions" and FASB Statement No. 88, "Employers' Accounting for Settlements and Curtailments of Defined Benefit Pension Plans and for Termination Benefits" were issued in late 1985. As indicated by their titles, these statements relate to employer plans and describe how the costs of these plans should be accounted for by the employer. This chapter deals primarily with this type of pension plan.

Regulation of Pension Plans—ERISA

The tremendous growth in pension plans led to many abuses by both employers and unions. Many pension plans did not have adequate funds to make the required pension payments, and the rights of employees who were terminated prior to retirement were often almost nonexistent. Employees counting on pension benefits when they retired often found assets lacking, or provisions changed.

As a result of pension plan irregularities and abuses, Congress enacted a massive piece of legislation in 1974 officially known as the **Employee Retirement Income Security Act of 1974 (ERISA)**. The act introduced a

---

[2]As reported by the Employee Benefit Research Institute, *DH + S Review* (April 28, 1986).

wide spectrum of reforms and regulations covering all types of pensions. The act included provisions requiring minimum funding of plans, minimum rights to employees upon termination of their employment, and minimum disclosure and audit requirements for trustees of pension plans. In addition to these provisions, the Act called for creation of a special federal agency, the **Pension Benefit Guaranty Corporation (PBGC)**, to help protect employee benefits when pension plans are terminated as a result of employer bankruptcy or other causes. When a plan is terminated, ERISA requires the employer to contribute up to 30% of its net assets to provide benefits for the employees covered by the plan. To enforce this provision, the PBGC is given the right to impose a lien on the employer's assets that gives it priority over most creditor claims. In effect, PBGC actually becomes the trustee for pension plans that terminate.

The PBGC also administers a fund supported by premiums charged to participating companies. The fund is used to pay retirement benefits if the employer is unable to do so. The economic recession of the early 1980s and the resultant business failures of many large U.S. companies led to a heavy drain on the PBGC fund. It has been estimated that at the end of 1985, the fund had a deficit of more than $1 billion. As a result of these deficits, the PBGC has been forced to increase significantly the premiums charged for covered employees. Effective January 1, 1986, the premium was increased from $2.60 to $8.50 per covered employee.[3]

A key element in all pension plans is the **vesting** provision. Vesting occurs when an employee has met certain specified requirements and is eligible to receive pension benefits at retirement regardless of whether the employee continues working for the employer. In early pension plans, vesting did not occur for many years. In extreme cases, vesting occurred only when an employee reached retirement. A major outcome of ERISA was much earlier vesting privileges for employees. This change has had a significant impact on accounting for pension costs.

NATURE AND CHARACTERISTICS OF EMPLOYER PENSION PLANS

The subject of employers' accounting for pensions is very complex, partly because of the many variations in plans that have been developed. Most pension plans are specifically designed for one employer and are known as **single-employer plans**. If several companies contribute to the

---

[3]Deloitte Haskins & Sells, "Premium Increase and New Termination Rules Set for Pension Plans," *DH + S Review* (April 28, 1986), p. 4.

same plan, it is called a **multiemployer plan**. This chapter, like the accounting standards, focuses on accounting for single-employer plans. Accounting and reporting considerations relating to multiemployer plans are discussed briefly near the end of the chapter.

Funding of Employer Pension Plans

The basic purpose of all employer pension plans is the same—to provide retirement benefits to employees. A principal issue concerning pension plans is how to provide sufficient funds to meet the needs of retirees. The social security system of the Federal Government has frequently been criticized because it is not a "funded" plan. FICA taxes (contributions) paid by employers and employees in the current year are used to pay benefits to individuals who are currently retired. This means that the current employees must have faith that a future generation will do the same for them. Such a system creates much doubt and uncertainty.

Private plans are not permitted to operate in this way. Federal legislation has been passed that requires companies to **fund** their pension plans in an orderly manner so that the employee is protected at retirement. Some pension plans are funded entirely by the employer and are referred to as **noncontributory plans**. In other cases, the employee also contributes to the cost of the pension plan, referred to as a **contributory plan**.[4] The amounts and timing of contributions depend on the particular circumstances and plan provisions. While the provisions of pension plans vary widely and in many cases are very complex, there are two basic classifications of pension plans: (1) defined contribution plans and (2) defined benefit plans.

Defined Contribution Plans

Defined contribution plans are relatively simple in their construction and raise very few accounting issues for employers. Under these plans, a periodic contribution amount is paid by the employer into a separate trust fund, which is administered by an independent third-party trustee. The contribution may be defined as a fixed amount each period, a percentage of the employer's income, a percentage of employee earnings, or a combination of these or other factors. As contributions to the fund are made, they are invested by the fund administrator. When an employee retires, the accumulated value in the fund is used to determine the pension payout to the employee. The employee's retirement income therefore depends on how the fund has been managed. If investments have been made wisely, the employee will fare better than if the investments were managed poorly.

---

[4]Employee contributions are not considered in subsequent discussions and examples, since the chapter is concerned with employers' accounting for pensions.

In effect, the investment risk is borne by the employee. The employer's obligation extends only to making the specified periodic contribution.

Defined Benefit Plans

Defined benefit pensions plans are much more complex in their construction than defined contribution plans. Under defined benefit plans, the employee is guaranteed a specified retirement income often related to his or her average salary over a certain number of years. The periodic amount of contribution is based on the future benefits to be received by the employees and is affected by a number of variables. Because the benefits are defined, the contributions (funding) must vary as conditions change. Exhibit 22–1 illustrates the basic nature of a defined benefit plan. A defined contribution plan could be illustrated in the same manner except that the contributions (rather than the benefits) would be defined. This difference, however, is significant and accounts for the complexity of defined benefit plans.

Exhibit 22–1 Defined Benefit Pension Plans

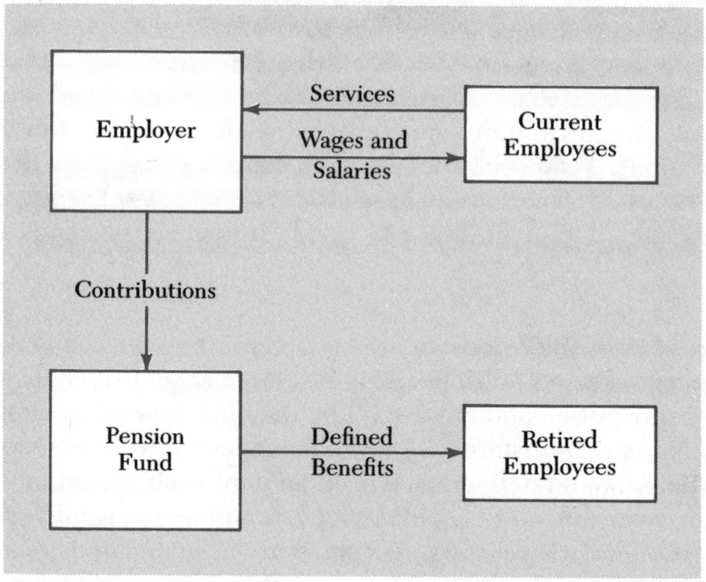

```
   ┌──────────────┐   Services      ┌──────────────┐
   │              │ ◄────────────   │              │
   │   Employer   │   Wages and     │   Current    │
   │              │   Salaries      │  Employees   │
   │              │ ───────────►    │              │
   └──────────────┘                 └──────────────┘
          │
    Contributions
          │
          ▼
   ┌──────────────┐   Defined       ┌──────────────┐
   │   Pension    │   Benefits      │   Retired    │
   │    Fund      │ ───────────►    │  Employees   │
   │              │                 │              │
   └──────────────┘                 └──────────────┘
```

Under defined benefit plans, the investment risk is, in substance, borne by the employer. While a separate trust fund is usually maintained for contributions and investment earnings, the employer is ultimately responsible to assure that employees receive the defined benefits provided by the plan. Pension fund assets may be viewed essentially as funds set aside to meet the employer's future pension obligation just as funds may be set aside for other purposes, e.g., to retire bonds at maturity. One major difference, however, is that a future obligation to retire bonds is a definite amount, while the employer's future obligation for retirement benefits is based on many estimates and assumptions.

Defined Benefits. Defined benefit plans provide for an increase in future retirement benefits as additional services are rendered by an employee. In effect, the employee's total compensation for a period consists of current wages or salaries plus the right to receive a defined amount of future benefits. The amount of future benefits earned by employees for a particular period is determined by actuaries, not accountants. However, an understanding of the basic concepts used in measuring future retirement benefits is necessary for understanding the accounting issues relating to pensions.

The amount of future benefits earned for a period is based on the plan's **benefit formula**, which specifies how benefits are **attributed** (assigned) to years of employee service. Some plans attribute equal benefits to each year of service rendered, e.g., a pension benefit of $20 per month for each year of employee service rendered. Thus an employee who retires after 30 years of service would be entitled to a monthly benefit of $600 ($20 per month × 30 years of service). The benefit attributed to each year of service would be $20 multiplied by the number of months of life expectancy after retirement. Some plans attribute different benefits to different years of service, e.g., a pension benefit of $20 per month for each year of service up to 20 years and $25 per month for each additional year of service. Many plans include a benefit formula based on current or future employee earnings. For example, a plan might provide monthly benefits of 2% of an employee's average annual earnings for the 5 years preceding retirement. This type of benefit formula requires an estimate of future earnings in determining the additional benefits earned in the current period.

Two different approaches are used to determine the amount of future benefits earned by employees under a defined benefit plan: (1) the accumulated benefit approach and (2) the projected benefit approach. The **accumulated benefit approach** is used when benefits are non-pay related (e.g., a fixed monthly benefit for each year of service) or based on current salary levels. When benefits are defined in terms of future salaries, the **projected benefit approach** is used.

Regardless of the approach used, the measurement of future benefits is highly subjective. The amount of benefits earned by employees for a period is based on many variables including the average age of employees, length of service, expected turnover, vesting provisions, and life expectancy. Thus, the actuaries must estimate how many of the current employees will retire and when they will retire, the number of employees who will leave the company prior to retirement, the number who will leave with vested benefits, the life expectancy of employees after retirement, and other relevant factors.

Funding of Defined Benefit Plans. The periodic amounts to be contributed to a defined benefit plan by the employer are directly related to the future benefits expected to be paid to current employees. The methods of funding pension plans vary widely. Most defined benefit plans require periodic contributions that accumulate to the balance needed to pay the promised retirement benefits to employees. Some plans specify an even amount each year. Others require a lower amount in the early years of employee service, with an accelerating schedule over the years. Still other plans provide for a higher amount at first, then a declining pattern of funding. The contribution amounts are determined by actuarial formulas and must be adjusted as estimates and assumptions are revised to reflect changing conditions.

All funding methods are based on present values. The additional future benefits earned by employees each year must be discounted to their present value, referred to as the **actuarial present value**, using an assumed rate of return on pension fund investments. In many cases, employers contribute an amount equal to the present value of future benefits attributed to current services. As noted above, however, funding patterns vary and the amount contributed for a particular period may be less than or greater than the present value of the additional benefits earned for the period. Assume, for example, that the present value of future benefits earned in the current period is determined to be $30,000 using a discount rate of 8%. If the funding method requires a contribution of only $25,000 for the period, the employer has an **unfunded** obligation of $5,000. At the end of the following year, this obligation will have increased to $5,400 to reflect the interest cost of 8%. When contributions exceed the present value of the future benefits, lower contributions will be required in subsequent periods as a result of earnings on the "overfunded" amount.

Thus far the discussion has focused on the additional future benefits earned by employees for **current services**. When a pension plan is first adopted, provision must be made to give credit to current employees for prior services rendered. Some of the current employees may be near retirement with few years of future service remaining, but they will still receive full retirement benefits. Actuaries analyze the extent of the additional benefits attributable to **prior services**, and negotiate with the employer as to how these benefits will be funded. The entire amount could be funded immediately by one contribution equal to the present value of the additional future benefits. In many cases, the amount is relatively large, and the employer is permitted to fund the benefits over several years.

To illustrate, assume that a pension plan is adopted on January 1, 1988. The current employees are granted benefits "retroactively" for services rendered prior to the plan adoption and the present value of those benefits, as measured by actuaries, is $825,000. This amount is to be funded by the employer over a 12-year period, with an equal amount being contributed at the end of each year. If the interest rate is 8%, the annual contribution amount can be determined using the formula for the present value of an ordinary annuity and Table IV from Chapter 6 (see page 233).

$$PV_n = R(PVAF_{\overline{n}|i})$$

$$R = \frac{PV_n}{PVAF_{\overline{n}|i}}$$

$$R = \frac{\$825,000}{\text{Table IV}_{\overline{12}|8\%}}$$

$$R = \frac{\$825,000}{7.5361}$$

$$R = \$109,473$$

As the computations indicate, 12 annual payments of $109,473 will liquidate the employer's prior service obligation by the end of 1999.

The problem of providing additional funds to cover prior services also arises whenever a plan amendment is adopted to provide for increased benefits. In recent years, a high inflation rate has made it necessary for many employers to amend their pension plans in order to provide an adequate retirement income for their employees. The additional benefits granted for services prior to the plan amendment must be measured and funded in some equitable manner as discussed previously in the context of plan adoption.

Scope of Pension Accounting Standards. Most individual retirement programs are defined contribution plans. Amounts are invested in IRAs, real estate, Keogh plans, etc. At retirement, the value of these assets is used to establish a payout program for the retiree. Employer programs may be either defined contribution or defined benefit plans. Because accounting for defined contribution plans merely involves charging the employer's periodic contribution to pension expense, the FASB focused its work, and Statement No. 87, on defined benefit plans. This chapter follows the same emphasis.

HISTORY OF PENSION ACCOUNTING STANDARDS

The first accounting pronouncement dealing with pension plans was *Accounting Research Bulletin No. 47*, "Accounting for Costs of Pension Plans," issued in 1956 by the Committee on Accounting Procedures. The Committee recommended an accrual approach that recognizes pension costs as expense over the period of active service of covered employees and that prior service costs be charged to future periods rather than revising prior years' income figures. Because of the large number of pension plans already in existence at that time, the standard did not specify any one method of determining pension cost. The standard did require, however, that the financial statements reflect the present value of pension obligations to employees to the extent the employees' rights to the benefits had vested.

The Accounting Principles Board addressed pensions in *APB Opinion No. 8*, "Accounting for the Cost of Pension Plans," issued in 1967. This standard reiterated the preference for an accrual approach to pension accounting, but it still did not require one particular method. Instead, a minimum and maximum amount was defined for determining the proper pension cost. As long as the employer's accrual for pension expense was within the defined range, it was acceptable. APB Opinion No. 8 governed accounting for pension costs for two decades.

Because there was still wide diversity in accounting for pension costs, and because the conceptual framework project raised questions as to the adequacy of APB Opinion No. 8 in dealing with pension assets and liabilities, the topic of pensions was added to the FASB's agenda in 1975. As indicated in Chapter 1 (see page 13), the project that resulted in the 1985 FASB standards lasted for more than ten years. No other accounting issue has generated greater debate and concern among companies and accountants than the issue of pensions.[5] Statements No. 87 and No. 88 are complete replacements of APB Opinion No. 8, and they continue "the evolutionary search for more meaningful and more useful pension accounting."[6] As this comment implies, the Board members recognize that additional standards may be required before all issues in the pension area are resolved.

The FASB also addressed accounting and reporting by pension plans (i.e., the pension trust funds) as separate entities during the ten-year study

---

[5]While studying the pension area, the FASB issued in 1980 *Statement of Financial Accounting Standards No. 36* "Disclosure of Pension Information" that required additional disclosures to supplement those required under APB Opinion No. 8. Like APB Opinion No. 8, FASB Statement No. 36 was superseded by FASB Statements No. 87 and 88.

[6]*Statement of Financial Accounting Standards No. 87*, "Employers' Accounting for Pensions," (Stamford: Financial Accounting Standards Board, 1985), par. 5.

period. This resulted in the issuance of *FASB Statement No. 35,* "Accounting and Reporting by Defined Benefit Plans" in 1980. This standard is not replaced by the new standards. This chapter does not discuss the specialized accounting issues relating to pension plans, but the impact such plans have on employers and their reporting.

ISSUES IN ACCOUNTING FOR DEFINED BENEFIT PLANS

Although the provisions of defined benefit pension plans can be extremely complex, and the application of accounting standards to a specific plan can be highly technical, the accounting issues themselves are more easily identified. Following is a list of these issues, all of which relate to accounting and reporting by employers:

1. The amount of net periodic pension cost to be recognized as expense
2. The amount of pension liability to be reported on the balance sheet
3. The amount of the pension fund assets to be reported on the balance sheet
4. Accounting for pension settlements, curtailments, and terminations
5. Disclosures needed to supplement the amounts reported in the financial statements

The issue of funding pension plans is purposely omitted from the list. Funding decisions are affected by tax laws, governmental regulations, actuarial computations, and contractual terms, not by accounting standards. They should not directly affect the amount that is reported as net periodic pension cost (expense) under the accrual concept. However, differences between the amount funded and the amount expensed do have an impact on the balance sheet, as explained in the subsequent section of the chapter.

The five issues identified are not new. They are the same ones previously addressed by the Committee on Accounting Procedures and by the APB prior to the FASB's decade-long study of pensions. As these issues were being considered by the FASB, there were many conflicting viewpoints, and the final pension standards differed in significant ways from the preliminary views and exposure drafts. In many instances, the final standards are not consistent with the FASB definitions of elements of financial statements as contained in the concepts statements. Three of the seven FASB members dissented from FASB Statement No. 87 and two dissented from FASB Statement No. 88. The dissenting members have documented the reasons for their dissent in Statements No. 87 and 88.

The next section of the chapter discusses accounting for pensions in the context of the five issues identified. Terms will be defined as they arise, and examples of how these issues have been resolved by the FASB will be presented. A glossary of pension terms is provided in the appendix to the chapter.

ACCOUNTING FOR PENSIONS

The basic accounting entries for pensions are very straightforward. An entry is made to accrue the pension cost computed according to the applicable accounting standards, and another entry is made to record the contribution to the pension fund. If the accrual and the contribution are equal in amount, as they have often been in the past, there is no effect on the balance sheet. However, if the amounts differ, as they frequently will under FASB Statement No. 87, the difference is reported on the balance sheet as either a **prepaid pension cost** or an **accrued pension cost**. A single account, often labelled Prepaid/Accrued Pension Cost, is used to reflect either a debit or credit balance.

To illustrate, assume the Robertson Company computed pension cost for 1988 of $230,000 and made a contribution to the pension fund of $190,000. The journal entries would be as follows:

Pension Cost...	230,000	
Prepaid/Accrued Pension Cost................................		230,000
To accrue 1988 pension cost.		
Prepaid/Accrued Pension Cost..................................	190,000	
Cash..		190,000
To record 1988 contribution to pension fund.		

As a result of these entries, pension cost of $230,000 would be reported as an expense on the income statement. Assuming there was a zero balance in the Prepaid/Accrued Pension Cost account at the beginning of the year, the balance sheet would report the accrued pension cost of $40,000 as a liability. If the contribution had exceeded the accrual, prepaid pension cost would be reported as an asset.

While the entries themselves are very simple, the determination of pension cost can be very complex. Likewise, there are many complexities that enter into the determination of amounts to be reported as liabilities or assets. These problems are discussed and illustrated in the following sections.

Determining Net Periodic Pension Cost

Net periodic pension cost is the annual expense recognized by the employer as a result of its pension plan.[7] The FASB identified four objectives of FASB Statement No. 87. Two of these objectives are directed to

---

[7]The FASB Statements dealing with pensions use the term "pension cost" rather than "pension expense" to recognize that the cost may be expensed immediately or capitalized as part of an asset such as inventory. Cost and expense may be used interchangeably. We have chosen to follow the FASB and refer to the periodic charge as pension cost.

the issue of determining the net periodic pension cost and are described as follows:

1. To provide a measure of net periodic pension cost that is more representationally faithful than those used in past practice because it reflects the terms of the underlying plan and because it better approximates the recognition of the cost of an employee's pension over that employee's service period
2. To provide a measure of the net periodic pension cost that is more understandable and comparable and is, therefore, more useful than those in past practice.[8]

The terms representationally faithful, understandable, comparable, and useful are all references to Concepts Statement No. 2 issued as part of the conceptual framework project.

The FASB recognized six different components of net periodic pension cost (alternatively referred to, for simplicity, as *pension cost*):

1. Service cost +
2. Interest cost +
3. Actual return on plan assets (if any) −
4. Amortization of unrecognized prior service cost (if any) +
5. Gain or loss (to the extent recognized) ±
6. Effects (if any) of transition to the revised standards +

Each of these components of pension cost is explained and illustrated in the subsequent sections of the chapter.

Service Cost. Defined benefit plans provide for an increase in future retirement benefits as additional services are rendered by an employee. That is, each year employees earn the right to receive additional retirement benefits as part of their total compensation. The cost to the employer of the additional benefits earned during a period is called **service cost**.[9] Because the retirement benefits will be paid in the future, the amount of service cost is the present value of the additional benefits. As explained earlier, the amount of future benefits is determined by actuaries based on the plan's benefit formula. The computation of service cost for accounting purposes, however, is not directly affected by funding decisions.

---

[8]*Statement of Financial Accounting Standards No. 87*, par. 6. The staff of the FASB responded to a myriad of implementation questions concerning this standard by issuing in late 1986 a special report, "A Guide to Implementation of Statement 87 on Employers' Accounting for Pensions — Questions and Answers" (Stamford: Financial Accounting Standards Board, 1986).

[9]This component of pension cost was referred to as *normal cost* in accounting standards prior to FASB Statement No. 87.

In order to determine the service cost for a particular year, several assumptions must be made about the plan and the economy. The FASB made the following assumptions about the computation of service cost.

1. The pension plan will continue in effect in the absence of evidence to the contrary.
2. The discount rate to be used is that rate at which the pension benefits could be effectively **settled**, e.g., the rate implicit in the current prices of annuity contracts that could be purchased to settle the benefits owed to employees.
3. If the pension plan provides for benefits that are determined by future salary levels, the pension cost shall also reflect estimated future salary levels rather than current salary levels. In estimating future salary levels, consideration shall be given to general price level changes, promotion, productivity, etc.
4. Any automatic benefit increases specified by the plan shall be included in the measurement of service costs.[10]

The amount of service cost is the actuarial present value of the benefits attributed by the plan's benefit formula to services rendered by employees during the current period.[11] One way to measure the amount of service cost for a period is to compute the present value of the expected future benefits at the beginning of a period and again at the end of a period using the same assumptions about discount rates and other factors such as future salary levels. This present value is defined as the **projected benefit obligation**. The difference between the projected benefit obligation at these two points in time, adjusted for the interest cost (discussed in the following section) on the beginning balance and any benefits paid to retirees, is the period's service cost (assuming no plan amendment occurred in the current year).

To illustrate this computation, assume that Thornton Electronics, Inc. computes the projected benefit obligation for its pension plan at the beginning and end of 1988 with the following results:

Projected benefit obligation, December 31, 1988	$1,580,000
Projected benefit obligation, January 1, 1988	1,495,000

Assume that the interest cost on the beginning balance is $156,975, and that the amount of benefits paid to retirees is $136,975. The service cost for 1988 would be computed as follows:

Projected benefit obligation, December 31, 1988	$1,580,000
Projected benefit obligation, January 1, 1988	1,495,000
Total increase in obligation	$ 85,000
Less interest cost	(156,975)
Plus benefits paid	136,975
Service cost—1988	$ 65,000

---

[10]*Statement of Financial Accounting Standards No. 87*, par. 43 – 48.
[11]*Ibid.*, par. 16.

Because there can be many complexities in an actual computation, service cost is usually determined by actuaries.

Many companies have changed or will have to change their method of determining service cost as a result of FASB Statement No. 87. If these companies previously used accrual methods that charged higher pension costs to an employee's early years, and if a company has a young and growing work force, service cost should decline as a result of changing to a more level benefit approach. For example, Phillips Petroleum adopted FASB Statement No. 87 in its 1985 financial statements and included the following note concerning the change in methods of computing service cost.

PHILLIPS PETROLEUM

Note 14 — Retirement Income Plans
The company elected to adopt FASB Statement No. 87, "Employers' Accounting for Pensions," with respect to its U.S. retirement plans, effective January 1, 1985. Application of FASB Statement No. 87 increased 1985 earnings $31 million ($.11 per common share).

Interest Cost. The interest component of net periodic pension cost is computed on the projected benefit obligation as of the beginning of the year. Previous pension standards defined interest in terms of the unfunded portion of the future benefits. The FASB, however, chose to identify interest cost and an offsetting return on plan assets as separate components of pension cost. As indicated previously, the **settlement rate** is used to compute the interest component. An interest cost of $156,975 was assumed in the preceding example for Thornton Electronics, Inc. demonstrating the computation of service cost. To compute interest cost for a period, the settlement rate is applied to the projected benefit obligation at the beginning of the period. The Thornton Electronics example assumed a rate of 10.5%, thus the interest cost is calculated as follows: $1,495,000 × 10.5% = $156,975.

Actual Return on Plan Assets. Offsetting the other components of pension cost is the **actual return on the fair value of the plan assets**. This amount can be computed by comparing the fair value of plan assets at the beginning and end of the year. After adjusting for current-year contributions and benefits paid to retirees, any increase is the actual return on plan assets.

To illustrate the determination of the actual return on plan assets, assume that the fair value of the plan assets at January 1, 1988, was $1,385,000 and at December 31, 1988, was $1,513,025 after benefits of $136,975 were paid from the plan assets and current-year contributions of

$115,000 were added to them. The actual return on plan assets would, therefore, be $150,000 computed as follows:

Fair value of plan assets December 31, 1988.................	$1,513,025
Fair value of plan assets January 1, 1988.....................	1,385,000
Increase in fair value	$ 128,025
Add benefits paid	136,975
Deduct contributions made	(115,000)
Actual return on plan assets...............................	$ 150,000

The actual return on plan assets is always computed in determining net periodic pension cost. However, as explained in a later section on the treatment of gains and losses under FASB Statement No. 87, the actual return may be adjusted to the expected return when there is a difference between the two amounts.

Amortization of Unrecognized Prior Service Cost. As explained earlier in the chapter, when a pension plan is initially adopted or amended to provide increased benefits, employees are granted additional benefits for services performed in years prior to the plan adoption or amendment. The cost of these additional benefits to the employer is called **prior service cost**. The amount of prior service cost can be computed as the increase in the projected benefit obligation arising from the adoption or amendment of the plan. As is true with service cost, the settlement discount rate is used to compute the prior service cost.

Although prior service cost arises from services rendered in prior periods, there has been general agreement in the accounting profession that the cost should be **amortized over future periods**. This is based on the assumption that the employer will receive future economic benefits accruing from the plan adoption or amendment in the form of improved employee morale, loyalty, and productivity. FASB Statement No. 87 states that prior service cost should be amortized by "assigning an equal amount to each future period of service of each employee active at the date of the amendment who is expected to receive benefits under the plan."[12] This is referred to as the **expected service period**. Because employees will have varying years of remaining service, this amortization method will result in a declining amortization charge. For example, assume a company has 4 employees at the time of a plan amendment. The prior service cost is $30,000. Assume further that the employees had the following expected remaining years of service life.

Employee 1	1 year
Employee 2	2 years
Employee 3	4 years
Employee 4	5 years

---

[12]*Ibid.*, par. 25.

The amortization fractions would be computed as follows:

Employee Number	Future Service Years	Year 1	Year 2	Year 3	Year 4	Year 5
1	1	1				
2	2	1	1			
3	4	1	1	1	1	
4	$\dfrac{5}{12}$	$\dfrac{1}{4}$	$\dfrac{1}{3}$	$\dfrac{1}{2}$	$\dfrac{1}{2}$	$\dfrac{1}{1}$
Amortization fraction		$\dfrac{4}{12}$	$\dfrac{3}{12}$	$\dfrac{2}{12}$	$\dfrac{2}{12}$	$\dfrac{1}{12}$
Amortization amount (fraction × $30,000)		$10,000	$7,500	$5,000	$5,000	$2,500

When a company has many employees retiring or terminating in a systematic pattern, a method similar to the sum-of-the-years-digits depreciation method can be used. The FASB included an illustration of how this computation would be made in Statement No. 87, Appendix B.[13] A simplified version of the Board's illustration is included in Exhibit 22–2. Assume that Thornton Electronics, Inc. has 150 employees who are expected to receive benefits for prior services under the plan amendment. Ten percent of the employees (15 employees) are expected to leave (either

---

Exhibit 22–2 Determination of Amortization Fraction Based on Service Years Rendered in Each Year

Employees	Future Service Yrs.	Year 1	2	3	4	5	6	7	8	9	10
A1-A15	15	15									
B1-B15	30	15	15								
C1-C15	45	15	15	15							
D1-D15	60	15	15	15	15						
E1-E15	75	15	15	15	15	15					
F1-F15	90	15	15	15	15	15	15				
G1-G15	105	15	15	15	15	15	15	15			
H1-H15	120	15	15	15	15	15	15	15	15		
I1-I15	135	15	15	15	15	15	15	15	15	15	
J1-J15	150	15	15	15	15	15	15	15	15	15	15
	825	150	135	120	105	90	75	60	45	30	15
Amortization fraction		$\dfrac{150}{825}$	$\dfrac{135}{825}$	$\dfrac{120}{825}$	$\dfrac{105}{825}$	$\dfrac{90}{825}$	$\dfrac{75}{825}$	$\dfrac{60}{825}$	$\dfrac{45}{825}$	$\dfrac{30}{825}$	$\dfrac{15}{825}$

---

[13]*Ibid.*, pp. 84–86.

retire or quit with vesting privileges) in each of the next 10 years. Employees hired after that date do not affect the amortization. Note that under these assumptions, 825 service years will be rendered. The fraction used to determine the amortization has a numerator that declines by 15 employees each year and a denominator that is the sum of the service years, or 825. If the increase in the projected benefit obligation, or prior service cost, arising from a plan amendment at the end of 1987 was $495,000, the amortization for 1988 would be 150/825 × $495,000, or $90,000. The annual amortization for the 10 years is shown in Exhibit 22–3.

Exhibit 22–3 Declining Amortization of Unrecognized Prior Service Cost

Year	Beginning-of-Year Balance	Amortization Rate	Amortization	End-of-Year Balance
1988	$495,000	150/825	$90,000	$405,000
1989	$405,000	135/825	$81,000	$324,000
1990	$324,000	120/825	$72,000	$252,000
1991	$252,000	105/825	$63,000	$189,000
1992	$189,000	90/825	$54,000	$135,000
1993	$135,000	75/825	$45,000	$90,000
1994	$90,000	60/825	$36,000	$54,000
1995	$54,000	45/825	$27,000	$27,000
1996	$27,000	30/825	$18,000	$9,000
1997	$9,000	15/825	$9,000	$0

It is not necessary to construct a future years of service table (Exhibit 22–2) each time an amortization schedule is desired. The formula for the sum-of-the-years-digits method illustrated on page 498 can be used with a slight modification to reflect the decreased number of employees each period. Thus, the total service years for Thornton Electronics, Inc. could be computed with the following formula:

$$\frac{N(N + 1)}{2} \times D = \text{Total future years of service}$$

where N = number of remaining years of service
D = decrease in number of employees working each year.

or,

$$\frac{10(11)}{2} \times 15 = 825$$

The numerator would begin with the total employees at the time of the plan amendment, and decline by D each period.

Although the FASB indicated a preference for this method, it also indicated that consistent use of an alternative amortization approach that more rapidly reduces the unrecognized prior service cost is acceptable.[14] As an example of such an alternative, a straight-line amortization of prior service cost over the average remaining service period of employees was presented in Statement No. 87, Appendix B.[15] To illustrate the straight-line approach using the Thornton Electronics example, the average remaining service life would be 5.5 years (825/150 employees), and the amortization schedule would be as shown in Exhibit 22–4.[16]

Exhibit 22–4 Straight-Line Amortization of Unrecognized
Prior Service Cost

Year	Beginning-of-Year Balance	Amortization	End-of-Year Balance
1988	$495,000	$90,000	$405,000
1989	$405,000	$90,000	$315,000
1990	$315,000	$90,000	$225,000
1991	$225,000	$90,000	$135,000
1992	$135,000	$90,000	$45,000
1993	$45,000	$45,000	$0

A separate amortization schedule is necessary for each plan amendment. There is no need to alter the schedule for new employees, as they would not receive benefits from prior services. If the planned termination pattern does not occur, adjustments may be necessary later to completely amortize the prior service cost.

Under previous standards, prior service costs were allocated over fairly long periods of time. FASB Statement No. 87 tends to charge these costs to expense over much shorter periods. Thus, this component of net periodic pension cost will probably increase for many companies as a result of the new standard.

Gains and Losses. Because pension costs include many assumptions and estimates, frequent adjustments must be made for variations between the actual results and the estimates or projections that were used in deter-

---

[14]*Ibid.*, par. 26.

[15]*Ibid.*, p. 88.

[16]The straight-line amortization rate can be obtained more directly by using the simplified version of the formula on page 972. Since the number of employees is equal to DN in the formula, simplification results in

$$\text{Average life} = (N + 1) \div 2.$$

Thus, for Thornton it would be $11 \div 2 = 5.5$ years. If N were 15, the average life would be $16 \div 2$ or 8 years.

mining net periodic pension cost for previous periods. For example, the market value of pension fund assets may increase at a much higher or lower rate than anticipated, the employee turnover rate may differ from that projected in earlier periods, or changes in the interest rate may differ significantly from expectations. Such differences between expected results and actual experience give rise to **gains and losses**.

Recognition of these gains and losses was a subject of controversy during the FASB's study of pensions. Immediate recognition was opposed by many accountants who were concerned about the volatility of pension expense. Like its predecessors, the FASB decided to minimize the volatility of net periodic pension cost by allowing deferral of some gains and losses over future periods rather than requiring recognition of gains and losses in the period they arise.[17] The FASB's position, as reflected in FASB Statement No. 87, represented a compromise and created some unusual and complex accounting practices.

The gain or loss component of net periodic pension cost is comprised of two items: (1) the difference between the actual and expected return on plan assets, or deferred gain or loss, and (2) amortization of any unrecognized gain or loss from a previous period.

Deferral of Difference Between Actual and Expected Return on Plan Assets. Because using the actual return on plan assets can result in significant fluctuations in pension cost as economic conditions change, FASB Statement No. 87 permits a deferral of the difference between the actual return and the expected return on plan assets through the gain or loss component. If the actual return exceeds the expected return, the difference is a deferred gain; if the expected return exceeds the actual return, the difference is a deferred loss.

The amount of any deferred gain was potentially increased by the Board's decision that allowed employers to use a flexible **market-related value** for determining the expected return on plan assets as an alternative to the **fair value** (current market value). The market-related value may be based on a maximum averaging period of five years. Thus, when market values are increasing, the use of an average market rate will smooth the fair values and always result in a lower expected return on plan assets than if

---

[17]Alternately, a company may elect to recognize all gains or losses immediately. If this election is made, the company must (1) apply the immediate recognition method consistently, (2) recognize all gains or losses immediately, and (3) disclose the fact that immediate recognition is being followed. *Special Report*, "A Guide to Implementation of Statement 87 on Employers' Accounting for Pensions—Questions and Answers," FASB, *op. cit.*, p. 23. For purposes of this chapter, all illustrations and end-of-chapter material will assume the deferred recognition method is used.

the more current, and higher, fair value were used. The accumulated gain or loss deferral that has not yet been recognized as part of net pension cost through the amortization computation discussed below is a significant part of unrecognized net gain or loss.

To illustrate the adjustment of the actual return to the expected return, assume that Thornton Electronics expected a 10% return on its plan assets, and that the market-related value of the assets at January 1, 1988 was $1,200,000. Based on these figures, the expected return on plan assets for 1988 is $120,000. Since the actual return for the year as computed on page 970 is $150,000, the $30,000 difference is treated as a deferred gain. In effect, this amount is added to pension cost through the gain or loss component in the current period. When the $30,000 difference is combined with the actual return on plan assets reported as a separate component above, the net result is to include the lower expected return, rather than the actual return, in net periodic pension cost. The unrecognized gain will be added to other unrecognized gains and losses from prior years and amortized over future years.

Amortization of Unrecognized Gains and Losses. The impact of amortizing unrecognized gains and losses on pension cost was lessened when the FASB established a **corridor amount** within which amortization is not required. Amortization is required only for unrecognized gains and losses that exceed 10% of the greater of the projected benefit obligation or the market-related asset value as of the beginning of the year. The Board indicated that any systematic method of amortization that equalled or exceeded the use of expected service years would be acceptable as long as the procedure is applied consistently to both gains and losses.

To illustrate the computation of the corridor amount, recall that Thornton Electronics has a projected benefit obligation of $1,495,000 at January 1, 1988. The market-related asset value at the same date is $1,200,000. The corridor amount is computed using the higher amount of $1,495,000 × 10%, or $149,500. If the unrecognized gain carried over from the previous year was $200,000, and if the average service life of the employees was 5.5 years, the minimum amortization for 1988 would be $9,182 [($200,000 − $149,500) ÷ 5.5 years.]

Summary of Gains and Losses. The amount of gains and losses to be reported as a component of net periodic pension cost is the sum of the gain or loss deferral for the current period and the amortization of unrecognized gains and losses from previous periods. Because there can be different combinations of gains and losses, care must be taken when including the gain or loss component in the computation of net pension cost. The following table summarizes the possible combinations that can occur.

	Added in Computing Net Pension Cost	Deducted in Computing Net Pension Cost
Deferred gain in current year	X	
Deferred loss in current year		X
Amortization of deferred gain from prior years		X
Amortization of deferred loss from prior years	X	

In the Thorton Electronics example, the $9,182 amortization of the gain is deducted from the $30,000 gain deferral, and the net deferred gain of $20,818 is added to pension cost. Thornton would now have $220,818 to carry forward as an unrecognized net gain for the next year ($200,000 + $30,000 − $9,182).[18]

Amortization of Transition Amount. The last component of service cost arises as a result of the transition between accounting for pensions under previous standards and those required under FASB Statement No. 87. The **transition amount** is defined as the difference between the projected benefit obligation and the fair value of the plan assets at the time FASB Statement No. 87 is adopted by a company. If the projected benefit obligation is the larger of the two values, the difference is a loss. If the fair value of the plan assets is the larger value, the difference is a gain. This indicated gain or loss is further adjusted by any balance sheet pension liability or asset recorded under previous accounting standards. The net result is a **transition gain** or **transition loss.** This amount is not recorded on the books, but the gain or loss is periodically recognized through amortization on a straight-line basis over the average remaining service life of the participating employees. (See the straight-line amortization method illustrated for prior service cost on page 973). Alternatively, if the average service life is less than 15 years, the employer is permitted to use a 15-year amortization period. Amortized losses are increases in net periodic pension cost, while amortized gains are decreases in net periodic pension cost.

The use of a transition adjustment provides employers' pension plans with a fresh start. Any previously unrecognized prior service cost or actuarial gains or losses are included in this one adjustment amount. A company would have no unrecognized prior service cost to amortize unless plan amendments were adopted after the transition date. Likewise, unre-

---

[18]This simplified example has stressed the gain or loss arising from the change in the value and return on plan assets. Additional gains or losses can also arise from changes in other pension variables such as a change in the expected projected benefit obligation arising from changes in such variables as employee turnover, mortality of retirees, interest rates, etc. The amount of unrecognized net gain or loss to be used in pension computations will usually be furnished to the employer by actuaries.

cognized gains and losses would be only those arising for subsequent years.[19] Any accrued/prepaid pension costs would still be reported on the financial statements and would not be affected by the transition adjustment.

Exhibit 22–5 illustrates the computation of the transition gain or loss and amortization under four different, independent conditions.

Exhibit 22–5 Illustrative Computations of Transition Gain or Loss and Annual Amortization Amount

	Condition			
	1	2	3	4
Projected benefit obligation at transition date.............	$15,315,000	$ 9,630,000	$8,720,000	$11,260,000
Fair market value of plan assets at transition date...........	9,600,000	10,756,000	6,950,000	13,500,000
Difference — transition amount ..	$ 5,715,000	$(1,126,000)	$1,770,000	$(2,240,000)
Prepaid/(accrued) pension cost at transition date...........	—	500,000	(300,000)	(600,000)
Transition (gain) or loss to be amortized..................	$ 5,715,000	$ (626,000)	$1,470,000	$(2,840,000)
Average remaining service life (amortization period)	15 years	12 years*	10 years*	20 years
Annual amortization of transition (gain) or loss to be (deducted) or added in computing net periodic pension cost........	$ 381,000	$ (52,167)	$ 147,000	$ (142,000)

*Alternatively, an amortization period of 15 years could be used.

To complete the illustration for Thornton Electronics, Inc., assume that at the time FASB Statement No. 87 is adopted, January 1, 1987, the projected benefit obligation is $940,000 and the fair value of the plan assets is $1,240,000. Assume further that there is no liability or prepayment for pension costs at the time of adoption. Because the average remaining service life is 5.5 years, Thornton elects to amortize the transition gain over 15 years. The annual amortization would thus be ($20,000), computed as follows:

$$(\$940,000 - \$1,240,000) \div 15 = \$(20,000)$$

---

[19]*Special Report,* "A Guide to Implementation of Statement 87 on Employers' Accounting for Pensions — Questions and Answers" (Stamford: Financial Accounting Standards Board, 1986) p. 18.

Summary of Pension Cost. The net periodic pension cost is determined by combining the six components. Throughout the preceding discussion, Thornton Electronics, Inc. was used to illustrate the computation of the individual components. A summary of the information and the amount that would be reported as the pension cost for 1988 is presented below.

Thornton Electronics, Inc.
Summary of Net Periodic Pension Cost—1988

Information Used to Compute Net Periodic Pension Cost:

January 1, 1988	Projected benefit obligation	$1,495,000
December 31, 1988	Projected benefit obligation	$1,580,000
January 1, 1988	Fair value of plan assets..............	$1,385,000
January 1, 1988	Market-related value of plan assets	$1,200,000
	Settlement discount rate..............	10.5%
	Average remaining service life of employees........................	5.5 years
	Unamortized gain—prior years........	$ 200,000
	Actual return on plan assets	$ 150,000
	Expected rate of return	10%

Components of Net Periodic Pension Cost:

Service cost	$ 65,000
Interest cost	156,975
Actual return on plan assets	(150,000)
Amortization of prior service cost	90,000
Gain or (loss)	20,818
Amortization of transition (gain) or loss........	(20,000)
Net periodic pension cost....................	$ 162,793

The journal entry on Thornton's books to record the pension cost for 1988 would be as follows:

Pension Cost...	162,793	
Prepaid/Accrued Pension Cost		162,793
To record accrual of net pension cost for 1988.		

The funding for 1988 would be determined by the plan provisions, and would not necessarily be related to the determination of the pension cost. Assume the funding provisions require a payment of $135,000 for 1988. The following journal entry would made to record the payment.

Prepaid/Accrued Pension Cost	135,000	
Cash..		135,000
To record funding of pension plan.		

As a result of these two entries, the balance sheet for Thornton Electronics, Inc. would report an accrued liability for pension cost of $27,793 and the income statement would report net pension cost of $162,793. If the contributions exceed the accrual of pension cost, the difference would be reported as a prepaid pension cost. In most cases, these accounts would be reported in the noncurrent section of the balance sheet unless the facts indicated that the amounts would be settled within the next fiscal year.

Determining Pension Liability

As described earlier, an employer under a defined benefit plan assumes the responsibility for making pension payments to retired employees based on the pension formula in the plan. The exact amount of these future payments is not known until they occur. Most plans provide for pension payments that are related to the salary levels in the years preceding retirement. For example, in the authors' pension plan at their University, the formula is based on an average salary computed on the highest five consecutive salary years before retirement. The exact amount of the payments also depends on how long the retiree lives after retirement, and what option for payment is selected.

The greatest controversy in employers' accounting for pensions concerns how the employer's obligation for these highly uncertain future payments should be reported — more specifically, how the employer should report the obligation for future benefits that have been earned by employees but not yet funded by the employer. There are two conditions giving rise to these unfunded benefits: (1) when the annual net periodic pension cost exceeds the amount of the annual pension fund contribution, and (2) when the present value of the future benefits for services already rendered exceeds the amount of pension fund assets.

The liability for **unfunded accrued pension cost** arising from the first condition has been recognized in financial statements for many years. This situation was illustrated in the previous example on page 978. However, the existence of the second condition has seldom been recognized as a liability. The principal causes of the second condition are unrecognized prior service cost and unrecognized losses. Because these costs are amortized over future periods, there was seldom any recorded liability for these unfunded costs under accounting standards prior to FASB Statement No. 87. The failure to record a liability to reflect unfunded prior service cost has disturbed an increasing number of accountants and users of financial statements over the years. For example, in an article entitled "Pension Accounting: The Liability Question," the authors concluded that:

> Based on our work to date, we are not convinced by the arguments against recording a liability when a pension plan is established or amended. We believe that an accounting liability does exist and that

including it with other liabilities in the balance sheet will significantly improve the usefulness of financial statements.[20]

As the Board members considered the issues involved, they were influenced by the conceptual framework they had established, especially its definitions of the elements and the qualitative characteristics. They were convinced that an improvement in reporting financial position was required. Some proponents of maintaining the existing standards argued that increased benefits provided by plan amendments are granted by the employer in exchange for future services and that a liability should be recognized only as the future services are rendered. They cited the FASB definition of liabilities which stresses that the obligation has to arise as a result of *past* transactions and events. The Board agreed that a plan amendment "is undertaken by the employer with the expectation of future economic benefits . . ." and "to the extent that an amendment increases benefits that will be attributable to future services . . . ," no recognition of a liability is necessary.[21]

However, the Board members felt that prior service costs are more directly related to past services than to future periods. They recognized that for matching purposes, the prior service cost is assigned to future periods through the amortization process. They also recognized, however, that the historical policy of allocating prior service costs to future periods rather than past periods is at least partially done to avoid the continual changing of previously issued financial statements.

This analysis led the Board to accept the view that some recognition of a liability for unfunded prior service cost was warranted. FASB Statement No. 87 identified the concept of a **minimum liability** to reflect existing unfunded pension costs. The Board adopted rules for an employer to apply in determining if an entry to record a minimum liability is required. Since the pension benefit payments are future amounts, any reporting of a liability for future payments must be discounted to its present value. The FASB adopted the settlement rate as the rate to be used for discounting. In determining the minimum liability, the Board continued the practice of previous standards by allowing the rule of **offset** to be applied. This means that the discounted future benefits payable can be offset by plan assets in determining the liability to be reported.

The major question remaining was how to measure both the liabilities and the assets. The Board had already decided to use the projected benefit

---

[20]Thomas S. Lucas and Betsy Ann Hollowell, "Pension Accounting: The Liability Question," *Journal of Accountancy* (October 1981), p. 66.
[21]*Statement of Financial Accounting Standards No. 87,* par. 145.

obligation to determine the periodic service cost. This amount includes all the variables affecting the future payment of benefits, including estimates of future salary levels. Several respondents to the exposure draft of the pension standard argued that these values were unknown and highly subjective. The Board acknowledged this, but several Board members felt that a liability using these amounts would be more representationally faithful than one that used only historical salary levels. This issue became the most controversial one in the entire study, and was finally resolved by identifying a new obligation referred to as the **accumulated benefit obligation (ABO)**. The ABO is similar to the projected benefit obligation (PBO) except that current, rather than future, salary levels are used in computing the ABO. The result is an amount lower than the projected benefit obligation.[22] The accumulated benefit obligation was identified as the amount to be used in computing the minimum pension liability to be reported on the employer's financial statements.

As indicated in the discussion of return on plan assets, there were also two measurement methods under consideration to determine the value of the plan assets: the **fair value of the assets** as of a given date and the **market-related value of the assets** that can be determined by averaging values over a period up to five years. In an inflationary economy, the fair value of the assets at any given date would be higher than the market-related value. Because one of the concerns expressed by respondents to the pension exposure drafts was the impact that a large increase in liabilities would have on employers, their financial statements, and their other contractual agreements, the Board selected the higher of the two asset values, or the fair value, as the amount to be offset against the liability. When combined with the lower alternative for computing the liability (the accumulated benefit obligation), the most conservative, or lowest, minimum liability possible was obtained. While this compromise position was agreed to by a majority of the FASB, a strong opposing view was included in the dissents to the standard.

The employer must report a net pension liability that is at least equal to the **unfunded accumulated benefit obligation (ABO)**, which is determined as follows:

Unfunded ABO = ABO − Fair value of plan assets

If the employer already has an accrued pension liability resulting from accrued pension costs in excess of the amount funded, no **additional liability** is recognized if the accrued pension cost is equal to or greater than

---

[22]Under plans where benefits are not defined in terms of future salaries, the accumulated benefit obligation is the same as the projected benefit obligation.

the minimum liability (unfunded ABO). If accrued pension costs are less than the minimum liability, then an additional liability is recognized for the difference. In this situation, the additional liability equals the minimum liability minus the accrued pension cost.

If a prepaid pension cost balance exists because funding has exceeded the accrual, the *total* amount of the liability to be reported is the minimum liability (unfunded ABO) plus the prepaid balance reported as an asset. Thus, the *net* pension liability reported is the minimum liability. To illustrate, assume that the unfunded ABO at December 31 is determined to be $250,000 and the accounts reflect prepaid pension cost of $60,000. The prepaid cost of $60,000 would be reported with the assets on the balance sheet, and a separate liability of $310,000 would be reported. The result is a net pension liability equal to the minimum liability required by Statement No. 87.

Exhibit 22–6 illustrates the computation of the pension liability under four different conditions. The entries to record the liability are discussed and illustrated in the next section.

Exhibit 22–6 Pension Liability Computation

Case	(1) Accumulated Benefit Obligation	(2) Fair Value of Plan Assets	(3) Minimum Liability	(4) Prepaid Pension Costs	(5) Accrued Pension Costs	(6) Adjustment for Minimum Liability	(7) Total Pension Liability
1	2,564,500	1,685,600	878,900		125,000	753,900	878,900
2	2,564,500	2,480,000	84,500		125,000	0	125,000
3	2,150,000	2,480,000	0		125,000	0	125,000
4	2,564,500	2,480,000	84,500	32,000		116,500	116,500

(1) Present value of future benefits attributable to services already rendered by employees. The measurement of future benefits is based on current, rather than future, salary levels.
(2) Fair market value of pension fund assets.
(3) The minimum amount of net pension liability to be reported on the balance sheet (ABO − Fair value of plan assets).
(4) Excess of pension fund contributions over accrued pension costs reported as an asset.
(5) Excess of accrued pension costs over pension fund contributions reported as a liability.
(6) Additional liability, if any, necessary to reflect the minimum liability required by FASB Statement No. 87.
(7) Total amount of pension liability to be reported on the balance sheet.

Determining Pension Assets

There are two distinct types of assets related to defined benefit pension plans: (1) pension fund assets arising from employer contributions and earnings from investment of the contributions and (2) prepaid or deferred amounts arising from the recognition of pension costs or liabilities.

Pension Fund Assets. When the value of the pension fund assets is less than the present value of the pension obligation, the pension plan is said to be **underfunded**. In this situation, the rule of offset is applied and a net pension liability is reported. As indicated in the previous section, if the accumulated benefit obligation exceeds the fair value of the pension fund assets, a minimum liability equal to the unfunded obligation must be reported on the employer's balance sheet.

When the value of the pension fund assets is greater than the present value of the pension obligation, the pension plan is said to be **overfunded**. In this situation, however, **no recognition of the net asset position on the balance sheet is permitted**. The FASB's decision to exclude the reporting of net pension fund assets under these circumstances is another reflection of inconsistency in the interest of conservatism, and reflects the intense pressure that was exerted on the Board by various groups. In Appendix A of Statement No. 87, the Board stated that it "believes that . . . an employer with . . . an overfunded pension obligation has an asset."[23] The Board concluded, however, that recognition of all changes in fund asset values and in the present value of the obligation would not be practical at the present time and would be too drastic a change from previous reporting practices.

Prepaid Net Pension Cost. As has been discussed previously, if the amount funded for a pension plan exceeds the amount accrued, a prepaid net pension cost arises. Each year the total cumulative amount funded is compared to the cumulative amount accrued, and either an accrued liability or a prepaid cost is reported. As discussed previously, to simplify the accounting for these differences, a single account entitled **Prepaid/Accrued Pension Cost** can be used. If this account has a credit balance, it is reported as a liability; if it has a debit balance, it is reported as an asset.

Deferred Pension Cost. If an employer is required to record an additional pension liability as a result of applying the minimum liability provisions, the Board indicated that the offsetting charge should be to a **deferred pension cost** account (intangible asset) to the extent of any unrecognized prior service cost or any unamortized transition loss. If the additional liability exceeds these unrecognized amounts, the Board indicated the excess should be recorded as a separate **contra-equity adjustment**. The deferred account represents that portion of the additional liability that can be related to prior periods because of either the adoption of a plan or a plan amendment, or because of the transition to the new standards. These unrecognized costs will be recognized in future periods through the amortization procedures discussed earlier, and thus the deferred account is not

---

[23]*Statement of Financial Accounting Standards No. 87,* par. 98.

directly amortized. It is adjusted each period to reflect the increases or decreases in the recorded minimum liability.

The contra-equity adjustment account represents that portion of the additional liability that reflects either changes in the value of fund assets or changes in the benefit obligation that are not related to unrecognized prior service costs or to the transition adjustment. These unrecognized losses are recognized through the gains and losses component of pension cost. The contra-equity account is also adjusted each period when the minimum liability is recorded.

To illustrate accounting for the minimum liability and its offsetting asset or equity adjustment, assume the Clapton Corporation computes the following balances as of December 31, 1988:

Accumulated benefit obligation	$1,250,000
Fair value of plan assets	$1,140,000
Accrued pension cost	$ 16,000
Unrecognized prior service cost	$ 80,000
Unamortized transition adjustment	-0-

The additional liability of $94,000 would be recorded as follows:

Deferred Pension Cost	80,000	
Excess of Additional Pension Liability over Unrecognized Prior Service Cost	14,000	
Additional Pension Liability		94,000
To recognize additional pension liability.		

For reporting purposes, the $16,000 accrued pension cost and the $94,000 additional pension liability may be combined into one pension liability of $110,000 on the balance sheet.

The minimum liability is accounted for in subsequent periods in a similar manner. For example, assume that the computed minimum liability at December 31, 1989, is $104,000 and accrued pension cost at that date is $18,000. The balance in the additional pension liability account would be adjusted to $86,000 ($104,000 − $18,000). If the unrecognized prior service cost at December 31, 1989 has declined to $70,000, the following entry would be made at the end of 1989:

Additional Pension Liability	8,000	
Excess of Additional Pension Liability over Unrecognized Prior Service Cost	2,000	
Deferred Pension Cost		10,000
To adjust additional pension liability and related asset and contra-equity accounts.		

The deferred pension cost account would have a balance of $70,000 (the amount of unrecognized prior service cost) and would be reported on the balance sheet as an intangible asset. The contra-equity account balance of $16,000 would be deducted in the stockholders' equity section. A combined pension liability of $104,000 ($18,000 accrued pension cost + $86,000 additional liability) would be reported as a liability, usually under the noncurrent liabilities section. If Clapton Corporation had an unamortized transition loss, that amount would be treated the same as unrecognized prior service cost in recording the minimum pension liability.

One of the more difficult aspects of the pension standards is identifying which obligation and asset values are used for the different pension amounts. It is important to note that the "accumulated benefit obligation" is used only in determining the minimum liability. In all other determinations involving future benefits discussed in this chapter, the "projected benefit obligation" is used.

Pension Settlements and Curtailments and Termination Benefits

If a pension plan is settled or the benefits are curtailed, a question arises as to how a resulting gain or loss should be treated by the employer. **Settlement** of a pension plan occurs when an employer takes an irrevocable action that relieves the employer of primary responsibility for all or part of the obligation. Examples of a settlement transaction include the purchase by the employer of an annuity from an insurance company that would cover vested benefits, or a lump-sum cash payment to the employees in exchange for their rights to receive specified pension benefits. A **curtailment** of a plan arises from an event that significantly reduces the benefits that will be provided for present employees' future services. Curtailments include: (1) the termination of employees' services earlier than expected, for example, as a result of closing a plant or discontinuing a segment of the business and (2) the termination or suspension of a pension plan so that employees do not earn additional benefits for future services.[24]

As discussed throughout this chapter, FASB Statement No. 87 provides for delayed recognition of gains and losses arising from the ordinary operations of the pension plan. In addition, the statement provides for delayed recognition of prior service costs and transition adjustments. Thus, at any given time there are usually amounts of gains, losses, and prior service costs unrecognized in an employer's financial statements.

The FASB felt it was clear that if a pension plan is completely terminated and all pension obligations are settled and plan assets are disbursed, then previously unrecognized pension amounts should be recognized. What wasn't clear, however, is what happens when partial settlements or

---

[24]*Statement of Financial Accounting Standards No. 88,* "Employers' Accounting for Settlements and Curtailments of Defined Benefit Pension Plans and for Termination Benefits" (Stamford: Financial Accounting Standards Board, 1985), par. 6.

curtailments take place. The FASB considered this issue and presented their recommendations in FASB Statement No. 88. The statement also addresses the issue of *termination benefits*, i.e., benefits provided to employees in connection with the termination of their employment.

Settlements. In recent years, many pension plans have become overfunded because of the rising stock market. To take advantage of this situation, many companies have **settled** their pension plans by purchasing annuity contracts from insurance companies for less than the amount in the pension fund. Subject to regulations such as ERISA, the excess funds can then be used for other corporate purposes.

The accounting issue surrounding settlements centers on whether the gain should be recognized immediately or deferred and recognized in future periods. Prior to Statement No. 88, settlement gains that were accompanied by asset withdrawals from the pension fund, referred to as "asset reversion transactions," were deferred and offset against future pension costs. The Board, however, decided that if the settlement was (1) an irrevocable action, (2) relieved the employer of primary responsibility for the pension benefit obligation, and (3) eliminated significant risks related to the obligation and the assets used to effect the settlement, the previously unrecognized net gain or loss should be recognized in the current period. If only part of the projected benefit obligation is settled, a pro rata portion of the gain should be recognized currently.[25] The Board further required that any unamortized asset reversion existing from a prior settlement be recognized in the year when Statement No. 87 is first adopted.[26]

Many companies began to take advantage of this provision as early as 1985. For example, the following companies were among the many that reported significant gains arising from pension settlements and other pension-related gains in their 1985 financial statements.[27]

Company	1985 EPS	Portion from Pension Gain	Percentage
Morrison-Knudsen	$3.84	$1.49	39%
Marine Midland	6.06	1.50	25
Phillips Petroleum	1.44	.29	20
DuPont	4.61	.65	14
Manufacturers Hanover	8.38	.86	10

[25]*Ibid.*, par. 9.
[26]*Ibid.*, par. 20.
[27]Lee Berton, "Profit Volatility Rises After Rule Change," *Wall Street Journal* (May 6, 1986), p. 6.

The note accompanying the Manufacturers Hanover Corporation statement describing the effect of applying FASB Statement No. 88 to a settlement is reproduced below:

MANUFACTURERS HANOVER CORPORATION

During 1985, the Corporation also adopted Statement of Financial Accounting Standards No. 88 (SFAS No. 88) which deals with the accounting for "settlements." In accordance with SFAS No. 88, the Retirement Plan purchased annuity contracts for approximately 4,100 members of the pension plan guaranteeing the payment of their future pension benefits. In connection with this transaction, no Retirement Plan assets were reverted and no cash was received. A gain was recognized in other revenue of approximately $53.5 million, which was equal to a pro-rata portion of the excess of the Retirement Plan's assets over the projected benefit obligation at January 1, 1985.

Curtailments. As indicated previously, a pension plan curtailment is an event that significantly reduces the expected years of future service of present employees or eliminates for a significant number of employees the accrual of defined benefits for their future services. Examples include termination of employees' services earlier than expected, such as occurs when a segment of the business is discontinued, or termination or suspension of a plan so that no further benefits are earned for future services.

Any unrecognized prior service cost or transition adjustment associated with years of service no longer expected to be rendered as a result of the curtailment is recognized as a loss. In addition, the projected benefit obligation of the pension plan may be changed as a result of the curtailment, giving rise to an additional gain or loss. The Board provided for offsetting previously unrecognized pension gains and losses against the gain or loss from changes in the projected benefit obligation and called the difference curtailment gains or losses. If the sum of all gains and losses attributed to the curtailment, including the write-off of unrecognized prior service cost, is a loss, it is recognized in the period when it is probable that the curtailment will occur and the effects are estimable. If the sum of all gains and losses attributed to the curtailment is a gain, it is recognized when the related employees terminate or when the plan suspension or amendment is adopted.[28]

These rules were adopted by the Board to allow consistency between this standard and other standards related to disposal of a business segment

---

[28]*Statement of Financial Accounting Standards No. 88*, par. 12–14.

and accounting for contingencies, both of which affect the concept of accounting for pension curtailments. They do, however, result in a conflict with the delayed recognition of gains and losses and prior service costs adopted in Statement No. 87. This latter inconsistency led to a strong dissent by one of the Board members.[29]

Termination Benefits. Termination benefits to employees may be either **special termination benefits** arising from a plan amendment that covers only a short period of time, or **contractual termination benefits** provided in the original pension contract only if a certain event, such as a plant closing, occurs. In the case of special benefits, a loss and liability are recognized by the employer when the employees accept the offer of the special benefits. The loss and liability relating to contractual benefits should be recognized when it is both probable that the employees will be entitled to termination benefits because of the occurrence of the triggering event and the amount can be reasonably estimated. If the termination benefits are payable immediately, the entire amount is recognized as a loss. If they are to be paid in the future, the present value of the termination benefits is recognized.[30]

The rules relating to these changes in pension plans are complex and are often in conflict with one or more parts of the conceptual framework. A careful reading of the Statements No. 87 and No. 88, including the dissents and the appendices, reveals the continual trade-offs that were required in arriving at the final pension standards. Permitting unrecognized gains to be reported in the income statement earlier than previously allowed has created concern about how the increase in earnings will be interpreted by users. The transition periods may be especially volatile, and the financial statements for these periods must be studied carefully.

Disclosure of Pension Plans

The FASB recognized that all of the useful information concerning an employer's pension plans cannot be provided in the body of the financial statements. The Board identified as a major objective:

> To provide disclosures that will allow users to understand better the extent and effect of an employer's undertaking to provide employee pensions and related financial arrangements.[31]

---

[29]*Ibid.*, p. 8.
[30]*Ibid.*, par. 15.
[31]*Statement of Financial Accounting Standards No. 87*, par. 6c.

Statement No. 87 therefore requires extensive disclosure in the notes accompanying the general purpose financial statements. Following is a list of the required disclosures for defined benefit plans.

1. A description of the plan including employee groups covered, type of benefit formula, funding policy, types of assets held and significant non-benefit liabilities, if any, and the nature and effect of significant matters affecting comparability of information for all periods presented
2. The amount of the net periodic pension cost for the period showing separately the service cost component, the interest cost component, the actual return on assets for the period, and the net total of the other components
3. A schedule reconciling the funded status of the plan with amounts shown in the employer's statement of financial position, showing separately,
   (a) The fair value of plan assets
   (b) The projected benefit obligation, the accumulated benefit obligation, and the vested benefit obligation
   (c) The amount of unrecognized prior service cost
   (d) The amount of unrecognized net gain or loss, including differences between the fair and market-related value of plan assets
   (e) The amount of any remaining unrecognized transition adjustment, either net obligation or net asset
   (f) The amount of any additional liability arising from application of the minimum liability provision
   (g) The net result of the preceding items recognized in the statement of financial position
4. The discount rate and rate of compensation increase used to measure the projected benefit obligation and the weighted-average expected average long-term rate of return on plan assets
5. The amounts and types of securities included in plan assets and approximate amount of annual benefits to employees covered by annuity contracts.[32]

As indicated in item (3), the required disclosures include a reconciliation of the funded status of the plan with amounts reported in the employer's statement of financial position. Illustrations of the required reconciliation are included in Appendix B of FASB Statement No. 87. Essentially, the reconciliation is prepared in two parts: (1) Compute the funded status of the pension plan as the difference between the projected benefit obligation and the fair value of plan assets. (2) Identify the unrecognized items that have not yet been included on the employer's balance sheet, such as unrecognized prior service cost, unrecognized transition adjustments, and unrecognized gains and losses. The difference between

---

[32]*Ibid.*, par. 54.

the funding status and the unrecognized items should reconcile with the pension assets and liabilities reported on the balance sheet.

To illustrate the reconciliation, assume that an employer computed the following amounts related to its pension plan at December 31, 1988 (parentheses indicate credit balances):

	000s omitted
Projected benefit obligation.	$ (6,500)
Plan assets at fair value	10,000
Unrecognized transition gain	(2,000)
Unrecognized net (gain) loss	(1,250)
Unrecognized prior service cost	500
Prepaid/(accrued) pension cost	750

The reconciliation that would be included in the pension note to the 1988 financial statements would appear as follows:

Projected benefit obligation.	$ (6,500)
Plan assets at fair value	10,000
Funding status.	$ 3,500
Unrecognized transition gain	(2,000)
Unrecognized net gain.	(1,250)
Unrecognized prior service cost.	500
Prepaid/(accrued) pension cost	$ 750

Care must be taken in the use of the parentheses. They can be viewed as credit balances, and thus the projected benefit obligation and the unrecognized gains are shown as credits, and the assets, unrecognized losses, and unrecognized prior service cost are shown as debits.

An illustration of how Manufacturers Hanover Corporation reported its pension plan under the disclosure requirements of FASB Statement No. 87 is included on pages 992 and 993. Although not part of the reconciliation itself, both vested benefits and the accumulated benefit obligation are usually reported "short" before the projected benefit obligation, as shown in the illustration. The reconciliation includes reference to "Unrecognized Net Asset being Amortized over 10.5 years." This item is the net asset existing at transition, and is thus the transition adjustment. The only pension-related item appearing on the balance sheet of Manufacturers Hanover is the Prepaid Pension Cost of $64,263 included in Other Assets. Note that because of a significant overfunding of the pension plan, no minimum liability is required. Also, because of the high rate of return on plan assets, the company had net pension income in 1985 rather than pension cost. The difference between 1984 pension cost of $27 million and the 1985 pension income of $15 million is a swing of $42 million. Another illustration of pension disclosure is included in Case 22–2 for Dupont Company.

MULTIEMPLOYER PENSION PLANS

As noted earlier in the chapter, when several companies contribute to the same plan, it is known as a **multiemployer plan**. For example, university professors at many schools belong to a nation-wide multiemployer plan known as the TIAA/CREF plan. Schools place a certain percentage of a professor's salary into the fund, and at retirement, the employee receives a share of the plan assets.

When an employer contributes to a multiemployer plan, the employer recognizes as net pension cost the required contribution for the period and recognizes as a liability any contributions due and unpaid. The following disclosures for multiemployer plans are required by the FASB:

a. A description of the multiemployer plan(s) including the employee groups covered, the type of benefits provided (defined benefit or defined contribution), and the nature and effect of significant matters affecting comparability of information for all periods presented

b. The amount of cost recognized during the period.[33]

While the accounting issues relating to multiemployer plans are not as complex as for single-employer plans, a problem does arise when an employer withdraws from a multiemployer plan. As a result of the Multiemployer Pension Plan Act Amendment of 1980, a substantial obligation is imposed on the withdrawing employer for any unfunded vested benefits. The provisions of FASB Statement No. 5, *Accounting for Contingencies*, governs the accounting for this obligation.

POSTRETIREMENT BENEFITS OTHER THAN PENSIONS

Although pension benefits that are related to an employee's services rendered are the most significant postretirement[34] benefits provided by employers, there often are other benefits that accrue to an employee upon retirement. These include such items as continuation of medical insurance programs, life insurance contracts, and other special corporate privileges such as country club dues, special transportation privileges, or special discounts on items produced or sold by the employer. These amounts can often be very material. In a 1983 speech to the Economic Club of Detroit,

---

[33]*Ibid.*, par. 69.

[34]Also referred to as postemployment benefits in the literature. Since the FASB used the term postretirement in Statement 81, we have used this term in the text.

MANUFACTURERS HANOVER CORPORATION

---

12. POST-RETIREMENT BENEFITS

PENSION PLAN

The Corporation and its U.S. subsidiaries have several noncontributory defined benefit pension plans covering substantially all domestic employees. The employees of certain foreign operations participate in various local plans.

The pension plans' benefit formulas generally base payments to retired employees upon their length of service and a percentage of qualifying compensation during the final years of employment. The Corporation's funding policy is to contribute annually the amount necessary to satisfy the Internal Revenue Service's funding standards. Contributions are intended to provide not only for benefits attributed to service to date but also for those expected to be earned in the future.

Effective January 1, 1985, the Corporation amended the benefits formula of its principal domestic pension plan (the Retirement Plan) in connection with amendments effective the same date which resulted in an increase in the benefits payable under the Employees' Profit Sharing Plan (the Profit Sharing Plan). The change in the benefits formula for the Retirement Plan caused 1985 pension plan expense to decrease by approximately $7 million. Recognized actuarial gains, primarily from changes in assumptions and amortization periods, resulted in an additional reduction of approximately $13 million from 1984. These reductions were substantially offset by the increased expense resulting from the amendments to the Profit Sharing Plan.

With regard to all domestic pension plans, the Corporation also adopted Statement of Financial Accounting Standards No. 87, "Employers' Accounting for Pensions" (SFAS No. 87) effective January 1, 1985. As a result, 1985 pension expense was reduced by an additional $22.4 million.

As of January 1, 1985, the retirement plan assets were $580,691,000, the projected benefit obligation was $398,329,000 and the accumulated benefit obligation was $321,275,000. The following table sets forth the Retirement Plan's funded status and amounts recognized in the Corporation's consolidated financial statements at December 31, 1985:

Joseph A. Califano, Jr., former secretary of Health, Education, and Welfare, estimated that United States companies would pay $77 billion in health insurance premiums for their employees and retirees, as well as their dependents, in 1983. This would be more than these same companies would pay to their stockholders in dividends.[35]

---

[35]Joseph A. Califano, Jr., "Can We Afford One Trillion Dollars for Health Care?" as reported in Judith R. Vejlupek and Betsy Hollowell Cropsey, "The Hidden Costs of Post-employment Benefits," *The Journal of Accountancy* (October 1984), p. 85.

(In Thousands)

Actuarial present value of benefit obligations:

Accumulated Benefit Obligation, including Vested Benefits of $191,792	$(234,299)

Projected Benefit Obligation for Service Rendered to Date	$(305,194)
Plan Assets at Fair Value, Primarily Listed Stocks, Fixed Income Securities and Immediate Participation Guarantee Contracts	566,052

Excess of Plan Assets over the Projected Benefit Obligation	260,858
Unrecognized Net Gain from Past Experience Different from that Assumed and Effects of Changes in Assumptions	(83,792)
Unrecognized Net Asset being Amortized over 10.5 years	(112,803)
Prepaid Pension Cost included in Other Assets	$ 64,263

Net Pension Income for 1985 included the following Income/(Expense) components:

Service Cost — Benefits Earned During the Period	$ (21,709)
Interest Cost on Projected Benefit Obligation	(36,079)
Actual Return on Plan Assets	135,737
Net Amortization and Deferral	(63,065)

Net Periodic Pension Income Included in Employee Benefits	$ 14,884

The weighted-average discount rate and rate of increase in future compensation levels used in determining the actuarial present value of the projected benefit obligation were 9% and 7%, respectively. The expected long-term rate of return on retirement plan assets was 9%.

For 1984 and 1983, pension cost for the Retirement Plan was determined by the Entry Age–Frozen Initial Liability Method. Cost under this method is the level amount that would result in a pension fund equal to the present value of the pensions at retirement for employees who retire at the normal retirement age. The earnings rate assumed on plan assets was 7%. Total pension expense, which approximated the amounts funded, amounted to $27,130,000 in 1984 and $25,605,000 in 1983.

When the FASB began considering accounting for pension costs, these other postretirement benefits were included in the discussions. As the project developed, the Board decided to consider these items separately. The primary issue involved was whether these costs should be recorded as they were paid (a pay-as-you-go approach), or whether they should be estimated in advance and charged to the service-producing periods like pension costs.

The standards for determining when to record a liability seem to apply to this area. If it is probable that postretirement benefits will be paid, and the amount can be reasonably measured in advance, then an accrual of these benefits seems appropriate. Otherwise, the pay-as-you-go basis that is most commonly followed is acceptable.

In 1984, the FASB issued Statement No. 81 that prescribed the disclosures required for certain postretirement benefits pending a Board decision as to whether to require, where feasible, an accrual of these benefits. The following are the required disclosures:

1. A description of the benefits provided and the employee groups covered
2. A description of the accounting and funding policies followed
3. The cost of the benefits recognized for the period
4. The effect of significant matters affecting the comparability of the costs recognized for all the periods presented[36]

The determination of the amount of these postretirement benefits is complicated by the fact that many employers do not record separately the cost of those benefits related to retired employees. Under these circumstances, the employer should disclose the total cost as well as the number of active and retired employees covered by the plan. Disclosure of postretirement benefits by Phillips-Van Heusen Corp. in 1985 is reproduced below.

PHILLIPS-VAN HEUSEN CORP.

Postretirement Benefits — The Company and its domestic subsidiaries provide certain health care and life insurance benefits for retired employees. Employees will become eligible for these benefits if they reach normal retirement age while working for the Company. The Company recognizes the cost of providing these benefits by expensing the annual insurance premiums. The estimated cost of retiree health care and life insurance benefits was approximately $215,000 in 1986 and $225,000 in 1985.

CONCLUSION

The provisions of FASB Statements No. 87 and 88 will have a significant impact on the financial statements of almost all companies. The Board

---

[36]*Statement of Financial Accounting Standards No. 81*, "Disclosure of Postretirement Health Care and Life Insurance Benefits" (Stamford: Financial Accounting Standards Board, 1984), par. 6.

specified that the standard would generally be effective for fiscal years beginning after December 15, 1986. Because the minimum liability provision was likely to have the greatest impact on the financial statements of companies, the effective date for that provision is two years later, or December 15, 1988. This means that the widespread use of the standard will first apply to 1987 financial statements, and the impact of additional liabilities won't be noticed until 1989. Companies were encouraged to adopt the provisions of the standards earlier, and, as illustrated in this chapter, some companies incorporated the standard as early as 1985. This occurred primarily in situations where companies had large unrecognized gains that created overfunded pension conditions. Through settlements, these gains could be recognized and included in income. In addition, the use of higher discount rates and higher rates of return gave rise to significant reductions in periodic pension costs.

It is too early to tell what the overall impact of the standards will be on financial statements and on their usefulness to decision makers. The failure to recognize completely market changes as they occur will conceivably lead to management actions to recognize gains earlier and defer losses longer. Unless carefully monitored, this could lead to abuses of pension plans and leave employees with less protection than they had expected. The Board had to compromise from exposure drafts in which it had recommended earlier and more complete recognition of the impact of economic change on pension plans. This led to a more complicated standard, and one that leaves considerable doubt as to its ultimate effects.

The Board included the following conclusion in Appendix A of Statement No. 87.

> After considering the range of comments . . . , the Board concluded that the changes required by this Statement represent a worthwhile improvement in financial reporting. Opinion 8 noted in 1966 that "accounting for pension cost is in a transitional stage" (paragraph 17). The Board believes that is still true in 1985. FASB Concepts Statement No. 5, *Recognition and Measurement in Financial Statements of Business Enterprises,* paragraph 2, indicates that "the Board intends future change [in practice] to occur in the gradual, evolutionary way that has characterized past change." The Board realizes that the evolutionary change in some areas may have to be slower than in others. The Board believes that it would be conceptually appropriate and preferable to recognize a net pension liability or asset measured as the difference between the projected benefit obligation and plan assets, either with no delay in recognition of gains and losses, or perhaps with gains and losses reported currently in comprehensive income but not in earnings. However, it concluded that those approaches would be too great a change from past practice to be adopted at the present time. In light

of the differences in respondents' views and the practical considerations noted, the Board concluded that the provisions of this Statement as a whole represent an improvement in financial reporting.[37]

Early reaction to the standards is less positive as to the ultimate improvement. Certainly its complexity will require careful study by accountants, actuaries, auditors, and users. It is likely that many refinements and modifications to the standards will be required during its first few years of implementation. The impact of pensions on our society has made these standards more visible than perhaps any others. As indicated in the Board's conclusion, evolutionary changes in the pension area will undoubtedly continue.

APPENDIX

GLOSSARY OF PENSION TERMS

Accrued pension cost. A liability account that arises when the net periodic pension cost for a period exceeds the pension amount funded in the period. Once established, it is adjusted each year for the difference in the same two factors. It is classified as a current or noncurrent liability depending on the ultimate date of payment. It is related to prepaid pension cost and often only one account is maintained for both accrued and prepaid pension costs. If the account has a credit balance, it is a liability account; if it has a debit balance, it is an asset.

Accumulated benefit obligation. The actuarial present value of pension benefits based on the plan formula for employee service earned to date using existing salary structure. It is used to compute the minimum liability.

Actuarial funding methods. Methods determined by actuaries to fund the prospective benefit obligation taking into consideration income tax requirements, interest rates, employer desires, etc. Some methods provide for smaller initial payments and larger payments later. Others provide for a level payment pattern.

---

[37] *Statement of Financial Accounting Standards No. 87,* par. 107.

Amortization of unrecognized prior service cost. The component of net periodic pension cost relating to prior service cost arising from initial adoption or amendment of the plan. Amortization may be computed on a declining-balance or straight-line basis. The FASB prefers the declining-balance method that recognizes that employees will retire or leave the firm on a staggered basis. The FASB also permits the straight-line basis using average remaining service life of employees.

Amortization of unrecognized net gain or loss. The component of net periodic pension cost relating to the excess of unrecognized gain or loss over a corridor amount. A straight-line basis using average remaining service life of employees is used for amortization purposes.

Average remaining service life of employees. An average computed life based on the total expected future years of service divided by the number of employees. The expected future years of service may be computed by the formula $[N(N + 1) \div 2] \times D$, where N equals the number of years over which service is to be performed and D is the decrease in number of employees through retirement or termination of services per year.

Corridor approach. A technique used to reduce the amounts of gains and losses recognized as part of the net periodic pension cost. Only amortization of unrecognized gains and losses that exceed 10% of the greater of the projected benefit obligation or the market-related asset value as of the beginning of the period is included in the net periodic pension cost. Any systematic method of amortization that exceeds the minimum may be used as long as it is consistently applied to both gains and losses and it is disclosed in the statements.

Curtailment. An event that significantly reduces the expected years of future services of present employees or eliminates for a significant number of employees the accrual of defined benefits for their future services.

Deferred pension cost. A noncurrent asset arising whenever it is necessary to adjust the accounts for a minimum pension liability. It represents a portion of unrecognized prior service cost. If this balance exceeds unrecognized prior service cost, the excess should be reported as a contra owners' equity account.

Defined benefit plan. A pension plan that defines the benefits the employee will receive at retirement. In these plans, it is necessary to determine what the contributions should be to meet the future benefit requirements. FASB Statement No. 87 deals primarily with this type of pension plan.

Defined contribution plan. A pension plan that specifies the employer's contributions based on a formula that includes such factors as age, length of service, employer's profits, and compensation levels. FASB Statement No. 87 does not deal with these types of plans except for disclosure requirements. The pension expense is the amount funded each year.

Fair value of plan assets. The amount that could be received from the sale of plan assets in a current sale between a willing buyer and seller. Fair value is used to determine the minimum liability and the transition amount.

Funded pension plan. A plan in which an employer sets aside funds for future pension payments by making payments (contributions) to a separate funding agency who is responsible for managing the assets of the pension fund and for making payments to recipients as the benefits come due.

Gains and losses. Component of net periodic pension cost arising from amortization of a change in either the projected benefit obligation or value of plan assets resulting from experience different from that assumed or from a change in an actuarial assumption. Includes (a) difference between actual and expected return on plan assets and (b) amortization of unrecognized net gain or losses from prior periods. Amortization is required only if a corridor amount is exceeded.

Interest. The amount of interest computed on the projected benefit obligation outstanding for the period (beginning-of-year projected benefit obligation is used for the computation). The interest rate used should be the rate at which pension benefits could be effectively settled. This amount is offset by the return on plan assets in computing net periodic pension cost. If the projected benefit obligation is completely funded, and if the interest rate used is equal to the expected return on plan assets, the interest component and return on plan assets component will exactly offset each other.

Market-related asset value. A method for valuing plan assets that generally reflects an average of fair values over a period of time. Used to compute expected return on plan assets and the corridor amount for amortizing gains and losses.

Minimum pension liability. The net amount of pension liability that must be reported when a plan is underfunded. The minimum liability is measured as the difference between the accumulated benefit obligation and the fair value of the plan assets. If an accrued pension cost is already reported and the accrual is less than the minimum liability, an additional liability to reach the minimum amount is recorded. If a prepaid pension cost is reported, an additional liability equal to the minimum liability plus the prepaid amount is recorded. The result is a *net* pension liability equal to the minimum liability.

Multiemployer plan. Pension plans sponsored by two or more different employers. FASB Statement No. 87 does not include detailed accounting for multiemployer plans.

Net periodic pension cost. An amount that consists of the following six components: (1) **Service cost** component, (2) **interest cost** on beginning of year projected benefit obligation component, (3) **actual return on fair value of assets** component (a credit component), (4) **amortization of unrecognized prior service cost**, (5) (a) **gains or losses** arising from the difference between actual and expected return on plan assets plus (b) **amortization of gains and losses** resulting from experience different from assumed or from a change in actuarial assumption (recognized only if gains or losses exceed a computed corridor amount), and (6) **amortization of transition** amount, or the unrecognized net obligation or unrecognized net asset existing at date of initial application of the FASB Statement No. 87.

Noncontributory pension plan. A plan in which the employer bears the total cost of the plan.

Pension plan assets. Assets attributed to the pension plan arising from contributions to the plan. Generally comprised of cash and investments that have been segregated and designated for use of the pension plan only.

Postretirement benefits. Benefits other than pensions provided by an employer to former employees. Includes health insurance, life insurance, and disability payments. Some companies charge these costs to accounts on a pay-as-you-go basis. Others accrue them. FASB still considering this area, but has specified disclosure requirements.

Prepaid pension cost. An asset account that arises when the current amount funded for a pension plan exceeds the net periodic pension cost for a period. It is classified as a current or noncurrent asset depending on when the benefits from the prepayment are expected to be realized. Related to accrued pension cost.

Prior service cost. Cost of credit given to employees for service rendered prior to initiation or amendment of a pension plan. Often called retroactive benefits. Cost of benefits is measured by the increase in projected benefits arising from initiation of plan or by plan amendment. Usually amortized over future service life of employees as part of net periodic pension cost.

Private pension plan. An arrangement whereby a company undertakes to provide its employees retirement benefits that can be determined or estimated in advance from the provisions of a document or from the company's past practices.

Projected benefit obligation. The actuarial present value of benefits using the benefits/years of service approach that requires assumptions about future compensation levels. Increases over time by interest, amendments to plan, additional service years, and changes in discount rate. Used to compute service cost, prior service cost, transition and corridor amount.

Return on plan assets-actual. Actual earnings on fair value of pension plan assets. FASB Statement No. 87 uses actual return and adjusts to expected return through the gains and losses.

Return on plan assets-expected. Expected earnings on market-related value of pension plan assets.

Service cost component. The actuarial present value of pension benefits attributed by the pension benefit formula to employee service during the period. Formerly referred to as normal cost. A component of net periodic pension cost. Benefit/years-of-service approach recommended by FASB.

Settlement. An irrevocable action that relieves the employer of primary responsibility for the pension benefit obligation and eliminates significant employer risks related to the obligation and the assets used to effect the settlement.

Single-employer plan. A pension plan established for a single employer. FASB Statement No. 87 primarily refers to this type of plan.

Termination benefits. Benefits that arise either from a special amendment to the pension plan that covers only a short period of time, or from the original pension contract that provides special benefits if a certain event, such as a plant closing, occurs.

Transition amount. The difference between the projected benefit obligation and the fair value of pension fund assets existing at the time FASB Statement No. 87 is adopted, adjusted by any accrued pension cost or prepaid pension cost at the time of transition. This amount is amortized over the average remaining service life of employees. If average service life is less than 15 years, the employer may use 15 years for amortization purposes.

Unfunded pension plan. A plan in which no funds are set aside by the employer. Pension payments are made directly by the employer to the employees as they come due.

Unrecognized gains and losses. The amount of gains and losses not yet recognized as a component of periodic pension cost.

Unrecognized prior service costs. The amount of prior service costs not yet recognized as a component of periodic pension cost.

Vested benefits. The amount of pension benefits an employee will retain if employment with the employer is terminated.

QUESTIONS

1. What conditions led to a growth in private pension plans in America?
2. (a) What conditions led to the enactment in 1974 of the Employee Retirement Income Security Act (ERISA)? (b) What provisions in ERISA affected the safety of pension benefits for employees?
3. What is meant by the term "vesting"?
4. Distinguish between: (a) a defined benefit plan and a defined contribution plan, (b) a contributory plan and a noncontributory plan, (c) a single-employer and a multiemployer plan.
5. Distinguish between the accumulated benefit approach and the projected benefit approach in determining the amount of future benefits earned by employees under a defined benefit pension plan.
6. What factors must be considered by actuaries in determining the amount of future benefits under a defined benefit plan?
7. Explain how prior period pension costs arise (a) at the inception of a pension plan, and (b) at the time of a plan amendment.
8. How were pension costs computed prior to FASB Statement No. 87?
9. What 5 accounting issues were addressed by the FASB in relation to defined benefit plans?
10. List and briefly describe the 6 basic components of net periodic pension cost.
11. How is the service cost portion of net periodic pension cost to be measured according to FASB Statement No. 87?
12. Why will the service cost of many plans be lower under FASB Statement No. 87 than was true under earlier standards?
13. Assume the following measurements related to Danish Company for 1988:

	January 1, 1988	December 31, 1988
Projected benefit obligation	$1,300,000	$1,550,000
Accumulated benefit obligation . . .	$1,100,000	$1,365,000
Settlement rate.		9.5%
Accrued pension liability	$100,000	$115,000

Compute the interest component of pension cost for 1988.
14. Since prior service costs are related to years of service already rendered, why are they considered to be a future pension cost?
15. How does the FASB recommend that prior service cost be amortized?
16. Does pension cost include the actual return on plan assets or the expected return? Explain.
17. The FASB identified 2 parts to the gain or loss component of pension cost. Identify the parts and explain how they are computed and used.

18. Why is a corridor amount identified in recognizing gain or loss from pension plans?
19. (a) How is the transition amount arising from adoption of FASB Statements No. 87 and 88 computed? (b) How is the transition amount amortized?
20. What 2 types of liabilities can be identified as arising from pension plans?
21. (a) What conditions give rise to recognizing a minimum liability according to FASB Statement No. 87? (b) What conditions give rise to recognizing assets in a pension plan on the employer's books according to FASB Statement No. 87?
22. The FASB identified 2 measurement methods for valuing the assets in a pension plan: (1) the fair value of plan assets, and (2) a market-related value of plan assets. According to the FASB, under what conditions would you use these methods? Explain.
23. (a) Under what conditions does FASB Statement No. 87 provide for recording a contra-equity account? (b) How is it adjusted from period to period?
24. Distinguish between a pension settlement and a pension curtailment.
25. How are gains and losses arising from pension settlements recognized according to FASB Statement No. 88?
26. What is the function of the pension disclosure requirement included in the pension standards?
27. What is meant by postretirement benefits, and what is the primary issue in accounting for their costs?

DISCUSSION CASES

CASE 22–1   (What will FASB Statements No. 87 and 88 do to us?)

Atlantic Company has had a pension plan for its employees for the past 10 years. During this time the Company has followed carefully the provisions of the accounting pension standards, and has reported a minimum pension expense each year. The funding provisions of the plan have been flexible, and the company has funded the same amount of pension cost each year. No asset or liability appears on Atlantic's financial statements for pension costs. This is true even though the company has vested obligations that exceed the cost of the investment assets acquired by the pension fund trustee. The market value of these assets, however, exceeds the vested liability. Management is concerned about Atlantic's debt-to-equity ratio, which has been about 1.5 over the past 5 years.

The controller, Anthony Kroll, is particularly concerned as to the impact FASB Statements No. 87 and 88 will have on Atlantic's financial statements, including the debt ratios. He does not think any additional liability should be required since the fair value of the plan assets exceeds the vested obligations of the plan.

As Atlantic's CPA, you are approached for your opinion. How would you respond to Kroll?

CASE 22–2   (I don't understand the note!)

The following excerpts from a note were included with the 1985 financial statements for Dupont (E.I.) de Nemours at December 31, 1985, and presented to stockholders at the annual stockholders' meeting in early 1986. Dupont elected to apply FASB Statements No. 87 and 88 to their financial statements effective January 1, 1985. The amounts presented in the note are in millions of dollars.

The Company has noncontributory defined benefit plans covering most U.S. employees. The benefits for these plans are based primarily on years of service and employees' pay near retirement. The company's funding policy is consistent with the funding requirements of Federal law and regulations. Plan assets consist principally of common stocks and U.S. governmental obligations.

1985	Pension costs include the following components:		
	Service cost—benefits earned during the period..		$ 111
	Interest cost on projected benefit obligation.......		587
	Return on assets—actual.....................	$(2,214)	
	—deferred gain	1,525	(689)
	Amortization of net gain at January 1, 1985		(167)
	Net pension cost		$(158)

The funded status of U.S. plans at December 31, 1985, was as follows:

Actuarial present value of vested benefit obligation	$(5,165)	
Accumulated benefit obligation	$(5,502)	
Projected benefit obligation		$(5,763)
Plan assets at fair value............................		9,401
Excess of assets over projected benefit obligation		$3,638
Unrecognized net gain at January 1, 1985............		(2,720)
Unrecognized 1985 gain............................		(840)
Prepaid pension cost at December 31, 1985..........		$ 78

The projected benefit obligation was determined using an assumed discount rate of 11% (12.25% at January 1, 1985), and an assumed long-term rate of compensation increase of 5%. The assumed long-term rate of return on plan assets is 9%.

As the external auditor, you were present at the meeting and were asked the following questions. How would you respond to the queries?

(1) Since the plan assets' value exceeds the vested benefit obligation, why isn't there an asset on the balance sheet for the excess?

(2) What does the note mean by "net gain"?

(3) Explain the 2 components of return on assets, actual and deferred gain.

(4) How does the return on assets of $(689) relate to the amortization of net gain of $(167)?

(5) How is the interest cost on projected benefit obligation computed?

(continued)

(6) What is the difference between the accumulated benefit obligation and the projected benefit obligation?

(7) Does the DuPont note disclosure meet the requirements of FASB Statement No. 87?

CASE 22–3   (Why fix something that isn't broken?)

The FASB's study of pension accounting for employers generated considerable interest among business executives. During the extended discussion period, pressure was brought to bear against the FASB by several individuals and the companies they represented to leave pension accounting alone. These business executives felt that the existing standards (APB Opinion No. 8) were adequate, and that further tinkering with the pension provisions was unnecessary.

What are some of the factors that caused the FASB to "hold on" to the pension issue until a standard was released?

CASE 22–4
(What theoretical support is there for the pension standards?)

The topic of pensions was considered at length in an accounting theory class. The discussion centered around the following terms:

(a) Representational faithfulness
(b) Substance over form
(c) Verifiability
(d) Usefulness
(e) Present value
(f) Conservatism
(g) Adequate disclosure

How would these terms be helpful in resolving the issue of how to account for pension plans on the employer's books? Based on your understanding of these terms, assess the treatment of pension plans by the FASB in Statements No. 87 and 88.

EXERCISES

EXERCISE 22–1   (Computation of pension service cost)

Pension plan information for Dallas Metro Company is as follows:

January 1, 1988	Projected benefit obligation	$3,690,000
	Accumulated benefit obligation	$2,850,000
1988 transactions	Pension benefits paid to retired employees	$136,000
December 31, 1988	Projected benefit obligation	$4,150,000
	Accumulated benefit obligation	$3,125,000
Discount rate at which pension benefits could be effectively settled...		11.5%

What is the pension service cost for 1988?

EXERCISE 22-2
(Amortization of prior service cost — plan amendment)

Caledonia Company has 5 employees belonging to its pension plan. Expected years of future service for these employees are as follows:

Employee	Future Service Years
1	2
2	5
3	7
4	8
5	10

On January 1, 1988, Caledonia initiated an amendment to its pension plan that increased the projected benefit obligation for the plan by $260,000. If Caledonia amortizes the prior service cost of the pension plan by assigning an equal amount to each future period of service of each employee active at the date of the amendment who is expected to receive benefits under the plan, determine the amortization for the years 1988, 1990, 1994, and 1997.

EXERCISE 22-3
(Amount of funding and amortization of prior service cost)

Skyways Unlimited has a work force of 200 employees. A new pension plan is negotiated on January 1, 1988, with the labor union. Based on the provisions of the pension agreement, prior service cost related to the new plan amounts to $2,360,000. The cost is to be funded evenly with annual contributions over a 10-year period, with the first payment due at the end of 1988. The interest rate for funding purposes is 10%. It is anticipated that, on the average, 10 employees will retire each year over the next 20 years.
   (1) Compute the annual amount Skyways will pay to fund its prior service cost.
   (2) Compute the amount of amortization of prior service cost for 1988, 1990, and 1995.

EXERCISE 22-4
(Amortization of prior service cost; straight-line method)

Hernandez Awning Co. has unrecognized prior service cost of $896,000 arising from a pension plan amendment. The board of directors decided to amortize this cost over the average remaining service period for its 45 employees on a straight-line basis. It is assumed that employees will retire at the rate of 3 employees each year over a 15-year period. (1) Compute the average remaining service life and the annual amortization of prior service cost for Hernandez. (2) Assuming that pension cost other than amortization of prior service cost was $370,000 for the year, and $400,000 was contributed by the employer to the pension fund, prepare the journal entries relating to the pension plan for the current year.

EXERCISE 22–5 (Computation of actual return on plan assets)

The Escort Hardware Company maintains a fund to cover its pension plan. The following data relate to the fund for 1988.

January 1	Fair value of plan assets.	$875,000
	Market-related value of plan assets	$715,000
During year	Pension benefits paid	$62,000
	Contributions made to the fund	$50,000
December 31	Fair value of plan assets.	$960,000
	Market-related value of plan assets	$730,000

Compute the 1988 actual return on plan assets for Escort Hardware.

EXERCISE 22–6 (Return on plan assets — expected and actual)

Dyer and Dyer Originals has a pension plan covering its 75 employees. Dyer anticipates a 12% return on its pension plan assets. The fund trustee furnishes Dyer with the following information relating to the pension fund for 1988.

January 1	Fair value of plan assets	$1,350,000
	Market-related value of plan assets	$1,100,000
During year	Actual return on plan assets	$150,000
December 31	Fair value of plan assets	$1,470,000
	Market-related value of plan assets	$1,210,000

Compute the difference between the actual and expected return on plan assets. How should the difference be treated in determining pension cost for 1988?

EXERCISE 22–7 (Amortization of unrecognized gain on plan assets)

Hillburn Enterprises has an unrecognized gain of $350,000 relating to its pension plan as of January 1, 1988. Management has chosen to amortize this deferral on a straight-line basis over the 9-year average remaining service life of its employees, subject to the limitation of the corridor amount. Additional facts about the pension plan as of January 1, 1988, are as follows:

Projected benefit obligation.	$2,100,000
Accumulated benefit obligation	$1,850,000
Fair value of plan assets	$1,500,000
Market-related value of plan assets	$1,350,000

Compute the minimum amortization of unrecognized gain to be recognized by Hillburn in 1988.

EXERCISE 22–8 (Computation of gain or loss component)

The gain or loss component of pension cost consists of (a) a deferral of the difference between actual and expected return on plan assets and (b) amortization of unrecognized gains and losses. Determine the proper addition (deduction) to pension cost related to the gain or loss component under each of the following independent conditions.

	a	b	c	d
1. Actual return on plan assets	$200,000	$200,000	$ 500,000	$500,000
2. Expected return on plan assets	$180,000	$230,000	$ 400,000	$550,000
3. Unrecognized (gain) loss at beginning of year	$200,000	$50,000	$(100,000)	$ (75,000)
4. Average service life of employees used for amortization	10 years	5 years	8 years	12 years
5. Corridor amount.........	$100,000	$250,000	$50,000	$175,000

EXERCISE 22–9   (Amortization of transition gain or loss)

Karrass Industrial Inc. adopts FASB Statement No. 87 at January 1, 1988 to account for its pension plan. The following values relate to the plan at that date.

Projected benefit obligation............................	$895,000
Accumulated benefit obligation	$763,000
Fair value of plan assets...............................	$520,000
Market-related value of plan assets	$470,000
Accrued pension cost..................................	$52,000
Average remaining service life of employees	15 years

(a) Compute the amortization of the transition (gain) or loss for 1988.
(b) Assume the fair value of plan assets was $975,000, the market-related value was $852,000, and other balances remained the same. Compute the amortization of the transition (gain) or loss for 1988.

EXERCISE 22–10   (Computation of pension cost and journal entries)

The accountants for Lander Financial Services provide you with the following detailed information at December 31, 1988. Based on these data, prepare the journal entries related to the accrual and funding of pension cost for 1988.

Service cost...	$45,000
Actual return on plan assets...........................	$75,000
Interest cost...	$60,000
Excess of actual return over expected return on plan assets	$20,000
Amortization of deferred loss from prior years	$15,000
Amortization of transition loss	$8,000
Amortization of prior service cost	$30,000
Contribution to pension fund..........................	$120,000

EXERCISE 22–11
(Computing and recording minimum pension liability)

Barbizon Energy Corp. has had a retirement program for its employees for several years. It has adopted the new FASB pension standards beginning January 1, 1988, and must now determine if the minimum liability requirements of the standards will affect its financial statements. The following information relates to the plan for 1988.

Balances at December 31, 1988:
Projected benefit obligation.......................... $967,500
Accumulated benefit obligation $825,000
Fair value of plan assets............................ $775,000
Market-related value of plan assets $610,000
Prepaid pension cost................................. $28,000
Unamortized transition loss.......................... $76,000
Unrecognized prior service cost .... -0-

Compute the minimum liability, if any, and prepare any necessary journal entries to record the liability.

EXERCISE 22–12   (Computing minimum pension liability)

Craig Furniture and Cabinet Mfg. Co. computes the following balances for its defined benefit pension plan as of the end of its fiscal year (000's omitted).

Projected benefit obligation................................ $1,625
Accumulated benefit obligation $1,380
Fair value of plan assets.................................. $1,475
Market-related value of plan assets $1,336
Accrued pension cost....................................... $61
Unamortized transition loss................................ $115
Unrecognized prior service cost............................ $180

(a) According to FASB Statement No. 87, what is the amount of additional liability, if any, required to reflect the minimum liability?
(b) Some FASB members felt that the minimum liability should consider expected future salary levels rather than the current levels. If this approach had been adopted in the standard, what additional liability adjustment, if any, would have been required?

EXERCISE 22–13   (Settlement of pension plan)

The Golightly Company pension plan has been overfunded for several years. In 1984, Golightly entered into an asset reversion transaction that resulted in a partial settlement of its pension obligation. The transaction resulted in a gain of $5,400,000 that was deferred over a 10-year period beginning in 1984. An additional settlement was completed in 1986 that resulted in an additional $3,700,000 gain. Golightly decided to adopt FASB Statements No. 87 and 88 as of January 1, 1986. How much settlement gain should Golightly have reported in 1986 under the provisions of FASB Statement No. 88?

EXERCISE 22–14   (Reconciliation of funding status)

From the following information for each of three independent cases, prepare the reconciliation that would be included in the pension note according to FASB Statement No. 87.

	Case 1	Case 2	Case 3
Projected benefit obligation...................	$12,500	$6,290	$890
Accumulated benefit obligation	9,700	5,400	700
Fair value of plan assets....................	15,300	4,200	750
Market-related value of plan assets	12,800	5,000	560
Unrecognized transition (gain) or loss	(400)	1,200	(75)
Unrecognized net (gain) or loss from prior years......................................	(200)	(500)	100
Unrecognized prior service cost..............	1,200	1,100	200
Recorded additional liability	-0-	-0-	100
Prepaid/(accrued) pension cost..............	3,400	(290)	85

EXERCISE 22–15 (Postretirement benefits)

The Boulding Company has decided to continue paying medical and life insurance premiums for its retired employees beginning with employees retiring after 4 more years. No funds will be accumulated for these premiums. The Company presently has only 6 employees. It is anticipated that, on the average, $10,000 in insurance premiums will be paid for each retired employee. The remaining years to retirement for the 6 employees are as follows:

Employee Name	Remaining Years to Retirement
Sandra Millward	8
Roger Palmer	5
Don Larsen	16
Jayne Mitchell	3
Greg Gee	12
Warren Clyde	7

The company has chosen to accrue the liability for postretirement benefits based on the remaining years of service. Give the entry required to accrue postretirement benefits as of the end of the first year. (Ignore present value considerations.)

PROBLEMS

PROBLEM 22–1
(Entries to record accrual and funding of pension costs)

The Continental Rental Company reported the following information related to its pension plan for the years 1988–1991. The fund is administered by a separate outside trustee.

Year	Pension Cost Accrual	Funding	Benefit Payments to Retirees	Actual Return on Plan Assets
1988	$560,700	$625,000	$250,000	$350,000
1989	725,000	670,000	300,000	400,000
1990	685,000	650,000	275,000	500,000
1991	726,500	625,000	400,000	525,000

Instructions:

(1) Prepare the summary journal entries for each year that would be required on Continental's books to record applicable pension items.
(2) Assuming Continental had an accrued pension liability of $25,000 at January 1, 1988, compute the prepaid/accrued pension account balance at December 31, 1991.
(3) Assuming that the fair value of the plan assets at January 1, 1988, was $2,600,000, compute the fair value of the plan assets at December 31, 1991.

PROBLEM 22–2
(Computation of prior service cost funding and amortization)

The Paradise Leisure Co. amended its pension plan effective January 1, 1988. The increase in the pension benefit obligation occurring as a result of the plan amendment is $5,320,000. Paradise arranged to fund the prior service cost by equal annual contributions over the next 15 years at 10% interest. The first payment will be made December 31, 1988. The company decides to amortize the prior service cost on a straight-line basis over the average remaining service life of its employees. The company has 225 employees at January 1, 1988, who are entitled to the benefits of the amendment. It is estimated that, on the average, 15 employees will retire each year.

Instructions:

(1) Compute the amount Continental will pay each year to fund the prior service cost arising from the plan amendment.
(2) Compute Continental's annual prior service cost amortization.

PROBLEM 22–3 (Computation of gain or loss component)

The Ponderosa Equipment Co. has a defined benefit pension plan. As of January 1, 1988, the following balances were computed for the pension plan.

Unrecognized gain since company adoption of FASB Statement No. 87	$500,000
Fair value of plan assets	$3,100,000
Market-related value of plan assets	$2,600,000
Projected benefit obligation	$3,750,000
Accumulated benefit obligation	$3,300,000

It was anticipated that the plan assets would earn 11% in 1988. The actual return on plan assets was $325,000. The company has elected to amortize the unrecognized gains and losses over 10 years.

Instructions:

(1) Compute the amount of gain or loss deferral for 1988.
(2) Compute the amount of amortization of unrecognized gain or loss for 1988.
(3) If net periodic pension cost, exclusive of the gain or loss component, is $525,000, what is the net periodic pension cost after including the gain or loss component.
(4) What is the unrecognized gain or loss that Ponderosa will carry forward to 1989 as a result of changes in the return on plan assets?

PROBLEM 22–4
(Computation, recording, and funding of pension cost)

Carnival Rockies, Inc. computed the following components of pension cost for the years 1988–1990.

| | (000's omitted) | | |
Components of Pension Cost	1988	1989	1990
Service cost.	$320	$415	$580
Interest cost.	150	180	220
Actual return on plan assets	35)5	50)5	60)10
Expected return on plan assets.	30	45	50
Amortization of unrecognized (gain) or loss—above corridor amount	(15)	(10)	18
Amortization of unrecognized prior service cost	90	105	105
Amortization of transition (gain) or loss	(20)	(15)	(15)
Amount funded	520	580	800

Instructions:
(1) Compute the net periodic pension cost for the years 1988–1990.
(2) Prepare the journal entries to record the computed pension cost in (1) and the funding of the pension plan.
(3) If the prepaid pension cost balance at January 1, 1988, was $75, compute the balance of the prepaid/(accrued) pension cost account at December 31, 1990.

PROBLEM 22–5
(Computation of transition gain or loss and minimum liability)

All-Star Wholesale Company adopted FASB Statement No. 87 as of January 1, 1987, for its defined benefit pension plan. The following information was provided relative to the plan over a 3-year period.

	January 1, 1987	December 31, 1987	December 31, 1988	December 31, 1989
Accrued pension cost	$ 625			
Projected benefit obligation	27,525	$29,700	$32,600	$34,300
Accumulated benefit obligation	22,900	23,800	29,300	34,750
Fair value of plan assets	20,600	24,200	27,900	32,600
Market-related value of plan assets	17,900	18,600	21,300	26,950
Net pension cost exclusive of transition amortization		2,016	2,410	2,470
Contributions made to pension fund		1,970	3,510	2,410

Assume the average remaining service life of employees in the pension plan is 15 years.

Instructions:
(1) Compute the transition (gain) or loss at January 1, 1987.
(2) Compute the amount of net periodic pension cost for each of the 3 years.
(3) Prepare the journal entries for recording the net pension cost and the pension funding for the 3 years.
(4) Compute any additional liability to be recorded for each of the 3 years under the minimum liability requirements of FASB Statement No. 87.
(5) Identify the pension balance sheet accounts and their amounts as of December 31, 1989.

PROBLEM 22–6   (Adjusting additional liability)

The Howell Corporation adopted FASB Statement No. 87 in 1985. A transition loss of $1,500,000 was calculated at the transition date. At the end of 1985, an additional pension liability of $1,200,000 was recorded, the offset being charged to Deferred Pension Cost. Minimum liability computations for 1986–89 indicated the following additional liability amounts

December 31, 1986	$1,300,000
December 31, 1987	$1,600,000
December 31, 1988	$900,000
December 31, 1989	$1,100,000

The transition loss is being amortized over a 10-year period, and no plan amendments occurred during these years. For each of the 4 years, prepare the journal entry to adjust the minimum liability account to the balance indicated above.

PROBLEM 22–7   (Journal entries and minimum liability)

Marcella Transportation Co. decides to adopt the provisions of FASB Statements No. 87 and 88 effective January 1, 1987. The following balances relate to the pension plan at that date and at December 31, 1987 and 1988.

	(000's omitted)		
	January 1, 1987	December 31, 1987	December 31, 1988
Projected benefit obligation	$2,620	$3,075	$3,160
Accumulated benefit obligation	2,370	2,700	2,775
Fair value of plan assets	2,875	2,600	2,500
Market-related value of plan assets . . .	2,570	2,550	2,750
Unrecognized prior service cost	—	240	215
Prepaid/(accrued) pension cost.	75	15	(30)

Instructions:
(1) Compute the transition adjustment at January 1, 1987. What entry, if any, is required for the transition adjustment?
(2) Determine if a minimum liability adjustment is required at December 31, 1987 and 1988.

(3) Prepare journal entries at December 31, 1987 and 1988, to record any additional liability assuming the transition adjustment is amortized over a 10-year period.

PROBLEM 22–8
(Comprehensive computation of pension cost components)

The actuaries for Cassel Cable Company provided Cassel's accountants with the following information related to the company's pension plan. Cassel decided to adopt FASB Statements No. 87 and 88 effective January 1, 1987.

	(000's omitted)
January 1, 1987:	
Projected benefit obligation (PBO)	$2,950
Accumulated benefit obligation (ABO)	$2,400
Fair value of plan assets	$2,680
Prepaid/(accrued) pension cost.......................	$(50)
December 31, 1987:	
Increase in PBO arising from plan amendment..........	$732
January 1, 1988:	
Projected benefit obligation	$3,800
Accumulated benefit obligation	$3,420
Fair value of plan assets	$2,530
Market-related value of plan assets	$2,100
Settlement discount rate.............................	12%
Average service life for amortization of transition amount..	10 years
Average service life for amortization of gain and prior service costs.......................................	12 years
Unamortized gain — prior year........................	$60
Expected rate of return..............................	10%
For year 1988:	
Benefit payments to retirees	$185
Contributions to pension fund	$300
December 31, 1988:	
Projected benefit obligation	$4,161
Fair value of plan assets	$2,865

Instructions:
(1) Compute the transition gain or loss at January 1, 1987, the 1988 service cost, and the 1988 actual return on plan assets.
(2) Based on the data provided and computations in (1), compute the net periodic pension cost for 1988. Show clearly all computations.

PROBLEM 22–9 (Disclosure of pension plan information)

The following information relates to the pension plan of Diamond Battery Company at December 31, 1988. Assume that Diamond adopted FASB Statement No. 87 effective January 1, 1988, the beginning of the current fiscal year.

Balances at December 31, 1988:	(000's omitted)
Projected benefit obligation.........................	$11,750
Fair value of plan assets...........................	$10,800
Accumulated benefit obligation	$9,900
Vested benefit obligation...........................	$7,400
Unrecognized transition loss........................	$850
Unrecognized net loss (arose in 1988)...............	$60
Accrued pension cost..............................	$40
1988 activity:	
Service cost......................................	$875
Interest cost.....................................	$1,100
Actual return on assets	$1,250
Expected return on assets	$1,310
Amortization of transition loss	$75

Instructions: Prepare the pension note at December 31, 1988 that discloses the component parts of pension cost and the reconciliation of the funded status of the plan.

To Find Fair Value of Plan Assets:

Previous Year's Ending Value
+ Employer's Contribution
+ Actual Return on Fund Assets
- Benefits Paid
_____
Fair Value of Plan Assets

23

Accounting Changes and Error Corrections

The financial statements of companies sometimes report significantly different results from year to year. This may be due to changes in economic circumstances as reflected in the statements. But it may also be due to changes in accounting methods or to corrections of errors in recording past transactions. As an example, a change in accounting for pension costs caused Sears, Roebuck and Co., to report a 7.3% increase (almost $28 million) in net income for the second quarter of 1986. Without this change in accounting method, Sears' earnings would have actually declined about 3% during that quarter. As another example, in 1985 Texas Eastern Corp. switched its method of oil and gas accounting from "full cost" to "successful efforts." This accounting change resulted in a $139 million write off to retained earnings. While lowering prior years' earnings, the change increased 1986 first-quarter profits to $37 million, up from $6 million reported earlier.

As these examples show, an accounting change can have a dramatic impact on the financial statements of a company. Because of this impact, one can argue that accounting changes detract from the informational characteristics of *comparability* and *consistency* discussed in Chapter 2. So why are these accounting changes made? The main reasons for such changes may be summarized as follows:

1. A company, as a result of experience or new information, may change its estimates of revenues or expenses, for example, the estimate of uncollectible accounts receivable, or the estimated service lives of depreciable assets.
2. Due to changes in economic conditions, companies may need to change methods of accounting to more nearly reflect the current economic situation.

1015

3. Accounting standard-setting bodies may require the use of a new accounting method or principle, such as the new pension requirements as noted in the Sears example.
4. The acquisition or divestiture of companies, which has been particularly prevalent in the mid 1980's, may cause a change in the reporting entity.

Whatever the reason, accountants must keep the primary qualitative characteristic of *usefulness* in mind. They must determine if the reasons for accounting changes are appropriate, and then how best to report the changes to facilitate understanding of the financial statements.

The detection of errors in accounting for past transactions presents a similar problem. The errors must be corrected and appropriate disclosures made so that the readers of the financial statements will clearly understand what has happened. The purpose of this chapter is to discuss the different types of accounting changes and error corrections, and the appropriate accounting procedures that should be used.

TREATMENT OF ACCOUNTING CHANGES AND ERROR CORRECTIONS

The accounting profession has identified three main categories of accounting changes:[1]

1. Change in accounting estimate
2. Change in accounting principle
3. Change in reporting entity

In addition, while not an accounting change, past accounting errors resulting from mathematical mistakes, improper application of accounting principles, or omissions of material facts must be corrected.

As pointed out in Chapter 1, a major objective of published financial statements is to provide users with information to help them predict, compare, and evaluate future earning power and cash flows to the reporting entity. When a reporting entity adjusts its past estimates of revenues earned or costs incurred, changes its accounting principles from one method to another, changes its nature as a reporting entity, or corrects past errors, it becomes more difficult for a user to predict the future from past historical statements. The basic accounting issue is whether these changes and error corrections should be reported as adjustments of the

---

[1] *Opinions of the Accounting Principles Board, No. 20,* "Accounting Changes" (New York: American Institute of Certified Public Accountants, 1971).

prior periods' statements and thus increase their comparability with the current and future statements, or whether the changes and error corrections should affect only the current and future years?

Several alternatives have been suggested for reporting accounting changes and correction of errors.

1. Restate the financial statements presented for prior periods to reflect the effect of the change or correction. Adjust the beginning Retained Earnings balance for the current period for the cumulative effect of the change or correction.

2. Make no adjustment to statements presented for prior periods. Report the cumulative effect of the change or correction in the current year as a direct entry to Retained Earnings.

3. Same as (2) except report the cumulative effect of the change or correction as a special item in the income statement instead of directly to Retained Earnings.

4. Report the cumulative effect in the current year as in (3), but also present limited pro forma information for all prior periods included in the financial statements reporting "what might have been" if the change or correction had been made in the prior years.

5. Make the change effective only for current and future periods with no catch-up adjustment. Correct errors only if they still affect the statements.

Each of these methods for reporting an accounting change or correcting an error has been used by companies in the past, and arguments can be made for each of the various approaches. For example, some accountants argue that accounting principles should be applied consistently for all reported periods. Therefore, if a new accounting principle is used in the current period, the financial statements presented for prior periods should be restated so that the results shown for all reported periods are based on the same accounting principles. Other accountants contend that restating financial statements may dilute public confidence in those statements. Principles applied in earlier periods were presumably appropriate at that time and should be considered final. The only exceptions would be for changes in a reporting entity or for corrections of errors. In addition, restating financial statements is costly, requires considerable effort, and is sometimes impossible due to lack of data.

Because of the diversity of practice and the resulting difficulty in user understandability of the financial statements, the Accounting Principles Board issued Opinion No. 20 to bring increased uniformity to reporting practice. Evidence of compromise exists in the final opinion, as the Board attempted to reflect both its desire to increase comparability of financial statements and to improve user confidence in published financial statements. Depending on the type of accounting change or error correction, different accounting treatment is required, as explained in the following sections.

Change in Accounting Estimate

Contrary to what many people believe, accounting information cannot always be measured and reported precisely. Also, to be reported on a timely basis for decision making, accounting data often must be based on estimates of future events. The financial statements incorporate these estimates, which are based on the best professional judgment given the information available at that time. At a later date, however, additional experience or new facts sometimes make it clear that the estimates need to be changed or revised to more accurately reflect the existing business circumstances. When this happens, a change in accounting estimate occurs.

Examples of areas where changes in accounting estimates often are needed include:

1. Uncollectible receivables
2. Useful lives of depreciable or intangible assets
3. Residual values for depreciable assets
4. Warranty obligations
5. Quantities of mineral reserves to be depleted
6. Actuarial assumptions for pensions
7. Number of periods benefited by deferred costs

Accounting for a change in estimate has already been discussed in Chapter 4 and throughout the text in areas where changes in estimates are common. By way of review, all changes in estimates should be reflected either in the current period or in current and future periods. No retroactive adjustments or pro forma statements are to be prepared for a change in accounting estimate. Changes in estimates are considered to be part of the normal accounting process and not corrections or changes of past periods.

Change in Accounting Principles[2]

As indicated in previous chapters, companies may select among several alternative accounting principles to account for a business transaction. For example, a company may depreciate its buildings and equipment using the straight-line depreciation method, the double-declining-balance method, the sum-of-the-years-digits method, or any other consistent and rational

---

[2] The classification "change in accounting principle" includes changes in methods used to account for transactions. No attempt was made by the Accounting Principles Board in Opinion No. 20 to distinguish between a principle and a method.

allocation procedure. Long-term construction contracts may be accounted for by the percentage-of-completion or the completed-contract method. Inventory may be accounted for using FIFO, LIFO, or other acceptable methods. These alternative methods are often equally available to a given company but in most instances criteria for selection among the methods is inadequate. As a result, companies have found it rather easy to justify changing from one method to another.

Current Recognition of Cumulative Effect. The APB concluded that, in general, companies should not change their accounting principles from one period to the next. "Consistent use of accounting principles from one period to another enhances the utility of financial statements to users by facilitating analysis and understanding of comparative accounting data."[3] However, a company may change its accounting principles if it can justify a change because of a new pronouncement by the authoritative accounting standard-setting body, or because of a change in its economic circumstances. Just what constitutes an acceptable change in economic circumstances is not clear. However, it presumably could include a change in the competitive structure of an industry, a significant change in the rate of inflation in the economy, a change resulting from government restrictions due to economic or political crisis, and so forth.

In general, the effect of a change from one accepted accounting principle to another is reflected by **reporting the cumulative effect of the change in the income statement** in the period of the change. This cumulative adjustment is shown as a separate item on the income statement after extraordinary items and before net income. The financial statements for all prior periods reported for comparative purposes with the current year financial statements are presented as previously reported. However, to enhance trend analysis, pro forma income information is also required wherever possible to reflect the income before extraordinary items and net income that would have been reported if the new accounting principle had been in effect for the respective prior years. The pro forma information should include not only the direct effects of the change in method, but also the indirect effect of any nondiscretionary adjustment that would have been necessary if the new principle had been in effect for the prior periods. The indirect adjustments include items such as bonuses, profit sharing, or royalty agreements based on income. Related tax effects should be recognized for both direct and indirect adjustments. Pro forma earnings per share figures should also be reported.

---

[3] *Opinions of the Accounting Principles Board, No. 20,* par. 15.

The cumulative effect of a change in accounting principle must usually be adjusted for the effect of interperiod tax allocation. The change is often from a method that was used for both tax and reporting purposes to a different method for reporting purposes. Retroactive changes in methods for tax purposes are generally not permitted. Thus, the current income tax payable is usually not affected by the change; however, an adjustment is usually necessary to the deferred income tax account. For example, if a company has been using an accelerated method of depreciation for both reporting and tax purposes but changes to the straight-line method for reporting purposes, the tax effect should be reflected as a reduction in the cumulative change account and as a credit to Deferred Income Tax. If the change for reporting purposes is to a method used for tax purposes, the books and the tax return would be in agreement after the change; and previously recorded amounts in Deferred Income Tax would be reversed. An exception arises when the change is made from LIFO inventory to another method. This is because the income tax regulations require consistency between the books and the tax return whenever LIFO inventory is involved. Thus, a change on the books must also be made on the tax return. Any additional tax arising from the change must be paid, although the income tax regulations provide for some spreading of the liability over several future years.

To illustrate the general treatment of a change in accounting principle, assume Brubaker Company elected in 1988 to change from an accelerated method of depreciation used for both reporting and tax purposes to the straight-line method to make its reporting practice consistent with the majority of its competitors. The income tax rate is 40%, and the company pays a 20% management bonus on operating income before tax. The following information was gathered reflecting the impact of the change on net income.

Year	Excess of Accelerated Depreciation Over Straight-Line Depreciation	Effect of Change	
		Direct Effect Less Tax (40% Tax Rate)	Direct and Indirect Effect After 20% Management Bonus, Pro Forma Data
Prior to 1983	$ 80,000	$ 48,000 [.60($80,000)]*	$ 38,400 {.60[$80,000 − .20($80,000)]}
1983	25,000	15,000 [.60($25,000)]	12,000 {.60[$25,000 − .20($25,000)]}
1984	30,000	18,000 [.60($30,000)]	14,400 {.60[$30,000 − .20($30,000)]}
1985	28,000	16,800 [.60($28,000)]	13,440 {.60[$28,000 − .20($28,000)]}
1986	22,000	13,200 [.60($22,000)]	10,560 {.60[$22,000 − .20($22,000)]}
1987	25,000	15,000 [.60($25,000)]	12,000 {.60[$25,000 − .20($25,000)]}
	$210,000	$126,000	$100,800

*The direct effect could be computed as $80,000 − .40($80,000), or simply as the complement of the tax rate .60($80,000). The complement computation is used in this illustration.

The net income for prior years as originally reported was:

1983.	$350,000	1986.	$450,000
1984.	400,000	1987.	500,000
1985.	410,000		

The cumulative direct effect would be recorded on the books and reported in the income statement for 1988, the year of the change. The following journal entry would be made to record the $126,000 cumulative adjustment:

Accumulated Depreciation.	126,000	
Cumulative Effect of Change in Accounting Principle.		126,000

The partial income statement for 1988 would report the $126,000 after-tax, direct effect as a separate item after any extraordinary items as follows:

Income from continuing operations.	$560,000
Extraordinary gain on refunding of long-term debt (less applicable income tax of $60,000).	90,000
Cumulative effect on prior years of changing from accelerated depreciation to the straight-line method (less applicable income tax of $84,000).	126,000
Net income.	$776,000

Pro forma income information for prior years would be disclosed by adding both direct and indirect effects to the net income as originally reported. These pro forma income amounts would be included on the face of the income statements presented for prior periods.

	Pro Forma Income Data				
	1987	1986	1985	1984	1983
Net income as previously reported.	$500,000	$450,000	$410,000	$400,000	$350,000
Effect of change in principle — direct and indirect.	12,000	10,560	13,440	14,400	12,000
Pro forma net income.	$512,000	$460,560	$423,440	$414,400	$362,000

Revised earnings per share figures would also be computed and disclosed reflecting the revised net income amounts. It is recognized that in rare instances, past records are inadequate to prepare the pro forma statements for individual years. This fact should be disclosed when applicable. For example, a change to the LIFO method of inventory valuation is usually made effective with the beginning inventory in the year of change rather than with some prior year because of the difficulty in identifying prior year layers or dollar-value pools. Thus, the beginning inventory in the year of change is the same as the previous inventory valued at cost, and this becomes the base LIFO layer. No cumulative effect adjustment is required.

Restatement of Prior Periods. The APB generally favored the reporting procedures described in the preceding section. However, the Board identified three specific changes in accounting principle and one general condition change as being of such a nature that the "advantages of retroactive treatment in prior period reports outweigh the disadvantages."[4] These special exceptions are:

1. Change from LIFO method of inventory pricing to another method.
2. Change in the method of accounting for long-term construction contracts.
3. Change to or from the "full cost" method of accounting used in the extractive industries.
4. Changes made at the time of an initial distribution of company stock.[5]

In these cases, the APB required the cumulative effect of the change to be recorded directly as an adjustment to the beginning Retained Earnings balance and all prior income statement data reported for comparative purposes to be adjusted to reflect the new principle. No justification was given by the Board for selecting these items for special treatment; however, these items usually would be material and data would generally be available to adjust the prior years' statements.

To illustrate the exceptions, assume that the Frankfort Company compiles the following information concerning its change in 1988 from the completed-contract method of valuing long-term construction contracts to the percentage-of-completion method. The assumed tax rate is 40%.

Year	Net Income— Completed Contract Method	Net Income— Percentage-of-Completion Method
1983.	$ 20,000	45,000
1984.	60,000	70,000
1985.	80,000	75,000
1986.	75,000	110,000
1987.	90,000	85,000
Total at beginning of 1988.	$325,000	$385,000

The retained earnings statement for 1988 would reflect the effect of the change on prior years as shown at the top of the next page:

All prior period income statements presented for comparative purposes would be adjusted to the amounts that would have been reported using the new principle. If the prior statements could not be adjusted because of inadequate data, this fact should be disclosed and the cumulative impact

---

[4] *Ibid.*, par. 27.

[5] This exception is available only once for a company, and may be used whenever a company first issues financial statements for (a) obtaining additional equity capital from investors, (b) effecting business combinations, or (c) registering securities, *Ibid.*, par. 29.

Frankfort Company Retained Earnings Statement For Year Ended December 31, 1988	
Retained earnings, January 1, 1988, as previously reported	$ 900,000
Add adjustment for the cumulative effect on prior years of applying retroactively the percentage-of-completion method of accounting for long-term construction contracts as opposed to the com-pleted-contract method (less applicable income tax of $40,000)	60,000
January 1, 1988, balance, as adjusted	$ 960,000
Add net income per income statement	660,000
	$1,620,000
Deduct dividends declared	400,000
Retained earnings, December 31, 1988	$1,220,000

would be reported only on the retained earnings statement. No pro forma information is required for these exceptions because the prior periods' statements are changed directly; however, full disclosure of the effect of the change should be made for all periods presented. The earnings per share data would be recomputed taking into consideration any impact the new income amount would have on the computations.

If comparative retained earnings statements are prepared for 1987 and 1988, the cumulative adjustment to beginning retained earnings for the earliest reported year would reflect only those years prior to that particular year. Thus, in the example, the 1987 beginning retained earnings balance would be adjusted by $65,000, the difference in net income under the two methods for the years 1983–1986 ($300,000 − 235,000).

If a change in accounting principle is caused by a new pronouncement of an authoritative accounting body, the cumulative effect may be reported retroactively or currently, depending on the instructions contained in the pronouncement. Even though APB Opinion No. 20 supports current rec-ognition of the cumulative effect in most cases, many FASB Statements require retroactive restatement.

If an asset is affected by both a change in principle and a change in estimate during the same period, APB Opinion No. 20 requires that the change be treated as a change in estimate rather than a change in principle.[6] For example, if a company changes its depreciation method at the same time it recognizes a change in estimated asset life, this would involve both a change in method and a change in estimate. According to

---

[6] *Opinions of the Accounting Principles Board, No. 20*, par. 32.

APB Opinion No. 20, such circumstances would be treated as a change in estimate.

Change in Reporting Entity

Companies sometimes change their nature or report their operations in such a way that the financial statements are in effect those of a different reporting entity. These changes include: (a) presenting consolidated or combined statements in place of statements of individual companies; (b) changing specific subsidiaries comprising the group of companies for which consolidated statements are presented; (c) changing the companies included in combined financial statements; and (d) a business combination accounted for as a pooling of interest.[7]

Because of the basic objective of preparing statements that assist in predicting future cash flows, the APB recommended that financial statements be adjusted retroactively to disclose what the statements would have looked like if the current entity had been in existence in the prior years. Of course, this requirement assumes that the companies acting as a unit would have made the same decisions as they did while acting alone. While this assumption is probably invalid, the retroactive adjustment will probably come closer to providing useful information for trend analysis than would statements clearly noncomparable because of the different components of the entity.

In the period of the change, the financial statements should describe the nature and reason for the change. They should also clearly show the effect of the change on income from continuing operations, net income, and the related earnings per share amounts for all periods presented. Subsequent years' statements do not need to repeat the disclosure.[8]

Error Corrections

As noted earlier, error corrections are not considered accounting changes, but their treatment is specified in APB Opinion No. 20 and reaffirmed in FASB Statement No. 16.[9] In effect, accounting errors made in prior years that have not already been "counterbalanced" or reversed are reported as prior period adjustments and recorded directly to Retained Earnings.

Kinds of Errors. There are a number of different kinds of errors. Some errors are discovered in the period in which they are made, and these are

---

[7] *Ibid.*, par. 12.

[8] *Ibid.*, par. 35.

[9] *Statement of Financial Accounting Standards No. 16*, "Prior Period Adjustments" (Stamford: Financial Accounting Standards Board, 1977), p. 5.

easily corrected. Others may not be discovered currently and are reflected on the financial statements until discovered. Some errors are never discovered; however, the effects of these errors may be counterbalanced in subsequent periods and after this takes place, account balances are again accurately stated. Errors may be classified as follows.

1. **Errors discovered currently in the course of normal accounting procedures.** Examples of this type of error are clerical errors, such as an addition error, posting to the wrong account, or misstating or omitting an account from the trial balance. These types of errors usually are detected during the regular summarizing process of the accounting cycle and are readily corrected.

2. **Errors limited to balance sheet accounts.** Examples include debiting Marketable Securities instead of Notes Receivable, crediting Interest Payable instead of Notes Payable, or crediting Interest Payable instead of Salaries Payable. Another example is not recording the exchange of convertible bonds for stock. Such errors are frequently discovered and corrected in the period in which they are made. When such errors are not found until a subsequent period, corrections must be made at that time and balance sheet data subsequently restated for comparative reporting purposes.

3. **Errors limited to income statement accounts.** The examples and correcting procedures for this type of error are similar to those in (2). For example, Office Salaries may be debited instead of Sales Salaries. This type of error should be corrected as soon as it is discovered. Even though the error would not affect net income, the misstated accounts should be restated for analysis purposes and comparative reporting.

4. **Errors affecting both income statement accounts and balance sheet accounts.** Certain errors, when not discovered currently, result in the misstatement of net income and thus affect both the income statement accounts and the balance sheet accounts. The balance sheet accounts are carried into the succeeding period; hence, an error made currently and not detected will affect earnings of the future. Such errors may be classified into two groups:

   (a) **Errors in net income that, when not detected, are automatically counterbalanced in the following fiscal period.** Net income amounts on the income statements for two successive periods are inaccurately stated; certain account balances on the balance sheet at the end of the first period are inaccurately stated, but the account balances in the balance sheet at the end of the succeeding period are accurately stated. In this class are errors such as the misstatement of inventories and the omission of adjustments for prepaid and accrued items at the end of the period.

   (b) **Errors in net income that, when not detected, are not automatically counterbalanced in the following fiscal period.** Account balances on successive balance sheets are inaccurately stated until such time as entries are made compensating for or correcting the errors. In this class are errors such as the recognition of capital expenditures as revenue expenditures and the omission of charges for depreciation and amortization.

When errors affecting income are discovered, careful analysis is necessary to determine the required action to correct the account balances. As indicated, most errors will be caught and corrected prior to closing the books. The few material errors not detected until subsequent periods, and that have not already been counterbalanced, must be treated as prior period adjustments.

The following sections describe and illustrate the procedures to be applied when error corrections require prior period adjustments. It is assumed that each of the errors is material. When errors are discovered, they usually affect the income tax liability for a prior period. Amended tax returns are usually prepared either to claim a refund or to pay any additional tax assessment. For simplicity, the examples on the following pages and the exercises and problems ignore the income tax effect of errors.

Illustrative Example of Error Correction. Assume the Dexter Co. began operations at the beginning of 1986. An auditing firm is engaged for the first time in 1988. Before the accounts are adjusted and closed for 1988, the auditor reviews the books and accounts and discovers the errors summarized on pages 1028 and 1029. Effects of these errors on the financial statements, before any correcting entries, are indicated as follows: a plus sign (+) indicates an overstatement; a minus sign (−) indicates an understatement. Each error correction is discussed in the following paragraphs.

(1) **Understatement of merchandise inventory.** It is discovered that the merchandise inventory as of December 31, 1986, was understated by $1,000. The effects of the misstatement were as follows:

	Income Statement	Balance Sheet
For 1986:	Cost of goods sold overstated (ending inventory too low)	Assets understated (inventory too low)
	Net income understated	Retained earnings understated
For 1987:	Cost of goods sold understated (beginning inventory too low)	Balance sheet items not affected, retained earnings understatement for 1986 being corrected by net income overstatement for 1987.
	Net income overstated	

Since this type of error counterbalances after two years, no correcting entry is required in 1988.

If the error had been discovered in 1987 instead of 1988, an entry should have been made to correct the account balances so that operations for 1987 would be reported accurately. The beginning inventory for 1987 would have been increased by $1,000, the asset understatement, and

Retained Earnings would have been credited for this amount representing the income understatement in 1986. The correcting entry in 1987 would have been:

```
Merchandise Inventory ..........................................  1,000
    Retained Earnings ..............................................       1,000
```

(2) **Failure to record merchandise purchases.** It is discovered that purchase invoices as of December 28, 1986, for $850 were not recorded until 1987. The goods were included in the inventory at the end of 1986. The effects of failure to record the purchases were as follows:

	Income Statement	Balance Sheet
For 1986:	Cost of goods sold understated (purchases too low) Net income overstated	Liabilities understated (accounts payable too low) Retained earnings overstated
For 1987:	Cost of goods sold overstated (purchases too high) Net income understated	Balance sheet items not affected, retained earnings overstatement for 1986 being corrected by net income understatement for 1987

Since this is a counterbalancing error, no correcting entry is required in 1988.

If the error had been discovered in 1987 instead of 1988, a correcting entry would have been necessary. In 1987, Purchases was debited and Accounts Payable credited for $850 for merchandise acquired in 1986 and included in the ending inventory of 1986. Retained Earnings would have to be debited for $850, representing the net income overstatement for 1986, and Purchases would have to be credited for a similar amount to reduce the Purchases balance in 1987. The correcting entry in 1987 would have been:

```
Retained Earnings ..............................................  850
    Purchases .....................................................       850
```

(3) **Failure to record merchandise sales.** It is discovered that sales on account for the last week of December, 1987, for $1,800 were not recorded until 1988. The goods sold were not included in the inventory at the end of 1987. The effects of the failure to report the revenue in 1987 were:

	Income Statement	Balance Sheet
For 1987:	Revenue understated (sales too low) Net income understated	Assets understated (accounts receivable too low) Retained earnings understated

When the error is discovered in 1988, Sales is debited for $1,800 and Retained Earnings is credited for this amount representing the net income understatement for 1987. The following entry is made:

```
Sales .........................................................  1,800
    Retained Earnings ..............................................       1,800
```

Analysis Sheet to Show Effects

	At End of 1986			
	Income Statement		Balance Sheet	
	Section	Net Income	Section	Retained Earnings
(1) Understatement of merchandise inventory of $1,000 on December 31, 1986.	Cost of Goods Sold +	−	Current Assets −	−
(2) Failure to record merchandise purchases on account of $850 in 1986, purchases were recorded in 1987.	Cost of Goods Sold −	+	Current Liabilities −	+
(3) Failure to record merchandise sales on account of $1,800 in 1987. (It is assumed that the sales for 1987 were recognized as revenue in 1988.)				
(4) Failure to record accrued sales salaries; expense was recognized when payment was made. On December 31, 1986, $450.	Selling Expense −	+	Current Liabilities −	+
On December 31, 1987, $300.				
(5) Failure to record prepaid taxes of $275 on December 31, 1986, amount was included as miscellaneous general expense.	General Expense +	−	Current Assets −	−
(6) Failure to record accrued interest on notes receivable of $150 on December 31, 1986, revenue was recognized on collection in 1987.	Other Revenue −	−	Current Assets −	−
(7) Failure to record unearned service fees; amounts received were included in Miscellaneous Revenue. On December 31, 1986, $175.	Other Revenue +	+	Current Liabilities −	+
On December 31, 1987, $225.				
(8) Failure to record depreciation of delivery equipment. On December 31, 1986, $1,200.	Selling Expense −	+	Noncurrent Assets +	+
On December 31, 1987, $1,200.				

(4) Failure to record accrued expense. Accrued sales salaries of $450 as of December 31, 1986, and $300 as of December 31, 1987, were overlooked in adjusting the accounts on each of these dates. Sales Salaries is debited for salary payments. The effects of the failure to record the accrued expense of $450 as of December 31, 1986, were as follows:

of Errors on Financial Statements

	At End of 1987				At End of 1988		
Income Statement		Balance Sheet		Income Statement		Balance Sheet	
Section	Net Income	Section	Retained Earnings	Section	Net Income	Section	Retained Earnings
Cost of Goods Sold −	+						
Cost of Goods Sold +	−						
Sales −	−	Accounts Receivable −	−	Sales +	+		
Selling Expense +	−						
Selling Expense −	+	Current Liabilities −	+	Selling Expense +	−		
General Expense −	+						
Other Revenue +	+						
Other Revenue −	−						
Other Revenue +	+	Current Liabilities −	+	Other Revenue −	−		
		Non-current Assets +	+			Non-current Assets +	+
Selling Expense −	+	Non-current Assets +	+			Non-current Assets +	+

	Income Statement	Balance Sheet
For 1986:	Expenses understated (sales salaries too low)	Liabilities understated (accrued sales salaries not reported)
	Net income overstated	Retained earnings overstated
For 1987:	Expenses overstated (sales salaries too high)	Balance sheet items not affected, retained earnings overstatement for 1986 being corrrected by net income understatement for 1987.
	Net income understated	

The effects of failure to recognize the accrued expense of $300 on December 31, 1987, were as follows:

	Income Statement	Balance Sheet
For 1987:	Expenses understated (sales salaries too low)	Liabilities understated (accrued sales salaries not reported)
	Net income overstated	Retained earnings overstated

No entry is required in 1988 to correct the accounts for the failure to record the accrued expense at the end of 1986, the misstatement in 1986 having been counterbalanced by the misstatement in 1987. An entry is required, however, to correct the accounts for the failure to record the accrued expense at the end of 1987 if the net income for 1988 is not to be misstated. If accrued expenses were properly recorded at the end of 1988, Retained Earnings would be debited for $300, representing the net income overstatement for 1987, and Sales Salaries would be credited for a similar amount, representing the amount to be subtracted from salary payments in 1988. The correcting entry is:

Retained Earnings...	300	
Sales Salaries..		300

If the failure to adjust the accounts for the accrued expense of 1986 had been recognized in 1987, an entry similar to the preceding one would have been required in 1987 to correct the account balances. The entry in 1987 would have been:

Retained Earnings...	450	
Sales Salaries..		450

The accrued salaries of $300 as of the end of 1987 would be recorded at the end of that year by an appropriate adjustment.

(5) **Failure to record prepaid expense.** It is discovered that Miscellaneous General Expense for 1986 included taxes of $275 that should have been deferred in adjusting the accounts on December 31, 1986. The effects of the failure to record the prepaid expense were as follows:

	Income Statement	Balance Sheet
For 1986:	Expenses overstated (miscellaneous general expense too high)	Assets understated (prepaid taxes not reported)
	Net income understated	Retained earnings understated
For 1987:	Expenses understated (miscellaneous general expense too low)	Balance sheet items not affected, retained earnings understatement for 1986 being corrected by net income overstatement for 1987.
	Net income overstated	

Since this is a counterbalancing error, no entry to correct the accounts is required in 1988.

If the error had been discovered in 1987 instead of 1988, a correcting entry would have been necessary. If prepaid taxes were properly recorded at the end of 1987, Miscellaneous General Expense would have to be debited for $275, the expense relating to operations of 1987, and Retained Earnings would have to be credited for a similar amount representing the net income understatement for 1986. The correcting entry in 1987 would have been:

Miscellaneous General Expense	275	
Retained Earnings		275

(6) Failure to record accrued revenue. Accrued interest on notes receivable of $150 was overlooked in adjusting the accounts on December 31, 1986. The revenue was recognized when the interest was collected in 1987. The effects of the failure to record the accrued revenue were:

	Income Statement	Balance Sheet
For 1986:	Revenue understated (interest revenue too low) Net income understated	Assets understated (interest receivable not reported) Retained earnings understated
For 1987:	Revenue overstated (interest revenue too high) Net income overstated	Balance sheet items not affected, retained earnings understatement for 1986 being corrected by net income overstatement for 1987.

Since the balance sheet items at the end of 1987 were correctly stated, no entry to correct the accounts is required in 1988.

If the error had been discovered in 1987 instead of 1988, an entry would have been necessary to correct the account balances. If accrued interest on notes receivable had been properly recorded at the end of 1987, Interest Revenue would have to be debited for $150, the amount to be subtracted from receipts of 1987, and Retained Earnings would have to be credited for a similar amount representing the net income understatement for 1986. The correcting entry in 1987 would have been:

Interest Revenue	150	
Retained Earnings		150

(7) Failure to record unearned revenue. Fees received in advance for miscellaneous services of $175 as of December 31, 1986, and $225 as of December 31, 1987, were overlooked in adjusting the accounts on each of these dates. Miscellaneous Revenue had been credited when fees were received. The effects of the failure to recognize the unearned revenue of $175 at the end of 1986 were as follows:

	Income Statement	Balance Sheet
For 1986:	Revenue overstated (miscellaneous revenue too high) Net income overstated	Liabilities understated (unearned service fees not reported) Retained earnings overstated
For 1987:	Revenue understated (miscellaneous revenue too low) Net income understated	Balance sheet items not affected, retained earnings overstatement for 1986 being corrected by net income understatement for 1987.

The effects of the failure to recognize the unearned revenue of $225 at the end of 1987 were as follows:

	Income Statement	Balance Sheet
For 1987:	Revenue overstated (miscellaneous revenue too high)	Liabilities understated (unearned service fees not reported)
	Net income overstated	Retained earnings overstated

No entry is required in 1988 to correct the accounts for the failure to record the unearned revenue at the end of 1986, the misstatement in 1986 having been counterbalanced by the misstatement in 1987. An entry is required, however, to correct the accounts for the failure to record the unearned revenue at the end of 1987 if the net income for 1988 is not to be misstated. If the unearned revenue were properly recorded at the end of 1988, Retained Earnings would be debited for $225, representing the net income overstatement for 1987, and Miscellaneous Revenue would be credited for the same amount, representing the revenue that is to be identified with 1988. The correcting entry is:

```
Retained Earnings..................................................  225
    Miscellaneous Revenue .........................................       225
```

If the failure to adjust the accounts for the unearned revenue of 1986 had been recognized in 1987, instead of 1988, an entry similar to the preceding one would have been required in 1987 to correct the account balances. The entry at that time would have been:

```
Retained Earnings..................................................  175
    Miscellaneous Revenue .........................................       175
```

The unearned service fees of $225 as of the end of 1987 would be recorded at the end of that year by an appropriate adjustment.

(8) **Failure to record depreciation.** Delivery equipment was acquired at the beginning of 1986 at a cost of $6,000. The equipment has an estimated 5-year life, and depreciation of $1,200 was overlooked at the end of 1986 and 1987. The effects of the failure to record depreciation for 1986 were as follows:

	Income Statement	Balance Sheet
For 1986:	Expenses understated (depreciation of delivery equipment too low)	Assets overstated (accumulated depreciation of delivery equipment too low)
	Net income overstated	Retained earnings overstated
For 1987:	Expenses not affected	Assets overstated (accumulated depreciation of delivery equipment too low)
	Net income not affected	Retained earnings overstated

It should be observed that the misstatements arising from the failure to record depreciation are not counterbalanced in the succeeding year.

Failure to record depreciation for 1987 affected the statements as shown below:

	Income Statement	Balance Sheet
For 1987:	Expenses understated (depreciation of delivery equipment too low)	Assets overstated (accumulated depreciation of delivery equipment too low)
	Net income overstated	Retained earnings overstated

When the omission is recognized, Retained Earnings must be decreased by the net income overstatements of prior years and accumulated depreciation must be increased by the depreciation that should have been recorded. The correcting entry in 1988 for depreciation that should have been recognized for 1986 and 1987 is as follows:

| Retained Earnings.. | 2,400 | |
| Accumulated Depreciation—Delivery Equipment.................... | | 2,400 |

Working Papers to Summarize Corrections. It is assumed in this section that the errors previously discussed are discovered in 1988 before the accounts for 1988 are adjusted and closed. Accounts are corrected so that revenue and expense accounts report the balances identified with the current period and asset, liability, and retained earnings accounts are accurately stated. Instead of preparing a separate entry for each correction, a single compound entry may be made for all of the errors discovered. The entry to correct earnings of prior years as well as to correct current earnings may be developed by the preparation of working papers. Assume the following retained earnings account for the Dexter Co.:

Account   **Retained Earnings**

Date		Item	Debit	Credit	Balance Debit	Balance Credit
1986 Dec.	31	Balance				12,000
1987 Dec.	20	Dividends declared ..	5,000			7,000
	31	Net income		15,000		22,000

The working papers to determine the corrected retained earnings balance on December 31, 1986, and the corrected net income for 1987 are shown on page 1034. As indicated earlier, no adjustment is made for income tax effects in this example.

Dexter Co.
Working Papers for Correction of Account Balances
December 31, 1988

Explanation	Retained Earnings Dec. 31, 1986		Net Income Year Ended Dec. 31, 1987		Accounts Requiring Correction in 1988		
	Debit	Credit	Debit	Credit	Debit	Credit	Account
Reported retained earnings balance, Dec. 31, 1986		12,000					
Reported net income for year ended Dec. 31, 1987				15,000			
Corrections:*							
(1) Understatement of inventory on Dec. 31, 1986, $1,000		1,000	1,000				
(2) Failure to record merchandise purchases in 1986, $850	850			850			
(3) Failure to record merchandise sales in 1987, $1,800				1,800	1,800		Sales
(4) Failure to record accrued sales salaries: (a) On Dec. 31, 1986, $450	450			450			
(b) On Dec. 31, 1987, $300			300			300	Sales Salaries
(5) Failure to record prepaid taxes on Dec. 31, 1986, $275		275	275				
(6) Failure to record accrued interest on notes receivable on Dec. 31, 1986, $150		150	150				
(7) Failure to record unearned service fees: (a) On Dec. 31, 1986, $175	175			175			
(b) On Dec. 31, 1987, $225			225			225	Misc. Revenue
(8) Failure to record depreciation of delivery equipment: (a) On Dec. 31, 1986, $1,200	1,200					1,200 ⎱	Accumulated
(b) On Dec. 31, 1987, $1,200			1,200			1,200 ⎰	Depr.—Delivery Equipment
Corrected retained earnings balance, Dec. 31, 1986	10,750						
	13,425	13,425					
Corrected net income for 1987			15,125				
			18,275	18,275			
Net correction to retained earnings as of Jan. 1, 1988					1,125		Retained Earnings
					2,925	2,925	

*For a more detailed description of the individual errors and their correction, refer to pages 1026–1033.

The working papers indicate that Retained Earnings is to be decreased by $1,125 as of January 1, 1988, as shown below.

```
Retained earnings overstatement as of December 31, 1986:
    Retained earnings as originally reported.......................   $12,000
    Retained earnings as corrected ............................      10,750    $1,250
Retained earnings understatement in 1987:
    Net income as corrected......................................   $15,125
    Net income as originally reported............................     15,000        125
Retained earnings overstatement as of January 1, 1988............                $1,125
```

The following entry is prepared from the working papers to correct the account balances in 1988:

```
Retained Earnings...............................................   1,125
Sales...........................................................   1,800
    Sales Salaries..............................................              300
    Miscellaneous Revenue ......................................              225
    Accumulated Depreciation — Delivery Equipment...............            2,400
```

The retained earnings account after correction will appear with a balance of $20,875, as follows:

Account **Retained Earnings**

Date	Item	Debit	Credit	Balance Debit	Balance Credit
1988 Jan. 1 Dec. 31	Balance .... Corrections in net incomes of prior periods discovered during the course of the audit	1,125			22,000 20,875

SUMMARY OF ACCOUNTING CHANGES AND CORRECTION OF ERRORS

The following summary presents the appropriate accounting procedures applicable to each of the four main categories covered in APB Opinion No. 20. Naturally, accountants must apply these guidelines with judgment and should seek to provide the most relevant and reliable information possible.

Summary of Procedures for Reporting Accounting Changes and Corrections of Errors

Category	Accounting Procedures
I. Change in estimate	1. Adjust only current period results or current and future periods.
	2. No separate, cumulative adjustment or restated financial statements.
	3. No pro forma disclosure needed.
II. Change in accounting principle	
a. Current recognition of cumulative effect	1. Adjust for cumulative effect, i.e., a "catch-up" adjustment in current period as special item in income statement.
	2. No restated financial statements.
	3. Pro forma data required showing income and EPS information for all periods presented.
b. Restatement of prior periods	1. Direct cumulative adjustment to beginning Retained Earnings balance.
	2. Restate financial statements to reflect new principle for comparative purposes.
	3. No pro forma information required because prior period statements are changed directly.
III. Change in reporting entity	1. Restate financial statements as though new entity had been in existence for all periods presented.
IV. Error correction	1. If detected in period error occurred, correct accounts through normal accounting cycle adjustments.
	2. If detected in a subsequent period, adjust for effect of material errors by prior period adjustments directly to Retained Earnings.

QUESTIONS

1. How do accounting changes detract from the informational characteristics of comparability and consistency as described in FASB Concepts Statement No. 2?

2. List the three categories of accounting changes and explain briefly why such changes are made.

3. What alternative procedures have been suggested as solutions for reporting accounting changes and corrections of errors?

4. (a) List several examples of areas where changes in accounting estimates are often made. (b) Explain briefly the proper accounting treatment for a change

in estimate. (c) Why is this procedure considered proper for recording changes in accounting estimates?

5. (a) List several examples of changes in accounting principle that a company may make. (b) Explain briefly the proper accounting treatment for a change in accounting principle.

6. What information should pro-forma statements include?

7. Why does a change in accounting principle require justification?

8. (a) When should the effects of a change in accounting principle be reported as a restatement of prior periods? (b) Although no justification was given by the APB for selecting these items for special treatment, what might be a possible reason?

9. The Cannon Manufacturing Company purchased a delivery van in 1985. At the time of purchase, the van's service life was estimated to be 7 years with a salvage value of $500. The company has been using the straight-line method of depreciation. In 1988, the company determined that because of extensive use, the van's service life would be only 5 years with no salvage value. Also, the company has decided to change the depreciation method used from straight-line to the sum-of-the-years digits method. How would these changes be treated?

10. (a) List the 4 types of changes in reporting entities that might occur. (b) How are these changes treated? (c) What assumption does the treatment of a change in reporting entity make?

11. Describe the effect on current net income, beginning retained earnings, individual asset accounts, and contra-asset accounts when:
    (a) Depreciation is changed from the straight-line method to an accelerated method.
    (b) Depreciation is changed from an accelerated method to the straight-line method.
    (c) Income on construction contracts that had been reported on a completed-contract basis is now reported on the percentage-of-completion basis.
    (d) The valuation of inventories is changed from a FIFO to a LIFO basis.
    (e) It is determined that warranty expenses in prior years should have been 5% of sales instead of 4%.
    (f) The valuation of inventories is changed from a LIFO to a FIFO basis.
    (g) Your accounts receivable clerk has learned that a major customer has declared bankruptcy.
    (h) Your patent lawyer informs you that your rival has perfected and patented a new invention making your product obsolete.

12. (a) How are accounting errors to be treated? (b) What are the basic types of errors? (c) What are counterbalancing errors?

13. The Berkliner Manufacturing Co. failed to record accrued interest for 1985, $800; 1986, $700; and 1987, $950. What is the amount of overstatement or understatement of retained earnings at December 31, 1988?

14. Goods purchased F.O.B. shipping point were shipped to Merkley & Co. on December 30, 1987. The purchase was recorded in 1987, but the goods were not included in ending inventory. (a) What effect would this error have had on reported income for 1987 had it not been discovered? (b) What entry should be made on the books to correct this error assuming the books have not yet been closed for 1987?

DISCUSSION CASES

CASE 23–1   (Accounting changes)

Situation 1

Randall Company has determined that the depreciable lives of several operating machines are too long and therefore do not fairly match the cost of the assets with the revenues produced. Randall therefore decides to reduce the depreciable lives of these machines by 3 years.

Situation 2

Darton Company decides that at the beginning of the year they will adopt the straight-line method of depreciation for plant equipment. The straight-line method will be used for new acquisitions as well as for the previously acquired plant equipment, which had been accounted for on an accelerated depreciation method.

What types of accounting changes were involved in the two situations? Describe the method of reporting the changes under current GAAP. Where applicable, explain how the reported amounts are computed.   (AICPA Adapted)

CASE 23–2   (What disclosures should be made?)

Lang Inc. has always used an accelerated depreciation method for its depreciable assets both for federal income taxes and for financial reporting. At the start of the current year, Lang changed to the straight-line method for financial reporting. As a result the depreciation expense was $50,000 less for financial reporting than for income tax reporting. This amount is considered material to net income for the year. Lang failed to use interperiod income tax allocation in the current year even though timing differences existed. Explain what disclosures should be made in the financial statements of Lang Inc. with respect to the accounting changes.   (AICPA Adapted)

CASE 23–3   (Change in principle or change in estimate?)

Jack Debbos, President of North Company, is confused about why your accounting firm has recommended that he report certain events as changes in principle instead of changes in estimate, which is what Jack thought they should be. He has asked you for an explanation. Describe a change in an accounting principle and a change in accounting estimate. Explain how each would be reported in the income statement of the period of change.

EXERCISES

EXERCISE 23–1   (Change in estimate and in accounting principle)

Raspberry Manufacturing purchased a machine on January 1, 1984, for $100,000. At the time it was determined that the machine had an estimated useful life of 20 years and an estimated residual value of $5,000. The company used the double-declining-balance method of depreciation. On January 1, 1988, the company decided to change its depreciation method from double-declining-balance to straight-line. The machine's remaining useful life was estimated to be 12 years with a residual value of $3,000.

(1) Give the entry required to record Raspberry's depreciation expense for 1988.
(2) Give the entry, if any, to record the effect of the change in depreciation methods.

EXERCISE 23–2   (Change in estimate)

The Glue Company purchased a machine on January 1, 1985, for $3,000,000. At the date of acquisition, the machine had an estimated useful life of 6 years with no residual value. The machine is being depreciated on a straight-line basis. On January 1, 1988, Glue determined, as a result of additional information, that the machine had an estimated useful life of 8 years from the date of acquisition with no residual value.

(1) Assuming that the direct effects of this change are limited to the effect on depreciation and the related income tax expense, and that the income tax rate was 40% in 1985, 1986, 1987, and 1988, give the journal entry, if any, to record the cumulative effect on prior years of changing the estimated useful life of the machine.
(2) What is the amount of depreciation expense on the machine that should be charged to Glue Company's income statement for the year ended December 31, 1988?

EXERCISE 23–3   (Change in principle)

Blanchard Corporation began operations in January of 1983 and uses the FIFO method for inventory valuation. In 1988, management is considering changing from FIFO to LIFO and wants to determine the effects of such a change on net income.

Ending inventories	1987	1988
FIFO	$360,000	$405,000
LIFO	300,000	315,000
Net income (using FIFO)	180,000	255,000

Based on the information for Blanchard, compute net income for 1988, assuming that the change from FIFO to LIFO was made beginning January 1, 1988. The income tax rate is 40%.

EXERCISE 23–4   (Change in accounting principle)

The Old Timers Construction Company has used the completed-contract method of accounting since it began operations in 1981. In 1988, for justifiable reasons, management decided to adopt the percentage-of-completion method.

The following schedule, reporting income for the past 3 years, has been prepared by the company.

	1985	1986	1987
Total revenues from completed contracts...	$500,000	$1,200,000	$1,000,000
Less cost of completed contracts....	350,000	925,000	760,000
Income from operations	$150,000	$ 275,000	$ 240,000
Extraordinary loss			45,000
Income before taxes	$150,000	$ 275,000	$ 195,000

Analysis of the accounting records disclosed the following income by projects, earned in the years 1985–1987 using the percentage-of-completion method.

	1985	1986	1987
Project A.....................	$150,000		
Project B.....................	100,000	$175,000	
Project C.....................	70,000	200,000	$ 10,000
Project D.....................		10,000	60,000
Project E.....................			(40,000)

Give the journal entry required in 1988 to reflect the change in accounting principle. Use a 40% income tax rate.

EXERCISE 23–5 (Change in accounting principle)

United Wholesale Company decides to change from an accelerated depreciation method it has used for both reporting and tax purposes to the straight-line method for reporting purposes. From the following information, prepare the income statement for 1988. Assume a 40% tax rate.

Year	Net Income As Reported	Excess of Accelerated Depreciation Over Straight-Line Depreciation	Direct Effect Less Tax (40%)
Prior to 1985		$12,500	$ 7,500
1985	$62,500	6,250	3,750
1986	54,500	7,500	4,500
1987	78,000	11,250	6,750
		$37,500	$22,500

In 1988, net sales were $190,000; cost of goods sold, $92,500; selling expenses, $47,500, and general and administrative expenses, $14,000. In addition, United had a tax deductible extraordinary loss of $22,500. Assume the fiscal year ends on December 31.

EXERCISE 23–6 (Change in accounting principle involving LIFO)

Assume the change in net income as shown in Exercise 23–5 is the result of a change from the LIFO method of inventory pricing to another method. During 1988, dividends of $17,500 were paid. Based on this information, prepare the retained earnings statement for 1988. The December 31, 1987 retained earnings balance as reported was $260,000.

EXERCISE 23–7   (Accounting errors)

The following errors in the accounting records of the Wiley & James Partnership were discovered on January 10, 1988.

Year of Error	Ending Inventories Overstated	Depreciation Understated	Accrued Rent Revenue Not Recorded	Accrued Interest Expense Not Recorded
1985	$20,000		$ 6,000	
1986		$5,000	22,000	
1987	28,000			$3,000

The partners share net income and losses as follows: 40%, Wiley; 60%, James.
(1) Prepare a correcting journal entry on January 10, 1988, assuming that the books were closed for 1987.
(2) Prepare a correcting journal entry on January 10, 1988, assuming that the books are still open for 1987 and that the partnership uses the perpetual inventory system.

EXERCISE 23–8   (Analysis of errors)

State the effect of each of the following errors made in 1987 upon the balance sheets and the income statements prepared in 1987 and 1988:

(a) The ending inventory is understated as a result of an error in the count of goods on hand.

(b) The ending inventory is overstated as a result of the inclusion of goods acquired and held on a consignment basis. No purchase was recorded on the books.

(c) A purchase of merchandise at the end of 1987 is not recorded until payment is made for the goods in 1988; the goods purchased were included in the inventory at the end of 1987.

(d) A sale of merchandise at the end of 1987 is not recorded until cash is received for the goods in 1988; the goods sold were excluded from the inventory at the end of 1987.

(e) Goods shipped to consignees in 1987 were reported as sales; goods in the hands of consignees at the end of 1987 were not recognized for inventory purposes; sale of such goods in 1988 and collections on such sales were recorded as credits to the receivables established with consignees in 1987.

(f) One week's sales total during 1987 was credited to Gain on Sales — Machinery.

(g) No depreciation is taken in 1987 for machinery sold in April, 1987. The company is on a calendar year and computes depreciation to the nearest month.

(h) No depreciation is taken in 1987 for machinery purchased in October, 1987. The company is on a calendar year and computes depreciation to the nearest month.

(i) Customers' notes receivable are debited to Accounts Receivable.

EXERCISE 23–9   (Correction of errors — work papers)

The Hanson Co. reports net incomes for a 3-year period as follows: 1985, $18,000; 1986, $10,500; 1987, $12,500.

In reviewing the accounts in 1988, after the books for the prior year have been closed, you find that the following errors have been made in summarizing activities:

	1985	1986	1987
Overstatement of ending inventories as a result of errors in count	$1,600	$2,800	$1,800
Understatement of advertising expense payable	300	600	450
Overstatement of interest receivable	250	—	200
Omission of depreciation on property items still in use	900	800	750

(1) Prepare working papers summarizing corrections and reporting corrected net incomes for 1985, 1986, and 1987.
(2) Give the entry to bring the books of the company up to date in 1988.

EXERCISE 23–10 (Journal entries to correct accounts)

The first audit of the books for the Booker Corporation was made for the year ended December 31, 1988. In reviewing the books, the auditor discovered that certain adjustments had been overlooked at the end of 1987 and 1988, and also that other items had been improperly recorded. Omissions and other failures for each year are summarized below:

	December 31	
	1987	1988
Sales salaries payable	$1,300	1,100
Interest receivable	325	215
Prepaid insurance	450	300
Advances from customers	1,750	2,500
(Collections from customers had been included in sales but should have been recognized as advances from customers since goods were not shipped until the following year.)		
Equipment	1,400	1,200
(Expenditures had been recognized as repairs but should have been recognized as cost of equipment; the depreciation rate on such equipment is 10% per year, but depreciation in the year of the expenditure is to be recognized at 5%.)		

Prepare journal entries to correct revenue and expense accounts for 1988 and record assets and liabilities that require recognition on the balance sheet as of December 31, 1988. Assume the nominal accounts for 1988 have not yet been closed into the income summary account.

PROBLEMS

PROBLEM 23–1 (Change in accounting principle)

Giovani, Inc. acquired the following assets on January 3, 1985:

Equipment, estimated service life 5 years; residual value $13,000	$513,000
Building, estimated service life 40 years; no residual value	900,000

The equipment has been depreciated using the sum-of-the-years-digits method for the first 3 years. In 1988, the company decided to change the method of depreciation to straight-line. No change was made in the estimated service life or residual value. The company also decided to change the total estimated service life of the building from 40 to 45 years with no change in the estimated residual value. The building is depreciated on the straight-line method.

The company has 200,000 shares of capital stock outstanding. Partial results of operations for 1988 and 1987 are as follows:

	1988	1987
Income before cumulative effect of change in computing depreciation for 1988; depreciation for 1988 was computed on a straight-line basis for equipment and building.*.......................................	$890,000	$856,000
Income per share before cumulative effect of change in computing depreciation for 1988	$4.45	$4.28

*The computations for depreciation expense for 1988 and 1987 for the building were based on the original estimate of service life of 40 years.

Instructions:
(1) Compute the cumulative effect of the change in accounting principle to be reported in the income statement for 1988, and prepare the journal entry to record the change (ignore tax effects).
(2) Present comparative data for the years 1987 and 1988, starting with income before cumulative effect of accounting change. Prepare pro-forma data. (Ignore tax effects).

PROBLEM 23–2   (Accounting changes)

Mecham Corporation has released the following condensed financial statements for 1986 and 1987 and has prepared the following proposed statements for 1988.

Mecham Corporation
Comparative Balance Sheet
December 31

Assets	1988	1987	1986
Current assets	$249,000	$219,000	$165,000
Land	60,000	45,000	30,000
Equipment..................................	150,000	150,000	150,000
Accumulated depreciation — equipment	(45,000)	(30,000)	(15,000)
Total assets.................................	$414,000	$384,000	$330,000
Liabilities and Stockholders' Equity			
Current liabilities............................	$177,000	$177,000	$147,000
Common stock	60,000	60,000	60,000
Retained earnings	177,000	147,000	123,000
Total liabilities and stockholders' equity........	$414,000	$384,000	$330,000

Mecham Corporation
Comparative Income Statement
For Years Ended December 31

	1988	1987	1986
Sales.	$315,000	$300,000	$255,000
Cost of goods sold.	$240,000	$225,000	$189,000
Other expenses except depreciation	30,000	36,000	33,000
Depreciation expense — equipment	15,000	15,000	15,000
Total costs	$285,000	$276,000	$237,000
Net income	$ 30,000	$ 24,000	$ 18,000

Mecham Corporation acquired the equipment for $150,000 on January 1, 1986, and began depreciating the equipment over a 10-year estimated useful life with no salvage value, using the straight-line method of depreciation. The double-declining-balance method of depreciation, under the same assumptions, would have required the following depreciation expense:

1986	20% × $150,000 = $30,000
1987	20% × $120,000 = $24,000
1988	20% × $ 96,000 = $19,200

Instructions: In comparative format, prepare a balance sheet and a combined statement of income and retained earnings for 1988, giving effect to the following changes. Ignore any income tax effect. Mecham Corporation has 10,000 shares of common stock outstanding. The following situations are independent of each other.

(1) For justifiable reasons, Mecham Corporation changed to the double-declining-balance method of depreciation in 1988. The effect of the change should be included in the net income of the period in which the change was made.

(2) During 1988, Mecham Corporation found the equipment was fast becoming obsolete and decided to change the estimated useful life from 10 years to 5 years. The books for 1988 had not yet been closed.

(3) During 1988, Mecham Corporation found additional equipment, also acquired on January 1, 1986, costing $24,000, had been recorded in the land account and had not been depreciated. This error should be corrected using straight-line depreciation over a 10-year period.

PROBLEM 23–3 (Change in accounting estimate and principle)

The following information relates to depreciable assets of Data Electronics:

(a) Machine A was purchased for $60,000 on January 1, 1983. The entire cost was expensed in the year of purchase. The machine had a 15-year useful life and no residual value.

(b) Machine B cost $105,000 and was purchased January 1, 1984. The straight-line method of depreciation was used. At the time of purchase the expected useful life was 12 years with no residual value. In 1988, it was estimated that the total useful life of the asset would be only 8 years and that there would be a $5,000 residual value.

(c) Building A was purchased January 1, 1985, for $600,000. The straight-line method of depreciation was originally chosen. The building was expected to be useful for 20 years and to have zero residual value. In 1988, a change was made from the straight-line depreciation method to the sum-of-the-years-digits method. Estimates relating to the useful life and residual value remained the same.

Income before depreciation expense was $520,000 for 1988. Depreciation on assets other than those described totaled $50,000. Net income for 1987 was $415,000.

Instructions: (Ignore all income tax effects)
(1) Prepare all entries for 1988 relating to depreciable assets.
(2) Prepare partial income statements for 1987 and 1988. Begin with income before the cumulative effects of any accounting changes. Show all computations.

PROBLEM 23–4   (Change to generally accepted accounting principle)

City Loan Company is in the consumer finance business. In the past, City Loan has used the direct write-off method for uncollectible loans. City also provided for uncollectible loans by an appropriation of retained earnings.

In 1988 City decided to change to the generally accepted allowance method of recognizing loss due to uncollectible loans. The direct write-off method was continued for tax purposes only. City's tax rate is 40%. Experience shows that approximately 5% of the loans outstanding at the end of each year are uncollectible. Loans receivable at January 1, 1987, amounted to $800,000.

City Loan Corporation trial balances for December 31, 1987 and 1988, are shown below.

City Loan Company
Trial Balance
December 31, 1988 and 1987

	1988		1987	
	Debits	Credits	Debits	Credits
Cash.	$ 78,880		$ 138,400	
Loans Receivable.	1,140,000		1,100,000	
Other Assets	50,016		46,080	
Income Taxes Payable		$ 827,776		$ 869,600
Other Liabilities.		27,264		25,920
Capital Stock.		160,000		160,000
Retained Earnings		173,960		147,880
Appropriated Retained Earnings — Uncollectible Loans		55,000		55,000
Dividends.	16,000		12,800	
Interest Revenue		264,000		208,000
Operating Expenses	79,200		58,240	
Uncollectible Loans Written Off.	21,440		17,600	
Interest Expense	95,200		67,360	
Income Tax Expense.	27,264		25,920	
Totals	$1,508,000	$1,508,000	$1,466,400	$1,466,400

Instructions:
(1) Prepare journal entries at December 31, 1988, to discontinue the appropriation of retained earnings and to record the change in accounting principle occurring in that year.
(2) Prepare an income statement and statement of retained earnings for City Loan Company for the year ended December 31, 1988, showing comparative information for 1987. (AICPA adapted)

PROBLEM 23–5 (Reporting accounting changes)

Listed below are three independent, unrelated sets of facts concerning accounting changes.

Case 1. The Seamons Company determined that the amortization rate on its patents is unacceptably low due to current advances in technology. The company decided at the beginning of 1988, the current year, to increase the amortization rate on all existing patents from 10% to 20%. Patents purchased on January 1, 1983, for $2,400,000 had a book value of $1,200,000 on January 1, 1988.

Case 2. Berrett Enterprises decided on January 1, 1988, to change its depreciation method on manufacturing equipment from an accelerated method to the straight-line method. The straight-line method is to be used for new acquisitions as well as for previously acquired equipment. It has been determined that the excess of accelerated depreciation over straight-line depreciation for the years 1985 through 1987 totals $634,000.

Case 3. On December 31, 1987, Hostex Inc. owned 27% of the Box Company, at which time Hostex reported its investment using the equity method. During 1988, Hostex has increased its ownership in Box by 24%. Accordingly, Hostex is planning to prepare consolidated financial statements for Hostex and Box for the year ended December 31, 1988.

Instructions: For each of the situations described:
(1) Explain the type of accounting change.
(2) Explain how the accounting change should be reported under current generally accepted accounting principles, and provide, where applicable, the journal entries to effect the accounting change. (Ignore the effect of income taxes.)
(3) Explain the effect of the change on the statement of financial position and earnings statement. (AICPA adapted)

PROBLEM 23–6 (Change in accounting principle)

In 1988, Hastings Inc. changed its method of depreciating equipment from an accelerated depreciation method, used for both reporting and tax purposes, to the straight-line method. The following information shows the effect of this change on the amount of depreciation to be shown on the income statement.

Assume the company has a tax rate of 40%. Employees have been given a 20% cash bonus on operating income during these years.

Year	Net Income as Reported	Excess of Accelerated Depreciation Over Straight-Line Depreciation
Prior to 1984................		$40,000
1984........................	$200,000	15,000
1985........................	182,500	13,000
1986........................	190,000	14,000
1987........................	210,000	17,000
		$99,000

Instructions:
(1) Compute the effect of the change in accounting principle on income as follows: (a) the direct effect less the tax effect; (b) the direct and indirect effects.
(2) Prepare (a) a partial income statement for 1988 if income before extraordinary items was $225,000 and an extraordinary loss of $36,000 before tax was incurred, and (b) pro forma income data for the years 1984–1987.

PROBLEM 23–7 (Change in accounting principle — LIFO to FIFO)

On January 1, 1988, Hanover Inc. decided to change from the LIFO method of inventory pricing to the FIFO method. The reported income for the 4 years Hanover had been in business was as follows:

1984..................	$250,000	1986..................	$310,000
1985..................	260,000	1987..................	330,000

Analysis of the inventory records disclosed that the following inventories were on hand at the end of each year as valued under both the LIFO and FIFO methods.

	LIFO Method	FIFO Method
January 1, 1984..........................	0	0
December 31, 1984.......................	$228,000	$256,000
December 31, 1985.......................	240,000	238,000
December 31, 1986.......................	270,000	302,000
December 31, 1987.......................	288,000	352,000

The income tax rate is 40%.

Instructions:
(1) Compute the restated net income for the years 1984–1987.
(2) Prepare the retained earnings statement for Hanover Inc. for 1988 if the 1987 ending balance had been previously reported at $600,000, 1988 net income using the FIFO method is $360,000, and dividends of $200,000 were paid during 1988.

PROBLEM 23–8 (Correction of errors)

Harrison Textile Corporation is planning an expansion of its current plant facilities. Harrison is in the process of obtaining a loan at City Bank. The bank has requested audited financial statements. Harrison has never been audited before. It has prepared the following comparative financial statements for the years ended December 31, 1988, and 1987.

Harrison Textile Corporation
Balance Sheet
December 31, 1988 and 1987

	1988	1987
Assets		
Current assets:		
Cash......	$ 407,500	$ 205,000
Accounts receivable.....	980,000	740,000
Allowance for doubtful accounts.....	(92,500)	(45,000)
Marketable securities (at cost).....	195,000	195,000
Inventory.....	517,500	505,000
Total current assets.....	$2,007,500	$1,600,000
Plant assets:		
Property, plant and equipment.....	$ 417,500	$ 423,750
Accumulated depreciation.....	(304,000)	(266,000)
Total plant assets.....	113,500	157,750
Total assets.....	$2,121,000	$1,757,750
Liabilities and Stockholder's Equity		
Liabilities:		
Accounts payable.....	$ 303,500	$ 490,250
Stockholder's equity:		
Common stock, par value $25; authorized, 30,000 shares; issued and outstanding, 26,000 shares.....	$ 650,000	$ 650,000
Retained earnings.....	1,167,500	617,500
Total stockholders' equity.....	$1,817,500	$1,267,500
Total liabilities and stockholders equity.....	$2,121,000	$1,757,750

Harrison Textile Corporation
Income Statement
For Years Ended December 31, 1988 and 1987

	1988	1987
Sales......	$2,500,000	$2,250,000
Cost of good sold.....	1,075,000	987,500
Gross margin.....	$1,425,000	$1,262,500
Operating expenses.....	$ 575,000	$ 512,500
General and administrative expense.....	300,000	262,500
	$ 875,000	$ 775,000
Net income.....	$ 550,000	$ 487,500

The following facts were disclosed during the audit.

(a) On January 20, 1987, Harrison had charged a 5-year fire insurance premium to expense. The total premium amounted to $15,500.

(b) All marketable securities were purchased in 1987. The entire portfolio was properly classified as current and includes only equity securities. The market valuation at the end of each year was as follows:

1987 $202,500
1988 $178,250

(c) Over the last two years, the amount of loss due to bad debts has steadily decreased. Harrison has decided to reduce the amount of bad debt expense from 2% to 1½% of sales, beginning with 1988. (A charge of 2% has already been made for 1988.)

(d) The inventory account (maintained on a periodic basis) has been in error the last 2 years. The errors were as follows:

1987:   Ending inventory overstated $37,750
1988:   Ending inventory overstated $49,500

(e) A machine costing $75,000, purchased on January 4, 1987, was incorrectly charged to operating expense. The machine had a useful life of 10 years and a residual value of $12,500. The straight-line depreciation method is used by Harrison.

Instructions:

(1) Prepare the journal entries to correct the books at December 31, 1988. The books for 1988 have not been closed. Ignore income taxes.

(2) Prepare a schedule showing the computation of corrected net income for the years ended December 31, 1988 and 1987, assuming that any adjustments are to be reported on the comparative statements for the two years. Begin your schedule with the net income for each year. Ignore income taxes.

(AICPA adapted)

PROBLEM 23–9   (Correction of errors — work papers)

The auditors for the Albrecht Co. in inspecting accounts on December 31, 1988, the end of the fiscal year, find that certain prepaid and accrued items had been overlooked in prior years and in the current year as follows:

	End of			
	1985	1986	1987	1988
Prepaid expenses......	$700	$600	$750	$1,900
Expenses payable	500	800	950	1,000
Prepaid revenues	140			420
Revenues receivable ...		150	125	200

Retained earnings on December 31, 1985, had been reported at $25,600; and net income for 1986 and for 1987 were reported at $9,500 and $12,250 respectively. Revenue and expense balances for 1988 were transferred to the income summary account and the latter shows a credit balance of $12,500 prior to correction by the auditors. No dividends had been declared in the 3-year period.

Instructions:

(1) Prepare working papers to develop a corrected retained earnings balance as of

December 31, 1985, and corrected earnings for 1986, 1987, and 1988. Disregard effects of corrections on income tax.

(2) Prepare a corrected statement of retained earnings for the 3-year period ending December 31, 1988.

(3) Give the entry or entries required as of December 31, 1988, to correct the income summary account and retained earnings account and to establish the appropriate balance sheet accounts as of this date.

PROBLEM 23–10 (Analysis and correction of errors)

An auditor is engaged by the SW Corp. in 1988 to examine the books and records and to make whatever corrections are necessary.

An examination of the accounts discloses the following:

(a) Dividends had been declared on December 15 in 1985 and 1986 but had not been entered in the books until paid.

(b) Improvements in buildings and equipment of $4,800 had been debited to expense at the end of April, 1984. Improvements are estimated to have an 8-year life. The company uses the straight-line method in recording depreciation.

(c) The physical inventory of merchandise had been understated by $1,500 at the end of 1985 and by $2,150 at the end of 1987.

(d) The merchandise inventories at the end of 1986 and 1987 did not include merchandise that was then in transit and to which the company had title. These shipments of $1,900 and $2,750 were recorded as purchases in January of 1987 and 1988 respectively.

(e) The company had failed to record sales commissions payable of $1,050 and $850 at the end of 1986 and 1987 respectively.

(f) The company had failed to recognize supplies on hand of $600 and $1,250 at the end of 1986 and 1987 respectively.

The retained earnings account on the date of the audit is as follows:

Account **Retained Earnings**

Date		Item	Debit	Credit	Balance Debit	Balance Credit
1985						
Jan.	1	Balance.................				40,500
Dec.	31	Net income for year		9,000		49,500
1986						
Jan.	10	Dividends paid...........	7,500			42,000
Mar.	6	Stock sold — excess over par		16,000		58,000
Dec.	31	Net loss for year	5,600			52,400
1987						
Jan.	10	Dividends paid...........	7,500			44,900
Dec.	31	Net loss for year	6,200			38,700

Instructions:

(1) Prepare working papers for the correction of account balances using the following columns (disregard effects of corrections on income tax and assume 1987 books are closed):

Explanation	Retained Earnings Jan. 1, 1985		Net Income Year Ended Dec. 31, 1985		Net Income Year Ended Dec. 31, 1986		Net Income Year Ended Dec. 31, 1987		Accounts Requiring Correction in 1988		
	Debit	Credit	Debit	Credit	Debit	Credit	Debit	Credit	Debit	Credit	Account

(2) Journalize corrections required in March, 1988, in compound form.

(3) Prepare a statement of retained earnings covering the 3-year period beginning January 1, 1985. The statement should report the corrected retained earnings balance on January 1, 1985, the annual changes in the account, and the corrected retained earnings balances as of December 31, 1985, 1986, and 1987.

(4) Set up an account for retained earnings before correction, and post correcting data to this account for part (2). Balance the account, showing the corrected retained earnings as of December 31, 1987.

PART FIVE
FINANCIAL REPORTING

24   Statement of Cash Flows

25   Reporting the Impact of Changing Prices

26   Financial Statement Analysis

24
Statement of Cash Flows

Assessing the amounts, timing, and uncertainty of future cash flows is one of the primary objectives of financial reporting.[1] The statement that provides information needed to meet this objective is a **statement of cash flows**. Previously, this objective was met by presenting a **statement of changes in financial position** or **funds statement**. Chapter 5 provided an overview of reporting cash flows; in this chapter, we discuss in detail the techniques for preparing and analyzing a cash flow statement.

HISTORICAL PERSPECTIVE

As discussed in Chapters 4 and 5, the primary financial statements for a business unit traditionally have consisted of the balance sheet, the income statement, and the statement of changes in financial position. The balance sheet reports the financial position of a business at a given time. The income statement reports the operating results for the period and may be accompanied by a statement summarizing the changes in retained earnings in successive periods. The funds statement or statement of changes in financial position provided a summary not only of the operations of a business, but also of any significant financing and investing activities for the period. Thus, it accounted for all the changes in financial position as reported on successive balance sheets.

The funds statement went through several years of development in becoming one of the primary financial statements. In 1961, Accounting Research Study No. 2, sponsored by the AICPA, recommended that a

---

[1] *Statement of Financial Accounting Concepts No. 1,* "Objectives of Financial Reporting by Business Enterprises" (Stamford: Financial Accounting Standards Board, 1978), par 37.

funds statement be prepared and included with the income statement and balance sheet in annual reports to shareholders.[2] Two years later APB Opinion No. 3 was issued to provide guidelines for the preparation of the funds statement.[3] Even though Opinion No. 3 did not require a funds statement, most businesses sensed the value of the funds statement and included it in their annual reports. Thus, it was somewhat anticlimactic when, in 1971, the APB issued Opinion No. 19 officially requiring that a funds statement be included as one of the three primary financial statements in annual reports to shareholders and be covered by the auditor's opinion.[4]

Prior to the issuance of Opinion No. 19, the funds statement was referred to by a variety of titles including: *the statement of sources and uses of funds, the source and application of funds statement, and the statement of resources provided and applied.* The Accounting Principles Board in Opinion No. 19 recommended that the funds statement be called the statement of changes in financial position. In this chapter and in practice, the term "funds statement" is often used as a general term encompassing cash flow statements as well as funds statements prepared using working capital or some other concept of funds.

Opinion No. 19 did not specify a definition or concept of funds to be used in preparing the funds statement or a required format for the statement. Thus, companies were allowed considerable flexibility in the reporting of funds flow information. In late 1987, the FASB issued Statement No. 95, which supersedes APB Opinion No. 19. Instead of allowing various definitions of funds, such as cash or working capital, and a variety of formats, the FASB called for a statement of cash flows to replace the more general statement of changes in financial position. In addition, the FASB specified a format that highlights cash flows from operating, investing, and financing activities.[5] A major reason for the FASB's actions is to better help investors and creditors predict future cash flows, which is considered an important financial reporting objective. While the discussion in the remainder of the chapter focuses on reporting cash flows, the working capital concept of funds is also discussed briefly to provide a historical perspective of past accounting practice.

---

[2] Perry Mason, *Accounting Research Study No. 2,* "'Cash Flow' Analysis and the Funds Statement" (New York: American Institute of Certified Public Accountants, 1961).

[3] *Opinions of the Accounting Principles Board, No. 3,* "The Statement of Source and Application of Funds" (New York: American Institute of Certified Public Accountants, 1963).

[4] *Opinions of the Accounting Principles Board, No. 19,* "Reporting Changes in Financial Position" (New York: American Institute of Certified Public Accountants, 1971).

[5] *Statement of Financial Accounting Standards No. 95,* "Statement of Cash Flows" (Stamford: Financial Accounting Standards Board, November 1987).

OBJECTIVES AND LIMITATIONS
OF THE FUNDS STATEMENT

As indicated in Chapter 5, a funds statement provides a summary of the sources from which funds became available during a period and the purposes to which funds were applied. Essentially, there are two main sources of funds: (1) those provided internally from the operations of a business and (2) those provided from external sources through borrowing or the sale of stock. The main uses of funds are for day-to-day operating expenditures, plant and equipment purchases, dividend payments, debt retirement, and treasury stock acquisitions. These primary inflows and outflows were illustrated in Exhibit 5–1 on page 185.

The funds statement is based on data taken from comparative balance sheets and the income statement. However, it is not intended to be a duplicate of or a substitute for those statements. Instead, the funds statement is intended to help investors, creditors, and other external users better understand the financing and investing activities of a company for a period of time. Thus, the funds statement highlights important relationships and helps answer questions such as: What was the total amount of funds used during the period? Where did they come from? How much was generated from normal operations that can be expected to continue in the future? What amount of funds came from long-term debt that will have to be repaid in the future? Does the amount of dividends paid seem reasonable in light of other outlays and total funds available? These questions and others require answers if the readers of financial statements are to be fully informed and in the best position to evaluate the operations of a company and its management.

THE "ALL FINANCIAL RESOURCES" CONCEPT OF FUNDS

Funds have been defined in a variety of ways, and the definition used determines the type of funds statement prepared. The two most common definitions of funds have been cash and working capital. However, if these definitions were to be applied literally, a number of transactions involving highly significant information relative to financing and investing activities would be omitted from the funds statement and thus might not be considered by the user. For example, debt and equity securities may be issued in exchange for land and buildings; shares of stock may be issued in payment of long-term debt; properties may be acquired by donation.

Transactions such as these carry significant implications in analyzing the change in financial position even though they are not factors in reconciling the change in funds defined either as cash or working capital. This suggests that in order to make the funds statement more useful, the funds interpretation should be broadened to recognize all financing and investing transactions, such as those mentioned. The broadened view, for example, would recognize the issuance of capital stock for a plant asset as funds provided by the issuance of stock offset by funds applied to the acquisition of the asset. This treatment assumes that the transfer of an item in an exchange effectively provides a company with funds that are immediately applied to the acquisition of property, the liquidation of debt, or the retirement of capital stock. This broadened interpretation of funds, often referred to as the **all financial resources concept**, was required under APB Opinion No. 19, and is retained by the FASB as an underlying concept in preparing a cash flow statement.

PREPARATION OF FUNDS STATEMENTS

Regardless of how funds may be defined, the funds statement is prepared from comparative balance sheets supplemented by operating income data from the income statement and by other explanatory data concerning individual account balance changes. The preparation of a funds statement calls for three specific steps:

1. Select a definition for "funds."
2. Compute the total net change in funds by analyzing the fund accounts as listed on the comparative balance sheets. This amount should be the same balancing figure as that determined in step 3.
3. Analyze the changes in each nonfund account on the comparative balance sheets in conjunction with the other explanatory data available in order to classify the changes as funds flow from operating, investing, and financing activities. The resulting net increase or decrease should be the same amount as that computed in step 2. Through this analysis, the formal funds statement can be prepared.

To illustrate the process of analyzing accounts and preparing funds statements, a simple example will be considered. The mechanics of preparing a cash flow statement will be explained first, followed by an illustration of a funds statement on a working capital basis. The balance sheets and additional information for the Taylor Company provide the necessary data for preparing the statements. To emphasize the nature of the account analysis required in preparing a funds statement, it is assumed that no other information is available. In practice, however, the data for preparing a funds statement can be taken directly from the accounting records.

Taylor Company Comparative Balance Sheets December 31, 1988 and 1987		
Assets	1988	1987
Cash	$ 82,000	$ 40,000
Receivables (net)	180,000	150,000
Inventory.	170,000	200,000
Equipment	200,000	140,000
Accumulated depreciation.	(72,000)	(60,000)
	$560,000	$470,000
Liabilities and Stockholders' Equity		
Accounts payable	$100,000	$ 80,000
Long-term notes payable.	100,000	50,000
Common stock	250,000	250,000
Retained earnings.	110,000	90,000
	$560,000	$470,000

Net income for the year as reported on the income statement was $100,000. Equipment that cost $30,000 and had a book value of $2,000 was sold during the year for $7,000.

Funds Defined as Cash

Defining funds as cash is the first step in preparing a cash flow statement. Normally, cash is used in the same sense as that employed for cash recognized as a current asset — cash on hand and unrestricted deposits in banks. Also, items that are considered cash equivalents, i.e., Treasury bills and other highly liquid temporary investments, are also included. The second step is to compute the net change in cash, which is the difference between beginning and ending cash balances. The Taylor Company's December 31, 1988, cash balance shows a $42,000 increase over its December 31, 1987, cash balance.

The next step is to analyze the changes in all noncash accounts to determine the effect on cash flow. The statement of cash flows might be developed by simply classifying and summarizing cash receipts and disbursements as reported in the cash account. However, the statement is intended to highlight the major categories of cash flow, and such items as cash collected from customers, cash paid for merchandise, and cash paid for operating expenses are generally better disclosed in a "net cash flow from operations" category.

The purpose of a cash flow statement is to explain the change in the cash balance. Thus the statement can be prepared by analyzing all non-cash

accounts (step 3) to see what operating, investing, and financing transactions took place and what effect they had on cash flows. For example,
cash flows from operations are determined from net income as adjusted for
noncash items and also adjustments to a cash basis income measurement.
Cash provided or used for investing activities includes transactions such as
the sale or purchase of equipment. Cash flow from financing activities
includes proceeds from the issuance of bonds or the payment of dividends.

To assist in the analysis of accounts, it is often helpful to use T-accounts,
especially for certain accounts such as Retained Earnings where the net
change in the balance does not clearly show the total picture of the inflows
and outflows of cash. To illustrate, the December 31, 1987, balance in
Retained Earnings for the Taylor Company was $90,000. It has increased
$20,000 during 1988. Since net income was $100,000 for the year, there
must have been reductions in Retained Earnings totaling $80,000. The
probable explanation for the $80,000 decrease is the payment of dividends.
The following T-account illustrates this situation.

Retained Earnings

Dividends	80,000	Beginning balance	90,000
		Net income	100,000
		Ending balance	110,000

Based on this analysis, the $100,000 of net income, prior to any adjustments,
would be shown as an operating source of cash and the $80,000 of dividends
as a use of cash for financing activities. These items would appear on the
partially completed cash flow statement as shown below.

Cash flows from operating activities:
Net income. $100,000
Cash flows from financing activities:
Payment of dividends. . . . . (80,000)

An indirect or direct approach may be used in presenting the amount
of net cash flow from operations. The **indirect approach**, illustrated on
page 1073, reconciles the amount of net income (or loss) from the income
statement with the amount of cash provided (or used) by operations. Such
information may be presented in the cash flow statement itself (again, as
illustrated on page 1073) or in a separate schedule. The **direct approach**
shows the operating cash receipts (e.g., from customers) and cash payments
(e.g., to suppliers). This approach to presenting operating cash flows, illustrated on page 1074, usually requires a separate schedule due to the
amount of detail.

Continuing the example, Taylor Company's net income of $100,000
must be adjusted for two items. First, the $5,000 gain from the sale of

equipment (selling price of $7,000 less book value of $2,000) must be subtracted from net income since it does not reflect the amount of cash received in the transaction. It is the proceeds from the sale of equipment, $7,000 in this illustration, that provide the cash, and this amount should be included in the cash flow statement as part of cash flows from investing activities. Since the gain on the sale is included in the net income ($100,000), it must be subtracted from net income to avoid overstating cash provided by the sale. This adjustment to eliminate the gain on the sale and to recognize separately the increase in cash from the total proceeds of the sale is illustrated in a partially completed funds statement as follows:

Cash flows from operating activities:
Net income.. $100,000
Adjustments:
   Gain on sale of equipment .... (5,000)

Cash flows from investing activities:
Sale of equipment... $ 7,000

Cash flows from financing activities:
Payment of dividends...................................... $ (80,000)

If a loss had been recognized on the sale (i.e., selling price was less than book value), net income would be adjusted by adding the amount of loss reported, and the proceeds would be reported in cash flows from investing activities.

The approach described and illustrated in this section highlights the amount of cash generated by normal, recurring operations. It also recognizes cash provided from other activities such as the sale of assets, which may not occur with regularity. A similar approach would be followed in reporting any gains or losses from the disposal of a business segment or from an extraordinary item.

The second adjustment to net income is for depreciation. The entries for depreciation and amortization have no effect on cash. However, they are valid expenses that are deducted from revenues in arriving at net income. Therefore, such noncash items must be added to net income to arrive at cash provided by operations.

The amount of depreciation expense for the period can be determined from the income statement. However, because of the limited information provided in this example, an analysis of Accumulated Depreciation and the related equipment account is necessary. The following T-accounts facilitate the analysis.

Equipment

Beginning balance	140,000	Sale of equipment	30,000
Purchase of equipment	90,000		
Ending balance	200,000		

Accumulated Depreciation

Sale of equipment	28,000	Beginning balance	60,000
		Depreciation expense	40,000
		Ending balance	72,000

When information is limited to that reported in financial statements, assumptions must be made as to the logical reasons for increases or decreases in accounts. The $40,000 increase in Accumulated Depreciation presumably represents the amount of depreciation expense for the period. Because depreciation is a noncash item, this amount must be added to net income as an adjustment to derive the cash from operations figure. Similarly, the T-account analysis shows an increase of $90,000 in the equipment account. The logical assumption is that additional equipment has been purchased, and this should be reflected on the cash flow statement. Now two more entries can be added to the developing statement of cash flows.

Cash flows from operating activities:

Net income.	$100,000
Adjustments:	
Gain on sale of equipment	(5,000)
Depreciation expense.	40,000

Cash flows from investing activities:

Sale of equipment.	$ 7,000
Purchase of equipment	(90,000)

Cash flows from financing activities:

Payment of dividends.	$ (80,000)

In the preceding example, the amount of net income adjusted for items not requiring cash is $135,000 ($100,000 net income − $5,000 gain + $40,000 depreciation). When preparing a cash flow statement, this amount must be further adjusted to reflect net income measured on a cash basis. The changes in current assets other than cash and in current liabilities are recognized as adjustments to accrual net income in deriving cash from operations.

Net income is adjusted as follows:

1. All increases in current assets other than cash and decreases in current liabilities are deducted from net income.
2. All decreases in current assets other than cash and increases in current liabilities are added to net income.

An exception to this adjusting process applies to accounting for changes in marketable securities. Purchases and sales of marketable securities are recognized with cash flows from investing activities, since marketable securities transactions are not operating activities unless the entity is a financing institution.

T-accounts for the noncash current asset accounts and the current liability account of Taylor Company are presented below:

Receivables (net)

Beginning balance	150,000	
Net increase	30,000	
Ending balance	180,000	

Inventory

Beginning balance	200,000	Net decrease	30,000
Ending balance	170,000		

Accounts Payable

		Beginning balance	80,000
		Net increase	20,000
		Ending balance	100,000

The $30,000 increase in receivables is deducted from net income, since cash receipts for goods and services sold were less than the revenue recognized in arriving at accrual net income. The $30,000 decrease in inventory is added to net income since purchases were less than the charge made against revenue for cost of sales in arriving at net income. The $20,000 increase in accounts payable requires an addition to net income since the cash disbursements for goods and services purchased were less than the charges made for these items in arriving at net income. These adjustments would result in the following presentation of the net cash flow provided by operations for Taylor Company.

Cash flows from operating activities:

Net income.....................................	$100,000
Adjustments:	
Gain on sale of equipment	(5,000)
Depreciation expense.........................	40,000
Increase in receivables	(30,000)
Decrease in inventories.......................	30,000
Increase in accounts payable..................	20,000
Net cash flow provided (used) by operations	$155,000

At this point all noncash accounts have been analyzed except Long-Term Notes Payable and Common Stock. In the Taylor Company example, there is no change in the common stock account, but there is an increase of $50,000 in the long-term notes payable account, presumably due to additional borrowing. Thus, the complete cash flow statement would appear as follows:

Taylor Company
Statement of Cash Flows
For the Year Ended December 31, 1988

Cash flows from operating activities:

Net income..	$100,000	
Adjustments:		
Gain on sale of equipment......................	(5,000)	
Depreciation expense	40,000	
Increase in receivables	(30,000)	
Decrease in inventories.........................	30,000	
Increase in accounts payable...................	20,000	
Net cash flow provided (used) by operations		$155,000

Cash flows from investing activities:

Sale of equipment...............................	$ 7,000	
Purchase of equipment	(90,000)	
Net cash flow provided (used) by investing activities ..		(83,000)

Cash flows from financing activities:

Payment of dividends.............................	$ (80,000)	
Increase in long-term notes payable..............	50,000	
Net cash flow provided (used) by financing activities ..		(30,000)
Net increase (decrease) in cash..................		$ 42,000

The completed statement highlights the major categories of inflows and outflows of cash. Taylor Company generated $155,000 from its operations. It used $83,000 for investments and another $30,000 for financing activities. The remaining $42,000 represents the increase in the cash balance.

Funds Defined as Working Capital

Preparing a funds statement on a working capital basis follows the same three general steps as for a cash flow statement. Step 1 would be to define funds as working capital, which is current assets minus current liabilities. The second step is to compute the net change in working capital. A schedule of changes in working capital, such as the one shown on page 1063, accomplishes this step and provides useful information that might be disclosed to the reader along with a formal funds statement on a working capital basis. This supporting schedule is important because it highlights changes within the working capital pool. For example, a significant increase in receivables without a corresponding increase in sales may indicate a serious credit and collection problem.

As shown in the schedule on page 1063, the Taylor Company has experienced a net increase in working capital of $22,000 for the period. A funds statement, prepared on a working capital basis, would show why this change has occurred. Since all working capital account changes are already included in the $22,000 number, only nonworking capital accounts need be analyzed as part of step 3. The analysis is similar to that already explained for a cash flow statement. An illustration of the resulting funds statement on a working capital basis for Taylor Company follows:

Taylor Company
Funds Statement — Working Capital Basis
For the Year Ended December 31, 1988

Working capital from operating activities:		
Net income....................................	$100,000	
Adjustments:		
Gain on sale of equipment.....................	(5,000)	
Depreciation expense	40,000	
Net working capital provided (used) by operations		$135,000
Working capital from investing activities:		
Sale of equipment.............................	$ 7,000	
Purchase of equipment	(90,000)	
Net working capital provided (used) by investing activities......................................		(83,000)
Working capital from financing activities:		
Payment of dividends..........................	$ (80,000)	
Increase in long-term notes payable...............	50,000	
Net working capital provided (used) by financing activities......................................		(30,000)
Net increase (decrease) in working capital		$ 22,000

Schedule of Changes in Working Capital

Working Capital Items	December 31, 1988	December 31, 1987	Working Capital Increase (Decrease)
Current assets:			
Cash	$ 82,000	$ 40,000	$ 42,000
Receivables (net)	180,000	150,000	30,000
Inventory......................	170,000	200,000	(30,000)
	$432,000	$390,000	$ 42,000
Current liabilities:			
Accounts payable	$100,000	$ 80,000	$(20,000)
Working capital	$332,000	$310,000	$ 22,000

The funds statement for Taylor Company indicates that working capital of $135,000 was provided by normal operations, $83,000 was used for investments, and $30,000 was used for financing activities. The remainder of the funds generated increased the amount of working capital available to Taylor Company.

COMPREHENSIVE ILLUSTRATION
OF CASH FLOW STATEMENT

Examples in the preceding sections were relatively simple. Ordinarily, however, more complex circumstances are encountered and it is not possible to rely on the net change in an account balance for a full explanation of the effect of that item on a company's funds flow. To illustrate, assume that comparative balance sheets report a $50,000 increase in bonds payable. Without further investigation, this might be interpreted as cash provided by a financing activity of $50,000. However, reference to the liability account may disclose that bonds of $100,000 were retired during the period while new bonds of $150,000 were issued. A further analysis of the transactions affecting the liability account may reveal that a call premium of $2,000 was paid on bonds retired and a discount of $7,500 was identified with the new issue. Thus, a cash flow statement, based on these data, should report a net cash flow of $142,500 provided by the new bond issue, a financing activity, and cash of $102,000 used to retire the old bond issue.

Work Sheet Approach to Preparing a Cash Flow Statement

The use of a work sheet, such as that illustrated on page 1068, facilitates the analysis of account changes. The format of the work sheet is straightforward. The first column contains the beginning balances, then there are two columns for analysis of transactions to arrive at the ending balances in the fourth column.

In preparing a work sheet, accumulated depreciation balances, instead of being reported as credit balances in the debit (asset) section, may be more conveniently listed with liability and owners' equity balances in the credit section. Similarly, contra liability accounts and contra owners' equity balances may be separately recognized and more conveniently listed with assets in the debit section.

The lower portion of the work sheet shows the major categories of cash flow: operations, investing, and financing. A debit in the lower section means an increase in cash, while a credit reflects a decrease in cash. It is from the lower section of the work sheet that the formal cash flow statement may be prepared. Remaining pages of this chapter describe and illustrate the nature of the analysis required and the procedures employed in developing a more complex cash flow statement using a work sheet. The appendix to this chapter illustrates a T-account approach to preparing a cash flow statement. Both the worksheet approach and the T-account approach are illustrated using the comparative balance sheet data for Parker Inc. shown on page 1066 and the following information.

- Changes in retained earnings during the year were as follows:

Balance, December 31, 1987..............................		$234,300
Add net income..		44,000
		$278,300
Deduct:		
Cash dividends..	$ 25,100	
40% stock dividend on common stock....................	100,000	
Prior period adjustment resulting from understatement of depreciation on equipment............................	3,500	128,600
Balance, December 31, 1988..........................		$149,700

- The income statement for 1988 summarizes operations as follows:

Income from continuing operations......................................	$36,000
Extraordinary gain on involuntary conversion of building (net of income taxes)...	8,000
Net income..	$44,000

- Marketable securities were purchased at a cost of $2,000.

- A building costing $40,000 with a book value of $2,000 was completely destroyed in an extraordinary disaster. The insurance company paid $10,000 cash; a new building was then constructed at a cost of $105,000.

- Long-term investments, cost $96,000, were sold for $102,500.

- Land was acquired for $108,500, the seller accepting in payment $40,000 of common stock and cash of $68,500.

- New machinery was purchased for $12,000 cash. Additional machinery and equipment were overhauled, extending the useful life at a cost of $26,000, the cost being debited to the accumulated depreciation account.

- The amortization of patent cost and depreciation expense on buildings and equipment were recorded as follows:

Buildings.....................................	$ 5,600
Machinery and equipment.....................	15,300
Patents	5,000
Total.....................................	$25,900

- Ten-year bonds of $60,000 were issued at a discount of $3,000 at the beginning of the year; discount amortization for the year was $300.

- The company recognizes depreciation for tax purposes by the ACRS method, and for accounting purposes by the straight-line method. This depreciation timing difference caused income taxes payable on 1988 taxable income to be $6,000 less than the income tax expense based on financial income.

Parker Inc. Comparative Balance Sheets December 31, 1988 and 1987				
	1988		1987	
Assets				
Current assets:				
Cash	$ 47,300		$ 55,000	
Marketable securities...................	12,000		10,000	
Accounts receivable (net)..............	60,000		70,500	
Inventories...........................	75,000		76,500	
Prepaid operating expenses............	16,500	$210,800	12,000	$224,000
Investments (at cost)....................		10,000		106,000
Land, buildings, and equipment:				
Land	$183,500		$ 75,000	
Buildings............................	290,000		225,000	
Less accumulated depreciation........	(122,600)		(155,000)	
Machinery and equipment..............	132,000		120,000	
Less accumulated depreciation........	(36,300)	446,600	(43,500)	221,500
Patents.................................		35,000		40,000
Total assets		$702,400		$591,500
Liabilities				
Current liabilities:				
Accounts payable......................	$ 65,000		$ 81,200	
Income taxes payable	10,000		9,500	
Salaries payable.......................	5,000		1,500	
Dividends payable	4,400	$ 84,400	—	$ 92,200
Bonds payable...........................	$ 60,000			
Less discount on bonds payable........	2,700	57,300		
Deferred income taxes...................		21,000		15,000
Total liabilities		$162,700		$107,200
Stockholders' Equity				
Common stock	$390,000		$250,000	
Retained earnings......................	149,700	539,700	234,300	484,300
Total liabilities and stockholders' equity		$702,400		$591,500

In preparing a cash flow statement for Parker Inc., we begin by determining the change in fund balance, in this case a $7,700 decrease in cash. All noncash accounts may now be analyzed using the work sheet illustrated on page 1068. The cash flow statement is prepared directly from the work sheet and is illustrated on page 1073.

Generally, the most efficient approach to developing a work sheet for a statement of cash flows is to begin with an analysis of the change in Retained Earnings (see items (a) through (d) on the work sheet). In the process, the income from continuing operations and other income components should be separately reported (item (a)). After the change in Retained

Earnings has been accounted for, the remaining noncash accounts should be reviewed in conjunction with the income statement and supplementary information to determine what additional adjustments are required. Operating income and any other income components should be adjusted (items (e), (g), (l), (n), and (o)) to determine the actual amount of cash provided from each separately identified source; or, in the case of a loss, the amount of cash used. Analysis must also be made to determine all other cash flows (items (f), (h), (j), and (k)) and to reflect significant financing and investing activities that have no effect on cash (item (i)).

Explanations for individual adjustments recorded on the work sheet for Parker Inc. follow. The letter preceding each explanation corresponds with that used on the work sheet.

(a) Net income included in the ending retained earnings balance is composed of income from continuing operations and an extraordinary gain. Net income, then, is recorded on the work sheet as follows:

Cash Provided by Income from Continuing Operations	36,000	
Cash Provided by Involuntary Conversion of Building	8,000	
Retained Earnings		44,000

The operating income must be adjusted to arrive at the total cash provided by operations; the extraordinary item requires separate recognition and must also be adjusted to reflect the amount of cash provided. Since a number of adjustments are usually required in arriving at the actual amount of net cash flow from operating activities, adequate space should be allowed below this line on the work sheet.

(b) The cash dividends declared and deducted from retained earnings are adjusted for the change in the dividends payable balance in arriving at the amount of dividends actually paid during the year. The work sheet adjustment would be as follows:

Retained Earnings	25,100	
Dividends Payable		4,400
Cash Used for Payment of Dividends		20,700

(c) The transfer of retained earnings to common stock as a result of a stock dividend has no effect on cash, and the changes in the account balances are reconciled by the following adjustment:

Retained Earnings	100,000	
Common Stock		100,000

(d) The recognition that depreciation had been understated on equipment in prior periods is recorded by a debit to retained earnings and a credit to accumulated depreciation — machinery and equipment. The correction of earnings of prior periods has no effect on cash, and the changes in the account balances may be reconciled as follows:

Retained Earnings	3,500	
Accumulated Depreciation — Machinery and Equipment		3,500

Parker Inc.
Work Sheet for Statement of Cash Flows
For the Year Ended December 31, 1988

Accounts	Balance Dec. 31, 1987	Adjustments DR		Adjustments CR		Balance Dec. 31, 1988
Debits						
Cash..................................	55,000			(w)	7,700	47,300
Marketable Securities	10,000	(v)	2,000			12,000
Accounts Receivable (net)..............	70,500			(p)	10,500	60,000
Inventories...........................	76,500			(q)	1,500	75,000
Prepaid Operating Expenses...........	12,000	(r)	4,500			16,500
Investments..........................	106,000			(g)	96,000	10,000
Land.................................	75,000	(h)	108,500			183,500
Buildings	225,000	(f)	105,000	(e)	40,000	290,000
Machinery and Equipment	120,000	(j)	12,000			132,000
Patents..............................	40,000			(l)	5,000	35,000
Discount on Bonds Payable............		(m)	3,000	(n)	300	2,700
Total	790,000					864,000
Credits						
Accum. Depr.—Buildings..............	155,000	(e)	38,000	(l)	5,600	122,600
Accum. Depr.—Mach. and Equip........	43,500	(k)	26,000	(d)	3,500	36,300
				(l)	15,300	
Accounts Payable	81,200	(t)	16,200			65,000
Income Taxes Payable	9,500			(s)	500	10,000
Salaries Payable	1,500			(u)	3,500	5,000
Dividends Payable....................				(b)	4,400	4,400
Bonds Payable.......................				(m)	60,000	60,000
Deferred Income Taxes................	15,000			(o)	6,000	21,000
Common Stock.......................	250,000			(c)	100,000	
				(i)	40,000	390,000
Retained Earnings....................	234,300	(b)	25,100	(a)	44,000	
		(c)	100,000			
		(d)	3,500			149,700
	790,000		443,800		443,800	864,000
Cash flows from operating activities:						
Income from continuing operations.....		(a)	36,000			
Adjustments:						
Gain on sale of investments				(g)	6,500	
Amortization of patents.............		(l)	5,000			
Depreciation expense		(l)	20,900			
Amortization of bond discount.......		(n)	300			
Increase in deferred income taxes ...		(o)	6,000			
Decrease in accounts receivable (net)		(p)	10,500			
Decrease in inventories		(q)	1,500			
Increase in prepaid operating expenses..........................				(r)	4,500	
Increase in income taxes payable ...		(s)	500			
Increase in salaries payable		(u)	3,500			
Decrease in accounts payable				(t)	16,200	
Cash flows from investing activities:						
Involuntary conversion of building......		(a)	8,000			
		(e)	2,000			
Construction of building				(f)	105,000	

Work Sheet (continued)				
Sale of long-term investments.........	(g)	102,500		
Purchase of land			(h)	108,500
Issuance of common stock as partial payment for land	(i)	40,000		
Purchase of machinery and equipment			(j)	12,000
Overhaul of machinery and equipment			(k)	26,000
Purchase of marketable securities			(v)	2,000
Cash flows from financing activities:				
Issuance of bonds at discount.........	(m)	57,000		
Payment of cash dividends			(b)	20,700
		293,700		301,400
Net decrease in cash	(w)	7,700		
		301,400		301,400

(e) The destruction of the building and the subsequent insurance reimbursement produced an extraordinary gain of $8,000. This gain was recorded as "Cash Provided by Involuntary Conversion of Building," in entry (a), as the result of the earlier recognition of the individual component of net income. Since the effect of the destruction was to provide cash of $10,000, the proceeds from the insurance company, the cash of $8,000 recognized in entry (a) must be adjusted to show the full amount of cash received:

Accumulated Depreciation—Buildings..........................	38,000	
Cash Provided by Involuntary Conversion of Building.............	2,000	
Buildings..		40,000

(f) The buildings account was increased by the cost of constructing a new building, $105,000. The cost of the new building is reported separately as an investment of cash by the following entry:

Buildings..	105,000	
Cash Used for Construction of Building		105,000

(g) The sale of long-term investments was recorded by a credit to the asset account at cost $96,000, and a credit to a gain on sale of investment account. At the end of the period, the gain account was closed to retained earnings as part of income from continuing operations. Since the effect of the sale was to provide cash of $102,500, this amount is reported as cash provided by investing activities. The investments account balance is reduced, and cash provided by operations is decreased by the amount of the gain. The following adjustment is made on the work sheet:

Cash Provided by Sale of Long-Term Investments	102,500	
Long-Term Investments....................................		96,000
Income from Continuing Operations—Gain on Sale of Investments..		6,500

(h) and (i) Land was acquired at a price of $108,500; payment was made in common stock valued at $40,000 and cash of $68,500. The analysis on the work sheet is as follows: (h) the increase in the land balance, $108,500, is reported separately as a use of cash for investing purposes; (i) the increase in the common stock balance is reported separately and deducted from the $108,500 on the statement of cash flows to show the net cash used to purchase land. The entries are:

Land...	108,500	
Cash Used to Purchase Land		108,500
Cash Provided by Issuance of Common Stock as Partial Payment for Land	40,000	
Common Stock		40,000

Although the issuance of common stock for land has no effect on cash, it is a significant transaction that should be disclosed under the all financial resources concept. Thus the cash flow statement reports both the total purchase price of the land and the value of the stock issued rather than reporting only the amount of cash paid for the land. An alternative to the procedures illustrated would be to present the issuance of common stock as a financing activity rather than offsetting the common stock value against the purchase price of the land.

(j) and (k) Machinery costing $12,000 was acquired during the year. Payment was made in cash and is reported as cash used for investing purposes. The cost of overhauling other machinery and equipment also represents a use of cash for investing purposes. The cost of overhauling, $26,000, was debited to the accumulated depreciation account. The work sheet adjustments for the acquisition (j) and overhauling (k) of machinery and equipment are:

Machinery and Equipment.....................................	12,000	
Cash Used to Purchase Machinery and Equipment		12,000
Accumulated Depreciation — Machinery and Equipment	26,000	
Cash Used to Overhaul Machinery and Equipment.............		26,000

(l) The changes in the patents account and in the accumulated depreciation accounts result from the recognition of amortization of the patents and depreciation on the plant assets. Cash provided by operations is increased by the charges against earnings not involving current cash outflows by the following adjustment:

Income from Continuing Operations — Amortization of Patents.....	5,000	
Income from Continuing Operations — Depreciation Expense......	20,900	
Patents		5,000
Accumulated Depreciation — Buildings........................		5,600
Accumulated Depreciation — Machinery and Equipment		15,300

(m) and (n) During the year, bonds were issued at a discount. The result of this transaction was to credit Bonds Payable for $60,000 and debit Discount on Bonds Payable for $3,000. The net cash provided by financing through the bond issuance of $57,000 is recognized by entry (m). Subsequently, the bond discount was amortized by reducing the bond discount account. This decrease in the discount account is explained by increasing cash provided by operations by the amount of the charge against earnings not involving the use of cash — entry (n). The entries are as follows:

Discount on Bonds Payable	3,000	
Cash Provided by Issuance of Bonds..........................	57,000	
Bonds Payable		60,000
Income from Continuing Operations — Amortization of Bond Discount	300	
Discount on Bonds Payable		300

(o) The depreciation timing difference was recognized by a debit to Income Tax Expense and a credit to Deferred Income Taxes. The timing difference for 1988 is $6,000 and is shown on the work sheet as an increase in Deferred Income Taxes and an increase in cash provided by operations. The $6,000 is thus added back to income from operations because it represents income taxes recognized as expense of the current period but not paid. Thus the increase in deferred taxes did not involve an outflow of cash. The following entry is made:

Income from Continuing Operations — Increase in Deferred Income Taxes...	6,000	
Deferred Income Taxes		6,000

(p)–(u) In preparing a cash flow statement, operating income must be adjusted from an accrual basis to a cash basis. For example, if sales of $80,000 reported on an accrual basis on the income statement, and the beginning and ending accounts receivable balances are $25,000 and $20,000 respectively, the cash provided by sales would be $85,000. The beginning accounts receivable balance reflects sales of the previous period, but cash collected in the current period; thus, the beginning balance should be added to the $80,000 sales figures. The ending balance, however, reflects current-year sales included in the $80,000 amount, but cash will not be collected on these receivables until the subsequent period; therefore, the ending accounts receivable balance should be subtracted. Thus, the net decrease in accounts receivable should be added to the reported sales figure of $80,000 to arrive at the total cash provided during the period from sales. Other noncash working capital accounts except marketable securities, as explained in item (v), require a similar analysis. The entries (p) through (u) reflect that analysis for Parker Inc. A compound entry to reflect these adjustments might be made as follows:

Prepaid Operating Expenses (r)..............................	4,500	
Accounts Payable (t)	16,200	
Accounts Receivable (p)		10,500
Inventories (q)		1,500
Income Taxes Payable (s)...................................		500
Salaries Payable (u).......................................		3,500
Income from Continuing Operations — Net Adjustment to Cash Basis		4,700

(v) As noted earlier in the chapter, marketable securities are treated differently from other current assets in preparing a cash flow statement, since marketable securities transactions are investing rather than operating activities. The adjustment to reflect the purchase of $2,000 of marketable securities would be:

Marketable Securities...	2,000	
Cash Used to Purchase Marketable Securities....................		2,000

(w) After all changes in account balances have been reconciled and the effects of the changes on cash flow have been recorded in the work sheet, the total debits and credits in the Adjustments columns are $293,700 and $301,400, respectively. The excess of credits (decreases in cash) over debits (increases in cash) is equal to the net change in the cash balance for the period of $7,700. The following entry is made to reflect the net decrease in cash and balance the work sheet:

Net Decrease in Cash	7,700	
Cash		7,700

The work sheet is now complete, and a statement of cash flows for Parker, Inc. can be prepared in an appropriate format, such as that presented on page 1073.

A reader analyzing the cash flow statement for Parker Inc. can readily see that $57,000 cash was provided internally from operating activities. This amount was not sufficient to satisfy the investment needs of the company, and so additional cash was generated from external financing activities involving the issuance of bonds. External financing was also obtained by the issuance of common stock as partial payment for the acquisition of land. Although the issuance of common stock could be shown as a separate financing activity, it is presented in the Parker Inc. illustration as an offset to the purchase price of land. This approach enables the user to readily identify all aspects of the land acquisition and the net outflow of cash from the purchase. The cash generated from operations clearly met the need for payment of cash dividends, but when other cash needs are considered, the total cash outflow exceeded the total inflow of cash for the period, causing the cash balance to decrease by $7,700, or 14%.

The indirect approach, explained previously, was used in presenting cash flows from operating activities for Parker Inc. When a more detailed explanation of the cash provided (used) by operations is desired, the **direct approach** can be applied. Under this approach, adjustments are made to the individual revenue and expense items rather than to income from operations. The operating activities section of the work sheet will require expansion in developing this detail as illustrated on page 1074. Adjustment (a), instead of reporting income from continuing operations as

Parker Inc.
Statement of Cash Flows
For the Year Ended December 31, 1988

Cash flows from operating activities:

Income from continuing operations....	$ 36,000	
Adjustments:		
Gain on sale of investments........	(6,500)	
Amortization of patents	5,000	
Depreciation expense	20,900	
Amortization of bond discount	300	
Increase in deferred income taxes ..	6,000	
Decrease in accounts receivable		
(net).........................	10,500	
Decrease in inventories............	1,500	
Increase in prepaid operating		
expenses	(4,500)	
Increase in income taxes payable...	500	
Increase in salaries payable........	3,500	
Decrease in accounts payable......	(16,200)	
Net cash flow provided (used) by opera-		
tions............................		$ 57,000

Cash flows from investing activities:

Involuntary conversion of building.....		$ 10,000	
Construction of building.............		(105,000)	
Sale of long-term investments........		102,500	
Purchase of land...................	$(108,500)		
Less: Issuance of common stock in par-			
tial payment for land..............	40,000	(68,500)	
Purchase of machinery and equip-			
ment		(12,000)	
Overhaul of machinery and equip-			
ment		(26,000)	
Purchase of marketable securities		(2,000)	
Net cash flow provided (used) by			
investing activities................			(101,000)

Cash flows from financing activities:

Issuance of bonds at discount........	$ 57,000	
Payment of cash dividends..........	(20,700)	
Net cash flow provided (used) by		
financing activities................		36,300
Net increase (decrease) in cash.......		$ (7,700)

summarized on the income statement, lists the individual revenue and expense items. The adjustments required in developing the cash flow from operations are then applied to the revenue and expense balances.

| | Adjustments | |
Item	Debit	Credit
Cash flows from operating activities:		
Sales...	(a) 753,800 ⎫	
Add decrease in accounts receivable	(p) 10,500 ⎭	
Cost of goods sold....................................		(a) 550,000 ⎫
Add decrease in accounts payable.................		(t) 16,200
Deduct:		
Depreciation of building, machinery, and equipment,		
amortization of patents	(l) 25,900	
Decrease in inventories	(q) 1,500	
Selling and general expenses........................		(a) 146,400 ⎫
Add increase in prepaid operating expenses........		(r) 4,500 ⎭
Deduct increase in salaries payable................	(u) 3,500	
Other expense—interest expense....................		(a) 3,900 ⎭
Deduct bond discount amortization	(n) 300	
Income tax expense		(a) 24,000 ⎫
Deduct:		
Increase in income taxes payable	(s) 500	
Increase in deferred income taxes..............	(o) 6,000	
Gain on sale of long-term investments	(a) 6,500	
To cancel gain		(g) 6,500 ⎭

Cash flows from operations, as summarized above, may be presented on the statement as follows:

Cash flows from operating activities:		
Receipts—Sales		$764,300
Payments—Cost of goods sold	$538,800	
Selling and general expenses	147,400	
Interest expense	3,600	
Income taxes	17,500	707,300
Net cash flow provided (used) by operations...................		$ 57,000

REPORTING CASH FLOWS

The cash flow statements presented in this chapter highlighted three major categories of cash flows: operating activities, investing activities, and financing activities. This approach is consistent with the recommendations of the FASB. The Board recognizes, however, that the form, terminology, and content of cash flow statements will not be exactly the same for all companies. For example, as explained in the chapter, noncash investing and financing activities may be reported separately in the cash flows from financing activities section or offset against the related investing activity. The offset approach was illustrated for the issuance of stock by Parker Inc. as partial payment for land. Another alternative is to present a separate schedule of noncash investing and financing activities rather than disclosing them in the body of the statement.

In addition, there are several alternatives for presenting net cash flows from operations. In the chapter illustrations, the adjustments required to arrive at net cash flows provided or used by operations were presented in the body of the statement. Both the indirect approach and the direct approach were illustrated. Alternatively, net cash flows from operations could be presented in a separate schedule — using either the indirect or direct approach — and only the net amount would be reported in the statement of cash flows.

The statements of General Mills, Inc., reproduced in Appendix A at the end of the book provide an example of one of the many variations in funds statement formats that are found in practice. In addition to presenting cash flows from operating, investing, and financing activities, the General Mills funds statement also presents a schedule of increases and decreases in working capital.

Frequently, in published financial statements, much of the detail is omitted. For example, a single amount may be shown for land, building, and equipment additions, and a number of individual items may be combined and presented as "Other sources" or "Other uses" of cash.

Regardless of the format used, the funds statement is considered essential for fully reporting the activities of a business enterprise. Even though not officially required for external reporting until APB Opinion No. 19 was issued in 1971, the funds statement has a long history of use. Many companies prepared the statement for management purposes long before actually presenting this information to external users. Now, as noted earlier, the FASB's conceptual framework calls for a cash flow statement to meet the objectives of financial reporting. The Board's proposed standard for a statement of cash flows provides more specific guidelines than earlier standards and should bring greater uniformity and comparability to reporting practices in this area.

APPENDIX

T-ACCOUNT APPROACH TO PREPARING
A CASH FLOW STATEMENT

This appendix illustrates a T-account approach to preparing a cash flow statement. As shown, this approach produces the same results as the columnar work sheet illustrated in the chapter; only the format is different. To highlight the similarities in the two approaches, the information and account analysis used in the work sheet illustration for Parker Inc. (pages 1065–1072) will also be used for the T-account illustration.

With the T-account approach, special "Cash Flows" T-accounts may be established. These accounts are used to summarize cash flows from operations and from significant investing and financing activities during the period and provide the basis for preparing the formal cash flow statement. Individual T-accounts are also established for Cash and all other balance sheet accounts.

During the process of analysis, the change in each account is explained as providing or using cash. In following the illustration, it may be helpful to refer to the detailed explanations for individual adjustments described on pages 1067–1072 of the text. Once the changes in all accounts have been reconciled and the Cash Flows T-accounts balanced, the formal cash flow statement can be prepared as illustrated on page 1073 of the chapter.

Cash Flows — Operating

	(a)	36,000		
			(g)	6,500
	(l)	5,000		
	(l)	20,900		
	(n)	300		
	(o)	6,000		
	(p)	10,500		
	(q)	1,500	(r)	4,500
	(s)	500	(t)	16,200
	(u)	3,500		
Net cash provided by operations		57,000		

Cash Flows — Investing

	(a)	8,000	(f)	105,000
	(e)	2,000	(h)	108,500
	(g)	102,500	(j)	12,000
	(i)	40,000	(k)	26,000
			(v)	2,000
Net cash used by investing activities				101,000

Cash Flows — Financing

	(m)	57,000	(b)	20,700
Net cash provided by financing activities		36,300		

Cash Flows — Summary

Net cash provided by operations		57,000	
Net cash used by investing			101,000
Net cash provided by financing		36,300	
Net decrease in cash	(w)	7,700	
		101,000	101,000

Cash

Beginning Bal.	55,000	(w)	7,700
Ending Bal.	47,300		

Marketable Securities

Beginning Bal.	10,000		
(v)	2,000		
Ending Bal.	12,000		

Accounts Receivable (net)

Beginning Bal.	70,500	(p)	10,500
Ending Bal.	60,000		

Inventories

Beginning Bal.	76,500	(g)	1,500
Ending Bal.	75,000		

Prepaid Operating Expenses

Beginning Bal.	12,000		
(r)	4,500		
Ending Bal.	16,500		

Investments

Beginning Bal.	106,000	(g)	96,000
Ending Bal.	10,000		

Land

Beginning Bal.	75,000		
(h)	108,500		
Ending Bal.	183,500		

Buildings

Beginning Bal.	225,000	(e)	40,000
(f)	105,000		
Ending Bal.	290,000		

Accumulated Depreciation—Buildings

(e)	38,000	Beginning Bal.	155,000
		(l)	5,600
		Ending Bal.	122,600

Machinery and Equipment

Beginning Bal.	120,000		
(j)	12,000		
Ending Bal.	132,000		

Accumulated Depreciation—Machinery and Equipment

(k)	26,000	Beginning Bal.	43,500
		(d)	3,500
		(l)	15,300
		Ending Bal.	36,300

Patents

Beginning Bal.	40,000	(l)	5,000
Ending Bal.	35,000		

Accounts Payable

		Beginning Bal.	81,200
(t)	16,200		
		Ending Bal.	65,000

Income Taxes Payable

		Beginning Bal.	9,500
		(s)	500
		Ending Bal.	10,000

Salaries Payable

		Beginning Bal.	1,500
		(u)	3,500
		Ending Bal.	5,000

Dividends Payable

		Beginning Bal.	0
		(b)	4,400
		Ending Bal.	4,400

Deferred Income Taxes

		Beginning Bal.	15,000
		(o)	6,000
		Ending Bal.	21,000

Bonds Payable		
	Beginning Bal.	0
	(m)	60,000
	Ending Bal.	60,000

Common Stock		
	Beginning Bal.	250,000
	(c)	100,000
	(i)	40,000
	Ending Bal.	390,000

Discount on Bonds Payable			
Beginning Bal.	0		
(m)	3,000	(n)	300
Ending Bal.	2,700		

Retained Earnings			
(b)	25,100	Beginning Bal.	234,300
(c)	100,000	(a)	44,000
(d)	3,500		
		Ending Bal.	149,700

QUESTIONS

1. (a) Describe the funds statement. (b) What information does it offer that is not provided by the income statement? (c) What information does it offer that is not provided by comparative balance sheets?
2. (a) What is the "all financial resources" concept of funds? (b) Why is use of this concept important?
3. Why must all "nonfund" account balances be analyzed in preparing a funds statement?
4. Name a source of funds originating from a transaction involving (a) noncurrent assets, (b) noncurrent liabilities, (c) capital stock, (d) retained earnings. Name a use of funds identified with each group.
5. Why is the statement of cash flows being recommended by the FASB?
6. What uses might each of the following find for a cash flow statement?
   (a) Manager of a small laundry.
   (b) Stockholder interested in regular dividends.
   (c) Bank granting short-term loans.
   (d) Officer of a labor union.
7. Indicate how each of the following would be reported in a cash flow statement.
   (a) Increases in inventories and short-term prepayments.
   (b) Increases in accrued liabilities (including income taxes payable).
   (c) Decreases in accounts and notes payable to suppliers.
   (d) Increases in dividends payable.
8. (a) Why is it important to disclose separately the amount of cash provided from continuing operations?
   (b) To compute "net cash flow from operations" what adjustments are applied to net income on a cash flow statement?
9. In presenting a funds statement on a working capital basis, why is it important to also include a supporting schedule showing the changes in working capital?
10. What alternatives exist to using work sheets in developing funds statements?

DISCUSSION CASES

CASE 24–1 (Is depreciation a source of funds?)

Brad Berrett and Jim Davis are roommates in college. Berrett is an accounting major while Davis is a finance major. Both have recently studied the "funds statement" in their classes. Davis's finance professor stated that depreciation is a major source of funds for some companies. Berrett's accounting professor indicated in class that depreciation cannot be a source of funds because no funds are involved.

Berrett and Davis wonder which professor is correct. Explain the positions taken by both professors and indicate which viewpoint you support and why?

CASE 24–2 (The most useful concept of funds)

At a recent luncheon, DeLance Jones, Lauretta Squires, and Merlin Hawkins, all CPAs, were discussing the funds statement. Jones favors a cash flow statement based on the premise that cash flows are of most interest to investors and creditors. Squires prefers a working capital funds statement because it is commonly understood by many financial statement readers. Hawkins feels strongly that the all financial resources concept should be used in preparing a funds statement. Should these three concepts of funds be considered as alternatives? Which concept do you prefer and why?

CASE 24–3 (Where does all the money go?)

Price Brothers Auto Parts has hired you as a consultant to analyze the company's financial position. One of the owners, David Price, is in charge of the financial affairs of the company. He makes all the deposits and pays the bills, but has an accountant prepare a balance sheet and an income statement once a year. The business has been quite profitable over the years. In fact, 2 years ago Price Brothers opened a second store and is considering a third outlet. However, the economy has slowed and the cash position has become very tight. The company is having an increasingly difficult time paying its bills. David has not been able to satisfactorily explain to his brothers what is happening. What factors should you consider and what recommendations might you make to Price Brothers?

CASE 24–4 (Why do we have more cash?)

Hot Lunch Delivery Service has always had a policy to pay stockholders annual dividends in an amount exactly equal to net income for the year. Joe Alberg, the company's president, is confused because the cash balance has been consistently increasing ever since Hot Lunch began operations 5 years ago, in spite of their faithful adherence to the dividend policy. Assuming no errors have been made in the bookkeeping process, explain why this situation might occur. Which basis for the funds statement, cash or working capital, provides the best explanation of what is happening to the cash balance?

EXERCISES

EXERCISE 24-1   (Cash flow analysis)

State how each of the following items would be reflected on a statement of cash flows.
(a) Marketable securities were purchased for $5,000.
(b) At the beginning of the year, equipment with a book value of $2,000 was traded for dissimilar equipment costing $3,500; a trade-in value of $700 was allowed on the old equipment; the balance of the purchase price is to be paid in 12 monthly installments.
(c) Buildings were acquired for $187,500, the company paying $50,000 cash and signing a 12% mortgage note payable in 5 years for the balance.
(d) Uncollectible accounts of $225 were written off against the allowance for doubtful accounts.
(e) Cash of $62,500 was paid to purchase business assets consisting of: merchandise, $22,500; furniture and fixtures, $7,500; land and buildings, $23,750; and goodwill, $8,750.
(f) A cash dividend of $1,250 was declared in the current period, payable at the beginning of the next period.
(g) An adjustment was made increasing Deferred Income Tax by $5,000.
(h) Accounts payable shows a decrease for the period of $3,750.

EXERCISE 24-2   (Net cash flow provided by operations)

The following data were taken from the books of Sweetwater Company. Compute the amount of net cash flow provided by operations during 1988.

	December 31, 1988	January 1, 1988
Accounts receivable	18,900	16,750
Accounts payable	11,500	14,000
Accumulated depreciation (no plant assets were retired during the year)	26,000	22,000
Inventories	26,500	22,000
Other current liabilities	5,000	3,000
Short-term prepayment	1,200	2,000
Net income	35,500	

EXERCISE 24-3   (Net cash flow provided by operations)

Net income for Boman Industrial Supply for 1988 is $540,000. Compute the net cash flow provided by operations, given the following information.
(a) Machinery costing $30,000 with a book value of $10,000 was stolen. The insurance company reimbursed Boman for $7,500, and new equipment was purchased for $42,500.
(b) Two delivery trucks were traded in for two new vans that are considered dissimilar from the trucks. Book value of the old trucks was $3,000 each. Cash of $9,000 was paid for each of the new vans and $3,500 was allowed on each trade-in. Cash price of the new vans was $12,500 each.

(c) Boman uses accelerated depreciation for income tax purposes and straight-line depreciation of $110,000 for book purposes. This resulted in an increase in Deferred Income Taxes of $13,500.

EXERCISE 24–4 (Cash computations)

Comparative balance sheets and income statement data for the Xavier Metals Company are presented below.

	December 31,	
	1988	1987
Assets		
Current assets:		
Cash	$ 119,000	$ 98,000
Marketable securities.........................	59,000	
Accounts receivable (net)	312,000	254,000
Inventory......................................	278,000	239,000
Prepaid expenses.............................	35,000	21,000
Total current assets	$ 803,000	$ 612,000
Property, plant, and equipment	$ 536,000	$ 409,000
Less accumulated depreciation	76,000	53,000
	$ 460,000	$ 356,000
Total assets	$1,263,000	$ 968,000
Liabilities and Equity		
Current liabilities:		
Accounts payable	$ 212,000	$ 198,000
Accrued expenses	98,000	76,000
Dividends payable	40,000	
Total current liabilities	$ 350,000	$ 274,000
Notes payable-due 1990	125,000	—
Total liabilities	$ 475,000	$ 274,000
Stockholders Equity:		
Common stock	$ 600,000	$ 550,000
Retained earnings............................	188,000	144,000
Total stockholders equity.....................	$ 788,000	$ 694,000
Total liabilities and equity	$1,263,000	$ 968,000

	Year Ended December 31,	
	1988	1987
Net sales	$3,561,000	$3,254,000
Cost of goods sold.............................	2,789,000	2,568,000
Gross profit	$ 772,000	$ 686,000
Expenses	521,000	486,000
Net income....................................	$ 251,000	$ 200,000

Additional information for Xavier:
(1) All accounts receivable and accounts payable relate to trade merchandise.
(2) The proceeds from the notes payable were used to finance plant expansion.
(3) Capital stock was sold to provide additional working capital.
Compute the following for 1988:
   (a) Cash collected from accounts receivable, assuming all sales are on account.
   (b) Cash payments made on accounts payable to suppliers, assuming that all purchases of inventory are on account.
   (c) Cash dividend payment.
   (d) Cash receipts that were not provided by operations.
   (e) Cash payments for assets that were not reflected in operations.

EXERCISE 24–5
(Net cash flow provided by operations — direct approach)

A summary of revenues and expenses for Stanton Company for 1988 follows:

Sales..	$6,000,000
Cost of goods manufactured and sold.........................	2,800,000
Gross profit..	$3,200,000
Selling, general, and administrative expenses.................	2,000,000
Income before income tax......................................	$1,200,000
Income tax..	520,000
Net income..	$ 680,000

Net changes in working capital items for 1988 were as follows:

	Debit	Credit
Cash..	$104,000	
Trade accounts receivable (net)....................	400,000	
Inventories......................................		$ 60,000
Prepaid expenses (selling and general)...............	10,000	
Accrued expenses (75% of increase related to manufacturing activities and 25% to general operating activities.......................................		32,000
Income taxes payable.............................		48,000
Trade accounts payable...........................		140,000

Depreciation on plant and equipment for the year totaled $600,000; 70% was related to manufacturing activities and 30% to general and administrative activities.
   Prepare a schedule of net cash flow provided by operations for the year using the direct approach.

EXERCISE 24–6   (Statement of cash flows)

Below is information and a schedule of changes in working capital for Boswell Manufacturing Company.

Schedule of Changes in Working Capital

	January 1, 1988	December 31, 1988	Working Capital Changes
Current assets:			
Cash	80,000	108,100	28,100
Inventory.	162,000	192,000	30,000
Accounts receivable (net) . . .	200,000	213,000	13,000
Marketable securities (LCM) . .	60,000	39,000	(21,000)
Current liabilities:			
Accounts payable	85,800	51,000	34,800
Dividends payable	18,000	27,000	(9,000)
Interest payable	3,000	11,100	(8,100)
Wages payable	12,000	84,000	(72,000)
Net change in working capital . .			(4,200)

(a) Long-term debt of $450,000 was retired at face value.
(b) New machinery was purchased for $48,000.
(c) Common stock with a par value of $120,000 was sold for $150,000.
(d) Dividends of $18,000 declared in 1987 were paid in January 1988, and new dividends of $27,000 were declared in December 1988 to be paid in 1989.
(e) Included in net income for 1988 was an unrealized loss on the short-term marketable equity securities portfolio in the amount of $21,000.
(f) Income of $19,200 was recognized from an investment accounted for by the equity method even though no cash dividends were received during the year.
(g) Net income was $300,000. Included in the computation was depreciation expense of $60,000 and goodwill amortization of $30,000.

Prepare a statement of cash flows for the year ended December 31, 1988.

EXERCISE 24–7   (Statement of cash flows)

A comparative balance sheet for Wheeler Trucking Co. and a funds statement on a working capital basis, including a schedule of working capital changes, are presented on pages 1084 and 1085. From the information provided prepare a cash flow statement for 1988.

Wheeler Trucking Co.
Comparative Balance Sheet
December 31, 1988 and 1987

Assets	1988	1987
Cash.	$ 50,000	$ 65,000
Accounts receivable.	170,000	143,000
Inventory	200,000	210,000
Prepaid items	60,000	40,000
Total current assets	$ 480,000	$458,000
Land, building and equipment (net)	690,000	510,000
Total assets	$1,170,000	$968,000
Liabilities and Equity		
Accounts payable.	$ 145,000	$155,000
Cash dividends payable	70,000	50,000
Total current liabilities	$ 215,000	$205,000
Bonds payable	300,000	200,000
Total liabilities	$ 515,000	$405,000
Stockholders' equity.	655,000	563,000
Total liabilities and equity	$1,170,000	$968,000

Wheeler Trucking Co.
Funds Statement — Working Capital Basis
For Year Ended December 31, 1988

Working capital from operating activities:		
Net income	$162,000	
Add depreciation	20,000	
Working capital provided by operations		$182,000
Working capital from investing activities:		
Purchase of equipment	$(200,000)	
Working capital used for investing activities		(200,000)
Working capital from financing activities:		
Issuance of bonds payable	$ 100,000	
Dividends	(70,000)	
Working capital used for financing activities		30,000
Net increase in working capital		$ 12,000

Schedule of Changes in Working Capital

	December 31, 1988	December 31, 1987	Working Capital Increase (Decrease)
Current assets:			
Cash	$ 50,000	$ 65,000	$(15,000)
Accounts receivable.........	170,000	143,000	27,000
Inventory..................	200,000	210,000	(10,000)
Prepaid items	60,000	40,000	20,000
Current liabilities:			
Accounts payable...........	145,000	155,000	10,000
Cash dividends payable	70,000	50,000	(20,000)
Increase in working capital.....			$ 12,000

EXERCISE 24–8 (Sources and uses of cash)

The accountant for Alpine Hobby Stores prepared the following selected information for the year ended December 31, 1988.

	December 31, 1988	December 31, 1987
a. Equipment....................	$25,000	$30,000
b. Accumulated depreciation	11,000	9,500
c. Long-term debt...............	11,000	20,000
d. Common stock...............	20,000	15,000

Equipment with a book value of $20,000 was sold for $17,000. The original cost of the equipment was $25,000.

What is the amount of cash provided or used by each item listed?

EXERCISE 24–9 (Sources and uses of working capital)

Determine how each of the following items would be reported on a working capital funds statement.

(a) New equipment with a fair market value of $12,500 was acquired on August 1 with an issuance of common stock.

(b) Inventory showed a decrease of $9,000 during the period.

(c) Stock dividends were paid during the year. The fair market value of the dividends was $8,000.

(d) A machine with an original cost of $25,000 and a book value of $8,000 was sold for $5,500.

(e) A long-term investment in Timo Co. bonds was exchanged during the year for a long-term investment in Emo Co. common stock. The fair market value and the cost of each of the exchanged securities was $11,000.

EXERCISE 24–10   (Work sheet adjustments)

Analyze the retained earnings account below, and give the adjustments, in journal entry form, needed for a work sheet for a cash flow statement.

Account   **Retained Earnings**

Date		Item	Debit	Credit	Balance Debit	Balance Credit
1988						
Jan.	1	Balance				532,000
Mar.	20	Correction for error in inventory at end of 1988		10,500		542,500
June	1	Stock dividend	140,000			402,500
Aug.	5	Sale of treasury stock (cost $150,000) for $132,500....	17,500			385,000
Dec.	5	Cash dividends............	35,000			350,000
	31	Appropriation for loss contingencies.................	70,000			280,000
	31	Net income		52,500		332,500

EXERCISE 24–11   (Statement of cash flows)

The Sunset Corporation prepared for 1988 and 1987 the following balance sheet data:

	December 31 1988	December 31 1987
Cash...	$ 349,500	$ 255,000
Marketable securities	69,000	420,000
Accounts receivable (net)	360,000	345,000
Merchandise inventory.........................	750,000	654,000
Prepaid insurance..............................	4,500	6,000
Buildings and equipment........................	5,515,500	4,350,000
Accumulated depreciation — buildings and equipment......................................	(2,235,000)	(1,995,000)
Total.....................................	$ 4,813,500	$ 4,035,000
Accounts payable	$ 613,500	$ 945,000
Salaries payable	75,000	105,000
Notes payable — bank (current)	150,000	600,000
Mortgage payable	1,500,000	0
Capital stock, $5 par..........................	2,400,000	2,400,000
Retained earnings (deficit)......................	75,000	(15,000)
Total.....................................	$ 4,813,500	$ 4,035,000

Cash needed to purchase new equipment and to improve the company's working capital position was raised by selling marketable securities costing $351,000 for $360,000 and by issuing a mortgage. Equipment costing $75,000 with a book value of $15,000 was sold for $18,000; the gain on sale was included in net income. The company paid cash dividends of $90,000 during the year and reported earnings of $180,000 for 1987. There were no entries in the retained earnings account other than to record the dividend and the net income for the year. Marketable securities are carried at cost which is lower than market.

Prepare a statement of cash flows without use of a work sheet.

PROBLEMS

PROBLEM 24–1   (Statement of cash flows)

Comparative balance sheet data for the Amber Company are presented below.

	1988	1987
Cash...	$ 2,000	$ 10,000
Marketable securities	9,000	18,000
Accounts receivable	94,000	86,000
Inventory...	110,000	100,000
Property, plant and equipment	550,000	500,000
Accumulated depreciation on property, plant and equipment..	(277,500)	(250,000)
Total...	$ 487,500	$ 464,000
Short-term notes payable...........................		$ 20,000
Accounts payable	$ 105,000	80,000
Long-term notes payable...........................	100,000	75,000
Bonds payable....................................	50,000	100,000
Common stock, $5 par.............................	100,000	100,000
Additional paid-in capital	75,000	75,000
Retained earnings.................................	57,500	14,000
Total...	$ 487,500	$ 464,000

Marketable securities costing $9,000 were sold for $9,000. New equipment was purchased for $50,000, consisting of $25,000 cash and a long-term note for $25,000. Proceeds from the short-term notes payable were used for operating purposes. Cash dividends of $10,000 were paid in 1988, all other changes to retained earnings were caused by the net income for 1988, which amounted to $53,500.

Instructions: Prepare a statement of cash flows for the year ended December 31, 1988.

PROBLEM 24–2 (Changing from working capital to cash flows)

Presented below are the funds statement on a working capital basis for the Perk Building Company for the year ended December 31, 1988, and a schedule of changes in working capital.

The balance sheet for December 31, 1987, appears at the top of the next page.

Perk Building Company
Statement of Changes in Financial Position — Working Capital Basis
For the Year Ended December 31, 1988

Working capital was provided by:		
Net income	$188,500	
Adjustments:		
Depreciation	37,500	
Amortization of patent	3,750	
Gain on sale of investments	(21,750)	
Working capital provided by operations		$208,000
Proceeds from sale of investments		78,000
Proceeds from sale of common stock		108,300
Long-term borrowing		79,200
Total working capital provided		$473,500
Working capital was applied to:		
Purchase of land	$ 57,250	
Dividends declared	37,500	
Reclassification of portion of long-term debt as current	7,500	
Purchase of machinery	225,000	
Total working capital applied		$327,250
Net increase in working capital		$146,250

Schedule of Changes in
Working Capital Components

	Working Capital Changes
Cash	$ 33,750
Accounts receivable	(7,500)
Inventory	60,000
Prepaid insurance	15,000
Accounts payable	22,500
Dividends payable	18,750
Current portion of long-term debt	3,750
	$146,250

Perk Building Company
Balance Sheet
December 31, 1987

Assets

Cash...		$ 22,500
Accounts receivable................................		33,750
Inventory		15,000
Prepaid insurance		7,500
Land		6,500
Machinery	$150,000	
Accumulated depreciation	(37,500)	112,500
Patents..		30,000
Investments (at cost)..............................		75,000
Total assets.......................................		$302,750

Liabilities and Stockholders' Equity

Accounts payable......................................	$ 60,000
Dividends payable	56,250
Current portion of long-term debt	11,250
Long-term debt.......................................	37,500
Common stock	112,500
Retained earnings	25,250
Total liabilities and stockholders' equity....................	$302,750

Instructions:
(1) Convert the funds statement on a working capital basis to a cash flow statement.
(2) Prepare a classified balance sheet for Perk Building Company as of December 31, 1988.

PROBLEM 24–3 (Cash flow statement)

Comparative balance sheet data for the firm of Young and Jones are as follows:

	December 31,	
	1988	1987
Cash...	$ 14,000	$ 10,500
Accounts receivable...........................	22,000	25,500
Inventory	112,500	85,000
Prepaid expenses	3,500	4,250
Furniture and fixtures	64,500	42,000
Accumulated depreciation	(33,875)	(25,425)
Total	$182,625	$141,825
Accrued expenses.............................	$ 7,000	$ 5,200
Accounts payable.............................	19,425	28,875
Long-term note...............................	17,700	-0-
Charles Young, capital	51,375	50,875
Diane Jones, capital	87,125	56,875
Total	$182,625	$141,825

Income from operations for the year was $43,000 and this was transferred in equal amounts to the partners' capital accounts. Further changes in the capital accounts arose from additional investments and withdrawals by the partners. The change in the furniture and fixtures account arose from a purchase of additional furniture; part of the purchase price was paid in cash and a long-term note was issued for the balance.

Instructions: Prepare a statement of cash flows for 1988 (worksheets are not required).

PROBLEM 24–4 (Cash flow statement with worksheet)

The following data are provided for the Dallas Department Store:

	Dr. (Cr.)	
	December 31, 1987 Post-Closing Trial Balance	December 31, 1988 Trial Balance
Cash....................................	12,000	28,800
Accounts receivable (net)...............	36,000	24,000
Inventory	96,000	144,000
Prepaid expenses	6,000	7,200
Plant assets..........................	480,000	624,000
Accumulated depreciation — plant assets ..	(48,000)	(122,400)
Accounts payable......................	(24,000)	(30,000)
Accrued liabilities	(9,600)	(12,000)
Mortgage payable	(60,000)	(84,000)
Bonds payable	(240,000)	(240,000)
Common stock	(180,000)	(210,000)
Capital in excess of par	(30,000)	(36,000)
Retained earnings	(38,400)	(26,400)
Sales.................................	—	(840,000)
Cost of goods sold.....................	—	480,000
Operating expenses	—	252,000
Gain on sale of plant assets	—	(12,000)
Income tax expense	—	52,800
Total	0	0

The following additional information was obtained from Dallas Department Store's accounting records:
(a) All accounts receivable were from sales to customers.
(b) The inventory and accounts payable were for merchandise purchased for resale.
(c) The prepaid expenses and accrued liabilities were for operating expenses.
(d) During the year, plant assets were purchased by paying $180,000 cash and signing a $24,000 mortgage.
(e) Plant assets with a cost of $60,000 and accumulated depreciation of $24,000 were sold for $48,000 cash.
(f) Depreciation expense for the year was included in operating expenses.

(g) Common stock was sold for $36,000 cash.

(h) Cash dividends of $12,000 were paid during the year.

Instructions: Using a worksheet, prepare a cash flow statement for the year ended December 31, 1988.   (AICPA adapted)

PROBLEM 24–5 (Cash flow statement)

Berclay Tile Co. reported net income of $6,160 for 1988 but has been showing an overdraft in its bank account in recent months. The manager has contracted you as the auditor for an explanation. The information below was given to you for examination.

Berclay Tile Company
Comparative Balance Sheet
December 31, 1988 and 1987

	1988		1987	
Assets				
Current assets:				
Cash	$ (960)		$ 4,780	
Accounts receivable	4,000		1,000	
Inventory	2,350		750	
Prepaid insurance	70		195	
Total current assets		$ 5,460		$ 6,725
Land, buildings, and equipment:				
Land	$12,500		$12,500	
Buildings	$25,000		$25,000	
Less accumulated depreciation	15,000	10,000	14,000	11,000
Equipment	$37,250		$30,850	
Less accumulated depreciation	22,500	14,750	18,400	12,450
Total land, buildings, and equipment		37,250		35,950
Total assets		$42,710		$42,675
Liabilities and Stockholders' Equity				
Current liabilities:				
Accounts payable	$ 4,250		$ 3,500	
Taxes payable	1,400		2,350	
Wages payable	750		1,675	
Notes payable—current portion	1,500		3,500	
Total current liabilities		$ 7,900		$11,025
Long-term liabilities:				
Notes payable		10,500		11,500
Capital stock	$17,500		$15,000	
Retained earnings	6,810		5,150	
Total stockholders' equity		24,310		20,150
Total liabilities and stockholders' equity		$42,710		$42,675

You also determine the following:
  (a) Equipment was sold for $1,500, its cost was $2,500 and its book value was $500. The gain was reported as Other Revenue.
  (b) Cash dividends of $4,500 were paid.

Instructions: Prepare a statement of cash flows (work sheets are not required).

PROBLEM 24–6 (Working capital funds statement)

The Kimball Company has prepared its financial statements for the year ended December 31, 1987, and for the 3 months ended March 31, 1988. You have been asked to prepare a statement of changes in financial position on a working capital basis for the 3 months ended March 31, 1988. The company's balance sheet data at December 31, 1987, and March 31, 1988, and its income statement data for the 3 months ended March 31, 1988, follow. You have previously satisfied yourself as to the correctness of the amounts presented. The balance sheet data are as follows:

	March 31, 1988	December 31, 1987
Cash....................................	$ 85,200	$ 29,600
Marketable securities.......................	7,300	16,500
Accounts receivable (net)...................	38,700	26,900
Inventory	48,800	28,000
Total current assets......................	$180,000	$101,000
Land....................................	18,700	40,000
Buildings	250,000	250,000
Equipment................................	75,000	0
Accumulated depreciation	(16,000)	(15,000)
Investment in 30% owned company...........	67,100	61,220
Other assets	25,000	25,000
Total assets...........................	$599,800	$462,220
Accounts payable..........................	$ 14,988	$ 26,528
Dividends payable	8,000	0
Income taxes payable.....................	34,616	0
Total current liabilities	$ 57,604	$ 26,528
Other liabilities	186,000	186,000
Bonds payable	110,000	60,000
Discount on bonds payable	(2,150)	(2,300)
Deferred income tax	846	510
Preferred stock...........................	0	30,000
Common stock............................	110,000	80,000
Dividends declared	(8,000)	0
Retained earnings	145,500	81,482
Total liabilities and equity.................	$599,800	$462,220

Income statement data for the 3 months ended March 31, 1988, are as follows:

Sales.	$242,807
Gain on sale of marketable securities	2,400
Equity in earnings of 30% owned company	5,880
Extraordinary gain on condemnation of land	10,700
	$261,787
Cost of goods sold.	$138,407
General and administrative expenses	22,010
Depreciation	1,250
Interest expense.	1,150
Income taxes.	34,952
	$197,769
Net income	$ 64,018

Your discussion with the company's controller and a review of the financial records revealed the following information:

(a) On January 8, 1988, the company sold marketable securities for cash.

(b) The company's preferred stock is convertible into common stock at a rate of 1 share of preferred for 2 shares of common. The preferred stock and common stock have par values of $2 and $1 respectively.

(c) On January 17, 1988, three acres of land were condemned. An award of $32,000 in cash was received on March 22, 1988. Purchase of additional land as a replacement is not contemplated by the company.

(d) On March 25, 1988, the company purchased equipment for cash.

(e) On March 29, 1988, bonds payable were issued by the company at par for cash.

(f) The company's tax rate is 40%.

Instructions: Prepare a funds statement of changes in financial position on a working capital basis for the Kimball Company for the 3 months ended March 31, 1988.

(AICPA adapted)

PROBLEM 24–7 (Comprehensive cash flow statement)

The following schedule showing net changes in balance sheet accounts at December 31, 1987, compared to December 31, 1988, was prepared from the records of the Willard Company. The statement of cash flows for the year ended December 31, 1988 has not yet been prepared.

	Increase (Decrease)
Assets	
Cash..	$ 60,000
Accounts receivable (net).....................	66,000
Inventories..................................	37,000
Prepaid expenses	2,000
Property, plant, and equipment (net)	63,000
Total assets............................	$228,000
Liabilities	
Accounts payable..........................	$ (46,000)
Short-term notes payable...................	(20,000)
Accrued liabilities.........................	28,500
Bonds payable	(28,000)
Less unamortized bond discount	1,200
Total liabilities........................	$ (64,300)
Stockholders' Equity	
Common stock, $10 par	$500,000
Paid-in capital in excess of par............	200,000
Retained earnings	(437,700)
Appropriation of retained earnings for possible future inventory price decline	30,000
Total stockholders' equity................	$292,300

Additional information includes:
(a) The net income for the year ended December 31, 1988, was $172,300. There were no extraordinary items.
(b) During the year ended December 31, 1988, uncollectible accounts receivable of $26,400 were written off by a debit to Allowance for Doubtful Accounts.
(c) A comparison of Property, Plant, and Equipment, as of the end of each year follows:

	December 31 1988	December 31 1987	Increase (Decrease)
Property, plant, and equipment...	$570,500	$510,000	$60,500
Less accumulated depreciation...	225,500	228,000	(2,500)
Property, plant and equipment...	$345,000	$282,000	$63,000

During 1988, machinery was purchased at a cost of $45,000. In addition, machinery that was acquired in 1981 at a cost of $48,000 was sold for $3,600. At the date of sale, the machinery has an undepreciated cost of $4,200. The remaining increase in property, plant and equipment resulted from the acquisition of a tract of land for a new plant site.
(d) The bonds payable mature at the rate of $28,000 every year.
(e) In January 1988, the company issued an additional 10,000 shares of its common stock at $14 per share upon the exercise of outstanding stock options held by key employees. In May, 1988, the company declared and issued a 5% stock dividend on its outstanding stock. During the year, a cash dividend was paid on the common stock. On December 31, 1988, there were 840,000 shares of common stock outstanding.

(f) The appropriation of retained earnings for possible future inventory price declines was provided by a debit to Retained Earnings, in anticipation of an expected future drop in the market related to goods in inventory.

(g) The notes payable relate to operating activities.

Instructions: Prepare a statement of cash flows for the year ended December 31, 1988, based on the information presented. (AICPA adapted)

PROBLEM 24–8 (Analysis of cash flows)

The following schedule shows the account balances of the Tundra Corporation at the beginning and end of the fiscal year ended October 31, 1988.

Debits	October 31, 1988	November 1, 1987	Increase (Decrease)
Cash.............................	$ 226,000	$ 50,000	$176,000
Accounts Receivable	148,000	100,000	48,000
Inventories	291,000	300,000	(9,000)
Prepaid Insurance....................	2,500	2,000	500
Long-Term Investments (at cost)	10,000	40,000	(30,000)
Sinking Fund	90,000	80,000	10,000
Land and Building...................	195,000	195,000	
Equipment..........................	215,000	90,000	125,000
Discount on Bonds Payable	8,500	9,000	(500)
Treasury Stock (at cost)..............	5,000	10,000	(5,000)
Cost of Goods Sold..................	539,000		
Selling and General Expenses........	287,000		
Income Taxes......................	35,000		
Loss on Sale of Equipment...........	1,000		
Total debits......................	$2,053,000	$876,000	

Credits			
Allowance for Doubtful Accounts	$ 8,000	$ 5,000	$ 3,000
Accumulated Depreciation—Building...	26,250	22,500	3,750
Accumulated Depreciation—Equipment..............................	39,750	27,500	12,250
Accounts Payable	55,000	60,000	(5,000)
Notes Payable—current	70,000	20,000	50,000
Miscellaneous Expenses Payable	18,000	15,000	3,000
Taxes Payable......................	35,000	10,000	25,000
Unearned Revenue..................	1,000	9,000	(8,000)
Notes Payable—Long-Term..........	40,000	60,000	(20,000)
Bonds Payable—Long-Term	250,000	250,000	
Common Stock	300,000	200,000	100,000
Retained Earnings Appropriated for Sinking Fund	90,000	80,000	10,000
Unappropriated Retained Earnings	94,000	112,000	(18,000)
Paid-In Capital in Excess of Par Value	116,000	5,000	111,000
Sales	898,000		
Gain on Sale of Investments..........	12,000		
Total credits	$2,053,000	$876,000	

The following information was also available:
    (a) All purchases and sales were on account.
    (b) The sinking fund will be used to retire the long-term bonds.
    (c) Equipment with an original cost of $15,000 was sold for $7,000.
    (d) Selling and general expenses include the following expenses:

Building depreciation	$ 3,750
Equipment depreciation	19,250
Doubtful accounts expense	4,000
Interest expense	18,000

    (e) A 6-months note payable for $50,000 was issued toward the purchase of new equipment.
    (f) The long-term note payable requires the payment of $20,000 per year plus interest until paid.
    (g) Treasury stock was sold for $1,000 more than its cost.
    (h) All dividends were paid by cash.

Instructions:
(1) Prepare schedules computing: (a) collections of accounts receivable: (b) payments of accounts payable.
(2) Prepare a statement of cash flows using the direct approach. Supporting computations should be in good form.   (AICPA adapted)

25

Reporting the Impact of Changing Prices

A troublesome problem for individuals and businesses alike is how to deal with changing prices. Most consumers are well aware that the prices of goods and services have risen significantly over the past fifty years. This increase in the general price level is called **inflation**. The following schedule shows the general price level in the U.S. for selected years since 1920, as measured by the consumer price index. The schedule illustrates the long-term inflationary trend that has characterized the U.S. economy in the post-Depression years. In some parts of the world, for example in South America, the rate of inflation has been much higher, at times over 1,000% a year.

Consumer Price Index for All Urban Consumers (CPI-U)
(1967 = 100)

Selected Years	Average for Year
1920	60.0
1930	50.0
1940	42.0
1950	72.1
1960	88.7
1965	94.5
1967*	100.0
1970	116.3
1972	125.3
1974	147.7
1976	170.5
1978	195.4
1980	246.8
1981	272.4
1982	289.1
1983	298.4
1984	311.1
1985	322.2

*Currently the base year.

Source: U.S. Department of Labor, Bureau of Labor Statistics

Financial statements of business enterprises have traditionally reflected transactions in terms of the number of dollars exchanged. These statements are often referred to as **historical cost/nominal dollar** or simply **historical cost** statements, meaning statements reporting unadjusted original dollar amounts. The justification for reporting original dollar amounts is objectivity. Historical costs generally are based on arm's-length transactions that are considered to measure appropriate exchange values at a transaction date.

The problem is that historical cost statements do not reflect the impact of price changes subsequent to the transaction date. To some, this is a serious limitation of traditional accounting, especially in periods of high inflation or rapidly increasing replacement costs for certain assets. When the inflation rate is low, the concern over accounting for changing prices tends to diminish.

Regardless of existing economic conditions, and the related level of interest in accounting for changing prices, there are some basic concepts that should be understood. This chapter explains these concepts and provides simple examples to illustrate the procedures involved in accounting for changing prices. For many students this conceptual understanding will be sufficient exposure to this important topic. Others may want to study carefully the appendix at the end of the chapter, which provides a comprehensive illustration of financial statements prepared under each of three approaches to reporting the impact of changing prices on business enterprises: *historical cost/constant dollar, current cost/nominal dollar,* and *current cost/constant dollar*. In addition, the appendix compares the results of these approaches to the currently generally accepted method of *historical cost/nominal dollar* accounting.

REPORTING THE EFFECTS OF CHANGING PRICES

Two kinds of price changes have been identified. The first deals with changes in the general price level for all commodities and services. The second kind of price change relates to changes in prices of particular items. Prices for individual items may fluctuate up or down and by differing magnitudes; the average of all specific price changes determines the change in the general price level. With respect to terminology, accounting for the first kind of price change is referred to as **constant dollar accounting** or general price-level adjusted accounting. Accounting for the second kind of price change is referred to as **current cost accounting** or current value accounting. This distinction is important in order to understand the reporting alternatives identified in the next section.

Reporting Alternatives

The major financial reporting alternatives, including the currently used historical cost/nominal dollar basis, may be classified as follows:

	Historical Cost Valuation	Current Cost Valuation
Nominal Dollar Measurement	HC/ND Historical Cost/ Nominal Dollar	CC/ND Current Cost/ Nominal Dollar
Constant Dollar Measurement	HC/CD Historical Cost/ Constant Dollar	CC/CD Current Cost/ Constant Dollar

The two distinct aspects of changing prices are highlighted by the matrix: the change in the unit of measurement (nominal and constant dollars) and the change in basis of valuation (historical and current costs). These distinctions are important since the accounting for and the effects on the financial statements are significantly different.

The first cell reflects financial statements that are currently reported in terms of nominal dollars using historical cost valuation. The dollar measurement is not adjusted for changes in the general price level, and the valuation basis represents the historical exchange prices of transactions, not current costs or values of the items reported. This is contrasted to the cell labeled HC/CD. Reporting on this basis maintains historical cost valuation but measures the items in terms of constant dollars. This means that the original or nominal dollars are adjusted to constant dollars — dollars of equivalent purchasing power. Sometimes constant dollars are referred to as **general purchasing power dollars** because they represent quantities of goods or services that can be purchased given a general price level. This concept is explained in greater detail later in this chapter.

The cell identified as CC/ND does not adjust the dollar measurement; it reports nominal dollars. However, it changes the valuation basis from historical costs to current costs. This basis of reporting reflects changes in specific prices but does not account for changes in the general price level. The term **current cost** is used throughout this chapter in a general sense to mean the current value of an asset as well as other measures of current cost: replacement cost, reproduction cost, sales value, net realizable value, and net present value of expected cash flows. Current costs and current values are used interchangeably.

The cell identified as CC/CD combines current cost valuation with constant dollar measurement. Reporting on this basis reflects both specific price changes and general purchasing power changes.

In summary, reporting on the traditional basis (represented by HC/ND) does not reflect the impact of general price changes or specific price changes until assets are sold or otherwise disposed of. Reporting on the HC/CD basis considers general purchasing power changes but not specific price changes. The CC/ND basis is just the opposite. It reports the impact of specific price changes because of its current cost valuation but does not reflect changes in the general purchasing power of the dollar. Only by reporting on a CC/CD basis are both types of price changes accounted for.

The extent and manner of reporting the impact of changing prices is also an issue. One possibility is to choose one of the three nontraditional cells and require preparation of primary financial statements on the basis selected. Another alternative is to continue reporting the primary financial statements on the historical cost/nominal dollar basis, but to provide supplemental information adjusted to constant dollars and/or reflecting current costs. If the latter alternative were chosen, a remaining question is whether to restate all items or only selected items.

Historical Perspective

The issues involved and the proposed alternatives for reporting the effects of changing prices are not new. In the 1920s and 1930s Henry Sweeney and others advocated constant dollar accounting under the names of "stabilized" or price-level accounting.[1]

In 1963, the AICPA published Accounting Research Study No. 6, "Reporting the Financial Effects of Price-Level Changes." This study recommended that supplementary data be presented showing comprehensive restatement of all elements of financial statements using a general price index.[2] Later, in 1969, the APB issued Statement No. 3, which again recognized the potential benefits of general price-level adjusted information and suggested supplemental disclosure of such data.[3]

At the end of 1974, the FASB issued an exposure draft entitled "Financial Reporting in Units of General Purchasing Power." This pro-

---

[1] See, for example, Henry W. Sweeney, *Stabilized Accounting*, (New York: Harper & Brothers, 1936).

[2] *Accounting Research Study No. 6*, "Reporting the Financial Effects of Price-Level Changes" (New York: American Institute of Certified Public Accountants, 1963).

[3] *Statement of the Accounting Principles Board, No. 3*, "Financial Statements Restated for General Price-Level Change" (New York, American Institute of Certified Public Accountants, 1969).

posed statement would have required constant dollar accounting, although still as supplemental information.[4] However, before the FASB adopted a final statement, the SEC issued ASR No. 190, which required many companies to disclose current replacement costs of selected assets.[5] Because this conflicted with the FASB's constant dollar exposure draft, the Board withdrew its proposal.

In 1979, after careful evaluation, the FASB decided to experiment with alternative ways of reporting the impact of changing prices by issuing Statement No. 33, "Financial Reporting and Changing Prices.[6] This statement required certain companies to disclose supplemental information for selected items on *both* a constant dollar and a current cost basis. Subsequently, the SEC modified its requirements, as established in ASR No. 190, to comply with the more comprehensive FASB Statement No. 33.

In December 1986, after careful review of the Statement No. 33 experiment, the FASB issued Statement No. 89 which supersedes Statement No. 33 and various related amendments to that statement. The FASB has made voluntary the supplementary disclosure of current cost/constant dollar information after concluding that such disclosure should be encouraged, but not required.[7]

Since some companies will continue to report changing price data and since this topic will no doubt continue to be debated, accounting students should be familiar with the underlying concepts of constant dollar accounting and current cost accounting.

CONSTANT DOLLAR ACCOUNTING

Recording transactions in terms of the number of nominal dollars exchanged ignores the fact that the dollar is *not* a stable monetary unit. As a unit of measurement, the dollar has significance only in reference to a particular price level. Thus, nominal dollar measurements represent diverse amounts of purchasing power. Unless statements are adjusted, readers are likely to regard dollars in terms of current general purchasing

---

[4] *FASB Exposure Draft*, "Financial Reporting in Units of General Purchasing Power" (Stamford: Financial Accounting Standards Board, 1974).

[5] Securities and Exchange Commission, *Accounting Series Release No. 190*, "Disclosure of Certain Replacement Cost Data" (Washington: U.S. Government Printing Office, 1976).

[6] *Statement of Financial Accounting Standards No. 33*, "Financial Reporting and Changing Prices" (Stamford: Financial Accounting Standards Board, 1979); Also see, Robert W. Berliner and Dale L. Gerboth, "FASB Statement No. 33 'The Great Experiment,'" *Journal of Accountancy* (May 1980), pp. 48–54.

[7] *Statement of Financial Accounting Standards No. 89*, "Financial Reporting and Changing Prices" (Stamford: Financial Accounting Standards Board, 1986).

power rather than the general purchasing power at the time the dollars were exchanged. The objective of constant dollar accounting is to convert all dollar measurements into **equivalent purchasing power units** so that a company's position and progress may be viewed in proper perspective.

To illustrate, it would not seem proper to add 100 U.S. dollars to 100 British pounds. It would seem necessary to first convert one of the figures to its exchange equivalent before adding, subtracting, or comparing amounts. Similarly, the number of dollars spent years ago for land or buildings should be converted into current equivalent purchasing power units to arrive at meaningful asset totals. This conversion of nominal dollar amounts to equivalent purchasing power units is the essence of constant dollar accounting. Historical costs, the original exchange values, are maintained as the valuation basis, but are adjusted for changes in the general price level. The basis of measurement changes from nominal dollar amounts to constant dollar amounts or equivalent purchasing power units. The conversion is accomplished using a general price index.

Price Indexes

The value or purchasing power of a monetary unit is inversely related to the price of goods or services for which it can be exchanged. Over a period of time, the prices of specific goods or services will move up or down depending on the relative scarcity and desirability of the goods or services. It would be possible to adjust for specific items, but those price changes may be different than changes in the general price level.

The general price level cannot be measured in absolute terms, but relative changes from period to period and the direction of change can be determined. To measure changes in the general price level, a sample of commodities and services is selected and the current prices of these items are compared with their prices during a base period. The prices during the base period are assigned a value of 100, and the prices of all other periods are expressed as percentages of this amount. The resulting series of numbers is called a **price index**.

Price indexes are valuable aids in measuring inflation or deflation. However, these measurements do have limitations. In the first place, all price indexes are based on samples. Since all prices do not fluctuate in the same degree or direction, the selection of commodities to be included in the sample affects the computed amounts. In addition, improvements in products affect the general level of prices, but such qualitative changes are difficult to measure.

Although there is no perfect way to measure the changing value of the dollar, indexes have been developed that provide reasonable estimates of changes in the dollar's general purchasing power. Among these are the

Consumer Price Index and the Wholesale Price Index, both provided by the Bureau of Labor Statistics, and the GNP (Gross National Product) Implicit Price Deflator provided by the Department of Commerce.

Each of these indexes exhibits a similar pattern of price-level change, but reports different values. This is because each index is based on a different sample. The index recommended by the FASB is the Consumer Price Index for all Urban Consumers (CPI-U), which is published monthly.

Mechanics of Constant Dollar Restatement

Constant dollar accounting requires that nominal dollar amounts be restated to equivalent purchasing power units, i.e., constant dollars, usually for the current period. The general formula for restatement is:

$$\text{Nominal dollar amount} \times \frac{\text{Price index converting \textbf{to}}}{\text{Price index converting \textbf{from}}} = \text{Constant dollar amount}$$

To illustrate the conversion process, assume that a company issued capital stock worth $50,000 in exchange for inventory valued at $50,000. Further assume that the current end-of-year price index is 105 and that the exchange took place when the general price index was 100. The company holds inventory during the year without engaging in any other activities. A conventional balance sheet prepared at the end of the year will show both inventory and invested capital at their nominal amounts, $50,000. In preparing a constant dollar balance sheet at the end of the year, however, inventory and capital stock will be reported as follows:

1. Inventory needs to be restated for the change in the general price level since its acquisition. Inventory, with a nominal acquisition cost of $50,000, is expressed in constant dollars as $52,500:

$$\$50,000 \times \frac{\text{Index converting to (105)}}{\text{Index converting from (100)}} = \$52,500$$

2. Capital stock also requires restatement so that it expresses the stockholders' investment in terms of the current general price level. The capital stock balance is expressed in constant dollars as $52,500:

$$\$50,000 \times \frac{\text{Index converting to (105)}}{\text{Index converting from (100)}} = \$52,500$$

Conversion ratios may be used that express the relationship of one index to another. Thus, in the example cited, 105/100 may be stated as a conversion ratio of 1.05.

In the example presented, the price index converted "to" was the end-of-year index. Alternatively, an average index for the current year could have been used. If such an approach were taken, the conversion factor would have been 102.5/100 rather than 105/100. Another approach would be to restate all amounts in terms of the price level of an earlier period, e.g., the year of purchase of an item or a base year. Then events occurring during the current year would be restated in terms of constant dollars of the earlier period selected. Nominal dollars can be restated to constant dollars of any period by modifying the indexes used for the conversion factor.

If current-year constant dollars are used to prepare comparative summaries, all past year data, including monetary assets and liabilities (defined in the next section), must be "rolled forward" to the current year. In this manner, data presented for several years will all be stated in terms of the same purchasing power units. To illustrate, assume that land was purchased in 1981 for $100,000. Assume further that the general price level was 150 when the land was purchased, 200 at the end of 1986, and 215 at the end of 1987. In reporting the land on the balance sheet at the end of 1986, the land would be reported in current end-of-year constant dollars as follows:

$$\text{Land}\left(\$100,000 \times \frac{200}{150}\right) = \$133,333$$

However, in reporting comparative amounts at the end of 1987 in current end-of-year constant dollars, the 1986 amount would have to be rolled forward as follows:

$$\text{Land}\left(\$133,333 \times \frac{215}{200}\right) = \$143,333$$

Alternatively, the 1987 amount could be computed directly as follows:

$$\$100,000 \times \frac{215}{150} = \$143,333$$

Thus, the comparative balance sheet at December 31, 1987, would show the following:

	1986	1987
Land...........................	$143,333	$143,333

This correctly shows no increase in the land account during 1986 and 1987 when amounts are all stated in terms of the same constant dollars. For comparative balance sheet purposes at the end of 1988, the $143,333 would again have to be rolled forward to reflect 1988 dollars.

As indicated earlier, all items may be reported in terms of constant dollars of an earlier base year. This would eliminate the need for a roll-forward adjustment because all items would be stated in terms of a base year's constant dollars. Even though restating amounts to current-year constant dollars requires a roll-forward procedure, it provides information that relates to the current general price level as opposed to some earlier price level. Current price levels are usually more understandable and relevant for decision-making purposes.

To illustrate the application of constant dollar accounting to the balance sheet, consider a simple example — Campus Supply. All amounts are restated to current end-of-year constant dollars. Assume that the beginning-of-year index was 220; the end-of-year index was 260. The entire ending inventory was all purchased when the index was 225; the land was bought when the index was 125; all capital stock was issued when the index was 110.

	Campus Supply Balance Sheet December 31, 1987 (Constant Dollar Basis)		
Assets	HC/ND Amounts	Conversion Factor	HC/CD Amounts
Cash	$22,000		$22,000
Accounts receivable...................	14,000		14,000
Inventory...........................	9,000	260/225	10,400
Land	20,000	260/125	41,600
Total assets........................	$65,000		$88,000
Liabilities and Stockholders' Equity			
Accounts payable.....................	$ 4,000		$ 4,000
Mortgage payable.....................	15,000		15,000
Capital stock	22,000	260/110	52,000
Retained earnings....................	24,000		17,000*
Total liabilities and stockholders' equity ...	$65,000		$88,000
*$88,000 − ($4,000 + $15,000 + $52,000)			

Note that conversion is not made for cash, receivables, and payables. As explained in the next section, these "monetary items" are fixed in amount regardless of changes in the price level, except when rolling forward past year data for comparative statements. It also should be observed that Retained Earnings cannot be converted directly, since it represents a composite of many different price levels.

A comprehensive illustration for this and other reporting alternatives is presented in the appendix to this chapter. But even this simple example shows the potentially significant impact of changing price levels on a balance sheet.

Purchasing Power Gains and Losses

In preparing an income statement on the historical cost/constant dollar basis, revenues and expenses are restated by applying the appropriate indexes in the same manner as illustrated in the preceding section. In addition, reported income is adjusted for any **purchasing power gain or loss** that results from holding monetary items. **Monetary items** are assets, liabilities, and equities whose balances are fixed in terms of numbers of dollars regardless of changes in the general price level. All items not representing a right to receive or an obligation to pay a fixed sum are **nonmonetary items**.

Monetary assets include cash and items such as accounts and notes receivable, loans to employees, cash surrender value of life insurance, and certain marketable securities, such as bonds, that are expected to be held to maturity and redeemed at a fixed number of dollars. Regardless of changes in the general price level, these balances are fixed and provide for the recovery of neither more nor less than the stated amounts. Monetary liabilities include such items as accounts and notes payable, cash dividends payable, and fixed payments for accruals under pension plans. Regardless of changes in the price level, these balances are fixed and call for the payment of neither more nor less than the stated amounts. Nonconvertible preferred stock is a monetary equity item while common stock is a nonmonetary item. (For a more extensive classification of monetary and nonmonetary items, see Appendix D of FASB Statement No. 33.)

To illustrate the concept of purchasing power gain or loss, assume that a person placed $1,000 cash under the mattress for "safekeeping" when the price index was 100. If the price index were to rise to 110 a year later, the individual would have suffered a purchasing-power loss because it would require $1,100 to purchase the same amount of goods that $1,000 would have bought a year ago. On the other hand, a debt of $1,000 payable a year later, again assuming an increase in the price index to 110 from 100, would result in a purchasing power gain. The equivalent purchasing power would be $1,100 yet the debt can be settled for the fixed amount of $1,000.

Nonmonetary assets include such items as inventories and supplies; land, buildings, and equipment; and intangible assets. These items are nonmonetary because with changes in the general price level, the nominal dollar amounts at which they are reported on the conventional financial statements will differ from the resources they actually represent. On the other hand, nonmonetary liabilities generally include such items as obligations to furnish goods or services, advances on sales contracts, and warranties on goods sold. These items are nonmonetary because with changes in the general price level, the dollar demands they actually make will differ from the dollar amounts reported on conventional financial statements.

The difference between a company's monetary assets and its monetary liabilities and equities is referred to as its **net monetary position**. With the number of dollars relating to monetary items remaining fixed, and reflecting current dollars regardless of the change in the price level, purchasing power gains and losses arise as prices change. In any given period, the gain or loss from holding monetary assets is offset by the loss or gain from maintaining monetary liabilities and equities. The net gain or loss for a period, then, depends on whether a company's position in net monetary items is positive — monetary assets exceeding monetary liabilities and equities — or negative — monetary liabilities and equities exceeding monetary assets. Gains and losses are associated with a company's net monetary position as follows:

	Rising Prices	Declining Prices
Positive Net Monetary Position	Loss	Gain
Negative Net Monetary Position	Gain	Loss

Constant dollar accounting requires that purchasing power gains and losses be determined. The steps to be followed in determining these gains and losses are explained and illustrated using the financial information for Campus Supply on page 1105 and the following additional information.

Sales for the year were $90,000, purchases were $60,000, and other expenses were $24,000. These revenues and expenses were incurred evenly throughout the year.

The net monetary positions as of January 1, 1987, and December 31, 1987, are as follows:

	January 1, 1987	December 31, 1987
Cash................................	$19,000	$22,000
Accounts receivable...................	11,000	14,000
Accounts payable.....................	(3,000)	(4,000)
Mortgage payable	(16,000)	(15,000)
Net monetary position.................	$11,000	$17,000

The purchasing power gain or loss is calculated as follows assuming conversion to end-of-year constant dollars:

1. The company's net monetary position at the beginning of the period is restated to end-of-year constant dollars. Campus Supply's net monetary position as of January 1, 1987, is $11,000. This amount can be restated to end-of-year dollars by multiplying it by the ratio of the year-end price index to the index at the beginning of the year: $11,000 \times 260/220 = $13,000.

2. Transactions involving monetary items during the year are expressed in terms of year-end constant dollars and are added to or subtracted from the beginning net monetary position. For Campus Supply, monetary items were increased by sales and decreased by purchases and other expenses. Because these items were incurred evenly during the year, the ratio of the

year-end price index to the average index for 1987 can be used to restate them to end-of-year dollars.

	HC/ND	Conversion Factor	HC/CD
Sales	$90,000	260/240	$97,500
Purchases	(60,000)	260/240	(65,000)
Other expenses	(24,000)	260/240	(26,000)
Increase in net monetary position	$ 6,000	260/240	$ 6,500

If no gain or loss in purchasing power had occurred during the year, the ending net monetary position would be $19,500 computed as follows:

	HC/CD
Net monetary position, January 1, 1987	$13,000
Increase in net monetary position	6,500
Net monetary position, December 31, 1987	$19,500

3. The actual net monetary position at the end of the year is compared with the results from Step 2. If the actual net monetary position is less than the amount computed in Step 2, the company has sustained a loss in purchasing power. If it is greater, the company has experienced a gain. Campus Supply's actual net monetary position at the end of 1987 is $17,000. Since this amount is less than the $19,500 computed above, the company has sustained a $2,500 purchasing power loss. The foregoing calculations can be summarized in the following schedule:

Campus Supply Schedule of Purchasing Power Loss For the Year Ended December 31, 1987			
	HC/ND	Conversion Factor	HC/CD*
Net monetary position, January 1, 1987	$11,000	260/220	$13,000
Increase in net monetary position	6,000	260/240	6,500
			$19,500
Net monetary position, December 31, 1987	$17,000		17,000
Purchasing power loss			$ 2,500
*End of year dollars			

This schedule shows several things. First, the beginning net monetary position plus the net increase (or less the net decrease) will always equal the ending net monetary position, all stated in nominal dollars. This amount can be computed directly from the balance sheet data. Second, the $19,500 represents the amount that the ending monetary position should be in terms of current end-of-year purchasing power units (constant dollars) if no gain or loss had occurred. However, the actual net monetary position is $17,000 because monetary items are fixed in amount. The result is a purchasing power loss of $2,500, the difference between what the monetary position would be if purchasing power had been maintained and the actual amount. On a constant dollar income statement, the purchasing power gain or loss is added to or subtracted from the constant dollar operating income and becomes a part of the ending retained earnings balance, as illustrated in the appendix at the end of the chapter.

As indicated earlier, the objective of constant dollar accounting is to convert all nominal dollar amounts to dollars of equivalent purchasing power. Thus, nominal dollars may be converted to constant dollars of a prior period or to average dollars for the current year. The latter approach is frequently encountered in practice and is illustrated in the following schedule for Campus Supply.

	HC/ND	Conversion Factor	HC/CD*
Campus Supply Schedule of Purchasing Power Loss For the Year Ended December 31, 1987			
Net monetary position, January 1, 1987.....	$11,000	240/220	$12,000
Increase in net monetary position..........	6,000		6,000
			$18,000
Net monetary position, December 31, 1987...	$17,000	240/260	15,692
Purchasing power loss....................			$ 2,308
*Average dollars			

When average-for-the-year constant dollars are used to determine purchasing power gain or loss, both beginning and ending amounts must be restated in terms of the average price index. No restatement was required for the ending balance in the previous example since this amount reflected end-of-year dollars. When using an average current-year index, the net increase or decrease in monetary position is not converted since revenues and expenses are assumed to occur evenly throughout the period; therefore, these amounts already reflect average price levels for the year. The purchasing power loss of $2,308 differs from the $2,500 loss in the previous example because it reflects a different price level. The $2,308 can be restated to end-of-year dollars as follows: $2,308 × 260/240 = $2,500.

Arguments For and Against Constant Dollar Accounting

Proponents of constant dollar accounting maintain that meaningful comparisons of accounting data are not possible unless the measuring units are comparable. They argue that the purchasing power of the dollar is not stable, fluctuating with changes in the general price level. Constant dollar accounting corrects this deficiency by measuring transactions in terms of equivalent purchasing power units, thus giving proper recognition to changes in the general price level. Those in favor of constant dollar accounting also point out that recognition of purchasing power gains and losses highlights the impact of inflation with respect to monetary assets, liabilities, and equities. They conclude that constant dollar information is relevant to decision makers and can be provided on a reliable basis without undue cost.

Those opposed to constant dollar accounting note that changes in specific prices of goods are not considered. Constant dollar accounting reflects only changes in the general price level. It ignores many underlying reasons for specific price changes — for example, those due to improvements in quality and specialized industry circumstances. In addition, the general price index used may not be relevant to particular industries. Constant dollar opponents also point out that price indexes are based on statistical averages and have many weaknesses. They question the reliability of the data, especially if used indiscriminately. Many accountants also question whether the benefits exceed the costs of providing constant dollar data. They fear companies will incur substantial costs, only to have users of the data be confused by or uninterested in the information.

CURRENT COST ACCOUNTING

The objective of **current cost accounting** is different from constant dollar accounting. Constant dollar accounting seeks to use comparable measuring units to reflect equivalent purchasing power for a specified general price level. Current cost accounting attempts to measure the current values of assets, liabilities, and equities. The current values may be measured in nominal dollars or in constant dollars, but they are intended to represent the current exchange prices of goods or services, not historical costs.

Current cost accounting measures changes in specific prices rather than changes in the general price level. While the general price level may have increased an average 12% during the past year, the current values of land may be up 22%, inventories may be up only 8%, and certain types of equipment, perhaps due to technological advancements, may have even decreased in value.

Concept of Well-Offness

From an income measurement perspective, current cost accounting is based on a concept of *well-offness*. This concept is attributed to an economist, J. R. Hicks, and maintains that operating gross profit, often called economic income, is the amount a firm can spend during a period and be as well-off at the end of the period as at the beginning. Operationalized, economic income (loss) is the difference between the sales price of an item and the cost to replace that item. Alternatively, it may be viewed as the change in net assets during a period measured on a current value basis. For example, if an entity's net assets, in terms of current costs, equaled $250,000 at the beginning of a period, and $300,000 at the end of the period, given no additional investments or withdrawals and holding the general price level constant, economic income would be $50,000.

Current costs may be defined in several ways. Among the most common are: (1) input prices, i.e., replacement costs; (2) exit prices, i.e., sales values; (3) net realizable values, i.e., expected sales prices less costs to complete and sell; and (4) economic values, i.e., present values of future cash flows. These distinctions are technical refinements in implementing the general approach of reflecting current values in financial statements.

Different circumstances may require different approaches to presenting current cost information. For example, the current cost of inventory or plant assets is generally thought of as the cost to replace or reproduce those assets at the balance sheet date. However, assets such as timber can be replaced only over a long period of time; minerals and oil and gas reserves may not be renewable at all. In these circumstances, economic values probably offer better representations of current costs than do replacement costs. This again points out the need for accountants to use judgment, within the guidelines established by the profession, in applying accounting principles.

Holding Gains or Losses

Current cost accounting not only emphasizes economic income but also makes it possible to isolate any gains or losses resulting from holding nonmonetary assets. Traditionally, accountants have recognized income at the point of sale, measuring the difference between the sales price and the historical cost of the item sold. Under current cost accounting, changes in asset values during a period would be recognized whether the assets were sold or not. The recognition of **holding gains or losses** is therefore an essential ingredient of current cost accounting.

Two types of gains and losses from holding assets need to be accounted for. **Realized holding gains and losses** indicate the differences between the current costs and the historical costs of assets sold or used during a period. **Unrealized holding gains and losses** are increases (or decreases) in the current values of assets held during a period but not sold or used. For example, in the earlier illustration assume that the land of Campus Supply had a current value of $60,000 at the end of 1987. On a December 31, 1987, current cost balance sheet, the land would be reported at its current value of $60,000 rather than its historical cost of $20,000 or its end-of-year constant dollar value of $41,600, thus disclosing a $40,000 unrealized holding gain.

To further illustrate the concept of holding gains or losses, assume that Current Value Company made a sale of $100,000. The cost of goods sold was $65,000, and the cost to replace the inventory sold was $80,000. The total gross profit recognized under historical cost accounting is $35,000 (sales price minus historical cost of inventory sold). However, the $35,000 includes an operating gross profit of $20,000 (sales price minus current cost of inventory sold) and an inventory holding gain of $15,000. The realized holding gain of $15,000 represents the difference between the historical cost and the replacement cost of the inventory sold. This may be illustrated as follows:

Sales............................	$100,000	$20,000 Operating gross profit
Current cost of inventory............	80,000	15,000 Realized holding gain
Cost of goods sold.................	65,000	
Total gross profit..................		$35,000

If, in the example, Current Value Company had additional inventory that was not sold but that had a change in value, it would have an unrealized holding gain or loss. Assume inventory that was not sold cost $50,000 and had a replacement cost of $75,000. There would be a $25,000 unrealized holding gain on the inventory.

To show how these concepts would be applied over time, assume $10,000 of inventory was purchased by a company at the beginning of Year 1. At the end of Year 1 no inventory had been sold but its current cost was $12,000. At the end of Year 2, the inventory was sold for $18,000 and was replaced at a cost of $15,000. A comparison of the historical cost and current cost approaches over time is shown in the following illustration. For simplicity, assume that the only expense is cost of goods sold.

	Historical Cost			Current Cost		
	Year 1	Year 2	Total	Year 1	Year 2	Total
Sales revenue	-0-	$18,000	$18,000	-0-	$18,000	$18,000
Cost of goods sold	-0-	10,000	10,000	-0-	15,000	15,000
Operating income	-0-	$ 8,000	$ 8,000	-0-	$ 3,000	$ 3,000
Holding gain (loss)	-0-	-0-	-0-	$2,000	3,000	5,000
Net income	-0-	$ 8,000	$ 8,000	$2,000	$ 6,000	$ 8,000

Note that total income recognized is the same under either method. Under current cost accounting, however, changes in the prices of inventory are recognized as they occur. The $2,000 increase in the value of the inventory during Year 1 was an unrealized holding gain, since the inventory had not been sold.

In Year 2, the difference between the current cost of the inventory and its historical cost, $5,000, is a realized holding gain. Note that this realized holding gain includes the $2,000 unrealized holding gain recognized in Year 1 as well as $3,000 realized in Year 2. There is no unrealized holding gain on the inventory in Year 2, since the ending inventory was acquired at the end of Year 2.

Current cost net income in this example consists of operating income and holding gains, both realized and unrealized. The total net income would be reflected in retained earnings and would offset changes in net asset values shown on the balance sheet. Some accountants argue, however, that holding gains and losses should be reported as a special account in the owners' equity section of the balance sheet and should not be included in the determination of net income. Another position is that only realized holding gains and losses should be reported as income, and unrealized gains or losses should be reported in an owners' equity account.

Mechanics of Current Cost Accounting

The major problem in current cost accounting is determining appropriate current values. There are two recommended approaches: (1) **Indexing** through internally or externally developed specific price indexes for the class of goods or services being measured, and (2) **direct pricing** from current invoice prices, vendors' price lists, or standard manufacturing costs that reflect current costs. If indexing is used, restatement is mechanically the same as for constant dollar accounting. The difference is that specific price indexes are used rather than a general price index. The direct pricing approach assigns current values, determined by analysis and estimate, to particular assets.

Arguments for and Against Current Cost Accounting

Many accountants were not in favor of the replacement cost reporting requirements of ASR 190. Some were opposed to FASB Statement No. 33, being especially critical of its complexity and the confusion it might cause. However, proponents of current cost accounting argue that historical cost financial statements, even if adjusted for general price-level changes, do not adequately reflect the economic circumstances of a business. The balance sheet is deficient because only historical costs are presented, and these measurements do not reflect the current financial picture of an enterprise. The income statement is deficient because charges against revenues are based on historical costs that may differ from current costs. Also, increases in net asset values are not recognized at the time of a change in asset value but must await realization at time of sale. Under current cost accounting, assets are reported at their current values, thus more closely reflecting the actual financial position of a business. Expenses are based on the expiration of current costs of assets utilized, thus providing a more meaningful income measure, and changes in values of assets held are recognized as they occur.

Opponents of current cost accounting argue that determining current values is too subjective. For example, the current cost of a particular item may not be readily available and may have to be determined by appraisal or estimation. It may be difficult or impossible to even find an identical replacement item to consider its replacement cost. If an identical asset is not used, a subjective adjustment for differences in the quality of a similar but not identical item would have to be made.

Another disadvantage is the increased subjectivity of the income measurement if changes in current values are recognized as income prior to transactions that confirm arm's-length exchange values.

Additional arguments against current cost accounting include the lack of understanding of current cost financial statements; the question of whether the benefits are worth the extra costs involved; and the uncertainty of whether financial statement users will be better served by current cost accounting.

CURRENT COST/CONSTANT DOLLAR ACCOUNTING

A number of accountants argue against both constant dollar and current cost accounting, pointing out that each approach solves only one of the problems of accounting for changing prices. Constant dollar accounting adjusts for general price changes; current cost accounting recognizes the impact of specific price changes. Current cost/constant dollar accounting combines both approaches and reflects current cost valuation on a constant dollar basis. Such an approach recognizes that adjustments for specific and general price changes are neither mutually exclusive nor competing alternatives. Conceptually, this is the best reporting alternative if the objective is to give full effect to the impact of changing prices on business enterprises. Its primary disadvantage, in addition to the shortcomings ascribed to the other approaches considered separately, is its complexity.

Again referring to the Campus Supply example, on a December 31, 1987, current cost/constant dollar balance sheet, the land would be reported at its current cost stated in end-of-year constant dollars of $60,000. Note that this is the same amount as reported under the current cost/nominal dollar approach. For the $60,000 to be a current cost it would have to be a year-end amount. Conversion would be required, however, if average-year or base-year dollars were used.

In the example, the $60,000 current cost/constant dollar land amount is $40,000 higher than the $20,000 reported under the historical cost/nominal dollar approach. As explained earlier, this is an unrealized holding gain. However, only part of the $40,000 total unrealized holding gain is real; a portion of it is an inflationary component or fictitious holding gain due to changes in the general purchasing power of the dollar. This concept can be illustrated by the following diagram:

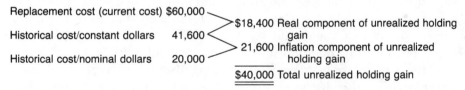

Replacement cost (current cost) $60,000
$18,400 Real component of unrealized holding gain
Historical cost/constant dollars   41,600
21,600 Inflation component of unrealized holding gain
Historical cost/nominal dollars   20,000
$40,000 Total unrealized holding gain

However, it should be noted that in presenting financial statements on a current cost/constant dollar basis, the inflationary component is not reported separately. The constant dollar adjustment is made for all non-monetary items, and only the real component of unrealized holding gains is shown as a separate item. In the Campus Supply example, only the $18,400 holding gain on the land would be disclosed.

This example shows the impact of both general and specific price changes on only one item. It is indeed a complex problem to determine and report such information for all items on a balance sheet as well as to trace the impact of real and inflationary and realized and unrealized holding gains and losses through the income and retained earnings statements.

THE FASB EXPERIMENT

FASB Statement No. 33 was published in September 1979 as an experiment in requiring supplementary information concerning the effects of changing prices on business enterprises. The statement initially required large, public companies to disclose both constant dollar and current cost information for the current year as well as summary data for the most recent five-year period. Subsequently, requirements for the disclosure of certain constant dollar data were eliminated, and other disclosure requirements were modified.

As an illustration of how one company met the disclosure requirements of FASB Statement No. 33, see Note Seventeen of the financial statements in Appendix A. In the note, General Mills explains the purpose of presenting inflation-adjusted data; provides supplementary income statement and balance sheet data on a current cost basis; discloses selected information as required by FASB No. 33 for its five most recent fiscal years; and explains briefly the significance and limitations of the information presented. As a matter of interest, for the period ending May 26, 1985, General Mills' net earnings were $115 million as reported using unadjusted historical costs and $94 million using current costs. The effective tax rate changed from 41.1% based on income as reported on the traditional income statement to 46.3% using the current cost method.

When Statement No. 33 was issued, the FASB indicated that it would review the results of the reporting requirements after five years. The Board has now completed that review and has concluded that further supplementary disclosures should be encouraged, but are not required. The primary basis for this decision seems to be a lack of public interest in and use of the supplemental data and a feeling that whatever benefits may be derived from the disclosures are not equal to the costs of providing the information.

The decision of the FASB to, in effect, rescind Statement No. 33 was not unanimous. Some members of the Board, and no doubt others, believe that inflation and specific price changes cause historical cost statements to show illusory profits and to hide the erosion of capital. These accountants view supplemental disclosures of changing prices as being relevant information necessary to prevent users from making incorrect economic decisions.

PROSPECTS FOR THE FUTURE

It is likely that some companies will continue to disclose supplemental information concerning changing prices. Other companies, however, will probably discontinue the supplementary disclosures since there is no reporting requirement and little public interest. If inflation rates increase to higher levels, however, this topic may again become controversial, with increased pressure to consider additional reporting on a basis other than historical cost/nominal dollar.

APPENDIX

COMPREHENSIVE ILLUSTRATION

The purpose of this appendix is to provide a comprehensive illustration that compares financial statements presented on historical cost/nominal dollar, historical cost/constant dollar, current cost/nominal dollar, and current cost/constant dollar bases. Throughout this appendix, the financial data for Young Corporation will be used. This company began operations on January 1, 1987. The results of operations and year-end financial position for 1987 for Young Corporation are shown at the top of pages 1118 and 1119 using the four reporting alternatives. An explanation of how the numbers were derived is provided in the sections that follow.

	Historical Cost (HC/ND)	Historical Cost/Constant Dollar (HC/CD) (End-of-Year)	Current Cost/ Nominal Dollar (CC/ND)	Current Cost/Constant Dollar (CC/CD) (End-of-Year)
	Young Corporation Statement of Income and Retained Earnings For Year Ended December 31, 1987			
Sales......................	$300,000	$305,882	$300,000	$305,882
Cost of goods sold	190,000	194,847	230,000	234,510
Gross profit on sales	$110,000	$111,035	$ 70,000	$ 71,372
Expenses:				
Depreciation................	$ 5,000	$ 5,200	$ 6,750	$ 6,882
Other expenses............	90,000	91,765	90,000	91,765
Total expenses	$ 95,000	$ 96,965	$ 96,750	$ 98,647
Income (loss) from continuing operations.................	$ 15,000	$ 14,070	$ (26,750)	$ (27,275)
Holding gains...............			163,250	158,370
Purchasing power gain (loss) on net monetary items.........		(595)		(595)
Net income..................	$ 15,000	$ 13,475	$136,500	$130,500
Retained earnings, 1/1/87......	-0-	-0-	-0-	-0-
	$ 15,000	$ 13,475	$136,500	$130,500
Dividends	5,000	5,000	5,000	5,000
Retained earnings, 12/31/87....	$ 10,000	$ 8,475	$131,500	$125,500

HISTORICAL COST/CONSTANT DOLLAR BASIS

The following assumptions are made in restating Young Corporation's financial statements to reflect general price-level changes.

1. Price indexes were:

January 1, 1987......................	200
December 31, 1987	208

The price level rose evenly throughout the year. The average index for 1987 was 204.

	Young Corporation Balance Sheet December 31, 1987			
Assets	Historical Cost (HC/ND)	Historical Cost/Constant Dollar (HC/CD)	Current Cost/Nominal Dollar (CC/ND)	Current Cost/Constant Dollar (CC/CD)
Cash	$ 30,000	$ 30,000	$ 30,000	$ 30,000
Accounts receivable...........	40,000	40,000	40,000	40,000
Inventory.....................	65,000	66,275	90,000	90,000
Land	35,000	36,400	100,000	100,000
Buildings (net)...............	45,000	46,800	76,500	76,500
Total assets	$215,000	$219,475	$336,500	$336,500
Liabilities and Stockholders' Equity				
Accounts payable.............	$ 25,000	$ 25,000	$ 25,000	$ 25,000
Mortgage payable.............	30,000	30,000	30,000	30,000
Total liabilities	$ 55,000	$ 55,000	$ 55,000	$ 55,000
Capital stock	$150,000	$156,000	$150,000	$156,000
Retained earnings............	10,000	8,475	131,500	125,500
Total stockholders' equity	$160,000	$164,475	$281,500	$281,500
Total liabilities and stockholders' equity.....................	$215,000	$219,475	$336,500	$336,500

2. Sales and purchases were made evenly and expenses were incurred evenly throughout the year.
3. Inventories are valued at cost using the first-in, first-out method. The beginning inventory was acquired at the beginning of 1987. For simplicity, it is assumed that the entire ending inventory was acquired when the price index was 204.
4. Dividends were declared and paid at the end of the year.
5. Land and buildings were acquired on January 1, 1987. The buildings have a 10-year useful life and are depreciated at $5,000 per year.

A historical cost/nominal dollar statement of income and retained earnings and a balance sheet for Young Corporation are presented on the following page (income taxes are ignored).

Young Corporation
Statement of Income and Retained Earnings
For the Year Ended December 31, 1987
(Historical Cost/Nominal Dollar Basis)

Sales...		$300,000
Cost of goods sold:		
Beginning inventory	$ 55,000	
Purchases	200,000	
Goods available for sale	$255,000	
Ending inventory................................	65,000	
Cost of goods sold		190,000
Gross profit on sales		$110,000
Expenses:		
Depreciation....................................	$ 5,000	
Other expenses.................................	90,000	95,000
Net income..		$ 15,000
Retained earnings, January 1, 1987..................		—
		$ 15,000
Dividends		5,000
Retained earnings, December 31, 1987..............		$ 10,000

Young Corporation
Comparative Balance Sheet
As of January 1, 1987 and December 31, 1987
(Historical Cost/Nominal Dollar Basis)

Assets	January 1, 1987	December 31, 1987
Cash	$ 60,000	$ 30,000
Accounts receivable.................	—	40,000
Inventory..........................	55,000	65,000
Land	35,000	35,000
Buildings (net)	50,000	45,000
Total assets	$200,000	$215,000
Liabilities and stockholders' equity		
Accounts payable...................	$ 20,000	$ 25,000
Mortgage payable..................	30,000	30,000
Total liabilities	$ 50,000	$ 55,000
Capital stock	$150,000	$150,000
Retained earnings	—	10,000
Total stockholders' equity	$150,000	$160,000
Total liabilities and stockholders'		
equity.............................	$200,000	$215,000

Historical Cost/Constant Dollar Statement
of Income and Retained Earnings

A statement of income and retained earnings for 1987, restated to end-of-year constant dollars, and a schedule reporting the purchasing power loss are presented below and on the following page.

Young Corporation
Statement of Income and Retained Earnings
For the Year Ended December 31, 1987
(Historical Cost/Constant Dollar Basis)

	HC/ND	Conversion Factor	HC/CD
Sales.....................................	$300,000	208/204	$305,882
Cost of goods sold:			
Beginning inventory..................	$ 55,000	208/200	$ 57,200
Purchases	200,000	208/204	203,922
Goods available for sale	$255,000		$261,122
Ending inventory.....................	65,000	208/204	66,275
Cost of goods sold...................	$190,000		$194,847
Gross profit on sales	$110,000		$111,035
Expenses:			
Depreciation........................	$ 5,000	208/200	$ 5,200
Other expenses.....................	90,000	208/204	91,765
Total expenses	$ 95,000		$ 96,965
Income from continuing operations.......	$ 15,000		$ 14,070
Purchasing power loss (see schedule)....	—		595
Net income...........................	$ 15,000		$ 13,475
Retained earnings, January 1, 1987......	-0-		-0-
	$ 15,000		$ 13,475
Dividends	5,000		5,000
Retained earnings, December 31, 1987...	$ 10,000		$ 8,475

In preparing a historical cost/constant dollar income statement, the following items should be noted.

Sales. Since sales were made evenly throughout the year, the sales balance reflects the average price index for the year. To restate the sales balance to end-of-year dollars, it is multiplied by the ratio of the year-end price index to the average index.

$$\text{Sales: } \$300,000 \times \frac{208}{204} = \$305,882$$

Young Corporation Schedule of Purchasing Power Loss For the Year Ended December 31, 1987				
		HC/ND	Conversion Factor	HC/CD
Net monetary position, January 1, 1987:				
Monetary assets (cash).................	$60,000			
Monetary liabilities (accounts payable and mortgage payable)	50,000	$ 10,000	208/200	$ 10,400
Increase in net monetary position:				
Sales.....................................		300,000	208/204	305,882
		$310,000		$316,282
Decrease in net monetary position:				
Purchases		$200,000	208/204	$203,922
Other expenses.........................		90,000	208/204	91,765
Dividends		5,000		5,000
		$295,000		$300,687
				$ 15,595
Net monetary position, December 31, 1987:				
Monetary assets (cash and accounts receivable)	$70,000			
Monetary liabilities (accounts payable and mortgage payable)	55,000	$ 15,000		15,000
Purchasing power loss....................				$ 595

Cost of Goods Sold. Young Corporation reports its inventory on the first-in, first-out basis. To restate cost of goods sold to end-of-year dollars, the following adjustments must be made:

1. The beginning inventory balance reports purchases made when the business was organized, and reflects the price level at the beginning of the year. To restate the beginning inventory to end-of-year dollars, it is multiplied by the ratio of the year-end index to the index at the beginning of the year.

$$\text{Beginning inventory: } \$55,000 \times \frac{208}{200} = \$57,200$$

2. Purchases were made evenly throughout the year. To restate the purchases balance to end-of-the-year dollars, it is multiplied by the ratio of the year-end price index to the average index.

$$\text{Purchases: } \$200,000 \times \frac{208}{204} = \$203,922$$

3. The ending inventory was acquired when the price index was 204, the average index for the year. To restate the ending inventory balance to year-end dollars, it is multiplied by the ratio of the year-end index to the average index.

$$\text{Ending inventory: } \$65,000 \times \frac{208}{204} = \$66,275$$

Depreciation. Since depreciation expense represents the allocation of the cost of depreciable assets to operations, the adjustment for depreciation expense must be consistent with the adjustment applicable to the related assets. To restate buildings to year-end dollars, the balance in the buildings account is multiplied by the ratio of the year-end price index to the price index at the time the assets were acquired. Thus, depreciation expense for buildings is multiplied by the same ratio to be restated to year-end dollars. In the case of Young Corporation, the buildings were acquired when the price index was 200. The depreciation expense is restated to year-end constant dollars as follows:

$$\text{Depreciation: } \$5,000 \times \frac{208}{200} = \$5,200$$

Other Expenses. The other expenses were incurred evenly throughout the year. To restate the total of other expenses to year-end dollars, it is multiplied by the ratio of the year-end price index to the average index for the year.

$$\text{Other expenses: } \$90,000 \times \frac{208}{204} = \$91,765$$

Purchasing Power Gain or Loss. The purchasing power loss reported in the statement of income and retained earnings is supported by a schedule reporting the gain or loss from holding monetary items in a period of changing prices. As shown in the schedule, the net monetary position for Young Corporation at the end of the year would have been $15,595 if the company had not experienced a gain or loss in purchasing power. Since the net monetary position is actually only $15,000, a loss in purchasing power of $595 was sustained by the company.

Dividends. Since dividends were declared and paid at the end of the year, the dividends balance reflects end-of-year dollars and does not have to be converted.

Historical Cost/Constant Dollar Balance Sheet

A balance sheet for Young Corporation as of December 31, 1987, restated to end-of-year constant dollars, appears below.

Young Corporation Balance Sheet December 31, 1987 (Historical Cost/Constant Dollar Basis)			
Assets	HC/ND	Conversion Factor	HC/CD
Cash	$ 30,000		$ 30,000
Accounts receivable..................	40,000		40,000
Inventory...........................	65,000	208/204	66,275
Land	35,000	208/200	36,400
Buildings (net)	45,000	208/200	46,800
Total assets	$215,000		$219,475
Liabilities and stockholders' equity			
Accounts payable....................	$ 25,000		$ 25,000
Mortgage payable....................	30,000		30,000
Total liabilities	$ 55,000		$ 55,000
Capital stock	$150,000	208/200	$156,000
Retained earnings...................	10,000		8,475*
Total stockholders' equity	$160,000		$164,475
Total liabilities and stockholders' equity ..	$215,000		$219,475

*See the Statement of Income and Retained Earnings on page 1121.

In preparing a historical cost/constant dollar balance sheet, monetary assets and liabilities do not require restatement and are reported without change.[8] The restatement of ending inventory was explained and illustrated on page 1123 in conjunction with cost of goods sold. The following additional items should be noted.

Land and Buildings. The land and buildings accounts reflect the price level at the time the assets were acquired. To restate land and buildings to end-of-year dollars, they are multiplied by the ratio of the year-end price index to the price index at the time of acquisition.

---

[8] If comparative statements were being prepared at the end of 1988, the 1987 monetary items would be adjusted (rolled forward) to reflect 1988 purchasing power units.

$$\text{Land:} \qquad \$35,000 \times \frac{208}{200} = \$36,400$$

$$\text{Buildings (net): } \$45,000 \times \frac{208}{200} = \$46,800$$

Capital Stock. The capital stock account reports the dollars received by the firm when it issued its stock. To restate the capital stock balance to year-end dollars, it is multiplied by the ratio of the year-end price index to the price index at the time the stock was issued.

$$\text{Capital stock: } \$150,000 \times \frac{208}{200} = \$156,000$$

Retained Earnings. No single conversion factor is appropriate for retained earnings. The year-end retained earnings on the balance sheet is the same amount that appears as the ending retained earnings balance on the statement of income and retained earnings. If the procedures and assumptions used to develop the historical cost/constant dollar balance sheet and statement of income and retained earnings are consistent, the retained earnings amount computed on the statement of income and retained earnings should bring the balance sheet into balance. If the balance sheet does not balance, the errors or inconsistencies must be found and corrected.

CURRENT COST/NOMINAL DOLLAR BASIS

To illustrate restatement on a current cost/nominal dollar basis, consider again the historical cost/nominal dollar financial statements of Young Corporation presented on pages 1121 and 1124 and the following additional information.

1. The cost of goods sold, based on the average current costs of units sold during the year, is $230,000.
2. Current costs at the end of 1987 are:

Inventory	$ 90,000
Land	100,000
Buildings (before depreciation)	85,000

Current Cost/Nominal Dollar Statement of Income and Retained Earnings

A current cost/nominal dollar income statement generally reports two major sources of income:

1. Current cost income (loss) from operations
2. Holding gains (losses)

Current cost operating income is the difference between revenues and the current costs of expenses. Holding gains (losses) result from increases (decreases) in current costs of inventory and property, plant, and equipment. Total holding gains include both realized and unrealized holding gains.

The following illustration is a current cost/nominal dollar statement of income and retained earnings for Young Corporation for the year ended December 31, 1987.

Young Corporation Statement of Income and Retained Earnings For the Year Ended December 31, 1987 (Current Cost/Nominal Dollar Basis)		
Sales...		$300,000
Cost of goods sold...................................		230,000
Gross profit on sales		$ 70,000
Less expenses:		
Depreciation......................................	$ 6,750	
Other expenses..................................	90,000	96,750
Loss from operations		$ (26,750)
Holding gains:		
Increase in current cost of inventories	$65,000	
Increase in current cost of land and buildings	98,250	163,250
Current cost net income		$136,500
Retained earnings, January 1, 1987.................		-0-
		$136,500
Dividends		5,000
Retained earnings, December 31, 1987...............		$131,500

In preparing a current cost/nominal dollar income statement, the following items should be noted.

Sales. Since sales revenue is stated at current sales prices during the period, it reflects current values and is not restated.

Sales	$300,000

Cost of Goods Sold. The current cost of goods sold given on page 1125 is the result of adjusting the historical cost of the goods sold to their current costs as of the dates they were sold.

Cost of goods sold (current cost).....................	$230,000

Depreciation Expense. Current costs of depreciable assets must be used to compute depreciation expense. If depreciation is incurred evenly throughout the year, the depreciation expense can be calculated from the average current costs of the depreciable assets.

Young Corporation's buildings had current values before depreciation of $50,000 and $85,000 at the beginning and the end of 1987, respectively. The 1987 current cost/nominal dollar depreciation expense can be calculated as follows:

$$\text{Average current cost of buildings:} \quad \frac{\$50,000 + \$85,000}{2} = \$67,500$$

$$\text{Depreciation expense:} \quad \frac{\$67,500}{\text{10-year useful life}} = \$6,750$$

Other Expenses. Other expenses are usually reported at their current costs when paid, and do not need to be restated on a current cost/nominal dollar income statement. Thus, the other expenses on the current cost/nominal dollar income statement are the same as on the historical cost/nominal dollar income statement.

Other expenses..................................	$90,000

Holding Gains and Losses. The holding gain on inventory is made up of two parts: the realized holding gain on the difference between historical cost of goods sold and current cost of goods sold, and the unrealized holding gain on the difference between the historical cost of the ending inventory and the current cost of the ending inventory. For the Young Corporation, the holding gains would be computed as follows:

	HC/ND	CC/ND	Holding Gain	
Cost of goods sold........................	$190,000	$230,000	$40,000	(Realized)
Inventory, December 31, 1987..............	65,000	90,000	25,000	(Unrealized)
Total holding gain........................			$65,000	

The holding gain on land is an unrealized gain, while the holding gain on buildings is composed of a realized component and an unrealized component. The realized holding gain on buildings is the difference between historical cost depreciation and current cost depreciation. This difference is a realized holding gain, because a portion of the increase in value has been charged against revenue on the current cost income statement. The unrealized holding gain on buildings is the difference between historical cost net book value and current cost net book value. For the Young Corporation, the holding gains on land and buildings would be computed as follows:

	HC/ND	CC/ND	Holding Gain	
Land, December 31, 1987	$35,000	$100,000	$65,000	(Unrealized)
Buildings (net) December 31, 1987	45,000	76,500	31,500	(Unrealized)
Depreciation expense, 1987.	5,000	6,750	1,750	(Realized)
Total holding gain.			$98,250	

Alternatively, the unrealized portion of the holding gain on the buildings could be computed as follows:

	December 31, 1987		
	HC/ND	CC/ND	Increase (Decrease)
Buildings (gross).	$50,000	$85,000	$35,000
Accumulated depreciation	(5,000)	(8,500)	(3,500)
Buildings (net).	$45,000	$76,500	$31,500

The difference between the current cost depreciation expense of $6,750 and the accumulated depreciation of $8,500 used to compute the current cost net book value is a **depreciation catch-up adjustment** that is reflected in a reduced unrealized holding gain for the year. If the current cost net book value had been computed using the $6,750 depreciation expense as the amount of accumulated depreciation for the first year, the holding gain would have been increased by $1,750, or to a total of $33,250. The catch-up adjustment is caused by using the current value of the building at year-end to compute accumulated depreciation but the average current value of the building for the year to compute depreciation expense. In subsequent years, a further difference between the changing current value of the building and the depreciation expense computed in earlier years would add to this catch-up adjustment.

Dividends. Since the dividends were declared and paid at the end of the year, the $5,000 dividends balance is stated at current cost and does not need to be restated.

Current Cost/Nominal Dollar Balance Sheet

A current cost/nominal dollar balance sheet for Young Corporation as of December 31, 1987, is presented as follows.

Young Corporation
Balance Sheet
December 31, 1987
(Current Cost/Nominal Dollar Basis)

Assets	HC/ND	CC/ND
Cash	$ 30,000	$ 30,000
Accounts receivable	40,000	40,000
Inventory	65,000	90,000
Land	35,000	100,000
Buildings (net)	45,000	76,500
Total assets	$215,000	$336,500
Liabilities and stockholders' equity		
Accounts payable	$ 25,000	$ 25,000
Mortgage payable	30,000	30,000
Total liabilities	$ 55,000	$ 55,000
Capital stock	$150,000	$150,000
Retained earnings	10,000	131,500*
Total stockholders' equity	$160,000	$281,500
Total liabilities and stockholders' equity	$215,000	$336,500

*See Statement of Income and Retained Earnings on page 1126.

Since monetary assets and liabilities are reported at their face values, which are the same as their current values, they do not require restatement on a current cost/nominal dollar balance sheet. Inventory on hand at the end of the year is reported on the current cost/nominal dollar balance sheet at its year-end value of $90,000. Land and buildings are also reported at their respective year-end values: land, $100,000 and buildings (net), $76,500. Capital stock is not adjusted on a current cost/nominal dollar balance sheet since the purchasing power of the dollar is assumed constant.

Retained Earnings

The ending retained earnings balance is derived from the statement of income and retained earnings on page 1126. The beginning retained earnings ($0) plus current cost net income ($136,500) minus dividends ($5,000) equals the ending balance ($131,500). The $121,500 difference between the $131,500 current cost amount and the $10,000 historical cost amount is the unrealized portion of the total holding gain (inventory $25,000 + land $65,000 + buildings $31,500 = $121,500), which is recognized prior to realization on a current cost basis but usually not until the point of sale on a historical cost basis. Obviously, the ending retained earnings balance may be computed as the difference between total assets and total liabilities less capital stock [$336,500 − ($55,000 + $150,000) = $131,500].

CURRENT COST/CONSTANT DOLLAR BASIS

To illustrate restatement on a current cost/constant dollar basis, consider again the financial statements of the Young Corporation.

Historical cost/constant dollar financial statements account for purchasing power gains and losses on net monetary items but do not take into account holding gains and losses. Current cost/nominal dollar financial statements account for holding gains and losses but do not account for purchasing power gains and losses. Current cost/constant dollar financial statements take into account both types of gains and losses. All amounts are stated on current cost/constant dollar statements at their current costs in end-of-year constant dollars.

Current Cost/Constant Dollar Statement of Income and Retained Earnings

A current cost/constant dollar (end-of-year dollars) statement of income and retained earnings for Young Corporation for the year ended December 31, 1987, is presented at the top of the next page.

In preparing a current cost/constant dollar statement of income and retained earnings, the following items should be noted.

Operating Revenues and Expenses. On the current cost/nominal dollar income statement, sales revenues, cost of goods sold, depreciation expense, and other expenses reflect average current values for the year assuming an even flow of activities during the year. Each of these amounts can be restated to end-of-year constant dollars by multiplying the current cost/nominal dollar amount by the ratio of the year-end price index to the average price index.

Holding Gains (Losses). On a current cost/constant dollar income statement, holding gains (losses) are reported net of the impact of general price-level changes. The increase in current values of inventories for Young Corporation, adjusted to eliminate the inflation component can be computed as follows:

	HC/CD	CC/CD	Holding Gain	
Cost of goods sold..........................	$194,847	$234,510	$39,663	(Realized)
Inventory, December 31, 1987...............	66,275	90,000	23,725	(Unrealized)
Total holding gain..........................			$63,388	

Young Corporation
Statement of Income and Retained Earnings
For Year Ended December 31, 1987
(Current Cost/Constant Dollar Basis)

Sales..		$305,882
Cost of goods sold...............................		234,510
Gross profit on sales		$ 71,372
Less expenses:		
Depreciation..................................	$ 6,882	
Other expenses...............................	91,765	98,647
Loss from operations		$ (27,275)
Holding gains:		
Increase in current cost of inventories	$63,388	
Increase in current cost of land and buildings	94,982	158,370
		$131,095
Purchasing power loss on net monetary items..........		(595)
Current cost/constant dollar net income...............		$130,500
Retained earnings, January 1, 1987...................		-0-
		$130,500
Dividends		5,000
Retained earnings, December 31, 1987...............		$125,500

Sales:	$300,000 $\times \dfrac{208}{204} =$ $305,882
Cost of goods sold:	$230,000 $\times \dfrac{208}{204} =$ $234,510
Depreciation expense:	$ 6,750* $\times \dfrac{208}{204} =$ $ 6,882
Other expenses:	$ 90,000 $\times \dfrac{208}{204} =$ $ 91,765

*Assumed to be in average 1987 dollars

The increase in the value of the ending inventory, $23,725, is an unrealized holding gain. The $39,663 increase in the value of the cost of goods sold is a realized holding gain.

The holding gain on land and buildings, net of the effect of changes in the general price level, can be computed as follows:

	HC/CD	CC/CD	Holding Gain	
Land, December 31, 1987	$36,400	$100,000	$63,600	(Unrealized)
Buildings (net), December 31, 1987	46,800	76,500	29,700	(Unrealized)
Depreciation expense	5,200	6,882	1,682	(Realized)
Total holding gain.			$94,982	

The appreciation in the value of the land, $63,600, is an unrealized holding gain. The increase in the value of the buildings, $29,700, is also an unrealized holding gain. The difference between the current cost/constant dollar and historical cost/constant dollar depreciation expenses, $1,682, is a realized holding gain.

Purchasing Power Gain or Loss. The purchasing power gain or loss on net monetary items computed on a current cost/constant dollar basis is the same as the purchasing power gain or loss computed on a historical cost/constant dollar basis, since net monetary items are always stated at their current values.

Dividends. Since dividends are already stated at their year-end current value of $5,000, they do not require restatement on the current cost/constant dollar financial statements.

Current Cost/Constant Dollar Balance Sheet

A current cost/constant dollar balance sheet for the Young Corporation as of December 31, 1987, is presented at the top of the next page.

All amounts on the current cost/constant dollar balance sheet are the same as those on the current cost/nominal dollar balance sheet except capital stock and retained earnings.

Capital Stock. Since the capital stock account balance represents the dollars received by the firm when the stock was first issued, the capital stock balance must be restated to year-end dollars. This is done by multiplying the balance by the ratio of the year-end price index to the price index at the time the stock was issued.

$$\text{Capital stock: } \$150,000 \times \frac{208}{200} = \$156,000$$

Retained Earnings. The ending retained earnings balance is explained by the statement of income and retained earnings on page 1131. The beginning balance plus net income on a current cost/constant dollar basis less dividends equals the ending balance of $125,500. Since both a different valuation basis (current costs) and measuring unit (constant dollars) are used

Young Corporation
Balance Sheet
December 31, 1987
(Current Cost/Constant Dollar Basis)

Assets	HC/ND	CC/CD
Cash	$ 30,000	$ 30,000
Accounts receivable	40,000	40,000
Inventory	65,000	90,000
Land	35,000	100,000
Buildings (net)	45,000	76,500
Total assets	$215,000	$336,500
Liabilities and stockholders' equity		
Accounts payable	$ 25,000	$ 25,000
Mortgage payable	30,000	30,000
Total liabilities	$ 55,000	$ 55,000
Capital stock	$150,000	$156,000
Retained earnings	10,000	125,500*
Total stockholders' equity	$160,000	$281,500
Total liabilities and stockholders' equity	$215,000	$336,500

*See Statement of Income and Retained Earnings on page 1131.

under this approach, the ending retained earnings balance is affected by the purchasing power gain or loss for monetary items and by the adjustments to operating income (loss) and to realized and unrealized holding gains (losses).

The statements on pages 1118 and 1119 summarize the information presented in this appendix and contrast the amounts that would be reported under the alternatives discussed and according to the assumptions made.

QUESTIONS

1. (a) Why have accountants traditionally preferred to report historical costs rather than current costs in conventional statements? (b) What are some of the limitations of historical cost statements?

2. What are the 3 alternatives to reporting historical cost/nominal dollar financial statements and how do they differ from conventional reporting practice.

3. (a) What are general purchasing power dollars? (b) How are they different from equivalent purchasing power units?

4. Historically, what has caused an increased interest in reporting financial statements adjusted for price changes?

5. (a) How does constant dollar reporting differ from current cost reporting? (b) What is the objective of constant dollar reporting and how is this objective accomplished?

6. (a) How are general price indexes computed? (b) What are some of their limitations? (c) Which index was required by FASB Statement No. 33?

7. If equipment was purchased for $85,000 at the beginning of the year when the CPI-U was 160, how would the equipment be recorded on a constant dollar end-of-year balance sheet if the year-end CPI-U was 180?

8. (a) Distinguish between monetary assets and nonmonetary assets. (b) Which of the following are monetary assets?
   (1) Cash
   (2) Investment in common stock
   (3) Investment in bonds
   (4) Merchandise on hand
   (5) Prepaid expenses
   (6) Buildings
   (7) Patents
   (8) Sinking fund — uninvested cash
   (9) Sinking fund — investments in real estate
   (10) Deferred development costs

9. Assume a company holds property or maintains the obligations listed below during a year in which there is an increase in the general price level. State in each case whether the real position of the company at the end of the year is better, worse, or unchanged.
   (a) Cash
   (b) Cash surrender value of life insurance
   (c) Land
   (d) Unearned subscription revenue
   (e) Accounts receivable
   (f) Notes payable
   (g) Inventory
   (h) Long-term warranties on sales

10. Indicate whether a company sustains a gain or loss in purchasing power under each of the following conditions.
    (a) A company maintains an excess of monetary assets over monetary liabilities during a period of general price-level increase.
    (b) A company maintains an excess of monetary liabilities over monetary assets during a period of general price-level increase.
    (c) A company maintains an excess of monetary assets over monetary liabilities during a period of general price-level decrease.
    (d) A company maintains an excess of monetary liabilities over monetary assets during a period of general price-level decrease.

11. (a) What is the objective of current cost accounting? (b) Give examples of definitions of current costs?

12. Define the concept of well-offness.

13. (a) Distinguish between realized and unrealized holding gains and losses. (b) Distinguish between the real and inflationary components of total holding gains and losses.

14. What are the two recommended approaches used to determine appropriate current values?

15. Briefly explain the advantages and disadvantages of current cost accounting as compared to constant dollar and historical cost accounting.

16. Distinguish between the current cost/constant dollar approach and the current cost/nominal dollar approach to financial reporting.

*17. In analyzing sales as reported under the various alternatives for Young Corporation (page 1118), what assumptions would produce the same number ($300,000) for all columns?

*18. Why is a "catch-up adjustment" often needed in computing the unrealized holding gain or loss on depreciable assets in conjunction with the accumulated depreciation on those assets?

Relates to Appendix

DISCUSSION CASES

CASE 25–1   (Which reporting alternative is best?)

At a recent executive committee meeting, the officers of SavTex Corporation entered into a lively discussion concerning changing prices in the economy and financial reporting. Kyle Jones, the controller, argued that the FASB is smart to experiment with reporting alternatives in Statement No. 33 since something must be done to reflect price changes. The economic analyst, Marie Colton, argued strongly for a current cost approach. Colton had little good to say about "irrelevant" historical costs, even if adjusted to constant dollars. Ted Starley, the marketing V.P., on the other hand, felt comfortable with historical cost data. Starley understands that approach and has confidence in the objectivity of the numbers reported. As president of the company, what position do you take?

CASE 25–2   (Constant dollar theory)

Published financial statements of United States companies are currently prepared on a "stable-dollar" assumption even though the general purchasing power of the dollar has declined considerably because of inflation over the past several years. To account for this changing value of the dollar, many accountants suggest that financial statements should be adjusted for general price-level changes. Two independent statements regarding constant dollar financial statements follow. Each statement contains some fallacious reasoning.

Statement 1

The accounting profession has not seriously considered constant dollar financial statements before because the rate of inflation usually has been so small from year-to-year that the adjustments would have been immaterial in amount. Constant dollar financial statements represent a departure from the historical-cost basis of accounting. Financial statements should be prepared from facts, not estimates.

Statement 2

If financial statements were adjusted for general price-level changes, depreciation changes in the earnings statement would permit the recovery of dollars of current purchasing power and, thereby, equal the cost of net assets to replace the old ones. Constant dollar adjusted data would yield balance sheet amounts closely approximating current values. Furthermore, management can make better decisions if constant dollar financial statements are published.

Evaluate each of the independent statements and identify the areas of fallacious reasoning in each and explain why the reasoning is incorrect. Complete your discussion of statement 1 before proceeding to statement 2.   (AICPA adapted)

CASE 25–3   (Current valuation of assets)

The financial statements of a business entity could be prepared by using historical cost or current value as a measurement basis. In addition, the basis could be stated in terms of unadjusted dollars or dollars restated for changes in purchasing power. The various combinations of these two separate and distinct areas are shown in the following matrix:

	Unadjusted dollars	Dollars restated for changes in purchasing power
Historical cost	1	2
Current value	3	4

Block number 1 of the matrix represents the traditional method of accounting for transactions in accounting today, wherein the absolute (unadjusted) amount of dollars given up or received is recorded for the asset or liability obtained (relationship between resources). Amounts recorded in the method described in block 1 reflect the original cost of the asset or liability and do not give effect to any change in value of the unit of measure (standard of comparison). This method assumes the validity of the accounting concepts of going concern and stable monetary unit. Any gain or loss (including holding and purchasing power gains or losses) resulting from the sale or satisfaction of amounts recorded under this method is deferred in its entirety until sale or satisfaction.

For each of the remaining matrix blocks respond to the following questions. Limit your discussion to nonmonetary assets only.

(1) How will this method of recording assets affect the relationship between resources and the standard of comparison?

(2) What is the theoretic justification for using each method?

Complete your discussion of each matrix block before proceeding to the discussion of the next matrix block.   (AICPA adapted)

EXERCISES

EXERCISE 25–1   (Classification of monetary and nonmonetary items)

Classify the following accounts as either monetary or nonmonetary.

Assets

Current assets:
  Cash
  Marketable securities (stocks)
  Receivables (net of allowance)
  Inventories
  Prepaid rent
  Discount on notes payable
  Deferred income tax expense
Long-term investments:
  Affiliated companies, at cost
  Cash surrender value of life
    insurance
  Bond sinking fund
  Investment in bonds
Land, buildings, and equipment:
  Land
  Buildings
  Equipment
Intangible assets:
  Patents
  Goodwill
Advances paid on purchase
  contracts

Liabilities and Stockholders' Equity

Current liabilities:
  Accounts and notes payable
  Dividends payable
  Refundable deposits on return-
    able containers
  Advances on sales contracts
Long-term liabilities:
  Bonds payable
  Premium on bonds payable
Stockholders' equity:
  Preferred stock (at fixed liqui-
    dation price)
  Common stock
  Retained earnings

EXERCISE 25–2   (Computing purchasing power gains or losses)

On January 1, 1988, Beehive Corporation had monetary assets of $5,000,000 and monetary liabilities of $2,000,000. During 1988, Beehive's monetary inflows and outflows were relatively constant and equal so that it ended the year with net monetary assets of $3,000,000.
  (1) Assume that the CPI-U was 200 on January 1, 1988, and 220 on December 31, 1988. In end-of-year constant dollars, what is Beehive's purchasing power gain or loss for 1988?
  (2) Assume that the CPI-U was 200 on January 1, 1988, and 180 on December 31, 1988. In average-year constant dollars, what is Beehive's purchasing power gain or loss for 1988?   (AICPA adapted)

EXERCISE 25–3   (Adjusting expenses to constant dollars)

Assuming prices rise evenly by 6% during the year, compute the amount of expenses stated in terms of year-end constant dollars in each of the following independent cases:
  (a) Expenses of $1,000,000 were paid at the beginning of the year for services received during the first half of the year.

(b) Expenses of $250,000 were paid at the end of each quarter for services received during the quarter.

(c) Expenses of $250,000 were paid at the beginning of each quarter for services received during the quarter.

(d) Expenses of $1,000,000 were paid evenly throughout the year for services received during the year.

In terms of year-end constant dollars, when is it the best time to pay for services received in periods of rising prices?

EXERCISE 25–4   (Constant dollar depreciation)

The financial statements for Super Mining Corp. showed the original cost of depreciable assets purchased over the years as $3,500,000 at December 31, 1986, and $4,200,000 at December 31, 1987. These assets are being depreciated on a straight-line basis over a 10-year period with no residual value. Acquisitions of $700,000 were made on January 1, 1987. A full year's depreciation was taken in the year of acquisition.

Super Mining presents constant dollar financial statements as supplemental information to its historical cost financial statements. The December 31, 1987, depreciable asset balance (before accumulated depreciation) restated to reflect 1987 average purchasing power was $4,060,000.

Compute the amount of depreciation expense that should be shown in the constant dollar income statement for 1987 if the general price-level index was 110 at December 31, 1986, and 130 at December 31, 1987. Assume that the constant dollar financial statements are to be expressed in average 1987 dollars.

EXERCISE 25–5
(Constant dollar restatement of income and retained earnings statement)

A comparative income statement for the Scott Company for the first 2 years of operations appears below.

	Results of Operations			
	First Year		Second Year	
Sales		$750,000		$900,000
Cost of goods sold:				
Beginning inventory	—		$300,000	
Purchases.	$750,000		500,000	
Goods available for sale	$750,000		$800,000	
Ending inventory	300,000	450,000	400,000	400,000
Gross profit on sales.		$300,000		$500,000
Operating expenses:				
Depreciation	$ 30,000		$ 30,000	
Other	240,000	270,000	350,000	380,000
Net income		$ 30,000		$120,000
Dividends		15,000		30,000
Increase in retained earnings		$ 15,000		$ 90,000

Prepare a comparative income and retained earnings statement expressing items in constant dollars at the end of the second year, considering the following data:

(a) Prices rose evenly and index numbers expressing the general price-level changes were:

Beginning of first year	100
End of first year	110
End of second year	140

(b) Sales and purchases were made and expenses were incurred evenly each year.

(c) Inventories were reported at cost using first-in, first-out pricing; average indexes for the year are applicable in restating inventories.

(d) Depreciation relates to equipment acquired at the beginning of the first year.

(e) Dividends were paid at the middle of each year.

(f) Assume no purchasing power gain or loss in either year.

EXERCISE 25–6   (Constant dollar restatement of balance sheet)

Comparative balance sheet data for Fortune Industries Inc., since its formation, appear below. The general price level during the 2-year period went up steadily; index numbers expressing the general price-level changes are listed following the balance sheet. Restate the comparative balance sheet data in terms of constant dollars at the end of the second year.

	End of First Year	End of Second Year
Cash	$ 90,000	$ 75,000
Receivables	60,000	84,000
*Land, buildings, and equipment (net)	156,000	138,000
	$306,000	$297,000
Payables	$ 81,000	$ 54,000
Capital stock	192,000	192,000
Retained earnings	33,000	51,000
	$306,000	$297,000

*Acquired at the beginning of the first year.

General Price Index

At the beginning of the first year	106
At the end of the first year	120
At the end of the second year	130

EXERCISE 25–7   (Adjustment to average-year constant dollars)

The historical cost/constant dollar income statement of the Heros Corporation shows a purchasing power loss of $3,000 based on end-of-year constant dollars. Price indexes were as follows:

Beginning of year..................................	120
Average	145
End of year	170

Calculate the purchasing power loss in average-year dollars.

EXERCISE 25–8 (Current cost income)

On January 1, 1987, Weyland's Toy Store purchased 1,000 robots at $25 per robot. As of December 31, 1987, Weyland's had sold three-fourths of the robots at $32 per robot, and the robot manufacturer (supplier) was selling to retailers (Weyland) at $28 per robot.

Compute the operating gross profit for 1987 on a current-cost basis. Also identify the amount of realized holding gain and unrealized holding gain. Ignore income taxes.

EXERCISE 25–9 (Current cost depreciation)

Young Company began operating on December 31, 1985, at which time it purchased operating machinery for $3,000,000. These assets were expected to have a 15-year life with no residual value and are to be depreciated using the straight-line method:

The following information is available:

(a) Current value of assets (as if new)

December 31, 1987	$5,000,000
December 31, 1988	5,500,000

(b) General price-level index values:

December 31, 1985	120
December 31, 1987	140
December 31, 1988	155
1988 average..................................	148

Compute the following:

(1) Current value depreciation expense for 1988 in terms of average dollars from 1988.

(2) Realized holding gains from the use (and depreciation) of the asset during 1988 measured in terms of average dollars from 1988.

EXERCISE 25–10 (Current cost/constant dollar balance sheet)

The current cost/nominal dollar balance sheet for the Grant Corporation at December 31, 1987, is shown at the top of the next page.

The equipment and land were purchased at year end. The inventory is valued at year-end current prices.

The capital stock was issued when the consumer price index was 240. The consumer price index at December 31, 1987 was 270.

Prepare a current cost/constant dollar balance sheet for the Grant Corporation at December 31, 1987, stated in end-of-year constant dollars.

Grant Corporation
Balance Sheet
December 31, 1987
(Current Cost/Nominal Dollar Basis)

Assets		Liabilities and Stockholders' Equity	
Cash	$ 10,000	Accounts payable	$ 20,000
Accounts receivable	15,000	Interest payable	10,000
Inventory	30,000	Total liabilities	$ 30,000
Equipment (net)	50,000		
Land	45,000	Capital stock	$ 80,000
		Retained earnings	40,000
		Total stockholders' equity	$120,000
		Total liabilities and stockholders'	
Total assets	$150,000	equity	$150,000

EXERCISE 25–11   (Reporting alternatives)

Presto Company purchased land for $150,000 in 1986 when the price index was 150. At the end of 1987 when the price index was 175, the land had a fair market value of $180,000. How would the land be reported on the balance sheet under each of the following approaches?

(a) Historical cost/nominal dollar
(b) Historical cost/constant dollar
(c) Current cost/nominal dollar
(d) Current cost/constant dollar (year-end dollars)

EXERCISE 25–12   (Multiple choice)

1. In preparing constant dollar financial statements, monetary items consist of:
   a. Cash items plus all receivables with a fixed maturity date.
   b. Cash, other assets expected to be converted into cash and current liabilities.
   c. Assets and liabilities whose amounts are fixed by contract or otherwise in terms of dollars regardless of price-level changes.
   d. Assets and liabilities that are classified as current on the balance sheet.
2. When computing information on a historical cost/constant dollar basis, which of the following is classified as monetary?
   a. Equity investments in unconsolidated subsidiaries.
   b. Obligations under warranties.
   c. Unamortized discount on bonds payable.
   d. Deferred income tax credits.
3. A method of accounting based on measures of current cost or lower recoverable amount, without restatement into units having the same general purchasing power is:
   a. Historical cost/constant dollar accounting.
   b. Historical cost/nominal dollar accounting.
   c. Current cost/constant dollar accounting.
   d. Current cost/nominal dollar accounting.

4. In current cost financial statements:
   a. Purchasing power gains or losses are recognized on net monetary items.
   b. Amounts are always stated in common purchasing power units of measurements.
   c. All balance sheet items are different in amount than they would be in a historical cost balance sheet.
   d. Holding gains are recognized.

*EXERCISE 25–13
(Computation of holding gains or losses and current cost income statement)

The historical cost/nominal dollar income statement for the Junior Corporation for the first year of operations ended June 30, 1988, is presented below in partially complete form. Historical cost/constant dollar and current cost/constant dollar values for selected items are also presented. Determine the realized and unrealized holding gains or losses, net of inflation, and prepare the income statement using the current cost/constant dollar basis.

Junior Corporation
Income Statement
For the Year Ended June 30, 1988
Historical Cost/Nominal Dollar Basis

Sales	$1,700,000
Cost of goods sold	800,000
Gross profit	$ 900,000
Depreciation expense	100,000
Other expenses	400,000
Income from continuing operations	$ 400,000

Junior Corporation
Historical Cost/Constant Dollar and Current Cost/Constant Dollar Values
for Selected Items

	HC/CD	CC/CD
Inventory June 30, 1988	$600,000	$720,000
Inventory July 1, 1987	750,000	750,000
Cost of goods sold	840,000	870,000
Purchases	800,000	800,000
Equipment (net) June 30, 1988	350,000	450,000
Equipment (net) July 1, 1987	400,000	400,000
Depreciation expense	150,000	200,000
Land June 30, 1988	350,000	400,000
Land July 1, 1987	200,000	200,000
Other expenses	430,000	430,000

Purchasing power loss on net monetary items, $50,000.

*EXERCISE 25–14
(The inflation component of realized holding gains)

Davis Company reports the following selected information for its first year of operation.

	Historical Costs	Current Costs
Sales............................	$1,450,000	$1,450,000
Cost of goods sold...............	870,000	950,000
Gross profit	580,000	500,000

Assume sales and cost of goods sold are incurred evenly. During the past year, the general price level rose from 100 to 110, or an average of 5%. Based on the information provided and adjusting to end-of-year prices, determine:

(a) The amount of operating gross profit (economic profit).
(b) The real component of the realized holding gain.
(c) Recognizing that the inflation component of the holding gain is not reported separately under current cost/constant dollar accounting, compute the amount of the inflation component implied by the data.

The appendix to this chapter may be helpful in completing this exercise.

PROBLEMS

PROBLEM 25–1
(Constant dollar adjustments and replacement costs)

Valuation to reflect constant dollar adjustments would yield differing amounts on a firm's financial statements as opposed to replacement costs.

Transactions regarding one asset of a company whose calendar year is from January 1 to December 31 are as follows:

1986 Purchased land for $48,000 cash on December 31. Replacement cost at year-end was $48,000.

1987 Held land all year. Replacement cost at year-end was $62,400.

1988 December 31 — sold land for $81,600.

General price-level index as:
December 31, 1985 120
December 31, 1986 132
December 31, 1987 144

Instructions: Duplicate the following schedules and complete the information required based on the foregoing transactions. Express all constant dollar amounts in year-end dollars. Do not distinguish between realized and unrealized holding gains.

	Historical Cost		Replacement Costs	
	Nominal Dollar	Constant Dollar	Unadjusted for Inflation	Adjusted for Inflation
Valuation of land:				
December 31, 1986				
December 31, 1987				
Gain on income statement:				
1986.....................				
1987.....................				
1988.....................				
Total.....................				

(AICPA adapted)

PROBLEM 25–2
(Constant dollar adjustment for cost of goods sold and depreciation)

The following information was taken from the books of the High Value Company during its first 2 years of operations:

	Useful Life	1986	1987
Beginning inventory.......................		$150,000	$200,000
Purchases...............................		550,000	500,000
Ending inventory..........................		200,000	160,000
Building (acquired 1/1/86)	25 years	400,000	—
Office equipment (acquired 7/1/86)	12 years	30,000	—
Machinery (acquired 10/1/86)	8 years	16,000	—
Price index (1/1)..........................		190	202
Price index (12/31)*......................		202	214

*Assume prices rose evenly throughout the year.

Instructions:
(1) Calculate the cost of goods sold for 1986 and 1987 in terms of respective year-end dollars assuming a LIFO inventory cost flow with average costs used for any increments. Assume the 1986 beginning inventory was purchased on January 1, 1986. Round to the nearest dollar amount.
(2) Restate depreciable assets and accumulated depreciation (straight-line, ignore salvage values) reporting the depreciation for 1986 and 1987 in terms of 1986 and 1987 year-end dollars respectively.

PROBLEM 25–3
(Converting nominal dollar financial data to constant dollars)

O'Brien, Inc., a retailer, was organized during 1984. O'Brien's management has decided to supplement its December 31, 1987, historical dollar financial statement with constant dollar financial statements. The following general ledger trial balance (historical dollar) and additional information have been furnished.

O'Brien, Inc.
Trial Balance
December 31, 1987

	Debits	Credits
Cash and Receivables (net).............................	432,000	
Marketable Securities (common stock)	320,000	
Inventory	352,000	
Equipment..	520,000	
Equipment—Accumulated Depreciation...................		131,200
Accounts Payable		240,000
6% First-Mortgage Bonds, Due 1992.....................		400,000
Common Stock, $8 par.................................		800,000
Retained Earnings, December 31, 1986 (Deficit)............	36,800	
Sales..		1,520,000
Cost of Sales	1,206,400	
Depreciation	52,000	
Other Operating Expenses and Interest	172,000	
Total	3,091,200	3,091,200

(a) Monetary assets (cash and receivables) exceeded monetary liabilities (accounts payable and bonds payable) by $356,000 at December 31, 1986.

(b) Purchases ($1,152,000 in 1987) and sales are made evenly throughout the year.

(c) Depreciation is computed on a straight-line basis, with a full year's depreciation being taken in the year of acquisition and none in the year of retirement. The depreciation rate is 10%, and no residual value is anticipated. Acquisitions and retirements have been made fairly evenly over each year, and the retirements in 1987 consisted of assets purchased during 1985 that were scrapped. No cash was received.

An analysis of the equipment account reveals the following:

Year	Beginning Balance	Additions	Retirements	Ending Balance
1985		440,000		440,000
1986	440,000	8,000		448,000
1987	448,000	120,000	48,000	520,000

(d) The bonds were issued in 1985, and the marketable securities were purchased fairly evenly over 1987. Other operating expenses and interest were incurred evenly throughout the year and paid with cash.

(e) Assume that the relevant price-index values were as follows:

Annual Average		Quarterly Average	
1985	110	1986	
1986	122	Fourth	123
1987	128	1987	
		First	124
		Second	128
		Third	127
		Fourth	130

Instructions: In completing the following requirements, use constant dollars from the fourth quarter of 1987.

(1) Prepare a schedule to convert the equipment account balance at December 31, 1987, from nominal to constant dollars.

(2) Prepare (in nominal dollars) an analysis of the Accumulated Depreciation–Equipment account for the years 1985 through 1987.

(3) Prepare a schedule to express the Accumulated Depreciation–Equipment account balance as of December 31, 1987, in terms of constant dollars.

(4) Prepare a schedule to compute O'Brien's purchasing power gain or loss on its net holdings or monetary assets for 1987. (AICPA adapted)

PROBLEM 25–4
(Analysis of EPS & ROI in terms of constant dollars)

To obtain a more realistic appraisal of her investment, Nina Richards, your client, has asked you to adjust certain financial data on the World Company for general price-level changes. On January 1, 1986, Richards invested $50,000 in the World Company in return for 10,000 shares of common stock. Immediately after her investment, the trial balance data appeared as follows:

Cash and Receivables	65,200	
Merchandise Inventory	4,000	
Building	50,000	
Accumulated Depreciation — Building		8,000
Equipment	36,000	
Accumulated Depreciation — Equipment		7,200
Land	10,000	
Current Liabilities		50,000
Capital Stock, $5 par		100,000
	165,200	165,200

Balances in certain selected accounts as of December 31, 1986–1988, were as follows:

	1986	1987	1988
Sales	$39,650	$39,000	$42,350
Inventory	4,500	5,600	5,347
Purchases	14,475	16,350	18,150
Operating expenses (excluding depreciation)	10,050	9,050	9,075

Assume the 1986 price level as the base year and all changes in the price level take place at the beginning of each year. Further assume the 1987 price level is 10% above the 1986 price level and the 1988 price level is 10% above the 1987 level.

The building was constructed in 1982 at a cost of $50,000 with an estimated life of 25 years. The price level at that time was 80% of the 1986 price level.

The equipment was purchased in 1984 at a cost of $36,000 with an estimated life of 10 years. The price level at that time was 90% of the 1986 price level.

The LIFO method of inventory valuation is used. The original inventory was acquired in the same year the building was constructed and was maintained at a constant $4,000 until 1986. In 1986 a gradual buildup of the inventory was begun in anticipation of an increase in the volume of business.

Richards considers the return on her investment as the dividend she actually receives. In 1986 and also in 1988 the World Company paid cash dividends in the amount of $4,000.

Instructions:
(1) Compute the 1988 earnings per share of common stock in terms of 1986 dollars.
(2) Compute the percentage return on the investment for 1986 and 1988 in terms of 1986 dollars.   (AICPA adapted)

PROBLEM 25–5   (Restatement of balance sheet to constant dollars)

The Stanforth Co. began operations in 1956. At the end of 1987 it was decided to furnish stockholders with a balance sheet restated in terms of constant 1987 dollars such as a supplement to the conventional financial statements. This is the first time such a statement was prepared. The balance sheet prepared in conventional form at the end of 1987 follows.

Stanforth Co.
Balance Sheet
December 31, 1987

Cash............................	$ 187,600	Accounts payable	$ 379,900
Accounts receivable............	342,400	Mortgage note payable.......	450,000
Inventory	742,300	Bonds payable..............	1,250,000
Land...........................	1,720,000	Capital stock...............	1,000,000
Building	2,115,000	Additional paid-in capital	200,000
Less accumulated depreciation ..	(705,000)	Retained earnings...........	1,122,400
		Total liabilities and stockholders'	
Total assets....................	$4,402,300	equity....................	$4,402,300

All the stock was issued in 1956. Land was purchased subject to a mortgage note of $1,000,000 at the time the company was formed. The present building is being depreciated on a straight-line basis with a 30-year life and no salvage value. The bonds were issued in 1966. The company uses the first-in, first-out method in pricing inventories.

Instructions: Prepare a balance sheet for the Stanforth Co. restated in terms of 1987 constant dollars. Use the following indexes in making adjustments; assume the index for each year is regarded as representative of the price level for the entire year.

Year	Price Index	Year	Price Index
1956	54.9	1984............	160.1
1966	70.7	1985............	168.0
1976	93.0	1986............	178.6
1978	100.0	1987............	185.2
1983	146.5		

PROBLEM 25-6

(Restatement of income statement to constant dollars)

The income statement prepared at the end of the year for Shur-Shot Corporation follows:

Shur-Shot Corporation
Income Statement
For Year Ended December 31, 1988

Sales..		$350,000
Less sales discount		15,000
Net sales		$335,000
Cost of goods sold:		
Inventory, January 1............................	$125,000	
Purchases	180,000	
Goods available for sale	$305,000	
Inventory, December 31	120,000	
Cost of goods sold............................		185,000
Gross profit on sales		$150,000
Operating expenses:		
Depreciation.....................................	$ 21,250	
Other operating expenses........................	50,000	
Total operating expenses		71,250
Income before income tax...........................		$ 78,750
Income tax......................................		31,300
Net income......................................		$ 47,450

The following additional data are available:

(a) The price index rose evenly throughout the year from 120 on January 1 to 130 on December 31.

(b) Sales were made evenly throughout the year; expenses were incurred evenly throughout the year.

(c) The inventory was valued at cost using first-in, first-out pricing; average indexes for the year are used in restating inventories. The beginning inventory was acquired in the preceding period when the average index was 122.

(d) The depreciation charge related to the following items:

	Asset Cost	Index at Date of Acquisition	Depreciation Rate
Building	$75,000	95	3 %
Equipment.............	80,000	95	12½%
Equipment.............	20,000	98	12½%
Equipment*	39,000	120	16⅔%

*Acquired at the beginning of the current year.

(e) Semiannual dividends of $7,500 were declared and paid at the end of June and at the end of December.

(f) The balance sheet position for the company changed during the year as follows:

	January 1	December 31
Current assets	$180,000	$174,700
Building and equipment (net)	120,000	137,750
	$300,000	$312,450
Current liabilities	$ 55,000	$ 35,000
Capital stock	200,000	200,000
Retained earnings	45,000	77,450
	$300,000	$312,450

Instructions: Prepare an income statement in which items are stated in end-of-year dollars accompanied by a schedule summarizing the purchasing power gain or loss for 1988.

PROBLEM 25–7
(Restatement of financial statements to constant dollars)

Financial statements are prepared for the Silvoso Company at the end of each year in nominal dollars and are also measured in constant dollars. Balance sheet data summarized in nominal dollars and in constant dollars at the end of 1987 are given below.

	Nominal Dollars		Constant Dollars (Reporting Purchasing Power at End of Year)	
Assets:				
Cash		$ 23,000		$ 23,000
Accounts receivable		70,000		70,000
Inventory		105,000		106,500
Buildings and equipment	$120,000		$153,600	
Less accumulated depreciation	48,000	72,000	61,440	92,160
Land		50,000		64,000
Total assets		$320,000		$355,660
Liabilities:				
Accounts payable		$ 48,000		$ 48,000
Long-term liabilities		40,000		40,000
Total liabilities		$ 88,000		$ 88,000
Stockholders' equity:				
Capital stock		$150,000		$192,000
Retained earnings		82,000		75,660
Total stockholders' equity		$232,000		$267,660
Total liabilities and stockholders' equity		$320,000		$355,660

Data from statements measured in nominal dollars at the end of 1988 are given below:

Balance Sheet		Income and Retained Earnings Statement	
Assets		Sales	$1,100,000
Cash..........................	$ 83,840	Cost of goods sold	600,000
Accounts receivable.............	72,500	Gross profit on sales..............	$ 500,000
Inventory	125,000	Operating expenses	308,000
Buildings and equipment	120,000	Income before income tax..........	$ 192,000
Accumulated depreciation	(56,000)	Income tax	85,660
Land..........................	50,000	Net income	$ 106,340
	$395,340	Dividends	20,000
Liabilities and Stockholders' Equity		Increase in retained earnings	$ 86,340
Accounts payable................	$ 37,000		
Long-term liabilities	40,000		
Capital stock...................	150,000		
Retained earnings	168,340		
	$395,340		

The following additional data are available at the end of 1988:
(a) Price indexes were as follows for the year:

January 1	150
December 31	153

(b) Sales and purchases were made evenly, and expenses were incurred evenly throughout the year.
(c) The first-in, first-out method was used to compute inventory cost; average indexes for the year are used in restating inventories.
(d) All the land, buildings, and equipment were acquired when the company was formed.
(e) Dividends were declared and paid at the end of the year.

Instructions: Prepare in terms of end-of-year constant dollars: (1) an income and retained earnings statement accompanied by a schedule summarizing the purchasing power gain or loss for 1988, (2) a balance sheet as of December 31, 1988.

PROBLEM 25–8 (Reporting constant dollar information)

The historical cost income statement for the MacKay Company is presented at the top of the next page.

The following additional information is provided:
(a) Sales, purchases, and other expenses were incurred evenly over the year.
(b) The beginning inventory was purchased when the price index was 180. Assume the ending inventory was acquired when the price index was 220.

MacKay Company
Income Statement
For the Year Ended December 31, 1988

Sales.		$180,000
Cost of goods sold:		
Beginning inventory	$ 20,000	
Purchases	140,000	
Goods available for sale	$160,000	
Ending inventory.	50,000	
Cost of goods sold.		110,000
Gross profit		$ 70,000
Operating expenses:		
Depreciation expense	$ 10,000	
Other expenses.	20,000	30,000
Net income.		$ 40,000

(c) Price indexes were as follows:

Beginning of year	200
Average for year	220
End of year.	240

(d) The equipment on which the depreciation expense is computed was purchased when the price index was 110.

Instructions: Prepare a statement showing income from continuing operations in average-year constant dollars.

PROBLEM 25–9   (Current cost accounting)

Heartland, Inc. adopted a current cost system in its first year of operations. At the start of the first year, 1988, the company purchased $168,000 of inventory, and at the end of the year had an inventory of $100,800 on a historical cost basis and $164,500 on a current cost basis. At the time the inventory was sold, the current cost of the inventory was $107,800. Sales for the year were $182,000. Ignore all tax effects and assume that the CPI-U did not change over this period. Other expenses were $8,400 on both historical cost and current cost basis.

Instructions:
(1) Prepare a current cost income statement.
(2) What is the increase in the specific price of inventory during the year?

*PROBLEM 25–10   (Current cost accounting)

The Riverton Company's statements of financial position at December 31, 1987 and 1986, were as follows:

	1987	1986
Cash	$ 930,000	$ 150,000
Accounts receivable.........................	270,000	240,000
Inventory (FIFO)	750,000	825,000
Operating assets (net).......................	1,320,000	1,650,000
Land	300,000	300,000
Total assets	$3,570,000	$3,165,000
Accounts payable...........................	$ 615,000	$ 562,000
Bonds payable..............................	1,125,000	1,125,000
Total liabilities	$1,740,000	$1,687,000
Net assets	$1,830,000	$1,478,000

The income statement for 1987 was as follows:

Sales...	$4,500,000
Cost of goods sold	(1,800,000)
Salaries expense	(1,410,000)
Interest expense...	(112,500)
Depreciation expense	(330,000)
Net income before taxes....................................	$ 847,500
Income taxes (40%)...	(339,000)
Net income..	$ 508,500

Additional facts about Riverton are as follows:
(a) The current values of the accounts receivable, inventory, and accounts payable were approximately the same as their book values.
(b) The operating assets had been purchased at the end of 1981 for $3,300,000. They have a 10-year service life with no residual value and are being depreciated with the straight-line method. The specific price index for this type of asset was 110 at their date of purchase. At the end of 1986, the index was 200 and it was 225 at the end of 1987.
(c) The land was reliably appraised at $937,500 on December 31, 1986, and at $1,087,500 on December 31, 1987. It was purchased on December 31, 1981.
(d) Because interest rates had continued to increase since their issuance, the bonds payable had a current discharge value of $1,031,250 at the end of 1986 and $975,000 at the end of 1987.
(e) On a replacement cost basis, the cost of goods sold for 1987 was $2,062,500.
(f) Cash dividends of $156,000 were declared and paid during 1987.

Instructions:
(1) Prepare a schedule to estimate the current value of the operating assets in their existing condition at the end of 1986 and 1987.
(2) Prepare a schedule that computes the current value depreciation expense for 1987, using the method that allocates the average current cost over the assets' estimated service life.
(3) Prepare a schedule that computes the realized holding gains derived from the sales of inventory and the depreciation of the operating assets for 1987.

(4) Prepare a schedule that computes the change in the accumulated unrealized holding gains between the end of 1986 and the end of 1987. The schedule should identify each component of the gain.
(5) Prepare a current cost income statement for 1987 that shows the net after tax operating income, the net after-tax realized holding gains, the total after-tax realized income, the change in the accumulated holding gain, and comprehensive income.

The appendix to the chapter may be helpful in completing this problem.

*PROBLEM 25–11 (Comparison of four reporting alternatives)

Inventory information for the Hilton Company is presented below.

	Historical Cost/ Nominal Dollar	Current Cost/ Nominal Dollar
Beginning inventory	$ 60,000	—
Purchases	240,000	—
Ending inventory	75,000	90,000

The Hilton Company uses the FIFO inventory method.

The beginning inventory was purchased when the price index was 100. The ending inventory was purchased when the index was 120. Purchases and sales were made evenly throughout the year. The current value of the goods sold was $270,000 based on average current costs.

General price indexes were as follows:

Beginning of year	100
Average index	120
End of year	140

Instructions: Compute the cost of goods sold and ending inventory under each of the following accounting methods.
  (a) Historical cost/nominal dollar
  (b) Historical cost/end-of-year constant dollar
  (c) Current cost/nominal dollar
  (d) Current cost/end-of-year constant dollar

The appendix to the chapter may be helpful in completing this problem.

26

Financial Statement Analysis

Accounting provides information to assist various individuals in making economic decisions. A significant amount of information relevant to this purpose is presented in the primary financial statements of companies. Additional useful information is provided by financial data reported by means other than the financial statements. However, as explained in Chapter 2, financial data are only part of the total information needed by decision makers. Nonfinancial information may also be relevant. Thus, the total information spectrum is broader than just financial reporting. It encompasses financial statements, financial reporting by means other than the financial statements, and additional nonfinancial information.

The Financial Accounting Standards Board has restricted its focus to general-purpose external financial reporting by business enterprises. This chapter concentrates on analysis of information in the primary financial statements. Notes are an integral part of financial statements, and significant accounting policies and other information included in notes should be considered carefully in performing an analysis and in evaluating results. Supplementary information should also be considered in interpreting financial statement data.

OBJECTIVES OF FINANCIAL STATEMENT ANALYSIS

Nearly all businesses prepare financial statements of some type; the form and complexity of the statements vary according to the needs of those who prepare and use them. The owner of a small business might simply list the firm's cash receipts and disbursements and prepare an income tax return. On the other hand, a large corporation's accounting staff spends considerable time in preparing the company's complex financial statements.

Whatever their form, financial statements provide information about a business and its operations to interested users. For example, questions may be raised by external users concerning matters such as a company's sales, net income, and trends for these items; the amount of working capital and changes in working capital; the relationship of income to sales, and of income to investments. Identifying these relationships requires analysis of data reported on the income statement, the balance sheet, and the statement of cash flows. Internal management is also concerned with analyzing the general-purpose financial statements, but requires additional special information in setting policies and making decisions. Questions may arise on matters such as the performance of various company divisions, the income from sales of individual products, and whether to make or buy product parts and equipment. These questions can be answered by establishing internal information systems to provide the necessary data. Thus, in analyzing financial data, the nature of analysis and the information needed depend on the requirements of users and the issues involved.

The analyses of financial data described in this chapter are directed primarily to the information needs of external users who must generally rely on the financial reports issued by a company. Many groups are interested in the data found in financial statements, including:

1. Owners — sole proprietor, partners, or stockholders.
2. Management, including board of directors.
3. Creditors.
4. Government — local, state, and federal (including regulatory, taxing, and statistical units).
5. Prospective owners and prospective creditors.
6. Stock exchanges, investment bankers, and stockbrokers.
7. Trade associations.
8. Employees of a business and their labor unions.
9. The general public.

Questions raised by these groups can generally be answered by analyses that develop comparisons and measure relationships between components of financial statements. The analyses will form a basis for decisions made by the user.

Analysis is generally directed toward evaluating four aspects of a business: (1) liquidity, (2) stability, (3) profitability, and (4) growth potential.

Liquidity relates to the ability of an enterprise to pay its liabilities as they mature. Financial statements are analyzed to determine whether a business is currently liquid and whether it could retain its liquidity in a period of adversity. The analysis includes studies of the relationship of current assets to current liabilities, the size and nature of creditor and ownership interests, the protection afforded creditors and owners through sound asset values, and the amounts and trends of net income.

Stability is measured by the ability of a business to make interest and principal payments on outstanding debt and to pay regular dividends to its stockholders. In judging stability, data concerning operations and financial position are studied. For example, there must be a regular demand for the goods or services sold, and the gross profit on sales must be sufficient to cover operating expenses, interest, and dividends. There should be a satisfactory turnover of assets, and all business resources should be productively employed.

Profitability is measured by the ability of a business to maintain a satisfactory dividend policy while at the same time steadily increasing ownership equity. The nature and amount of income, as well as its regularity and trend, are significant factors affecting profitability.

The **growth potential** of a company is also of primary importance. This element, along with profitability, directly affects future cash flows, derived from increased income and/or appreciation in stock values. Growth potential is measured by the expansion and growth into new markets, the rate of growth in existing markets, the rate of growth in earnings per share, and the amount of expenditures for research and development.

An analysis must serve the needs of those for whom it is made. For example, owners are interested in a company's ability to obtain additional capital for current needs and possible expansion. Creditors are interested not only in the position of a business as a going concern but also in its position should it be forced to liquidate.

ANALYTICAL PROCEDURES

Analytical procedures fall into two main categories: (1) comparisons and measurements based on financial data for two or more periods, and (2) comparisons and measurements based on financial data of only the current fiscal period. The first category includes comparative statements, ratios and trends for data on successive statements, and analyses of changes in the balance sheet, income statement, and statement of changes in financial position. The second category includes determining current balance sheet and income statement relationships and analyzing earnings and earning power. A review of financial data usually requires both types of analysis.

The analytical procedures commonly employed may be identified as: comparative statements, index-number trend series, common-size statements, and analysis of financial statement components. These techniques are described and illustrated in the following sections. It should be emphasized that the analyses illustrated herein are simply guides to the evaluation of financial data. Sound conclusions can be reached only through intelligent use and interpretation of such data. The Wycat Corporation is used as an example throughout the chapter.

Comparative Statements

Financial data become more meaningful when compared with similar data for preceding periods. Statements reflecting financial data for two or more periods are called **comparative statements**. Annual data can be compared with similar data for prior years. Monthly or quarterly data can be compared with similar data for previous months or quarters or with similar data for the same months or quarters of previous years.

Comparative data allow statement users to analyze trends in a company, thus enhancing the usefulness of information for decision making. The Accounting Principles Board stated that comparisons between financial statements are most informative and useful under the following conditions:

1. The presentations are in good form; that is, the arrangement within the statements is identical.
2. The content of the statements is identical; that is, the same items from the underlying accounting records are classified under the same captions.
3. Accounting principles are not changed or, if they are changed, the financial effects of the changes are disclosed.
4. Changes in circumstances or in the nature of the underlying transactions are disclosed.[1]

To the extent that the foregoing criteria are not met, comparisons may be misleading. Consistent practices and procedures and reporting periods of equal and regular lengths are also important, especially when comparisons are made for a single enterprise.

Comparative financial statements may be even more useful to investors and others when the reporting format highlights absolute changes in dollar amounts as well as relative percentage changes. Statement users will benefit by considering both amounts as they make their analyses. For example, an investor may decide that any change in a financial statement amount of 10% or more should be investigated further. A 10% change in an amount

---

[1]*Statements of the Accounting Principles Board, No. 4,* "Basic Concepts and Accounting Principles Underlying Financial Statements of Business Enterprises" (New York: American Institute of Certified Public Accountants, 1970), par. 95–99.

of $1,000, however, is not as significant as a 5% change in an amount of $100,000. When absolute or relative amounts appear out of line, conclusions, favorable or unfavorable, are not justified until investigation has disclosed reasons for the changes.

The development of data measuring changes taking place over a number of periods is known as **horizontal analysis**. Using the Wycat Corporation's income statement as an example, and a reporting format that discloses both dollar and percentage changes, horizontal analysis is illustrated below.

				Increase (Decrease)			
				1987–1988		1986–1987	
	1988	1987	1986	Amount	Percent	Amount	Percent
Gross sales	$1,500,000	$1,750,000	$1,000,000	$(250,000)	(14%)	$750,000	75%
Sales returns	75,000	100,000	50,000	(25,000)	(25%)	50,000	100%
Net sales..............	$1,425,000	$1,650,000	$ 950,000	$(225,000)	(14%)	$700,000	74%
Cost of goods sold	1,000,000	1,200,000	630,000	(200,000)	(17%)	570,000	90%
Gross profit on sales ...	$ 425,000	$ 450,000	$ 320,000	$ (25,000)	(6%)	$130,000	41%
Selling expense........	$ 280,000	$ 300,000	$ 240,000	$ (20,000)	(7%)	$ 60,000	25%
General expense.......	100,000	110,000	100,000	(10,000)	(9%)	10,000	10%
Total operating expenses	$ 380,000	$ 410,000	$ 340,000	$ (30,000)	(7%)	$ 70,000	21%
Operating income (loss) .	$ 45,000	$ 40,000	$ (20,000)	$ 5,000	13%	$ 60,000	—
Other revenue items....	85,000	75,000	50,000	10,000	13%	25,000	50%
	$ 130,000	$ 115,000	$ 30,000	$ 15,000	13%	$ 85,000	283%
Other expense items ...	30,000	30,000	10,000	—	—	20,000	200%
Income before income tax	$ 100,000	$ 85,000	$ 20,000	$ 15,000	18%	$ 65,000	325%
Income tax	30,000	25,000	5,000	5,000	20%	20,000	400%
Net income............	$ 70,000	$ 60,000	$ 15,000	$ 10,000	17%	$ 45,000	300%

Wycat Corporation
Comparative Income Statement
For Years Ended December 31

Index-Number Trend Series

When comparative financial statements present information for more than two or three years, they become cumbersome and potentially confusing. A technique used to overcome this problem is referred to as an **index-number trend series**.

To compute index numbers, the statement preparer must first choose a base year. This may be the earliest year presented or some other year considered particularly appropriate. Next, the base year amounts are all expressed as 100%. The amounts for all other years are then stated as a percentage of the base year amounts. Index numbers can only be computed when amounts are positive. The set of percentages for several years may thus be interpreted as trend values or as a series of index numbers relating to a particular item. For example, Wycat Corporation had gross sales of $1,000,000 in 1986, $1,750,000 in 1987, and $1,500,000 in 1988. These amounts, expressed in an index-number trend series with 1986 as the base year, would be 100, 175, and 150, respectively.

The index-number trend series technique is a type of horizontal analysis. It can give statement users a long-range view of a firm's financial position, earnings, and sources and uses of funds. The user needs to recognize, however, that long-range trend series are particularly sensitive to changing price levels.

Data expressed in terms of a base year are frequently useful for comparisons with similar data provided by business or industry sources or government agencies. When information used for making comparisons does not employ the same base period, it will have to be restated. Restatement of a base year calls for the expressing of each value as a percentage of the value for the base-year period.

To illustrate, assume the net sales data for the Wycat Corporation for 1986–1988 are to be compared with a sales index for its particular industry. The industry sales indexes are as follows:

	1988	1987	1986
(1980 − 1984 = 100)	146	157	124

Recognizing 1986 as the base year, industry sales are restated as follows:

1986	100
1987 (157 ÷ 124)	127
1988 (146 ÷ 124)	118

Industry sales and net sales for the Wycat Corporation can now be expressed in comparative form as follows:

	1988	1987	1986
Industry sales index	118	127	100
Wycat Corporation sales index*	150	174	100

*From comparative income statement on page 1158.

Common-Size Financial Statements

Horizontal analysis measures changes over a number of accounting periods. Statement users also need data that express relationships within a single period, which is known as **vertical analysis**. Preparation of **common-size financial statements** is a widely used vertical analysis technique. The common-size relationships may be stated in terms of percentages or in terms of ratios. Common-size statements may be prepared for the same business as of different dates or periods, or for two or more business units as of the same date or for the same period.

Common-size financial statements are useful in analyzing the internal structure of a financial statement. For example, a common-size balance sheet expresses each amount as a percentage of total assets usually expressed as a decimal fraction. A common-size income statement usually shows each revenue or expense item as a percentage of net sales. As an illustration, a comparative balance sheet for Wycat Corporation with each item expressed in both dollar amounts and percentages is shown below. Other types of common-size financial statements, e.g., a common-size retained earnings statement or statement of changes in financial position, may be prepared. When a supporting schedule shows the detail for a group total, individual items may be expressed as percentages of either the base figure or the group total.

	Wycat Corporation Comparative Balance Sheet December 31					
	1988		1987		1986	
	Amount	Common Size Ratio	Amount	Common Size Ratio	Amount	Common Size Ratio
Assets						
Current assets..............	$ 855,000	.38	$ 955,500	.40	$ 673,500	.38
Long-term investments.......	500,000	.22	400,000	.17	250,000	.14
Land, buildings, and equipment						
(net).....................	775,000	.34	875,000	.37	675,000	.38
Intangible assets............	100,000	.04	100,000	.04	100,000	.06
Other assets................	48,000	.02	60,500	.02	61,500	.04
Total assets	$2,278,000	1.00	$2,391,000	1.00	$1,760,000	1.00
Liabilities						
Current liabilities	$ 410,000	.18	$ 546,000	.23	$ 130,000	.07
Long-term liabilities — 10%						
bonds...................	400,000	.18	400,000	.17	300,000	.17
Total liabilities	$ 810,000	.36	$ 946,000	.40	$ 430,000	.24
Stockholders' Equity						
Preferred 6% stock..........	$ 350,000	.15	$ 350,000	.15	$ 250,000	.14
Common stock..............	750,000	.33	750,000	.31	750,000	.43
Additional paid-in capital	100,000	.04	100,000	.04	100,000	.06
Retained earnings...........	268,000	.12	245,000	.10	230,000	.13
Total stockholders' equity	$1,468,000	.64	$1,445,000	.60	$1,330,000	.76
Total liabilities and stock-						
holders' equity	$2,278,000	1.00	$2,391,000	1.00	$1,760,000	1.00

Common-size analysis can also be used when comparing a company with other companies or with an entire industry. Differences in sizes of numbers in the financial statement are neutralized by reducing them to common-size ratios. Industry statistics are frequently published in common-size form, which facilitates making these types of comparisons. When comparing a company with other companies or with industry figures, it is important that the financial data for each company reflect comparable price levels. Furthermore, the financial data should be developed using comparable accounting methods, classification procedures, and valuation bases. Comparisons should be limited to companies engaged in similar activities. When the financial policies of two companies are different, these differences should be recognized in evaluating comparative reports. For example, one company may lease its properties while the other may purchase such items; one company may finance its operations using long-term borrowing while the other may rely primarily on funds supplied by stockholders and by earnings. Financial statements for two companies under these circumstances cannot be wholly comparable.

All this suggests that comparisons between different companies should be evaluated with care, and should be made with a full understanding of the inherent limitations. Reference was made earlier to the criteria that the Accounting Principles Board identified if comparisons are to be meaningful. Comparability between enterprises is more difficult to obtain than comparability within a single enterprise. Ideally, differences in companies' financial reports should arise from basic differences in the companies themselves or from the nature of their transactions and not from differences in accounting practices and procedures.

Other Analytical Procedures

In addition to the financial statement analysis procedures described in the preceding sections, various measures may be developed with respect to specific components of financial statements. Some measurements are of general interest, while others have special significance to particular groups. Creditors, for example, are concerned with the ability of a company to pay its current obligations and seek information about the relationship of current assets to current liabilities. Stockholders are concerned with dividends and seek information relating to earnings that will form the basis for dividends. Managements are concerned with the activity of the merchandise stock and seek information relating to the number of times goods have turned over during the period. All users are vitally interested in profitability and wish to be informed about the relationship of income to both liabilities and owners' equity.

The computation of percentages, ratios, turnovers, and other measures of financial position and operating results for a period is a form of vertical analysis. Comparison with the same measures for other periods is a form of horizontal analysis. These comparisons can be made within a company's financial statements or with other companies, individually or in industry groups. The measures described and illustrated in the following sections should not be considered all-inclusive; other measures may be useful to various groups, depending on their particular needs. It should be emphasized again that sound conclusions cannot be reached from an individual measurement. But this information, together with adequate investigation and study, may lead to a satisfactory evaluation of financial data.

Liquidity Analysis

Generally, the first concern of a financial analyst is a firm's liquidity. Will the firm be able to meet its current obligations? If a firm cannot meet its obligations in the short run, it may not have a chance to be profitable or to experience growth in the long run. The two most commonly used measures of liquidity are the current ratio and the acid-test ratio.

Current Ratio. The comparison of current assets with current liabilities is regarded as a fundamental measurement of a company's liquidity. Known as the **current ratio** or **working capital ratio**, this measurement is computed by dividing total current assets by total current liabilities.

The current ratio is a measure of the ability to meet current obligations. Since it measures liquidity, care must be taken to determine that proper items have been included in the current asset and current liability categories. A ratio of current assets to current liabilities of less than 2 to 1 for a trading or manufacturing unit has frequently been considered unsatisfactory. However, because liquidity needs are different for different industries and companies, any such arbitrary measure should not be viewed as meaningful or appropriate in all cases. A comfortable margin of current assets over current liabilities suggests that a company will be able to meet maturing obligations even in the event of unfavorable business conditions or losses on such assets as marketable securities, receivables, and inventories.

For the Wycat Corporation, current ratios for 1988 and 1987 are developed as follows[2]:

---

[2] Comparative data for more than two years are generally required in evaluating financial trends. Analyses for only two years are given in the examples in this chapter, since these are sufficient to illustrate the analytical procedures involved.

	1988	1987
Current assets	$855,000	$955,500
Current liabilities.....................................	$410,000	$546,000
Current ratio	2.1:1	1.8:1

A current ratio of 2.1 to 1 means that Wycat could liquidate its total current liabilities 2.1 times using only its current assets.

Ratio calculations are sometimes carried out to two or more decimal places; however, ratios do not need to be carried beyond one place unless some particularly significant interpretative value is afforded by the more refined measurement.

It is possible to overemphasize the importance of a high current ratio. Assume a company is normally able to carry on its operations with current assets of $200,000 and current liabilities of $100,000. If the company has current assets of $500,000 and current liabilities remain at $100,000, its current ratio has increased from 2:1 to 5:1. The company now has considerably more working capital than it requires. It should also be observed that certain unfavorable conditions may be accompanied by an improving ratio. For example, a company's cash balance may rise due to a slowdown in business and the postponement of advertising and research programs or building and equipment repairs and replacements. At the same time, slower customer collections may result in rising trade receivables, and reduced sales volume may result in rising inventories.

Acid-Test Ratio. A test of a company's immediate liquidity is made by comparing the sum of cash, marketable securities, notes receivable, and accounts receivable, commonly referred to as **quick assets**, with current liabilities. The total quick assets divided by current liabilities gives the **acid-test ratio** or **quick ratio**. Considerable time may be required to convert raw materials, goods in process, and finished goods into receivables and then into cash. A company with a satisfactory current ratio may be in a relatively poor liquidity position when inventories comprise most of the total current assets. This is revealed by the acid-test ratio. In developing the ratio, the receivables and securities included in the total quick assets should be examined closely. In some cases these items may actually be less liquid than inventories.

Usually, a ratio of quick assets to current liabilities of at least 1 to 1 is considered desirable. Again, however, special conditions of the particular business must be evaluated. Questions such as the following should be considered: What is the composition of the quick assets? What special requirements are made by current activities upon these assets? How soon are current payables due?

Acid-test ratios for Wycat Corporation are computed as follows:

	1988	1987
Quick assets:		
Cash...	$ 60,000	$100,500
Marketable securities................................	150,000	150,000
Receivables (net)...................................	420,000	375,000
Total quick assets	$630,000	$625,500
Total current liabilities	$410,000	$546,000
Acid-test ratio	1.5:1	1.1:1

Other Measures of Liquidity. Other ratios may help to analyze a company's liquidity. For example, it may be useful to show the relationship of total current assets to total assets, and of individual current assets, such as receivables and inventories, to total current assets. In the case of liabilities, it may be useful to show the relationship of total current liabilities to total liabilities, and of individual current liabilities to total current liabilities.

The foregoing comparisons may provide information concerning the relative liquidity of total assets and the maturity of total obligations as well as the structure of working capital and shifts within the working capital group. The latter data are significant, since all items within the current classification are not equally current.

Activity Analysis

There are special tests that may be applied to measure how efficiently a firm is utilizing its assets. Several of these measures also relate to liquidity because they involve significant working capital elements, such as receivables, inventories, and accounts payable.

Accounts Receivable Turnover. The amount of receivables usually bears a close relationship to the volume of credit sales. The receivable position and approximate collection time may be evaluated by computing the **accounts receivable turnover**. This rate is determined by dividing net credit sales (or total net sales if credit sales are unknown) by the average trade notes and accounts receivable outstanding. In developing an average receivables amount, monthly balances should be used if available.

Assume in the case of Wycat Corporation that all sales are made on credit, that receivables arise only from sales, and that receivable totals for only the beginning and the end of the year are available. Receivable turnover rates are computed as follows:

	1988	1987
Net credit sales...............................	$1,425,000	$1,650,000
Net receivables:		
Beginning of year................................	$ 375,000	$ 333,500
End of year.....................................	$ 420,000	$ 375,000
Average receivables	$ 397,500	$ 354,250
Receivables turnover for year......................	3.6	4.7

Number of Days' Sales in Receivables. Average receivables are sometimes expressed in terms of the **number of days' sales in receivables**, which shows the average time required to collect receivables. Assume for convenience that there are 360 days per year. Annual sales divided by 360 equals average daily sales. Average receivables divided by average daily sales then gives the number of days' sales in average receivables. This procedure for Wycat Corporation is illustrated below.

	1988	1987
Average receivables	$ 397,500	$ 354,250
Net credit sales.................................	$1,425,000	$1,650,000
Average daily credit sales (net credit sales ÷ 360)	$ 3,958	$ 4,583
Number of days' sales in average receivables (average receivables ÷ average daily credit sales)...........	100	77

This same measurement can be obtained by dividing the number of days in the year by the receivable turnover. The same number of days for each year should be used in developing comparisons. Computations are generally based on the calendar year, consisting of 365 days, often rounded to 360 days, or a business year consisting of 300 days (365 days less Sundays and holidays). The calendar year basis, rounded to 360 days, is used here.

In some cases, instead of developing the number of days' sales in average receivables, it may be more useful to report the number of days' credit sales in receivables at the end of the period. This information would be significant in evaluating current position, and particularly the receivable position as of a given date. This information for Wycat Corporation is presented below:

	1988	1987
Receivables at end of year	$420,000	$375,000
Average daily credit sales	$ 3,958	$ 4,583
Number of days' sales in receivables at end of year	106	82

What constitutes a reasonable number of days in receivables varies with individual businesses. For example, if merchandise is sold on terms of net 60 days, 40 days' sales in receivables would be reasonable; but if terms are net 30 days, a receivable balance equal to 40 days' sales would indicate slow collections.

Sales activity just before the close of a period should be considered when interpreting accounts receivable measurements. If sales are unusually light or heavy just before the end of the fiscal period, this affects total receivables as well as the related measurements. When such unevenness prevails, it may be better to analyze accounts receivable according to their due dates, as was illustrated in Chapter 8.

The problem of minimizing accounts receivable without losing desirable business is important. Receivables often do not earn interest revenue, and the cost of carrying them must be covered by the profit margin. The longer accounts are carried, the smaller will be the percentage return realized on invested capital. In addition, heavier bookkeeping and collection charges and increased bad debts must be considered.

To attract business, credit is frequently granted for relatively long periods. The cost of granting long-term credit should be considered. Assume that a business has average daily credit sales of $5,000 and average accounts receivable of $250,000, which represents 50 days' credit sales. If collections and the credit period can be improved so that accounts receivable represent only 30 days' sales, then accounts receivable will be reduced to $150,000. Assuming a total cost of 10% to carry and service the accounts, the $100,000 decrease would yield annual savings of $10,000.

Inventory Turnover. The amount of inventory carried frequently relates closely to sales volume. The inventory position and the appropriateness of its size may be evaluated by computing the **inventory turnover**. The inventory turnover is computed by dividing cost of goods sold by average inventory. Whenever possible, monthly figures should be used to develop the average inventory balance.

Assume that for Wycat Corporation the inventory balances for only the beginning and the end of the year are available. Inventory turnover rates are computed as follows:

	1988	1987
Cost of goods sold	$1,000,000	$1,200,000
Inventory:		
Beginning of year	$ 330,000	$ 125,000
End of year	$ 225,000	$ 330,000
Average inventory	$ 277,500	$ 227,500
Inventory turnover for year	3.6	5.3

Number of Days' Sales in Inventories. Average inventories are sometimes expressed as the **number of days' sales in inventories**. Information is thus afforded concerning the average time it takes to turn over the inventory.

The number of days' sales in inventories is calculated by dividing average inventory by average daily cost of goods sold. The number of days' sales can also be obtained by dividing the number of days in the year by the inventory turnover rate. The latter procedure for Wycat Corporation is illustrated below:

	1988	1987
Inventory turnover for year.....................................	3.6	5.3
Number of days' sales in average inventory (assuming a year of 360 days)...	100	68

As was the case with receivables, instead of developing the number of days' sales in average inventories, it may be more useful to report the number of days' sales in ending inventories. The latter measurement is determined by dividing ending inventory by average daily cost of goods sold. This information is helpful in evaluating the current asset position and particularly the inventory position as of a given date.

A company with departmental classifications for inventories will find it desirable to support the company's inventory measurements with individual department measurements, since there may be considerable variation among departments. A manufacturing company may compute separate turnover rates for finished goods, goods in process, and raw materials. The finished goods turnover is computed by dividing cost of goods sold by average finished goods inventory. Goods in process turnover is computed by dividing cost of goods manufactured by average goods in process inventory. Raw materials turnover is computed by dividing the cost of raw materials used by average raw materials inventory.

The same valuation methods must be employed for inventories in successive periods if the inventory measurements are to be comparable. Maximum accuracy is possible if information relating to inventories and amount of goods sold is available in terms of physical units rather than dollar costs.

The effect of seasonal factors on the size of year-end inventories should be considered in inventory analyses. Inventories may be abnormally high or low at the end of a period. Many companies adopt a fiscal year ending when operations are at their lowest point. This is called a **natural business year**. Inventories will normally be lowest at the end of such a period, so that the organization can take inventory and complete year-end closing most conveniently. Under these circumstances, monthly inventory balances should be used to arrive at a representative average inventory figure. When a periodic inventory system is employed, monthly inventories may be estimated using the gross profit method as explained in Chapter 10.

With an increased inventory turnover, the investment necessary for a given volume of business is smaller, and consequently the return on invested capital is higher. This conclusion assumes an enterprise can acquire goods in smaller quantities sufficiently often at no price disadvantage. If merchandise must be bought in very large quantities in order to get favorable prices, then the savings on quantity purchases must be weighed against the additional investment, increased costs of storage, and other carrying charges.

The financial advantage of an increased turnover rate may be illustrated as follows. Assuming cost of goods sold of $1,000,000 and average inventory at cost of $250,000, inventory turnover is 4 times. Assume further that, through careful buying, the same business volume can be maintained with turnover of 5 times, or an average inventory of only $200,000. If interest on money invested in inventory is 10%, the savings on the $50,000 will be $5,000 annually. Other advantages include decreased inventory spoilage and obsolescence, savings in storage cost, taxes, and insurance, and reduction in risk of losses from price declines.

Inventory investments and turnover rates vary among businesses, and each business must be judged in terms of its financial structure and operations. Management must establish an inventory policy that will avoid the extremes of a dangerously low stock, which may impair sales, and an overstocking of goods involving a heavy capital investment and risks of spoilage and obsolescence, price declines, and difficulties in meeting purchase obligations.

Total Asset Turnover. A measure of the overall efficiency of asset utilization is the ratio of net sales to total assets, sometimes called the **asset turnover rate**. This ratio is calculated by dividing net sales by total assets. The resulting figure indicates the contribution made by total assets to sales. With comparative data, judgments can be made concerning the relative effectiveness of asset utilization. A ratio increase may suggest more efficient asset utilization, although a point may be reached where there is a strain on assets and a company is unable to achieve its full sales potential. An increase in total assets accompanied by a ratio decrease may suggest overinvestment in assets or inefficient utilization.

In developing the asset turnover rate, long-term investments should be excluded from total assets when they make no contribution to sales. On the other hand, a valuation for leased property should be added to total assets to permit comparability between companies owning their properties and those that lease them. If monthly figures for assets are available, they may be used in developing a representative average for total assets employed. Often the year-end asset total is used for the computation. When sales can be expressed in terms of units sold, ratios of sales units to total assets offer more reliable interpretations than sales dollars, since unit sales are not affected by price changes.

Assume that for Wycat Corporation only asset totals for the beginning and end of the year are available, and that sales cannot be expressed in terms of units. Ratios of net sales to total assets are computed as follows:

	1988	1987
Net sales	$1,425,000	$1,650,000
Total assets (excluding long-term investments):		
Beginning of year	$1,991,000	$1,510,000
End of year	$1,778,000	$1,991,000
Average total assets	$1,884,500	$1,750,500
Ratio of net sales to average total assets	0.8:1	0.9:1

Other Measures of Activity. Turnover analysis, as illustrated for receivables, inventories, and total assets, can also be applied to other assets or groups of assets. For example, current asset turnover is calculated by dividing net sales by average current assets. This figure may be viewed as the number of times current assets are replenished, or as the number of sales dollars generated per dollar of current assets. Similarly, if net sales are divided by plant assets, a plant asset turnover can be computed. This figure measures the efficiency of plant asset management and indicates the volume of sales generated by the operating assets of a company. Increases in turnover rates generally indicate more efficient utilization of assets.

Similar procedures may also be used to analyze specific liabilities. An accounts payable turnover, for example, may be computed by dividing purchases by average payables; the number of days' purchases in accounts payable may be computed by dividing accounts payable by average daily purchases.

Analysis of liabilities in terms of due dates may assist management in cash planning. Useful relationships may also be obtained by comparing specific assets or liabilities with other assets or liabilities, or with asset or liability totals. For example, data concerning the relationship of cash to accounts payable or of cash to total liabilities may be useful.

Profitability Analysis

Profitability analysis provides evidence concerning the earnings potential of a company and how effectively a firm is being managed. Since the reason most firms exist is to earn profits, the profitability ratios are among the most significant financial ratios. The adequacy of earnings may be measured in terms of (1) the rate earned on sales, (2) the rate earned on total assets, (3) the rate earned on stockholders' equity, and (4) the availability of earnings to common stockholders. Thus, the most popular profitability measurements are profit margin on sales, return on investment ratios, and earnings per share.

Profit Margin on Sales. The ratio of net income to sales determines the **net profit margin on sales**. This measurement represents the net income percentage per dollar of sales. The percentage is computed by dividing net income by net sales for a period. For Wycat Corporation, the net profit margin on sales is:

	1988	1987
Net income	$ 70,000	$ 60,000
Net sales	$1,425,000	$1,650,000
Net profit margin rate	4.9%	3.6%

This means that for 1988, Wycat generated almost five cents of profit per dollar of sales revenue. Because net income is used in the computation, any extraordinary or irregular items may distort the profit margin rate with respect to normal operating activities. Adjustments may be needed in the analysis to account for such items.

For merchandising and manufacturing companies, the **gross profit margin on sales** is often a significant ratio for evaluating the profitability of a company. In these companies, cost of goods sold is the most significant expense, and careful inventory control is necessary to assure profitable operations. For Wycat, the gross profit margin on sales is:

	1988	1987
Gross profit on sales	$ 425,000	$ 450,000
Net sales	$1,425,000	$1,650,000
Gross profit margin rate	29.8%	27.3%

Rate Earned on Total Assets. Overall asset productivity may be expressed as the **rate earned on total assets**, also referred to as the **return on investment (ROI)** or the **asset productivity rate**. The rate is computed by dividing net income by the total assets used to produce net income. This rate measures the efficiency in using resources to generate net income. If total assets by months are available, they should be used to develop an average for the year. Frequently, however, the assets at the beginning of the year or the assets at the end of the year are used. In some cases it may be desirable to use net income from operations by excluding revenue from investments, such as interest, dividends, and rents, or from gains or losses resulting from nonoperating transactions. When this is the case, total assets should be reduced by the investments or other assets. Sometimes comparisons are developed for the rate of operating income to total assets or the rate of pretax income to total assets, so that results are not affected by financial management items or by changes in income tax rates.

Rates earned on total assets for Wycat Corporation are determined as follows:

	1988	1987
Net income	$ 70,000	$ 60,000
Total assets:		
Beginning of year	$2,391,000	$1,760,000
End of year	$2,278,000	$2,391,000
Average total assets	$2,334,500	$2,075,500
Rate earned on average total assets	3.0%	2.9%

Rate Earned on Stockholders' Equity. Net income may be expressed as the **rate earned on stockholders' equity** (or return on stockholders' equity) by dividing net income by stockholders' equity. In developing this rate, it is preferable to calculate the average stockholders' equity for a year from monthly data, particularly when significant changes have occurred during the year, such as the sale of additional stock, retirement of stock, and accumulation of earnings. Sometimes the beginning or the ending stockholders' equity is used.

For Wycat Corporation, rates earned on stockholders' equity are as follows:

	1988	1987
Net income	$ 70,000	$ 60,000
Stockholders' equity:		
Beginning of year	$1,445,000	$1,330,000
End of year	$1,468,000	$1,445,000
Average stockholders' equity	$1,456,500	$1,387,500
Rate returned on average stockholders' equity	4.8%	4.3%

As a company's liabilities increase in relationship to stockholders' equity, the spread between the rate earned on stockholders' equity and the rate earned on total assets rises. The rate earned on stockholders' equity is important to investors who must reconcile the risk of debt financing with the potentially greater profitability.

Rate Earned on Common Stockholders' Equity. As a refinement to the rate earned on total stockholders' equity, earnings may be measured in terms of the residual common stockholders' equity. The **rate earned on common stockholders' equity** is computed by dividing net income after preferred dividend requirements by common stockholders' equity. The average equity for common stockholders should be determined, although the rate is frequently based on beginning or ending common equity.

In the case of Wycat Corporation, preferred dividend requirements are 6%. The rate earned on common stockholders' equity, then, is calculated as follows:

	1988	1987
Net income	$ 70,000	$ 60,000
Less dividend requirements on preferred stock........	21,000	21,000
Net income related to common stockholders' equity....	$ 49,000	$ 39,000
Common stockholders' equity:		
Beginning of year...............................	$1,095,000	$1,080,000
End of year.....................................	$1,118,000	$1,095,000
Average common stockholders' equity	$1,106,500	$1,087,500
Rate earned on average common stockholders' equity..	4.4%	3.6%

Earnings per Share. Earnings per share calculations were described in detail in Chapter 18. Recall that the Accounting Principles Board in Opinion No. 15 indicated that earnings per share data were of such importance to investors and others that such data should be presented prominently on the income statement. In computing earnings per share on common stock, earnings are first reduced by the prior dividend rights of preferred stock. Computations are made in terms of the weighted average number of common shares outstanding for each period presented. Adjustments are required when a corporation's capital structure includes potentially dilutive securities. If the total potential dilution is material, both primary earnings per share and fully diluted earnings per share must be disclosed. When net income includes below-the-line items, earnings per share should be reported for each major component of income as well as for net income.

For Wycat Corporation, there are no potentially dilutive securities. Earnings per share on common stock is calculated as follows.

	1988	1987
Net income	$70,000	$60,000
Less dividend requirements on preferred stock..............	21,000	21,000
Income related to common stockholders' equity	$49,000	$39,000
Number of shares of common stock outstanding	75,000	75,000
Earnings per share on common stock......................	$.65	$.52

Dividends per Share. In addition to earnings per share, many companies report **dividends per share** in the financial statements. This amount is computed simply by dividing cash dividends for the year by the number of shares of common stock outstanding. When a significant number of common shares have been issued or retired during a period, an average should be computed; otherwise, the number of common shares outstanding at the end of the period is normally used. For Wycat Corporation, the number of shares of common stock outstanding has remained constant for the past 3 years. Therefore, the dividends per share are $.35 for 1988 and $.32 for 1987. Another way of analyzing dividends is to compute the **dividend payout rate**, or the percentage of net income paid out in dividends. This may be computed by dividing the earnings per share by the dividends per share, or by dividing dividends paid by net income. The dividend payout rates for Wycat are 54% in 1988 and 62% in 1987.

Yield on Common Stock. Dividends per share may be used to compute a rate of return on the market value of common stock. Such a rate, referred to as the **yield on common stock**, is found by dividing the annual dividends per common share by the latest market price per common share. For Wycat Corporation the yield on the common stock is computed as follows:

	1988	1987
Dividends for year per common share.........................	$ .35	$ .32
Market value per common share at end of year	$10.00	$6.50
Yield on common stock......................................	3.5%	4.9%

Price-Earnings Ratio. The market price of common stock may be expressed as a multiple of earnings to evaluate the attractiveness of common stock as an investment. This measurement is referred to as the **price-earnings ratio** and is computed by dividing the market price per share of stock by the annual earnings per share. Instead of using the average market value of shares for the period covered by earnings, the latest market value is normally used. The lower the price-earnings ratio, the more attractive the investment. Assuming market values per common share of Wycat Corporation stock at the end of 1988 of $10 and at the end of 1987 of $6.50, price-earnings ratios would be computed as follows:

	1988	1987
Market value per common share at end of year	$10.00	$6.50
Earnings per share (calculated on page 1172)	$ .65	$ .52
Price-earnings ratio	15.4	12.5

As an alternative to the price-earnings ratio, earnings per share can be presented as a percentage of the market price of the stock.

Capital Structure Analysis

The composition of a company's capital structure has significant implications for stockholders, creditors, and potential investors and creditors. First, a company's creditors look to stockholders' equity as a margin of safety. To the extent that creditors supply the funds used in a business, they, rather than investors, bear the risks of the business. Second, when funds are obtained by borrowing, the stockholders retain control of a business; when funds are obtained by issuing additional stock, the existing shareholders must share the ownership rights with new investors. Third, as long as the return on investment of borrowed funds exceeds the cost of the debt (interest), the use of debt financing is advantageous. If, however, the return is less than the cost of borrowing, the use of debt is unfavorable. Fourth, there is a legal obligation to pay the interest on borrowed funds and to repay the principal. Dividends, however, are paid at the discretion of the board, and there is no obligation to return contributed capital to investors. Interest payments, unlike dividends, are deductible for tax purposes.

As stockholders' equity increases in relation to total liabilities, the margin of protection to the creditors also increases. From the stockholders' point of view, such an increase makes the organization less vulnerable to declines in business and an inability to meet obligations, and also serves to minimize the cost of carrying debt.

However, it is often advantageous to supplement funds invested by stockholders with borrowed capital. The effects of debt financing can be illustrated as follows. Assume that a company with 10,000 shares of stock outstanding is able to borrow $1,000,000 at 10% interest. The company estimates that pretax earnings will be $80,000 if it operates without the borrowed capital. Income tax is estimated at 40% of earnings. The following summary reports the effects upon net income and earnings per share, assuming a return on borrowed capital of (1) 20%, and (2) 8%.

	Results of Operations Without Borrowed Capital	Results of Operations If Borrowed Capital Earns 20%	Results of Operations If Borrowed Capital Earns 8%
Operating income	$80,000	$280,000	$160,000
Interest expense		100,000	100,000
Income before income tax	$80,000	$180,000	$ 60,000
Income tax at 40%	32,000	72,000	24,000
Net income	$48,000	$108,000	$ 36,000
Number of shares outstanding	10,000	10,000	10,000
Earnings per share	$4.80	$10.80	$3.60

The use of borrowed funds is known as **trading on the equity** or **applying leverage**. A company that relies heavily on debt financing is said to be "highly leveraged." Common leverage measurements include the equity to debt ratio, times interest earned, and fixed charge coverage.

Ratio of Stockholders' Equity to Total Liabilities. Stockholders' and creditors' equities may be expressed in terms of total assets or in terms of each other. For example, stockholders may have a 60% interest in total assets and creditors a 40% interest. This can be expressed as an **equity to debt ratio** of 1.5 to 1.

For Wycat Corporation, the relationships of stockholders' equity to total liabilities are calculated as follows:

	1988	1987
Stockholders' equity...............................	$1,468,000	$1,445,000
Total liabilities.....................................	$ 810,000	$ 946,000
Ratio of stockholders' equity to total liabilities.........	1.8:1	1.5:1

In analyzing the relationship of stockholders' equity to total liabilities, particular note should be made of lease arrangements. Both property rights provided under the leases and the accompanying liabilities should be considered in evaluating the equities and changes in equities from period to period.

Often the reciprocal of the equity to debt ratio is used. The **debt to equity ratio** is computed by dividing total liabilities by total stockholders' equity. This shows the reciprocal relationship to that just described. It is still a measure of the amount of leverage used by a company. Investors generally prefer a higher debt to equity ratio while creditors favor a lower ratio.

Number of Times Interest Earned. A measure of the debt position of a company in relation to its earnings ability is the **number of times interest is earned**. The calculation is made by dividing income before any charges for interest or income tax by the interest requirements for the period. The resulting figure reflects the company's ability to meet interest payments and the degree of safety afforded the creditors. The number of times interest was earned by Wycat Corporation follows:

	1988	1987
Income before income tax.............................	$100,000	$ 85,000
Add bond interest (10% of $400,000)...................	40,000	40,000
Amount available in meeting bond interest requirements..	$140,000	$125,000
Number of times bond interest requirements were earned..	3.5	3.1

Pretax income was used in the computation since income tax applies only after interest is deducted, and it is pretax income that protects creditors. However, the calculation is frequently based on net income since it is consistent with other measures employing net income, and offers a more conservative approach in measuring ability to meet interest requirements. For Wycat Corporation, net income was $70,000 for 1988 and $60,000 for 1987. These amounts would be increased by interest requirements net of tax for each year and then divided by the bond interest expense to derive times interest earned.

A computation similar to times interest earned, but more inclusive, is the **fixed charge coverage**. Fixed charges include such obligations as interest on bonds and notes, lease obligations, and any other recurring financial commitments. The number of times fixed charges are covered is calculated by adding the fixed charges to pretax income and then dividing the total by the fixed charges.

Book Value Per Share. Stockholders' equity can be measured by calculating the **book value per share**, which is the dollar equity in corporate capital of each share of stock. This amount is frequently used by investors in conjunction with the market value per share to evaluate the attractiveness of the stock for investment purposes.

When there is only one class of stock outstanding, the calculation of book value is relatively simple; the total stockholders' equity is divided by the number of shares of stock outstanding at the close of the reporting period. When a company is holding treasury stock, its cost is deducted from stockholders' equity and the treasury shares are deducted from the shares outstanding. When more than one class of stock is outstanding, a portion of the stockholders' equity must be allocated to the other classes of stock before the book value of the common stock is computed. Usually the par or liquidation value of the other classes of stock is used to make this allocation.

In the case of Wycat Corporation, the par value of the preferred stock is equal to the liquidation value, and there are no preferred dividends in arrears. The book value per share is computed as follows:

	1988	1987
Common stockholders' equity	$1,118,000	$1,095,000
Number of shares of common stock outstanding	75,000	75,000
Book value per share on common stock	$14.91	$14.60

Since the market value of the stock is lower than the book value, many investors would consider Wycat an attractive investment. However, the nature and limitations of the per share book value measurements must be considered in using these data. Carrying values of assets may vary significantly from their present fair values or immediate realizable values. This would directly affect the per share amount that could be realized in the event of a company liquidation.

Summary of Analytical Measures

Financial ratios, percentages, and other measures are useful tools for analyzing financial statements. They enable statement users to make meaningful judgments about an enterprise's financial condition and operating results. These measures, like financial statements, are more meaningful when compared with similar data for more than one period and with industry averages or other available data. A summary of the major analytical measures discussed in this chapter is presented below and on the following page.

Summary of Major Analytical Measures

Liquidity Analysis

(1) Current ratio	$\dfrac{\text{Current assets}}{\text{Current liabilities}}$	Measures ability to pay short-term debts.
(2) Acid-test ratio	$\dfrac{\text{Quick assets}}{\text{Current liabilities}}$	Measures immediate ability to pay short-term debts.

Activity Analysis

(3) Accounts receivable turnover	$\dfrac{\text{Net credit sales}}{\text{Average accounts receivable}}$	Measures receivable position and approximate average collection time.
(4) Number of days' sales in receivables	$\dfrac{\text{Average accounts receivable}}{\text{Average daily credit sales}}$	Measures receivable position and approximate average collection time.
(5) Inventory turnover	$\dfrac{\text{Cost of goods sold}}{\text{Average inventory}}$	Measures appropriateness of inventory levels in terms of time required to sell or "turn over" goods.
(6) Number of days' sales in inventories	$\dfrac{\text{Average inventory}}{\text{Average daily cost of goods sold}}$	Measures appropriateness of inventory levels in terms of time required to sell or "turn over" goods.
(7) Total asset turnover	$\dfrac{\text{Net sales}}{\text{Average total assets}}$	Measures effectiveness of asset utilization.

Profitability Analysis

(8) Net profit margin on sales	$\dfrac{\text{Net income}}{\text{Net sales}}$	Measures profit percentage per dollar of sales.
(9) Gross profit margin on sales	$\dfrac{\text{Gross profit}}{\text{Net sales}}$	Measures gross profit percentage per dollar of sales.
(10) Rate earned on total assets	$\dfrac{\text{Net income}}{\text{Average total assets}}$	Measures overall asset productivity.
(11) Rate earned on stockholders' equity	$\dfrac{\text{Net income}}{\text{Average stockholders' equity}}$	Measures rate of return on average stockholders' equity.

(12) Rate earned on common stockholders' equity.	$$\frac{\text{Net income — preferred dividend requirements}}{\text{Average common stockholders' equity}}$$	Measures rate of return on average common stockholders' equity.
(13) Earnings per share	$$\frac{\text{Net income — preferred dividend requirements}}{\text{Average number of shares of common stock outstanding}}$$	Measures net income per share of common stock.
(14) Dividends per share	$$\frac{\text{Dividends on common stock}}{\text{Average number of shares of common stock outstanding}}$$	Measures dividends per share of common stock.
(15) Yield on common stock	$$\frac{\text{Dividends per share of common stock}}{\text{Market value per share of common stock}}$$	Measures rate of cash return to stockholders.
(16) Price-earnings ratio	$$\frac{\text{Market price per share of common stock}}{\text{Earnings per share of common stock}}$$	Measures attractiveness of stock as an investment.

Capital Structure Analysis

(17) Equity-to-debt ratio	$$\frac{\text{Stockholders' equity}}{\text{Total liabilities}}$$	Measures use of debt to finance operations.
(18) Times interest earned	$$\frac{\text{Income before taxes and interest expense}}{\text{Interest expense}}$$	Measures ability to meet interest payments.
(19) Book value per share	$$\frac{\text{Common stockholders' equity}}{\text{Number of shares of common stock outstanding}}$$	Measures equity per share of common stock.

USE OF INDUSTRY DATA FOR COMPARATIVE ANALYSIS

As indicated earlier in the chapter, comparisons of common-size information or other measurements may be made over time within a company or with similar companies individually or in industry groups. There are many general and industry sources that can be used to obtain comparative information. The major difficulty in using comparative data is the selection of specific companies or an industry that is similar to the company being examined. The government has established a standard for classifying industries known as the **Standard Industrial Code (SIC)**. Over 800 industries are identified, and general survey information is compiled according to these codes.

If the company being analyzed operates only in one general business area, it usually isn't difficult to find a category for comparison. However, many businesses today are large, complex organizations engaged in a variety of activities that bear little relationship to each other. For example, a company might manufacture airplane engines, operate a real estate business, and manage a professional hockey team. Such companies, referred to as **diversified companies** or **conglomerates**, operate in multiple industries and do not fit any one specific industry category. Thus, comparative analysis for a highly diversified company requires either an assumption that the company operates primarily in one area or separate data for each subindustry or segment. Generally, comparisons are more meaningful when separate data for segments are analyzed, and many companies are required to include such data with their financial statements.

Segment Reporting

When a company is diversified, the different segments of the company often operate in distinct and separate markets, involve different management teams, and experience different growth patterns, profit potentials, and degrees of risk. In effect, the segments of the company behave almost like, and in some cases are, separate companies within an overall corporate structure. Yet, if only total company information is presented for a highly diversified company, the different degrees of risk, profitability, and growth potential for major segments of the company cannot be analyzed and compared.

Recognizing this problem, the FASB issued Statement No. 14, which requires disclosure of selected information for segments of diversified companies.[3] Information to be reported includes revenues, operating profit, and identifiable assets for each significant industry segment of a company. Essentially, a **segment** is considered significant if its sales, profits, or assets are 10% or more of the respective total company amounts. A practical limit of 10 segments is suggested, and at least 75% of total company sales must be accounted for. The segment data may be reported in the audited financial statements, or in a separate schedule considered an integral part of the statements. Other provisions of Statement No. 14 require disclosure of revenues from major customers and information about foreign operations and export sales.

---

[3]*Statement of Financial Accounting Standards No. 14,* "Financial Reporting for Segments of a Business Enterprise" (Stamford: Financial Accounting Standards Board, 1976).

Reporting by lines of business presents several problems. For example, how does one determine which business segments should be reported on? Certainly not all companies are organized in the same manner, even if they are engaged in similar business activities. Reporting on a particular division or profit-center in one company may not be comparable to another company. Another problem relates to transfer pricing. Not all companies use the same method of pricing goods or services that are "sold" among the different divisions or units of a company. This could lead to distorted segment profit data. Another related problem is the allocation of common costs among segments of a company. Certain costs, such as general and administrative expenses, are very difficult to assign to particular segments of a company on anything other than an arbitrary basis. This, again, could result in misleading information.

In spite of these difficulties, the accounting profession has concluded that segment reporting is necessary to assist readers of financial statements in analyzing and understanding an enterprise's past performance and future prospects and making comparisons with other companies. An example of segment reporting, from the 1985 annual report of Monsanto Company, is presented on pages 1182 and 1183. The disclosures made by General Mills in Appendix A provide another illustration of segment reporting by a diversified company.

Sources of Industry Data

Whether a company operates in one industry or in several different industries, financial analysis is enhanced if company data can be compared with industry statistics. Ratio information concerning various industries is available from different sources. These sources can be divided into two categories: (1) general sources and (2) specific industry sources. The following two general sources are kept reasonably current and are quite comprehensive:

1. Dun and Bradstreet, Inc., "Key Business Ratios"
2. Robert Morris and Associates, "Annual Statement Studies"

"Key Business Ratios" features 14 financial ratios for over 800 retailing, wholesaling, and manufacturing lines of business. The computations are made using data for over 400,000 companies. In addition, common-size statement information is provided for each line of business. "Key business ratios" is published annually, but data are collected continuously throughout the year. A sampling of data for 118 companies is contained in *Dun's Review* each November.

The second general source is Robert Morris Associates "Annual Statement Studies." Ratios for about 300 lines of business are prepared based on data furnished by member banks of Robert Morris Associates from customer-submitted financial reports. The ratios are presented for 5 years, and additional trend data are also provided. In contrast, the Dun and Bradstreet ratios and common-size data are presented for a single year. Because the submission of data for the Robert Morris publication is on a voluntary basis, the number of companies included in "Annual Statement Studies" is much lower than the number included in Dun and Bradstreet's "Key Business Ratios."

Other general sources of information include limited ratio information published occasionally in business periodicals such as *Forbes*, *Business Week*, and *Fortune*. This information is usually classified by industry and often includes rankings of factors such as growth and profitability. The annual "Fortune 500" listing and analysis of the 500 largest American companies is perhaps the best known of these sources.

Specific industry sources for comparative data include a large number of industry associations that collect, summarize, and disseminate information about their members. Often this information is of greater use in financial analysis than information from general sources because of its greater detail and more current data.

INTERPRETATION OF ANALYSES

The analyses discussed in this chapter are designed to help an analyst arrive at certain conclusions with regard to a business. As previously stated, these are merely guides to intelligent interpretation of financial data.

All ratios and measurements need not be used, but only those that will actually assist in arriving at informed conclusions with respect to questions raised. The measurements developed need to be interpreted in terms of the circumstances of a particular enterprise, the conditions of the particular industry in which the enterprise operates, and the general business and economic environment. If measurements are to be of maximum value, they need to be compared with similar data developed for the particular enterprise for past periods, with standard measurements for the industry as a whole, and with pertinent data relating to general business conditions and price fluctuations affecting the individual enterprise. Only through intelligent use and integration of the foregoing sources of data can financial weaknesses and strengths be identified and reliable opinions be developed concerning business structure, operations, and growth.

Operating Unit Segment Data

	Net Sales			Operating Income (Loss)			Research and Development		
	1985	1984	1983	1985	1984	1983	1985	1984	1983
Agricultural Products:									
Crop Chemicals	$1,073	$1,256	$1,167	$298	$438	$400	$110	$107	$ 78
Animal Sciences	79	82	83	(55)	(49)	(33)	32	22	14
Chemicals	4,051	4,360	4,148	234	336	230	128	131	112
Electronic Materials	137	220	120	(67)	4	(56)	16	14	14
Fisher Controls	652	550	535	36	27	24	20	23	13
NutraSweet	317			58			11		
Pharmaceuticals	262	15		(84)	(30)	(15)	96	24	15
Oil and Gas	172	203	241	16	27	41			
Biotechnology Product									
Discovery				(31)	(24)	(21)	31	24	21
Corporate Items and									
Eliminations	4	5	5	(54)	(52)	(49)	26*	25*	23*
Total consolidated	**$6,747**	**$6,691**	**$6,299**	**$351**	**$677**	**$521**	**$470**	**$370**	**$290**

Corporate R&D expenses are allocated on a weighted average basis of investment to operating units in determining operating income (loss).

	Total Assets			Capital Expenditures			Depreciation and Amortization		
	1985	1984	1983	1985	1984	1983	1985	1984	1983
Agricultural Products:									
Crop Chemicals	$1,061	$1,236	$1,214	$ 84	$ 88	$109	$ 89	$ 80	$ 73
Animal Sciences	174	184	187	31	31	60	21	20	16
Chemicals	2,982	3,222	3,201	291	279	213	248	273	298
Electronic Materials	302	280	253	55	47	26	37	30	28
Fisher Controls	636	536	503	53	32	29	28	21	20
NutraSweet	1,862			4			73		
Pharmaceuticals	1,438	80	3	33	7	4	39	7	1
Oil and Gas		578	543	85	107	101	59	69	85
Biotechnology Product									
Discovery	33	31	15	3	17	15	2	1	1
Nonoperating Assets	389	226	508	6	6	3	3	2	1
Total consolidated	**$8,877**	**$6,373**	**$6,427**	**$645**	**$614**	**$560**	**$599**	**$503**	**$523**

The above data should be read in conjunction with the "Segment Information" note to the financial statements on page 44.

The Company realigned its financial reporting of Operating Unit Segments to closely align with the recent reorganization and to better reflect the future direction of Monsanto's operations following the acquisition of G. D. Searle & Co. The fibers and intermediates, industrial chemicals, polymer products and most of the fabricated products businesses have been combined to form a new Chemicals segment. Two new segments, Pharmaceuticals and NutraSweet, include the acquired operations of G. D. Searle & Co. The Electronic Materials business has been made a separate segment and the separations business, previously part of fabricated products, has been transferred to and combined with Fisher Controls, because they serve similar markets. The businesses in the former Biological Sciences segment have been realigned with the animal products now being separately reported as Animal Sciences, the Health Care Division has been merged with Searle and included in the Pharmaceuticals segment and other products have been transferred to the Chemicals segment. Biotechnology Product Discovery represents the Corporate basic R&D effort in biotechnology, a major thrust of the Company.

▰▰▰Segment Information

Certain operating unit segment data for 1985–1983 appear on page 27 and are integral parts of the accompanying financial statements. The principal product lines included in each operating unit are shown in this segment data.

Sales between operating units are not significant. Inter-area sales, which are sales from one Monsanto location to another Monsanto location in a different world area, were made on a market price basis. Net sales in 1985 of businesses divested or discontinued that are included in the Chemicals segment were $645 million.

Certain corporate expenses, primarily those related to the overall management of the Company, were not allocated to the operating units or world areas. Restructuring cost — net, interest expense, interest income and other income — net, as shown in the Statement of Consolidated Income, are the only reconciling items between operating income and income before income taxes. Nonoperating assets principally include investments, a portion of cash, time deposits and certificates of deposit, short-term securities and certain miscellaneous receivables.

Net sales by entities in each world area were:

	Unaffiliated Customers			Inter-Area Between Monsanto Entities		
	1985	1984	1983	1985	1984	1983
United States	$4,824	$4,914	$4,596	$ 529	$ 534	$ 526
Europe-Africa	1,076	945	924	163	207	188
Canada	268	278	259	5	9	6
Latin America	220	203	192	2	6	4
Asia-Pacific	359	351	328	21	33	25
Eliminations				(720)	(789)	(749)
Total consolidated	**$6,747**	**$6,691**	**$6,299**	**$ —**	**$ —**	**$ —**

Operating income and total assets by entities in each world area were:

	Operating Income (Loss)			Total Assets		
	1985	1984	1983	1985	1984	1983
United States	$ 177	$ 475	$ 433	$7,077	$5,088	$5,110
Europe-Africa	164	192	137	1,019	772	696
Canada	34	25	24	120	105	92
Latin America	6	4	(4)	232	178	180
Asia-Pacific	12	31	15	299	257	203
Eliminations	12	2	(35)	(259)	(253)	(362)
Corporate expenses	(54)	(52)	(49)			
Nonoperating assets				389	226	508
Total consolidated	**$ 351**	**$ 677**	**$ 521**	**$8,877**	**$6,373**	**$6,427**

Following is a reconciliation of ex-U.S. operating income and total assets to the Company's equity in the net income and net assets of consolidated ex-U.S. subsidiaries:

	1985	1984	1983
Operating income	$ 216	$ 252	$ 172
Restructuring cost — net	14		
Interest expense	(26)	(53)	(65)
Interest income	38	36	28
Other income — net	(20)	29	36
Income taxes (including extraordinary tax benefits of loss carryforwards)	(70)	(108)	(45)
Net income of consolidated ex-U.S. subsidiaries	**$ 152**	**$ 156**	**$ 126**
Total operating assets	$1,670	$1,312	$1,171
Total liabilities	847	519	470
Net assets of consolidated ex-U.S. subsidiaries	**$ 823**	**$ 793**	**$ 701**

QUESTIONS

1. What groups may be interested in a company's financial statements?
2. What types of questions requiring financial statement analysis might be raised by external users, such as investors and creditors, as contrasted to internal management?
3. What are the factors that one would look for in judging a company's (a) liquidity, (b) stability, (c) profitability, (d) growth potential?
4. Why are comparative financial statements considered more meaningful than statements prepared for a single period? What conditions increase the usefulness of comparative statements?
5. Distinguish between horizontal and vertical analysis. What special purpose does each serve?
6. What information is provided by analysis of comparative statement of cash flows that is not available from analysis of comparative balance sheets and income statements?
7. What is meant by a *common-size* statement? What are its advantages?
8. Mention some factors that may limit the comparability of financial statements of two companies in the same industry.
9. What factors may be responsible for a change in a company's net income from one year to the next?
10. The Black Co. develops the following measurements for 1988 as compared with the year 1987. What additional information would you require before arriving at favorable or unfavorable conclusions for each item?
    (a) Net income has increased $70,000.
    (b) Sales returns and allowances have increased by $25,000.
    (c) The gross profit rate has increased by 5%.
    (d) Purchase discounts have increased by $5,000.
    (e) Working capital has increased by $85,000.
    (f) Accounts receivable have increased by $150,000.
    (g) Inventories have decreased by $100,000.
    (h) Retained earnings have decreased by $300,000.
11. Define working capital and appraise its significance.
12. Distinguish between the current ratio and the acid-test ratio.
13. Balance sheets for the Rich Corporation and the Poor Corporation each show a working capital total of $500,000. Does this indicate that the short-term liquidity of the two corporations is approximately the same? Explain.
14. (a) How is the accounts receivable turnover computed? (b) How is the number of days' purchases in accounts payable computed?
15. (a) How is the merchandise inventory turnover computed? (b) What precautions are necessary in arriving at the basis for the turnover calculation? (c) How would you interpret a rising inventory turnover rate?
16. The ratio of stockholders' equity to total liabilities offers information about the long-term stability of a business. Explain.
17. Indicate how each of the following measurements is calculated and appraise its significance:

(a) The number of times bond interest requirements were earned.
(b) The number of times preferred dividend requirements were earned.
(c) The rate of earnings on the common stockholders' equity.
(d) The earnings per share on common stock.
(e) The price-earnings ratio on common stock.
(f) The dividends per share on common stock.
(g) The yield on common stock.

18. Under what circumstances is the use of industry ratios beneficial in analyzing a company's activity?

19. (a) What are the principal sources of industry data for use in comparative analysis? (b) What are the advantages and disadvantages of each source?

20. In what ways can segment information assist in the analysis of a company's financial statements?

DISCUSSION CASES

CASE 26–1   (How should we finance our expansion?)

The Krogstad Co. is considering expanding its operations. The company's balance sheet at December 31, 1987, is presented below.

Krogstad Co.
Balance Sheet
December 31, 1987

Assets		Liabilities		
Cash	$ 335,000	Accounts payable	$ 300,000	
Accounts receivable	385,000	Bonds payable	1,100,000	
Inventory	420,000	Total liabilities		$1,400,000
Land	800,000	Stockholders' Equity		
Buildings and equipment (net)	460,000	Preferred stock, 8% cumu-		
		lative, par $100	$ 300,000	
		Common stock, par $25	400,000	
		Retained earnings	300,000	
		Total stockholders' equity		1,000,000
		Total liabilities and stock-		
Total assets	$2,400,000	holders' equity		$2,400,000

Each $1,000 bond is convertible at the option of the bondholder to 40 shares of common stock. The bonds carry an interest rate of 12%, and are callable at 100. The company's 1987 income before taxes was $825,000 and was $500,000 after taxes. The preferred stock is callable at par. The common stock has a market price of $60 per share.

The company's management has identified several alternatives to raise $1,000,000.

(a) Issue additional bonds.
(b) Call in the convertible bonds to force conversion and then issue additional bonds.

(c) Issue additional 8% cumulative preferred stock.
(d) Issue additional common stock.

Evaluate the company's leverage position and discuss the advantages and disadvantages of each alternative.

CASE 26–2   (Analyzing earnings)

Marty Feldman owns two businesses: a drug store and a retail department store. The investment in land, buildings, and equipment is approximately the same in either business.

Drug Store		Department Store	
Net sales................	$1,050,000	Net sales................	$670,000
Cost of goods sold........	1,000,000	Cost of goods sold	600,000
Average inventory	50,000	Average inventory	200,000
Operating expenses.......	39,500	Operating expenses	36,500

Which business earns more income? Which business earns a higher return on its investment in inventory? Which business would you consider more profitable?

CASE 26–3   (Evaluating alternative investments)

Dana Oman is considering investing $10,000 and wishes to know which of two companies offers the better alternative.

The Astro Company earned net income of $63,000 last year on average total assets of $280,000, and average stockholders' equity of $210,000. The company's shares are selling on the market at $100 per share; 6,300 shares of common stock are outstanding.

The Bellini Company earned $24,375 last year on average total assets of $125,000 and average stockholders' equity of $100,000. The company's common shares are selling on the market at $78 per share; 2,500 shares are outstanding.

Which stock should Oman buy?

CASE 26–4   (Should the FASB set standards for financial ratios?)

Financial ratios can be computed using many different formulas. In an article in the *CPA Journal*, the author recommends that the FASB become involved in identifying common formulas and ratios that would be included in all financial statements. What are the advantages in pursuing such a recommendation? What are the difficulties?

EXERCISES

EXERCISE 26–1   (Index numbers)

Sales for the Genovese Company for a 5-year period and an industry sales index for this period are listed at the top of the next page. Convert both series into indexes employing 1984 as the base year.

	1988	1987	1986	1985	1984
Sales of Genovese Company (in thousands of dollars)	$8,400	$9,030	$8,710	$8,850	$8,530
Industry sales index (1974–78 = 100)	190	212	210	170	158

EXERCISE 26–2 (Comparative cost of goods sold schedule)

Cost of goods sold data for J. Ellis and Sons are presented below:

	1987–88	1986–87
Inventory, July 1	$ 75,000	$ 60,000
Purchases	410,000	320,000
Goods available for sale	$485,000	$380,000
Less inventory, June 30	55,000	75,000
Cost of goods sold	$430,000	$305,000

Prepare a comparative schedule of cost of goods sold showing dollar and percentage changes. Round to nearest whole percentage.

EXERCISE 26–3 (Vertical analysis)

The financial position of the Harnick Co. at the end of 1988 and 1987 is as follows:

	1988	1987
Assets		
Current assets	$ 70,000	$ 60,000
Long-term investments	15,000	14,000
Land, buildings, and equipment (net)	100,000	75,000
Intangible assets	10,000	10,000
Other assets	5,000	6,000
Total assets	$200,000	$165,000
Liabilities		
Current liabilities	$ 30,000	$ 35,000
Long-term liabilities	88,000	62,000
Total liabilities	$118,000	$ 97,000
Stockholders' Equity		
Preferred 8% stock	$ 10,000	$ 9,000
Common stock	54,000	42,000
Additional paid-in capital	5,000	5,000
Retained earnings	13,000	12,000
Total stockholders' equity	$ 82,000	$ 68,000
Total liabilities and stockholders' equity	$200,000	$165,000

Prepare a comparative balance sheet including a percentage analysis of component items in terms of total assets and total liabilities and stockholders' equity for each year. (Common-size statement) Round to nearest whole percentage.

EXERCISE 26–4   (Liquidity ratios)

The following data are taken from the comparative balance sheet prepared for the Meyer Company:

	1988	1987
Cash	$ 20,000	$ 10,000
Marketable securities (net)	9,000	35,000
Trade receivables (net)	43,000	30,000
Inventories	65,000	50,000
Prepaid expenses	3,000	2,000
Land, buildings, and equipment (net)	79,000	75,000
Intangible assets	10,000	15,000
Other assets	7,000	8,000
	$236,000	$225,000
Current liabilities	$ 80,000	$ 60,000

(1) From the data given, compute for 1988 and 1987: (a) the working capital, (b) the current ratio, (c) the acid-test ratio, (d) the ratio of current assets to total assets, (e) the ratio of cash to current liabilities.
(2) Evaluate each of the changes.

EXERCISE 26–5   (Analysis of inventory position)

Income statements for the Marion Sales Co. show the following:

	1988	1987	1986
Sales	$125,000	$100,000	$75,000
Cost of goods sold:			
Beginning inventory	$ 30,000	$ 25,000	$ 5,000
Purchases	105,000	80,000	85,000
	$135,000	$105,000	$90,000
Ending inventory	45,000	30,000	25,000
	$ 90,000	$ 75,000	$65,000
Gross profit on sales	$ 35,000	$ 25,000	$10,000

Give whatever measurements may be developed in analyzing the inventory position at the end of each year. What conclusions would you make concerning the inventory trend?

EXERCISE 26–6   (Analysis of accounts payable)

The total purchases of goods by The Wallace Company during 1987 were $720,000. All purchases were on a 2/10, n/30 basis. The average balance in the vouchers payable account was $76,000. Was the company prompt, slow, or average in paying for goods? How many days' average purchases were there in accounts payable, assuming a 360-day year?

EXERCISE 26–7   (Inventory turnover)

The following data are taken from the Kiger Corporation records for the years ending December 31, 1988, 1987, and 1986.

	1988	1987	1986
Finished goods inventory	$ 60,000	$ 40,000	$ 30,000
Goods in process inventory	60,000	65,000	60,000
Raw materials inventory	60,000	40,000	35,000
Sales...................................	400,000	340,000	300,000
Cost of goods sold.....................	225,000	230,000	210,000
Cost of good manufactured	260,000	250,000	200,000
Raw materials used in production........	150,000	130,000	120,000

(1) Compute turnover rates for 1988 and for 1987 for (a) finished goods, (b) goods in process, and (c) raw materials.
(2) Analyze the turnover results as to reasonableness, and the message they provide to a statement reader.

EXERCISE 26–8   (Analysis of capital structure)

The McMillan Corporation estimates that pretax earnings for the year ended December 31, 1987, will be $200,000 if it operates without borrowed capital. Income tax is 40% of earnings. There are 15,000 shares of common stock outstanding for the entire year. Assuming that the company is able to borrow $1,200,000 at 12% interest, indicate the effects on net income if borrowed capital earns (1) 20%, and (2) 10%. Explain the cause of the variations.

EXERCISE 26–9   (Profitability analysis)

The balance sheets for the Marquis Corp. showed long-term liabilities and stockholders' equity balances at the end of each year as given below:

	1988	1987	1986
10% Bonds payable	$ 600,000	$600,000	$600,000
Preferred 8% stock, $100 par...........	600,000	400,000	400,000
Common stock, $25 par	1,200,000	900,000	900,000
Additional paid-in capital	150,000	100,000	100,000
Retained earnings.....................	300,000	100,000	50,000

Net income after income tax was: 1988, $260,000; 1987, $160,000. Using the foregoing data, compute for each year:
(a) The rate of earnings on average total stockholders' equity.
(b) The number of times bond interest requirements were earned (income after tax).
(c) The number of times preferred dividend requirements were earned.
(d) The rate earned on average common stockholders' equity.
(e) The earnings per share on common stock.

EXERCISE 26–10   (Inventory turnover)

The controller of the Chou Manufacturing Co. wishes to analyze the activity of the finished goods, goods in process, and raw materials inventories. The following information is produced for the analysis.

Finished goods inventory, 12/31/87.........................	$112,500
Finished goods inventory, 12/31/88.........................	215,000
Goods in process inventory, 12/31/87......................	211,000
Goods in process inventory, 12/31/88......................	239,000
Raw materials inventory, 12/31/87.........................	140,000

Raw materials inventory, 12/31/88..........................	$175,000
Cost of goods sold, 1988...................................	245,000
Cost of goods manufactured, 1988	306,000
Cost of materials used, 1988	250,000

(1) Compute the inventory turnovers.
(2) Based upon the foregoing data and the turnover computations, evaluate the company's control over inventories.

EXERCISE 26–11 (Return on stockholders' equity)

Fay Cutler wishes to know which of two companies will yield the greater rate of return on an investment in common stock. Financial information for 1987 for the Carter Company and the Lujan Company is presented below:

	Carter Co.	Lujan Co.
Net income.....................................	$ 140,000	$ 293,000
Preferred stock (7%)	600,000	970,000
Common stockholders' equity:		
January 1, 1987	1,450,000	2,505,000
December 31, 1987	1,350,000	2,670,000

Determine which company earned the greater return on common stockholders' equity in 1987.

EXERCISE 26–12 (Analysis of financial data)

For each of the following numbered items, you are to select the letter items that indicate its effects on the corporation's statements. Indicate your choice by giving the letters identifying the effects that you select. If there is no appropriate response among the effects listed, leave the item blank. If more than one effect is applicable to a particular item, be sure to list *all* applicable letters. (Assume the state statutes do not permit declaration of nonliquidating dividends except from earnings.)

Item

(1) Declaration of a cash dividend due in one month on preferred stock.
(2) Declaration and payment of an ordinary stock dividend.
(3) Receipt of a cash dividend, not previously recorded, on stock of another corporation.
(4) Passing of a dividend on preferred stock.
(5) Receipt of preferred shares as a dividend on stock held as a temporary investment. This was not a regularly recurring dividend.
(6) Payment of dividend mentioned in (1).
(7) Issue of new common shares in a 5-for-1 stock split.

Effect

A. Reduces working capital.
B. Increases working capital.
C. Reduces current ratio.
D. Increases current ratio.
E. Reduces the dollar amount of total capital stock.
F. Increases the dollar amount of total capital stock.
G. Reduces total retained earnings.
H. Increases total retained earnings.
I. Reduces equity per share of common stock.
J. Reduces equity of each common stockholder.

(AICPA adapted)

EXERCISE 26–13   (Analysis of financial data)

The December 31, 1987 balance sheet of Kroton Inc. is presented on the next page. These are the only accounts in Kroton's balance sheet. Amounts indicated by a question mark (?) can be calculated from the additional information given.

Assets		Liabilities and Stockholders' Equity	
Cash	$ 25,000	Accounts payable (trade)	$?
Accounts receivable (net)	?	Income taxes payable (current)..........	25,000
Inventory...............................	?	Long-term debt........................	?
Property, plant, and equipment (net)......	294,000	Common stock	300,000
		Retained earnings	?
	$432,000		$?

Additional information:

Current ratio (at year end)	1.5 to 1
Total liabilities divided by total stockholders' equity	.8
Inventory turnover based on sales and ending inventory....................	15 times
Inventory turnover based on cost of goods sold and ending inventory........	10.5 times
Gross margin for 1987	$315,000

(1) What was Kroton's December 31, 1987 balance in trade accounts payable?
    (a) $67,000.   (b) $92,000.   (c) $182,000.   (d) $207,000.
(2) What was Kroton's December 31, 1987 balance in retained earnings?
    (a) $60,000 deficit.   (b) $60,000.   (c) $132,000 deficit.   (d) $132,000.
(3) What was Kroton's December 31, 1987 balance in the inventory account?
    (a) $21,000.   (b) $30,000.   (c) $70,000.   (d) $135,000.

(AICPA adapted)

PROBLEMS

PROBLEM 26–1   (Comparative statements)

Operations for the Nyman Company for 1988 and 1987 are summarized below:

	1988	1987
Sales...	$500,000	$450,000
Sales returns..................................	20,000	10,000
Net sales	$480,000	$440,000
Cost of goods sold	350,000	240,000
Gross profit on sales	$130,000	$200,000
Selling and general expenses	100,000	120,000
Operating income..............................	$ 30,000	$ 80,000
Other expenses................................	35,000	30,000
Income (loss) before income tax.................	$ (5,000)	$ 50,000
Income tax (refund)	(2,000)	20,000
Net income (loss)	$ (3,000)	$ 30,000

Instructions:
(1) Prepare a comparative income statement showing dollar changes and percentage changes for 1988 as compared with 1987.
(2) Prepare a comparative income statement offering a percentage analysis of component revenue and expense items of net sales for each year.
(3) Based on the above percentages, prepare an analysis of Nyman's operations for 1987 and 1988.

PROBLEM 26–2 (Common-size statements)

Balance sheet data for the Stay-Trim Company and the Tone-Up Company are as follows:

	Stay-Trim Company	Tone-Up Company
Assets		
Current assets.	$ 51,000	$ 240,000
Long-term investments	5,000	280,000
Land, buildings, and equipment (net).	48,000	520,000
Intangible assets.	6,000	100,000
Other assets	5,000	60,000
Total assets	$115,000	$1,200,000
Liabilities		
Current liabilities	$ 15,000	$ 180,000
Long-term liabilities.	25,000	300,000
Deferred revenues	5,000	70,000
Total liabilities	$ 45,000	$ 550,000
Stockholders' Equity		
Preferred stock	$ 5,000	$ 100,000
Common stock	30,000	200,000
Additional paid-in capital	25,000	185,000
Retained earnings.	10,000	165,000
Total stockholders' equity	$ 70,000	$ 650,000
Total liabilities and stockholders' equity	$115,000	$1,200,000

Instructions:
(1) Prepare a common-size statement comparing balance sheet data for the year.
(2) What analytical conclusions can be drawn from this comparative common-size statement?

PROBLEM 26–3 (Index numbers)

Sales for Tsai Mfg. Co. and its chief competitor, the Fuota Company, and the sales index for the industry, are as follows:

	1988	1987	1986	1985	1984
Sales of Tsai Mfg. Co. (in thousands of dollars) . . .	$ 7,000	$7,280	$7,735	$8,450	$8,385
Sales of Fuota Company (in thousands of dollars).	$10,100	$9,690	$9,975	$9,785	$9,880
Industry sales index (1979 = 100)	140	152	161	144	133

Instructions:
(1) Convert the three series to index numbers using 1984 as the base year.
(2) Prepare a short report for the management of Tsai Mfg. Co. summarizing your findings.

PROBLEM 26–4 (Computation of various ratios)

The balance sheet data for the Outboard Marine Corp. on December 31, 1987, are as follows:

Assets		Liabilities and Stockholders' Equity	
Cash	$ 120,000	Notes and accounts payable	$ 130,000
Marketable securities	25,000	Income tax payable	40,000
Notes and accounts receivable (net)	175,000	Wages and interest payable	10,000
Inventories	600,000	Dividends payable	25,000
Prepaid expenses	15,000	Bonds payable	400,000
Bond redemption fund (securities of		Deferred revenues	30,000
other companies	400,000	Common stock $20 par	1,200,000
Land, buildings, and equipment (net)	730,000	Preferred 6% stock, $20 par (noncumu-	
Intangible assets	420,000	lative, liquidating value at par)	200,000
	$2,485,000	Retained earnings appropriated for plant	
		expansion	200,000
		Retained earnings	250,000
			$2,485,000

Instructions: From the balance sheet data, compute the following:
(1) The amount of working capital.
(2) The current ratio.
(3) The acid-test ratio.
(4) The ratio of current assets to total assets.
(5) The ratio of stockholders' equity to total liabilities.
(6) The ratio of land, buildings, and equipment to bonds payable.
(7) The book value per share of common stock.

PROBLEM 26–5 (Liquidity analysis)

The following are comparative data for Silver State Equipment, Inc. for the 3-year period 1986–1988.

Income Statement Data

	1988	1987	1986
Net sales	$1,200,000	$900,000	$1,020,000
Cost of goods sold	760,000	600,000	610,000
Gross profit on sales	$ 440,000	$300,000	$ 410,000
Selling, general, and other expenses	340,000	280,000	250,000
Operating income	$ 100,000	$ 20,000	$ 160,000
Income tax	40,000	9,000	72,000
Net income	$ 60,000	$ 11,000	$ 88,000
Dividends paid	35,000	30,000	30,000
Net increase (decrease in retained earnings	$ 25,000	$ (19,000)	$ 58,000

Balance Sheet Data

	1988	1987	1986
Assets			
Cash.................................	$ 50,000	$ 40,000	$ 75,000
Trade notes and accounts receivable			
(net)	300,000	320,000	250,000
Inventory (at cost)	380,000	420,000	350,000
Prepaid expenses	30,000	10,000	40,000
Land, buildings, and equipment (net).......	760,000	600,000	690,000
Intangible assets	110,000	100,000	125,000
Other assets	70,000	10,000	20,000
	$1,700,000	$1,500,000	$1,550,000
Liabilities and Stockholders' Equity			
Trade notes and accounts payable	$ 120,000	$ 185,000	$ 220,000
Wages, interest, dividends payable	25,000	25,000	25,000
Income tax payable	29,000	5,000	30,000
Miscellaneous current liabilities............	10,000	4,000	10,000
8% bonds payable.......................	300,000	300,000	250,000
Deferred revenues......................	10,000	10,000	25,000
Preferred 6% stock, cumulative, $100 par			
and liquidating value	200,000	200,000	200,000
No-par common stock, $10 stated value....	500,000	400,000	400,000
Additional paid-in capital..................	310,000	200,000	200,000
Retained earnings — appropriated	90,500	60,000	60,000
Retained earnings — unappropriated	105,500	111,000	130,000
	$1,700,000	$1,500,000	$1,550,000

Instructions:

(1) From the foregoing data, calculate comparative measurements for 3 years, 1986–1988 as follows: (for ratios using averages, assume 1985 figures are the same as 1986)
   (a) The amount of working capital.
   (b) The current ratio.
   (c) The acid-test ratio.
   (d) The average days' sales in trade receivables at the end of the year (assume a 360-day year and all sales on a credit basis).
   (e) The trade payables turnover rate for the year.
   (f) The inventory turnover rate.
   (g) The number of days' sales in the inventory at the end of the year.
   (h) The ratio of stockholders' equity to total liabilities.
   (i) The ratio of land, buildings, and equipment to bonds payable.
   (j) The ratio of stockholders' equity to land, buildings, and equipment.
   (k) The book value per share of common stock.
(2) Based on the measurements made in (1), evaluate the liquidity position of Silver State Equipment, Inc. at the end 1988 as compared with the end of 1987.

PROBLEM 26–6 (Profitability analysis)

Use the comparative data for Silver State Equipment, Inc. as given in Problem 26–5.

Instructions:
(1) Compute comparative measurements for the 3 years 1986–1988 as follows:
   (a) The ratio of net sales to average total assets.
   (b) The ratio of net sales to average land, buildings, and equipment.
   (c) The rate earned on net sales.
   (d) The gross profit rate on net sales.
   (e) The rate earned on average total assets.
   (f) The rate earned on average stockholders' equity.
   (g) The number of times bond interest requirements were earned (before income tax).
   (h) The number of times preferred dividend requirements were earned.
   (i) The rate earned on average common stockholders' equity.
   (j) The earnings per share on common stock.
(2) Based on the measurements made in (1), evaluate the profitability of Silver State Equipment, Inc. for 1988 as compared with 1987 and 1986.

PROBLEM 26–7   (Analysis of inventory, receivables, and payables)

Inventory and receivable balances and also gross profit data for Golden Arrow Co. appear below:

	1988	1987	1986
Balance sheet data:			
Inventory, December 31	$100,000	$ 90,000	$ 80,000
Accounts receivable, December 31........	60,000	50,000	20,000
Accounts payable, December 31..........	70,000	60,000	45,000
Net purchases..........................	140,000	110,000	80,000
Income statement data:			
Net sales	$320,000	$270,000	$250,000
Cost of goods sold.....................	225,000	200,000	180,000
Gross profit on sales	$ 95,000	$ 70,000	$ 70,000

Instructions: Assuming a 300-day business year and all sales on a credit basis, compute the following measurements for 1988 and 1987.
(1) The receivables turnover rate.
(2) The average days' sales in receivables at the end of the year.
(3) The inventory turnover rate.
(4) The number of days' sales in inventory at the end of the year.
(5) The accounts payable turnover rate.

PROBLEM 26–8   (Comprehensive analysis of financial data)

The partially condensed financial statements for Variety Company are shown on pages 1196 and 1197.

Variety Company
Balance Sheet
December 31, 1987

Cash......	$ 63,000
Trade receivables, less estimated uncollectibles of $12,000............	238,000
Inventories......	170,000
Prepaid expenses	7,000
Land, buildings, and equipment, cost less $182,000 charged to operations	390,000
Other assets	13,000
	$881,000

Liabilities and Stockholders' Equity

Accounts and notes payable — trade......	$ 98,000
Accrued liabilities payable	17,000
Income tax payable......	18,000
First-mortgage, 7% bonds, due in 1994......	150,000
$7 Preferred stock — no par value (entitled to $110 per share in liquidation); authorized 1,000 shares; in treasury 400 shares; outstanding 600 shares......	108,000
Common stock — no par; authorized 100,000 shares, issued and outstanding 10,000 shares stated at a nominal value of $10 per share......	100,000
Paid-in capital from sale of common stock at more than stated value	242,000
Retained earnings appropriated for plant expansion......	50,000
Retained earnings appropriated for cost of treasure stock	47,000
Retained earnings	98,000
Cost of 400 shares of treasury stock......	(47,000)
	$881,000

Notes: (1) Working capital — December 31, 1986, was $205,000. (2) Trade receivables — December 31, 1986, were $220,000 gross, $206,000 net. (3) Dividends for 1987 have been declared and paid. (4) There has been no change in amount of bonds outstanding during 1987.

Instructions: For each item listed below select the best answer from the approximate answers. Indicate your choice by giving the appropriate letter for each. Give the calculations in support of each choice.

Items To Be Computed	Approximate Answers				
	(a)	(b)	(c)	(d)	(e)
(1) Acid test ratio	3.2:1	2.3:1	2.9:1	2.4:1	3.07:1
(2) Average number of days' charge sales uncollected......	86	94	103	100	105
(3) Average finished goods turnover......	7	10.1	10.3	9.7	6.7
(4) Number of times bond interest was earned (before tax)	4.81	6.83	6.52	10.3	5.92
(5) Number of times preferred dividend was earned.......	5.71	8.3	13.8	9.52	8.52

Variety Company
Income Statement
For the Year Ended December 31, 1987

	Cash	Credit	Total
Gross sales................................	$116,000	$876,000	$992,000
Less: Sales discount.........................	$ 3,000	$ 12,000	$ 15,000
Sales returns and allowances............	1,000	6,000	7,000
	$ 4,000	$ 18,000	$ 22,000
Net sales..................................	$112,000	$858,000	$970,000
Cost of goods sold:			
Inventory of finished goods, January 1		$ 92,000	
Cost of goods manufactured		680,000	
Inventory of finished goods, December 31		(100,000)	672,000
Gross profit on sales........................			$298,000
Selling expenses		$173,000	
General expenses		70,000	243,000
Income from operations			$ 55,000
Other additions and deductions (net)...........			3,000
Income before income tax			$ 58,000
Income tax (estimated)......................			18,000
Net income			$ 40,000

Items To Be Computed	Approximate Answers				
	(a)	(b)	(c)	(d)	(e)
(6) Earnings per share of common stock	$4.00	$3.30	$3.58	$5.10	$5.38
(7) Book value per share of common stock...............	$33.80	$35.00	$49.80	$48.80	$53.20
(8) Current ratio	3.6:1	1:2.7	2.7:1	4.2:1	1:3.6

(AICPA adapted)

PROBLEM 26–9 (Financial statement analysis)

Gro-More Corporations management is concerned over the corporation's current financial position and return on investment. They request your assistance in analyzing their financial statements and furnish the following information:

Schedule of Working Capital — December 31, 1987

Current liabilities....................................		$223,050
Less current assets:		
Cash..	$ 5,973	
Accounts receivable (net)	70,952	
Inventory......................................	113,125	190,050
Working capital deficit		$ 33,000

Gro-More
Income Statement
For Year Ended December 31, 1987

Sales (90,500 units)...	$760,200
Cost of goods sold...	452,500
Gross profit	$307,700
Selling and general expenses, including depreciation of $22,980 ...	155,660
Income before income tax....................................	$152,040
Income tax...	68,418
Net income...	$ 83,622

Assets other than current assets consist of land, buildings, and equipment with a book value of $352,950 on December 31, 1987.

Sales of 100,000 units are forecasted for 1988. Within this relevant range of activity, costs are estimated as follows (excluding income tax):

	Fixed Costs	Variable Costs per Unit
Cost of goods sold.......................................		$4.90
Selling and general expenses, including depreciation of		
$15,450	$129,720	1.10
Total	$129,720	$6.00

The income tax rate is expected to be 40%. Past experience indicates that current assets vary in direct proportion to sales.

Instructions:
(1) Assuming Gro-More Corporation operates 360 days per year, compute the following (show your computations):
   (a) Number of days' sales uncollected.
   (b) Inventory turnover.
   (c) Number of days' operations to cover the working capital deficit.
   (d) Return on total assets as a product of asset turnover and the net income ratio (sometimes called profit margin).
(2) Management feels that in 1988 the market will support a sales price of $8.30 at a sales volume of 100,000 units. Compute the rate of return on book value of total assets after income tax assuming management's expectations are realized.   (AICPA adapted)

PROBLEM 26–10   (Comprehensive financial statement analysis)

Financial analysis is often applied to test the reasonableness of the relationships among current financial data against those of prior financial data. Given prior financial relationships and a few key amounts, a CPA could prepare estimates of current financial data to test the reasonableness of data furnished by a client. Four Seasons Corporation has in recent years maintained the following relationships among the data on its financial statements.

Gross profit on net sales....................................	40%
Net profit rate on net sales..................................	10%
Rate of selling expenses to net sales........................	20%
Accounts receivable turnover................................	8 per year
Inventory turnover...	6 per year
Acid-test ratio..	2 to 1
Current ratio...	3 to 1
Quick-asset composition: 8% cash, 32% marketable securities, 60% accounts receivable	
Asset turnover...	2 per year
Ratio of total assets to intangible assets......................	20 to 1
Ratio of accumulated depreciation to cost of fixed assets.........	1 to 3
Ratio of accounts receivable to accounts payable...............	1.5 to 1
Ratio of working capital to stockholders' equity.................	1 to 1.6
Ratio of total liabilities to stockholders' equity..................	1 to 2

The corporation had a net income of $120,000 for 1987, which resulted in earnings of $5.20 per share of common stock. Additional information includes the following:

(a) Capital stock authorized, issued (all in 1979), and outstanding: Common, $10 per share par value, issued at 10% premium; 8% Preferred, $100 per share par value, issued at a 10% premium.

(b) Market value per share of common at December 31, 1987, $78.

(c) Preferred dividends paid in 1987, $3,000.

(d) Number of times interest earned in 1987, 21.

(e) The amounts of the following were the same at December 31, 1987 as at January 1, 1987. Inventory, accounts receivable, 10% bonds payable — due 1989, and total stockholders' equity.

(f) All purchases and sales were "on account."

Instructions:

(1) Prepare in good form: (a) the condensed balance sheet and (b) the condensed income statement for the year ending December 31, 1987, presenting the amounts you would expect to appear on Four Seasons' financial statements (ignoring income tax). Major captions appearing on Four Seasons' balance sheet are: Current assets, Fixed assets, Intangible assets, Current liabilities, Long-term liabilities, and Stockholders' equity. In addition to the accounts divulged in the problem, you should include accounts for prepaid expenses, miscellaneous expenses payable, and administrative expenses. Supporting computations should be in good form.

(2) Compute the following for 1987 (show your computations):

(a) Rate of return on stockholders' equity.

(b) Price-earnings ratio for common stock.

(c) Dividends paid per share of common stock.

(d) Dividends paid per share of preferred stock.

(e) Yield on common stock.   (AICPA adapted)

APPENDIX A
Illustrative Financial Statements

Report of Management Responsibilities

The management of General Mills, Inc., includes corporate executives, operating managers, controllers and other personnel working full time on company business. These people are responsible for the fairness and accuracy of our financial statements. The statements have been prepared in accordance with generally accepted accounting principles, using management's best estimates and judgments where appropriate. The financial information throughout this report is consistent with our financial statements.

Management has established a system of internal control which we believe provides reasonable assurance that, in all material respects, assets are maintained and accounted for in accordance with management's authorizations, and transactions are recorded accurately on our books.

Our internal audit program is designed for constant evaluation of the adequacy and effectiveness of the internal controls. Audits measure adherence to established policies and procedures. Our formally stated and communicated policies demand high ethical standards of employees.

The Audit Committee of the Board of Directors is composed solely of outside directors. The Committee meets periodically with management, internal auditors and independent public accountants to review the work of each and to satisfy itself that the respective parties are properly discharging their responsibilities. Independent public accountants, internal auditors and the Controller have full and free access to the Audit Committee at any time.

Peat, Marwick, Mitchell & Co., independent certified public accountants, are retained to examine the con-solidated financial statements. Their opinion follows.

H. B. Atwater, Jr.
H. B. Atwater, Jr.
Chairman of the Board of Directors and Chief Executive Officer

Mark H. Willes
Mark H. Willes
Executive Vice President and Chief Financial Officer

Auditors' Report

The Stockholders and the Board of Directors of General Mills, Inc.:

We have examined the consolidated balance sheets of General Mills, Inc. and subsidiaries as of May 26, 1985 and May 27, 1984 and the related consolidated statements of earnings, retained earnings and changes in financial position for each of the fiscal years in the three-year period ended May 26, 1985. Our examinations were made in accord-ance with generally accepted auditing standards and, accordingly, included such tests of the accounting records and such other auditing procedures as we considered necessary in the circumstances.

In our opinion, the aforementioned consolidated financial statements present fairly the financial position of General Mills, Inc. and subsidiaries at May 26, 1985 and May 27, 1984 and the results of their operations and the changes in their financial position for each of the fiscal years in the three-year period ended May 26, 1985, in conformity with generally accepted accounting principles applied on a consistent basis.

Peat, Marwick, Mitchell & Co.
Minneapolis, Minnesota
July 19, 1985

Consolidated Statements of Earnings

General Mills, Inc., and Subsidiaries

(Amounts in Millions, Except Per Share Data)		Fiscal Year Ended		
		May 26, 1985 (52 Weeks)	May 27, 1984 (52 Weeks)	May 29, 1983 (52 Weeks)
CONTINUING OPERATIONS: SALES		$4,285.2	$4,118.4	$4,082.3
COSTS AND EXPENSES:	Cost of sales, exclusive of items below	2,474.8	2,432.8	2,394.8
	Selling, general and administrative expenses	1,368.1	1,251.5	1,288.3
	Depreciation and amortization expenses	110.4	99.0	94.2
	Interest expense	60.2	31.5	39.5
	TOTAL COSTS AND EXPENSES	4,013.5	3,814.8	3,816.8
EARNINGS FROM CONTINUING OPERATIONS—PRETAX		271.7	303.6	265.5
GAIN (LOSS) FROM REDEPLOYMENTS		(75.8)	53.0	2.7
EARNINGS FROM CONTINUING OPERATIONS AFTER REDEPLOYMENTS—PRETAX		195.9	356.6	268.2
INCOME TAXES		80.5	153.9	106.1
EARNINGS FROM CONTINUING OPERATIONS AFTER REDEPLOYMENTS		115.4	202.7	162.1
EARNINGS PER SHARE—CONTINUING OPERATIONS AFTER REDEPLOYMENTS		$ 2.58	$ 4.32	$ 3.24
DISCONTINUED OPERATIONS AFTER TAX		(188.3)	30.7	83.0
NET EARNINGS (LOSS)		$ (72.9)	$ 233.4	$ 245.1
NET EARNINGS (LOSS) PER SHARE		$ (1.63)	$ 4.98	$ 4.89
AVERAGE NUMBER OF COMMON SHARES		44.7	46.9	50.1

Consolidated Statements of Retained Earnings

(Amounts in Millions, Except Per Share Data)	Fiscal Year Ended		
	May 26, 1985 (52 Weeks)	May 27, 1984 (52 Weeks)	May 29, 1983 (52 Weeks)
RETAINED EARNINGS AT BEGINNING OF YEAR	$1,375.0	$1,237.6	$1,085.2
Net earnings (loss)	(72.9)	233.4	245.1
Deduct dividends of $2.24 per share in 1985, $2.04 per share in 1984 and $1.84 per share in 1983	(100.4)	(96.0)	(92.7)
RETAINED EARNINGS AT END OF YEAR	$1,201.7	$1,375.0	$1,237.6

See accompanying notes to consolidated financial statements.

Consolidated Balance Sheets
General Mills, Inc., and Subsidiaries

Assets	(In Millions)	Fiscal Year Ended	
		May 26, 1985	May 27, 1984
CURRENT ASSETS:	Cash and short-term investments	$ 66.8	$ 66.0
	Receivables, less allowance for doubtful accounts of $4.0 in 1985 and $18.8 in 1984	284.5	550.6
	Inventories	377.7	661.7
	Investments in tax leases	—	49.6
	Prepaid expenses	40.1	43.6
	Net assets of discontinued operations and redeployments	517.5	18.4
	TOTAL CURRENT ASSETS	1,286.6	1,389.9
LAND, BUILDINGS AND EQUIPMENT, AT COST:	Land	93.3	125.9
	Buildings	524.4	668.6
	Equipment	788.1	904.7
	Construction in progress	80.2	130.0
	Total Land, Buildings and Equipment	1,486.0	1,829.2
	Less accumulated depreciation	(530.0)	(599.8)
	NET LAND, BUILDINGS AND EQUIPMENT	956.0	1,229.4
OTHER ASSETS:	Net noncurrent assets of businesses to be spun off	206.5	—
	Intangible assets, principally goodwill	50.8	146.0
	Investments and miscellaneous assets	162.7	92.8
	TOTAL OTHER ASSETS	420.0	238.8
TOTAL ASSETS		$2,662.6	$2,858.1

Liabilities and Stockholders' Equity			
CURRENT LIABILITIES:	Accounts payable	$ 360.8	$ 477.8
	Current portion of long-term debt	59.4	60.3
	Notes payable	379.8	251.0
	Accrued taxes	1.4	74.3
	Accrued payroll	91.8	119.1
	Other current liabilities	164.0	162.9
	TOTAL CURRENT LIABILITIES	1,057.2	1,145.4
LONG-TERM DEBT		449.5	362.6
DEFERRED INCOME TAXES		29.8	76.5
DEFERRED INCOME TAXES—TAX LEASES		60.8	—
OTHER LIABILITIES AND DEFERRED CREDITS		42.0	49.0
	TOTAL LIABILITIES	1,639.3	1,633.5
STOCKHOLDERS' EQUITY:	Common stock	213.7	215.4
	Retained earnings	1,201.7	1,375.0
	Less common stock in treasury, at cost	(333.9)	(291.8)
	Cumulative foreign currency adjustment	(58.2)	(74.0)
	TOTAL STOCKHOLDERS' EQUITY	1,023.3	1,224.6
TOTAL LIABILITIES AND STOCKHOLDERS' EQUITY		$2,662.6	$2,858.1

See accompanying notes to consolidated financial statements.

Consolidated Statements of Changes in Financial Position
General Mills, Inc., and Subsidiaries

(In Millions)		May 26, 1985 (52 Weeks)	Fiscal Year Ended May 27, 1984 (52 Weeks)	May 29, 1983 (52 Weeks)
FUNDS PROVIDED FROM (USED FOR) OPERATIONS:	Net earnings from continuing operations after redeployments	$ 115.4	$ 202.7	$ 162.1
	Depreciation and amortization	110.4	99.0	94.2
	Deferred income taxes	(19.4)	(17.2)	26.4
	(Gain) loss from redeployment program, net	44.0	(28.5)	(.8)
	Other	(9.1)	.4	2.6
	Funds provided from continuing operations before redeployments	241.3	256.4	284.5
	(Increase) decrease in working capital used in continuing operations	(90.9)	(4.4)	33.3
	Cash provided from continuing operations	150.4	252.0	317.8
	Cash provided from (used for) discontinued operations	(86.1)	(15.9)	121.0
	CASH PROVIDED FROM OPERATIONS	64.3	236.1	438.8
FUNDS PROVIDED FROM (USED FOR) INVESTMENTS:	Purchase of land, buildings and equipment	(209.7)	(282.4)	(308.0)
	Purchase price of businesses acquired, net of cash received	(10.2)	—	(1.1)
	Cash provided from disposal of land, buildings and equipment	22.3	11.7	19.0
	Proceeds from dispositions	11.6	268.8	10.7
	Other	(2.9)	11.9	13.4
	NET CASH PROVIDED FROM (USED FOR) INVESTMENTS	(188.9)	10.0	(266.0)
FUNDS USED FOR DIVIDENDS		(100.4)	(96.0)	(92.7)
FUNDS PROVIDED FROM (USED FOR) FINANCING:	Increase (decrease) in notes payable	129.6	(147.2)	(6.8)
	Issuance of long-term debt and debt warrants	197.7	15.5	164.1
	Reduction of long-term debt	(103.2)	(59.1)	(31.5)
	Investment in U.S. Treasury securities	(65.5)	—	—
	Investments in tax leases	(3.2)	(14.6)	(200.6)
	Income tax cash flows from tax leases	114.2	194.3	151.8
	Purchase of treasury stock	(53.8)	(141.4)	(161.4)
	Common stock issued	10.0	10.4	28.9
	NET CASH PROVIDED FROM (USED FOR) FINANCING	225.8	(142.1)	(55.5)
NET INCREASE IN CASH AND SHORT-TERM INVESTMENTS		0.8	8.0	24.6
CASH AND SHORT-TERM INVESTMENTS AT BEGINNING OF YEAR		66.0	58.0	33.4
CASH AND SHORT-TERM INVESTMENTS AT END OF YEAR		$ 66.8	$ 66.0	$ 58.0
(INCREASE) DECREASE IN WORKING CAPITAL USED IN CONTINUING OPERATIONS:	Receivables	$ (9.4)	$ (17.5)	$ (23.2)
	Inventories	(63.5)	9.3	(13.3)
	Prepaid expenses and other current assets	6.7	1.9	(2.7)
	Accrued taxes	(98.7)	(5.8)	13.2
	Accounts payable and other current liabilities	74.0	7.7	59.3
(INCREASE) DECREASE IN WORKING CAPITAL USED IN CONTINUING OPERATIONS		$ (90.9)	$ (4.4)	$ 33.3

See accompanying notes to consolidated financial statements.

Notes to Consolidated Financial Statements
General Mills, Inc., and Subsidiaries

Note One: Summary of Significant Accounting Policies

A. Principles of Consolidation

The consolidated financial statements include the following domestic and foreign operations: (1) parent company and 100% owned subsidiaries other than General Mills Finance, Inc.; (2) majority-owned subsidiaries; and (3) General Mills' investment in and share of net earnings or losses of 20-50% owned companies. General Mills Finance, Inc., is accounted for by the equity method because of the different nature of its operations. The Toy, Fashion, and Non-apparel Specialty Retailing operations are reflected in the accompanying consolidated financial statements as discontinued operations (see Note Two). Accordingly, where considered appropriate, the following notes relate to continuing operations only.

The fiscal years of foreign operations generally end in April.

Certain 1984 and 1983 amounts have been reclassified to conform to 1985's presentation.

B. Land, Buildings, Equipment and Depreciation

Buildings and equipment are depreciated over estimated useful lives ranging from 3-50 years, primarily using the straight-line method. Accelerated depreciation methods are generally used for income tax purposes.

When an item is sold or retired, the accounts are relieved of cost and the related accumulated depreciation; the resulting gains and losses, if any, are recognized.

C. Capitalization of Construction Interest

Interest costs related to certain construction projects are capitalized. This capitalization decreased interest expense from continuing operations by $2.5 million, $5.5 million and $6.5 million in fiscal 1985, 1984 and 1983, respectively.

D. Inventories

Inventories are valued at the lower of cost or market. Certain domestic inventories are valued using the LIFO method, while other inventories are generally valued using the FIFO method.

E. Amortization of Intangibles

Goodwill represents the difference between purchase prices of acquired companies and the related fair values of net assets acquired and accounted for by the purchase method of accounting. Any goodwill acquired after October 1970 is amortized on a straight-line basis over 40 years or less.

The costs of patents, copyrights and other intangible assets are amortized evenly over their estimated useful lives. Most of these costs were incurred through purchases of businesses.

Annually, the Audit Committee of the Board of Directors reviews goodwill and other intangibles. At its meeting on April 22, 1985, the Board of Directors confirmed that the remaining amounts of these assets have continuing value.

F. Research and Development

All expenditures for research and development are charged against earnings in the year incurred. The charges

to continuing operations for fiscal 1985, 1984 and 1983 were $38.7 million, $32.3 million and $32.1 million, respectively.

G. Income Taxes

Income taxes include deferred income taxes, which result from timing differences between earnings for financial reporting and tax purposes. Investment tax credits are reflected as reductions of income taxes in the year eligible purchases are placed in service.

H. Earnings (Loss) Per Share

Earnings (loss) per share has been determined by dividing net earnings (loss) by the weighted average number of common shares outstanding during the year. Common share equivalents were not material.

I. Foreign Currency Translation

For most foreign operations, local currencies are considered the functional currency. Assets and liabilities are translated using the exchange rates in effect at the balance sheet date. Results of operations are translated using the average exchange rates prevailing throughout the period. Translation effects are accumulated as part of the foreign currency adjustment in stockholders' equity.

Gains and losses from foreign currency transactions are generally included in net earnings for the period.

Note Two: Discontinued Operations
In the third quarter of fiscal 1985, the Board of Directors authorized disposition of the Toy and Fashion segments of our business. Plans are to spin off the Fashion businesses, excluding Foot-Joy (which has been sold), and the Toy businesses, excluding the Mexican operations, as two separate freestanding companies to our shareholders. We are presently negotiating to dispose of Fundimensions and the Mexican operations.

In the fourth quarter of fiscal 1985, the Board of Directors authorized disposition of the Leewards and Wallpapers To Go companies. These companies make up the non-apparel retailing line of business within our Specialty Retailing segment. Present plans are to sell these companies.

The net impact of these discontinued operations on fiscal 1985, including disposal reserves and operating losses, was a $188.3 million ($4.21 per share) loss after an income tax benefit of $87.2 million. Part of the estimated disposal loss is a $31.1 million after-tax noncash transfer from the cumulative foreign currency adjustment component of equity. Operating earnings for the Toy and Fashion businesses for the first two quarters of fiscal 1985 and for the Non-apparel Specialty Retailing businesses for all of fiscal 1985, net of income tax expense of $4.5 million, were $19.2 million ($.43 per share).

The net assets of the discontinued operations included on the balance sheet as of May 26, 1985, amounted to $613.1 million and represent their estimated net realizable value for those companies to be sold and net book values for those companies to be spun off. The net assets consist primarily of receivables, inventory, fixed assets, certain intangibles and miscellaneous liabilities. Prior year balance sheets have not been restated.

The Consolidated Statements of Earnings have been restated to show continuing operations for the periods presented. The discontinued Toy, Fashion, and Non-apparel Specialty Retailing operations are shown separately from continuing operations and include both operating results and the estimated reserve for loss upon disposal of these activities.

Sales for the discontinued operations were $1,368.9 million, $1,482.4 million and $1,468.5 million for fiscal 1985, 1984 and 1983, respectively.

Note Three: Redeployment Program
During fiscal 1985, we continued our redeployment program. The net results of the redeployment program decreased fiscal 1985 net earnings by $44.0 million ($.98 per share). This resulted from the decisions to dispose of We Are Sportswear, a Specialty Retailing operation, and Casa Gallardo, Darryl's and the Good Earth restaurant chains; other restructuring costs; and adjustments to previously established redeployment items.

Operations involved in the fiscal 1985 dispositions represented approximately 4.2% of fiscal 1984 sales and approximately .1% of fiscal 1984 operating profits.

Fiscal 1984 results included an after-tax gain of $28.5 million ($.60 per share) in connection with the redeployment program. The most significant item was the sale of the net assets of Tom's Foods, which resulted in an after-tax gain of $73.7 million. This was offset by losses associated with the disposition of assets that did not fit our ongoing strategy, the closing of certain low volume or marginal Specialty Retailing and Restaurant operations, and the undertaking of a major, chain-wide Red Lobster restaurant market repositioning and store renovation program.

Operations involved in the fiscal 1984 dispositions represented approximately 8.2% of fiscal 1983 sales and approximately 10.4% of fiscal 1983 operating profits.

Fiscal 1983 results included an after-tax gain of $.8 million ($.02 per share) resulting from adjustments to fiscal

1982 amounts recorded due to the redeployment program.

These redeployment results relate only to continuing operations and exclude redeployment actions in the Toy, Fashion, and Non-apparel Specialty Retailing operations prior to their being discontinued. Redeployment program charges for the Toy, Fashion, and Non-apparel Specialty Retailing operations are included in the discontinued operations amount in the Consolidated Statements of Earnings.

Note Four: Foreign Currency Translation
The following is an analysis of the changes in the cumulative foreign currency adjustment equity account:

(In Millions)	Fiscal Year 1985	1984
Balance, beginning of year	$74.0	$64.8
Adjustments during the year, including applicable income taxes of $5.3 in 1985 and $2.7 in 1984	15.3	9.2
Amount transferred to discontinued operations loss as a result of the planned divestiture of certain foreign operations (see Note Two)	(31.1)	—
Balance, end of year	$58.2	$74.0

$28.1 million of the $58.2 million balance as of the end of fiscal 1985 relates to the Toy and Fashion businesses, which will be spun off in fiscal 1986.

Note Five: Inventories
The components of year-end inventories are as follows:

(In Millions)	May 26, 1985	May 27, 1984
Raw materials, work in process, finished goods and supplies:		
Valued at LIFO	$170.4	$262.6
Valued primarily at FIFO	207.3	399.1
Total inventories	$377.7	$661.7

The above amounts include both continuing and discontinued operations for fiscal 1984, but only the continuing operations for fiscal 1985.

If the FIFO method of inventory accounting had been used in place of LIFO, inventories would have been $47.5 million and $79.7 million higher than reported at May 26, 1985, and May 27, 1984, respectively. Reported earnings per share of continuing operations would have been lower by $.07 in fiscal 1985, and higher by $.05 in fiscal 1984 and $.04 in fiscal 1983.

Note Six: Tax Leases
In fiscal 1982 and 1983 we purchased certain income tax items from other companies through tax lease transactions. These transactions resulted in income tax cash flows during fiscal 1985, which recovered the net investment in tax leases at May 27, 1984, and provided an additional $60.8 million that will be repaid over the remaining life of the arrangements. This liability is classified as "Deferred Income Taxes—Tax Leases."

Note Seven: Short-Term Borrowings

The components of notes payable are as follows:

(In Millions)	May 26, 1985	May 27, 1984
U.S. commercial paper	$314.6	$165.3
Banks	65.0	85.0
Miscellaneous	.2	.7
Total	$379.8	$251.0

To ensure the availability of funds during the year, we maintained bank credit lines sufficient to cover our outstanding commercial paper. As of May 26, 1985, we had $365.0 million of such domestic lines available. These lines are on a fee-paid basis. As of May 26, 1985, foreign subsidiaries of continuing operations had $12.4 million of unused credit lines. The amount and cost of the credit lines are generally renegotiated each year.

Note Eight: Long-Term Debt

(In Millions)	May 26, 1985	May 27, 1984
Zero coupon notes, yield 11.14%, $1,000 due August 15, 2013	$ 48.1	$ —
9⅜% sinking fund debentures, due March 1, 2009	113.3	113.3
Zero coupon notes, yield 11.73%, $250 due August 15, 2004	28.3	—
8% sinking fund debentures, due February 15, 1999	—	48.5
12% notes due December 19, 1991	100.0	—
Zero coupon notes, yield 14⅝%, $102.5 due June 30, 1991	43.4	37.7
Zero coupon notes, yield 13.3%, $100 due January 4, 1988	71.5	62.9
12⅛% notes due August 15, 1985	50.0	50.0
10⅜% notes due October 15, 1984	—	50.0
Other, no individual item larger than $4.7	54.3	60.5
	508.9	422.9
Less amounts due within one year	(59.4)	(60.3)
Total long-term debt	$449.5	$362.6

In fiscal 1985, we filed a shelf registration statement with the Securities and Exchange Commission for the issuance of up to $150 million net proceeds in unsecured debt securities to reduce short-term debt and for other general corporate purposes. In addition, $50 million net proceeds in unsecured debt securities is still available for issuance under a previously filed shelf registration statement.

Also in fiscal 1985, we issued outside of the United States $250 million face amount, $26.3 million net value, of zero coupon notes yielding 11.73% that will mature on August 15, 2004, and $1 billion face amount, $45.4 million net value of zero coupon notes yielding 11.14% that will mature on August 15, 2013. We also issued outside of the United States $100 million principal amount of 12% notes maturing on December 19, 1991. In the same offering we issued 100,000 warrants, net value $4 million, which expire on December 19, 1989, to purchase an additional $100 million principal amount of 12% notes maturing on December 19, 1991. All warrants were still outstanding on May 26, 1985.

In fiscal 1985, we satisfied the future requirements of certain sinking fund debentures through the deposit of U.S. obligations in an irrevocable trust. This transaction increased fiscal 1985 net earnings by $6.7 million ($.15 per share). In fiscal 1984, we satisfied the future requirements of certain sinking fund debentures through the deposit of primarily U.S. obligations in an irrevocable trust. This transaction increased fiscal 1984 net earnings by $4.0 million ($.09 per share). In fiscal 1983, we exchanged 239,331 shares of our stock held in treasury for $15 million of our sinking fund debentures. This transaction increased fiscal 1983 net earnings by $3.2 million ($.06 per share).

The sinking fund and principal payments due on long-term debt are (in millions) $59.4, $10.3, $73.5, $1.8 and $6.8 in fiscal years ending 1986, 1987, 1988, 1989 and 1990, respectively.

Note Nine: Changes in Capital Stock

(Dollars in Millions)	$.75 Par Value Common Stock (70,000,000 Shares Authorized)			
	Issued		In Treasury	
	Shares	Amount	Shares	Amount
Balance at May 30, 1982	50,860,525	$206.6	575,026	$ 19.5
Stock option, profit sharing and employee stock ownership plans	177,808	7.9	(188,695)	(7.8)
Shares issued for acquisitions and other	—	.2	(36,154)	(1.3)
Shares issued for debentures	—	3.2	(239,331)	(8.5)
Shares repurchased on open market	—	—	3,127,414	161.4
Balance at May 29, 1983	51,038,333	217.9	3,238,260	163.3
Stock option, profit sharing and employee stock ownership plans	—	(2.5)	(246,752)	(12.4)
Shares issued for acquisitions and other	—	—	(10,619)	(.5)
Shares repurchased on open market	—	—	2,793,524	141.4
Balance at May 27, 1984	51,038,033	215.4	5,774,413	291.8
Stock option, profit sharing and employee stock ownership plans	—	(1.7)	(228,990)	(11.5)
Shares issued for acquisitions and other	—	—	(2,938)	(.2)
Shares repurchased on open market	—	—	1,055,024	53.8
Balance at May 26, 1985	51,038,033	$213.7	6,597,509	$333.9

Cumulative preferred stock of 5,000,000 shares, without par value, is authorized but unissued.

The Board of Directors has authorized the repurchase, from time to time, of common stock for our treasury, provided that the number of shares in the treasury shall not exceed 8,500,000.

Shares of common stock are potentially issuable for the following purposes:

	Number of Shares as of May 26, 1985
Stock options outstanding	1,710,592
Stock options available for grant	1,771,000
Incentive plans	20,460

Note Ten: Stock Options

The following table contains information on stock options:

	Shares	Average Option Price Per Share
Granted:		
1985	512,150	$52.48
1984	250,000	51.82
1983	464,750	45.45
Exercised:		
1985	273,193	$31.19
1984	272,182	29.08
1983	220,318	27.87
Expired:		
1985	143,946	$36.12
1984	65,881	33.64
1983	74,665	27.98
Outstanding at year-end:		
1985	1,710,592	$42.33
1984	1,615,581	36.67
1983	1,703,644	33.12
Exercisable at year-end:		
1985	926,495	$34.84
1984	1,008,943	30.52
1983	966,058	28.01

Options for a total of 1,771,000 shares are available for grant to officers and key employees under our 1984 stock option plan, under which grants may be made until September 30, 1988. The options may be granted subject to approval of the Compensation Committee of the Board of Directors at a price not less than 100% of the fair market value on the date the option is granted. Options now outstanding include some granted under the 1975 and 1980 option plans, under which no further options may be granted. All options expire within 10 years plus 30 days after date of grant.

The 1975 plan permitted the granting of stock appreciation rights (SARs) in tandem with some options granted to certain individuals. Upon exercise of an SAR, the option for a corresponding number of shares of stock is cancelled and the holder receives in cash or stock an amount equal to the appreciation between the option price and the market value of the stock on the date of exercise. This amount may not exceed the option price. On May 26, 1985, there were 57,150 SARs outstanding. The weighted average option price of the related stock options was $28.80.

The 1980 and 1984 plans permit the granting of performance units corresponding to stock options granted. The value of performance units will be determined by return on equity and growth in earnings per share measured against preset goals over three-year performance periods. For seven years after a performance period, holders may elect to receive the value of performance units (with interest) as an alternative to exercising corresponding stock options. On May 26, 1985, there were 1,017,854 outstanding options with corresponding performance units or performance unit accounts.

The 1984 plan provides for granting of incentive stock options as well as non-qualified options. No incentive stock options have yet been granted.

**Note Eleven: Employees'
Retirement Plans**
We have retirement plans covering most employees. Our contributions to these plans, which are expensed and funded on a current basis, were $39.2 million in fiscal 1985, $36.9 million in fiscal 1984 and $53.6 million in fiscal 1983. Most of the 1984 expense reduction was due to smaller contributions to our employee stock ownership plan (ESOP), with additional reductions because of actuarial changes described below.

Certain retirement plans (and the related costs) associated with the Toy and Fashion operations will be included with the spun-off businesses. Also the net plan assets available for benefits and the actuarial present value of accumulated benefits, as disclosed below, will be adjusted for plans included with the spun-off businesses.

Most of our plans are defined benefit plans, which provide for retirement benefits based on employees' length of service and earnings. The following table contains aggregated information about our defined benefit plans, determined as of January 1, 1985, and January 1, 1984, for the principal plans:

(In Millions)	1985	1984
Net plan assets available for benefits	$456	$429
Actuarial present value of accumulated benefits:		
Vested	$318	$296
Nonvested	34	31
Total	$352	$327

Actuarial present values of accumulated benefits were determined using discount rates established by the Pension Benefit Guaranty Corporation (PBGC) for valuing plan benefits. The PBGC rates ranged from 4% to 9.75% for 1985 and 4% to 9.5% for 1984, with

the latter of each range being the principal rate.

Contributions to our defined benefit plans are determined by independent actuaries using assumptions and methods reflecting plan experience and expectations. During fiscal 1984, a study by management and plan actuaries of the principal plan covering salaried employees resulted in changes to reflect fund performance, current status and more realistically portray future expectations. The investment return assumption was changed from 7½% to 8½%, and the actuarial cost method was changed from the aggregate method to the entry age normal method. These changes in actuarial procedures do not affect participant benefits under the plan and continue adequate funding of future payments. Under the previous actuarial practices, 1984 pension expense would have been $5.9 million higher.

In fiscal 1983, we adopted the ESOP. Our contributions to the plan expensed in fiscal 1985, 1984 and 1983 were $3.6 million, $1.8 million and $12.1 million, respectively (included in the $39.2 million, $36.9 million and $53.6 million above). Our contributions to this plan are made primarily in shares of General Mills common stock. We receive an equivalent federal income tax credit as a result of the contribution.

We have a few defined contribution plans that provide for benefits based on accumulated contributions and investment income. Such plans, including the ESOP, had net assets of $217.9 million at May 26, 1985.

We have a variety of plans that provide health care benefits to the majority of our retirees. Some of these plans require contributions from the retirees. In fiscal 1985, we recognized total costs of $4.3 million for these benefits on a pay-as-you-go basis.

Note Twelve: Profit-Sharing Plans

We have profit-sharing plans to provide incentives to key individuals who have the greatest opportunity to contribute to current earnings and successful future operations.

These plans were approved by the Board of Directors upon recommendation of the Compensation Committee. The awards under these plans depend on profit performance in relation to pre-established goals. The plans are administered by the Compensation Committee, which consists of directors who are not members of our management. Profit-sharing expense, including performance unit accruals, was $2.9 million in fiscal 1985, $6.8 million in fiscal 1984 and $10.0 million in fiscal 1983.

Note Thirteen: Income Taxes

The components of continuing operations' earnings before income taxes and the income taxes thereon are as follows:

(In Millions)	1985	Fiscal Year 1984	1983
Earnings before income taxes:			
U.S.	**$181.0**	$334.5	$242.0
Outside U.S.	**14.9**	22.1	26.2
Total earnings before income taxes	**$195.9**	$356.6	$268.2
Income taxes:			
Current:			
Federal taxes	**$ 95.7**	$161.9	$ 66.8
U.S. investment tax credit	**(10.1)**	(10.3)	(11.6)
State and local taxes	**8.2**	12.1	11.7
Foreign taxes	**6.1**	7.4	12.8
Total current income taxes	**99.9**	171.1	79.7
Deferred income taxes (principally U.S.)	**(19.4)**	(17.2)	26.4
Total income taxes	**$ 80.5**	$153.9	$106.1

Total current income taxes charged to earnings in fiscal 1985, 1984 and 1983 reflect the amounts attributable to our operations and have not been materially affected by tax leases. Actual current taxes payable on fiscal 1985, fiscal 1984 and fiscal 1983 operations were reduced by approximately $113 million, $118 million and $175 million, respectively, due to the effect of tax leases. These tax benefits are temporary in nature and do not affect taxes for statement of earnings purposes since the amount of benefits (net of the consideration paid to the sellers) will be repaid to the government in future years over the terms of the leases.

Deferred income taxes result from timing differences in the recognition of revenue and expense for tax and financial statement purposes. The tax effects of these differences follow.

(In Millions)	1985	Fiscal Year 1984	1983
Depreciation	$ 23.9	$ 9.4	$ 16.8
Interest	3.0	5.5	5.9
Provision for losses on dispositions and redeployments	(28.1)	(19.5)	10.0
Accrued expenses	(17.5)	0.9	(9.7)
Other	(0.7)	(13.5)	3.4
Total deferred income taxes	$(19.4)	$(17.2)	$26.4

The following table reconciles the U.S. statutory income tax rate with the effective income tax rate:

	1985	Fiscal Year 1984	1983
U.S. statutory rate	46.0%	46.0%	46.0%
U.S. investment tax credit	(5.1)	(2.9)	(4.3)
Credit for employee stock ownership plan	(1.0)	(.3)	(2.4)
State and local income taxes, net of federal tax benefits	2.9	1.8	3.1
Other	(1.7)	(1.4)	(2.8)
Effective income tax rate	41.1%	43.2%	39.6%

Unremitted earnings of foreign operations amounting to $65.3 million are expected by management to be permanently reinvested. Accordingly, no provision has been made for additional foreign or U.S. taxes that would be payable if such earnings were to be remitted to the parent company as dividends.

Income taxes have been allocated to the discontinued operations as if each had prepared a separate income tax return. These allocated income taxes are included in the "Discontinued Operations After Tax" line on the Consolidated Statement of Earnings.

Note Fourteen: Leases

An analysis of rent expense of continuing operations by property leased follows:

(In Millions)	1985	Fiscal Year 1984	1983
Retail and restaurant space	$20.6	$19.9	$19.7
Office space	5.3	4.0	3.7
Warehouse space	5.3	5.2	5.6
Transportation	2.2	2.9	4.1
Computers	1.5	2.7	4.4
All other	2.2	3.1	3.3
Total rent expense	$37.1	$37.8	$40.8

Some leases require payment of property taxes, insurance and maintenance costs in addition to the rent payments. Contingent and escalation rent in excess of minimum rent payments for continuing operations totaled approximately $3.7 million in fiscal 1985, $2.5 million in fiscal 1984 and $2.6 million in fiscal 1983. Sublease income netted in rent expense was insignificant.

Noncancelable future lease commitments are (in millions) $23.7 in 1986, $22.4 in 1987, $20.7 in 1988, $19.5 in 1989, $18.2 in 1990 and $77.5 after 1990, or a cumulative total of $182.0. Of this total, restaurant and retail leases account for 83%. Future lease commitments of our discontinued operations, which aggregate approximately $150 million, are not included in these amounts.

Note Fifteen: Segment Information

(In Millions)	Consumer Foods	Restaurants	Specialty Retailing and Other	Unallocated Corporate Items (b)	Consoli-dated Total
Sales (a)					
1985	$2,771.3	$1,140.1	$373.8		$4,285.2
1984	2,713.4	1,079.7	325.3		4,118.4
1983	2,792.6	984.5	305.2		4,082.3
Operating Profits before Redeployments					
1985	265.6	91.5	(1.7)	$ (83.7)	271.7
1984	275.3	70.0	19.8	(61.5)	303.6
1983	269.4	80.0	10.4	(94.3)	265.5
Operating Profits after Redeployments					
1985	261.5	52.2	(34.1)	(83.7)	195.9
1984	383.0	37.3	(3.1)	(60.6)	356.6
1983	268.2	80.0	14.3	(94.3)	268.2
Identifiable Assets					
1985	1,008.7	424.6	204.9	1,024.4	2,662.6
1984	934.1	585.3	153.1	1,185.6	2,858.1
1983	983.8	572.7	176.5	1,210.9	2,943.9
Capital Expenditures					
1985	103.2	40.5	27.9	38.1	209.7
1984	130.3	82.3	10.1	59.7	282.4
1983	123.8	107.6	13.2	63.4	308.0
Depreciation Expense					
1985	60.9	37.5	7.5	1.7	107.6
1984	53.9	34.7	6.5	1.2	96.3
1983	51.9	30.6	6.3	1.8	90.6

(a) Both inter-segment sales and export sales are immaterial.

(b) Corporate expenses include interest expense, profit sharing, employee stock ownership plan, balance sheet related foreign currency effects and general corporate expenses. Corporate assets consist mainly of cash and short-term investments, investments in tax leases, other miscellaneous investments and the identifiable assets of discontinued and redeployed operations. Corporate capital expenditures include capital expenditures of discontinued operations through the date disposition was authorized.

Note Sixteen: Quarterly Data (unaudited)

Summarized quarterly data for fiscal 1985 and 1984 follows. Fiscal 1984 and the first three quarters of fiscal 1985 are restated to segregate discontinued operations (see Note Two).

(In Millions, Except Per Share and Market Price Amounts)	First Quarter		Second Quarter		Third Quarter		Fourth Quarter		Total Year	
	1985	1984	**1985**	1984	**1985**	1984	**1985**	1984	**1985**	1984
Sales	**$1,017.4**	$1,041.9	**$1,128.3**	$1,036.7	**$1,069.1**	$1,021.6	**$1,070.4**	$1,018.2	**$4,285.2**	$4,118.4
Gross profit*	**427.6**	441.8	**474.0**	428.0	**444.4**	418.1	**464.4**	397.7	**1,810.4**	1,685.6
Earnings after tax–Continuing operations after redeployments	**43.1**	79.7	**41.0**	51.6	**31.2**	41.1	**0.1**	30.3	**115.4**	202.7
Earnings per share– Continuing operations after redeployments	**.96**	1.67	**.91**	1.09	**.70**	.89	**.01**	.67	**2.58**	4.32
Discontinued operations after tax	**11.0**	(7.2)	**14.6**	30.1	**(105.3)**	(2.4)	**(108.6)**	10.2	**(188.3)**	30.7
Net earnings (loss)	**54.1**	72.5	**55.6**	81.7	**(74.1)**	38.7	**(108.5)**	40.5	**(72.9)**	233.4
Net earnings (loss) per share	**1.20**	1.52	**1.23**	1.71	**(1.64)**	.85	**(2.42)**	.90	**(1.63)**	4.98
Dividends per share	**.56**	.51	**.56**	.51	**.56**	.51	**.56**	.51	**2.24**	2.04
Redeployment gain (loss), after tax	**(0.1)**	36.6	**(0.8)**	3.3	**(8.5)**	(2.4)	**(34.6)**	(9.0)	**(44.0)**	28.5
Market price of common stock: High	**55¾**	57⅛	**60**	57	**59½**	54⅝	**60⅝**	51½	**60⅝**	57⅛
Low	**49⅜**	47⅝	**49½**	46¾	**47¾**	41⅝	**52**	45½	**47¾**	41⅝

*Before charges for depreciation.

Note Seventeen: Accounting for Inflation (unaudited)

During the last decade, an increased rate of inflation became a significant factor in both the U.S. economy and world economies. Traditional accounting procedures are based on the "historical cost" method, where generally each individual transaction is recorded at its original cash value, and is not subsequently adjusted to a different value.

In periods of continuing rapid inflation, use of traditional accounting may cause two major concerns: (1) prior years' financial statements lose some comparability to the current year's; and (2) recent financial statements may not be a meaningful guide for tomorrow's requirements.

In September 1979, experimental accounting procedures were prescribed by the Financial Accounting Standards Board. They required that limited amounts of accounting data (prepared according to traditional procedures) be adjusted for inflation by the current cost method.

The current cost method of adjustment revalues selected past years' cost data by an estimate of what each item would cost at the current time. We used a combination of specific indices, current price lists, and appraisals to estimate current cost amounts. The U.S. Consumer Price Index is used to adjust current costs of both United States and non-United States operations to reflect the effects of general inflation.

Statement of Earnings, Adjusted for Inflation

The experimental regulations prescribe that current cost calculations include most statement of earnings items at historical costs. Only fixed asset depreciation and cost of sales are modified for the effects of inflation. Earnings from continuing operations, as adjusted for inflation under these regulations for our fiscal year ended May 26, 1985, are shown in the following table:

(In Millions)	Historical Cost Statement of Earnings	Current Cost Statement of Earnings
Sales	$4,285	$4,285
Cost of sales (excluding depreciation)	2,475	2,465
Depreciation	108	139
All other expenses	1,506	1,506
Earnings before income taxes	196	175
Income taxes	81	81
Net earnings	$ 115	$ 94
Effective income tax rate	41.1%	46.3%

Effects of Holding Assets and Liabilities

We maintain a net liability position with our "monetary" assets and liabilities (items that have a fixed amount of cash receivable or payable). In the same sense that a homeowner "benefits" in a time of inflation by repaying a home mortgage loan with "cheaper" dollars, we had an unrealized fiscal 1985 "gain" of approximately $38 million on our average net liability position.

Foreign investments resulted in an unrealized current cost translation loss for fiscal 1985 of $9.1 million. This amount includes income taxes of $4.0 million.

We estimate that the inflation-adjusted amounts of our May 26, 1985 inventories and fixed assets are as follows:

(In Millions)	Historical Cost	Current Cost
Inventories	$ 378	$ 425
Fixed assets	956	1,368
Total	$1,334	$1,793

Five-Year Statistics

Some of the above information, plus additional statistics, are summarized in the following five-year table. Current cost information is expressed in current costs of each year, inflated to average fiscal 1985 dollars.

(Dollar Amounts In Millions, Except Per Share Data)	Fiscal Year 1985	1984	1983	1982	1981
Sales					
Historical amounts	$4,285	$4,118	$4,082	$3,861	$3,466
Constant purchasing power	4,285	4,279	4,394	4,350	4,251
Earnings from continuing operations					
Historical cost	115	203	162	142	128
Current costs	94	179	119	106	108
Earnings per share from continuing operations					
Historical cost	2.58	4.32	3.24	2.81	2.54
Current costs	2.10	3.82	2.38	2.09	2.14
Net assets at year-end					
Historical cost	1,023	1,225	1,227	1,232	1,132
Current costs	1,481	1,910	2,011	2,167	2,137
Current cost translation adjustment	(9)	(19)	(35)	(42)	*
Market price per share at year-end					
Historical cost	58.13	50.13	56.38	39.88	34.62
Constant purchasing power	57.13	51.12	59.93	44.08	40.56
Dividends per share					
Historical cost	2.24	2.04	1.84	1.64	1.44
Constant purchasing power	2.24	2.12	1.98	1.85	1.77
Unrealized "gains" from decline in purchasing power of average net amounts owed	38	48	47	55	82
Increases in current cost of fixed assets (land, buildings and equipment) and inventories:					
Pro forma increase, due to general inflation as measured by the U.S. Urban Consumer Price Index	$ 64	107	104	148	239
Compare to: estimated actual increases in specific prices of assets held by General Mills	$ 18	125	70	212	195
Difference: excess (deficiency) of pro forma general inflationary increase over estimated actual specific increase	$ 46	(18)	34	(64)	44
Average consumer price index for fiscal year (calendar 1967 = 100)	315.8	303.9	293.4	280.3	257.5

*Neither required nor available for 1981.

Management Comments
Inflation accounting advocates claim inflation-adjusted data (1) provides better displays of real growth, (2) gives improved insight into future cash needs, and (3) promotes the concept that profit has not been earned until current costs have been recovered. The adjusted data also highlights the heavy tax burden imposed by government when tax rates are not adjusted for inflation.

We continue to caution that the value of inflation accounting is still unproven and that the inflation-adjusted data should be used only to indicate general trends rather than as a precise measurement. We have not found this data useful for operational decisions because:
1. Current costs cannot be used mechanically to forecast actual replacements of assets due to uncertain timing, technological change, financing and other considerations.

2. Different assumptions and estimating procedures by individual companies may affect the comparability of the current cost data.

We continue to combat the effects of inflation through our planning and operating philosophy and practices.

Eleven-Year Financial Summary As Reported
General Mills, Inc., and Subsidiaries

(Amounts in Millions, Except Per Share Data)		May 26, 1985	May 27, 1984
FINANCIAL RESULTS	Earnings (loss) per share	$ (1.63)	$ 4.98
	Return on average equity	(6.5)%	19.0%
	Dividends per share	$ 2.24	2.04
	Sales	$4,285.2(a)	5,600.8
	Costs and expenses:		
	Cost of sales, exclusive of items below	$2,474.8(a)	3,165.9
	Selling, general and administrative (b)	$1,443.9(a)	1,841.7
	Depreciation and amortization	$ 110.4(a)	133.1
	Interest	$ 60.2(a)	61.4
	Earnings before income taxes	$ 195.9(a)(c)	398.7
	Net earnings (loss)	$ (72.9)(e)	233.4
	Net earnings (loss) as a percent of sales	(1.7)%	4.2%
	Weighted average number of common shares (f)	44.7	46.9
	Taxes (income, payroll, property, etc.) per share	$ 4.02(a)	6.22
FINANCIAL POSITION	Total assets	$2,662.6	2,858.1
	Land, buildings and equipment, net	$ 956.0(a)	1,229.4
	Working capital at year-end	$ 229.4	244.5
	Long-term debt, excluding current portion	$ 449.5	362.6
	Stockholders' equity	$1,023.3	1,224.6
	Stockholders' equity per share	$ 23.05	27.03
OTHER STATISTICS	Working capital provided from operations before redeployments	$ 241.3(a)	348.3
	Total dividends	$ 100.4	96.0
	Gross capital expenditures	$ 209.7(g)	282.4
	Research and development	$ 38.7(a)	63.5
	Advertising media expenditures	$ 274.3(a)	349.6
	Wages, salaries and employee benefits	$ 860.2(a)	1,121.6
	Number of employees	63,162(a)	80,297
	Accumulated LIFO charge	$ 47.5(a)	79.7
	Common stock price range	$60⅝-47¾	57⅛-41⅝

Fiscal 1975 per share and share amounts have been adjusted for the two-for-one stock split in October of 1975.

Financial Data For Continuing Operations Years Prior to Fiscal 1985 Restated

(Amounts in Millions, Except Per Share Data)	Fiscal Year Ended				
	May 26, 1985	May 27, 1984	May 29, 1983	May 30, 1982	May 31, 1981
Sales	$4,285.2	$4,118.4	$4,082.3	$3,860.5	$3,466.4
Earnings after tax, before redeployments	$ 159.4	174.2	161.3	157.2	127.9
Earnings per share	$ 3.56	3.72	3.22	3.11	2.54
Earnings after tax, after redeployments	$ 115.4	202.7	162.1	142.2	127.9
Earnings per share	$ 2.58	4.32	3.24	2.81	2.54

May 29, 1983	May 30, 1982	May 31, 1981	May 25, 1980	May 27, 1979	May 28, 1978	May 29, 1977	May 30, 1976	May 25, 1975
$ 4.89	$ 4.46	$ 3.90	$ 3.37	$ 2.92	$ 2.72	$ 2.36	$ 2.04	$ 1.59
19.9%	19.1%	18.2%	17.6%	17.0%	17.6%	17.1%	16.7%	14.6%
1.84	1.64	1.44	1.28	1.12	.97	.79	.66	.58½
5,550.8	5,312.1	4,852.4	4,170.3	3,745.0	3,243.0	2,909.4	2,645.0	2,308.9
3,123.3	3,081.6	2,936.9	2,578.5	2,347.7	2,026.1	1,797.5	1,663.9	1,537.7
1,831.6	1,635.5	1,384.0	1,145.5	1,021.3	883.8	807.9	704.5	546.3
127.5	113.2	99.5	81.1	73.3	58.6	48.1	46.7	41.8
58.7	75.1	57.6	48.6	38.8	29.3	26.7	29.4	36.2
409.7	406.7	374.4	316.6	263.9	245.2(d)	229.2	200.5	146.9
245.1	225.5	196.6	170.0	147.0	135.8	117.0	100.5	76.2
4.4%	4.2%	4.1%	4.1%	3.9%	4.2%	4.0%	3.8%	3.3%
50.1	50.6	50.4	50.5	50.4	49.9	49.6	49.2	47.8
5.70	5.88	5.59	4.66	3.99	3.71	3.43	3.02	2.35
2,943.9	2,701.7	2,301.3	2,012.4	1,835.2	1,612.7	1,447.3	1,328.2	1,205.6
1,197.5	1,054.1	920.6	747.5	643.7	587.0	540.1	471.5	441.0
235.6	210.7	337.3	416.3	441.6	285.1	298.2	295.1	276.8
464.0	331.9	348.6	377.5	384.8	259.9	276.1	281.8	304.9
1,227.4	1,232.2	1,145.4	1,020.7	916.2	815.1	724.9	640.2	560.5
25.68	24.50	22.75	20.32	18.23	16.38	14.60	12.98	11.50
401.6	353.6	317.8	262.7	237.5	197.9	174.2	153.2	124.2
92.7	82.3	72.3	64.4	56.1	48.2	39.1	32.4	27.8
308.0	287.3	246.6	196.5	154.1	140.5	117.1	94.4	99.8
60.6	53.8	45.4	44.4	37.3	30.5	29.9	25.7	22.9
336.2	284.9	222.0	213.1	188.9	170.5	145.6	111.4	70.5
1,115.2	1,028.4	907.0	781.2	717.1	622.0	541.2	479.4	402.7
81,186	75,893	71,225	66,032	64,229	66,574	61,797	51,778	47,969
79.7	75.5	73.7	60.3	46.5	29.3	18.7	12.5	15.9
57¾-38⅝	42⅛-32⅝	35¾-23⅜	28¼-19	34⅛-24	31½-26¼	35⅜-26½	34⅛-23⅜	27¾-14⅛

(a) Includes continuing operations only.
(b) Includes redeployment gains or losses.
(c) Includes pretax redeployment charge of $75.8 million.
(d) Before discontinued Chemical operations; earnings before income taxes for years prior to fiscal 1978 include this operation.
(e) Includes after-tax discontinued operations charge of $188.3 million.
(f) Years prior to fiscal 1983 include common share equivalents.
(g) Includes capital expenditures of continuing operations and capital expenditures of discontinued operations through the date disposition was authorized.

APPENDIX B
Index of References to APB and FASB Pronouncements

The following list of pronouncements by the Accounting Principles Board and the Financial Accounting Standards Board (as of December 31, 1986) is provided to give students an overview of the standards issued since 1962 and to reference these standards to the relevant chapters in this book. Earlier pronouncements by the Committee on Accounting Procedure of the AICPA have been largely superseded or amended. In those cases where no change has been made by subsequent standard-setting bodies, the earlier pronouncements are still accepted as official.

ACCOUNTING PRINCIPLES BOARD OPINIONS

Date issued	Opinion Number	Title	Chapters to Which References Most Applicable
November 1962	1	*New Depreciation Guidelines and Rules*	12
December 1962	2	*Accounting for the "Investment Credit"; addendum to Opinion No. 2—Accounting Principles for Regulated Industries*	N/A
October 1963	3	*The Statement of Source and Application of Funds*	24
March 1964	4	*Accounting for the "Investment Credit"*	20
September 1964	5	*Reporting of Leases in Financial Statements of Lessee*	21
October 1965	6	*Status of Accounting in Research Bulletins*	16
May 1966	7	*Accounting for Leases in Financial Statements of Lessors*	21
November 1966	8	*Accounting for the Cost of Pension Plans*	22
December 1966	9	*Reporting the Results of Operations*	4
December 1966	10	*Omnibus Opinion—1966*	20
December 1967	11	*Accounting for Income Taxes*	20
December 1967	12	*Omnibus Opinion—1967*	12

APB OPINIONS (concluded)

Date issued	Opinion Number	Title	Chapters to Which References Most Applicable
March 1969	13	Amending Paragraph 6 of ABP Opinion No. 9, Application to Commercial Banks	N/A
March 1969	14	Accounting for Convertible Debt and Debt Issued with Stock Purchase Warrants	15, 16
May 1969	15	Earnings per Share	18
August 1970	16	Business Combinations	N/A
August 1970	17	Intangible Assets	11, 12
March 1971	18	The Equity Method of Accounting for Investments in Common Stock	13
March 1971	19	Reporting Changes in Financial Position	24
July 1971	20	Accounting Changes	23
August 1971	21	Interest on Receivables and Payables	8, 14
April 1972	22	Disclosure of Accounting Policies	5
April 1972	23	Accounting for Income Taxes — Special Areas	20
April 1972	24	Accounting for Income Taxes — Investments in Common Stock Accounted for by the Equity Method (Other than Subsidiaries and Corporate Joint Ventures)	20
October 1972	25	Accounting for Stock Issued to Employees	16, 18
October 1972	26	Early Extinguishment of Debt	15
November 1972	27	Accounting for Lease Transactions by Manufacturer or Dealer Lessors	21
May 1973	28	Interim Financial Reporting	N/A
May 1973	29	Accounting for Nonmonetary Transactions	11, 13, 15
June 1973	30	Reporting the Results of Operations	4, 23
June 1973	31	Disclosure of Lease Commitments by Lessees	21

ACCOUNTING PRINCIPLES BOARD STATEMENTS

Date Issued	Statement Number	Title	Chapters to Which References Most Applicable
April 1962	1	Statement by the Accounting Principles Board (on Accounting Research Studies Nos. 1 and 3)	2
September 1967	2	Disclosure of Supplemental Financial Information by Diversified Companies	26
June 1969	3	Financial Statements Restated for General Price-Level Changes	25
October 1970	4	Basic Concepts and Accounting Principles Underlying Financial Statements of Business Enterprises	2

FINANCIAL ACCOUNTING STANDARDS BOARD STATEMENTS OF FINANCIAL ACCOUNTING STANDARDS

Date Issued	Statement Number	Title	Chapters to Which References Most Applicable
December 1973	1	Disclosure of Foreign Currency Translation Information	N/A
October 1974	2	Accounting for Research and Development Costs	11
December 1974	3	Reporting Accounting Changes in Interim Financial Statements	N/A
March 1975	4	Reporting Gains and Losses from Extinquishment of Debt	4, 15
March 1975	5	Accounting for Contingencies	14
May 1975	6	Classification of Short-Term Obligations Expected to be Refinanced	5, 14
June 1975	7	Accounting and Reporting by Development Stage Enterprises	11
October 1975	8	Accounting for the Translation of Foreign Currency Transactions and Foreign Currency Financial Statements	N/A
October 1975	9	Accounting for Income Taxes—Oil and Gas Producing Companies	N/A
October 1975	10	Extension of "Grandfather" Provisions for Business Combinations	N/A
December 1975	11	Accounting for Contingencies—Transition Method	14
December 1975	12	Accounting for Certain Marketable Securities	7, 13
November 1976	13	Accounting for Leases	21
December 1976	14	Financial Reporting for Segments of a Business Enterprise	26
June 1977	15	Accounting by Debtors and Creditors for Troubled Debt Restructurings	15
June 1977	16	Prior Period Adjustments	17, 23
November 1977	17	Accounting for Leases—Initial Direct Costs	21
November 1977	18	Financial Reporting for Segments of a Business Enterprise—Interim Financial Statements	N/A
December 1977	19	Financial Accounting and Reporting by Oil and Gas Producing Companies	12
December 1977	20	Accounting for Forward Exchange Contracts	N/A
April 1978	21	Suspension of the Reporting of Earnings per Share and Segment Information by Nonpublic Enterprises	18, 26
June 1978	22	Changes in the Provisions of Lease Agreements Resulting from Refundings of Tax-Exempt Debt	N/A
August 1978	23	Inception of the Lease	21

FASB STATEMENTS (continued)

Date Issued	Statement Number	Title	Chapters to Which References Most Applicable
December 1978	24	*Reporting Segment Information in Financial Statements That Are Presented in Another Enterprise's Financial Report*	N/A
February 1979	25	*Suspension of Certain Accounting Requirements for Oil and Gas Producing Companies*	12
April 1979	26	*Profit Recognition on Sales-Type Leases of Real Estate*	21
May 1979	27	*Classification of Renewals or Extensions of Existing Sales-Type or Direct Financing Leases*	21
May 1979	28	*Accounting for Sales with Leasebacks*	21
June 1979	29	*Determining Contingent Rentals*	21
August 1979	30	*Disclosure of Information About Major Customers*	26
September 1979	31	*Accounting for Tax Benefits Related to U.K. Tax Legislation Concerning Stock Relief*	N/A
September 1979	32	*Specialized Accounting and Reporting Principles and Practices in AICPA Statements of Position and Guides on Accounting and Auditing Matters*	19
September 1979	33	*Financial Reporting and Changing Prices*	25
October 1979	34	*Capitalization of Interest Cost*	11
March 1980	35	*Accounting and Reporting by Defined Benefit Pension Plans*	22
May 1980	36	*Disclosure of Pension Information*	22
July 1980	37	*Balance Sheet Classification of Deferred Income Taxes*	20
September 1980	38	*Accounting for Preacquisition Contingencies of Purchased Enterprises*	N/A
October 1980	39	*Financial Reporting and Changing Prices: Specialized Assets — Mining and Oil and Gas*	N/A
November 1980	40	*Financial Reporting and Changing Prices: Specialized Assets — Timberlands and Growing Timber*	N/A
November 1980	41	*Financial Reporting and Changing Prices: Specialized Assets — Income-Producing Real Estate*	N/A
November 1980	42	*Determining Materiality for Capitalization of Interest Cost*	11
November 1980	43	*Accounting for Compensated Absences*	14
December 1980	44	*Accounting for Intangible Assets of Motor Carriers*	N/A

FASB STATEMENTS (continued)

Date Issued	Statement Number	Title	Chapters to Which References Most Applicable
March 1981	45	Accounting for Franchise Fee Revenue	19
March 1981	46	Financial Reporting and Changing Prices: Motion Picture Films	N/A
March 1981	47	Disclosure of Long-Term Obligations	15
June 1981	48	Revenue Recognition When Right of Return Exists	19
June 1981	49	Accounting for Product Financing Arrangements	N/A
November 1981	50	Financial Reporting in the Record and Music Industry	N/A
November 1981	51	Financial Reporting by Cable Television Companies	N/A
December 1981	52	Foreign Currency Translation	N/A
December 1981	53	Financial Reporting by Producers and Distributors of Motion Picture Films	N/A
January 1982	54	Financial Reporting and Changing Prices: Investment Companies	N/A
February 1982	55	Determining Whether a Convertible Security Is a Common Stock Equivalent	18
February 1982	56	Designation of AICPA Guide and Statement of Position (SOP) 81-1 on Contractor Accounting and SOP 81-2 Concerning Hospital-Related Organizations as Preferable for Purposes of Applying APB Opinion 20	19
March 1982	57	Related Party Disclosures	N/A
April 1982	58	Capitalization of Interest Cost in Financial Statements that Include Investments Accounted for by the Equity Method	N/A
April 1982	59	Deferral of the Effective Date of Certain Accounting Requirements for Pension Plans of State and Local Governmental Units	N/A
June 1982	60	Accounting and Reporting by Insurance Enterprises	N/A
June 1982	61	Accounting for Title Plant	N/A
June 1982	62	Capitalization of Interest Cost in Situations Involving Certain Tax-Exempt Borrowings and Certain Gifts and Grants	N/A
June 1982	63	Financial Reporting by Broadcasters	N/A
September 1982	64	Extinguishments of Debt Made to Satisfy Sinking-Fund Requirements	15
September 1982	65	Accounting for Certain Mortgage Banking Activities	N/A

FASB STATEMENTS (continued)

Date Issued	Statement Number	Title	Chapters to Which References Most Applicable
October 1982	66	*Accounting for Sales of Real Estate*	19
October 1982	67	*Accounting for Costs and Initial Rental Operations of Real Estate Projects*	N/A
October 1982	68	*Research and Development Arrangements*	15
November 1982	69	*Disclosures About Oil and Gas Producing Activities*	N/A
December 1982	70	*Financial Reporting and Changing Prices: Foreign Currency Translation*	N/A
December 1982	71	*Accounting for the Effects of Certain Types of Regulation*	N/A
February 1983	72	*Accounting for Certain Acquisitions of Banking or Thrift Institutions*	N/A
August 1983	73	*Reporting a Change in Accounting for Railroad Track Structures*	N/A
August 1983	74	*Accounting for Special Termination Benefits Paid to Employees*	22
November 1983	75	*Deferral of the Effective Date of Certain Accounting Requirements for Pension Plans of State and Local Governmental Units*	N/A
November 1983	76	*Extinguishment of Debt*	15
December 1983	77	*Reporting by Transferors for Transfers of Receivables with Recourse*	8
December 1983	78	*Classification of Obligations That Are Callable by the Creditor*	5, 15
February 1984	79	*Elimination of Certain Disclosures for Business Combinations by Nonpublic Enterprises*	N/A
August 1984	80	*Accounting for Futures Contracts*	N/A
November 1984	81	*Disclosure of Postretirement Health Care and Life Insurance Benefits*	22
November 1984	82	*Financial Reporting and Changing Prices: Elimination of Certain Disclosures*	25
March 1985	83	*Designation of AICPA Guides and Statement of Position on Accounting by Brokers and Dealers in Securities, by Employee Benefit Plans, and by Banks as Preferable for Purposes of Applying APB Opinion 20*	N/A
March 1985	84	*Induced Conversions of Convertible Debt*	15
March 1985	85	*Yield Test for Determining Whether a Convertible Security Is a Common Stock Equivalent*	18

FASB STATEMENTS (concluded)

Date Issued	Statement Number	Title	Chapters to Which References Most Applicable
August 1985	86	Accounting for the Costs of Computer Software to Be Sold, Leased, or Otherwise Marketed	11
December 1985	87	Employers' Accounting for Pensions	22
December 1985	88	Employers' Accounting for Settlements and Curtailments of Defined Benefit Pension Plans and for Termination Benefits	22
December 1986	89	Financial Reporting and Changing Prices	25
December 1986	90	Regulated Enterprises—Accounting for Abandonments and Disallowances of Plant Costs	N/A
December 1986	91	Accounting for Nonrefundable Fees and Costs Associated with Originating or Acquiring Loans and Initial Direct Costs of Leases	21

FINANCIAL ACCOUNTING STANDARDS BOARD STATEMENTS OF FINANCIAL ACCOUNTING CONCEPTS

Date Issued	Statement Number	Title	Chapters to Which References Most Applicable
November 1978	1	Objectives of Financial Reporting by Business Enterprises	2
May 1980	2	Qualitative Characteristics of Accounting Information	2
December 1980	3	Elements of Financial Statements of Business Enterprises	2
December 1980	4	Objectives of Financial Reporting by Nonbusiness Organizations	N/A
December 1984	5	Recognition and Measurement in Financial Statements of Business Enterprises	2
December 1985	6	Elements of Financial Statements	2

SELECTED FASB EXPOSURE DRAFTS

Date Issued	Title	Chapters to Which References Most Applicable
July 1986	Statement of Cash Flows	24
September 1986	Accounting for Income Taxes	20

INDEX

A

Accelerated Cost Recovery System
(ACRS), 506
Acceleration clause, 167
objective, 168
subjective, 168
Account form of balance sheet, 175
Accounting
accrual, 85
and financial reporting, 3
cash-basis, 85
double entry, 66; illus., 68
financial, 5
management, 5
tax, 5
Accounting and Audit Guides, 15
Accounting and Auditing Enforcement Releases (AAER), 17
Accounting changes, 1016
summary of, 1035, 1036
Accounting cycle, 62
Accounting information,
users of, 3
qualities, hierarchy of, 39
Accounting model, assumptions of,
51
Accounting period, 53
Accounting principles,
change in, 1018
generally accepted, 10
Accounting Principles Board (APB),
14
Accounting process, 62
computers and, 85
illus., 67
overview of, 63
Accounting profession, 5
Accounting Research Bulletins
(ARB), 14
Accounting Series Releases (ASR),
17
Accounting standards,
development of, 9
impact of, 19

Accounting standard-setting bodies,
9
Accounting Standards Executive
Committee (AcSEC), 15
Accounting system, 62
Accounts, 70
adjunct, 73
chart of, 70
contra, 73
control, 71
nominal, 79
permanent, 79
real, 79
temporary, 79
Accounts payable, 596
Accounts receivable, 286, 287
as source of cash, 296
recognition of, 287
reporting, 289
uncollectible, 289
valuation of, 289
Accounts receivable ledger, 93
Accounts receivable turnover, 1164
Accrual accounting, 53, 85
vs. cash accounting, 93
Accumulated benefit approach, 961
Acid-test ratio, 1163
Acquisition,
by exchange of nonmonetary
assets, 446
by issuance of securities, 446
by self-construction, 447
costs, 435
expenditures subsequent to, 463
Activity analysis, 1164
Actuarial present value, 962
Additional paid-in capital, 173, 693
Additions, 465
Adjunct account, 73
Adjusting entries, 72
Administrative expenses, 132
Aging receivables, 292
All financial resources concept,
1055

Allocation of expense recognition,
rational, 124
systematic, 124
Allowance for doubtful accounts,
289
corrections to, 293
Allowance method, for
uncollectible accounts, 289
American Accounting Association
(AAA), 11, 17
American Institute of Certified
Public Accountants (AICPA),
11, 14
Amortization, 492, 513
bond premium or discount, 645
Analysis,
interpretation of, 1181
activity, 1164
capital structure, 1173
liquidity, 1162
profitability, 1169
Annuity, 213
ordinary, 222
Annuity due, 222
future value of, 224
present value of, 224
Antidilution of earnings, 773
short-cut test for, 787
Antidilutive securities, 773, 779
Appropriated retained earnings, 743
Appropriations, 174
Arms length transactions, 52
Articles of incorporation, 692
Asset-linked bonds, 639
Asset productivity rate, 1170
Assets, 162
balance sheet presentation, 529
current, 164
exchange of, 523
intangible, 429, 434
monetary, 163
noncurrent operating, 428
nonmonetary, 163
plant, 428

rate earned on, 1170
retirement, 522
    by exchange, 523
wasting, 516
Asset swap, 661
Asset turnover, total, 1168
Asset values, impairment of, 521
Assignment of receivables, 296
Audit function, external, 6
Auditors, internal, 6
Average cost methods of inventory costing, 337, 340
Average excess net earnings, capitalization of, 468
Average net earnings, capitalization of, 468

B

Balance sheet, 51
    additional disclosure to, 177
    assets on, 529
    classified, 163
    contributed capital on, 723
    elements of, 162
    form of, 175
    inventories on, 407
    liabilities on, 620
    limitations of, 183
    long-term investments on, 576
    long-term liabilities on, 670
    offsets on, 174
    stock dividends on, 750
    usefulness of, 161
Bank discounting of notes receivable, 307
Bank reconciliation, 249
Bargain purchase option, 905
Bargain renewal options, 905
Bearer bonds, 639
Benefit formula, 961
Betterments, 465
Board of directors, 692
Bond certificates, 637
Bond interest, 645
Bond issuance costs, 644
Bond redemption,
    by exercise of call provision, 651
    by purchase on market, 650
Bond refinancing, 656
Bond retirement, 649
Bonds,
    accounting for, 636
    as investments, 671
    as liabilities, 671
    asset-linked, 639
    bearer, 639
    callable, 640

collateral trust, 638
commodity-backed, 639
convertible, 639, 652
coupon, 639
debenture, 638
deep-discount, 639
first-mortgage, 638
issuance of, 642
market price of, 640
nature of, 637
registered, 639
second-mortgage, 638
secured, 638
serial, 638
term, 638
unsecured, 638
zero-interest, 639
Bonds-outstanding method, 673
Bonuses, 600
Books of original entry, 69
Book value per share, 1178
Borrowing rate, incremental, 907
Business documents, 69
Business year, natural, 1167
Bylaws, corporation 692

C

Callable bonds, 640
Call price, 697
Call provision, 651
Cancellation provision, 905
Capital, 172
    additional paid-in, 173, 693
    contributed, 173, 691
    corporate, 691
    legal, 173, 693
    paid-in, 173, 691
    permanent, 173
Capital expenditure, 456
Capital lease, 445, 902, 913
Capital stock, 173, 693
    issuance of, 699
Capital structure,
    analysis, 1173
    complex, 775, 779
    simple, 775, 776
Captive finance companies, 668
Carry back, net operating loss, 879
Carry forward, operating loss, 881
Cash, 242, 833
    control of, 247
    idle, 243
    proof of, 252
Cash basis accounting, 85
Cash disbursement journal, 88
    illus., 91
Cash discount, 294, 335
Cash dividends, 745

Cash flows,
    reporting, 1074
    statement of, 51, 184, 1053
        historical perspective, 1053
    to and from investors and creditors, 37
Cash flow statement,
    comprehensive illustration of, 1064
    format of, 187
    work sheet approach, 1064
Cash management, 247
Cash method, 841
Cash on hand, 243
Cash overdraft, 244
Cash receipts journal, 88
    illus., 90
Cash surrender value of life insurance, 574
Cash vs. accrual accounting, 93
Certificate of Management Accounting (CMA), 18
Certified public accountant (CPA), 6
    other services provided, 7
Change orders, 828
Changes in accounting principles, cumulative effect of, 137
Changes in financial position, statement of, 185, 1053
Changing prices,
    comprehensive illustration, 1117
    FASB experiment, 1116
    historical perspective, 1100
    prospects for, 1116
    reporting effects of, 1098
Changing tax rates, tax allocation with, 872
Characteristics, qualitative, 38
Charter, 692
Chart of accounts, 70
Check register, 88
Checks, outstanding, 250
Coinsurance clause, 531
Collateral trust bond, 638
Committee on Accounting Procedures (CAP), 14
Commodity backed bonds, 639
Common-size financial statements, 1159
Common stock, 692, 698
    equivalent, 779
Common stockholders' equity, rate earned on, 1171
Comparability of financial statements, 42, 1015
Comparative statements, 1157
Compensated absences, 614
Compensating balance, 245

Compensation expense, 716
Compensatory plans, 716
Compensatory stock options,
    fixed, 717
    variable, 719
Completed-contract method, 819
    income tax considerations, 829
Completed production, 122
Completion, percentage of, 123
Composite depreciation, 508, 510
Compound interest, 211
Comprehensive income, 51
Comprehensive income tax allo-
    cation, 878
Computers, personal, 86
Computer software development
    expenditures, 460
Computers, and accounting pro-
    cess, 85
Computer system, 86
Conceptual framework, 28
    illus., 32
    implications of, 143
    nature and components of, 30
    summary of, 54
Conditional sales, 333
Conglomerates, 1179
Conservatism, 45
Consignee, 845
Consignment, 333
Consignment sales, 845
Consignor, 845
Consistency, 43
Consolidation, 555
Constant dollar, 1098
Constant dollar accounting, 1101,
    1110
Constant dollar restatement, 1104
Construction, interest during, 449
Containers, returnable, 434
Contingencies,
    gain, 181
    loss, 181
Contingent liability, 596, 615
Contra account, 73
Contract change orders, 828
Contract losses, 827
Contract rate, 640
Contracts, executory, 593
Contra-equity adjustment, 983
Contra stockholders' equity
    account, 559
Contributed capital, 173, 691
    on balance sheet, 723
Contribution clause, 532
Contributory plans, 959
Control account, 71
Conventional retail inventory
    method, 387

Conversion,
    effect of, on EPS, 789
    involuntary, 528
    stock, 721
Convertible bonds, 639, 652
Convertible preferred stock, 697
Convertible securities, for EPS, 783
Copyright, 435
Corporate capital, 691
Corporation, 172, 692
Cost allocation methods, inventory,
    337
Cost and equity methods, changes
    between, 567
Cost effectiveness, 43
Cost method, 556, 557
    compared with equity method,
        564
    for treasury stock, 707
Cost of goods available for sale, 131
Cost of latest purchases, 360
Cost percentage, 385
Cost recovery method, 123, 833,
    840
Cost-to-cost method, 821
    income recognition using, 824
Cost variances, standard, 361
Coupon bonds, 639
Credit, 67
Cumulative effect of change, 1019
    in accounting principles, 137
Cumulative preferred stock, 696
Current, 286
Current and noncurrent, change in
    classification between, 561
Current assets, 164
Current cost, 511, 1098
Current cost accounting, 1110, 1114
    mechanics of, 1113
Current cost/constant dollar
    accounting, 1114
Current cost/constant dollar basis,
    1130
Current cost/nominal dollar basis,
    illustration of, 1125
Current liabilities, 166
Current market value, 49
Current ratio, 1162
Current replacement cost, 49
Current services, 962
Curtailments, 985
Customer premium offers, 611
Cycle, normal operating, 164

D

Debentures, 638
Debit, 67

Debit and credit relationships of
    accounts, 68
Debt,
    extinguishment of, prior to
        maturity, 650
    long-term, 635
    short-term, 597
Debt restructuring, 660
Debt securities, marketable, 257
Debt terms, modification of, 664
Debt to equity ratio, 1175
Decision usefulness, 39
Declining-balance methods, 498
Decreasing-charge depreciation,
    495
Deep-discount bonds, 639
Default, subscription, 701
Defeasance, in-substance, 650, 657
Deferred concept, 873
    evaluation of, 877
Deferred income taxes
    account, 868
    classification and reporting of,
        876
Deferred method, 883
Deferred payment contract, 443
Deferred pension cost, 983
Deficit, 174, 741
Defined benefit plans, 960
    funding, 962
    issues in accounting for, 965
Defined contribution plans, 959
Demand deposit, 243
Depletion, 492, 516
    oil and gas, 517
Deposit in transit, 250
Deposit method, 843
Deposits,
    demand, 243
    time, 243
Depreciation, 492
    changes in estimates, 519
    composite, 508, 510
    declining-balance, 498
    decreasing-charge, 495
    group, 507
    methods of, 496
    productive-output, 495, 507
    service hours, 495
    straight-line, 495, 497
    sum-of-the-years-digits, 498
    unit, 508
    rate, 497
Detachable warrants, 714
Discussion Memorandum, 12
Differences,
    originating, 869
    permanent, 864, 865
    reversing, 869

temporary, 864, 866
timing, 864, 866
Dilution, 773
    material, 775
Dilutive securities, 773
    multiple potentially, 787
Direct costing, 361
Direct-financing leases, 922, 923
Direct labor, 328
Direct matching, 123
Direct materials, 328
Directors, board of, 692
Direct pricing, 1113
Direct write-off method, 289
Disclosure, full, 50
Discontinued operations, 133
Discounted value, 49
Discounts, 212, 389, 640
    as reductions in cost, 334
    cash, 294, 335
    sales, 294
    trade, 294, 334
Discrete projects, 450
Dishonor, of note receivable, 309
Disposal date, 135, 716
Diversified companies, 1179
Dividend payout percentage, 772
Dividends, 741
    accounting for, 742
    cash, 745
    in arrears, 696
    liquidating, 750
    payment of, 744
    property, 745
    recognition of, 744
    stock, 746
Dividends per share, 1172
Documents, business, 69
    source, 69
Dollar value LIFO, 347
Donated treasury stock, 710
Double-declining balance, 499
Double-entry accounting, 66
    illus., 68
Double extension, 348
Double extension index, 363
Doubtful accounts, allowance for, 289
Draft, exposure, 13

E

Earnings, 143, 741
    antidilution of, 773
    dilution of, 773
Earnings per share (EPS), 141, 772, 1172
    financial statement presentation of, 792

fully diluted, 774, 787
historical, 774
primary, 774, 779
simple, 774
summary of computations, 791
Earnings process, 121
Economic approach, 119
Economic entity, 52
Effective-interest method, 302, 674
    of amortization, 647
Effective-interest rate, 211, 640
Efforts-expended methods, 822
Electronic data processing (EDP) system, 63
Employee Retirement Income Security Act of 1974, 957
Employees, stock options issued to, 715
Entries,
    adjusting, 72
    reversing, 83
Entry cost, 394
Equity, 162
    owners', 172
    shareholders', 172
    trading on, 1174
Equity method, 556, 563
    compared with cost method, 564
Equity securities,
    long-term investments in, 554
    marketable, 257
Equity swap, 663
Equity-to-debt ratio, 1174
Error corrections, 1024
    summary of, 1035, 1036
Escrow statement, 432
Estimated life, change in, 519
Estimated units of production, change in, 520
Estimates,
    change in, 1018
    revision of, 826
Excess earnings, number of years, 469
Exchange for other assets, retirement by, 523
Ex-dividend, 745
Executory contracts, 593
Executory costs, 906
Exercisable date, 716
Exercise date, 716
Exercise period, 710
Exercise price, 711
Exit values, 394
Expected cash value, 289
Expected service period, 970
Expenditure, capital, 456
Expenditure, revenue, 456
Expenditures, subsequent, 463

Expense recognition, 123
Expenses,
    administrative, 132
    general, 132
    operating, 132
    selling, 132
Exposure draft, 13
Ex-rights, 711
External indexes, 364
External user groups, 4
External audit function, 6
Extinguishment of debt prior to maturity, 650
Extraordinary items, 136

F

Face amount,
    of bonds, 637
    of notes receivable, 302
Factoring receivables, 296, 298
Factory overhead, 328
Factory supplies, 327
Fair market value, 455
Fair value, 974, 981
Federal Insurance Contributions Act (FICA), 602
Feedback value, 40
Financial accounting, 5
Financial Accounting Concepts, Statements of, 12
Financial Accounting Foundation (FAF), 10
    organization chart, illus., 11
Financial Accounting Standards, Statements of, 12
Financial Analysts Federation, 18
Financial Analysts Foundation (FAF), 11
Financial Accounting Standards Board (FASB), 10
Financial Executives Institute, 11, 18
Financial capital maintenance, 118
Financial flexibility, 162
Financial position, statement of changes in, 185, 1053
Financial reporting, 5
    objectives of, 32, 33
Financial Reporting Releases (FRR), 17
Financial statement analysis, 1154
    procedures, 1156
Financial statements, 78
    common-size, 1159
    elements of, 46, 47
Financing, off-balance-sheet, 667
Finished goods, 328
Fire insurance, 530

First-in, first-out (FIFO), 337, 338
First-mortgage bond, 638
First-mortgage notes, 257
Fixed charge coverage, 1175
Flexibility, financial, 162
Floating interest rates, 639
Floor values, 402
Flow-through method, 883
FOB destination, 332
FOB shipping point, 332
Fractional share warrants, 748
Franchises, 437
Franchising industry, deposit
    method, 843
Freight in, 389
Full cost approach, 517
Full disclosure principle, 50
Funding, 959
Funds, 572
    accounting for, 573
    all-financial resources concept,
        1055
    defined as cash, 1057
    defined as working capital, 1062
    long-term investments in, 572
    redemption, 572
    sinking, 572
Funds flow, 186
Funds statement, 185, 1053
    limitations of, 1055
    objectives of, 1055
    preparation of, 1056
Furniture and fixtures, 434
Future earnings, 466
Future value, 212

G

Gain, 522
    holding, 400, 1111
    contingencies, 181
    recognition, 121
    purchasing power, 1105
General expenses, 132
Generally accepted accounting prin-
    ciples (GAAP), 10
General journal, 70, 87
    illus., 92
General ledger, 71, 92
General purchasing power dollars,
    1099
Gift certificates, 613
Going concern, 52
Goods available for sale, cost of,
    131
Goods in process, 328
Goods in transit, 332
Goodwill, 438
    estimation, 465

    negative, 441
    valuation, 466, 467
Governmental Accounting Stan-
    dards Board (GASB), 11, 19
Government Finance Officers Asso-
    ciation (GFOA), 11, 19
Grant of equity swap, 663
Grantor, 437
Gross change method, 874
Gross profit margin on sales, 1170
Gross profit method, 382
Gross profit test, 382
Group depreciation, 507
Growth potential, 1156
Guarantees, loan, 620
Guides, Accounting and Audit, 15

H

Historical cost, 49, 511, 1098
Historical cost/constant dollar basis,
    illustration of, 1118
Holding gains and losses, 400, 1111
    realized, 1112
    unrealized, 400, 1112

I

Idle cash, 243
Immediate recognition, 124
Implicit interest, 302
    rate, 907
Imprest system, 248
Imputed interest rate, 305
Income, 117
    component elements, 121
    reporting of, 126
    taxable, 864
Income statement, 50
    form of, 127
    multiple-step, 130
Income Summary, 82
Income tax, 603, 606
    considerations for LIFO, 355
    disclosure of, 884
    expense, computation of, 867
Income tax allocation,
    interperiod, 864
    intra period, 863
    partial, 878
Income taxes payable, computation
    of, 867
Incorporation, articles of, 692
Incremental borrowing rate, 907
Incremental shares, 781
Indenture, trust, 572
Index,
    double extension, 363

    link-chain, 363
    price, 1102
    external, 364
    internal, 363
Indexing, 1113
Index-number trend series, 1158
Indirect materials, 328
Individual Retirement Accounts
    (IRA), 957
Industry Accounting Guides, 818
Industry Audit Guides, 818
Industry data, 1178
    sources of, 1180
Information,
    qualitative characteristics of, 38
    users of accounting, 3
Initial markup, 386
Input measures, 821
Installment sales, 123, 333, 833,
    834
    of merchandise, 835
    of real estate, 838
In-substance defeasance, 650, 657
Insurance,
    fire, 530
    self, 619
    recovery, 530
Intangible assets, 429, 434
    amortization of, 513
    valuation at, 429
Interest, 210
    bond, 645
    compound, 211
    number of times earned, 1175
    simple, 211
Interest-bearing notes, 302
Interest cost, 969
Interest rate,
    determining, 219
    effective, 211, 640
    floating, 639
    implicit, 907
    imputed, 305
Internal auditors, 6
Internal user groups, 4
Intra period income tax allocation,
    863, 864
    impact of, 868
Interperiod income tax allocation,
    with changing tax rates, 872
Interpolation, 226
Inventories,
    classes of, 327
    number of days' sales in, 1166
    on balance sheet, 407
Inventory, 326
    errors in recording, 404
    items included in, 332
    periodic, 77

perpetual, 78
physical, 329
Inventory cost,
    determination of, 333
    items included in, 334
Inventory methods,
    comparison of, 353
    selection of, 362
Inventory pools, 345
Inventory systems, 328
Inventory turnover, 1166
Inventory values, decline in, 397
Investments,
    long-term, 554
    noncurrent, 554
    temporary, 256
Investment tax credit, 882
    evaluation of accounting treat-
        ment of, 883
Involuntary conversion, 528
Issuance costs, bond, 644
Issuance of securities, acquisition
    by, 446
Items, extraordinary, 136

J

Journal, 69
    cash disbursement, 88; illus., 91
    cash receipts, 88; illus., 90
    general, 70, 87; illus., 92
    purchases, 88
    sales, 87; illus., 89
    special, 70, 87
Journal entries, illus., 68

K

Keough plans, 957

L

Labor, direct, 328
Land, 430
Last-in, first-out (LIFO), 337
    advantages of, 357
    disadvantages of, 357
    income tax considerations for,
        355
Lease accounting, historical devel-
    opment of, 903
Leases, 445, 901
    advantage of, 902
    capital, 901, 913
    classification of, 908
    direct-financing, 922, 923
    disclosure requirements for, 930
    leveraged, 936, 939

minimum payments, 906
    nature of, 904
    operating, 913, 921, 923
    sales, 922, 927
Lease term, 905
Ledger, 69, 70
    accounts receivable, 93
    general, 71, 92
    subsidiary, 71, 92
Legal capital, 173, 693
Lessee, 901
    accounting by, 913
    disclosure requirements for, 931
Lessor, 901
    accounting by, 921
    disclosure requirements for, 931
Leverage, 1174
Leveraged leases, 936, 939
Liabilities, 162, 593
    balance presentation of, 620
    contingent, 595, 615
    current, 166, 594
    estimated, 596, 608
    noncurrent, 594
Liability concept, 873, 875
    evaluation of, 877
LIFO, see Last-in, first-out
LIFO allowance, 342
LIFO conformity rule, 344
LIFO method, retail, 390
LIFO pools, specific-goods, 345
LIFO reserve, 342
LIFO-specific goods, 342
Link-chain index, 363
Liquidity analysis, 1155, 1162
Liquidating dividends, 750
Liquidation, asset and dividend
    preferences upon, 698
Loan guarantees, 620
Loan value, 575
Long-term construction contracts,
    accounting for, 823
Long-term debt, 635
Long-term investments, 554, 576
    in funds, 572
    in stocks, 555
        required disclosures for, 570
    other, 576
Long-term liabilities on balance
    sheet, 670
Long-term notes, as investments,
    671
Long-term service contracts, 829
Loss, 522
Loss contingencies, 181
Losses, contract, 827
    holding, 1111
    purchasing power, 1105
Loss recognition, 123

Lower of aggregate cost or market,
    259
Lower of average cost or market,
    387
Lower of cost or market (LCM),
    393
    and tax laws, 397
    rule, 398

M

Machinery, 433
Maintenance, 463
    financial capital, 118
    physical capital, 118
Maker, 301
Management accounting, 5
Management advisory services, 7
Manual system, 63
Manufacturing overhead, 328
Manufacturing supplies, 327
Marginal costing, 361
Markdown, 386
Mark on, 386
Mark up, 386
Market, 394
    valuation at, 399
Marketable equity securities, valu-
    ation of, illus., 562
Marketable securities, 257
    valuation of, 259
Market rate, 640
Market-related value, 974, 981
Market value,
    permanent, 560
    of noncurrent equity securities,
        temporary changes in, 558
Matching, direct, 123
Materiality, 44
Materials,
    direct, 328
    indirect, 328
    raw, 327
Maturity date, 302
Maturity value, 637
Measurement, 46
Measurement date, 135, 716
Minimum liability, 980
Monetary assets, 163
Monetary items, 1106
Monetary units, stable, 53
Money, time value of, 208
Moving average method, 341
Multiemployer plan, 959, 991
Multiple pools, 352
Multiple potentially dilutive securi-
    ties, 787
Multiple-step income statement,
    130
Municipal debt, 638

N

National Association of Accountants (NAA), 11, 18
National Association of State Auditors, Comptrollers, and Treasurers (NASACT), 11, 19
Natural business unit pools, 352
Natural business year, 1167
Negotiable, 301
Net change method, 874
Negative goodwill, 441
Net losses, effect of on EPS, 790
Net method, 335
Net operating losses,
    accounting for, 879
    carryback, 879
Net periodic pension cost, 966
Net profit margin on sales, 1170
Net realizable value, 49, 289, 394
Neutrality, 41
Nominal account, 79
Nominal dollar, 1098
Noncompensatory plans, 716
Noncontributory plans, 959
Noncumulative preferred stock, 696
Noncurrent assets, 168
Noncurrent equity securities,
    changes in temporary market value of, 558
Noncurrent investments, 554
Noncurrent liabilities, 168
Noncurrent operating assets, 428
Nondeductible expenses, 865
Nondetachable warrants, 714
Non-interest-bearing notes, 302
Nonmonetary assets, 163
Nonmonetary items, 1106
Nonreciprocal transfers,
    of nonmonetary asset, 455
    to owners, 745
Nontaxable revenues, 865
Nontrade notes payable, 597
Nontrade receivables, 286
No-par, 694
Normal earnings rate, 467
Normal operating cycle, 164
Notes,
    first-mortgage, 257
    promissory, 301, 597
    interest-bearing, 302
Notes payable, 597
    nontrade, 597
    trade, 597
Notes receivable, 286, 301
    as source of cash, 307
    exchanged for cash, 304
    exchanged for property, 304
    nontrade, 301
trade, 301
valuation of, 301
Not-sufficient-funds (NSF), 250
Number of days' sales in receivables, 1165
Number of times interest earned, 1175

O

Objective acceleration clauses, 167
Objectives of financial reporting, 32, 33
Off-balance sheet financing, 667
    reasons for, 669
Oil and gas depletion, 517
Operating lease, 913, 921, 923
Operating loss carry forward, 881
Operating expenses, 132
Operating profit, 400
Opinions of the Accounting Principles Board, 14
Option,
    bargain purchase, 905
    renewal, 905
    stock, 710, 715
Organization costs, 436
Original entry, books of, 69
Original retail, 386
Originating differences, 869
Output measures for percentage-of-completion method, 822
Outstanding checks, 250
Overdraft, 244
Overhead,
    factory, 328
    manufacturing, 328
Owners' equity, 172
    elements of, illus., 694
Ownership, rights of, 693

P

Paid-in capital, 173, 691, 693
Parent, 555
Partial income tax allocation, 878
Partnership, 172, 691
Par value, 637, 693
Par value method, 707, 709
Patent, 434
Pattern of use, 495
Patterns and dies, 434
Payout rate, 772
Payroll taxes, 602
    accounting for, 604
Pension accounting standards, history of, 964
Pension assets, 982
Pension Benefit Guaranty Corporation (PBGC), 958
Pension cost,
    net periodic, 966
    summary of, 978
    unfunded accrued, 979
Pension curtailments, 985, 987
Pension liability, 979
Pension plans, 956
    accounting for, 966
    disclosure of, 988
    employer, 958
    gains and losses, 974
Pension settlements, 985, 986
Per annum, 211
Percentage-of-completion,
    income recognition under, 824, 825
    income tax considerations, 829
    measuring, 821
    method, 123, 819, 820
Period costs, 334
Periodic inventory, 77
    system, 328
Periods,
    accounting, 53
    determining number of, 219
Permanent account, 79
Permanent capital, 173
Permanent differences, 864, 865
Perpetual inventory, 78
    system, 329
Personal computers (PC), 86
Personal property, 430
Petty cash fund, 248
Physical capital maintenance, 118
Physical inventory, 328
Plan date, 716
Planning, tax, 7
Plant assets, 428
    acquisition of, 442
    valuation at acquisition, 429
Point of completed production, 122
Point of sale, 122
Pooling of interest, 704
Post-closing trial balance, 82
Posting, 70
Postretirement benefits, 991
Predictive value of accounting information, 40
Preferable Accounting Principles, 15
Preferred stock, 693
    cumulative, 696
    noncumulative, 696
    redeemable, 698
Premium, 640
Premium offers, 611
Prepaid net pension cost, 983
Present value, 49, 212, 307

actuarial, 962
Present value method, 470
Price-earnings ratio, 772, 1173
Price indexes, 1102
Primary EPS, for partial year, 785
Prior period adjustment, 740
Prior periods, restatement of, 1022
Prior service cost, amortization of, 970
Prior services, 963
Private Companies Practice Section (PCPS), 15
Productive-output depreciation, 495, 507
Productivity rate, asset, 1170
Professional judgment, 19
Profit, operating, 400
Profitability, 1156
Profitability analysis, 1169
Profit margin on sales, 1170
Projected benefit approach, 961
Projected benefit obligation, 968
Project financing arrangements, 669
Promissory note, 301, 597
Proof of cash, 252
Property,
    personal, 430
    real, 430
Property dividends, 745
Property taxes, 605
Proportional performance methods, 123, 819, 829, 830
    evaluation of, 832
Proprietorship, 172, 691
Public accounting, practice of, 7
Purchase, 704
Purchase commitments, losses on, 401
Purchase option, bargain, 905
Purchase returns and allowances, 336
Purchases journals, 88
Purchasing power dollars, general, 1099
Purchasing power gains and losses, 1105

Q

Qualitative characteristics, 38
Quasi-reorganizations, 751
Quick assets, 1163
Quick ratio, 1163

R

Rate,
    contract, 640
    market, 640

stated, 640
Rate earned on common stock-holders' equity, 1171
Rate earned on total assets, 1170
Rate of return, appropriate, 467
Ratio of stockholders' equity to total liabilities, 1174
Raw materials, 327
Real account, 79
Real-estate leases, 936
Realizable value, net, 289
Realization, 121
Real property, 430
Receivables, 285
    accounts, 286, 287
    aging, 292
    classification of, 285
    nontrade, 286
    notes, 286, 301
    number of days' sales in, 1165
    presentation of, 310
    trade, 286
    transfer of, 296
Recognition, 46
    expense, 123
    gain, 121
    immediate, 124
    loss, 123
    revenue, 121
Reconciliations, bank, 249
Recording phase, 66
Recourse, 296
    sale of accounts receivable without, 298
    sale of receivables with, 667
    transfer of accounts receivable with, 300, 308
    transfer of accounts receivable without, 308
Recovery periods, 500
Redeemable preferred stock, 698
Redemption,
    bond, by purchase on market, 650
    by exercise of call provision, 651
Redemption funds, 572
Refundable deposits, 608
Refunding, 656
Register,
    check, 88
    voucher, 90
Registered bonds, 639
Relevance, 40
Reliability 40, 41
Renewal options, bargain, 905
Renewals, 464
Rental payment, determining, 219
Repairs, 464
Replacement, 464

Replacement cost, 394, 512
Report form of balance sheet, 175
Reporting, 46
    financial, 4
Reporting entity, change in, 1024
Reporting income, 126
Repossessions, 402
Representational faithfulness, 42
Research, 457
Research and development,
    arrangements, 668
    expenditures, 457
Reserve Recognition Accounting (RRA), 518
Residual value, 493
    guaranteed, 906
    of lease, 905
Retail inventory method, 385
    conventional, 387
Retail-lifo method, 390
Retail method with varying profit margin inventories, 390
Retained earnings, 174, 691, 739
    appropriated, 743
    changes in, 142
    free, 743
    restrictions on, 743
    unappropriated, 743
Retained earnings statement, 51
Retirement,
    asset, 522
    stock reacquired for, 705
Returnable containers, 434
Return on investment (ROI), 1170
Returns, 389
Returns and allowances,
    purchase, 336
    sales, 294
Revenue expenditure, 456
Revenue recognition, 121
    after delivery of goods or performance of services, 833
    principle of, 48
    prior to delivery of goods or performance of services, 819
Revenues, unearned, 607
Reverse stock split, 722
Reversing differences, 869
Reversing entries, 83
Rights,
    for earnings per share, 780
    stock, 710, 711
Rights-on, 711

S

Salaries, 600
Sale-leaseback, 932
Sales,

conditional, 333
    installment, 123, 333
    point of, 122
Sales discount, 294
Sales journal, 87; illus., 89
Sales returns and allowances, 294
Sales tax, 607
Sales-type leases, 922, 927
Salvage value, 493
Second-mortgage bond, 638
SEC Practice Section (SECPS), 15
Secret reserves, 703
Secured bonds, 638
Securities,
    antidilutive, 773
    dilutive, 773
    marketable, 257
Securities and Exchange Commis-
    sion, 16
Securities Industry Association
    (SIA), 11, 19
Segment reporting, 1179
Self-construction, 447
    overhead chargeable to, 448
    saving or loss on, 449
Self insurance, 619
Selling expenses, 132
Serial bonds, 638, 673
    redemption prior to maturity,
    675
Service charge, 250
Service contract, 610, 829
Service cost, 967
Service hours depreciation, 495,
    506
Settlement, 985, 986
    rate, 969
Shareholders' equity, 172
Shares, incremental, 781
Share warrants, fractional, 748
Short-term debt, 597
Short-term obligations expected to
    be refinanced, 598
Short-term paper, 257
Simple interest, 211
Single-employer plans, 958
Sinking funds, 572
Social security taxes, 602
Software development costs, 437
Software development ex-
    penditures, 460
Source documents, 69
Special journal, 70, 87
Specific goods LIFO pools, 345
Specific identification, 337, 338
Split-down, stock, 722
Stability, 1156
Stable monetary units, 53
Standard cost variances, 360

Standard Industrial Code (SIC),
    1779
Standard-setting bodies, 9
Standard-setting process, 12, 22
Standards, development of, 9
Stated rate, 640
Stated value, 693, 695
    method, 707, 709
Statement of cash flows, 51
    overview of, 184
Statement of changes in owners'
    equity, 51
Statement of changes in stock-
    holders' equity, 754
Statements of Financial Accounting
    Concepts, 12
Statement of Financial Accounting
    Standards, 12, 13
Statement of Position (SOP), 15,
    818
Statements,
    comparative, 1157
    financial, 78
Stock,
    capital, 173, 693
    common, 698
    issuance of, 699
    par value, 693, 694
    preferred, 695
    stated value, 693
    subscription, 700
    treasury, 173, 706
Stock certificates, 692
Stock conversions, 721
Stock dividends, 746
    small vs. large, 747
    vs. stock splits, 749
Stockholders' equity, 753
    rate earned on, 1171
Stock issuance in exchange for
    business, 704
Stock issued for consideration other
    than cash, 703
Stock options, 710, 715
    compensatory, 717
    disclosure of, 721
    for EPS, 780
Stock rights, 710, 711
Stock reacquisition, 704
    for retirement, 705
Stocks, acquisitions of, 554
Stock split, 722
    reverse, 722
    vs. stock dividend, 749
Stock split-down, 722
Stock warrants, 710, 711, 714
Straight-line depreciation, 495, 497
Straight-line method, of amortiza-
    tion, 645

Subjective acceleration clause, 168
Subscribers journal, 700
Subscribers ledger, 700
Subscription,
    default, 701
    stock sold on, 700
Subsequent events, 181
Subsidiary, 555
Subsidiary ledgers, 71, 92
Substantial performance, 844
Successful efforts approach, 517
Sum-of-the-years-digits method,
    498
Supplies,
    factory, 327
    manufacturing, 327
Swap,
    asset, 661
    equity, 663
System,
    computer, 86
    EDP, 63
    manual, 63
    voucher, 88
Systematic allocation, 124

T

Taxable income, 864
Tax accounting, 5
Taxes,
    income, 603, 606
    payroll, 602
    property, 605
Tax planning, 7
Technical Bulletins, 14
Technological feasibility, 462
Temporary account, 79
Temporary differences, 864, 866
Temporary investments, 256
Term bonds, 638
Termination benefits, 985, 987
Termination benefits,
    contractual, 988
    special, 988
Third-party financing, 432
Third-party long-term creditor, 939
Tickets, tokens, and gift certificates
    outstanding, 613
Time deposits, 243
Time-factor methods, 496
Time lines, 41
Time value of money, 208
Timing differences, 864, 866
Total asset turnover, 1168
Trade discounts, 294, 334
Trade-ins, 402
Trademarks, 435
Trade names, 435

Trade notes payable, 597
Trade notes receivable, 301
Trade receivables, 286
Transaction, 66
  illus., 68
Transaction approach, 119, 120
Transfer of assets in full settlement
  of debt, 661
Transition amount, amortization
  of, 976
Transition gain or loss, 976
Treasury stock, 173, 706
  donated, 710
Treasury stock method, 780
  limitation on use of, 782
Trend series, 1158
Trial balance, 72
  post-closing, 82
Troubled debt restructuring, 660
Trust indenture, 572
Turnover, 1166
  accounts receivable, 1164
  asset, 1168

U

Uncollectible accounts receivable,
  289
Uncollectibles, estimating, 291

Unearned revenues, 607
Unemployment insurance, 602
Unfunded accumulated benefit obli-
  gation (ABO), 981
Unfunded accrued pension cost,
  979
Unit depreciation, 508
Unrealized holding gain, 400
Unrecognized gains and losses,
  amortization of, 975
Unsecured bonds, 638
Use factor methods, 506
Useful life, 494
Usefulness, decision, 39
Users of accounting information, 3
  external, 3, 4
  internal, 3, 4
Use tax, 607

V

Valuation approach, 119
Value,
  future, 212
  present, 212
  residual, 493
  salvage, 493
Variable costing, 361
Verifiability, 41
Vertical analysis, 1159

Voucher register, 90
Voucher system, 88

W

Warranties, 609
Warrants, detachable, 714
  for EPS, 780
  fractional, 748
  nondetachable, 714
  stock, 710, 711, 714
Wasting assets, 516
Watered stock, 703
Weighted average method, 340
Well-offness, 1111
Working capital, 163, 1062
Working-capital ratio, 1162
Work in process, 328
Work sheet, 78
Write-off method, direct, 289

Y

Yield, 640
Yield on common stock, 1173

Z

Zero-interest bonds, 639

<u>EX 23-1</u>

DEPREC. EXP   5218

  ACCUM. DEPREC.   5218

B.V. - Salvage = Deprec Base ÷ 12 years = Annual Deprec

65,610 - 3,000 = 62,610   ÷ 12 = $5218

			EXP	A/D
1984	100,000	× 10% =	10,000	10,000
1985	90,000	× 10% =	9,000	19,000
1986	81,000	× 10% =	8,100	27,100
1987	72,900	× 10% =	7290	34,390

$$\frac{100\%}{20} = 5\% \times 2 = 10\%$$

New Rate

Change in estimate & principle so
treat as estimate → no entry

100,000 - 34,390 = 65,610 B.V.

Pension Cost
PREPAID/ACCRUED PENSION   } Net periodic pension cost

Prepaid/Accrued Pension
  Cash   } employer contribution

23-3

* FIFO   **LIFO**

Diff in beg. invent. $60,000   Beg. Inv.   360,000   300,000
Diff in End. invent.   (90,000)*   Purch. (make up) 1,000,000   1,000,000
CT on Pre tax Inc $(30,000)   COG Avail   1,360,000   1,300,000
me tax Effect   x 40%   End. Inv.   405,000   315,000
          $(12,000)   COGS
r tax Effect $(18,000) [30-12]   955,000 ← +30,000 → 985,000
Income FIFO $255,000 [GIVEN] ← show on current   ∴ Net Inc. (30,000)
Income LIFO $237,000 [255-18]   yrs. income statement   so subtract Diff in ending inventory

---

mum Lease Pay.   ⌐1,400,000⌐ (175,000 x 8)
    Financing Prof. 373,100 | | **EK 21-13**
          | 1,026,900 | $425,000
    Dealer Prof. 51,900 | | [2] 1,225,000 [Bal. of Min. Lease Pay Rec.
SALE'S TYPE LEASE ↗ └ 975,000 ┘   − 373,100 [unearned Int. Re] Acct.]
                            851,900
Lease Pay. Rec   1,400,000   x 10% Implicit Int. Rate
   Sale   1026,900   85,190 x 9/12 = $63,893
   Unearn. Int. Rev.   373,100
                                    ↗
s   975,000   partial
quip for Lease   975,000   year
                      Unearned Int. Rev.   63,893
h   115,000   Int. Rev.   63,893
in Lease Pay Rec.   175,000

Lease Pay.   ⌐3,450,000⌐ (230,000 x 15)
   Fin. Profit 1,525,659 | | **EK 21-9**
          | 1,924,341 | $1,525,659   ① DIRECT FIN. LEASE; defer profit over life
   Dealer Profit $∅ | | of lease → no dealer profit
         └ 1,924,341 ┘

Lease Pay.   3,450,000
   Unearned Int. Rev.   1,525,659   3,220,000 (bal min. lease pay rec. acct)
   Equip Purch for Lease   1,924,341   − 1,525,659 (bal. unearn. rent)
                             1,694,341
       230,000   x 10% implicit interest rate
n. Lease Pay. Rec   230,000   169,434

arned Int. Rev.   169,434
Int. Rev.   169,434

[CAPITAL LEASE p. 915]

EX 21-2 | DIANE (Lessor)   [OPERATING LEASE]   MELTON (LESSEE)

4/1/87 Machinery for lease 1,250,000   3/1/87 Prepaid Rent   300,000
           Cash   1,250,000   Cash   300,000
                                                         (12 mos rent)
3/1/87 Cash   300,000
           Unearned Rent   300,000   12/31/87 Rent Exp   250,000
                                                              Prepaid Rent   250,000
?/?/87 Various Exp.   15,000   (300,000 ÷ 12) × 10
           Cash   15,000

12/31/87 Deprec. Exp. Leased Machine 208,333
              Accum Deprec. Leased Machine 208,333   ┌─────┐ B/P   Premium
                 (1,250,000 ÷ 6)   │EX 15-9│ │400,000   │10,800
                                                         └─────┘
              Unearned Rent   250,000   ① 3/1/88 Interest Exp   3,000
                 Rental Income   250,000   Interest Pay   3,000
                                                            (200,000 × 9% × 2/12)
        Gross Profit = 250,000 − (15,000 + 208,333) = $26,667

③ Bonds Pay   200,000   ② Premium on B/P   90   10,800 ÷ 10 yrs.
   Int. Pay   3,000   Int. Exp.   90
   Premium on B/P   5310 [10,800 × 1/2 = 5400 − 90)   per year for →
              Gain on Retirement   9310   retired
              Cash   199,000 [200,000 × 98% = 196,000 + 3000 = 199,000]   X
                                                                    Interest
───
a) Cash   309,000 [300,000 ×103%) 12/31/86 Int. Exp   2500   B/P   Prem   │EX 15-3│
    Bonds Pay   300,000   ②   Int. Pay   2500   │300,000   75│9000   Int. E
  ① Premium   9,000   (9000÷120)   900│   2500│2
                            ③ Prem B/P 75 [300,000 × 10% × 1/12]   15000│
                               Int. Exp. 75   2500│90
b) 6/1/87 Int. Exp. 15,000   12/1 Int. Exp. 15,000   12/31 Int. Exp 2500
    ④   Cash   15,000 [300000 × 10% × 6/12] ③   Cash   15,000   ⑥ Int. Pay.   2500

   12/31 Prem on B/P   900   4/1 Prem. B/P   37 } 75 × 3 = 225
    ⑦   Int. Exp   900 [(9,000 ÷ 120)×12]   ⑧ Int. Exp.   37] 225 × 50,000/300,000 = 37

   ⑨ Int. Pay   417   ⑩ B/P   50,000
       Int. Exp   1250   Prem B/P   1300
          Int. Pay.   1667   Int. Pay   1667
       50,000 × 10% × 3/12 = 1250   Cash   50,667
                                        Gain on Retire   2300
       2500 × 50000/300,000 = 417
                                        50,000   9000
                                       + 1300   - 75
                                       − 49,000   - 900
                                        ──────   − 225
                                        2300   7800 × 50,000/300,000 = 1300

B 16-7	a) Land	450,000	

a) Land 450,000
  Common Stock .... 240,000 (40 x 8000)
  Prem. Common Stock 210,000

Cash 330,000
  Pref. Stock .... 300,000 (3000 x 100)
  Prem. Pref. Stock .... 39,000 (3000 x 10)

COST:
  Treasury Stock - Pref. .... 30,000 (300 @ 100)
    Cash 30,000

Treasury Stock - Common 27,500
  Cash .... 27,500 (500 @ 55)

Cash 15,000
  T.S. - Pref. .... 15,000 (100 @ 150)

Cash .... 17,100 (57 x 300)
  T.S. - C.S. .... 16,500 (55 x 300)
  Pd-In Cap. from Sale T.S. .... 600 ↑par

.- Common 5300
  Cash .... 5300 (53 x 100)

---

c) Cash 30,000
  Common Stock .... 15,000 (500 x 30)
  Prem. Common Stock 15,000

PAR VALUE:
a) Treasury Stock - Pref 30,000
  Prem on Pref. Stock .... 3,000 (10 @ 300) Issued @ 110
    Cash 30,000   so 10 premium
    Pd-In Cap. from Treas. Stock 3000

e) Treasury Stock Common .... 15,000 (500 @ 30)
  Prem. - C.S. .... 13,125 (500 @ 26.25)
    Cash .... 27,500 (500 @ 55)
    Pd-In Cap. from C.S. 625

f) Cash .... 15,300 (150 @ 102)
  T.S. - Pref. .... 15,000 (100 x 150)
  Prem - Pref. 300

g) Cash .... 17,100 (57 x 300)
  Pd-In Cap. .... 8100 (27 x 300)
  T.S. - C.S. .... 9000 (300 x 30) par

h) Cash .... 5300 (53 x 100)
  T.S. - C.S. .... 3000 (30 x 100)
  Prem - C.S. .... 2300 (23 x 100

17-4		

160,000 (10,000 x 16)
S. 160,000
648,000 (3000 x 216)
  600,000 (PAR)
In Cap. 48,000
h 305,100
C.S. 305,100
SOLD: [10,800 @ 22] + [2700 @ 25]
d (appraised) 400,000
P.S. .... 120,000 (600 x 200)
Pd-In Cap. .... 9,600 (600 x 16)
C.S. .... 270,400 (400,000 - 129,600)
147,750
Div Pay - P.S. 72,000
Div Pay - C.S. 75,750

000 x 20 = 72,000 (10% of 200 par)
500 x 1.50 = 75,750

12/29 Div Pay - P.S. 72,000
  Div Pay - C.S. 75,750
    Cash 147,750
12/31 Inc. Sum. 450,000
  R|E 450,000
2/27 T.S. .... 228,000 (12,000 x 19)
  Cash 228,000

R|E 228,000
  Approp. R|E 228,000
6/17 Cash (23 + 10,000) 230,000
  T.S. - Common (par) 190,000
  Pd-In Cap. 40,000

Approp. R|E 190,000
  R|E 190,000
7/31 Cash (2,000 x 20) 40,000
  T.S. 38,000
  Pd-In Cap 2,000

Approp. R|E 38,000
  R|E 38,000
9/30 Cash .... 231,000 (11,000 x 21)
  C.S. 231,000
12/16 R|E 121,200
  Div Pay - P.S. 72,000
  Div Pay - C.S. 49,200

3,600 x 20 = 72,000
61,500 x .80 = 49,200

Div Pay - P.S. 72,000
Div Pay - C.S. 49,200
  Cash 121,200

Inc. Sum. 425,000
  R|E 425,000

PROB 16-2 | 10/1   Comm. Stock Sub. Rec   12,600,000   (300,000 x 42)

        Comm Stock Sub.   9,000,000   (300,000 x 30)

        Pd-In Cap. in excess Value   3,600,000

    Cash   6,600,000

        Stock Sub. Rec.   6,600,000   (300,000 x 22)

       Land   210,000

       Building   250,000

       Equip.   50,000

       Inventory   110,000

           Mortgage Pay.   41,000

           A/P   11,000

           Int. Pay.   550

           C.S.   495,000   (30 x 16,500)

           Prem on C.S.   72,450

10/3   Stock Sub. Rec.   5,400,000   (45 x 120,000)

       Pref Stock Sub   4,800,000   (40 x 120,000)

       Prem. on Pref. Stock   600,000

    Cash   1,800,000

       Stock Sub. Rec.   1,800,000   (120,000 x 15)

11/1   Cash   4,800,000

       C.S. - Sub. Rec   3,000,000   (300,000 x10)   42-22 = 20 ÷ 2 =10

       P.S. - Sub Rec   1,800,000   (120,000 x 15)   45-15 = 30 ÷ 2 = 15

11/12   Stock Sub. Rec.   21,120,000   (44 x 480000)

       C.S. - Sub   14,400   (40 x 480,000)

       Prem on C.S.   6,720,000

    Cash   10,560,000

       Stock Sub Rec   10,560,000   (22 x 480,000)

12/1   Cash   3,000,000   Cash   1,791,000

       C.S. Rec   3,000,000   P.S. Sub Rec   1,791,000

    C.S. Sub   9,000,000

       C.S.   9,000,000   (30 x 300,000)

   Cash   1,791,000   due   1,800,000

      P.S. Sub Rec   1,791,000   <u>- 9,000</u> → not paying

                                      1,791,000

                 9,000 @ $15 = 600   120,000 - 600 = 119,400

                                               pd for.

Pref. Stock Sub.   4,776,000
    Pref. Stock   4,776,000   (119,400 × 40)

P.S. Sub   24,000   (40 × 600)
Pd-In Capital   3,000
                                    9,000 (default)   45
    P.S. Sub Rec   40
    Pay to Default Sub   18,000   (600 × 30 = 18,000)   5 × 600 = 3,000

Cash   21,600   (600 × 36)
Pay. to Default Sub   5400 ──────→ (600 × 45 = 27,000 − 21,600 = 5400)
    Pref. Stock   24,000
    Pd-In Cap   3,000

Pay to Default Sub.   12,600
    Cash   12,600   (18,000 − 5400)